Barry Garrison

I0820948

ALEUTIAN ISLANDS
Attu I. · Shemya I. · Unalaska I.
Buldir I. · Adak I.

ARCTIC OCEAN

GULF OF ALASKA

HUDSON BAY

ATLANTIC OCEAN

PACIFIC OCEAN

GULF OF MEXICO

CARIBBEAN SEA

SCALE OF KILOMETERS
0   500   1000   1500

SCALE OF MILES
0   200   400   600   800   1000

NORTH AMERICA
Relief Map

MODIFIED CONIC PROJECTION

SOUTH AMERICA

HAWAIIAN ISLANDS
Kure · Midway · Lisianski · Laysan · Kauai · Oahu · Molokai · Maui · Lanai · Hawaii

athene graphics

Barrett A. Garrison
20 October 1983

CHECK-LIST

OF

NORTH AMERICAN BIRDS

**

The Species of Birds of North America
from the Arctic through Panama,
Including the West Indies and Hawaiian Islands

**

PREPARED BY

THE COMMITTEE ON CLASSIFICATION AND NOMENCLATURE

OF THE

AMERICAN ORNITHOLOGISTS' UNION

**

SIXTH EDITION

1983

_____

Zoölogical nomenclature is a means, not an end, to Zoölogical Science

_____

PUBLISHED BY THE

AMERICAN ORNITHOLOGISTS' UNION

1983

ISBN Number: 0-943610-32-X

Preferred citation:

American Ornithologists' Union, 1983, *Check-list of North American birds,* 6th edition.

Printed by Allen Press, Inc.
Lawrence, Kansas, U.S.A.

CONTENTS

iv

DEDICATION

EUGENE EISENMANN
1906–1981

To Eugene Eisenmann, Chairman of the Committee on Classification and Nomenclature, our friend and colleague, who, as Chairman of the Committee from 1966 until his death in October 1981, directed our efforts toward production of this Check-list. His charisma and enthusiasm, the legal training that developed his skill as a moderator able to achieve fruitful compromise, and his broad knowledge of Neotropical birds made him a most effective Chairman. A warm and sensitive human being, he never failed to give the fullest attention to anyone approaching him seeking advice or help. We take pleasure in dedicating this work to his memory.

PREFACE TO THE SIXTH EDITION

HISTORICAL BACKGROUND

The five previous editions of the Check-list of North American Birds were published in 1886, 1895, 1910, 1931 and 1957. The present edition, the sixth, thus follows the first by almost a century. Each edition has included a preface, and the first edition was accompanied by a Code of Nomenclature which, in its introduction, outlined a 17-point "plan and form of the proposed American Ornithologists' Union 'List of North American Birds'." In the prefaces of all editions since the first, the respective Committees on Classification and Nomenclature reviewed to some extent the policies and procedures of their predecessors and discussed any changes considered. The various prefaces and the Code of Nomenclature in particular are important historical documents pertaining to traditions and points of view that have strongly influenced American systematic ornithology.

Of the 17 points of plan and form, the more important dealt with the geographical scope of the list, the inclusion of English vernacular names, a system of numbering and lettering species and subspecies, the composition of a hypothetical list, the addition of a list of fossil birds, the inclusion of some habitat information as well as geographic range, and the listing of taxa "in systematic order, to the end that the List may represent a classification as well as a nomenclature of the birds." The use of the subspecies category, expressed by trinomials, was also strongly affirmed. This plan and form for the first edition has been followed, with relatively minor changes, in the subsequent editions.

Check-lists, like living organisms, tend to evolve toward greater complexity, although there may be some simplifying deletions. There were no major changes in the second and third editions, but the number of forms included and details of range were greatly increased. In discussing classification in the preface to the third edition, the Committee noted that "it seemed best from the standpoint of convenience to continue the old Check-list system unchanged" although "a slight modification of the system proposed by Dr. Hans Gadow in 1892–93 would best reflect our present knowledge of the classification of birds." The fourth edition incorporated this change, adopting a modified Gadow classification for higher categories. The sequence of genera was largely determined by Alexander Wetmore and Waldron DeWitt Miller, and the sequence of species and subspecies arranged by Witmer Stone was based primarily on Robert Ridgway's "Birds of North and Middle America." The fifth edition followed essentially the same system of classification and sequence of taxa. English names for both species and subspecies were applied in the first four editions, but those for subspecies were dropped in the fifth. The list of fossil birds had grown so large by the fourth edition that it was not included as a separate appendix in the fifth; instead, only Pliocene and Pleistocene records of living species were mentioned along with the contemporary range. The "summary statement of the habitat of each species and subspecies" called for in the first edition was never more than perfunctory and had virtually disappeared by the fifth edition. The number of forms included in the list and the details of geographic ranges continued to expand, and the fifth edition was particularly detailed in the ranges of subspecies. Technical changes in nomenclature were incorporated in each new edition, but the numbering and lettering system for species and subspecies and criteria for the hypothetical list remained essentially the same.

The continuous flow of new information on avian relationships and distribution renders any check-list instantly obsolete in at least some respects, and the need for revision and addition inevitably increases through time. As the desirability of a sixth edition of the Check-list became more evident, the Council of the A.O.U. and its Committee on Classification and Nomenclature considered essentially two choices: either to follow the format of the fifth edition, revising and updating it, or to adopt a new and broader approach. The latter alternative was chosen, and the Committee was charged with developing an appropriate plan. In the plan that was accepted, the most important changes from previous editions include: (1) expansion of the geographic scope of the Check-list area to include the Hawaiian Islands, Middle America and the West Indies; (2) restriction of coverage to the species level, in view of the great increase in the number of species treated; and (3) adoption of those major changes in classification that are considered well-supported by published evidence and widely accepted. Details of these and other changes in plan, form and policy, and the rationale for each, are given in the following sections.

GEOGRAPHIC COVERAGE

The first point of plan and form of the first edition was "that the term 'North American,' as applied to the proposed List of Birds, be held to include the continent of North America north of the present United States and Mexican boundary, and Greenland; and the peninsula of Lower [Baja] California, with the islands naturally belonging thereto"; Bermuda was also included in the first edition. At that time, and until well into the 20th century the systematics and distribution of most Neotropical birds were too poorly known to be treated satisfactorily along with the comparatively well-studied Nearctic avifauna. The United States-Mexican border provided, for the most part, a convenient southern boundary that was reasonably close to the northern limit of the tropics, and a sea barrier separated the West Indies. Baja California was included because the avifauna of this peninsula, which lies mostly within the Temperate Zone, was relatively well known and of largely Nearctic affinities. Greenland was apparently included because it is geographically part of the Western Hemisphere and also to extend the usefulness of the Check-list. At the time there was no comprehensive work in English on the birds of Greenland, and its inclusion added relatively few forms to the list.

With the systematics and distribution of birds of the West Indies and of Middle America now reasonably well known, the Committee felt that the inclusion of those areas within the scope of the Check-list would greatly enhance its usefulness and would better express the zoogeographic relationship between these largely tropical regions and North America as it was defined in earlier editions of the Check-list. The area covered in the sixth edition is delimited as North America including all of the continental United States and Canada and their adjacent islands; the Hawaiian Islands; Clipperton Island; the Bermuda Islands; Middle America, consisting of Mexico and Central America, the latter including Guatemala, Belize (formerly British Honduras), El Salvador, Honduras, Nicaragua, Costa Rica and Panama, as well as all islands under their jurisdictions; the West Indies, including the Bahama Islands, Greater Antilles, Leeward and Windward islands of the Lesser Antilles, and Swan, Providencia and San Andrés islands. In the Bering Sea region the boundary corresponds to that delimiting the United

States from the U.S.S.R., which also corresponds to the International Date Line. Greenland is excluded from the Check-list area. The southern boundary in Middle America is the Panama-Colombia border; in the Lesser Antilles, Grenada is the southernmost island included. Excluded are those of the Lesser Antilles extending along the northern coast of South America and roughly parallel to it, from Aruba east to Tobago and Trinidad; the term "Netherlands Antilles" is used in the Check-list to refer only to Aruba, Curaçao and Bonaire, collectively, and does not include the Dutch islands of the Leeward group.

The geographic limits of a regional check-list are unavoidably arbitrary. Inclusion of all species of New World birds in one check-list would be highly desirable, but this is not now feasible considering the data, resources, and time available to this Committee. The Committee did, however, consider the historical biogeography of the New World in defining the area described in the preceding paragraph. The widely accepted current theory of plate tectonics and continental drift holds that, in post-Cretaceous time, South America was separated by sea barriers from all other continents until the end of the Pliocene, when it became connected with Middle America by the closing of the Panama Seaway. North America was separated from Europe in the North Atlantic region by a sea barrier, at least since the Eocene period. In the Bering Sea region, North America was probably connected intermittently with Asia in the Cenozoic Era (Miocene connection highly probable) and certainly connected in the Pleistocene. Throughout the Cenozoic Era there was a continuity of land from North America into Middle America at least as far south as northern Nicaragua and sometimes as far as central Panama. Until the land connection at the end of the Pliocene, Middle America was separated from South America by seaways of varying extent, duration and location. There were no land connections between the West Indies and North, Middle or South America from at least the early Cenozoic Era to the present. The details of this picture will undoubtedly be modified in the future, but the separation of the New World continents from each other and from the West Indies throughout most of the evolutionary history of modern birds appears to be well established. The present composition and distribution of the avifaunas of all of these regions have also been strongly influenced by Pleistocene events including glaciation, cooling and warming trends, and wet and dry cycles and changes in sea level associated with glacial and interglacial periods.

North and Middle America are part of a continuum in terms of physical geography, but the tradition in American ornithology has been to discuss these as distinguishable regions as previously defined, primarily for practical convenience. North America north of Mexico lies entirely in the Temperate to Arctic zones, but basically Temperate Zone conditions and habitats extend south in the higher altitudes into tropical latitudes in parts of the Greater Antilles and Middle America. The contemporary avifauna of Middle America consists of a complex mixture of taxa of temperate and tropical North or South American derivation along with endemic forms, the latter primarily in montane regions, and a few relatively recent colonizers from the West Indies. The contemporary avifauna of the West Indies appears to be largely derived from colonizations from temperate North America and tropical Middle America, with a lesser degree of direct colonization from South America. The insularity of the region has also resulted in a large number of endemic forms. South America, as the longest isolated of the continents and with a wide variety of climatic zones and habitat types, evolved a distinctive avifauna of great diversity. The contemporary avifauna of South America has been less influenced by post-Pliocene invasions from the north than it was by earlier, overwater invasions that introduced representatives of groups new to the continent.

Hawaii became the 50th state of the United States in 1959. Because state and federal government agencies and legislative bodies use the A.O.U. Check-list as a standard reference in matters pertaining to birds, the avifauna of all of the states should be included as a public service. Moreover, at least some members of the native Hawaiian avifauna were derived from ancestral populations of North or Middle American origin. Inclusion of the Hawaiian Islands within the Check-list area thus seems appropriate on all counts.

Greenland has no endemic species of birds. Its avifauna includes numerous species of otherwise entirely Old World distribution that have been included in previous A.O.U. check-lists solely on the basis of the Greenland records. Deletion of Greenland from the Check-list area eliminates such essentially Palearctic forms but does not exclude any species that occur in both North America and Greenland. The deleted forms that appeared in previous editions are found in Appendix B of this edition. Finn Salomonsen's "The Birds of Greenland" (1950–51) gives a complete check-list and bibliography to that date, and eastern Greenland is covered in Charles Vaurie's "The Birds of the Palearctic Fauna" (1959, 1965).

The Lesser Antilles along the northern coast of South America, and Tobago and Trinidad in particular, have avifaunas with moderate to strong South American affinities and for that reason are excluded from the Check-list area.

TAXONOMIC CATEGORIES

Because the A.O.U. Check-list is widely used as an official or quasi-official reference on the systematics and distribution of birds within its area, the Committee feels a special responsibility to avoid introducing sweeping changes in taxonomic concepts that would drastically affect the form and content of the list unless such proposed changes have been adequately debated and widely accepted on the basis of published evidence. This policy is not based on inertia or innate conservatism, but on what we believe to be sound historical perspective. The shortest interval between the publication of any two Check-lists was nine years, and the interval since the fifth edition has been 26 years. Boldly innovative proposals for changes in systematics that will stimulate discussion, debate, and testing should be introduced in scientific journals or books. Modifications and counter-proposals can then be published, and the original innovative ideas may undergo many alterations before a consensus develops. Because the Check-list cannot quickly be revised and republished as the weight of opinion shifts, the Committee feels that it should adopt major changes only when a consensus based on verifiable data has developed. The Committee is fully aware that many aspects of the present system of avian classification are based more on tradition than on comprehensive data, but this does not necessarily make the traditional arrangement wrong. In fact, in many cases, contemporary studies using sophisticated modern techniques have supported traditional classification. Our view of traditionally accepted avian classification may be expressed by a legal analogy—it is innocent until proven guilty; suspicion and accusation without verifiable supporting evidence are not sufficient grounds for corrective action, but responsible charges should be investigated, a fair trial given if the charges have substance, and rehabilitation attempted when mistakes or violations have demonstrably occurred.

Subspecies. The Committee strongly endorses the concept of the subspecies and the continued use of trinomials to express it, and we wish to make clear that the omission of separate listings of subspecies in this edition is not a rejection of the validity or utility of this systematic category. The omission of subspecies in this edition is based entirely on practical grounds, especially the need for publication of the Check-list within a reasonable period of time. Expansion of the geographic scope, which we consider of major importance, requires the treatment of more than 2000 species (1913 in the main text), many of which are considered polytypic. If we had emulated previous committees by evaluating critically all of the described subspecies within the Check-list area, there would be little hope of publishing the work before the 21st Century. The Committee therefore agreed, with some reservations, to proceed with a check-list dealing with taxa only down to the species level. References to subspecies have been included when necessary to clarify relationships or distribution, or where opinions differ as to specific or subspecific status.

The subspecies taxon is particularly useful in birds because of the great potential mobility of most species and the migratory habits of many. The availability of formal published descriptions of the characteristics of taxonomically recognizable, geographically circumscribed breeding populations within the overall range of a species facilitates determination of the area of origin of individuals found outside that range, and in particular facilitates the tracing of routes of passage and seasonal residences of migratory forms. The study of intraspecific variation in connection with subspecies has also resulted in the assembling of data that have been of great value in ecological studies and in the analysis of the early stages of the process of evolution.

It is the Committee's hope and intent that the species-level sixth edition will serve as a framework for future publications that will carry the taxonomy of the avifauna within the Check-list area to the subspecies level. We recognize that many people, including those in government agencies dealing with legislation, permits and law enforcement, need an authoritative list of subspecies within the A.O.U. Check-list area. For such purposes the Committee recommends continued use of the fifth edition plus the 32nd and 33rd supplements (Auk, 1973, 90, pp. 411–419, and 1976, 93, pp. 875–879, respectively) for the area covered therein. For Middle America and the West Indies, the Committee recommends use of the Peters' "Check-list of Birds of the World" (1931 *et seq.*) and those regional works that have critically evaluated subspecies included in their areas.

Species. Of all the taxonomic categories within the Linnaean system, the species has been the most controversial. This is not an appropriate place for a review of opinions—the differing views have been extensively debated in other publications. The Committee has considered only those arguments that apply to birds and not those dealing with quite dissimilar organisms. Our policy is that the species is a real and fundamental biological entity, and we follow the biological species concept of Ernst Mayr. Our preferred definition is: a species is a group of populations, actually or potentially interbreeding, that is reproductively isolated from all other such groups. This definition is adequate to determine the status of the overwhelming majority of forms within the Check-list area. The major problems in determining specific status are posed by those cases in which formerly allopatric populations are in contact with limited interbreeding, or in which presently allopatric

xiii

populations are spatially completely isolated from each other and perhaps potentially although not actually able to interbreed. From the 1940's through about the 1960's, the predominant trend in avian systematics was to treat such distinguishable allopatric populations as subspecies of a single polytypic species. In recent years there has been a trend away from relatively uncritical lumping as close study of some populations in zones of contact has shown that there may be assortative mating, reduced reproductive success in mixed pairs, and subtle (to the human investigator) behavioral, morphological, physiological or ecological differences that appear to constitute isolating mechanisms.

Cases of intermediacy between the subspecies and species levels of differentiation are to be expected since evolution is a dynamic and continuing process. The Linnaean system of nomenclature, originally based on the concept of fixed or immutable categories, cannot be adapted to the infinite degrees of difference between allopatric populations; there is therefore no absolutely right or wrong way to treat taxonomically those populations that are on the borderline between species and subspecies. The Committee has attempted to evaluate the evidence in each case, with the advice, when available, of specialists on the groups in question. Our tendency has been to consider closely related allopatric forms that differ substantially in ways that might be expected to effect reproductive isolation (such as visual and vocal signals, various aspects of behavior) as species unless there is strong evidence of a lack of reproductive isolation. In cases in which such populations are taxonomically distinguishable but not in ways that would appear to bring about reproductive isolation (such as small differences in size, color or form), our tendency has been to consider them conspecific. We have not always agreed within the Committee as to the treatment of individual cases, and we are aware that our collective judgment results in some compromise decisions that may ultimately prove wrong. In cases in which we felt reasonable doubt or in which contemporary authorities disagree, we have cited alternative opinions.

Superspecies. The study of allopatric taxa has made it clear that two or more such taxa may represent similar but distinct species of relatively recent monophyletic origin which are much more closely related to each other than to any other species. It is useful and informative to call attention to the particularly close relationship of such a group or groups of species within the genus. For this purpose we employ the category of superspecies, defined as a group of entirely or essentially allopatric populations that have differentiated into distinct biological species from a common ancestor. The species comprising a superspecies are called allospecies. This definition is essentially that of Amadon (1966, Syst. Zool., 15, pp. 246–249), who traced the history of the concept and discussed its utility. The superspecies category does not require new names or formal taxonomic description. In the "Notes" section of the accounts of allospecies, we have indicated those groups of species that appear to constitute superspecies as defined above.

A single example may help to clarify the Committee's approach in dealing with subspecies, species and superspecies. The genus *Sphyrapicus* (Picidae), comprising the sapsuckers, is a well-characterized genus with six taxa in at least two and possibly as many as four species. *Sphyrapicus thyroideus* is a distinct species which has been separated into two slightly different subspecies, *S. t. thyroideus* and *S. t. nataliae*. No modern authority considers these anything more than subspecies, and thus they are not individually mentioned or discussed in the Check-list. The fifth edition recognized only one other species, *Sphyrapicus varius*, divided into five subspecies: *S. v. varius, S. v. appalachiensis, S. v. nuchalis, S. v. daggetti,* and

S. v. ruber. Except for *appalachiensis,* which is but a weakly marked form of *varius,* they differ sufficiently in color as to be (usually) recognizable in the field, but they are extremely similar in behavior and ecology and, although essentially allopatric, are known to interbreed to varying extents. For these reasons they were considered a single polytypic species in the fifth edition. Studies since then have confirmed that *ruber* and *daggetti* interbreed freely where their ranges meet, but interbreeding otherwise varies from moderate over a narrow zone of contact (*nuchalis* and *daggetti, nuchalis* and *ruber*) to very rarely or not at all (*varius* and *nuchalis, varius* and *ruber*) in some other areas. The Committee considered a mass of complex evidence and decided (not unanimously) to recognize two species, *Sphyrapicus varius* (consisting of *S. v. varius* and *S. v. nuchalis*) and *Sphyrapicus ruber* (consisting of *S. r. ruber* and *S. r. daggetti*). We have noted that these are considered conspecific by some authorities, and that others would also recognize *nuchalis* as a distinct species. *Sphyrapicus ruber* and *S. varius* are considered to be allospecies of a superspecies, and if *nuchalis* is recognized as specifically distinct it would also be included as an allospecies. *S. thyroideus,* which is widely sympatric with the other forms in western North America, is not included in the superspecies.

Amadon (*loc. cit.*) proposed that superspecies status be symbolized by putting in brackets, following the name of the genus, the chronologically first-named species in the group of allospecies. The Committee endorses this procedure for well-studied cases, especially in simple lists; practical considerations preclude its usage in this Check-list. In the bracketing system, the species in the genus *Sphyrapicus* would be listed as follows:

Sphyrapicus [*varius*] *varius*
Sphyrapicus [*varius*] *ruber*
Sphyrapicus thyroideus.

Genera. The definition of a genus used by the Committee is: a group of species of common phylogenetic origin that are more closely related to one another than to any others and that differ from others by a decided gap. If a single species differs markedly from any others, it may constitute a monotypic genus. The limits of genera cannot be defined except by arbitrary criteria, yet many subjectively or arbitrarily defined genera appear to represent natural monophyletic assemblages. The accurate determination of generic limits is inherently one of the most difficult problems in taxonomy, but the Committee has attempted to follow certain guidelines in making its decisions. We have sought particularly to recognize as genera those species or groups of species that have reached different adaptive plateaus with the potential for further diversification in other evolutionary directions. We have adopted a middle course, avoiding recognition of monotypic genera that do not appear to meet this criterion but also avoiding submergence of adaptively distinct forms into large genera, thus obscuring their distinctiveness. We have also exercised practical judgment in some cases by recognizing more than one genus in very large groups of species which, even though there seem to be intermediate forms, appear to fall into two or more natural assemblages. For example, the parrot genera *Aratinga* and *Ara* are large and distinct multispecies groups, but the differences between them appear to be bridged by one or two species with intermediate characteristics. In our judgment, merging these genera would neither more accurately represent nor enhance understanding of the apparent relationship between them. We have placed them adjacent in sequence and noted that they are closely related. We have also retained the extinct monotypic genus *Conuropsis,* as some potentially important characteristics must remain unknown, but have noted its apparent close relationship to *Aratinga*.

Sequences of genera and species. The 17th point of the "plan and form" of the first edition called for sequences that "begin with the lowest or most generalized type, and end with the highest or most specialized." This was probably intended to refer to higher categories, but the principle can be logically extended to the lower ranking taxa as well. There are two obvious major problems in following this procedure: first, determining which taxa are more generalized and which more specialized; second, expressing this in a linear sequence of names. In attempting to decide sequences of generalized or primitive to specialized or derived, the Committee has followed what it considers to be the best published evidence and its own judgment. In many cases we simply lack sufficient evidence to make sound inferences about the phylogenetic history of a given taxon. The living forms may show a confusing mixture of presumably primitive and derived characters rather than a clear evolutionary trend. In the course of avian evolution there have been numerous and repeated branchings; even if these were all perfectly known, they could not be clearly represented by a linear sequence of names. We have attempted to cluster together those taxa which seem to be more closely related to one another than to any others, and within and among clusters have attempted to approximate a primitive to derived sequence. For example, the evolution of three contemporary species in the genus *Sphyrapicus* can be represented by the following diagram:

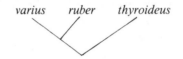

We further propose that *varius* is closest to the probable ancestral stock and that *thyroideus* is a more highly derived form whose ancestors diverged at an earlier time than those of *ruber*, which shares more derived characters with *varius*. The linear sequence that most closely represents this view is *varius-ruber-thyroideus*, but we do not intend to suggest thereby that *thyroideus* is derived from *ruber*-like ancestors. An alternative arrangement that lists *thyroideus* first would suggest that it was the most primitive, not the most derived form. When there is no convincing evidence for placing one taxon before or after another, we have either followed conventional arrangements or altered these somewhat to allow grouping of taxa that seem to show a primitive-derived sequence. When we found no secure basis for a primitive-derived sequence of species within a genus, we have followed the most widely used conventional geographic sequence of species, with roughly the northernmost form listed first and the southernmost last, or from west to east if the division of ranges is more oriented to that axis.

A frequently encountered problem in attempting to reflect primitive-derived sequences in a check-list occurs when a sequence is traced from a presumably primitive form to the end of a chain of related taxa, whereupon it becomes necessary to return to a second such chain, derived from the same or similar primitive taxa, and follow it out the same way. This procedure results in the admittedly awkward juxtaposition of a more derived taxon and a relatively primitive one in the sequence. For example, in the Carduelinae, a phyletic line of medium-sized finches is followed from the primitive rosy-finches (*Leucosticte*) to the highly derived crossbills (*Loxia*). The next form in the Check-list sequence is the Common Redpoll (*Carduelis flammea*). This is not meant to suggest that we believe *Carduelis* to be derived from *Loxia* or *Loxia*-like ancestors; we regard the Common Redpoll as the most primitive (within our area) of a second phyletic line that also arose from primitive medium-sized finches. This line is followed through the derived *Serinus,* where it terminates. The remaining genera, *Pyrrhula* and *Coccothraustes,* are both primarily Old World derivatives of still other phyletic lines originating from primitive carduelines. As listed in a Check-list sequence, the most derived species of one phyletic line thus immediately precedes the most primitive species of another line derived from a common ancestor.

Higher categories. Probably not since the time of the third edition, in which the Committee on Classification and Nomenclature chose not to use Gadow's relatively new system, has a Committee been faced with so many proposals for radical changes in the systematics of higher categories. As background on the bases for earlier arrangements, the historical introductions to avian classification in papers by Sibley (1970, Bull. Peabody Mus. Nat. Hist., 32, pp. 1–131) and Sibley and Ahlquist (1972, Peabody Mus. Nat. Hist., 39, pp. 1–276) provide an excellent review. Since publication of the fifth edition (and even before), the traditional arrangement of higher categories has been challenged at many points. In some cases the recent challenges have been based on new data, in others on new methods and philosophies of classification. The new data stem from discoveries in morphology and paleontology, biochemistry, genetics, behavior and related fields. The new methods and philosophies include numerical taxonomy (phenetics) and phylogenetic systematics (cladistics). We will not attempt to review all of these subjects and their consequences, a task that would require at least another volume. The virtues and shortcomings of the different methods and philosophies are being hotly debated in journals and symposia at the present time, and only true believers on the various sides consider the issues to be settled. Systematic revisions based on interpretations of new data, along with counter-proposals based on different data, are more frequent than ever. The dilemma that this poses for the Committee is well illustrated by the case of the flamingos (Phoenicopteridae). In the fifth edition, this group comprised a suborder Phoenicopteri in the order Ciconiiformes. This suborder was placed last in sequence, just before the Anseriformes, reflecting a belief that the flamingos also showed a close relationship to the latter. Subsequently, biochemical data from egg-white protein analysis were adjudged to support that classification, or at least not to refute it. An alternative arrangement was the placement of the flamingos in a separate order Phoenicopteriformes, indicative of their distinctiveness and the uncertainty as to their closest relationships. More recently, fossil evidence and anatomical studies led to various proposals, first that flamingos and anseriforms had a common ancestry, then that both those groups were derived from primitive charadriiform stock (with no close relationship to the Ciconiiformes), and next that the Phoenicopteridae be considered a family within the Charadriiformes, closest to the Recurvirostridae. The issue remains controversial. We cite this case not as a horrible example of unwelcome change but as a good example of how science advances—by the proposal of new hypotheses based on new evidence, and the testing of these for validity in the light of the same or different evidence. We feel, as stated earlier, that the Check-list is not the appropriate place for the testing of boldly innovative ideas in systematics and that the Committee's best course in this case is to retain the flamingos as a separate order, noting that their relationships remain uncertain and citing other treatments.

In other cases, there appears to be consensus for change from tradition. For example, the penguins (Sphenisciformes) were formerly placed at the beginning

xvii

of the sequence of Neognathae, implying that they were the most primitive living forms within that superorder. The present consensus is that the penguins are a specialized group derived from a volant marine ancestor and are best placed following the Procellariiformes.

A particular difficulty for the Committee was the arrangement and content of the families of passeriform birds, a matter that is still in ferment. The fourth and fifth editions both used the same arrangement of passerine families, and many ornithologists over several generations have come to think of that arrangement as standard. The Committee feels that the evidence has become overwhelmingly strong for changes in the traditional system even though all the issues are by no means settled. The major changes from either the fifth edition or general usage that are adopted in the sixth edition are described below, in the sequence in which they occur in the list.

1. The genera *Attila, Rhytipterna, Laniocera, Pachyramphus* (including *Platypsaris*) and *Tityra* (including *Erator*) are transferred from the Cotingidae to the Tyrannidae.

2. The genera *Auriparus* and *Psaltriparus* are removed from the Paridae and placed in the families Remizidae and Aegithalidae, respectively. Relationships of these chiefly Old World families remain uncertain; they follow the Paridae only because compelling evidence for their proper placement is not yet available.

3. The monotypic genus *Donacobius* is transferred from the Mimidae to the Troglodytidae.

4. A large family Muscicapidae is recognized, including in our area the subfamilies Sylviinae, Muscicapinae, Monarchinae, Turdinae and Timaliinae, most of which were formerly regarded as families. The genus *Chamaea,* formerly placed in the monotypic family Chamaeidae, is included in the Timaliinae.

5. The Vireolaniinae and Cyclarhinae, formerly given family rank, are included as subfamilies in the Vireonidae.

6. A large family Emberizidae is recognized, including the following divisions:
Subfamily Parulinae (formerly family Parulidae), including the genus *Zeledonia* (formerly in the monotypic family Zeledoniidae);
Subfamily Coerebinae, including only the genus *Coereba,* the former family Coerebidae being considered polyphyletic and other genera formerly included in it now being placed in either the Thraupinae or Emberizinae;
Subfamily Thraupinae, including the tribes Thraupini (including most genera in the former families Thraupidae and Coerebidae) and Tersini (formerly the monotypic family Tersinidae);
Subfamily Cardinalinae, formerly the subfamily Richmondeninae of the family Fringillidae, but with *Tiaris* transferred to the Emberizinae;
Subfamily Emberizinae, including the Emberizinae of the fifth edition plus *Sporophila, Tiaris* and other genera of the Emberizinae as used in Volume XIII of Peters' "Check-list of Birds of the World" (also including *Diglossa* and *Euneornis,* of the former Coerebidae);
Subfamily Icterinae, formerly the family Icteridae.

7. The family Fringillidae is revised to include the following divisions: Subfamily Fringillinae, including only the genus *Fringilla*; Subfamily Carduelinae, including the Carduelinae of the fifth edition plus *Serinus,* and excluding *Sporophila*; and Subfamily Drepanidinae (formerly the family Drepanididae).

8. The family Passeridae is recognized, in the Check-list area including only the introduced species of *Passer,* formerly included in the Ploceidae.

9. The family Ploceidae is represented in the Check-list area only by the in-

troduced species of *Ploceus* and *Euplectes.* Several introduced species, not listed in previous editions, were formerly placed in the family Ploceidae but are here assigned to the family Estrildidae.

10. The family Estrildidae, including the subfamilies Estrildinae and Viduinae, is represented in the Check-list area by several introduced species.

Classifications similar to the above are used in most recent comprehensive taxonomic works; the major differences among these are in the placement of relatively few genera and in the ranking of taxa as families, subfamilies or tribes.

The Committee feels that this arrangement expresses probable relationships much better than the traditional system and that the changes are necessary and desirable, although we recognize that new evidence will surely require modification of it. Other proposed changes will doubtless be validated in the future. In order to meet publications schedules, we have fixed 31 December 1981 as the latest date of publication of proposals for systematic changes to be considered by the Committee.

At the time of this writing, Joel Cracraft (1981, Auk, 98, pp. 681–714) has published a new classification of birds of the world down to the level of tribes, based on principles of phylogenetic systematics (cladistics); Cracraft points out that many of his proposals are tentative and intended to stimulate further testing. A series of papers by Charles G. Sibley (and co-authors) appearing in late 1981 and early 1982, with others in prospect, revises avian classification largely on the basis of data obtained from DNA-DNA hybridization. Many parts of these authors' new classifications differ considerably from each other and from those used in most current references, including the present Check-list. Adoption by the Committee of any or all of these major changes would be premature, as the Committee's publication deadline does not allow sufficient time for critical evaluation to be published; we can only recommend serious consideration of these new proposals in the future.

In summary, our interpretation of the original charge that the Check-list should represent "a classification as well as a nomenclature of the birds" is that it should constitute both a workable and a working hypothesis of avian systematics. By our recognition of the included taxa and our grouping and sequencing of them, we hypothesize a set of relationships and phylogenetic events. We have also attempted to point out the cases of greatest uncertainty and controversy, indicating alternative hypotheses that may be considered. We wish our hypothesis to be workable, in the sense of providing a classification that is as close as possible to a consensus of the views of authorities respected for their work in avian systematics, so that other scientists and interested persons in all fields may use it with reasonable confidence as a standard reference. While the Check-list should be authoritative, it should never be considered sacrosanct. The collective opinion of a committee frequently tends toward conservatism and tradition, which helps to avoid the risk of eccentricity or hasty and premature judgments but may result in overreluctance to accept new ideas. We also wish to have our classification regarded and evaluated as a working hypothesis—a set of proposals to be challenged and vigorously tested, then supported, modified, or rejected and replaced, all to the ultimate advancement of ornithological knowledge.

FORMAT

The basic format of the Check-list consists of headings of systematic categories above the species level (class to subgenus) and, following the heading for genus (or subgenus, if any), accounts of species included therein. The species accounts include the scientific name, the preferred English name, the original citation and type locality, a general summary of the habitat(s) occupied, the geographical distribution, and, when necessary, notes on relevant matters not covered in the foregoing. Fossil records are not listed; these may be found in Pierce Brodkorb's "Catalogue of Fossil Birds" (1963–1978, Bull. Fla. State Mus., Biol. Sci.). Policies followed for each of the portions of the species accounts are discussed beyond.

CRITERIA FOR INCLUSION

All species for which there is a published record of occurrence within the Check-list area are included, either in the main text or in the appendices. In general, only records which appeared in print by 31 December 1981 have been considered, although unpublished records new to the area have been included if the Committee was able to verify them. Records of occurrence within 160 kilometers (100 miles) offshore from any coast within the Check-list area are included unless the locality of the records lies outside the specified limits of that area. For example, no records of occurrence west of the United States-Russian boundary in the Bering Sea region are included even though these could be less than 160 kilometers from U.S. territory, but records within 160 kilometers of the Hawaiian Islands are included.

For inclusion of a species in the main text, records of occurrence must be documented either by a specimen or an unequivocally identifiable photograph. A recording of vocalizations diagnostic for a species could constitute equally valid documentation, but there are no cases in which inclusion in the Check-list is based solely on a recorded vocalization. Specimens provide by far the best evidence as they can be re-examined in many ways and may yield valuable data beyond a simple record of occurrence, but collecting of specimens is not always possible, practical or advisable. Photographs, preferably published, are the next best kind of evidence, and several species are included on the basis of photographic documentation. Much of the distributional data for species whose occurrence in the Check-list area is well documented is based on sight records. Distributional records based on band recoveries are treated in the same manner as observational records. Where such reports significantly extend the otherwise known range of a species, the nature of the record is specified in the text.

Established introductions. Introduced species (deliberate or inadvertent) are deemed to be established if there are persistent records for at least 10 years and satisfactory evidence of maintaining a reasonably stable or increasing population through successful reproduction. Dates of first introduction are given when known with reasonable certainty. All such established introduced species are included in the appropriate place in the main text.

Appendix A. Species recorded in the Check-list area only on the basis of observation are listed in Appendix A. The Committee recognizes that sight records, as they are usually called, can be as satisfactory as photographs for records of occurrence, and that many regional organizations have rigorous standards of acceptance for sightings. Unfortunately, not all sight records can be satisfactorily evaluated, and even some published sightings are rejected by groups concerned with validation of regional lists. The Committee could not assume the enormous task of evaluating all published sight records and decided that its best course was to place in Appendix A all species whose occurrence within our area is based entirely on observational data accepted by the appropriate regional group. The scientific and English names for these species are also included in the main text in brackets, with reference to Appendix A, at the appropriate place in the species sequence. Observational records considered noteworthy and valid are included in the species accounts in the primary list for those species that are also documented by specimens or photographs. However, Appendix A does not include records of occurrence that appear to be human-assisted in any important way; these are treated in other appendices.

Appendix B. This appendix is roughly equivalent to the single hypothetical list of earlier editions of the Check-list. Included in Appendix B are all species that are no longer accepted in the main text; see p. 777 for detailed criteria. The scientific and English names are included in the main text (in brackets) at the appropriate place in the species sequence, with reference to Appendix B.

Appendix C. This appendix includes forms of doubtful identity or of hybrid origin that have been given a formal scientific name. Forms of doubtful identity are those such as Audubon's *Sylvia carbonata,* which cannot be identified as belonging to any known species and of which no specimens exist, or those based on unique type specimens, such as *Emberiza townsendi.* These species do not appear in the main text but are indexed.

Appendix D. This appendix provides a simple list of deliberately introduced species or escaped captives of which there are records but that are deemed neither to have become established nor of sufficient importance to warrant treatment in Appendix B. They do not appear in the main text.

A.O.U. NUMBERS

The policy of providing A.O.U. Numbers for species is continued (see discussion on p. 797 preceding the List of A.O.U. numbers).

NAMES

Scientific names. The Check-list follows the International Code of Zoological Nomenclature adopted by the XV International Congress of Zoology, July 1958, effective on date of publication 6 November 1961, and subsequent amendments approved by the International Commission on Zoological Nomenclature. Unsettled questions on nomenclature are discussed in the Notes sections under the relevant taxonomic category.

Each scientific name is followed by the original citation (journal abbreviations in accordance with the BIOSIS List of Serials), the originally designated type locality, and any valid emendations or restrictions of the latter by subsequent revisers. The Committee has checked most but not all the citations in the original publications; scholars for whom these data are critical are advised to consult original sources.

English names. The Committee follows the policy guidelines of Eisenmann (1955, Trans. Linn. Soc. N.Y., 7, pp. 1–128) and Eisenmann *in* Meyer de Schauensee's "The Species of Birds of South America and Their Distribution" (1966) in regard to choice of names. With respect to orthography and related matters, we follow Cheesman and Oehser (1937, Auk, 54, pp. 333–340) and Parkes (1978, Auk, 95, pp. 324–326). Opinions were sought and received from the Check-list Committee of the American Birding Association and others with a major interest in English names, and we appreciate their cooperation and detailed analysis of English name problems. There is much concern about changes in both scientific and English names of birds. However, absolute stability is not possible in either set of names. Progress in systematic ornithology often dictates changes in scientific names in accordance with nomenclatural codes, and a broadening world-wide experience with birds has indicated that some changes in English names help to avoid confusion and promote uniformity.

In general, the policy guidelines are as follows:

1. Retain well established names for well known and widely distributed species, even if the group name or a modifier is not precisely accurate, universally appropriate, or descriptively the best possible. For example, the group names flycatcher, warbler and oriole are applied to New World species that are not confamilial with Old World taxa to which these same English group names are applied, but in both areas the names are so well established and the differences in relationship so well known that there is little confusion. Species such as the Common Tern are not everywhere "common," the Tennessee Warbler occurs in many other areas, and the Purple Finch is more red than purple. Changing such long established names would only contribute to confusion, not lessen it.

2. For species or groups with extensive extralimital distributions, use English names that are generally accepted on a world-wide basis, provided that such a name does not duplicate another well-established one and is not otherwise inappropriate. For example, we have adopted "Common Moorhen" for *Gallinula chloropus* and "moorhen" as the group name for all species of *Gallinula,* and likewise have adopted "harrier" as the group name for hawks of the genus *Circus.* These group names have long been established for these widely distributed forms in the rest of the English-speaking world. In a few cases of widely distributed species having long established, perhaps equally appropriate names in North America and in Eurasia (such as "Oldsquaw" and "Long-tailed Duck," respectively, for *Clangula hyemalis*), we have retained the American name.

3. Use modifiers for all single-word or group names that are applied to more than one species. For example, Gray Catbird, not simply Catbird, is used for *Dumetella carolinensis,* as the closely-related *Melanoptila glabrirostris* is called the Black Catbird. *Troglodytes troglodytes* is usually known as "The Wren" in English-speaking regions of the Old World where it is the only species of wren present; this unmodified name is inappropriate for the Check-list area, where there are other congeneric and confamilial species known as wrens. In general, modifiers that are comparative terms should have parallel construction, as in Greater Yellowlegs (*Tringa melanoleuca*) and Lesser Yellowlegs (*T. flavipes*); however, we have not rigidly adhered to this policy in cases of well established names such as Great Black-backed Gull (*Larus marinus*) and Lesser Black-backed Gull (*L. fuscus*).

4. In the New World tropics there are many species for which there are no well established English names. Some earlier authors of reference works on Neotropical birds knew some species only from a few study skins and coined names that often proved seriously inappropriate in the light of later knowledge. Previously published names should be used, however, if they are reasonably appropriate and/or well established. We have followed Eisenmann (*loc. cit.*) and Eisenmann *in* Meyer de Schauensee (*loc. cit.*) in conserving such names and in adopting newer ones to replace those that were not well established and were also descriptively inaccurate or suggested wrong relationships or distributions, or were obscure and uninformative patronyms. A new name should be informative about some distinctive aspect of the bird's appearance, habits, relationships or distribution, or some combination of these that is not too lengthy. For example, we have adopted

Chihuahuan Raven for *Corvus cryptoleucus,* a name suggested to us by several persons; normally, we would not replace a well known name such as White-necked Raven, no matter how inappropriate, but our policy would require the additional modifier "American" (because of an African species by the same name), producing a name cumbersome as well as inappropriate.

5. When two taxa previously recognized as different species with different English names are merged, a name applicable to both is needed. If neither taxon has an English name that is suitable for both, a new name must be provided. The few such names proposed by the Committee are intended to be informative rather than fanciful. For example, the taxa listed in the fifth edition as the Myrtle Warbler (*Dendroica coronata*) and Audubon's Warbler (*D. auduboni*) are considered conspecific in this Check-list under the scientific name *D. coronata,* which has priority. The preferred English name is Yellow-rumped Warbler, which has been used in recent years in most publications; this name is equally descriptive of all populations of both forms. Where we have merged two or more forms or divided one form into two or more, we have in the "Notes" section suggested appropriate English names for the taxa if treated in the other mode.

6. Vernacular names derived from a language other than English may be adopted when these are well established and not inappropriate. Many well known names are, of course, derived from classical or other European languages and some are based on verbal names from unwritten native languages. The endemic Hawaiian avifauna includes many species for which Hawaiian-language names are well established and used in English-language publications. We have generally followed authorities on Hawaiian birds in the use of these names, but for species belonging to widespread groups, we have chosen English names that we felt were more informative (e.g., Hawaiian Goose instead of Nene, Hawaiian Crow instead of Alala).

We are fully aware that it is impossible to achieve universal agreement on the best choices for English names, and some differences in preference are inevitable. The Committee hopes that its choices will be acceptable to those who use primarily English names; those requiring greater uniformity may use Linnaean nomenclature.

HABITAT AND DISTRIBUTION

Habitat. This section is intended to provide a concise overview of the kinds of habitats characteristically occupied by a given species. At the very least, this overview gives an indication of whether the species has broad or limited environmental tolerances, of its altitudinal range if relevant, and of the vegetational association usually frequented. The descriptions of habitats use similar phrasing but are not standardized. For many species detailed data on habitat occupancy can be found in regional works and monographs, especially those dealing with the Temperate Zone, and we have not attempted to be similarly exhaustive. For many other species, especially those in tropical regions, the range of habitats occupied is familiar only to specialists or little known to anyone. We believe that even generalized habitat information in conjunction with geographic range allows a better perception of the spatial and ecological distribution of a species than is otherwise possible, and for that reason we have included both kinds of data. If deficiencies in knowledge of habitat occupancy are made evident by the Check-list and this stimulates further study, so much the better.

Many tropical regions include a range of altitudes that support tropical, subtropical, temperate and paramo zones, and in such cases the zones occupied by a species are indicated with capital letters (e.g., Subtropical Zone). As the altitudinal limits of such zones vary with local conditions and especially with latitude, we use the designation "Zone" in a general sense and follow the approximations suggested by Meyer de Schauensee in "A Guide to the Birds of South America" (1970, p. xii) converted to metric units. These are: Tropical Zone, sea level to 1450–1600 m; Subtropical Zone, 1450–1600 to 2400–2800 m; Temperate Zone, 2400–2800 to 3000–3800 m; Paramo Zone, 3000–3800 m to snow line, if present. For migratory species, any distinct differences in habitats used for breeding and for wintering have been indicated in a general way. Emphasis is on the breeding habitat, particularly if the species is widely dispersed in a variety of habitats in winter or if the wintering habitat is poorly known.

Distribution. Geographic ranges are described in detail with the intent of leaving no doubt as to whether or not a species has been recorded within a particular geographic entity, down to the level of states or provinces in large countries and to portions of such units if they, too, are large. Such detailed range accounts are given only for regions within the Check-list area; detailed extralimital ranges are not given as these are better provided in works dealing specifically with those areas.

The Committee considered at length the use of maps to designate ranges for all or most of the included species and reluctantly concluded that this was not feasible within the constraints of time and budget. Written descriptions can be altogether sufficient for ranges of species confined to islands or isolated montane regions or highly restricted lowland habitats. Such descriptions are at least adequate for species with ranges of limited geographic extent even if varied habitats are included, but written descriptions do not provide the means for easy visualization of the ranges of widely distributed continental species. Nevertheless, a written description does provide the essential data for determining range (especially in conjunction with habitat information), and one can readily ascertain if some particular locality is within the overall distribution of the species.

The terms Gulf-Caribbean slope and Pacific slope are frequently used in the distributional accounts of Middle American birds. Throughout most of Middle America, there are mountain ranges that run generally parallel to the long axis of mainland Middle America and divide it into two slopes. The direction of prevailing winds from the Gulf of Mexico and the Caribbean Sea is roughly from northeast to southwest, so that moisture carried by these winds tends to be precipitated in lowlands on the Gulf-Caribbean side and in the mountains, leaving the Pacific slope relatively dry. This condition prevails, in general, from tropical Mexico to northern Costa Rica. The Gulf-Caribbean slope tends to be much wetter and to support more humid forests than the Pacific slope, which tends toward desert in northwestern Mexico and to thorn scrub and deciduous forest south to northwestern Costa Rica. Farther south, the axis of Middle America shifts to a more east-west configuration, and humid conditions occur on both slopes, although there are local areas of aridity. Especially from northern Costa Rica north through tropical Mexico, many species are found only on either the wetter or the drier slope. Belize lies entirely within the Caribbean slope, and El Salvador lies entirely within the Pacific slope, which accounts for the absence of some latitudinally wide-ranging species from one country or the other.

The sequence of localities in extensive geographic distributions within the Check-list area is as follows: northwest to northeast, defining the northern limit of the range; then south to the southwestern limit and east to the southeastern limit, defining the southern limit. A simplified example (omitting intermediate localities) for a wide-ranging continental species would be from northern Alaska east to Newfoundland, south to southern California, and east to the Atlantic coast of Georgia. This system defines a roughly quadrangular space, and the intermediate localities omitted in this example would fill in the details. Gaps or other complexities within the circumscribed range are mentioned parenthetically. Extralimital ranges, if any, follow the same sequence of compass directions.

Many species have smaller or more complex ranges that do not even approximate a quadrangle, but the same basic sequence of localities is used with modifications as needed. In Middle America many distributions follow the northwest to southeast axis of the isthmus, and the descriptive sequence accords well with this. This sequence is used purely for standardization and is not intended to suggest the course of distributional history of the species.

In the Hawaiian Islands, the sequence of localities is from northwest to southeast, roughly following the axis of the archipelago.

Ranges for intraspecific groups that are considered by some authors to represent separate species are given separately for each "group." For nonmigratory species, the geographic area of known and regular residence (*Resident* heading) is described, along with mention of any records of unusual occurrence outside that area. For migratory species, the distribution is described under two headings: *Breeds* and *Winters,* which are self-explanatory; in some cases where breeding and wintering ranges overlap, some sedentary (resident) populations of an otherwise migratory species may be included. For species that have distinct and easily defined sedentary populations (and especially if different "groups" are involved), separate breeding, wintering and resident sections may be included within the limits of these ranges. In migratory species in which breeding or wintering ranges do not encompass all geographic areas where transients occur, a separate migration paragraph is added following the wintering range section; it should be emphasized that this separate statement is primarily for the purpose of adding these areas and, although occasionally included for clarification of migratory patterns (especially if spring and fall routes are different), its omission does not necessarily imply absence of migration. These sections are followed by any records of casual or accidental occurrence outside the usual range.

For each species recorded in the Check-list area only accidentally, there is a a a brief and combined *Habitat & Distribution* account, followed by specific record(s) and citations pertaining to the Check-list area; species of casual occurrence are treated similarly, but citations are not given. For species listed in Appendices A, B and C, only those distributional data relevant to the actual or supposed occurrence of the species within the Check-list area are given.

"Accidental" is applied to a species whose inclusion is based on one or two (rarely more) records and which, on grounds of reasonable probability, is literally accidental within the Check-list area and unlikely to occur there regularly. An example is *Fregata ariel,* a tropical pelagic bird of the Southern Hemisphere that has been recorded in Maine.

"Casual" is applied to a species whose inclusion is based on two or a few records, not enough to constitute regular occurrence but for which subsequent records are not improbable. Examples would be some of the Siberian species recorded in the westernmost Aleutians, not far off their usual migration routes.

xxv

Geographic names. It is a practical impossibility to name all the localities referred to in the Check-list in the language of their country. It is not even practical to attempt complete consistency in the use of a given language; translating all names into English, for example, would lead to absurdities. The principal languages used within the Check-list area are English and Spanish, but there are a few localities where the official language is French or Dutch. The Committee's general policy is to give English place names for large geographical units (countries and larger), large physical features (major mountain ranges, islands, oceans, etc., especially if international in scope), and for other places with well established English names or spellings; examples include Germany (not Deutschland), Brazil (not Brasil), Mexico (not México), Panama (not Panamá), Mexico City (not Ciudad de México), the Isle of Pines (not Isla de Pinos) and the Caribbean Sea (not Mar Caribe). For smaller political units (states and smaller) and smaller geographical features (small islands, mountains, streams, etc.), place names are generally given in the language of the country (including appropriate diacritical marks); examples include Volcán Irazú (Costa Rica), Isla Tiburón (off Sonora) and Darién (province in Panama). In the case of state or province names that are the same as a larger political unit, the words "state of" or "province" are added for further clarification; examples include the state of México (in Mexico), the state of Yucatán (on the Yucatan Peninsula), and Panamá province (in Panama). In a few cases we attempt to conform to common usage as it appears in well known regional works; for example, in recent West Indian publications by James Bond, San Andrés, Providencia and St. Barthélemy are used instead of St. Andrew, Old Providence and St. Bartholomew islands, respectively, and we follow that format. In cases where various choices are available, we have referred to the Atlas Plate series of the National Geographic Society and followed the etymology therein.

Any policy is bound to involve compromises and exceptions that will not find unanimous favor. Our objective is to adopt names that will be clearly recognized and understood, regardless of language, by the greatest number of potential users of the list rather than to achieve a multilingual check-list. In no sense are we proposing a standardized format for place names within the area covered.

Procedure and Future Needs

. Following the publication of the fifth edition, a Special Committee to Study Problems Relating to Avian Classification and the A.O.U. Check-list was established in 1960, consisting of Alden H. Miller (Chairman), Dean Amadon, W. Earl Godfrey, George H. Lowery, Jr., and Robert W. Storer. As a result of their findings, the Committee on Classification and Nomenclature was reestablished in 1962 for the purpose of producing the sixth edition of the Check-list; Miller was named as Chairman, and in 1963, Amadon, Emmet R. Blake, Eugene Eisenmann, Ned K. Johnson, Lowery, Storer and Harrison B. Tordoff were named as members. After Miller's death in 1965, Lowery was appointed Chairman Pro-tem. In 1966, Eisenmann was named Chairman and Thomas R. Howell and Kenneth C. Parkes were added to the Committee, bringing the total membership to nine. Richard C. Banks replaced Tordoff, who resigned in 1972. In 1975, Parkes was named Vice-Chairman, and Lester L. Short was added to the Committee (and appointed Secretary) to replace Amadon, who had resigned. In 1976, Blake resigned and was replaced by Burt L. Monroe, Jr.; Lowery resigned in 1977 for reasons of health and was not replaced. In 1972, Lloyd F. Kiff began preparing a file of distributional records for the Committee, and his extensive data were later given to Monroe for use in preparation of the species accounts.

In the final years of the Committee's activities, the preparation of the manuscript by Monroe was the major factor ensuring production of the Check-list within the proposed time. The accuracy and consistency of the text reflect his time-consuming writing, proof-reading, checking of details, and handling of correspondence within and outside the Commitee, made possible through the generous allowance of time for these activities by the administration of the University of Louisville.

From 1977 through 1981, the Committee, consisting of Eisenmann, Banks, Howell, Johnson, Monroe, Parkes, Short and Storer, produced the final manuscript for the sixth edition. Each member had been assigned certain families and was charged with preparing a list of the included taxa in a preferred sequence, with rationale and discussion about controversial points. This required evaluation of the validity of all the taxa from the family to the species (including the informal category of superspecies) and evaluation of the status of taxa regarded as either species or subspecies by different authors. When the available data were inadequate to permit an estimate of a primitive to derived sequence, conventional arrangements were followed. The completed list and a memorandum discussing the basis for the arrangement were circulated to the entire Committee for review. Any matters of disagreement were discussed, and advice of specialists outside the Committee was solicited whenever appropriate. Differences of opinion were decided by majority vote of the Committee.

The preliminary and final drafts of the systematic and distributional parts of the Check-list, from higher categories to species accounts (including original citations, habitat description, geographic ranges and notes), as well as appendices A–C, the section on A.O.U. numbers, and the index, were prepared by Monroe; Howell composed the original draft of the Preface, and Banks and Monroe compiled the material for inclusion in Appendix D. Drafts of the species accounts were prepared and circulated to the Committee for criticism, and the substantive changes proposed were discussed in correspondence and at meetings and submitted to a vote. Early accounts requiring major revision were rewritten and recirculated, some groups going through as many as three preliminary drafts. A first draft of the entire Check-list was completed by August 1980 and was circulated to regional authorities and specialists in a variety of matters. Minor additions and corrections were routinely incorporated, but all substantive changes proposed were voted on by the Committee. A second complete draft was prepared in December 1981, and this and all still unresolved issues pertaining to the form and content of the list were discussed and voted on at a meeting of the Committee in Louisville, Kentucky, from 28 January to 1 February 1982.

Eisenmann as Chairman initiated the activities of the Committee, chaired its meetings, guided discussions on policy, and participated as a working member, sharing in all of the Committee's functions. Short as Secretary took minutes and kept records and assumed a large burden of responsibility for organizational matters as well as participating in all other Committee activities. Eisenmann died in October 1981, and Monroe was appointed Acting Chairman to oversee the final stages of Committee operation and publication of the Check-list.

The Committee was aided by information and advice from a large number of people. The names of all those who contributed something of value to the list would fill many pages, and the Committee acknowledges its debt to them and its appreciation for their assistance. We especially wish to thank the major regional reviewers (Keith A. Arnold, Andrew J. Berger, James Bond, Paul A. Buckley, John Bull, Jon Dunn, Charles A. Ely, Kimball Garrett, Daniel D. Gibson, W. Earl Godfrey, J. B. Gollop, George A. Hall, C. Stuart Houston, John P. Hubbard, H. Lee Jones, Brina Kessel, Douglas P. Kibbe, Robert L. Pyle, J. Van Remsen, Robert S. Ridgely, William B. Robertson, Arnold Small, Henry M. Stevenson, F. Gary Stiles, Max C. Thompson and Glen E. Woolfenden).

At the conclusion of its task, the Committee realized once again that a check-list of such magnitude will inevitably be incomplete or otherwise deficient in some aspects of virtually all areas. Even our general policies will not be approved by all potential users of the list. We offer the Check-list in its present form as a document containing, we hope, the maximum amount of essential and useful data for those seeking information on the systematics and distribution of birds within the prescribed geographic area, considering the limits of time and budget and the availability of data.

On the latter point, the Committee feels strongly and unanimously the need for continued collection of specimens to resolve unsettled questions of relationship and distribution. At the time of publication of the first A.O.U. Check-list, American ornithology was, in part, still in the pioneering stage, and specimens were needed for correct identification and locality documentation. This is still the situation in many areas included in the sixth edition, and in all regions specimens provide the basic data for studies of systematics and distribution. However, support for such studies is only one reason for continued collecting. Properly prepared and precisely labeled specimens are analogous to books in a library—some are more important and useful than others, but every one has value, each contributes to cumulative knowledge, and the whole constitutes an inexhaustible source of information for researchers now and in the future. Contemporary research requires specimens of many kinds, from traditional museum study skins and osteological and preserved whole-body preparations to samples of organs, tissues, cells, secretions, and intracellular structures and substances. Under the best of circumstances, a single specimen may provide data on all of these things. Fossil material is of continuously increasing importance, as are specimens of eggs, embryos and nests. Knowledge derived from specimens is essential to the accuracy and verifiability of purely observational field studies, and even the conception and planning of such studies require the data base provided by collections.

We wish to stress that judicious and ethical collecting is not only compatible with wise management practices but is ultimately essential for effective programs of wildlife conservation. Even with the most sophisticated instruments and mathematical procedures, analysis still requires sound original data. If data are not already available, they must be obtained—in the field or laboratory, or both—and collecting is an integral part of this process. The A.O.U. Committee on Scientific and Educational Uses of Wild Birds (1975, Auk, 92, pp. 1A–27A) proposed in its report a code of ethics for collectors, designed to prevent abuses and to assure the protection of endangered populations. We emphasize that the number of individual birds taken by scientific collecting in any given period of time is infinitesimally small compared to the numbers lost through natural mortality and human activities unrelated to ornithological research. The greatest threat to avian survival is the alteration of environmental conditions and destruction of habitats by man—primitive or technologically advanced—and the best hope for countering this threat is the presentation of scientifically valid reasons for an alternative course of action. We regard the advancement of ornithological knowledge to be of enormous importance for its inherent value and also for use in planning the maintenance of environmental conditions that will enhance the quality of human life. We therefore support the continued acquisition of such knowledge through appropriate scientific means consistent with these goals.

Committee: †EUGENE EISENMANN, *Chairman*
BURT L. MONROE, JR.,
Acting Chairman and
Editorial Coordinator
KENNETH C. PARKES, *Vice-Chairman*
LESTER L. SHORT, *Secretary*
RICHARD C. BANKS
THOMAS R. HOWELL
NED K. JOHNSON
ROBERT W. STORER

† Deceased.

THE CHECK-LIST: SPECIES

Class **AVES**: Birds

Subclass NEORNITHES: True Birds

Superorder PALEOGNATHAE: Ratites and Tinamous

Order **TINAMIFORMES**: Tinamous

Family **TINAMIDAE**: Tinamous

Genus **TINAMUS** Hermann

Tinamus Hermann, 1783, Tabula Affinit. Anim., pp. 164, 235. Type, by subsequent designation (Apstein, 1915), "Le Magoua" Buffon = *Tetrao major* Gmelin.

Tinamus major (Gmelin). GREAT TINAMOU.

> *Tetrao major* Gmelin, 1789, Syst. Nat., 1 (2), p. 767. Based largely on "Le Magoua" Buffon, Hist. Nat. Ois., 4, p. 507, pl. 24. (in Americae australis, praesertim Cayennae et Gujanae = Cayenne.)

Habitat.—Humid lowland and foothill forest (Tropical and lower Subtropical zones).

Distribution.—*Resident* from southeastern Puebla and central Veracruz south along the Gulf-Caribbean slope of northern Oaxaca, Tabasco, Chiapas, southern Quintana Roo, Guatemala, Belize, Honduras and Nicaragua, on both slopes of Costa Rica (absent from dry northwest) and Panama (except the drier central regions), and in South America from Colombia, Venezuela and the Guianas south, west of the Andes to western Ecuador and east of the Andes to eastern Peru, northern Bolivia and central Brazil.

Genus **NOTHOCERCUS** Bonaparte

Nothocercus Bonaparte, 1856, C. R. Acad. Sci. Paris, 42, p. 881. Type, by subsequent designation (Salvadori, 1895), *Tinamus julius* Bonaparte.

Nothocercus bonapartei (Gray). HIGHLAND TINAMOU.

> *Tinamus Bonapartei* G. R. Gray, 1867, List Birds Br. Mus., pt. 5, p. 97. (valley of Aragua, Venezuela.)

Habitat.—Humid foothill and montane forest, especially in ravines (upper Tropical and Subtropical zones).

Distribution.—*Resident* in the highlands of Costa Rica (north to Cordillera de Guanacaste) and extreme western Panama (Volcán de Chiriquí massif); and the mountains from Colombia and western and northern Venezuela south through Ecuador to northwestern Peru.

Genus CRYPTURELLUS Brabourne and Chubb

Crypturellus Brabourne and Chubb, 1914, Ann. Mag. Nat. Hist., ser. 8, 14, p. 322. Type, by original designation, *C. tataupa* (Temminck) = *Tinamus tataupa* Temminck.

Crypturellus soui (Hermann). LITTLE TINAMOU.

Tinamus soui Hermann, 1783, Tabula Affinit. Anim., p. 165. Based on "Le Soui" Buffon, Hist. Nat. Ois., 4, p. 512, and "Le Soui ou Petit Tinamou, de Cayenne" Daubenton, Planches Enlum., pl. 829. (Cayenne.)

Habitat.—Humid and subhumid forest edge, second growth, thickets, shrubbery bordering cultivated fields, and overgrown pastures (Tropical and lower Subtropical zones).

Distribution.—*Resident* on the Gulf-Caribbean slope from southern Veracruz and northern Oaxaca south through Tabasco, northern Chiapas, Campeche, southern Quintana Roo, Guatemala, Belize, Honduras and Nicaragua, on both slopes of Costa Rica (absent from dry northwest) and Panama (including Isla del Rey in the Pearl Islands, where probably introduced), and in South America (also Trinidad) from Colombia, Venezuela and the Guianas south, west of the Andes to western Ecuador and east of the Andes to eastern Peru, northern Bolivia and central and southeastern Brazil.

Crypturellus cinnamomeus (Lesson). THICKET TINAMOU.

Tinamus (*nothura*) *cinnamomea* Lesson, 1842, Rev. Zool. [Paris], 5, p. 210. (La Union, Centre Amérique = La Unión, El Salvador.)

Habitat.—Brushy forest edge, second growth, dense scrub and thickets, primarily in semi-arid regions but locally entering humid lowland forest (Tropical and lower Subtropical zones).

Distribution.—*Resident* on the Pacific slope of Middle America from central Sinaloa south to northwestern Costa Rica (Guanacaste), and on the Gulf-Caribbean slope from eastern San Luis Potosí and northern Tamaulipas south to the Yucatan Peninsula, northern Guatemala (Petén), Belize, and the interior valleys of eastern Chiapas, central Guatemala and northern Honduras.

Notes.—Also known as RUFESCENT TINAMOU. *C. cinnamomeus* and *C. boucardi,* while widely sympatric, hybridize along zones of habitat contact in the interior of Honduras (see Monroe, 1968, A.O.U. Ornithol. Monogr., no. 7, p. 42). The relationship of *C. cinnamomeus* to various South American forms remains uncertain. Frequently, *C. idoneus* (Todd, 1919), an isolate in northeastern Colombia and western Venezuela that is morphologically very similar, is treated as a subspecies of *C. cinnamomeus,* but others have included *idoneus* and the Middle American populations in a broader species, *C. noctivagus* (Wied, 1820), to include nominate *C. noctivagus* of southeastern Brazil, *C. atrocapillus* (Tschudi, 1844) of western Amazonia, *C. duidae* Zimmer, 1938, of the upper Orinoco, and other related forms. More recently, a superspecies relationship of *C. cinnamomeus* (and *idoneus*) with the wide-ranging, largely Amazonian *C. undulatus* (Temminck, 1815) has been suggested.

Crypturellus boucardi (Sclater). SLATY-BREASTED TINAMOU.

Tinamus boucardi (Sallé MS) Sclater, 1859, Proc. Zool. Soc. London, p. 391. (Playa Vicente and Teotalcingo = Teotalcingo, Oaxaca.)

Habitat.—Humid forest, advanced second growth and bordering thickets (Tropical and lower Subtropical zones).

Distribution.—*Resident* from southern Veracruz (Cerro de Tuxtla) south along the Gulf-Caribbean slope of northern Oaxaca, Tabasco, Chiapas, southern Quintana Roo, Guatemala, Belize, Honduras and Nicaragua to Costa Rica (to the latitude of Puerto Limón, occurring also on the Pacific slope of the Cordillera de Guanacaste).

Notes.—Also known as BOUCARD'S TINAMOU. *C. boucardi* and *C. kerriae* are closely allied and constitute a superspecies. The relationships of the northern Colombian *C. columbianus* (Salvadori, 1895), variously treated as a separate species, a race of *C. boucardi,* or a race of the South American *C. erythropus* (Pelzeln, 1863), remain uncertain (see Blake, 1977, Man. Neotrop. Birds, 1, pp. 41–44). See also comments under *C. cinnamomeus.*

Crypturellus kerriae (Chapman). CHOCO TINAMOU.

Crypturus kerriae Chapman, 1915, Bull. Am. Mus. Nat. Hist., 34, p. 636. (Baudó, Chocó, Colombia.)

Habitat.—Humid foothill forest (upper Tropical and lower Subtropical zones).

Distribution.—*Resident* in extreme eastern Panama (Río Mono to Cerro Quía in southeastern Darién) and northwestern Colombia (foothills of the Serranía de Baudó in Chocó).

Notes.—See comments under *C. boucardi.*

Superorder NEOGNATHAE: Typical Birds

Order GAVIIFORMES: Loons

Notes.—Evidence from fossils (Storer, 1956, Condor, 58, pp. 413–426) and from egg-white proteins (Sibley and Ahlquist, 1972, Peabody Mus. Nat. Hist. Bull., 39, pp. 53–58) suggests that the loons' closest living relatives are the Charadriiformes.

Family GAVIIDAE: Loons

Genus GAVIA Forster

Gavia J. R. Forster, 1788, Enchirid. Hist. Nat., p. 38. Type, by subsequent designation (Allen, 1908), *Colymbus imber* Gunnerus = *Colymbus immer* Brünnich.

Notes.—Authors in the Old World use the group name DIVER for this genus.

Colymbus Linnaeus, 1758, has been frequently used in Old World literature for *Gavia* but has now been suppressed (Int. Comm. Zool. Nomencl., 1956, Opin. Decl. Rend., 13, p. 3).

Gavia stellata (Pontoppidan). RED-THROATED LOON. [11.]

> *Colymbus stellatus* Pontoppidan, 1763, Dan. Atlas, 1, p. 621. Based on *Colymbus maximus stellatus* Willughby, Ornithology, p. 256, pl. 62. (Tame River, Warwickshire, England.)

Habitat.—Ponds and lakes in coastal and alpine tundra, and in coastal flats south of tundra (breeding); primarily bays, seacoasts and estuaries, less frequently on lakes and rivers (nonbreeding).

Distribution.—*Breeds* in North America from Arctic coasts and islands from Alaska to Greenland, south along the Pacific coast through the Aleutian Islands to the Queen Charlotte Islands and (formerly) Vancouver Island, in the interior of the continent to central Yukon, southern Mackenzie, northern Saskatchewan, northern Manitoba, James Bay and (formerly) the north shore of Lake Superior, and along the Atlantic coast to southeastern Quebec (including Anticosti Island), Miquelon Island and northern Newfoundland (Ball Island); and in Eurasia from Iceland and Arctic islands and coasts south to the British Isles, southern Scandinavia, northern Russia, Lake Baikal, Sakhalin, the Kurile Islands, Kamchatka and the Commander Islands. Recorded in summer (and probably breeding) in northeastern Alberta and Newfoundland.

Winters in North America primarily along the Pacific coast south to northern Baja California and northwestern Sonora, and on the Atlantic coast south to Florida, ranging regularly to the Gulf coast of Florida; and in Eurasia south to the Mediterranean, Black and Caspian seas, and along the western Pacific coast to China and Formosa.

Casual in inland areas of North America south through the Rocky Mountains to Colorado and New Mexico, and in the eastern states to Texas and the Gulf coast (sight reports for Arizona).

Gavia arctica (Linnaeus). ARCTIC LOON. [10.]

> *Colymbus arcticus* Linnaeus, 1758, Syst. Nat., ed. 10, 1, p. 135. (in Europa & America boreali = Sweden.)

Habitat.—Lakes in tundra and taiga (breeding); primarily seacoasts, bays and estuaries, less frequently on lakes and rivers (nonbreeding).

Distribution.—*Breeds* [*pacifica* group] in eastern Siberia from the Arctic coast (west to the Indigirka River) south to Anadyrland, and in North America from the Arctic coast of Alaska and Canada, and Banks, Prince of Wales, Victoria and northern Baffin islands, south to St. Lawrence Island, southern Alaska (the base of the Alaska Peninsula and Kodiak Island), southwestern Yukon, southern Mackenzie, northeastern Alberta, northern Manitoba, northwestern Ontario, Belcher Islands and northwestern Quebec; [*arctica* group] in Eurasia from the British Isles east across Arctic coasts to the Lena River, and south to southern Scandinavia, central Russia and Lake Baikal; and [*viridigularis* group] in eastern Siberia (east of *arctica* but not in the Arctic east of the Indigirka River) south to Transbaicalia, Amurland, Sakhalin and Kamchatka, and in western Alaska in the Cape Prince of Wales region. Recorded in summer and possibly breeding [*pacifica* group] in northwestern British Columbia, northern Alberta and northwestern Saskatchewan, and north to Melville Island.

Winters [*pacifica* group] south to Japan and along the Pacific coast of North America south to southern Baja California and southern Sonora, casually in the interior of western North America south to Arizona, New Mexico and Texas; [*arctica* group] in Eurasia south to the Mediterranean, Black, Caspian and Aral seas; and [*viridigularis* group] in Eurasia from the breeding range south to Manchuria, Ussuriland, Japan and the Kurile Islands, probably also to Korea and northern China, and casually in North America from western and southern Alaska south to British Columbia.

Casual [*pacifica* group] in central and eastern North America from the Great Lakes region, southern Ontario, southern Quebec, New Brunswick and Maine south to the Gulf coast and southern Florida, most frequently recorded along the Atlantic coast from Maine to New York (Long Island), also (group uncertain) in the Hawaiian Islands (Oahu); and [*arctica* group] north to the Faroe Islands, Bear Island and Spitsbergen.

Notes.—Known in Old World literature as BLACK-THROATED DIVER. The *pacifica* group is frequently treated as a separate species, *G. pacifica* (Lawrence, 1858) [PACIFIC LOON, 10], distinct from *G. arctica* [BLACK-THROATED LOON], because of reported sympatric breeding in eastern Siberia and western Alaska; however, since some specimens show intergradation between the *pacifica* and *viridigularis* groups, treatment as a single species is continued. A few authors would also consider *G. viridigularis* Dwight, 1918 [GREEN-THROATED LOON, 10.1], as a species distinct from *G. arctica*, but intergradation of the two forms occurs widely in eastern Siberia east of the Lena River and Lake Baikal.

Gavia immer (Brünnich). COMMON LOON. [7.]

Colymbus Immer Brünnich, 1764, Ornithol. Bor., p. 38. (Faeroes.)

Habitat.—Lakes and ponds, occasionally river banks, from tundra south to coniferous forest in either open or wooded situations (breeding); primarily seacoasts, bays and estuaries, in migration regularly along lakes and rivers (nonbreeding).

Distribution.—*Breeds* from western and central Alaska (Seward Peninsula, western Aleutian Islands, and the Brooks Range), northern Yukon, northwestern and southern Mackenzie, central Keewatin, northern Manitoba, northern Ontario, southern Baffin Island, Labrador and Newfoundland south to northern California (at least formerly), northwestern Montana, North Dakota, northern Iowa, northern Illinois, northern Indiana, northern Ohio, northern Pennsylvania, northern New York, southern New England and Nova Scotia; also both coasts of Greenland, Iceland, Scotland (in 1970) and (probably) Bear Island. Summers regularly outside the breeding range south, at least casually, to southern California, Sonora, Texas and the Gulf coast, and in northern Europe and on Jan Mayen.

Winters in North America primarily along the Pacific coast from the Aleutians south to Baja California and Sonora, and along the Atlantic and Gulf coasts from Newfoundland south to southern Florida and west to southern Texas; and in the western Palearctic along the Atlantic coast south to northwestern Africa, casually to the eastern Atlantic islands and through Europe to the Mediterranean and Black seas.

In migration occurs on inland waters through most of the continental United States.

Casual in Cuba (Havana).

Notes.—In the Old World known as GREAT NORTHERN DIVER. *G. immer* and the closely related *G. adamsii* constitute a superspecies; they are considered conspecific by some authors.

Gavia adamsii (Gray). YELLOW-BILLED LOON. [8.]

> *Colymbus adamsii* G. R. Gray, 1859, Proc. Zool. Soc. London, p. 167. (Russian America = Alaska.)

Habitat.—Tundra lakes (breeding); seacoasts, bays and estuaries, less frequently on lakes (nonbreeding).

Distribution.—*Breeds* in North America from northern and western Alaska (south to St. Lawrence Island and the southern Seward Peninsula) east to Banks, Victoria and Prince of Wales islands and northern Keewatin, and south to east-central Mackenzie and east-central Keewatin; and in Eurasia from extreme northwestern Russia east to Siberia (including Novaya Zemlya). Summers outside the breeding range east to northeastern Keewatin (Melville Peninsula) and northern Baffin Island, and south to southern Mackenzie (Great Slave Lake) and southern Keewatin.

Winters in North America along the Pacific coast of Alaska, casually south in coastal areas to California and extreme northern Baja California, and inland to Alberta; and in Eurasia in the breeding range, casually west to Greenland and south to southern Europe, China, Korea and Japan.

Casual or accidental in Saskatchewan, Nevada (Lake Tahoe), Minnesota (Duluth area) and New York (Long Island); a report from Colorado is based on a misidentified specimen of *G. immer*.

Notes.—Known in the Old World as WHITE-BILLED DIVER. See comments under *G. immer*.

Order **PODICIPEDIFORMES**: Grebes

Notes.—The relationships of the grebes are uncertain. Their similarities with the loons and fossil Hesperornithiformes are generally believed to be a result of convergent evolution. According to Sibley and Ahlquist (1972, Peabody Mus. Nat. Hist. Bull., 39, p. 58), the total available evidence indicates that the loons and grebes, while members of the large complex of aquatic nonpasserine birds, are probably more closely related to some other group than to each other.

Family **PODICIPEDIDAE**: Grebes

Genus **TACHYBAPTUS** Reichenbach

> *Tachybaptus* Reichenbach, 1853, Avium Syst. Nat. (1852), p. iii. Type, by monotypy, *Colymbus minor* Gmelin = *Colymbus ruficollis* Pallas.
> *Limnodytes* Oberholser, 1974, Bird Life Tex., 1, p. 63; 2, p. 970. Type, by original designation, *Colymbus dominicus* Linnaeus.

Notes.—For reasons for recognizing *Tachybaptus* as a genus distinct from *Podiceps,* see Storer, 1976, Trans. San Diego Soc. Nat. Hist., 18, pp. 113–126.

Tachybaptus dominicus (Linnaeus). LEAST GREBE. [5.]

Colymbus dominicus Linnaeus, 1766, Syst. Nat., ed. 12, 1, p. 223. Based on "La Grebe de riviere de S. Domingue" Brisson, Ornithologie, 6, p. 64, pl. 5, fig. 2. (in Dominica = Santo Domingo, Dominican Republic.)

Habitat.—Fresh-water lakes, streams, ponds, lagoons and temporary bodies of water, generally in sluggish or quiet situations (Tropical to lower Temperate zones).

Distribution.—*Resident* from southern Baja California, Sinaloa, east-central and southern Texas and the Bahamas (except Grand Bahama) south through most of Middle America (including Cozumel Island), the Greater Antilles (east to Puerto Rico, possibly the Virgin Islands) and South America (also Tobago and Trinidad) to southern Peru and northern Argentina.

Casual north to southern California (bred once, Imperial Dam, 1946), southern Arizona, Sonora, and central and eastern Texas. Accidental in Louisiana (Baton Rouge), sight reports for Florida.

Genus **PODILYMBUS** Lesson

Podilymbus Lesson, 1831, Traité Ornithol., livr. 8, p. 595. Type, by monotypy, *Podiceps carolinensis* Latham = *Colymbus podiceps* Linnaeus.

Podilymbus podiceps (Linnaeus). PIED-BILLED GREBE. [6.]

Colymbus Podiceps Linnaeus, 1758, Syst. Nat., ed. 10, 1, p. 136. Based on "The Pied-Bill Dopchick" Catesby, Nat. Hist. Carolina, p. 91, pl. 91. (in America septentrionali = South Carolina.)

Habitat.—Lakes, ponds, sluggish streams and marshes, in migration and winter also in brackish bays and estuaries.

Distribution.—*Breeds* in southeastern Alaska (Copper River region, at least formerly), and from southwestern and central British Columbia, south-central Mackenzie, northern Alberta, northern Saskatchewan, northern Manitoba, central Ontario, southwestern Quebec, central Maine, southern New Brunswick, Prince Edward Island and Nova Scotia south locally through temperate North America, Middle America, the West Indies and South America to central Chile and southern Argentina (Chubut).

Winters through most of the breeding range from southern British Columbia (west of the Rockies) and the central United States (east of the Rockies) southward, casually farther north. Northern populations are migratory, at least in part, and winter south to Panama; tropical populations are essentially sedentary.

Casual in the Hawaiian Islands; north to southern Alaska, southern Yukon, Baffin Island, Labrador and Newfoundland; and on Bermuda. Accidental in Great Britain and the Azores.

Notes.—*P. podiceps* and *P. gigas* are closely allied and may constitute a superspecies, although both are reported to breed on Lake Atitlán, Guatemala.

Podilymbus gigas Griscom. ATITLAN GREBE.

Podilymbus gigas Griscom, 1929, Am. Mus. Novit., no. 379, p. 5. (Panajachel, 5300 ft., north shore of Lake Atitlan, Guatemala.)

Habitat.—Reed and cattail beds, less frequently open water (Subtropical Zone).

Distribution.—*Resident* on Lake Atitlán, Guatemala (elevation, 1555 meters). **Notes.**—Also known as GIANT PIED-BILLED GREBE. See comments under *P. podiceps.*

Genus PODICEPS Latham

Podiceps Latham, 1787, Gen. Synop. Birds, suppl., 1, p. 294. Type, by subsequent designation (G. R. Gray, 1840), *Colymbus cristatus* Linnaeus.
Dytes Kaup, 1829, Skizz. Entw.-Ges. Eur. Thierw., p. 44. Type, by subsequent designation (G. R. Gray, 1841), *Dytes cornutus* Kaup = *Colymbus auritus* Linnaeus.
Pedetaithya Kaup, 1829, Skizz. Entw.-Ges. Eur. Thierw., p. 44. Type, by monotypy, *Colymbus subcristatus* Jacquin = *Colymbus grisegena* Boddaert.
Proctopus Kaup, 1829, Skizz. Entw.-Ges. Eur. Thierw., p. 49. Type, by monotypy, *Colymbus auritus* Linnaeus.

Notes.—*Podiceps* has been considered by many authors to be a junior synonym of *Colymbus* Linnaeus, 1758, but the latter name has been officially suppressed (see comments under *Gavia*).

Podiceps auritus (Linnaeus). HORNED GREBE. [3.]

Colymbus auritus Linnaeus, 1758, Syst. Nat., ed. 10, 1, p. 135. (in summis Europæ & Americæ lacubus = Vaasa, Finland.)

Habitat.—Marshes, ponds and lakes, occasionally along sluggish streams (breeding); bays, estuaries and seacoasts, and in migration commonly in inland freshwater habitats, especially lakes and rivers (nonbreeding).
Distribution.—*Breeds* in North America from central Alaska, northern Yukon, northwestern and southern Mackenzie, southern Keewatin and northern Manitoba south to eastern Washington, northeastern Idaho, southwestern and northern Montana, northern South Dakota, northwestern Minnesota, central Wisconsin and extreme western Ontario (formerly from northern Ontario, southern Quebec and New Brunswick south to northern Utah, northwestern Nebraska, northeastern Iowa, northern Illinois, northern Indiana and southern New England); and in Eurasia from Iceland, northern Scotland and Scandinavia east across northern Russia and northern Siberia, south to central Russia, Lake Baikal, Amurland, Sakhalin and Kamchatka.
Winters in North America on the Pacific coast from the Aleutians and south-coastal Alaska south to southern California and on the Atlantic and Gulf coasts from Nova Scotia south to southern Florida and west to southern Texas, rarely on inland waters from southern Canada and the Great Lakes southward; and in Eurasia from the seas off Iceland, the Faroe Islands, British Isles and Norway south to the northern Mediterranean, Black and Caspian seas, casually to Madeira, the Azores and northern Africa, and on the Pacific coast from Japan south to Korea.
In migration regularly in North America through the Mississippi and Ohio valleys, and in western Europe.
Casual or accidental in the Hawaiian Islands (Kauai), the Gulf of California, Bermuda, Greenland, Jan Mayen, Spitsbergen and the Commander Islands.
Notes.—In Old World literature known as SLAVONIAN GREBE.

Podiceps grisegena (Boddaert). RED-NECKED GREBE. [2.]

Colymbus grisegena Boddaert, 1783, Table Planches Enlum., p. 55. Based on "Le Jougris" Daubenton, Planches Enlum., pl. 931. (No locality given = France.)

Habitat.—Lakes and large ponds with margins of reeds or sedges, occasionally along quiet rivers (breeding); primarily seacoasts, bays and estuaries, less frequently large inland bodies of water, in migration regularly on lakes, ponds and rivers (nonbreeding).

Distribution.—*Breeds* in North America from western and central Alaska, central Yukon, northwestern and southern Mackenzie, northwestern Saskatchewan, central Manitoba and western and south-central Ontario south to St. Lawrence Island (at least formerly), the Alaska Peninsula, central Washington, northern Montana, northeastern South Dakota and south-central Minnesota, rarely to southwestern Oregon, northern Michigan, southern Quebec and New Hampshire; and in Eurasia from Scandinavia and western Russia south to eastern Europe and Asia Minor, and from eastern Siberia south to Japan.

Winters in North America from the Aleutians south on the Pacific coast to southern California (rarely), and from the Bay of Fundy south on the Atlantic coast to Florida, casually west along the Gulf coast to coastal Louisiana, and central and southeastern Texas; and in Eurasia primarily along the coasts of Norway and the North, Baltic, Caspian, Aegean, Adriatic and Black seas, rarely to the Mediterranean, and along the Pacific coast from Kamchatka south to Korea.

Migrates regularly through the Great Lakes region, rarely through the Ohio and upper Mississippi valleys, and casually elsewhere in interior North America.

Casual north to Hudson Bay, Labrador, Greenland, Iceland, the Faroe Islands and Spitsbergen.

Podiceps nigricollis Brehm. EARED GREBE. [4.]

Podiceps nigricollis C. L. Brehm, 1831, Handb. Naturgesch. Vögel Dtsch., p. 963. (Germany.)

Habitat.—Marshes, ponds and lakes, in migration and winter also salt lakes, bays, estuaries and seacoasts.

Distribution.—*Breeds* in North America from south-central British Columbia, central Alberta, central Saskatchewan, southwestern Manitoba and western Minnesota south to northern Baja California, central Arizona, central and northeastern New Mexico and south-central Texas, east to northeastern Illinois (Cook County), northern Iowa, eastern Nebraska, central Kansas and central Oklahoma, and south locally to central Mexico (recorded Chihuahua, Nayarit, Jalisco and Puebla); in South America (formerly) on temperate lakes in the Eastern Andes of Colombia; in Eurasia locally from the British Isles, southern Scandinavia, central Russia and eastern Siberia south to the Mediterranean region, northern Africa (formerly), Asia Minor and Ussuriland; and locally in eastern and southern Africa.

Winters inland in North America from central California, northern Nevada, northern Utah, northern New Mexico and central Texas, and on the Pacific coast from southern British Columbia, south through most of Mexico to Guatemala; in Eurasia from the British Isles south to the Mediterranean Sea, eastern Africa, Iran and northern India, and on the Pacific coast from Japan south to southern

China; and essentially in the breeding range in South America (formerly) and Africa.

Casual in southern Yukon, southern Mackenzie, and eastern North America from the Great Lakes and New England south to the Gulf coast and Florida; also in Madeira and the Canary Islands.

Notes.—Also known as BLACK-NECKED GREBE. The distinct, isolated, rufous-necked form in Colombia, now apparently extinct, has sometimes been recognized as a separate species, *P. andinus* (Meyer de Schauensee, 1959). *P. nigricollis* (including *andinus*), *P. taczanowskii* Berlepsch and Stolzmann, 1894, of Lago de Junín, Peru, and *P. occipitalis* Garnot, 1826, of the Andes and temperate South America, may constitute a superspecies. *P. caspicus* (Hablitzl, 1783), used by some authors for *P. nigricollis,* has been officially suppressed (Int. Comm. Zool. Nomencl., 1956, Opin. Decl. Rend., 13, p. 121).

Genus **AECHMOPHORUS** Coues

Aechmophorus Coues, 1862, Proc. Acad. Nat. Sci. Philadelphia, 14, p. 229. Type, by original designation, *Podiceps occidentalis* Lawrence.

Aechmophorus occidentalis (Lawrence). WESTERN GREBE. [1.]

Podiceps occidentalis Lawrence, 1858, *in* Baird, Cassin and Lawrence, Rep. Explor. Surv. R. R. Pac., 9, pp. liv, 892, 894. (Pacific coast from Washington Territory to California = Fort Steilacoom, Washington.)

Habitat.—Marshes, lakes and bays, in migration and winter also sheltered seacoasts, less frequently along rivers (Subtropical and Temperate zones).

Distribution.—*Breeds* from southeastern Alaska, south-central British Columbia, central Alberta, central Saskatchewan and southwestern Manitoba south to southern California, north-central Utah, southwestern Colorado, southwestern and northeastern New Mexico, western Nebraska, northwestern Iowa and western Minnesota; and locally in Mexico from Chihuahua and Durango south to northern Guerrero, Puebla and San Luis Potosí.

Winters along the Pacific coast from southern British Columbia, and from Utah, Colorado, New Mexico and western and southern Texas south to southern Baja California, northern Guerrero, Puebla and San Luis Potosí.

Casual north to southwestern and south-coastal Alaska (west to Adak in the Aleutians) and southern Yukon, and east to the Great Lakes, upper Mississippi Valley and southeastern Texas, very rarely to the Atlantic and Gulf coasts from New England to Florida.

Notes.—Two "color" morphs (referred to as "light-phase" and "dark-phase") exist in the populations of *A. occidentalis,* with light-phase birds becoming more scarce in the northern breeding populations. A high degree of assortative mating has been revealed in recent field studies (see Ratti, 1979, Auk, 96, pp. 573–586; Nuechterlein, 1981, Auk, 98, pp. 335–349), suggesting that further research may reveal the two forms to represent distinct species; if so, dark-phase birds will be called *A. occidentalis,* light-phased ones *A. clarkii* (Lawrence, 1858) [CLARK'S GREBE, 1.1] (see Dickerman, 1963, Condor, 65, pp. 66–67; lectotype from Chihuahua).

Order **PROCELLARIIFORMES**: Tube-nosed Swimmers

Notes.—We follow Alexander *et al.* (1965, Ibis, pp. 401–405) in the arrangement of families and genera of the order.

Family **DIOMEDEIDAE**: Albatrosses

Genus **DIOMEDEA** Linnaeus

Diomedea Linnaeus, 1758, Syst. Nat., ed. 10, 1, p. 132. Type, by subsequent designation (G. R. Gray, 1840), *Diomedea exulans* Linnaeus.

Diomedea exulans Linnaeus. WANDERING ALBATROSS. [81.1.]

Diomedea exulans Linnaeus, 1758, Syst. Nat., ed. 10, 1, p. 132. Based primarily on "The Albatross" Edwards, Nat. Hist. Birds, 2, p. 88, pl. 88. (intra tropicos Pelagi & ad Cap. b. Spei = Cape of Good Hope.)

Habitat & Distribution.—*Breeds* on Antarctic islands from the South Atlantic east to the Auckland and Antipodes islands in the South Pacific, and *ranges* at sea generally throughout the southern oceans north to lat. 30°S.

Accidental in California (The Sea Ranch, Sonoma County, 11–12 July 1967; Paxton, 1968, Auk, 85, pp. 502–504) and Panama (Bay of Panama, August 1937; Murphy, 1938, Condor, 40, p. 126); a report from Florida is unsatisfactory.

Notes.—While there will always be uncertainty as to the validity of the northern occurrences with respect to possible transport by man, vagrancies in our area by other southern albatrosses (*e.g., D. cauta* and *D. chlororhynchos*) lend support that the foregoing reports are based on natural wanderings.

[**Diomedea irrorata** Salvin. WAVED ALBATROSS.] See Appendix A.

Diomedea albatrus Pallas. SHORT-TAILED ALBATROSS. [82.]

Diomedea albatrus Pallas, 1769, Spic. Zool., 1, fasc. 5, p. 28. (ad oran Kamtschatcae orientalum . . . ad Insulam Beringii = in the Bering Sea off Kamchatka.)

Habitat.—Pelagic, breeding on the ground on small oceanic islands.

Distribution.—*Breeds* in small numbers on Torishima, in the Seven Islands of Izu; formerly bred on Kita-no-shima (in the Parry group), Kobishi (in the Senkaku Archipelago, southern Ryukyu Islands) and Nishi-no-shima, Tome-shima and Muko-shima (in the Bonin Islands). Reported breeding from Wake Island is erroneous, being based on *D. immutabilis*.

Ranges at sea (commonly prior to 1900, casually in the 20th Century) from Siberia, the Bering Sea and Gulf of Alaska south to the China coast and through the North Pacific to the Hawaiian Islands (primarily the Leeward chain) and southern Baja California.

Diomedea nigripes Audubon. BLACK-FOOTED ALBATROSS. [81.]

Diomedea nigripes Audubon, 1839, Ornithol. Biogr., 5, p. 327. (Pacific Ocean, lat. 30°44′N., long. 146°[W].)

Habitat.—Pelagic, breeding on the open sand on oceanic islands.

Distribution.—*Breeds* in the western Hawaiian Islands (Kure, Midway, Pearl and Hermes Reef, Lisianski, Laysan, French Frigate Shoals, Necker, Nihoa and Kaula), and on Torishima in the Seven Islands of Izu; bred formerly in the northern Bonin Islands (Muko-shima), Volcano Islands (Iwo Jima), Marianas (Agrihan), Marshall Islands (Taongi), and on Marcus, Wake and Johnston islands.

Ranges at sea in the Bering Sea, and in the North Pacific from the Gulf of Alaska south to Baja California and the Revillagigedo Islands, and from Kamchatka south to the coast of China and the Caroline Islands.

Notes.—Occasional hybrids between *D. nigripes* and *D. immutabilis* are reported from the Hawaiian Islands (Midway).

Diomedea immutabilis Rothschild. LAYSAN ALBATROSS. [82.1.]

Diomedea immutabilis Rothschild, 1893, Bull. Br. Ornithol. Club, 1, p. 48. (Laysan Island.)

Habitat.—Pelagic, breeding in open grassy areas on oceanic islands.

Distribution.—*Breeds* on most of the western Hawaiian Islands (Kure east to Nihoa, Niihau and Kauai, and rarely on Moku Manu off Oahu), in the Ogasawara Islands (on Torishima), and, at least formerly, in the Seven Islands of Izu (on Torishima), and on Marcus, Johnston and Wake islands.

Ranges at sea in the Bering Sea, and in the North Pacific from the Gulf of Alaska south (at least uncommonly) to the coast of California and Baja California, and from Kamchatka and the Kurile Islands south to the coast of Japan.

Accidental in Arizona (Yuma).

Notes.—See comments under *D. nigripes.*

Diomedea melanophris Temminck. BLACK-BROWED ALBATROSS. [82.2.]

Diomedea melanophris Temminck, 1828, Planches Color., livr. 77, p. 456 and text. (Cap. Nouvelle Hollande, et mers antarctiques = Cape of Good Hope.)

Habitat & Distribution.—*Breeds* on islands off southern South America, Kerguelen in the southern Indian Ocean, and islands off southern New Zealand, and *ranges* at sea in southern oceans generally north to the Tropic of Capricorn.

Accidental on Martinique (Vauclin, 12 November 1956; Bond, 1959, Birds W. Indies, 4th Suppl., p. 10), near Greenland, and in Iceland, the Faroe Islands, British Isles, Spitsbergen and Norway (sight records for waters off the Atlantic coast of North America from Newfoundland to Florida).

Notes.—Although emended to *D. melanophrys* by Temminck in 1839, the consistent use of the acceptable spelling *D. melanophris* by him in 1828 renders the former an unjustified emendation.

Diomedea cauta Gould. SHY ALBATROSS. [82.3.]

Diomedea cauta Gould, 1841, Proc. Zool. Soc. London (1840), p. 177. (Bass's Straits [off southeastern Australia].)

Habitat & Distribution.—*Breeds* on islands off southern Australia and New Zealand, and *ranges* at sea widely in the southern Pacific and Indian oceans, less commonly in the South Atlantic.

Accidental off the coast of Washington (lat. 47°55'N., long. 125°37'W., ca. 39 miles west of the mouth of Quillayute River, 1 September 1951; Slipp, 1952, Auk, 69, pp. 458–459).

Notes.—Also known as WHITE-CAPPED ALBATROSS. The specimen from off Washington has been referred to the race breeding in Australian waters, *D. c. cauta*.

Diomedea chlororhynchos Gmelin. YELLOW-NOSED ALBATROSS. [83.]

Diomedea chlororhynchos Gmelin, 1789, Syst. Nat., 1 (2), p. 568. Based on the "Yellow-nosed Albatross" Latham, Gen. Synop. Birds, 3 (1), p. 309, pl. 94. (Ad caput bonae spei, et in mari australi extra tropicos = off Cape of Good Hope.)

Habitat & Distribution.—*Breeds* on islands in the South Atlantic and southern Indian oceans, and *ranges* widely at sea in these southern oceans east to Australian and New Zealand waters.

Casual or accidental in Quebec (Gulf of St. Lawrence), New Brunswick (mouth of Bay of Fundy), Maine (East Freyburg, and off Machias Seal Island), New York (off Freeport, Long Island), Maryland (Ocean City), Louisiana (Holly Beach) and Texas (South Padre Island), also sight records offshore from Newfoundland and Maine south to Florida.

[Diomedea chrysostoma Forster. GRAY-HEADED ALBATROSS.] See Appendix B.

[Genus PHOEBETRIA Reichenbach]

Phoebetria Reichenbach, 1853, Avium Syst. Nat. (1852), p. v. Type, by original designation, *Diomedea fuliginosa* Gmelin = *Diomedea palpebrata* Forster.

[Phoebetria palpebrata (Forster). LIGHT-MANTLED ALBATROSS.] See Appendix B.

Family PROCELLARIIDAE: Shearwaters and Petrels

Notes.—See comments under Hydrobatidae.

[Genus MACRONECTES Richmond]

Ossifraga (not Wood, 1835) Hombron and Jacquinot, 1844, C. R. Acad. Sci. Paris, 18, p. 356. Type, by monotypy, *Procellaria gigantea* Gmelin.
Macronectes Richmond, 1905, Proc. Biol. Soc. Wash., 18, p. 76. New name for *Ossifraga* Hombron and Jacquinot, preoccupied.

[Macronectes giganteus (Gmelin). ANTARCTIC GIANT-PETREL.] See Appendix A.

Genus FULMARUS Stephens

Fulmarus Stephens, 1826, *in* Shaw, Gen. Zool., 13 (1), p. 233. Type, by subsequent designation (G. R. Gray, 1855), *Procellaria glacialis* Linnaeus.
Priocella Hombron and Jacquinot, 1844, C. R. Acad. Sci. Paris, 18, p. 357.

Fulmarus glacialis (Linnaeus). NORTHERN FULMAR. [86.]

> *Procellaria glacialis* Linnaeus, 1761, Fauna Svecica, ed. 2, p. 51. Based primarily on "Mallemucke" Martens, Spitsbergen Groenland Reise, p. 68, pl. N, fig. c. (in mari septentrionali intra circulum arcticum = Spitsbergen.)

Habitat.—Pelagic, breeding primarily on sea cliffs, less frequently on low and flat rocky islands.

Distribution.—*Breeds* in western North America on islands in the Bering Sea (Hall, St. Matthew and the Pribilofs), in the Aleutians (Buldir, Davidof, Gareloi, Bobrof and Chagulak islands) and in the northern Gulf of Alaska (on Seal, Semidi, Barren and Chiswell islands); in the Canadian Arctic on Devon Island, eastern Baffin Island (south to Cumberland Sound and Admiralty Bay) and Newfoundland (since 1973); and from coastal Greenland (north of Disko Bay and the Liverpool coast) east through Jan Mayen, Iceland, the Faroe Islands, British Isles, northwestern France, Norway, Bear Island, Spitsbergen, Franz Josef Land, northern Novaya Zemlya and the Chukotski Peninsula (Plover Bay). Summers regularly outside the breeding range in the Bering and Chukchi seas, in Arctic Canada west to Banks and Melville islands, in the Gulf of St. Lawrence, in the English Channel and North Sea, and along the coast of Kamchatka.

Winters at sea in the southern Bering Sea and Pacific Ocean from the Aleutians south to Japan, the Seven Islands of Izu, the Hawaiian Islands and southern Baja California; and in the Atlantic Ocean from Greenland, Labrador, Spitsbergen and northern Norway south to the Newfoundland Banks, Georges Bank off Massachusetts, and northern France, less commonly but regularly off the east coast of the United States to South Carolina.

Casual in Ontario, Quebec and continental Europe.

Notes.—Known in Old World literature as the FULMAR. *F. glacialis* and *F. glacialoides* may constitute a superspecies.

Fulmarus glacialoides (Smith). SOUTHERN FULMAR.

> *Procellaria glacialoides* Smith, 1840, Illus. Zool. S. Afr., pt. 11, pl. 51. (neighbourhood of the South African coast.)

Habitat & Distribution.—*Breeds* on cliffs around Antarctica and on Antarctic islands in the South Atlantic and southern Indian oceans, and *ranges* at sea in southern oceans north to southern Australia, New Zealand, central South America and South Africa.

Accidental off western Mexico (near Mazatlán, Sinaloa; Friedmann *et al.,* 1950, Pac. Coast Avifauna, no. 29, p. 15). The locality of Townsend's specimen reported from the "mouth of the Columbia River, Oregon" is deemed erroneous (Stone, 1930, Auk, 47, pp. 414–415).

Notes.—Also known as SLENDER-BILLED FULMAR. *F. antarcticus* Stephens, 1826, often used for this species, cannot be definitely identified as to species (Falla, 1937, Br. Aust. N. Z. Antarct. Res. Exped. Rep. (B), 2, pp. 158–164). See also comments under *F. glacialis.*

Genus **DAPTION** Stephens

> *Daption* Stephens, 1826, *in* Shaw, Gen. Zool., 13 (1), p. 239. Type, by original designation, *Procellaria capensis* Linnaeus.

Daption capense (Linnaeus). CAPE PETREL. [102.]

Procellaria capensis Linnaeus, 1758, Syst. Nat., ed. 10, 1, p. 132. Based primarily on "The white and black Spotted Peteril" Edwards, Nat. Hist. Birds, 2, p. 90, pl. 90, right fig. (ad Cap. b. Spei = Cape of Good Hope.)

Habitat & Distribution.—*Breeds* in cliff niches and burrows on Antarctic and subantarctic islands in the South Atlantic and southern Indian oceans and in New Zealand waters, and *ranges* at sea regularly in southern oceans north to the Tropic of Capricorn, less frequently to the Equator.

Accidental in Maine (Harpswell, Cumberland County, June 1873; Norton, 1922, Auk, 39, pp. 101–103), Ireland, continental Europe, Sicily and Ceylon. Sight reports in the Pacific Ocean off California have been questioned, although one (off Monterey, 1962) seems to be well documented; a record from off the coast of Acapulco, Guerrero, is regarded as "indefinite" (Friedmann *et al.*, 1957, Pac. Coast Avifauna, no. 33, p. 402), and an early California specimen ("coast of California, opposite Monterey," before 1853; Lawrence, 1853, Ann. Lyc. Nat. Hist. N.Y., 6, pp. 4–7) is regarded as of uncertain origin. Some authors question the origin of all Northern Hemisphere records.

Notes.—Also known as PINTADO PETREL and CAPE PIGEON.

Genus **PTERODROMA** Bonaparte

Pterodroma Bonaparte, 1856, C. R. Acad. Sci. Paris, 42, p. 768. Type, by subsequent designation (Coues, 1866), *Procellaria macroptera* Smith.

Pterodroma hasitata (Kuhl). BLACK-CAPPED PETREL. [98.]

Procellaria hasitata Kuhl, 1820, Beitr. Zool., abth. 1, p. 142. (No locality given = Dominica.)

Habitat.—Pelagic, breeding in burrows on mountain summits.

Distribution.—*Breeds* at high elevations on Hispaniola (Morne La Selle east to western end of Sierra de Baorucó), eastern Cuba (Monte La Bauja), Jamaica (Blue Mountains, formerly), Guadeloupe, Dominica (where probably extirpated) and (possibly) Martinique.

Ranges at sea in the Caribbean and western Atlantic Ocean from about the Tropic of Cancer south to eastern Brazil, rarely to the Atlantic coast of North America from Maine to Florida (although regular and sometimes in large numbers off North Carolina).

Accidental in Ontario, New York, western Virginia, Kentucky, Ohio, western Florida (Leon County) and England.

Notes.—The possibly extinct, dark form that bred on Jamaica has been regarded by some to represent a distinct species, *Pterodroma caribbaea* Carte, 1866 [JAMAICAN PETREL]. *P. hasitata* and *P. cahow* constitute a superspecies; they are considered conspecific by some authors. In addition, the Pacific forms *P. phaeopygia* and *P. externa* are considered by some to be representatives of the complex and conspecific with *P. hasitata*. All four species are best treated as constituting a superspecies.

Pterodroma cahow (Nichols and Mowbray). BERMUDA PETREL.

Æstrelata cahow Nichols and Mowbray, 1916, Auk, 33, p. 194. (Gurnet Head Rock, Bermuda.)

Habitat.—Pelagic, breeding in burrows in sandy areas on islets.

Distribution.—*Breeds* in Bermuda, persisting in small numbers on islets in Castle Roads, formerly also the Bahamas (Crooked Island, bone deposits in caves).

Ranges at sea but not definitely recorded away from the breeding grounds.

Notes.—Also known as the CAHOW. See comments under *P. hasitata.*

Pterodroma phaeopygia (Salvin). DARK-RUMPED PETREL. [98.5.]

Œstrelata phæopygia Salvin, 1876, Trans. Zool. Soc. London, 9, p. 507, pl. 88, figs. 1 and 2. (Chatham Island, Galapagos.)

Habitat.—Pelagic, breeding in burrows at higher elevations on islands.

Distribution.—*Breeds* [*sandwichensis* group] in the interior highlands of the Hawaiian Islands (Kauai, Maui and Hawaii, probably also on Molokai and Lanai, formerly also Oahu); and [*phaeopygia* group] in the Galapagos Islands (Isabela, San Salvador, Santa Cruz, Floreana and San Cristóbal.

Ranges at sea [*sandwichensis* group] in the vicinity of the Hawaiian Islands; and [*phaeopygia* group] along the Pacific coast of Middle America in the vicinity of Clipperton Island and off Costa Rica.

Notes.—The two groups are sometimes regarded as distinct species, *P. sandwichensis* (Ridgway, 1884) [HAWAIIAN PETREL, 98.5] and *P. phaeopygia* [GALAPAGOS PETREL]. See also comments under *P. hasitata.*

Pterodroma externa (Salvin). WHITE-NECKED PETREL. [98.7.]

Œstrelata externa Salvin, 1875, Ibis, p. 373. (Island of Masafuera and Juan Fernandez.)

Habitat & Distribution.—*Breeds* [*externa* group] on Más Afuera Island in the Juan Fernandez Islands off Chile, and [*cervicalis* group] on Raoul Island in the Kermadecs north of New Zealand, and *ranges* [both groups] primarily in the South Pacific, occasionally north as far as lat. 21°N.

Casual [*externa* group] off the Pacific coast of Middle America (ca. 20 miles northwest of Clipperton Island; Loomis, 1918, Proc. Calif. Acad. Sci., ser. 4, 2, p. 95); also near Hawaiian waters (lat. 19°45′N., long. 161°52′W., 135 miles southwest of Kaula, 16 November 1965, specimen USNM); also a sight record [*cervicalis* group] for Hawaiian waters (ca. 60 miles east of Hawaii, W. King and D. Husted), and others (not identified to group) from Hawaiian waters within 100 miles of island areas.

Notes.—The two widely isolated and distinct breeding groups are sometimes regarded as separate species, *P. externa* [JUAN FERNANDEZ PETREL] and *P. cervicalis* (Salvin, 1891) [WHITE-NECKED PETREL]. See also comments under *P. hasitata.*

[**Pterodroma rostrata** (Peale). TAHITI PETREL.] See Appendix A.

[**Pterodroma alba** (Gmelin). PHOENIX PETREL.] See Appendix A.

Pterodroma inexpectata (Forster). MOTTLED PETREL. [99.]

Procellaria inexpectata J. R. Forster, 1844, Descr. Anim., p. 204. (in Oceano antarctico = Antarctic Ocean.)

Habitat.—Pelagic, breeding primarily along inland mountain bluffs and in burrows on small islands.

Distribution.—*Breeds* in New Zealand (inland ranges of North and South islands, this population now much reduced) and on islands in the region (Curvier and Stewart islands, islets in Preservation Inlet and around Puysegue Point, and in the Snares, Auckland, Antipodes, Bounty and Chatham groups).

Ranges at sea in Antarctic waters between New Zealand and South America, and throughout much of the Pacific from Japan, the southern Bering Sea and Gulf of Alaska south to the Hawaiian Islands and California (mostly far-offshore waters).

Casual along the Pacific coast from British Columbia to California, and in the vicinity of the Galapagos Islands. Accidental in New York (Mount Morris, Livingston County, 1880).

Notes.—Also known as SCALED PETREL.

[**Pterodroma solandri** (Gould). SOLANDER'S PETREL.] See Appendix A.

Pterodroma ultima Murphy. MURPHY'S PETREL. [100.1.]

Pterodroma ultima Murphy, 1949, *in* Mayr and Schuz (eds.), Ornithol. Biol. Wiss., p. 89. (Oeno Island, south Pacific.)

Habitat & Distribution.—*Breeds* in burrows in the Austral, Tuamotu and other islands in the south-central Pacific Ocean, and *ranges* at sea north, possibly regularly, to the tropical North Pacific.

Casual in the Hawaiian Islands at Kure, French Frigate Shoals, and off Oahu (7 miles southwest of Barber's Point), in Oregon (Lincoln County, 15 June 1981; specimen USNM), and at sea ca. 350 miles west of Santa Barbara, California (lat. 34°19′N., long. 126°24′W.); a report of *P. solandri* from off California (between Cape Mendocino and Point Reyes, within 60 miles of shore, 21 May 1981, 20 individuals, photograph, R. Pitman; Am. Birds, 35: 973, 1981) apparently also pertains to *P. ultima*.

Pterodroma neglecta (Schlegel). KERMADEC PETREL. [98.4.]

Procellaria neglecta Schlegel, 1863, Mus. Hist. Nat. Pays-Bas, livr. 4, Procell., p. 10. (Kermadec and Sunday Islands.)

Habitat & Distribution.—*Breeds* in burrows on islands in the South Pacific (Kermadecs and Lord Howe east to the Juan Fernandez group), and *ranges* at sea generally through the South Pacific.

Accidental in the Hawaiian Islands (Kure, 30 April 1923, A. Wetmore; Gould and King, 1967, Auk, 84, pp. 592–593) and England.

The specific identity of a bird photographed in Pennsylvania (Heintzelman, 1961, Wilson Bull., 73, pp. 262–267) and reported as *P. neglecta* is uncertain (Palmer, 1962, Handb. North Am. Birds, 1, p. 211); the record may be referable to either *P. neglecta* or *P. arminjoniana*. Reports from Mexican waters are considered hypothetical (Friedmann *et al.,* 1957, Pac. Coast Avifauna, no. 33, p. 403).

Notes.—Also known as VARIABLE PETREL and sometimes treated under the name *P. phillipii* (G. R. Gray, 1862). *P. neglecta* and *P. arminjoniana* constitute a superspecies; they are considered conspecific by some authors.

Pterodroma arminjoniana (Giglioli and Salvadori). HERALD PETREL. [98.2.]

> *Æstrelata arminjoniana* Giglioli and Salvadori, 1869, Ibis, p. 62. (near Trinidad [= Trindade] Island, in the South Atlantic.)

Habitat & Distribution.—*Breeds* on islands on bare rock under overhanging ledges or plants [*arminjoniana* group] in the South Atlantic and Indian oceans, and [*heraldica* group] in the South Pacific, and *ranges* at sea generally in the oceans near the respective breeding grounds.

Casual [*arminjoniana* group] in the North Atlantic off North Carolina and east of the Lesser Antilles (lat. 21°51′N., long. 43°35′W.). Accidental [*arminjoniana* group] in New York (Caroline Center near Ithaca) and England; and [*heraldica* group] in the Hawaiian Islands (French Frigate Shoals, 14 March 1968; Amerson, 1971, Atoll Res. Bull., no. 150, p. 125).

Notes.—The two groups are sometimes regarded as separate species, *P. arminjoniana* [TRINDADE or SOUTH TRINIDAD PETREL, 98.2] and *P. heraldica* (Salvin, 1888) [HERALD PETREL, 98.7]. See also comments under *P. neglecta*.

Pterodroma cookii (Gray). COOK'S PETREL. [98.3.]

> *Procellaria Cookii* G. R. Gray, 1843, *in* Dieffenbach, Travels N. Z., 2, p. 199. (New Zealand.)

Habitat.—Pelagic, breeding in burrows on islands.

Distribution.—*Breeds* on islands off the coast of New Zealand (Little and Great Barrier, off North Island; and Codfish, off Stewart Island).

Ranges at sea from the northern and eastern Pacific Ocean south to New Zealand and Peru, and uncommonly but regularly to the Aleutians (near Adak), off California (especially Davidson Seamount), and off Mexico (between the Revillagigedo Islands and southern Baja California).

Notes.—Also known as BLUE-FOOTED PETREL. *P. cookii* and *P. defilippiana* (Giglioli and Salvadori, 1869), from the Juan Fernandez Islands, constitute a superspecies; they are considered conspecific by some authors.

Pterodroma hypoleuca (Salvin). BONIN PETREL. [99.1.]

> *Œstrelata hypoleuca* Salvin, 1888, Ibis, p. 359. (Krusenstern Is., in North Pacific Ocean = Hawaiian Leeward Islands, probably Laysan; see Murphy, 1951, Am. Mus. Novit., no. 1512, pp. 17–18.)

Habitat.—Pelagic, breeding in burrows in oceanic islands.

Distribution.—*Breeds* in the western Hawaiian Islands (Kure east to Nihoa), and in the Bonin and Volcano islands.

Ranges at sea in the western North Pacific in the vicinity of the breeding grounds and from Sakhalin south to Formosa and the Seven Islands of Izu.

Notes.—The relationships of this species and several closely allied forms that breed in southern waters from Australia and New Zealand east to South America, *P. nigripennis, P. axillaris* (Salvin, 1893), *P. leucoptera* (Gould, 1844) and *P.*

longirostris remain doubtful and controversial; some authors include *P. cookii* in the complex in addition to the above.

Pterodroma nigripennis (Rothschild). BLACK-WINGED PETREL. [100.2.]

Œstrelata nigripennis Rothschild, 1893, Bull. Br. Ornithol. Club, 1, p. 57. (Kermadec Islands.)

Habitat & Distribution.—*Breeds* in burrows in the Kermadec and Austral islands, off New Zealand, and *ranges* at sea, primarily in the South Pacific near the breeding grounds.

Accidental in Hawaiian waters (ca. 60 miles west of Hawaii, 12 November 1965; Berger, 1972, Hawaiian Birdlife, p. 239).

Notes.—See comments under *P. hypoleuca.*

[**Pterodroma longirostris** (Stejneger). STEJNEGER'S PETREL.] See Appendix A.

Genus **BULWERIA** Bonaparte

Bulweria Bonaparte, 1843, Nuovi Ann. Sci. Nat. Bologna (1842), 8, p. 426. Type, by monotypy, *Procellaria bulwerii* Jardine and Selby.

Bulweria bulwerii (Jardine and Selby). BULWER'S PETREL. [101.]

Procellaria bulwerii Jardine and Selby, 1828, Illus. Ornithol., 2, pl. 65. (Madeira or the small islands adjacent.)

Habitat.—Pelagic, breeding in rocky holes, crevices in cliffs, and on the ground under thick vegetation.

Distribution.—*Breeds* in the Pacific Ocean in the Hawaiian Islands (Midway east to Kaula Rock, and on small islets around the main islands), on small islands off the coast of China, in the Bonin, Volcano, Marquesas and Phoenix islands, and on Johnston Island; and in the Atlantic Ocean in the Azores, Madeira, Canary and Cape Verde islands.

Ranges at sea in the western Pacific Ocean in the breeding areas and from Japan to Formosa and the Moluccas; in the eastern Atlantic Ocean from England to the Cape Verde Islands, casually to the Mediterranean Sea and the western Atlantic (off Trinidad); and to the equatorial, western and central Indian Ocean. A sight report from Florida is unsatisfactory.

Notes.—*B. bulwerii* and *B. fallax* constitute a superspecies; they are sometimes considered conspecific.

Bulweria fallax Jouanin. JOUANIN'S PETREL. [101.1.]

Bulweria fallax Jouanin, 1955, Oiseau, 25, pp. 158, 159, 160. (en mer au point approximatif [lat.] 12°30′N., [long.] 55°E. [northwestern Indian Ocean].)

Habitat & Distribution.—*Breeds* presumably on small islands in the Indian Ocean off Arabia, and *ranges* at sea primarily in the northwestern Indian Ocean.

Accidental in the Hawaiian Islands (Lisianski Island, 4 September 1967; Clapp, 1971, Condor, 73, p. 490).

Notes.—See comments under *B. bulwerii.*

Genus **PROCELLARIA** Linnaeus

Procellaria Linnaeus, 1758, Syst. Nat., ed. 10, 1, p. 131. Type, by subsequent designation (G. R. Gray, 1840), *Procellaria aequinoctialis* Linnaeus.

Adamastor Bonaparte, 1856, C. R. Acad. Sci. Paris, 43, p. 594. Type, by original designation, *Procellaria haesitata* Forster = *Procellaria cinerea* Gmelin.

[Procellaria cinerea Gmelin. GRAY PETREL.] See Appendix B.

Procellaria parkinsoni Gray. BLACK PETREL.

Procellaria parkinsoni G. R. Gray, 1862, Ibis, p. 245. (New Zealand.)

Habitat.—Pelagic, breeding in burrows on islands and at high elevations in mountains.

Distribution.—*Breeds* on islands off New Zealand (Great Barrier and Little Barrier) and, at least formerly, in the mountainous interior ranges of both North and South islands, New Zealand.

Ranges at sea west to Australia and east, apparently regularly, to the vicinity of the Galapagos Islands and waters off the west coast of Middle America (ca. 50 miles off Guatemala, 14 April 1973, and 17 miles off the Nicoya Peninsula, Costa Rica, 21 April 1973, plus many sight records between Mexico and Panama probably referable to this species; Jehl, 1974, Auk, 91, pp. 687–689).

Notes.—Also known as PARKINSON'S PETREL. *P. parkinsoni, P. westlandica* Falla, 1946, of New Zealand, and *P. aequinoctialis* Linnaeus, 1758, of New Zealand and South American waters, constitute a superspecies; they are sometimes considered conspecific.

Genus **CALONECTRIS** Mathews and Iredale

Calonectris Mathews and Iredale, 1915, Ibis, pp. 590, 592. Type, by original designation, *Procellaria leucomelas* Temminck.

Notes.—For reasons for separation of *Calonectris* from *Puffinus,* see Kuroda, 1954, Class. Phyl. Tubinares, pp. 102–104, 117.

Calonectris leucomelas (Temminck). STREAKED SHEARWATER. [88.1.]

Procellaria leucomelas Temminck, 1835, Planches Color., livr. 99, pl. 587. (seas of Japan and Nagasaki Bay.)

Habitat & Distribution.—*Breeds* on small wooded islands from the Bonin and Pescadores groups to the coast of Japan, and *ranges* at sea in the western Pacific Ocean from Korea and Japan to Borneo and New Guinea, casually to Ceylon.

Accidental in Monterey Bay, California, 3 October 1975 (Morejohn, 1978, Auk, 95, p. 420), and 9 October 1977 (Roberson, Morlan and Small, 1977, Am. Birds, 31, pp. 1097–1098), also a sight record in October 1978. The inclusion of the Hawaiian Islands in the range by Vaurie (1965, Birds Palearctic, 1, p. 25) was based on an unsubstantiated report by a Japanese fishing vessel "in Hawaiian waters."

Calonectris diomedea (Scopoli). CORY'S SHEARWATER. [88.]

Procellaria diomedea Scopoli, 1769, Annus I, Hist.-Nat., p. 74. (No locality given = Tremiti Islands, Adriatic Sea.)

Habitat.—Pelagic, breeding in burrows and crevices on islands.

Distribution.—*Breeds* in the eastern Atlantic Ocean (in the Azores, on Berlenga Island off Portugal, and in the Madeira, Canary and Cape Verde islands) and the Mediterranean Sea (from Gibraltar locally east to the Adriatic Sea, the Balkans, Turkey and the Near East).

Ranges at sea in the Mediterranean and the Atlantic Ocean from about lat. 44°N. to lat. 36°S., reaching the coasts of North America (from Newfoundland and Nova Scotia south to Florida), Brazil and Europe (north irregularly to England and France).

Casual in the Gulf of Mexico (from Texas to Florida), the Bahamas (Grand Bahama), Cuba (off Gibara), Barbados, Trinidad, the Faroe Islands, continental Europe, Syria, South Africa and New Zealand.

Genus PUFFINUS Brisson

Puffinus Brisson, 1760, Ornithologie, 1, p. 56; 6, p. 130. Type, by tautonymy, *Puffinus* Brisson = *Procellaria puffinus* Brünnich.
Ardenna Reichenbach, 1853, Avium Syst. Nat. (1852), p. iv. Type, by original designation, *Procellaria minor* Faber = *Procellaria gravis* O'Reilly.
Thyellodroma Stejneger, 1889, Proc. U.S. Natl. Mus., 11 (1888), p. 93. Type, by original designation, *Puffinus sphenurus* Gould = *Puffinus chlororhynchus* Lesson.
Neonectris Mathews, 1913, Austral Avian Rec., 2, p. 12. Type, by original designation, *Puffinus brevicaudus* Gould = *Procellaria tenuirostris* Temminck.
Hemipuffinus Iredale, 1913, Austral Avian Rec., 2, p. 20. Type, by original designation, *Puffinus carneipes* Gould.

Puffinus creatopus Coues. PINK-FOOTED SHEARWATER. [91.]

Puffinus creatopus (Cooper MS) Coues, 1864, Proc. Acad. Nat. Sci. Philadelphia, 16, p. 131. (ex insula "San Nicholas" prope California = San Nicolas Island, California.)

Habitat.—Pelagic, breeding in burrows on islands.

Distribution.—*Breeds* on islands off Chile (Más a Tierra and Santa Clara in the Juan Fernandez group, and Isla Mocha in Arauco Bay).

Ranges at sea mostly adjacent to land masses off the Pacific coast of the Americas, north at least as far as the southern Bering Sea and Gulf of Alaska.

Notes.—*P. creatopus* and the closely allied *P. carneipes* constitute a superspecies and are sometimes considered to be conspecific.

Puffinus carneipes Gould. FLESH-FOOTED SHEARWATER. [95.1.]

Puffinus carneipes Gould, 1844, Ann. Mag. Nat. Hist., ser. 1, 13, p. 365. (Small islands off Cape Leeuwin, western Australia.)

Habitat.—Pelagic, breeding in burrows on islands.

Distribution.—*Breeds* on islands off the south coast of western Australia (from Cape Leeuwin to Archipelago of the Recherche), on Lord Howe Island, on islands off New Zealand (eastern coast of North Island), and on St. Paul Island in the Indian Ocean.

Ranges at sea from the breeding areas throughout most of the Pacific Ocean to the Hawaiian Islands, the west coast of North America (from the southern Bering Sea and Gulf of Alaska south, uncommonly, to California), waters off Japan and the Juan Fernandez Islands off Chile, and to the Indian Ocean (north to the Arabian Sea and Ceylon).

Notes.—Also known as PALE-FOOTED SHEARWATER. See comments under *P. creatopus*.

Puffinus gravis (O'Reilly). GREATER SHEARWATER. [89.]

> *Procellaria Gravis* O'Reilly, 1818, Voy. Greenland Adj. Seas, p. 140, pl. 12, fig. 1. (Latitude of Cape Farewell and Staten Hook, frequently Newfoundland in summer.)

Habitat.—Pelagic, breeding in burrows on oceanic islands.

Distribution.—*Breeds* in the South Atlantic Ocean on Tristan da Cunha (Nightingale and Inaccessible islands), on Gough Island, and in the Falkland Islands.

Ranges at sea throughout the Atlantic Ocean from Greenland and Iceland south to Tierra del Fuego and South Africa, occurring between May and September off the Atlantic coast of North America from Newfoundland to Florida, in June in the Davis Strait off Labrador and Greenland, and between August and October off Iceland, the Faroe Islands, and the west coast of Europe (including the western Mediterranean east to Algeria and Sardinia).

Casual in the Gulf of Mexico (from eastern Texas to Florida), West Indies (off Puerto Rico and St. Lucia), Costa Rica (Tortuguero), Trinidad and continental Europe, also sight reports for California (Monterey Bay) and the New Zealand region.

Notes.—Known in Old World literature as GREAT SHEARWATER.

Puffinus pacificus (Gmelin). WEDGE-TAILED SHEARWATER. [96.1.]

> *Procellaria pacifica* Gmelin, 1789, Syst. Nat., 1 (2), p. 560. Based on the "Pacific Petrel" Latham, Gen. Synop. Birds, 3 (2), p. 416. (circa insulam Europa aliasque maris pacifici = Kermadec Islands.)

Habitat.—Pelagic, breeding in burrows near sea level on islands.

Distribution.—*Breeds* on islands off the western coast of Mexico (on San Benedicto, in the Revillagigedo group), in the Hawaiian Islands (Kure east to Kauai and Oahu, and on small islets around the main islands), in the central and western Pacific Ocean (from the Pescadores and Bonin Islands south to the Tonga, Austral and Pitcairn groups), in waters off southern Australia and around New Zealand, and in the Indian Ocean (from the Seychelles and Cocos-Keeling south to the Mascarenes and Western Australia).

Ranges at sea in the Pacific Ocean off the west coast of Middle America and South America (from Baja California, the Tres Marias Islands and Nayarit south to Panama, Colombia and Ecuador) and throughout most of the central and western Pacific Ocean north to Japan and Formosa; and in the Indian Ocean north to the Arabian and southern Red seas.

Puffinus bulleri Salvin. BULLER'S SHEARWATER. [96.2.]

Puffinus bulleri Salvin, 1888, Ibis, p. 354. (New Zealand.)

Habitat.—Pelagic, breeding in burrows on islands.

Distribution.—*Breeds* on islands off North Island, New Zealand (Poor Knights, Whale, and possibly Three Kings and Mayor).

Ranges at sea in the Pacific Ocean off the west coast of North America (from the Aleutian Islands and Gulf of Alaska south to California), near the Hawaiian and Galapagos islands, off the Kurile Islands, and off the west coast of South America (Peru and Chile).

Accidental inland in southern California (Salton Sea).

Notes.—Also known as GRAY-BACKED or NEW ZEALAND SHEARWATER.

Puffinus griseus (Gmelin). SOOTY SHEARWATER. [95.]

Procellaria grisea Gmelin, 1789, Syst. Nat., 1 (2), p. 564. Based mainly on the "Grey Petrel" Latham, Gen. Synop. Birds, 3 (2), p. 399. (in hemisphaerio australi, inter 35° et 50° = New Zealand.)

Habitat.—Pelagic, breeding in burrows on small islands.

Distribution.—*Breeds* on islands off southeastern Australia (off New South Wales and Tasmania) and widely in New Zealand waters (including Stewart, Snakes, Auckland and Chatham islands); and off the southern coast of South America (Wollaston and Deceit, probably also Huafo and Mocha, off Chile; off Tierra del Fuego; and in the Falkland Islands).

Ranges at sea throughout the Pacific Ocean north to the southern Bering Sea, Aleutian Islands, Kamchatka, Formosa and the Hawaiian Islands, and along the entire Pacific coast of the Americas; in the Atlantic Ocean off the coast of North America from Labrador and Newfoundland south to Florida and Cuba (also in the Gulf of Mexico west to Texas), off eastern South America north to Brazil, off the west coast of Europe from Greenland, Iceland, Norway, Sweden and Denmark south to Portugal and the Mediterranean Sea (east to Algeria and Italy), and off the west coast of Africa north to Fernando Po and Angola.

Casual inland in the United States, mostly after storms; recorded from southern California, southern Arizona, Alabama (Attalla) and North Carolina (Twin Oaks).

Puffinus tenuirostris (Temminck). SHORT-TAILED SHEARWATER. [96.]

Procellaria tenuirostris Temminck, 1835, Planches Color., livr. 99, text facing pl. 587. (dans les mers au nord du Japon et sur les côtes de la Corée = Japan.)

Habitat.—Pelagic, breeding in burrows on small islands.

Distribution.—*Breeds* on islands off the coast (and locally along the mainland coast) of southeastern Australia from South Australia (Nuyts Archipelago) east to Victoria and Tasmania, and north to New South Wales (Bateman's Bay).

Ranges at sea in southern Australian and New Zealand waters, and north through the Pacific Ocean to the Bering and Chukchi seas, and south along the west coast of North America to Baja California (Los Coronados Islands).

Casual in Hawaiian waters, off Guerrero, and in the Indian Ocean (Ceylon, and the Mekran coast of Baluchistan, Pakistan), also questionable sight reports from the Gulf of California and Costa Rican waters.

Notes.—Also known as SLENDER-BILLED SHEARWATER.

Puffinus nativitatis Streets. CHRISTMAS SHEARWATER. [96.3.]

Puffinus (Nectris) nativitatis Streets, 1877, Bull. U.S. Natl. Mus., no. 7, p. 29. (Christmas Island [Pacific Ocean].)

Habitat.—Pelagic, breeding on oceanic islands on the ground beneath vegetation or in shallow tunnels.

Distribution.—*Breeds* in the Hawaiian Islands (east to Kauai and Moku Manu, off Oahu), in the Phoenix, Marquesas, Tuamotu and Austral islands, and on Wake, Christmas and Easter islands.

Ranges at sea in the tropical Pacific Ocean.

Accidental at sea between Clipperton Island and the mainland of Mexico.

Puffinus puffinus (Brünnich). MANX SHEARWATER. [90.]

Procellaria Puffinus Brünnich, 1764, Ornithol. Bor., p. 29. (E Feroa & Norvegia = Faroe Islands.)

Habitat.—Pelagic, breeding in burrows on turfy coastal islands, on cliffs of rocky islands, and occasionally inland in mountainous regions.

Distribution.—*Breeds* in the North Atlantic on islands off Newfoundland (since 1977) and Massachusetts (Penikese Island, 1973), and from Iceland and the Faroe and Shetland islands south around most of the British Isles to western France (Brittany), in Madeira and the Azores, and around much of the Mediterranean Sea (formerly also on Bermuda).

Ranges at sea to the western Atlantic along the coast of North America (recorded regularly at sea from Newfoundland south to Maryland and Bermuda, casually to Florida), to the eastern Atlantic from Iceland and Norway south to the Canary Islands, east throughout the Mediterranean and Black seas, and to the east coast of South America from Trinidad to Argentina.

Casual or accidental on the Gulf coast of Texas (Nueces County, North Padre Island) and Florida (Santa Rosa County), and in Greenland, continental Europe, South Africa and South Australia.

Notes.—Species limits in the superspecies complex, which includes *P. puffinus,* the two following species, and two species from the Australian-New Zealand region, *P. gavia* (Forster, 1844) and *P. huttoni* Mathews, 1912, are uncertain. Variable treatments include the entire complex as a single species, or with the recognition of three species (*P. puffinus, P. gavia* and *P. huttoni*), the other forms united with one of the three; Murphy (1952, Am. Mus. Novit., no. 1586, pp. 1–21) unites *auricularis* and *newelli* with the *puffinus* group, and *opisthomelas* with the *gavia* group. Except for *newelli,* it seems best to consider all as allospecies of a superspecies; see also comments under *P. auricularis.*

Puffinus opisthomelas Coues. BLACK-VENTED SHEARWATER. [93.]

Puffinus opisthomelas Coues, 1864, Proc. Acad. Nat. Sci. Philadelphia, 16, p. 139. (Cape San Lucas, Baja California.)

Habitat.—Pelagic, breeding in burrows and small caves on islands.

Distribution.—*Breeds* off the Pacific coast of Baja California (on Guadalupe, San Martín, San Benito and Natividad islands).

Ranges at sea along the Pacific coast of North America from central California (casually north to Vancouver Island and Washington) south to Baja California, Sonora and (at least casually) Guerrero.

Notes.—See comments under *P. puffinus.*

Puffinus auricularis Townsend. TOWNSEND'S SHEARWATER. [93.1.]

Puffinus auricularis C. H. Townsend, 1890, Proc. U.S. Natl. Mus., 13, p. 133. (Clarión Island, Revillagigedo Group.)

Habitat.—Pelagic, breeding in burrows on oceanic islands.

Distribution.—*Breeds* [*newelli* group] in the Hawaiian Islands (Kauai, possibly also on Molokai and Hawaii, and probably formerly on Maui); and [*auricularis* group] in the Revillagigedo Islands (on Clarión, San Benedicto and Socorro), off western Mexico.

Ranges at sea in the vicinity of the breeding grounds, recorded [*auricularis* group] north to southern Baja California (Cape San Lucas) and south to Clipperton Island and Oaxaca; a sight report for Panama requires confirmation.

Notes.—The two groups are occasionally regarded as distinct species, *P. auricularis* [TOWNSEND'S SHEARWATER, 93.1] and *P. newelli,* Henshaw, 1900 [NEWELL'S SHEARWATER, 93.2], but because of similar morphology and vocalizations, conspecific treatment seems warranted. See also comments under *P. puffinus.*

Puffinus assimilis Gould. LITTLE SHEARWATER. [92.1.]

Puffinus assimilis Gould, 1838, Synop. Birds Aust., pt. 4, app., p. 7. (New South Wales = Norfolk Island.)

Habitat & Distribution.—*Breeds* in burrows and crevices on coastal cliffs and islands in the eastern Atlantic (Azores south to Gough Island) and off Australia and New Zealand, and *ranges* at sea in the southern Atlantic and Indian oceans.

Accidental in the Hawaiian Islands (Midway, 18 February 1968; Clapp and Woodward, 1968, Proc. U.S. Natl. Mus., 124, p. 9), Nova Scotia (Sable Island, 1 September 1896), South Carolina (Sullivan's Island, August 1883) and continental Europe, also additional sight records from Puerto Rico and off the North Carolina coast.

Notes.—Also known as ALLIED SHEARWATER. See comments under *P. lherminieri.*

Puffinus lherminieri Lesson. AUDUBON'S SHEARWATER. [92.]

Puffinus [sic] *Lherminieri* Lesson, 1839, Rev. Zool. [Paris], 2, p. 102. (ad ripas Antillarum = Straits of Florida.)

Habitat.—Pelagic, breeding in rock crevices and on the ground under dense vegetation on islands.

Distribution.—*Breeds* in the Caribbean and western Atlantic region on Crab Cay (off Isla de Providencia, east of Nicaragua), on Tiger Rock (off Bocas del Toro, Panama), on Los Roques (off northern Venezuela), on Bermuda, in the Bahamas, off Puerto Rico (Mona Island, and Cayo del Agua off Culebra), in the Virgin Islands, and widely in the Lesser Antilles (from St. Martin south to islets off Tobago); in the eastern Atlantic on the Cape Verde Islands; in the Indian Ocean (islands in the southern Persian Gulf south to the Mascarene, Seychelles and

Maldive groups); and in the Pacific Ocean from the Bonin and Volcano islands south to the Palau, New Hebrides, Society, Tuamotu and Galapagos islands.

Ranges at sea in the western Atlantic from Massachusetts (at least casually, also sight reports north to Nova Scotia) south to Florida and throughout the West Indies to the Caribbean coast of Costa Rica and Panama, and in the Gulf of Mexico west (at least casually) to Louisiana and Texas; in the tropical Indian Ocean north to the Persian Gulf, Arabian Sea and India; and in the eastern Pacific along the coast of Middle America from Oaxaca south to Panama and Colombia, and in the tropical Pacific from the general breeding range south to Indonesia, New Guinea and northern Australia.

Accidental in Ontario (Almonte) and England.

Notes.—*P. lherminieri* and *P. assimilis* constitute a superspecies; they are considered conspecific by some authors.

Family HYDROBATIDAE: Storm-Petrels

Notes.—Some authors consider this group to be a subfamily of the Procellariidae.

Genus OCEANITES Keyserling and Blasius

Oceanites Keyserling and Blasius, 1840, Wirbelth. Eur., pp. xciii, 131, 238. Type, by monotypy, "*Thalassidroma*" (= *Procellaria*) *wilsonii* Bonaparte = *Procellaria oceanica* Kuhl.

Oceanites oceanicus (Kuhl). WILSON'S STORM-PETREL. [109.]

Procellaria oceanica Kuhl, 1820, Beitr. Zool., abth. 1, p. 136. (No locality given = South Georgia.)

Habitat.—Pelagic, breeding in burrows on islands and in coastal areas.

Distribution.—*Breeds* around the continent of Antarctica, on subantarctic islands off southern South America (Wollaston, Deceit, Herschel, South Georgia, South Orkneys, South Shetlands and probably other nearby islands) and on islands in the southern Indian Ocean (Crozets and Kerguelen).

Ranges at sea throughout the Atlantic Ocean and Gulf of Mexico north to Texas, the Gulf coast, Labrador and the British Isles, and east in the Mediterranean to Sardinia, throughout the Indian Ocean north to the Red Sea and Persian Gulf, in Australian and New Zealand waters north to Indonesia and New Guinea, and in the South Pacific north along the west coast of South America to Peru and occasionally Ecuador.

Casual north in the Pacific Ocean off North America (recorded from California, Oaxaca and Panama, also sight records from Washington, Michoacán, Guatemala and Costa Rica). Accidental in southern Ontario (Long Beach, Lake Muskoka), southwestern Quebec (Lake Deschênes), northern and western New York, Pennsylvania (Greensburg, Reading) and interior Florida (Gainesville).

[Oceanites gracilis (Elliot). WHITE-VENTED STORM-PETREL.] See Appendix A.

Genus PELAGODROMA Reichenbach

Pelagodroma Reichenbach, 1853, Avium Syst. Nat. (1852), p. iv. Type, by original designation, *Procellaria marina* Latham.

Pelagodroma marina (Latham). WHITE-FACED STORM-PETREL. [111.]

Procellaria marina Latham, 1790, Index Ornithol., 2, p. 826. Based on the "Frigate Petrel" Latham, Gen. Synop. Birds, 3 (2), p. 410. (in Mari australi; latitudine 37 = off the mouth of the Río de la Plata, lat. 35°–37°S.)

Habitat.—Pelagic, breeding in burrows beneath heavy vegetation on islands.

Distribution.—*Breeds* on islands off Australia (from Abrolhos east to Bass Strait and Broughton Islands) and in New Zealand waters (Kermadec, Chatham, Auckland, Antipodes and others near the mainland); in the Atlantic Ocean on Salvage, Canary (possibly) and Cape Verde islands, and on Tristan da Cunha and Gough Island in the South Atlantic; and in the southern Indian Ocean, at least formerly, on Amsterdam and St. Paul islands.

Ranges at sea in the Indian and Pacific oceans from the Arabian Sea south and east throughout the Australian and New Zealand breeding range across the Pacific to the Galapagos Islands and the west coast of South America (off Ecuador); in the Atlantic from the Azores (casually north to the British Isles) south along the west coast of Africa to the South Atlantic and southern Indian Oceans, occurring west to the coasts of Uruguay and Argentina.

Casual off the North American coast from Massachusetts south to North Carolina.

[Genus FREGETTA Bonaparte]

Fregetta Bonaparte, 1855, C. R. Acad. Sci. Paris, 41, p. 1113. Type, by original designation, *Thalassidroma leucogaster* Gould.

[Fregetta grallaria (Vieillot). WHITE-BELLIED STORM-PETREL.] See Appendix B.

Genus HYDROBATES Boie

Hydrobates Boie, 1822, Isis von Oken, col. 562. Type, by subsequent designation (Baird, Brewer and Ridgway, 1884), *Procellaria pelagica* Linnaeus.

Hydrobates pelagicus (Linnaeus). BRITISH STORM-PETREL. [104.]

Procellaria pelagica Linnaeus, 1758, Syst. Nat., ed. 10, 1, p. 131. (in albo Oceano = Sweden.)

Habitat & Distribution.—*Breeds* on small rocky islands in the northern and eastern Atlantic Ocean and western Mediterranean Sea, and *ranges* at sea throughout the Mediterranean and Black seas and the eastern Atlantic and western Indian oceans.

Accidental in Nova Scotia (Sable Island, 10 August 1970; McNeil and Burton, 1971, Auk, 88, pp. 671–672); there is also an old specimen (USNM) from the "Bay of Fundy" lacking further data. A specimen taken at McClellanville, South Carolina, in 1972 and reported as *H. pelagicus,* was subsequently identified as *Oceanodroma castro* (Am. Birds, 27: 44, 1973).

Notes.—Known in Old World literature as the STORM PETREL.

Genus OCEANODROMA Reichenbach

Oceanodroma Reichenbach, 1853, Avium Syst. Nat. (1852), p. iv. Type, by original designation, *Procellaria furcata* Gmelin.

Cymochorea Coues, 1864, Proc. Acad. Nat. Sci. Philadelphia, 16, p. 75. Type, by original designation, *Procellaria leucorhoa* Vieillot.
Halocyptena Coues, 1864, Proc. Acad. Nat. Sci. Philadelphia, 16, p. 78. Type, by original designation, *Halocyptena microsoma* Coues.
Loomelania Mathews, 1934, Bull. Br. Ornithol. Club, 54, p. 119. Type, by original designation, *Procellaria melania* Bonaparte.

[**Oceanodroma hornbyi** (Gray). RINGED STORM-PETREL.] See Appendix B.

Oceanodroma furcata (Gmelin). FORK-TAILED STORM-PETREL. [105.]

Procellaria furcata Gmelin, 1789, Syst. Nat., 1 (2), p. 561. Based on the "Fork-tail Petrel" Pennant, Arct. Zool., 2, p. 535. (in glacie maris, Americam & Asiam interfluentis = Bering Sea.)

Habitat.—Pelagic, breeding on islands in burrows or holes under rocks.
Distribution.—*Breeds* in the North Pacific from southern Alaska (the Aleutian Islands, islands in the Gulf of Alaska, and the Alexander Archipelago) south along the west coast of North America to islets off northern California (Del Norte and Humboldt counties), and from the Commander Islands south to the Kuriles.
Ranges at sea from western Alaska (the Bering Sea, casually the southern Chukchi Sea) south through the Bering Sea and North Pacific along the west coast of North America to central (casually southern) California, to the Hawaiian Islands and Marcus Island, and to Japan and the Volcano Islands.

Oceanodroma leucorhoa (Vieillot). LEACH'S STORM-PETREL. [106.]

Procellaria leucorhoa Vieillot, 1818, Nouv. Dict. Hist. Nat., nouv. éd., 25 (1817), p. 422. (sur les bords maritimes de la Picardie, se tient sur l'Ocean, jusqu'au Brésil = Picardy, France.)

Habitat.—Pelagic, breeding in burrows on islands.
Distribution.—*Breeds* in the North Pacific from the Shumagin and Aleutian islands and south-coastal Alaska south along the North American coast to Baja California (Los Coronados, San Benito and Guadalupe islands), and from the Commander Islands south to the Kuriles and northern Hokkaido, Japan; and in the North Atlantic from southern Labrador south to Newfoundland, Maine (Casco Bay) and Massachusetts (Penikese Islands), and from southern Iceland, the Faroe Islands and Norway to northern Scotland.
Ranges at sea in the Pacific Ocean from the breeding areas south to the Hawaiian, Revillagigedo and Galapagos islands, and in the western Pacific to Indonesia and New Guinea; and in the Atlantic Ocean south along both coasts to Florida, the West Indies, Caribbean Sea, South America (Venezuela east to eastern Brazil) and South Africa, casually to the eastern Atlantic islands, Mediterranean Sea and western Europe.
Casual or accidental in Ohio, southern Ontario, northern Quebec, Vermont, the District of Columbia, along the Gulf coast (from Texas east to Florida) and the Pacific coast of Costa Rica (Cabo Velas), and in Greenland and New Zealand.
Notes.—*O. leucorhoa* and the closely allied *O. monorhis* (Swinhoe, 1867), of Japan and Korea, probably constitute a superspecies; some authors consider them

to be conspecific. The breeding population on Guadalupe Island, here regarded as a race of *O. leucorhoa,* has been treated variously as a subspecies of *O. monorhis* or as a distinct species, *O. socorroensis* C. H. Townsend, 1890 [DUSKY-RUMPED STORM-PETREL, 105.2].

Oceanodroma homochroa (Coues). ASHY STORM-PETREL. [108.]

Cymochroa homochroa Coues, 1864, Proc. Acad. Nat. Sci. Philadelphia, 16, p. 77. (Farallone Islands, Pacific coast of North America = Farallon Islands, California.)

Habitat.—Pelagic, breeding on islands in natural cavities under rocks and in burrows.

Distribution.—*Breeds* on islands off the coast of California (on Bird in Marin County, in the Farallon Islands and on San Miguel and Santa Cruz in the Channel Islands) and, rarely, northern Baja California (in Los Coronados Islands).

Ranges at sea off the coast of California and Baja California from Marin County south to the San Benito Islands.

Oceanodroma castro (Harcourt). BAND-RUMPED STORM-PETREL. [106.2.]

Thalassidroma castro Harcourt, 1851, Sketch Madeira, p. 123. (Deserta Islets, near Madeira.)

Habitat.—Pelagic, breeding on islands in burrows and rocky crevices.

Distribution.—*Breeds* on islands in the Pacific Ocean in the Hawaiian Islands (no nest located, indirect evidence for nesting on Kauai, possibly also Maui), off Japan, in the Galapagos Islands, and possibly on Cocos Island, off Costa Rica; and in the Atlantic Ocean in the Azores (probably), Salvage, Madeira, Cape Verde, Ascension and St. Helena islands.

Ranges at sea primarily in the vicinity of the breeding grounds, occurring casually off the coast of Brazil and the British Isles.

Casual or accidental off the Pacific coast of California and Costa Rica, off the Atlantic coast of North America (Delaware to North Carolina), on the central coast of Texas, in Florida (Escambia, Gulf and Pinellas counties, and Key West) and Cuba, and inland in Missouri (Weldon Spring), Ontario (Ottawa), Indiana (Martinsville), Pennsylvania (Chambersburg) and the District of Columbia.

Notes.—Also known as MADEIRA or HARCOURT'S STORM-PETREL.

Oceanodroma tethys (Bonaparte). WEDGE-RUMPED STORM-PETREL. [106.3.]

Thalassidroma Tethys Bonaparte, 1852, Tagebl. Dtsch. Naturforsch. Aertze, Weisbaden, Beilage, no. 7, p. 89. (Galapagos Islands.)

Habitat.—Pelagic, breeding in burrows on islands.

Distribution.—*Breeds* in the Galapagos Islands (Tower and Pitt) and on islands off the coast of Peru (San Gallán and Pescadores).

Ranges at sea along the west coast of the Americas from Costa Rica south to the coast of Chile (lat. 20°S.), occasionally north as far as the Revillagigedo Islands and Guatemala.

Casual off California (Monterey region) and Baja California (Guadalupe Island).

Notes.—Also known as GALAPAGOS STORM-PETREL. The northern specimens have been referred to the Peruvian breeding race, *O. t. kelsalli* (Lowe, 1925); specimens of both *kelsalli* and nominate *O. t. tethys* from the Galapagos population have been reported from the Bay of Panama.

Oceanodroma melania (Bonaparte). BLACK STORM-PETREL. [107.]

Procellaria melania Bonaparte, 1854, C. R. Acad. Sci. Paris, 38, p. 662. (coast of California = vicinity of San Francisco.)

Habitat.—Pelagic, breeding on islands in burrows, crannies under rocks and crevices in cliffs.

Distribution.—*Breeds* on Sutil Island, adjacent to Santa Barbara Island in the Channel Islands, off southern California; on Los Coronados and San Benito islands, off the Pacific coast of Baja California; and on islands in the northern third of the Gulf of California (Consag Rock, San Luis Islands and Partida Island).

Ranges at sea along the Pacific coast of the Americas from central California (Marin County) south to Panama, Colombia, Ecuador and Peru (to lat. 8°S.).

Notes.—*O. melania* and the closely related *O. matsudariae* Kuroda, 1922, of the Volcano Islands and Japanese waters, constitute a superspecies; they are considered conspecific by some authors.

†Oceanodroma macrodactyla Bryant. GUADALUPE STORM-PETREL.

Oceanodroma leucorhoa macrodactyla W. E. Bryant, 1887, Bull. Calif. Acad. Sci., 2, p. 450. (Guadalupe Island, Baja California.)

Habitat.—Pelagic, breeding in burrows among coniferous trees at high elevations.

Distribution.—EXTINCT. *Bred* formerly on Guadalupe Island, Baja California; not certainly recorded since 1912. Known only from the vicinity of the breeding grounds.

Oceanodroma markhami (Salvin). MARKHAM'S STORM-PETREL.

Cymochorea markhami Salvin, 1883, Proc. Zool. Soc. London, p. 430. (coast of Peru, lat. 19°40′S., long. 75°W.)

Habitat & Distribution.—*Breeding* grounds unknown; *ranges* at sea along the Pacific coast of South America from northern Peru to central Chile, occasionally to the Galapagos Islands.

Accidental near Clipperton Island and off western Costa Rica (at Cocos Island).

Notes.—This species and *O. tristrami* constitute a superspecies; some authors consider them conspecific, in which case SOOTY STORM-PETREL may be used for the broader specific unit.

Oceanodroma tristrami Salvin. SOOTY STORM-PETREL. [107.1.]

Oceanodroma tristrami (Stejneger MS) Salvin, 1896, Cat. Birds Br. Mus., 25, pp. xiv, 347, 354. (Sendai Bay, [Honshu,] Japan.)

Habitat.—Pelagic, breeding on islands in burrows and rocky crevices.

Distribution.—*Breeds* in the western Hawaiian Islands (Pearl and Hermes Reef, Laysan, French Frigate Shoals, Nihoa, and possibly Kure and Midway), in the Seven Islands of Izu (Torishima) and in the Volcano Islands (Kita Iwo).

Ranges at sea from the Hawaiian Islands (east at least to Kauai) to Japanese waters and the Bonin Islands.

Notes.—See comments under *O. markhami.*

Oceanodroma microsoma (Coues). LEAST STORM-PETREL. [103.]

> *Halocyptena microsoma* Coues, 1864, Proc. Acad. Nat. Sci. Philadelphia, 16, p. 79. (San Jose del Caba [sic], Lower California = San José del Cabo, Baja California.)

Habitat.—Pelagic, breeding on islets in crevices or among loose stones.

Distribution.—*Breeds* on the Pacific side of Baja California in the San Benito Islands and in the northern third of the Gulf of California (Consag Rock, and San Luis and Partida islands).

Ranges at sea along the west coast of North America from southern California (San Diego County), south to Oaxaca, less frequently south as far as Panama and northern South America (Colombia and Ecuador, to lat. 2°S.).

Notes.—This species has formerly been treated in the monotypic genus *Halocyptena.*

[Order SPHENISCIFORMES: Penguins]

Notes.—Evidence from fossils, morphology and egg-white proteins, as summarized by Sibley and Ahlquist (1972, Peabody Mus. Nat. Hist. Bull., 39, pp. 36–43) indicates that the penguins are most closely related to the Procellariiformes.

[Family SPHENISCIDAE: Penguins]

[Genus SPHENISCUS Brisson]

> *Spheniscus* Brisson, 1760, Ornithologie, 1, p. 52; 6, p. 96. Type, by monotypy, *Diomedea demersa* Linnaeus.

[Spheniscus mendiculus Sundevall. GALAPAGOS PENGUIN.] See Appendix B.

Order PELECANIFORMES: Totipalmate Swimmers

Suborder PHAETHONTES: Tropicbirds

Family PHAETHONTIDAE: Tropicbirds

Genus PHAETHON Linnaeus

> *Phaëthon* Linnaeus, 1758, Syst. Nat., ed. 10, 1, p. 134. Type, by subsequent designation (G. R. Gray, 1840), *Phaethon aethereus* Linnaeus.

Phaethon lepturus Daudin. WHITE-TAILED TROPICBIRD. [112.]

> *Phaëton* [sic] *lepturus* Daudin, 1802, *in* Buffon, Hist. Nat., ed. Didot, Quadr., 14, p. 319. (Mauritius.)

Habitat.—Pelagic, breeding on tropical islands in rocky crevices, holes or caves, especially on cliffs, occasionally in trees.

Distribution.—*Breeds* on islands in the Atlantic Ocean and Caribbean Sea from Bermuda, the Bahamas and throughout the Greater and Lesser Antilles south to islets off Tobago, Fernando de Noronha (off Brazil), Ascension Island, and islands in the Gulf of Guinea; in the Pacific Ocean from the Hawaiian Islands (main islands west to Kauai, rarely on Midway) and the Bonin and Volcano islands south to New Caledonia and the Fiji, Marquesas and Tuamotu islands; and in the Indian Ocean from the Seychelles and Andaman Islands south to the Mascarenes and Christmas Island.

Ranges at sea throughout the breeding areas and tropical waters in the western Atlantic, rarely north along the east coast of North America to North Carolina (casually in the Gulf Stream to Nova Scotia), casually in the Gulf of Mexico (mostly recorded off Florida), and (probably) casually in the Caribbean Sea (recorded off Puerto Barrios, Guatemala, and northern Colombia); in the Pacific Ocean from Japan to Australia and (casually) New Zealand; and in the Indian Ocean south to South Africa.

Accidental in California (Newport Bay, Orange County), Arizona (Scottsdale), Pennsylvania (Gettysburg) and western New York.

Notes.—Also known as YELLOW-BILLED TROPICBIRD.

Phaethon aethereus Linnaeus. RED-BILLED TROPICBIRD. [113.]

> *Phaëthon æthereus* Linnaeus, 1758, Syst. Nat., ed. 10, 1, p. 134. (in Pelago inter tropicos = Ascension Island.)

Habitat.—Pelagic, breeding on tropical islands in crevices and holes, usually on cliffs.

Distribution.—*Breeds* on islands in the Caribbean region (on Culebra and Vieques off Puerto Rico, on small islets in the Virgin Islands and Lesser Antilles south to Tobago and Grenada, and on Swan Key in Almirante Bay, Panama, also on Los Hermanos and Los Roques off Venezuela), the eastern Atlantic (off Africa, including the Cape Verde Islands) and the South Atlantic (off Brazil); in the eastern Pacific off Mexico (Revillagigedo, Tres Marias and Isabela islands), in the Gulf of California (Consag Rock, and San Pedro Mártir and San Jorge islands) and northern South America (the Galapagos and islands off the coast from Colombia to Ecuador and Peru); and in the northern Indian Ocean, Red Sea and Persian Gulf.

Ranges at sea in the breeding areas in the western Atlantic region throughout the Lesser Antilles and off northern South America, less frequently through the Greater Antilles and south to Brazil, casually north off the Atlantic coast of North America from Florida to New York (Long Island) and Rhode Island; in the Pacific regularly from southern California and Baja California south to Peru, irregularly north to Washington, west to the Hawaiian Islands (recorded French Frigate Shoals and Nihoa) and south to Chile; and in the tropical Indian Ocean.

Casual or accidental in southern Arizona, Madeira and southern Africa; an old report from the Newfoundland Banks is unsubstantiated.

Phaethon rubricauda Boddaert. RED-TAILED TROPICBIRD. [113.1.]

> *Phaeton* [sic] *rubricauda* Boddaert, 1783, Table Planches Enlum., p. 57. Based on "Paille-en queue de l'Isle de France" Daubenton, Planches Enlum., pl. 979. (Mauritius.)

Habitat.—Pelagic, breeding on small islands on the ground, in crevices and under vegetation, occasionally on cliffs.

Distribution.—*Breeds* in the Pacific Ocean from the western Hawaiian (Kure east to Niihau, also on Lanai and Kahoolawe, irregularly on Manana Island off Oahu, and possibly on islets off Molokai), Bonin and Volcano islands south to northeastern Australia (Raine Island) and Lord Howe, Norfolk, Kermadec, Tuamotu and Pitcairn islands; and in the Indian Ocean near Mauritius, in the Cocos-Keeling Islands, and off the northwestern coast of Australia.

Ranges at sea throughout the breeding range and in the Pacific from Japan and the Hawaiian Islands (throughout) south to Australia and New Zealand; and in the Indian Ocean from the Red Sea and Persian Gulf south to South African and Australian waters.

Casual east in the Pacific to California, and to waters off Guadalupe, the Revillagigedo and Clipperton islands. Accidental off the coast of Chile.

Suborder PELECANI: Boobies, Pelicans, Cormorants and Darters

Family SULIDAE: Boobies and Gannets

Genus SULA Brisson

Sula Brisson, 1760, Ornithologie, 1, p. 60; 6, p. 494. Type, by tautonymy, *Sula* Brisson = *Sula leucogaster* Boddaert.

Subgenus SULA Brisson

Parasula Mathews, 1913, Austral Avian Rec., 2, p. 55. Type, by original designation, *Sula dactylatra bedouti* Mathews = *Sula dactylatra* Lesson.

Sula dactylatra Lesson. MASKED BOOBY. [114.]

Sula dactylatra Lesson, 1831, Traité Ornithol., livr. 8, p. 601. (L'île de l'Ascension = Ascension Island.)

Habitat.—Pelagic, breeding on open ground on oceanic islands.

Distribution.—*Breeds* in the Atlantic-Caribbean region off the Yucatan Peninsula (Cayo Arcas, Cayo Arenas and Alacrán reef), in the southern Bahamas (Santo Domingo Cay), southwest of Jamaica (the Pedro and Serranilla cays), off Puerto Rico (Monito Island), in the Virgin Islands (Cockroach and Sula cays), in the Lesser Antilles (Dog Island off Anguilla, and in the Grenadines), off Venezuela (Islas de Aves east to Los Hermanos), and on islands off Brazil east to Ascension Island; in the Pacific off Mexico (on Clarión and San Benedicto islands in the Revillagigedo group, and on Clipperton Island), from the Hawaiian (Kure east to Kaula Rock, and on Moku Manu off Oahu) and Ryukyu islands south to eastern Australia (New South Wales) and the Kermadec and Tuamotu islands, and in the Galapagos and on islands off Ecuador, Peru and Chile (San Ambrosia and San Félix); and in the Indian Ocean from the Gulf of Aden and Cocos-Keeling and Christmas islands south to the Mascarenes and northwestern Australia.

Ranges at sea in the Atlantic-Caribbean region from the Bahamas, Antilles and the Yucatan Peninsula south through the breeding range, casually north through the Gulf of Mexico from Tamaulipas and Texas east to Florida, along the Atlantic coast to North Carolina, and along the coast of Middle America; and in the Pacific and Indian oceans generally throughout the breeding range south to western Mexico (Oaxaca), eastern Australia and South Africa.

Casual off southern California (sight report).
Notes.—Also known as BLUE-FACED or WHITE BOOBY.

Sula nebouxii Milne-Edwards. BLUE-FOOTED BOOBY. [114.1.]

Sula Nebouxii Milne-Edwards, 1882, Ann. Sci. Nat. (Zool.), sér. 6, 13, p. 37, pl. 14. (la côté pacifique de l'Amérique = Pacific coast of America, presumably Chile.)

Habitat.—Pelagic, breeding on open ground on islands.
Distribution.—*Breeds* on islands in the Gulf of California (from Consag Rock and George Island southward), off western Mexico (Isabela, the Tres Marietas and the Tres Marias islands), in the Gulf of Panama (Isla Villa, Farallón del Chirú and Isla Pachequilla in the Pearl Islands, and Isla Boná), in the Galapagos Islands, and along the coast of South America from Colombia to northern Peru.
Ranges at sea in the eastern Pacific from Baja California and the Gulf of California south along the coast of Middle America and South America to the Galapagos Islands and central Peru, casually north to central and southeastern California and southwestern Arizona (Havasu Lake, Phoenix).
Accidental in Washington (Everett) and Texas (Cameron County).

Sula leucogaster (Boddaert). BROWN BOOBY. [115.]

Pelecanus Leucogaster Boddaert, 1783, Table Planches Enlum., p. 57. Based on "Le Fou, de Cayenne" Daubenton, Planches Enlum., pl. 973. (No locality given = Cayenne.)

Habitat.—Pelagic, breeding on the ground on islands.
Distribution.—*Breeds* on islands in the Atlantic-Caribbean region from islets off the Yucatan Peninsula, Florida Keys (formerly) and Bahamas south through the Antilles and along the coasts of Middle America and northern South America (east to Los Hermanos), and from the Cape Verde Islands and the Gulf of Guinea south to the coast of central Brazil and Ascension Islands; in the Pacific from Consag Rock and George Island in the Gulf of California south to Isabela, the Tres Marias, Revillagigedo and Clipperton islands, on islets off Costa Rica, in the Bay of Panama (Isla Boná, Farallon Rock and the Pearl Islands), off Colombia (Gorgona Island), and from the Hawaiian Islands (Kure east to Niihau and Moku Manu off Oahu), the Bonin and Volcano islands and the Seven Islands of Izu south to the South China Sea, northern Australia, New Caledonia and the Tonga and Tuamotu islands; and in the Indian Ocean from the Red Sea and the Malay Peninsula south to the Seychelles, Cocos-Keeling and Christmas islands.
Ranges at sea generally in the breeding range, and in the Atlantic-Caribbean region north, at least rarely, to the Gulf coast (Texas east to Florida), along the Atlantic coast north as far as New York and Massachusetts (casually Nova Scotia), and to Bermuda; in the Pacific from Baja California south to Ecuador, casually north to southern California, southern Nevada (Lake Mead) and southwestern Arizona (Havasu Lake), and from Hawaiian waters and Japan south to Australia and (rarely) New Zealand; and in the Indian Ocean south to South Africa.
Notes.—Also known as WHITE-BELLIED BOOBY.

Sula sula (Linnaeus). RED-FOOTED BOOBY. [116.]

Pelecanus Sula Linnaeus, 1766, Syst. Nat., ed. 12, 1, p. 218. Based in part on "The Booby" Catesby, Nat. Hist. Carolina, 1, p. 87, pl. 87. (in Pelago indico = Barbados, Lesser Antilles.)

Habitat.—Pelagic, breeding in small trees and bushes on islands.

Distribution.—*Breeds* on islands in the Atlantic-Caribbean region off Belize (Half Moon Cay), in the Swan Islands (Little Swan), off Puerto Rico (Mona, Monito, Desecheo and Culebra islands), in the Virgin Islands (Dutchcap and, formerly, Cockroach and Sula cays), in the Grenadines (Battowia and Kick-'em-Jenny), off Venezuela (Los Roques east to Los Hermanos) and off Brazil (Fernando de Noronha and Trindade islands); in the Pacific off Mexico (the Tres Marias islands, and Clarión and San Benedicto in the Revillagigedo group), off Costa Rica (Cocos Island), in the Galapagos Islands, and from the Hawaiian (Kure east to Kauai, Oahu and Moku Manu islet) and Bonin islands south to northern Australia, New Caledonia, and the Fiji, Samoa and Tuamotu islands; and in the Indian Ocean from Aldabra east to Cocos-Keeling Island.

Ranges at sea in the breeding areas in the Atlantic-Caribbean region from Quintana Roo and Belize south along the coasts of Middle America and South America to eastern Brazil, casually north to the Gulf coast (from Texas east to western Florida) and through the Greater Antilles to southern Florida; in the Pacific throughout the Hawaiian Islands (rare east of Oahu) and from Sinaloa south to Panama; and in the Indian Ocean north to the Bay of Bengal.

Accidental in California (Farallon Islands).

Subgenus MORUS Vieillot

Morus Vieillot, 1816, Analyse, p. 63. Type, by monotypy, "Fou de Bassan" Brisson = *Pelecanus bassanus* Linnaeus.

Sula bassanus (Linnaeus). NORTHERN GANNET. [117.]

Pelecanus Bassanus Linnaeus, 1758, Syst. Nat., ed. 10, 1, p. 133. (in Scotia, America = Bass Rock, Scotland.)

Habitat.—Pelagic, breeding primarily on open ground on flat-topped islands, less frequently on rocky slopes and cliffs along coasts.

Distribution.—*Breeds* on islands in eastern North America in the Gulf of St. Lawrence (on Bonaventure, Anticosti and Bird Rocks in the Magdalen Islands), off Quebec (Perroquet Island, formerly), in Newfoundland (Cape St. Mary, and on Baccalieu and Funk islands), in Nova Scotia (near Yarmouth, formerly) and off New Brunswick (Gannet Rock); and in Europe around Iceland, the Faroe Islands, British Isles, northern France and Norway.

Ranges at sea off eastern North America from southern Labrador, Greenland and areas near the breeding range south along the Atlantic coast to Florida, and west along the Gulf coast to southern Texas; and in Europe east and south to northern Russia, Scandinavia, the Baltic Sea, throughout the Mediterranean Sea, and along the Atlantic coast to northwestern Africa and (casually) the Cape Verde Islands.

Casual inland in the St. Lawrence Valley, New England and the Great Lakes

west to Michigan, Indiana and Ohio; and in Eurasia to Spitsbergen, Bear Island
and continental Europe. Accidental on Victoria Island (Holman) and in Kentucky.
Notes.—Known in most literature as the GANNET. The gannets of the world, *S.
bassanus, S. capensis* (Lichtenstein, 1823) of South Africa, and *S. serrator* (G. R.
Gray, 1843) of Australia and New Zealand, probably constitute a superspecies.

Family **PELECANIDAE**: Pelicans

Genus **PELECANUS** Linnaeus

Pelecanus Linnaeus, 1758, Syst. Nat., ed. 10, 1, p. 132. Type, by subsequent
designation (G. R. Gray, 1840), *Pelecanus onocrotalus* Linnaeus.
Cyrtopelicanus Reichenbach, 1853, Avium Syst. Nat. (1852), p. vii. Type, by
original designation, *Pelecanus trachyrhynchus* Latham = *Pelecanus erythrorhynchos* Gmelin.
Leptopelicanus Reichenbach, 1853, Avium Syst. Nat. (1852), p. vii. Type, by
original designation, *Pelecanus fuscus* Gmelin = *Pelecanus occidentalis*
Linnaeus.

Pelecanus erythrorhynchos Gmelin. AMERICAN WHITE PELICAN. [125.]

Pelecanus erythrorhynchos Gmelin, 1789, Syst. Nat., 1 (2), p. 571. Based on
the "Rough-billed Pelican" Latham, Gen. Synop. Birds, 3 (2), p. 586. (in
America septentrionali = Hudson Bay.)

Habitat.—Rivers, lakes, estuaries and bays, breeding on the ground, usually on
islands in inland lakes.
Distribution.—*Breeds* from south-central British Columbia (Stum Lake), northeastern Alberta, northwestern Saskatchewan, central Manitoba and southwestern
Ontario south locally to extreme northern California, western Nevada, northern
Utah, northern Colorado, northeastern South Dakota and southwestern (formerly
central) Minnesota, with sporadic breeding on the central coast of Texas and from
central to southern California (formerly on Salton Sea). Recorded in summer (and
possibly breeding) in southern Mackenzie (Great Slave Lake).
Winters along the Pacific coast from central California and southern Arizona
south along the western lowlands (less frequently in the interior) of Mexico to
Guatemala and Nicaragua (sight reports for Costa Rica), and from Florida and
the Gulf states south along the Gulf coast of Mexico to Tabasco and the state of
Yucatán, casually in the breeding range in western North America.
Wanders irregularly after the breeding season through most of eastern North
America from Hudson Bay, Quebec, New Brunswick and Nova Scotia south to
the Gulf coast and (rarely) the West Indies (Bimini and Great Inagua in the
Bahamas, Cuba and Puerto Rico). Accidental in Alaska (Petersburg), northern
Mackenzie (Liverpool Bay) and Victoria Island (Holman).
Notes.—In American literature usually known as the WHITE PELICAN.

Pelecanus occidentalis Linnaeus. BROWN PELICAN. [126.]

Pelecanus occidentalis Linnaeus, 1766, Syst. Nat., ed. 12, 1, p. 215. Based
mainly on "The Pelican of America" Edwards, Nat. Hist. Birds, 2, p. 93,
pl. 93. (in Africa, Asia, & in America = Jamaica.)

Habitat.—Open marine situations along coasts, breeding on islands on the ground or in small bushes and trees.

Distribution.—*Breeds* on islands along the Pacific coast from central California (the Channel Islands, formerly north to Monterey County) south to Isabela and the Tres Marias Islands (and including islands in the Gulf of California), in the Bay of Fonseca (Honduras), off Costa Rica (Guayabo and Bolaños) and Panama (mostly in the Pearl Islands, and islets off Isla Coiba and in the Bay of Panama), in the Galapagos Islands, and along the South American coast from Ecuador to Chile (Isla de Chiloé); and along the Atlantic, Gulf and Caribbean coasts from North Carolina south around Florida and west to southern Texas, in the West Indies in the southern Bahamas (Great Inagua and Caicos islands) and the Greater Antilles east to the Virgin Islands and St. Martin, off the Yucatan Peninsula and Belize (Man-of-war Cay), and off the north coast of Venezuela from Los Roques east to Tobago and Trinidad.

Ranges along the Pacific coast of the Americas from southern British Columbia south to Cape Horn; and throughout the Atlantic, Gulf and Caribbean coastal and insular areas from North Carolina (casually north to New England) south to eastern Venezuela (rarely to northern Brazil).

Casual in inland areas of North America north to Idaho, Wyoming, North Dakota, Wisconsin, Michigan and Ontario, and to Nova Scotia.

Notes.—The large South American form in Peru and Chile is sometimes regarded as a distinct species, *P. thagus* Molina, 1782.

Family **PHALACROCORACIDAE**: Cormorants

Notes.—See comments under Anhingidae.

Genus **PHALACROCORAX** Brisson

Phalacrocorax Brisson, 1760, Ornithologie, 1, p. 60; 6, p. 511. Type, by tautonymy, *Phalacrocorax* Brisson = *Pelecanus carbo* Linnaeus.

Phalacrocorax carbo (Linnaeus). GREAT CORMORANT. [119.]

Pelecanus Carbo Linnaeus, 1758, Syst. Nat., ed. 10, 1, p. 133. (in Europa = Sweden.)

Habitat.—Lakes, rivers and seacoasts, breeding primarily in trees, although in North America nesting mostly on cliffs and ranging along seacoasts.

Distribution.—*Breeds* in North America along the Atlantic coast from the north shore of the Gulf of St. Lawrence in Quebec (Lake, Outer Wapitagun, Anticosti, Magdalen and St. Mary islands) and southwestern Newfoundland (Guernsey Island, Coal River and Port au Prince Peninsula) south to Prince Edward Island (Cape Tryon and East Point) and Nova Scotia (south to Shelburne County), formerly south to the Bay of Fundy; in the Palearctic from southern Greenland, Iceland, the Faroe Islands and Scandinavia south to the Mediterranean and southern Europe, and across central Asia to Sakhalin, Japan, Formosa and China; and in New Guinea, Australia and New Zealand.

Winters in North America in the breeding range and south regularly to North

Carolina, casually to southern Florida, the Gulf coast west to Louisiana, and inland to Lake Ontario and West Virginia; in Eurasia from the breeding range south to the Mediterranean and Black seas, the Persian Gulf, India, the Malay Peninsula, Sumatra, the Philippines and Bonin Islands; and generally in the breeding range in the Australian region.

Notes.—Also known as BLACK or COMMON CORMORANT and, in Old World literature, as the CORMORANT. The African *P. lucidus* (Lichtenstein, 1823) is considered by some to be conspecific with *P. carbo*; these two, along with *P. capillatus* (Temminck and Schlegel, 1850) of Japan and Korea, constitute a superspecies.

Phalacrocorax auritus (Lesson). DOUBLE-CRESTED CORMORANT. [120.]

> *Carbo auritus* Lesson, 1831, Traité Ornithol., livr. 8, p. 605. Based on "Le Cormoran dilophe" Vieillot, *in* Vieillot and Oudart, Gal. Ois., 2, pl. 275. (in Nouvelle-Zélande, error = North America; restricted to upper Saskatchewan River by Todd, 1963, Birds Labrador Peninsula, p. 105.)

Habitat.—Lakes, rivers, swamps and seacoasts, breeding on the ground or in trees in fresh-water situations, and on coastal cliffs.

Distribution.—*Breeds* in the southeastern Bering Sea (Cape Peirce), southern Alaska (from Carlisle Island in the eastern Aleutians east to Yakutat Bay, and inland to Lake Louise), and from southwestern British Columbia, northern Alberta, central Saskatchewan, central Manitoba, southern James Bay, the north shore of the Gulf of St. Lawrence and Newfoundland south in coastal areas (on the Atlantic coast between New England and Florida in but a few isolated colonies) and very locally throughout interior of North America (in widely scattered colonies) to Baja California, coastal Sonora, southwestern Arizona, southern New Mexico, north-central and southeastern Texas, the Gulf coast and Florida, and in the northernmost Bahamas, Cuba, the Isle of Pines and (formerly) Man-of-war Cay off Belize.

Winters along the Pacific coast from the Aleutians and southern Alaska south to Baja California, the Revillagigedo Islands and Guerrero; and in the southern (casually central) United States from New Mexico and Texas east to the Gulf coast, north in the Mississippi Valley to Tennessee, and on the Atlantic coast from New England south to Florida, the Bahamas and Greater Antilles (east, at least casually, to the Virgin Islands).

In migration regularly through the Great Plains and Mississippi and Ohio valleys, irregularly north to southern Mackenzie and south to islands off the Yucatan Peninsula and Belize.

Casual north to Yukon, Hudson Bay, Baffin Island and Labrador, and in Bermuda and the Lesser Antilles (Guadeloupe).

Notes.—*P. auritus* probably constitutes a superspecies with *P. olivaceus,* with which it is marginally sympatric.

Phalacrocorax olivaceus (Humboldt). OLIVACEOUS CORMORANT. [121.]

> *Pelecanus olivaceus* Humboldt, 1805, *in* Humboldt and Bonpland, Rec. Observ. Zool. Anat. Comp., p. 6. (prope banco ad Magdalenas fluminis ripas, lat. 8°55' = El Banco, Magdalena, Colombia.)

Habitat.—Rivers, lakes, marshes and seacoasts, breeding in trees (Tropical to Temperate zones).

Distribution.—*Resident* from Sonora, southern New Mexico, north-central and eastern Texas, and western Louisiana south throughout Middle America (including islands off the Yucatan Peninsula) and South America (also islands north of Venezuela from Aruba to Trinidad) to Tierra del Fuego; and on Cuba, the Isle of Pines and in the Bahamas (Cat Island, San Salvador and Great Inagua).

Casual or accidental in southeastern California (Imperial Dam), southern Arizona, Colorado, western Texas, Oklahoma, Kansas, southern Illinois, Mississippi, Jamaica, Puerto Rico and the northern Lesser Antilles, also sight reports for southern Nevada.

Notes.—Also known as NEOTROPIC CORMORANT. The name *P. brasilianus* (Gmelin, 1789), sometimes used for this species, is regarded as indeterminate. See also comments under *P. auritus.*

Phalacrocorax penicillatus (Brandt). BRANDT'S CORMORANT. [122.]

Carbo penicillatus M. Brandt, 1837, Bull. Sci. Acad. Imp. Sci. St.-Petersbourg, 3, col. 55. (No locality given = Vancouver Island.)

Habitat.—Seacoasts, breeding on open ground in rocky areas, ranging primarily at sea and, less commonly, inshore on brackish bays.

Distribution.—*Breeds* along the Pacific coast in south-coastal Alaska (Seal Rocks, Hinchinbrook Entrance, Prince William Sound, since 1972), and from Washington (Matia Island) south to Baja California (Isla Natividad and in San Cristobal Bay, formerly on Guadalupe Island, Pacific coast; and San Pedro Mártir, Salsipuedes and Roca Blanca islands, Gulf of California).

Ranges generally near the breeding areas but occurs from southern Alaska south to southern Baja California (Cape San Lucas) and widely in the Gulf of California.

Phalacrocorax pelagicus Pallas. PELAGIC CORMORANT. [123.]

Phalacrocorax pelagicus Pallas, 1811, Zoogr. Rosso-Asiat., 2, p. 303. (maris Camtschatici orientalis et Americanarum insularum incola = Aleutian Islands.)

Habitat.—Primarily seacoasts, breeding on cliffs on islands and along rocky coasts.

Distribution.—*Breeds* from the southern Chukchi Sea (Cape Lisburne and Cape Thompson, Alaska) south through the Bering Sea to the Aleutian Islands, and along the Pacific coast of North America to northern Baja California (Los Coronados Islands), and from Wrangel Island east along the Arctic coast of Siberia to the Bering Strait, and south to northern Japan (Hondo).

Winters from the Aleutians and southern Alaska south to central Baja California (casually to Cape San Lucas), and from Kamchatka south to China.

Casual north to Point Barrow, Alaska; accidental in the Hawaiian Islands (Midway and Laysan).

[†Phalacrocorax perspicillatus Pallas. PALLAS' CORMORANT.] See Appendix B.

Phalacrocorax urile (Gmelin). RED-FACED CORMORANT. [124.]

Pelecanus Urile Gmelin, 1789, Syst. Nat., 1 (2), p. 575. Based on the "Red-faced Corvorant" Pennant, Arct. Zool., 2, p. 584, and the "Red-faced Shag"

Latham, Gen. Synop. Birds, 3 (2), p. 601. (in Camtschatcae rupestribus maritimis = Kamchatka.)

Habitat.—Seacoasts and rocky islands, breeding on cliffs.

Distribution.—*Breeds* in the southern Bering Sea (on St. Paul and St. George in the Pribilofs, on Cape Peirce, and in the Walrus Islands), in the Aleutian Islands (from Attu eastward), and along the coast of southern Alaska (east to Cape St. Elias); also in the Commander Islands and off Japan (Hokkaido).

Winters generally throughout the breeding range, occurring casually north to St. Michael in Norton Sound, Alaska, and south to southeastern Alaska (Sitka) and Japan (Honshu).

[**Phalacrocorax bougainvillii** (Lesson). GUANAY CORMORANT.] See Appendix A.

[**Phalacrocorax gaimardi** (Lesson and Garnot). RED-LEGGED CORMORANT.] See Appendix B.

Family ANHINGIDAE: Darters

Notes.—By some authors considered a subfamily of the Phalacrocoracidae.

Genus ANHINGA Brisson

Anhinga Brisson, 1760, Ornithologie, 1, p. 60; 6, p. 476. Type, by tautonymy, *Anhinga* Brisson = *Plotus anhinga* Linnaeus.

Anhinga anhinga (Linnaeus). ANHINGA. [118.]

Plotus Anhinga Linnaeus, 1766, Syst. Nat., ed. 12, 1, p. 218. Based on the "Anhinga" Marcgrave, Hist. Nat. Bras., p. 218, and Brisson, Ornithologie, 6, p. 476. (in America australi = Rio Tapajós, Pará, Brazil.)

Habitat.—Fresh-water swamps, lakes and sluggish streams at low elevations and, in tropical regions, primarily around brackish lagoons and in mangroves, nesting in trees (Tropical and lower Subtropical zones).

Distribution.—*Breeds* from central and eastern Texas, southeastern Oklahoma, southern and eastern Arkansas, southern Missouri (formerly), western Tennessee, southern Illinois (formerly), north-central Mississippi, southern Alabama, southern Georgia and coastal North Carolina south to southern Florida, Cuba and the Isle of Pines, and from Sinaloa and the Gulf coast south along both lowlands of Mexico and through Middle America and South America (also Tobago and Trinidad) west of the Andes to Ecuador and east of the Andes to eastern Peru, Bolivia, northern Argentina and Uruguay.

Winters in the southeastern United States from central South Carolina, southern Georgia, Florida and the Gulf coast southward, being essentially resident in the breeding range in Cuba, the Isle of Pines, Middle America and South America.

Casual after the breeding season north to southern California, Arizona, New Mexico, Nebraska, Michigan, southern Ontario, Ohio, New York and Maryland, and to the Florida Keys and Bahamas (Andros); the origin of some of these individuals, especially those reported in California, is questionable, and they may represent escapes from captivity.

Notes.—Also known as AMERICAN DARTER. The relationship of *A. anhinga* to the Old World forms *A. rufa* (Daudin, 1802) of Africa, *A. melanogaster* Pennant, 1769, of Southeast Asia, and *A. novaehollandiae* (Gould, 1847) of the Australian region, remains in doubt; some authors suggest that all forms constitute a single superspecies.

Suborder FREGATAE: Frigatebirds

Family FREGATIDAE: Frigatebirds

Genus FREGATA Lacépède

Fregata Lacépède, 1799, Tabl. Mamm. Ois., p. 15. Type, by subsequent designation (Daudin, 1802), *Pelecanus aquilus* Linnaeus.

Fregata magnificens Mathews. MAGNIFICENT FRIGATEBIRD. [128.]

Fregata minor magnificens Mathews, 1914, Austral Avian Rec., 2, p. 20. (Barrington, Indefatigable, Albemarle Islands = Barrington Island, Galapagos.)

Habitat.—Pelagic, breeding on islands in mangroves, low trees and shrubs.

Distribution.—*Breeds* along the Pacific coast off Baja California (Santa Margarita Island), Nayarit (Isabel and the Tres Marietas islands), Oaxaca (Natartiac Island in Laguna Superior, Juchitán), Honduras (Isla Pájaro in the Gulf of Fonseca), Costa Rica (Isla Bolaños), Panama (many islets in the Gulf of Chiriquí and Bay of Panama) and South America (Colombia, Ecuador and the Galapagos Islands); in the Atlantic-Caribbean region in Florida (Marquesas Key), on the central coast of Texas (Aransas county) and the coast of Veracruz (Laguna de Tamiahua), off the Yucatan Peninsula and Belize (Man-of-war Cay), widely in the Bahamas and Antilles (east to Barbuda in the northern Lesser Antilles), in the Cayman (Little Cayman) and Swan (Little Swan) islands, on islands north of Venezuela (Los Hermanos and Margarita east to Tobago), in the Grenadines of the southern Lesser Antilles, and locally along the South American coast to southern Brazil; and in the Cape Verde Islands, off western Africa.

Ranges at sea along the Pacific coast from northern California (casually from south-coastal Alaska) south to northern Peru; throughout the Gulf of Mexico, Caribbean Sea and western Atlantic from North Carolina (casually from New England and Nova Scotia) south to northern Argentina; and in the eastern Atlantic in the vicinity of the Cape Verde Islands.

Casual or accidental in the interior of North America, mostly after storms, north to Kansas, Iowa, Wisconsin, Indiana, Ohio, Quebec and Newfoundland, and in Arizona and New Mexico; also in the British Isles, on continental Europe and in the Azores.

Fregata minor (Gmelin). GREAT FRIGATEBIRD. [128.1.]

Pelecanus minor Gmelin, 1789, Syst. Nat., 1 (2), p. 572. Based mainly on the "Lesser Frigate" Latham, Gen. Synop. Birds, 3 (2), p. 590. (No locality given = Christmas Island, eastern Indian Ocean.)

Habitat.—Pelagic, breeding on islands in trees or on low vegetation.

Distribution.—*Breeds* in the Pacific Ocean in the Revillagigedo Islands (San Benedicto and Clarión), off Costa Rica (Cocos Island), in the Galapagos Islands, and from the Hawaiian Islands (Kure east to Nihoa, also one breeding record for Moku Manu islet off Oahu) and the South China Sea south to northeastern Australia (Raine Island) and the Fiji and Tuamotu islands; in the South Atlantic on Trindade Island, off Brazil; and in the Indian Ocean from Aldabra and the Seychelles east to Christmas Island.

Ranges at sea generally in the vicinity of the breeding areas, and occurring throughout the Hawaiian Islands, north to Japan and south to southeastern Australia and New Zealand; not certainly recorded from the Pacific coast of North or South America.

Accidental in Oklahoma (Perry, 3 November 1975).

Fregata ariel (Gray). LESSER FRIGATEBIRD. [128.2.]

> *Atagen Ariel* (Gould MS) G. R. Gray, 1845, Genera Birds, 3, p. [669], col. pl. [185]. (No locality given = Raine Island, Queensland.)

Habitat.—Pelagic, breeding on islands primarily in low bushes or trees.

Distribution.—*Breeds* in the South Pacific off northern Australia (Northwest Australia east to Raine Island, Queensland), in New Caledonia, and from the Howland, Line and Marquesas islands south to the Fiji, Tonga and Tuamotu islands; in the South Atlantic at Trindade Island, off Brazil; and in the western Indian Ocean in the Aldabra Islands.

Ranges widely at sea, especially in the Pacific Ocean, north regularly through Indonesia, the South China Sea and western Pacific to Korea, Japan and Kamchatka, and casually to the western Hawaiian Islands (Kure); also recorded in the South Atlantic not far from the breeding grounds, and in the Indian Ocean in the Mascarene Islands.

Accidental in Maine (Deer Island, Hancock County, 3 July 1960; Snyder, 1961, Auk, 78, p. 265) and Siberia.

Notes.—Also known as LEAST FRIGATEBIRD.

Order CICONIIFORMES: Herons, Ibises, Storks and Allies

Notes.—The monophyly of the Ciconiiformes, the relationships among the subgroups within it, and the relationships between this order and others are by no means clear. For a summary of these problems, see Sibley and Ahlquist (1972, Peabody Mus. Nat. Hist. Bull., 39, pp. 72–86).

Suborder ARDEAE: Bitterns, Herons and Allies

Family ARDEIDAE: Bitterns and Herons

Tribe BOTAURINI: Bitterns

Genus **BOTAURUS** Stephens

Botaurus Stephens, 1819, *in* Shaw, Gen. Zool., 11 (2), p. 592. Type, by subsequent designation (G. R. Gray, 1840), *Ardea stellaris* Linnaeus.

Botaurus pinnatus (Wagler). PINNATED BITTERN.

Ardea pinnata (Lichtenstein MS) Wagler, 1829, Isis von Oken, col. 662. (Bahia, Brazil.)

Habitat.—Fresh-water marshes (Tropical to Temperate zones).

Distribution.—*Breeds* locally in the lowlands of Middle America in southeastern Mexico (Veracruz, Tabasco, the state of Yucatán, and Quintana Roo), Belize, El Salvador (Laguna Jocotal) and Costa Rica (Río Frío district, Guanacaste, Turrialba); and widely in South America in central Colombia and western Ecuador, and east of the Andes from southern Venezuela and the Guianas south to northern Argentina, Uruguay and southern Brazil.

Botaurus lentiginosus (Rackett). AMERICAN BITTERN. [190.]

Ardea lentiginosa Rackett, 1813, *in* Pulteney, Cat. Birds Shells Plants Dorsetshire, ed. 2, p. 14. (Piddletown, Dorset, England.)

Habitat.—Fresh-water and brackish marshes, generally in tall vegetation.

Distribution.—*Breeds* from extreme southeastern Alaska, central British Columbia, southern Mackenzie, northern Manitoba, northern Ontario, central Quebec and Newfoundland south to southern California, central Arizona (formerly), southern New Mexico, central Kansas, central Missouri, central and western Tennessee, western Kentucky, central Ohio, southern Pennsylvania, northeastern West Virginia, eastern Maryland and eastern Virginia; and locally in Texas, Louisiana, Florida, and in Mexico south to Puebla and the state of México.

Winters from southwestern British Columbia, western Washington, western Oregon, northern Nevada, northern and central Utah, northern Arizona, central New Mexico, northern Texas, central Oklahoma, central Arkansas, the Ohio Valley (rarely) and New York (casually farther north) south to southern Mexico and Cuba, rarely (or formerly) to Costa Rica and Panama, and to the Swan and Cayman islands, Greater Antilles (east to the Virgin Islands), Bahamas and Bermuda.

Casual north to Keewatin and Labrador, and in Greenland, Iceland, the Faroe Islands, British Isles, continental Europe, the Azores and Canary Islands.

Genus **IXOBRYCHUS** Billberg

Ixobrychus Billberg, 1828, Synop. Faunae Scand., ed. 2, 1 (2), p. 166. Type, by subsequent designation (Stone, 1907), *Ardea minuta* Linnaeus.

Ixobrychus exilis (Gmelin). LEAST BITTERN. [191.]

Ardea exilis Gmelin, 1789, Syst. Nat., 1 (2), p. 645. Based on the "Minute Bittern" Latham, Gen. Synop. Birds, 3 (1), p. 66. (in Jamaica.)

Habitat.—Tall vegetation in marshes, primarily fresh-water, less commonly in coastal brackish marshes and mangrove swamps (Tropical to Temperate zones).

Distribution.—*Breeds* locally in western North America in southern Oregon, interior and southern coastal California, central Baja California and southern coastal Sonora; in eastern North America from southern Manitoba, northeastern North Dakota, northwestern Minnesota, central Wisconsin, northern Michigan, southern Ontario, extreme southern Quebec, eastern Maine and southern New

Brunswick south to western and southern Texas, the Gulf coast, Florida and the Greater Antilles, and west to central Montana, Utah (Great Salt Lake, formerly), eastern Colorado and south-central New Mexico; in Middle America in Guatemala (Dueñas and Atitlán), El Salvador (Lake Olomega), Honduras (Lake Yojoa, Copén), Nicaragua (Los Sabalos), Costa Rica (Guanacaste), Panama (Canal Zone) and undoubtedly elsewhere, especially in Mexico; and widely in South America in central Colombia (Temperate Zone), along the coast of Peru, and east of the Andes from Venezuela and the Guianas south to northern Argentina and southern Brazil. Recorded in summer (and probably breeding) in Nova Scotia.

Winters from southern California, southern Texas and northern Florida south throughout the Greater Antilles, Middle America and South America (south to the limits of the breeding range). Breeding populations south of the United States are mostly sedentary; North American breeding birds winter as far south as Panama and Colombia.

Casual north to southern British Columbia, southern Saskatchewan, southern Alberta, southern Quebec and Newfoundland, and throughout most of the western states where breeding has not been verified. Accidental in Bermuda, Iceland and the Azores.

Notes.—Two Old World species, *I. minutus* (Linnaeus, 1766) and *I. sinensis* (Gmelin, 1789), along with *I. exilis,* probably constitute a superspecies.

Tribe TIGRISOMATINI: Tiger-Herons

Genus **TIGRISOMA** Swainson

Tigrisoma Swainson, 1827, Zool. J., 3, p. 362. Type, by original designation, *Ardea tigrina* "Latham" [= Gmelin] = *Ardea lineata* Boddaert.
Heterocnus Sharpe, 1895, Bull. Br. Ornithol. Club, 5, p. xiv. Type, by original designation, *Tigrisoma cabanisi* Heine = *Tigrisoma mexicana* Swainson.

Notes.—Members of this genus are sometimes known under the group name TIGER-BITTERN.

Tigrisoma lineatum (Boddaert). RUFESCENT TIGER-HERON.

Ardea lineata Boddaert, 1783, Table Planches Enlum., p. 52. Based on "L'O-noré rayé, de Cayenne" Daubenton, Planches Enlum., p. 860. (Cayenne.)

Habitat.—Interior of shaded forests and along forest streams, less commonly in swamps and mangroves (Tropical Zone).

Distribution.—*Resident* in Middle America on the Caribbean slope of extreme eastern Honduras (Gracias a Dios), Nicaragua, Costa Rica and Panama (east to San Blas), and on the Pacific slope of Panama in Darién; and in South America from Colombia and Venezuela (also Trinidad) south, west of the Andes to western Ecuador and east of the Andes to northern Argentina, Uruguay and central Brazil.

Casual or accidental in northern Honduras (Lake Yojoa, sight record) and Chiapas (presumably a vagrant).

Tigrisoma fasciatum (Such). FASCIATED TIGER-HERON.

Ardea fasciata Such, 1825, Zool. J., 2, p. 117. (Brazil.)

Habitat.—Along forest streams in humid, hilly regions (Tropical and lower Subtropical zones).

Distribution.—*Resident* in Costa Rica (Caribbean slope foothills of the Cordillera Central and Cordillera Talamanca) and Panama (primarily Caribbean slope from Bocas del Toro to San Blas, and in Darién); and in South America east of the Andes from Colombia and Venezuela south to northern Argentina and southeastern Brazil.

Notes.—For use of *T. fasciatum* instead of *T. salmoni* Sclater and Salvin, 1875, see Eisenmann, 1965, Hornero, 10, pp. 225–234.

Tigrisoma mexicanum Swainson. BARE-THROATED TIGER-HERON.

Tigrisoma mexicanum Swainson, 1834, *in* Murray, Encycl. Geogr., p. 1383. (Real del Monte, [Hidalgo,] Mexico.)

Habitat.—Marshes, swamps, mangroves and occasionally moist woodland, primarily along the banks of streams and lagoons (Tropical Zone).

Distribution.—*Resident* from southern Sonora, southern San Luis Potosí and southern Tamaulipas south along both slopes of Middle America (including Cozumel Island and Isla Cancun) to eastern Panama (on the Pacific slope primarily, including the Pearl Islands, Isla Coiba and several smaller islets; on the Caribbean slope only in the San Blas area); also in the lower Atrato Valley of northwestern Colombia.

Notes.—Often placed in the monotypic genus *Heterocnus.*

Tribe ARDEINI: Typical Herons

Genus **ARDEA** Linnaeus

Ardea Linnaeus, 1758, Syst. Nat., ed. 10, 1, p. 141. Type, by subsequent designation (G. R. Gray, 1840), *Ardea cinerea* Linnaeus.

Ardea herodias Linnaeus. GREAT BLUE HERON. [194.]

Ardea Herodias Linnaeus, 1758, Syst. Nat., ed. 10, 1, p. 143. Based mainly on "The Ash-colour'd Heron of North-America" Edwards, Nat. Hist. Birds, 3, p. 135, pl. 135. (in America = Hudson Bay.)

Habitat.—Fresh-water and brackish marshes, along lakes, rivers and lagoons, and mangroves, breeding primarily in trees, less commonly on the ground, rock ledges and coastal cliffs (Tropical to Temperate zones).

Distribution.—*Breeds* [*herodias* group] from south-coastal and southeastern Alaska (west to Prince William Sound), coastal and southern British Columbia, northern Alberta, southern Keewatin, central Manitoba, southern Ontario, southern Quebec, New Brunswick, Prince Edward Island and Nova Scotia south, at least locally, throughout the United States and much of Mexico to Guerrero, Veracruz, the Gulf coast and interior southern Florida, also in the Galapagos Islands; and [*occidentalis* group] in southern coastal Florida (north to the Tampa area, and including the Florida Keys), Cuba, the Isle of Pines, St. Thomas, Anegada, the coast of the Yucatan Peninsula, and Los Roques off the northern coast of Venezuela, with breeding probably elsewhere in the Greater Antilles and on other islands off Venezuela.

Winters [*herodias* group] from south-coastal and southeastern Alaska, the coasts of British Columbia and Washington, central Oregon, southern Idaho, western Montana, northern Wyoming, central Nebraska, central Missouri, the Ohio Valley, southern Ontario and the southern New England coast south throughout the southern United States, Middle America, Bermuda and the West Indies to northern Colombia, northern Venezuela, western Ecuador and the Galapagos Islands; and [*occidentalis* group] primarily in the vicinity of the breeding range and along the coasts of Venezuela and on islands offshore (east to Tobago and Trinidad).

Wanders widely [*herodias* group] west to Cook Inlet, Alaska, and north to the Arctic coast of Alaska (rarely), central British Columbia, southern Keewatin, Hudson Bay (rarely), northern Quebec, Anticosti Island and Newfoundland; and [*occidentalis* group] north in peninsular Florida and casually along the Gulf coast west to Texas and the Atlantic coast to North Carolina, and in the Bahamas. Accidental [*herodias* group] in the Hawaiian Islands (Oahu, Maui, Hawaii), northwestern Alaska (Wainwright) and Greenland; and [*occidentalis* group] in Pennsylvania.

Notes.—The white and mixed white and blue forms have often been considered as a separate species, *A. occidentalis* Audubon, 1835 [GREAT WHITE HERON, 192], but are now generally regarded as being conspecific with *A. herodias*. *A. cinerea*, *A. cocoi* and *A. herodias* are closely related and constitute a superspecies; some authors consider them conspecific.

Ardea cinerea Linnaeus. GRAY HERON.

Ardea cinerea Linnaeus, 1758, Syst. Nat., ed. 10, 1, p. 143. (in Europa = Sweden.)

Habitat & Distribution.—*Breeds* in habitats similar to *A. herodias* from the British Isles and Scandinavia east to Sakhalin and throughout much of Eurasia south locally to South Africa and the East Indies, wandering within this range after the breeding season.

Casual in Greenland. Accidental in the Lesser Antilles (Cars Bay, Montserrat, 20 September 1959, bird banded at Lac de Grand-Lieu, France; Baudouin-Bodin, 1960, Oiseau, 30, p. 274) and Trinidad.

Notes.—Known in Old World literature as the HERON. See comments under *A. herodias*.

Ardea cocoi Linnaeus. WHITE-NECKED HERON.

Ardea Cocoi Linnaeus, 1766, Syst. Nat., ed. 12, 1, p. 237. Based in part on "Le Hérón hupé de Cayenne" Brisson, Ornithologie, 5, p. 400. (in Cayana = Cayenne.)

Habitat.—Along rivers, lagoons, marshes and swamps, breeding primarily in trees (Tropical to Temperate zones).

Distribution.—*Resident* in eastern Panama (eastern Panamá province and eastern Darién) and throughout South America (also Trinidad) south to southern Chile and southern Argentina.

Casual in central Panama (west to the Canal Zone). Accidental in the Falkland Islands.

Notes.—Also known as COCOI HERON. See comments under *A. herodias*.

Genus **CASMERODIUS** Gloger

Casmerodius Gloger, 1842, Gemein. Handb. Hilfsb. Naturgesch. (1841), p. 412. Type, by subsequent designation (Salvadori, 1882), *Ardea egretta* Gmelin.

Notes.—By some authors merged in *Egretta,* by others in *Ardea.*

Casmerodius albus (Linnaeus). GREAT EGRET. [196.]

Ardea alba Linnaeus, 1758, Syst. Nat., ed. 10, 1, p. 144. (in Europa = Sweden.)

Habitat.—Marshes, swampy woods, tidal estuaries, lagoons, mangroves and along streams, breeding primarily in tall trees (Tropical to Temperate zones).

Distribution.—*Breeds* in North America locally from southern Oregon and southern Idaho south through California, Nevada and southwestern Arizona, and from southeastern Saskatchewan, southwestern Manitoba, central Minnesota, southwestern Wisconsin, central Illinois, southern Indiana, southern Ontario, northern Ohio, Vermont (probably) and Maine south (west to eastern Colorado, southern New Mexico and south-central Texas) through the Gulf states, along both coasts of Mexico (also locally in the interior), and through the Bahamas, Antilles, Middle America and South America to southern Chile and southern Argentina; in the Old World from central Europe east to Ussuriland and Japan, and south to Turkey, Iran, India, China, most of Southeast Asia, the East Indies, the Philippines, New Guinea, Australia and New Zealand; and locally in Africa south of the Sahara and in Madagascar.

Winters in North America from northern California, central Nevada, central Arizona, central New Mexico, central Texas, the Gulf coast and coastal North Carolina south throughout Mexico and the remainder of the breeding range in the Americas to the Straits of Magellan; in the Old World from the Mediterranean coast of Africa, the Red Sea, Persian Gulf, central India, China, Korea and Japan south through the breeding range in Southeast Asia to Australia and New Zealand; and in the breeding range in Africa and Madagascar.

Wanders north irregularly in North America to southwestern British Columbia, southern Alberta, southern Saskatchewan, southeastern Manitoba, southern Quebec and Newfoundland; and in Europe to the British Isles, Scandinavia and the Baltic states. Casual in southeastern Alaska (Juneau), the Falkland and Canary islands, Mediterranean region and southern Africa; accidental in the Hawaiian Islands (Oahu).

Notes.—Also known as COMMON or AMERICAN EGRET and, in Old World literature, as GREAT WHITE HERON.

Genus **EGRETTA** Forster

Egretta T. Forster, 1817, Synop. Cat. Br. Birds, p. 59. Type, by monotypy, *Ardea garzetta* Linnaeus.

Florida Baird, 1858, *in* Baird, Cassin and Lawrence, Rep. Explor. Surv. R. R. Pac., 9, pp. xxi, xlv, 659, 671. Type, by monotypy, *Ardea caerulea* Linnaeus.

Hydranassa Baird, 1858, *in* Baird, Cassin and Lawrence, Rep. Explor. Surv. R. R. Pac., 9, p. 660. Type, by original designation, *Ardea ludoviciana* Wilson = *Egretta ruficollis* Gosse.

Dichromanassa Ridgway, 1878, Bull. U.S. Geol. Geogr. Surv. Terr., 4, pp.

224, 246. Type, by original designation, *Ardea rufa* Boddaert = *Ardea rufescens* Gmelin.

Mesophoyx Sharpe, 1894, Bull. Br. Ornithol. Club, 3, p. xxxviii. Type, by original designation, *Ardea intermedia* Wagler.

Leucophoyx Sharpe, 1894, Bull. Br. Ornithol. Club, 3, p. xxxix. Type, by original designation, *Ardea candidissima* Gmelin = *Ardea thula* Molina.

[Egretta intermedia (Wagler). INTERMEDIATE EGRET.] See Appendix B.

Egretta eulophotes (Swinhoe). CHINESE EGRET. [196.2.]

Herodias eulophotes Swinhoe, 1860, Ibis, p. 64. (Amoy, China.)

Habitat & Distribution. — *Breeds* in fresh-water habitats in northern Korea and southeastern China, and *winters* to Japan, wandering south to the Philippines and the East Indies.

Accidental in Alaska (Agattu Island in the Aleutians, 16 June 1974; Byrd, Trapp and Gibson, 1978, Condor, 80, p. 309).

Egretta garzetta (Linnaeus). LITTLE EGRET. [196.1.]

Ardea Garzetta Linnaeus, 1766, Syst. Nat., ed. 12, 1, p. 237. (in Oriente = northeastern Italy.)

Habitat & Distribution. — *Breeds* locally in marshy areas in southern Europe, Africa, Madagascar, and from Southeast Asia and Japan south to New Guinea, and *winters* principally in Southeast Asia and the African and Australian regions.

Accidental in Quebec (Cacouna area, 14 May–6 September 1980), Newfoundland (Flatrock, Conception Bay, 8 May 1954), Barbados (Graeme Hall Swamp, 16 April 1954), Martinique (6 October 1962), Trinidad and Surinam.

Notes. — *E. garzetta* and *E. thula* may constitute a superspecies.

Egretta thula (Molina). SNOWY EGRET. [197.]

Ardea Thula Molina, 1782, Saggio Stor. Nat. Chili, p. 235. (Chili = Chile.)

Habitat. — Marshes, lakes, ponds, lagoons, mangroves and shallow coastal habitats, breeding in bushes and trees (Tropical to Temperate zones).

Distribution. — *Breeds* from northern California, northern Nevada, southeastern Idaho, Montana, South Dakota, Nebraska (formerly), central Kansas, central Oklahoma, central and eastern (also locally in extreme western) Texas, the lower Mississippi Valley (north casually or formerly to southeastern Missouri and southern Illinois), and the Gulf and Atlantic coasts (north to Maine) south, primarily in coastal lowlands and locally in the interior, through the Greater Antilles (east to the Virgin Islands) and Middle America, and throughout South America to southern Chile and central Argentina.

Winters from northern California, southwestern Arizona, the Gulf coast and coastal South Carolina south throughout the breeding range in the West Indies, Middle America and South America.

Wanders irregularly north to southern British Columbia, southern Alberta, southern Saskatchewan, central Minnesota, southern Ontario, southern Quebec and Newfoundland (sight report from southwestern Mackenzie); also to the Bahamas and throughout the Lesser Antilles, casually to Bermuda and the Hawaiian Islands (Oahu, Maui, Hawaii). Accidental in southeastern Alaska (Juneau) and on Tristan da Cunha.

Notes.—This species is frequently placed in the monotypic genus *Leucophoyx*. See also comments under *E. garzetta*.

Egretta caerulea (Linnaeus). LITTLE BLUE HERON. [200.]

Ardea cærulea Linnaeus, 1758, Syst. Nat., ed. 10, 1, p. 143. Based mainly on "The Blew Heron" Catesby, Nat. Hist. Carolina, 1, p. 76, pl. 76. (in America septentrionali = South Carolina.)

Habitat.—Marshes, ponds, lakes, meadows, streams and mangroves, breeding in trees and low shrubs, primarily in fresh-water habitats (Tropical to Temperate zones).

Distribution.—*Breeds* from southern California (casually, since 1979), southern Sonora, southeastern New Mexico, north-central Texas, central Oklahoma, central Kansas, southern Arkansas, southeastern Missouri, southwestern Kentucky, northwestern Tennessee, central Alabama, southern Georgia and the Atlantic coast (north to Maine) south along both coasts of Mexico and Middle America, through the Gulf coast region and West Indies, and in South America (also Tobago and Trinidad) from Colombia, Venezuela and the Guianas west of the Andes to central Peru and east of the Andes to eastern Peru, central Brazil and Uruguay; also sporadically in central Minnesota (Pope and probably Grant counties).

Winters from southern Baja California, southern Sonora, the Gulf coast and coastal Virginia south throughout most of the breeding range.

Wanders irregularly north to central California, southeastern Saskatchewan, southern Minnesota, central Wisconsin, southern Michigan, southern Ontario, southern Quebec, southern Labrador, Newfoundland and Nova Scotia. Casual or accidental in the Hawaiian Islands (Oahu), southwestern British Columbia and northwestern Washington (same individual), Utah and Greenland.

Notes.—This species is often placed in the monotypic genus *Florida*.

Egretta tricolor (Müller). TRICOLORED HERON. [199.]

Ardea tricolor P. L. S. Müller, 1776, Natursyst., Suppl., p. 111. Based on "La Demi-Aigrette" Buffon, Hist. Nat. Ois. 7, p. 378, and "Herón bleuâtre a ventre blanc, de Cayenne" Daubenton, Planches Enlum., pl. 350. (America = Cayenne.)

Habitat.—Marshes, ponds and rivers, breeding primarily near salt water in mangroves, on trees and in grasses virtually on the ground, very rarely in inland fresh-water situations (Tropical and Subtropical zones).

Distribution.—*Breeds* from central Baja California, southern Sonora, southeastern New Mexico, north-central and northeastern Texas, the Gulf coast and the Atlantic coast (north to southern Maine) south along both coasts of Middle America to northern South America, on the Pacific coast to central Peru and on the Caribbean-Atlantic coast to northeastern Brazil (also islands off the north coast of Venezuela); and in the Bahamas, Greater Antilles (east to St. Thomas and St. Croix), and on Providencia and San Andrés islands in the western Caribbean Sea. Casual or rare breeding inland in North Dakota (Long Lake) and central Kansas (Cheyenne Bottoms).

Winters from southern Baja California, southern Sonora, southeastern Texas, the Gulf coast and the Atlantic coast (north to New Jersey, casually farther) south through the remainder of the breeding range.

Wanders irregularly north to Oregon, California, central Arizona, southern New Mexico, Colorado and, east of the Rockies, to southern Manitoba, northern Minnesota, central Wisconsin, northern Michigan, southern Ontario, southern Quebec, southern New Brunswick and Nova Scotia; also to the Lesser Antilles (south to Barbados).

Notes.—Also known as LOUISIANA HERON. This species is frequently placed in the monotypic genus *Hydranassa.*

Egretta rufescens (Gmelin). REDDISH EGRET. [198.]

> *Ardea rufescens* Gmelin, 1789, Syst. Nat., 1 (2), p. 628. Based on "Aigrette rousse" Buffon, Hist. Nat. Ois., 7, p. 378, and "L'Aigrette rousse, de la Louisiane" Daubenton, Planches Enlum., pl. 902. (in Louisiana.)

Habitat.—Brackish marshes and shallow coastal habitats, breeding in low trees, primarily in red mangrove (Tropical Zone).

Distribution.—*Breeds* in Baja California (north to San Quintín on the Pacific coast and Angel de la Guarda in the Gulf of California), Sonora (Tobari Bay), Sinaloa (Isla Las Tunas) and Oaxaca (Mar Muerto); along the Gulf coast of Texas (Cameron to Chambers counties), Louisiana (North Island) and Alabama (Cat Island); in southern Florida (north to Merritt Island and the Tampa area), the northwestern Bahamas (Grand Bahama, Abaco, Andros and Great Inagua), Cuba, the Isle of Pines and Hispaniola (formerly Jamaica); and on the coast of the Yucatan Peninsula, including offshore islands.

Winters primarily in coastal areas of the breeding range, north irregularly to central coastal and southern California, southwestern Arizona, the Gulf coast (from Texas to Florida) and Georgia (casually north to Virginia); and south along the Pacific coast to Costa Rica, and in the Caribbean to Belize, Puerto Rico and the northern coast of Venezuela (also the Netherlands Antilles east to Margarita Island).

Casual inland, generally as postbreeding wanderers, to southern Colorado, central Texas, southern Illinois and Kentucky, and to Costa Rica (Caribbean coast) and Isla Coiba (off Panama).

Notes.—This species is often placed in the monotypic genus *Dichromanassa.*

Genus BUBULCUS Bonaparte

> *Bubulcus* (Pucheran MS) Bonaparte, 1855, C. R. Acad. Sci. Paris, 40, p. 722. Type, by subsequent designation (G. R. Gray, 1871), *Ardea ibis* "Hasselquist" [= Linnaeus].

Notes.—By some merged in the Old World genus *Ardeola* Boie, 1822, or in *Egretta*; affinities remain uncertain.

Bubulcus ibis (Linnaeus). CATTLE EGRET. [200.1.]

> *Ardea Ibis* Linnaeus, 1758, Syst. Nat., ed. 10, 1, p. 144. Based on *Ardea Ibis* Hasselquist, Iter Palaestinum, p. 248. (in Ægypto = Egypt.)

Habitat.—Wet pasturelands and marshes, both fresh-water and brackish situations, also dry fields, nesting in trees (Tropical to Temperate zones).

Distribution.—*Breeds* in the Western Hemisphere locally from northwestern and central California, southern Idaho, northern Utah, Colorado, North Dakota, southern Saskatchewan, Minnesota, Wisconsin, southern Ontario, northern Ohio and Maine south, primarily in coastal lowlands (very scattered inland localities) through Middle America, the Gulf and Atlantic states, West Indies and South America (also Tobago and Trinidad) to northwestern Chile and northern Argentina; in southern Europe from the Mediterranean region east to the Caspian Sea, and south throughout most of Africa (except the Sahara), including Madagascar and islands in the Indian Ocean; and in Southeast Asia from India east to eastern China, Japan and the Ryukyu Islands, and south throughout the Philippines and East Indies to New Guinea and probably also northern Australia (introduced and established widely elsewhere in Australia).

Winters in the Americas through much of the breeding range from southern California, eastern Texas, the Gulf states and Florida south through the West Indies, Middle America and South America; and in the Old World from southern Spain and northern Africa south and east through the remainder of the breeding range in Africa, Asia and Australia.

Wanders north, at least casually, to southeastern Alaska (Ketchikan), southern Canada (British Columbia east to Nova Scotia and Newfoundland), and in Eurasia to Iceland, the British Isles, continental Europe and the eastern Atlantic islands.

Introduced (in 1959) and established on most of the larger Hawaiian Islands, wandering to Midway and Johnston Island.

Notes.—Also known as BUFF-BACKED HERON. This species apparently spread to the New World (Guianas in South America) in the late 1870's, reaching Florida by the early 1940's; the range is still expanding.

Genus **BUTORIDES** Blyth

Butorides Blyth, 1852, Cat. Birds Mus. Asiat. Soc. (1849), p. 281. Type, by monotypy, *Ardea javanica* Horsfield = *Ardea striata* Linnaeus.

Notes.—Some authors merge this genus in the Old World *Ardeola.*

Butorides striatus (Linnaeus). GREEN-BACKED HERON. [201.]

Ardea striata Linnaeus, 1758, Syst. Nat., ed. 10, 1, p. 144. (in Surinami = Surinam.)

Habitat.—Ponds, rivers, lakes, lagoons, marshes, swamps and mangroves, breeding in trees in wooded areas in both fresh-water and brackish habitats (Tropical to Temperate zones).

Distribution.—*Breeds* [*virescens* group] from southwestern British Columbia (including Vancouver Island), western Washington, western Oregon, northern California, west-central and southern Nevada, southern Utah, north-central New Mexico, the western edge of the Great Plains states (north to eastern Colorado and eastern South Dakota), central Minnesota, northern Wisconsin, north-central Michigan, southern Ontario, southern Quebec and southern New Brunswick south through Middle America, the eastern United States and West Indies to eastern Panama (including the Pearl Islands), islands off the north coast of Venezuela (Aruba east to La Tortuga and Blanquilla) and Tobago.

Winters [*virescens* group] from western Washington (rarely at Lake Washington), coastal and southeastern California, southern Arizona, southern Texas, southern Louisiana, northern Florida and South Carolina south throughout the breeding range to northern Colombia and northern Venezuela.

Resident [*striatus* group] in the Americas from eastern Panama (eastern Panamá province and Darién), Colombia and Venezuela (also Margarita Island and Trinidad) south to southern Peru, Chile (rarely), central Argentina and Uruguay, also in the Galapagos Islands; and in the Old World from the Red Sea to the Gulf of Aden, in Africa south of the Sahara, on islands in the Indian Ocean, and from northern China, the Amur Valley and Japan (northern populations in eastern Asia are migratory) south throughout southeast Asia, the East Indies and the Philippines to Australia and southern Polynesia.

Wanders [*virescens* group] north to eastern Washington, Idaho, southern Alberta, southern Saskatchewan, southern Manitoba, central Ontario, Nova Scotia and southwestern Newfoundland, and south to Surinam; and [*striatus* group] north to Costa Rica (Guanacaste and Cocos Island) and St. Vincent, in the Lesser Antilles. Accidental [*virescens* group] in Bermuda, Greenland and England, also a sight report from the Hawaiian Islands (Hawaii).

Notes.—Also known as LITTLE HERON. The two groups are sometimes regarded as separate species, *B. striatus* [STRIATED HERON] and *B. virescens* (Linnaeus, 1758) [GREEN HERON], but intergradation occurs in central Panama. Some authors also consider *B. striatus* and *B. sundevalli* (Reichenow, 1877), of the Galapagos Islands, as conspecific, since intermediate specimens (as well as both forms) have been obtained there; the extent of hybridization, however, has not been determined.

Genus **AGAMIA** Reichenbach

Agamia Reichenbach, 1853, Avium Syst. Nat. (1852), p. xvi. Type, by original designation, *Agamia picta* Reichenbach = *Ardea agami* Gmelin.

Agamia agami (Gmelin). CHESTNUT-BELLIED HERON.

Ardea Agami Gmelin, 1789, Syst. Nat., 1 (2), p. 629. Based on "Agami" Buffon, Hist. Nat. Ois., 7, p. 382, and "Le Heron Agami de Cayenne" Daubenton, Planches Enlum., pl. 859. (in Cayanna = Cayenne.)

Habitat.—Shady forest streams and ponds in humid forest (Tropical, occasionally to Subtropical and lower Temperate zones).

Distribution.—*Resident* locally from southeastern Mexico (Veracruz, Tabasco, Chiapas and Quintana Roo) south through eastern Guatemala (Petén), Belize, northern Honduras (La Ceiba), Costa Rica and Panama, and in South America from Colombia, Venezuela (also Trinidad) and the Guianas south, west of the Andes to northwestern Ecuador and east of the Andes to northern Bolivia and Amazonian Brazil.

Notes.—Also known as AGAMI HERON.

Genus **PILHERODIUS** Bonaparte

Pilherodius Bonaparte, 1855, Consp. Gen. Avium, 2 (1857), p. 139. Type, by monotypy, *Ardea alba* var. β Gmelin = *Ardea pileata* Boddaert.

Pilherodius pileatus (Boddaert). CAPPED HERON.

Ardea pileata Boddaert, 1783, Table Planches Enlum., p. 54. Based on "Heron blanc, hupé de Cayenne" Daubenton, Planches Enlum., pl. 907. (Cayenne.)

Habitat.—Forest regions near rivers and ponds, occasionally in wooded savanna and cultivated regions (Tropical Zone).

Distribution.—*Resident* from eastern Panama (primarily in Darién but recorded west to Canal Zone), Colombia, Venezuela, the Guianas and Surinam south, east of the Andes, to eastern Peru, central Bolivia, northern Paraguay and eastern Brazil (to Santa Catarina).

Tribe NYCTICORACINI: Night-Herons

Genus **NYCTICORAX** Forster

Nycticorax T. Forster, 1817, Synop. Cat. Br. Birds, p. 59. Type, by tautonymy, *Nycticorax infaustus* Forster = *Ardea nycticorax* Linnaeus.
Nyctanassa Stejneger, 1887, Proc. U.S. Natl. Mus., 10, p. 295, note. Type, by original designation, *Ardea violacea* Linnaeus.

Nycticorax nycticorax (Linnaeus). BLACK-CROWNED NIGHT-HERON. [202.]

Ardea Nycticorax Linnaeus, 1758, Syst. Nat., ed. 10, 1, p. 142. (in Europa australi = southern Europe.)

Habitat.—Marshes, swamps, ponds, lakes, lagoons and mangroves, breeding in trees in wooded areas near water, occasionally in reeds (Tropical to Temperate zones).

Distribution.—*Breeds* in the Western Hemisphere from central Washington, southern Idaho, central Wyoming, east-central Alberta, central Saskatchewan, southern Manitoba, northwestern and central Minnesota, central Wisconsin, southern Michigan, southern Ontario, southern Quebec, northeastern New Brunswick and Nova Scotia south locally through the United States, Middle America, the Bahamas, Greater Antilles and South America to Tierra del Fuego and the Falkland Islands; from the Hawaiian Islands (Niihau east to Hawaii) south locally through the islands of Polynesia; and in the Old World from the Netherlands, central and southern Europe and northwestern Africa east to south-central Russia, and south locally through East and South Africa, on Madagascar, and from Asia Minor east across Southeast Asia to eastern China and Japan, and south to the Philippines and East Indies.

Winters in the Western Hemisphere from southern Oregon, southern Nevada, northern Utah, central New Mexico, southern Texas, the lower Ohio Valley, Gulf coast and southern New England south throughout the breeding range, becoming more widespread in winter (including through the Lesser Antilles); in the Hawaiian Islands and Polynesia (sedentary population); and in the Old World in Africa south of the Sahara (most European populations), and from Asia Minor across Southeast Asia to Japan, and southward.

Wanders north in North America to southern British Columbia, northern Wisconsin, central Ontario, central Quebec and Newfoundland; and in Europe to Iceland, the Faroe Islands, British Isles, Scandinavia and the eastern Atlantic islands. Casual in the western Hawaiian Islands (Kure, Midway), southwestern Alaska (St. Paul Island in the Pribilofs, and Shemya and Atka in the Aleutians), Bermuda and Greenland.

Notes.—*N. nycticorax* and *N. caledonicus* (Gmelin, 1789), of Polynesia and the Australian region, may constitute a superspecies.

Nycticorax violaceus (Linnaeus). YELLOW-CROWNED NIGHT-HERON. [203.]

> *Ardea violacea* Linnaeus, 1758, Syst. Nat., ed. 10, 1, p. 143. Based on "The Crested Bittern" Catesby, Nat. Hist. Carolina, 1, p. 79, pl. 79. (in America septentrionali = South Carolina.)

Habitat.—Marshes, swamps, lakes, lagoons and mangroves, breeding in trees in wooded situations near water, occasionally in arid areas on islands (Tropical to lower Temperate zones).

Distribution.—*Breeds* from central Baja California (both coasts), central Sonora, central and northeastern Texas, central Oklahoma, northeastern Kansas, southeastern Nebraska, southern Iowa, southeastern Minnesota, southern Wisconsin, southern Michigan, extreme southern Ontario (questionably), the lower Ohio Valley, eastern Tennessee, eastern West Virginia, southeastern Pennsylvania and Massachusetts south along both coasts of Mexico (including Socorro Island in the Revillagigedo group, and Isla María Madre in the Tres Marias group), the Gulf coast, Bahamas, Antilles, Middle America and coastal South America on the Pacific to extreme northern Peru (including the Galapagos Islands) and on the Caribbean-Atlantic to eastern Brazil.

Winters from central Baja California, central Sonora, the Gulf coast and coastal South Carolina south throughout the remainder of the breeding range.

Wanders, at least casually, north as far as central California, southern Arizona, southern New Mexico, eastern Colorado, North Dakota, southeastern Saskatchewan, southern Manitoba, southern Ontario, southern Quebec, southern New Brunswick, Newfoundland and Nova Scotia, and to Bermuda (where recently also introduced).

Notes.—This species is placed by some authors in the genus *Nyctanassa*.

Tribe COCHLEARIINI: Boat-billed Herons

Notes.—Sometimes maintained as a separate family or subfamily.

Genus COCHLEARIUS Brisson

> *Cochlearius* Brisson, 1760, Ornithologie, 1, p. 48; 5, p. 506. Type, by tautonymy, *Cochlearius* Brisson = *Cancroma cochlearia* Linnaeus.

Cochlearius cochlearius (Linnaeus). BOAT-BILLED HERON.

> *Cancroma cochlearia* Linnaeus, 1766, Syst. Nat., ed. 10, 1, p. 233. Based on "La Cuilliere" Brisson, Ornithologie, 5, p. 506. (in Guiana = Cayenne.)

Habitat.—Marshes, mangroves and humid forest, usually near ponds or streams (Tropical Zone).

Distribution.—*Resident* from Sinaloa in the Pacific lowlands and Tamaulipas in the Gulf-Caribbean lowlands south through Middle America (including islands off the Yucatan Peninsula) and South America (also Trinidad) west of the Andes to western Ecuador and east of the Andes to eastern Peru, eastern Bolivia and northern Argentina.

Suborder THRESKIORNITHES: Ibises and Spoonbills

Family **THRESKIORNITHIDAE**: Ibises and Spoonbills

Subfamily THRESKIORNITHINAE: Ibises

Genus **EUDOCIMUS** Wagler

Eudocimus Wagler, 1832, Isis von Oken, col. 1232. Type, by subsequent designation (Reichenow, 1877), *Scolopax rubra* Linnaeus.

Eudocimus albus (Linnaeus). WHITE IBIS. [184.]

Scolopax alba Linnaeus, 1758, Syst. Nat., ed. 10, 1, p. 145. Based on "The White Curlew" Catesby, Nat. Hist. Carolina, 1, p. 82, pl. 82. (in America = South Carolina.)

Habitat.—Marshes, mangroves, lagoons and lakes, breeding in trees near water, especially in wooded swamps (Tropical and lower Subtropical zones).

Distribution.—*Resident* from central Baja California (lat. 27°N.), central Sinaloa, southern and eastern Texas, southern Louisiana, Florida, southeastern Georgia and coastal North Carolina (rarely Virginia) south along both slopes of Middle America, through the Greater Antilles (Cuba, the Isle of Pines, Jamaica and Hispaniola), and along the coasts of South America to northwestern Peru and French Guiana.

Wanders north, at least casually, to southern California, southern Arizona, central New Mexico, eastern Colorado, southeastern South Dakota, southern Michigan, southern Ontario, southern Quebec and Nova Scotia; reports from northern California are regarded as based on escapes. Casual in Puerto Rico, also a sight report from the Bahamas (New Providence).

Notes.—Despite slight overlap in mixed colonies in Venezuela, *E. albus* and *E. ruber* appear to constitute a superspecies. Hybridization between the two occurs in captivity and among the mixed Florida colony but has not been reported under natural conditions in South America.

Eudocimus ruber (Linnaeus). SCARLET IBIS. [185.]

Scolopax rubra Linnaeus, 1758, Syst. Nat., ed. 10, 1, p. 145. Based mainly on "The Red Curlew" Catesby, Nat. Hist. Carolina, 1, p. 84, pl. 84. (in America.)

Habitat.—Primarily in coastal swamps and lagoons, mangroves and occasionally along rivers and in drier interior areas, breeding in trees (Tropical Zone).

Distribution.—*Resident* from northern Colombia and Venezuela (also Margarita Island and Trinidad) south, east of the Andes, to eastern Ecuador and southern Brazil.

Accidental in Texas, Florida (1874), Alabama, Nova Scotia (possibly a man-assisted vagrant) and Grenada; reports from Louisiana, the Bahamas, Cuba, Jamaica, Honduras and Costa Rica are all open to question. Attempted introductions in southern Florida through eggs placed in nests of *E. albus* have been generally unsuccessful.

Notes.—See comments under *E. albus.*

Genus **PLEGADIS** Kaup

Plegadis Kaup, 1829, Skizz. Entw.-Ges. Eur. Thierw., p. 82. Type, by monotypy, *Tantalus falcinellus* Linnaeus.

Plegadis falcinellus (Linnaeus). GLOSSY IBIS. [186.]

Tantalus Falcinellus Linnaeus, 1766, Syst. Nat., ed. 12, 1, p. 241. Based mostly on *Numenius rostro arcuato* Kramer, Elench. Veget. Anim. Austriam Inf. Obsv., p. 350, and "Le Courly verd" Brisson, Ornithologie, 5, p. 326, pl. 27, fig. 2. (in Austria, Italia = Neusiedler See, Lower Austria.)

Habitat.—Marshes, swamps, lagoons and lakes, breeding in trees in wooded situations near water.

Distribution.—*Breeds* in North America locally from Maine (Stratton Island) and Rhode Island south to Florida, and west on the Gulf coast to Louisiana (Bird Island), also inland, at least casually, in Arkansas (Blytheville); in northwestern Costa Rica (Guanacaste, since 1978); in the Greater Antilles (Cuba, Hispaniola and Puerto Rico); in South America in northern Venezuela (Aragua); and locally in the Old World from southeastern Europe east to eastern China, India and the Malay Peninsula, and south through East Africa to South Africa and Madagascar, and through the East Indies to Australia. Reported breeding in eastern Texas has not been verified.

Winters in the Americas from northern Florida and (casually) the Gulf coast of Louisiana south through the Greater Antilles (casually the Bahamas and northern Lesser Antilles), in northwestern Costa Rica, and in northern Venezuela; and in the Old World from the Mediterranean region east to Southeast Asia and south widely through Africa, the East Indies and Australia.

Wanders north, at least casually, in North America to central Oklahoma, Missouri, Iowa, Wisconsin, southern Ontario, southern Quebec, Prince Edward Island, New Brunswick, Nova Scotia and Newfoundland, and in Eurasia to Iceland, the Faroe Islands, British Isles and Scandinavia. Casual in Bermuda, Panama, Colombia and the eastern Atlantic islands; sight reports from eastern Texas, Honduras and Costa Rica are not certainly identifiable to species.

Notes.—*P. falcinellus* and *P. chihi* are sometimes considered conspecific, but sympatric breeding occurs in Louisiana (Bird Island) and possibly in eastern Texas. Despite limited sympatry, the two probably constitute at least a superspecies.

Plegadis chihi (Vieillot). WHITE-FACED IBIS. [187.]

Numenius chihi Vieillot, 1817, Nouv. Dict. Hist. Nat., nouv. éd., 8, p. 303. Based on "Cuello jaspeado" Azara, Apunt. Hist. Nat. Páx. Parag., 3, p. 197 (no. 364). (Paraguay et dans les plaines de Buenos-Ayres = Paraguay and the campos of Buenos Aires, Argentina.)

Habitat.—Marshes, swamps, ponds and rivers, mostly in fresh-water areas, breeding in low trees or on the ground in marshes (Tropical to Temperate zones).

Distribution.—*Breeds* in North America locally from central California, eastern

Oregon, southern Idaho, Montana (probably), southern North Dakota and (formerly) southwestern Minnesota south to Colima, Zacatecas, the state of México, Veracruz, southern and eastern Texas, southern Louisiana (east to Bird Island), coastal Alabama, and occasionally (or formerly) in Florida (Brevard County and Lake Okeechobee); and in South America in northern Colombia and northern Venezuela, and from southwestern Peru, central Bolivia, Paraguay and extreme southern Brazil south to central Chile and central Argentina.

Winters from southern California, Baja California, and the Gulf coast of Texas and Louisiana south through both lowlands of Mexico to Guatemala and El Salvador; and in the general breeding range in South America.

Wanders north, at least casually, to southern British Columbia, southeastern Alberta, southern Saskatchewan, southern Manitoba and Minnesota. Casual in the Hawaiian Islands, and in North America east to Arkansas, Ohio, New York (Long Island, where breeding suspected) and Maryland, along the Gulf coast to Florida, and south, at least formerly, to Costa Rica (Térraba valley).

Notes.—See comments under *P. falcinellus.*

Genus **MESEMBRINIBIS** Peters

Mesembrinibis Peters, 1930, Occas. Pap. Boston Soc. Nat. Hist., 5, p. 256. Type, by original designation, *Tantalus cayennensis* Gmelin.

Mesembrinibis cayennensis (Gmelin). GREEN IBIS.

Tantalus cayennensis Gmelin, 1789, Syst. Nat., 1 (2), p. 652. Based mainly on "Courly verd de Cayenne" Daubenton, Planches Enlum., pl. 820. (in Cayanna = Cayenne.)

Habitat.—Swampy woods and along the banks of forest ponds and streams (Tropical Zone).

Distribution.—*Resident* from Panama, Colombia, southern Venezuela and the Guianas south, east of the Andes, to eastern Peru, northern Bolivia, Paraguay, northeastern Argentina and extreme southeastern Brazil.

Casual north to Costa Rica (Sarapiquí), also sight reports for northeastern Honduras (Río Platano).

Genus **THERISTICUS** Wagler

Theristicus Wagler, 1832, Isis von Oken, col. 1231. Type, by monotypy, *Tantalus melanopis* Gmelin.

Theristicus caudatus (Boddaert). BUFF-NECKED IBIS.

Scolopax caudatus Boddaert, 1783, Table Planches Enlum., p. 57. Based on "Courly à col blanc de Cayenne" Daubenton, Planches Enlum., pl. 976. (Cayenne.)

Habitat & Distribution.—*Resident* in marshes and wet fields through most of South America south to Cape Horn.

Accidental in Panama (near Pacora, eastern Panamá province; Wetmore, 1965, Smithson. Misc. Collect., 150 (1), p. 127) and the Falkland Islands.

Notes.—*T. caudatus* and the high Andean *T. melanopis* (Gmelin, 1789) constitute a superspecies; they have been considered conspecific by some authors.

Subfamily PLATALEINAE: Spoonbills

[Genus PLATALEA Linnaeus]

Platalea Linnaeus, 1758, Syst. Nat., ed. 10, 1, p. 139. Type, by subsequent designation (G. R. Gray, 1840), *Platalea leucorodia* Linnaeus.

[Platalea leucorodia Linnaeus. WHITE SPOONBILL.] See Appendix B.

Genus AJAIA Reichenbach

Ajaia Reichenbach, 1853, Avium Syst. Nat. (1852), p. xvi. Type, by original designation, *Ajaia rosea* Reichenbach = *Platalea ajaja* Linnaeus.

Ajaia ajaja (Linnaeus). ROSEATE SPOONBILL. [183.]

> *Platalea Ajaia* Linnaeus, 1758, Syst. Nat., ed. 10, 1, p. 140. Based mainly on *Ajaia Brasiliensibus* Marcgrave, Hist. Nat. Bras., p. 204. (in America australi = Rio São Francisco, eastern Brazil.)

Habitat.—Marshes, swamps, ponds, rivers and lagoons, breeding in low trees and bushes, occasionally on the ground (Tropical and Subtropical zones).

Distribution.—*Resident* locally from northern Sinaloa, the Gulf coast of Texas and southwestern Louisiana (Cameron Parish), and southern Florida south along both coasts of Middle America and through the Greater Antilles (Cuba, the Isle of Pines and Hispaniola), Bahamas (Great Inagua) and South America to central Chile and central Argentina.

Wanders north to central (rarely) and southern California, southwestern Arizona, the Gulf states from Louisiana to Florida, along the Atlantic coast to North Carolina; also widely through much of the West Indies (rare in Lesser Antilles). Casual or accidental north to southern Nevada, Colorado, Nebraska, southeastern Kansas, Arkansas, Indiana, Pennsylvania and Maryland, and south to southern Chile and the Falkland Islands.

Suborder CICONIAE: Storks

Family CICONIIDAE: Storks

Tribe LEPTOPTILINI: Jabirus and Allies

Genus JABIRU Hellmayr

Jabiru Hellmayr, 1906, Abh. Math. Phys. Kl. Bayr. Akad. Wiss., 22, p. 711. Type, by original designation, *Ciconia mycteria* Lichtenstein.

Jabiru mycteria (Lichtenstein). JABIRU. [189.]

> *Ciconia mycteria* Lichtenstein, 1819, Abh. Phys. Kl. Akad. Wiss. Berlin (1816–17), p. 163. Based on "Jabirú" Marcgrave, Hist. Nat. Bras., p. 200. (northeastern Brazil.)

Habitat.—Marshes, savanna, lagoons and coastal estuaries, breeding in trees (Tropical Zone).

Distribution.—*Resident* locally in Middle America in southeastern Mexico (Tabasco, Chiapas, Campeche and Quintana Roo), Belize, Honduras, El Salvador,

Nicaragua, Costa Rica and Panama, and in South America from Colombia, Venezuela and the Guianas south, mostly east of the Andes, to eastern Peru, central Bolivia, northeastern Argentina and Uruguay.

Wanders casually north to Veracruz (Cosamaloapan) and Texas (Kleberg and Brooks counties, Houston, Corpus Christi and Austin, the last an 1867 record possibly in error as to locality). Accidental in Oklahoma (near Tulsa).

Tribe MYCTERIINI: Wood Storks

Genus MYCTERIA Linnaeus

Mycteria Linnaeus, 1758, Syst. Nat., ed. 10, 1, p. 140. Type, by monotypy, *Mycteria americana* Linnaeus.

Mycteria americana Linnaeus. WOOD STORK. [188.]

Mycteria americana Linnaeus, 1758, Syst. Nat., ed. 10, 1, p. 140. Based mainly on "Jabiru-guaçu" Marcgrave, Hist. Nat. Bras., p. 201. (in America calidiore = Brazil.)

Habitat.—Marshes, swamps, lagoons and mangroves, breeding in trees (Tropical and lower Subtropical zones).

Distribution.—*Resident* from southern Sonora, the Mexican Plateau (rarely), the Gulf coast (from eastern Texas to Florida), and the Atlantic coast (from South Carolina to southern Florida) south locally along both lowlands of Middle America (including many offshore islands), in Cuba and Hispaniola (Dominican Republic), and through South America to western Ecuador, eastern Peru, Bolivia and northern Argentina.

Wanders north to southern California, southern Arizona, in the Gulf states to Arkansas and western Tennessee, and in the Atlantic states to Massachusetts, casually to northern California, southern Idaho, Montana, Colorado, Nebraska, southeastern South Dakota, Missouri, Illinois, southern Michigan, southern Ontario, New York, Maine and southern New Brunswick. Casual in Jamaica; accidental in northwestern British Columbia (Telegraph Creek).

Notes.—Formerly known as WOOD IBIS.

Order PHOENICOPTERIFORMES: Flamingos

Notes.—The taxonomic position of the flamingos is controversial; recent evidence suggests a relationship with the Charadrii of the Charadriiformes (see Olson and Feduccia, 1980, Smithson. Contrib. Zool., no. 316, pp. 1–73).

Family PHOENICOPTERIDAE: Flamingos

Genus PHOENICOPTERUS Linnaeus

Phoenicopterus Linnaeus, 1758, Syst. Nat., ed. 10, 1, p. 139. Type, by monotypy, *Phoenicopterus ruber* Linnaeus.

Phoenicopterus ruber Linnaeus. GREATER FLAMINGO. [182.]

Phoenicopterus ruber Linnaeus, 1758, Syst. Nat., ed. 10, 1, p. 139. Based largely on "The Flamingo" Catesby, Nat. Hist. Carolina, 1, p. 73, pl. 73. (in Africa, America, rarius in Europa = Bahamas.)

Habitat.—Mud flats, lagoons and lakes, generally of high salinity, breeding on mud mounds in shallow water.

Distribution.—*Resident* locally in the Americas along the Yucatan Peninsula (Río Lagartos), in the Greater Antilles (Cuba, Hispaniola, and probably Gonâve and Beata islands), in the southern Bahamas (Acklins Island and Great Inagua), in the Netherlands Antilles (Bonaire) and in the Galapagos Islands; and in the Old World locally along the Mediterranean and northwestern African coasts, in the rift lakes of East Africa, in South Africa, and from southern Russia and the Caspian Sea south to the Persian Gulf and northwestern India. Formerly bred in the Florida Keys (probably), widely in the Bahamas, along the north coast of South America from Colombia to the Guianas, and in the Cape Verde Islands.

Wanders to southern Florida (where a semi-domesticated flock is also established at Miami), widely through the Bahamas and Antilles, along the coasts of the Yucatan Peninsula (including Cozumel Island) and South America from Colombia to northern Brazil; and widely through Europe and to the Canary Islands. Casual or accidental along the Gulf coast from Texas to Florida, along the Atlantic coast north to New Brunswick and Nova Scotia, inland north to Kansas and Michigan, and to Bermuda; reports from California certainly pertain to escaped individuals, and some of the foregoing vagrant records (especially the northern ones) may likewise pertain to such escapes.

Notes.—Known in Old World literature as the FLAMINGO. The Old World populations have often been considered a separate species, *P. roseus* Pallas, 1811; with that viewpoint, *P. ruber* would be called AMERICAN FLAMINGO. *P. ruber* (including *roseus*) and the South American *P. chilensis* Molina, 1782, appear to constitute a superspecies.

Order **ANSERIFORMES**: Screamers, Swans, Geese and Ducks

Suborder ANSERES: Swans, Geese and Ducks

Family **ANATIDAE**: Swans, Geese and Ducks

Subfamily ANSERINAE: Whistling-Ducks, Swans and Geese

Tribe DENDROCYGNINI: Whistling-Ducks

Genus **DENDROCYGNA** Swainson

Dendrocygna Swainson, 1837, Class. Birds, 2, p. 365. Type, by subsequent designation (Eyton, 1838), *Anas arcuata* Horsfield.

Notes.—The group name TREE-DUCK was formerly used for members of this genus.

Dendrocygna bicolor (Vieillot). FULVOUS WHISTLING-DUCK. [178.]

Anas bicolor Vieillot, 1816, Nouv. Dict. Hist. Nat., nouv. éd., 5, p. 136. Based on "Pato roxo y negro" Azara, Apunt. Hist. Nat. Páx. Parag., 3, p. 443 (no. 436). (Paraguay.)

Habitat.—Shallow fresh and brackish waters, preferring marshes, lagoons, wet cultivated fields and occasionally forest, nesting on the ground among reeds and marshy vegetation (primarily Tropical Zone).

Distribution.—*Breeds* from southern California (locally north to Merced County, at least formerly), southwestern Arizona, central and eastern Texas, and the Gulf coast of Louisiana south to Nayarit, Jalisco (Lake Chapala), the valley of México and northern Veracruz; locally in southern Florida, Cuba, Hispaniola, Puerto Rico, central Honduras (Lake Yojoa) and, probably, northwestern Costa Rica; in South America from Colombia, northern Venezuela and the Guianas south to western Ecuador and eastern Peru, and from Paraguay and central and eastern Brazil south to central Chile and central Argentina; and in the Old World in East Africa, Madagascar, India, Ceylon and southwestern Burma.

Winters from southern California (at least formerly), southern Arizona (at least formerly), the Gulf coast and southern Florida south to Oaxaca and Tabasco, and in the breeding range elsewhere in the American tropics, South America and the Old World.

Casual north to southern British Columbia, western Washington, central Oregon, Nevada, Utah, North Dakota, Minnesota, Michigan, southern Ontario, southern Quebec, Maine, southern New Brunswick, Prince Edward Island and Nova Scotia; also to Guatemala (Lago de Retana), Bermuda, the Bahamas, Virgin Islands, Lesser Antilles (south to St. Vincent and Barbados) and Morocco. Accidental in Panama (La Jagua, eastern Panamá province), presumably from South America.

Notes.—*D. bicolor* and *D. arcuata* (Horsfield, 1824), of the Australian region, may constitute a superspecies.

Dendrocygna arborea (Linnaeus). WEST INDIAN WHISTLING-DUCK.

Anas arborea Linnaeus, 1758, Syst. Nat., ed. 10, 1, p. 128. Based mainly on "The Black-billed Whistling Duck" Edwards, Nat. Hist. Birds, 4, p. 193, pl. 193. (in America = Jamaica.)

Habitat.—Primarily mangroves and forested swamps, nesting on the ground in reedy areas, in cavities in trees, or among dense bromeliads in palm trees.

Distribution.—*Resident* throughout the Greater Antilles (including the Isle of Pines, Grand Cayman, and Île-à-Vache off Hispaniola), in the Bahamas (Andros, San Salvador and Inagua islands) and in the northern Lesser Antilles (at least on Barbuda and Antigua).

Accidental in Bermuda; a sight report from Florida (Belle Glade) may be based on an individual escaped from captivity.

Dendrocygna viduata (Linnaeus). WHITE-FACED WHISTLING-DUCK. [178.1.]

Anas viduata Linnaeus, 1766, Syst. Nat., ed. 12, 1, p. 205. (in Carthagenæ lacubus = Cartagena, Colombia.)

Habitat.—Marshes, swamps, lagoons (fresh-water and brackish) and rivers, nesting on the ground among reeds and grasses, occasionally in hollow trees (Tropical Zone).

Distribution.—*Resident* in Costa Rica (Guanacaste and the Gulf of Nicoya area) and irregularly in eastern Panama (eastern Panamá province, wandering casually to the Canal Zone); through most of South America from Colombia and Venezuela (also Curaçao and Trinidad) south to central Peru, Bolivia, northern Argentina and Uruguay; in Africa from the Sahara south to Angola in the west and Natal in the east; and in Madagascar and the Comoro Islands.

Casual in the Antilles (Cuba, the Dominican Republic on Hispaniola, and Barbados).

Dendrocygna autumnalis (Linnaeus). BLACK-BELLIED WHISTLING-DUCK. [177.]

Anas autumnalis Linnaeus, 1758, Syst. Nat., ed. 10, 1, p. 127. Based on "The Red-billed Whistling Duck" Edwards, Nat. Hist. Birds, 4, p. 194, pl. 194. (in America = West Indies.)

Habitat. — Marshes (fresh-water and brackish), lagoons and the borders of ponds and streams, nesting on the ground in grassy areas or in hollow trees, and often foraging in cultivated fields (Tropical and Subtropical zones).

Distribution. — *Resident* from central Sonora, southern Arizona, the valley of México (Distrito Federal), and central and southeastern Texas south through most of Middle America and South America (also Trinidad) west of the Andes to western Ecuador and east of the Andes to eastern Peru, Bolivia, northern Argentina, Paraguay and southern Brazil; also one breeding record for northwestern Tennessee (Reelfoot Lake, 1978), possibly based on escaped individuals.

Casual in southern California, Colorado, southern New Mexico, Kansas, Iowa, Michigan, Louisiana, Cuba, Puerto Rico, the Virgin Islands and the Lesser Antilles; records from southern Florida may pertain to escapes from captivity, and early records in the West Indies may be of birds introduced from South America.

Tribe CYGNINI: Swans

Genus **CYGNUS** Bechstein

Cygnus Bechstein, 1803, Ornithol. Taschenb. Dtsch., 2, p. 404, footnote. Type, by monotypy, *Anas olor* Gmelin.

Subgenus OLOR Wagler

Olor Wagler, 1832, Isis von Oken, col. 1234. Type, by subsequent designation (G. R. Gray, 1840), *Cygnus musicus* Bechstein = *Anas cygnus* Linnaeus.
Clangocycnus Oberholser, 1908, Emu, 8, p. 3. Type, by monotypy, *Cygnus buccinator* Richardson.

Cygnus columbianus (Ord). TUNDRA SWAN. [180.]

Anas Columbianus Ord, 1815, *in* Guthrie, Geogr., ed. 2 (Am.), 2, p. 319. Based on the "Whistling Swan" Lewis and Clark, Hist. Exped. Rocky Mount. Pac., 2, p. 192. (below the great narrows of the Columbia River = The Dalles, Oregon.)

Habitat. — Open tundra ponds, lakes and sluggish streams, occasionally swampy bogs, breeding mainly on islets, less frequently in raised areas along shores, wintering primarily in sheltered fresh-water situations, less frequently on bays and estuaries, in migration often in flooded fields.

Distribution. — *Breeds* [*columbianus* group] from northwestern Alaska (Point Barrow and Cape Prince of Wales) south to St. Lawrence Island and the Alaska Peninsula, and east near the Arctic coast to Baffin Island, thence south around Hudson Bay to Churchill and the Belcher Islands; and [*bewickii* group] from northern Russia east along the Arctic coast (including Novaya Zemlya and other islands) to northern Siberia.

Winters [*columbianus* group] on the Pacific coast of North America from southern British Columbia south to Oregon, and in the interior through the valleys of California to northern Baja California (casually), western Nevada, northern Utah, southern Arizona and southern New Mexico, also on the Gulf coast of southern Texas, and along the Atlantic coast from Maryland to North Carolina, casually north to Maine, south to Florida, and west along the Gulf coast to Louisiana, and in the interior of North America in the Great Lakes region; and [*bewickii* group] in Eurasia south to the British Isles, northern Europe, the Caspian Sea, Japan, Korea and the coast of China.

In migration occurs widely [*columbianus* group] through the interior of North America on large bodies of water, primarily in the Great Basin, upper Mississippi Valley and Great Lakes, also across the Appalachians in southern Pennsylvania and northern West Virginia.

Casual or accidental [*columbianus* group] in the Hawaiian Islands (Midway), Chihuahua, Guanajuato, Bermuda, Cuba, Puerto Rico, Newfoundland, England, Japan and the Commander Islands; and [*bewickii* group] in the Aleutians (Adak), Oregon, California, Saskatchewan and Maryland (some of these reports are probably based on escaped individuals, although the bird from Adak and one from California were recoveries of birds banded in Siberia), and in the Old World in Iceland, and south to the Mediterranean region.

Notes.—The two groups are sometimes considered full species, *C. columbianus* [Whistling Swan, 180] and *C. bewickii* Yarrell, 1830 [Bewick's Swan, 180.1], although free interbreeding occurs when the two are in contact. See also comments under *C. cygnus*.

Cygnus cygnus (Linnaeus). Whooper Swan. [179.]

Anas Cygnus Linnaeus, 1758, Syst. Nat., ed. 10, 1, p. 122. (in Europa, America septentrionali = Sweden.)

Habitat.—Lakes, ponds, marshes and quiet-flowing rivers, breeding in reed beds and weedy margins in the taiga zone (including in large bogs), more rarely in open tundra or steppe, wintering also in sheltered bays and estuaries.

Distribution.—*Breeds* from Greenland (formerly), Iceland, the Faroe Islands (formerly), Scotland, Scandinavia and northern Russia east to Anadyrland and Kamchatka, and south to Poland, the Caspian Sea, Turkestan and Ussuriland.

Winters south to central Europe, the eastern Mediterranean, Black and Caspian seas; and from Korea and Japan south to eastern China (casually to India and the Bonin Islands), and east to the central Aleutian Islands (at least as far as Atka).

Casual in the Pribilof Islands, western and south-coastal Alaska, Jan Mayen, Spitsbergen, Bear Island, and south to northern Africa. Accidental in Maine (Washington County, 1903).

Notes.—The relationships of *C. cygnus, C. columbianus* and *C. buccinator* are uncertain at the species level. *C. cygnus* and *C. buccinator* have been considered conspecific by some authors; an extreme view unites all three into a single species, despite geographical overlap in the ranges of the two Old World forms. For the present, it seems best to retain all three as distinct species.

Cygnus buccinator Richardson. Trumpeter Swan. [181.]

Cygnus buccinator Richardson, 1832, *in* Swainson and Richardson, Fauna Bor.-Am., 2 (1831), p. 464. (Hudson's Bay.)

Habitat.—Ponds, lakes and marshes, breeding in areas of reeds, sedges or similar emergent vegetation, primarily on fresh-water, occasionally in brackish situations, wintering on open ponds, lakes and sheltered bays.

Distribution.—*Breeds* in northern Alaska (casually, from the Canning River east to Demarcation Point), in western Alaska (Noatak River Valley, Seward Peninsula and Yukon-Kuskokwim Delta), widely in central and southern Alaska (from the middle Yukon River south to the Kenai Peninsula and Yakutat Bay), in southeastern Alaska (casually), and locally from southern British Columbia, west-central and southeastern Alberta, and southwestern Saskatchewan south to southeastern Oregon, eastern Idaho and northwestern Wyoming. Formerly bred from northern Yukon, northern Mackenzie, northern Manitoba and James Bay south to Nebraska, Iowa, Missouri and Indiana.

Winters from southern Alaska, western British Columbia, southern Alberta (rarely) and Montana south to northern (casually southern) California, occasionally to Utah, New Mexico and eastern Colorado; formerly wintered south to the Mexican border (one record from Tamaulipas), the Gulf coast of Texas and Louisiana, Mississippi Valley, and Atlantic coast to North Carolina.

Introduced and established in Nevada (Ruby Lake), and in southwestern South Dakota, with casual wintering from the latter population to Missouri (banding recovery and sight reports).

Notes.—See comments under *C. cygnus.*

Subgenus CYGNUS Bechstein

Cygnus olor (Gmelin). MUTE SWAN. [178.2.]

Anas Olor Gmelin, 1789, Syst. Nat., 1 (2), p. 501. Based in part on the "Mute Swan" Latham, Gen. Synop. Birds, 3 (2), p. 436, and Pennant, Arct. Zool., 2, p. 543. (in Russia, Sibiria, Persico etiam littore maris caspii = Russia.)

Habitat.—Open and quiet waters of lakes, ponds, marshes and sluggish rivers, breeding in reed beds and similar emergent vegetation primarily in fresh-water areas, wintering also in brackish and protected marine situations.

Distribution.—*Breeds* from the British Isles, southern Scandinavia and Russia southeast through central Europe to Asia Minor, and east to eastern Siberia and Ussuriland.

Winters from the breeding range south to the Mediterranean, Black and Caspian seas and northwestern India, and from Korea south to eastern China, wintering casually to the Azores, northern Africa, Japan and the Seven Islands of Izu.

Introduced and established in North America, with breeding recorded locally from southern Saskatchewan, northern Wisconsin, central Michigan, southern Ontario, southern New York and Connecticut south to central Missouri, northern Illinois, northwestern Indiana and, in the Atlantic region, Virginia; also in the Faroe Islands, South Africa, Australia and New Zealand. Recorded after the breeding season from the breeding range, Minnesota, the Great Lakes and Maine south to the Ohio Valley and Virginia. Some of these records, as well as isolated reports elsewhere in North America, may pertain to escapes from captivity.

Tribe ANSERINI: Geese

Genus **ANSER** Brisson

Anser Brisson, 1760, Ornithologie, 1, p. 58; 6, p. 261. Type, by tautonymy, *Anser domesticus* Brisson = *Anas anser* Linnaeus.

Notes.—See comments under *Chen.*

Anser fabalis (Latham). BEAN GOOSE. [171.1.]

Anas Fabalis Latham, 1787, Gen. Synop. Birds, suppl., 1, p. 297. (Great Britain.)

Habitat.—Lakes, ponds, bogs, sluggish rivers, swamps and wet meadows from the coastal tundra to the taiga, breeding along watercourses, on open heath and in open grassy plains, wintering in brackish and marine situations as well as on fresh-water lakes and ponds.

Distribution.—*Breeds* from Scandinavia, northern Russia (including Novaya Zemlya) and northern Siberia south to northern Mongolia, Lake Baikal, Amurland and Anadyrland.

Winters south to the Mediterranean Sea, Iran, China and Japan.

In migration ranges regularly in spring east to the western Aleutian Islands (east casually as far as Adak), and casually to St. Lawrence Island, in the Pribilofs, and on the Seward Peninsula (Safety Sound).

Casual to Iceland, the eastern Atlantic islands and northern Africa.

Notes.—*A. fabalis* and *A. brachyrhynchus* constitute a superspecies; they are regarded as conspecific by some authors.

Anser brachyrhynchus Baillon. PINK-FOOTED GOOSE. [171.2.]

Anser Brachyrhynchus Baillon, 1834, Mém. Soc. R. Émulation Abbeville, sér. 2, no. 1 (1833), p. 74. (Abbeville, lower Somme River, France.)

Habitat & Distribution.—*Breeds* in habitats similar to those of the preceding species in eastern Greenland, Iceland, Spitsbergen and possibly also Franz Josef Land and the Kola Peninsula, and *winters* in northwestern Europe.

Accidental in Newfoundland (St. Anthony, 10 May–3 June 1980, photograph; Am. Birds, 34: 755, 1980); a report from Massachusetts in 1924 is regarded as of dubious authenticity.

Anser erythropus (Linnaeus). LESSER WHITE-FRONTED GOOSE. [171.3.]

Anas erythropus Linnaeus, 1758, Syst. Nat., ed. 10, 1, p. 123. (in Europa septentrionali = northern Sweden.)

Habitat & Distribution.—*Breeds* in taiga from Scandinavia to eastern Siberia, and *winters* widely on marshes, lakes and ponds from Europe and the Mediterranean region east to India and eastern China.

Accidental in North Dakota (Mallard Island, Lake Sakakawea, McLean County), Ohio (Ottawa National and Magee wildlife refuges), western Pennsylvania and Delaware (Bombay Hook); some of these records may be of individuals escaped from captivity.

Anser albifrons (Scopoli). GREATER WHITE-FRONTED GOOSE. [171.]

Branta albifrons Scopoli, 1769, Annus I, Hist.-Nat., p. 69. (No locality given = northern Italy.)

Habitat.—Arctic tundra and open areas in subarctic forest zone, breeding along small lakes and ponds, in deltas and estuaries, and in relatively dry areas of open low vegetation (scrubby trees, heath, sedges and grasses), wintering in sheltered inland and coastal marshes, pastureland and open terrain with small bodies of water, in migration often in flooded fields.

Distribution.—*Breeds* in North America from northern Alaska south to Bristol Bay and Cook Inlet, and east across northern Yukon, northern Mackenzie and southern Victoria Island to northern Keewatin; in western Greenland; and in northern Eurasia from the Kanin Peninsula east to Anadyrland. Recorded in summer on Melville Island.

Winters in North America from southern British Columbia south in the coastal states and western Mexico to Jalisco, on the Mexican Plateau to the state of México, on the Gulf coast from Texas and Louisiana south to Veracruz and Campeche, and rarely in the lower Mississippi Valley from Missouri southward; and in Eurasia from the British Isles and southern Scandinavia south to the eastern Atlantic islands (rarely), Mediterranean Sea, Asia Minor, India, and from Manchuria and Japan south to eastern China.

In migration occurs in North America primarily west of the Mississippi River, casually in eastern North America from southern Ontario, southern Quebec and Labrador south to the Gulf coast (east to north-central Florida) and North Carolina, formerly to Cuba.

Casual in the Hawaiian Islands, Aleutians (Attu, Amchitka, Adak) and Pribilofs (St. Paul).

Notes.—Usually known as WHITE-FRONTED GOOSE. The Greenland race, *A. a. flavirostris* Dalgety and Scott, 1948, has been recorded from Quebec and the Atlantic seaboard south to Georgia; other North American records, including stragglers to the east coast, pertain to North American subspecies.

[**Anser anser** (Linnaeus). GRAYLAG GOOSE.] See Appendix B.

[**Anser indicus** Latham. BAR-HEADED GOOSE.] See Appendix B.

Genus CHEN Boie

Chen Boie, 1822, Isis von Oken, col. 563. Type, by monotypy, *Anser hyperboreus* Pallas = *Anas caerulescens* Linnaeus.

Exanthemops Elliot, 1868, Birds N. Am., 2 (9), pl. 44. Type, by monotypy, *Anser rossii* Cassin.

Philacte Bannister, 1870, Proc. Acad. Nat. Sci. Philadelphia, 22, p. 131. Type, by monotypy, *Anas canagica* Sevastianov.

Notes.—Some authors merge *Chen* in *Anser*; we retain *Chen* pending definition of generic limits in the geese.

Chen caerulescens (Linnaeus). SNOW GOOSE. [169.]

Anas cærulescens Linnaeus, 1758, Syst. Nat., ed. 10, 1, p. 124. Based on "The Blue-winged Goose" Edwards, Nat. Hist. Birds, 3, p. 152, pl. 152. (in Canada = Hudson Bay, northeastern Manitoba.) [Blue morph.]

Anser hyperboreus Pallas, 1769, Spic. Zool., 1, fasc. 6, p. 25. (in terris borealibus ad Orientem 130° longitudinis sive circa Lenam et Ianam fluvios = northeastern Siberia.) [White morph.]

Habitat.—Open tundra generally near water, breeding on raised hummocks and ridges, wintering in both fresh-water and salt marshes, wet prairies and extensive sandbars, foraging also in pastures, cultivated lands and flooded fields.

Distribution.—*Breeds* from northern Alaska (Point Barrow) east along the Arctic coast and islands of Canada to northwestern Greenland and Ellesmere and Baffin islands, south to Southampton Island and along both coasts of Hudson Bay to the head of James Bay, also in northeastern Siberia (Wrangel Island, possibly also on the Chukotski Peninsula); isolated breeding reports from Oregon (Malheur Lake) and North Dakota (Arrowwood).

Winters in western North America from the Puget Sound areas of British Columbia and Washington south to the interior valleys and (rarely) the southern coast of California, northern Baja California, northwestern Sonora and southwestern Arizona; from Chihuahua and southern (rarely northern) New Mexico south (locally and rarely) to Jalisco, Durango and Guanajuato (a report from Oaxaca is without foundation); from Kansas and Missouri south to the Gulf coast (from Florida to northern Veracruz), most commonly from Louisiana and Texas south to northern Tamaulipas; on the Atlantic coast from New York (Long Island) to Florida (primarily from Chesapeake Bay to North Carolina); and in eastern Asia in Japan and eastern China.

Migrates chiefly along the Pacific coast and through Alberta and western Saskatchewan, occurring widely in the United States west of the Rocky Mountains; through the Great Plains and Mississippi Valley, with large staging areas in the Dakotas, Minnesota, Nebraska and Iowa; and through Quebec and Ontario to the Atlantic wintering grounds.

Casual south to southern Mexico (Tabasco), the Greater Antilles (east to the Virgin Islands), Bahamas and Bermuda; also in the Hawaiian Islands (Oahu, Maui), Aleutians (Attu, Alaid), Pribilofs (St. Paul), New England (coastal area), eastern Greenland, Iceland, the British Isles, continental Europe, the Azores and Korea. Accidental in Honduras (Campín, near La Lima) and the Marshall Islands.

Notes.—The blue morph and white morph were formerly considered two distinct species, *C. caerulescens* [BLUE GOOSE, 169.1] and *C. hyperborea* [SNOW GOOSE, 169]; the name *caerulescens* has priority. Blue morphs are concentrated in the center of the range, breeding mostly in populations north and northeast of Hudson Bay and wintering primarily on the Gulf coast. Hybridization in the wild between this species and *C. rossii* occurs infrequently; also occasional hybrids between *C. caerulescens* and *Branta canadensis,* and between the former and *Anser albifrons,* have been reported.

Chen rossii (Cassin). ROSS' GOOSE. [170.]

Anser Rossii Cassin, 1861, Proc. Acad. Nat. Sci. Philadelphia, 13, p. 73. (Great Slave Lake.)

Habitat.—Arctic tundra lakes, usually breeding on islands therein, frequently associated with *C. caerulescens,* in migration and winter in both fresh-water and brackish marshes and wet prairies, foraging in grassy areas, pastures and cultivated fields.

Distribution.—*Breeds* primarily in the Queen Maud Gulf area of northern Mackenzie and northwestern Keewatin, with other colonies on southern Southampton Island and along the west coast of Hudson Bay south to Cape Churchill; probably also on Banks Island in northern Mackenzie.

Winters in the interior valleys of California (casually to southern Arizona), and to southern (casually northwestern) New Mexico, Texas and the Gulf coast of Louisiana.

Migrates primarily through Alberta and western Saskatchewan and the western states (casually west to British Columbia and Washington, and east to Wyoming, Colorado and Utah), and through the Great Plains (uncommonly east to southern Manitoba and the Dakotas, rarely to Minnesota, Illinois and Missouri).

Casual in northern Alaska (Barrow, Tashekpuk Lake, Canning River Delta), southeastern Alaska (Stikine River Delta), Chihuahua (Laguna Bustillos), Ontario, Quebec, and along the Atlantic coast from New Jersey to Florida.

Notes.—See comments under *C. caerulescens*.

Chen canagica (Sevastianov). EMPEROR GOOSE. [176.]

Anas Canagica Sevastianov, 1802, Nova Acta Acad. Sci. Imp. Petropolitanae, 13, p. 349, pl. 10. (Kanaga Island, Aleutian Islands.)

Habitat.—Lowland marsh areas of Arctic tundra, generally not far from the coast, nesting on the edges of ponds, lakes and potholes, migrating to upland areas to forage, and wintering in salt-water areas along reefs, rocky beaches and cliff shores.

Distribution.—*Breeds* along the coast of western Alaska from Kotzebue Sound south to Kuskokwim Bay, on St. Lawrence and Nunivak islands, and in northeastern Siberia from Koliutschin Bay east to East Cape and south to the Gulf of Anadyr.

Winters throughout the Aleutians, along the Alaska Peninsula (east to Sanak Island and Bristol Bay), on Kodiak Island, irregularly south along the Pacific coast from southeastern Alaska and British Columbia to California (casually, once as far south as Orange County), and in Kamchatka and the Commander Islands.

Casual in the Hawaiian Islands (Midway, Laysan, and the main islands from Kauai east to Hawaii) and northern Alaska (east to Barrow).

Notes.—This species is frequently placed in the monotypic genus *Philacte*.

Genus **BRANTA** Scopoli

Branta Scopoli, 1769, Annus I, Hist.-Nat., p. 67. Type, by subsequent designation (Bannister, 1870), *Anas bernicla* Linnaeus.

Leucopareia Reichenbach, 1853, Avium Syst. Nat. (1852), p. ix. Type, by monotypy, *Anas leucopsis* Bechstein.

Eubranta Verheyen, 1955, Bull. Inst. R. Sci. Nat. Belg., 31, no. 36, p. 9. Type, by subsequent designation (Parkes, 1958), *Anas leucopsis* Bechstein.

Branta bernicla (Linnaeus). BRANT. [173.]

Anas Bernicla Linnaeus, 1758, Syst. Nat., ed. 10, 1, p. 124. (in Europa boreali = Sweden.)

Habitat.—Arctic tundra, breeding in low and barren terrain, river deltas, sandy areas among puddles and shallows, wintering primarily in marine situations that are marshy, along lagoons and estuaries, and on shallow bays.

Distribution.—*Breeds* [*bernicla* group] in North America from Prince Patrick, Melville and Ellesmere islands south to northern Keewatin (Adelaide Peninsula), Prince of Wales Island (probably), and Southampton, Coats and western Baffin islands, and in the Palearctic in northern Greenland, Spitsbergen and Franz Josef Land; and [*nigricans* group] in North America from western (Kuskokwim Bay) and northern Alaska east to northern Mackenzie and Banks, Melville and Prince

Patrick islands (probably also Victoria Island), and in the Palearctic along the coast of Siberia east to the Chukotski Peninsula and Anadyrland.

Winters [*bernicla* group] in eastern North America on the Atlantic coast from Maine to North Carolina (rarely to Florida), and in Europe (formerly widespread, now local) from the British Isles and North Sea south to the Mediterranean region, casually the Azores; and [*nigricans* group] in western North America along the Pacific coast from southern British Columbia south to southern Baja California, casually north to southeastern Alaska, and in eastern Eurasia south, at least rarely, to the coast of northern China and Korea.

Casual [*bernicla* group] in the interior of North America from Manitoba and Ontario south to Texas and the Gulf coast, and in western North America (primarily coastal areas) from southeastern Yukon and southern British Columbia south to California; and [*nigricans* group] in the Hawaiian Islands, western North America east to Saskatchewan, Minnesota, the Dakotas, Colorado and Kansas, and south to Arizona, New Mexico, Texas and Louisiana, and along the Atlantic coast from Massachusetts to Virginia. Accidental [*bernicla* group] in Barbados.

Notes.—Known in Old World literature as BRENT GOOSE. The two groups have been regarded by some authors as separate species, *B. bernicla* [WHITE-BELLIED BRANT, 173] and *B. nigricans* (Lawrence, 1846) = *B. orientalis* Tougarinov, 1941 [BLACK BRANT, 174]; mixed pairs and intermediates have been reported from Prince Patrick and Melville islands, but the extent of interbreeding is not known.

Branta leucopsis (Bechstein). BARNACLE GOOSE. [175.]

> *Anas leucopsis* Bechstein, 1803, Ornithol. Taschenb. Dtsch., 2, p. 424. (auf dem Zuge, Deutschland = Germany.)

Habitat.—Rivers and marshes in Arctic regions, breeding primarily on rocky outcrops, ledges and crevices, less frequently on low islands, wintering in marshes and grasslands, generally near the coast.

Distribution.—*Breeds* in eastern Greenland, Spitsbergen and southern Novaya Zemlya.

Winters from the breeding range south to the British Isles, northern Europe and the Russian coast, casually to southern Europe and northern Africa.

Casual in North America, most frequently from Labrador west to Baffin Island and James Bay, and south to Quebec, New Brunswick and Nova Scotia, less frequently along the Atlantic coast south to South Carolina, and on rare occasions inland as far as Colorado, Nebraska, Oklahoma, Illinois and Tennessee, and south to the Gulf coast (recorded Texas and Alabama); and in the Old World to Bear Island, the Mediterranean region, the Azores and northern Africa. Some of these reports very likely pertain to escapes from captivity, but the majority of the northeastern North American and most of the Old World reports probably are of wild vagrants.

Branta canadensis (Linnaeus). CANADA GOOSE. [172.]

> *Anas canadensis* Linnaeus, 1758, Syst. Nat., ed. 10, 1, p. 123. Based mainly on "The Canada Goose" Catesby, Nat. Hist. Carolina, 1, p. 92, pl. 92. (in Canada = City of Quebec.)

Habitat.—A variety of habitats near water, from temperate regions to tundra, breeding on marshes, meadows, small islands, rivers and open situations commanding clear views in fresh-water or brackish areas, also on man-made structures and in vegetation, wintering from tidewater areas and marshes to inland refuges and flooded fields.

Distribution.—*Breeds* from the Arctic coast of Alaska and northern Canada east to Baffin Island, western Greenland and Labrador, and south to the Commander Islands (formerly), Aleutians (Buldir), central California (San Francisco Bay region), northern Utah, southern Kansas, northern Arkansas, western Tennessee, western Kentucky, central Ohio, southern Ontario, southern Quebec and Newfoundland, occasionally to Maine (formerly to Massachusetts and undoubtedly farther south on the Atlantic coast).

Winters from Kamchatka, south-coastal and southeastern Alaska (west to Prince William Sound), British Columbia, southern Alberta, southern Saskatchewan, southern Manitoba, the Great Lakes region and Atlantic coast of Newfoundland south to northern Baja California, the northern Mexican states (casually south to Jalisco and Veracruz), the Gulf coast and northern Florida (casually to the Florida Keys).

Introduced and established in Iceland, the British Isles, Sardinia and New Zealand; in addition, there are many feral, usually nonmigratory (although free-flying) populations in the United States, both within and outside the normal breeding range, and often of a subspecies other than that expected in the wild.

Casual north to Melville Island, and in the Hawaiian Islands, central Siberia and Japan. Accidental in Bermuda, the Bahamas (Andros, New Providence) and Cuba, questionably in Jamaica.

Notes.—The northern populations of small Canada Geese have been variously treated taxonomically as three separate species, *B. hutchinsii* (Richardson, 1832) [HUTCHINS' or RICHARDSON'S GOOSE, 172.3], *B. minima* Ridgway, 1885 [CACKLING GOOSE, 172.2], and *B. leucopareia* (Brandt, 1836) [TUNDRA GOOSE, 172.1]; as a single species under the name *B. hutchinsii* [CACKLING GOOSE]; or as one or more subspecies of *B. canadensis*. Consideration of the entire complex as a single species seems best for the present.

[Branta ruficollis (Pallas). RED-BREASTED GOOSE.] See Appendix B.

Genus **NESOCHEN** Salvadori

Nesochen Salvadori, 1895, Cat. Birds Br. Mus., 27, pp. xii, 81, 126. Type, by original designation, *Anser sandvicensis* Vigors.

Notes.—Some authors merge this genus in *Branta*.

Nesochen sandvicensis (Vigors). HAWAIIAN GOOSE. [175.1.]

Anser sandvicensis Vigors, 1833, List Anim. Garden Zool. Soc., ed. 3, p. 4. (Hawaiian Islands.)

Habitat.—Uplands, primarily sparsely vegetated lava flows with no standing water.

Distribution.—*Resident* in the Hawaiian Islands on Hawaii (population small and locally distributed, the surviving native populations having been increased by introductions from captive stock); recently reintroduced in the Haleakala area of Maui, where it may formerly have bred.

Notes.—Also known as NENE.

Subfamily ANATINAE: Ducks

Tribe TADORNINI: Shelducks

[Genus TADORNA Lorenz von Oken]

Tadorna Lorenz von Oken, 1817, Isis von Oken, 1, p. 1183. Type, by tautonymy, *Anas tadorna* Linnaeus.
Casarca Bonaparte, 1828, Geogr. Comp. List, p. 56. Type, by monotypy, *Anas rutila* Pallas = *Anas ferruginea* Pallas.

[Tadorna ferruginea (Pallas). RUDDY SHELDUCK.] See Appendix B.

[Tadorna tadorna (Linnaeus). COMMON SHELDUCK.] See Appendix B.

Tribe CAIRININI: Muscovy Ducks and Allies

Genus CAIRINA Fleming

Cairina Fleming, 1822, Philos. Zool., 2, p. 260. Type, by monotypy, *Anas moschata* Linnaeus.

Cairina moschata (Linnaeus). MUSCOVY DUCK.

Anas moschata Linnaeus, 1758, Syst. Nat., ed. 10, 1, p. 124. (in India, error = Brazil.)

Habitat.—Forest streams, ponds, marshes and swamps, nesting primarily in hollow trees (Tropical Zone).

Distribution.—*Resident* in the lowlands from Sinaloa and Tamaulipas south through most of Middle America (including Cozumel Island) and South America west of the Andes to western Colombia and east of the Andes to eastern Peru, Bolivia, northern Argentina and Uruguay.

Casual in Trinidad. This species is widely domesticated, and reports of stragglers in North America north of Mexico likely pertain to escapes or individuals from attempted but unsuccessful introductions (especially those in Texas and Florida).

Notes.—Also known as the MUSCOVY.

Genus SARKIDIORNIS Eyton

Sarkidiornis Eyton, 1838, Monogr. Anatidae, p. 20. Type, by original designation, *Anser melanotos* Pennant.

Sarkidiornis melanotos (Pennant). COMB DUCK.

Anser melanotos Pennant, 1769, Indian Zool., p. 12, pl. 11. (Ceylon.)

Habitat.—Primarily ponds, wooded swamps, savanna lagoons and forested streams (Tropical to Temperate zones).

Distribution.—*Resident* in tropical America from eastern Panama (Río Chucunaque in eastern Darién, casually west to La Jagua, eastern Panamá province) south through northern South America to central Peru, Bolivia, northern Argentina and Uruguay; and in the Old World in Africa (south of the Sahara), Madagascar, and from India east to southeastern China and Ceylon.

Notes.—The tropical American form has sometimes been treated as a species, *S. sylvicola* Ihering and Ihering, 1907 [AMERICAN COMB-DUCK], distinct from the Old World *S. melanotos.*

Genus AIX Boie

Aix Boie, 1828, Isis von Oken, col. 329. Type, by subsequent designation (Eyton, 1838), *Anas sponsa* Linnaeus.

Aix sponsa (Linnaeus). WOOD DUCK. [144.]

Anas Sponsa Linnaeus, 1758, Syst. Nat., ed. 10, 1, p. 128. Based mainly on "The Summer Duck" Catesby, Nat. Hist. Carolina, 1, p. 97, pl. 97. (in America septentrionali = South Carolina.)

Habitat.—Quiet inland waters near woodland, such as wooded swamps, flooded forest, ponds, marshes and along streams, where nesting in holes in trees and bird boxes, wintering on both fresh-water and brackish marshes, ponds, streams and estuaries.

Distribution.—*Breeds* in western North America from southern British Columbia and southwestern Alberta south to central (rarely southern) coastal California and the interior valleys (Sacramento and San Joaquin) of that state, west-central Nevada, southern Oregon, northern Idaho and western Montana; and in eastern North America from east-central Saskatchewan, central and southeastern Manitoba, southern Ontario, southern Quebec, New Brunswick, Prince Edward Island and Nova Scotia south (east of the Rockies) to central and southeastern Texas, the Gulf coast, southern Florida and Cuba.

Winters at least irregularly throughout the breeding range in western North America (most commonly near coastal areas and in the interior valleys of California, casually east to central Montana, northern Utah and southeastern Arizona); in eastern North America primarily in the southern parts of the breeding range north to southern Kansas, southern Iowa, the Ohio Valley and New England (occasionally farther north), and west to southern New Mexico; and in Cuba and the Bahamas.

Casual in southeastern Alaska (Juneau, Stikine River), Newfoundland, northern Mexico (recorded Sinaloa, Durango and Distrito Federal) and Jamaica (at least formerly). Accidental in Puerto Rico, the Lesser Antilles (Saba) and Azores; European reports are likely based on escapes or on small, local, unestablished flocks.

Tribe ANATINI: Dabbling Ducks

Genus ANAS Linnaeus

Anas Linnaeus, 1758, Syst. Nat., ed. 10, 1, p. 122. Type, by subsequent designation (Lesson, 1828), *Anas boschas* Linnaeus = *Anas platyrhynchos* Linnaeus.

Spatula Boie, 1822, Isis von Oken, col. 564. Type, by monotypy, *Anas clypeata* Linnaeus.

Dafila Stephens, 1824, *in* Shaw, Gen. Zool., 12 (2), p. 126. Type, by monotypy, *Dafila caudacuta* Stephens = *Anas acuta* Linnaeus.

Mareca Stephens, 1824, *in* Shaw, Gen. Zool., 12 (2), p. 130. Type, by subsequent designation (Eyton, 1838), *Mareca fistularis* Stephens = *Anas penelope* Linnaeus.

Querquedula Stephens, 1824, *in* Shaw, Gen. Zool., 12 (2), p. 142. Type, by tautonymy, *Anas circia* Linnaeus = *Anas querquedula* Linnaeus.
Nettion Kaup, 1829, Skizz. Entw.-Ges. Eur. Thierw., p. 95. Type, by monotypy, *Anas crecca* Linnaeus.
Chaulelasmus "G. R. Gray" Bonaparte, 1838, Geogr. Comp. List, p. 56. Type, by monotypy, *Anas strepera* Linnaeus.
Eunetta Bonaparte, 1856, C. R. Acad. Sci. Paris, 43, p. 650. Type, by monotypy, *Anas falcata* Georgi.

Anas crecca Linnaeus. GREEN-WINGED TEAL. [139.]

Anas Crecca Linnaeus, 1758, Syst. Nat., ed. 10, 11, p. 126. (in Europæ aquis dulcibus = Sweden.)

Habitat.—Lakes, marshes, ponds, pools and shallow streams, breeding in inland fresh-water areas with dense rushes or other emergent vegetation, in migration and winter in both fresh-water and brackish situations around marshes, lakes, estuaries and rice fields.

Distribution.—*Breeds* [*crecca* group] in North America in the Pribilof (group uncertain) and Aleutian islands (east to Akutan), and in Eurasia from the British Isles east to eastern Siberia and the Commander, Kurile and Bering islands, and south to the Mediterranean, Black and Caspian seas, Mongolia, Manchuria, Ussuriland and Japan; and [*carolinensis* group] in North America from western and northern Alaska (including the eastern Aleutians), northern Yukon, northwestern and southern Mackenzie, southern Keewatin, northeastern Manitoba, northern Ontario, northern Quebec, north-central Labrador and Newfoundland south to central Oregon, northern Nevada, northern Utah, Colorado, central South Dakota, southern Minnesota, southern Ontario, southern Quebec, northern Maine and Nova Scotia, with sporadic local breeding south to southern California, eastern Arizona, southern New Mexico, Kansas, Iowa, northern Illinois, northern Indiana, northern Ohio, Pennsylvania, northeastern West Virginia, and on the Atlantic coast to Delaware.

Winters [*crecca* group] in North America in the Aleutians, and in Eurasia from Iceland, the British Isles, northern Europe, the Black and Caspian seas, Korea and Japan south to tropical Africa, India, Ceylon, the Malay Peninsula, southeastern China and the Philippines; and [*carolinensis* group] in the Hawaiian Islands, and in North America from southern Alaska (Kodiak Island), southern British Columbia, central Montana, South Dakota, southern Minnesota, southern Wisconsin, the Great Lakes, New York, New England, New Brunswick and Nova Scotia south to Baja California, central Mexico, the Gulf coast, southern Florida and the Bahamas, rarely to northern Central America (Belize and northern Honduras), the Antilles (recorded south to Tobago) and Bermuda.

Casual [*crecca* group] in the Hawaiian Islands (Midway, Oahu), on continental North America from Alaska and Labrador south on the Pacific coast to southern California, in the interior to Nevada, Ohio and Pennsylvania, and on the Atlantic coast to Florida, and in Micronesia, Greenland, Jan Mayen, Spitsbergen and the eastern Atlantic islands; and [*carolinensis* group] in Colombia, Greenland, the British Isles, continental Europe, Morocco and Japan. *Accidental* [*carolinensis* group] in Costa Rica.

Notes.—Known in Old World literature as the TEAL. The two groups within the species have often been considered as separate species, *A. crecca* [COMMON

TEAL, 138] and *A. carolinensis* Gmelin, 1789 [GREEN-WINGED TEAL, 139]; intergradation between the two groups occurs in the Aleutians.

Anas formosa Georgi. BAIKAL TEAL. [139.1.]

> *Anas formosa* Georgi, 1775, Bemerk. Reise Russ. Reich., 1, p. 168. (um Irkutsk . . . und dem ganzen südlichen Baikal = Lake Baikal, Siberia.)

Habitat.—Small ponds, pools or edges of streams, generally in forested areas, breeding in marshy areas with reeds and emergent vegetation.

Distribution.—*Breeds* in eastern Siberia from the Yenisei River east to western Anadyrland and Kamchatka, and south to Lake Baikal, Transbaicalia and the Sea of Okhotsk.

Winters from eastern China, Korea and Japan south to India and Burma.

Casual in western and northern Alaska from Wainwright south to the Pribilofs and Nanvak Bay, and in fall and winter on the Pacific coast from British Columbia south to southern California, although more southerly reports may be based on escapes. Birds reported from Ohio, Pennsylvania, New Jersey, North Carolina and Europe are almost certainly based on escaped individuals.

Anas falcata Georgi. FALCATED TEAL. [137.1.]

> *Anas falcata* Georgi, 1775, Bemerk. Reise Russ. Reich., 1, p. 167. (Baikal region, Siberia.)

Habitat.—Primarily in fresh-water on and around ponds, small lakes and quiet rivers, foraging and wintering also in rice fields.

Distribution.—*Breeds* in eastern Siberia from the Yenisei River east to the Sea of Okhotsk and Kamchatka, and south to Lake Baikal, Mongolia, Amurland, Sakhalin and Japan.

Winters from Japan south to Korea and eastern China, less frequently to Iran, India, Burma, Viet Nam and southeastern China.

Casual in Alaska in the Pribilof (St. George, St. Paul) and Aleutian islands (Attu, Shemya, Amchitka, Adak), and in the Commander Islands. Reports from British Columbia (Vernon), Washington (Willapa Bay) and California (San Francisco, Newport Bay) may pertain to escaped individuals; records from Virginia, North Carolina and Europe almost certainly do.

Anas rubripes Brewster. AMERICAN BLACK DUCK. [133.]

> *Anas obscura rubripes* Brewster, 1902, Auk, 19, p. 184. (Lake Umbagog, New Hampshire shore.)

Habitat.—A wide variety of wetland habitats in both fresh-water and marine situations, in and around marshes, swamps, ponds, lakes, bays, estuaries and tidal flats, favoring wooded swamps for breeding.

Distribution.—*Breeds* from northern Saskatchewan, northern Manitoba, northern Ontario, northern Quebec, Labrador and Newfoundland south to northern South Dakota, southern Minnesota, southern Wisconsin, northern Illinois, central Indiana, central Ohio, central West Virginia, and on the Atlantic coast to North Carolina; also sporadic breeding west to southern Alberta and south to the northern Gulf states and Georgia.

Winters from southeastern Minnesota, central Wisconsin, central Michigan, southern Ontario, southern Quebec, New Brunswick and Nova Scotia south to southern Texas, the Gulf coast and south-central Florida.

Casual visitant (in summer in the northern areas, in migration and winter in western and southern localities) from central Alaska, northern Mackenzie, Keewatin and Baffin Island south to northern California, northern Utah, Colorado and western Texas. Accidental in Puerto Rico, the British Isles, Sweden and the Azores; some of the extralimital records (especially one from Puerto Rico) and peripheral reports in the southwest (e.g., California) may pertain to escaped or released individuals.

Notes.—Formerly known in American literature as the BLACK DUCK. See comments under *A. platyrhynchos.*

Anas fulvigula Ridgway. MOTTLED DUCK. [134.]

Anas obscura, var. *fulvigula* Ridgway, 1874, Am. Nat., 8, p. 111. (St. John's river, Florida = Dummits, Brevard County.)

Habitat.—Primarily in coastal wetlands, both fresh-water and brackish situations, in marshes and ponds, foraging also in ungrazed fields and in rice.

Distribution.—*Breeds* along the Gulf coast from southern Louisiana and Texas south to Tamaulipas; in peninsular Florida from Alachua County south to Cape Sable; and locally inland in southeastern Colorado, western Kansas, Oklahoma (rarely) and northeastern Texas.

Winters in the breeding range and, at least casually, along the entire Gulf coast from western Florida to central Texas and south to Veracruz.

Casual in the Great Plains region from Kansas and Oklahoma south to northern Texas, and in the Florida Keys (Key Largo).

Notes.—Some individuals taken in the Great Plains region from Colorado to Oklahoma show indications of hybridization with *A. platyrhynchos* (Hubbard, 1977, Bull. N.M. Dept. Game Fish, no. 16, pp. 31–34). See also comments under *A. platyrhynchos.*

Anas platyrhynchos Linnaeus. MALLARD. [132.]

Anas platyrhynchos Linnaeus, 1758, Syst. Nat., ed. 10, 1, p. 125. (in Europæ maritimis = Sweden.)

Habitat.—Primarily shallow waters such as ponds, lakes, marshes and flooded fields, nesting on the ground and occasionally in trees in old crow nests, in migration and winter mostly in fresh-water and cultivated fields, less commonly in brackish situations.

Distribution.—*Breeds* [*platyrhynchos* group] in North America from northern Alaska, northern Yukon, northwestern and southern Mackenzie, southern Keewatin, northeastern Manitoba, northern Ontario, southern Quebec and southern Maine south to the Aleutian and Pribilof islands, southern California, the southern Great Basin, southern New Mexico, and from Oklahoma east through the Ohio Valley to Virginia, with local breeding (possibly through introduction or semi-domestic stock) to the Gulf coast and Florida, and in the Palearctic in southwestern Greenland, Iceland, and from Scandinavia east to eastern Siberia and south to the Mediterranean region, central Asia and Japan; and [*diazi* group] from southeastern Arizona, southern New Mexico and west-central Texas south in the highlands of Mexico to Jalisco, Michoacán, the state of México, Distrito Federal, Tlaxcala and Puebla.

Winters [*platyrhynchos* group] in North America generally from southern Alaska (west coastally to the Aleutian Islands, rare in central Alaska) and southern Canada south to central Mexico (at least to Michoacán, the state of México and Veracruz), the Gulf coast, southern Florida and western Cuba, and in Eurasia from Iceland, the British Isles, southern Scandinavia and the southern part of the breeding range south to the eastern Atlantic islands, northern Africa, India, Burma and Borneo; and [*diazi* group] generally in the region of the breeding range.

Introduced and established [*platyrhynchos* group] in the Hawaiian Islands, Australia and New Zealand; in addition, wild populations throughout most of the normal range are supplemented frequently by escapes from captivity.

Casual or accidental [*platyrhynchos* group] in Guatemala, Honduras, Nicaragua, Costa Rica (near Turrialba), Panama (Canal Zone), the Bahamas (Andros, New Providence), Puerto Rico, the Virgin Islands (St. Croix), Trinidad, Spitsbergen, Bear Island, and the Marshall and Gilbert [=Kiribati] islands.

Notes.—Extensive hybridization in southeastern Arizona, southern New Mexico and west-central Texas compels merger of the two groups, formerly recognized as distinct species, *A. platyrhynchos* and *A. diazi* Ridgway, 1886 [MEXICAN DUCK, 133.1]. *A. platyrhynchos* (including *diazi*), *A. fulvigula*, *A. rubripes*, *A. wyvilliana*, *A. laysanensis* and possibly several Old World forms are all closely related; at least the first three appear to constitute a superspecies. In various treatments, some or even all the taxa mentioned are treated as conspecific under the name *A. platyrhynchos*. *A. rubripes* hybridizes frequently with *A. platyrhynchos* in an area of broad overlap, largely the result of introductions of the latter in the range of the former, but these two forms differ somewhat behaviorally and they tend to segregate as species.

Anas wyvilliana Sclater. HAWAIIAN DUCK. [132.1.]

Anas wyvilliana Sclater, 1878, Proc. Zool. Soc. London, p. 350. (Hawaiian Islands.)

Habitat.—Coastal lagoons, marshes and mountain streams, nesting (at least at present) primarily on small islets.

Distribution.—*Resident* in the Hawaiian Islands (Kauai and possibly Niihau, formerly on all main islands except Lanai and Kahoolawe); recent introductions from captive stocks to Oahu and Hawaii have bred successfully.

Accidental in Sinaloa (Mazatlán, prior to 1859 = type of *A. aberti* Ridgway, 1878); the validity of this record has been questioned.

Notes.—Also known as the KOLOA. See comments under *A. platyrhynchos*.

Anas laysanensis Rothschild. LAYSAN DUCK. [132.2.]

Anas laysanensis Rothschild, 1892, Bull. Br. Ornithol. Club, 1, p. 17. (Island of Laysan.)

Habitat.—Brackish lagoons, and adjacent dense brush and sedges.

Distribution.—*Resident* in small numbers on Laysan Island, in the Hawaiian Islands.

Notes.—Also known as LAYSAN TEAL. See comments under *A. platyrhynchos*.

Anas poecilorhyncha Forster. SPOT-BILLED DUCK. [134.1.]

Anas poecilorhyncha J. R. Forster, 1781, Zool. Indica, p. 23, pl. 13, fig. 1. (Ceylon.)

Habitat & Distribution.—*Breeds* on small streams and ponds in eastern Asia from Siberia and Sakhalin south to India, Ceylon and Southeast Asia, and *winters* south to the Philippines.

Accidental in Alaska in the Aleutians (Adak, 10 April 1970–18 April 1971; Byrd, Gibson and Johnson, 1974, Condor, 76, p. 290) and on Kodiak Island (30 October–1 November 1977; Trapp and MacIntosh, 1978, W. Birds, 9, pp. 127–128).

Anas bahamensis Linnaeus. WHITE-CHEEKED PINTAIL. [143.1.]

Anas bahamensis Linnaeus, 1758, Syst. Nat., ed. 10, 1, p. 124. Based on the "Ilathera Duck" Catesby, Nat. Hist. Carolina, 1, p. 93, pl. 93. (in Bahama = Bahama Islands.)

Habitat.—Shallow ponds, lakes, lagoons and inlets in fresh-water or brackish situations, usually with dense vegetation bordering water, sometimes foraging in cultivated fields.

Distribution.—*Resident* in the Bahamas (from Abaco south to the Caicos), Greater Antilles, northern Lesser Antilles (south to Guadeloupe), islands off the north coast of Venezuela (Netherlands Antilles east to Tobago and Trinidad), northern Colombia (Magdalena Valley), coast of northern Venezuela, Galapagos Islands, Pacific coast of South America from Ecuador to northern Chile, and eastern South America from the Guianas south through eastern Brazil to central Argentina and Uruguay.

Casual in peninsular Florida. Accidental in Wisconsin (Lake Winnecone), Illinois (Steward Lake), Texas (Laguna Atascosa), Alabama (Magnolia Springs), Virginia (Pungo, Chincoteague) and Delaware (Assawoman); some of these reports, as well as one from New Jersey representing a South American race, probably pertain to escapes from captivity.

Notes.—Also known as BAHAMA PINTAIL or DUCK.

Anas acuta Linnaeus. NORTHERN PINTAIL. [143.]

Anas acuta Linnaeus, 1758, Syst. Nat., ed. 10, 1, p. 126. (in Europæ maritimis = Sweden.)

Habitat.—Lakes, rivers, marshes and ponds in grasslands, barrens, dry tundra, open boreal forest or cultivated fields, in migration and winter in both fresh-water and brackish situations.

Distribution.—*Breeds* [*acuta* group] in North America from northern Alaska, northern Yukon, northern Mackenzie, southern Victoria Island, northern Keewatin, Southampton Island, northern and eastern Quebec, New Brunswick and Nova Scotia south, at least locally, to southwestern and south-coastal Alaska, along the Pacific coast to southern California, and to northern Arizona, southern New Mexico, Kansas, central Iowa, northern Illinois, northern Indiana, northern Ohio, northern New York and Massachusetts, casually or sporadically to western Kentucky, Maryland and Virginia, also once on Ellesmere Island; and in the

Palearctic from western Greenland, Iceland, the Faroe Islands, Spitsbergen and Scandinavia east across Arctic areas to the Chukotski Peninsula, Kamchatka and the Commander Islands, and south to the British Isles, central Europe, Caspian Sea, Transcaucasia and the Kurile Islands. In summer recorded casually to Banks and Baffin islands, and in Newfoundland.

Winters [*acuta* group] in the Hawaiian Islands; in the Americas from southern Alaska (coastal areas west to the Aleutian and Kodiak islands), coastal British Columbia, central Washington, southern Idaho, central Utah, northern Arizona, northern New Mexico, eastern Colorado, Kansas, central Missouri, the Ohio Valley (uncommonly), and along the Atlantic coast from Massachusetts, south throughout the southern United States, Middle America, Bermuda and the West Indies (south at least to Guadeloupe) to northern Colombia, northern Venezuela and the Guianas; and in the Old World from the British Isles, southern Scandinavia, southern Russia, Turkestan and Japan south to northern and eastern Africa, the Indian Ocean, Borneo, the Philippines and islands of Micronesia.

In migration occurs regularly in the Aleutians, Labrador and Newfoundland.

Resident [*eatoni* group] in the southern Indian Ocean on the Crozets and Kerguelen Island.

Casual [*acuta* group] to Bear Island, Madeira and the Azores.

Notes.—Also known as COMMON PINTAIL and, in Old World literature, as the PINTAIL. The two groups are sometimes treated as separate species, *A. acuta* and *A. eatoni* (Sharpe, 1875), or with *A. eatoni* split as two additional species, *A. eatoni* on Kerguelen and *A. drygalskii* Reichenow, 1904, in the Crozets. Some authors consider the South American *A. georgica* Gmelin, 1789, and *A. acuta* as comprising a superspecies.

Anas querquedula Linnaeus. GARGANEY. [139.2.]

Anas Querquedula Linnaeus, 1758, Syst. Nat., ed. 10, 1, p. 126. (in Europæ aquis dulcibus = Sweden.)

Habitat.—Shallow inland lakes, ponds and streams bordered with dense emergent vegetation, reed beds or marshes, wintering primarily on fresh-water but also in marine or brackish situations.

Distribution.—*Breeds* from the British Isles, southern Scandinavia, central Russia and eastern Siberia (east to Amurland and Kamchatka) south to southern Europe, the Black and Caspian seas, Turkey. Transcaucasia, Mongolia and Ussuriland.

Winters from the Mediterranean Sea (rarely), Iraq, Arabia, India, eastern China, Formosa and Japan south to southern Africa, the Maldive Islands, Ceylon, Greater Sunda Islands, New Guinea and Australia.

In migration occurs rarely (but regularly) in the western Aleutians (casually east to Adak).

Casual in the Hawaiian Islands, the Pribilofs (St. Paul Island), Iceland and the Faroe Islands. Accidental in British Columbia (Sea and Iona islands), Alberta (Two Hills, Galahad), Manitoba (St. Ambroise), New Brunswick (St. John), Barbados and the Azores, also additional sight reports of drakes from California, Prince Edward Island, Massachusetts, Delaware and North Carolina; some of these vagrants, particularly those in eastern North America, may pertain to escaped individuals.

Anas discors Linnaeus. BLUE-WINGED TEAL. [140.]

> *Anas discors* Linnaeus, 1766, Syst. Nat., ed. 12, 1, p. 205. Based mainly on "The White-face Teal" Catesby, Nat. Hist. Carolina, 1, p. 100, pl. 100. (in America septentrionali = South Carolina.)

Habitat.—Marshes, ponds, sloughs, lakes and sluggish streams, in migration and winter in both fresh-water and brackish situations.

Distribution.—*Breeds* from east-central Alaska, southern Yukon, southern Mackenzie, northern Saskatchewan, central Manitoba, central Ontario, southern Quebec, New Brunswick, Prince Edward Island, Nova Scotia and southwestern Newfoundland south to northeastern California, central Nevada, central Utah, southern New Mexico, western and southern Texas, central Louisiana, western Arkansas, central Tennessee and eastern North Carolina, locally also to southern California, the Gulf coast and central Florida.

Winters from southern California, southwestern Arizona, western and southern Texas, the Gulf coast and North Carolina on the Atlantic coast (casually north to the southern Ohio Valley and Chesapeake Bay) south throughout Middle America and the West Indies to central Peru, central Argentina and southern Brazil.

Casual in the Hawaiian and Aleutian (Adak) islands; north to northern Alaska, northern Mackenzie, Anticosti Island and southern Labrador; and to Bermuda and Uruguay. Accidental in Greenland and Europe.

Notes.—*A. discors* and *A. cyanoptera* are closely related and natural hybrids are known; some authors have suggested superspecific status for the two despite rather broad overlap of breeding range.

Anas cyanoptera Vieillot. CINNAMON TEAL. [141.]

> *Anas cyanoptera* Vieillot, 1816, Nouv. Dict. Hist. Nat., nouv. éd., 5, p. 104. Based on "Pato Alas azules" Azara, Apunt. Hist. Nat. Páx. Parag., 3, p. 437 (no. 434). (dans l'Amérique meridionale sur la rivière de la Plata et à Buenos Ayres = Río de la Plata and Buenos Aires, Argentina.)

Habitat.—Shallow lake margins, reed beds, ponds, lagoons, sluggish streams and marshes, primarily in fresh-water but found in winter occasionally in marine situations (Tropical to Temperate zones).

Distribution.—*Breeds* in North America from southern British Columbia, southern Alberta, southwestern Saskatchewan (probably), eastern Montana, central North Dakota, southwestern South Dakota (probably), western Nebraska and central Kansas south to northern Baja California, Jalisco, Chihuahua, Tamaulipas and central Texas.

Winters from central California, southern Nevada, central Utah, southeastern Arizona, southern New Mexico and central Texas south through Middle America to Colombia, northern Venezuela and northern Ecuador.

Resident in South America in Colombia (Eastern Andes, and the Cauca and Magdalena valleys), and from central Peru, Bolivia, Paraguay and southern Brazil south to the Straits of Magellan.

Casual in the Hawaiian Islands (Kauai, Maui, Hawaii); north to south-central and southeastern Alaska, southern Yukon, central British Columbia, central Alberta, central Saskatchewan, southern Manitoba and Minnesota; and in eastern North America from southern Ontario, southern Quebec, New York and New Jersey south to the Gulf coast, Florida, the Bahamas (Grand Bahama), Cuba and Jamaica.

Notes.—See comments under *A. discors.*

Anas clypeata Linnaeus. NORTHERN SHOVELER. [142.]

Anas clypeata Linnaeus, 1758, Syst. Nat., ed. 10, 1, p. 124. (in Europæ maritimis = southern Sweden.)

Habitat.—Shallow fresh-water areas with surrounding marsh, reed beds and other types of emergent vegetation, especially in muddy, sluggish water situations, in migration and winter in both fresh-water and brackish habitats, and in cultivated fields.

Distribution.—*Breeds* in North America from northern Alaska, northern Yukon, northwestern and southern Mackenzie, and northern Manitoba south to northwestern and eastern Oregon (absent west of the coast ranges from central British Columbia southward), northern Utah, northern Colorado, northern Nebraska, northern Missouri and central Wisconsin, casually (or formerly) east to southern Ontario, southern Quebec, Prince Edward Island and New Brunswick, and south to southern California, central Arizona (probably), southern New Mexico, southeastern Texas, central Kansas, northern Illinois, northern Indiana, northern Ohio, western Pennsylvania, New York and Delaware, and casually to northern Alabama; and in Eurasia from Iceland, the British Isles and Scandinavia east across northern Russia and Siberia to Kamchatka and the Commander Islands, and south to the Mediterranean, Black and Caspian seas, southern Russia, Mongolia, Transbaicalia and Sakhalin.

Winters in the Hawaiian Islands; in the Americas from the coast of southern British Columbia, central Arizona, northern New Mexico, central Texas, the Gulf coast and South Carolina on the Atlantic coast south through Middle America and the West Indies to Colombia, the Netherlands Antilles and Trinidad, rarely in southern Alaska (in the Aleutians, on Kodiak Island, and in southeastern Alaska), and north to Minnesota, the Great Lakes, New England and Nova Scotia; and in the Old World from the British Isles, central Europe, southern Russia, eastern China and Japan south to northern and eastern Africa, the Indian Ocean, Malay Peninsula, Borneo, the Philippines and Micronesia.

In migration occurs regularly in the Aleutian Islands.

Casual or accidental in northern Alaska, Labrador, Newfoundland, Bermuda, Spitsbergen, Bear Island, the eastern Atlantic islands, South Africa and the Gilbert Islands [=Kiribati].

Notes.—Known in Old World literature as the SHOVELER. Interrelationships of the shovelers of the world remain to be determined.

Anas strepera Linnaeus. GADWALL. [135.]

Anas strepera Linnaeus, 1758, Syst. Nat., ed. 10, 1, p. 125. (in Europæ aquis dulcibus = Sweden.)

Habitat.—Marshes and grassy areas in both fresh-water and brackish situations, casually breeding in brushy or grassy areas away from water or on islands in lakes, in migration and winter on open water of any kind (but preferring marshy fresh-water situations to other types).

Distribution.—*Breeds* [*strepera* group] in North America from southern Alaska (the Alaska Peninsula, and east to Prince William Sound and, rarely, southeastern Alaska), southern Yukon, southwestern Mackenzie, northern Saskatchewan, central Manitoba, southern Ontario, southwestern Quebec, Prince Edward Island, Anticosti Island (rarely) and the New Brunswick-Nova Scotia border south locally to southern California, southern Nevada, northern Arizona, southern New Mexico, northern Texas, southern Kansas, Iowa, central Minnesota, southern Wisconsin, northern Ohio, northern Pennsylvania (formerly) and, on the Atlantic coast, to North Carolina, with one isolated breeding in northern Alabama (Wheeler Refuge); and in Eurasia from Iceland, the British Isles and southern Scandinavia east to eastern Siberia, and south to the Mediterranean region, Algeria, Turkey, Iran, Afghanistan, northern China and Sakhalin.

Winters [*strepera* group] in North America from southern Alaska (west to the Aleutian and Kodiak islands), southern British Columbia, Idaho, Colorado, southern South Dakota, Iowa, the southern Great Lakes and Chesapeake Bay on the Atlantic coast (rarely from New Brunswick and Nova Scotia) south to northern Baja California, Oaxaca, the state of México, Puebla, Veracruz, Tabasco, the state of Yucatán, the Gulf coast throughout, Florida, the Bahamas (New Providence), western Cuba and (formerly) Jamaica; and in Eurasia from the British Isles, central Europe, and the Black and Caspian seas south to northern and eastern Africa, and east to India, Burma, Thailand, eastern China and Japan.

Formerly *resident* [*couesi* group] in the northern Line Islands (Washington and New York islands); now extinct.

Casual or accidental [*strepera* group] in the Hawaiian Islands, Pribilofs, western and northern Alaska, northern Manitoba, Bermuda, Greenland, the Faroe Islands, Nigeria, Ceylon and the Marshall Islands.

Notes.—The two groups have sometimes been regarded as separate species, *A. strepera* [COMMON GADWALL] and *A. couesi* (Streets, 1876) [COUES' GADWALL].

Anas penelope Linnaeus. EURASIAN WIGEON. [136.]

Anas penelope Linnaeus, 1758, Syst. Nat., ed. 10, 1, p. 126. Based on "The Wigeon or Whewer" Albin, Nat. Hist. Birds, 2, p. 88, pl. 99. (in Europæ maritimis & paludibis = Sweden.)

Habitat.—Extensive marshes and lakes with good vegetation along shores, breeding in fresh-water in taiga, forested areas, less commonly in open moors and cultivated country, wintering primarily in fresh-water and brackish situations in coastal areas but migrating extensively through inland regions.

Distribution.—*Breeds* in Eurasia from Iceland, the British Isles and Scandinavia east to eastern Siberia and Kamchatka, south to northern Europe, central Russia and Transcaucasia.

Winters in the Old World from Iceland, the British Isles, northern Europe, southern Russia and Japan south to the eastern Atlantic islands, northern and eastern Africa, Arabia, India, the Malay Peninsula, southern China, Formosa and the Philippines, casually to Ceylon, Borneo, Celebes and Greenland; and regularly in North America on the Pacific coast from southeastern Alaska south to northern Baja California, and on the Atlantic-Gulf coast from Labrador and Newfoundland south to Florida and west to southern Texas, casually in the Hawaiian Islands.

In migration occurs regularly (primarily in the spring) in southeastern Alaska (rare elsewhere in Alaska), and irregularly in the interior of North America from the southern parts of the Canadian provinces south to Arizona, Texas and the Gulf coast.

Casual or accidental in Bermuda, the Antilles (Hispaniola, Puerto Rico, Barbuda and Barbados), Jan Mayen, Spitsbergen, Bear Island, and the Caroline and Marshall Islands.

Notes.—Also known as EUROPEAN WIGEON and, in Old World literature, as the WIGEON. *A. penelope* and *A. americana* constitute a superspecies; occasional hybrids between the two species have been reported.

Anas americana Gmelin. AMERICAN WIGEON. [137.]

> *Anas americana* Gmelin, 1789, Syst. Nat., 1 (2), p. 526. Based on "Le Canard jensen, de la Louisiane" Daubenton, Planches Enlum., pl. 955, and the "American Wigeon" Pennant, Arct. Zool., 2, p. 567. (in America a Cayenna insulisque vicini Oceani ad sinum Hudsonis usque = New York.)

Habitat.—Large marshes and lakes, breeding in fresh-water situations with exposed shorelines, wintering in both fresh-water and brackish areas and foraging in marsh edges, sloughs and sheltered bays.

Distribution.—*Breeds* from central (rarely western) Alaska, central Yukon, northwestern and central Mackenzie, southern Keewatin, northeastern Manitoba, northern Ontario, southern Quebec, New Brunswick, Prince Edward Island and southern Nova Scotia south to south-coastal Alaska (Cook Inlet east to Yakutat Bay), in the interior through much of British Columbia, northwestern and eastern Washington and eastern Oregon to northeastern California, northern Nevada, northern Utah, northern New Mexico, central Colorado, South Dakota, northwestern Minnesota, northern Michigan, southern Ontario and northern New York, sporadically to the Atlantic coast (recorded breeding in Maine, Massachusetts and Delaware); the breeding range east of Manitoba and Minnesota is highly local.

Winters in the Hawaiian Islands; and from southern Alaska, southwestern British Columbia, Oregon, southern Nevada, southwestern Utah, sporadically across the central United States to the southern Great Lakes and Ohio Valley, and on the Atlantic coast from Nova Scotia south throughout the southern United States, Middle America and the West Indies to Panama, northern Colombia, northern Venezuela (rarely), Tobago and Trinidad.

Casual or accidental in the Aleutians, islands in the Bering Sea, Banks Island, Newfoundland, Greenland, Iceland, Europe, the Azores, Japan, and the Commander, Caroline and Marshall islands.

Notes.—See comments under *A. penelope.*

Tribe AYTHYINI: Pochards and Allies

[Genus NETTA Kaup]

> *Netta* Kaup, 1829, Skizz. Entw.-Ges. Eur. Thierw., p. 102. Type, by monotypy, *Anas rufina* Pallas.

[Netta rufina (Pallas). RED-CRESTED POCHARD.] See Appendix B.

Genus AYTHYA Boie

> *Aythya* Boie, (before May) 1822, Tageb. Reise Norwegen, p. 351. Type, by monotypy, *Anas marila* Linnaeus.
> *Nyroca* Fleming, (June) 1822, Philos. Zool., 2, p. 260. Type, by tautonymy, *Anas nyroca* Güldenstädt.
> *Aristonetta* Baird, 1858, *in* Baird, Cassin and Lawrence, Rep. Explor. Surv. R. R. Pac., 9, p. 793. Type, by original designation, *Anas valisineria* Wilson.

Perissonetta Oberholser, 1921, Proc. Ind. Acad. Sci. (1920), p. 110. Type, by original designation, *Anas collaris* Donovan.

Aythya ferina (Linnaeus). COMMON POCHARD. [146.1.]

Anas ferina Linnaeus, 1758, Syst. Nat., ed. 10, 1, p. 126. (in Europæ maritimis = Sweden.)

Habitat.—Lakes, ponds and sluggish streams, breeding in fresh-water situations bordered with emergent vegetation, wintering in sheltered fresh-water and brackish areas, rarely in bays and estuaries.

Distribution.—*Breeds* from Iceland, the British Isles, southern Scandinavia, central Russia and southern Siberia south to Spain, central Europe, Tunisia (formerly), the Black and Caspian seas, Turkey and Lake Baikal.

Winters from the British Isles, central Europe, southern Sweden and southern Russia south to the Mediterranean region, northern Africa, Arabia, India, Burma, eastern China and Japan, rarely to the eastern Atlantic islands, Formosa and the Philippines.

In migration occurs rarely (but regularly) in the Aleutians (east to Adak), casually in the Pribilofs (St. Paul, St. George).

Casual or accidental in south-coastal Alaska (Homer), the Faroe Islands and Guam, also a sight report from Saskatchewan.

Notes.—Known in Old World literature as the POCHARD. Relationships among *A. ferina, A. valisineria* and *A. americana* are close, and some authors have suggested that the first two form a superspecies.

Aythya valisineria (Wilson). CANVASBACK. [147.]

Anas valisineria Wilson, 1814, Am. Ornithol., 8, p. 103, pl. 70, fig. 5. (United States.)

Habitat.—Marshes, ponds, lakes, rivers and bays, breeding in fresh-water marshes bordered by emergent vegetation, and wintering on deep, fresh-water lakes and rivers as well as on sheltered bays and estuaries.

Distribution.—*Breeds* from central Alaska, northern Yukon, western and southern Mackenzie, northern Saskatchewan, central and northeastern Manitoba, and western Ontario south to south-coastal Alaska (Anchorage area east to Bering River delta), and locally in inland areas to northeastern California, northern Nevada, northern Utah, central New Mexico, central Kansas, northwestern Iowa and extreme southern Ontario (Walpole Island).

Winters along the Pacific coast from the central Aleutians (in small numbers west to Adak) and south-coastal Alaska south to Baja California, and from Arizona, New Mexico, Colorado, Nebraska, Iowa, the Great Lakes and, on the Atlantic coast, from New England (sporadically north in the western states to southern Canada) south to southern Mexico (Oaxaca, Veracruz and the Yucatan Peninsula), the Gulf coast and Florida.

In migration occurs in southern Ontario and (rarely) southwestern Quebec.

Casual or accidental in the Hawaiian Islands, western Aleutians, Pribilofs (St. Paul), Clipperton Island, Guatemala, Honduras, eastern Canada (north to New Brunswick and Nova Scotia), Bermuda, Cuba and the Marshall Islands, also sight reports from Puerto Rico and the Swan Islands.

Notes.—See comments under *A. ferina.*

Aythya americana (Eyton). REDHEAD. [146.]

Fuligula americana Eyton, 1838, Monogr. Anatidae, p. 155. (North America.)

Habitat.—Large marshes, lakes, lagoons, rivers and bays, breeding in extensive fresh-water marshy areas, wintering mostly in brackish and marine lagoons and bays, less frequently in inland fresh-water situations.

Distribution.—*Breeds* locally in south-central and southeastern Alaska, and from central British Columbia, southwestern Mackenzie, northern Saskatchewan, west-central and southern Manitoba, and northwestern and central Minnesota south to southern California, southern Arizona, central New Mexico, northern Texas (Panhandle), central Kansas and northern Iowa, sporadically in eastern North America from Michigan, southern Ontario, southern Quebec, New Brunswick and Nova Scotia south to Illinois, northwestern Indiana, northern Ohio, western Pennsylvania (formerly) and central New York.

Winters from British Columbia on the Pacific coast, in the interior from Nevada, Utah, Colorado, Kansas, the middle Mississippi and Ohio valleys, and the Great Lakes (occasionally north to the upper Great Lakes and southern Ontario), and from New England on the Atlantic coast south throughout the southern United States and most of Mexico to Guatemala, Cuba, Jamaica and the Bahamas.

Casual in the Hawaiian Islands, Pribilofs (St. Paul), northern and western Alaska, Kodiak Island, southern Yukon, Nova Scotia, Bermuda, Greenland and Sweden, also a sight report for Guam.

Notes.—See comments under *A. ferina.*

[**Aythya baeri** (Radde). BAER'S POCHARD.] See Appendix B.

Aythya collaris (Donovan). RING-NECKED DUCK. [150.]

Anas collaris Donovan, 1809, Nat. Hist. Br. Birds, 6, p. 147 and text. (Lincolnshire, England, specimen found in Leadenhall market, London.)

Habitat.—Marshes, lakes, rivers and swamps, breeding in fresh-water marshes, sloughs, bogs and swamps with relatively dense vegetation, wintering primarily on fresh-water and brackish situations of larger lakes, rivers and estuaries.

Distribution.—*Breeds* in east-central and southeastern Alaska, and from central British Columbia, southern Yukon, northwestern and southern Mackenzie, northern Saskatchewan, central Manitoba, northern Ontario, southern Quebec, Newfoundland and Nova Scotia south to northwestern Washington, eastern Oregon, northeastern California, central Nevada, southeastern Arizona, southern Colorado, northern Nebraska, northern Iowa, northern Illinois, central Michigan, southern Ontario, western Pennsylvania (formerly), northern New York and Massachusetts; also north-central Florida (Alachua County).

Winters on the Pacific coast from southeastern Alaska, in the interior from southern Nevada, southern Arizona, northern New Mexico, northern Texas, and the lower Mississippi and Ohio valleys, and on the Atlantic coast from New England south through the southern United States, Middle America and the West Indies to Panama (east to Canal Zone and eastern Panamá province) and Grenada.

Casual in northern, western and southern Alaska, and in the Hawaiian Islands, Bermuda, Venezuela (also Margarita Island and Trinidad), Iceland, Europe and the Azores.

Aythya fuligula (Linnaeus). TUFTED DUCK. [149.1.]

Anas Fuligula Linnaeus, 1758, Syst. Nat., ed. 10, 1, p. 128. (in Europæ maritimis = Sweden.)

Habitat.—Marshes, ponds, lakes, swamps, bays and estuaries, breeding primarily near marshy ponds and small lakes, wintering mostly in marine and brackish areas, less commonly in fresh-water.

Distribution.—*Breeds* from Iceland, the Faroe Islands, Bear Island (probably) and Scandinavia east to Ussuriland, Sakhalin and the Commander Islands, and south to central Europe, the Mediterranean Sea (rarely), Syria, Transcaucasia, northern Mongolia and Japan.

Winters from Iceland, the British Isles, southern Scandinavia and Japan south to northern Africa, Arabia, India, the Malay Peninsula, eastern China and the Philippines.

In migration ranges regularly to the western and central Aleutians, casually north to the Pribilofs, St. Lawrence Island and Barrow, and east in southern Alaska to Unalaska and Kodiak islands, and to Cordova.

Casual in the Hawaiian Islands; elsewhere along the Pacific coast of North America from southern British Columbia south to southern California; on the Atlantic coast from Massachusetts to New Jersey and inland to Lake Michigan, southern Ontario, southern Quebec and central New York; and in Greenland, Spitsbergen, the eastern Atlantic islands, Seychelles, the Greater Sunda Islands and Micronesia.

Aythya marila (Linnaeus). GREATER SCAUP. [148.]

Anas Marila Linnaeus, 1861, Fauna Svecica, ed. 2, p. 39. (in Lapponica = Lapland.)

Habitat.—Large lakes, rivers, bays and estuaries, breeding near small ponds and lakes primarily in forested tundra and northern borders of the taiga, frequently in open tundra and moors, and wintering mostly in open marine or brackish situations, less commonly on open inland fresh water.

Distribution.—*Breeds* in North America from western Alaska (Kotzebue Sound south locally to the Aleutians, Alaska Peninsula and Kodiak Island) east across northern Yukon, northwestern, north-central and southern Mackenzie, southern Keewatin, around Hudson and James bays, and northern Quebec (possibly also Labrador), casually or irregularly south to southeastern Alaska (Copper-Bering River deltas), northwestern British Columbia, central Manitoba, southeastern Michigan (St. Clair Flats), Anticosti and Magdalen islands, and Newfoundland (other southern reports open to question); and in Eurasia from Iceland, the Faroe Islands (formerly) and Scandinavia east across Arctic Russia to eastern Siberia, Kamchatka and the Commander Islands.

Winters in North America along the Pacific coast from the Aleutians and southeastern Alaska south to Baja California, in the eastern Great Lakes, from the Ohio and lower Mississippi valleys south to the Gulf coast (southern Texas east to Florida), and on the Atlantic coast from Newfoundland south to Florida; and in Eurasia from the British Isles, southern Scandinavia and the Baltic and North seas south to the Mediterranean, Black and Caspian seas, the Persian Gulf and northwestern India, and on the Pacific coast from Sakhalin and Japan south to Korea and eastern China, rarely to Formosa and the Philippines.

Casual in the Hawaiian Islands, throughout most of interior North America, in Sinaloa, the Bahamas (New Providence), Greenland, Jan Mayen and Bear Island, and south to the Azores and northern Africa; a sight report from Costa Rica requires confirmation.

Notes.—Known in Old World literature as the SCAUP. The extent of overlap in breeding range of the closely related *A. marila* and *A. affinis* may not adequately reflect their actual sympatry, as they are easily confused in the field.

Aythya affinis (Eyton). LESSER SCAUP. [149.]

Fuligula affinis Eyton, 1838, Monogr. Anatidae, p. 157. (North America.)

Habitat.—Lakes, rivers, bays, estuaries and marshes, breeding mostly near grass-margined ponds and small lakes, sometimes in grassy areas away from water, wintering in both fresh-water and marine situations, generally in sheltered areas.

Distribution.—*Breeds* from central Alaska, central Yukon, northwestern and southern Mackenzie, northern Manitoba and western Ontario south to southern interior British Columbia, northern Idaho, northern Wyoming, northern North Dakota, and northwestern and (formerly) central Minnesota, casually or irregularly east to southern Ontario and west-central Quebec, and south to western Washington (Everett), northeastern California, southern Idaho, northeastern Colorado, central Nebraska, eastern Iowa, northern Illinois and northern Ohio.

Winters in the Hawaiian Islands and southern Alaska (rare at Kodiak and Cordova), and from southern British Columbia, southern Idaho, Utah, northeastern Colorado, Kansas, Iowa, the southern Great Lakes region and New England south throughout the southern United States, Middle America and the West Indies (uncommon in Lesser Antilles) to northern Colombia, northern Venezuela, Tobago and Trinidad.

In migration occurs regularly east to New Brunswick, Nova Scotia and Newfoundland.

Casual in Bermuda, western Ecuador and Greenland, also a sight report for Surinam.

Tribe MERGINI: Eiders, Scoters, Mergansers and Allies

Genus **SOMATERIA** Leach

Somateria Leach, 1819, *in* Ross, Voy. Discovery, app., p. xlviii. Type, by monotypy, *Anas spectabilis* Linnaeus.
Eider Jarocki, 1819, Spis. Ptakow Gab. Zool. Krol. Warsz. Uniw., p. 62. Type, by monotypy, *Anas mollissima* "Gmelin" [= Linnaeus].
Lampronetta J. F. Brandt, 1847, Fuligulam (Lampronettam) Fischeri Nov. Avium Rossicarum Spec., pp. 18, 19 and plate. Type, by monotypy, *Fuligula* (*Lampronetta*) *fischeri* Brandt.

Somateria mollissima (Linnaeus). COMMON EIDER. [159.]

Anas mollissima Linnaeus, 1758, Syst. Nat., ed. 10, 1, p. 124. Based on "The Great Black and White Duck" Edwards, Nat. Hist. Birds, 2, p. 98, pl. 98. (in Europa boreali, pelagica = Island of Gotland, Sweden.)

Habitat.—Rocky seacoasts and islands, breeding on shores of ponds and lagoons with outlets to the sea, wintering primarily along seacoasts, and in bays or estuaries, occurring rarely on open fresh-water.

Distribution.—*Breeds* in western North America from the Arctic coast of Alaska and Canada east to northeastern Mackenzie, on southern Banks and southern Victoria islands, and south (locally) in Alaska to the Aleutians, Alaska Peninsula and south-coastal Alaska (east probably to Glacier Bay); in eastern North America on southern Ellesmere, Cornwallis, Devon, Somerset and Baffin Islands, along coasts and on islands in Hudson and James Bays, and along coasts from northern Quebec, Labrador and Newfoundland south to eastern Quebec (mouth of St. Lawrence River), New Hampshire, Maine and Nova Scotia; in the western Palearctic from Greenland (both coasts), Iceland, the Faroe Islands, Spitsbergen and Franz Josef Land south to the northern British Isles, northern Europe and southern Scandinavia; and in the eastern Palearctic from Wrangel Island, the New Siberian Islands and northeastern coast of Siberia south to Kamchatka and the Commander Islands.

Winters in western North America from the Bering Sea ice pack south to the Aleutians and Cook Inlet, and on the Pacific coast south (rarely) to Washington and Oregon; in eastern North America in open water of Hudson and James bays, and from Labrador south along the Atlantic coast to New York (Long Island), casually south as far as Florida and inland to the Great Lakes; in the western Palearctic from the breeding range south to central Europe, casually to the Azores and southern Europe; and in eastern Eurasia south to Kamchatka.

Casual in interior North America south to Colorado, Kansas and Iowa.

Notes.—Known in Old World literature as the EIDER.

Somateria spectabilis (Linnaeus). KING EIDER. [162.]

Anas spectabilis Linnaeus, 1758, Syst. Nat., ed. 10, 1, p. 123. Based mainly on "The Gray-headed Duck" Edwards, Nat. Hist. Birds, 3, p. 154, pl. 154. (in Canada, Svecia = Sweden.)

Habitat.—Seacoasts and large river valleys, breeding in the Arctic near freshwater ponds and pools, usually in open tundra, rarely in rocky situations, and wintering primarily offshore along rocky coasts.

Distribution.—*Breeds* in North America along the Arctic coast and islands from northern Alaska east to Greenland, the west coast of Hudson Bay, James Bay and (probably) northern Labrador; and in Eurasia along the Arctic coast from northern Russia (including Spitsbergen and Novaya Zemlya) east to the Chukotski Peninsula and St. Lawrence and St. Matthews islands.

Winters in the Pacific region from Kamchatka and the Bering Sea south to the Kurile, Aleutian and Shumagin islands, rarely to the southern mainland coast of Alaska, casually as far south on the Pacific coast as southern California; in the Atlantic from Labrador and Greenland south to New England, less frequently to New York (Long Island) and New Jersey, and casually as far south as Florida; in the interior of North America uncommonly to the Great Lakes, casually to Kansas, Iowa, Illinois, Indiana, Kentucky, West Virginia and central South Carolina; and in western Eurasia to Iceland and the Scandinavian and northern Russian coasts.

Casual in Alberta, the Faroe Islands, British Isles, Jan Mayen, Bear Island, continental Europe and Japan.

Somateria fischeri (Brandt). SPECTACLED EIDER. [158.]

Fuligula Fischeri J. F. Brandt, 1847, Fuligulam (Lampronettam) Fischeri Nov. Avium Rossicarum Spec., p. 18, pl. 1. (St. Michael, Alaska.)

Habitat.—Ponds, lakes and open sea, breeding around sedgy or grassy ponds, lakes, deltas and tidal inlets, and wintering in marine situations near coasts.

Distribution.—*Breeds* on the Arctic coast of Alaska from Point Barrow south to St. Lawrence Island and the mouth of the Kuskokwim River, and along the Arctic coast of Siberia from the Yana Delta east to the Chukotski Peninsula.

Winters probably offshore in the western Bering Sea; recorded irregularly in coastal Alaska, and south casually to southern British Columbia (Vancouver Island).

Accidental in Norway; the origin of the individual supposedly taken at Bitterwater Lake, San Benito County, California, in 1893 is questionable.

Genus **POLYSTICTA** Eyton

Polysticta Eyton, 1836, Cat. Br. Birds, p. 58. Type, by monotypy, *Anas stelleri* Pallas.

Polysticta stelleri (Pallas). STELLER'S EIDER. [157.]

Anas Stelleri Pallas, 1769, Spic. Zool., 1, fasc. 6, p. 35, pl. v. (E. Kamtschatka = Kamchatka.)

Habitat.—Arctic ponds, lakes and seacoasts, breeding in grassy edges of tundra ponds and lakes, occasionally on barren rocky tundra, wintering in shallow marine habitats around bays, reefs, lagoons and inlets.

Distribution.—*Breeds* in North America along the Arctic coast of Alaska from Point Barrow eastward, and south to St. Lawrence Island and Hooper Bay; and in Eurasia along the Arctic coast of Siberia from the New Siberian Islands and Lena Delta (casually Scandinavia and Novaya Zemlya) east to the Chukotski Peninsula. Recorded in summer (and possibly breeding) in northern Yukon and northwestern Mackenzie.

Winters in North America in the Pribilof and Aleutian islands, and east along the southern coast of Alaska to Cook Inlet (rarely to Prince William Sound), casually along the Pacific coast to southern British Columbia (Vancouver Island); and in Eurasia from Scandinavia and northern Siberia south to the Baltic Sea, southern Kamchatka, and the Commander and Kurile islands.

Casual or accidental in Quebec (Godbout), Maine (Scarborough), Massachusetts (off Scituate), Baffin Island, Greenland, the British Isles, Spitsbergen and continental Europe.

Genus **CAMPTORHYNCHUS** Bonaparte

Camptorhynchus "Eyton" Bonaparte, 1838, Geogr. Comp. List, p. 58. Type, by monotypy, *Anas labradoria* Gmelin.

†**Camptorhynchus labradorius** (Gmelin). LABRADOR DUCK. [156.]

Anas labradoria Gmelin, 1789, Syst. Nat., 1 (2), p. 537. Based on "The Pied Duck" Pennant, Arct. Zool., 2, p. 559, and Edwards, Nat. Hist. Birds, 2, p. 99, pl. 99. (in America boreali = Labrador.)

Habitat.—Breeding unknown; winter habitat included sandy bays and estuaries.

Distribution.—EXTINCT. Alleged to have bred in Labrador. Recorded along the Atlantic coast from Nova Scotia and New Brunswick south to New York (Long Island) and New Jersey (also one report from Chesapeake Bay); and inland in Quebec (Laprairie near Montreal) and New York (Elmira), where the last known individual was allegedly taken on 12 December 1878.

Genus HISTRIONICUS Lesson

Histrionicus Lesson, 1828, Man. Ornithol., 2, p. 415. Type, by original designation, *Anas histrionica* Linnaeus.

Histrionicus histrionicus (Linnaeus). HARLEQUIN DUCK. [155.]

Anas histrionica Linnaeus, 1758, Syst. Nat., ed. 10, 1, p. 127. Based on "The Dusky and Spotted Duck" Edwards, Nat. Hist. Birds, 2, p. 99, pl. 99. (in America = Newfoundland.)

Habitat.—Seacoasts, shallow fast-flowing water and rocky islets, breeding along mountain streams in forested regions, in rocky coastal areas, and occasionally on open tundra, wintering primarily in turbulent coastal waters, especially in rocky regions.

Distribution.—*Breeds* in western North America from western Alaska, northern Yukon, northern British Columbia and southern Alberta south to the Alaska Peninsula, southeastern Alaska, Vancouver Island, eastern Oregon (also in the Sierra Nevada of California), central Idaho, western Wyoming and (formerly) southwestern Colorado; in eastern North America from southern Baffin Island south to central and eastern Quebec and eastern Labrador, possibly also northern New Brunswick and Newfoundland; and in the Palearctic in Greenland and Iceland, and from the Lena River in Siberia east to Kamchatka, and south to northern Mongolia and the Kurile Islands.

Winters along the Pacific coast of North America from the Pribilof and Aleutian islands south to central (rarely southern) California; on the Atlantic coast from southern Labrador, Newfoundland and Nova Scotia south to New York (Long Island), less commonly to the Great Lakes, casually farther inland south to northern New Mexico, Nebraska, Missouri, Kentucky and West Virginia, on the Atlantic coast to Florida, and on the Gulf coast from western Florida to Texas; and in eastern Eurasia from Manchuria and Kamchatka south to Korea and southern Japan.

Casual or accidental in the Hawaiian Islands (Midway, Laysan), western Mackenzie, southern Canada (Alberta east to Manitoba), Sonora (Puerto Peñasco), and widely through Europe.

Notes.—Known in Old World literature as the HARLEQUIN.

Genus CLANGULA Leach

Clangula Leach, 1819, *in* Ross, Voy. Discovery, app., p. xlviii. Type, by monotypy, *Anas glacialis* Linnaeus = *Anas hyemalis* Linnaeus.

Clangula hyemalis (Linnaeus). OLDSQUAW. [154.]

Anas hyemalis Linnaeus, 1758, Syst. Nat., ed. 10, 11, p. 126. Based mainly on "The Long-tailed Duck from Hudson's-Bay" Edwards, Nat. Hist. Birds, 3, p. 156, pl. 156. (in Europa & America arctica = northern Sweden.)

Habitat.—Mostly around shallow fresh-water lakes, primarily in taiga but also in tundra and along coasts and fjords (breeding); primarily open sea along coastal areas and large inland lakes, less commonly along rivers and on smaller lakes (nonbreeding).

Distribution.—*Breeds* in North America from the Arctic coast of Alaska east across northern Canada and throughout the Arctic islands to Ellesmere and Baffin islands and northern Labrador, south to southern and central Alaska and north-western British Columbia, and from eastern and south-central Mackenzie and most of Keewatin south around Hudson and James bays; and in the Palearctic from Greenland, Iceland, Spitsbergen and Scandinavia east across Arctic Russia to the Chukotski Peninsula, Anadyrland, Kamchatka and the Commander Islands.

Winters along the Pacific coast of North America from the Bering Sea south to central (rarely southern) California; along the Atlantic coast from Greenland and Labrador south to South Carolina; in the interior of North America on the Great Lakes; in Europe from Iceland, the Faroe Islands, Scandinavia and western Russia south to central Europe and the Black Sea, casually to southern Europe, Madeira and the Azores; and in Asia from Caucasia to Iran, Lake Baikal, Korea, eastern China and Japan.

Casual throughout the interior of North America from southern Canada south to southern Arizona, New Mexico, southern Texas, the Gulf coast, and the Atlantic coast to southern Florida. Accidental in the Hawaiian Islands (Midway) and northwestern Sinaloa (near Guamuchil), also sight reports for Baja California and Sonora.

Notes.—Known in Old World literature as LONG-TAILED DUCK.

Genus MELANITTA Boie

Melanitta Boie, 1822 (before May), Isis von Oken, col. 564. Type, by subsequent designation (Eyton, 1838), *Anas fusca* Linnaeus.

Oidemia Fleming, 1822 (May), Philos. Zool., 2, p. 260. Type, by subsequent designation (G. R. Gray, 1840), *Anas nigra* Linnaeus.

Pelionetta Kaup, 1829, Skizz. Entw.-Ges. Eur. Thierw., p. 107. Type, by monotypy, *Anas perspicillata* Linnaeus.

Melanitta nigra (Linnaeus). BLACK SCOTER. [163.]

Anas nigra Linnaeus, 1758, Syst. Nat., ed. 10, 1, p. 123. (in Lapponia, Anglia = Lapland and England.)

Habitat.—Fresh-water lakes and pools on grassy or bushy tundra and in the northern taiga (breeding); mostly coastal waters, less commonly on large inland lakes and rivers (nonbreeding).

Distribution.—*Breeds* in North America in Alaska (from Cape Lisburne and the Alaska Range south to the Alaska Peninsula and Kodiak Island) and scattered localities in central and eastern Canada (southern Keewatin, northern Quebec and Newfoundland); and in Eurasia from Iceland, the British Isles, Spitsbergen and Scandinavia east across northern Russia and Siberia to Anadyrland, Sakhalin and Kamchatka. Summers widely (and possibly breeds) from southern Yukon and southern Mackenzie east to Labrador and Newfoundland.

Winters in North America primarily on the Pacific coast from the Pribilof and Aleutian islands south to southern California and (rarely) northern Baja California, on the Great Lakes, and on the Atlantic coast from Newfoundland south to South

Carolina and Florida; and in Eurasia from the breeding regions south to the Mediterranean, Black and Caspian seas (casually to Greenland, northern Africa and the eastern Atlantic islands), Korea, eastern China and Japan.

Casual throughout the interior of North America south to Arizona, New Mexico, Texas and the Gulf coast (from southern Texas east to Florida).

Notes.—Also known as COMMON SCOTER.

Melanitta perspicillata (Linnaeus). SURF SCOTER. [166.]

Anas perspicillata Linnaeus, 1758, Syst. Nat., ed. 10, 1, p. 125. Based on "The Great Black Duck from Hudson's-Bay" Edwards, Nat. Hist. Birds, 2, p. 155, pl. 155. (in Canada = Hudson Bay.)

Habitat.—Brushy or forested areas near bogs, ponds or sluggish streams (breeding); primarily marine littoral areas, less frequently in bays or on fresh-water lakes and rivers (nonbreeding).

Distribution.—*Breeds* from the Mackenzie River delta east across central Mackenzie and northern Manitoba to Hudson Bay in northern Ontario and west-central Quebec, and south to western (from Kotzebue Sound to the Alaska Peninsula) and central Alaska, southern Yukon, central British Columbia, central Alberta and northern Saskatchewan; also in eastern Quebec and Labrador. Summers widely in northern Alaska, and across northern Canada from southern Keewatin east to Newfoundland.

Winters primarily along the Pacific coast from the eastern Aleutian Islands and southeastern Alaska south to central Baja California and Sonora, on the Great Lakes, on the Atlantic coast from the Bay of Fundy south to Florida, and rarely (but regularly) to the Gulf coast (Texas east to Florida).

Casual throughout the interior of North America south to Arizona, New Mexico, Texas and the Gulf states, and in Bermuda, Greenland, the Faroe Islands, British Isles, continental Europe and eastern Siberia. Accidental in the Hawaiian Islands (Oahu) and Japan.

Melanitta fusca (Linnaeus). WHITE-WINGED SCOTER. [165.]

Anas fusca Linnaeus, 1758, Syst. Nat., ed. 10, 1, p. 123. (in oceano Europæo = Swedish coast.)

Habitat.—Ponds, lakes and sluggish streams, primarily in open tundra or prairie with dense ground cover, less frequently in mixed tundra-taiga (breeding); mostly open sea and brackish waters along coasts, less frequently on open fresh water in inland areas (nonbreeding).

Distribution.—*Breeds* [*deglandi* group] in North America from northern Alaska, northern Yukon, northwestern and southern Mackenzie, southern Keewatin and northern Manitoba south to central Alaska, southern Yukon, south-central British Columbia, northeastern Washington, southeastern Alberta, southern Saskatchewan, northern North Dakota, southern Manitoba and northern Ontario, occurring in summer (and possibly breeding) to northeastern Mackenzie and from Hudson Bay east to Labrador and Newfoundland, and in Asia from central and eastern Siberia south to Lake Baikal, Amurland, Sakhalin and Kamchatka; and [*fusca* group] in Eurasia from Spitsbergen (formerly) and Scandinavia east across northern Russia to central Siberia, and south to west-central Russia.

Winters [*deglandi* group] in North America primarily on the Pacific coast from the Aleutians and Alaska Peninsula south to northern Baja California, on the Great Lakes, and on the Atlantic coast from the Gulf of St. Lawrence and Newfoundland south to South Carolina (rarely to Florida), and in Asia from Kamchatka south to Korea, eastern China and Japan; and [*fusca* group] in Eurasia from the breeding grounds south to the Mediterranean, Black and Caspian seas.

Casual [*deglandi* group] on Melville Island, through the interior to North America south to Arizona, New Mexico, southern Texas and the Gulf coast (east to Florida), and in Greenland; and [*fusca* group] in Greenland, Iceland, the Faroe Islands, Bear Island, the Azores, northern Africa and Afghanistan.

Notes.—Some authors regard the two groups as separate species, *M. fusca* [VELVET SCOTER] and *M. deglandi* (Bonaparte, 1850) [WHITE-WINGED SCOTER], the latter also including the eastern Asiatic form *M. f. stejnegeri* (Ridgway, 1887), whose relationships appear to be with *deglandi* but whose status is uncertain.

Genus **BUCEPHALA** Baird

Bucephala Baird, 1858, *in* Baird, Cassin and Lawrence, Rep. Explor. Surv. R. R. Pac., 9, pp. xxiii, L, 787, 788, 795. Type, by original designation, *Anas albeola* Linnaeus.

Glaucionetta Stejneger, 1885, Proc. U.S. Natl. Mus., 8, p. 409. Type, by original designation, *Anas clangula* Linnaeus.

Clanganas Oberholser, 1974, Bird Life Texas, 2, p. 974. Type, by original designation, *Anas islandica* Gmelin.

Bucephala clangula (Linnaeus). COMMON GOLDENEYE. [151.]

Anas Clangula Linnaeus, 1758, Syst. Nat., ed. 10, 1, p. 125. (in Europa; sæpius maritima = Sweden.)

Habitat.—Ponds, lakes, rivers and coastal bays, nesting in hollow trees and stubs near water, and in bird boxes, wintering primarily in bays and estuaries, less commonly on rivers and lakes.

Distribution.—*Breeds* in North America from western Alaska (Kotzebue Sound), northern Yukon, northwestern and southern Mackenzie, southwestern Keewatin, northern Manitoba, northern Ontario, northern Quebec, central Labrador and Newfoundland south to central Alaska, southern British Columbia, northern Washington, central Montana, southern Saskatchewan (absent from grassland region of Alberta and most of Saskatchewan), northern North Dakota, northern Minnesota, northern Wisconsin, northern Michigan, southern Ontario, northern New York, northern Vermont, Maine, New Brunswick and Nova Scotia; and in Eurasia from Scandinavia east across Russia and Siberia to Kamchatka, and south to northern Europe, Lake Baikal, Manchuria and Sakhalin.

Winters in North America primarily on the Pacific coast from the Aleutians and southeastern Alaska south to southern California (casually to northern Baja California, Sinaloa and Durango), on the Great Lakes, in the interior in the Mississippi and Ohio valleys and south to the Gulf coast (southern Texas east to western Florida), and on the Atlantic coast from Newfoundland and Nova Scotia south to Florida, also irregularly elsewhere in the interior of the United States south to Arizona, New Mexico and western Texas; and in Eurasia from the breeding range south to the Mediterranean Sea, Turkey, Iran, southeastern China and Japan.

Casual in Bermuda, Greenland, the Faroe Islands, Azores and northern Africa. **Notes.**—Known in Old World literature as the GOLDENEYE.

Bucephala islandica (Gmelin). BARROW'S GOLDENEYE. [152.]

Anas islandica Gmelin, 1789, Syst. Nat., 1 (2), p. 541. Based on "Hravn Oend" O. F. Müller, Zool. Dan. Prodromus, p. 16. (in Islandia = Iceland.)

Habitat.—Lakes, ponds, rivers and seacoasts, breeding in tree cavities (occasionally on the ground) generally near lakes and ponds having borders of dense emergent vegetation, wintering mostly on lakes and rivers, and in coastal estuaries and bays, especially where rocky.

Distribution.—*Breeds* from central and southwestern Alaska (base of the Alaska Peninsula), southern Yukon, western Mackenzie (probably), northern British Columbia and southwestern Alberta south to south-coastal and southeastern Alaska, southern British Columbia and northern Washington, locally at higher elevations to the Sierra Nevada of eastern California (at least formerly), eastern Oregon, northern Montana, northwestern Wyoming and (formerly) southwestern Colorado; in northeastern Quebec and northern Labrador; and in southwestern Greenland and Iceland.

Winters primarily along the Pacific coast from south-coastal and southeastern Alaska (west to Kodiak Island) south to central (casually southern) California; in the interior of western North America locally from southern British Columbia and northern Montana to the Colorado River Valley of southeastern California and southwestern Arizona, and to Utah and Colorado; and in the Atlantic region (primarily coastal) from the upper St. Lawrence drainage, Gulf of St. Lawrence and Nova Scotia south to New York (Long Island), rarely to South Carolina.

Casual in the Aleutian and Pribilof islands, to the eastern shore of Hudson Bay and Newfoundland, in the interior of North America from southern Canada south to southern New Mexico, Texas, Kansas, Missouri, Tennessee and western North Carolina; also in the Faroe Islands, British Isles, Spitsbergen and continental Europe.

Bucephala albeola (Linnaeus). BUFFLEHEAD. [153.]

Anas Albeola Linnaeus, 1758, Syst. Nat., ed. 10, 1, p. 124. Based on the "Little Black and White Duck" Edwards, Nat. Hist. Birds, p. 100, pl. 100. (in America = Newfoundland.)

Habitat.—Lakes, ponds, rivers and seacoasts, breeding in tree cavities in mixed coniferous-deciduous woodland near lakes and ponds, wintering on sheltered bays and estuaries as well as open fresh-water situations.

Distribution.—*Breeds* from central Alaska, southern Yukon, western and southern Mackenzie, southern Keewatin, northeastern Manitoba and northern Ontario south to southern British Columbia, northern Washington, northern Montana, southern Alberta, southern Saskatchewan, southern Manitoba and (locally) southern Ontario; also locally (or formerly) south to the mountains of Oregon and northern California, and to northwestern Wyoming, northern Iowa and southeastern Wisconsin.

Winters from the Aleutian Islands and the Alaska Peninsula on the Pacific coast, the Great Lakes in the interior, and New Brunswick, Nova Scotia and Newfoundland on the Atlantic, south in coastal states and the Ohio and Mississippi valleys (irregularly elsewhere in the interior) to the southern United States, northern Baja California, the interior of Mexico (to Jalisco, the state of México, Distrito Federal and Tamaulipas), the Gulf coast and Florida, casually to the Greater Antilles (Cuba, Jamaica and Puerto Rico) and the Hawaiian Islands.

Casual in the Yucatan Peninsula, Bermuda, Greenland, Iceland, the British Isles, continental Europe, Japan, and the Kurile and Commander islands.

Genus MERGELLUS Selby

Mergellus Selby, 1840, Cat. Generic Sub-Generic Types Aves, p. 47. Type, by monotypy, *Mergus albellus* Linnaeus.

Notes.—*Mergellus* and *Lophodytes* are sometimes merged in *Mergus*.

Mergellus albellus (Linnaeus). SMEW. [131.1.]

Mergus albellus Linneaus, 1758, Syst. Nat., ed. 10, 1, p. 129. (in Europa = Mediterranean, near Izmir, Turkey.)

Habitat.—Lakes, ponds, bays and rivers, breeding in the taiga in cavities in trees (rarely on the ground) near water, wintering on lakes, sheltered bays and rivers.

Distribution.—*Breeds* from Scandinavia east through northern Russia and Siberia to Kamchatka, south to southern Russia, Amurland, the Sea of Okhotsk and northern Sakhalin.

Winters from Iceland, the British Isles, Scandinavia, Russia and Kamchatka south to northwestern Africa, the Mediterranean Sea, Persian Gulf, eastern China, Korea and Japan.

In migration (and casually at other seasons) ranges rarely but regularly to the Aleutian Islands (Attu east to Adak), casually north to the Pribilofs (St. Paul and St. George islands) and east to Kodiak Island and the coast of British Columbia (Vancouver Island), also a sight report from Washington.

Casual or accidental in California (San Mateo), southern Ontario, New York (Buffalo), Rhode Island (Newport), Iceland, northern Africa and Burma; some of the eastern North American reports may pertain to escaped individuals.

Genus LOPHODYTES Reiche `bach

Lophodytes Reichenbach, 1853, Avium Syst. Nat. (1852), p. ix. Type, by original designation, *Mergus cucullatus* Linnaeus.

Notes.—See comments under *Mergellus*.

Lophodytes cucullatus (Linnaeus). HOODED MERGANSER. [131.]

Mergus cucullatus Linnaeus, 1758, Syst. Nat., ed. 10, 1, p. 129. Based on "The round-crested Duck" Catesby, Nat. Hist. Carolina, 1, p. 94, pl. 94. (in America = South Carolina.)

Habitat.—Streams, lakes, swamps, marshes and estuaries, breeding in tree cavities in forested regions near water, often near fast-flowing streams, wintering mostly in fresh-water areas but also regularly in estuaries and sheltered bays.

Distribution.—*Breeds* from southeastern Alaska (north to the Taku and Chilkat rivers, casually to the Copper River delta), central British Columbia and southwestern Alberta south to southwestern Oregon, central Idaho and northwestern Montana (casually to northern Colorado); and from central Saskatchewan, central Manitoba, central Ontario, southern Quebec, New Brunswick and southern Nova Scotia south (primarily from the mountains of New England, New York and the Appalachians westward) through eastern North Dakota, central Iowa, southeastern Kansas and central Arkansas to northern Louisiana, central Mississippi, northern Alabama, northern Georgia and (rarely) central Florida. Occurs in summer (and probably breeds) north to southern Mackenzie, northern Ontario and northern Quebec.

Winters along the Pacific coast in south-coastal Alaska (rarely, Prince William Sound), and from southern British Columbia south to northern Baja California, on the Atlantic and Gulf coasts from New England south to Florida and west to Texas and Tamaulipas, irregularly in the interior from southern Canada south to the Mexican border, casually farther (recorded Distrito Federal and Veracruz), and in the northern Bahamas and Greater Antilles (recorded regularly in Cuba, casually in Puerto Rico and the Virgin Islands).

In migration occurs casually in southwestern Alaska (including the Aleutian and Pribilof islands) and Newfoundland.

Casual or accidental in the Hawaiian Islands (Oahu, Hawaii), Bermuda, Martinique, the British Isles and continental Europe.

Genus **MERGUS** Linnaeus

Mergus Linnaeus, 1758, Syst. Nat., ed. 10, 1, p. 129. Type, by subsequent designation (Eyton, 1838), *Mergus castor* Linnaeus = *Mergus serrator* Linnaeus.

Notes.—See comments under *Mergellus*.

Mergus merganser Linnaeus. COMMON MERGANSER. [129.]

Mergus Merganser Linnaeus, 1758, Syst. Nat., ed. 10, 1, p. 129. (in Europa = Sweden.)

Habitat.—Mostly lakes and rivers, nesting in tree cavities, nest boxes or cliff crevices, generally near clear waters in forested regions and mountainous terrain, wintering primarily on open lakes and rivers or brackish lagoons, rarely in marine coastal situations.

Distribution.—*Breeds* in North America from central and south-coastal Alaska (west to the lower Kuskokwim River and Kodiak Island), southern Yukon, southern Mackenzie, northern Saskatchewan, northern Manitoba, northern Ontario, central Quebec, central Labrador and Newfoundland south to the mountains of central California, central Nevada, central Arizona, and southwestern and northern New Mexico (also once in northern Chihuahua), and east of the Rocky Mountains south to southern Saskatchewan, southwestern South Dakota (at least formerly), northeastern Minnesota, central Wisconsin, central Michigan, southern Ontario, New York, eastern Pennsylvania (probably), northwestern New Jersey, central Massachusetts, southern Maine and west-central Nova Scotia, locally and casually farther south (recorded breeding in Virginia and North Carolina); and in Eurasia from Iceland, the British Isles and Scandinavia east across Russia and Siberia to Anadyrland and Kamchatka, and south to northern Europe, central Russia, the northern Himalayas, northern Mongolia, Ussuriland and Sakhalin.

Recorded in summer (and probably breeding) north to central Mackenzie, southern Keewatin and northern Quebec.

Winters in North America from the Aleutian Islands, central (rarely) and south-coastal Alaska, and British Columbia east across southern Canada to Newfoundland, and south to southern California, northern Baja California (rarely), northern Mexico (Sonora east to Tamaulipas, casually to Jalisco, Guanajuato and Distrito Federal) and the Gulf coast from southern Texas east to central Florida; and in Eurasia from Iceland, the British Isles, Scandinavia, Japan and the Kurile Islands south to the northern Mediterranean region, Black Sea, Iran, northern India and eastern China.

Casual or accidental in the Pribilof Islands, Bermuda, Greenland, the Faroe Islands, Spitbergen, Bear Island, northwestern Africa, Formosa and the Ryukyu Islands; a report from Puerto Rico is erroneous.

Notes.—Known in Old World literature as the GOOSANDER.

Mergus serrator Linnaeus. RED-BREASTED MERGANSER. [130.]

Mergus Serrator Linnaeus, 1758, Syst. Nat., ed. 10, 1, p. 129. (in Europa = Sweden.)

Habitat.—Rivers, ponds, lakes and coastal areas, breeding along inland waters, generally on small islands with low shrubby growth, wintering mainly in estuaries and sheltered bays, less frequently on inland fresh waters.

Distribution.—*Breeds* in North America from northern Alaska, northern Yukon, northern Mackenzie, central Keewatin, northern Baffin Island, Labrador and Newfoundland south to the Aleutian Islands, southern and southeastern Alaska, northern British Columbia, northern Alberta, southwestern and central Saskatchewan, southern Manitoba, central Minnesota, central Wisconsin, central Michigan, southern Ontario, northern New York, southern Quebec, northern Vermont, Maine, New Brunswick and Nova Scotia, casually south along the Atlantic coast to New York (Long Island); and in the Palearctic from Greenland, Iceland, the Faroe Islands, British Isles, Scandinavia and northern Europe east across northern Russia and Siberia to Kamchatka and the Commander Islands.

Winters in North America primarily along coasts and on large inland bodies of water from southern Alaska (west to the Aleutian Islands), the Great Lakes and Nova Scotia south to southern Baja California, southern Texas and the Gulf coast (east to Florida), casually also elsewhere in the interior from southern Canada south to northern Sonora, southern Arizona, northern Chihuahua and southern New Mexico; and in the Old World from Iceland, the Faroe Islands, British Isles, Scandinavia, Kamchatka and the Kurile Islands south to the Mediterranean, Black and Caspian seas, southern Russia, eastern China and Japan.

Casual or accidental in the Hawaiian Islands (Oahu, Molokai, Hawaii), Pribilofs, Bermuda, the Bahamas (Andros, New Providence), Cuba, Puerto Rico, Jan Mayen, Spitsbergen, the eastern Atlantic islands and northern Africa; a report from St. Croix, in the Virgin Islands, is erroneous.

Tribe OXYURINI: Stiff-tailed Ducks

Genus OXYURA Bonaparte

Oxyura Bonaparte, 1828, Ann. Lyc. Nat. Hist. N.Y., 2, p. 390. Type, by monotypy, *Anas rubidus* Wilson = *Anas jamaicensis* Gmelin.

Nomonyx Ridgway, 1880, Proc. U.S. Natl. Mus., 3, p. 15. Type, by original designation, *Anas dominica* Linnaeus.

Oxyura jamaicensis (Gmelin). RUDDY DUCK. [167.]

Anas jamaicensis Gmelin, 1789, Syst. Nat., 1 (2), p. 519. Based on the "Jamaica Shoveler" Latham, Gen. Synop. Birds, 3 (2), p. 513. (in Jamaica.)

Habitat.—Marshes, lakes and coastal areas, breeding mostly on fresh-water marshes with dense emergent vegetation, wintering on sheltered brackish and marine coastal areas as well as lakes and rivers (Temperate Zone).

Distribution.—*Breeds* in North America in east-central Alaska (casually), and from central and northeastern British Columbia, southwestern Mackenzie, northern Alberta, northern Saskatchewan, central Manitoba and western Ontario south to southern California, central Arizona, southern New Mexico, western and southern Texas, and southwestern Louisiana, with scattered, sporadic or former breeding from southern Ontario, southern Quebec and Nova Scotia south to northern Iowa, southwestern Illinois, northern Ohio, western Pennsylvania, Delaware, South Carolina and northern Florida, also in Mexico in southern Baja California and the valley of México (and once at Dueñas, Guatemala); in the West Indies in the Bahamas (New Providence), throughout the Greater Antilles, and in the Lesser Antilles south to Grenada; and in South America in the Andes from Colombia south to western Argentina and southern Chile.

Winters in North America from southern British Columbia, Idaho, Colorado, Kansas, the Great Lakes and on the Atlantic coast from Massachusetts south throughout the southern United States and most of Mexico to Honduras (also a sight record from Nicaragua and a doubtful record from Costa Rica), and throughout the Bahamas; and in the Antilles and South America generally resident within the breeding range.

In migration occurs rarely east to the Maritime Provinces and Newfoundland. Introduced and established in England.

Casual in the Hawaiian Islands (Oahu, Hawaii), southeastern Alaska, southern Yukon and Bermuda.

Oxyura dominica (Linnaeus). MASKED DUCK. [168.]

Anas dominica Linnaeus, 1766, Syst. Nat., ed. 12, 1, p. 201. Based mainly on "La Sarcelle de S. Domingue" Brisson, Ornithologie, 6, p. 472, pl. 41, fig. 2. (in America meridionali = Santo Domingo, Hispaniola.)

Habitat.—Fresh-water and brackish pools, ponds, lagoons, swamps and sluggish streams, generally with dense aquatic vegetation (primarily Tropical Zone, ranging locally to Temperate Zone).

Distribution.—*Resident* locally from Nayarit, the Gulf coast of Texas and the Greater Antilles (including Grand Cayman) south through Middle America (both slopes, but not recorded Nicaragua) and the Lesser Antilles, and in South America from Colombia, Venezuela (also Trinidad) and the Guianas south, east of the Andes, to southeastern Peru, southern Bolivia, northern Argentina and Uruguay.

Casual inland in central Texas, and in southern Louisiana, Florida, the Bahamas and Tobago. Accidental in Wisconsin, Vermont, Massachusetts, Maryland and Tennessee.

Order FALCONIFORMES: Diurnal Birds of Prey

Notes.—That the diurnal birds of prey form a natural group has been questioned. The Cathartidae share several characters with the Ciconiidae (Ligon, 1967, Univ. Mich. Mus. Zool., Occas. Pap., no. 651). Other authors consider the Accipitridae and Falconidae to be convergent. With a few exceptions, we follow the arrangement of Amadon (*in* Peters, 1979, Birds World, 1, ed. 2).

Suborder CATHARTAE: American Vultures

Superfamily CATHARTOIDEA: American Vultures

Family CATHARTIDAE: American Vultures

Genus CORAGYPS Geoffroy

Coragyps Geoffroy, 1853, *in* Le Maout, Hist. Nat. Ois., p. 66. Type, by monotypy, *Vultur urubu* Vieillot = *Vultur atratus* Bechstein.

Coragyps atratus (Bechstein). BLACK VULTURE. [326.]

Vultur atratus Bechstein, 1793, *in* Latham, Allg. Uebers. Vögel, 1, Anh., p. 655. Based on "The black vulture or carrion crow" Bartram, Travels Carolina, pp. 152, 289. (St. John's River, Florida.)

Habitat.—Nearly ubiquitous except in heavily forested regions, more commonly in lowland than highland habitats (Tropical to Temperate zones).
Distribution.—*Resident* from southern Arizona, Chihuahua, western Texas, eastern Oklahoma, eastern Kansas (formerly), Missouri, southern Illinois, southern Indiana, central Ohio, south-central Pennsylvania and New Jersey south to the Gulf coast and southern Florida, and throughout Middle America and South America (also Trinidad and Margarita Island, off Venezuela) to central Chile and central Argentina. Recorded in summer (and possibly breeding) north to New Jersey, New York (Long Island) and southern Maine.

Wanders casually north to Colorado, North Dakota, Wisconsin, southern Ontario, southern Quebec, New Brunswick, Prince Edward Island and Nova Scotia; also questionably recorded (sight reports only) from southern California and the Antilles (Cuba, Jamaica, Barbados, Grenada). Some populations appear to be partly migratory, especially the northernmost ones in the eastern United States and those in Middle America.

Genus CATHARTES Illiger

Cathartes Illiger ,1811, Prodromus, p. 236. Type, by subsequent designation (Vigors, 1825), *Vultur aura* Linnaeus.

Cathartes aura (Linnaeus). TURKEY VULTURE. [325.]

Vultur aura Linnaeus, 1758, Syst. Nat., ed. 10, 1, p. 86. Based mainly on the "Tzopilotle s. Aura" Hernandez, Nova Plant Anim. Min. Mex. Hist., p. 331. (in America calidiore = state of Veracruz.)

Habitat.—Forested and open situations, more commonly in the latter, from lowlands to mountains (Tropical to Temperate zones).

Distribution.—*Breeds* from southern British Columbia, central Alberta, central Saskatchewan, southern Manitoba, western Ontario, northern Minnesota, southern Wisconsin, southern Michigan, extreme southern Ontario, New York, southern Vermont, southwestern New Hampshire and Massachusetts south throughout the remaining continental United States, Middle America and South America (also Trinidad and Margarita Island, off Venezuela) to the Straits of Magellan; also in the Greater Antilles (Cuba, the Isle of Pines and Jamaica). Recorded in summer (and possibly breeding) north to northern Manitoba, east-central Ontario, southern Quebec, northern Vermont and Maine.

Winters mainly from northern California, Arizona, Chihuahua, Texas, the Great Plains (north to Nebraska), Ohio Valley and Maryland (casually north to southern Canada) south to the Gulf coast, Florida and the northern Bahamas (casually to Bimini and New Providence), and through the breeding range in Middle America, the Greater Antilles and South America.

Introduced and established in Puerto Rico.

Casual north to east-central Alaska, northern Ontario, central Quebec, Labrador and Newfoundland, and on Bermuda, Hispaniola, St. Croix (in the Virgin Islands) and the Cayman Islands.

Cathartes burrovianus Cassin. LESSER YELLOW-HEADED VULTURE.

Cathartes Burrovianus Cassin, 1845, Proc. Acad. Nat. Sci. Philadelphia, 2, p. 212. (in the vicinity of Vera Cruz = near Veracruz Llave, Veracruz.)

Habitat.—Lowland savanna, grasslands, marshy areas and open woodland (Tropical Zone).

Distribution.—*Resident* locally in eastern and southern Mexico (southern Tamaulipas, Veracruz, Tabasco, northern Chiapas, the Yucatan Peninsula, and on both slopes of Oaxaca), Belize, eastern Honduras (Mosquitia), northeastern Nicaragua (Puerto Cabezas) and Costa Rica (Río Frío region, recorded rarely elsewhere), and from Panama (both slopes) south through most of South America east of the Andes to northern Argentina and Uruguay.

Genus GYMNOGYPS Lesson

Gymnogyps Lesson, 1842, Echo Monde Savant, sér. 2, 6, col. 1037. Type, by monotypy, *Vultur californianus* Shaw.

Gymnogyps californianus (Shaw). CALIFORNIA CONDOR. [324.]

Vultur californianus Shaw, 1798, *in* Shaw and Nodder, Naturalists' Misc., 9, pl. 301 and text. (coast of California = San Francisco or Monterey.)

Habitat.—Mountainous country at low and moderate elevations, especially rocky and brushy areas with cliffs available for nest sites, foraging also in grasslands, oak savanna, mountain plateaus, ridges and canyons.

Distribution.—*Resident* at present in very small numbers in the coastal ranges of California from Monterey and San Benito counties south to Ventura County, ranging, at least casually, north to Santa Clara and San Mateo counties, and east to the western slope of the Sierra Nevada (north as far as Fresno County) and the Tehachapi Mountains, with breeding sites apparently confined to Los Padres National Forest in Santa Barbara, Ventura and extreme northern Los Angeles counties. Formerly resident along the Pacific coast and in part inland west of the Cascade-Sierra Nevada ranges, apparently from southern British Columbia south to northern Baja California (although there are no confirmed breeding records outside of California). Recent reports of condors east to southwestern Utah and southeastern Arizona, as well as within or around the former range in Baja California, seem to be without foundation.

Genus SARCORAMPHUS Duméril

Sarcoramphus Duméril, 1806, Zool. Anal., p. 32. Type, by subsequent designation (Vigors, 1825), *Vultur papa* Linnaeus.

Sarcoramphus papa (Linnaeus). KING VULTURE.

Vultur Papa Linnaeus, 1758, Syst. Nat., ed. 10, 1, p. 86. Based on "The Warwovwen, or Indian Vulture" Albin, Nat. Hist. Birds, 2, p. 4, pl. 4, and "The King of the Vultures" Edwards, Nat. Hist. Birds, 1, p. 2, pl. 2. (in India occidentali, error = Surinam.)

Habitat.—Primarily lowland forested regions, locally from densely forested situations to open country in moist to arid habitats (Tropical and lower Subtropical zones).

Distribution.—*Resident* from Sinaloa, Puebla and Veracruz south through Middle America and South America, mostly east of the Andes, to northern Argentina and Uruguay. Former reports from Florida (St. Johns River) probably pertain to *Polyborus plancus.*

Casual in Trinidad.

Suborder ACCIPITRES: Secretarybirds, Kites, Eagles, Hawks and Allies

Superfamily ACCIPITROIDEA: Kites, Eagles, Hawks and Allies

Family ACCIPITRIDAE: Kites, Eagles, Hawks and Allies

Subfamily PANDIONINAE: Ospreys

Notes.—Sometimes regarded as a family, the Pandionidae.

Genus PANDION Savigny

Pandion Savigny, 1809, Descr. Egypte, 1, pp. 69, 95. Type, by monotypy, *Pandion fluvialis* Savigny = *Falco haliaetus* Linnaeus.

Pandion haliaetus (Linnaeus). OSPREY. [364.]

Falco Haliætus Linnaeus, 1758, Syst. Nat., ed. 10, 1, p. 91. (in Europa = Sweden.)

Habitat.—Primarily along rivers, lakes and seacoasts, occurring widely in migration, often crossing land areas between bodies of water (Tropical and Temperate zones).

Distribution.—*Breeds* in North America from northwestern Alaska, northern Yukon, western and southern Mackenzie, northern Saskatchewan, northern Manitoba, northern Ontario, central Quebec, central Labrador and Newfoundland south locally to Baja California (both coasts), the Tres Marias Islands (off Nayarit), Sinaloa, central Arizona, southwestern and central New Mexico, southern Texas, the Gulf coast and southern Florida, and in the Bahamas, on small cays off Cuba, in the Virgin Islands, and along the coasts and on islands off the Yucatan Peninsula and Belize; and in the Old World from the British Isles, Scandinavia, northern Russia and northern Siberia south, at least locally, through much of Eurasia and most of Africa and Australia to South Africa, the Himalayas, Tasmania, New Caledonia and the Solomon Islands.

Winters in the Americas from central California, southern Texas, the Gulf coast, Florida and Bermuda south through Middle America (including Cocos Island off Costa Rica, and in the Revillagigedos), the West Indies and South America (also the Galapagos Islands) to southern Chile, northern Argentina and Uruguay; and in the Old World from the Mediterranean, Black and Caspian seas, India and eastern China south throughout the remainder of the breeding range.

In migration occurs regularly on islands in the western Pacific from the Ryukyu and Bonin chains southward.

Casual in the Hawaiian Islands (Kauai eastward), Aleutians and Pribilofs, north to northern Yukon and northern Quebec, on Guadalupe Island (off Baja California), and in Greenland, Iceland, the Faroe Islands and the eastern Atlantic islands.

Subfamily ACCIPITRINAE: Kites, Eagles, Hawks and Allies

Genus **LEPTODON** Sundevall

Leptodon Sundevall, 1836, Vetensk.-Akad. Handl. (1835), p. 114. Type, by monotypy, "*Falco cayanensis* et *palliatus* auct." = *Falco cayanensis* Latham.

Leptodon cayanensis (Latham). GRAY-HEADED KITE.

Falco cayanensis Latham, 1790, Index Ornithol., 1, p. 28. Based on the "Cayenne Falcon" Latham, Gen. Synop. Birds, 1 (1), p. 59. (in Cayana = Bahia, Brazil.)

Habitat.—Primarily heavily forested humid lowlands, often near marshes and streams, less frequently open woodland or arid situations (Tropical and Subtropical zones).

Distribution.—*Resident* locally from Oaxaca and southern Tamaulipas south through Middle America and South America (also Trinidad) west of the Andes to western Ecuador and east of the Andes to Paraguay, northern Argentina and southern Brazil.

Genus **CHONDROHIERAX** Lesson

Chondrohierax Lesson, 1843, Echo Monde Savant, sér. 2, 7, col. 61. Type, by monotypy, *Chondrohierax erythrofrons* Lesson = *Falco uncinatus* Temminck.

Chondrohierax uncinatus (Temminck). HOOK-BILLED KITE. [327.1.]

Falco uncinatus (Illiger MS) Temminck, 1822, Planches Color., livr. 18, pls. 103–104. (Rio de Janeiro and Bahia, Brazil = Bahia.)

Habitat.—Lowland forests, especially in swampy situations, ranging over open marsh and in open woodland (Tropical to lower Subtropical zones).

Distribution.—*Resident* [*uncinatus* group] from southern Sinaloa, Distrito Federal, southern Texas (Falcon Dam, Santa Ana) and Tamaulipas south through Middle America and South America (also on Grenada in the Lesser Antilles, and on Trinidad) east of the Andes to central Peru, southern Bolivia, northern Argentina and southern Brazil; and [*wilsonii* group] in eastern Cuba.

Notes.—The two groups are often regarded as distinct species, *C. uncinatus* [HOOK-BILLED KITE] and *C. wilsonii* (Cassin, 1847) [CUBAN KITE].

Genus ELANOIDES Vieillot

Elanoïdes Vieillot, 1818, Nouv. Dict. Hist. Nat., nouv. éd., 24 (1817), p. 101. Type, by monotypy, "Milan de la Caroline" = *Falco forficatus* Linnaeus.

Elanoides forficatus (Linnaeus). AMERICAN SWALLOW-TAILED KITE. [327.]

Falco forficatus Linnaeus, 1758, Syst. Nat., ed. 10, 1, p. 89. Based on "The Swallow tail'd Hawk" Catesby, Nat. Hist. Carolina, 1, p. 4, pl. 4. (in America = South Carolina.)

Habitat.—Lowland forested regions, especially swampy areas, ranging into open woodland (Tropical and Subtropical zones).

Distribution.—*Breeds* locally from South Carolina south to Florida, and west to Louisiana and (formerly) central Texas; and from southeastern Mexico (Campeche and Quintana Roo) south through most of Middle America (except El Salvador) and South America (also Trinidad) to eastern Peru, southern Bolivia, northern Argentina, Uruguay and southern Brazil. Formerly bred north to Oklahoma, eastern Kansas, eastern Nebraska, northwestern Minnesota and southern Wisconsin.

Winters primarily in South America from Colombia and Venezuela southward; recorded occasionally in winter in Middle America, casually in Florida.

In migration occurs regularly in the western Greater Antilles (Cuba, Jamaica), and in Mexico from Nuevo León and Tamaulipas south to the Distrito Federal and Oaxaca, and eastward through the Yucatan Peninsula.

Casual west and north to southeastern Arizona (sight record), New Mexico, eastern Colorado, southern Saskatchewan, southern Manitoba, southern Ontario, New York, Vermont, New Hampshire, Massachusetts and Nova Scotia, also a sight report from the Bahama Islands (west of Grand Bahama). Accidental in Bermuda, Tobago and England.

Notes.—In American literature usually known as the SWALLOW-TAILED KITE.

Genus GAMPSONYX Vigors

Gampsonyx Vigors, 1825, Zool. J., 2, p. 69. Type, by monotypy, *Gampsonyx swainsonii* Vigors.

Notes.—For inclusion of this genus is the Accipitridae, see Brodkorb, 1960, Auk, 77, pp. 88–89.

Gampsonyx swainsonii Vigors. PEARL KITE.

Gampsonyx swainsonii Vigors, 1825, Zool. J., 2, p. 69. (tableland of Bahia, about ten leagues west-southwest from the Bay of San Salvador, Brazil.)

Habitat.—Open, primarily deciduous woodland and savanna, mostly in semi-arid regions (Tropical Zone).

Distribution.—*Resident* on the Pacific slope of western Nicaragua (from near Chinandega to Granada); and in South America west of the Andes from western Colombia south to extreme northwestern Peru, and east of the Andes from northern Colombia, northern Venezuela (also Trinidad) and the Guianas south to southeastern Peru, eastern Bolivia, northern Argentina and southern Brazil.

Casual (possibly resident) in Panama (west to Bocas del Toro and Coclé).

Genus ELANUS Savigny

Elanus Savigny, 1809, Descr. Egypte, 1, pp. 69, 97. Type, by monotypy, *Elanus caesius* Savigny = *Falco caeruleus* Desfontaines.

Elanus caeruleus (Desfontaines). BLACK-SHOULDERED KITE. [328.]

Falco cœruleus Desfontaines, 1789, Hist. Acad. R. Sci. Paris (1787), p. 502, pl. 15. (Algiers.)

Habitat.—Savanna, open woodland, marshes, partially cleared lands and cultivated fields, mostly in lowland situations (Tropical to Temperate zones).

Distribution.—*Resident* [*leucurus* group] locally from northwestern Oregon south (west of the deserts) to northwestern Baja California, in peninsular Florida (formerly), from southern Oklahoma, western Louisiana, east-central and southeastern Texas, Tamaulipas and Oaxaca south through Middle America (both slopes) to eastern Panama, thence eastward in northern South America to Surinam, from southern Bolivia and central and eastern Brazil south to central Argentina, and in central Chile; [*caeruleus* group] from southern Europe, southern Arabia, India, Southeast Asia, southern China and the Philippines south to southern Africa, Ceylon, the East Indies and New Guinea; and [*notatus* group] throughout Australia. The range [*leucurus* group], especially in Middle America, has greatly expanded since 1960.

Casual straggler [*leucurus* group] north and east to Washington (where possibly breeding), eastern Oregon, Idaho, Nevada, Arizona, New Mexico and northern and western Texas, in the Mississippi Valley north to Missouri and southern Illinois, east through the southeastern United States from Louisiana to South Carolina, Georgia and Florida, and to Trinidad. Accidental [*leucurus* group] in Massachusetts.

Notes.—The three groups are sometimes considered as three allospecies, *E. caeruleus* [BLACK-WINGED KITE], *E. leucurus* (Vieillot, 1818) [WHITE-TAILED KITE] and *E. notatus* Gould, 1838 [BLACK-SHOULDERED KITE], of a superspecies.

Genus ROSTRHAMUS Lesson

Rostrhamus Lesson, 1830, Traité Ornithol., livr. 1, p. 55. Type, by monotypy, *Rostrhamus niger* Lesson = *Herpetotheres sociabilis* Vieillot.

Helicolestes Bangs and Penard, 1918, Bull. Mus. Comp. Zool. Harv., 62, p. 38. Type, by original designation, *Falco hamatus* Illinger = Temminck.

Rostrhamus sociabilis (Vieillot). SNAIL KITE. [330.]

> *Herpetotheres sociabilis* Vieillot, 1817, Nouv. Dict. Hist. Nat., nouv. éd., 18, p. 318. Based on "Gavilan de Estero Sociable" Azara, Apunt. Hist. Nat. Páx. Parag., 1, p. 84 (no. 16). (Corrientes, near Río de la Plata, Argentina.)

Habitat.—Fresh-water marshes, primarily in lowlands (Tropical, rarely Subtropical and lower Temperate zones).

Distribution.—*Resident* in Florida (Lake Okeechobee region, and locally throughout the Everglades basin and the upper St. John's River, formerly more widely in peninsular Florida), Cuba and the Isle of Pines; in the Pacific lowlands of Oaxaca; locally on the Gulf-Caribbean slope from Veracruz, Campeche and Quintana Roo south to Nicaragua; in northwestern Costa Rica (Pacific lowlands around Gulf of Nicoya and Guanacaste); locally in Panama (recorded Chiriquí, eastern Panamá province and San Blas); and in South America from Colombia, Venezuela and the Guianas south, west of the Andes to western Ecuador and east of the Andes throughout to northern Argentina, Uruguay and southern Brazil.

Casual or accidental in southern Texas (Jim Wells County) and Trinidad; and north casually in Florida (primarily dispersal due to drought) to Wakulla, Sumter and Putnam counties.

Notes.—Also known as EVERGLADE KITE.

Rostrhamus hamatus (Temminck). SLENDER-BILLED KITE.

> *Falco hamatus* (Illiger MS) Temminck, 1821, Planches Color., livr. 11, pl. 61 and text. (Brazil.)

Habitat.—Lowland forests, usually near ponds, swamps or sluggish streams (Tropical Zone).

Distribution.—*Resident* in eastern Panama (Tuira Valley, along the Río Paya, Darién); and locally in South America east of the Andes from northern Colombia, northern Venezuela and Surinam south to eastern Peru, Bolivia and Amazonian Brazil.

Genus **HARPAGUS** Vigors

> *Harpagus* Vigors, 1824, Zool. J., 1, p. 338. Type, by subsequent designation (G. R. Gray, 1840), *Falco bidentatus* Latham.

Harpagus bidentatus (Latham). DOUBLE-TOOTHED KITE.

> *Falco bidentatus* Latham, 1790, Index Ornithol., 1, p. 38. Based on the "Notched Falcon" Latham, Gen. Synop. Birds, suppl., 1, p. 34. (in Cayana = Cayenne.)

Habitat.—Forests and open woodland, primarily in humid lowlands (Tropical and lower Subtropical zones).

Distribution.—*Resident* from Veracruz, Oaxaca and Quintana Roo south in the Gulf-Caribbean lowlands to Nicaragua, on both slopes of Costa Rica (absent from dry northwest) and Panama, and in South America from Colombia, Venezuela (also Trinidad) and the Guianas south, east of the Andes, to eastern Peru, eastern Bolivia and east-central Brazil.

Genus **ICTINIA** Vieillot

Ictinia Vieillot, 1816, Analyse, p. 24. Type, by monotypy, "Milan cresserelle" Vieillot = *Falco plumbeus* Gmelin.

Ictinia mississippiensis (Wilson). Mississippi Kite. [329.]

Falco misisippiensis [sic] Wilson, 1811, Am. Ornithol., 3, p. 80, pl. 25, fig. 1. (a few miles below Natchez [Mississippi].)

Habitat.—Forest, open woodland and prairies, breeding in trees, usually near watercourses.

Distribution.—*Breeds* from central Arizona, northern New Mexico, southeastern Colorado, north-central Kansas, central Arkansas, southern Missouri, southern Illinois, western Kentucky, western Tennessee, the northern portions of the Gulf states, South Carolina and (probably) North Carolina south to central and southeastern New Mexico, western and south-central Texas, the Gulf coast and north-central Florida, the range expanding along its northern border in recent years; formerly bred north to central Colorado, Iowa, southern Indiana and southern Ohio.

Winters apparently for the most part in central South America, where recorded from Paraguay and northern Argentina (in Chaco and Formosa); scattered reports indicate casual or occasional wintering north as far as southern Texas.

In migration occurs regularly from Tamaulipas and Chiapas south through Middle America and Colombia.

Casual straggler north to central California, southern Nevada, northern Colorado, South Dakota, Minnesota, Wisconsin, southern Ontario, Ohio, Pennsylvania, New Jersey, New York (Staten Island) and Massachusetts.

Notes.—*I. mississippiensis* and *I. plumbea* constitute a superspecies; some authors regard them as conspecific. If merged into a single species, Plumbeous Kite would be the most suitable English name, although some authors have proposed Gray Kite.

Ictinia plumbea (Gmelin). Plumbeous Kite.

Falco plumbeus Gmelin, 1788, Syst. Nat., 1 (1), p. 283. Based on the "Spotted-tailed Hawk" Latham, Gen. Synop. Birds, 1 (1), p. 106. (in Cayenne = Cayenne.)

Habitat.—Primarily forested lowlands, including moist forest, pines and mangroves, mainly in edge situations or in open woodland (Tropical and Subtropical zones).

Distribution.—*Breeds* from Tamaulipas, eastern San Luis Potosí, Veracruz and Oaxaca south along both slopes of Middle America (including the Pearl Islands, where perhaps only a migrant), and in South America from Colombia, Venezuela (also Trinidad) and the Guianas south, east of the Andes, to southern Peru, southern Bolivia, northern Argentina and southeastern Brazil.

Winters primarily in the South American portion of the breeding range, casually south to Buenos Aires. Winter reports from Middle America have not been substantiated.

Notes.—See comments under *I. mississippiensis*.

Genus HALIAEETUS Savigny

Haliaeetus Savigny, 1809, Descr. Egypte, 1, pp. 68, 85. Type, by monotypy, *Haliaeetus nisus* Savigny = *Falco albicilla* Linnaeus.

Notes.—See comments under *Busarellus.*

Haliaeetus leucocephalus (Linnaeus). BALD EAGLE. [352.]

Falco leucocephalus Linnaeus, 1766, Syst. Nat., ed. 12, 1, p. 124. Based on "The Bald Eagle" Catesby, Nat. Hist. Carolina, 1, p. 1, pl. 1. (in America, Europa = South Carolina.)

Habitat.—Primarily near seacoasts, rivers and large lakes, breeding in tall trees or on cliffs.

Distribution.—*Breeds* from central Alaska (southern Brooks Range), northern Yukon, northwestern and southern Mackenzie, northern Saskatchewan, northern Manitoba, central Ontario, central Quebec, Labrador and Newfoundland south locally to the Commander (formerly) and Aleutian islands (west to Buldir), southern Alaska, Baja California (both coasts), central Arizona, southwestern and central New Mexico, and the Gulf coast from southeastern Texas east to southern Florida (including the Florida Keys); absent as a breeding bird through much of the Great Basin (bred formerly) and most of the prairie and plains regions, also very locally distributed in interior North America, with populations reduced in recent years.

Winters generally throughout the breeding range but most frequently from southern Alaska and southern Canada southward.

In migration occurs widely but sporadically over most of the North American continent.

Casual along the Arctic coast of northeastern Siberia, also a sight report from Puerto Rico.

Notes.—*H. leucocephalus* and *H. albicilla* constitute a superspecies.

Haliaeetus albicilla (Linnaeus). WHITE-TAILED EAGLE. [351.]

Falco Albicilla Linnaeus, 1758, Syst. Nat., ed. 10, 1, p. 89. (in Europa, America = Sweden.)

Habitat.—Rocky coasts, rivers and large lakes, in regions of tundra, forests, deserts or mountains.

Distribution.—*Breeds* from western Greenland, Iceland, Scandinavia, northern Russia and northern Siberia south to northern Europe (formerly to northeastern Africa), Syria, Iran, Turkestan and Kamchatka; a report of breeding on Baffin Island (Cumberland Sound) has not been confirmed.

Winters in the breeding range and south, at least casually, to the Mediterranean and Red seas, India, Formosa, Japan and the Seven Islands of Izu.

Casual in the Aleutian Islands (Attu, where probably breeding, and Unalaska), off Massachusetts (near Nantucket Lightship) and in eastern Greenland.

Notes.—Also known as WHITE-TAILED or GRAY SEA-EAGLE. See comments under *H. leucocephalus.*

Haliaeetus pelagicus (Pallas). STELLER'S SEA-EAGLE. [352.1]

Aquila pelagica Pallas, 1811, Zoogr. Rosso-Asiat., 1, p. 343 and plate. (in Insulis inter Camtshatcam et Continentem Americes, praesertim in infami naufragio et monte Beringii insula = Tauisk, on Sea of Okhotsk.)

Habitat.—Sea coasts and the lower portions of coastal rivers.

Distribution.—*Breeds* from northwestern Siberia (west to Yakutsk) and Kamchatka south to Sakhalin, possibly also in Korea.

Winters from the breeding range south to Korea, Japan and the Seven Islands of Izu.

Casual or accidental in the Hawaiian Islands (Kure, Midway), the Aleutians (Attu, Unalaska, Unmak), the Pribilofs (St. Paul), Kodiak Island, Bering Island and eastern China.

Genus **CIRCUS** Lacépède

Circus Lacépède, 1799, Tabl. Mamm. Ois., p. 4. Type, by subsequent designation (Lesson, 1828), *Falco aeruginosus* Linnaeus.

Circus cyaneus (Linnaeus). NORTHERN HARRIER. [331.]

Falco cyaneus Linnaeus, 1766, Syst. Nat., ed. 12, 1, p. 126. Based on "The Blue Hawk" Edwards, Glean. Nat. Hist., 1, p. 33, pl. 225. (in Europa, Africa = vicinity of London, England.)

Habitat.—Prairies, moorlands, steppe and marshes (breeding); coastal marshes, meadows, grasslands and cultivated fields (nonbreeding).

Distribution.—*Breeds* [*hudsonius* group] in North America from northern Alaska, northern Yukon, northwestern and southern Mackenzie, northern Saskatchewan, northern Manitoba, central (and probably northern) Ontario, southern Quebec and Newfoundland (probably) south to northern Baja California, southern Arizona, southern New Mexico, southern and eastern Texas, western Oklahoma, southeastern Kansas, southern Missouri, southern Illinois, central Kentucky, West Virginia, southeastern Virginia and (formerly) Florida; and [*cyaneus* group] in Eurasia from the British Isles, Scandinavia, northern Russia and northern Siberia south to the northern Mediterranean region, southern Russia, Turkestan, Amurland, Ussuriland, Sakhalin and the Kurile Islands.

Winters [*hudsonius* group] in the Americas from Alaska (casually), southern British Columbia, southern Alberta, southern Saskatchewan (rarely), South Dakota, Minnesota, southern Wisconsin, southern Michigan, southern Ontario, New York and Massachusetts (casually farther north) south through the United States, Middle America and the Antilles (rare in Lesser Antilles) to northern Colombia, northern Venezuela and Barbados; and [*cyaneus* group] in Eurasia from the British Isles, southern Scandinavia and southern Japan south to northwestern Africa, Asia Minor, India, Burma, eastern China, Formosa and the Ryukyu Islands.

In migration occurs casually [group unknown] in the Aleutian and Commander islands.

Casual or accidental [*hudsonius* group] in the Hawaiian Islands (Midway, Oahu), Labrador, Bermuda and the Bahamas; and [*cyaneus* group] in Iceland and the Faroe Islands.

Notes.—The two groups are sometimes regarded as separate species, *C. cyaneus* [HEN HARRIER] and *C. hudsonius* (Linnaeus, 1766) [AMERICAN HARRIER or MARSH HAWK]. *C. cyaneus* and the South American *C. cinereus* Vieillot, 1816, constitute a superspecies; they are considered conspecific by some authors.

Genus **ACCIPITER** Brisson

Accipiter Brisson, 1760, Ornithologie, 1, p. 28; 6, p. 310. Type, by tautonymy, *Accipiter* Brisson = *Falco nisus* Linnaeus.

Accipiter superciliosus (Linnaeus). TINY HAWK.

Falco superciliosus Linnaeus, 1766, Syst. Nat., ed. 12, 1, p. 128. (in Surinamo = Surinam.)

Habitat.—Lowland forest, especially in forest edge and open woodland (Tropical and lower Subtropical zones).

Distribution.—*Resident* from eastern Nicaragua (vicinity of Waspam and Greytown) south through Costa Rica, Panama and South America west of the Andes to western Ecuador and east of the Andes to eastern Peru, central Bolivia, northern and eastern Brazil, eastern Paraguay and extreme northeastern Argentina.

[**Accipiter nisus** (Linnaeus). EURASIAN SPARROWHAWK.] See Appendix B.

Accipiter striatus Vieillot. SHARP-SHINNED HAWK. [332.]

Accipiter striatus Vieillot, 1808, Hist. Nat. Ois. Am. Sept., 1 (1807), p. 42, pl. 14. (Santo Domingo = Haiti.)

Habitat.—Forest and open woodland, either coniferous or deciduous, primarily the former in more northern and mountainous sections of the range (Tropical to Temperate zones).

Distribution.—*Breeds* [*striatus* group] from western and central Alaska, northern Yukon, western and southern Mackenzie, northern Saskatchewan, central Manitoba, central Ontario, central Quebec, southern Labrador and Newfoundland south to central California, central Arizona, southern New Mexico, southern Texas, the northern parts of the Gulf states, and South Carolina, and south through the highlands of Mexico to Oaxaca; also in the Greater Antilles (Cuba, Hispaniola and Puerto Rico).

Winters [*striatus* group] from southern Alaska, the southernmost portions of the Canadian provinces (casually), and Nova Scotia south through the United States and Middle America to central Panama, casually to the Bahamas, Jamaica and (probably) Mona Island off Puerto Rico; also in the breeding range in the Greater Antilles.

Resident [*chionogaster* group] in the highlands of Chiapas, Guatemala, El Salvador, Honduras and north-central Nicaragua; and [*erythronemius* group] in South America in the mountains of Venezuela, the Andes from Colombia to Bolivia, and from central Brazil and Paraguay south to northern Argentina and Uruguay.

Casual or accidental [*striatus* group] in northern Alaska and Bermuda.

Notes.—The three groups are sometimes regarded as distinct species, *A. striatus*

[SHARP-SHINNED HAWK], *A. chionogaster* (Kaup, 1852) [WHITE-BREASTED HAWK] and *A. erythronemius* (Kaup, 1850) [RUFOUS-THIGHED HAWK]; others would recognize *A. erythronemius* as a species, including *chionogaster* as a subspecies thereof.

Accipiter bicolor (Vieillot). BICOLORED HAWK.

Sparvius bicolor Vieillot, 1817, Nouv. Dict. Hist. Nat., nouv. éd., 10, p. 325. (Cayenne.)

Habitat.—Lowland forest and forest edge (Tropical and lower Subtropical zones, in southern South America to Temperate Zone).

Distribution.—*Resident* from Oaxaca, Veracruz and the Yucatan Peninsula south through Middle America and South America west of the Andes to northwestern Peru and east of the Andes to northern Argentina, Paraguay and southern Brazil; and in Chile and extreme western Argentina north to about lat. 34°S.

Notes.—The distinct form from Bolivia and western Brazil south to northern Argentina has sometimes been treated as a separate species, *A guttifer* Hellmayr, 1917, as has the isolated *A. chilensis* R. A. Philippi and Landbeck, 1864, of Chile and western Argentina. See also comments under *A. cooperii*.

Accipiter cooperii (Bonaparte). COOPER'S HAWK. [333.]

Falco Cooperii Bonaparte, 1828, Am. Ornithol., 2, p. 1, pl. 10, fig. 1. (near Bordentown, New Jersey.)

Habitat.—Primarily mature forest, either broadleaf or coniferous, mostly the former, foraging and wintering in open woodland and forest edge as well.

Distribution.—*Breeds* from southern British Columbia, central Alberta, central Saskatchewan, central Manitoba, western and southern Ontario, southern Quebec, Maine, New Brunswick (rarely), Prince Edward Island and (rarely) Nova Scotia south to Baja California, Sinaloa, Chihuahua, Nuevo León, southern Texas, Louisiana, central Mississippi, central Alabama and central Florida.

Winters from Washington, Colorado, Nebraska, southern Minnesota, southern Wisconsin, southern Michigan, southern Ontario, New York and New England south through the southern United States and Mexico to Guatemala and Honduras, casually to Costa Rica and Colombia (Cundinamarca).

Notes.—*A. cooperii* and *A. gundlachi* may constitute a superspecies; some authors also consider *A. bicolor* as part of this same superspecies.

Accipiter gundlachi Lawrence. GUNDLACH'S HAWK.

Accipiter Gundlachi Lawrence, 1860, Ann. Lyc. Nat. Hist. N.Y., 7, p. 252. (Hanabana, Cuba.)

Habitat.—Forest, open woodland and mangroves, primarily in the lowlands but ranging into the highlands.
Distribution.—*Resident* on Cuba.
Notes.—See comments under *A. cooperii*.

Accipiter gentilis (Linnaeus). NORTHERN GOSHAWK. [334.]

Falco gentilis Linnaeus, 1758, Syst. Nat., ed. 10, 1, p. 89. (in Alpibus = Dalecarlian Alps, Sweden.)

Habitat.—Deciduous and coniferous forest, forest edge and open woodland, foraging also in cultivated regions, primarily in mountains towards the south.

Distribution.—*Breeds* in North America from western and central Alaska, northern Yukon, western and southern Mackenzie, southern Keewatin (probably), northeastern Manitoba, northern Ontario, central and northeastern Quebec, Labrador and Newfoundland south to southern Alaska (west to the base of the Alaska Peninsula), central California, southern Nevada, southeastern Arizona, southern New Mexico, the eastern foothills of the Rockies (including the Black Hills of western South Dakota), central Alberta, central Saskatchewan, southern Manitoba, northern Minnesota, central Michigan, Pennsylvania, central New York and northwestern Connecticut, and in the Appalachian and (probably) Great Smoky mountains south to eastern Tennessee and western North Carolina; locally in central Mexico (Jalisco and probably elsewhere); and in Eurasia from the British Isles (rarely), Scandinavia, northern Russia and northern Siberia south to the Mediterranean region, Asia Minor, Iran, the Himalayas, eastern China and Japan.

Winters throughout the breeding range, and in North America south irregularly or casually as far as southern California, northern Mexico (recorded Sonora, Sinaloa, Durango and Chihuahua), south-central Texas, the northern portions of the Gulf states, and west-central Florida, and in Eurasia casually to northern Africa, India and Burma.

Casual on southeastern Baffin Island.

Notes.—Known in Old World literature as the GOSHAWK. The following species are closely allied to *A. gentilis* and may form a superspecies; *A. henstii* (Schlegel, 1873) of Madagascar; *A. melanoleucus* Smith, 1830, of Africa; and *A. meyerianus* (Sharpe, 1878) of the Papuan region.

Genus GERANOSPIZA Kaup

Ischnosceles (not *Ischnoscelis* Burmeister, 1842) Strickland, 1844, Ann. Mag. Nat. Hist., ser. 1, 13, p. 409. Type, by original designation, *Falco gracilis* Temminck = *Sparvius caerulescens* Vieillot.
Geranospiza Kaup, 1847, Isis von Oken, col. 143. New name for *Ischnosceles* Strickland.

Geranospiza caerulescens (Vieillot). CRANE HAWK.

Sparvius cœrulescens Vieillot, 1817, Nouv. Dict. Hist. Nat., nouv. éd., 10, p. 318. (L'Amérique méridionale = Cayenne.)

Habitat.—Humid forest and open woodland, including swamps and borders of marshes, almost always near water (Tropical and lower Subtropical zones).

Distribution.—*Resident* from Mexico (Sonora on the Pacific slope and Tamaulipas on the Gulf-Caribbean) south through Middle America and South America west of the Andes to northwestern Peru and east of the Andes to eastern Peru, Bolivia, northern Argentina and Uruguay.

Notes.—Middle American birds have been considered a separate species, *G. nigra* (Du Bus de Gisignies, 1847) [BLACKISH CRANE-HAWK], by some authors but populations in Panama and northwestern South America are intermediate between *nigra* and *caerulescens*.

Genus LEUCOPTERNIS Kaup

Leucopternis Kaup, 1847, Isis von Oken, col. 210. Type, by subsequent designation (G. R. Gray, 1844), *Falco melanops* Latham.

Leucopternis plumbea Salvin. PLUMBEOUS HAWK.

Leucopternis plumbea Salvin, 1872, Ibis, p. 240, pl. 8. (Ecuador.)

Habitat.—Humid lowland forest (Tropical Zone).
Distribution.—*Resident* from Panama (from Veraguas eastward on the Caribbean slope, and on both slopes in Darién) south on the Pacific coast of South America to extreme northwestern Peru.
Notes.—*L. plumbea* and the South American *L. schistacea* (Sundevall, 1851) [SLATE-COLORED HAWK], constitute a superspecies; they are regarded as conspecific by some authors.

Leucopternis princeps Sclater. BARRED HAWK.

Leucopternis princeps Sclater, 1866, Proc. Zool. Soc. London (1865), p. 429, pl. 24. (Costa Rica, in montibus = Tucurrique, Costa Rica.)

Habitat.—Moist mountain forests (upper Tropical and Subtropical zones).
Distribution.—*Resident* from Costa Rica (cordilleras Central and Talamanca) and Panama south through western Colombia to northern Ecuador.

Leucopternis semiplumbea Lawrence. SEMIPLUMBEOUS HAWK.

Leucopternis semiplumbeus Lawrence, 1861, Ann. Lyc. Nat. Hist. N.Y., 7, p. 288. (Atlantic side of the Isthmus of Panama, along the line of the Panama Railroad.)

Habitat.—Humid lowland and foothill forest (Tropical and lower Subtropical zones).
Distribution.—*Resident* locally in northeastern Honduras (Gracias a Dios), Costa Rica, Panama, northern Colombia and northwestern Ecuador.

Leucopternis albicollis (Latham). WHITE HAWK.

Falco albicollis Latham, 1790, Index Ornithol., 1, p. 36. Based on the "White-necked Falcon" Latham, Gen. Synop. Birds, suppl., 1, p. 30. (Cayenne.)

Habitat.—Humid forest, forest edge and, less frequently, open woodland (Tropical and Subtropical zones).
Distribution.—*Resident* from northern Oaxaca, Veracruz, Tabasco and Chiapas south mostly on the Caribbean drainage of Guatemala, Belize, Honduras and Nicaragua, and both slopes of Costa Rica and Panama to South America, from Colombia, Venezuela (also Trinidad) and the Guianas south, east of the Andes, to eastern Peru, northern Bolivia and Amazonian Brazil.

Genus BUTEOGALLUS Lesson

Buteogallus Lesson, 1830, Traité Ornithol., livr. 2, p. 83. Type, by monotypy, *Buteogallus cathartoides* Lesson = *Falco aequinoctialis* Gmelin.

Urubitinga Lafresnaye, 1842, Dict. Univ. Hist. Nat., 2, p. 786. Type, by tautonymy, *Falco urubitinga* Gmelin.
Hypomorphnus Cabanis, 1844, Arch. Naturgesch., 10, p. 263. Type, by original designation, *Falco urubitinga* Gmelin.
Heterospizias Sharpe, 1874, Cat. Birds Br. Mus., 1, pp. x, 158, 160. Type, by monotypy, *Falco meridionalis* Latham.

Buteogallus anthracinus (Deppe). COMMON BLACK-HAWK. [345.]

Falco anthracinus W. Deppe, 1830, Preis.-Verz. Säugeth. Vögel, etc., Mex., p. 3. (Veracruz.)

Habitat.—Lowland forest, swamps and mangroves, in both moist and arid habitats but generally near water, foraging often on tidal flats or in open woodland (Tropical and lower Subtropical zones).

Distribution.—*Resident* [*anthracinus* group] from central Arizona, southwestern Utah, southern New Mexico, and western and (formerly) southern Texas south through Middle America (including Cozumel and Cancun islands off Quintana Roo, and Utila and Guanaja islands off Caribbean Honduras) to northern Colombia, and east through coastal Venezuela (also Trinidad) to Guyana, and in the Lesser Antilles on St. Vincent; and [*gundlachii* group] in Cuba (including small coastal cays) and the Isle of Pines. Northernmost breeding populations in the southwestern United States usually migrate southward in nonbreeding season.

Casual or accidental [*anthracinus* group] in southern Nevada (breeding attempted), Puerto Rico and the Lesser Antilles (St. Lucia, the Grenadines and Grenada), also a sight report for Colorado; reports from southern Florida (Miami area) are probably on escaped individuals, and may pertain in part to *B. urubitinga*.

Notes.—Also known as BLACK HAWK. Some authors treat the Cuban form as a distinct species, *B. gundlachii* (Cabanis, 1855) [CUBAN BLACK-HAWK]; others would consider *B. subtilis* to be conspecific with *B. anthracinus* (and *gundlachii*). It appears that *B. anthracinus* (with *gundlachii*), *B. subtilis* and the South American *B. aequinoctialis* (Gmelin, 1788) constitute a superspecies.

Buteogallus subtilis (Thayer and Bangs). MANGROVE BLACK-HAWK.

Urubitinga subtilis Thayer and Bangs, 1905, Bull. Mus. Comp. Zool. Harv., 46, p. 94. (Gorgona Island, Colombia.)

Habitat.—Mangroves (Tropical Zone).
Distribution.—*Resident* along the Pacific coast of El Salvador (possibly north to Chiapas), Honduras, Costa Rica, Panama (including the Pearl Islands), Colombia (including coastal islands), Ecuador and extreme northwestern Peru (Tumbes).
Notes.—See comments under *B. anthracinus*.

Buteogallus urubitinga (Gmelin). GREAT BLACK-HAWK.

Falco Urubitinga Gmelin, 1788, Syst. Nat., 1 (1), p. 265. Based in part on the "Brasilian Eagle" Latham, Gen. Synop. Birds, 1 (1), p. 41. (in Brasilia = northeastern Brazil.)

Habitat.—Moist lowland forest and open woodland, primarily near large streams, lakes, ponds or marshes (Tropical and occasionally lower Subtropical zones).

Distribution.—*Resident* from northern Mexico (central Sonora on the Pacific slope and southern Tamaulipas on the Gulf-Caribbean) south through Middle America and South America (also Tobago and Trinidad) west of the Andes to northwestern Peru and east of the Andes to eastern Peru, eastern Bolivia, northern Argentina and Uruguay.

Buteogallus meridionalis (Latham). SAVANNA HAWK.

Falco meridionalis Latham, 1790, Index Ornithol., 1, p. 36. Based on the "Rufous-headed Falcon" Latham, Gen. Synop. Birds, suppl., 1, p. 33. (in Cayana = Cayenne.)

Habitat.—Wet savanna, marshes with scattered trees, and open swamps, rarely in drier savanna away from water (Tropical Zone).

Distribution.—*Resident* from western Panama (from Chiriquí eastward, rare or absent from Darién) south in South America (also Trinidad) west of the Andes to northwestern Peru and east of the Andes to eastern Bolivia, northern Argentina and Uruguay.

Notes.—Usually placed in the monotypic genus *Heterospizias*.

Genus PARABUTEO Ridgway

Parabuteo Ridgway, 1874, *in* Baird, Brewer and Ridgway, Hist. N. Am. Birds, 3, pp. 248, 250. Type, by monotypy, *Buteo harrisi* Audubon = *Falco unicinctus* Temminck.

Parabuteo unicinctus (Temminck). HARRIS' HAWK. [335.]

Falco unicinctus Temminck, 1824, Planches Color., livr. 53, p. 313. (Brésil ... dans les environs du Rio-Grande, près Boa-Vista = Boa Vista, western Minas Gerais, Brazil.)

Habitat.—Primarily savanna, open woodland and semi-desert, especially in the vicinity of marshes, swamps and large bodies of water (Tropical and Subtropical zones).

Distribution.—*Resident* in southern Kansas (Meade County and vicinity, casually or formerly), and from northern Baja California, southeastern California (formerly, recently reintroduced), southern Arizona, southern New Mexico and central Texas south through Middle America (rare and local from Chiapas to Nicaragua, unrecorded in Belize and Honduras) and South America (including Margarita Island off Venezuela) to central Chile and central Argentina.

Casual in northern and eastern Texas, Oklahoma and Louisiana (sight reports from southern Nevada and southern Utah). Stragglers reported from southwestern California, Iowa (Hillsboro), Ohio (Harrisburg), New York (Westchester County) and several localities in Florida likely pertain to escapes from captivity.

Notes.—Also known as BAY-WINGED HAWK.

Genus BUSARELLUS Lesson

Busarellus "Lafresnaye" Lesson, 1843, Echo Monde Savant, sér. 2, 7, col. 468. Type, by original designation, *Circus busarellus* Vieillot = *Falco nigricollis* Latham.

Notes.—Some authors suggest that this genus is closely related to *Haliaeetus*.

Busarellus nigricollis (Latham). BLACK-COLLARED HAWK.

Falco nigricollis Latham, 1790, Index Ornithol., 1, p. 35. Based on the "Black-necked Falcon" Latham, Gen. Synop. Birds, suppl., 1, p. 30. (in Cayana = Cayenne.)

Habitat.—Fresh-water marshes, wet savanna and swamps, less frequently around lakes and lagoons (Tropical Zone).

Distribution.—*Resident* from Sinaloa and Veracruz south along both slopes of Middle America, and in South America from Colombia, Venezuela (also Trinidad) and the Guianas south, east of the Andes, to southern Bolivia, northern Argentina and Uruguay.

Genus **HARPYHALIAETUS** Lafresnaye

Harpyhaliætus Lafresnaye, 1842, Rev. Zool. [Paris], 5, p. 173. Type, by original designation, *Harpyia coronata* Vieillot.

Urbitornis J. Verreaux, 1856, Proc. Zool. Soc. London, p. 145. Type, by original designation, *Circaetus solitarius* Tschudi.

Harpyhaliaetus solitarius (Tschudi). SOLITARY EAGLE.

Circaëtus solitarius Tschudi, 1844, Arch. Naturgesch., 10, p. 264. (Republica Peruana = Río Chanchamayo, Junín, Peru.)

Habitat.—Heavily wooded foothills and mountains, both in moist forest and pines (upper Tropical and Subtropical zones).

Distribution.—*Resident* locally in Mexico (recorded southeastern Sonora, Jalisco and Oaxaca), Guatemala (San Gerónimo), Honduras (Valle de Talanga), Costa Rica (Volcán de Poás, Cordillera Talamanca and Golfo Dulce), Panama (Veraguas, eastern Panamá province and Darién) and South America from Colombia and northern Venezuela south to central Peru, Bolivia and northwestern Argentina. Although often listed for Nicaragua, there is no specific record.

Notes.—*H. solitarius* is sometimes considered to be conspecific with the South American *H. coronatus* (Vieillot, 1817) [AMERICAN CROWNED or CROWNED EAGLE].

Genus **BUTEO** Lacépède

Buteo Lacépède, 1799, Tabl. Mamm. Ois., p. 4. Type, by tautonymy, *Falco buteo* Linnaeus.

Asturina Vieillot, 1816, Analyse, pp. 24, 68. Type, by original designation, *Asturia* [sic] *cinerea* Vieillot = *Falco nitidus* Latham.

Craxirex Gould, 1839, *in* Darwin, Zool. Voy. Beagle, 3 (6), p. 22. Type, by subsequent designation (G. R. Gray, 1840), *Polyborus galapagoensis* Gould.

Tachytriorchis Kaup, 1844, Class. Säugeth. Vögel, p. 123. Type, by monotypy, *Buteo pterocles* Temminck = *Buteo albicaudatus* Vieillot.

Notes.—Species of this genus are known in Old World literature under the group name BUZZARD.

Buteo nitidus (Latham). GRAY HAWK. [346.]

Falco nitidus Latham, 1790, Index Ornithol., 1, p. 41. Based on the "Plumbeous Falcon" Latham, Gen. Synop. Birds, suppl., 1, p. 37. (in Cayana = Cayenne.)

Habitat.—Open woodland, pasturelands, and generally open country with scattered trees, primarily in arid situations (Tropical and Subtropical zones).

Distribution.—*Resident* from southern Arizona, Sonora, Jalisco, Hidalgo, Tamaulipas and (casually) southern Texas south through Middle America, and in South America from Colombia, Venezuela (also Tobago and Trinidad) and the Guianas south, west of the Andes to western Ecuador and east of the Andes to eastern Peru, northern and eastern Bolivia, northern Argentina, Paraguay and southern Brazil. Northernmost breeding populations in Arizona and Texas are usually migratory southward in nonbreeding season.

Casual in southern New Mexico, and western and southeastern Texas.

Notes.—Some authors have suggested that populations south to northwestern Costa Rica constitute a species, *B. plagiatus* (Schlegel, 1862), distinct from *B. nitidus* [GRAY-LINED HAWK], which ranges from southwestern Costa Rica southward. Sometimes treated in the monotypic genus *Asturina.*

Buteo magnirostris (Gmelin). ROADSIDE HAWK. [343.1.]

Falco magnirostris Gmelin, 1788, Syst. Nat., 1 (1), p. 282. Based mainly on "Éspervier à gros bec de Cayenne" Daubenton, Planches Enlum., pl. 464. (in Cayenna = Cayenne.)

Habitat.—Open woodland, second growth, pastureland, savanna and, less frequently, the canopy of denser moist forest (Tropical and Subtropical zones).

Distribution.—*Resident* from Jalisco, southern Nuevo León and southern Tamaulipas south through Middle America (including Cozumel and Holbox islands off Quintana Roo; Roatán, Barbareta and Guanaja in the Bay Islands, off Caribbean Honduras; and Coiba, Taboguilla, Iguana and the Pearl islands off Panama), and in South America from Colombia, Venezuela and the Guianas south, west of the Andes to western Ecuador and east of the Andes to eastern Bolivia, northern Argentina and Uruguay.

Accidental in southern Texas (Cameron County).

Buteo lineatus (Gmelin). RED-SHOULDERED HAWK. [339.]

Falco lineatus Gmelin, 1788, Syst. Nat., 1 (1), p. 268. Based on the "Barred-breasted Buzzard" Latham, Gen. Synop. Birds, 1 (1), p. 56, and the "Red-shouldered Falcon" Pennant, Arct. Zool., 2, p. 206. (in insula Longa = Long Island, New York.)

Habitat.—Moist and riverine forest, and in eastern North America in wooded swamps, foraging in forest edge and open woodland (Tropical to Temperate zones).

Distribution.—*Breeds* from northern California south, west of the Sierran divide, to northern Baja California; and from eastern Nebraska, Iowa, central Minnesota, northern Wisconsin, northern Michigan, southern Ontario, southwestern Quebec and southern New Brunswick south to Veracruz, Tamaulipas, central and southern Texas, the Gulf coast and Florida (to Florida Keys); also locally in the valley of México (recorded Zacatecas and Distrito Federal).

Winters, at least sporadically, through the breeding range, but in eastern North America primarily from eastern Kansas, central Missouri, the Ohio Valley, northwestern Pennsylvania, New York and southern New England southward.

Casual north to Washington (Nisqually), southern Oregon, Colorado, North Dakota and southern Manitoba, and in southern Arizona, Sinaloa and Jalisco. Accidental in Scotland; a report from Jamaica is highly questionable.

Notes.—*B. lineatus* and *B. ridgwayi* may constitute a superspecies.

Buteo ridgwayi (Cory). RIDGWAY'S HAWK.

> *Rupornis ridgwayi* Cory, 1883, Q. J. Boston Zool. Soc., 2, p. 46. (Santo Domingo = Samana, Dominican Republic.)

Habitat.—Lowland forest edge and open woodland, foraging frequently in relatively open country.

Distribution.—*Resident* on Hispaniola and surrounding small islands (Beata, Gonâve, Île-à-Vache, Alto Velo, Grand Cayemite and Petite Cayemite).

Notes.—See comments under *B. lineatus.*

Buteo platypterus (Vieillot). BROAD-WINGED HAWK. [343.]

> *Falco pennsylvanicus* Wilson, 1812, Am. Ornithol., 6, p. 92, pl. 54, fig. 1. (l'Amérique septentrionale = near the Schuylkill River, Pennsylvania.) [Not *Falco pennsylvanicus* Wilson, 1812, *ibid.*, p. 13 = *Falco velox* Wilson.]
> *Sparvius platypterus* Vieillot, 1823, *in* Bonnaterre and Vieillot, Tabl. Encycl. Méth., Ornithol., 3, livr. 93, p. 1273. New name for *Falco pennsylvanicus* Wilson, preoccupied.

Habitat.—Broad-leaved and mixed forest, preferring denser situations, less frequently in open woodland, in migration also in open country.

Distribution.—*Breeds* in central Alberta and central Saskatchewan, and from central Manitoba, central Ontario, southern Quebec, New Brunswick and Nova Scotia south to eastern Texas, the Gulf coast and Florida.

Winters primarily in southern Florida (mostly coasts and the Florida Keys, casually farther north), and from Guatemala (casually from Sinaloa and southern Texas) south through Middle America and South America to eastern Peru, Bolivia and southern Brazil, occasionally also in the breeding range in eastern North America.

In migration occurs regularly in the eastern Plains states, eastern New Mexico, eastern and southern Mexico, and western Cuba, casually west to California, Utah, Arizona, Colorado and western New Mexico; in recent years reported regularly in fall and winter in coastal California.

Resident in the Antilles on Cuba and Puerto Rico, and from Antigua south to Grenada and Tobago.

Casual north to northern British Columbia, northern Alberta, northern Saskatchewan and northern Ontario, and to Hispaniola (questionably) and Barbados.

Buteo brachyurus Vieillot. SHORT-TAILED HAWK. [344.]

> *Buteo brachyurus* Vieillot, 1816, Nouv. Dict. Hist. Nat., nouv. éd., 4, p. 477. (No locality given = Cayenne.)

Habitat.—Generally open country, from mangrove and cypress swamps to open pine-oak woodland, avoiding heavily forested situations (Tropical and Subtropical zones).

Distribution.—*Resident* locally in peninsular Florida (from St. Marks and San Mateo south to Lake Okeechobee, in winter mostly south of Lake Okeechobee), and from Sinaloa and Tamaulipas south through Middle America (including Cozumel Island off Quintana Roo) and South America west of the Andes to western Ecuador and east of the Andes to eastern Peru, Bolivia, northern Argentina,

Paraguay and southern Brazil; a sight report from Hispaniola (Dominican Republic) is doubtful.

Notes.—Suggestions that *B. albigula* Philippi, 1899, of the South American Andes, and *B. brachyurus* are conspecific require confirmation.

Buteo swainsoni Bonaparte. SWAINSON'S HAWK. [342.]

Buteo vulgaris (not Swainson, 1832) Audubon, 1837, Birds Am. (folio), 4, pl. 372. (near the Columbia River = Fort Vancouver, Washington.)
Buteo Swainsoni Bonaparte, 1838, Geogr. Comp. List, p. 3. New name for *Buteo vulgaris* Audubon, preoccupied.

Habitat.—Savanna, open pine-oak woodland and cultivated lands with scattered trees, in migration and winter also in grasslands and other open country.

Distribution.—*Breeds* locally in east-central Alaska, Yukon and Mackenzie, and from central Alberta, central Saskatchewan, southern Manitoba, western and southern Minnesota and western Illinois south to southern California (rarely), Baja California (formerly), Sonora, Durango, Chihuahua, central and southern Texas, and western Missouri.

Winters primarily on the pampas of southern South America (south to Uruguay and Argentina), irregularly north to Costa Rica and Panama, casually north to the southwestern United States and southeastern Florida.

In migration occurs regularly in most of Middle America, and rarely east along the Gulf coast to Florida; occasionally a common fall migrant through the Florida Keys.

Casual in northeastern North America from southern Ontario, southern Quebec, New York and Massachusetts south to Pennsylvania and Virginia; a report from Jamaica is highly questionable.

Buteo albicaudatus Vieillot. WHITE-TAILED HAWK. [341.]

Buteo albicaudatus Vieillot, 1816, Nouv. Dict. Hist. Nat., nouv. éd., 4, p. 477. (l'Amérique meridionale = Rio de Janeiro, Brazil.)

Habitat.—Open country, primarily savanna, prairie and arid habitats of mesquite, cacti and bushes, very rarely in open forest (Tropical and Subtropical zones).

Distribution.—*Resident* from southern Arizona (formerly, one breeding record in 1897), Sonora, Durango, Zacatecas and central and southeastern Texas south through Middle America (including Isla Taboga off Panama), and in South America from Colombia, Venezuela (also the Netherlands Antilles, Margarita Island and Trinidad) and the Guianas south, east of the Andes, to extreme eastern Peru, Bolivia and central Argentina.

Casual in southwestern Louisiana, also a sight report for St. Vincent, in the Lesser Antilles.

Notes.—The relationship between *B. albicaudatus* and the South American *B. polyosoma* (Quoy and Gaimard, 1824) and *B. poecilochrous* Gurney, 1879, needs clarification.

Buteo albonotatus Kaup. ZONE-TAILED HAWK. [340.]

Buteo albonotatus "G. R. Gray" Kaup, 1847, Isis von Oken, col. 329. (No locality given = Mexico.)

Habitat.—Arid semi-open country, especially open deciduous or pine-oak woodland, often nesting in tall trees along streams (Tropical and Subtropical zones).

Distribution.—*Resident* (although partly migratory in northern part of breeding range) from northern Baja California, central Arizona, southern New Mexico and western Texas south locally through Middle America (including the Pearl Islands off Panama, but not recorded Belize), and in South America from Colombia, Venezuela (also Trinidad) and the Guianas south, east of the Andes, to eastern Bolivia, Paraguay and southeastern Brazil; also recorded in western Peru (Lima area).

Casual north to southern California (where breeding attempted in Santa Rosa Mountains in 1979 and 1980) and southern Nevada (sight record).

Buteo solitarius Peale. HAWAIIAN HAWK. [344.1.]

> *Buteo solitarius* Peale, 1848, U.S. Explor. Exped., 8, p. 62. (Island of Hawaii.)

Habitat.—Open forest and forest edge from sea level to highlands.
Distribution.—*Resident* in small numbers on Hawaii, in the Hawaiian Islands. Accidental on Oahu (Pearl Harbor), also sight reports for Kauai and Maui.

Buteo jamaicensis (Gmelin). RED-TAILED HAWK. [337.]

> *Falco jamaicensis* Gmelin, 1788, Syst. Nat., 1 (1), p. 266. Based on the "Cream-colored Buzzard" Latham, Gen. Synop. Birds, 1 (1), p. 49. (in Jamaica.)

Habitat.—A wide variety of open woodland and open country with scattered trees, rarely in denser forest (Subtropical and Temperate zones).

Distribution.—*Breeds* from western and central Alaska, central Yukon, western Mackenzie, northern Saskatchewan, northern Manitoba, central Ontario, southern Quebec, New Brunswick, Prince Edward Island and Nova Scotia south to southeastern Alaska, Baja California, Sonora, Chihuahua, Nuevo León, southern Texas, the Gulf coast and Florida, and in the highlands of Middle America to Costa Rica and western Panama (east to Canal Zone); in the Tres Marias and Socorro islands off western Mexico; and in the northern Bahamas (Grand Bahamas, Abaco, Andros), Greater Antilles and northern Lesser Antilles (Saba south to Nevis).

Winters from southern Canada south throughout the remainder of the breeding range, occurring also in the lowlands of Middle America.

Accidental in Bermuda and England.

Notes.—The dark and variable populations breeding in western, central and south-coastal Alaska, and in western Canada have sometimes been regarded as a distinct species, *B. harlani* (Audubon, 1831) [HARLAN'S HAWK, 338]. Relationships between *B. jamaicensis,* the South American *B. ventralis* Gould, 1837, and the Old World *B. buteo* (Linnaeus, 1758) complex are uncertain.

Buteo regalis (Gray). FERRUGINOUS HAWK. [348.]

> *Archibuteo regalis* G. R. Gray, 1844, Genera Birds, 1, pl. vi. (No locality given = Real del Monte, Hidalgo.)

Habitat.—Open country, primarily prairies, plains and badlands, breeding in trees near streams or on steep slopes, sometimes on mounds in open desert.

Distribution.—*Breeds* from eastern Washington, southern Alberta, southern Saskatchewan and (formerly) southwestern Manitoba south to eastern Oregon, Nevada, northern and southeastern Arizona, northern and (formerly) southwestern New Mexico, north-central Texas, western Oklahoma and western Kansas. Recorded in summer (and probably breeding) in northeastern California.

Winters primarily from the central and southern parts of the breeding range (casually north to Alberta and Saskatchewan, and east to western Missouri) south to Baja California, Chihuahua, Durango, Guanajuato, Hidalgo and Tamaulipas.

In migration occurs east to western Minnesota.

Casual east to Wisconsin, Michigan, Illinois, New Jersey, Arkansas, Louisiana, Mississippi and Alabama.

Notes.—Also known as FERRUGINOUS ROUGHLEG.

Buteo lagopus (Pontoppidan). ROUGH-LEGGED HAWK. [347.]

> *Falco lagopus* Pontoppidan, 1763, Dan. Atlas, 1, p. 616. (No locality given = Denmark.)

Habitat.—Open coniferous forest, tundra and generally barren country, breeding on cliffs or in trees, wintering also in grasslands and open cultivated areas.

Distribution.—*Breeds* in North America from western and northern Alaska (also Kodiak Island, and Umnak in the eastern Aleutians), northern Yukon, the Arctic islands (north to Prince Patrick, Victoria, Bylot and southwestern Baffin islands) and northern Labrador south to northern and southeastern Mackenzie, northern Manitoba, northern Ontario, northern Quebec and Newfoundland; and in Eurasia in the Arctic from Scandinavia east to northern Siberia, Kamchatka and the Sea of Okhotsk.

Winters in North America from south-central Alaska (casually), southern Canada (southern British Columbia east to southern Quebec and Newfoundland) south to southern California, southern Arizona, southern New Mexico, southern Texas, Missouri, Tennessee and Virginia, casually to eastern Texas and the Gulf coast (sight records from northeastern Sonora, northern Chihuahua and Florida); and in Eurasia from the British Isles, southern Scandinavia and central Russia south to southern Europe, southern Russia, Manchuria, Ussuriland and Japan.

Casual or accidental in the central and western Aleutians, Bermuda, Iceland, the Faroe Islands, southern Europe and northern Africa.

Genus **MORPHNUS** Dumont

> *Morphnus* Dumont, 1816, Dict. Sci. Nat., 1, suppl., p. 88. Type, by subsequent designation (Chubb, 1816), *Falco guianensis* Daudin.

Morphnus guianensis (Daudin). CRESTED EAGLE.

> *Falco guianensis* Daudin, 1800, Traité Ornithol., 2, p. 78. Based on "Petit Aigle de la Guiane" Mauduyt, Encycl. Méth., Hist. Nat. Ois., 1, p. 475. (Guiane = Cayenne.)

Habitat.—Humid lowland and foothill forest (Tropical and lower Subtropical zones).

Distribution.—*Resident* locally in northern Guatemala (Petén), northern Honduras (San Pedro Sula, La Ceiba), Costa Rica (Cuabre and Cañas Gordas region) and Panama (both slopes, but doubtfully on Isla Coiba), and in South America from Colombia, Venezuela and the Guianas south, primarily east of the Andes, to eastern Peru, eastern Bolivia, eastern Paraguay, northeastern Argentina (possibly) and southeastern Brazil. Although listed for Nicaragua, there are no specific records.

Genus HARPIA Vieillot

Harpia Vieillot, 1816, Analyse, p. 24. Type, by monotypy, "Aigle destructeur" Buffon = *Vultur harpyja* Linnaeus.

Harpia harpyja (Linnaeus). HARPY EAGLE.

Vultur Harpyja Linnaeus, 1758, Syst. Nat., ed. 10, 1, p. 86. Based on "Yzquauhtli" Hernandez, Nova Plant Anim. Min. Mex. Hist., p. 34. (in Mexico.)

Habitat.—Dense lowland forest (Tropical Zone).
Distribution.—*Resident* from southern Mexico (Oaxaca, Veracruz, Tabasco, Campeche and Chiapas) south through Middle America (excluding El Salvador, primarily occurring on the Caribbean slope north of Costa Rica), and in South America, from Colombia, Venezuela and the Guianas south, primarily east of the Andes, to eastern Peru, eastern Bolivia, northern Argentina and southeastern Brazil.

Genus AQUILA Brisson

Aquila Brisson, 1760, Ornithologie, 1, p. 28; 6, p. 419. Type, by tautonymy, *Aquila* Brisson = *Falco chrysaetos* Linnaeus.

Aquila chrysaetos (Linnaeus). GOLDEN EAGLE. [349.]

Falco Chrysaëtos Linnaeus, 1758, Syst. Nat., ed. 10, 1, p. 88. (in Europa = Sweden.)

Habitat.—Generally open country, in prairies, tundra, open coniferous forest and barren areas, especially in hilly or mountainous regions, nesting on cliff ledges and in trees.
Distribution.—*Breeds* in North America from northern and western Alaska east across Yukon, western and southern Mackenzie, northwestern Manitoba, northern Ontario and northern Quebec to Labrador, and south to southern Alaska (west to Unalaska in the eastern Aleutians), northern Baja California, the highlands of northern Mexico (south to Durango, Guanajuato and Nuevo León), western and central Texas (at least formerly), western Oklahoma and western Kansas, and in eastern North America to New York and New England, probably also in the Appalachian Mountains to eastern Tennessee and western North Carolina; and in Eurasia from the British Isles, Scandinavia, northern Russia and northern Siberia south to northern Africa, Arabia, Iran, the Himalayas, central China, Korea and Japan.

Winters in North America from south-central Alaska (casually, the Alaska Range) and the southern portions of the Canadian provinces south throughout the breeding range, casually to Sonora, Sinaloa, Hidalgo and the Gulf coast from Texas east to central Florida (sight reports to Florida Keys); and in Eurasia generally in the breeding range, casually south to eastern China.

Accidental in the Hawaiian Islands (Kauai), possibly an escaped or released individual.

Genus SPIZASTUR Gray

Spizastur G. R. Gray, 1841, List Genera Birds, ed. 2, p. 3. Type, by original designation, *S. atricapillus* (Cuv.) = *Buteo melanoleucus* Vieillot.

Spizastur melanoleucus (Vieillot). BLACK-AND-WHITE HAWK-EAGLE.

Buteo melanoleucus Vieillot, 1816, Nouv. Dict. Hist. Nat., nouv. éd., 4, p. 482. (la Guyane = Guyana.)

Habitat.—Dense lowland and foothill forest (Tropical and Subtropical zones).
Distribution.—*Resident* from southern Mexico (Oaxaca, Veracruz, Chiapas and the state of Yucatán) south through Middle America (except El Salvador), and in South America from Colombia, Venezuela and the Guianas south, west of the Andes to western Ecuador and east of the Andes to eastern Peru, Bolivia, northern Argentina and southeastern Brazil.

Genus SPIZAETUS Vieillot

Spizaëtus Vieillot, 1816, Analyse, p. 24. Type, by subsequent designation (G. R. Gray, 1840), "L'Autout huppé" Levaillant = *Falco ornatus* Daudin.

Spizaetus tyrannus (Wied). BLACK HAWK-EAGLE.

Falco tyrannus Wied, 1820, Reise Bras., 1, p. 360. (Ilha do Chave, below Quartel dos Arcos, Rio Belmonte, Bahia, Brazil.)

Habitat.—Lowland forest, primarily open woodland, forest edge or partially cleared woods (Tropical and lower Subtropical zones).
Distribution.—*Resident* from southern San Luis Potosí, Veracruz and Oaxaca south through Middle America (not recorded from the state of Yucatán or El Salvador), and in South America from Colombia, Venezuela (also Trinidad) and the Guianas south, west of the Andes to western Ecuador and east of the Andes to eastern Peru, eastern Bolivia, eastern Paraguay, northeastern Argentina and southeastern Brazil.

Spizaetus ornatus (Daudin). ORNATE HAWK-EAGLE.

Falco ornatus Daudin, 1800, Traité Ornithol., 2, p. 77. Based on "L'Aigle Moyen de la Guiane" Mauduyt, Encycl. Méth., Hist. Nat. Ois., 1, p. 475, and "L'Autour Huppé" Levaillant, Hist. Nat. Ois. Afr., 1, p. 76, pl. 2. (Cayenne.)

Habitat.—Heavy moist forest, occasionally forest edge (Tropical and Subtropical zones).
Distribution.—*Resident* from Tamaulipas, Veracruz and Oaxaca south through Middle America (including Isla Coiba off Panama), and in South America from Colombia, Venezuela (also Tobago and Trinidad) and the Guianas south, west of the Andes to northwestern Peru and east of the Andes to eastern Peru, eastern Bolivia, northern Argentina and southeastern Brazil.

Suborder FALCONES: Caracaras and Falcons

Family FALCONIDAE: Caracaras and Falcons

Tribe POLYBORINI: Caracaras

Genus DAPTRIUS Vieillot

Daptrius Vieillot, 1816, Analyse, p. 22. Type, by monotypy, *Daptrius ater* Vieillot.

Daptrius americanus (Boddaert). RED-THROATED CARACARA.

Falco americanus Boddaert, 1783, Table Planches Enlum., p. 25. Based on "Le Petit Aigle d'Amerique" Daubenton, Planches Enlum., pl. 417. (Cayenne.)

Habitat.—Primarily humid lowland forest, especially along forest edge and in clearings, less commonly deciduous forest (Tropical and lower Subtropical zones).

Distribution.—*Resident,* at least formerly, from southern Mexico (Chiapas) south through Middle America (not reported Belize or El Salvador), and in South America from Colombia, Venezuela and the Guianas south, west of the Andes to western Ecuador and east of the Andes to eastern Peru, east-central Bolivia and central Brazil; in recent years has disappeared from most of its Middle American range.

Genus POLYBORUS Vieillot

Polyborus Vieillot, 1816, Analyse, p. 22. Type, by monotypy, "Caracara" Buffon = *Falco plancus* Miller.

Caracara Merrem, 1826, *in* Ersch and Gruber, Allg. Encycl. Wiss. Künste, 15, p. 159. Type, by subsequent designation (Hellmary and Conover, 1949), *Falco plancus* Miller.

Notes.—For use of *Polyborus* instead of *Caracara,* see Amadon, 1954, Auk, 71, pp. 203–204. See also comments under *Milvago.*

Polyborus plancus (Miller). CRESTED CARACARA. [362.]

Falco plancus J. F. Miller, 1777, Var. Subj. Nat. Hist., pt. 3, pl. 17. (Tierra del Fuego.)

Habitat.—Open country, including pastureland, cultivated areas and semi-desert, both arid and moist habitats but more commonly in the former (Tropical and Subtropical zones, also Temperate Zone in South America).

Distribution.—*Resident* [*plancus* group] in central and southern Florida (north to Brevard County, formerly to Enterprise and St. Augustine), Cuba and the Isle of Pines, and from northern Baja California, southern Arizona, Sonora, Sinaloa, Zacatecas, Nuevo León, central and southern Texas, and (rarely) southwestern Louisiana south locally through Middle America (including the Tres Marias Islands off Nayarit, but not reported Belize), and throughout most of South America (also islands off Venezuela from Aruba east to Trinidad) south to Tierra del Fuego and the Falkland Islands; and [*lutosus* group] formerly on Guadalupe Island, off Baja California (now extinct).

Casual [*plancus* group] north to central New Mexico and Oklahoma, and to islands off Panama (Taboga and Pearl) and Jamaica. Individuals reported from Oregon, Ontario, Pennsylvania, New Jersey and North Carolina are almost certainly escapes from captivity.

Notes.—The Guadalupe Island form is recognized by many authors as a distinct species, *P. lutosus* Ridgway, 1876 [GUADALUPE CARACARA]. The northern forms south to central South America are also considered by some as *P. cheriway* (Jacquin, 1784) [CRESTED CARACARA], distinct from *P. plancus* [SOUTHERN CARACARA], although they intergrade near the mouth of the Amazon.

Genus **MILVAGO** Spix

Milvago Spix, 1824, Avium Spec. Nov. Bras., 1, p. 12. Type, by monotypy, *Milvago ochrocephalus* Spix = *Polyborus chimachima* Vieillot.

Notes.—Sometimes merged in *Polyborus.*

Milvago chimachima (Vieillot). YELLOW-HEADED CARACARA.

Polyborus chimachima Vieillot, 1816, Nouv. Dict. Hist. Nat., nouv. éd., 5, p. 259. Based on "Chimachima" Azara, Apunt. Hist. Nat. Páx. Parag., 1, p. 50 (no. 6). (Paraguay.)

Habitat.—Open country, savanna, pasturelands and cultivated areas, especially frequent near cattle (Tropical and lower Subtropical zones).

Distribution.—*Resident* in southwestern Costa Rica (north to San José province) and Panama (including the Pearl Islands), and in South America from Colombia, Venezuela (also Trinidad) and the Guianas south, mostly east of the Andes, to eastern Peru, southern Bolivia, northern Argentina and Uruguay.

Notes.—*M. chimachima* and the South American *M. chimango* (Vieillot, 1816) appear to constitute a superspecies.

Tribe HERPETOTHERINI: Laughing Falcons

Genus **HERPETOTHERES** Vieillot

Herpetotheres Vieillot, 1817, Nouv. Dict. Hist. Nat., nouv. éd., 18, p. 317. Type, by subsequent designation (G. R. Gray, 1840), *Falco cachinnans* Linnaeus.

Herpetotheres cachinnans (Linnaeus). LAUGHING FALCON.

Falco cachinnans (Rolander MS) Linnaeus, 1758, Syst. Nat., ed. 10, 1, p. 90. (in America meridionali = Surinam.)

Habitat.—Forest, most frequently in humid situations, primarily in forest edge and open woodland, nesting in tree cavities (Tropical and Subtropical zones).

Distribution.—*Resident* from Sonora and Tamaulipas south along both slopes of Middle America, and in South America from Colombia, Venezuela and the Guianas south, west of the Andes to northwestern Peru and east of Andes to eastern Peru, eastern Bolivia, northern Argentina and southern Brazil.

Tribe MICRASTURINI: Forest-Falcons

Genus **MICRASTUR** Gray

Brachypterus (not Kugelmann, 1794, nor Latreille, 1819) Lesson, 1836, Compl. Oeuvres Buffon, 7, p. 113. Type, by monotypy, *Falco brachypterus* Temminck = *Sparvius semitorquatus* Vieillot.
Micrastur G. R. Gray, 1841, List Genera Birds, ed. 2, p. 6. New name for *Brachypterus* Lesson, preoccupied.

Micrastur ruficollis (Vieillot). BARRED FOREST-FALCON.

Sparvius ruficollis Vieillot, 1817, Nouv. Dict. Hist. Nat., nouv. éd., 10, p. 322. (l'Amérique méridionale = Rio de Janeiro, Brazil.)

Habitat.—Moist forest (Tropical and Subtropical zones).
Distribution.—*Resident* from Guerrero, Puebla and Veracruz south through Middle America (except the state of Yucatán), and in South America west of the Andes from Colombia south to western Ecuador, and east of the Andes in northern Venezuela, and from eastern Peru and central and eastern Brazil (south of the Amazon) south to northern Argentina and southern Brazil.
Notes.—The South American *M. gilvicollis* (Vieillot, 1817) is sometimes considered conspecific with *M. ruficollis,* but see Schwartz, 1972, Condor, 74, pp. 399–415.

Micrastur mirandollei (Schlegel). SLATY-BACKED FOREST-FALCON

Astur mirandollei Schlegel, 1862, Mus. Hist. Nat. Pays-Bas, livr. 1, Astures, p. 27. (Surinam.)

Habitat.—Heavy moist lowland forest (Tropical Zone).
Distribution.—*Resident,* primarily in the Caribbean lowlands, in Costa Rica and Panama; and in South America from central Colombia, southern Venezuela and the Guianas south, east of the Andes, to eastern Peru, northern Bolivia and Amazonian and eastern Brazil.

Micrastur semitorquatus (Vieillot). COLLARED FOREST-FALCON.

Sparvius semi-torquatus Vieillot, 1817, Nouv. Dict. Hist. Nat., nouv. éd., 10, p. 322. Based on "Esparvero Faxado" Azara, Apunt. Hist. Nat. Páx. Parag., 1, p. 126 (no. 29). (Paraguay.)

Habitat.—Heavy forest, especially in thickets and dense areas, and mangroves (Tropical and Subtropical zones).
Distribution.—*Resident* from Sinaloa, San Luis Potosí and Tamaulipas south through Middle America, and in South America from Colombia, Venezuela and the Guianas south, west of the Andes to northwestern Peru and east of the Andes to eastern Peru, southern Bolivia, northern Argentina and southern Brazil.

Tribe FALCONINI: True Falcons

Genus **FALCO** Linnaeus

Falco Linnaeus, 1758, Syst. Nat., ed. 10, 1, p. 88. Type, by subsequent designation (G. R. Gray, 1840), "*F. peregrinus* L." = *Falco peregrinus* Tunstall.

Tinnunculus Vieillot, 1808, Hist. Nat. Ois. Am. Sept., 1 (1807), p. 39. Type, by subsequent designation (Walden, 1872), *Falco columbarius* Linnaeus.

Hierofalco Cuvier, 1817, Règne Anim., 1 (1816), p. 312. Type, by monotypy, *Falco subbuteo* Gmelin = *Falco rusticolus* Linnaeus.

Cerchneis Boie, 1826, Isis von Oken, col. 970. Type, by monotypy, *Falco rupicolus* Daudin = *Falco tinnunculus* Linnaeus.

Hypotriorchis Boie, 1826, Isis von Oken, col. 970. Type, by original designation, *Falco subbuteo* Linnaeus.

Aësalon Kaup, 1829, Skizz. Entw.-Ges. Eur. Thierw., pp. 40, 190. Type, by tautonymy, *Falco aesalon* Tunstall = *Falco columbarius* Linnaeus.

Rhynchodon Nitzsch, 1829, Observ. Avium Art. Carot. Comm., p. 20. Type, by subsequent designation (A.O.U. Comm., 1886), *Falco peregrinus* Tunstall.

Rhynchofalco Ridgway, 1873, Proc. Boston Soc. Nat. Hist., 16, p. 46. Type, by original designation, *Falco femoralis* Temminck.

Planofalco Oberholser, 1974, Bird Life Texas, 2, p. 976. Type, by original designation, *Falco mexicanus* Schlegel.

Falco tinnunculus Linnaeus. EURASIAN KESTREL. [359.1.]

Falco Tinnunculus Linnaeus, 1758, Syst. Nat., ed. 10, 1, p. 90. (in Europæ turribus, etc. = Sweden.)

Habitat & Distribution.—*Breeds* in open country and partly open situations from the British Isles and northern Eurasia south to southern Africa, India, eastern China and Japan, and *winters* south to the East Indies and Philippines.

Casual in Alaska (Attu and Shemya, in the Aleutians). Accidental in Massachusetts (Nantasket Beach), New Jersey (Cape May Point), the Lesser Antilles (Martinique), Greenland, Iceland and the Faroe Islands.

Notes.—Also known as EUROPEAN KESTREL and, in Old World literature, as the KESTREL. See comments under *F. sparverius*.

Falco sparverius Linnaeus. AMERICAN KESTREL. [360.]

Falco sparverius Linnaeus, 1758, Syst. Nat., ed. 10, 1, p. 90. Based on "The Little Hawk" Catesby, Nat. Hist. Carolina, 1, p. 5, pl. 5. (in America = South Carolina.)

Habitat.—Open and partly open country with scattered trees, cultivated lands and urban areas, nesting in holes in trees, on cliffs and in crevices of buildings (Tropical or Temperate zones).

Distribution.—*Breeds* from western and central Alaska, southern Yukon, western (and probably northwestern) Mackenzie, northern Alberta, northern Saskatchewan, northern Manitoba, northern Ontario, southern Quebec, New Brunswick,

Prince Edward Island, Nova Scotia and southern Newfoundland south to southern Baja California (including Guadalupe Island), Sinaloa, the highlands of Middle America (to central Honduras), the Gulf coast and (at least formerly) southern Florida; in the Bahamas (north to Long Island, Rum Cay and San Salvador) and the Antilles (rare south of Guadeloupe); the lowland pine savannas of eastern Honduras and northeastern Nicaragua; and through most of South America (also the Netherlands Antilles and Trinidad, but absent from heavily forested regions such as the Amazon basin) south to Tierra del Fuego (including the Juan Fernandez Islands off Chile).

Winters from south-central Alaska (casually), southern British Columbia, the northern United States, southern Ontario, southwestern Quebec and Nova Scotia south throughout the breeding range, and including the northern Bahamas and virtually all of Middle America, the northern populations migrating as far south as Panama.

Casual or accidental in northern and southwestern Alaska, District of Franklin (Jenny Lind Island), Barbados, the Falkland Islands, British Isles, Denmark, the Azores and Malta.

Notes.—Formerly known in American literature as SPARROW HAWK. Various Old World taxa, including *F. tinnunculus,* have been considered to form a superspecies with *F. sparverius,* but relationships are uncertain.

Falco columbarius Linnaeus. MERLIN. [357.]

> *Falco columbarius* Linnaeus, 1758, Syst. Nat., ed. 10, 1, p. 90., Based on "The Pigeon-Hawk" Catesby, Nat. Hist. Carolina, 1, p. 3, pl. 3. (in America = South Carolina.)

Habitat.—Open country, nesting in and adjacent to grasslands (using mostly old crow and magpie nests) in scattered trees and bushes, on the ground under shrubs, on cliffs, and in cities, in migration and winter also in open woodland, moorlands, marshes and deserts, and along seacoasts.

Distribution.—*Breeds* in North America from northwestern Alaska, northern Yukon, northwestern and central Mackenzie, southeastern Keewatin, northern Manitoba, northern Ontario, northern Quebec, Labrador and Newfoundland south to southern Alaska, southwestern British Columbia, central Washington, eastern Oregon, Idaho, northern Montana, northern North Γ ɔota, northern Minnesota, Iowa (formerly), northern Wisconsin, northern Michigan, southern Ontario, northern Ohio, southern Quebec, New Brunswick and Nova Scotia; and in Eurasia from Iceland, the Faroe Islands, British Isles and Scandinavia east across Russia and Siberia to the Sea of Okhotsk, and south to Lake Baikal, Mongolia and Sakhalin.

Winters in North America west of the Rockies from south-central Alaska, southern (primarily coastal) British Columbia, Wyoming and Colorado southward, locally across southern Canada (mostly in cities) in Alberta, Saskatchewan, Manitoba, southern Ontario, southwestern Quebec, New Brunswick, Nova Scotia and Newfoundland, and in the eastern United States from southern Texas, the Gulf coast and South Carolina (casually elsewhere north to the Canadian border) south through Middle America and the West Indies to northwestern Peru, western Ecuador, northern Colombia, northern Venezuela and Trinidad; and in Eurasia from Iceland, the British Isles, southern Scandinavia, southern Russia and southern

Japan south to the Mediterranean region, northern Africa, Asia Minor, northern India, eastern China and Korea.
Casual in Spitsbergen.
Notes.—Formerly known as PIGEON HAWK.

Falco femoralis Temminck. APLOMADO FALCON. [359.]

Falco femoralis Temminck, 1822, Planches Color., livr. 21, pl. 121 and text. (Brazil.)

Habitat.—Open country, especially savanna and open woodland, and sometimes in very barren situations (Tropical Zone, in South America to Temperate Zone).

Distribution.—*Resident* from Sinaloa, Chihuahua (possibly) and Tamaulipas (formerly north to southeastern Arizona, southern New Mexico, and west-central and southern Texas, the last documented breeding in the United States in 1952 in New Mexico, with an unverified report from southeastern Arizona in the late 1960's) south locally to Chiapas, the Yucatan Peninsula and Belize; in the pine savanna of eastern Honduras and northeastern Nicaragua; and from western Panama south generally throughout South America to Tierra del Fuego and the Falkland Islands.

Casual in Guatemala (San Agustín), western Nicaragua, Costa Rica, and, in recent years, in the former breeding range in the southwestern United States.

[**Falco subbuteo** Linnaeus. NORTHERN HOBBY.] See Appendix B.

Falco rufigularis Daudin. BAT FALCON.

Falco rufigularis Daudin, 1800, Traité Ornithol., 2, p. 131. Based on the "Orange-breasted Hobby" Latham, Gen. Synop. Birds, suppl., 1, p. 28. (in Cayana = Cayenne.)

Habitat.—Open woodland, forest edge and savanna, primarily in humid regions (Tropical and Subtropical zones).

Distribution.—*Resident* from southern Sonora and Tamaulipas south along both slopes through Middle America (including Coiba, Taboga and the Pearl islands off Panama), and in South America from Colombia, Venezuela (also Tobago and Trinidad) and the Guianas south, west of the Andes to western Ecuador and east of the Andes to eastern Peru, eastern Bolivia, northern Argentina and southern Brazil.

Notes.—For use of *F. rufigularis* instead of *F. albigularis* Daudin, 1800, see Eisenmann, 1966, Condor, 68, pp. 208–209.

Falco deiroleucus Temminck. ORANGE-BREASTED FALCON.

Falco deiroleucus Temminck, 1825, Planches Color., livr. 59, pl. 348. (Dans l'île Saint Francois, partie méridionale du Brésil = São Francisco Island, Santa Catarina, Brazil.)

Habitat.—Primarily open forest and forest edge, usually in humid lowlands (Tropical and Subtropical zones).

Distribution.—*Resident* locally in southern Mexico (recorded Veracruz and Campeche), northeastern Guatemala (primarily Petén), Honduras (El Hatillo), Nicaragua (Matagalpa and the northeastern lowlands), Costa Rica and Panama (Chiriquí, Coclé and Darién), and in South America from Colombia, Venezuela (also Trinidad) and the Guianas south, mostly east of the Andes, to eastern Peru, Bolivia, northern Argentina and southern Brazil.

Falco peregrinus Tunstall. PEREGRINE FALCON. [356.]

Falco Peregrinus Tunstall, 1771, Ornithol. Br., p. 1. (No locality given = Northamptonshire, England.)

Habitat.—A variety of open situations from tundra, moorlands, steppe and seacoasts, especially where there are suitable nesting cliffs, to high mountains, more open forested regions, and even human population centers where large buildings provide nesting sites.

Distribution.—*Breeds* in North America from northern Alaska, northern Mackenzie, Banks, Victoria, southern Melville, Somerset and northern Baffin islands, and Labrador south to southern Baja California, the coast of Sonora, southern Arizona, New Mexico, western and central Texas, and Colorado, occasionally in the Sierra Madre Occidental and Sierra Madre Oriental of northern Mexico, and, at least formerly, Kansas, Arkansas, northeastern Louisiana, Tennessee, northern Alabama and northwestern Georgia; in South America in central and southern Argentina, and central and southern Chile; and in much of the Old World from Greenland, the British Isles, Scandinavia, northern Russia, northern Siberia and the Chukotski Peninsula south, at least locally, through Eurasia and Africa to South Africa, Arabia, India, Ceylon, the East Indies, Australia (including Tasmania), New Hebrides, and the Fiji and Loyalty islands. Absent as a breeding bird through much of continental North America, especially in the eastern part south of the Canadian Arctic, since the 1950's; recently re-established as a breeding bird through introductions in parts of the northeastern United States.

Winters in the Americas from southern Alaska (the Aleutians and Prince William Sound), the Queen Charlotte Islands, coastal British Columbia, the central and southern United States (rarely farther north) and New Brunswick south through Middle America, the West Indies and South America to Tierra del Fuego; and in the Old World generally through the breeding range, with northernmost populations usually migrating to tropical regions.

Casual in the Hawaiian Islands, Iceland, the Faroe Islands and Canary Islands.

Notes.—Also known as the PEREGRINE. The North African and Asiatic form is sometimes regarded as a distinct species, *F. pelegrinoides* Temminck, 1829. The South American *F. kreyenborgi* Kleinschmidt, 1929, appears to be a color morph of *F. peregrinus.*

Falco rusticolus Linnaeus. GYRFALCON. [354.]

Falco rusticolus Linnaeus, 1758, Syst. Nat., ed. 10, 1, p. 88. (in Svecia = Sweden.)

Habitat.—Primarily open country in the Arctic, including tundra, open coniferous forest, mountainous regions and rocky seacoasts, nesting on cliffs and, occasionally, in trees.

Distribution.—*Breeds* in North America from northern Alaska, northern Yukon, and Banks, Prince Patrick and Ellesmere islands south to central Alaska (including the Aleutians west to Umnak), northwestern British Columbia, southern Yukon, northern Mackenzie, southern Keewatin, Southampton Island, northern Quebec and northern Labrador; and in the Palearctic from Greenland, Iceland and northern Scandinavia east across northern Russia and northern Siberia to the Chukotski Peninsula, and south to Anadyrland, Kamchatka and Bering Island.

Winters in North America from the breeding range south irregularly to the Pribilof and Aleutian islands, southern Alaska, southern Canada and the extreme northern United States; and in Eurasia from the breeding range south to the British Isles, western (casually central) Europe, southern Russia, Lake Baikal, Manchuria, Sakhalin, the Kurile Islands and Japan.

Casual in winter south as far as northern California, Oregon, Idaho, Wyoming, Oklahoma, Kansas, Illinois, Indiana, northern Ohio, Pennsylvania and Delaware.

Notes.—Known in Old World literature as GYR FALCON. *F. rusticolus* and the Asiatic *F. altaicus* (Menzbier, 1891) appear to constitute a superspecies.

Falco mexicanus Schlegel. PRAIRIE FALCON. [355.]

Falco mexicanus Schlegel, 1851, Abh. Geb. Zool. Bergl. Anat., 3, p. 15. (Mexico = Monterrey, Nuevo León.)

Habitat.—Primarily open situations, especially in mountainous areas, steppe, plains or prairies, nesting on cliffs.

Distribution.—*Breeds* from southeastern British Columbia, southern Alberta, southern Saskatchewan and northern North Dakota south to Baja California, southern Arizona, southern New Mexico, southeastern Coahuila, western and northern Texas, and (formerly) northwestern Missouri.

Winters from the breeding range in southern Canada south to Baja California, Sonora, Durango, Zacatecas, Aguascalientes, Nuevo León and Tamaulipas.

Casual north and east to Manitoba, Minnesota, Illinois, Indiana and Tennessee, and south to Hidalgo. Reports of accidentals in Alabama, Georgia and South Carolina may pertain to escaped individuals.

Order **GALLIFORMES**: Gallinaceous Birds

Superfamily CRACOIDEA: Megapodes, Curassows and Guans

Family **CRACIDAE**: Curassows and Guans

Genus **ORTALIS** Merrem

Ortalida [accusative case] = *Ortalis* [nominative] Merrem, 1786, Avium Rar. Icones Descr., 2, p. 40. Type, by original designation, *Phasianus motmot* Linnaeus.

Ortalis ruficauda Jardine. RUFOUS-VENTED CHACHALACA.

Ortalida ruficauda Jardine, 1847, Ann. Mag. Nat. Hist., ser. 1, 20, p. 374. (Tobago.)

Habitat.—Scrub, second growth and dense forest (Tropical Zone).

Distribution.—*Resident* in northeastern Colombia, northern Venezuela (south to the Arauca and Orinoco rivers), and on Margarita Island and Tobago.

Introduced in the Lesser Antilles in the Grenadines (on Union and Bequia), where apparently established by the late 17th Century, but there have been no recent reports from Bequia. Early writings also alluded to its presence on St. Vincent in the late 17th Century.

Notes.—Also known as RUFOUS-TAILED CHACHALACA. The populations in Colombia and northwestern Venezuela are sometimes recognized as a distinct species, *O. ruficrissa* Sclater and Salvin, 1870; with this treatment, *O. ruficauda* is called RUFOUS-TIPPED CHACHALACA.

Ortalis vetula (Wagler). PLAIN CHACHALACA. [311.]

> *Penelope vetula* Wagler, 1830, Isis von Oken, col. 1112. (Mexico = Tampico, Tamaulipas.)

Habitat.—Thickets, dense second growth, scrub and forest, primarily in semi-arid regions (Tropical Zone).

Distribution.—*Resident* [*vetula* group] on the Gulf-Caribbean slope from southern Texas (lower Rio Grande Valley) and Nuevo León south through the lowlands of eastern Mexico (including the Yucatan Peninsula and Isla Cancun), Belize and eastern Guatemala to northern Honduras (including Isla Utila in the Bay Islands), and in the interior valleys of Chiapas, central Honduras and north-central Nicaragua; and [*leucogastra* group] in the Pacific lowlands from western Chiapas (vicinity of Pijijiapan) south to northwestern Costa Rica (Guanacaste). Reports from Cozumel, Mujeres and Holbox islands are regarded as doubtful.

Introduced and established [*vetula* group] on islands off the coast of Georgia (Sapelo, Blackbeard and Little St. Simons).

Notes.—The distinct Pacific lowland populations have often been regarded as a separate species, *O. leucogastra* (Gould, 1843) [WHITE-BELLIED CHACHALACA].

Ortalis cinereiceps Gray. GRAY-HEADED CHACHALACA.

> *Ortalida cinereiceps* G. R. Gray, 1867, List Birds Br. Mus., pt. 5, p. 12. (northwest coast of America = Pearl Islands, Panama.)

Habitat.—Thickets, second growth and forest, especially near streams (Tropical Zone).

Distribution.—*Resident* in eastern Honduras (Olancho, Mosquitia), eastern and central Nicaragua, Costa Rica (except the dry northwest), Panama (including Isla del Rey in the Pearl Islands) and northwestern Colombia.

Notes.—The South American *O. garrula* (Humboldt, 1805) and *O. cinereiceps* constitute a superspecies; they are considered by some as conspecific. With the broader species concept, CHESTNUT-WINGED CHACHALACA may be used.

Ortalis poliocephala (Wagler). WAGLER'S CHACHALACA.

> *Penelope poliocephala* Wagler, 1830, Isis von Oken, col. 1112. (Mexico.)

Habitat.—Dense scrub, second growth and forest in semi-arid regions, generally found near water (Tropical Zone).

Distribution.—*Resident* from southern Sonora, Sinaloa and western Durango south to Morelos, western Puebla, Oaxaca and extreme western Chiapas (vicinity of Tonalá).

Notes.—Also known as WEST MEXICAN CHACHALACA. Includes *O. wagleri* G.

R. Gray, 1867 [RUFOUS-BELLIED CHACHALACA], formerly recognized as a distinct species but now known to intergrade with *poliocephala* (see Vaurie, 1965, Am. Mus. Novit., no. 2222, pp. 17–19).

Genus CHAMAEPETES Wagler

Chamaepetes Wagler, 1832, Isis von Oken, col. 1227. Type, by monotypy, *Ortalida goudotii* Lesson.

Chamaepetes unicolor Salvin. BLACK GUAN.

Chamaepetes unicolor Salvin, 1867, Proc. Zool. Soc. London, p. 159. (Veragua, Panama = Calovévora, Panama.)

Habitat.—Primarily dense, undisturbed, moist montane forest (upper Tropical and Subtropical zones).
Distribution.—*Resident* in the mountains of Costa Rica (north to Cordillera de Guanacaste) and western Panama (east to Veraguas).

Genus PENELOPINA Reichenbach

Penelopina Reichenbach, 1862, Avium Syst. Nat., Columbariae, p. 152. Type, by monotypy, *Penelope niger* Fraser.

Penelopina nigra (Fraser). HIGHLAND GUAN.

Penelope niger Fraser, 1852, Proc. Zool. Soc. London (1850), p. 246, pl. 29. (No locality given.)

Habitat.—Humid montane forest, less frequently in deciduous woodland (upper Tropical and Subtropical zones).
Distribution.—*Resident* in the mountains of extreme eastern Oaxaca (Sierra Madre de Chiapas), Chiapas, Guatemala, El Salvador (at least formerly), Honduras and north-central Nicaragua.
Notes.—Also known as BLACK CHACHALACA.

Genus PENELOPE Merrem

Penelope Merrem, 1786, Avium Rar. Icones Descr., 2, p. 39. Type, by subsequent designation (Lesson, 1828), *Penelope marail* "Linnaeus" [=Gmelin] = *Penelope jacupema* Merrem = *Phasianus marail* Müller.

Penelope purpurascens Wagler. CRESTED GUAN.

Penelope purpurascens Wagler, 1830, Isis von Oken, col. 1110. (Mexico = probably Veracruz.)

Habitat.—Humid forest, occasionally in scrub (Tropical and lower Subtropical zones).
Distribution.—*Resident* from Sinaloa and Tamaulipas south along both slopes of Middle America to Colombia, western Ecuador and northern Venezuela.
Notes.—*P. purpurascens, P. jacquacu* Spix, 1825, and *P. obscura* Temminck, 1815, the latter two South American, may constitute a superspecies.

Genus OREOPHASIS Gray

Oreophasis G. R. Gray, 1844, Genera Birds, 3, p. [485], col. pl. 121 and pl. [121]. Type, by monotypy, *Oreophasis derbianus* Gray.

Oreophasis derbianus Gray. HORNED GUAN.

Oreophasis derbianus G. R. Gray, 1844, Genera Birds, 3, p. [485], col. pl. 121 and pl. [121]. (Guatemala.)

Habitat.—Humid montane forest (Subtropical and lower Temperate zones).
Distribution.—*Resident* in the mountains of Chiapas (possibly also extreme eastern Oaxaca) and Guatemala.

Genus CRAX Linnaeus

Crax Linnaeus, 1758, Syst. Nat., ed. 10, 1, p. 157. Type, by subsequent designation (Ridgway, 1896), *Crax rubra* Linnaeus.

Crax rubra Linnaeus. GREAT CURASSOW.

Crax rubra Linnaeus, 1758, Syst. Nat., ed. 10, 1, p. 157. Based on "The Red Peruvian Hen" Albin, Nat. Hist. Birds, 3, p. 37, pl. 40. (in America = western Ecuador.)

Habitat.—Primarily undisturbed, mature forest, mostly humid but also in semi-arid regions, occasionally in partially cleared areas and scrubby woodland (Tropical and lower Subtropical zones).
Distribution.—*Resident* from southern San Luis Potosí, southern Tamaulipas, Veracruz and Oaxaca south along both slopes of Middle America (including Cozumel Island) to western Colombia and western Ecuador.
Notes.—*C. rubra* is part of a large complex that probably constitutes a super-species, including the South American *C. alberti* Fraser, 1852, *C. alector* Linnaeus, 1766, *C. fasciolata* Spix, 1825, *C. daubentoni* G. R. Gray, 1867, *C. globulosa* Spix, 1815, and *C. blumenbachii* Spix, 1825.

Superfamily PHASIANOIDEA: Partridges, Grouse, Turkeys and Quail

Family PHASIANIDAE: Partridges, Grouse, Turkeys and Quail

Subfamily PHASIANINAE: Partridges and Pheasants

Tribe PERDICINI: Partridges

Genus PERDIX Brisson

Perdix Brisson, 1760, Ornithologie, 1, pp. 26, 219. Type, by tautonymy, *Perdix cinerea* Brisson = *Tetrao perdix* Linnaeus.

Perdix perdix (Linnaeus). GRAY PARTRIDGE. [288.1.]

Tetrao Perdix Linnaeus, 1758, Syst. Nat., ed. 10, 1, p. 160. (in Europæ agris = southern Sweden.)

Habitat.—Primarily cultivated regions with marginal cover of bushes, undergrowth or hedgerows, and pastures, steppe and meadows.

Distribution.—*Resident* in Eurasia from the British Isles, southern Scandinavia and northern Russia south to southern Europe, Turkey, northern Iran, Turkestan and Mongolia.

Widely introduced in North America and established locally from southern British Columbia, central Alberta, central Saskatchewan, southern Manitoba, southern Ontario, southwestern Quebec, New Brunswick, Prince Edward Island and Nova Scotia south to northeastern California (formerly), northern Nevada, northern Utah, northern Wyoming, northern South Dakota, northwestern Iowa, extreme northern Illinois, central Indiana, west-central Ohio, northern New York and northern Vermont.

Notes.—Also known as HUNGARIAN or COMMON PARTRIDGE and, in Old World literature, as the PARTRIDGE.

Genus **FRANCOLINUS** Stephens

Francolinus Stephens, 1819, *in* Shaw, Gen. Zool., 11 (2), p. 316. Type, by tautonymy, *Francolinus vulgaris* Stephens = *Tetrao francolinus* Linnaeus.

Francolinus francolinus (Linnaeus). BLACK FRANCOLIN. [288.3.]

Tetrao Francolinus Linnaeus, 1766, Syst. Nat., ed. 12, 1, p. 275. (in Italia, Orienta, Africa, Asia = Cyprus.)

Habitat.—Grasslands (primarily tall grass), scrubby and brushy areas, marshes and, locally, clearings in open forest.

Distribution.—*Resident* from Cyprus, Asia Minor and the Near East east to southern Afghanistan, India and Assam.

Introduced and established in the Hawaiian Islands (in 1959, presently on Kauai, Molokai, Maui and Hawaii), southwestern Louisiana (Calcasieu and Cameron parishes), and southern Florida (Palm Beach County).

Francolinus pondicerianus (Gmelin). GRAY FRANCOLIN. [288.4.]

Tetrao pondicerianus Gmelin, 1789, Syst. Nat., 1 (2), p. 760. Based on the "Pondicherry Partridge" Latham, Gen. Synop. Birds, 2 (2), p. 774. (in Coromandel = Pondicherry, India.)

Habitat.—Open dry country with scrub or grass, cultivated fields and desert scrub.

Distribution.—*Resident* from eastern Iran east to India and Ceylon.

Introduced and established in the Hawaiian Islands (in 1958, presently on Molokai, Lanai, Maui and Hawaii), southern Arabia, and the Andaman, Seychelles, Amirante and Mascarene islands.

Francolinus erckelii (Rüppell). ERCKEL'S FRANCOLIN. [288.5.]

Perdix Erckelii Rüppell, 1835, Neue Wirbelth., Vögel, p. 12, pl. 6. (Taranta Mts., northeastern Ethiopia.)

Habitat.—Scrub, brush and open areas with scattered trees, primarily in hilly or mountainous country.

Distribution.—*Resident* in eastern Sudan (Red Sea Province), northern Ethiopia and Eritrea.

Introduced and established in the Hawaiian Islands (in 1957, now on all main islands from Kauai eastward).

Genus ALECTORIS Kaup

Alectoris Kaup, 1829, Skizz. Entw.-Ges. Eur. Thierw., pp. 180, 193. Type, by monotypy, *Perdix petrosa* Auct. (not Gmelin) = *Perdix barbara* Bonnaterre.

Alectoris chukar (Gray). CHUKAR. [288.2.]

Perdix Chukar J. E. Gray, 1830, *in* Hardwicke, Illus. Indian Zool., 1 (2), pl. 54. (India = Srinagar, Kumaon, India.)

Habitat.—Rocky hillsides, mountain slopes with grassy vegetation, open and flat desert with sparse grasses, and barren plateaus.

Distribution.—*Resident* in Eurasia from southeastern Europe and Asia Minor east to southern Manchuria, northern China, Turkestan and the western Himalayas.

Introduced widely in North America and established, at least locally, from south-central British Columbia, northern Idaho, and central and eastern Montana south to extreme northern Baja California, southern Nevada, northern Arizona, extreme northwestern New Mexico and south-central Colorado; also in the Hawaiian Islands (main islands from Kauai eastward, but no longer on Oahu).

Notes.—*A. chukar* was long regarded as a subspecies of *A. graeca* (Meisner, 1804) [ROCK PARTRIDGE] of Europe, but see Watson, 1962, Evolution, 16, pp. 11–19, and 1962, Ibis, pp. 353–367.

Genus COTURNIX Bonnaterre

Coturnix Bonnaterre, 1791, Tabl. Encycl. Méth., Ornithol., 1, livr. 47, pl. lxxxvii. Type, by tautonymy, "Caille" Bonnaterre = *Tetrao coturnix* Linnaeus.

Coturnix japonica Temminck and Schlegel. JAPANESE QUAIL. [288.6.]

Coturnix vulgaris japonica Temminck and Schlegel, 1849, *in* Siebold, Fauna Jpn., Aves, p. 103, pl. 61. (Japan.)

Habitat.—Grasslands, marshes, cultivated fields and pastures.

Distribution.—*Breeds* from northern Mongolia and Transbaicalia east through Amurland to Ussuriland, Sakhalin and the Kurile Islands, and south to Manchuria, Korea and Japan.

Winters from Transbaicalia (rarely) and central Japan south to the northern Indochina region, southern China and the Ryukyu Islands.

Introduced and established in the Hawaiian Islands (in 1921, presently on main islands from Kauai eastward, except Oahu).

Notes.—Regarded by some authors as conspecific with *C. coturnix* (Linnaeus, 1758), a widespread Eurasian species, but differences in vocalizations and sympatric breeding in northern Mongolia indicate specific status of *C. japonica*; the two species constitute a superspecies.

Tribe PHASIANINI: Pheasants

Genus **LOPHURA** Fleming

Lophura Fleming, 1822, Philos. Zool., 2, p. 230. Type, by monotypy, *Phasianus ignitus* [Shaw].
Gennaeus Wagler, 1832, Isis von Oken, col. 1228. Type, by monotypy, *Phasianus nycthemerus* Linnaeus.

Lophura leucomelana (Latham). KALIJ PHEASANT. [309.3.]

Phasianus leucomelanos Latham, 1790, Index Ornithol., 2, p. 633. (India = Nepal.)

Habitat.—Dense scrub, forest undergrowth, thickets and wooded ravines, in Hawaii in ohia-tree fern and koa forest, and on plantations.
Distribution.—*Resident* in the Himalayas from Nepal east to northern Assam and Bhutan.
Introduced and established in the Hawaiian Islands (on Hawaii in 1962, now in the North Kona district and on the slopes of Mauna Loa and Mauna Kea).

Genus **GALLUS** Brisson

Gallus Brisson, 1760, Ornithologie, 1, pp. 26, 166. Type, by tautonymy, *Gallus* Brisson = *Phasianus gallus* Linnaeus.

Gallus gallus (Linnaeus). RED JUNGLEFOWL. [309.4.]

Phasianus Gallus Linnaeus, 1758, Syst. Nat., ed. 10, 1, p. 158. (in India Orientali: Pouli candor etc. = Island of Pulo Condor, off the mouth of the Mekong River.)

Habitat.—Forest undergrowth, second growth, scrub and cultivated lands.
Distribution.—*Resident* from the Himalayas, southern China and Hainan south to central India, Southeast Asia, Sumatra and Java.
Introduced in the Hawaiian Islands (by early Polynesians, probably about 500 A.D.), established presently on Kauai, formerly on other main islands, with recent reintroductions not known to have become established except at Waimea Falls Park, on Oahu; on islands off Puerto Rico (Mona, and possibly Culebra); and in the Philippines, and on many islands of the East Indies and Polynesia.

Genus **PHASIANUS** Linnaeus

Phasianus Linnaeus, 1758, Syst. Nat., ed. 10, 1, p. 158. Type, by tautonymy, *Phasianus colchicus* Linnaeus (*Phasianus,* prebinomial specific name, in synonymy).

Phasianus colchicus Linnaeus. RING-NECKED PHEASANT. [309.1.]

Phasianus colchicus Linnaeus, 1758, Syst. Nat., ed. 10, 1, p. 158. (in Africa, Asia = Rion, formerly Phasis, Georgian S.S.R.)

Habitat.—Open country (especially cultivated areas, scrubby wastes, open woodland and edges of woods), grassy steppe, desert oases, riverside thickets, swamps and open mountain forest.

Distribution.—*Resident* [*colchicus* group] from central Russia, Transcaucasia, Turkestan, Mongolia and Ussuriland south to northern Iran, northern Burma, China and Korea; and [*versicolor* group] in Japan, and the Seven Islands of Izu.

Introduced and established [*colchicus* group] in the Hawaiian Islands (about 1865, presently on all main islands from Kauai eastward), widely in North America from southern British Columbia (and the Queen Charlotte Islands), central Alberta, central Saskatchewan, southwestern Manitoba, northern Minnesota, northern Wisconsin, central Michigan, southern Ontario, southwestern Quebec, New Brunswick, Prince Edward Island and Nova Scotia south, at least locally, to southern interior California, northern Baja California, Utah, southern New Mexico, northern and southeastern Texas, northwestern Oklahoma, Kansas, northern Missouri, southern Illinois, central Indiana, southern Ohio, Pennsylvania, northern Maryland, New Jersey and North Carolina (Outer Banks), and in Japan, New Zealand and Europe; and [*versicolor* group] in the Hawaiian Islands (common on Hawaii, with smaller numbers on Kauai, Lanai and possibly Maui).

Notes.—Known in Old World literature as the PHEASANT. The two groups are sometimes considered as separate species, *P. colchicus* [RING-NECKED PHEASANT, 309.1] and *P. versicolor* Vieillot, 1825 [GREEN or JAPANESE PHEASANT, 309.2]. Within the *colchicus* group, the Asiatic complex is sometimes treated as a species, *P. torquatus* Gmelin, 1789 [RING-NECKED PHEASANT], distinct from the more western *P. colchicus* [COMMON or ENGLISH PHEASANT]; most North American populations are from *P. torquatus* stock, although birds from European *P. colchicus* are mixed with *torquatus* in many areas.

Genus **PAVO** Linnaeus

Pavo Linnaeus, 1758, Syst. Nat., ed. 10, 1, p. 156. Type, by tautonymy, *Pavo cristatus* Linnaeus (*Pavo,* prebinomial specific name, in synonymy).

Pavo cristatus Linnaeus. COMMON PEAFOWL. [309.5.]

Pavo cristatus Linnaeus, 1758, Syst. Nat., ed. 10, 1, p. 156. (in India orientali, Zeylona = India.)

Habitat.—Open forest, forest edge, second growth, scrub, open areas with scattered trees, and cultivated lands.

Distribution.—*Resident* throughout India and on Ceylon.

Introduced in the Hawaiian Islands (initially in 1860, presently established on Oahu and Hawaii, doubtfully so on Molokai and Maui); local, semi-domesticated populations have also persisted for years in various parts of the North American continent.

Subfamily TETRAONINAE: Grouse

Notes.—Sometimes regarded as a family, the Tetraonidae.

Genus **DENDRAGAPUS** Elliot

Dendragapus Elliot, 1864, Proc. Acad. Nat. Sci. Philadelphia, 16, p. 23. Type, by subsequent designation (Baird, Brewer and Ridgway, 1874), *Tetrao obscurus* Say.

Canachites Stejneger, 1885, Proc. U.S. Natl. Mus., 8, p. 410. Type, by original designation, *Tetrao canadensis* Linnaeus.

Dendragapus canadensis (Linnaeus). SPRUCE GROUSE. [298.]

Tetrao canadensis Linnaeus, 1758, Syst. Nat., ed. 10, 1, p. 159. Based on "The Black and Spotted Heath-cock" Edwards, Nat. Hist. Birds, 3, p. 118, pl. 118. (in Canada = Hudson Bay.)

Habitat.—Coniferous forest, primarily spruce and pine, especially with dense understory of grasses and shrubs.

Distribution.—*Resident* from northern Alaska, northern Yukon, western and southern Mackenzie, southern Keewatin, northeastern Manitoba, northern Ontario, northern Quebec, Labrador, New Brunswick and Nova Scotia south to south-coastal and southeastern Alaska (west to the base of the Alaska Peninsula), northern Oregon, central and southeastern Idaho, northwestern Wyoming, western Montana, southeastern and central Alberta, central Saskatchewan, southern Manitoba, northern Minnesota, northern Wisconsin, north-central Michigan, southern Ontario, northern New York, northern Vermont, northern New Hampshire and eastern Maine.

Introduced and established in Newfoundland.

Notes.—The form resident from southeastern Alaska, central British Columbia and west-central Alberta south to northern Oregon, central Idaho, western Montana and northwestern Wyoming was formerly regarded as a separate species, *D. franklinii* (Douglas, 1829) [FRANKLIN'S GROUSE, 299].

Dendragapus obscurus (Say). BLUE GROUSE. [297.]

Tetrao obscurus Say, 1823, *in* Long, Exped. Rocky Mount., 2, p. 14. (near Defile Creek = about 20 miles north of Colorado Springs, Colorado.)

Habitat.—Coniferous forest, especially fir, mostly in open situations with a mixture of deciduous trees and shrubs.

Distribution.—*Resident* [*obscurus* group] from southeastern Alaska (except coastal areas), southern Yukon and extreme southwestern Mackenzie south through the mountains of interior British Columbia, southwestern Alberta, eastern Washington and the Rocky Mountains to eastern Nevada, northern and eastern Arizona, southwestern and north-central New Mexico, eastern Colorado and (formerly) western South Dakota; and [*fuliginosus* group] from coastal southeastern Alaska (north to Yakutat) and coastal British Columbia (including the Queen Charlotte and Vancouver islands) south in coastal ranges and the Cascades to northwestern California, and in the Sierra Nevada to southern California (Ventura County) and extreme western Nevada.

Notes.—The two groups are sometimes treated as separate species, *D. obscurus* [DUSKY GROUSE, 297] and *D. fuliginosus* (Ridgway, 1873) [SOOTY GROUSE, 297.1].

Genus **LAGOPUS** Brisson

Lagopus Brisson, 1760, Ornithologie, 1, pp. 26, 181. Type, by tautonymy, *Lagopus* Brisson = *Tetrao lagopus* Linnaeus.

Lagopus lagopus (Linnaeus). WILLOW PTARMIGAN. [301.]

Tetrao Lagopus Linnaeus, 1758, Syst. Nat., ed. 10, 1, p. 159. (in Europæ alpinis = Swedish Lapland.)

Habitat.—Open tundra, especially in areas heavily vegetated with grasses, mosses, herbs and shrubs, less frequently in openings in boreal coniferous forest.

Distribution.—*Breeds* in North America across the Arctic from northern Alaska east through Banks, southern Melville and Bathurst islands to western Baffin Island, and south to the central and eastern Aleutian Islands, southern Alaska, central British Columbia, extreme west-central Alberta, central Mackenzie, southern Keewatin, northeastern Manitoba, extreme northern Ontario, the Belcher Islands (in Hudson Bay), central Quebec, Labrador and Newfoundland; and in Eurasia from the British Isles and Scandinavia east across Russia and Siberia, and south to Mongolia, Ussuriland and Sakhalin.

Winters mostly in the breeding range, in North America wandering irregularly (or casually) south to Montana, North Dakota, Minnesota, Wisconsin, central Ontario and Maine; and in Eurasia south to northern Europe.

Introduced and established (in 1968, from the Newfoundland population) in Nova Scotia.

Accidental on Vancouver Island and (prior to introduction) in Nova Scotia.

Notes.—In the Old World known as WILLOW GROUSE.

Lagopus mutus (Montin). ROCK PTARMIGAN. [302.]

> *Tetrao mutus* Montin, 1776, Phys. Sälskap. Handl., 1, p. 155. (Alpibus lapponicus = Sweden.)

Habitat.—Open tundra, barren and rocky slopes in Arctic and alpine areas, and relatively barren heaths and moors.

Distribution.—*Breeds* in North America from northern Alaska east through the Canadian Arctic islands to Ellesmere and Baffin islands, and south to the Aleutians, southern Alaska (including Kodiak Island), western British Columbia, central Mackenzie, central Keewatin, Southampton Island, northern Quebec, northern Labrador and Newfoundland; and in the Palearctic from Greenland, Iceland, Scotland and Scandinavia east across northern Russia and northern Siberia to Kamchatka, and at high elevations in the Pyrenees and Alps of southern Europe, the mountain ranges of central Asia, and in the Kurile Islands and Japan (Honshu).

Winters regularly in North America from the breeding range south to southern Mackenzie, northern Saskatchewan, northern Manitoba, northwestern Ontario and central Quebec, casually to southwestern British Columbia (Vancouver Island); and in the Palearctic primarily resident in the breeding range.

Notes.—Known in Old World literature as the PTARMIGAN.

Lagopus leucurus (Richardson). WHITE-TAILED PTARMIGAN. [304.]

> *Tetrao (Lagopus) leucurus* Richardson, 1831, *in* Wilson and Bonaparte, Am. Ornithol., Jameson ed., 4, p. 330. (Rocky Mountains, lat. 54°N.)

Habitat.—Alpine tundra, especially in rocky areas with sparse vegetation.

Distribution.—*Resident* from south-central Alaska (Alaska Range), central Yukon and southwestern Mackenzie south to southern Alaska (west to the Kenai Peninsula and Lake Clark), southern British Columbia (including Vancouver Island) and the Cascade Mountains of Washington, and along the Rocky Mountains (locally, mostly on alpine summits) from southeastern British Columbia and southwestern Alberta south through Montana, Wyoming and Colorado to northern New Mexico.

Introduced and established in California (high central Sierra Nevada).

Genus **BONASA** Stephens

Bonasa Stephens, 1819, *in* Shaw, Gen. Zool., 11 (2), p. 298. Type, by subsequent designation (A.O.U. Comm., 1886), *Tetrao umbellus* Linnaeus.

Bonasa umbellus (Linnaeus). RUFFED GROUSE. [300.]

Tetrao umbellus Linnaeus, 1766, Syst. Nat., ed. 12, 1, p. 275. Based on "The Ruffed Heath-cock or Grous" Edwards, Glean. Nat. Hist., 1, p. 79, pl. 248. (in Pensylvania = eastern Pennsylvania.)

Habitat.—Heavy forest, both coniferous and deciduous, although the presence of deciduous trees seems essential, in both wet and relatively dry situations from boreal forest and northern hardwood-ecotone to eastern deciduous forest and oak-savanna woodland.

Distribution.—*Resident* from central Alaska, northern Yukon, southwestern Mackenzie, northern Saskatchewan, northern Manitoba, northern Ontario, southern Quebec, southern Labrador, New Brunswick, Prince Edward Island and Nova Scotia south to northwestern California, northeastern Oregon, central and eastern Idaho, central Utah, central Wyoming, central Montana, southern Alberta, southern Saskatchewan, southern Manitoba (absent from prairie regions of three preceding provinces), central and southeastern Minnesota, northern Illinois, central Indiana, northern Ohio, in the Appalachians to northern Georgia, western South Carolina and western North Carolina, and to northeastern Virginia; also locally south to western South Dakota (Black Hills), eastern Kansas (formerly), central Arkansas, western Tennessee and northeastern Alabama (formerly).

Introduced and established in Iowa and Newfoundland.

Genus **CENTROCERCUS** Swainson

Centrocercus [subgenus] Swainson, 1832, *in* Swainson and Richardson, Fauna Bor.-Am., 2 (1831), pp. 358, 496. Type, by original designation, *Tetrao urophasianus* Bonaparte.

Centrocercus urophasianus (Bonaparte). SAGE GROUSE. [309.]

Tetrao urophasianus Bonaparte, 1827, Zool. J., 3, p. 213. (Northwestern countries beyond the Mississippi, especially on the Missouri = North Dakota.)

Habitat.—Foothills, plains and mountain slopes where sagebrush is present.
Distribution.—*Resident* locally (formerly widespread) from central Washington, southern Idaho, Montana, southeastern Alberta, southwestern Saskatchewan, southwestern North Dakota and western South Dakota south to eastern California, south-central Nevada, southern Utah, western Colorado and northern New Mexico, formerly north to southern British Columbia and southeast to the Oklahoma Panhandle.

Genus **TYMPANUCHUS** Gloger

Tympanuchus Gloger, 1842, Gemein. Handb. Hilfsb. Naturgesch. (1841), p. 396. Type, by monotypy, *Tetrao cupido* Linnaeus.
Pedioecetes Baird, 1858, *in* Baird, Cassin and Lawrence, Rep. Explor. Surv. R. R. Pac., 9, pp. xxi, xliv. Type, by monotypy, *Tetrao phasianellus* Linnaeus.

Tympanuchus cupido (Linnaeus). GREATER PRAIRIE-CHICKEN. [305.]

Tetrao Cupido Linnaeus, 1758, Syst. Nat., ed. 10, 1, p. 160. Based on "Le Cocq de bois d'Amérique" Catesby, Nat. Hist. Carolina, 2, app., p. 1, pl. 1. (in Virginia = Pennsylvania.)

Habitat.—Tall grasslands (prairie), occasionally cultivated lands of similar types, formerly in eastern (fire-produced) grassland and blueberry barrens.

Distribution.—*Resident* locally and in much reduced numbers from eastern North Dakota, northwestern and central Minnesota, northern Wisconsin and northern Michigan south to northeastern Colorado, Kansas (except southwestern), southern and northeastern Oklahoma, central Missouri and southern Illinois; also in southeastern Texas. Formerly occurred (now extirpated or nearly so) from east-central Alberta, central Saskatchewan, southern Manitoba and southern Ontario south, east of the Rocky Mountains, to eastern Texas, southwestern Louisiana, east-central Arkansas, central Indiana, western Kentucky and western Ohio; and in the east from Massachusetts south to Maryland, after 1835 confined to the island of Martha's Vineyard, Massachusetts (where last reported in 1932).

Notes.—Also known as PINNATED GROUSE; the extinct eastern population was called HEATH HEN. This species and *T. pallidicinctus* constitute a superspecies and are considered to be conspecific by some authors; with this concept, PRAIRIE CHICKEN or PINNATED GROUSE may be used. *T. cupido* and *T. phasianellus* hybridize sporadically, but occasionally they interbreed extensively on a local level.

Tympanuchus pallidicinctus (Ridgway). LESSER PRAIRIE-CHICKEN. [307.]

Cupidonia cupido var. *pallidicinctus* Ridgeway [sic], 1873, For. Stream, 1, p. 289. (prairie of Texas [near lat. 32°N.].)

Habitat.—Arid grasslands, generally interspersed with shrubs and dwarf trees.

Distribution.—*Resident* locally and in reduced numbers from southeastern Colorado, south-central Kansas and western Oklahoma to extreme eastern New Mexico and northern Texas (Panhandle), formerly north to southwestern Nebraska.

Notes.—See comments under *T. cupido*.

Tympanuchus phasianellus (Linnaeus). SHARP-TAILED GROUSE. [308.]

Tetrao Phasianellus Linnaeus, 1758, Syst. Nat., ed. 10, 1, p. 160. Based on "The Long-tailed Grous from Hudson's-Bay" Edwards, Nat. Hist. Birds, 3, p. 117, pl. 117. (in Canada = Hudson Bay.)

Habitat.—Grasslands, especially with scattered woodlands, arid sagebrush, brushy hills, oak savanna and edges of riparian woodland.

Distribution.—*Resident,* at least locally, from central Alaska, central Yukon, northwestern Mackenzie, northern Saskatchewan, northern Manitoba, northern Ontario and west-central Quebec south to eastern Washington, eastern Oregon, southern Idaho, central Utah, central Colorado, extreme northeastern New Mexico (at least formerly), central Nebraska, eastern South Dakota, eastern North Dakota, central Minnesota, central Wisconsin, northern Michigan and southern Ontario; formerly occurred south to southern Oregon, northeastern California, northeastern Nevada, western Kansas, southern Iowa and northern Illinois, probably also northern Texas.

Notes.—See comments under *T. cupido*.

Subfamily MELEAGRIDINAE: Turkeys

Notes.—Sometimes regarded as a family, the Meleagrididae.

Genus MELEAGRIS Linnaeus

Meleagris Linnaeus, 1758, Syst. Nat., ed. 10, 1, p. 156. Type, by tautonymy, *Meleagris gallopavo* Linnaeus (*Meleagris,* prebinomial specific name, in synonymy).

Notes.—See comments under *Agriocharis.*

Meleagris gallopavo Linnaeus. WILD TURKEY. [310.]

Meleagris Gallopavo Linnaeus, 1758, Syst. Nat., ed. 10, 1, p. 156. Based mainly on the "Wild Turkey" Catesby, Nat. Hist. Carolina, 1, p. 44, pl. 44. (in America septentrionali = Mirador, Veracruz.)

Habitat.—Forest and open woodland, deciduous or mixed deciduous-coniferous areas, especially in mountainous regions (Subtropical and Temperate zones).

Distribution.—*Resident* locally and generally in reduced numbers (formerly widespread) from central Arizona, central Colorado, northern Kansas, eastern Nebraska, southeastern South Dakota, northern Iowa, southern and eastern Wisconsin, central Michigan, southern Ontario (formerly), northern New York, southern Vermont, southern New Hampshire and southwestern Maine south to Guerrero (possibly Oaxaca), Veracruz, southern Texas, the Gulf coast and Florida.

Reintroduced widely through its former breeding range, and introduced and established locally north to central California, west-central and southern Nevada, eastern Utah, central Wyoming, southern Alberta, southern Saskatchewan, southwestern Manitoba and southern Ontario (probably); also in the Hawaiian Islands (initially in 1788, now on Niihau, Lanai, Maui and Hawaii) and New Zealand.

Notes.—Also known as COMMON or PLAIN TURKEY.

Genus AGRIOCHARIS Chapman

Agriocharis Chapman, 1896, Bull. Am. Mus. Nat. Hist., 6, pp. 287, 288. Type, by monotypy, *Meleagris ocellata* "Temminck" [= Cuvier].

Notes.—By some authors merged in *Meleagris.*

Agriocharis ocellata (Cuvier). OCELLATED TURKEY.

Meleagris ocellata Cuvier, 1820, Mém. Mus. Hist. Nat., 6, pp. 1, 4, pl. 1. (Gulf of Honduras = Belize.)

Habitat.—Lowland forest edge and tall second growth (Tropical Zone).

Distribution.—*Resident* in southeastern Mexico (Tabasco and the Yucatan Peninsula), northern Guatemala (Petén) and northern Belize.

Subfamily ODONTOPHORINAE: Quail

Genus DENDRORTYX Gould

Dendrortyx Gould, 1844, Monogr. Odontoph., 1, pl. [3] and text. Type, by monotypy, *Ortyx macroura* Jardine and Selby.

Dendrortyx macroura (Jardine and Selby). LONG-TAILED WOOD-PARTRIDGE.

Ortyx macroura Jardine and Selby, 1828, Illus. Ornithol., 1, text to pl. 38 (in "Ortyx synopsis specierum"), and pl. 49 and text. (Mexico = mountains about valley of México.)

Habitat.—Dense underbrush of mountain slopes and relatively undisturbed humid pine-oak forests (Subtropical and Temperate zones).

Distribution.—*Resident* in the mountains of Jalisco, Michoacán, state of México, Distrito Federal, Morelos, Guerrero, Puebla, Veracruz and Oaxaca.

Dendrortyx barbatus Gould. BEARDED WOOD-PARTRIDGE.

Dendrortyx barbatus (Lichtenstein MS) Gould, 1846, Monogr. Odontoph., 2, pl. [2] and text. (Jalapa, Veracruz.)

Habitat.—Humid montane forests (Subtropical Zone).

Distribution.—*Resident* in eastern San Luis Potosí, eastern Hidalgo, eastern Puebla and Veracruz.

Dendrortyx leucophrys (Gould). BUFFY-CROWNED WOOD-PARTRIDGE.

Ortyx leucophrys Gould, 1844, Proc. Zool. Soc. London (1843), p. 132. (Cobán, Guatemala.)

Habitat.—Humid montane forest, primarily in dense undergrowth of clearings, open forest and forest edge (upper Tropical and Subtropical zones).

Distribution.—*Resident* locally in the mountains of Chiapas (Sierra Madre de Chiapas), Guatemala, El Salvador, Honduras, north-central Nicaragua and Costa Rica (central highlands, including Dota Mountains).

Genus **ODONTOPHORUS** Vieillot

Odontophorus Vieillot, 1816, Analyse, p. 51. Type, by monotypy, "Tocro" Buffon = *Tetrao gujanensis* Gmelin.

Odontophorus gujanensis (Gmelin). MARBLED WOOD-QUAIL.

Tetrao gujanensis Gmelin, 1789, Syst. Nat., 1 (2), p. 767. Based in part on the "Guiana Partridge" Latham, Gen. Synop. Birds, 2 (2), p. 776. (in Cayenna et Gujana = Cayenne.)

Habitat.—Humid forest and shaded second growth (Tropical and lower Subtropical zones).

Distribution.—*Resident* in southern and southwestern Costa Rica (Pacific slope from Gulf of Nicoya eastward) and Panama (Caribbean lowlands from Coclé eastward, and Pacific slope in Chiriquí, where probably now extirpated, and from eastern Panamá province eastward), and in South America from northern Colombia, Venezuela and the Guianas south, mostly east of the Andes, to eastern Bolivia and central and northeastern Brazil.

Odontophorus erythrops Gould. RUFOUS-FRONTED WOOD-QUAIL.

Odontophorus erythrops Gould, 1859, Proc. Zool. Soc. London, p. 99. (Pallatanga, Ecuador.)

Habitat.—Humid lowland and foothill forests, generally in dense forest or heavy second growth (Tropical and lower Subtropical zones).

Distribution.—*Resident* [*melanotis* group] locally in northern and eastern Honduras (Caribbean slope west to the Sula Valley), Nicaragua (Caribbean slope), Costa Rica (mostly Caribbean slope) and Panama (both slopes); and [*erythrops* group] in western Colombia and western Ecuador.

Notes.—The two groups are sometimes regarded as separate species, *O. melanotis* Salvin, 1865 [BLACK-EARED WOOD-QUAIL] and *O. erythrops*.

Odontophorus leucolaemus Salvin. BLACK-BREASTED WOOD-QUAIL.

Odontophorus leucolaemus Salvin, 1867, Proc. Zool. Soc. London, p. 161. (Cordillera de Tolé, Veraguas, Panama.)

Habitat.—Humid highland forest, especially on steep wooded slopes (upper Tropical and Subtropical zones).

Distribution.—*Resident* in the central highlands of Costa Rica (west to Cordillera de Guanacaste) and western Panama (east to Coclé, mostly on the Caribbean drainage).

Notes.—Also known as WHITE-THROATED WOOD-QUAIL.

Odontophorus dialeucos Wetmore. TACARCUNA WOOD-QUAIL.

Odontophorus dialeucos Wetmore, 1963, Smithson. Misc. Collect., 145, no. 6, p. 5. (1,450 meters elevation, 6½ kilometers west of the summit of Cerro Malí, Serranía del Darién, Darién, Panama.)

Habitat.—Humid montane forest (Subtropical Zone).

Distribution.—*Resident* in eastern Panama (on Cerro Malí and Cerro Tacarcuna, at the southern end of the Serranía del Darién, in Darién).

Odontophorus guttatus (Gould). SPOTTED WOOD-QUAIL.

Ortyx guttata Gould, 1838, Proc. Zool. Soc. London (1837), p. 79. (Bay of Honduras = Belize.)

Habitat.—Humid lowland and foothill forest, especially dense forest with open understory (Tropical and Subtropical zones).

Distribution.—*Resident* in southern Mexico (Veracruz, northern Oaxaca, Tabasco, Chipas, Campeche and Quintana Roo), northern Guatemala (Petén and the Caribbean lowlands) and Belize, and in the highlands of central Guatemala, Honduras, north-central Nicaragua, Costa Rica and extreme western Panama (western Chiriquí).

Genus **DACTYLORTYX** Ogilvie-Grant

Dactylortyx Ogilvie-Grant, 1893, Cat. Birds Br. Mus., 22, pp. xiv, 99, 429. Type, by monotypy, *Ortyx thoracicus* Gambel.

Dactylortyx thoracicus (Gambel). SINGING QUAIL.

Ortyx thoracicus Gambel, 1848, Proc. Acad. Nat. Sci. Philadelphia, 4, p. 77. (Jalapa, [Veracruz,] Mexico.)

Habitat.—Primarily humid montane (cloud) forest, less frequently tropical deciduous forest, pine-oak association and humid gallery forest (Tropical and Subtropical zones).

Distribution.—*Resident* locally in southwestern Tamaulipas, southeastern San Luis Potosí, northeastern Puebla and central Veracruz; in western Jalisco and probably also Colima; in central Guerrero; in the Yucatan Peninsula; and from extreme eastern Oaxaca (Sierra Madre de Chiapas) south through the mountains of Chiapas, Guatemala and El Salvador to central Honduras.

Genus CYRTONYX Gould

Cyrtonyx Gould, 1844, Monogr. Odontoph., 1, pl. [2] and text. Type, by monotypy, *Ortyx massena* Lesson = *Ortyx montezumae* Vigors.

Cyrtonyx montezumae (Vigors). MONTEZUMA QUAIL. [296.]

Ortyx Montezumae Vigors, 1830, Zool. J., 5, p. 275. (Mexico.)

Habitat.—Pine-oak and oak scrub in the highlands, especially in open woodland with grass understory (Subtropical and lower Temperate zones).

Distribution.—*Resident,* at least locally, from central and southeastern Arizona, southern New Mexico, western and central Texas, northern Coahuila, central Nuevo León and central Tamaulipas south in the mountains of Mexico to west-central Veracruz and central Oaxaca (La Cieneguilla).

Notes.—Also known as HARLEQUIN QUAIL. *C. montezumae* and *C. ocellatus* constitute a superspecies; conspecificity has been suggested by some authors.

Cyrtonyx ocellatus (Gould). OCELLATED QUAIL.

Ortyx ocellatus Gould, 1837, Proc. Zool. Soc. London (1836), p. 75. (No locality given = Guatemala.)

Habitat.—Highland pine and pine-oak woodland, occurring in heavy undergrowth or grassy areas, also on grassy slopes and in weedy fields adjacent to forest (Subtropical Zone).

Distribution.—*Resident* in the mountains of eastern Oaxaca (Sierra Madre de Chiapas), Chiapas, Guatemala, El Salvador, Honduras and north-central Nicaragua.

Notes.—See comments under *C. montezumae.*

Genus RHYNCHORTYX Ogilvie-Grant

Rhynchortyx Ogilvie-Grant, 1893, Cat. Birds Br. Mus., 22, pp. xv, 100, 443. Type, by monotypy, *Odontophorus spodiostethus* Salvin [=male] and *Odontophorus cinctus* Salvin [=female].

Rhynchortyx cinctus (Salvin). TAWNY-FACED QUAIL.

Odontophorus cinctus Salvin, 1876, Ibis, p. 379. (Veragua = Panama.)

Habitat.—Humid lowland and foothill forest (Tropical and lower Subtropical zones).

Distribution.—*Resident* locally on the Caribbean slope of northern and eastern Honduras (west to the Sula Valley), Nicaragua and Costa Rica, on both slopes of

Panama (rare west of the Canal Zone), and in northwestern Colombia and north-western Ecaudor.

Genus COLINUS Goldfuss

Colinus Goldfuss, 1820, Handb. Zool., 2, p. 220. Type, by monotypy, *Perdix mexicanus,* Caille de la Louisiane, Planches enlum. 149 = *Tetrao virginianus* Linnaeus.

Colinus cristatus (Linnaeus). CRESTED BOBWHITE.

Tetrao cristatus Linnaeus, 1766, Syst. Nat., ed. 12, 1, p. 277. Based mainly on "La Caille hupée du Mexique" Brisson, Ornithologie, 1, p. 260, pl. 25, fig. 2. (in Mexico, Guiania, error = Curaçao.)

Habitat.—Thickets, grasslands, cultivated areas and forest edge, generally in arid habitats north of South America (Tropical Zone, in South America to Temperate Zone).

Distribution.—*Resident* [*leucopogon* group] on the Pacific slope from western Guatemala (including the upper Motagua Valley on the Caribbean drainage) south through El Salvador, Honduras (including the Sula, Comayagua and Quimistán valleys on the Caribbean slope) and Nicaragua to central Costa Rica; and [*cristatus* group] on the Pacific slope of southwestern Costa Rica (Golfo Dulce region) and western Panama (east to western Panamá province), and from western Colombia east through most of Venezuela (also Aruba, Curaçao and Margarita Island) to the Guianas and eastern Brazil.

Introduced and established [*cristatus* group] in the Virgin Islands (St. Thomas, now extirpated) and the Grenadines (Mustique).

Notes.—The northern Middle American populations are sometimes recognized as a separate species, *C. leucopogon* (Lesson, 1842) [SPOT-BELLIED BOBWHITE]. *C. cristatus* may be an allospecies of a superspecies also including *C. virginianus* and *C. nigrogularis.*

Colinus virginianus (Linnaeus). NORTHERN BOBWHITE. [289.]

Tetrao virginianus Linnaeus, 1758, Syst. Nat., ed. 10, 1, p. 161. Based on "The American Partridge" Catesby, Nat. Hist. Carolina, 3, p. 12, pl. 12. (in America = Virginia.)

Habitat.—Brushy fields, grasslands (primarily long grass), cultivated lands and open woodland, in both humid and semi-arid situations (Tropical to Temperate zones).

Distribution.—*Resident* from southeastern Wyoming, central South Dakota, southern Minnesota, southern Wisconsin, central Michigan, southern Ontario, southern New York, southern Vermont, southern New Hampshire and southern Maine south through the central and eastern United States (west to eastern Colorado, eastern New Mexico and west-central Texas) to Florida (except the Florida Keys), Cuba, the Isle of Pines, Gulf coast, and eastern and southern Mexico, west to eastern Coahuila, western San Luis Potosí, southeastern Nayarit, eastern Jalisco, Guanajuato, the state of México, Puebla and Oaxaca, east to Tabasco, eastern Chiapas and extreme northwestern Guatemala (Nenton-Comitán valley), and in the Pacific lowlands from central Guerrero to southern Chiapas; also in southeastern Arizona (formerly, extirpated late 1890's, reintroduction attempts not certainly successful) and eastern Sonora.

Introduced and established in western North America (southwestern British Columbia, Washington, Oregon, Idaho and Montana), the West Indies (Hispaniola, Puerto Rico, St. Croix, and Andros and New Providence in the Bahamas) and New Zealand. Attempted introductions elsewhere (widely in the Hawaiian Islands, West Indies and Europe) have been unsuccessful as permanently established populations.

Notes.—Known also as COMMON BOBWHITE and, in earlier literature, as the BOBWHITE. *C. virginianus* and *C. nigrogularis* constitute a superspecies; they are considered conspecific by some authors. See also comments under *C. cristatus*.

Colinus nigrogularis (Gould). BLACK-THROATED BOBWHITE.

Ortyx nigrogularis Gould, 1843, Proc. Zool. Soc. London (1842), p. 181. (Mexico = state of Yucatán.)

Habitat.—Pine savanna, forest clearings, weedy fields, sisal plantations, cultivated areas and coastal scrub forest, mostly in arid regions (Tropical Zone).

Distribution.—*Resident* in the Yucatan Peninsula (northern Campeche, the state of Yucatán, and northwestern Quintana Roo), northern Guatemala (Petén) and Belize; and in the Mosquitia of eastern Honduras and northeastern Nicaragua.

Notes.—See comments under *C. virginianus* and *C. cristatus*.

Genus **PHILORTYX** Gould

Philortyx Gould, 1846, Monogr. Odontoph., 2, pl. 6 and text. Type, by monotypy, *Ortyx fasciatus* Gould.

Philortyx fasciatus (Gould). BANDED QUAIL.

Ortyx fasciatus Gould, 1843, Proc. Zool. Soc. London (1842), p. 133. (California, error = Mexico.)

Habitat.—Open lowland thorn forest, thickets and weedy fields, especially near cultivated areas (Tropical and lower Subtropical zones.)

Distribution.—*Resident* in southwestern Jalisco, Colima, Michoacán, Guerrero, the state of México, Morelos and Puebla.

Notes.—Also known as BARRED QUAIL.

Genus **CALLIPEPLA** Wagler

Callipepla Wagler, 1832, Isis von Oken, col. 277. Type, by monotypy, *Callipepla strenua* Wagler = *Ortyx squamatus* Vigors.
Lophortyx Bonaparte, 1838, Geogr. Comp. List, p. 42. Type, by subsequent designation (G. R. Gray, 1840), *Tetrao californicus* Shaw.

Callipepla squamata (Vigors). SCALED QUAIL. [293.]

Ortyx squamatus Vigors, 1830, Zool. J., 5, p. 275. (Mexico.)

Habitat.—Desert grasslands, deserts with spiny or shrubby ground cover, thorn scrub, and secondary deserts produced by man (Subtropical and lower Temperate zones).

Distribution.—*Resident* from south-central Arizona, northern New Mexico, east-central Colorado and southwestern Kansas south through western Oklahoma, the western half of Texas, and the interior of Mexico to northeastern Jalisco, Guanajuato, Querétaro, Hidalgo and western Tamaulipas.

Introduced and established in central Washington (Yakima and Grant counties) and eastern Nevada.

Notes.—*C. squamata* and *C. gambelii* occasionally hybridize.

Callipepla douglasii (Vigors). ELEGANT QUAIL.

Ortyx douglasii Vigors, 1829, Zool. J., 4 (1828), p. 354. (Monterey, error = Mazatlán, Sinaloa.)

Habitat.—Thorn forest, especially in foothill regions, scrubby thickets and deciduous forest, primarily in river valleys (Tropical Zone).

Distribution.—*Resident* from northern Sonora and southwestern Chihuahua south through Sinaloa, northwestern Durango and Nayarit to northwestern Jalisco.

The small population present near Nogales, Arizona, from 1964 to the early 1970's apparently originated from escaped individuals.

Notes.—This and the next two species previously have been separated from *Callipepla* in the genus *Lophortyx*.

Callipepla gambelii (Gambel). GAMBEL'S QUAIL. [295.]

Lophortyx Gambelii "Nutt." Gambel, 1843, Proc. Acad. Nat. Sci. Philadelphia, 1, p. 260. (some distance west [=east] of California = southern Nevada.)

Habitat.—Deserts, primarily with brushy or thorny growth such as mesquite, desert thorn and yucca, also in adjacent cultivated regions (Tropical and Subtropical zones).

Distribution.—*Resident* from east-central California, southern Nevada, southern Utah, western Colorado and northwestern New Mexico south to northeastern Baja California, Sonora (including Isla Tiburón in the Gulf of California), coastal Sinaloa, northern Chihuahua and the Rio Grande Valley of western Texas.

Introduced and established in the Hawaiian Islands (in 1928, now on Lanai, Kahoolawe and possibly Hawaii), on San Clemente Island (off California), and in north-central Idaho.

Notes.—*C. gambelii* and *C. californica* constitute a superspecies. See also comments under *C. squamata* and *C. douglasii*.

Callipepla californica (Shaw). CALIFORNIA QUAIL. [294.]

Tetrao californicus Shaw, 1798, *in* Shaw and Nodder, Naturalists' Misc., 9, text to pl. 345. (California = Monterey.)

Habitat.—Brushy, grassy and weedy areas in both humid and arid regions, including chaparral, forest edge, cultivated lands, semi-desert scrub, thickets, sagebrush and, less frequently, open second-growth woodland.

Distribution.—*Resident* from southern British Columbia (including Vancouver Island), Washington and western Idaho south through most of Oregon, California (including Santa Catalina Island) and Utah to southern Baja California. Most of the populations north of southern Oregon and east of California are apparently the result of introductions.

Introduced and established in the Hawaiian Islands (by 1855, presently on Kauai and Hawaii), on Santa Cruz and Santa Rosa islands (off California), and in central Chile, Australia (King Island) and New Zealand.

Notes.—See comments under *C. douglasii* and *C. gambelii.*

Genus OREORTYX Baird

Oreortyx Baird, 1858, *in* Baird, Cassin and Lawrence, Rep. Explor. Surv. R. R. Pac., 9, pp. xlv, 638, 642. Type, by monotypy, *Ortyx picta* Douglas.

Oreortyx pictus (Douglas). MOUNTAIN QUAIL. [292.]

Ortyx picta Douglas, 1829, Trans. Linn. Soc. London, 16, p. 143. (No locality given = junction of Willamette and Santiam rivers, Linn County, Oregon; see Browning, 1977, Proc. Biol. Soc. Wash., 90, p. 809.)

Habitat.—Brushy mountainsides, coniferous forest, forest and meadow edges, dense undergrowth, and in more arid conditions in sagebrush, pinyon and juniper.

Distribution.—*Resident* from southwestern British Columbia (on Vancouver Island, where introduced but perhaps also native), western and southern Washington, and central Idaho south through the mountains of California and northern and western Nevada to northern Baja California (Sierra Juárez and Sierra San Pedro Martír).

Subfamily NUMIDINAE: Guineafowl

Notes.—Sometimes regarded as a family, the Numididae.

Genus NUMIDA Linnaeus

Numida Linnaeus, 1766, Syst. Nat., ed. 12, 1, p. 273. Type, by monotypy, *Numida meleagris* Linnaeus = *Phasianus meleagris* Linnaeus.

Numida meleagris (Linnaeus). HELMETED GUINEAFOWL. [296.1.]

Phasianus Meleagris Linnaeus, 1758, Syst. Nat., ed. 10, 1, p. 158. (in Africa = Nubia, upper Nile.)

Habitat.—Open woodland, cultivated lands and grasslands.

Distribution.—*Resident* generally throughout Africa south of the Sahara.

Widely domesticated throughout the world, and escaped individuals are frequently reported. Introduced and established in the Hawaiian Islands (in 1874 on Hawaii and possibly other main islands, perhaps not well established), in the West Indies (on Cuba, the Isle of Pines, Hispaniola, Puerto Rico and Barbuda), and on Ascension, Trindade, and the Cape Verde islands.

Notes.—There are three distinctive groups, the West African *galeata* group, the northeastern African *meleagris* group, and the central and southern African *mitrata* group (see Crowe, 1978, Ann. S. Afr. Mus., 16, pp. 41–136), that intergrade where their ranges meet. Of these, *N. mitrata* Pallas, 1767 [HELMETED GUINEAFOWL], and *N. meleagris* [TUFTED GUINEAFOWL] have been considered specifically distinct. Introductions in the Hawaiian Islands and West Indies are of the West African race, *N. m. galeata* Pallas, 1767.

Order **GRUIFORMES**: Cranes, Rails and Allies

Family **RALLIDAE**: Rails, Gallinules and Coots

Notes.—The sequence and placement of genera used in this family is essentially that of Olson (1973, Wilson Bull., 85, pp. 381–416).

Subfamily RALLINAE: Rails, Gallinules and Coots

Genus **COTURNICOPS** Gray

Coturnicops G. R. Gray, 1855, Cat. Genera Subgenera Birds, p. 120. Type, by monotypy, *Rallus noveboracensis* Gmelin = *Fulica noveboracensis* Gmelin.

Notes.—See comments under *Micropygia.*

Coturnicops noveboracensis (Gmelin). YELLOW RAIL. [215.]

Fulica noveboracensis Gmelin, 1789, Syst. Nat., 1 (2), p. 701. Based on the "Yellow-breasted Gallinule" Pennant, Arct. Zool., 2, p. 491. (in Noveboraco = New York.)

Habitat.—Marshes and wet meadows, breeding in fresh-water situations, wintering in both fresh-water and brackish marshes, as well as in dense, deep grass and grain fields.

Distribution.—*Breeds* locally from northwestern Alberta, southern Mackenzie, central Saskatchewan, northern Manitoba, northern Ontario, southern Quebec, New Brunswick and (probably) Nova Scotia south to southern Alberta, southern Saskatchewan, North Dakota, central Minnesota, southern Wisconsin, northern Michigan, southern Ontario, Massachusetts and Connecticut (formerly in east-central California, and to northern Illinois and southern Ohio); and around Lerma in the valley of Toluca, state of México. Reported in summer in southeastern Alaska, southern British Columbia, Montana and Colorado.

Winters from coastal North Carolina south to southern Florida, west along the Gulf coast to central and southeastern Texas, and in the breeding range in Mexico; also (locally and casually) from Oregon south to southern California.

In migration recorded in Washington, Arizona and New Mexico, and irregularly through most of the United States east of the Rocky Mountains.

Casual in Labrador.

Notes.—Relationships with the Asiatic *C. exquisita* (Swinhoe, 1873) are uncertain, but that form and *C. noveboracensis* may constitute a superspecies.

Genus **MICROPYGIA** Bonaparte

Micropygia Bonaparte, 1856, C. R. Acad. Sci. Paris, 43, p. 599. Type, by virtual monotypy, *Micropygia schomburgi* "Cabanis" = *Crex schomburgkii* Schomburgk.

Notes.—Some authors merge this genus in *Coturnicops.*

Micropygia schomburgkii (Schomburgk). OCELLATED CRAKE.

Crex Schomburgkii (Cabanis MS) Schomburgk, 1848, Reisen Br.-Guiana, 2, p. 245. (Our Village, on the upper Kukenaam River, Terr. Yuruari, Venezuela.)

Habitat & Distribution.—*Resident* in savanna and marshes of South America from southeastern Colombia, southern Venezuela and the Guianas south, east of the Andes, to extreme eastern Peru, Bolivia and southeastern Brazil.

One record from Costa Rica (Buenos Aires, Puntarenas province, 9 March 1967; Dickerman, 1968, Bull. Br. Ornithol. Club, 88, pp. 25–30).

Genus LATERALLUS Gray

Laterallus G. R. Gray, 1855, Cat. Genera Subgenera Birds, p. 120. Type, by monotypy, *Rallus melanophaius* Vieillot.

Laterallus ruber (Sclater and Salvin). RUDDY CRAKE.

Corethrura rubra Sclater and Salvin, 1860, Proc. Zool. Soc. London, p. 300. (in provincia Veræ Pacis = Cobán, Vera Paz, Guatemala.)

Habitat.—Marshes and wet fields, primarily in fresh-water situations (Tropical and lower Subtropical zones).

Distribution.—*Resident* in the lowlands from Oaxaca on the Pacific and Tamaulipas on the Gulf-Caribbean south along both slopes of Middle America (including Cozumel Island off Quintana Roo) to Honduras and northern Nicaragua, also a sight report for northwestern Costa Rica (Guanacaste).

Laterallus albigularis (Lawrence). WHITE-THROATED CRAKE.

Corethrura albigularis Lawrence, 1861, Ann. Lyc. Nat. Hist. N.Y., 7, p. 302. (Atlantic side of the Isthmus of Panama, along the line of the Panama Railroad.)

Habitat.—Marshes and wet meadows, primarily in fresh-water situations (Tropical and lower Subtropical zones).

Distribution.—*Resident* from southeastern Honduras (Río Segovia [=Coco]) south through Nicaragua (Caribbean lowlands), Costa Rica (Caribbean lowlands and Pacific region around Golfo Dulce), Panama and northern and western Colombia to western Ecuador.

Notes.—Some authors consider *L. albigularis* to be conspecific with the South American *L. melanophaius* (Vieillot, 1819) [RUFOUS-SIDED CRAKE], although its closest relationships may be with *L. exilis*.

Laterallus exilis (Temminck). GRAY-BREASTED CRAKE.

Rallus exilis Temminck, 1831, Planches Color., livr. 87, pl. 523. (No locality given = Cayenne.)

Habitat.—Lowland marshes, mostly fresh-water situations (Tropical and lower Subtropical zones).

Distribution.—*Resident* locally in Belize (Middlesex), southeastern Honduras (Río Segovia [=Coco]), southeastern Nicaragua (Río Escondido), Costa Rica (sight reports), Panama (Isla Coiba, San Blas and the Canal Zone) and South America (scattered reports from Colombia, Venezuela, Trinidad, the Guianas, northern Brazil, eastern Ecuador, eastern Peru and southern Paraguay).

Laterallus jamaicensis (Gmelin). BLACK RAIL. [216.]

> *Rallus jamaicensis* Gmelin, 1789, Syst. Nat., 1 (2), p. 718. Based on "The Least Water-Hen" Edwards, Glean. Nat. Hist., 2, p. 142, pl. 278, lower fig. (in Jamaica.)

Habitat.—Salt marshes, less frequently in wet savanna and fresh-water marshes.

Distribution.—*Breeds* locally in California (recorded from the San Francisco Bay area and San Luis Obispo County, formerly also San Diego County); in Kansas (Finney, Franklin, Barton and Riley counties); along the Atlantic coast from New York south to central Florida; on the Gulf coast in eastern Texas (Brazoria Refuge, possibly also Galveston) and western Florida (St. Marks to Clearwater); in Belize (vicinity of Monkey River); and in western Peru, Chile and western Argentina. Recorded in summer (and possibly breeding) south to extreme northern Baja California, Veracruz (Tecolutla), and southern Florida (Everglades), and in Cuba and, at least formerly, Puerto Rico and Jamaica.

Winters along the coast of California from the breeding range north to Tomales Bay; in the Imperial and lower Colorado River valleys of southeastern California; along the Gulf coast from southeastern Texas east to Florida; and in the breeding range in Belize and South America.

In migration recorded sporadically east of the Rocky Mountains from Colorado, Nebraska, Iowa, Minnesota, Wisconsin, Michigan and Pennsylvania south to western Texas, San Luis Potosí and the Gulf coast.

Casual or accidental in Arizona, Guatemala (Dueñas) and Bermuda. Reports from Honduras and Costa Rica require confirmation.

Genus **CREX** Bechstein

> *Crex* Bechstein, 1803, Ornithol. Taschenb. Dtsch., 2, p. 336. Type, by tautonymy, *Crex pratensis* Bechstein = *Rallus crex* Linnaeus.

Crex crex (Linnaeus). CORN CRAKE. [217.]

> *Rallus Crex* Linnaeus, 1758, Syst. Nat., ed. 10, 1, p. 153. (in Europæ agris, carectis = Sweden.)

Habitat.—Grasslands, meadows and cultivated grain fields, mostly in lowland and mountain valleys, occasionally in marshy locations.

Distribution.—*Breeds* from the Faroe Islands, British Isles, Scandinavia, northern Russia and central Siberia south to the northern Mediterranean region, Turkey, Iran and Lake Baikal.

Winters from the Mediterranean region (rarely), south throughout most of Africa, Madagascar and Arabia.

Casual (at least formerly) on Baffin Island, along the Atlantic coast of North America (recorded from Newfoundland, Nova Scotia, Maine, Rhode Island, Connecticut, New York, New Jersey, eastern Pennsylvania and Maryland), Bermuda, Greenland, Iceland, the eastern Atlantic islands, India, Australia and New Zealand.

Genus **RALLUS** Linnaeus

> *Rallus* Linnaeus, 1758, Syst. Nat., ed. 10, 1, p. 153. Type, by subsequent designation (Fleming, 1821), *Rallus aquaticus* Linnaeus.

Rallus longirostris Boddaert. CLAPPER RAIL. [211.]

Rallus longirostris Boddaert, 1783, Table Planches Enlum., p. 52. Based on "Râle à long bec, de Cayenne" Daubenton, Planches Enlum., pl. 849. (Cayenne.)

Habitat.—Salt and brackish marshes and mangrove swamps, locally (mostly in the lower Colorado River Valley) in fresh-water marshes (Tropical and Subtropical zones).

Distribution.—*Resident* [*obseoletus* group] locally along the Pacific coast from central California (Marin County) south to central Baja California (Magdalena Bay), on the Gulf coast of southern Baja California (near La Paz, and on San José and Espíritu Santo islands), in the interior of southeastern California and southwestern Arizona at the southern end of the Salton Sea and in the lower Colorado River Valley (where absent in winter), and along the Pacific coast from Sonora to Nayarit; and [*longirostris* group] along the Atlantic and Gulf coasts from Connecticut south to southern Florida and west to southern Texas (Brownsville), in the Bahamas and Antilles (south to Antigua, also on Guadeloupe), in Quintana Roo (Chinchorro Reef, possibly also Cayo Culebra and Holbox Island), the state of Yucatán (Río Lagartos) and Belize (Ycacos Lagoon), and along both coasts of South America (also Margarita Island and Trinidad) south to northwestern Peru and southeastern Brazil. Northernmost populations tend to be partially migratory.

Wanders casually [*obseoletus* group] on the Pacific coast to the Farallon Islands, north to northern California (Humboldt Bay), and south to southern Baja California (Todos Santos); and [*longirostris* group] on the Atlantic coast north to New Brunswick, Prince Edward Island, Nova Scotia and Newfoundland, and inland to central Nebraska (near Stapleton), central New York, Vermont, West Virginia and central Virginia.

Notes.—*R. longirostris* and *R. elegans* constitute a superspecies; some authors consider them to be conspecific. The populations along the Pacific coast of North America and in the Colorado River Valley region have variously been treated as races of *R. longirostris,* races of *R. elegans,* or a separate species, *R. obsoletus* Ridgway, 1874 [WESTERN RAIL, 210]. See also comments under *R. elegans.*

Rallus elegans Audubon. KING RAIL. [208.]

Rallus elegans Audubon, 1834, Birds Am. (folio), 3, pl. 203; 1835, Ornithol. Biogr., 3, p. 27. (Kentucky, South Carolina, Louisiana and north to Camden, N. J. and Philadelphia = Charleston, South Carolina.)

Habitat.—Fresh-water and, locally, brackish marshes.

Distribution.—*Breeds* locally from eastern Nebraska, Iowa, central Minnesota, southern Wisconsin, southern Michigan, extreme southern Ontario, central New York, Connecticut and (rarely) Massachusetts south through northwestern and central Kansas, central Oklahoma and most of the eastern United States to western and southern Texas, southern Louisiana, central Mississippi, central Alabama and southern Florida; in the Greater Antilles (Cuba and the Isle of Pines); and in the interior of Mexico (from Nayarit, Jalisco, Guanajuato and San Luis Potosí south to Guerrero, Morelos and Puebla).

Winters primarily from southern Georgia, Florida, the southern portions of the Gulf states, and southern Texas south to Guerrero, Puebla and Veracruz, and in Cuba and the Isle of Pines; occurs less frequently in winter in the central portions of the breeding range, and casually to the northern limits.

Casual or accidental in eastern Colorado (Pueblo), North Dakota, southern Manitoba, east-central Ontario, southern Quebec, Maine and Newfoundland.

Notes.—The breeding population in the interior of Mexico has been treated as a race of *R. longirostris* by some authors. See also comments under *R. longirostris*.

Rallus limicola Vieillot. VIRGINIA RAIL. [212.]

> *Rallus limicola* Vieillot, 1819, Nouv. Dict. Hist. Nat., nouv. éd., 28, p. 558. (États Unis = Pennsylvania.)

Habitat.—Fresh-water and occasionally brackish marshes, mostly in cattails, reeds and deep grasses (Subtropical and Temperate zones).

Distribution.—*Breeds* locally in North America from southern British Columbia, northwestern Alberta, central Saskatchewan, central Manitoba, western and southern Ontario, southern Quebec, New Brunswick, Prince Edward Island (probably), Nova Scotia and southwestern Newfoundland south to northwestern Baja California, southern Arizona, southern New Mexico, west-central Texas, western Oklahoma, Kansas, Missouri, Illinois, northern Indiana, central Ohio, western Virginia, northern Georgia and coastal North Carolina, also in central Louisiana and northern Alabama; in the interior of central Mexico (Puebla, Tlaxcala and the state of México, probably also central Veracruz, Oaxaca and western Chiapas); and in South America from southwestern Colombia to western Peru, and in southern Chile and southern Argentina south to the Straits of Magellan.

Winters in North America from southern British Columbia and western Washington south to northern Baja California, and from northern Sonora, Chihuahua, central Texas, the Gulf coast and coastal North Carolina south locally through most of Mexico to central Guatemala, casually in interior North America north to Montana, Colorado, Illinois, Michigan, southern Ontario, New York and Massachusetts; and in the breeding range in Mexico and South America.

Casual or accidental in Bermuda, Cuba and Greenland, also a sight report for Puerto Rico.

[Rallus aquaticus Linnaeus. WATER RAIL.] See Appendix B.

Genus **ARAMIDES** Pucheran

> *Aramides* Pucheran, 1845, Rev. Zool. [Paris], 8, p. 277. Type, by subsequent designation (Sclater and Salvin, 1869), *Fulica cayennensis* Gmelin = *Fulica cajanea* Müller.

Notes.—Ripley (1977, Rails World, p. 44) merges this genus with the Old World *Eulabeornis* Gould, 1844.

Aramides cajanea (Müller). GRAY-NECKED WOOD-RAIL.

> *Fulica cajanea* P. L. S. Müller, 1776, Natursyst., Suppl., p. 119. Based on "Poule d'eau, de Cayenne" Daubenton, Planches Enlum., pl. 352. (Cayenne.)

Habitat.—Marshes, mangrove swamps and wet lowland forest (Tropical and lower Subtropical zones).

Distribution.—*Resident* from southern Tamaulipas, Hidalgo, Distrito Federal and Oaxaca south along both slopes of Middle America (including Cozumel Island off Quintana Roo, and the Pearl Islands off Panama), and in South America from northern Colombia, Venezuela (also Trinidad) and the Guinas south, east of the Andes, to eastern Peru, eastern Bolivia, northern Argentina and Uruguay.

Aramides axillaris Lawrence. RUFOUS-NECKED WOOD-RAIL.

Aramides axillaris Lawrence, 1863, Proc. Acad. Nat. Sci. Philadelphia, 15, p. 107. (Barranquilla, New Granada [=Colombia].)

Habitat.—Mangroves and coastal lagoons, rarely in wet forest (Tropical and lower Subtropical zones).

Distribution.—*Resident* locally on the Pacific slope of central Mexico (recorded Sinaloa, Nayarit and Guerrero), in the state of Yucatán (Isla Mujeres and Las Bocas de Silán), Belize, Honduras (Isla Guanaja in the Bay Islands, and Pacific coast of Bay of Fonseca), western Nicaragua (San Cristóbal and Volcán Mombacho) and Panama (on the Caribbean coast in northwestern Bocas del Toro and the Canal Zone, and on the Pacific in southern Coclé), and along the coasts of northern South America (also Trinidad and Isla Los Roques, off northern Venezuela) south to Ecuador and east to Surinam.

Genus **AMAUROLIMNAS** Sharpe

Amaurolimnas Sharpe, 1893, Bull. Br. Ornithol. Club, 1, p. xxviii. Type, by original designation, *A. concolor* (Gosse) = *Rallus concolor* Gosse.

Amaurolimnas concolor (Gosse). UNIFORM CRAKE.

Rallus concolor Gosse, 1847, Birds Jamaica, p. 369. (Basin Spring, and the neighbourhood of the Black River, in St. Elizabeth's, Jamaica.)

Habitat.—Swamps, dense thickets along forested streams, humid lowland forest and dense second growth (Tropical Zone).

Distribution.—*Resident* locally from southern Mexico (recorded Veracruz, Oaxaca, Tabasco and Chiapas) south through Middle America (not recorded El Salvador), and in South America very locally in western Ecuador, Guyana, and from eastern Colombia and Amazonian Brazil south to eastern Peru, northern Bolivia and southeastern Brazil; also formerly in Jamaica (last reported in 1881).

Genus **PORZANA** Vieillot

Porzana Vieillot, 1816, Analyse, p. 61. Type, by tautonymy, "Marouette" Buffon = *Rallus porzana* Linnaeus.
Pennula Dole, 1878, *in* Thrum, Hawaii. Almanac Annual (1879), p. 54. Type, by monotypy, *Pennula millei* [sic] Dole = *Rallus sandwichensis* Gmelin.
Porzanula Frohawk, 1892, Ann. Mag. Nat. Hist., ser. 6, 9, p. 247. Type, by monotypy, *Porzanula palmeri* Frohawk.

Porzana porzana (Linnaeus). SPOTTED CRAKE.

Rallus Porzana Linnaeus, 1766, Syst. Nat., ed. 12, 1, p. 262. (in Europa ad ripas = France.)

Habitat & Distribution.—*Breeds* in swamps, wet meadows and marshes throughout Europe east to northern Russia and Lake Baikal, and *winters* south to central Africa and the Bay of Bengal, rarely to the eastern Atlantic islands and southern Africa.

Accidental in the Lesser Antilles (Marigot, St. Martin, 8 October 1956; Voous, 1957, Ardea, pp. 89–90) and Greenland.

Porzana carolina (Linnaeus). SORA. [214.]

Rallus carolinus Linnaeus, 1758, Syst. Nat., ed. 10, 1, p. 153. Based on "The Little American Water Hen" Edwards, Nat. Hist. Birds, 3, p. 144, pl. 144, and the "Soree" Catesby, Nat. Hist. Carolina, 1, p. 70, pl. 70. (in America septentrionali = Hudson Bay.)

Habitat.—Primarily fresh-water marshes, less frequently in flooded fields, sometimes foraging on open mudflats adjacent to marshy habitat.

Distribution.—*Breeds* from southeastern Alaska (Stikine River), northwestern British Columbia, southern Yukon, west-central and southwestern Mackenzie, northern Saskatchewan, northern Manitoba, northern Ontario, west-central and southern Quebec, New Brunswick, Prince Edward Island, Nova Scotia and southwestern Newfoundland south locally to northwestern Baja California, central Nevada, central Arizona, southern New Mexico, eastern Colorado, central Oklahoma, southern Missouri, central Illinois, central Indiana, central Ohio, West Virginia and Maryland.

Winters regularly from central California, central Arizona, northern New Mexico, southern Texas, the Gulf coast and southern South Carolina south through Middle America (including Cozumel Island and Chinchorro Reef, but not recorded El Salvador), the West Indies and northern South America (also the Netherlands Antilles, Tobago and Trinidad) west of the Andes to central Peru and east of the Andes to eastern Colombia, eastern Ecuador, Venezuela and Guyana; occasionally occurs in winter north to extreme southern Canada and the northern United States.

Casual or accidental in east-central Alaska, the Queen Charlotte Islands, southern Labrador, Bermuda, Greenland and the British Isles.

Porzana flaviventer (Boddaert). YELLOW-BREASTED CRAKE.

Rallus flaviventer Boddaert, 1783, Table Planches Enlum., p. 52. Based on "Petit Râle, de Cayenne" Daubenton, Planches Enlum., pl. 847. (Cayenne.)

Habitat.—Fresh-water marshes, borders of lakes and ponds, and, less frequently, swamps (Tropical and lower Subtropical zones).

Distribution.—*Resident* locally in the Greater Antilles (Cuba, Jamaica, Hispaniola and Puerto Rico), and from southern Mexico (Michoacán, Guerrero, Puebla, Veracruz and Chiapas) south through Guatemala (La Avellana), El Salvador (Lake Olomega), Nicaragua (Río San Juan) and Costa Rica (Guanacaste) to Panama (east to eastern Panamá province, and on Isla Coiba), and in South America from Colombia, Venezuela (also Trinidad) and the Guianas south, east of the Andes, to northern Argentina, Paraguay and eastern Brazil.

Notes.—Some authors place this species in the Old World genus *Poliolimnas* Sharpe, 1893.

†**Porzana sandwichensis** (Gmelin). HAWAIIAN RAIL. [214.1.]

> *Rallus sandwichensis* Gmelin, 1789, Syst. Nat., 1 (2), p. 717. Based on the "Sandwich Rail" Latham, Gen. Synop. Birds, 3 (1), p. 236. (in insulis Sandwich = Hawaii.)

Habitat.—Open country below the forest belt, presumably in grassy areas.
Distribution.—EXTINCT. Formerly *resident* on Hawaii in the Hawaiian Islands; last specimen taken in 1864, last reported in 1884.
Notes.—*Porzana millsi* (Dole, 1878) is a synonym.

†**Porzana palmeri** (Frohawk). LAYSAN RAIL. [214.2]

> *Porzanula Palmeri* Frohawk, 1892, Ann. Mag. Nat. Hist., ser. 6, 9, p. 247. (Laysan Island, lat. 25°46′N., long. 171°49′W.)

Habitat.—Grass tussocks and scattered vegetation in sandy areas, foraging often in more open areas.
Distribution.—EXTINCT. Formerly *resident* on Laysan Island, in the Hawaiian Islands, where it disappeared between 1923 and 1936.
Introduced and established in the Midway group on Eastern Island (between 1887 and 1891, extirpated around 1944) and subsequently on Sand Island (in 1910, last reported 1943); attempted introductions elsewhere in the western Hawaiian Islands were unsuccessful.

Genus **NEOCREX** Sclater and Salvin

> *Neocrex* Sclater and Salvin, 1869, Proc. Zool. Soc. London (1868), p. 457. Type, by monotypy, *Porzana erythrops* Sclater.

Neocrex columbianus Bangs. COLOMBIAN CRAKE.

> *Neocrex columbianus* Bangs, 1898, Proc. Biol. Soc. Wash., 12, p. 171. (Palomina, Santa Marta Mountains, Colombia.)

Habitat.—Fresh-water marshes, swamps and wet savanna (Tropical and Subtropical zones).
Distribution.—*Resident* in western Colombia and western Ecuador. Recorded from (and probably resident in) central Panama (Achiote Road just beyond the Canal Zone border in western Colón, 8 November 1965; Wetmore, 1967, Proc. Biol. Soc. Wash., 80, p. 229).
Notes.—Considered by some authors to be conspecific with *N. erythrops,* with which it constitutes a superspecies.

Neocrex erythrops (Sclater). PAINT-BILLED CRAKE. [217.1.]

> *Porzana erythrops* Sclater, 1867, Proc. Zool. Soc. London, p. 343, pl. 21. (Lima, Peru.)

Habitat & Distribution.—*Resident* in marshes, swamps and wet savanna in South America in the Galapagos Islands, western Peru, and from eastern Colombia, Venezuela and the Guianas south, east of the Andes, to northwestern Argentina, Paraguay and eastern Brazil.
Accidental in Panama (Bocas del Toro, November 1981, specimen, N. Smith), Texas (near College Station, Brazos County, 17 February 1972; Arnold, 1978,

Auk, 95, pp. 745–746) and Virginia (western Henrico County, 15 December 1978; Blem, 1980, Wilson Bull., 92, pp. 393–394); some of these individuals may have been transported by man.

Notes.—See comments under *N. columbianus.*

Genus CYANOLIMNAS Barbour and Peters

Cyanolimnas Barbour and Peters, 1927, Proc. N. Engl. Zool. Club, 9, p. 95. Type, by monotypy, *Cyanolimnas cerverai* Barbour and Peters.

Cyanolimnas cerverai Barbour and Peters. ZAPATA RAIL.

Cyanolimnas cerverai Barbour and Peters, 1927, Proc. N. Engl. Zool. Club, 9, p. 95. (Santo Tomás, Zapata Peninsula, Cuba, Greater Antilles.)

Habitat.—Fresh-water swamps.

Distribution.—*Resident* only in the Zapata Swamp in the vicinity of Santo Tomás and north of Cochinos Bay, in western Cuba.

Genus PARDIRALLUS Bonaparte

Pardirallus Bonaparte, 1856, C. R. Acad. Sci. Paris, 43, p. 599. Type, by monotypy, *Rallus variegatus* Gmelin = *Rallus maculatus* Boddaert.

Notes.—Some authors merge this genus in *Rallus.*

Pardirallus maculatus (Boddaert). SPOTTED RAIL. [212.2.]

Rallus maculatus Boddaert, 1783, Table Planches Enlum., p. 48. Based on "Le Râle tacheté, de Cayenne" Daubenton, Planches Enlum., pl. 775. (Cayenne.)

Habitat.—Fresh-water marshes, swamps, irrigated fields and wet grasslands (Tropical Zone).

Distribution.—*Resident* locally in Cuba (Havana, Matanzas and Las Villas provinces), the Isle of Pines (probably), Hispaniola (Dominican Republic) and Jamaica (at least formerly, a recent sight record from the Black River marshes); in Mexico, where recorded from Nayarit (near Laguna Agua Brava), Michoacán (Lake Patzcuaro, sight record), Puebla (Laguna San Felipe), Veracruz (Tecolutla and near Tlacotalpan), Guerrero (near Acapulco), Oaxaca (near Putla) and Chiapas (Tuxtla Gutiérrez and San Cristóbal); in Belize (Ycacos Lagoon), Costa Rica (Guanacaste, Turrialba and near Cartago) and Panama (San Blas and eastern Panamá provinces); and in South America from Colombia, Venezuela (also Tobago and Trinidad) and the Guianas south, west of the Andes to northwestern Peru and east of the Andes to east-central Bolivia, northern Argentina, Uruguay and southern Brazil.

Accidental in Pennsylvania (Shippingport, Beaver County), Texas (Brownwood, Brown County) and the Juan Fernandez Islands (off Chile); the North American vagrants may have been man-assisted.

Genus PORPHYRULA Blyth

Porphyrula Blyth, 1852, Cat. Birds Mus. Asiat. Soc. (1849), p. 283. Type, by monotypy, *Porphyrula chloronotus* Blyth = *Porphyrio alleni* Thomson.

Notes.—Sometimes merged in the Old World genus *Porphyrio* Brisson, 1760.

Porphyrula martinica (Linnaeus). PURPLE GALLINULE. [218.]

Fulica martinica Linnaeus, 1766, Syst. Nat., ed. 12, 1, p. 259. (in Martinicæ inundatis = Martinique, West Indies.)

Habitat.—Marshes, especially in areas of rank vegetation, primarily in lowlands, less frequently in highlands in South America (Tropical to Temperate zones).

Distribution.—*Breeds* locally in the interior of the eastern United States in southern Illinois (formerly), western Tennessee and central Ohio, and, primarily in lowlands, on the Pacific coast from Nayarit and on the Atlantic-Gulf-Caribbean coast from Maryland and Delaware south through Middle America, eastern and southern Texas, the Gulf states, Florida, the Greater Antilles and southern Lesser Antilles (Guadeloupe southward) to South America, where found virtually throughout south at least to northern Chile and northern Argentina.

Winters from Nayarit, southern Texas, Louisiana and Florida south throughout the remainder of the breeding range.

Wanders widely but irregularly north to southern California (San Diego), southern Nevada, central Arizona, Utah, Colorado, South Dakota, Minnesota, Wisconsin, Michigan, southern Ontario, southern Quebec, New Brunswick, Nova Scotia, Labrador and Newfoundland, and to the Bahamas and northern Lesser Antilles (north to Barbuda). Casual or accidental in Bermuda, the Galapagos and Falkland islands, Tristan da Cunha, Ascension, St. Helena, the British Isles, continental Europe, the Azores and South Africa.

Notes.—*P. martinica* and the African *P. alleni* Thomson, 1842, appear to constitute a superspecies.

Genus **GALLINULA** Brisson

Gallinula Brisson, 1760, Ornithologie, 1, p. 50; 6, p. 2. Type, by tautonymy, *Gallinula* Brisson = *Fulica chloropus* Linnaeus.

Gallinula chloropus (Linnaeus). COMMON MOORHEN. [219.]

Fulica Chloropus Linnaeus, 1758, Syst. Nat., ed. 10, 1, p. 152. (in Europa = England.)

Habitat.—Fresh-water marshes, lakes and ponds, pr˙ narily in areas of emergent vegetation and grassy borders (Tropical to Temperate zones).

Distribution.—*Breeds* in the Western Hemisphere locally from central California, central Arizona, northern New Mexico, western and north-central Texas, Oklahoma, Kansas, Nebraska, Iowa, central Minnesota, southern Wisconsin, north-central Michigan, southern Ontario, southwestern Quebec, Vermont and Massachusetts (also in New Brunswick and Nova Scotia) south, most frequently in lowlands, throughout Middle America, Bermuda, the West Indies and most of South America (also the Galapagos Islands, Netherlands Antilles, Tobago and Trinidad) to northern Chile and northern Argentina; and in the Old World from the British Isles, Shetlands, southern Scandinavia, central Russia, southern Siberia, Sakhalin and Japan south throughout most of Eurasia and Africa to the eastern Atlantic islands, South Africa, the borders of the northern Indian Ocean (including Ceylon), the East Indies (to Sumbawa and Celebes), Philippines, Formosa, and the Ryukyu, Bonin and Volcano islands.

Winters in eastern North America primarily from South Carolina and the Gulf coast southward, elsewhere in the Americas throughout the breeding range, occasionally north to Utah, Minnesota, southern Ontario and New England; and in the Old World from the British Isles, southern Scandinavia, southern Russia and eastern China south throughout the remainder of the breeding range, casually to the Seven Islands of Izu.

Resident in the Hawaiian Islands (presently resident on Kauai, Oahu and Molokai, formerly on all main islands from Kauai eastward, except Lanai).

Casual north to southern Manitoba, central Ontario, eastern Quebec, New Brunswick, Nova Scotia and Newfoundland. Accidental in Greenland, Iceland, the Faroe Islands, Spitsbergen and the Commander Islands.

Notes.—Also known as COMMON GALLINULE, in New World literature as the FLORIDA GALLINULE, and in Old World literature as the MOORHEN. *G. chloropus* and the Australian *G. tenebrosa* Gould, 1846, constitute a superspecies; they are sometimes considered to be conspecific.

Genus **FULICA** Linnaeus

Fulica Linnaeus, 1758, Syst. Nat., ed. 10, 1, p. 152. Type, by tautonymy, *Fulica atra* Linnaeus (*Fulica,* prebinomial specific name, in synonymy).

Fulica atra Linnaeus. EURASIAN COOT. [220.]

Fulica atra Linnaeus, 1758, Syst. Nat., ed. 10, 1, p. 152. (in Europa = Sweden.)

Habitat & Distribution.—*Breeds* in habitats similar to those of *F. americana* from Iceland, the British Isles and northern Eurasia south to northern Africa, India and eastern China, also in New Guinea and Australia, and *winters* throughout the breeding range and south to the East Indies and Philippines.

Casual or accidental in Alaska (St. Paul, in the Pribilof Islands), Labrador (Tangnaivik Island in Anaktalak Bay, and Separation Point in Sandwich Bay), Newfoundland (Exploits Harbour), Greenland and the Faroe Islands.

Notes.—Also known as EUROPEAN COOT and, in Old World literature, as the COOT.

Fulica americana Gmelin. AMERICAN COOT. [221.]

Fulica americana Gmelin, 1789, Syst. Nat., 1 (2), p. 704. Based on the "Cinereous Coot" Latham, Gen. Synop. Birds, 3 (1), p. 279. (in America septentrionali = North America.)

Habitat.—Fresh-water lakes, ponds, marshes and larger rivers, wintering also on brackish estuaries and bays.

Distribution.—*Breeds* in North America from east-central Alaska (casually), southern Yukon, southern Mackenzie, northwestern and central Saskatchewan, central Manitoba, western and southern Ontario, southwestern Quebec, southern New Brunswick, Prince Edward Island and Nova Scotia south locally to southern Baja California, through Middle America to Nicaragua and northwestern Costa Rica (Guanacaste), and to the Gulf coast, southern Florida, the Bahamas, Greater Antilles (Cuba, the Isle of Pines, Jamaica and Hispaniola) and Grand Cayman.

Winters widely from southeastern Alaska and British Columbia south through the Pacific States, and from northern Arizona, northern New Mexico, central Texas, the lower Mississippi and Ohio valleys, and Maryland (casually north to the Canadian border east of the Rockies) south throughout Middle America, the southeastern United States and West Indies (south to Grenada) to eastern Panama and (apparently) northern Colombia.

Resident in the Hawaiian Islands (all main islands from Niihau eastward, except Lanai); and in the Andes of South America from Colombia south to western Bolivia, northern Chile and northwestern Argentina.

Casual west to the eastern Aleutians, and north to western Alaska (Seward Peninsula), Franklin District, northern Ontario, central Quebec, Labrador, Newfoundland and western Greenland; also to Clipperton Island, islands of the western Caribbean sea (Corn and Providencia), Bermuda and Iceland.

Notes.—The Andean *F. ardesiaca* Tschudi, 1843, has sometimes been treated as a separate species, but it apparently is a color morph of *F. americana* (see Gill, 1964, Condor, 66, pp. 109–111). See also comments under *F. caribaea.*

Fulica caribaea Ridgway. CARIBBEAN COOT. [221.1.]

> *Fulica caribæa* Ridgway, 1884, Proc. U.S. Natl. Mus., 7, p. 358. (St. John, Virgin Islands.)

Habitat.—Fresh-water lakes and ponds, less frequently in coastal brackish lagoons (Tropical Zone).

Distribution.—*Resident* throughout most of the Antilles (south to Grenada and Barbados, but absent from the Isle of Pines and unreported from some of the Lesser Antilles), on Trinidad (questionably on Tobago), on Curaçao, and in northwestern Venezuela.

Since 1974 reported from southern Florida (Broward County), primarily in nonbreeding season. Accidental in Tennessee (Chattanooga).

Notes.—The relationships of *F. americana* and *F. caribaea* are not fully understood; the latter may eventually prove to be a morph of *F. americana.* Individuals with intermediate characteristics have been reported from southern Florida, Cuba, Hispaniola and St. Croix.

Family HELIORNITHIDAE: Sungrebes

Genus HELIORNIS Bonnaterre

> *Heliornis* Bonnaterre, 1791, Tabl. Encycl. Méth., Ornithol., 1, livr. 47, pp. lxxxiv, 64. Type, by monotypy, *Heliornis fulicarius* Bonnaterre = *Colymbus fulica* Boddaert.

Heliornis fulica (Boddaert). SUNGREBE.

> *Colymbus fulica* Boddaert, 1783, Table Planches Enlum., p. 54. Based on "Le Grebifoulque, de Cayenne" Daubenton, Planches Enlum., pl. 893. (Cayenne.)

Habitat.—Fresh-water lakes, sluggish streams and lagoons, especially where overhanging vegetation is dense (Tropical Zone).

Distribution.—*Resident* from San Luis Potosí, central Veracruz, Campeche, northern Chiapas and Quintana Roo south in the Gulf-Caribbean lowlands of Central America to Costa Rica (locally also on the Pacific slope around the Gulf of Nicoya), in Panama (both slopes), and in South America from Colombia, Venezuela and the Guianas south, west of the Andes to western Ecuador and east of the Andes to eastern Peru, east-central Bolivia, Paraguay and southeastern Brazil.

Accidental in Trinidad.

Notes.—Also known as AMERICAN FINFOOT.

Family **EURYPYGIDAE**: Sunbitterns

Genus **EURYPYGA** Illiger

Eurypyga Illiger, 1811, Prodromus, p. 257. Type, by monotypy, *Ardea helias* "Lin. Gm." [=Pallas].

Eurypyga helias (Pallas). SUNBITTERN.

Ardea Helias Pallas, 1781, Neue Nord. Beytr., 2, p. 48, pl. 3. (Brazil.)

Habitat.—Humid lowland and foothill forest, primarily along streams, less frequently in swamps (Tropical and lower Subtropical zones).

Distribution.—*Resident* locally on the Gulf-Caribbean slope of southern Mexico (recorded Tabasco and Chiapas), Guatemala, Honduras and Nicaragua, on both slopes of Costa Rica and Panama, and in the lowlands of South America from Colombia, Venezuela and the Guianas south to northwestern and eastern Peru, central Bolivia and Amazonian Brazil.

Family **ARAMIDAE**: Limpkins

Genus **ARAMUS** Vieillot

Aramus Vieillot, 1816, Analyse, p. 58. Type, by monotypy, "Courliri" Buffon = *Scolopax guarauna* Linnaeus.

Aramus guarauna (Linnaeus). LIMPKIN. [207.]

Scopolax [sic] *Guarauna* Linnaeus, 1766, Syst. Nat., ed. 12, 1, p. 242. Based on "Le Courly brun d'Amérique" Brisson, Ornithologie, 5, p. 330, and "Guarauna" Marcgrave, Hist. Nat. Bras., p. 204. (in America australi = Cayenne.)

Habitat.—Swampy forest, mangroves and marshy lagoons (Tropical Zone).

Distribution.—*Resident* in southeastern Georgia (north to the Altamaha River), Florida (absent from the Panhandle west of Wakulla County, and a visitant only in the Florida Keys) and the Greater Antilles (Cuba, the Isle of Pines, Jamaica, Hispaniola and Puerto Rico, including Gonâve and Tortue islands), and from Veracruz, Oaxaca, Tabasco, Campeche and Quintana Roo (including Cozumel Island) south along both slopes of Middle America, and in South America from Colombia, Venezuela (also Trinidad) and the Guianas south, west of the Andes to western Ecuador and east of the Andes to eastern Peru, Bolivia, northern Argentina and Uruguay.

Casual or accidental in Texas (Jefferson and Cameron counties), Maryland and the Bahamas.

Family **GRUIDAE**: Cranes

Subfamily GRUINAE: Typical Cranes

Genus **GRUS** Pallas

Grus Pallas, 1766, Misc. Zool. p. 66. Type, by tautonymy, *Ardea grus* Linnaeus.
Limnogeranus Sharpe, 1893, Bull. Br. Ornithol. Club, 1, p. xxxvii. Type, by original designation, *Limnogeranus americanus* (L.) = *Ardea americana* Linnaeus.

Grus canadensis (Linnaeus). SANDHILL CRANE. [206.]

Ardea canadensis Linnaeus, 1758, Syst. Nat., ed. 10, 1, p. 141. Based on "The Brown and Ash-colour'd Crane" Edwards, Nat. Hist. Birds, 3, p. 133, pl. 133. (in America septentrionali = Hudson Bay.)

Habitat.—Open grasslands, marshes, swampy edges of lakes and ponds, river banks, and occasionally pine savanna.
Distribution.—*Breeds* from western and central Alaska, northern Yukon, northern Mackenzie, Banks Island, northern Keewatin (Boothia Peninsula), southern Devon Island and Baffin Island south locally to the Chukotski Peninsula, Wrangel and St. Lawrence islands, southern Alaska (the Alaska Peninsula and Cook Inlet), Oregon, northeastern California, northeastern Nevada, north-central Utah, southern Idaho, Wyoming, Colorado, South Dakota, Nebraska (formerly), southern Minnesota, northern Illinois, southern Michigan, northern Ohio (formerly), western (formerly southern) Ontario and western Quebec (James Bay); also locally from northeastern Siberia south to the Chukotski Peninsula.
Winters from central California, Sonora, southeastern Arizona, central New Mexico, western and southern Texas, the Gulf coast and southern Georgia south to northern Baja California, Sinaloa, Jalisco, the state of México, Distrito Federal, Veracruz and central Florida.
In migration recorded regularly throughout North America east to the Great Lakes, Appalachians and northeastern Mexico.
Resident from southern Mississippi, southern Alabama and southern Georgia south through Florida to Cuba and the Isle of Pines, formerly also in southeastern Texas.
Casual in the Pribilof and Aleutian islands, and in eastern North America from Quebec, New Brunswick, Prince Edward Island and Nova Scotia south throughout the eastern United States. Accidental in Quintana Roo (Chinchorro Reef), Ireland and Japan.

Grus grus (Linnaeus). COMMON CRANE. [206.1.]

Ardea Grus Linnaeus, 1758, Syst. Nat., ed. 10, 1, p. 141. (in Europæ, Africæ = Sweden.)

Habitat & Distribution.—*Breeds* in marshes and open areas near water from northern Eurasia south to central Europe, Mongolia and Manchuria, and *winters* from the Mediterranean region east to India, and in Southeast Asia.
Accidental in Alaska (Fairbanks), Alberta (Cavendish, Lethbridge and Athabaska) and Nebraska (Buffalo and Kearney counties, also sight reports North Platte

and Elm Creek), and sight reports for New Mexico (Bitter Lake) and Texas (near Brownfield).

Notes.—Also known as EUROPEAN CRANE and, in Old World literature, as the CRANE.

Grus americana (Linnaeus). WHOOPING CRANE. [204.]

Ardea americana Linnaeus, 1758, Syst. Nat., ed. 10, 1, p. 142. Based on "The Hooping Crane" Catesby, Nat. Hist. Carolina, 1, p. 75, pl. 75, and "The Hooping-Crane from Hudson's Bay" Edwards, Nat. Hist. Birds, 3, p. 132, pl. 132. (in America septentrionali = Hudson Bay.)

Habitat.—Fresh-water marshes and wet prairies, in migration and winter also in grain and stubble fields and on shallow lakes and lagoons.

Distribution.—*Breeds* in south-central Mackenzie (vicinity of Wood Buffalo National Park) and adjacent northern Alberta; formerly bred from southern Mackenzie, northeastern Alberta, northern Saskatchewan and northern Manitoba south to North Dakota, Minnesota and Iowa, and in southeastern Texas and southern Louisiana.

Winters primarily near the coast of southern Texas (mostly in the vicinity of the Aransas National Wildlife Refuge), occasionally northeast to southern Louisiana; formerly wintered from southern Texas and the Gulf coast (east, at least casually, to Georgia and Florida), south to Jalisco, Guanajuato and northern Tamaulipas.

Migrates primarily through the Great Plains from southern Canada and the Dakotas south to Texas; formerly ranged west to Wyoming, Colorado and New Mexico, and east to Ontario, New York, Pennsylvania, New Jersey and South Carolina.

Introduced (through introduction of eggs in nests of *G. canadensis,* not yet breeding) in Idaho (Grays Lake), these birds summering also in Utah, Montana and Wyoming, with wintering primarily in central New Mexico (upper Rio Grande Valley), casually to southeastern Arizona and northwestern Chihuahua (Janos), in migration also through western Colorado and northern New Mexico.

Casual in migration recently east to Illinois (Pike County) and Missouri (Mingo National Wildlife Refuge).

Order CHARADRIIFORMES: Shorebirds, Gulls, Auks and Allies

Notes.—Some authors suggest that various other orders, such as Gaviiformes, Phoenicopteriformes and Columbiformes, or taxa therein, are closely related to or should be included in the Charadriiformes.

Suborder CHARADRII: Plovers and Allies

Family BURHINIDAE: Thick-knees

Genus BURHINUS Illiger

Burhinus Illiger, 1811, Prodromus, p. 250. Type, by monotypy, *Charadrius magnirostris* Latham.

Burhinus bistriatus (Wagler). DOUBLE-STRIPED THICK-KNEE. [269.2.]

Charadrius bistriatus Wagler, 1829, Isis von Oken, col. 648. (Mexico.)

Habitat.—Arid semi-open country, savanna and openings in dry woodland (Tropical Zone).

Distribution.—*Resident* in Middle America from southern Mexico (Veracruz, Tabasco, Oaxaca and Chiapas) south through the Pacific lowlands of Central America to nothwestern Costa Rica (Guanacaste); in the Greater Antilles (Hispaniola); and in South America from northern Colombia east through Venezuela (also Margarita Island) to Guyana and extreme northwestern Brazil.

Casual or accidental in Texas (King Ranch, Kleberg County, 5 December 1961), Barbados (perhaps not a natural vagrant) and Curaçao.

Family CHARADRIIDAE: Plovers and Lapwings

Subfamily VANELLINAE: Lapwings

Tribe HOPLOXYPTERINI: Spur-winged Lapwings

[Genus HOPLOXYPTERUS Bonaparte]

Hoploxypterus Bonaparte, 1856, C. R. Acad. Sci. Paris, 43, p. 418. Type, by monotypy, *Charadrius cayanus* Latham.

Notes.—Often merged in *Vanellus*.

[Hoploxypterus cayanus (Latham). PIED LAPWING.] See Appendix B.

Tribe VANELLINI: Typical Lapwings

Genus VANELLUS Brisson

Vanellus Brisson, 1760, Ornithologie, 1, p. 48; 5, p. 94. Type, by tautonymy, *Vanellus* Brisson = *Tringa vanellus* Linnaeus.
Belonopterus Reichenbach, 1853, Avium Syst. Nat. (1852), p. xviii. Type, by original designation, *Tringa cajennensis* Latham = *Parra cayennensis* Gmelin.

Notes.—See comments under *Hoploxypterus*.

Vanellus vanellus (Linnaeus). NORTHERN LAPWING. [269.]

Tringa Vanellus Linnaeus, 1758, Syst. Nat., ed. 10, 1, p. 148. (in Europa, Africa = Sweden.)

Habitat.—Open fields, pastures, wet meadows, bogs, and grassy banks of ponds and lakes, in migration and winter also cultivated fields, seacoasts and mudflats.

Distribution.—*Breeds* from the Faroe Islands (rarely), British Isles, northern Scandinavia, northern Russia, Transbaicalia and Ussuriland south to Morocco, the northern Mediterranean region, Black Sea, Iran, Turkestan and northern Mongolia.

Winters from the British Isles, central Europe, southern Russia, Asia Minor, Iraq, Iran, India, Burma, China and Japan south to Madeira, the Canary Islands, northern Africa, Southeast Asia, Formosa and the Ryukyu Islands.

Casual to northeastern North America from Baffin Island, Labrador and New-
foundland south through southern Quebec, New Brunswick, Prince Edward Island,
Nova Scotia and New England to New York (Long Island). Accidental in North
Carolina, South Carolina, Bermuda, the Bahamas (Hog Island), Puerto Rico and
Barbados.
Notes.—Known in Old World literature as the LAPWING.

Vanellus chilensis (Molina). SOUTHERN LAPWING.

Parra Chilensis Molina, 1782, Saggio Stor. Nat. Chili, p. 258. (Chile.)

Habitat.—Open country, preferring savanna, short grassy areas and fields, less
commonly in marshes (Tropical to Temperate zones).
Distribution.—*Resident* in South America mostly east of the Andes from Colombia, Venezuela and the Guianas south to Tierra del Fuego.
Casual or irregular visitant to eastern Panama (Chiriquí, eastern Panamá province, eastern San Blas and eastern Darién), Trinidad and the Falkland Islands.
Accidental in the Juan Fernandez Islands.
Reports of individuals of this species from southern Florida (north to Collier
and Palm Beach counties) from 1959 to 1962 are apparently based on escaped
birds.
Notes.—Also known as SPUR-WINGED LAPWING.

Subfamily CHARADRIINAE: Plovers

Genus **PLUVIALIS** Brisson

Pluvialis Brisson, 1760, Ornithologie, 1, p. 46; 5, p. 42. Type, by tautonymy,
Pluvialis aurea Brisson = *Charadrius pluvialis* Linnaeus = *Charadrius
apricarius* Linnaeus.
Squatarola Cuvier, 1817, Règne Anim., 1 (1816), p. 467. Type, by tautonymy,
Tringa squatarola Linnaeus.

Pluvialis squatarola (Linnaeus). BLACK-BELLIED PLOVER. [270.]

Tringa Squatarola Linnaeus, 1758, Syst. Nat., ed. 10, 1, p. 149. (in Europa =
Sweden.)

Habitat.—Tundra (breeding); mudflats, beaches, wet savanna, shores of ponds
and lakes, and flooded fields (nonbreeding).
Distribution.—*Breeds* in North America from northern Alaska (Barrow eastward) south to western Alaska (Hooper Bay, Nelson Island), and from northwestern Mackenzie and Banks, southern Melville, Bathurst, Devon, Bylot and
western and southern Baffin islands south to the Yukon River, north-central
Mackenzie (Cockburn Point), southern Victoria Island, northern Keewatin (Adelaide and Melville peninsulas), and Southampton and Coats islands; and in Eurasia
from north-central Russia east across northern Siberia (including Kolguyev Island,
southern Novaya Zemlya, the New Siberian Islands and Wrangel Island) to the
Gulf of Anadyr. Nonbreeding individuals frequently summer in the wintering
range.
Winters in the Americas primarily in coastal areas from southern British Columbia and New Jersey (rarely New England) south along both coasts of the United
States and Middle America, through the West Indies, and along both coasts of

South America (also the Galapagos and other offshore islands) to central Chile and northern Argentina, also casually throughout the Hawaiian Islands; and in the Old World from the British Isles, southern Europe, northern India, Southeast Asia, southeastern China, southern Japan and the Solomon Islands south to southern Africa, islands of the Indian Ocean, the Malay Peninsula, Australia and New Zealand.

Migrates primarily along coasts in the Northern Hemisphere from western and southern Alaska (casually the Aleutians), Labrador (casually) and Newfoundland southward, and locally through interior North America, especially in the Mississippi and Ohio valleys.

Casual in northern Ellesmere Island, Greenland, Iceland, the Faroe Islands, Azores and Madeira.

Notes.—In Old World literature known as GRAY PLOVER.

Pluvialis apricaria (Linnaeus). GREATER GOLDEN-PLOVER. [271.]

> *Charadrius apricarius* Linnaeus, 1758, Syst. Nat., ed. 10, 1, p. 150. (in Oelandia, Canada = Lapland.)

Habitat & Distribution.—*Breeds,* with habitat requirements similar to those of *P. dominica,* from northern Eurasia south to the British Isles, northern Europe, the Baltic states and Taimyr Peninsula, and *winters* south to northern Africa, the Caspian Sea and eastern India, in migration regularly in Greenland.

Casual in Newfoundland (St. John's, Avalon Peninsula and Cappahayden, 18–20 April 1961; Stephenville Crossing, 24 May 1963; L'Anse-aux-Meadows, 26 April–14 May 1978).

Notes.—Also known as EURASIAN GOLDEN-PLOVER and, in Old World literature, as the GOLDEN PLOVER. *P. apricaria* and *P. dominica* constitute a superspecies.

Pluvialis dominica (Müller). LESSER GOLDEN-PLOVER. [272.]

> *Charadrius Dominicus* P. L. S. Müller, 1776, Natursyst., Suppl., p. 116. Based on "Le Pluvier doré de S. Dominigue" Brisson, Ornithologie, 5, p. 48. (St. Domingo = Hispaniola.)

Habitat.—Grassy tundra (breeding); short grasslands, pastures, mudflats, sandy beaches and flooded fields (nonbreeding).

Distribution.—*Breeds* [*dominica* group] in North America from northern Alaska, northern Yukon, northern Mackenzie, and Banks, southern Melville (probably), Bathurst, Devon and northern Baffin islands south to central Alaska (interior mountain ranges), southern Yukon, northwestern British Columbia, central Mackenzie, southern Keewatin, northeastern Manitoba, northern Ontario (Cape Henrietta Maria), and Southampton and southern Baffin islands; and [*fulva* group] along the Bering coast of Alaska (Wales south to Kuskokwim River, including St. Lawrence, Nunivak and Nelson islands), and in Eurasia from the Arctic coast of Siberia (Yamal Peninsula eastward) south to the Stanovoi and Koryak mountains and the Gulf of Anadyr. Nonbreeding individuals summer in the wintering range [*dominica* group] south to northern South America and [*fulva* group] in the Hawaiian Islands.

Winters [*dominica* group] in South America from Bolivia, Uruguay and southern Brazil south to northern Chile and northern Argentina; and [*fulva* group] in the Old World from northeastern Africa, the Red Sea, India, southern China, Formosa and islands of Polynesia south to the Malay Peninsula, Australia, Tasmania, New Zealand, the Tonga and Tuamotu islands and, casually, in coastal southern California.

Migrates [*dominica* group] in spring through Middle America and the interior of North America (from the Rockies to the Mississippi Valley), casually to the Pacific and Atlantic coasts, and in fall mostly from Newfoundland and Nova Scotia to New England, thence southward over the Atlantic, rarely through the West Indies and the interior of North America; and [*fulva* group] in the Hawaiian Islands, through the Aleutians, along the Pacific coast of North America south to California, and in Eurasia primarily in eastern Asia and over oceanic islands of the Pacific.

Casual or accidental [*dominica* group] in Bermuda, Greenland, the British Isles and continental Europe; and [*fulva* group] inland in western North America (to Alberta and Idaho), on Isla Clarión (in the Revillagigedo group), and in Maine, Chile, Greenland, Europe, the Cape Verde Islands, Mediterranean region, eastern Africa and Arabia.

Notes.—Also known as AMERICAN GOLDEN-PLOVER. Recent studies suggest that the two groups breed sympatrically in western Alaska and may represent separate species, *P. dominica* [AMERICAN GOLDEN-PLOVER, 272] and *P. fulva* (Gmelin, 1789) [ASIATIC GOLDEN-PLOVER, 272.1]. See also comments under *P. apricaria.*

Genus **CHARADRIUS** Linnaeus

Charadrius Linnaeus, 1758, Syst. Nat., ed. 10, 1, p. 150. Type, by tautonymy, *Charadrius hiaticula* Linnaeus (*Charadrius s. Hiaticula,* prebinomial specific name, in synonymy).
Eudromias C. L. Brehm, 1830, Isis von Oken, col. 987. Type, by monotypy, *Charadrius morinellus* Linnaeus.
Eupoda J. F. Brandt, 1845, *in* Tchihatchev, Voy. Sci. Altai Orient., p. 444. Type, by monotypy, *Charadrius asiaticus* Pallas.
Aegialeus Reichenbach, 1853, Avium Syst. Nat. (1852), p. 18. Type, by original designation, *Charadrius semipalmatus* "Aud." [=Bonaparte].
Oxyechus Reichenbach, 1853, Avium Syst. Nat. (1852), p. 18. Type, by original designation, *Charadrius vociferus* Linnaeus.
Ochthodromus (not *Ochthedromus* Le Conte, 1848, Coleoptera) Reichenbach, 1853, Avium Syst. Nat. (1852), p. 18. Type, by original designation, *Charadrius wilsonia* Ord.
Leucopolius Bonaparte, 1856, C. R. Acad. Sci. Paris, 43, p. 417. Type, by tautonymy, *Charadrius niveifrons* Cuvier = *Charadrius leucopolius* Wagler = *Charadrius marginatus* Vieillot.
Podasocys Coues, 1866, Proc. Acad. Nat. Sci. Philadelphia, 18, p. 96. Type, by original designation, *Charadrius montanus* Townsend.
Pagolla Mathews, 1913, Birds Aust., 3, p. 83. New name for *Ochthodromus* Reichenbach, preoccupied.

Charadrius mongolus Pallas. MONGOLIAN PLOVER. [279.]

Charadrius mongolus Pallas, 1776, Reise Versch. Prov. Russ. Reichs, 3, p. 700. (circa lacus salsos versus Mongoliae fines = Kulussutai, probably on the Onon River, eastern Siberia.)

Habitat.—Mudflats, beaches and shores of lakes and ponds, breeding on barren flats and steppe along sandy and stony banks of rivers, lakes and ponds.

Distribution.—*Breeds* in central and northeastern Asia from the Pamirs east to western Sinkiang and through Tibet to the Nan Shan ranges, and on the Chukotski Peninsula, Kamchatka and the Commander Islands; also has bred in North America in northern and western Alaska (Brooks Range, Choris Peninsula, Goodnews Bay, Seward Peninsula).

Winters in the Old World from the Red Sea, Iran, India, Southeast Asia, southeastern China and the Philippines south to southern Africa, the Seychelles, Ceylon, the Andaman Islands, Java, New Guinea and Australia.

In migration occurs regularly in the Aleutians (east to Adak), on islands in the Bering Sea (St. Lawrence and the Pribilofs), and in coastal western Alaska, casually to northern Alaska (Barrow) and south-coastal Alaska (Cook Inlet).

Accidental in the Hawaiian Islands (Lisianski), Oregon (Tillamook Bay, Columbia River), California (Moss Landing) and Louisiana (Grand Isle).

Charadrius collaris Vieillot. COLLARED PLOVER.

Charadrius collaris Vieillot, 1818, Nouv. Dict. Hist. Nat., nouv. éd., 27, p. 136. Based on "Mbatuitui Collar negro" Azara, Apunt. Hist. Nat. Páx. Parag., 3, p. 291 (no. 392). (Paraguay.)

Habitat.—Beaches, sandy savanna, and shores of rivers, lakes and ponds (Tropical Zone).

Distribution.—*Resident* primarily in coastal areas from Sinaloa and Veracruz south through Middle America, in the southern Lesser Antilles (Mustique in the Grenadines, and Grenada), and in South America from Colombia, Venezuela (also the Netherlands Antilles, Margarita Island, Tobago and Trinidad) and the Guianas south, west of the Andes to western Ecuador and east of the Andes to central Argentina, also occasionally in central Chile.

Charadrius alexandrinus Linnaeus. SNOWY PLOVER. [278.]

Charadrius alexandrinus Linnaeus, 1758, Syst. Nat., ed. 10, 1, p. 150. (ad Ægypti ex Nilo canalem = Egypt.)

Habitat.—Beaches, dry mud or salt flats, and sandy shores of rivers, lakes and ponds (Tropical to Temperate zones).

Distribution.—*Breeds* in western and central North America along the Pacific coast from southern Washington to southern Baja California, and locally from interior southern Oregon, northeastern California, western Nevada, Utah, southwestern Montana, Colorado, central Kansas and north-central Oklahoma south to southeastern California, southern Arizona, southern New Mexico and north-central Texas; along the Gulf coast from Florida (south locally to Marco Island and, probably, the Florida Keys) west to Texas and northeastern Tamaulipas; in the southern Bahamas (north to Andros, Exuma and San Salvador), Greater Antilles (east to the Virgin Islands) and Lesser Antilles (St. Martin); on islands off the north coast of Venezuela (Curaçao east to Margarita Island); on the Pacific coast of Oaxaca (Laguna Superior); along the Pacific coast of South America in Peru and Chile; and in Eurasia from southern Sweden, central Russia, central Siberia and Japan south to the Cape Verde Islands, Mauritania, North Africa, the Red

Sea, northwestern India, Ceylon, Java, southeastern China and the southern Ryukyu Islands.

Winters on islands and in coastal areas of North America from northern Oregon, the Gulf coast and Bahamas south to southern Mexico (casually to Guatemala, Honduras, Costa Rica and Panama) and the Greater Antilles; in the breeding range in South America; and in the Old World from the Mediterranean region and breeding range in Asia south to tropical Africa, Arabia, Ceylon, Southeast Asia, the East Indies, Philippines, Formosa and the Bonin Islands, casually from Sakhalin to the Palau Islands.

Casual in the interior of North America north to southern British Columbia (in coastal regions to the Queen Charlotte Islands), Idaho, Montana, southern Saskatchewan, Minnesota, Wisconsin and southern Ontario, to the Atlantic coast of Florida (Merritt Island), and in the Florida Keys; a sight record from the Hawaiian Islands (Oahu) is questionable.

Notes.—Known in Old World literature as KENTISH PLOVER. The western South American form is sometimes considered as a separate species, *C. occidentalis* (Cabanis, 1872); *C. alexandrinus,* the Australian *C. ruficapillus* Temminck, 1822, and the African *C. marginatus* Vieillot, 1818, constitute a superspecies and are treated as conspecific by some authors.

Charadrius wilsonia Ord. WILSON'S PLOVER. [280.]

Charadrius wilsonia Ord, 1814, *in* Wilson, Am. Ornithol., 9, p. 77, pl. 73, fig. 5. (shore of Cape Island [=Cape May], New Jersey.)

Habitat.—Sandy beaches, tidal mudflats and savanna pools, rarely far from coastal areas.

Distribution.—*Breeds* from central Baja California, northern Sonora and southern New Jersey south along the Pacific and Atlantic-Gulf-Caribbean coasts of Middle America (not recorded Nicaragua), the southeastern United States and West Indies (absent in Lesser Antilles south of Dominica, except for the Grenadines, where present) to Panama (including the Pearl Islands) and northern South America east to northeastern Brazil (including islands off the coast of Venezuela); also one breeding record for southeastern California (Salton Sea).

Winters from Baja California, Sonora, the Gulf coast of Louisiana and Texas, and Florida south along the Pacific coast to northwestern Peru and in the Caribbean-Gulf-Atlantic region throughout the breeding range to northern South America.

Casual north to southern California (Ventura and San Diego counties), in the interior to Minnesota (Duluth), Illinois (Glencoe) and the Lake Erie region (southern Ontario, Ohio and Pennsylvania), along the Atlantic coast to Nova Scotia, and on Barbados.

Notes.—Also known THICK-BILLED PLOVER.

Charadrius hiaticula Linnaeus. COMMON RINGED PLOVER. [275.]

Charadrius Hiaticula Linnaeus, 1758, Syst. Nat., ed. 10, 1, p. 150. (in Europa & America ad ripas = Sweden.)

Habitat.—Sandy areas with scattered low vegetation, cultivated fields, shortgrass areas near water, and grassy tundra, in migration and winter also mudflats, beaches and shores of lakes, ponds and rivers.

Distribution.—*Breeds* in North America in western Alaska (St. Lawrence Island), and on Ellesmere, Bylot and eastern Baffin islands; and in the Palearctic in Greenland, Iceland and the Faroe Islands, and from Scandinavia, northern Russia and northern Siberia south to the northern Mediterranean region, the Chukotski Peninsula, Anadyrland and the Sea of Okhotsk.

Winters from the British Isles, western Europe, the Mediterranean region, Persian Gulf, western India and Sakhalin south to the eastern Atlantic islands, the Canary Islands, southern Africa, the Maldive Islands, northern China, Japan, the Volcano Islands and (casually) to Australia.

In migration ranges casually to St. Lawrence and the Aleutian islands (Amchitka, Adak), and the mainland of western Alaska (Wales).

Accidental in the Lesser Antilles (Barbados).

Notes.—Also known as the RINGED PLOVER. *C. hiaticula* and *C. semipalmatus* constitute a superspecies; they are considered conspecific by some authors.

Charadrius semipalmatus Bonaparte. SEMIPALMATED PLOVER. [274.]

Tringa hiaticula (not *Charadrius hiaticula* Linnaeus) Ord, 1824, *in* Wilson, Am. Ornithol., Ord reprint, 7, p. 65. (coast of New Jersey.)
Charadrius semipalmatus Bonaparte, 1825, J. Acad. Nat. Sci. Philadelphia, 5, p. 98. New name for *Tringa hiaticula* Ord, preoccupied.

Habitat.—Sandy areas, and grassy or mossy tundra (breeding); mudflats, shallow marshes, beaches, flooded fields, and shores of lakes and ponds (nonbreeding).

Distribution.—*Breeds* from northern Alaska, northern Yukon, northern Mackenzie, Banks, Victoria and southern Somerset islands, northern Keewatin (Melville Peninsula), central Baffin Island and the northern Labrador coast south to the Pribilof and eastern Aleutian islands, western Alaska (the Alaska Peninsula), the Queen Charlotte Islands, southwestern and central British Columbia, southeastern Yukon, southern Mackenzie, northeastern Alberta, northern Saskatchewan, northern Manitoba, northern Ontario (coast of Hudson and James bays), central Quebec and, coastally, the Gulf of St. Lawrence, southern New Brunswick, southern Nova Scotia, and Newfoundland. Nonbreeding birds often summer in the wintering areas south to Panama.

Winters primarily in coastal areas from central California, central Sonora, the Gulf coast and South Carolina south through the West Indies, and along both coasts of Middle America and South America (also the Galapagos Islands, Tobago and Trinidad) to central Chile and Argentina (Patagonia).

Migrates along both coasts of North America and commonly through the interior, rarely or casually in the intermountain region from Idaho and Montana to Arizona, and casually to the Hawaiian Islands and western Aleutians.

Casual in Bermuda, Greenland, the British Isles, eastern Siberia, and Johnston and Baker islands in the Pacific.

Notes.—See comments under *C. hiaticula*.

Charadrius melodus Ord. PIPING PLOVER. [277.]

Charadrius melodus Ord, 1824, *in* Wilson, Am. Ornithol., Ord reprint, 7, p. 71. (Great Egg Harbor, New Jersey.)

Habitat.—Sandy beaches, especially where scattered grass tufts are present, in migration and winter also mudflats, flooded fields and shores of lakes and ponds.

Distribution.—*Breeds* locally in the interior of North America from south-central Alberta, southern Saskatchewan and south-central Manitoba south to eastern Montana, northwestern North Dakota, southeastern South Dakota (Union County), and central and eastern Nebraska; in the Great Lakes region (locally, formerly more widespread) from northern Michigan (Schoolcraft and Alger counties) and southern Ontario south to the southern shores of lakes Michigan (in northeastern Illinois and Michigan), Erie (formerly) and Ontario; and in the coastal areas from northern New Brunswick, Prince Edward Island, southern Nova Scotia, southeastern Quebec (including Magdalen Islands) and Newfoundland south along the Atlantic coast to Virginia and (formerly) North Carolina.

Winters primarily on the Atlantic-Gulf coast from South Carolina south to Florida and west to eastern Texas, and, less commonly, throughout the Bahamas and Greater Antilles (east to the Virgin Islands).

Migrates through the interior of North America east of the Rockies (especially in the Mississippi Valley) as well as along the Atlantic coast.

Casual in southern California, southern Arizona, northwestern Sonora (Puerto Peñasco), southern New Mexico (sight reports), the interior of Texas, Bermuda and Barbados.

Charadrius dubius Scopoli. LITTLE RINGED PLOVER. [276.]

> *Charadrius (dubius)* Scopoli, 1786, Del Flor. Faun. Insubr., fasc. 2, p. 93. (Luzon, Philippines.)

Habitat & Distribution.—*Breeds* along inland fresh-water areas from northern Eurasia south to the eastern Atlantic islands, northern Africa, Ceylon, Southeast Asia, the East Indies, New Guinea and the Bismarck Archipelago, and *winters* from southern Europe, the Caspian and Black seas, India, eastern China and Japan south to tropical Africa and Australia.

Accidental in the Aleutian Islands (Buldir, 15–16 June 1974; Byrd, Trapp and Gibson, 1978, Condor, 80, p. 310); earlier reports from Alaska (Kodiak Island) and California (San Francisco) are regarded as unsatisfactory.

Charadrius vociferus Linnaeus. KILLDEER. [273.]

> *Charadrius vociferus* Linnaeus, 1758, Syst. Nat., ed. 10, 1, p. 150. Based on "The Chattering Plover" Catesby, Nat. Hist. Carolina, 1, p. 71, pl. 71. (in America septentrionali = South Carolina.)

Habitat.—Fields, meadows, pastures, mudflats, and shores of lakes, ponds and rivers, less commonly along seacoasts, breeding in open dry or gravelly situations.

Distribution.—*Breeds* in North America from east-central and southeastern Alaska, southern Yukon, western and southern Mackenzie, northern Saskatchewan, northern Manitoba, northern Ontario, central Quebec (including the Magdalen Islands), New Brunswick, Prince Edward Island, western Nova Scotia and western Newfoundland south to southern Baja California, central Mexico (recorded breeding to Guerrero and Guanajuato), Tamaulipas, the Gulf coast and southern Florida; in the southern Bahamas (Inagua, Caicos and Turks islands, probably also New Providence) and the Greater Antilles (east to the Virgin Islands); and in western South America along the coast of Peru and extreme northwestern Chile.

Winters from southeastern Alaska (rarely), southern British Columbia, Oregon, the central United States from Utah east to the Ohio Valley (casually from southern

Canada east of British Columbia), and New England south throughout the remainder of North America, Middle America, Bermuda, the West Indies and northern South America (also most islands offshore) west of the Andes to western Ecuador and eastward to northern Venezuela; also in the breeding range in Peru and Chile.

Casual in the Hawaiian Islands (Oahu, Maui) and Pribilofs; north to western and northern Alaska, northern Yukon, northern Mackenzie, southern Keewatin and central Labrador; and to Greenland, Iceland, the Faroe Islands, British Isles, Azores and Madeira.

Charadrius montanus Townsend. MOUNTAIN PLOVER. [281.]

Charadrius montanus J. K. Townsend, 1837, J. Acad. Nat. Sci. Philadelphia, 7, p. 192. (tableland of the Rocky Mountains = near Sweetwater River, Wyoming.)

Habitat.—Open plains at moderate elevations (breeding); short-grass plains and fields, plowed fields and sandy deserts (nonbreeding).

Distribution.—*Breeds* from extreme southern Alberta (Milk River), northern Montana and northeastern North Dakota (rarely) south through eastern Wyoming, western Nebraska, Colorado and western Kansas to central and southeastern New Mexico, western Texas (Brewster County, Davis Mountains), western Oklahoma (Cimarron County) and western Missouri (Jackson County, formerly).

Winters from central (rarely northern) California, southern Arizona, and central and coastal Texas south to southern Baja California and northern Mexico (Sonora east to Tamaulipas), rarely farther south (recorded Zacatecas).

Casual north to western Washington, southwestern Alberta and southwestern Saskatchewan. Accidental in Massachusetts (Chatham), Virginia (Chincoteague) and Florida, also sight reports from Minnesota and Georgia.

Notes.—Often placed in the genus *Eupoda*. *C. montanus* and the Old World *C. veredus* and *C. asiaticus* Pallas, 1773, appear to constitute a superspecies.

[**Charadrius veredus** Gould. ORIENTAL PLOVER.] See Appendix B.

Charadrius morinellus Linnaeus. EURASIAN DOTTEREL. [269.1.]

Charadrius Morinellus Linnaeus, 1758, Syst. Nat., ed. 10, 1, p. 150. (in Europa = Sweden.)

Habitat.—Stony steppes, plains, newly plowed fields and marginal grassland (breeding); open stony or sandy areas, less frequently marshes, mudflats and seacoasts (nonbreeding).

Distribution.—*Breeds* in North America in northern and western Alaska (Barrow to the Seward Peninsula and St. Lawrence Island); and in Eurasia locally in the mountains of the British Isles, Scandinavia and central Europe, and scattered across northern Russia and Siberia from the Ural Mountains to the Verkhoyansk Mountains and the Kolyma, and in northern Mongolia.

Winters in southern Europe, North Africa, Arabia, Iraq and Iran, casually in the Canary Islands, Madeira, Sakhalin, the Kuriles and Japan.

In migration occurs in coastal western Alaska and the western Aleutians, casually east along the northern coast of Alaska.

Accidental in the Hawaiian Islands (Kure), Washington (Ocean Shores, Westport), California (Farallon Islands) and the Commander Islands.

Notes.—In Old World literature known as the DOTTEREL. Often placed in the monotypic genus *Eudromias*.

Family HAEMATOPODIDAE: Oystercatchers

Genus HAEMATOPUS Linnaeus

Hæmatopus Linnaeus, 1758, Syst. Nat., ed. 10, 1, p. 152. Type, by monotypy, *Haematopus ostralegus* Linnaeus.

[**Haematopus ostralegus** Linnaeus. EURASIAN OYSTERCATCHER.] See Appendix B.

Haematopus palliatus Temminck. AMERICAN OYSTERCATCHER. [286.]

> *Hæmatopus palliatus* Temminck, 1820, Man. Ornithol., ed. 2, 2, p. 532. (à l'Amérique méridionale = Venezuela.)

Habitat.—Rocky and sandy seacoasts and islands.

Distribution.—*Breeds* locally along the Atlantic coast from Massachusetts (Monomoy) south to Florida, and along the Gulf coast west to central Texas and south to the Yucatan Peninsula (including Cozumel Island); in the Bahamas, Greater Antilles and Lesser Antilles (St. Barthélemy, Guadeloupe and the Grenadines); along the Pacific coast from central Baja California (San Benito Islands, possibly also Los Coronados Islands in northern Baja California) and the Gulf of California south to Guerrero (also the Revillagigedo, Tres Marias and Tres Marietas islands), along the coast of Costa Rica, and from the Bay of Panama (Pearl Islands and Los Santos) south to central Chile (Isla de Chiloé); and along the Caribbean-Atlantic coast of South America (also most islands off Venezuela, possibly also Tobago and Trinidad) south to south-central Argentina; recorded in summer and possibly breeding north to Labrador.

Winters on the Atlantic-Gulf coast from North Carolina (casually from New Brunswick) south to southeastern Mexico, casually to Honduras; on the Pacific coast of North America from central Baja California (casually from San Luis Obispo County, California) south to Guatemala and Honduras; and generally in the breeding range in the West Indies and along the South American coast, casually on the Caribbean coast north to the Canal Zone and on the Pacific to Costa Rica.

Casual in southern California (north to Point Reyes, and Salton Sea area), southern Ontario, southern Quebec, Maine and western Argentina.

Notes.—*H. palliatus* and *H. bachmani* are closely related and considered conspecific by some authors [AMERICAN OYSTERCATCHER]; they form a hybrid zone about 200 miles in width in central Baja California. *H. ostralegus* is also considered by some as conspecific with the preceding two; the entire complex constitutes a superspecies. Under a single species treatment, PIED OYSTERCATCHER may be used as the English name.

Haematopus bachmani Audubon. AMERICAN BLACK OYSTERCATCHER. [287.]

> *Hæmatopus Bachmani* Audubon, 1838, Birds Am. (folio), 4, pl. 427, fig. 1 (1839, Ornithol. Biogr., 5, p. 245). (Mouth of the Columbia River.)

Habitat.—Rocky seacoasts and islands, less commonly sandy beaches.

Distribution.—*Resident* from the western Aleutians (Kiska eastward) south along the Pacific coast of North America (including most islands offshore) to central Baja California (Punta Abreojos and Isla de Natividad); also has bred on Round Island, in the southern Bering Sea.

Casual in the Pribilof Islands.

Notes.—Known in American literature as the BLACK OYSTERCATCHER. See comments under *H. palliatus*.

Family RECURVIROSTRIDAE: Stilts and Avocets

Genus HIMANTOPUS Brisson

Himantopus Brisson, 1760, Ornithologie, 1, p. 46; 5, p. 33. Type, by tautonymy, *Himantopus* Brisson = *Charadrius himantopus* Linnaeus.

Himantopus mexicanus (Müller). BLACK-NECKED STILT. [226.]

Charadrius Mexicanus P. L. S. Müller, 1776, Natursyst., Suppl., p. 117. Based on the "Echasse de Mexique" Brisson, Ornithologie, 5, p. 36. (in Mexico.)

Habitat.—Grassy marshes, wet savanna, mudflats, shallow ponds and flooded fields (Tropical to Temperate zones).

Distribution.—*Breeds* [*mexicanus* group] locally on the Atlantic coast from southern New Jersey (formerly), Delaware and Virginia south to southern Florida, and from southern Oregon, Idaho, northern Utah, southern Colorado, eastern New Mexico, central Kansas, the Gulf coast of Texas and southern Louisiana, and the Bahamas south through Middle America, the Antilles (south to Antigua and Montserrat) and most of South America (also the Galapagos Islands, islands off Venezuela, and Tobago and Trinidad) to southern Chile and southern Argentina. Recorded in summer and probably breeding [*mexicanus* group] in eastern Montana and western South Dakota.

Winters [*mexicanus* group] from central California, Sonora, the Gulf coast of Texas and Louisiana, and southern Florida south through Middle America, the West Indies and South America to the limits of the breeding range.

Resident [*knudseni* group] in the Hawaiian Islands (main islands from Niihau eastward, except Lanai and Kahoolawe).

Casual [*mexicanus* group] north to southern British Columbia, southern Alberta, southern Saskatchewan, southern Manitoba, Wisconsin, southern Ontario, and, in the Atlantic coastal region, to New Brunswick, Nova Scotia and Newfoundland, and on Bermuda.

Notes.—The two groups are sometimes regarded as distinct species, *H. mexicanus* [BLACK-NECKED STILT, 226] and *H. knudseni* Stejneger, 1887 [HAWAIIAN STILT, 226.1.]. *H. mexicanus* (including *knudseni*) is sometimes considered conspecific with the Old World *H. himantopus* (Linnaeus, 1758) [PIED or BLACK-WINGED STILT]; they constitute a superspecies, and indeed all members of this genus may form a single superspecies.

Genus RECURVIROSTRA Linnaeus

Recurvirostra Linnaeus, 1758, Syst. Nat., ed. 10, 1, p. 151. Type, by monotypy, *Recurvirostra avosetta* Linnaeus.

Recurvirostra americana Gmelin. AMERICAN AVOCET. [225.]

> *Recurvirostra americana* Gmelin, 1789, Syst. Nat., 1 (2), p. 693. Based mainly on the "American Avoset" Pennant, Arct. Zool., 2, p. 502, pl. 21. (in America septentrionali et nova Hollandia = North America.)

Habitat.—Lowland marshes, mudflats, ponds, alkaline lakes, and estuaries, nesting colonially (usually) on open flats or areas with scattered tufts of grass along lakes (especially alkaline) and marshes.

Distribution.—*Breeds* from southeastern British Columbia, central Alberta, southern Saskatchewan, southwestern Manitoba, southwestern Ontario and Minnesota south locally to southern California, central Nevada, northern Utah, south-central Colorado, southern New Mexico and San Luis Potosí, and east to central Kansas and coastal Texas; also one breeding record for North Carolina (Pea Island, 1968). Formerly bred north to southern Mackenzie. Nonbreeding individuals frequently summer in the wintering range.

Winters mostly in coastal lowlands from northern California and southern Texas south to southern Mexico, casually to Guatemala (Pacific lowlands), Belize, Honduras (Copén and Cedeño) and Costa Rica (Chomes), also locally in southern Florida.

Migrates primarily throughout the western half of the United States, rarely in eastern North America from southern Ontario, southern Quebec, New Brunswick, Prince Edward Island and Nova Scotia south to the Gulf coast and Florida.

Casual or accidental in Alaska (Valdez), the Bahamas (Andros, San Salvador), Cuba, Jamacia, Puerto Rico, St. Croix (in the Virgin Islands), Barbados, Tobago and Greenland.

Notes.—Some authors consider all species of this genus as constituting a single superspecies.

Suborder SCOLOPACI: Sandpipers, Jacanas and Allies

Superfamily JACANOIDEA: Jacanas

Family **JACANIDAE**: Jacanas

Genus **JACANA** Brisson

> *Jacana* Brisson, 1760, Ornithologie, 1, p. 48; 5, p. 121. Type, by tautonymy, *Jacana* Brisson = *Parra jacana* Linnaeus.
> *Asarcia* Sharpe, 1896, Cat. Birds Br. Mus., 24, pp. ix, 68, 86. Type, by monotypy, *Parra variabilis* Linnaeus = *Fulica spinosa* Linnaeus.

Jacana spinosa (Linnaeus). NORTHERN JACANA. [288.]

> *Fulica spinosa* Linnaeus, 1758, Syst. Nat., ed. 10, 1, p. 152. Based on "The Spur-winged Water Hen" Edwards, Nat. Hist. Birds, 1, p. 48, pl. 48. (in America australi = Panama.)

Habitat.—Fresh-water marshes, floating vegetation, wet pastures and meadows, and edges of ponds, lakes and streams (Tropical and lower Subtropical zones).

Distribution.—*Resident* from southern Sinaloa, southern Texas (rarely north to Brazoria County) and Tamaulipas south along both slopes of Middle America (including Cozumel Island) to western Panama (east to Veraguas); also in the Greater Antilles (Cuba, the Isle of Pines, Jamaica and Hispaniola).

Casual in central Texas (north to Mitchell, Bexar and Victoria counties) and Puerto Rico; reports from Florida are unsubstantiated.

Notes.—Limited hybridization with *J. jacana* occurs in western Panama, and some authors treat *J. jacana* and *J. spinosa* as conspecific; they constitute a superspecies. If combined into a single species, AMERICAN JACANA may be used for the English name.

Jacana jacana (Linnaeus). WATTLED JACANA.

Parra Jacana Linnaeus, 1766, Syst. Nat., ed. 12, 1, p. 259. Based mainly on "Jacana quarta species" Marcgrave, Hist. Nat. Bras., p. 191, and "Le Chirurgien brun" Brisson, Ornithologie, 5, p. 125, pl. 11, fig. 1. (in America australi = Surinam.)

Habitat.—Fresh-water marshes, wet grassy areas, and shores of ponds, lakes and rivers (Tropical Zone).

Distribution.—*Resident* from western Panama (eastern Chiriquí and Veraguas eastward) south through South America (also Trinidad) to eastern Peru, eastern Bolivia, northern Argentina and Uruguay.

Notes.—See comments under *J. spinosa.*

Superfamily SCOLOPACOIDEA: Sandpipers, Phalaropes and Allies

Family **SCOLOPACIDAE**: Sandpipers, Phalaropes and Allies

Subfamily SCOLOPACINAE: Sandpipers and Allies

Tribe TRINGINI: Tringine Sandpipers

Genus **TRINGA** Linnaeus

Tringa Linnaeus, 1758, Syst. Nat., ed. 10, 1, p. 148. Type, by tautonymy, *Tringa ocrophus* Linnaeus (*Tringa,* prebinomial specific name, in synonymy).

Totanus Bechstein, 1803, Ornithol. Taschenb. Dtsch., 2, p. 282. Type, by tautonymy, *Totanus maculatus* Bechstein = *Scolopax totanus* Linnaeus.

Glottis Koch, 1816, Syst. Baier. Zool., 1, pp. xlii, 304. Type, by tautonymy, *Totanus glottis* Bechstein = *Scolopax nebularia* Gunnerus.

Notes.—Some authors would merge all the genera of the Tringini in *Tringa.*

Tringa nebularia (Gunnerus). COMMON GREENSHANK. [253.]

Scolopax nebularia Gunnerus, 1767, *in* Leem, Beskr. Finm. Lapper, p. 251. (district of Trondhjem, Norway.)

Habitat.—Marshes, bogs and wet meadows in the taiga or high moorlands (breeding); marshes, ponds, lakes and mudflats (nonbreeding).

Distribution.—*Breeds* from Scotland and Scandinavia east across Russia and Siberia to Anadyrland, Kamchatka and the Sea of Okhotsk, and south to Lake Baikal.

Winters from the Mediterranean region, Iraq, the Persian Gulf, eastern China and Formosa south to southern Africa, India, Ceylon, the Maldive Islands, East Indies, New Guinea and Australia, straggling to the eastern Atlantic islands and New Zealand.

In migration ranges regularly to the western Aleutians (Near Islands) and casually to the Pribilofs (St. Paul).

Audubon's record from Sand Key, near Cape Sable, Florida, is regarded as questionable.

Notes.—Known in Old World literature as the GREENSHANK. Some authors have suggested that *T. nebularia* and *T. melanoleuca* constitute a superspecies.

Tringa melanoleuca (Gmelin). GREATER YELLOWLEGS. [254.]

Scolopax melanoleuca Gmelin, 1789, Syst. Nat., 1 (2), p. 659. Based on the "Stone Snipe" Pennant, Arct. Zool., 2, p. 468. (auctumno in arenis littoris Labrador = Chateaux Bay, Labrador.)

Habitat.—Muskeg and tundra (breeding); marshes, ponds, lakes, stream margins, lagoons and coastal mudflats (nonbreeding).

Distribution.—*Breeds* from southern Alaska (the lower Kuskokwim River, and from the Alaska Peninsula eastward), southwestern Mackenzie and south-central British Columbia east across the northern and central portions of the Canadian provinces to central and southern Labrador, Newfoundland, northeastern Nova Scotia and southern Quebec (Anticosti Island). Nonbreeding individuals sometimes summer on the wintering grounds, especially along the coasts of the United States and in the West Indies.

Winters from Oregon (rarely from southwestern British Columbia), central California, southern Nevada, central Arizona, central New Mexico, southern Texas, the Gulf coast and coastal South Carolina (rarely from Long Island, New York) south through Middle America, the West Indies and South America to Tierra del Fuego.

In migration occurs regularly throughout the North American continent south of the breeding range.

Casual north to northern Alaska (Barrow), southern Mackenzie, southern Keewatin, Southampton and Baffin islands, and northern Quebec, and in the Hawaiian, Pribilof (St. George), Aleutian (Shemya, Adak) and Galapagos islands, and in Bermuda. Accidental in Greenland, the British Isles, Japan and the Marshall Islands.

Notes.—See comments under *T. nebularia*.

Tringa flavipes (Gmelin). LESSER YELLOWLEGS. [255.]

Scolopax flavipes Gmelin, 1789, Syst. Nat., 1 (2), p. 659. Based on the "Yellowshank" Pennant, Arct. Zool., 2, p. 468. (auctumno in Noveboraco = New York.)

Habitat.—Tundra and muskeg (breeding); marshes, ponds, wet meadows, lakes and mudflats (nonbreeding).

Distribution.—*Breeds* from western (rarely) and central Alaska, central Yukon, northwestern and east-central Mackenzie, southern Keewatin, northern Manitoba, northern Ontario and extreme west-central Quebec south to east-central British

Columbia, central Alberta, central Saskatchewan and southeastern Manitoba, with unconfirmed breeding reported south to southern Wisconsin and northern Illinois. Nonbreeding birds occasionally are reported in summer south from the breeding range as far as Argentina.

Winters from the lowlands of Mexico (most commonly the Gulf-Caribbean, less frequently the Pacific lowlands and the interior, uncommonly from southern California), central New Mexico (casually), southern Texas, the Gulf coast and coastal South Carolina (rarely from Long Island, New York) south through Middle America, the West Indies and South America (also the Galapagos Islands) to Tierra del Fuego.

In migration occurs regularly throughout North America south of the breeding range and east to southern Ontario, southern Quebec, New Brunswick and Nova Scotia, less commonly in western North America.

Casual in the Hawaiian, Pribilof and Aleutian islands, Labrador, Newfoundland, Bermuda, the Azores and New Zealand. Accidental in Greenland, the British Isles, continental Europe, Zambia and the Falkland Islands.

Tringa stagnatilis (Bechstein). MARSH SANDPIPER. [255.1.]

> *Totanus stagnatilis* Bechstein, 1803, Ornithol. Taschenb. Dtsch., 2, p. 292, pl. 29. (Germany.)

Habitat & Distribution.—*Breeds* in marshes and wet meadows from eastern Europe east to western Siberia, and *winters* from the Mediterranean region, Persian Gulf and Southeast Asia south to southern Africa, India, the East Indies and Australia.

Accidental in the Aleutian Islands (Buldir, 2 September 1974; Byrd, Trapp and Gibson, 1978, Condor, 80, p. 310).

[Tringa totanus (Linnaeus). COMMON REDSHANK.] See Appendix B.

Tringa erythropus (Pallas). SPOTTED REDSHANK. [253.2.]

> *Scolopax erythropus* Pallas, 1764, *in* Vroeg, Cat. Raissoné Ois., Adumbr., p. 6. (Holland.)

Habitat.—Marshy sites in bushy tundra and edge of the taiga (breeding); marshes, ponds, wet meadows and mudflats (nonbreeding).

Distribution.—*Breeds* from Scandinavia, northern Russia and northern Siberia south to central Russia, central Siberia, Anadyrland and Kamchatka.

Winters from the Mediterranean region, Persian Gulf, India and eastern China south to equatorial Africa, Ceylon and Southeast Asia.

In migration ranges (primarily in fall) regularly in the western and central Aleutians (Attu, Alaid, Shemya, Buldir, Adak) and, casually, the Pribilofs (St. Paul).

Accidental in British Columbia (Vancouver), Oregon (Columbia River), Newfoundland (Terra Nova), Massachusetts (Plum Island), Connecticut (New Haven), New Jersey (Brigantine) and Barbados, also sight records also for Nevada, Ontario, Ohio, New Jersey and Texas.

Notes.—See comments under *T. totanus* in Appendix B.

Tringa glareola Linnaeus. WOOD SANDPIPER. [257.1.]

Tringa Glareola Linnaeus, 1758, Syst. Nat., ed. 10, 1, p. 149. (in Europa = Sweden.)

Habitat.—Edges of ponds in the taiga (breeding); lakes, ponds, streams, wet meadows, bogs and shallow pools, frequently in wooded regions (nonbreeding).

Distribution.—*Breeds* in North America, at least rarely, in the western and central Aleutian Islands (Amchitka, probably also Adak and elsewhere); and in Eurasia from Scandinavia, northern Russia and northern Siberia south to southern Europe, Turkestan, northern Mongolia, Kamchatka, the Kurile and Commander islands, and the Chukotski Peninsula.

Winters from the Mediterranean region, Iran, India, northern Thailand and southern China south to southern Africa, Ceylon, the Malay Peninsula, East Indies and Australia.

In migration occurs rarely but regularly on St. Lawrence Island, in the Pribilof and western and central Aleutian islands, and on mainland western Alaska.

Casual to northern Alaska, on western Pacific islands, and in the Faroe and eastern Atlantic islands. Accidental in the Hawaiian Islands (Kure, Midway), New York (Gaines, Orleans County) and Barbados.

[**Tringa ocrophus** Linnaeus. GREEN SANDPIPER.] See Appendix A.

Tringa solitaria Wilson. SOLITARY SANDPIPER. [256.]

Tringa solitaria Wilson, 1813, Am. Ornithol., 7, p. 53, pl. 58, fig. 3. (Pocano Mt., Pa., Kentucky, and New York = Pocono Mountains, Pennsylvania.)

Habitat.—Taiga, nesting in trees in deserted passerine nests (breeding); freshwater ponds, stream edges, temporary pools, flooded ditches and fields, more commonly in wooded regions, less frequently on mudflats and open marshes (nonbreeding).

Distribution.—*Breeds* from central and south-coastal Alaska, northern Yukon, western and southern Mackenzie, northern Saskatchewan, northern Manitoba, and northern and central Ontario east through central Quebec to central and southern Labrador, and south to northwestern and central British Columbia, central Alberta, central Saskatchewan, southern Manitoba and northern Minnesota; also probably in west-central Oregon (Lane County).

Winters from northern Baja California (at least casually), the Gulf coast, southeastern Georgia, Florida and the Bahamas south through Middle America, the Antilles and South America to Peru, south-central Argentina and Uruguay.

In migration occurs from the southern portions of the breeding range south over most of the North American continent (rare on the Pacific coast north of central California).

Casual or accidental in northern and western Alaska, Bermuda, the Galapagos Islands, Greenland, Iceland, the British Isles, France and South Africa.

Notes.—*T. solitaria* and *T. ocrophus* may constitute a superspecies.

Genus **CATOPTROPHORUS** Bonaparte

Catoptrophorus Bonaparte, 1827, Ann. Lyc. Nat. Hist. N.Y., 2, p. 323. Type, by monotypy, *Totanus semipalmatus* Temminck = *Scolopax semipalmata* Gmelin.

Notes.—See comments under *Tringa*.

Catoptrophorus semipalmatus (Gmelin). WILLET. [258.]

Scolopax semipalmata Gmelin, 1789, Syst. Nat., 1 (2), p. 659. Based on the "Semipalmated Snipe" Pennant, Arct. Zool., 2, p. 469. (in Noveboraco = New York.)

Habitat.—Marshy lake margins in western North America, salt marshes in eastern North America (breeding); marshes, tidal mudflats, beaches, lake margins and, less frequently, open grassland (nonbreeding).

Distribution.—*Breeds* in western North America locally from eastern Oregon, Idaho, central Alberta, southern Saskatchewan and southwestern Manitoba south to northeastern and east-central California, western Nevada, central Utah, northern Colorado, western and northern Nebraska, and eastern South Dakota, formerly in western and southeastern Minnesota and Iowa; in eastern North America locally along the Atlantic-Gulf coast from southern New Brunswick, Prince Edward Island and Nova Scotia south to southern Florida and west to southern Texas (possibly Tamaulipas); in the Bahamas, Antilles (Cuba, Beata Island off Hispaniola, Anegada and St. Croix in the Virgin Islands, and Antigua, possibly also Barbuda, St. Martin and Anguilla); on Grand Cayman (in the Caribbean Sea); and on Los Roques, off northern Venezuela. Nonbreeding individuals occur sporadically in summer as far south as northern South America.

Winters from northern California (casually from southwestern British Columbia and western Washington) south along the Pacific coast (including offshore islands) to the Galapagos Islands and northern Chile; and from Virginia and the Gulf coast south along the Atlantic-Gulf-Caribbean coast of the Americas and throughout the West Indies to northern Brazil.

In migration occurs primarily in coastal areas but also irregularly throughout most of the interior United States, casually around the Great Lakes.

Casual north to northern Manitoba, southern Ontario, southwestern Quebec and Newfoundland. Accidental in Alaska (Minto Lakes), Bermuda and Europe, also sight reports from the Hawaiian Islands (Oahu, Maui).

Genus HETEROSCELUS Baird

Heteroscelus Baird, 1858, *in* Baird, Cassin and Lawrence, Rep. Explor. Surv. R. R. Pac., 9, pp. xxii, xlvii, 728, 734. Type, by monotypy, *Totanus brevipes* Vieillot.

Notes.—See comments under *Tringa.*

Heteroscelus incanus (Gmelin). WANDERING TATTLER. [259.]

Scolopax incana Gmelin, 1789, Syst. Nat., 1 (2), p. 658. Based on the "Ash-coloured Snipe" Latham, Gen. Synop. Birds. 3 (1), p. 154. (in insulis Eimeo et Palmerston = Eimeo [Moorea] Island, Society Group, Pacific Ocean.)

Habitat.—Mountains and hilly regions, primarily along streams and lakes in areas that are rocky, mossy, or covered with scrubby vegetation, in damp meadows, and in creek bottoms, occasionally in forest clearings away from water (breeding); rocky seacoasts and islands, and sandy beaches of oceanic islands (nonbreeding).

Distribution.—*Breeds* in North America in mountains of western, central and south-coastal Alaska, central and southern Yukon, and northwestern British Columbia; and in Eurasia in northeastern Siberia, Anadyrland and the Chukotski Peninsula. Nonbreeding individuals sometimes occur in summer on the wintering grounds.

Winters along the Pacific coast of the Americas from southern California (rarely Oregon and Washington) south regularly to the Revillagigedo Islands and the coast of Mexico, and locally to Honduras (Bay of Fonseca), Costa Rica (Cocos Island), Panama (Isla Coiba, Bay of Panama, and rarely to the Caribbean coast of the Canal Zone), Colombia (Malpelo Island), the Galapagos Islands, Ecuador and Peru (Punta Salinas); and in the Pacific from the Hawaiian Islands, Marianas and Philippines south to the Fiji, Samoa, Society and Tuamotu islands.

In migration occurs regularly in the Aleutian Islands and along the Pacific coast of Central America.

Casual inland in North America (recorded northwestern Mackenzie, east-central British Columbia, Alberta, eastern Oregon, eastern California, northeastern Baja California, southwestern Utah and southern Arizona), and in the Pacific from the Bonin, Volcano and Ryukyu islands, Japan and Formosa south to New Guinea, Australia and New Zealand. Accidental in Manitoba (Churchill), southern Ontario (Windmill Point, Fort Erie) and Massachusetts (Monomoy).

Notes.—*H. incanus* and *H. brevipes* constitute a superspecies; they are considered conspecific by some authors, although the breeding ranges seem to overlap in eastern Siberia.

Heteroscelus brevipes (Vieillot). GRAY-TAILED TATTLER. [259.1.]

Totanus brevipes Vieillot, 1816, Nouv. Dict. Hist. Nat., nouv. éd., 6, p. 410. (Pays inconnu = Timor.)

Habitat.—Mountains and hilly regions, primarily along streams or lakes in stony, mossy or scrubby situations, occasionally in clearings away from water (breeding); rocky seacoasts and islets, and sandy beaches on oceanic islands (nonbreeding).

Distribution.—*Breeds* apparently in eastern Siberian mountains from Lake Baikal to the Verkhoyansk Mountains and Anadyrland, possibly also in Kamchatka and the Kurile Islands; nest and eggs unknown.

Winters from the Malay Peninsula, Philippines, and the Caroline, Mariana and Marshall islands south to Christmas Island (in the Indian Ocean), Java, New Guinea, Australia and Norfolk Island.

In migration occurs regularly in the Aleutian (east to Unalaska) and Pribilof islands, on St. Lawrence Island, and along the coasts of Japan and China, casually along the coast to northern Alaska (Barrow).

Accidental in the Hawaiian Islands (Midway) and California (Los Angeles County).

Notes.—Also known as POLYNESIAN TATTLER. See comments under *H. incanus*.

Genus ACTITIS Illiger

Actitis Illiger, 1811, Prodromus, p. 262. Type, by subsequent designation (Stejneger, 1885), *Tringa hypoleucos* Linnaeus.

Notes.—See comments under *Tringa*.

Actitis hypoleucos (Linnaeus). COMMON SANDPIPER. [263.1.]

Tringa Hypoleucos Linnaeus, 1758, Syst. Nat., ed. 10, 1, p. 149. (in Europa = Sweden.)

Habitat.—Streams, ponds, lakes and seacoasts, generally with sandy or rocky margins, less frequently in marshes, breeding along banks of fresh-water habitats.

Distribution.—*Breeds* from the British Isles, Scandinavia, northern Russia and northern Siberia south to the Mediterranean region, northern Iran, Afghanistan, the Himalayas, Mongolia, Manchuria, Ussuriland, Kamchatka, the Kurile Islands and Japan; also in East Africa (Uganda).

Winters from southern Europe, the Mediterranean region, Iraq, eastern China and southern Japan south to southern Africa, Madagascar, Ceylon, islands in the eastern Indian Ocean, Australia, New Guinea and islands of the western Pacific.

In migration occurs regularly in the western Aleutians (Near Islands), casually in the Pribilof Islands (St. George), on St. Lawrence Island, and in the Aleutians east to Adak.

Notes.—*A. hypoleucos* and *A. macularia* constitute a superspecies; they are considered by some authors to be conspecific.

Actitis macularia (Linnaeus). SPOTTED SANDPIPER. [263.]

Tringa macularia Linnaeus, 1766, Syst. Nat., ed. 12, 1, p. 249. Based mainly on the "Spotted Tringa" Edwards, Glean. Nat. Hist., 2, p. 139, pl. 277. (in Europa & America septentrionali = Pennsylvania.)

Distribution.—*Breeds* from central Alaska, central Yukon, northwestern and central Mackenzie, southern Keewatin, northeastern Manitoba, northern Ontario, northern Quebec, Labrador and Newfoundland south to southern Alaska (west to the base of the Alaska Peninsula), Oregon, southern California (in interior mountains), central Arizona, southern New Mexico, central Texas, the northern portions of the Gulf states, North Carolina, Virginia and eastern Maryland. Occasional nonbreeding individuals remain in summer on the wintering grounds.

Winters from southwestern British Columbia, western Washington, southern Arizona, southern New Mexico, southern Texas, the southern portions of the Gulf states, and coastal South Carolina south through Middle America, the West Indies and South America (also the Galapagos Islands, and all islands off the Caribbean coast) to northern Chile, northern Argentina and Uruguay.

In migration occurs regularly along both coasts and throughout interior North America, and on Bermuda.

Casual or accidental in Tristan da Cunha, Greenland, the British Isles, continental Europe, the eastern Atlantic islands, Johnston Island and the Marshall Islands, also a sight report from the Hawaiian Islands (Oahu).

Notes.—See comments under *A. hypoleucos.*

Genus **XENUS** Kaup

Xenus Kaup, 1829, Skizz. Entw.-Ges. Eur. Thierw., p. 115. Type, by monotypy, *Scolopax cinerea* Güldenstädt.

Notes.—See comments under *Tringa.*

Xenus cinereus (Güldenstädt). TEREK SANDPIPER. [263.2.]

Scolopax cinerea Güldenstädt, 1775, Novi Comm. Acad. Sci. Petropol., 19 (1774), p. 473, pl. 19. (ad mare caspium, circa ostium fluuii Terek = shores of the Caspian Sea at the mouth of the Terek River.)

Habitat.—River meadows, marshes, grassy banks of streams, ponds and lakes, especially in wooded regions, wintering also on mudflats and shallow estuaries and bays.

Distribution.—*Breeds* from Finland, northern Russia and northern Siberia south to central Russia, Lake Baikal and Anadyrland.

Winters from the Persian Gulf, southern Red Sea, Southeast Asia and Hainan south to South Africa (along the coast of eastern Africa), Madagascar, India, Ceylon, the Andaman Islands, East Indies, New Guinea and Australia.

In migration occurs casually in the western Aleutians (Attu, Agattu, Shemya, Buldir), on St. Lawrence Island, in western and south-coastal Alaska (Nanvak Bay, Anchorage), and to western Europe, North Africa and New Zealand, also a sight report for northeastern Manitoba (Churchill).

Tribe NUMENIINI: Curlews

Genus **BARTRAMIA** Lesson

Bartramia Lesson, 1831, Traité Ornithol., livr. 7, p. 553. Type, by monotypy, *Bartramia laticauda* Lesson = *Tringa longicauda* Bechstein.

Bartramia longicauda (Bechstein). UPLAND SANDPIPER. [261.]

Tringa longicauda Bechstein, 1812, *in* Latham, Allg. Uebers. Vögel, 4 (2), p. 452. (Nordamerika = North America.)

Habitat.—Grasslands, especially prairies, dry meadows, pastures, and (in Alaska) scattered woodlands at timberline, very rarely in migration along shores and mudflats.

Distribution.—*Breeds* locally from north-central Alaska (Brooks Range, Alaska Range and Wrangell Mountains), northern Yukon, northwestern British Columbia, extreme southwestern Mackenzie, northern Alberta, west-central and southern Saskatchewan, southern Manitoba, northern Minnesota, southern Ontario, southern Quebec, central Maine and southern New Brunswick south in the interior to eastern Washington, northeastern Oregon, Idaho, central Colorado, northwestern Oklahoma, north-central Texas, central Missouri, southern Illinois, northern Kentucky, southern Ohio, West Virginia, central Virginia and Maryland, possibly also to central Tennessee and (formerly) northern Utah.

Winters in South America from Surinam and northern Brazil south to central Argentina and Uruguay.

Migrates south through North America (rare along Pacific coast from southern Alaska to Washington, casually to California, and rare in Arizona, Nova Scotia and the South Atlantic coastal region), Middle America (not reported northwestern Mexico), the West Indies and most of South America (also Tobago and Trinidad) east of the Andes.

Casual or accidental in eastern Quebec, Bermuda, Chile, the Falkland Islands,

Tristan da Cunha, Greenland, the British Isles, continental Europe, the Azores and Australia.

Notes.—Also known in Old World literature as BARTRAM'S SANDPIPER; formerly known as UPLAND PLOVER.

Genus NUMENIUS Brisson

Numenius Brisson, 1760, Ornithologie, 1, p. 48; 5, p. 311. Type, by tautonymy, *Numenius* Brisson = *Scolopax arquata* Linnaeus.
Phæopus Cuvier, 1817, Règne Anim., 1 (1816), p. 485. Type, by tautonymy, *Scolopax phaeopus* Linnaeus.

Numenius borealis (Forster). ESKIMO CURLEW. [266.]

Scolopax borealis J. R. Forster, 1772, Philos. Trans. R. Soc. London, 62, p. 431. (Fort Albany [on James Bay], Hudson Bay).

Habitat.—Open tundra (breeding); grasslands, pastures, plowed fields and, less frequently, marshes and mudflats (nonbreeding).

Distribution.—Nearly extinct. *Bred* formerly in northwestern Mackenzie, possibly west to western Alaska (Norton Sound).

Wintered formerly from south-central Brazil south through Paraguay and Uruguay to southern Argentina and Chile (Isla Chiloé); last sight report in winter from Argentina (near General Lavalle, Province of Buenos Aires, 17 January 1939).

In migration recorded in spring from Guatemala (San Gerónimo), Chihuahua (Lake Palomas) and regularly north from Texas and Louisiana through the Mississippi and Missouri river drainages and west of the Great Lakes and Hudson Bay to the breeding grounds; recorded in fall west of Hudson Bay and regularly from southern Labrador and the Gulf of St. Lawrence to the New England coast, casually to the lower Great Lakes (Michigan and southern Ontario), along the Atlantic coast (to South Carolina), and in Bermuda and the West Indies (recorded Puerto Rico, Guadeloupe, Carriacou in the Grenadines, Grenada and Barbados).

Since the mid-1950's recorded (primarily sight reports) in spring from Texas (Galveston to Rockport, 1959–1963, with photographs from Galveston in March–April 1962, and on Padre Island, 1972) and Manitoba (Lake Manitoba, May 1980), and in fall from the west coast of James Bay (1976), Massachusetts (Plymouth Beach, 1970), New Jersey (Cape May, 1959) and South Carolina (Charleston area, 1956); last recorded specimen from Barbados (4 September 1963).

Casual formerly on the Pribilofs, Colorado, Montana, Baffin Island, Tobago, Trinidad, the Falkland Islands, Greenland, Iceland and the British Isles.

Notes.—*N. borealis* and the Asiatic *N. minutus* Gould, 1841, constitute a superspecies and are regarded as conspecific by some authors.

Numenius phaeopus (Linnaeus). WHIMBREL. [265.]

Scolopax Phæopus Linnaeus, 1758, Syst. Nat., ed. 10, 1, p. 146. (in Europa = Sweden).

Habitat.—Sedge-dwarf shrub tundra, moorlands and heath (breeding); beaches, tidal mudflats, marshes, estuaries, flooded fields and pastures (nonbreeding).

Distribution.—*Breeds* [*hudsonicus* group] in North America from northern Alaska, northern Yukon and northwestern Mackenzie south to western and central

Alaska (Norton Sound, Alaska Range, Susitna River highlands) and southwestern Yukon, and along the western side of Hudson Bay from southern Keewatin south to northwestern James Bay (Lake River, Ontario); and [*phaeopus* group] in Eurasia from Iceland, the Faroe Islands, northern Scandinavia, northern Russia and northern Siberia south to the Orkney and Shetland islands, southern Scandinavia, central Russia, central Siberia, Anadyrland and the Sea of Okhotsk. Recorded in summer and possibly breeding [*hudsonicus* group] on Banks and Southampton islands; nonbreeding birds also may summer in the wintering range, especially along the Atlantic coast of the United States, in the West Indies, and along the coasts of California and western South America.

Winters [*hudsonicus* group] in the Americas in coastal areas from central California, the Gulf coast and South Carolina (rarely farther north) south through Middle America, the West Indies and South America (also the Galapagos Islands) to southern Chile and southern Brazil (casually to extreme northern Argentina); and [*phaeopus* group] in the Old World from the Mediterranean region (occasionally the British Isles), Arabia, India, Southeast Asia and eastern China south to southern Africa, Madagascar, islands in the Indian Ocean, Australia, New Zealand, and the Fiji and Phoenix islands.

In migration occurs [*hudsonicus* group] primarily along the coast from southern Alaska (from Bristol Bay eastward, most commonly in spring), around Hudson and James bays, and (in fall) from Labrador and Newfoundland southward, casually recorded through interior North America from southern Canada south to Arizona, New Mexico and the Gulf states; and [*phaeopus* group] through the eastern Aleutians (Near Islands) and the eastern Atlantic islands, rarely to the Pribilof and St. Lawrence islands.

Casual [*hudsonicus* group] in Europe and New Zealand; and [*phaeopus* group] in the Hawaiian Islands (Midway, Oahu), mainland Alaska (Point Barrow), southern Labrador, Newfoundland, Nova Scotia, Massachusetts, New York (Long Island), New Jersey and Barbados, also sight reports from California, Virginia and southern Florida.

Notes.—The American populations have sometimes been regarded as a separate species, *N. hudsonicus* Latham, 1790 [HUDSONIAN CURLEW, 265], distinct from *N. phaeopus* [WHIMBREL, 267].

Numenius tahitiensis (Gmelin). BRISTLE-THIGHED CURLEW. [268.]

> *Scolopax tahitiensis* Gmelin, 1789, Syst. Nat., 1 (2), p. 656. Based on the "Otaheite Curlew" Latham, Gen. Synop. Birds, 3 (1), p. 122. (in Tahiti [Society Islands].)

Habitat.—Montane tundra (breeding); coastal tundra, grassy fields, tidal mudflats and beaches (nonbreeding).

Distribution.—*Breeds* in western Alaska (near the mouth of the Yukon River and on the Seward Peninsula); nonbreeding birds occur in summer on coastal tundra from Kotzebue Sound south to Hooper Bay, occasionally in the Hawaiian Islands.

Winters on Pacific islands from the Hawaiian (most commonly from Midway east to French Frigate Shoals) and Marshall islands south to the Fiji, Tonga, Samoa, Marquesas and Tuamotu islands.

In migration occurs regularly in south-coastal Alaska (Cook Inlet to Prince William Sound), casually in the Pribilof and Aleutian islands.

Casual west to the Mariana and Caroline islands. Accidental in British Columbia (Vancouver Island) and Japan.

Numenius tenuirostris Vieillot. SLENDER-BILLED CURLEW. [268.1.]

Numenius tenuirostris Vieillot, 1817, Nouv. Dict. Hist. Nat., nouv. éd., 8, p. 302. (Egypt.)

Habitat & Distribution. — *Breeds* in boggy areas in steppe country in southwestern Siberia and *winters* along beaches and mudflats west to the Mediterranean region, straggling to the British Isles and northwestern Africa.

Accidental in Ontario (Crescent Beach, fall, "about 1925"; Beardslee and Mitchell, 1965, Bull. Buffalo Soc. Nat. Hist., 22, pp. 212–213); a sight report for North Carolina is open to question.

Numenius madagascariensis (Linnaeus). FAR EASTERN CURLEW. [268.2.]

Scolopax madagascariensis Linnaeus, 1766, Syst. Nat., ed. 12, 1, p. 242. Based on "Le Courly de Madagascar" Brisson, Ornithologie, 5, p. 321, pl. 28. (in Madagascar, error = Macassar, Celebes.)

Habitat. — Moorlands and wet meadows (breeding); mudflats, beaches and occasionally marshes (nonbreeding).

Distribution. — *Breeds* from eastern Siberia and Kamchatka south to Transbaicalia, northern Mongolia, northern Manchuria and Ussuriland.

Winters from Formosa and the Philippines south to the East Indies, New Guinea, Australia and (rarely) New Zealand.

In migration ranges casually to the Aleutian (Amchitka, Adak) and Pribilof (St. Paul, St. George) islands, and to western Alaska (Wales).

Numenius arquata (Linnaeus). EURASIAN CURLEW. [264.1.]

Scolopax Arquata Linnaeus, 1758, Syst. Nat., ed. 10, 1, p. 145. (in Europa = Sweden.)

Habitat & Distribution. — *Breeds* in grasslands and marshes from northern Eurasia south to southern Europe and the Gobi Desert region, and *winters* along beaches, on mudflats and in wet meadows from the southern parts of the breeding range south to southern Africa, Madagascar, the Indian Ocean, Southeast Asia and the East Indies.

Accidental in Ontario (Crescent Beach, near Buffalo, New York), New York (Long Island, 1853), Massachusetts (Monomoy, 19 September 1976, and Martha's Vineyard, 18 February–18 March 1978) and Greenland, also a sight report for Nova Scotia.

Notes. — Also known as COMMON CURLEW and, in Old World literature, as the CURLEW. *N. arquata* and *N. americanus* may constitute a superspecies.

Numenius americanus Bechstein. LONG-BILLED CURLEW. [264.]

Numenius americanus Bechstein, 1812, *in* Latham, Allg. Uebers. Vögel, 4 (2), p. 432. (New York.)

Habitat.—Prairies and grassy meadows, generally near water, in migration and winter occurring also on beaches and mudflats.

Distribution.—*Breeds* from south-central British Columbia, southern Alberta, southern Saskatchewan and southern Manitoba south to eastern Washington, northeastern California, central Nevada, central Utah, southern Colorado, central New Mexico and northern Texas (possibly also Jeff Davis County and along the Gulf coast), and east to southwestern Kansas.

Winters from central California, southern Arizona (rarely), extreme northern Mexico, southern Texas, southern Louisiana and coastal South Carolina south to southern Mexico (Oaxaca, Veracruz and the Yucatan Peninsula) and southern Florida, irregularly to Guatemala, Honduras and Costa Rica.

Casual in southern Mackenzie, New Brunswick, Missouri and the Greater Antilles (Cuba, Jamaica), also sight reports for eastern James Bay (Brae Island) and southern Ontario. Accidental in Panama (Canal Zone).

Notes.—See comments under *N. arquata.*

Tribe LIMOSINI: Godwits

Genus LIMOSA Brisson

Limosa Brisson, 1760, Ornithologie, 1, p. 48; 5, p. 261. Type, by tautonymy, *Limosa* Brisson = *Scolopax limosa* Linnaeus.

Vetola Mathews, 1913, Birds Aust., 3 (2), p. 191. Type, by original designation, *Scolopax lapponicus* Linnaeus.

Limosa limosa (Linnaeus). BLACK-TAILED GODWIT. [252.]

Scolopax Limosa Linnaeus, 1758, Syst. Nat., ed. 10, 1, p. 147. (in Europa = Sweden.)

Habitat.—Marshy grasslands, wet meadows, steppe and moorlands (breeding); marshes, flooded fields, beaches and mudflats (nonbreeding).

Distribution.—*Breeds* from Iceland, the Faroe Islands, southern Scandinavia, the Baltic states, central Russia, central Siberia and Kamchatka south to southern Europe, southern Russia, Lake Baikal, Mongolia and the Sea of Okhotsk.

Winters from the British Isles, Mediterranean region, India, Burma, China and the Philippines south to east-central Africa, Ceylon (rarely), Malaysia, the East Indies, Australia and Tasmania.

In migration occurs casually in spring in the Aleutian (east to Adak), Pribilof (St. Paul), St. Lawrence and Little Diomede islands.

Casual or accidental in Newfoundland, on Miquelon Island, and in Massachusetts (Dartmouth), Pennsylvania (Philadelphia), New Jersey (Brigantine), North Carolina (Bodie Island) and Florida (Merritt Island).

Notes.—*L. limosa* and *L. haemastica* appear to constitute a superspecies.

Limosa haemastica (Linnaeus). HUDSONIAN GODWIT. [251.]

Scolopax Hæmastica Linnaeus, 1758, Syst. Nat., ed. 10, 1, p. 147. Based on "The Red-breasted Godwit" Edwards, Nat. Hist. Birds, 3, p. 138, pl. 138. (in America septentrionali = Hudson Bay.)

Habitat.—Grassy tundra near water (breeding); marshes, beaches, flooded fields and tidal mudflats (nonbreeding).

Distribution.—*Breeds* locally in south-coastal Alaska (Cook Inlet area) and probably also in western Alaska (Kotzebue Sound and Norton Bay); in Mackenzie (Fort Anderson and mouth of Mackenzie River area) and northwestern British Columbia (Chilcat Pass); and around Hudson Bay (in northeastern Manitoba and northwestern Ontario). Recorded in summer in central and northern Alaska,in the interior of Southampton Island, and on Akimiski Island in James Bay.

Winters in South America on the coast of Chile (from Isla Chiloé south to the Straits of Magellan), and from Paraguay, southern Brazil and Uruguay south to Tierra del Fuego and the Falkland Islands, casually also in New Zealand.

In migration primarily recorded in spring in the interior of North America from Texas and Louisiana north to Alberta, Saskatchewan and the west side of Hudson Bay, rarely on the Pacific coast of Guatemala and Costa Rica; in fall mostly southeastward from James Bay to the Maritime Provinces and New England, thence by sea southward, regularly recorded on Barbados and casually on Guadeloupe.

Casual (primarily in migratory periods) along the Pacific coast of North America (recorded British Columbia to California), in the interior of the western United States (from Idaho and Wyoming south to Arizona and New Mexico), in the interior of the eastern United States (mostly in spring), in Newfoundland, along the Atlantic coast (south to Florida, primarily in fall), in Mexico (recorded Tamaulipas, Veracruz and Oaxaca), the Bahamas (Eleuthera), Greater Antilles (recorded definitely from Cuba, Hispaniola and Puerto Rico), coastal Venezuela (also Curaçao and Trinidad), Bolivia and Peru.

Notes.—See comments under *L. limosa.*

Limosa lapponica (Linnaeus). BAR-TAILED GODWIT. [250.]

Scolopax lapponica Linnaeus, 1758, Syst. Nat., ed. 10, 1, p. 147. (in Lapponia = Lapland.)

Habitat.—Coastal tundra and sedge-dwarf shrub tundra of foothills, in migration and winter also marshes, flooded fields, estuarine areas and beaches.

Distribution.—*Breeds* in North America in Alaska (Wales east to Point Barrow, and south to the Yukon River Delta); and in Eurasia from northern Scandinavia east across northern Russia and northern Siberia to the Chukotski Peninsula and northern Anadyrland.

Winters from the British Isles, North Sea, Mediterranean region, Black Sea, Iraq and the Persian Gulf south to central Africa, islands of the northern Indian Ocean and Ceylon, casually to the Azores, Canary Islands, southern Africa, Madagascar, the Seychelles and Maldive Islands; and from southeastern China, Formosa and the Philippines south to the East Indies, western Polynesia, Australia, New Zealand and the Chatham Islands.

Migrates through the Hawaiian, Aleutian and Pribilof islands, along the Bering Sea coast of the Alaska Peninsula, through Europe, and in the Pacific from the coast of Japan south through the islands of Polynesia to the Gilbert, Samoa and Tonga islands.

Casual along the Pacific coast from south-coastal Alaska (west to Kodiak) and British Columbia south to southern California, in the Atlantic coastal region (recorded Newfoundland, Maine, Massachusetts, New York, New Jersey, Virginia, North Carolina and Florida), and in Iceland and the Faroe Islands.

Limosa fedoa (Linnaeus). MARBLED GODWIT. [249.]

Scolopax Fedoa Linnaeus, 1758, Syst. Nat., ed. 10, 1, p. 146. Based on "The Greater American Godwit" Edwards, Nat. Hist. Birds, 3, p. 137, pl. 137. (in America septentrionali = Hudson Bay.)

Habitat.—Marshes and flooded plains, in migration and winter also on mudflats and beaches.

Distribution.—*Breeds* from central Alberta, central Saskatchewan, southern Manitoba and northern Ontario (west coast and islands of James Bay) south to central Montana, central North Dakota, northeastern South Dakota and northwestern Minnesota, formerly to central Iowa, east-central Minnesota and southern Wisconsin; recorded in summer (and probably breeding) in southwestern Alaska (Bristol Bay). Nonbreeding birds occur in summer in the winter range.

Winters from central California, western Nevada, the Gulf coast and coastal South Carolina south to Florida, and along both coasts of Middle America (irregular or local south of Mexico) to Colombia, Ecuador, Peru and northern Chile.

Migrates primarily through interior western North America and along the California coast, regularly north on the Pacific coast to British Columbia and southeastern and south-coastal Alaska, and, primarily in fall, casually through interior eastern North America and along the Atlantic coast from southern Ontario, Quebec and Nova Scotia south to the Greater Antilles (east to Anegada in the Virgin Islands).

Casual or accidental in the Hawaiian (Laysan) and Galapagos islands; reports from the Lesser Antilles, Tobago and Trinidad are questionable.

Tribe ARENARIINI: Turnstones

Notes.—Formerly considered a subfamily, the Arenariinae, and included the genus *Aphriza,* now regarded as related to the knots (*Calidris*).

Genus **ARENARIA** Brisson

Arenaria Brisson, 1760, Ornithologie, 1, p. 48; 5, p. 132. Type, by tautonymy, *Arenaria* Brisson = *Tringa interpres* Linnaeus.

Arenaria interpres (Linnaeus). RUDDY TURNSTONE. [283.]

Tringa Interpres Linnaeus, 1758, Syst. Nat., ed. 10, 1, p. 148. (in Europa & America septentrionali = Gotland, Sweden.)

Habitat.—Dry, dwarf-shrub tundra, usually near water (breeding); rocky, barren or pebbly coasts, sandy beaches, mudflats and shores of lakes (nonbreeding).

Distribution.—*Breeds* in North America from northern Alaska and the Canadian Arctic islands (Banks east to Ellesmere and southwestern Baffin islands) south to western Alaska (St. Lawrence Island and the Yukon River delta), and Southampton, Coats and Mansel islands, probably also the northern portions of Mackenzie and Keewatin; and in the Palearctic from northern Greenland, Iceland, northern Scandinavia, Spitsbergen, Novaya Zemlya and the New Siberian Islands south to central Greenland, the west coast of Norway, islands in the Baltic Sea, and the northern Siberian coast (east to the Bering Sea). Nonbreeding birds may be found in summer through the winter range.

Winters throughout the islands of the Pacific from the Hawaiian Islands southward; in North America in coastal areas from central California, the Gulf coast and New York (Long Island) south along both coasts of Middle America (including Mujeres, Cozumel and the Revillagigedo islands, Mexico), through the West Indies, and along both coasts of South America (also the Galapagos Islands, Netherlands Antilles, Tobago and Trinidad) to Tierra del Fuego; and in the Old World from the British Isles, southern Scandinavia, the Mediterranean region, Canary Islands and southeastern China south to southern Africa, India, Indonesia, Australia and New Zealand.

Migrates in North America regularly through the Aleutian and Pribilof islands, from Hudson Bay east to Labrador and Newfoundland (mostly in fall), and along the Atlantic coast from the Maritime Provinces southward, also in the Old World primarily along coastal areas between breeding and wintering ranges; in small numbers through the prairie areas of the Canadian provinces, the lower Great Lakes, and the Mississippi and Ohio valleys; rarely along the Pacific coast from southeastern Alaska south to northern California; and casually elsewhere through the interior of central and western North America, and to Bermuda, Jan Mayen and Franz Josef Land.

Notes.—Known in Old World literature as the TURNSTONE. Some authors suggest that *A. interpres* and *A. melanocephala* constitute a superspecies.

Arenaria melanocephala (Vigors). BLACK TURNSTONE. [284.]

Strepsilas melanocephalus Vigors, 1829, Zool. J., 4 (1828), p. 356. (northwest coast of [North] America.)

Habitat.—Coastal salt-grass tundra (breeding); rocky seacoasts and offshore islets, less frequently in seaweed on sandy beaches and tidal mudflats (nonbreeding).

Distribution.—*Breeds* locally along the coast of western and southern Alaska, from southern Kotzebue Sound south to the Yukon-Kuskokwim delta, rarely to the north side of the Alaska Peninsula. Nonbreeding birds may be found in summer through the wintering range.

Winters from south-coastal and southeastern Alas (west to Kodiak) south along the Pacific coast to southern Baja California and central Sonora.

Casual in the central Aleutians (Amchitka), and inland in central Alaska, Yukon (Watson Lake), British Columbia (Atlin region and Nulki Lake), Montana (Glacier National Park), Oregon (Washington County) and California (Salton Sea, Needles, Volta Wildlife Area). Accidental in Wisconsin (Winnebago County).

Notes.—See comments under *A. interpres*.

Tribe CALIDRIDINI: Calidridine Sandpipers

Genus **APHRIZA** Audubon

Aphriza Audubon, 1839, Ornithol. Biogr., 5, p. 249. Type, by monotypy, *Aphriza townsendi* Audubon = *Tringa virgata* Gmelin.

Notes.—See comments under Arenariini.

Aphriza virgata (Gmelin). SURFBIRD. [282.]

Tringa virgata Gmelin, 1789, Syst. Nat., 1 (2), p. 674. Based on the "Streaked Sandpiper" Latham, Gen. Synop. Birds, 3 (1), p. 180. (in sinu Sandwich = Prince William Sound, Alaska.)

Habitat.—Open rocky ground above treeline in interior mountains (breeding); rocky seacoasts and islands (nonbreeding).

Distribution.—*Breeds* in central Alaska (Alaska Range and Fortymile River system) and Yukon (except southeastern part). Occasional nonbreeding individuals summer as far south as Panama, and others have been recorded in summer (and possibly breeding) in western Alaska (from Kotzebue Sound south to Hooper and Goodnews bays).

Winters along the Pacific coast from south-coastal and southeastern Alaska (west to Kodiak) south along the Pacific coast of North America, Middle America (not recorded El Salvador, Honduras or Nicaragua) and South America to the Straits of Magellan.

Casual in central Alberta (Beaverhill Lake), and on the Gulf coast of Texas (Port Aransas, Padre Island) and Florida (Escambia and Lee counties), also a sight report for western Pennsylvania (Presque Isle).

Genus CALIDRIS Merrem

Calidris Anonymous [=Merrem], 1804, Allg. Lit. Ztg., 2, no. 168, col. 542. Type, by tautonymy, *Tringa calidris* Gmelin = *Tringa canutus* Linnaeus.

Ereunetes Illiger, 1811, Prodromus, p. 262. Type, by monotypy, *Ereunetes petrificatus* Illiger = *Tringa pusilla* Linnaeus.

Erolia Vieillot, 1816, Analyse, p. 55. Type, by monotypy, *Erolia variegata* Vieillot = *Scolopax testacea* Pallas.

Pelidna Cuvier, 1817, Règne Anim., 1 (1816), p. 490. Type, by subsequent designation (G. R. Gray, 1840), *Tringa cinclus* Linnaeus = *Tringa alpina* Linnaeus.

Crocethia Billberg, 1828, Synop. Faunae Scand., ed. 2, 1 (2), p. 132. Type, by monotypy, *Charadrius calidris* Linnaeus = *Trynga alba* Pallas.

Pisobia Billberg, 1828, Synop. Faunae Scand., ed. 2, 1 (2), p. 136, tab. A. Type, by subsequent designation (A.O.U. Committee, 1908), *Tringa minuta* Leisler.

Arquatella Baird, 1858, in Baird, Cassin and Lawrence, Rep. Explor. Surv. R. R. Pac., 9, pp. 714, 717. Type, by original designation, *Tringa maritima* Brünnich.

Micropalama Baird, 1858, *in* Baird, Cassin and Lawrence, Rep. Explor. Surv. R. R. Pac., 9, pp. xxii, xlvii, 714. 726. Type, by monotypy, *Tringa himantopus* Bonaparte.

Notes.—See comments under *Eurynorhynchus.*

Calidris tenuirostris (Horsfield). GREAT KNOT. [234.1.]

Totanus tenuirostris Horsfield, 1821, Trans. Linn. Soc. London, 13 (1), p. 192. (Java.)

Habitat.—Barren or stony mountain tundra (breeding); rocky seacoasts, sandy beaches and tidal mudflats (nonbreeding).

Distribution.—*Breeds* in the mountains of northeastern Siberia from the lower Kolyma to Anadyrland, probably also from the Verhoyansk Mountains east to the Sea of Okhotsk.

Winters from the Persian Gulf, India and Malaysia east and south to the Philippines, East Indies, New Guinea and Australia.

Migrates regularly along the coast of eastern Asia from Kamchatka south to Formosa and the Ryukyu Islands, rarely in the interior of Siberia, and casually in spring through southwestern and western Alaska in the Aleutians (Shemya, Adak), Pribilofs (St. Paul), and on St. Lawrence Island and the Seward Peninsula.

Calidris canutus (Linnaeus). RED KNOT. [234.]

Tringa Canutus Linnaeus, 1758, Syst. Nat., ed. 10, 1, p. 149. (in Europa = Sweden.)

Habitat.—Barren or stony tundra (breeding); primarily seacoasts on tidal mudflats and beaches, less frequently in marshes and flooded fields (nonbreeding).

Distribution.—*Breeds* in North America in northwestern and northern Alaska (Seward Peninsula and Delong Mountains, rarely at Point Barrow and Cooper Island) and the Canadian Arctic islands east to Ellesmere and south to southern Victoria and Southampton islands, probably also on the Adelaide Peninsula and Mansel Island; and in the Palearctic from northern Greenland and Spitsbergen east to the New Siberian and Wrangel islands. Nonbreeding individuals occasionally summer in the wintering range, especially on the Atlantic and Gulf coasts of the United States and in the British Isles.

Winters in the Americas in coastal regions from southern California, the Gulf coast and Massachusetts south to Tierra del Fuego, generally rare and irregular north of southern South America; and in the Old World from the British Isles, southern Europe, the Black Sea, India, Southeast Asia and the Philippines south to central Africa, Australia and New Zealand, casually to the Azores and Ceylon.

Migrates in North America primarily along the Atlantic coast from New Brunswick and Nova Scotia south to Florida (rarely in fall in southern Labrador and Newfoundland), through the Great Lakes region (mostly in spring), along the Pacific coast from western and southern Alaska and British Columbia southward, irregularly along the coasts of Middle America (not recorded Belize, El Salvador or Nicaragua) and South America (also Trinidad), casually elsewhere through the interior of North America and through the Pribilofs, Aleutians and West Indies (recorded Greater Antilles except Cuba, the Virgin Islands, Martinique and Barbados); and in the Old World generally in coastal areas through regions between the breeding and wintering ranges, casually through the eastern Atlantic islands.

Casual in the Hawaiian and Aleutian islands, on islands in the Bering Sea, and in Bermuda. Accidental in the Galapagos Islands.

Notes.—Known in Old World literature as the KNOT.

Calidris alba (Pallas). SANDERLING. [248.]

Trynga alba Pallas, 1764, *in* Vroeg, Cat. Raissoné Ois., Adumbr., p. 7. (de Noordsche Zeekusten = coast of the North Sea.)

Habitat.—Dry sedge, barren or stony tundra (breeding); primarily sandy beaches, less frequently on mudflats and shores of lakes or rivers (nonbreeding).

Distribution.—*Breeds* in North America in northern Alaska (Barrow), and from

Prince Patrick, Lougheed and northern Ellesmere islands south to northern Mackenzie, western Victoria Island, northern Keewatin (Melville Peninsula), the northwest coast of Hudson Bay (Cape Fullerton), and Southampton and northern Baffin islands; and in the Palearctic in northern Greenland, Spitsbergen, the Taimyr Peninsula, Severnaya Zemlya, mouth of the Lena River, and the New Siberian Islands. Nonbreeding birds occur in summer in the winter range.

Winters in the Hawaiian Islands; in the Americas in the Aleutians (locally), and from southern Alaska (west to the Aleutians), the Gulf coast and Massachusetts south along the coasts of North America and Middle America, through the West Indies, and along the coasts of South America to Tierra del Fuego; in the Old World from the British Isles, Outer Hebrides, Mediterranean region, Caspian Sea, Gulf of Oman, northern India, Burma and China south to South Africa, Madagascar, southern India, the Maldive Islands, Ceylon, the East Indies and Australia; and on Pacific islands from the Mariana and Marshall islands south to the Phoenix, Union and Galapagos islands.

In migration occurs in North America along the Pacific coast from the Aleutians and southern Alaska, the Atlantic coast from Newfoundland, and in the interior in the prairie areas of the Canadian provinces and from the Great Lakes southward, rarely elsewhere in the interior and north to Labrador.

Casual in Jan Mayen, Franz Josef Land and New Zealand.

Notes.—Often placed in the monotypic genus *Crocethia.*

Calidris pusilla (Linnaeus). SEMIPALMATED SANDPIPER. [245.]

> *Tringa pusilla* Linnaeus, 1766, Syst. Nat., ed. 12, 1, p. 252. Based on "La petite Alouette-de-mer de S. Domingue" Brisson, Ornithologie, 5, p. 222, pl. 25, fig. 2. (in Domingo = Hispaniola.)

Habitat.—Open tundra, generally near water (breeding); mudflats, sandy beaches, shores of lakes and ponds, and wet meadows (nonbreeding).

Distribution.—*Breeds* from the Arctic coast of western and northern Alaska (south to Norton Bay), northern Yukon, northern Mackenzie, Canadian Arctic islands (Banks, Victoria, King William, central Baffin, and probably also Melville and Somerset islands), and northern Labrador south to western Alaska (mouth of the Yukon River), east-central Mackenzie, southeastern Keewatin, northeastern Manitoba, Southampton Island, northern Ontario (Cape Henrietta Maria), northern Quebec and coastal Labrador. Nonbreeding individuals often summer in coastal North America south to the Gulf coast and Panama.

Winters from southern Florida and the Bahamas south through the West Indies (possibly along the Gulf-Caribbean coast of Middle America) and along the Caribbean-Atlantic coast of South America (also Tobago and Trinidad) to Paraguay and southern Brazil, casually to southern Argentina; and along the Pacific coast of Middle America and South America from Guatemala (casually Oaxaca) south to northern Chile.

Migrates primarily along the Atlantic-Gulf coast of North America from Newfoundland southward, through the interior of North America east of the Rockies, and rarely but regularly through the Pribilofs, along the Pacific coast from British Columbia southward, and through the interior of western North America.

Casual in the Pribilof and Aleutian islands, Bermuda, the Galapagos Islands, British Isles, continental Europe and the Azores.

Notes.—*C. pusilla* and *C. mauri* are often placed in the genus *Ereunetes.*

Calidris mauri (Cabanis). WESTERN SANDPIPER. [246.]

Ereunetes Mauri Cabanis, 1857, J. Ornithol., 4 (1856), p. 419. (South Carolina.)

Habitat.—Coastal sedge-dwarf tundra (breeding); mudflats, beaches, shores or lakes and ponds, and flooded fields (nonbreeding).

Distribution.—*Breeds* on islands in the Bering Sea (St. Lawrence, Nunivak) and along the coasts of western and northern Alaska (from Bristol Bay and the Kashunuk River to the Seward Peninsula and, less frequently, Point Barrow and Camden Bay), and in northeastern Siberia. Nonbreeding birds summer south at least to Panama.

Winters from the coast of California (rarely from southern Alaska) and North Carolina (rarely New Jersey) south along both coasts of North America and Middle America, and through the West Indies to South America (also the Netherlands Antilles and Trinidad), on the Pacific coast to northern Peru and the Atlantic coast east to Surinam.

Migrates most commonly along the Pacific coast from Alaska to South America, less commonly through the interior from central Alberta, southern Saskatchewan, southern (casually northeastern) Manitoba and southern Ontario southward, regularly in small numbers (especially in fall) through the Pribilofs, along the Atlantic coast from New England (rarely Quebec, New Brunswick and Nova Scotia) southward, and casually to the Aleutians.

Casual in the Hawaiian Islands (Kure, Kauai, Oahu, Maui) and the Galapagos Islands. Accidental in the Canary Islands, Tasmania and Japan.

Notes.—See comments under *C. pusilla.*

Calidris ruficollis (Pallas). RUFOUS-NECKED STINT. [242.2.]

Trynga ruficollis Pallas, 1776, Reise Versch. Prov. Russ. Reichs, 3, p. 700. (circa Lacus salsos Dauuriae campestris = Kulussutai, eastern Siberia.)

Habitat.—Swampy or mossy rundra, especially with scattered willow scrub (breeding); tidal mudflats and beaches (nonbreeding).

Distribution.—*Breeds* in North America in northern and western Alaska (Point Barrow and Seward Peninsula); and in Eurasia in northeastern Siberia (Chukotski Peninsula to Anadyrland and Koryakland). Recorded in summer (and possibly breeding) elsewhere in Alaska (Kotzebue Sound, St. Lawrence Island and Alaska Peninsula).

Winters from southern China south to the Andaman and Nicobar islands, East Indies, New Guinea, the Bismarck and Solomon islands, Australia, Tasmania and New Zealand.

In migration occurs in coastal northern Alaska (east to the Colville River), through the Pribilofs and Aleutians, and widely in coastal western, south-coastal and (casually) southeastern Alaska, also casually along the Pacific coast of British Columbia (Vancouver Island) and in California (south to San Diego County and Salton Sea).

Casual or accidental in Maine (Biddeford Pool), Massachusetts (Monomoy, Scituate), Connecticut (Guilford) and Ohio (Ashtabula).

Notes.—Also known as RED-NECKED STINT or RUFOUS-NECKED SANDPIPER. *C. ruficollis* and *C. minuta* may constitute a superspecies.

Calidris minuta (Leisler). LITTLE STINT. [242.3.]

> *Tringa minuta* Leisler, 1812, Nactr. Bechsteins Naturgesch. Dtsch., pt. 1, p. 74. (region of Hanau au Main, Germany.)

Habitat & Distribution.—*Breeds* on the tundra from northern Scandinavia east to the New Siberian Islands, and *winters* in marshes, flooded fields and mudflats in Africa and the Indian region.

Casual or accidental in the Aleutians (Buldir), on islands in the Bering Sea (St. Lawrence Island, and St. Paul and St. George in the Pribilofs), and in northern Alaska (Point Barrow), Ontario (North Bay on James Bay), New Brunswick (Grand Manan), Massachusetts (Monomoy), Delaware (Kent County) and Bermuda; a report from Attu in the Aleutians is erroneous.

Notes.—See comments under *C. ruficollis*.

Calidris temminckii (Leisler). TEMMINCK'S STINT. [241.1.]

> *Tringa Temminckii* Leisler, 1812, Nachtr. Bechsteins Naturgesch. Dtsch., pt. 1, p. 64. (region of Hanau au Main, Germany.)

Habitat.—Mossy or wet tundra, and grassy meadows in the taiga (breeding); mudflats, shallow marshes, shores of lakes and ponds, flooded fields and, rarely, tidal flats (nonbreeding).

Distribution.—*Breeds* from northern Scandinavia east across northern Russia to northern Siberia, and south to the Chukotski Peninsula and Anadyrland. Nonbreeding individuals summer south to Lake Baikal.

Winters from the Mediterranean region, Arabia, Iraq, Iran, India, southeastern China and Formosa south to central Africa, Ceylon, the Maldive Islands, Southeast Asia and Borneo, casually in Japan and the Philippines.

In migration ranges rarely (or casually) to western Alaska (Wales), and to St. Matthew, St. Lawrence, the Pribilof (St. George) and western Aleutian (Attu, Shemya, Buldir) islands.

Calidris subminuta (Middendorff). LONG-TOED STINT. [242.1.]

> *Tringa subminuta* Middendorff, 1851, Reise Sib., 2 (2), p. 222. (Höhen des Westabhanges vom Stanowoi Gebirge und des Nähe des Ausflusses des Uda = Stanovoi Mountains, Siberia.)

Habitat.—Mossy or wet tundra (breeding); sandy beaches, mudflats and shores of lakes and ponds (nonbreeding).

Distribution.—*Breeds* in the Commander Islands, in Anadyrland and (probably) Kamchatka, and on Sakhalin and the northern Kurile Islands.

Winters from eastern India, southeastern China, Formosa and the Philippines south to Ceylon, the East Indies and northern Australia.

In migration ranges rarely but regularly to the Aleutians (east to Adak), casually to the Pribilofs (Otter, St. Paul, St. George), St. Lawrence Island and western mainland Alaska (Wales).

Accidental in the western Hawaiian Islands (Midway) and Oregon (South Jetty, Columbia River); reports from British Columbia (Vancouver area) require confirmation.

Notes.—*C. subminuta* and *C. minutilla* appear to constitute a superspecies.

Calidris minutilla (Vieillot). LEAST SANDPIPER. [242.]

Tringa minutilla Vieillot, 1819, Nouv. Dict. Hist. Nat., nouv. éd., 34, p. 466. (Amérique jusq'au delà du Canada = Halifax, Nova Scotia.)

Habitat.—Mossy or wet grassy tundra, occasionally in drier areas with scattered scrubby bushes (breeding); wet meadows, mudflats, flooded fields, shores of pools and lakes, and, less frequently, sandy beaches (nonbreeding).

Distribution.—*Breeds* from western Alaska (Kobuk River), northern Yukon, northern Mackenzie, southern Keewatin, Southampton Island, northern Quebec and northern Labrador south to the eastern Aleutians (Unalaska), Alaska Peninsula, southeastern Alaska, northwestern British Columbia, northern Saskatchewan, northeastern Manitoba, northern Ontario, eastern Quebec (Anticosti and Magdalen islands), Nova Scotia (Sable Island) and Newfoundland, with an isolated breeding in Massachusetts (Monomoy). Nonbreeding birds summer in the wintering range, primarily in North America south to California and the Gulf coast.

Winters from coastal Oregon, California, southern Nevada, central Arizona, southern Utah, central New Mexico, central Texas, the Gulf states and North Carolina (casually north to Long Island) south through Middle America, the West Indies and South America (also all islands off the north coast) to the Galapagos Islands, northern Chile, and central and eastern Peru.

Migrates regularly along coastal areas and through interior North America, west to the Pribilof and eastern Aleutian islands, and east to western Greenland.

Casual in the Hawaiian Islands (Oahu, Maui), north to southern Victoria, Melville and southern Baffin islands, and in Bermuda, Europe and the Azores.

Notes.—See comments under *C. subminuta.*

Calidris fuscicollis (Vieillot). WHITE-RUMPED SANDPIPER. [240.]

Tringa fuscicollis Vieillot, 1819, Nouv. Dict. Hist. Nat., nouv. éd., 34, p. 461. (Paraguay.)

Habitat.—Mossy or grassy tundra near water (breeding); grassy marshes, mudflats, sandy beaches, flooded fields, and shores of ponds and lakes (nonbreeding).

Distribution.—*Breeds* from northern Alaska, northern Yukon (possibly), northwestern Mackenzie, and Banks, Melville, Bathurst and northern Bylot islands south to the mainland coasts of Mackenzie and Keewatin, northwestern Hudson Bay (Chesterfield Inlet), and Southampton and southern Baffin islands.

Winters extensively in South America, primarily east of the Andes, south to Cape Horn and Tierra del Fuego, casually west of the Andes to Chile.

Migrates in spring primarily through Central America, eastern Mexico (recorded Tamaulipas, Veracruz, the state of Yucatán, and Cozumel Island) and the interior of North America from the Rockies east to the Mississippi and Ohio valleys, less commonly on the Atlantic seaboard north to the Maritime Provinces; and in fall from Hudson Bay through the interior and along the Atlantic coast from Labrador and Newfoundland south through the West Indies and northern South America (also most islands off Venezuela).

Casual on Prince Patrick Island, and in western North America from south-coastal Alaska (Copper River delta) and British Columbia south to southern California and Arizona (also recorded Montana). Accidental in the Galapagos Islands, Franz Josef Land, the British Isles, continental Europe, the Azores and Australia.

Calidris bairdii (Coues). BAIRD'S SANDPIPER. [241.]

Actodromus Bairdii Coues, 1861, Proc. Acad. Nat. Sci. Philadelphia, 13, p. 194. (Fort Resolution [Great Slave Lake, Mackenzie].)

Habitat.—Dry coastal and alpine tundra (breeding); mudflats, estuaries, grassy marshes, and dry grassy areas near lakes and ponds, rarely dry pastures and prairies away from water (nonbreeding).

Distribution.—*Breeds* from western and northern Alaska (Wales and Point Barrow eastward), northern Yukon, and Melville, Ellef Ringnes and Ellesmere islands south to central Alaska (Ashinuk Mountains and Susitna River highlands), northern Mackenzie, northern Keewatin, southern Melville Peninsula, and Southampton and south-central Baffin islands; also in northwestern Greenland, and on the Chukotski Peninsula in northeastern Siberia.

Winters in South America locally in the Andes of Ecuador, and from central Peru, Bolivia, Paraguay and Uruguay south through Chile and Argentina to Tierra del Fuego.

Migrates primarily through the central interior of Canada and the central plains of the United States, and, in spring only, through Venezuela, Colombia, Central America (rarely, recorded Costa Rica, El Salvador and Guatemala) and Mexico (casually, recorded Oaxaca and the Tres Marias Islands); less frequently (primarily juveniles) and mostly in fall through the Pacific region (the entire Pacific coast of Alaska south to Baja California and Arizona, rarely in Middle America) and along the Atlantic coast (Prince Edward Island, Nova Scotia and, rarely, Newfoundland south to Florida and the Gulf coast); and rarely elsewhere in interior North America.

Casual in the Hawaiian Islands (Laysan, Oahu), the Outer Hebrides, Faroe Islands, British Isles, continental Europe, and the Kurile and Galapagos islands. Accidental in South West Africa and Tasmania.

Calidris melanotos (Vieillot). PECTORAL SANDPIPER. [239.]

Tringa melanotos Vieillot, 1819, Nouv. Dict. Hist. Nat., nouv. éd., 34, p. 462. (Paraguay.)

Habitat.—Wet coastal tundra (breeding); wet meadows, mudflats, flooded fields, and shores of ponds and pools (nonbreeding).

Distribution.—*Breeds* from western and northern Alaska (Wales and Point Barrow eastward), northern Yukon, northern Mackenzie, and Banks, Victoria, Bathurst, Devon, northern Baffin and Southampton islands south to western Alaska (Goodnews Bay), central Mackenzie, southeastern Keewatin, and the south coast of Hudson Bay (locally to Cape Henrietta Maria); and along the Arctic coast of central and eastern Siberia from the Taimyr Peninsula eastward.

Winters in southern South America from Peru, Bolivia and southern Brazil south to central Chile and southern Argentina, casually north to the Gulf coast and Florida.

Migrates chiefly through interior North America, Middle America and northern South America, and in fall (uncommon in spring) through eastern North America (north to Labrador and Newfoundland) and the West Indies, including most islands off the north coast of South America; also rarely (mostly in fall) through the Hawaiian, Pribilof and Aleutian islands, to the Pacific coast from British

Columbia southward, and along the coast of eastern Asia from the Kurile Islands and Sakhalin south to Japan.

Casual north to Prince Patrick Island, and in western Greenland, Iceland, the British Isles, continental Europe, the Azores, Zambia, Australia, New Zealand and Polynesia. Accidental in the Galapagos Islands.

Calidris acuminata (Horsfield). SHARP-TAILED SANDPIPER. [238.]

Totanus acuminatus Horsfield, 1821, Trans. Linn. Soc. London, 13 (1), p. 192. (Java.)

Habitat.—Grassy tundra (breeding); wet grassy areas, marshes, flooded fields, mudflats, and shores of lakes and ponds (nonbreeding).

Distribution.—*Breeds* in northern Siberia from the Indigirka to the Kolyma, probably also on the Chukotski Peninsula. Recorded rarely in summer (and possibly breeding) in western Alaska (Barrow, Kivalina).

Winters from New Guinea, New Caledonia and the Tonga Islands south to Australia, Tasmania and (rarely) New Zealand.

Migrates regularly through the Hawaiian Islands (mostly in western chain), western Alaska (north to Cape Seppings and Kotzebue Sound), islands in the Bering Sea, the Aleutians, and east to Kodiak Island, and from eastern Siberia, Sakhalin and Japan south through eastern China, the Philippines, East Indies (occasionally) and Ryukyu Islands; and rarely but regularly (primarily in fall) from south-coastal and southeastern Alaska south along the Pacific coast to southern California, and through Pacific islands from Johnston and the Marshall islands south to the Gilbert and Phoenix islands.

Casual elsewhere in North America, mostly in fall (recorded Alberta, Saskatchewan, Arizona, Colorado, Iowa, Illinois, Ontario, New York, Massachusetts, Connecticut, Maryland and Florida). Accidental on Tristan da Cunha, and in the British Isles and northern India; a record from Vera Paz, Guatemala, is an error.

Calidris maritima (Brünnich). PURPLE SANDPIPER. [235.]

Tringa Maritima Brünnich, 1764, Ornithol. Bor., p. 54. (E Christiansöe & Norvegia = Christiansöe, Denmark.)

Habitat.—Mossy tundra, moorlands and heath, and coastal barren flats (breeding); rocky seacoasts and jetties, rarely along shores of large inland bodies of water, usually in rocky areas (nonbreeding).

Distribution.—*Breeds* in North America from Melville, Bathurst, Devon, Bylot and Baffin islands south to Southampton and Belcher islands, and James Bay (North Twin Island); and in the Palearctic from western and southeastern Greenland, Iceland, Spitsbergen, Bear Island, Franz Josef Land, Novaya Zemlya, the New Siberian Islands and Taimyr Peninsula south to the Faroe Islands, northern Scandinavia, northern Russia and northern Siberia. Recorded in summer (and possibly breeding) west to Banks and Prince Patrick Islands.

Winters in North America from southern New Brunswick, Prince Edward Island, Nova Scotia and Newfoundland south along the Atlantic coast to Maryland, rarely south to Florida, and casually inland to the Great Lakes (west to Minnesota, Iowa, Wisconsin and Indiana) and along the Gulf coast to southeastern Texas.

In migration occurs on Prince of Wales Island and in coastal areas from Labrador southward.

Casual in Manitoba and the Azores.

Notes.—*C. maritima* and *C. ptilocnemis* constitute a superspecies; they are regarded as conspecific by some authors.

Calidris ptilocnemis (Coues). ROCK SANDPIPER. [236.]

Tringa ptilocnemis Coues, 1873, *in* Elliott, Rep. Seal Islands [*in* Affairs in Alaska], (not paged). (St. George Island, Pribilof Islands.)

Habitat.—Grassy or mossy tundra in coastal or montane areas (breeding); rocky seacoasts, breakwaters and mudflats (nonbreeding).

Distribution.—*Breeds* in central western Alaska (from Wales south probably to Hooper Bay), on islands in the Bering Sea (St. Lawrence, St. Matthew, Nunivak and the Pribilofs), in the Aleutian and Shumagin islands (Sanak), and in eastern Siberia on the Chukotski Peninsula and in the Commander Islands.

Winters from southern Alaska (west to the Aleutians and Alaska Peninsula) south along the Pacific coast to central (casually southern, at least formerly) California; and in Eurasia from the Commander Islands south to the northern Kurile Islands. A report from northwestern Baja California is probably erroneous.

Notes.—See comments under *C. maritima.*

Calidris alpina (Linnaeus). DUNLIN. [243.]

Tringa alpina Linnaeus, 1758, Syst. Nat., ed. 10, 1, p. 149. (in Lapponia = Lapland.)

Habitat.—Wet coastal tundra (breeding); mudflats, estuaries, marshes, flooded fields, sandy beaches, and shores of lakes and ponds (nonbreeding).

Distribution.—*Breeds* in North America from northern Alaska, northern Mackenzie (Baillie Island), northeastern Keewatin and southern Somerset Island south to coastal western Alaska (Nunivak Island, Hooper Bay and Cook Inlet), Southampton Island, northeastern Manitoba (Churchill) and northern Ontario (Cape Henrietta Maria), rarely to south-coastal Alaska (Cook Inlet and Cooper River delta); and in the Palearctic from eastern Greenland, Iceland, Spitsbergen, Novaya Zemlya and the Arctic coast of Siberia south to the British Isles, Baltic region, northern Russia and northern China. Recorded in summer (and possibly breeding) north to Melville Island and east to Baffin Island; nonbreeding individuals are often recorded in summer in the winter range.

Winters in the Hawaiian Islands (in smaller numbers), and in North America along the Pacific coast from southeastern Alaska south to Baja California and Sonora, and on the Atlantic-Gulf-Caribbean coast from Massachusetts south to Florida, west to Texas, and south to the Yucatan Peninsula; and in the Old World from the British Isles, Mediterranean and Red seas, Gulf of Aden, India, southeastern China and Japan south to the Cape Verde Islands, northern Africa, Arabia, the Indian coast and Formosa.

Migrates primarily along the Bering Sea coast of Alaska, the Pacific coast from the Aleutians and southern Alaska southward, the Atlantic coast from eastern Quebec and Nova Scotia southward, and in smaller numbers through the interior of North America from southern Canada south to Arizona, New Mexico and the Gulf coast, most frequently through the Mississippi Valley and Great Lakes region.

Casual in the Pribilof Islands, Newfoundland, Oaxaca, Guatemala, Costa Rica,

Panama, and the West Indies (irregularly south to Barbados); a report from Nicaragua is considered an error. Accidental in Peru (sight report).

Notes.—Also known as RED-BACKED SANDPIPER.

Calidris ferruginea (Pontoppidan). CURLEW SANDPIPER. [244.]

> *Tringa Ferruginea* Pontoppidan, 1763, Dan. Atlas, 1, p. 624. (Iceland and Christiansöe [Denmark].)

Habitat.—Drier portions of Arctic tundra (breeding); mudflats, marshes and beaches (nonbreeding).

Distribution.—*Breeds* in North America rarely in northern Alaska (Barrow); and in Eurasia in northern Siberia from the Yenisei Delta east through the Taimyr Peninsula and New Siberian Islands to Cape Baranov. Recorded in summer on Bering Island.

Winters from the British Isles (rarely), Mediterranean region, Iraq, India, Burma, southern Thailand and the Philippines (rarely) south to southern Africa, Madagascar, Mauritius, Ceylon, the Malay Peninsula, southern Australia, Tasmania and New Zealand.

In migration occurs casually in western Alaska and the Aleutian Islands.

Casual along the Pacific coast of North America from south-coastal Alaska south to California, and to eastern North America from southern Ontario, Quebec, New Brunswick and Nova Scotia south to Florida and west along the Gulf coast to Louisiana (sight reports also from Texas); recorded in interior North America in Alberta, Utah, Kansas, Illinois and Indiana (sight records from Montana, Wisconsin and Michigan), and in the Lesser Antilles (Grenada, Carriacou and Barbados, also sight records from Antigua and the Virgin Islands). Accidental in Peru and Argentina.

Calidris himantopus (Bonaparte). STILT SANDPIPER. [233.]

> *Tringa himantopus* Bonaparte, 1826, Ann. Lyc. Nat. Hist. N.Y., 2, p. 157. (Long Branch, New-Jersey.)

Habitat.—Sedge tundra near water, often near wooded borders of the taiga (breeding); mudflats, flooded fields, shallow ponds and pools, and marshes (nonbreeding).

Distribution.—*Breeds* from northern Alaska (west to Prudhoe Bay, probably rarely Colville River), northern Yukon (probably), northern Mackenzie (Cockburn Point, Perry River) and southern Victoria Island southeast to southeastern Keewatin, northeastern Manitoba and northern Ontario (Cape Henrietta Maria), probably also south locally in Canada to borders of the taiga.

Winters primarily in South America from Bolivia and south-central Brazil south to northern Chile and northern Argentina, casually northward through Middle America (regularly around the Gulf of Nicoya in Costa Rica) and the West Indies to southeastern California, the Gulf coast and Florida.

Migrates mostly through central North America (from the Rockies east to the Mississippi and Ohio valleys) and Middle America (not recorded Belize), in the fall also regularly along the Atlantic coast from New Brunswick and Nova Scotia southward (including the West Indies), and rarely in both migration periods west of the Rockies primarily along the Pacific coast from southeastern Alaska southward, but casually through western Alaska, the Pribilof Islands and south-coastal Alaska.

Casual on Bathurst Island, and in Bermuda and the Galapagos Islands. Accidental in the British Isles.

Notes.—Often placed in the monotypic genus *Micropalama.*

Genus EURYNORHYNCHUS Nilsson

Eurynorhynchus Nilsson, 1821, Ornithol. Svecica, 2, p. 29. Type, by monotypy, *Eurynorhynchus griseus* Nilsson = *Platalea pygmea* Linnaeus.

Notes.—This monotypic genus is distinguished from *Calidris* primarily by its highly specialized bill; some authors would merge *Eurynorhynchus* in *Calidris.*

Eurynorhynchus pygmeus (Linnaeus). SPOONBILL SANDPIPER. [245.]

Platalea pygmea Linnaeus, 1758, Syst. Nat., ed. 10, 1, p. 140. Based on *Platalea corpore supra fusco, subtus albo* Linnaeus, Mus. Adolphi Friderici, 2, p. . . . . (in Surinami, error = eastern Asia.)

Habitat & Distribution.—*Breeds* on stone or shell banks in northeastern Siberia, and *winters* on mudflats and beaches from southeastern China south to Southeast Asia.

Accidental in northwestern Alaska (Wainwright Inlet, 15 August 1914), the Aleutians (Buldir, 2 June 1977) and British Columbia (Vancouver, 31 July–3 August 1978).

Genus LIMICOLA Koch

Limicola C. L. Koch, 1816, Syst. Baier. Zool., 1, p. 316. Type, by monotypy, *Numenius pygmaeus* Bechstein = *Scolopax falcinellus* Pontoppidan.

Limicola falcinellus (Pontoppidan). BROAD-BILLED SANDPIPER. [248.1.]

Scolopax Falcinellus Pontoppidan, 1763, Dan. Atlas, 1, p. 263. (No locality given = Denmark.)

Habitat & Distribution.—*Breeds* on tundra in northern Scandinavia, the Kola Peninsula and probably also northern Siberia, and *winters* on marshes, mudflats and beaches from the Mediterranean region, India and southeastern China south to the East Indies, Australia and New Zealand.

Casual in the Aleutians on Adak (19 August 1977; Day, *et al.,* 1979, Auk, 96, pp. 189–190) and Shemya (30 August–6 September 1978, five individuals; Gibson, 1981, Condor, 83, p. 70).

Genus TRYNGITES Cabanis

Tryngites Cabanis, 1857, J. Ornithol., 4 (1856), p. 418. Type, by original designation, *Tringa rufescens* Vieillot = *Tringa subruficollis* Vieillot.

Tryngites subruficollis (Vieillot). BUFF-BREASTED SANDPIPER. [262.]

Tringa subruficollis Vieillot, 1819, Nouv. Dict. Hist. Nat., nouv. éd., 34, p. 465. (Paraguay.)

Habitat.—Dry, grassy tundra (breeding); dry grasslands (usually short grass), pastures, plowed fields and, rarely, mudflats (nonbreeding).

Distribution.—*Breeds* from northern Alaska (Barrow and Atkasuk eastward), northern Yukon, northwestern Mackenzie, and Banks, Melville, Bathurst and Devon islands south to southern Victoria, Jenny Lind (in Queen Maud Gulf) and King William islands.

Winters in South America in Paraguay, Uruguay and northern Argentina.

Migrates primarily through the interior of North America (between the Rocky Mountains and the Mississippi Valley), eastern Mexico (recorded Tamaulipas and Guanajuato), Central America (not recorded Belize) and northern South America (also Trinidad) east to Guyana and Surinam, rarely (mostly in fall) through eastern North America from southern Ontario, eastern Quebec and Nova Scotia south to southern Florida, and through the West Indies, casually in western North America from western Alaska, the Pribilof and Aleutian islands, and southern Alaska south to California.

Casual or accidental in the Hawaiian Islands (Kauai, Oahu), Labrador, Newfoundland, the British Isles, continental Europe, Egypt, eastern Siberia, the Kurile Islands, Japan and Australia.

Genus **PHILOMACHUS** Merrem

Philomachus Anonymous [=Merrem], 1804, Allg. Lit. Ztg., 2, no. 168, col. 542. Type, by monotypy, *Tringa pugnax* Linnaeus.

Philomachus pugnax (Linnaeus). RUFF. [260.]

Tringa Pugnax Linnaeus, 1758, Syst. Nat., ed. 10, 1, p. 148. (in Europa minus boreali = southern Sweden.)

Habitat.—Grassy tundra, along shores of lakes and ponds, in swampy meadows and marshes, and rarely in hayfields, in migration and winter also mudflats and flooded fields.

Distribution.—*Breeds* in Eurasia from northern Scandinavia, northern Russia and northern Siberia south to the British Isles (at least formerly), western and southern Europe, southern Russia, southern Siberia and the Chukotski Peninsula; also has nested in North America in northwestern Alaska (Point Lay). Occasional nonbreeding individuals are recorded in summer in the wintering range.

Winters from the British Isles, southern Europe, Iraq, Arabia, the Persian Gulf, southeastern China and Formosa south to southern Africa, India, Ceylon, the East Indies, Philippines and Australia.

In migration occurs rarely but regularly in the Hawaiian Islands, through western and southwestern Alaska (including St. Lawrence, Pribilof and Aleutian islands), along the east coast of North America (from Massachusetts to North Carolina), and in the Lesser Antilles (mostly in fall, recorded Guadeloupe, Barbados, St. Lucia and Grenada).

Casual in western North America (primarily along the Pacific coast) from southcoastal Alaska south to southern California and Arizona; throughout most of North America east of the Rockies from southern Alberta, southern Saskatchewan, northeastern Manitoba, Minnesota, Wisconsin, Michigan, southern Ontario, Quebec and Nova Scotia south to Texas, the Gulf coast and Florida; and in northeastern Manitoba (Churchill), Guatemala (Dpto. de Santa Rosa), Costa Rica (Chomes, sight reports), Panama (Canal Zone), Jamaica, Puerto Rico, the Virgin

Islands, Trinidad, Greenland, Iceland, the Faroe Islands, Johnston Island, and the Marshall Islands.

Tribe LIMNODROMINI: Dowitchers

Genus LIMNODROMUS Wied

Limnodromus Wied, 1833, Beitr. Naturgesch. Bras., 4, p. 716. Type, by monotypy, *Scolopax noveboracensis* Gmelin = *Scolopax grisea* Gmelin.

Limnodromus griseus (Gmelin). SHORT-BILLED DOWITCHER. [231.]

Scolopax grisea Gmelin, 1789, Syst. Nat., 1 (2), p. 658. Based on the "Brown Snipe" Pennant, Arct. Zool., 2, p. 464. (in Noveboraci maritimis = Long Island, New York.)

Habitat.—Grassy or mossy tundra and wet meadows (breeding); mudflats, estuaries, shallow marshes, pools, ponds, flooded fields and sandy beaches (nonbreeding).

Distribution.—*Breeds* in coastal regions of southern Alaska (Bristol Bay east to the Stikine River mouth); in central Canada from southern Yukon, southern Mackenzie and northeastern Manitoba south to east-central British Columbia, central Alberta and central Saskatchewan; and from the interior of the Ungava Peninsula south (probably) to northern Ontario (vicinity of Fort Albany). Nonbreeding individuals often occur in summer south to the wintering grounds.

Winters from central California, southern Arizona, the Gulf coast and coastal South Carolina south through Middle America, the West Indies and South America to central Peru and east-central Brazil.

Migrates regularly along the Pacific coast of North America from southeastern Alaska southward, through the interior of North America in the prairie regions of the Canadian provinces and from the Great Lakes region south through the Mississippi Valley, and along the Atlantic coast from southern Quebec, New Brunswick, Nova Scotia and Newfoundland southward, occurring casually elsewhere in the interior of the United States.

Casual or accidental in the Hawaiian Islands (Midway), Pribilof Islands, Bermuda, Greenland, the British Isles and continental Europe.

Notes.—*L. griseus* and *L. scolopaceus* constitute a superspecies.

Limnodromus scolopaceus (Say). LONG-BILLED DOWITCHER. [232.]

Limosa scolopacea Say, 1823, *in* Long, Exped. Rocky Mount., 1, p. 170. (near Boyer Creek = Council Bluffs, Iowa.)

Habitat.—Grassy tundra and wet meadows (breeding); marshes, shores of ponds and lakes, mudflats and flooded fields, primarily in fresh-water situations (nonbreeding).

Distribution.—*Breeds* in North America in coastal western and northern Alaska (Hooper Bay, and Point Barrow eastward), northern Yukon and northwestern Mackenzie; and in Eurasia in northeastern Siberia on the Chukotski Peninsula and in Anadyrland.

Winters from central California, southern Arizona, southern New Mexico, central Texas, the Gulf coast and southern Florida south through Mexico (mostly the western part) to Guatemala, rarely to Costa Rica, and casually to Panama (Bocas del Toro, and probably Canal Zone).

Migrates primarily through western North America west of the Rocky Mountains, less frequently (and primarily in fall) east of the Rockies from southern Canada (Alberta east to Quebec and, rarely, Nova Scotia) south to Florida, casually through the Aleutians and to the Antilles (recorded Cuba, Jamaica and Anegada).

Casual in the Hawaiian Islands (Kure, with many other records of "dowitchers" from throughout the islands attributed to this species). A record of an individual of this species in breeding plumage taken in October in Argentina (Buenos Aires) is open to question; sight records from South America likely pertain to *L. griseus.*

Notes.—See comments under *L. griseus.*

Tribe GALLINAGOINI: Snipe

Genus **LYMNOCRYPTES** Kaup

Lymnocryptes Kaup, 1829, Skizz. Entw.-Ges. Eur. Thierw., p. 118. Type, by monotypy, *Scolopax gallinula* Linnaeus = *Scolopax minima* Brünnich.

Lymnocryptes minimus (Brünnich). JACK SNIPE. [230.2.]

Scolopax Minima Brünnich, 1764, Ornithol. Bor., p. 49. (E Christiansöe [Island, Denmark].)

Habitat & Distribution.—*Breeds* on the tundra from northern Eurasia south to central Russia and central Siberia, and *winters* in swamps and flooded fields from the British Isles, southern Europe, India and southeastern China south to central Africa, Ceylon and Formosa.

Casual in Iceland, the Faroe Islands, Madeira, the Azores, Kurile Islands and Japan. Accidental in Alaska (St. Paul in the Pribilof Islands, Spring 1919), California (Gridley, Butte County, 20 November 1938), Labrador (Makkovik Bay, 24 December 1927) and Barbados (12 November 1960).

Notes.—Also known as EUROPEAN JACKSNIPE.

Genus **GALLINAGO** Brisson

Gallinago Brisson, 1760, Ornithologie, 5, p. 298. Type, by tautonymy, *Gallinago* Brisson = *Scolopax gallinago* Linnaeus.
Capella Frenzel, 1801, Beschr. Vögel Eyer Wittenberg, p. 58. Type, by monotypy, *Scolopax coelestis* Frenzel = *Scolopax gallinago* Linnaeus.

Notes.—For use of *Gallinago* instead of *Capella,* see Mayr, 1963, Ibis, pp. 402–403.

Gallinago gallinago (Linnaeus). COMMON SNIPE. [230.]

Scolopax Gallinago Linnaeus, 1758, Syst. Nat., ed. 10, 1, p. 147. (in Europa = Sweden.)

Habitat.—Wet, grassy areas from tundra to temperate lowlands and hilly regions, in winter and migration also wet meadows, flooded fields, bogs, swamps, moorlands, and marshy banks of rivers and lakes (Temperate Zone, in migration and winter also to Tropical and Subtropical zones).

Distribution.—*Breeds* in North America from northern Alaska, northern Yukon, northwestern and central Mackenzie, southern Keewatin, northeastern Manitoba, northern Ontario, northern Quebec and central Labrador south to southern Alaska (west to Unalaska in the Aleutians, probably to Shemya and Attu), central California, east-central Arizona, northern New Mexico (probably), northern Colorado, western Nebraska, central Iowa, northeastern Illinois, northern Indiana, northern Ohio, northern West Virginia, northwestern Pennsylvania, northern New Jersey, New England and the Maritime Provinces; in South America from Colombia, Venezuela (also Trinidad) and the Guianas south to Tierra del Fuego; and in Eurasia from the British Isles, Scandinavia, northern Russia, northern Siberia and Bering Isles, Scandinavia, northern Russia, northern Siberia and Bering Island south to southern Europe, southern Russia, the Himalayas and Kurile Islands. Reported breeding in central Mexico (Jalisco and Guanajuato) and the Azores is open to question.

Winters in the Hawaiian Islands (rarely); in the Americas from southern (rarely) and southeastern Alaska, southern British Columbia, eastern Washington, Oregon, Utah, the central United States (Colorado east to western Kentucky and the northern Gulf states) and Virginia (casually from southern Canada) south through Middle America, the West Indies and South America to Tierra del Fuego, the North American breeding populations reaching Colombia, Venezuela, Surinam and Ecuador; and in the Old World from the British Isles, southern Europe, Madeira (casually), southern Russia and Japan south to south-central Africa, Ceylon, the Andaman Islands, Java and the Philippines.

In migration occurs regularly in the central and western Aleutian Islands.

Notes.—Known in Old World literature as the SNIPE; the North American breeding populations are sometimes called WILSON'S SNIPE. The Eurasian race *G. g. gallinago* occurs in the Aleutians (east to Buldir, with probable breeding on Attu and Shemya), and casually in the Hawaiian Islands (Kauai), Pribilofs, Labrador (Jack Lane's Bay) and Bermuda. South American forms are sometimes separated as a distinct species, *G. paraguaiae* (Vieillot, 1816). The African *G. nigripennis* Bonaparte, 1839, is considered conspecific with *G. gallinago* by some authors; they constitute at least a superspecies.

[Gallinago media (Latham). GREAT SNIPE.] See Appendix B.

Gallinago stenura (Bonaparte). PIN-TAILED SNIPE. [229.1.]

Scolopax stenura (Kuhl MS) Bonaparte, 1830, Ann. Stor. Nat. Bologna, 4, p. 335. (Sunda Archipelago.)

Habitat & Distribution.—*Breeds* in wet meadows and marshes from northeastern Russia and northern Siberia south to central Russia, northern Manchuria and the Sea of Okhotsk, and *winters* from India, Southeast Asia, southeastern China and Formosa south to the East Indies, casually to northeastern Africa.

Accidental in the Hawaiian Islands (Green Island, Kure, 13 January 1964; Clapp and Woodward, 1968, Proc. U.S. Natl. Mus., 124, p. 21).

Tribe SCOLOPACINI: Woodcocks

Genus **SCOLOPAX** Linnaeus

Scolopax Linnaeus, 1758, Syst. Nat., ed. 10, 1, p. 145. Type, by tautonymy, *Scolopax rusticola* Linnaeus (*Scolopax,* prebinomial specific name, in synonymy).

Subgenus SCOLOPAX Linnaeus

Scolopax rusticola Linnaeus. EURASIAN WOODCOCK. [227.]

Scolopax Rusticola Linnaeus, 1758, Syst. Nat., ed. 10, 1, p. 146. (in Europa = Sweden.)

Habitat.—Moist woodland, both deciduous and coniferous, generally with ground cover of brackens and bushes, also in bogs, heath and moorlands.

Distribution.—*Breeds* locally from the British Isles, Scandinavia and the area of the Arctic Circle in Russia and Siberia south to the eastern Atlantic islands, northern Mediterranean region, southern Russia, northern India, the Himalayas, Turkestan, Transcaucasia, Japan, the Seven Islands of Izu, Kurile Islands and Sakhalin.

Winters from the British Isles, southern Europe, Iraq, Iran, India, southeastern China and Japan south to the Cape Verde Islands, northern Africa, southern India, the Malay Peninsula, Philippines (rarely) and Ryukyu Islands.

Casual in eastern North America (recorded from Newfoundland, southwestern Quebec, New Jersey, Pennsylvania, Ohio, Virginia and Alabama, mostly in the 19th century), and in Greenland, Iceland, the Faroe Islands and Spitsbergen.

Notes.—Also known as EUROPEAN WOODCOCK and, in Old World literature, as the WOODCOCK.

Subgenus PHILOHELA Gray

Philohela G. R. Gray, 1841, List Genera Birds, ed. 2, p. 90. Type, by original designation, *Scolopax minor* Gmelin.

Scolopax minor Gmelin. AMERICAN WOODCOCK. [228.]

Scolopax minor Gmelin, 1789, Syst. Nat., 1 (2), p. 661. Based on the "Little Woodcock" Pennant, Arct. Zool., 2, p. 463, pl. 19, upper fig. (in Americae, . . . in Carolinae, . . . in Noveboraci silvis humidis = New York.)

Habitat.—Moist woodland, primarily deciduous or mixed, thickets along streams or in boggy areas, and less frequently in wet grassy meadows and flooded fields.

Distribution.—*Breeds* from southern Manitoba, northern Minnesota, south-central and southern Ontario, southern Quebec, northern New Brunswick, Prince Edward Island, Nova Scotia and Newfoundland south throughout eastern North America west to southeastern Minnesota, central Iowa, eastern Kansas (probably also to the eastern Dakotas and eastern Nebraska), eastern Oklahoma and east-central Texas, and south to the Gulf states and southern Florida.

Winters in the southeastern United States from eastern Oklahoma, southern Missouri, Tennessee, the northern portions of the Gulf states, and Virginia south to east-central Texas, the Gulf coast and southern Florida, rarely wintering farther north in the breeding range.

Casual or accidental in Montana, Colorado, New Mexico, Manitoba, northeastern Ontario, eastern Quebec and Bermuda, also sight records for the Yucatan Peninsula and Isla Cancun, Mexico.

Subfamily PHALAROPODINAE: Phalaropes

Notes.—Sometimes considered a family, the Phalaropodidae.

Genus **PHALAROPUS** Brisson

Phalaropus Brisson, 1760, Ornithologie, 1, p. 50; 6, p. 12. Type, by tautonymy, *Phalaropus* Brisson = *Tringa fulicaria* Linnaeus.

Lobipes Cuvier, 1817, Règne Anim., 1 (1816), p. 495. Type, by original designation, *Tringa hyperborea* Linnaeus = *Tringa lobata* Linnaeus.

Steganopus Vieillot, 1818, Nouv. Dict. Hist. Nat., nouv. éd., 24 (1817), p. 124. Type, by monotypy, "Chorlito del tarso comprimeido" Azara = *Steganopus tricolor* Vieillot.

Phalaropus tricolor (Vieillot). WILSON'S PHALAROPE. [224.]

Steganopus tricolor Vieillot, 1819, Nouv. Dict. Hist. Nat., nouv. éd., 32, p. 136. Based on "Chorlito Tarso comprimido" Azara, Apunt. Hist. Nat. Páx. Parag., 3, p. 327 (no. 407). (Paraguay.)

Habitat.—Fresh-water marshes and wet meadows, in migration and winter also on lakes, mudflats and salt marshes, and along seacoasts.

Distribution.—*Breeds* in coastal British Columbia (Vancouver Island), and from southern Yukon, northern British Columbia, northern Alberta, central Saskatchewan, west-central and southern Manitoba, central Minnesota, southern Wisconsin, southern Michigan, southern Ontario and southwestern Quebec south in the interior to south-central California, central Nevada, central Utah, east-central Arizona, west-central New Mexico, northern Texas, central Kansas, western Nebraska, eastern South Dakota, northern Iowa (formerly), northern Illinois, northern Indiana and northern Ohio, with isolated breeding in Massachusetts (Plum Island). Recorded in summer (nonbreeding) north to central Alaska, central Mackenzie, northern Saskatchewan, New Brunswick and Nova Scotia.

Winters primarily in western South America from Peru, Bolivia, Paraguay and Uruguay south through Chile and Argentina, casually as far north as southern California and southern Texas.

Migrates regularly through western North America (east to the Great Plains, Texas and southwestern Louisiana), Middle America, Colombia and Ecuador, and uncommonly through eastern North America from Quebec (including Anticosti Island) and New Brunswick south to Florida and the Gulf coast; also recorded regularly in fall on Barbados.

Casual or accidental in the Hawaiian Islands, western and northern Alaska, elsewhere in the West Indies (recorded Grand Cayman, Jamaica, Puerto Rico, Guadeloupe and Martinique), the Galapagos and Falkland islands, British Isles, continental Europe, Africa, islands of the central Pacific (Johnston and Easter), Australia and Antarctica.

Notes.—Often placed in the monotypic genus *Steganopus*.

Phalaropus lobatus (Linnaeus). RED-NECKED PHALAROPE. [223.]

Tringa tobata [sic] Linnaeus, 1758, Syst. Nat., ed. 10, 1, p. 148 [*lobata* in Emendanda, p. 824]. Based on "The Cock Coot-footed Tringa" Edwards, Nat. Hist. Birds, 3, p. 143, pl. 143. (in America septentrionali, Lapponia = Hudson Bay.)

Habitat.—Grass-sedge borders of ponds and lakes (breeding); in winter primarily pelagic, occurring in migration on ponds, lakes, open marshes, estuaries and bays.

Distribution.—*Breeds* in North America from northern Alaska, northern Mackenzie, southern Victoria Island, central Keewatin, and Southampton and southern Baffin islands south to the Pribilof and Aleutian islands, southern Alaska, northwestern British Columbia, southern Yukon, southern Mackenzie, northern Alberta, northern Saskatchewan, northern Manitoba, northern Ontario, islands in southern James Bay, northern Quebec, and locally along the Labrador coast; and in the Palearctic from Greenland, Iceland, the northern British Isles, Faroe and Shetland islands, and Spitsbergen east across Scandinavia, northern Russia and northern Siberia to the Bering Sea, Kamchatka and the Commander Islands. Nonbreeding individuals occur in summer along the cost of Newfoundland and on Miquelon Island.

Winters at sea, in the Pacific from the Ryukyu Islands, central equatorial islands and the Galapagos south to the Lesser Sunda Islands, New Guinea, Australia (rarely), New Zealand and southern South America, casually north to southern California; in the South Atlantic off southern South America and Africa, casually north to the Azores; and in the Indian Ocean from East Africa east to Malaya.

Migrates regularly through the North Pacific and North Atlantic oceans along North American, Middle American and Eurasian coasts, also regularly through western Europe; less commonly but regularly through interior western North America from British Columbia and the prairie regions of Alberta, Saskatchewan and Manitoba south to southern Arizona; rarely or irregularly through the interior central and eastern North America south to San Luis Potosí, southern Texas, the Gulf coast and Florida; and casually through Central America (not recorded Belize or Nicaragua), Cuba and Bermuda, also sight reports from Jamaica, Puerto Rico and the Bahamas (New Providence).

Accidental in the Hawaiian Islands (Laysan, Kauai).

Notes.—Also known as NORTHERN PHALAROPE. This species is often placed in the monotypic genus *Lobipes*.

Phalaropus fulicaria (Linnaeus). RED PHALAROPE. [222.]

Tringa Fulicaria Linnaeus, 1758, Syst. Nat., ed. 10, 1, p. 148. Based on "The Red Coot-footed Tringa" Edwards, Nat Hist. Birds, 3, p. 142, pl. 142. (in America = Hudson Bay.)

Habitat.—Coastal tundra (breeding); in winter primarily pelagic, occurring in migration on bays and estuaries, less frequently on ponds, lakes and marshes.

Distribution.—*Breeds* in North America from western Alaska (Yukon delta and St. Lawrence Island) east across northern Alaska, northern Yukon, northern Mackenzie, and Banks, Melville, Ellesmere, Bylot, Dundas and northern Baffin islands, and south to eastern Keewatin, Southampton and Mansel islands, northern Quebec, and (probably) northern Labrador; and in the Palearctic from Greenland and

Iceland east through Arctic islands (Spitsbergen, Bear, Novaya Zemlya and New Siberian) to northern Siberia. Nonbreeding individuals summer off the coasts of California and Newfoundland.

Winters at sea off the Pacific coast of South America from Colombia and Ecuador south to Chile (also regularly off southern California); in the South Atlantic off Patagonia and the Falkland Islands, and off western Africa; and in the western Pacific from Japan south, at least casually to New Zealand.

Migrates regularly through the Aleutians and along both coasts of North America (recorded south to Baja California, Oaxaca, Texas, the Gulf coast and Florida), irregularly through the interior but casually recorded virtually throughout the continent north of Mexico; also through the North Atlantic, western Mediterranean Sea, western Europe, and the Pacific Ocean off Japan.

Casual in the Hawaiian Islands and Cuba, also sight records from Barbados. Accidental in India and Antarctica.

Notes.—In Old World literature known as GRAY PHALAROPE.

Suborder LARI: Skuas, Gulls, Terns and Skimmers

Family **LARIDAE**: Skuas, Gulls, Terns and Skimmers

Subfamily STERCORARIINAE: Skuas and Jaegers

Notes.—The subfamilies of the Laridae are given family rank by some authors, as the Stercorariidae, Sternidae and Rynchopidae.

Genus **STERCORARIUS** Brisson

Stercorarius Brisson, 1760, Ornithologie, 1, p. 56; 6, p. 149. Type, by tautonymy, *Stercorarius* Brisson = *Larus parasiticus* Linnaeus.
Coprotheres Reichenbach, 1853, Avium Syst. Nat. (1852), p. v. Type, by original designation, *Lestris pomarinus* Temminck.

Stercorarius pomarinus (Temminck). POMARINE JAEGER. [36.]

Lestris pomarinus Temminck, 1815, Man. Ornithol., ed. 1 (1814), p. 514. (les régions du cercle arcticuq; de passage accidentel sur les côtes de Hollande et de France = Arctic regions of Europe.)

Habitat.—Swampy or mossy tundra, and flats near seacoasts (breeding); primarily pelagic, casually on large inland bodies of water (nonbreeding).

Distribution.—*Breeds* in North America in western and northern Alaska (south to Hooper Bay) east across the Canadian Arctic islands (north to Melville, Bathurst, Devon and Baffin islands), and south to northern Mackenzie, Southampton Island and northwestern Quebec; and in the Palearctic in western Greenland, Spitsbergen, Bear Island, Novaya Zemlya, and in northern Russia and northern Siberia from the Taimyr Peninsula to Anadyrland. Nonbreeding birds occur in summer off Alaska and British Columbia (Bering Sea and Aleutians south to Queen Charlotte Islands), in central Canada (south to northern Alberta and Hudson Bay), and in the Atlantic from Labrador and Newfoundland south to New England; also off Scandinavia.

Winters primarily at sea in the Pacific near the Hawaiian Islands (primarily off Oahu), from central California south to Peru and the Galapagos Islands, and off eastern Australia; and in the Atlantic off Florida (possibly as far north as North Carolina) and the West Indies, and off the coasts of northern South America (Colombia to Guyana) and Africa.

In migration occurs regularly off both coasts of North America and along the Gulf coast (west to Texas); not recorded off the Caribbean coast of Middle America between southern Mexico and Costa Rica.

Casual in the interior of North America (from southern Canada south to Arizona, New Mexico and the Gulf states), and in central Europe, Japan, New Zealand and Antarctica.

Notes.—Also known as POMARINE or POMATORHINE SKUA.

Stercorarius parasiticus (Linnaeus). PARASITIC JAEGER. [37.]

Larus parasiticus Linnaeus, 1758, Syst. Nat., ed. 10, 1, p. 136. (intra tropicum Cancri, Europæ, Americæ, Asiæ = coast of Sweden.)

Habitat.—Barren and dwarf-shrub coastal tundra (breeding); mostly pelagic, less frequently along seacoasts, casually on large inland bodies of water (nonbreeding).

Distribution.—*Breeds* in North America from western and northern Alaska (Point Barrow eastward), northwestern Mackenzie, and Banks, southern Melville, Cornwallis, southern Ellesmere and Baffin islands south to the Aleutians, Alaska Peninsula, Kodiak Island, central Mackenzie, southern Keewatin, northeastern Manitoba, Southampton Island, northern Ontario (Cape Henrietta Maria), northern Quebec and northern Labrador; and in the Palearctic from Greenland, Jan Mayen, Spitsbergen, Bear Island and Franz Josef Land south to Iceland, the northern British Isles, northern Scandinavia, northern Russia, Novaya Zemlya, northern Siberia, the Commander Islands, Kamchatka and the Sea of Okhotsk. Nonbreeding birds occur in summer off the Pacific coast of North America south to British Columbia, off the Atlantic coast to Newfoundland, and in the interior to southern Canada; also along the northern coasts of Europe.

Winters mostly in offshore areas in the Pacific from southern California to southern Chile, and west to eastern Australia and New Zealand; in the Atlantic from Maine and the British Isles south to Brazil, eastern Argentina, the west coast of Africa, and the Mediterranean region, occurring west in the Gulf-Caribbean area to Texas; and in the Indian Ocean in the Persian Gulf and Arabian Sea.

In migration occurs regularly off the Pacific coast of North America, and along the Atlantic coast from Newfoundland to Florida, the Bahamas and Cuba, rarely to the Lesser Antilles (Barbados and the Grenadines), and casually through the interior of North America from southern Canada south to Arizona, Texas and the Gulf states (most frequently recorded in the Great Lakes region), and along both coasts of Middle America.

Notes.—Known in Old World literature as ARCTIC SKUA.

Stercorarius longicaudus Vieillot. LONG-TAILED JAEGER. [38.]

Stercorarius longicaudus Vieillot, 1819, Nouv. Dict. Hist. Nat., nouv. éd., 32, p. 157. (le Nord de l'Europe, de l'Asie et de l'Amérique = northern Europe.)

Habitat.—Open or alpine tundra, flats with sparse vegetation and moorlands (breeding); pelagic, casually along seacoasts and on inland waters (nonbreeding).

Distribution.—*Breeds* in North America in western Alaska (St. Matthew, St. Lawrence and Nunivak islands, and Hooper Bay), and from northern Alaska, northern Yukon, northern Mackenzie, northern Keewatin and throughout the Canadian Arctic islands south to central interior Alaska (Brooks Range, Alaska Range, Susitna River highlands), southwestern Yukon, southern Keewatin, Southampton Island and northern Quebec; and in the Palearctic from Greenland, Iceland, Jan Mayen, Spitsbergen, Bear Island and Novaya Zemlya south to northern Scandinavia, northern Russia, northern Siberia, Anadyrland, Kamchatka and the Sea of Okhotsk. Nonbreeding birds occur rarely in summer south to the Aleutian Islands, south-coastal Alaska, southern Mackenzie and southern Hudson Bay.

Winters mostly at sea in the Pacific off South America from Ecuador to Chile, and in the Atlantic from about lat. 40° N. south to Argentina (more commonly in the southern areas).

Migrates primarily well offshore, rarely along the Pacific coast from southeastern Alaska to Middle America (recorded south to Oaxaca, and off Costa Rica) and the Atlantic coast from Newfoundland to New Jersey (casually to Florida), and casually through the interior of North America (mostly in the Great Lakes region, reported occasionally from the prairie regions of the Canadian provinces, the Great Plains states and Mississippi Valley), along the Gulf coast (Texas to Florida) and through the Antilles (recorded Cuba, Martinique and Barbados); also off the coasts of Europe and Africa, casually in the Mediterranean region.

Notes.—In Old World literature known as LONG-TAILED SKUA.

Genus CATHARACTA Brünnich

Catharacta Brünnich, 1764, Ornithol. Bor., p. 32. Type, by subsequent designation (Reichenbach, 1852), *Catharacta skua* Brünnich.

Catharacta skua Brünich. GREAT SKUA. [35.]

Catharacta skua Brünnich, 1764, Ornithol. Bor., p. 33. (E. Feroa Islandia = Iceland.)

Habitat.—Rocky points, moors or pastures near the sea, occasionally sandy flats in estuaries (breeding); mostly pelagic (nonbreeding).

Distribution.—*Breeds* [*skua* group] in Iceland, and the Faroe, Shetland and Orkney islands; [*antarctica* group] in the Falkland Islands and along the coast of southern Argentina; and [*lonnbergi* group] widely on southern oceanic islands such as the South Shetlands, South Orkneys, South Georgia, Bouvet, Marion, Prince Edward, Crozets, Kerguelen, Heard, Macquarie, Auckland, Campbell and Antipodes. Nonbreeding birds [*skua* group] have been recorded in summer from Franklin District (Barrow Straits, Lancaster Sound, Baffin Bay), northern Quebec, southern Labrador, Newfoundland, Nova Scotia, Massachusetts (Georges Bank), Greenland, Jan Mayen, Spitsbergen and the northern European coast.

Winters at sea [*skua* group] in the eastern North Atlantic, from lat. 60°N. south to the Tropic of Cancer, regularly on the Newfoundland Banks and off the coast from Nova Scotia to Massachusetts, casually south to Florida, and rarely to the Canary Islands and Mediterranean region; [*antarctica* group] primarily in the South Atlantic and along eastern South America from Brazil to the Straits of Magellan; and [*lonnbergi* group] in southern oceans, most regularly off Australia.

Accidental [*skua* group] in Missouri (Kansas City), New York (Niagara Gorge between Ontario and New York), Belize (Ambergris Cay), Guyana, Novaya Zemlya and continental Europe; and [*lonnbergi* group] off Îles des Saintes (near Guadeloupe, Lesser Antilles, recovery of bird banded in South Shetlands, but see Devillers, 1977, Auk, 94, p. 427, for doubt as to identity) and near Kerala, India. Reports of *C. s. antarctica* and *C. s. lonnbergi* off the west coast of North America all pertain to *C. maccormicki* (see Devillers, *op. cit.*, pp. 417–429), and those from Barbados and off Puerto Rico may pertain to species other than *C. skua*.

Notes.—Also known as BROWN SKUA. Some authors prefer to treat the two southern forms as full species, *C. antarctica* (Lesson, 1831) [FALKLAND SKUA] and *C. lonnbergi* Mathews, 1912 [SOUTHERN SKUA], distinct from *C. skua* [NORTHERN SKUA]. *C. skua antarctica* and *C. chilensis* exhibit limited hybridization in areas where both breed on the coast of Argentina and have been considered conspecific by earlier authors. Although some have treated *C. maccormicki* as a race of *C. skua*, *C. s. lonnbergi* and *C. maccormicki* breed sympatrically without hybridization in the South Shetlands.

[**Catharacta chilensis** (Bonaparte). CHILEAN SKUA.] See Appendix B.

Catharacta maccormicki (Saunders). SOUTH POLAR SKUA. [35.2.]

Stercorarius maccormicki Saunders, 1893, Bull. Br. Ornithol. Club, 3, p. 12. (Possession Island, Victoria Land, lat. 71°14′S., long. 171°15′W.)

Habitat.—Pelagic, breeding on barren promontories and islands.

Distribution.—*Breeds* on the South Shetland Islands, and along the coast of Antarctica.

Ranges at sea regularly to the North Pacific, occurring in the northern spring, summer and fall from the Gulf of Alaska south to California (occasional reports of skuas off Mexico and Panama probably pertain to this species), in the Hawaiian waters (at least casually), and off Japan; and to the North Atlantic, where recorded certainly off Massachusetts (Georges Bank), New York (Hudson Canyon), North Carolina (several records, spring only) and Greenland. It is likely that most skua reports in the central North Atlantic in the northern summer pertain to this species.

Accidental in northern Alaska (off Icy Cape).

Notes.—See comments under *C. skua*.

Subfamily LARINAE: Gulls

Genus **LARUS** Linnaeus

Larus Linnaeus, 1758, Syst. Nat., ed. 10, 1, p. 136. Type, by subsequent designation (Selby, 1840), *Larus marinus* Linnaeus.

Hydrocoloeus Kaup, 1829, Skizz. Entw.-Ges. Eur. Thierw., pp. 113, 196. Type, by subsequent designation (G. R. Gray, 1841), *Larus minutus* Linnaeus.

Microlarus Oberholser, 1974, Bird Life Texas, 2, p. 982. Type, by original designation, *Sterna philadelphia* Ord.

Notes.—The genera *Rissa*, *Rhodostethia*, *Xema*, *Creagrus* and *Pagophila* are merged in *Larus* by some authors.

Larus atricilla Linnaeus. LAUGHING GULL. [58.]

Larus Atricilla Linnaeus, 1758, Syst. Nat., ed. 10, 1, p. 136. Based on the "Laughing Gull" Catesby, Nat. Hist. Carolina, 1, p. 89, pl. 89. (in America = Bahamas.)

Habitat.—Sandy islands with scattered patches of long grass (breeding); seacoasts, bays and estuaries, rarely on large inland bodies of water (nonbreeding).

Distribution.—*Breeds* on the Pacific coast of western Mexico in Sonora and Sinaloa (formerly bred at the southern end of the Salton Sea, southern California); and in the Atlantic-Gulf-Caribbean region from southern New Brunswick and southern Nova Scotia south locally along the coast to Florida and west to southern Texas, through the West Indies to islands off the north coast of Venezuela (Las Aves east to Tobago and Trinidad) and to French Guiana, and on islands off Campeche (Cayo Arcas) and the state of Yucatán (Alacrán reef). Nonbreeding birds occur in summer regularly in southern California (Salton Sea), on the Great Lakes (especially Erie and Michigan), along the Gulf-Caribbean coast of Middle America, and along the west coast of Mexico.

Winters along the Pacific coast from southern Mexico south to northern Peru (casually north to northern California and south to the Galapagos Islands); and from the Gulf coast and North Carolina south throughout the Gulf-Caribbean region to the coast of South America (Colombia east to the Amazon delta).

Casual in the Hawaiian Islands; to the interior lakes of Middle America; in interior North America from Arizona, Colorado, North Dakota, the Great Lakes region and West Virginia southward; and in Greenland.

Larus pipixcan Wagler. FRANKLIN'S GULL. [59.]

Larus pipixcan Wagler, 1831, Isis von Oken, col. 515. (Advena est, neque educat stagnis Mexicanis Prolem = Mexico.)

Habitat.—Fresh-water marshes in prairie and steppe (breeding); seacoasts, bays, estuaries, lakes, rivers, marshes, ponds and irrigated fields (nonbreeding).

Distribution.—*Breeds* from eastern Alberta, central Saskatchewan, southwestern Manitoba, eastern North Dakota and western Minnesota south locally to east-central Oregon, southern Idaho, northwestern Utah, northwestern Wyoming, northeastern South Dakota and northwestern Iowa. Nonbreeding birds occur in summer from east-central British Columbia and northeastern Manitoba south to northern New Mexico, southeastern Wyoming, Kansas, central Iowa and the Great Lakes (especially Lake Michigan).

Winters primarily along the Pacific coast of South America south to southern Chile (also the Galapagos Islands), less commonly from Guatemala southward, and on high Andean lakes in Peru and Bolivia; also rarely in southern coastal California, and casually along the Gulf coast of Texas and Louisiana.

Migrates regularly through western North America from southern British Columbia and the Rocky Mountains south to southern California, and through Texas and eastern Mexico to Veracruz and Oaxaca (casually to the Yucatan Peninsula), rarely to the Great Lakes region and the Mississippi and Ohio valleys, and casually elsewhere in the Pacific region from southwestern Arizona southward, and to the Atlantic coast from southern Quebec, New Brunswick, Nova Scotia and Newfoundland south to Florida.

Casual in the Hawaiian Islands, and southwestern and south-coastal Alaska (Cook Inlet, Kodiak Island, and St. Paul Island in the Pribilofs). Accidental in the Revillagigedo Islands (Socorro Island), on northern Baffin Island, in the Antilles (Puerto Rico and St. Barthélemy), on Tristan da Cunha, and in Sweden and the Marshall Islands.

Larus minutus Pallas. LITTLE GULL. [60.1.]

> *Larus minutus* Pallas, 1776, Reise Versch. Prov. Russ. Reichs, 3, p. 702. (Circa alueos majorum Sibiriae fluminum = Berezovo, Tobolsk, Siberia.)

Habitat.—Grassy marshes (breeding); seacoasts, bays, estuaries, rivers, lakes, ponds, marshes and flooded fields (nonbreeding).

Distribution.—*Breeds* locally in North America along the Great Lakes in northern Wisconsin (Manitowoc and Brown counties), northern Michigan (Upper Peninsula) and southern Ontario (Rondeau, Pickering, Toronto and Parry Sound, since 1962), also in Manitoba (Churchill, 1981); and in Eurasia from southern Scandinavia and northwestern Russia south to northern Europe, south-central Russia, central Siberia and Lake Baikal.

Winters in North America on the Great Lakes (especially Erie and Ontario), and along the Atlantic coast from Massachusetts to Virginia; and in the Old World from Iceland, the Faroe Islands, British Isles, southern Scandinavia and the Baltic coast south to the Mediterranean, Black and Caspian seas, questionably also in eastern China.

Migrates primarily through central Europe and western Asia.

Casual along the Atlantic coast north to New Brunswick and south to Florida; in the interior from northern Saskatchewan, northern Manitoba, Minnesota and the Great Lakes south to the Gulf coast (Texas east to western Florida), reported west to Colorado, Kansas and Missouri; along the Pacific coast from southern British Columbia south to southern California; and in Sierra Leone and Kenya.

Larus ridibundus Linnaeus. COMMON BLACK-HEADED GULL. [55.1.]

> *Larus ridibundus* Linnaeus, 1766, Syst. Nat., ed. 12, 1, p. 225. (in Mari Europæo = England.)

Habitat.—Lakes, rivers, bogs, moors, grasslands, swamps and coastal marshes, in winter also seacoasts, estuaries and bays.

Distribution.—*Breeds* from Iceland, the Faroe Islands, central Scandinavia, northern Russia and northern Siberia south to the Mediterranean Sea, central Russia, central Siberia, northwestern Mongolia and Kamchatka; also in Newfoundland (Stephenville Crossing, 1977). Nonbreeding birds occur north to Jan Mayen Island and northern Scandinavia, occasionally south in the wintering regions.

Winters in North America along the Atlantic coast from Labrador, Newfoundland, New Brunswick and Nova Scotia south to New York (Long Island), casually to Florida and inland in the Great Lakes region (especially Erie and Ontario); and in the Old World from the southern part of the breeding range south to the eastern Atlantic islands, central Africa, the Persian Gulf, northern India, Malay Peninsula, eastern China, Formosa and the Philippines.

In migration occurs regularly in western and southwestern Alaska from Nome south to the Aleutians, including St. Lawrence Island and the Pribilofs.

Casual in the Hawaiian Islands (Midway, Oahu), along the Pacific coast of North America from south-coastal Alaska to southern California, and in Missouri, Veracruz, the Antilles (Puerto Rico and many of the Lesser Antilles), Greenland and Guam, also sight reports from Manitoba (Churchill), Kansas and Surinam.

Notes.—Often called the BLACK-HEADED GULL. *L. ridibundus* and the South American *L. maculipennis* Lichtenstein, 1823, constitute a superspecies; they are considered conspecific by some authors.

[**Larus cirrocephalus** Vieillot. GRAY-HOODED GULL.] See Appendix A.

Larus philadelphia (Ord). BONAPARTE'S GULL. [60.]

> *Sterna Philadelphia* Ord, 1815, *in* Guthrie, Geogr., ed. 2 (Am.), 2, p. 319. (No locality given = near Philadelphia, Pennsylvania.)

Habitat.—Old birds' nests in trees in open coniferous woodland (occasionally on the ground) near ponds and lakes (breeding); seacoasts, bays, estuaries, mudflats, marshes, rivers, lakes, ponds and flooded fields (nonbreeding).

Distribution.—*Breeds* from western and central Alaska, central Yukon, northwestern and central Mackenzie and northern Manitoba south to the base of the Alaska Peninsula, south-coastal and (rarely) southeastern Alaska, southern British Columbia, central and southwestern Alberta, central Saskatchewan, southern Manitoba and central Ontario (southern James Bay). Nonbreeding birds occur in summer south in coastal areas to California and New England, and in the interior to the Great Lakes.

Winters from Washington (casually from south-coastal Alaska) south along the Pacific coast to southern Baja California, Sonora and Sinaloa; in the interior of Mexico south to western Jalisco and Guanajuato; from the Great Lakes (primarily Erie and Ontario) south through the Ohio and lower Mississippi valleys to the Gulf coast from southern Texas east to Florida (rare in the southern part), Bermuda, the Bahamas and Greater Antilles (Cuba, Hispaniola, Puerto Rico), casually also in southern New Mexico.

Migrates most commonly through eastern North America from the Mississippi Valley east to the Appalachians, but casually or sporadically elsewhere throughout the continent from southern Canada and Newfoundland southward.

Casual or accidental in the Hawaiian Islands, Lesser Antilles (Martinique, Barbados), the British Isles and continental Europe, also sight reports from the Yucatan Peninsula and Costa Rica.

Larus heermanni Cassin. HEERMANN'S GULL. [57.]

> *Larus Heermanni* Cassin, 1852, Proc. Acad. Nat. Sci. Philadelphia, 6, p. 187. (San Diego, California.)

Habitat.—Flat rocky islets or isolated coasts, often with scattered grass clumps present (breeding); seacoasts, beaches, bays and estuaries (nonbreeding).

Distribution.—*Breeds* on islets off the Pacific coast of Baja California (Isla Benito del Centro in the San Benito Islands, and Isla San Roque), in the Gulf of California (George, Raza, Salsipuedes, Ildefonso and Monserrate islands), locally on islets off Mexico south to Isla Isabela (off Nayarit), and elsewhere along the coast of Sinaloa; isolated breeding reports in coastal California (1980) north to Alcatraz

Island. Nonbreeding individuals often spend the breeding season in the post-breeding range.

Ranges after the breeding season north to southern British Columbia (Vancouver Island) and south to the Pacific coast of Guatemala.

Casual or accidental in the Revillagigedo Islands (Socorro Island), southeastern California, western Nevada (Pyramid Lake), southern Arizona, New Mexico (Pinos Altos Mountains), Oklahoma (Tulsa), Texas (Reagan County), Michigan (Lake St. Clair) and Ohio (Lorain).

Larus modestus Tschudi. GRAY GULL.

> *Larus modestus* Tschudi, 1843, Arch. Naturgesch., 9, p. 389. (in Oceani pacifici littoribus = Lurín, south of Lima, Peru.)

Habitat & Distribution.—*Breeds* on interior deserts in Chile and *ranges* in nonbreeding season along the Pacific coast of South America from Ecuador to central Chile.

Accidental off Costa Rica (Cocos Island, 22 May 1925, W. Beebe; Slud, 1967, Bull. Am. Mus. Nat. Hist., 134, p. 279) and off Colombia (Gorgona Island), also sight reports for Panama (Pacific entrance to Canal, and south of Isla Otoque in the Bay of Panama).

Larus belcheri Vigors. BAND-TAILED GULL. [54.2.]

> *Larus belcheri* Vigors, 1829, Zool. J., 4 (1828), p. 358. (No locality given = Peru.)

Habitat & Distribution.—*Breeds* [*belcheri* group] along the Pacific coast of South America in Peru and northwestern Chile, and [*atlanticus* group] on the Atlantic coast in northern Argentina, and *winters* along seacoasts and in bays and estuaries from western Ecuador to central Chile, and from Uruguay to central Argentina, respectively.

Casual in Panama (Pacific coast of Canal Zone, several sight records, one adult photographed) and Florida (near Pensacola, September 1968, weakened individual caught, photographed and kept in captivity for more than a decade; Marco Island, 6 June 1970, adult photographed; Cape Romano, 11 November 1974–29 January 1975, photographed; and near Marco, January–11 February 1976, adult photographed).

Notes.—Recent evidence points to the specific status of the two South American populations, *L. belcheri* [BELCHER'S GULL] and *L. atlanticus* Olrog, 1958 [OLROG'S GULL] (see Devillers, 1977, Le Gerfaut, 67, pp. 22–43). Photographs of birds in nonbreeding plumage (Pensacola and Cape Romano individuals) have been identified as the Pacific *L. b. belcheri*; other reports and photographs of birds in breeding plumage cannot be identified to group. The possibility of the Florida birds being escaped captives or man-assisted vagrants remains.

[Larus crassirostris Vieillot. BLACK-TAILED GULL.] See Appendix A.

Larus canus Linnaeus. MEW GULL. [55.]

> *Larus canus* Linnaeus, 1758, Syst. Nat., ed. 10, 1, p. 136. (in Europa = Sweden.)

Habitat.—Seacoasts, beaches, bays and mudflats, breeding along rocky or sandy coasts or inland along large lakes and rivers.

Distribution.—*Breeds* in North America from western and central Alaska (Brooks Range and Kotzebue Sound), central Yukon, and northwestern and southern Mackenzie south to the Alaska Peninsula, southern Alaska, coastal British Columbia (to Vancouver Island), southern Yukon, northern Alberta (probably) and central Saskatchewan, also in northeastern Manitoba (Churchill); and in Eurasia from the Faroe Islands, British Isles, Scandinavia, northern Russia and northern Siberia south to northern Europe, the Black and Caspian seas, Lake Baikal, northern Mongolia, Anadyrland, the Sea of Okhotsk, Kamchatka and the Kurile Islands. Nonbreeding birds occur in summer north to the northern coast of Alaska and northern Keewatin, and south to Washington, central Alberta and central Saskatchewan.

Winters in North America from southern Alaska (west to the Aleutians) south along the Pacific coast to northern Baja California, casually inland to eastern Washington, eastern Oregon, interior California, southern Nevada and Arizona, and casually to the Atlantic coast from New Brunswick, Nova Scotia and Newfoundland south to Massachusetts (sight records farther south); and in the Old World from the breeding range south to the Mediterranean region, northern Africa, Iraq, the Persian Gulf, Afghanistan, Southeast Asia, coastal China and Japan.

In migration occurs regularly in interior British Columbia and northern Yukon.

Casual in the western Aleutians, southern Ontario (lakes Erie and Ontario), Greenland, Iceland, Spitsbergen, Bear Island and the eastern Atlantic islands. Accidental in Wyoming (Lake Fork River) and Colorado (Denver); a report from Florida is questionable.

Notes.—Also known as COMMON or SHORT-BILLED GULL. Some authors suggest that the larger Asiatic form, which has been reported from the western Aleutians, is a separate species, *L. kamtschatschensis* Bonaparte, 1857 [KAMCHATKA GULL, 56.1]. Some (possibly most) Atlantic coast records are referable to the European *L. c. canus* Linnaeus (photographs).

Larus delawarensis Ord. RING-BILLED GULL. [54.]

Larus Delawarensis Ord, 1815, *in* Guthrie, Geogr., ed. 2 (Am.), 2, p. 319. (Delaware River, below Philadelphia, Pennsylvania.)

Habitat.—Seacoasts, bays, estuaries, rivers, lakes, ponds, irrigated fields and plowed lands, breeding on rocky, grassy and sandy islets or isolated shores, occasionally on marshy lands.

Distribution.—*Breeds* in western North America from southern interior British Columbia (Lake Okanagan), western and central Washington, northeastern Alberta, northwestern and central Saskatchewan, and north-central Manitoba south to northeastern California (Honey Lake), south-central Idaho, south-central Colorado, southeastern Wyoming and northeastern South Dakota (Waubay Lake); and in eastern North America from north-central Ontario, southern Quebec, Prince Edward Island, southern Labrador and northeastern Newfoundland south to eastern Wisconsin, northern Illinois (Lake Calumet), northern Michigan, southern Ontario, northern Ohio (Lucas County), northern New York (Little Galloo Island), central New Hampshire and New Brunswick. Nonbreeding individuals occur in summer north to central Alaska, southern Yukon, southern Mackenzie and southeastern Keewatin, and south through the wintering range.

Winters from southern British Columbia south along the Pacific coast to southern Mexico (casually to El Salvador), in the interior from the Great Lakes to central Mexico and the Gulf coast (Texas to Florida, casually south to the state of Yucatán), and along the Atlantic coast from the Gulf of St. Lawrence to Florida, the Bahamas and Greater Antilles (east to the Virgin Islands).

Casual in the Hawaiian Islands, Costa Rica (Chomes) and the Lesser Antilles (south to Barbados), also sight reports from Caribbean Honduras.

Larus californicus Lawrence. CALIFORNIA GULL. [53.]

Larus Californicus Lawrence, 1854, Ann. Lyc. Nat. Hist. N.Y., 6, p. 79. (near Stockton, California.)

Habitat.—Seacoasts, bays, estuaries, mudflats, marshes, irrigated fields, lakes, ponds and agricultural lands, nesting on open sandy or gravelly areas on islands or along shores of lakes and ponds, generally with scattered grasses present.

Distribution.—*Breeds* from southern Mackenzie south through eastern Alberta, Saskatchewan, southwestern Manitoba, central Montana, east-central North Dakota and northeastern South Dakota to north-central Colorado (Weld County), and west to southern interior British Columbia, south-central Washington, southeastern Oregon, northeastern California, western Nevada and northern Utah. Nonbreeding birds occur in summer north to southeastern Alaska and northern British Columbia, in northern New Mexico, and casually south through the wintering range.

Winters from southern Washington and eastern Idaho south, mostly along the Pacific coast, to southern Baja California, the Pacific coast of Mexico (to Colima), and locally in the interior of Mexico (to the state of México).

In migration occurs regularly in western North America south of the breeding range and east to New Mexico.

Casual or accidental in the Hawaiian Islands and Revillagigedos (Socorro Island), east to the Great Lakes and Mississippi Valley regions (recorded Minnesota, Illinois, Missouri, Michigan, Indiana, Ohio and New York), and to the Gulf coast of Texas, also questionable sight reports from the Atlantic coast (south to Virginia) and Florida. Reports from Guatemala are erroneous.

Notes.—The species listed from *L. californicus* through *L. marinus* are closely interrelated; this complex poses one of the most complicated problems in ornithological systematics today.

Larus argentatus Pontoppidan. HERRING GULL. [51.]

Larus Argentatus Pontoppidan, 1763, Dan. Atlas, 1, p. 622. (No locality given = Christiansöe, Denmark.)

Habitat.—Seacoasts, bays, estuaries, lakes and rivers, nesting along rocky or sandy coasts, on tundra, on islands in larger lakes and rivers, and on cliffs.

Distribution.—*Breeds* in North America from northern Alaska, northern Yukon, northern Mackenzie, central Keewatin, Southampton and western Baffin islands, northern Quebec and northern Labrador south to southwestern, southern and southeastern Alaska, south-central British Columbia, central Alberta, central Saskatchewan, southern Manitoba, northern Minnesota, northern Wisconsin, northeastern Illinois, central Michigan, southern Ontario, northern Ohio, northern New York, and along the Atlantic coast to northeastern South Carolina; and in the

Palearctic from Iceland, the Faroe Islands, British Isles, Scandinavia and northern Europe east across northern Russia and northern Siberia to Kamchatka, the Chukotski Peninsula, Anadyrland and the Sea of Okhotsk, and south locally to Italy. Nonbreeding birds summer south through much of the wintering range, especially in coastal areas.

Winters in the Americas from the Aleutian Islands, southern Alaska, the Great Lakes region and Newfoundland south (mostly at sea and along coasts, large rivers and lakes) through North America, Middle America (rare south of Mexico) and the West Indies to Panama and Barbados; and in the Old World mostly in the breeding range south to central Europe, the Mediterranean region, Black and Caspian seas, Gulf of Aden, Persian Gulf, India, central China, Formosa, and the Ryukyu and Bonin islands.

Casual in the Hawaiian Islands and Greenland.

Notes.—The central and southern Eurasian *L. cachinnans* Pallas, 1811, is considered conspecific with *L. argentatus* by some authors. For other comments on relationships or hybridization, see notes under *L. californicus, L. thayeri, L. fuscus, L. schistisagus, L. glaucescens, L. hyperboreus* and *L. marinus*.

Larus thayeri Brooks. THAYER'S GULL. [43.1.]

Larus thayeri Brooks, 1915, Bull. Mus. Comp. Zool. Harv., 59, p. 373. (Buchanan Bay, Ellesmere Land.)

Habitat.—Seacoasts, estuaries and bays, less commonly on large inland lakes and rivers, nesting on cliffs facing sounds.

Distribution.—*Breeds* from Banks, southern Melville, Bathurst, Axel Heiberg and central Ellesmere islands south to southern Victoria Island, northern Keewatin, and northern Southampton, Coats (formerly) and northwestern Baffin islands. Nonbreeding birds sometimes summer in the wintering range.

Winters primarily on the Pacific coast from southern British Columbia south to central Baja California, less commonly in south-coastal and southeastern Alaska, the Gulf of St. Lawrence and the eastern Great Lakes (Erie and Ontario), casually in the interior south to southern Arizona, southern New Mexico, and the Gulf coast of Texas and west-central Florida (St. Petersburg), and casually on the Atlantic coast to Maryland, also sight reports south to central Florida.

Notes.—*L. thayeri* was formerly regarded as a race of *L. argentatus* but is now generally regarded as a distinct species (see N. Smith, 1966, A. O. U. Ornithol. Monogr., no. 4, pp. 1–97); recent field studies indicate that *L. thayeri* and *L. glaucoides kumlieni* (once also regarded as a separate species, *L. kumlieni* Brewster, 1883 [KUMLIEN'S GULL]), interbreed in mixed colonies on Baffin Island, but the extent and nature of this interbreeding has not yet been determined (see Weber, 1981, Cont. Birdlife, 2, pp. 6–8).

Larus glaucoides Meyer. ICELAND GULL. [43.]

Larus glaucoides "Temm." Meyer, 1822, *in* Meyer and Wolf, Taschenb. Dtsch. Vögelkd., p. 197. (Meere der arktischen Zone, z. B. in Island, zuweilen im Herbst an den Küsten der Ost- und Nordsee = Iceland.)

Habitat.—Primarily coastal waters, casually on large inland bodies of water, nesting on steep cliffs and ledges facing sounds and fjords.

Distribution.—*Breeds* in North America on southern Baffin Island (Foxe Peninsula and Home Bay southward) and in extreme northwestern Quebec (Erik Cove, Digges Island), and in the Palearctic in Greenland, Iceland and Jan Mayen. Non-breeding birds summer south, at least casually, to British Columbia, Saskatchewan, the Great Lakes and New Jersey, and west to northern Alaska.

Winters in North America from Newfoundland and the Gulf of St. Lawrence south on the Atlantic coast to Virginia (casually to Florida), and inland (rarely) to the Great Lakes (especially Lake Erie), and in the Palearctic from Iceland, the Faroe Islands and Scandinavia south, at least rarely, to the British Isles, northern Europe and the Baltic region.

Casual in Idaho, Alberta, Saskatchewan, Manitoba, Nebraska, Novaya Zemlya, southern Europe and Madeira; also sight reports west to British Columbia and Washington, and south, east of the Rockies, to the Gulf coast (from southeastern Texas east to western Florida, but some or perhaps most of these reports probably pertain to *L. thayeri*).

Notes.—See comments under *L. californicus* and *L. thayeri.*

Larus fuscus Linnaeus. LESSER BLACK-BACKED GULL. [50.]

Larus fuscus Linnaeus, 1758, Syst. Nat., ed. 10, 1, p. 136. (in Europa = Sweden.)

Habitat.—Coastal regions, bays, estuaries, and inland on lakes and rivers, nesting on tundra, along sandy or rocky coasts, and on islands in lakes and larger rivers.

Distribution.—*Breeds* from Iceland, the Faroe Islands, northern Scandinavia and northern Russia south to the British Isles and France. Nonbreeding individuals often summer in the wintering range.

Winters from the British Isles, southern Scandinavia and the Baltic south to central Africa, the Red Sea and Persian Gulf; also in small numbers (but regularly and apparently increasing) in North America from the Great Lakes region, Labrador, eastern Quebec, Newfoundland and Nova Scotia south to the Gulf coast (west to Texas) and Florida.

Casual in northwestern Mackenzie, Victoria Island, northeastern Manitoba, Colorado, Puerto Rico and St. Martin (in the Lesser Antilles). Accidental in Alaska (Icy Cape), California (Monterey), Panama (Canal Zone) and Greenland; a report from Australia is erroneous.

Notes.—Some authors have considered *L. argentatus* and *L. fuscus* as conspecific, but they are widely sympatric with only local hybridization. See also comments under *L. californicus.*

Larus schistisagus Stejneger. SLATY-BACKED GULL. [48.]

Larus schistisagus Stejneger, 1884, Auk, 1, p. 231. (Bering Island and Petropaulski, Kamtschatka = Bering Island, Commander Islands.)

Habitat.—Mostly rocky seacoasts, breeding on cliffs and rocky islands, occasionally on flat sandy shores with bushes.

Distribution.—*Breeds* from the Gulf of Anadyr and the western Bering Sea coast south through Kamchatka and the Kurile Islands to Sakhalin and Japan. Reported breeding at Harrowby Bay, northwestern Mackenzie, has been seriously questioned (see Höhn, 1958, Can. Field Nat., 72, pp. 5–6).

Winters from the Bering Sea and Kamchatka south to Japan, the Seven Islands of Izu, Volcano and Ryukyu islands, and the coast of eastern China. Wanders rarely in nonbreeding season to western Alaska (Point Barrow south to St. Lawrence, Nunivak, and the Pribilof and Aleutian islands).

Casual in south-coastal Alaska (Anchorage, Kodiak, Homer). Accidental in the Hawaiian Islands (Kure) and British Columbia (Victoria).

Notes.—Occasional hybrids between *L. argentatus* and *L. schistisagus* are reported; some authors consider the two conspecific. See also comments under *L. californicus.*

Larus livens Dwight. YELLOW-FOOTED GULL. [49.1.]

Larus occidentalis livens Dwight, 1919, Proc. Biol. Soc. Wash., 32, p. 11. (San Jose Island, Lower [=Baja] California.)

Habitat.—Seacoasts, bays and estuaries, breeding on islands.

Distribution.—*Breeds* in the Gulf of California from George Island and Consag Rock south to Espíritu Santo and San Pedro Nolasco islands.

Winters in southwestern California (Salton Sea), the Gulf of California, and along the coast of Sonora, casually north to coastal southern California (San Diego County).

Casual off Guerrero.

Notes.—This species was formerly considered a race of *L. occidentalis,* but differences in morphology, behavior and vocalizations indicate that it is specifically distinct. Some authors feel *L. livens* is closely related to the Southern Hemisphere *L. dominicanus* Lichtenstein, 1823. See also comments under *L. californicus.*

Larus occidentalis Audubon. WESTERN GULL. [49.]

Larus occidentalis Audubon, 1839, Ornithol. Biogr., 5, p. 320. (Cape Disappointment [Washington].)

Habitat.—Seacoasts, bays and estuaries, breeding on rocky islands and coastal cliffs.

Distribution.—*Breeds* along the Pacific coast from southwestern British Columbia south to west-central Baja California (Isla Asunción) and Guadalupe Island.

Winters from southern British Columbia south to southern Baja California, casually to the coast of Sonora, Sinaloa and Nayarit.

Casual in the Hawaiian Islands (French Frigate Shoals, Oahu) and southwestern Arizona; a report from the Revillagigedo Islands (Isla Clarión) probably pertains to this species. Accidental in southwestern Alaska (Bristol Bay) and Illinois (Chicago).

Notes.—See comments under *L. californicus, L. livens, L. glaucescens* and *L. marinus.*

Larus glaucescens Naumann. GLAUCOUS-WINGED GULL. [44.]

Larus glaucescens J. F. Naumann, 1840, Naturgesch. Vögel Dtsch., 10, p. 351. (Nord-Amerika = North America.)

Habitat.—Primarily coastal waters, nesting on cliffs, rock ledges, grassy slopes or barren flats.

Distribution.—*Breeds* in North America from the southern Bering Sea (including the Pribilof and Aleutian islands), and southern and southeastern Alaska south along the Pacific coast to northwestern Oregon; and in the Commander Islands. Nonbreeding birds often summer in the wintering range.

Winters in North America from the southern Bering Sea and southern Alaska south along the Pacific coast to southern Baja California and the Gulf of California, casually to Sonora, and inland to Idaho and southwestern Arizona; and in Asia from Bering Island to Kamchatka, the Kurile Islands and Japan.

In migration occurs casually inland to Alberta.

Casual in the Hawaiian Islands. Accidental in the Revillagigedo Islands (Socorro Island), Yukon (Windy Pass), Manitoba (Churchill) and Oklahoma (Capron).

Notes.—Frequent hybridization between *L. glaucescens* and *L. occidentalis* occurs in mixed colonies from southern British Columbia to western Oregon, and these two will probably prove to be conspecific; hybridization also occurs between *L. glaucescens* and *L. argentatus,* at least on a limited basis, in south-coastal and southeastern Alaska. See additional comments under *L. californicus.*

Larus hyperboreus Gunnerus. GLAUCOUS GULL. [42.]

> *Larus hyperboreus* Gunnerus, 1767, *in* Leem, Beskr. Finm. Lapper. p. 226 (note). (Northern Norway.)

Habitat.—Primarily in coastal waters, less commonly along large inland bodies of water, breeding on sea cliffs, rocky coasts or borders of tundra lakes.

Distribution.—*Breeds* in North America on Arctic coasts and islands from western and northern Alaska (south to Hooper Bay, and St. Matthew, Hall and, at least formerly, the Pribilof islands), northern Yukon, northern Mackenzie, and Prince Patrick, Ellef Ringnes and northern Ellesmere islands south to northern Keewatin, northern Quebec, northern Labrador (south to Hopedale), and to Southampton, Coats, Belcher and southern Baffin islands; and in the Palearctic from northern Greenland, Iceland, Jan Mayen, Spitsbergen, Bear Island and Franz Josef Land east across northern Russia and northern Siberia (including Novaya Zemlya and the New Siberian Islands) to Anadyrland. Nonbreeding individuals often occur in the wintering range, and in summer south casually to northern Manitoba, northern Ontario, southeastern Quebec and New England.

Winters in North America from the southern Chukchi Sea (rarely) and Bering Sea south along the Pacific coast to Oregon (casually to southern California), and on the Atlantic coast from Labrador south to Virgi_ _ (rarely but regularly to Florida, and inland to the Great Lakes); and in the Palearctic from the breeding range south to the British Isles, northern Europe and central Siberia, casually to the Mediterranean, Black and Caspian seas.

Casual in the Hawaiian Islands; in coastal Baja California (San Benito Islands); in the interior of North America from southern Canada (where more regular in occurrence) south to Nevada, Utah, New Mexico, Texas and the Gulf coast; and in the eastern Atlantic islands.

Notes.—Extensive hybridization occurs between *L. hyperboreus* and *L. argentatus* in Iceland (although sympatry without interbreeding exists in Canada), and between *L. hyperboreus* and *L. glaucescens* in the eastern Bering Sea region. See also comments under *L. californicus.*

Larus marinus Linnaeus. GREAT BLACK-BACKED GULL. [47.]

> *Larus marinus* Linnaeus, 1758, Syst. Nat., ed. 10, 1, p. 136. (in Europa = Gotland, Sweden.)

Habitat.—Primarily seacoasts, less commonly on large inland bodies of water, nesting on rocky coasts and islands, occasionally on inland lakes.

Distribution.—*Breeds* in North America along the Atlantic coast from northern Quebec, northern Labrador and Newfoundland south to the St. Lawrence River, Anticosti Island, and (along the coast) to North Carolina, also in southern Ontario on Lake Huron (Little Haystack Island, Presquile Park); and in the Palearctic from Greenland, Iceland, the Faroe Islands, Shetlands, Spitsbergen, Bear Island, northern Scandinavia and northern Russia south to the British Isles, northern Europe and central Russia. Nonbreeding individuals occasionally summer north to southern Baffin Island, west to Hudson Bay, and south through the wintering range.

Winters in North America along the Atlantic coast from Newfoundland south to North Carolina, less commonly but regularly to Florida, Bermuda and inland on the Great Lakes; and in Eurasia from Iceland, the Faroe Islands, British Isles, Scandinavia and northern Europe south to the Mediterranean, Black and Caspian seas, casually to the eastern Atlantic islands.

Casual or accidental in northeastern Manitoba, Montana, Colorado, Nebraska, the Ohio Valley (south to Kentucky), along the Gulf coast (Florida west to eastern Texas), and to the Bahamas (San Salvador) and Antilles (Cuba, Hispaniola, Mona Island, Puerto Rico, St. Barthélemy and Barbados).

Notes.—Occasional hybridization between *L. marinus* and *L. argentatus* has been reported. Some authors consider *L. marinus* and *L. dominicanus* as constituting a superspecies, but others ally the former to *L. occidentalis*; see further comments under *L. californicus* and *L. occidentalis*.

Genus **RISSA** Stephens

Rissa Stephens, 1826, *in* Shaw, Gen. Zool., 13 (1), p. 180. Type, by monotypy, *Rissa brunnichii* Stephens = *Larus tridactylus* Linnaeus.

Notes.—See comments under *Larus*.

Rissa tridactyla (Linnaeus). BLACK-LEGGED KITTIWAKE. [40.]

Larus tridactylus Linnaeus, 1758, Syst. Nat., ed. 10, 1, p. 136. (in Europa septentrionali = Great Britain.)

Habitat.—Steep cliffs along coasts or on islands, occasionally on ledges of buildings (breeding); primarily pelagic, sometimes along seacoasts, bays and estuaries, casually on large inland bodies of water (nonbreeding).

Distribution.—*Breeds* in Alaska along the Chukchi and Bering seacoasts from Cape Lisburne south to the Aleutians, and east along the Pacific coast to Glacier Bay and Dixon Harbor; in northeastern North America from eastern Somerset, Prince Leopold, Bylot and Cobourg islands south locally through northern and central Baffin Island, Labrador (probably) and Newfoundland to southeastern Quebec (Gulf of St. Lawrence, Anticosti and Bonaventure islands, and Percé and Bird rocks); and in the Palearctic from Greenland, Iceland, the Faroe Islands, Jan Mayen, Spitsbergen, Franz Josef Land, Novaya Zemlya, and the New Siberian, Bennet and Wrangel islands south to the British Isles, northern Europe, the northern Russian coast, Sakhalin, Kamchatka, and the Kurile and Commander islands. Nonbreeding birds occur in summer along the Arctic coast of Alaska and Canada, occasionally south along the Pacific coast to California.

Winters along the Pacific coast of North America from the southern Bering Sea and southern Alaska south to northwestern Baja California, casually to Nayarit (San Blas); along the Atlantic coast (mostly offshore) from Newfoundland, Nova Scotia and the Gulf of St. Lawrence south to North Carolina, less frequently to Bermuda and eastern Florida; and in the Old World from the breeding range south to northwestern Africa, the Mediterranean region and Japan, casually to the Cape Verde Islands, West Africa and the Baltic Sea.

Casual in the Hawaiian Islands (Kure east to Laysan); and in the interior of North America from Alberta, Idaho, Montana, Manitoba, Minnesota and the Great Lakes region south to the Gulf coast (Texas east to western Florida), and in Nevada, Utah, Arizona and New Mexico. Accidental in the Bahamas (Andros), Cuba, and off Jamaica.

Rissa brevirostris (Bruch). RED-LEGGED KITTIWAKE. [41.]

Larus (Rissa) brevirostris "Brandt" Bruch, 1853, J. Ornithol., 1, p. 103. (Nord-Westküste von Amerika = Northwestern America.)

Habitat.—Steep cliffs on islands (breeding); primarily pelagic (nonbreeding).

Distribution.—*Breeds* in Alaska in the Pribilof (St. George, St. Paul) and Aleutian (Buldir, Bogoslof and Fire) islands, probably also the Commander Islands.

Winters in the northern North Pacific Ocean, occurring east to the Gulf of Alaska (Kodiak and Middleton islands).

Casual or accidental in east-central Alaska (near junction of Kandik and Yukon rivers), west-central Yukon (Fortymile), northwestern Oregon and Nevada (near Las Vegas), also a sight report for southwestern Washington.

Genus **RHODOSTETHIA** MacGillivray

Rhodostethia MacGillivray, 1842, Man. Br. Ornithol., 2, p. 252. Type, by original designation, *Larus rossii* Richardson = *Larus roseus* MacGillivray.

Notes.—See comments under *Larus*.

Rhodostethia rosea (MacGillivray). ROSS' GULL. [61.]

Larus roseus MacGillivray, 1824, Mem. Wernerian Soc., 5, p. 249. (Igloolik, Melville Peninsula.)

Habitat.—Arctic coasts, river deltas and swampy tundra (breeding); mostly pelagic in Arctic waters (nonbreeding).

Distribution.—*Breeds* in northern Siberia from the Kolyma Delta to Aby, Malaya (on the Alazeya River), Sredne Kolymsk and the Chaun River, also along the lower Indigirka River and on the southern Taymyr Peninsula; bred in 1977 and 1978 in the Cheyne Islands (east of Bathurst Island), in 1980 in northeastern Manitoba (Churchill, three nests located), and once in west-central Greenland (Disko Bay).

Winter range unknown, probably pelagic in open Arctic waters.

In migration occurs along the Arctic coast of Alaska (primarily at Point Barrow), rarely on St. Lawrence Island, and casually in the Pribilofs; also recorded in migration on the Boothia and Melville peninsulas, on Cornwallis and eastern Baffin islands, in Keewatin (McConnell River), and in Greenland and the Arctic islands of the Old World, casually to the Faroe Islands, British Isles and continental Europe.

Accidental in southwestern British Columbia (Victoria), Illinois (Chicago), Newfoundland (Fogo Island), Massachusetts (Newburyport) and Japan.

Genus XEMA Leach

Xema Leach, 1819, *in* Ross, Voy. Discovery, app. 2, p. lvii. Type, by monotypy, *Larus sabini* Sabine.

Notes.—See comments under *Larus.*

Xema sabini (Sabine). SABINE'S GULL. [62.]

Larus sabini J. Sabine, 1819, Trans. Linn. Soc. London, 12, p. 522, pl. 29. (Sabine Islands near Melville Bay, west coast of Greenland.)

Habitat.—Coastal wet meadows and salt-grass flats (breeding); primarily pelagic, casually along coasts or in inland waters (nonbreeding).

Distribution.—*Breeds* in North America from coastal western Alaska (Kotzebue Sound to Bristol Bay), northwestern Mackenzie, and Banks, Victoria, Bathurst, northwestern Devon and Bylot islands south locally to King William, southern Southampton and southwestern Baffin islands, and northern Keewatin; and in the Palearctic in northern Greenland and Spitsbergen, and from the New Siberian Islands and northern Siberia south to the Taimyr Peninsula and Lena Delta. Nonbreeding birds occur in summer to northern Ellesmere Island (probably breeding), central Alberta, southern Saskatchewan, central Manitoba, northern Ontario and northeastern Quebec, casually at sea south to wintering areas.

Winters at sea in the eastern Pacific from Panama south to central Chile; and, less commonly, in the Atlantic (primarily tropical areas, rarely the North Atlantic).

In migration recorded regularly along the Pacific coast of North America from Alaska to northern Baja California and Costa Rica; along the Atlantic coast from Labrador to New England (casually to Florida); and around Iceland and the coasts of Europe.

Casual through the interior of North America (mostly in migration but occasionally in winter) from Alberta, Montana, North Dakota and the Great Lakes south to Arizona, New Mexico, Texas, the Gulf coast and Cuba; in Caribbean Panama (Canal Zone); and to Japan and the North Sea.

[Genus CREAGRUS Bonaparte]

Creagrus Bonaparte, 1854, Naumannia, 4, p. 213. Type, by original designation, *Larus furcatus* Néboux.

Notes.—See comments under *Larus.*

[Creagrus furcatus (Néboux). SWALLOW-TAILED GULL.] See Appendix A.

Genus PAGOPHILA Kaup

Pagophila Kaup, 1829, Skizz. Entw.-Ges. Eur. Thierw., pp. 69, 196. Type, by monotypy, *Larus eburneus* Phipps.

Notes.—See comments under *Larus.*

Pagophila eburnea (Phipps). IVORY GULL. [39.]

Larus eburneus Phipps, 1774, Voy. North Pole, App., p. 187. (Spitsbergen.)

Habitat.—Associated with the Arctic ice pack and drift ice, nesting on steep cliffs or low rocky islets near ice or snow.

Distribution.—*Breeds* in Arctic North America on Seymour, southeastern Ellesmere, northern Baffin and, at least formerly, Prince Patrick, the Polynia and Meighen islands; and in the Palearctic in northern Greenland, Spitsbergen, Franz Josef Land, northern Novaya Zemlya and North Land.

Winters in North America primarily over drift ice south to the southern Bering Sea (Pribilof Islands) and northern Canada, casually south to south-coastal and southeastern Alaska and British Columbia, the Great Lakes (primarily Superior, Erie and Ontario), and along the Atlantic coast from Labrador, Newfoundland, eastern Quebec and Nova Scotia south to New Jersey; and in the Palearctic from southern Greenland, Iceland, the Faroe Islands, Scandinavia, northern Russia and northern Siberia south to the Commander Islands, casually to the British Isles and northern Europe.

Casual or accidental in southern Alberta, central Saskatchewan, Manitoba, Minnesota, Iowa (Appanoose County) and Ontario, also sight reports for Washington and North Carolina.

Subfamily STERNINAE: Terns

Notes.—See comments under Stercorariinae.

Genus **STERNA** Linnaeus

Sterna Linnaeus, 1758, Syst. Nat., ed. 10, 1, p. 137. Type, by tautonymy, *Sterna hirundo* Linnaeus (*Sterna,* prebinomial specific name, in synonymy).

Thalasseus Boie, 1822, Isis von Oken, col. 563. Type, by subsequent designation (Wagler, 1832), "*Th. cantiacus*" = *Sterna cantiaca* Gmelin = *Sterna sandvicensis* Latham.

Sternula Boie, 1822, Isis von Oken, col. 563. Type, by monotypy, *Sterna minuta* Linnaeus = *Sterna albifrons* Pallas.

Hydroprogne Kaup, 1829, Skizz. Entw.-Ges. Eur. Thierw., p. 91. Type, by subsequent designation (G. R. Gray, 1846), *Sterna caspia* Pallas.

Gelochelidon C. L. Brehm, 1830, Isis von Oken, col. 994. Type, by monotypy, *Gelochelidon meridionalis* Brehm = *Sterna nilotica* Gmelin.

Sterna nilotica Gmelin. GULL-BILLED TERN. [63.]

Sterna nilotica Gmelin, 1789, Syst. Nat., 1 (2), p. 606. Based on the "Egyptian Tern" Latham, Gen. Synop. Birds, 3 (2), p. 356. (in Aegypto = Egypt.)

Habitat.—Gravelly or sandy beaches (breeding); salt marshes, estuaries, lagoons and plowed fields, less frequently along rivers, around lakes and in fresh-water marshes (nonbreeding).

Distribution.—*Breeds* locally in western North America in southern California (at southern end of Salton Sea), and on the coasts of Sonora (Bahía de Tobarí) and Sinaloa, probably also on Montague Island (Baja California) and elsewhere in the Gulf of California; in eastern North America along the Atlantic-Gulf coast from New York (Long Island) south to Florida (occasionally also inland at Lake

Okeechobee and Haulover) and west to southern Texas, probably also to Tamaulipas and Veracruz; in the Bahamas (Great Inagua, Harbour Island), the Virgin Islands (probably Anegada and Sombrero, formerly Cockroach Cay); in South America on the Pacific coast of Ecuador, and on the Atlantic coast of Brazil, Uruguay and northern Argentina; and in the Old World from northern Europe, central Russia, southern Mongolia and eastern China south to Mauritania, northwestern Africa, Asia Minor, Iran, India, Ceylon and southern China, also in Australia. Nonbreeding birds often summer in the wintering range.

Winters in the Americas in coastal areas from Oaxaca, the Gulf coast and northern Florida south through Middle America, the West Indies and South America to Peru on the Pacific coast and northern Argentina on the Atlantic (including most islands off the north coast of Venezuela); and in the Old World from tropical Africa, the Persian Gulf, India, Southeast Asia, eastern China and the Philippines south to southern Africa, Java and Borneo, also in Australia and Tasmania.

Casual north to southern Arizona, Illinois, Ohio, New Brunswick and Nova Scotia, and to Bermuda, the British Isles, southern Scandinavia and Japan; sight reports from northern California are open to question.

Notes.—Often placed in the monotypic genus *Gelochelidon*.

Sterna caspia Pallas. CASPIAN TERN. [64.]

Sterna caspia Pallas, 1770, Novi Comm. Acad. Sci. Petropol., 14, p. 582, pl. 22. (Mare Caspium = Caspian Sea, southern Russia.)

Habitat.—Sandy or gravelly beaches and shell banks (breeding); seacoasts, bays, estuaries, lakes, marshes and rivers (nonbreeding).

Distribution.—*Breeds* locally in western North America from coastal and eastern Washington, eastern Oregon, northern Utah and northwestern Wyoming south (mostly in the interior) to southern California (San Diego Bay, Salton Sea) and western Nevada (Lahontan Reservoir); in western Mexico in Baja California (Scammon Lagoon) and on the coast of Sinaloa (Isla Larición); in the interior of North America from northeastern Alberta, southern Mackenzie, central Saskatchewan, north-central Manitoba and southern James Bay south to North Dakota (McLean County), northeastern Wisconsin, northeastern Illinois, central Michigan, southern Ontario, northwestern Pennsylvania (formerly) and New Jersey (probably); at scattered localities along the Atlantic coast in Newfoundland (Long Harbour River), southeastern Quebec (Fog Island, Natashquam), Virginia (Metomkin and formerly Cobbs islands), North Carolina (Oregon Inlet) and South Carolina (Cape Romain); along the Gulf coast from Texas east to Florida; and in the Old World from southern Scandinavia, northern Europe, southern Russia, the Black and Caspian seas, northern Mongolia, Ussuriland and eastern China south to the Mediterranean region, Persian Gulf, Ceylon, Australia and New Zealand, also along the coasts of Africa and in the interior at Lake Rudolph. Nonbreeding birds often summer in the James Bay and Great Lakes regions, and along both coasts of the United States, less frequently south in Middle America to Costa Rica.

Winters in the Americas primarily in coastal areas from central California south to Baja California and Oaxaca, and from North Carolina south along the Atlantic-Gulf coasts to eastern Mexico, less frequently along both coasts and on inland lakes of Middle America (not recorded El Salvador) to northern Colombia and

Venezuela, and rarely to the Bahamas and Greater Antilles (east to Puerto Rico); and in the Old World from the breeding range south to tropical Africa, the Persian Gulf, India and (rarely) Southeast Asia.

Migrates in North America primarily along coasts from British Columbia (rarely) and Nova Scotia southward, less frequently along large rivers in the interior.

Casual in the Hawaiian Islands (Oahu, Maui); in southeastern Alaska; in the interior of western North America from central Alberta and southern Saskatchewan south to Colorado and New Mexico; and in the Old World north to the Faroe Islands, British Isles and Japan.

Notes.—Often placed in the monotypic genus *Hydroprogne.*

Sterna maxima Boddaert. ROYAL TERN. [65.]

Sterna maxima Boddaert, 1783, Table Planches Enlum., p. 58. Based on the "Hirondelle de Mer de Cayenne" Daubenton, Planches Enlum., pl. 988. (Cayenne.)

Habitat.—Open sandy beaches (breeding); seacoasts, lagoons and estuaries, rarely on lakes (nonbreeding).

Distribution.—*Breeds* locally on the Pacific coast in southern California (San Diego Bay, rarely), in west-central Baja California (Scammon Lagoon, Isla San Roque), along the coast of Sonora and Sinaloa, and in the Tres Marias Islands (erroneously reported from Isla Isabela); in the Atlantic-Gulf-Caribbean region from the Gulf coast (west to southern Texas) and Maryland (Chesapeake Bay) south through the West Indies to islands off the north coast of Venezuela (Netherlands Antilles east to Los Roques, and Trinidad) and French Guiana, also in the state of Yucatán (Cayo Arcas and Alacrán reef); in South America on the coast of Uruguay; and in West Africa (islands off Mauritania). Nonbreeding individuals occur in summer in coastal areas in the Americas north to central California and New York, and south throughout the wintering range (rarely on the Pacific coast south of Mexico).

Winters from central California, the Gulf coast and North Carolina south along both coasts of the Americas to Peru, Uruguay and Argentina; and on the west coast of Africa from Morocco to Angola.

Casual north on the Atlantic coast to Maine and Nova Scotia. Accidental in the British Isles and Mozambique.

Notes.—This and the following two species are often placed in the genus *Thalasseus.*

Sterna elegans Gambel. ELEGANT TERN. [66.]

Sterna elegans Gambel, 1849, Proc. Acad. Nat. Sci. Philadelphia, 4 (1848), p. 129. (Mazatlan [Sinaloa], Pacific coast of Mexico.)

Habitat.—Sandy beaches and flats (breeding); seacoasts, bays, estuaries and mudflats (nonbreeding).

Distribution.—*Breeds* along the Pacific coast from southern California (San Diego Bay) south to central Baja California (Scammon Lagoon, Isla San Roque), and from the Gulf of California (Raza, Trinidad and George islands) south along the coast of Sonora and Sinaloa to (probably) Nayarit (Isabela Island). Nonbreeding birds occur in summer along the Pacific coast from central California to Costa Rica.

Winters along the Pacific coast from Guatemala south to central Chile (most commonly from Ecuador south, rare north of Panama).

Wanders north regularly to central (rarely northern) California. Accidental in Texas (Corpus Christi).

Notes.—See comments under *S. maxima.*

Sterna sandvicensis Latham. SANDWICH TERN. [67.]

Sterna Sandvicensis Latham, 1787, Gen. Synop. Birds, suppl., 1, p. 296. (Sandwich, Kent, England.)

Habitat.—Sandy beaches and flats (breeding); seacoasts, bays, estuaries and mudflats (nonbreeding).

Distribution.—*Breeds* [*sandvicensis* group] locally on the Atlantic coast of North America in Virginia (Fisherman's Island), North Carolina (Oregon Inlet) and South Carolina; along the Gulf coast from southern Texas east to southern Mississippi (Petit Bois Island), Alabama (formerly) and Florida; in the Bahamas, off southern Cuba (Cayo Los Ballenatos), and on islets in the Virgin Islands (off Culebra, St. Thomas and Anegada); off the state of Yucatán (Cayo Arcas, Alacrán reef), formerly off Belize (Northern Two Cays); and in the Old World from the British Isles and southern Scandinavia south to the Mediterranean, Black and Caspian seas; and [*eurygnatha* group] on islands off the coast of Venezuela (Netherlands Antilles, Las Aves, Los Roques, and on Soldado Rock off northern Trinidad, the latter colony assigned by some authors to the *sandvicensis* group) and French Guiana, and along the coast of northern Argentina. Nonbreeding individuals occur in summer throughout the wintering range, most commonly in the Atlantic-Gulf-Caribbean region.

Winters [*sandvicensis* group] along the Pacific coast from Oaxaca to Ecuador and Peru, in the Atlantic-Gulf-Caribbean region from Florida (casually from Virginia) and the Gulf coast south throughout the West Indies, and along coasts to southern Brazil and Uruguay, and in the Old World generally from the southern portions of the breeding range south to the eastern Atlantic islands, southern Africa, the Persian Gulf and India; and [*eurygnatha* group] from the islands off Venezuela (including Tobago and Trinidad) and the Colombian coast south along the Atlantic coast to northern Argentina.

Casual [*sandvicensis* group] north along the Atlantic coast to Massachusetts. Accidental [*sandvicensis* group] in southern California (San Diego Bay) and southern Ontario (Lucknow), also sight reports [*eurygnatha* group] for Puerto Rico, the Virgin Islands, and northern Lesser Antilles (St. Martin).

Notes.—The North American form is also known as CABOT'S TERN. The South American breeding form is usually regarded as a separate species, *S. eurygnatha* Saunders, 1876 [CAYENNE TERN], but interbreeding with *S. sandvicensis* occurs (see Junge and Voous, 1955, Ardea, 43, pp. 226–247). See also comments under *S. maxima.*

Sterna dougallii Montagu. ROSEATE TERN. [72.]

Sterna Dougallii Montagu, 1813, Suppl. Ornithol. Dict., [not paged], see under Tern, Roseate (with plate). (The Cumbrey Islands in Firth of Clyde [Scotland].)

Habitat.—Sandy beaches, open bare ground, grassy areas and under tumbled boulders, primarily on islands (breeding); seacoasts, bays and estuaries (nonbreeding).

Distribution.—*Breeds* locally along the Atlantic coast of North America from Maine and Nova Scotia south to North Carolina (Core Bank); in the Florida Keys (Dry Tortugas), the Bahamas, Jamaica (Pedro Cays), Hispaniola (Beata Island, Cayos de los Pájaros), Puerto Rico, the Virgin Islands, Lesser Antilles and islands off Venezuela (Netherlands Antilles, Las Aves and Los Roques); off Caribbean Honduras (on Sandy Cay near Utila in the Bay Islands); in Bermuda (formerly); and in the Old World locally from the British Isles and northern Europe south to the Azores, Madeira and southern Africa, and from Ceylon and the Andaman Islands south in the Indian Ocean along the east coast of Africa and to the Seychelles and western Australia, also in the Pacific Ocean from China and the Ryukyu Islands south to the Philippines, Solomon Islands, New Caledonia, and northern and eastern Australia. Breeding populations in the Northern Hemisphere show serious declines in recent years.

Winters in the Americas primarily in the eastern Caribbean from the West Indies southward, ranging along the Atlantic coast of South America to eastern Brazil; and in the Old World from the eastern Atlantic islands and northern Africa south through the breeding range, and in the Indian and Pacific ocean areas generally near the breeding grounds.

In migration occurs along the Atlantic coast of North America south to Florida, casually on the Gulf coast west to Texas; also in western Europe and the western Mediterranean region.

Accidental in Indiana (Miller), western New York (Niagara River), Gorgona Island (off Pacific coast of Colombia, recovery of a bird banded on Long Island, New York), and central and southern Europe. An old report from the Pacific coast of Oaxaca is questionable.

Sterna hirundo Linnaeus. COMMON TERN. [70.]

> *Sterna Hirundo* Linnaeus, 1758, Syst. Nat., ed. 10, 1, p. 137. (in Europa = Sweden.)

Habitat.—Sandy, pebbly or stony beaches, matted vegetation (including tops of muskrat houses) and grassy areas (breeding); seacoasts, estuaries, bays, lakes, rivers and marshes (nonbreeding).

Distribution.—*Breeds* in the interior of North America from northern Alberta, south-central Mackenzie, northern Saskatchewan, northwestern and central Manitoba, central Ontario (including southern James Bay), southern Quebec, southern Labrador, Newfoundland and Nova Scotia south to eastern Washington, southeastern Alberta, northeastern Montana, North Dakota, northeastern South Dakota, central Minnesota, northeastern Illinois, northwestern Indiana (Lake County), southern Michigan, northern Ohio, northwestern Pennsylvania (Presque Isle), central and northern New York, and northwestern Vermont, and locally along the Atlantic coast to North Carolina (to Wrightsville Beach); locally on the Gulf coast in Texas (Port Isabel to Galveston Bay), Mississippi (Petit Bois Island) and western Florida (St. George Island); in Bermuda, the Greater Antilles (islets off Hispaniola east to the Virgin Islands) and the Netherlands Antilles; and in the Old World from the British Isles, northern Europe, northern Russia, north-central Siberia and Mongolia south to the eastern Atlantic islands, Mediterranean region, Black and Caspian seas, Asia Minor, Iraq, Iran, Turkestan, Ladakh and Tibet. Nonbreeding individuals occur in summer on James Bay, throughout the Great

Lakes region, along the Atlantic-Gulf coast (west to southern Texas), south in Middle America to Costa Rica, and throughout the West Indies.

Winters in the Americas from southern California (casually) and Baja California (rarely) south along the Pacific coast of Middle America and South America to Peru, and from South Carolina, Florida and the Gulf coast (rarely) south through the West Indies and along the Caribbean-Atlantic coast of Middle America and South America to northern Argentina; and in the Old World from the southern portions of the breeding range south to southern Africa, Madagascar, Ceylon, the Malay Peninsula, New Guinea, and the Louisiade and Solomon islands.

In migration occurs regularly in interior North America in the Mississippi and Ohio valleys, casually elsewhere (reported north to Yukon, and south to Arizona and New Mexico), and on the Pacific coast north to British Columbia; also regular in western Alaska (the western Aleutian, Pribilof and St. Lawrence islands).

Casual or accidental in the Hawaiian Islands (main islands from Kauai eastward), Labrador, and interior South America (Ecuador, Bolivia).

Sterna paradisaea Pontoppidan. ARCTIC TERN. [71.]

> *Sterna paradisæa* Pontoppidan, 1763, Dan. Atlas, 1, p. 622. (Christiansöe, Denmark.)

Habitat.—Rocky or grass-covered coasts and islands, tundra, and sometimes along inland lakes and rivers (breeding); mostly pelagic, rarely in coastal bays and estuaries (nonbreeding).

Distribution.—*Breeds* in North America from northern Alaska, northern Yukon, northern Mackenzie, Banks, Bathurst and northern Ellesmere islands, Labrador and Newfoundland south to the Aleutian Islands, southern Alaska, southern Yukon, northwestern British Columbia, southern Mackenzie, northwestern Saskatchewan, northern Manitoba, extreme northern Ontario (including James Bay), central Quebec, New Brunswick and, along the Atlantic coast, locally to Maine (Casco Bay) and Massachusetts, also in Washington (Puget Sound, since 1977); and in the Palearctic from Greenland, Iceland, the British Isles, southern Scandinavia, northern Russia and northern Siberia south to northern Europe, Anadyrland, the Commander Islands and Gulf of Shelekhova.

Winters primarily in the Southern Hemisphere in subantarctic and Antarctic waters of the Pacific, Atlantic and Indian oceans, from off central Chile, central Argentina and South Africa to the Weddell Sea and (rarely) Antarctic continent.

Migrates primarily at sea, casually through the Hawaiian Islands, along the Pacific coast from Alaska to southern California, along the Atlantic coast from New England to Florida (and west along the Gulf coast to Texas), and off the Pacific coast of South America from Colombia to Chile.

Casual or accidental in interior California, northern and central Alberta, Idaho, Colorado (near Denver), Minnesota (Duluth), southern Ontario (Toronto), New York (Cayuga Lake), Georgia (Okefenokee Swamp), Cuba, the Black Sea and New Zealand.

[Sterna sumatrana Raffles. BLACK-NAPED TERN.] See Appendix B.

Sterna forsteri Nuttall. FORSTER'S TERN. [69.]

> *Sterna hirundo* (not Linnaeus) Richardson, 1832, *in* Swainson and Richardson, Fauna Bor.-Am., 2 (1831), p. 412. (on the banks of the Saskatchewan

[River] = about 10–50 miles west of Cumberland House, Saskatchewan.) *Sterna Forsteri* Nuttall, 1834, Man. Ornithol. U.S. Can., ed. 1, 2, p. 274. New name for *Sterna hirundo* Richardson, preoccupied.

Habitat.—Fresh-water and salt marshes, in migration and winter also seacoasts, bays, estuaries, rivers and lakes.

Distribution.—*Breeds* in the interior of North America from southeastern British Columbia, central Alberta, central Saskatchewan, central Manitoba and southern Ontario (formerly) south through east-central Washington and eastern and south-central Oregon to southern California (San Diego Bay), western Nevada, south-central Idaho, north-central Utah, northern and eastern Colorado, central Kansas, western Nebraska, northern Iowa, northeastern Illinois (at least formerly), north-western Indiana and east-central Michigan (Bay County); along the Atlantic coast from southern New York (Long Island) south locally to North Carolina and, formerly, South Carolina (Bulls Bay); and along the Gulf coast from northern Tamaulipas and Texas east to southern Louisiana.

Winters along the Pacific coast from central California and Baja California south to Oaxaca and Guatemala (Dueñas), casually to Costa Rica (Gulf of Nicoya); and along the Atlantic-Gulf coast from Virginia (casually farther north) south to Florida, west to Texas, south to northern Veracruz, casually to Costa Rica (Chomes); and in the Bahamas and Greater Antilles (east to Puerto Rico, also a questionable sight report from the Virgin Islands).

Migrates primarily through interior North America, casually to the Pacific coast (north to southern British Columbia) and Atlantic coast (north to southern Quebec, New Brunswick and Nova Scotia); birds from the Atlantic coast breeding populations apparently disperse northward, at least to New England, prior to fall migration.

Accidental at sea several hundred miles east of Pernambuco, Brazil.

[Sterna trudeaui Audubon. TRUDEAU'S TERN.] See Appendix B.

Sterna antillarum (Lesson). LEAST TERN. [74.]

> *Sterna antillarum* Lesson, 1847, Compl. Oeuvres Buffon, 20, p. 256. (Guadeloupe, West Indies.)

Habitat.—Seacoasts, beaches, bays, estuaries, lagoons, lakes and rivers, breeding on sandy or gravelly beaches and banks of rivers or lakes, rarely on flat rooftops of buildings.

Distribution.—*Breeds* along the Pacific coast from central California (southern San Francisco Bay) south to southern Baja California and Chiapas; in the interior of North America locally along the Colorado, Red, Missouri, Mississippi and Ohio river systems from southern South Dakota, western Iowa, southwestern Missouri, northwestern Indiana, central Kentucky and northwestern Ohio south to central New Mexico, western Kansas, central Oklahoma, northeastern Texas, central Louisiana and western Tennessee; along the Atlantic-Gulf coast from Maine (Scarborough) south to Florida and west to Texas (Port Isabel); in the Atlantic-Caribbean region in Bermuda, throughout the Bahamas and Greater Antilles, in the Lesser Antilles (St. Martin, St. Kitts and Antigua), off Belize (Grassy Cay), in Honduras (on Sandy Cay near Utila Island, and at Puerto Caxinas), and on islands off Venezuela (Netherlands Antilles, Los Roques and Margarita, possibly also Trinidad). Nonbreeding birds occur in summer north, at least casually, to west-central California (San Francisco Bay), eastern Wyoming, central Colorado, Minnesota, southern Wisconsin, northeastern Illinois and central Michigan, and south through the wintering range.

Winters along the Pacific coast from Baja California south to southern Mexico, probably also to northwestern South America, and along the coast of South America from Colombia east to eastern Brazil.

In migration occurs throughout the Gulf-Caribbean region (including the Lesser Antilles and Trinidad), and along both coasts of Middle America (not recorded El Salvador or Nicaragua).

Casual in the Hawaiian Islands, Washington (Ocean Shores), northwestern Oregon (mouth of Columbia River), southwestern Arizona, Minnesota, Nova Scotia and northeastern Argentina.

Notes.—*S. antillarum* and the Old World *S. albifrons* Pallas, 1764 [LITTLE TERN], are often considered conspecific, but see Massey, 1976, Auk, 93, pp. 760–773). The two species, in addition to *S. superciliaris* and *S. lorata* Philippi and Landbeck, 1861, of South America, *S. saundersi* Hume, 1877, of the northwestern Indian Ocean region, and *S. nereis* (Gould, 1843), of Australia, appear to constitute a superspecies.

Sterna superciliaris Vieillot. YELLOW-BILLED TERN.

Sterna superciliaris Vieillot, 1819, Nouv. Dist. Hist. Nat., nouv. éd., 32, p. 176. Based on "Hatí Ceja blanca" Azara, Apunt. Hist. Nat. Páx. Parag., 3, p. 377 (no. 415). (Paraguay.)

Habitat and Distribution.—*Breeds* along rivers and lakes in South America east of the Andes from Colombia, Venezuela and the Guianas south to southern Peru, central Bolivia, Paraguay, northeastern Argentina and Uruguuay, and *winters* in the breeding range, wandering to coastal areas, Tobago and Trinidad.

Accidental in Panama (Coco Solo, Canal Zone, 17–20 October 1977, J. Pujals, photograph; Ridgely, 1981, Birds Panama, rev. ed., p. 366).

Notes.—See comments under *S. antillarum.*

Sterna aleutica Baird. ALEUTIAN TERN. [73.]

Sterna aleutica Baird, 1869, Trans. Chicago Acad. Sci., 1, p. 321. (Kadiak = Kodiak Island, Alaska.)

Habitat.—Grassy or mossy flats, on small offshore islands and coastal spits, around lagoons or near river mouths (breeding); pelagic (nonbreeding).

Distribution.—*Breeds* in Alaska from the Chukchi Sea coast (Cape Krusenstern and Kotzebue Sound) south along the western coast to the Aleutians (west to Attu) and Alaska Peninsula, and east along the southern coast (including Kodiak Island) to Yakutat and Dry bays; and in Asia on the east coast of Kamchatka and Sakhalin.

Winters at sea, range unknown.

Casual in the Commander Islands and Japan.

Sterna lunata Peale. GRAY-BACKED TERN. [76.1.]

Sterna lunata Peale, 1848, U.S. Explor. Exped., 8, p. 277. (Vincennes Island, Paumotu Group, Kauehi Island, Tuamotu Islands.)

Habitat.—Sandy beaches or bare ground on islands (breeding); mostly pelagic (nonbreeding).

Distribution.—*Breeds* from the Hawaiian Islands (most of the western chain east to Kaula and Moku Manu off Oahu) and Wake Island south to the Phoenix, Fiji, Line and Tuamotu islands.

Winters at sea in the central Pacific Ocean, wandering casually to the Moluccas.

Sterna anaethetus Scopoli. BRIDLED TERN. [76.]

Sterna (*Anaethetus*) Scopoli, 1786, Del. Flor. Faun. Insubr., fasc. 2, p. 92. (in Guinea = Panay, Philippine Islands.)

Habitat.—Mostly pelagic, breeding on islands usually in rocky areas or on coral, occasionally on sand, but generally in crevices, on ledges or partially concealed.

Distribution.—*Breeds* in the Pacific Ocean on islets in northwestern Costa Rica (off Nicoya Peninsula) and possibly Panama (Frailes del Sur, off Azuero Peninsula), and from Formosa south to the East Indies, New Guinea and Australia; in the Atlantic-Caribbean region in the Bahamas, Cuba (Cayo Mono Grande), Jamaica (Morant and Pedro cays, and off Port Royal), Hispaniola (Navassa, Seven Brothers and Beata islands), Puerto Rico (Mona Island, and Desecheo Island off Culebra), the Virgin Islands, Lesser Antilles, Belize (Saddle, Ellen and Curlew cays, at least formerly), off Venezuela (Las Aves and Los Roques, formerly on Aruba and off Tobago), off Mauritania, and on islands in the Gulf of Guinea; and in the Indian Ocean from off western India south to the Seychelles, Mauritius, and the Laccadive and Maldive islands.

Ranges at sea in the Pacific off Middle America (recorded off Guerrero and Panama), and widely in the western Pacific from the breeding range north to Japan, Marcus Island, and the Volcano and Ryukyu islands; in the Atlantic-Caribbean region widely in the West Indies, north along the Atlantic coast (most abundantly after storms) from Florida to North Carolina (casually to Massachusetts), casually along the Gulf coast from Florida west to Texas, and rarely along the north coast of Venezuela; and in the Indian Ocean from India and Ceylon south in the breeding range, and to the east coast of Africa.

Accidental in Caribbean Costa Rica and Newfoundland, and at Cape Horn.

Notes.—Also known as BROWN-WINGED TERN.

Sterna fuscata Linnaeus. SOOTY TERN. [75.]

Sterna fuscata Linnaeus, 1766, Syst. Nat., ed. 12, 1, p. 228. Based mainly on "L'Hirondelle-de-mer brune" Brisson, Ornithologie, 6, p. 220, pl. 21, fig. 2. (in Insula Domincensi = Hispaniola.)

Habitat.—Primarily pelagic, nesting in colonies on islands on sandy beaches, bare ground or coral, most often with scattered grasses present, less commonly on rocky ledges.

Distribution.—*Breeds* in the Pacific from the Hawaiian Islands (Kure east to Moku Manu and Manana off Oahu), islands off western Mexico (Clipperton, Revillagigedo, Tres Marias and Isabela), and the Ryukyu, Bonin, Marcus and Wake islands south to Australia, and Lord Howe, Norfolk, Kermadec and Tuamotu islands, also in the Galapagos Islands and on San Felix Island off Chile; in the Atlantic-Gulf-Caribbean region on small islands along the Gulf coast of Texas (Matagorda Bay to Kleberg County), Louisiana (Chandeleur Islands) and the Yucatan Peninsula (Cayos Arcas, Alacrán reef, and formerly Mujeres and Cancun islands), in North Carolina (Morgan Island, 1978), in Florida (Franklin County,

Tampa region, Dry Tortugas, Key West), throughout the Bahamas, off Cuba (Cayo Mono Grande and Cayo de la Piedras), in the Virgin Islands and Lesser Antilles, off Belize (Round Cay) and probably also Honduras (Isla Roatán), off the north coast of Venezuela (Isla de Aves, islets off Tobago and Trinidad, and formerly Margarita), off Brazil (Rocas Reef, Fernando de Noronha, Trindade, Martin Vas Rocks) and in the tropical Atlantic (Ascension, and islets off St. Helena and Principe); and in the Indian Ocean from the Mascarene, Seychelles, Laccadive, Maldive and Andaman islands to western Australia.

Ranges at sea in the Pacific throughout the Hawaiian Islands, off the west coast of Middle America from Sinaloa to Panama, and widely in the tropical and subtropical Pacific Ocean, throughout most of the Caribbean-Gulf region, regularly from Texas east to Florida (especially after storms) and casually north along the Atlantic coast to New England and Nova Scotia, also to Bermuda and along the coast of South America east to the Guianas; and widely throughout the tropical and subtropical Indian Ocean.

Casual inland after storms in the Atlantic states north to New York, and to western Texas, Tennessee and West Virginia.

Genus PHAETUSA Wagler

Phaetusa Wagler, 1832, Isis von Oken, col. 1224. Type, by monotypy, *Sterna magnirostris* Lichtenstein = *Sterna simplex* Gmelin.

Phaetusa simplex (Gmelin). LARGE-BILLED TERN.

Sterna simplex Gmelin, 1789, Syst. Nat., 1 (2), p. 606. Based on the "Simple Tern" Latham, Gen. Synop. Birds, 3 (2), p. 355. (in Cayenna = Cayenne.)

Habitat & Distribution.—*Breeds* along rivers and lakes in South America in western Ecuador, and from Colombia, Venezuela (also Margarita Island and Trinidad) and the Guianas south, east of the Andes, to eastern Peru, Bolivia, Paraguay, northern Argentina and Uruguay, and *ranges* to seacoasts in the nonbreeding season.

Casual in Panama (Coco Solo, Canal Zone, and vicinity; and near El Rincón, Herrera). Accidental in Bermuda, Cuba (Nipe Bay) and Aruba, also records (of individuals whose origin has been questioned) for Illinois (photograph, Lake Calumet, Chicago) and Ohio (sight report, Evans Lake, near Youngstown).

Genus CHLIDONIAS Rafinesque

Chlidonias Rafinesque, 1822, Ky. Gazette, new ser., 1, no. 8, p. 3, col. 5. Type, by monotypy, *Sterna melanops* Rafinesque = *Sterna surinamensis* Gmelin = *Sterna nigra* Linnaeus.

[Chlidonias hybridus (Pallas). WHISKERED TERN.] See Appendix B.

Chlidonias leucopterus (Temminck). WHITE-WINGED TERN. [78.]

Sterna leucoptera Temminck, 1815, Man. Ornithol., ed. 1 (1814), p. 483. (les bords de la Méditerranée, etc. = Mediterranean Sea.)

Habitat & Distribution.—*Breeds* on marshes from eastern Europe east to southern Siberia, Sakhalin and Manchuria, and *winters* along coasts, rivers and lakes from tropical Africa, India, Southeast Asia and eastern China south to southern Africa, Madagascar, Ceylon, the East Indies, New Guinea, Australia and, rarely, New Zealand, migrating through Europe, Korea and Japan.

Casual or accidental in Alaska (Nizki Island in the Aleutians), Wisconsin (Lake Koshkonong), Indiana (Gary), New Brunswick (Grand Point, Portobello Creek and Miscou Island), Massachusetts (Salisbury), Delaware (Little Creek and Port Mahon), Virginia (Chincoteague), the Bahamas (Great Inagua), Barbados and Guam, also a sight report for Georgia.

Notes.—Also known as WHITE-WINGED BLACK TERN.

Chlidonias niger (Linnaeus). BLACK TERN. [77.]

> *Sterna nigra* Linnaeus, 1758, Syst. Nat., ed. 10, 1, p. 137. (in Europa = near Uppsala, Sweden.)

Habitat.—Marshes, sloughs and wet meadows, primarily fresh-water (breeding); pelagic, as well as along seacoasts, bays, estuaries, lagoons, lakes and rivers (non-breeding).

Distribution.—*Breeds* in North America from southwestern and east-central British Columbia, northern Alberta, south-central Mackenzie, northwestern Saskatchewan, northern Manitoba, northern Ontario (probably), southern Quebec, southern New Brunswick and Nova Scotia south locally to south-central California, northern Nevada, northern Utah, Colorado, Nebraska, Missouri (formerly), south-central Illinois, Kentucky (formerly), Ohio, Pennsylvania, western New York, northwestern Vermont and Maine (one old record from Fort Yukon, east-central Alaska); and in the Old World from northern Europe, north-central Russia and central Siberia south to the Mediterranean Sea, Asia Minor, Turkestan, and the Caspian and Aral seas. Nonbreeding birds occur in summer south on the Pacific coast to Panama, and in eastern North America to the Gulf coast.

Winters in the Americas along both coasts from Panama south to Peru and Surinam; and in the Old World primarily in tropical Africa south to Angola and Tanzania, casually to Madeira and northern China.

In migration occurs throughout the interior of North America south of the breeding range; along both coasts and through the interior of Middle America; along the Atlantic coast from Nova Scotia south to Florida and the West Indies (rarely south to Barbados); and often far at sea.

Casual in the Hawaiian Islands and Bermuda. Accidental in Alaska (Wrangell, and Walker Lake in the Brooks Range), southern Yukon, Chile and northern Argentina.

Genus ANOUS Stephens

> *Anoüs* Stephens, 1826, *in* Shaw, Gen. Zool., 13 (1), p. 139. Type, by subsequent designation (G. R. Gray, 1840), *Anoüs niger* Stephens = *Sterna stolida* Linnaeus.

Anous stolidus (Linnaeus). BROWN NODDY. [79.]

> *Sterna stolida* Linnaeus, 1758, Syst. Nat., ed. 10, 1, p. 137. Based mainly on *Hirundo marina minor, capite albo* Sloane, Voy. Jamaica, 1, p. 31, pl. 6, fig. 2, and "The Noddy" Catesby, Nat. Hist. Carolina, 1, p. 88, pl. 88. (in Americæ Pelago = West Indies.)

Habitat.—Primarily pelagic, nesting on islands on bare ground, rock ledges, sandy beaches or in trees.

Distribution.—*Breeds* in the Pacific Ocean from the Hawaiian (Kure east to Moku Manu and Manana islets off Oahu), Ryukyu and Bonin islands south to northern Australia, Norfolk Island and the Taumotu Archipelago, and from islands off western Mexico (Revillagigedo, Tres Marias, Tres Marietas and Isabela) south to Costa Rica (Cocos Island, possibly also on the Santa Elena Peninsula) and the Galapagos Islands; in the Gulf-Caribbean region from the Bahamas and Florida Keys (Dry Tortugas) south through most of the Antilles to islands off the coasts of the Yucatan Peninsula (Alacrán reef), Belize, Venezuela (Las Aves east to Margarita, Tobago and Trinidad) and French Guiana; in the Atlantic Ocean on Trindade, Ascension, St. Helena, Tristan da Cunha and Gough, also islands in the Gulf of Guinea; and in the Indian Ocean region from the Red Sea, Gulf of Aden and Laccadive Islands south to Madagascar and the Seychelles.

Winters at sea, generally in the vicinity of the breeding grounds, ranging casually (mostly after storms) to the Gulf coast (west to Texas), the Atlantic coast (north to North Carolina), and the coasts of Middle America (Caribbean coast and islands off Honduras and Nicaragua, and both coasts of Panama).

Casual in Bermuda. Accidental in Massachusetts.

Notes.—Also known as NODDY TERN and COMMON NODDY.

Anous minutus Boie. BLACK NODDY. [79.1.]

Anous minutus Boie, 1844, Isis von Oken, col. 188. (New Holland = Raine Island, Australia.)

Habitat.—Primarily pelagic, breeding on islands in trees or on rock ledges.

Distribution.—*Breeds* in the tropical Pacific Ocean from the Hawaiian Islands (throughout), and Marcus and Wake islands south to New Guinea, northeastern Australia and the Tuamotu Archipelago, also off the coast of Middle America on Clipperton Island, and on Cocos Island (off Costa Rica); in the Caribbean region off Belize (formerly on Southwest Cay in Glover's Reef, no recent records) and off Venezuela (Los Roques and possibly Las Aves); and in the tropical South Atlantic from St. Paul's Rocks and Fernando de Noronha to St. Helana and (formerly) Inaccessible Island.

Winters at sea in the vicinity of the breeding grounds.

Casual in the Florida Keys (Dry Tortugas, summers since 1962), also a sight report from Honduras (Isla Utila). Accidental on the central coast of Texas (Nueces County).

Notes.—Some authors treat *A. tenuirostris* (Temminck, 1823) [LESSER NODDY] of the Indian Ocean as conspecific with *A. minutus*; they constitute a superspecies. With a single species concept, WHITE-CAPPED NODDY is the appropriate English name.

Genus **PROCELSTERNA** Lafresnaye

Procelsterna [subgenus] Lafresnaye, 1842, Mag. Zool. [Paris], ser. 2, 4, Ois., pl. 29, p. 1. Type, by monotypy, *Procelsterna tereticollis* Lafresnaye = *Sterna cerulea* Bennett.

Procelsterna cerulea (Bennett). BLUE-GRAY NODDY. [79.2.]

> *Sterna cerulea* F. D. Bennett, 1840, Narr. Whaling Voy., 2, p. 248. (Christmas Island, Pacific Ocean.)

Habitat.—Primarily pelagic, nesting in recesses and shallow cavities on rocky islands, and in the open on sandy islets.

Distribution.—*Breeds* in the tropical Pacific Ocean from the Hawaiian Islands (Gardner Pinnacles, French Frigate Shoals, Necker, Nihoa and Kaula) south to the Samoa and Tuamotu archipelagos, and to Henderson, Easter and San Ambrosia (off Chile) islands; also on Lord Howe, Norfolk and the Kermadec islands north of New Zealand.

Winters at sea in the general vicinity of the breeding grounds.

Notes.—Also known as GRAY TERNLET. The southwestern Pacific populations are sometimes recognized as a distinct species, *P. albivittata* Bonaparte, 1856.

Genus GYGIS Wagler

> *Gygis* Wagler, 1832, Isis von Oken, col. 1223. Type, by monotypy, *Sterna candida* Gmelin = *Sterna alba* Sparrman.

Gygis alba (Sparrman). WHITE TERN. [79.3.]

> *Sterna alba* Sparrman, 1786, Mus. Carlson., fasc. 1, pl. 11. (in India orientali, ad promontorium Bonae Spet Insulasquae maris pacifici = Ascension Island.)

Habitat.—Primarily pelagic, breeding on islands on bare limbs or crotches in branches of trees (no nest), less commonly on rocky ledges or coral, sometimes in old nests of *Anous minutus* and on various man-made structures.

Distribution.—*Breeds* [*candida* group] on islands in the tropical Pacific Ocean from the Hawaiian (Kure east to Kaula, and on Oahu), Caroline and Marshall islands south to Norfolk, the Kermadec, Tonga and Society islands, also on Clipperton Island, Cocos Island (off Costa Rica), in the Galapagos Islands, and on Easter and Sala-y-Gomez islands, and in the Indian Ocean in the Seychelles; and [*alba* group] in the Pacific in the Marquesas Islands, and in the South Atlantic on Fernando de Noronha, Trindade, Martin Vas Rocks, Ascension and St. Helena.

Winters at sea generally near the respective breeding ranges.

Accidental [*candida* group] in the Revillagigedo Islands (Oneal Rock near Socorro) and on Bermuda (photograph of individual referable to this group).

Notes.—Also known as WHITE NODDY or FAIRY TERN, the latter name now restricted to *Sterna nereis* (Gould, 1843) of the southwest Pacific. Some authors suggest that the two groups may represent distinct species, *G. alba* and *G. candida* (Gmelin, 1789).

Subfamily RYNCHOPINAE: Skimmers

Notes.—See comments under Stercorariinae.

Genus RYNCHOPS Linnaeus

> *Rynchops* Linnaeus, 1758, Syst. Nat., ed. 10, 1, p. 138. Type, by subsequent designation (G. R. Gray, 1840), *Rynchops nigra* Linnaeus.

Notes.—Treatment of *Rynchops* as masculine results from a decision by the International Commission of Zoological Nomenclature ruling that all genera ending in *-ops* are to be considered as of masculine gender.

Rynchops niger Linnaeus. BLACK SKIMMER. [80.]

Rynchops nigra Linnaeus, 1758, Syst. Nat., ed. 10, 1, p. 138. Based mainly on the "Cut Water" Catesby, Nat. Hist. Carolina, 1, p. 90, pl. 90. (in America = coast of South Carolina.)

Habitat.—Primarily near coasts on sandy beaches, shell banks, coastal islands, tropical rivers, and locally, gravelly rooftops, in migration and winter also bays, estuaries, lagoons and mudflats (Tropical to Temperate zones).

Distribution.—*Breeds* in western North America in southern California (San Diego, Salton Sea) and along the coast of Sonora, Sinaloa and Nayarit; locally on the Atlantic-Gulf coast from Massachusetts (Plymouth), New York (Long Island) and New Jersey south to southern Florida (Miami area), and from western Florida (south to the Tampa Bay region) along the Gulf coast to Texas and south to Tabasco (possibly also the Yucatan Peninsula); and in South America along the Pacific coast in western Ecuador, and on the Caribbean-Atlantic coast from Colombia south (including in the larger rivers) to northern Argentina.

Winters from southern California and Sonora south along the Pacific coast of Middle America and South America to southern Chile; and in the Atlantic-Caribbean region from Florida (rarely from North Carolina) west along the Gulf coast to Texas and south along the coast of Middle America and South America (also Margarita Island and Trinidad) to central Argentina. Postbreeding individuals wander rarely north to central California and (usually following storms) to New Brunswick, Nova Scotia and Newfoundland.

Casual inland in coastal states, on the Mexican Plateau, and to Arizona, New Mexico, Kansas, Oklahoma, Tennessee, southern Ontario and Quebec; also to Bermuda, the Bahamas (Bimini, Great Inagua), Cuba, Hispaniola (off the coast), the Virgin Islands, Guadeloupe and Grenada.

Notes.—The morphologically distinct South American race, *R. n. cinerascens* Spix, 1825, has been recorded as a vagrant in Costa Rica and Panama. Some authors consider all species of the genus *Rynchops* to constitute a superspecies.

Suborder ALCAE: Auks and Allies

Family ALCIDAE: Auks, Murres and Puffins

Tribe ALLINI: Dovekies

Genus ALLE Link

Plautus Gunnerus, 1761, Trondheimske Selks. Skr., 1, p. 263, pl. 6. Type, by monotypy, *Plotus* eller *Plautus columbarius* Gunnerus = *Alca alle* Linnaeus. (Unavailable name; see Wetmore and Watson, 1969, Bull. Br. Ornithol. Club, 89, pp. 6–7.)

Alle Link, 1806, Beschr. Naturh. Samml. Univ. Rostock, 1, p. 46. Type, by monotypy, *Alle nigricans* Link = *Alca alle* Linnaeus.

Alle alle (Linnaeus). DOVEKIE. [34.]

> *Alca Alle* Linnaeus, 1758, Syst. Nat., ed. 10, 1, p. 131. (in Europæ Americæ arcticæ oceano = Scotland.)

Habitat.—Crevices on steep coastal cliffs (breeding); mostly pelagic, less frequently along seacoasts (nonbreeding).

Distribution.—*Breeds* in the Palearctic in Greenland, Iceland, Jan Mayen, Spitsbergen, Bear Island, Franz Josef Land, Novaya Zemlya and North Land; also probably islands in the Bering Sea (St. Lawrence and Little Diomede), and possibly in North America on eastern Ellesmere Island. Nonbreeding birds occur in summer south to Baffin Island, and along the Atlantic coast to Maine.

Winters offshore from the breeding range south to Southampton Island, Ungava Bay, the Gulf of St. Lawrence and Bay of Fundy (irregularly along the Atlantic coast as far as North Carolina), and in the eastern Atlantic to the Canary Islands, Azores, France and the Baltic Sea, also casually south to southern Florida, Cuba, the Bahamas (Grand Bahama), Bermuda, Madeira and the western Mediterranean Sea.

Casual along the Arctic coast of Alaska and Canada (Point Barrow), Melville Island and Keewatin, and in the interior of northeastern North America west to central Manitoba, Minnesota, Wisconsin, Michigan, Ontario and New York; also in the British Isles and interior of Europe. Accidental in western Florida (Bay County) and the Pribilof Islands (St. George).

Notes.—Also known as LITTLE AUK.

Tribe ALCINI: Murres and Auks

Genus **URIA** Brisson

> *Uria* Brisson, 1760, Ornithologie, 1, p. 52; 6, p. 70. Type, by tautonymy, *Uria* Brisson = *Colymbus aalge* Pontoppidan.

Uria aalge (Pontoppidan). COMMON MURRE. [30.]

> *Colymbus aalge* Pontoppidan, 1763, Dan. Atlas, 1, p. 621, pl. 26. (Island = Iceland.)

Habitat.—Coastal cliff ledges (breeding); pelagic and along rocky seacoasts (nonbreeding).

Distribution.—*Breeds* in North America along the Pacific coast from western Alaska (Cape Lisburne, Kotzebue Sound, Diomede Islands) south through Norton Sound and the Bering Sea (St. Matthew, Nunivak and the Pribilof islands) to the Aleutians, and from south-coastal Alaska to central California (including the Farallon Islands, and south to Monterey County, formerly Santa Barbara County); in eastern North America from Labrador (locally) and southeastern Quebec (north shore of Gulf of St. Lawrence, Anticosti and Bonaventure islands, and Bird Rocks) south to Newfoundland and Nova Scotia (at least formerly); and in the Palearctic from Greenland, Iceland, Bear Island and Novaya Zemlya south to northern France and central Norway, and from the Commander Islands and Kamchatka south to southern Sakhalin, eastern Korea and Japan.

Winters primarily offshore in areas near the breeding grounds, in the Pacific south regularly to southern California and (rarely) northern Baja California; in eastern North America south to Maine, casually as far as Virginia (Back Bay); and in the Palearctic to northern Europe.

Accidental in Florida (Fort Pierce).

Notes.—Also known as THIN-BILLED MURRE and, in Old World literature, as the GUILLEMOT.

Uria lomvia (Linnaeus). THICK-BILLED MURRE. [31.]

Alca Lomvia Linnaeus, 1758, Syst. Nat., ed. 10, 1, p. 130. (in Europa boreali = Greenland.)

Habitat.—Steep, coastal cliffs (breeding); mostly pelagic, less frequently along rocky coasts (nonbreeding).

Distribution.—*Breeds* in North America from northern Alaska (Cape Lisburne, Kotzebue Sound, Diomede Islands) south through the Pribilofs to the Aleutians, east to Kodiak, Middleton and St. Lazaria islands, in northwestern Mackenzie (Cape Parry), and from Prince Leopold, Cobourg, Bylot and eastern Baffin islands south to northern Hudson Bay (Coats Island and Chesterfield Inlet), northern Quebec (Ungava Bay to Cape Chidley), Labrador, the Gulf of St. Lawrence and Newfoundland (Bird Rock), formerly to Maine (Penobscot Bay); and in the Palearctic from Greenland, Iceland, Jan Mayen, Spitsbergen, Novaya Zemlya, the New Siberian Islands, Wrangel Island and northern Siberia south to northern Russia, Kamchatka, and the Commander and Kurile islands.

Winters primarily offshore from the breeding range in North America south to southeastern Alaska, casually to central California (Monterey Bay), in northern Canada south to Hudson Bay, casually to northern Yukon; along the Atlantic coast to New Jersey, casually south to South Carolina (sight reports for Florida) and inland to the Great Lakes region (recorded from Michigan, Ontario and Quebec south to Iowa, Indiana, Ohio and Pennsylvania); and in the Palearctic south to northern Europe and Japan.

Notes.—Also known as BRUNNICH'S MURRE and, in Old World literature, as BRUNNICH'S GUILLEMOT.

Genus ALCA Linnaeus

Alca Linnaeus, 1758, Syst. Nat., ed. 10, 1, p. 130. Type, by tautonymy, *Alca torda* Linnaeus (*Alca,* prebinomial specific name, in synonymy).

Alca torda Linnaeus. RAZORBILL. [32.]

Alca Torda Linnaeus, 1758, Syst. Nat., ed. 10, 1, p. 130. (in Europæ borealis oceano = Stora Karlsö, Baltic Sea.)

Habitat.—Coastal cliffs and on rocky shores and islands (breeding); mostly pelagic, less commonly along rocky seacoasts (nonbreeding).

Distribution.—*Breeds* in North America from extreme southeastern Baffin Island and the coast of Labrador south to southeastern Quebec (north shore of Gulf of St. Lawrence, Cape Whittle, Bird Rocks, and Anticosti, Bonaventure and Magdalen islands), eastern Newfoundland, southern New Brunswick (Grand Manan), eastern Maine (Machias Seal Island and Matinicus Rock) and Nova Scotia; and in the Palearctic from Greenland east to the British Isles, Scandinavia and northern Russia. Recorded in summer (and possibly breeding) on Digges Island, off northwestern Quebec.

Winters offshore from the breeding grounds in North America south to New York (Long Island), casually to South Carolina and Florida (Brevard County); and in the Palearctic from southern Scandinavia and the Baltic to the western Mediterranean Sea, casually to the Canary Islands.

Casual on Lake Ontario and the Gulf coast of Florida (St. George and Santa Rosa islands). Accidental in Pennsylvania (Pittston).

Notes.—Also known as RAZOR-BILLED AUK.

Genus PINGUINUS Bonnaterre

Plautus (not Gunnerus) Brünnich, 1771, Zool. Fund., p. 78. Type, by monotypy, "Brillefuglen" = *Alca impennis* Linnaeus.
Pinguinus Bonnaterre, 1791, Tabl. Encycl. Méth., Ornithol., livr. 47, pp. lxxxiii, 28. Type, by subsequent designation (Ogilvie-Grant, 1898), *Alca impennis* Linnaeus.

†Pinguinus impennis (Linnaeus). GREAT AUK. [33.]

Alca impennis Linnaeus, 1758, Syst. Nat., ed. 10, 1, p. 130. (in Europa arctica = Norwegian Sea.)

Habitat.—Low coastal rocky islands (breeding); mostly at sea (nonbreeding).
Distribution.—EXTINCT. Formerly *bred* in the Gulf of St. Lawrence (Bird Rocks), Newfoundland (Funk Island), Greenland, Iceland and the Outer Hebrides (St. Kilda), possibly in the Faroe Islands and on Lundy, doubtfully on the Isle of Man.

Wintered from the breeding grounds south to Maine and Massachusetts, casually to South Carolina; and to the British Isles, France, Spain, Denmark and Scandinavia.

Last verified record, two taken in Iceland on 3 June 1844.

Tribe CEPPHINI: Guillemots

Genus CEPPHUS Pallas

Cepphus Pallas, 1769, Spic. Zool., 1, fasc. 5, p. 33. Type, by monotypy, *Cepphus lacteolus* Pallas = *Alca grylle* Linnaeus.

Cepphus grylle (Linnaeus). BLACK GUILLEMOT. [26.]

Alca Grylle Linnaeus, 1758, Syst. Nat., ed. 10, 1, p. 130. (in Europæ borealis oceano = Gotland, Sweden.)

Habitat.—Holes under rocks (rarely in ground) on rocky islands, in crevices in base of coastal cliffs, and (in Alaska) in or under beach flotsam (breeding); mostly pelagic, less frequently along rocky seacoasts (nonbreeding).
Distribution.—*Breeds* in northern Alaska (along the Chukchi and Beaufort seacoasts from Cape Thompson east at least to Barter Island, probably also on St. Lawrence Island in the Bering Sea) and northern Yukon (Herschel Island); in eastern North America from Ellesmere, Devon, Somerset, Bylot and eastern Baffin islands south to the Melville Peninsula, Southampton Island, northern Ontario (Cape Henrietta Maria), the eastern shore of Hudson and James bays, northern Labrador, Newfoundland, shores and islands of the Gulf of St. Lawrence, New

Brunswick, Maine and southern Nova Scotia; and in the Palearctic from Greenland, Iceland, Scandinavia, northern Russia, Novaya Zemlya and the New Siberian, Wrangel and Herald islands south to the British Isles, southern Scandinavia and the coast of northern Siberia. Recorded in summer west to Banks Island and northern Keewatin.

Winters mostly at sea from the breeding grounds south in the Bering Sea ice front to the Pribilof Islands, and in eastern North America from the breeding grounds south to New England, rarely New York (Long Island) and New Jersey; and in the Palearctic to northern Europe.

Casual or accidental in Mackenzie, southern Manitoba, southern Ontario, eastern Pennsylvania (Delaware River near Chester) and South Carolina.

Notes.—*C. grylle* and *C. columba* constitute a superspecies.

Cepphus columba Pallas. PIGEON GUILLEMOT. [29.]

Cepphus Columba Pallas, 1811, Zoogr. Rosso-Asiat., 2, p. 348. (in oceano arctico pariterque circa Camtschatcam et in omni freto inter Sibiriam et Americam = Kamchatka and Bering Strait.)

Habitat.—Crevices in coastal cliffs or among rocks along shores, also under old docks and piers (breeding); mostly pelagic and along rocky seacoasts (nonbreeding).

Distribution.—*Breeds* in western North America from northern Alaska (Cape Lisburne and Cape Thompson) south through Norton Sound and the Bering Sea (Diomede, St. Lawrence, St. Matthew, Hall and Bogoslof islands, and Cape Newenham and Cape Peirce) to the Aleutians, and south along the Pacific coast to southern California (to Santa Barbara Island, and on the mainland to San Luis Obispo County); and in Eurasia from the Chukotski Peninsula south to the Kurile Islands. Nonbreeding individuals occur in summer elsewhere in the Bering Sea (Nunivak and Pribilof islands).

Winters in North America from the Pribilof and Aleutian islands south to central California (casually to San Diego County); and in Eurasia generally near the breeding grounds, casually to Sakhalin and Japan (Hokkaido).

Notes.—See comments under *C. grylle*.

[Cepphus carbo Pallas. SPECTACLED GUILLEMOT.] See Appendix B.

Tribe BRACHYRAMPHINI: Brachyramphine Murrelets

Genus BRACHYRAMPHUS Brandt

Brachyramphus M. Brandt, 1837, Bull. Sci. Acad. Imp. Sci. St.-Petersbourg, 2, no. 22, col. 346. Type, by subsequent designation (G. R. Gray, 1840), *Colymbus marmoratus* Gmelin.

Brachyramphus marmoratus (Gmelin). MARBLED MURRELET. [23.]

Colymbus marmoratus Gmelin, 1789, Syst. Nat., 1 (2), p. 583. Based on the "Marbled Guillemot" Pennant, Arct. Zool., 2, p. 517, pl. 22, right fig. (in America occidentali et Camtschatca = Prince William Sound, Alaska.)

Habitat.—Coniferous forests near coasts, nesting on large horizontal branches high up in trees, or on islands on open barren ground (breeding); mostly pelagic (nonbreeding).

Distribution.—*Breeds* in Alaska (Kenai Peninsula, Barren Islands), central California (Santa Cruz County) and Siberia (Okhotsk); few nests known. Occurs in summer and probably breeds in North America from southern Alaska (the Aleutians, Alaska Peninsula and south-coastal region) south to central California, and in Asia from the Sea of Okhotsk, Kamchatka and the Commander Islands south to Korea, Japan and the Kurile Islands.

Winters offshore in North America from southern Alaska (casually the Aleutians and Pribilofs) south to central (casually southern) California; and in Eurasia from the summer range south regularly to Japan.

Accidental in Indiana (Brown County) and Quebec (near Montreal).

Brachyramphus brevirostris (Vigors). KITTLITZ'S MURRELET. [24.]

> *Uria brevirostris* Vigors, 1829, Zool. J., 4 (1828), p. 357. (San Blas [Mexico], error = North Pacific.)

Habitat.—Coastal cliffs, and barren ground, rock ledges and talus above timberline in coastal mountains, generally near glaciers (breeding); mostly pelagic and along rocky seacoasts (nonbreeding).

Distribution.—*Breeds* in Alaska in mountains, primarily coastal, from Port Hope south to the Aleutians and east to Glacier Bay.

Winters generally offshore from the Aleutians east to Glacier Bay.

Casual in northeastern Siberia and the Kurile Islands. Accidental in southern California (La Jolla, possibly not a natural vagrant).

Tribe SYNTHLIBORAMPHINI: Synthliboramphine Murrelets

Genus **SYNTHLIBORAMPHUS** Brandt

> *Synthliboramphus* M. Brandt, 1837, Bull. Sci. Acad. Imp. Sci. St.-Petersbourg, 2, no. 22, col. 347. Type, by subsequent designation (G. R. Gray, 1840), *Alca antiqua* Gmelin.
>
> *Endomychura* Oberholser, 1899, Proc. Acad. Nat. Sci. Philadelphia, 51, p. 201. Type, by original designation, *Brachyramphus hypoleucus* Xántus de Vesey.

Synthliboramphus hypoleucus (Xántus de Vesey). XANTUS' MURRELET. [25.]

> *Brachyramphus hypoleucus* Xántus de Vesey, 1860, Proc. Acad. Nat. Sci. Philadelphia, 11 (1859), p. 299. (Cape St. Lucas, Lower California = 14 miles off the coast of Cape San Lucas, Baja California.)

Habitat.—On islands on the ground, in crevices beneath large rocks, or under dense clumps of vegetation (breeding); mostly pelagic (nonbreeding).

Distribution.—*Breeds* on islands off southern California (San Miguel, Anacapa and Santa Barbara, possibly other of the Channel Islands) and western Baja California (Los Coronados, Todos Santos, San Benito, Natividad and Guadalupe).

Winters primarily from central California (Monterey Bay) south to southern Baja California, casually farther north (recorded from the Farallon Islands, Oregon, Washington, and off Moresby Island, British Columbia).

Notes.—Breeding populations on Guadalupe Island, presently known as *S. h. scrippsi* (Green and Arnold, 1939), may represent a species distinct from *S. hypoleucus,* as there is some evidence that both breed in the San Benito Islands and on Santa Barbara Island (with limited hybridization). *S. hypoleucus* and *S. craveri* appear to constitute a superspecies; the two are considered conspecific by some authors, but both apparently breed in the San Benito Islands with very little hybridization. These two species were formerly placed in the genus *Endomychura.*

Synthliboramphus craveri (Salvadori). CRAVERI'S MURRELET. [26.]

Uria Craveri Salvadori, 1865, Atti Soc. Ital. Sci. Nat., Mus. Civ. Stor. Nat. Milano, 8, p. 387. (Golfo della California, Lat. 27°50′12″ Long. 110°10′45″ = Raza Island, Gulf of California.)

Habitat.—In rock crevices on islands (breeding); mostly pelagic (nonbreeding).
Distribution.—*Breeds* on most islands in the Gulf of California (north to Consag Rock), and probably north along the west coast of Baja California to Magdalena Bay and the San Benito Islands.

Winters at sea in the Gulf of California and to the coast of Sonora (possibly farther south off western Mexico). Wanders after the breeding season north along the Pacific coast of Baja California and southern California to Monterey Bay.

Accidental in Oregon (Lane County).
Notes.—See comments under *S. hypoleucus.*

Synthliboramphus antiquus (Gmelin). ANCIENT MURRELET. [21.]

Alca antiqua Gmelin, 1789, Syst. Nat., 1 (2), p. 554. Based on the "Antient Auk" Pennant, Arct. Zool., 2, p. 512. (in mari inter Camtschatcam, insulas Kuriles et Americam intermedio = Bering Sea.)

Habitat.—Rocky seacoasts in crevices, under rocks, and occasionally in burrows in the ground (breeding); mostly pelagic, casually on large inland bodies of water (nonbreeding).
Distribution.—*Breeds* in western North America from southern Alaska (the Aleutian, Sanak and Kodiak islands) south to British Columbia (Queen Charlotte Islands), casually to northwestern Washington (Carroll Island); and in eastern Asia from the Commander Islands and Kamchatka south to Amurland, Sakhalin, the Kurile Islands, Korea and Dagelet Island.

Winters primarily offshore in North America from the Pribilof and Aleutian islands south to central (rarely southern) California and (casually) northern Baja California (Ensenada); and in Asia from the Commander Islands south to Formosa and the Ryukyu Islands.

Casual in the interior of western North America (in southern Yukon, and from southern British Columbia, Alberta, Idaho, Montana and southern Manitoba south to Nevada, Utah, Colorado and Nebraska) and in the upper Midwest and Great Lakes region (from Minnesota, Wisconsin, Michigan, southern Ontario and southern Quebec south to central Illinois and northern Ohio). Accidental in Louisiana (Lake Pontchartrain).
Notes.—*S. antiquus* and the Japanese *S. wumizusume* (Temminck, 1835) [JAPANESE or TEMMINCK'S MURRELET] constitute a superspecies.

Tribe AETHIINI: Auklets

Genus **PTYCHORAMPHUS** Brandt

Ptychoramphus M. Brandt, 1837, Bull. Sci. Acad. Imp. Sci. St.-Petersbourg, 2, no. 22, col. 347. Type, by monotypy, *Uria aleutica* Pallas.

Ptychoramphus aleuticus (Pallas). CASSIN'S AUKLET. [16.]

Uria Aleutica Pallas, 1811, Zoogr., Rosso-Asiat., 2, p. 370. (Russia ad Oceanum orientalem = North Pacific Ocean.)

Habitat.—On islands in burrows in the ground (breeding); mostly pelagic, less frequently along rocky seacoasts (nonbreeding).

Distribution.—*Breeds* locally on coastal islands from southern Alaska (west to Buldir in the Aleutians) south to southern Baja California (Asunción, San Roque and Guadalupe islands).

Winters along the Pacific coast from southern British Columbia (Vancouver Island), rarely from southeastern Alaska, south to southern Baja California.

Casual inland in Washington and Oregon.

Genus **CYCLORRHYNCHUS** Kaup

Cyclorrhynchus Kaup, 1829, Skizz. Entw.-Ges. Eur. Thierw., p. 155. Type, by monotypy, *Alca psittacula* Pallas.

Cyclorrhynchus psittacula (Pallas). PARAKEET AUKLET. [17.]

Alca psittacula Pallas, 1769, Spic. Zool, 1, fasc. 5, p. 13, pl. ii; pl. v, figs. 4–6. (in mari Kamtschatkam . . . et circa insulas partim versus Iaponiam partim versus Americam septentrionalem sparsas = Kamchatka.)

Habitat.—Rocky seacoasts in cliff crevices, among boulders on beaches, and on rocky slopes with dense vegetation (breeding); mostly pelagic, less commonly in coastal regions (nonbreeding).

Distribution.—*Breeds* in western Alaska from the Diomede Islands, Fairway Rock, Sledge Island and Norton Sound south through the Bering Sea (St. Lawrence, St. Matthew and the Pribilof islands) to the Aleutians, and east to islands in Prince William Sound; and in eastern Siberia along the Gulf of Anadyr and the in the Commander Islands.

Winters off the Pacific coast of North America from the Pribilof and Aleutian islands south, at least formerly, to southern California; and in Eurasia from the Bering Sea south to Sakhalin, the Kurile Islands and Japan.

Casual in the Hawaiian Islands (Kure, Midway) and northern Alaska (Point Barrow). Accidental in Sweden.

Genus **AETHIA** Merrem

Aethia Merrem, 1788, Vers. Grundr. Allg. Ges. Nat. Eintheil. Vögel, 1, Tentamen Nat. Syst. Avium, pp. 7, 13, 20. Type, by monotypy, *Alca cristatella* Pallas.

Aethia pusilla (Pallas). LEAST AUKLET. [20.]

Uria pusilla Pallas, 1811, Zoogr. Rosso-Asiat., 2, p. 373. (circa Camtschatcam = Kamchatka.)

Habitat.—Talus slopes and beach rock rubble, occasionally in small crevices in coastal cliffs (breeding); mostly pelagic, and at upwellings along rocky seacoasts and islands (nonbreeding).

Distribution.—*Breeds* in western Alaska from the Diomede Islands south through islands of the Bering Sea (including the Pribilofs) to the Aleutian, Shumagin and Semidi islands; and in eastern Siberia along the Chukotski Peninsula.

Winters in the southern Bering Sea, at sea off the Aleutians, and from the coast of eastern Siberia south to Kamchatka, Sakhalin, the Kurile Islands and northern Japan.

Casual north to northern Alaska (Point Barrow) and east to northern Mackenzie (Kittigazuit). Accidental in California (San Mateo County).

Aethia pygmaea (Gmelin). WHISKERED AUKLET. [19.]

Alca pygmaea Gmelin, 1789, Syst. Nat., 1 (2), p. 555. Based on the "Pygmy Auk" Pennant, Arct. Zool., 2, p. 513. (circa insulam avium, inter Asiam septentrionalem et Americam = islands in the Bering Sea.)

Habitat.—Crevices in talus slopes, among boulders along beaches, and on lava flows on high slopes (breeding); mostly pelagic, occurring off rocky seacoasts and islands (nonbreeding).

Distribution.—*Breeds* in southwestern Alaska in the Aleutians (east at least to Unimak Pass and west to Buldir), possibly also in the Near Islands; and in eastern Siberia in the Commander and southern Kurile islands.

Winters at sea off the Aleutians, and from the Commander Islands and Kamchatka south to the Kurile Islands, casually to Japan.

Casual north in the Bering Sea to St. Lawrence Island and Bristol Bay.

Aethia cristatella (Pallas). CRESTED AUKLET. [18.]

Alca cristatella Pallas, 1769, Spic. Zool., 1, fasc. 5, p. 18, pl. iii; pl. v, figs. 7–9. (Ultimarum versus Japoniam maxime incola et circa insulam Matmey = Hokkaido to Kamchatka.)

Habitat.—Talus slopes and beach boulder rubble, occasionally in crevices in cliffs (breeding); mostly pelagic, occurring off rocky islands and seacoasts (nonbreeding).

Distribution.—*Breeds* in western Alaska on Bering Sea islands (from the Diomedes south, including King, St. Lawrence and St. Matthew, to the Pribilofs), and in the Aleutians east at least to the Shumagin and Semidi islands, but not in the Near Islands); and in eastern Siberia from the Chukotski Peninsula south to Sakhalin and the central Kurile Islands. Nonbreeding birds occur in summer north to northern Alaska (Wainwright and Barrow), and to the Wrangel and Herald islands, off northern Siberia.

Winters in open waters of the Bering Sea and around the Aleutians, east to the vicinity of Kodiak; and in Asia south to Japan.

Accidental inland in Alaska (Nulato), in California (Marin County), and in the North Atlantic off the northeastern coast of Iceland.

Tribe FRATERCULINI: Puffins

Genus CERORHINCA Bonaparte

Cerorhinca Bonaparte, 1828, Ann. Lyc. Nat. Hist. N.Y., 2, p. 427. Type, by monotypy, *Cerorhinca occidentalis* Bonaparte = *Alca monocerata* Pallas.

Cerorhinca monocerata (Pallas). RHINOCEROS AUKLET. [15.]

Alca monocerata Pallas, 1811, Zoogr. Rosso-Asiat., 2, p. 362. (circa promontorium S. Eliae Americae et ad littora insulae Kadiak = Cape St. Elias, Alaska.)

Habitat.—On wooded islands in ground burrows (breeding); mostly pelagic, less frequently along rocky seacoasts (nonbreeding).

Distribution.—*Breeds* on islands along the Pacific coast of North America from south-coastal and southeastern Alaska (Barren, Middleton, St. Lazaria and Forrester islands) south to western Washington (Destruction Island, formerly Whidbey and Smith islands) and northern California (Castle Island in Del Norte County, and the Farallons); and in eastern Asia from southern Sakhalin and the southern Kurile Islands south to Korea and Japan. Nonbreeding birds occur in summer south casually to southern California (San Pedro).

Winters off the Pacific coast of North America from southern British Columbia (casually from southern Alaska) south to Baja California (Santa Margarita Island); and in Asia in the southern part of the breeding range.

Casual in the Aleutian and Commander islands.

Notes.—Also known as HORN-BILLED PUFFIN.

Genus FRATERCULA Brisson

Fratercula Brisson, 1760, Ornithologie, 1, p. 52; 6, p. 81. Type, by tautonymy, *Fratercula* Brisson = *Alca arctica* Linnaeus.
Lunda Pallas, 1811, Zoogr. Rosso-Asiat., 2, p. 363. Type, by subsequent designation (G. R. Gray, 1840), *Alca cirrhata* Pallas.

Fratercula cirrhata (Pallas). TUFTED PUFFIN. [12.]

Alca cirrhata Pallas, 1769, Spic. Zool., 1, fasc. 5, p. 7, pl. i; pl. v, figs. 1–3. (in Mari inter Kamtschatcam et Americam Archipelagumque Kurilum = Bering Sea.)

Habitat.—Coastal slopes in ground burrows, sometimes under boulders and piles of rocks, occasionally under dense vegetation (breeding); primarily pelagic (nonbreeding).

Distribution.—*Breeds* along the Pacific coast of North America from the Diomede Islands and Cape Thompson south through islands of the Bering Sea (including the Pribilofs) to the Aleutians, and east from Kodiak Island, the Alaska Peninsula and southeastern Alaska south to central California (to the Farallons, formerly to Anacapa Island); and in eastern Asia from the Kolyuchin Islands and East Cape south to Kamchatka, the Commander and Kurile islands, Sea of Okhotsk, Sakhalin and northern Japan.

Winters offshore from southern Alaska and Kamchatka south through the breeding range to central (rarely southern) California and southern Japan.

Accidental in the Hawaiian Islands (Laysan) and Maine.

Notes.—Often placed in the monotypic genus *Lunda.*

Fratercula arctica (Linnaeus). ATLANTIC PUFFIN. [13.]

Alca arctica Linnaeus, 1758, Syst. Nat., ed. 10, 1, p. 130. (in Europæ borealis oceano = northern Norway.)

Habitat.—Rocky island slopes and seacoasts, usually in burrows, rarely in cliff crevices (breeding); primarily pelagic (nonbreeding).

Distribution.—*Breeds* in eastern North America from Labrador south in coastal areas to southeastern Quebec (Mingan, Anticosti, Bonaventure and Magdalen islands, and Gaspé Peninsula), Newfoundland, southwestern New Brunswick (Machias Seal Island) and eastern Maine (Seal Island and Matinicus Rock), also on Digges Island off northwestern Quebec; and in the Palearctic from Greenland, Iceland, the Faroe Islands, Spitsbergen, Bear Island and Novaya Zemlya south to the British Isles, northern Europe, southern Scandinavia and the coast of northern Russia.

Winters in the North Atlantic off North America from Labrador south to Massachusetts, casually to New Jersey, Maryland and Virginia; and in Eurasia from the breeding range south to the eastern Atlantic islands, northwestern Africa, the western Mediterranean region, and southern Europe.

Accidental in Ohio (Toledo area), Ontario (Ottawa), southwestern Quebec (Lake St. Peter) and Vermont (Rutland).

Notes.—Also known as COMMON PUFFIN and, in Old World literature, as the PUFFIN. *F. arctica* and *F. corniculata* constitute a superspecies.

Fratercula corniculata (Naumann). HORNED PUFFIN. [14.]

Mormon corniculata Naumann, 1821, Isis von Oken, col. 782. (Kamchatka.)

Habitat.—On rocky islands in cliff crevices and among boulders, rarely in ground burrows (breeding); mostly pelagic (nonbreeding).

Distribution.—*Breeds* on islands and along coasts of the Chukchi and Bering seas from the Diomede Islands and Cape Lisburne south to the Aleutian Islands, and along the Pacific coast of western North America from the Alaska Peninsula and south-coastal Alaska south to British Columbia (Queen Charlotte Islands, and probably elsewhere along the coast); and in Asia from northeastern Siberia (Kolyuchin Bay) south to the Commander Islands, Kamchatka, Sakhalin and the northern Kurile Islands. Nonbreeding birds occur in late spring and summer south along the Pacific coast of North America to southern California, and north in Siberia to Wrangel and Heard islands.

Winters from the Bering Sea and Aleutians south, at least casually, to the western Hawaiian Islands (Kure east to Laysan), and off North America to southern California; and in Asia from northeastern Siberia south to Japan.

Accidental in Mackenzie (Basil Bay) and inland in Washington (Coolee City).

Notes.—See comments under *F. arctica.*

Order COLUMBIFORMES: Sandgrouse, Pigeons and Doves

Notes.—Various taxa within this order have sometimes been included within the Charadriiformes.

Suborder PTEROCLETES: Sandgrouse

Family PTEROCLIDIDAE: Sandgrouse

Genus PTEROCLES Temminck

Pterocles Temminck, 1815, Pig. Gall., 3, pp. 238, 712. Type, by subsequent designation (G. R. Gray, 1840), *Tetrao alchata* Linnaeus.

Pterocles exustus Temminck. CHESTNUT-BELLIED SANDGROUSE. [311.1.]

Pterocles exustus Temminck, 1825, Planches Color., livr. 60, pls. 354, 360. (west coast of Africa, Egypt and Nubia = Senegal.)

Habitat.—Deserts and arid scrub, in the Hawaiian Islands in dry keawe scrub forest and rocky grasslands at low and moderate elevations.

Distribution.—*Resident* across northern Africa (south of the Sahara) from Senegal east to Somalia and Kenya, and from Arabia and Syria east to Baluchistan and India.

Introduced and established in the Hawaiian Islands (North Kona district of Hawaii, since 1961).

Suborder COLUMBAE: Pigeons and Doves

Family COLUMBIDAE: Pigeons and Doves

Genus COLUMBA Linnaeus

Columba Linnaeus, 1758, Syst. Nat., ed. 10, 1, p. 162. Type, by subsequent designation (Vigors, 1825), *Columba oenas* Linnaeus.
Patagioenas Reichenbach, 1853, Avium Syst. Nat. (1852), p. xxv. Type, by monotypy, *Columba leucocephala* Linnaeus.
Lithoenas Reichenbach, 1853, Avium Syst. Nat. (1852), p. xxv. Type, by monotypy, *Columba livia* "Linnaeus" = Gmelin.
Chloroenas Reichenbach, 1853, Avium Syst. Nat. (1852), p. xxv. Type, by monotypy, *Columba monilis* Vigors = *Columba fasciata* Say.
Œnoenas [subgenus] Salvadori, 1893, Cat. Birds Br. Mus., 21, p. 248. Type, by subsequent designation (Ridgway, 1916), *Columba nigrirostris* Sclater.

Notes.—For modern usage of *Patagioenas* and *Oenoenas* as genera distinct from *Columba,* see Johnston, 1962, Condor, 64, pp. 69–74; for contrary opinion, see Corbin, 1968, Condor, 70, pp. 1–13.

Columba livia Gmelin. ROCK DOVE. [313.1.]

Columba domestica β livia Gmelin, 1789, Syst. Nat., 1 (2), p. 769. (No locality given = southern Europe.)

Habitat.—In the wild state along rocky seacoasts or inland in gorges, river valleys, caves and desert oases, nesting on cliff ledges or in holes and fissures; feral birds in the Western Hemisphere occasionally in natural habitats, more abundantly near human settlement, especially in cities, nesting on building ledges, bridge structures, monuments, and in abandoned houses and barns.

Distribution.—*Resident* from the Faroe Islands, southern Scandinavia, Russia, western Siberia, Manchuria and northern China south through the British Isles, western Europe and the Mediterranean region to Madeira, the Canary Islands, Azores, Sahara region, Egypt, Saudi Arabia, Iran, India, Ceylon and Burma.

Introduced and established in most inhabited portions of the world, especially around larger cities, including virtually all of the Western Hemisphere, West Indies and Hawaiian Islands.

Notes.—Also known as ROCK PIGEON; established, feral populations are sometimes called FERAL or COMMON PIGEON.

Columba cayennensis Bonnaterre. PALE-VENTED PIGEON.

Columba cayennensis Bonnaterre, 1792, Tabl. Encycl. Méth., Ornithol., 1, livr. 51, p. 234. Based on "Le Pigeon Ramier de Cayenne" Holandre, Abrege Hist. Nat., 2, p. 214. (Cayenne.)

Habitat.—Savanna, open woodland and mangrove swamps, both in humid and semi-arid situations (Tropical Zone, in South America to Temperate Zone).

Distribution.—*Resident* from Veracruz, Tabasco, the Yucatan Peninsula and eastern Chiapas south in the Gulf-Caribbean lowlands of Middle America to Nicaragua, on both slopes of Costa Rica and Panama, and in South America from Colombia, Venezuela (also Tobago and Trinidad) and the Guianas south, west of the Andes to southwestern Ecuador and east of the Andes to eastern Peru, southern Bolivia, northern Argentina and Uruguay.

Notes.—Also known as RUFOUS PIGEON.

Columba speciosa Gmelin. SCALED PIGEON.

Columba speciosa Gmelin, 1789, Syst. Nat., 1 (2), p. 783. Based primarily on "Pigeon ramier, de Cayenne" Daubenton, Planches Enlum., pl. 213. (in Cayenna = Cayenne.)

Habitat.—Humid forest edge, open woodland and forest clearings, foraging occasionally in open areas near forest (Tropical and lower Subtropical zones).

Distribution.—*Resident* from Veracruz and Oaxaca south on the Gulf-Caribbean slope of Middle America to Nicaragua, on both slopes of Costa Rica (absent from dry northwest) and Panama, and in South America from Colombia, Venezuela (also Trinidad) and the Guianas south, west of the Andes to western Ecuador and east of the Andes to eastern Peru, Bolivia, northern Argentina and southeastern Brazil.

Columba squamosa Bonnaterre. SCALY-NAPED PIGEON. [314.1.]

Columba squamosa Bonnaterre, 1792, Tabl. Encycl. Méth., Ornithol., 1, livr. 51, p. 234. Based on "Le Pigeon Ramier de la Guadeloupe" Holandre, Abrege Hist. Nat., 2, p. 214. (Guadeloupe.)

Habitat.—Humid forest and woodland, occasionally in drier areas.

Distribution.—*Resident* in the Greater Antilles (rare on Jamaica), Lesser Antilles (not recorded Anguilla, St. Barthélemy or Désirade), and islands off the north coast of Venezuela (Curaçao, Bonaire, Los Testigos and Los Frailes, formerly also Aruba).

Casual in southern Florida (Key West).

Notes.—Also known as RED-NECKED PIGEON.

Columba leucocephala Linnaeus. WHITE-CROWNED PIGEON. [314.]

> *Columba leucocephala* Linnaeus, 1758, Syst. Nat., ed. 10, 1, p. 164. Based mainly on "The White-crown'd Pigeon" Catesby, Nat. Hist. Carolina, 1, p. 25, pl. 25. (in America septentrionali = Bahama Islands.)

Habitat.—Mangroves (breeding), foraging in open forest, woodland and scrub.

Distribution.—*Breeds* in southern Florida (mangrove islets in the Florida Keys from Elliott to Marquesas keys, and throughout Florida Bay), the Bahamas, Antilles (south to Barbuda and Antigua), Cayman Islands, and islands of the western Caribbean Sea (Cozumel off Quintana Roo, cays off Belize, the Bay and Hog islands off Honduras, Providencia and Corn islands, and possibly on Swan Cay, Veraguas, Panama). Nonbreeding individuals occur in summer in southern peninsular Florida (southern Dade and Monroe counties).

Winters throughout most of the breeding range, regularly in southern peninsular Florida, the Florida Keys and northern Bahamas, ranging in Middle America to coastal areas (recorded Quintana Roo, Belize, Honduras and western Panama), and in the Lesser Antilles south to St. Lucia.

Casual on the mainland of southern Florida (north to Fort Pierce region); a report from Oaxaca (Salina Cruz) is questionable.

Columba flavirostris Wagler. RED-BILLED PIGEON. [313.]

> *Columba flavirostris* Wagler, 1831, Isis von Oken, col. 519. (Mexico = Veracruz.)

Habitat.—Most frequently in semi-arid or arid woodland near water, less commonly in more humid regions (usually at higher elevations), foraging in open pastureland and areas with scattered trees (Tropical and lower Subtropical zones).

Distribution.—*Resident* from southern Sonora, Durango, San Luis Potosí, Nuevo León and southern Texas (lower and middle Rio Grande Valley) south mostly in the lowlands (less commonly in interior regions below 4000 feet) through Middle America (including the Tres Marias Islands, but absent or rare on most of the Caribbean slope from Guatemala southward) to central Costa Rica.

Notes.—*C. flavirostris* and *C. inornata* appear to constitute a superspecies.

Columba inornata Vigors. PLAIN PIGEON.

> *Columba inornata* Vigors, 1827, Zool. J., 3, p. 446. (near Havana, Cuba.)

Habitat.—Primarily woodland, including pine and rain forests, and open areas with scattered trees, foraging also in cultivated areas.

Distribution.—*Resident* in the Greater Antilles (including Tortue Island off Hispaniola, but now rare and surviving in reduced numbers everywhere except on Hispaniola, where locally common).

Notes.—See comments under *C. flavirostris.*

Columba fasciata Say. BAND-TAILED PIGEON. [312.]

> *Columba fasciata* Say, 1823, *in* Long, Exped. Rocky Mount., 2, p. 10 (note). (small tributary of the Platte = Plum Creek, near Castle Rock, Douglas County, Colorado.)

Habitat.—Temperate and mountain forests, primarily in oaks, less commonly in coniferous forest, and locally in lowlands, foraging also in cultivated areas (Subtropical and Temperate zones).

Distribution.—*Breeds* [*fasciata* group] from southwestern British Columbia (including Vancouver Island) south through the mountains of Washington, Oregon, California and extreme western Nevada to southern Baja California; from southern Nevada, Arizona, central Utah, north-central Colorado, New Mexico and western Texas south through the mountains of Mexico, Guatemala, El Salvador and Honduras to (at least formerly) north-central Nicaragua. Regular in summer (and probably breeding) north to southeastern Alaska (south of Thomas Bay) and west-central British Columbia.

Winters [*fasciata* group] from central California, central Arizona, central New Mexico (rarely) and western Texas southward through the breeding range, occurring widely in Mexico in foothills at lower elevations than in the breeding season, rarely north to southwestern British Columbia, west to islands off the coast of California, and east to Nevada.

Resident [*albilinea* group] in the mountains of Costa Rica and western Panama (east to eastern Veraguas); and in South America in the mountains from Venezuela (also Trinidad) and Colombia south to Peru, Bolivia and northwestern Argentina.

Casual [*fasciata* group] in western and northern Alaska (near Nome, upper Ikpikpuk River), and from central Alberta, southern Saskatchewan, Idaho, Montana and North Dakota south to Wyoming, western Kansas, Oklahoma and western Texas; many reports exist for eastern North America (from Minnesota, Michigan, southern Ontario, New Hampshire, New Brunswick, Maine and Nova Scotia south to Louisiana, Mississippi, Alabama and Florida), but these may pertain largely or entirely to individuals escaped from captivity.

Notes.—The two groups have sometimes been considered as distinct species, *C. fasciata* and *C. albilinea* Bonaparte, 1854 [WHITE-NAPED PIGEON]. *C. fasciata, C. caribaea* and the South American *C. araucana* Lesson, 1827, may constitute a superspecies.

Columba caribaea Jacquin. RING-TAILED PIGEON.

> *Columba (caribæa)* Jacquin, 1784, Beytr. Ges. Vögel, p. 30. Based on "Pigeon à queue annelée de la Jamaique" Brisson, Ornithologie, 1, p. 138. (Karibäische Inseln = Jamaica.)

Habitat.—Forested mountains and hills.

Distribution.—*Resident* on Jamaica.

Notes.—See comments under *C. fasciata.*

Columba subvinacea (Lawrence). RUDDY PIGEON.

Chloroenas subvinacea Lawrence, 1868, Ann. Lyc. Nat. Hist. N.Y., 9, p. 135. (Dota, Costa Rica.)

Habitat.—Humid forests, in mountains (Costa Rica and western Panama) or primarily in lowlands (eastern Panama and South America), occurring both in dense forest and along forest edge (Tropical and Subtropical zones).

Distribution.—*Resident* in the mountains of Costa Rica and western Panama (east to Veraguas); and from eastern Panama (eastern Panamá province, San Blas and eastern Darién), Colombia, Venezuela and the Guianas south, west of the Andes to western Ecuador and east of the Andes to east-central Bolivia and Amazonian Brazil.

Notes.—It has been suggested by Wetmore (1968, Smithson. Misc. Coll., 150 (2), pp. 17–18) that the small lowland race in eastern Panama, *C. s. berlepschi* Hartert, 1898, may represent a distinct species.

Columba nigrirostris Sclater. SHORT-BILLED PIGEON.

Columba nigrirostris Sclater, 1859, Proc. Zool. Soc. London, p. 390. (In statu Oaxaca reipubl. Mexicanæ = Oaxaca.)

Habitat.—Humid lowland and foothill forest, primarily dense forest but foraging in clearings and second growth (Tropical and lower Subtropical zones).

Distribution.—*Resident* from southern Veracruz, eastern Oaxaca, Tabasco, eastern Chiapas and Quintana Roo south on the Gulf-Caribbean slope of Central America to Costa Rica (including southwestern portion on the Pacific slope), Panama (both slopes) and northwestern Colombia (Chocó).

Notes.—The specimen described as *C. chiriquensis* (Ridgway, 1915) pertains to *C. nigrirostris* (see Wetmore, 1968, Smithson. Misc. Collect., 150 (2), p. 15). *C. nigrirostris* and *C. goodsoni* appear to constitute a superspecies.

[Columba goodsoni Hartert. DUSKY PIGEON.] See Appendix A.

Genus **STREPTOPELIA** Bonaparte

Streptopelia Bonaparte, 1855, C. R. Acad. Sci. ιris, 40, p. 17. Type, by subsequent designation (G. R. Gray, 1840), *Columba risoria* Linnaeus.

Streptopelia risoria (Linnaeus). RINGED TURTLE-DOVE. [315.2.]

Columba risoria Linnaeus, 1758, Syst. Nat., ed. 10, 1, p. 165. (in India.)

Habitat.—Feral populations occur in open woodland and parks around human habitation; related species in the wild state inhabit arid country with trees and shrubs, often near human habitation.

Distribution.—Origin and native country uncertain; long domesticated and worldwide in captivity.

Introduced and established in southern California (Los Angeles region), west-central Florida (Pinellas County), the Bahamas (New Providence), Puerto Rico, and apparently also in eastern Texas (Houston region).

Notes.—Also known as BARBARY DOVE. The use of the name *S. risoria* is tentative; the domestic stock, from which the introductions were made, may have been derived from either *S. roseogrisea* (Sundevall, 1857) of Africa or *S. decaocto* (Frivaldszky, 1838) of Eurasia, these two forms considered conspecific by some authors. For the present, it seems best to retain the usage of *S. risoria*.

Streptopelia chinensis (Scopoli). SPOTTED DOVE. [315.1.]

> *Columba* (*chinensis*) Scopoli, 1786, Del Flor. Faun. Insubr., fasc. 2, p. 94. (China = Canton.)

Habitat.—Woodland, forest edge, agricultural country with trees, and especially in suburban residential areas and cultivated lands around human habitation.

Distribution.—*Resident* from eastern Afghanistan, the Himalayas and eastern China south to Ceylon, the Malay Peninsula, East Indies and Philippines.

Introduced and established in the Hawaiian Islands (main islands from Kauai eastward); in southern California (primarily from Santa Barbara and Bakersfield south to San Diego and the Salton Sea) and extreme northwestern Baja California (Tijuana area); and in Mauritius, Celebes, Australia, New Zealand, and various islands of Polynesia. A small population still persists on St. Croix, in the Virgin Islands (introduced in 1964).

Genus GEOPELIA Swainson

> *Geopelia* Swainson, 1837, Class. Birds, 2, p. 348. Type, by monotypy, *Geopelia lineata* Mus. Carl. pl. 67 = *Columba striata* Linnaeus.

Geopelia striata (Linnaeus). ZEBRA DOVE. [315.3.]

> *Columba striata* Linnaeus, 1766, Syst. Nat., ed. 12, 1, p. 282. Based on "La Tourterelle rayée des Indes" Brisson, Ornithologie, 1, p. 109, and "The Transverse Striped or Bared Dove" Edwards, 1, p. 16, pl. 16. (in India orientali = Java.)

Habitat.—Open country with trees and shrubby growth, parks, gardens and cultivated areas, especially near human habitation.

Distribution.—*Resident* from the Malay Peninsula and Philippines south to the East Indies (east to Tanimbar and the Kei Islands).

Introduced and established in the Hawaiian Islands (in 1922, now on all main islands from Kauai eastward).

Notes.—Also known as BARRED DOVE. Often considered conspecific with the Australian *G. placida* Gould, 1844 [PEACEFUL DOVE], but now regarded as specifically distinct.

Genus ZENAIDA Bonaparte

> *Zenaida* Bonaparte, 1838, Geogr. Comp. List, p. 41. Type, by tautonymy, *Zenaida amabilis* Bonaparte = *Columba zenaida* Bonaparte = *Columba aurita* Temminck.
>
> *Zenaidura* Bonaparte, 1855, C. R. Acad. Sci. Paris, 40, p. 96. Type, by original designation, *Columba carolinensis* Linnaeus = *Columba macroura* Linnaeus.
>
> *Melopelia* Bonaparte, 1855, C. R. Acad. Sci. Paris, 40, p. 98. Type, by subsequent designation (G. R. Gray, 1855), *Columba meloda* Tschudi = *Columba asiatica* Linnaeus.

Zenaida asiatica (Linnaeus). WHITE-WINGED DOVE. [319.]

Columba asiatica Linnaeus, 1758, Syst. Nat., ed. 10, 1, p. 163. Based on "The Brown Indian Dove" Edwards, Nat. Hist. Birds, 2, p. 76, pl. 76. (in Indiis = Jamaica.)

Habitat.—Generally arid regions with scrubby thickets or riverine forest, open cultivated lands with scattered trees, and mangroves (Tropical and Subtropical zones).

Distribution.—*Breeds* from southeastern California, southern Nevada, central Arizona, central New Mexico, northern Chihuahua and southwestern Texas south to southern Baja California, through most of Middle America (including Isla Tiburón off Sonora, and Cozumel and Cancun islands off Quintana Roo) to Honduras, and locally in the Pacific lowlands to western Panama (Herrera and southwestern Coclé, breeding presumed); in the Bahamas (Great Inagua, Caicos and Turks islands) and Greater Antilles (east to Puerto Rico, and Mona and Vieques islands); on islands of the western Caribbean Sea (Providencia and San Andrés); and along the western coast of South America from southwestern Ecuador south to northern Chile.

Winters generally in the breeding range, but northern birds are mostly migratory (individuals from the western United States have been recovered south to Costa Rica), casually ranging north to northern California (Humboldt County) and Colorado, and occurring regularly along the Gulf coast east to Florida; West Indian, Middle American and South American breeding populations are mostly sedentary, although stragglers have been recorded from the northern Bahamas (Grand Bahama, Acklin's Island), and in the Virgin Islands (St. Croix).

In migration occurs rarely but regularly (in fall) in southeastern Alaska.

Introduced and established in southern Florida.

Casual in the Pacific Northwest (north to southwestern British Columbia, also a sight report for Montana), in northeastern North America (from northern Ontario, New Brunswick, Maine and Nova Scotia south to New York, Connecticut and Massachusetts) and along the Atlantic coast (in the Carolinas).

Zenaida aurita (Temminck). ZENAIDA DOVE. [317.]

Columba Aurita Temminck, 1810, *in* Knip, Les Pigeons, Les Colombes, p. 60, pl. 25. (Martinique.)

Habitat.—Open woodland, second growth, scrub, cultivated lands and, locally, around human habitation (Tropical Zone).

Distribution.—*Resident* in the Bahamas, Greater Antilles (also the Cayman Islands), Lesser Antilles (south to Grenada), and formerly in the Florida Keys (reportedly common in Audubon's day a century ago, nesting on islands near Indian Key); also along the coast of the Yucatan Peninsula (in the state of Yucatán and Quintana Roo), and on Holbox, Cancun and Mujeres islands. A specimen from Belize and reports from Cozumel Island are of dubious authenticity.

Casual in southern Florida (Key West, also sight reports north to Osceola County).

Zenaida auriculata (Des Murs). EARED DOVE.

Peristera auriculata Des Murs, 1847, *in* Gay, Hist. Fis. Pol. Chile, Zool., 1, p. 381, pl. 6. (central provinces of Chile.)

Habitat.—Arid or semi-arid country, usually with some trees or bushes, open woodland and areas of cultivation (Tropical to Temperate zones).

Distribution.—*Resident* in the southern Lesser Antilles (Grenada and the Grenadines), and throughout most of South America from Colombia, Venezuela (including islands from the Netherlands Antilles east to Tobago and Trinidad) and the Guianas south to Tierra del Fuego.

Casual on Barbados, St. Lucia and Martinique; accidental in the Falkland Islands. An individual photographed in Panama (Coco Solo, Canal Zone) may have been an escape from captivity.

Notes.—*Z. auriculata* and *Z. macroura* constitute a superspecies.

Zenaida macroura (Linnaeus). MOURNING DOVE. [316.]

> *Columba macroura* Linnaeus, 1758, Syst. Nat., ed. 10, 1, p. 164. Based mainly on "The Long-tailed Dove" Edwards, Nat. Hist. Birds, 1, p. 15, pl. 15. (in Canada, error = Cuba.)

Habitat.—Open woodland, cultivated lands with scattered trees and bushes, arid and desert country (generally near water) and second growth (Tropical to Temperate zones).

Distribution.—*Breeds* from southern British Columbia, central Alberta, south-central Saskatchewan, southern Manitoba, northern Minnesota, northern Wisconsin, northern Michigan, southern Ontario, southwestern Quebec, Maine, southern New Brunswick, Prince Edward Island and Nova Scotia south to southern Baja California, Sonora (in Pacific lowlands), in the interior mountains and Central Plateau of Mexico to Oaxaca and Puebla, and to northern Tamaulipas (in the Caribbean lowlands), Texas, the Gulf coast and southern Florida; in the Bahamas and Greater Antilles (east to Puerto Rico, and Culebra and Vieques islands); in the Revillagigedo (Clarión and Socorro) and Tres Marías islands off western Mexico; and in Costa Rica and Panama (east to western Panamá province), probably also elsewhere in northern Middle America. Occurs casually in summer (and possibly breeding) in southeastern Alaska.

Winters primarily from northern California east across the central United States to Iowa, southern Michigan, southern Ontario, New York and New England (uncommonly to the northern limits of the breeding range), and south throughout the breeding range and over most of Middle America to central Panama.

Casual north to western and central Alaska, southern Yukon, southern Mackenzie, northern Manitoba, northern Ontario, central Quebec, Labrador and Newfoundland. Accidental in Greenland and Colombia.

Introduced and established in the Hawaiian Islands (on Hawaii in 1963, presently a small population in the North Kona region).

Notes.—See comments under *Z. auriculata* and *Z. graysoni.*

Zenaida graysoni (Lawrence). SOCORRO DOVE.

> *Zenaidura graysoni* (Baird MS) Lawrence, 1871, Ann. Lyc. Nat. Hist. N.Y., 10, p. 17. (Socorro Island, Mexico.)

Habitat.—Open woodland and scrub.

Distribution.—EXTINCT in the wild. Formerly *resident* on Socorro Island, in the Revillagigedo Islands, off western Mexico; several recent searches (April 1978, April 1981) found only *Z. macroura* (a new invader to Socorro) and confirm the extirpation in the wild of *Z. graysoni,* although there are still living birds in captivity at this time.

Notes.—The taxonomic status of this form is in doubt. Although considered by many authors as conspecific with *Z. macroura,* differences in morphology, vocalizations and behavior support the maintenance of specific status for *Z. graysoni.*

Genus **ECTOPISTES** Swainson

Ectopistes Swainson, 1827, Zool. J., 3, p. 362. Type, by subsequent designation (Swainson, 1837), *Columba migratoria* Linnaeus.

†**Ectopistes migratorius** (Linnaeus). PASSENGER PIGEON. [315.]

Columba migratoria Linnaeus, 1766, Syst. Nat., ed. 12, 1, p. 285. Based mainly on "The Pigeon of Passage" Catesby, Nat. Hist. Carolina, 1, p. 23, pl. 23. (in America septentrionali = South Carolina.)

Habitat.—Forest, foraging in open country and cultivated lands adjacent to forest.

Distribution.—EXTINCT. *Bred* formerly from central Montana, east-central Saskatchewan, southern Manitoba, Minnesota, Wisconsin, Michigan, Ontario, southern Quebec, New Brunswick and Nova Scotia south to eastern Kansas, Oklahoma, Mississippi and Georgia.

Wintered from Arkansas, southeastern Missouri, Tennessee and North Carolina south to Texas, the Gulf coast and northern Florida, occasionally north to Indiana, southern Pennsylvania and Connecticut.

Casual or accidental to Nevada, Idaho, Wyoming, British Columbia, Mackenzie, Alberta, northern Saskatchewan, northern Manitoba, Baffin Bay, northern Quebec, Labrador, Prince Edward Island, Bermuda, Cuba (Havana market) and Mexico (recorded Puebla, Veracruz, Distrito Federal and Tabasco); also in Scotland, Ireland and France, although the European individuals may have been escapes from captivity. Last specimen obtained in the wild taken at Sargento, Pike County, Ohio, on 24 March 1900; last living individual died in captivity in the Cincinnati Zoological Gardens, Cincinnati, Ohio, on 1 September 1914.

Genus **COLUMBINA** Spix

Columbina Spix, 1825, Avium Spec. Nov. Bras., 2, p. 57. Type, by subsequent designation (G. R. Gray, 1841), *Columbina strepitans* Spix = *Columba picui* Temminck.

Columbigallina Boie, 1826, Isis von Oken, col. 977. Type, by monotypy, *Columba passerina* Linnaeus.

Scardafella Bonaparte, 1855, C. R. Acad. Sci. Paris, 40, p. 24. Type, by original designation, *Columba squamosa* Temminck (not Bonnaterre) = *Columba squammata* Lesson.

Columbina inca (Lesson). INCA DOVE. [321.]

Chamæpelia inca Lesson, 1847, Descr. Mamm. Ois., p. 211. (Mexico [probably west coast].)

Habitat.—Open country with scattered trees or scrubby growth, most frequently in arid or semi-arid situations, and around cultivated areas, farmlands, parks and gardens (Tropical, less frequently Subtropical zones).

Distribution.—*Resident* from extreme southeastern California (Parker Dam area), central Arizona, southern New Mexico and central Texas south through Mexico (except the Yucatan Peninsula), Guatemala (rare in Petén and Caribbean lowlands), Honduras (Pacific lowlands and arid interior valleys) and Nicaragua (highlands and Pacific lowlands) to northwestern Costa Rica (Guanacaste and highlands to vicinity of San José); and, at least formerly, in the Florida Keys (Key West), where now apparently extirpated.

Wanders casually to southern California, southern Nevada, Kansas, Oklahoma, Arkansas and Louisiana. The origin of some of the vagrants and of the Key West breeding populations may have been individuals escaped from captivity.

Notes.—Often placed in the genus *Scardafella*. Some authors consider *C. inca* and the South American *C. squammata* (Lesson, 1831) [SCALED DOVE] to be conspecific; they constitute a superspecies.

Columbina passerina (Linnaeus). COMMON GROUND-DOVE. [320.]

Columba passerina Linnaeus, 1758, Syst. Nat., ed. 10, 1, p. 165. Based mainly on "The Ground Dove" Catesby, Nat. Hist. Carolina, 1, p. 26, pl. 26. (in America inter tropicos = South Carolina.)

Habitat.—Open country with trees and bushes, sandy reefs, open sandy areas in forest and savanna, cultivated lands, and around human habitation in villages and towns (Tropical and Subtropical zones).

Distribution.—*Resident* from southern California (north to Orange County), central Arizona, southern New Mexico, central Texas, the Gulf coast, South Carolina, Bermuda and the Bahamas south through Mexico (including Socorro Island in the Revillagigedos, the Tres Marias and Tres Marietas islands off western Mexico, and islands off the Yucatan Peninsula, but rare in the central highlands), the Antilles and Central America (mostly in the highlands and arid interior, but also in the Caribbean lowland savanna, and in the Bay Islands off Honduras) to central Costa Rica (Guanacaste and the arid central highlands); in western Panama (Azuero Peninsula region); and in northern South America from Colombia, Venezuela (including islands from the Netherlands Antilles east to Trinidad) and the Guianas south to Ecuador and eastern Brazil.

Wanders casually north to northern California, southern Nevada, Wyoming, Kansas, Iowa, Illinois, Indiana, southern Ontario, Pennsylvania and New York.

Notes.—Also known as SCALY-BREASTED GROUND-DOVE.

Columbina minuta (Linnaeus). PLAIN-BREASTED GROUND-DOVE.

Columba minuta Linnaeus, 1766, Syst. Nat., ed. 12, 1, p. 285. Based on "La petite Tourterelle brun d'Amérique" Brisson, Ornithologie, 1, p. 116, pl. 8, fig. 2. (in America = Cayenne.)

Habitat.—Savanna (including pine savanna), open country with scattered trees, second-growth woodland and cultivated areas (Tropical Zone).

Distribution.—*Resident* on the Gulf-Caribbean slope of Middle America in Veracruz, northern Oaxaca, Tabasco, Chiapas, Campeche, Belize, Guatemala, and, locally, northeastern Nicaragua (probably also in eastern Honduras) and extreme northeastern Costa Rica; along the Pacific coast of Middle America locally from central Oaxaca south to Costa Rica (not recorded Honduras or Pacific lowlands of Nicaragua, but present in the central highlands of Nicaragua) and Panama (east to eastern Panamá province, also recorded on Caribbean slope in Canal Zone); and disjunctly in South America in northern Colombia, Venezuela (also Trinidad), the Guianas, both slopes of Peru, eastern and central Brazil, east-central Bolivia and northern Paraguay.

Columbina talpacoti (Temminck). RUDDY GROUND-DOVE. [320.1.]

Columba talpacoti Temminck, 1811, *in* Knip, Les Pigeons, Les Colombigallines, p. 22. (l'Amérique méridionale = Brazil.)

Habitat.—Open second growth, cultivated lands, savanna, scrubby areas, and around human habitation (Tropical, less frequently Subtropical zones).

Distribution.—*Resident* from southern Sinaloa, eastern San Luis Potosí and Tamaulipas south through Middle America (including Cozumel and Cancun islands off Quintana Roo, and Coiba and Pearl islands off Panama), and in South America from Colombia, Venezuela (also Margarita Island, Tobago and Trinidad) and the Guianas south, west of the Andes to northwestern Peru and east of the Andes to eastern Peru, Bolivia, northern Argentina and northern Uruguay.

Casual in southern Texas (lower Rio Grande Valley north to San Patricio County) and Chile.

Notes.—South American populations in western Ecuador and northwestern Peru have sometimes been treated as a separate species, *C. buckleyi* (Sclater and Salvin, 1877).

Genus CLARAVIS Oberholser

Peristera (not Rafinesque, 1815) Swainson, 1827, Zool. J., 3, p. 360. Type, by original designation, *Columba cinerea* Temminck = *Peristera pretiosa* Ferrari-Perez.
Claravis Oberholser, 1899, Proc. Acad. Nat. Sci. Philadelphia, 51, p. 203. New name for *Peristera* Swainson, preoccupied.

Claravis pretiosa (Ferrari-Perez). BLUE GROUND-DOVE.

Columba cinerea (not Scopoli, 1786) Temminck, 1811, *in* Knip, Les Pigeons, Les Colombes, p. 126, pl. 58. (au Brésil = Brazil.)
Peristera pretiosa Ferrari-Perez, 1886, Proc. U.S. Natl. Mus., 9, p. 175. New name for *Columba cinerea* Temminck, preoccupied.

Habitat.—Forest edge, second-growth woodland and forest clearings, generally in humid lowlands and foothills (Tropical and lower Subtropical zones).

Distribution.—*Resident* from Chiapas on the Pacific slope, and from eastern San Luis Potosí and southern Tamaulipas on the Gulf-Caribbean slope south through Middle America, and in South America from Colombia, Venezuela (also Trinidad) and the Guianas south, west of the Andes to central Peru and east of the Andes to eastern Peru, Bolivia, northern Argentina, Paraguay and southeastern Brazil.

A sight report from southern Texas (lower Rio Grande Valley) is unverified.

Claravis mondetoura (Bonaparte). MAROON-CHESTED GROUND-DOVE.

Peristera mondetoura Bonaparte, 1856, C. R. Acad. Sci. Paris, 42, p. 765. (Caracas, Venezuela.)

Habitat.—Humid montane forest, especially with heavy undergrowth or bamboo (Subtropical Zone).

Distribution.—*Resident* locally in the mountains of Middle America in Veracruz, Chiapas, Guatemala, El Salvador, Honduras, Costa Rica and western Panama (Chiriquí); and in the Andes of South America from Colombia and northwestern Venezuela south to Peru and western Bolivia.

Notes.—*C. mondetoura* and *C. godefrida* (Temminck, 1811), of eastern South America, constitute a superspecies; some authors regard them as conspecific.

Genus **LEPTOTILA** Swainson

Leptotila Swainson, 1837, Class. Birds, 2, p. 349. Type, by monotypy, *P*[*eristera*]. *rufaxilla* Nat. Lib. v. pl. 24 = *Columba jamaicensis* Linnaeus.

Leptotila verreauxi Bonaparte. WHITE-TIPPED DOVE. [318.]

Leptotila verreauxi Bonaparte, 1855, C. R. Acad. Sci. Paris, 40, p. 99. (de la Nouvelle-Grenade = Colombia.)

Habitat.—Open woodland, forest edge, second growth, clearings and, less frequently, cultivated areas around human habitation, primarily in arid or semi-arid regions (Tropical to lower Temperate zones).

Distribution.—*Resident* from southern Sonora, southwestern Chihuahua, western Durango, Nayarit (including the Tres Marias Islands), Jalisco, San Luis Potosí, Nuevo León and southern Texas (lower Rio Grande Valley) south through Middle America (including the Pearl Islands and many other small islands off Panama), and in South America from Colombia, Venezuela (also Netherlands Antilles east to Tobago and Trinidad) and the Guianas south to Peru, eastern Bolivia, central Argentina and Uruguay.

Notes.—Also known as WHITE-FRONTED DOVE. Includes the South America *L. brasiliensis* (Bonaparte, 1856), regarded by some as a separate species. *L. verreauxi* and the South American *L. megalura* Sclater and Salvin, 1879, appear to constitute a superspecies.

Leptotila rufaxilla (Richard and Bernard). GRAY-FRONTED DOVE.

Columba Rufaxilla Richard and Bernard, 1792, Actes Soc. Hist. Nat. Paris, 1, p. 118. (Cayenne.)

Habitat.—Humid lowland and foothill forest, occurring in forest edge, clearings, heavy undergrowth, and occasionally open situations adjacent to forest, in South America frequently also in open woodland, and on Grenada commonly in arid scrub (Tropical and lower Subtropical zones).

Distribution.—*Resident* [*plumbeiceps* group] from southern Tamaulipas, eastern San Luis Potosí, Veracruz, the state of México, Puebla and northern Oaxaca south on the Gulf-Caribbean slope (except the state of Yucatán) through Belize, northern Guatemala, Honduras, Nicaragua (also Pacific slope in southwest) and Costa Rica (both slopes) to northwestern Panama (Bocas del Toro), and in the Western Andes and Cauca Valley of Colombia; [*battyi* group] on the Pacific slope of western Panama (southern Veraguas and western Herrera), and on Cébaco and Coiba islands; [*wellsi* group] on Grenada (where surviving in small numbers), formerly also on offshore islands (Glover's and Green), possibly also on Tobago but not known from St. Vincent, although sometimes listed for that island; and [*rufaxilla* group] in South America from eastern Colombia, Venezuela and the Guianas south, east of the Andes, to eastern Peru, central Bolivia, Paraguay, northeastern Argentina and southern Brazil.

Notes.—Three groups in this species are often considered distinct species, *L. plumbeiceps* Sclater and Salvin, 1868 [GRAY-HEADED DOVE], which includes *battyi*, *L. wellsi* (Lawrence, 1884) [GRENADA DOVE], and *L. rufaxilla* [GRAY-FRONTED DOVE]; Wetmore (1968, Smithson. Misc. Collect., 150 (2), pp. 42–44) would also recognize *L. battyi* Rothschild, 1901 [BROWN-BACKED DOVE], as a distinct species. See also comments under *L. jamaicensis.*

Leptotila jamaicensis (Linnaeus). CARIBBEAN DOVE.

Columba jamaicensis Linnaeus, 1766, Syst. Nat., ed. 12, 1, p. 283. Based on *Columba minor ventre candido* Sloane, Voy. Jamaica, 2, p. 303, pl. 262, fig. 1, and "Le Pigeon de la Jamaïque" Brisson, Ornithologie, 1, p. 134. (in Jamaica.)

Habitat.—Open situations with shrubs or scattered trees, and arid woodland.

Distribution.—*Resident* on Jamaica, Grand Cayman, the Yucatan Peninsula (including Holbox, Mujeres, Cancun and Cozumel islands), islands off Caribbean Honduras (Barbareta in the Bay Islands, and Little Hog Island), and Isla San Andrés in the western Caribbean Sea.

Introduced and established in the Bahamas (New Providence).

Notes.—Also known as WHITE-BELLIED DOVE. *L. jamaicensis* and *L. rufaxilla* appear to constitute a superspecies.

Leptotila cassinii Lawrence. GRAY-CHESTED DOVE.

Leptotila cassinii Lawrence, 1867, Proc. Acad. Nat. Sci. Philadelphia, 19, p. 94. (Line of the Panama Railroad, New Granada = Atlantic slope, Canal Zone.)

Habitat.—Humid lowland forest, second-growth woodland, forest edge, thickets and, locally, shady pastures and gardens (Tropical and lower Subtropical zones).

Distribution.—*Resident* on the Gulf-Caribbean slope from Tabasco and northern Chiapas south through Belize, northern Guatemala, Honduras and Nicaragua, and on both slopes from Costa Rica through Panama to northern Colombia.

Notes.—Also known as CASSIN'S DOVE.

Genus GEOTRYGON Gosse

Geotrygon Gosse, 1847, Birds Jamaica, p. 316 (footnote). Type, by subsequent designation (Reichenbach, 1853), *Columba cristata* Latham [=Gmelin, not Temminck] = *Geotrygon sylvatica* Gosse = *Columbigallina versicolor* Lafresnaye.

Oreopeleia Reichenbach, 1853, Avium Syst. Nat. (1852), p. xxv. Type, by original designation, "Columba martinicana" Brisson = *Columba martinica* Linnaeus.

Notes.—See comments under *Starnoenas*.

Geotrygon veraguensis Lawrence. OLIVE-BACKED QUAIL-DOVE.

Geotrygon veraguensis Lawrence, 1867, Ann. Lyc. Nat. Hist. N.Y., 8, p. 349. (Veragua [Panama].)

Habitat.—Humid lowland forest and adjacent second-growth woodland (Tropical Zone).

Distribution.—*Resident* in the Caribbean lowlands of Costa Rica and Panama (also on Pacific slope in eastern Panamá province), and in western Colombia and northwestern Ecuador.

Notes.—Also known as VERAGUAS QUAIL-DOVE.

Geotrygon chrysia Bonaparte. KEY WEST QUAIL-DOVE. [322.]

Geotrygon chrysia Bonaparte, 1855, C. R. Acad. Sci. Paris, 40, p. 100. (Floride = Florida.)

Habitat.—Lowland forest and scrub, primarily in semi-arid situations.

Distribution.—*Resident* in the Bahamas (Grand Bahama, Great Abaco, Andros, New Providence, Eleuthera, San Salvador and North Caicos), Cuba, the Isle of Pines, Hispaniola (including Gonâve, Tortue and Catalina islands), Puerto Rico and Vieques Island (possibly also Mona Island).

Casual in southern Florida (the Florida Keys, and southern mainland in Monroe and Palm Beach counties, mostly near coasts). Formerly reported as common and breeding at Key West (Audubon, 1830's).

Notes.—*G. chrysia* and *G. mystacea* constitute a superspecies; they are considered conspecific by some authors.

Geotrygon mystacea (Temminck). BRIDLED QUAIL-DOVE.

Columba mystacea Temminck, 1811, *in* Knip, Les Pigeons, Les Colombes, p. 124, pl. 56. (l'Amerique = probably Lesser Antilles.)

Habitat.—Lowland forest and woodland, generally in undergrowth, usually in semi-arid situations.

Distribution.—*Resident* on Puerto Rico (including Vieques and, probably, Culebra islands), in the Virgin Islands (except Anegada), and in the Lesser Antilles (from Saba and Barbuda south to St. Lucia).

Notes.—See comments under *G. chrysia*.

Geotrygon albifacies Sclater. WHITE-FACED QUAIL-DOVE.

Geotrygon albifacies Sclater, 1858, Proc. Zool. Soc. London, p. 98. (environs of Jalapa, [Veracruz,] Southern Mexico.)

Habitat.—Humid montane forest (Subtropical Zone).

Distribution.—*Resident* in the mountains of Mexico (San Luis Potosí, Veracruz, Guerrero, Oaxaca and Chiapas), Guatemala, El Salvador, Honduras and north-central Nicaragua.

Notes.—*G. albifacies* and *G. chiriquensis* are often considered as conspecific with the South American *G. linearis* (Prévost, 1843), but retention of three species constituting a superspecies complex seems more satisfactory. In the event all are combined into a single species, *G. linearis,* the name WHITE-FACED QUAIL-DOVE would still be appropriate.

Geotrygon chiriquensis Sclater. CHIRIQUI QUAIL-DOVE.

Geotrygon chiriquensis Sclater, 1856, Proc. Zool. Soc. London, p. 143. (vicinity of the Town of David in the Province of Chiriqui in the State of Panama.)

Habitat.—Humid mountain forest undergrowth and coffee plantations (upper Tropical and Subtropical zones).

Distribution.—*Resident* in the mountains of Costa Rica and western Panama (Chiriquí and Veraguas).

Notes.—See comments under *G. albifacies.*

Geotrygon lawrencii Salvin. PURPLISH-BACKED QUAIL-DOVE.

Geotrygon lawrencii Salvin, 1874, Ibis, p. 329. (Calóbre, Veraguas, Panama.)

Habitat.—Humid foothill forest (upper Tropical and lower Subtropical zones).

Distribution.—*Resident* in southeastern Veracruz (Cerro de Tuxtla and Volcán San Martín, in the Sierra de Tuxtla); and in the mountains of Costa Rica and Panama (east to Darién).

Notes.—*G. lawrencii, G. costaricensis* and *G. goldmani* are closely related, but the degree of relationship is uncertain; *G. lawrencii* and *G. costaricensis* are reportedly sympatric in Costa Rica, while *G. lawrencii* and *G. goldmani* overlap in eastern Panama.

Geotrygon costaricensis Lawrence. BUFF-FRONTED QUAIL-DOVE.

Geotrygon costaricensis Lawrence, 1868, Ann. Lyc. Nat. Hist. N.Y., 9, p. 136. (Costa Rica = Las Cruces de la Candelaria, Costa Rica.)

Habitat.—Humid montane forest, especially in heavy undergrowth (Subtropical Zone).

Distribution.—*Resident* in the mountains of Costa Rica and western Panama (east to Veraguas).

Notes.—Also known as COSTA RICAN QUAIL-DOVE. See comments under *G. lawrencii.*

Geotrygon goldmani Nelson. RUSSET-CROWNED QUAIL-DOVE.

Geotrygon goldmani Nelson, 1912, Smithson. Misc. Collect., 60, no. 3, p. 2. (Mount Pirri, at 5000 feet altitude, head of Rio Limon, eastern Panama.)

Habitat.—Humid foothill and montane forest in dense undergrowth (upper Tropical and lower Subtropical zones).

Distribution.—*Resident* in the mountains of eastern Panama (eastern Panamá province and Darién) and extreme northwestern Colombia (Juradó).

Notes.—Also known as GOLDMAN'S QUAIL-DOVE. See comments under *G. lawrencii.*

Geotrygon caniceps (Gundlach). GRAY-HEADED QUAIL-DOVE.

Columba caniceps Gundlach, 1852, J. Boston Soc. Nat. Hist., 6, p. 315. (Cuba.)

Habitat.—Lowland forest (Cuba) and mountain forest (Hispaniola).

Distribution.—*Resident* in Cuba and Hispaniola (mountains of the Dominican Republic, not known from Haiti).

Notes.—Also known as MOUSTACHED QUAIL-DOVE.

Geotrygon violacea (Temminck). VIOLACEOUS QUAIL-DOVE.

Columba violacea Temminck, 1810, *in* Knip, Les Pigeons, Les Colombes, p. 67, pl. 29. (le Nouveau Monde = Rio de Janeiro, Brazil.)

Habitat.—Humid lowland and foothill forest, less frequently in semi-arid forest (Tropical and lower Subtropical zones).

Distribution.—*Resident* in eastern Nicaragua (Caribbean lowlands), Costa Rica (humid Caribbean lowlands and foothills, also in semi-arid Guanacaste lowlands on Pacific slope) and Panama (from Colón eastward), and in South America from northern Colombia, Venezuela and Surinam south, east of the Andes, to Bolivia, northeastern Argentina, eastern Paraguay and eastern Brazil.

Geotrygon montana (Linnaeus). RUDDY QUAIL-DOVE. [322.1.]

Columba montana Linnaeus, 1758, Syst. Nat., ed. 10, 1, p. 163. Based mainly on "The Mountain Partridge" Sloane, Voy. Jamaica, 2, p. 304, pl. 261, fig. 1. (in Jamaica.)

Habitat.—Humid lowland and foothill forest, second-growth woodland, coffee and cacao plantations, and occasionally semi-arid woodland (Tropical and lower Subtropical, locally to lower Temperate zones).

Distribution.—*Resident* in the Antilles (south to Grenada, but absent from Barbados and the Grenadines); and from southern Sinaloa and Veracruz south along both slopes of Middle America (including Isla Coiba and San José, in the Pearl Islands, but not recorded El Salvador), and in South America from Colombia, Venezuela (also Trinidad) and the Guianas south, east of the Andes to eastern Peru, Bolivia, northeastern Argentina, northern Paraguay and southeastern Brazil. Casual in southern Florida (Florida Keys, Dry Tortugas).

Geotrygon versicolor (Lafresnaye). CRESTED QUAIL-DOVE.

Columbigallina versicolor Lafresnaye, 1846, Rev. Zool. [Paris], 9, p. 321. (Jamaïque = Jamaica.)

Habitat.—Undergrowth of mountain forest.

Distribution.—*Resident* in the mountains of Jamaica.

Genus STARNOENAS Bonaparte.

Starnœnas Bonaparte, 1838, Geogr. Comp. List, p. 41. Type, by monotypy, *Columba cyanocephala* Linnaeus.

Notes.—Some authors merge *Starnoenas* in *Geotrygon*.

Starnoenas cyanocephala (Linnaeus). BLUE-HEADED QUAIL-DOVE. [323.]

Columba cyanocephala Linnaeus, 1758, Syst. Nat., ed. 10, 1, p. 163. Based on "The Turtle-Dove from Jamaica" Albin, Nat. Hist. Birds, 2, p. 45, pl. 49. (in America = Jamaica.)

Habitat.—Lowland forest undergrowth, occasionally highland forest.
Distribution.—*Resident* on Cuba.

Recorded from the Isle of Pines (one specimen, 1909), Jamaica (apparently through attempted introduction) and southern Florida (Key West and Miami, specimens, American Museum of Natural History and San Diego Natural History Museum, respectively), but these reports are likely based on introductions or escaped individuals.

Order PSITTACIFORMES: Parrots and Allies

Notes.—The Psittaciformes are sometimes divided into a various number of families.

Family PSITTACIDAE: Lories, Parakeets, Macaws and Parrots

Subfamily PLATYCERCINAE: Australian Parakeets and Rosellas

. Genus MELOPSITTACUS Gould

Melopsittacus Gould, 1840, Birds Aust., pt. 1, pl. [10] (=5, pl. 44 of bound volume). Type, by monotypy, *Psittacus undulatus* Shaw.

Melopsittacus undulatus (Shaw). BUDGERIGAR. [382.2.]

Psittacus undulatus Shaw, 1805, *in* Shaw and Nodder, Naturalists' Misc., 16, pl. 673. (New Holland = New South Wales, Australia.)

Habitat.—Open woodland and scrubby areas, especially in semi-arid habitats, suburban areas and parks.
Distribution.—*Resident* (though nomadic) through most of the interior of Australia, rarely ranging to coastal areas.

Introduced and established in west-central Florida (Charlotte to Citrus counties); recently escaped cage birds may be seen almost anywhere in North America.
Notes.—Also known as SHELL PARAKEET or BUDGERYGAH.

Subfamily PSITTACINAE: Typical Parrots

Genus PSITTACULA Cuvier

Psittacula Cuvier, 1800, Leçons Anat. Comp., 1, table at end. Type, by subsequent designation (Mathews, 1917), *Psittacus alexandri* Linnaeus.

Psittacula krameri (Scopoli). ROSE-RINGED PARAKEET. [382.3.]

Psittacus krameri Scopoli, 1769, Annus I, Hist.-Nat., p. 31. (No locality given = Senegal.)

Habitat.—Open woodland, savanna, cultivated lands, and areas around human habitation.

Distribution.—*Resident* in North Africa from Senegal east (south of the Sahara) to Eritrea, Ethiopia and Sudan; and in southern Asia from Afghanistan, India and Nepal south to Ceylon and Burma.

Introduced and established in small numbers in southern Florida (Dade County, since 1950's), Egypt, the Near East, Zanzibar, Mauritius, Singapore, Hong Kong and Macao; small introduced groups have also persisted in the Hawaiian Islands (on Oahu since 1971, breeding reported on Hawaii in 1981, and sight reports from Kauai), southern California (Los Angeles area, since 1956), and Virginia (Hampton, since 1973).

Subfamily ARINAE: New World Parakeets, Macaws and Parrots

Genus **PYRRHURA** Bonaparte

Pyrrhura Bonaparte, 1856, Naumannia, 6, Consp. Gen. Psittacorum, gen. 14. Type, by subsequent designation (Salvadori, 1891), *Psittacus vittatus* Shaw [not Boddaert] = *Psittacus frontalis* Vieillot.

Pyrrhura picta (Müller). PAINTED PARAKEET.

Psittacus pictus P. L. S. Müller, 1776, Natursyst., Suppl., pl. 75. (Cayenne.)

Habitat.—Humid lowland forest and forest edge (Tropical Zone).

Distribution.—*Resident* in western Panama (Azuero Peninsula); and in South America from northern Colombia, southern Venezuela and the Guianas south, east of the Andes, to eastern Peru and Amazonian Brazil.

Pyrrhura hoffmanni (Cabanis). SULPHUR-WINGED PARAKEET.

Conurus hoffmanni Cabanis, 1861, Sitzungber. Ges. Naturforsch. Freunde Berlin, 13 November. (Costa Rica.)

Habitat.—Humid montane forest, secondary forest, wooded ridges and hillsides, occasionally wandering to lowland forest (Subtropical, rarely Tropical zones).

Distribution.—*Resident* in the mountains of Costa Rica (from Cordillera de Talamanca and Dota Mountains southward, including to Volcán Irazú) and western Panama (Chiriquí and Bocas del Toro, occurring also in the lowlands of the latter).

Notes.—Also known as HOFFMANN'S CONURE.

Genus **MYIOPSITTA** Bonaparte

Myiopsitta Bonaparte, 1854, Rev. Mag. Zool., ser. 2, 6, p. 150. Type, by subsequent designation (G. R. Gray, 1855), *Psittacus monachus* Boddaert.

Myiopsitta monachus (Boddaert). MONK PARAKEET. [382.4.]

Psittacus monachus Boddaert, 1783, Table Planches Enlum., p. 48. Based on Daubenton, Planches Enlum., pl. 768. (No locality given = Montevideo, Uruguay.)

Habitat.—Open woodland, savanna, arid scrubland, riverine forest, cultivated lands and orchards, especially around human habitation (Tropical and Subtropical zones).

Distribution.—*Resident* from central Bolivia, Paraguay and southern Brazil south to central Argentina.

Introduced and established in Puerto Rico; in the northeastern United States from southern New York and Connecticut south to New Jersey, with individual reports south and west to Kentucky and Virginia, but the present distribution in North America is very local and its status in doubt, particularly since control measures are in progress; and possibly also in Texas (Austin) and southern Florida (Dade County and Key Largo, present status in doubt).

[Genus **NANDAYUS** Bonaparte]

Nandayus Bonaparte, 1854, Rev. Mag. Zool., ser. 2, 6, p. 150. Type, by monotypy, *Psittacus melanocephalus* (not Linnaeus) Vieillot = *Psittacus nenday* Vieillot.

[**Nandayus nenday** (Vieillot). BLACK-HOODED PARAKEET.] See Appendix B.

Genus **CONUROPSIS** Salvadori

Conuropsis Salvadori, 1891, Cat. Birds Br. Mus., 20, pp. xiii, 146, 203. Type, by original designation, *Psittacus carolinensis* Linnaeus.

Notes.—Some authors merge this genus in *Aratinga*.

†**Conuropsis carolinensis** (Linnaeus). CAROLINA PARAKEET. [382.]

Psittacus carolinensis Linnaeus, 1758, Syst. Nat., ed. 10, 1, p. 97. Based on the "Parrot of Carolina" Catesby, Nat. Hist. Carolina, 1, p. 11, pl. 11. (in Carolina, Virginia = South Carolina.)

Habitat.—Riverine forest, cypress swamps and deciduous woodland, foraging in open situations including cultivated lands and gardens.

Distribution.—EXTINCT. Formerly *ranged* from eastern Nebraska (reports from the Dakotas questionable), Iowa, southeastern Wisconsin, southern Michigan (probably), Ohio, Pennsylvania and central New York south to southern Oklahoma (Texas records doubtful), the Gulf states (Louisiana eastward) and south-central Florida. Last specimen taken in the wild on the north fork of the Sebastian River, Brevard County, Florida, on 12 March 1913; last known living individual died in the Cincinnati Zoo, 21 February 1918, although there are questionable sight reports for Florida in 1926 and South Carolina in 1936.

Genus **ARATINGA** Spix

Aratinga Spix, 1824, Avium Spec. Nov. Bras., 1, p. 29. Type, by subsequent designation (G. R. Gray, 1855), *Psittacus luteus* Boddaert = *Psittacus solstitialis* Linnaeus.

Notes.—Members of *Aratinga* and other related genera are sometimes referred to by the group name CONURE. See also comments under *Conuropsis*.

Aratinga holochlora (Sclater). GREEN PARAKEET.

Conurus holochlorus Sclater, 1859, Ann. Mag. Nat. Hist., ser. 3, 4, p. 224. (Jalapa, Vera Cruz, Mexico.)

Habitat.—Open woodland, most frequently highland pine forest, less frequently humid montane forest or lowland forest, locally arid scrub, foraging also in farmlands and plantations (Tropical and Subtropical zones).

Distribution.—*Resident* [*holochlora* group] in southwestern Chihuahua and northeastern Sinaloa, wandering to southern Sonora; on Socorro Island, in the Revillagigedos; and from southern Nuevo León and Tamaulipas south to Guanajuato, the state of México, Puebla, Oaxaca, Veracruz and Chiapas; and [*rubritorquis* group] in the highlands of central and eastern Guatemala, El Salvador, Honduras and northern Nicaragua.

Reports from southern Florida are based on escaped individuals.

Notes.—The distinct Central American populations are often treated as a separate species, *A. rubritorquis* (Sclater, 1887) [RED-THROATED PARAKEET]. *A. holochlora* and *A. strenua* constitute a superspecies; they are sometimes considered conspecific, but differences are retained in areas of sympatry.

Aratinga strenua (Ridgway). PACIFIC PARAKEET.

Conurus holochlorus strenuus Ridgway, 1915, Proc. Biol. Soc. Wash., 28, p. 106. (Ometepe, Nicaragua.)

Habitat.—Open woodland, primarily in arid lowland areas, less commonly to highland forest, foraging often in cultivated lands (Tropical, less frequently Subtropical zones).

Distribution.—*Resident* on the Pacific slope of Middle America from Oaxaca and Chiapas south to southwestern Nicaragua.

Notes.—See comments under *A. holochlora.*

Aratinga finschi (Salvin). CRIMSON-FRONTED PARAKEET.

Conurus finschi Salvin, 1871, Ibis, p. 91, pl. 4. (Bugaba, Chiriqui, Veragua [=Panama].)

Habitat.—Open humid woodland, forest edge, cultivated lands and pastures (Tropical and Subtropical zones).

Distribution.—*Resident* in southeastern Nicaragua (Caribbean lowlands), Costa Rica (primarily Caribbean slope and Golfo Dulce lowlands on Pacific slope, wandering elsewhere on latter in dry season on cordilleras Guanacaste and Central) and western Panama (Caribbean slope in western Bocas del Toro and western Chiriquí, and Pacific lowlands in western Veraguas).

Notes.—*A. finschi* and the South American *A. leucophthalmus* (P. L. S. Müller, 1776) [WHITE-EYED PARAKEET] constitute a superspecies; they are sometimes regarded as conspecific.

Aratinga chloroptera (de Souancé). HISPANIOLAN PARAKEET.

Psittacara chloroptera de Souancé, 1856, Rev. Mag. Zool., ser. 2, 8, p. 59. (Saint-Domingue = Hispaniola.)

Habitat.—Mountain forest, ranging also to open woodland and second growth in the lowlands.

Distribution.—*Resident* on Hispaniola, on Mona Island (formerly, last individual taken in 1892), and probably also on Puerto Rico (based on hearsay evidence, but certainly not there after 1883).

Introduced (but not certainly established) in southern Florida and Puerto Rico.

Notes.—*A. chloroptera* and *A. euops* constitute a superspecies.

Aratinga euops (Wagler). CUBAN PARAKEET.

Sittace euops Wagler, 1832, Abh. Math. Phys. Kl. Bayr. Akad. Wiss., 1, p. 638, pl. 24, fig. 2. (Cuba.)

Habitat.—Heavy forest, sometimes foraging in open country.

Distribution.—*Resident* on Cuba (widespread, most common in remote forested areas) and the Isle of Pines (apparently surviving in small numbers).

Notes.—See comments under *A. chloroptera.*

Aratinga nana (Vigors). OLIVE-THROATED PARAKEET.

Psittacara nana Vigors, 1830, Zool. J., 5, p. 273. (Jamaica.)

Habitat.—Lowland and foothill forest, clearings, scrub, second growth, cultivated lands and plantations, in both humid and semi-arid habitats (Tropical and lower Subtropical zones).

Distribution.—*Resident* [*astec* group] on the Gulf-Caribbean slope of Middle America from southern Tamaulipas and Veracruz south (including Holbox Island, off Quintana Roo) to extreme western Panama (western Bocas del Toro); and [*nana* group] on Jamaica.

Notes.—The two groups are often considered as separate species, *A. astec* (de Souancé, 1875) [AZTEC PARAKEET] and *A. nana* [JAMAICAN PARAKEET].

Aratinga canicularis (Linnaeus). ORANGE-FRONTED PARAKEET.

Psittacus canicularis Linnaeus, 1758, Syst. Nat., ed. 10, 1, p. 98. Based mainly on "The Red and Blue-headed Parakeet" Edwards, Nat. Hist. Birds, 4, p. 176, pl. 176. (in America = northwestern Costa Rica.)

Habitat.—Deciduous forest, arid scrubland, swamps, open woodland, forest edge and, occasionally, around towns and villages, mostly in arid or semi-arid situations, usually nesting in excavations in termitaria (Tropical and lower Subtropical zones).

Distribution.—*Resident* on the Pacific slope of Middle America from central Sinaloa and western Durango south to northwestern Costa Rica (to the Gulf of Nicoya and San José region), also in the arid Comayagua Valley on the Caribbean slope of Honduras.

An individual photographed in New Mexico (Las Cruces, July–August 1971) was almost certainly a bird escaped from captivity.

Introduced (but not certainly established) in southern Florida and Puerto Rico.

Notes.—Relationship of *A. canicularis* and the South American *A. azurea* (Gmelin, 1789) at the superspecies level has been suggested by some authors.

Aratinga pertinax (Linnaeus). BROWN-THROATED PARAKEET.

Psittacus pertinax Linnaeus, 1758, Syst. Nat., ed. 10, 1, p. 98. Based mainly on "The Brown-throated Parrakeet" Edwards, Nat. Hist. Birds, 4, p. 177, pl. 177. (in Indiis = Curaçao.)

Habitat.—Arid scrub, semi-desert, mangrove, savanna, cultivated lands and plantations, most frequently in the dry habitats (Tropical Zone).

Distribution.—*Resident* in western Panama (Pacific slope from western Chiriquí to eastern Panamá province, ranging to Caribbean slope in the Canal Zone); and along the north coast of South America (including islands from the Netherlands Antilles east to Margarita) from northern Colombia east to the Guianas and northern Brazil.

Introduced and established (before 1860) on St. Thomas, in the Virgin Islands (from the population on Curaçao), spreading in recent years to eastern Puerto Rico, Culebra Island and St. John.

Notes.—Known on St. Thomas as the CARIBBEAN PARAKEET. The isolated Panama population is sometimes regarded as a distinct species, *A. ocularis* (Sclater and Salvin, 1865) [VERAGUAS PARAKEET].

Genus ARA Lacépède

Ara Lacépède, 1799, Tabl. Mamm. Ois., p. 1. Type, by subsequent designation (Ridgway, 1916), *Psittacus macao* Linnaeus.

Ara severa (Linnaeus). CHESTNUT-FRONTED MACAW.

Psittacus severus Linnaeus, 1758, Syst. Nat., ed. 10, 1, p. 97. Based on *Psittacus severus* Linnaeus, Mus. Adolphi Friderici, 1, p. 13. (in Indiis = Amazon River.)

Habitat.—Forested lowlands and foothills, riverine woodland, swamps and coffee plantations (Tropical and lower Subtropical zones).

Distribution.—*Resident* from eastern Panama (Darién, ranging, at least formerly, west to eastern Panamá province and the Canal Zone), Colombia, Venezuela and the Guianas south, east of the Andes, to eastern Peru, Bolivia, and Amazonian and central Brazil.

An individual existing for several years in the wild state at Austin, Texas, was undoubtedly an escaped bird.

Ara militaris (Linnaeus). MILITARY MACAW.

Psittacus militaris Linnaeus, 1766, Syst. Nat., ed. 12, 1, p. 139. (No locality given = Colombia.)

Habitat.—Open woodland, riverine forest, and dry forest, especially pine-oak, primarily in arid or semi-arid habitats (Tropical, less commonly Subtropical and lower Temperate zones).

Distribution.—*Resident* in Mexico from southeastern Sonora, southwestern Chihuahua, Sinaloa, Nayarit, Zacatecas, San Luis Potosí, southern Nuevo León and central Tamaulipas south to the state of México, Guerrero and Oaxaca (west of the Isthmus of Tehuantepec); and in South America in a series of isolated populations in northern Venezuela, Colombia (east and south of the range of *A. ambigua*), eastern Ecuador, eastern Peru, eastern Bolivia and northwestern Argentina.

Notes.—*A. militaris* and *A. ambigua* may constitute a superspecies.

Ara ambigua (Bechstein). GREAT GREEN MACAW.

Psittacus ambiguus Bechstein, 1811, *in* Latham, Allg. Uebers. Vögel, 4 (1), p. 65. Based on "Le Grand Ara Militaire" Levaillant, Hist. Nat. Perr., 1, p. 15, pl. 6. (South America = northwestern Colombia.)

Habitat.—Humid forest, clearings, forest edge and open country near forests (Tropical and Subtropical zones).

Distribution.—*Resident* on the Caribbean slope of eastern Honduras (Olancho, Mosquitia), Nicaragua and Costa Rica, locally on both slopes of Panama, and in northwestern Colombia, with an isolated population in western Ecuador.

Notes.—Also known as GREEN or BUFFON'S MACAW. See comments under *A. militaris*.

Ara chloroptera Gray. RED-AND-GREEN MACAW.

Macrocercus macao (not *Psittacus macao* Linnaeus) Vieillot, 1816, Nouv. Dict. Hist. Nat., nouv. éd., 2, p. 262. (British Guiana.)
Ara chloroptera G. R. Gray, 1859, List Birds Br. Mus., pt. 3 (2), p. 26. New name for *Macrocercus macao* Vieillot, preoccupied.

Habitat.—Humid lowland and foothill forest (Tropical and lower Subtropical zones).

Distribution.—*Resident* in eastern Panama (eastern Panamá province, San Blas and Darién, formerly also Canal Zone), and in South America from northern and eastern Colombia, Venezuela and the Guianas south, east of the Andes, to eastern Peru and eastern Bolivia, thence eastward across Paraguay and northern Argentina to southeastern Brazil.

Notes.—Also known as GREEN-WINGED or RED-BLUE-AND-GREEN MACAW.

Ara macao (Linnaeus). SCARLET MACAW.

Psittacus Macao Linnaeus, 1758, Syst. Nat., ed. 10, 1, p. 96. Based mainly on "The Red and Blue Maccaw" Edwards, Nat. Hist. Birds, 4, p. 158, pl. 158. (in America meridionali = Pernambuco, eastern Brazil.)

Habitat.—Forest edge, open woodland, clearings, open country with scattered trees, and cultivated lands, in both humid and arid situations (Tropical and lower Subtropical zones.)

Distribution.—*Resident* locally from Tamaulipas, Veracruz, northern Oaxaca, Tabasco, Chiapas and southern Campeche south along both slopes of Middle America (including Isla Coiba, off Panama), and in South America from Colombia, Venezuela (also Trinidad) and the Guianas south, east of the Andes, to eastern Peru, Bolivia and Amazonian Brazil. Now much reduced in numbers or extirpated throughout most of its Middle American range.

†**Ara tricolor** Bechstein. CUBAN MACAW.

Ara tricolor Bechstein, 1811, *in* Latham, Allg. Uebers. Vögel, 4 (1), p. 64, pl. 1. Based on "L'Ara tricolor" Levaillant, Hist. Nat. Perr., 1, p. 13, pl. 5. (South America, error = Cuba.)

Habitat.—Forest edge and open country with scattered trees, especially palms.
Distribution.—EXTINCT. Formerly *resident* on Cuba (except Oriente Province), possibly also the Isle of Pines; last specimen taken in the Ciénaga de Zapata in 1864.
Notes.—Early accounts indicate that there may have been additional species of *Ara* on other West Indian islands; some scientific names have been proposed (see Appendix C) although no specimens exist.

Ara ararauna (Linnaeus). BLUE-AND-YELLOW MACAW.

Psittacus Ararauna Linnaeus, 1758, Syst. Nat., ed. 10, 1, p. 96. Based mainly on "The Blue and Yellow Maccaw" Edwards, Nat. Hist. Birds, 4, p. 159, pl. 159. (in America meridionali = Pernambuco, eastern Brazil.)

Habitat.—Lowland forest, riverine forest, swamps and savanna, foraging in open areas near forested regions (Tropical Zone).
Distribution.—*Resident* from eastern Panama (Pacific slope in eastern Panamá province and Darién), Colombia, southern Venezuela (also Trinidad) and the Guianas south, east of the Andes, to eastern Peru, northern and eastern Bolivia, Paraguay, and central and eastern Brazil.

Genus **RHYNCHOPSITTA** Bonaparte

Rhynchopsitta Bonaparte, 1854, Rev. Mag. Zool., ser. 2, 6, p. 149. Type, by monotypy, *Macrocercus pachyrhynchus* Swainson.

Rhynchopsitta pachyrhyncha (Swainson). THICK-BILLED PARROT. [382.1.]

Macrocercus pachyrhynchus Swainson, 1827, Philos. Mag., new ser., 1, p. 439. (Table land, Mexico.)

Habitat.—Highland pine-oak forest, foraging less frequently in pine forest at low elevations or in deciduous forest (Subtropical and Temperate zones).
Distribution.—*Breeds* in the mountains of Chihuahua and Durango, probably elsewhere in the Sierra Madre Occidental of central and northern Mexico.
Wanders widely, recorded from central Sonora south to Jalisco, Michoacán, the state of México (Popocatépetl) and central Veracruz (Cofre de Perote and Jalapa); recorded formerly north to south-central and southeastern Arizona (Chiricahua, Dragoon, Galiuro and Patagonia mountains) and, possibly, southwestern New Mexico (unverified reports from the Animas Mountains).
Notes.—Often considered conspecific with *R. terrisi* (but see Hardy, 1967, Condor, 69, pp. 537–538); they constitute a superspecies.

Rhynchopsitta terrisi Moore. MAROON-FRONTED PARROT.

Rhynchopsitta terrisi Moore, 1947, Proc. Biol. Soc. Wash., 60, p. 27. (Sierra Potosí, about 7500 feet, Nuevo León, Mexico.)

Habitat.—Highland pine-oak forest (upper Subtropical and Temperate zones).
Distribution.—*Resident* in the Sierra Madre Oriental of southeastern Coahuila, Nuevo León and western Tamaulipas.
Notes.—See comments under *R. pachyrhyncha.*

Genus BOLBORHYNCHUS Bonaparte

Bolborhynchus Bonaparte, 1857, Rem. Observ. Blanchard, Psittacides, p. 6. Type, by subsequent designation (Richmond, 1915), *Myiopsitta catharina* Bonaparte = *Psittacula lineola* Cassin.

Bolborhynchus lineola (Cassin). BARRED PARAKEET.

Psittacula lineola Cassin, 1853, Proc. Acad. Nat. Sci. Philadelphia, 6, p. 372. (vicinity of the National bridge, Mexico = Puerto Nacional, Veracruz.)

Habitat.—Primarily montane humid forest, wandering to lowland moist forest and open woodland, in South America regularly in open forest and savanna (Subtropical, less commonly upper Tropical zones).
Distribution.—*Resident* locally in the highlands of Middle America from southern Mexico (Guerrero, Oaxaca, Veracruz and Chiapas) south through Guatemala, Honduras and Costa Rica to western Panama (Chiriquí, Bocas del Toro and Veraguas); and in the Andes of South America from Colombia and northwestern Venezuela south to central Peru.

Genus FORPUS Boie

Forpus Boie, 1858, J. Ornithol., 6, p. 363. Type, by subsequent designation (Hellmayr, 1929), *Psittacus passerinus* Linnaeus.

Forpus passerinus (Linnaeus). GREEN-RUMPED PARROTLET.

Psittacus passerinus Linnaeus, 1758, Syst. Nat., ed. 10, 1, p. 103. Based on *Psittacus minimus* Linnaeus, Mus. Adolphi Friderici, 1, p. 14. (in America = Surinam.)

Habitat.—Semi-arid scrubland, savanna, cultivated lands, forest edge, mangroves, gardens and parks (Tropical and Subtropical zones).
Distribution.—*Resident* in northeastern Colombia, northern Venezuela (also Trinidad), the Guianas and Brazil south to the Amazon basin; also recorded from Curaçao, where possibly introduced.
Introduced and established on Jamaica (common) and Barbados (rare and apparently decreasing); attempted introduction on Martinique was unsuccessful.
Notes.—Also known as GUIANA PARROTLET. *F. passerinus* and *F. xanthopterygius* constitute a superspecies; they are sometimes considered conspecific. If the broad treatment is used, COMMON PARROTLET would be an appropriate name.

[Forpus xanthopterygius (Spix). BLUE-WINGED PARROTLET.] See Appendix B.

Forpus cyanopygius (de Souancé). BLUE-RUMPED PARROTLET.

Psittacula cyanopygia de Souancé, 1856, Rev. Mag. Zool., ser. 2, 8, p. 157. (No locality given = northwestern Mexico.)

Habitat.—Deciduous forest, open woodland and open country with scattered trees, mostly in arid regions (Tropical and lower Subtropical zones).

Distribution.—*Resident* in southern Sonora, Sinaloa, western Durango, Zacatecas, Nayarit (including the Tres Marias Islands), Jalisco and Colima.

Notes.—Also known as MEXICAN PARROTLET.

Forpus conspicillatus (Lafresnaye). SPECTACLED PARROTLET.

Psittacula conspicillata Lafresnaye, 1848, Rev. Zool. [Paris], 11, p. 172. (in Colombia aut Mexico = Honda, upper Magdalena River, Tolima, Colombia.)

Habitat.—Open woodland, forest edge, savanna and forest clearings (Tropical and lower Subtropical zones).

Distribution.—*Resident* in eastern Panama (eastern Panamá province and eastern Darién), Colombia and southwestern Venezuela.

Genus **BROTOGERIS** Vigors

Brotogeris Vigors, 1825, Zool. J., 2, p. 400. Type, by original designation, *Psittacus pyrrhopterus* Latham.

Brotogeris jugularis (Müller). ORANGE-CHINNED PARAKEET.

Psittacus jugularis P. L. S. Müller, 1776, Natursyst., Suppl., p. 80. Based on "Petit Perruche à gorge jaune d'Amerique" Daubenton, Planches Enlum., pl. 190, fig. 1. (in America = Bonda, Santa Marta, Colombia.)

Habitat.—Open woodland, secondary forest, forest edge, arid scrub and plantations, most commonly in arid regions, less frequently wandering into humid forest (Tropical and lower Subtropical zones).

Distribution.—*Resident* in southwestern Mexico (Pacific lowlands of Guerrero, Oaxaca and Chiapas), Guatemala (Pacific lowlands), El Salvador, Honduras (Pacific lowlands and arid interior valleys), Nicaragua (Pacific drainage, and locally in cleared areas on Caribbean slope), Costa Rica (Pacific lowlands and humid Caribbean region south at least to Limón), Panama (both slopes, including Coiba and Taboga islands), northern Colombia and northern Venezuela.

Notes.—Also known as TOVI PARAKEET.

Brotogeris versicolurus (Müller). CANARY-WINGED PARAKEET. [382.5.]

Psittacus versicolurus P. L. S. Müller, 1776, Natursyst., Suppl., p. 75. (No locality given = Cayenne.)

Habitat.—Open woodland, scrubland and open areas with scattered trees, less frequently in dense forest, in both arid and humid situations (Tropical and lower Subtropical zones).

Distribution.—*Resident* from eastern Colombia, northern Brazil and French Guiana south, east of the Andes, to eastern Peru, central Bolivia, northern Argentina, Paraguay and southern Brazil.

Introduced and established in southern California (Los Angeles County), west-central (Pinellas County) and southeastern Florida, Puerto Rico and western Peru (Lima).

Genus TOUIT Gray

Touit G. R. Gray, 1855, Cat. Genera Subgenera Birds, p. 89. Type, by original designation, *Psittacus huetii* Temminck.

Touit costaricensis (Cory). RED-FRONTED PARROTLET.

Urochroma costaricensis Cory, 1913, Field Mus. Nat. Hist. Publ., Ornithol. Ser., 1, p. 283. (vicinity of Puerto Limón, Costa Rica.)

Habitat.—Humid forest (Tropical and Subtropical zones).

Distribution.—*Resident* in Costa Rica (Turrialba to Puerto Limón, and Cordillera de Talamanca) and western Panama (Chiriquí and Bocas del Toro).

Notes.—*T. costaricensis* and *T. dilectissima* constitute a superspecies; they are frequently considered conspecific. If combined, the broad species *T. dilectissima* is called RED-WINGED PARROTLET.

Touit dilectissima (Sclater and Salvin). BLUE-FRONTED PARROTLET.

Urochroma dilectissima Sclater and Salvin, 1871, Proc. Zool. Soc. London (1870), p. 788, pl. 47. (south of Mérida, Venezuela.)

Habitat.—Humid lowland and foothill forest and open woodland (Tropical and lower Subtropical zones).

Distribution.—*Resident* in eastern Panama (eastern Panamá province and Darién), northern and western Colombia, northwestern Venezuela and northwestern Ecuador.

Notes.—See comments under *T. costaricensis*.

Genus PIONOPSITTA Bonaparte

Pionopsitta Bonaparte, 1854, Rev. Mag. Zool., ser. 2, 6, p. 152. Type, by monotypy, *Psittacus pileatus* Scopoli.

Pionopsitta pyrilia (Bonaparte). SAFFRON-HEADED PARROT.

Psittacula pyrilia Bonaparte, 1853, C. R. Acad. Sci. Paris, 37, p. 807, note. (Rio Hacha, Santa Marta, Colombia.)

Habitat.—Humid lowland and foothill forest (Tropical and lower Subtropical zones).

Distribution.—*Resident* in extreme eastern Panama (eastern Darién), northern Colombia and western Venezuela.

Pionopsitta haematotis (Sclater and Salvin). BROWN-HOODED PARROT.

Pionus hæmatotis Sclater and Salvin, 1860, Proc. Zool. Soc. London, p. 300. (In prov. Veræ Pacis regione calida = Vera Paz, Guatemala.)

Habitat.—Humid lowland and montane forest, forest edge and coffee plantations (Tropical and Subtropical zones).

Distribution.—*Resident* on the Gulf-Caribbean slope from southeastern Mexico (recorded Veracruz, Oaxaca, northern Chiapas, southern Campeche and Quintana

Roo) south to Nicaragua, on both slopes of Costa Rica and Panama, and from western Colombia to western Ecuador.

Genus PIONUS Wagler

Pionus Wagler, 1832, Abh. Math. Phys. Kl. Bayr. Akad. Wiss., 1, p. 497. Type, by subsequent designation (G. R. Gray, 1840), *Psittacus menstruus* Linnaeus.

Pionus menstruus (Linnaeus). BLUE-HEADED PARROT.

Psittacus menstruus Linnaeus, 1766, Syst. Nat., ed. 12, 1, p. 148. Based mainly on "The Blue-headed Parrot" Edwards, Glean. Nat. Hist., 3, p. 226, pl. 314. (in Surinamo = Surinam.)

Habitat.—Humid lowland and foothill forest, open woodland, forest edge and clearings, foraging also in cultivated lands (Tropical and lower Subtropical zones).

Distribution.—*Resident* in eastern Costa Rica (from Río Pacuare on the Caribbean slope eastward and, rarely, in the Golfo Dulce region on the Pacific) and Panama (both slopes, including Coiba and the Pearl islands), and in South America from Colombia, Venezuela (also Trinidad) and the Guianas south, west of the Andes to western Ecuador and east of the Andes to eastern Peru, central Bolivia, and Amazonian and southeastern Brazil.

Pionus senilis (Spix). WHITE-CROWNED PARROT.

Psittacus senilis Spix, 1824, Avium Spec. Nov. Bras., 1, p. 42, pl. 31, fig. 1. (No locality given = Veracruz, Mexico.)

Habitat.—Humid forest, open woodland (including pine-oak), forest edge, secondary woodland, savanna, and open country with scattered trees (Tropical and Subtropical zones).

Distribution.—*Resident* on the Gulf-Caribbean slope of Middle America from San Luis Potosí and southern Tamaulipas south through eastern Mexico (including Campeche and Quintana Roo) and Central America to Costa Rica (both slopes) and western Panama (western Chiriquí and western Bocas del Toro).

Genus AMAZONA Lesson

Amazona Lesson, 1830, Traité Ornithol., livr. 3, p. 189. Type, by subsequent designation (Salvadori, 1891), *C. farinosa* = *Psittacus farinosus* Boddaert.

Notes.—Members of the genus *Amazona* are sometimes referred to under the group name AMAZON.

Amazona albifrons (Sparrman). WHITE-FRONTED PARROT.

Psittacus albifrons Sparrman, 1788, Mus. Carlson., fasc. 3, pl. 52. Based on the "White-crowned Parrot" Latham, Gen. Synop. Birds, 1 (1), p. 281. (No locality given = southwestern Mexico.)

Habitat.—Deciduous forest, open woodland, secondary forest, scrub and savanna, more frequently in arid situations, occasionally in humid forest, foraging also in cultivated lands (Tropical and Subtropical zones).

Distribution.—*Resident* from southern Sonora, Sinaloa, western Durango and southeastern Veracruz south on the Gulf-Caribbean slope of Middle America (including the Yucatan Peninsula) to Honduras and on the Pacific slope to northwestern Costa Rica (Guanacaste).

Notes.—See comments under *A. xantholora.*

Amazona xantholora (Gray). YELLOW-LORED PARROT.

Psittacus albifrons (not Sparrman) Kuhl, 1820, Consp. Psittacorum, p. 80. (No locality given.)

Chrysotis xantholora G. R. Gray, 1859, List Birds Br. Mus., pt. 3 (2), p. 83. New name for *Psittacus albifrons* "Latham" [=Kuhl], preoccupied. (Honduras = probably Belize.)

Habitat.—Deciduous forest and second-growth woodland in arid situations, very rarely in humid forest (Tropical Zone).

Distribution.—*Resident* throughout the Yucatan Peninsula (including Cozumel Island), in Belize, and on Isla Roatán (in the Bay Islands, Honduras).

Notes.—Although superficially similar to *A. albifrons, A. xantholora* appears more closely related to the *A. leucocephala* superspecies of the West Indies.

Amazona leucocephala (Linnaeus). CUBAN PARROT.

Psittacus leucocephalus Linnaeus, 1758, Syst. Nat., ed. 10, 1 p. 100. Based mainly on "The White-headed Parrot" Edwards, Nat. Hist. Birds, 4, p. 166, pl. 166. (in America = eastern Cuba.)

Habitat.—Forested areas, open woodland and arid scrub.

Distribution.—*Resident* in the Bahamas (Great Inagua and Abaco, formerly also on Long, Crooked, Acklin and Fortune islands), Cuba, the Isle of Pines, and the Cayman Islands (Grand Cayman and Cayman Brac, formerly also Little Cayman).

Notes.—*A. leucocephala, A. collaria* and *A. ventralis* are closely related and constitute a superspecies; some authors consider them to be conspecific. See also comments under *A. xantholora.*

Amazona collaria (Linnaeus). YELLOW-BILLED PARROT.

Psittacus collarius Linnaeus, 1758, Syst. Nat., ed. 10, 1, p. 102. Based on *Psittacus minor, collo miniaceo* Sloane, Voy. Jamaica, 2, p. 297. (in America = Jamaica.)

Habitat.—Humid forest at higher elevations, foraging in cultivated lands.

Distribution.—*Resident* on Jamaica.

Notes.—See comments under *A. leucocephala.*

Amazona ventralis (Müller). HISPANIOLAN PARROT.

Psittacus ventralis P. L. S. Müller, 1776, Natursyst., Suppl., p. 79. Based on "Perroquet à ventre pourpre, de la Martinique" Daubenton, Planches Enlum., pl. 548. (Martinique, error = Hispaniola.)

Habitat.—Forested regions, foraging in cultivated lands.

Distribution.—*Resident* on Hispaniola (including Gonâve, Grand Cayemite, Beata and Saona islands).

Introduced and established on Puerto Rico and in the Virgin Islands (St. Croix and St. Thomas).

Notes.—See comments under *A. leucocephala.*

Amazona vittata (Boddaert). PUERTO RICAN PARROT.

Psittacus vittatus Boddaert, 1783, Table Planches Enlum., p. 49. Based on "Perroquet de St. Domingue" Daubenton, Planches Enlum., pl. 792. (Santo Domingo, error = Puerto Rico.)

Habitat.—Forested regions and open woodland.

Distribution.—*Resident* on Puerto Rico (a small population surviving in the Luquillo National Forest and vicinity), and formerly also Culebra Island.

Amazona agilis (Linnaeus). BLACK-BILLED PARROT.

Psittacus agilis Linnaeus, 1758, Syst. Nat., ed. 10, 1, p. 99. Based on "The Little Green Parrot" Edwards, Nat. Hist. Birds, 4, p. 168, pl. 168. (in America = Jamaica.)

Habitat.—Forested areas in hills and mountains.

Distribution.—*Resident* at higher elevations in western Jamaica (absent from Blue and John Crow mountains in eastern Jamaica).

Amazona viridigenalis (Cassin). RED-CROWNED PARROT. [382.6.]

Chrysotis viridigenalis Cassin, 1853, Proc. Acad. Nat. Sci. Philadelphia, 6, p. 371. (South America, error = northeastern Mexico.)

Habitat.—Forested regions, especially lowland deciduous forest and pine-oak woodland, foraging also in cultivated lands (Tropical and lower Subtropical zones).

Distribution.—*Resident* in Nuevo León, Tamaulipas, San Luis Potosí and extreme northeastern Veracruz.

Introduced and established in southern California (Los Angeles area, breeding in San Gabriel Valley, Los Angeles County), southern Florida (Dade County), and Puerto Rico; a small group has also persisted since 1970 in the Hawaiian Islands (on Oahu).

Casual (probably) in southern Texas (several sight records, lower Rio Grande Valley northwest to Falcon Dam, apparently based on wild vagrants although the possibility of escaped cage birds cannot be excluded).

Notes.—Also known as GREEN-CHEEKED PARROT. *A. viridigenalis* and *A. finschi* are closely related and constitute a superspecies.

Amazona finschi (Sclater). LILAC-CROWNED PARROT.

Chrysotis finschi Sclater, 1864, Proc. Zool. Soc. London, p. 298. (Mexico.)

Habitat.—Deciduous forest, pine-oak woodland and secondary forest, in both semi-arid and humid situations, foraging also in cultivated lands (Tropical and Subtropical zones).

Distribution.—*Resident* on the Pacific slope of western Mexico from southeastern Sonora and southwestern Chihuahua south to Oaxaca (the Isthmus of Tehuantepec).

Introduced and possibly established in southern California (Los Angeles County).

Notes.—See comments under *A. viridigenalis.*

Amazona autumnalis (Linnaeus). RED-LORED PARROT.

Psittacus autumnalis Linnaeus, 1758, Syst. Nat., ed. 10, 1, p. 102. Based on "The Lesser Green Parrot" Edwards, Nat. Hist. Birds, 4, p. 164, pl. 164. (in America = southern Mexico.)

Habitat.—Humid lowland and foothill forest, mangrove swamps and secondary forest, less frequently in deciduous woodland, pine-oak forest or pine savanna, foraging also in cultivated lands (Tropical and lower Subtropical zones).

Distribution.—*Resident* from Tamaulipas and San Luis Potosí south on the Gulf-Caribbean slope (including the Bay Islands off Honduras, but absent from the Yucatan Peninsula) to Nicaragua, on both slopes of Costa Rica (on the Pacific mainly in the southwestern region) and Panama (including Coiba and the Pearl islands), and in South America in northern and western Colombia, western Ecuador, northwestern Venezuela, and the upper Amazon basin of Brazil.

Notes.—Also known as YELLOW-CHEEKED PARROT. The population isolated in the Amazon basin is sometimes treated as a separate species, *A. diadema* (Spix, 1824).

Amazona farinosa (Boddaert). MEALY PARROT.

Psittacus farinosus Boddaert, 1783, Table Planches Enlum., p. 52. Based on "Le Perroquet Meunier de Cayenne" Daubenton, Planches Enlum., pl. 861. (Cayenne.)

Habitat.—Humid lowland and foothill forest (Tropical and lower Subtropical zones).

Distribution.—*Resident* from southern Veracruz and northern Oaxaca south on the Gulf-Caribbean slope (except the Yucatan Peninsula) to Nicaragua, on both slopes of Costa Rica and Panama (including Isla Coiba and other islets), and in South America from Colombia and Venezuela south, east of the Andes, to eastern Peru, Bolivia and central Brazil.

Notes.—Also known as BLUE-CROWNED PARROT.

[Amazona amazonica (Linnaeus). ORANGE-WINGED PARROT.] See Appendix B.

Amazona oratrix Ridgway. YELLOW-HEADED PARROT.

Chrysotis levaillantii (not *Amazona levaillantii* Lesson, 1831) G. R. Gray, 1859, List Birds Br. Mus., pt. 3 (2), p. 79. (Petapa, Oaxaca.)

Amazona oratrix Ridgway, 1887, Man. N. Am. Birds, p. 587. New name for *Chrysotis levaillantii* Gray, preoccupied.

Habitat.—Deciduous forest, open woodland and pine ridges (Tropical Zone).

Distribution.—*Resident* on the Pacific slope of Mexico (including the Tres Marias Islands) from Colima south to Oaxaca (the Isthmus of Tehuantepec); on the Gulf-Caribbean slope of Mexico from southern Nuevo León and Tamaulipas south to Veracruz and Tabasco; and in Belize.

Introduced and possibly established in southern California (Los Angeles region) and southern Florida (Dade County).

Notes. — Although *A. oratrix* and *A. auropalliata* are frequently considered conspecific with *A. ochrocephala,* the close approach of *A. oratrix* and *A. auropalliata* in Pacific Oaxaca without evidence of interbreeding, and the presence of both *A. auropalliata* and *A. ochrocephala* in Caribbean Honduras, suggest that the best treatment would be as allospecies of a superspecies complex. With a single species, YELLOW-HEADED PARROT is the appropriate name.

Amazona auropalliata (Lesson). YELLOW-NAPED PARROT.

Psittacus (amazona) auro-palliatus Lesson, 1842, Rev. Zool. [Paris], 5, p. 135. (Realejo, centre Amérique [=Nicaragua].)

Habitat. — Deciduous forest, thorn scrub, open woodland and pine savanna, primarily in dry or semi-arid regions, foraging also in coffee plantations and cultivated lands (Tropical Zone).

Distribution. — *Resident* on the Pacific slope of Middle America from extreme eastern Oaxaca south to northwestern Costa Rica (Guanacaste); in the Sula Valley of northern Honduras (where possibly introduced); in the Bay Islands off Caribbean Honduras (Roatán, Barbareta and Guanaja); and in the Mosquitia of eastern Honduras and northeastern Nicaragua.

Notes. — See comments under *A. oratrix.*

Amazona ochrocephala (Gmelin). YELLOW-CROWNED PARROT.

Psittacus ochrocephalus Gmelin, 1788, Syst. Nat., 1 (1), p. 339. Based in part on "Le Perroquet Amazone du Brésil" Brisson, Ornithologie, 4, p. 272, pl. 26, fig. 1. (in America australi = Venezuela.)

Habitat. — Deciduous and humid lowland forest, savanna, plantations and cultivated lands (Tropical and lower Subtropical zones).

Distribution. — *Resident* in the Sula Valley of northern Honduras (where present since at least mid-19th Century, probably a native population); and from western Panama (including Coiba and the Pearl islands), Colombia, Venezuela (probably also Trinidad) and the Guianas south, east of the Andes, to eastern Peru, Bolivia and Amazonian Brazil.

Notes. — See comments under *A. oratrix.*

Amazona arausiaca (Müller). RED-NECKED PARROT.

Psittacus arausiacus P. L. S. Müller, 1766, Natursyst., Suppl., p. 79. Based on the "Blue-faced Green Parrot" Edwards, Glean. Nat. Hist., 1, p. 43, pl. 230. (Dominica.)

Habitat. — Mountain forest.

Distribution. — *Resident* on Dominica, in the Lesser Antilles, surviving in reduced numbers.

Notes. — *A. arausiaca* and *A. versicolor* may constitute a superspecies. Species of *Amazona* may also have been present on Martinique and Guadeloupe, for which names have been proposed although no specimens exist (see Appendix C).

Amazona versicolor (Müller). ST. LUCIA PARROT.

Psittacus versicolor P. L. S. Müller, 1776, Natursyst., Suppl., p. 78. Based on "Perroquet, de la Havane" Daubenton, Planches Enlum., pl. 360. (Havana, error = St. Lucia.)

Habitat.—Mountain forest.
Distribution.—*Resident* on St. Lucia, in the Lesser Antilles, where surviving in much reduced numbers.
Notes.—See comments under *A. arausiaca.*

Amazona guildingii (Vigors). ST. VINCENT PARROT.

Psittacus Guildingii Vigors, 1837, Proc. Zool. Soc. London (1836), p. 80. (St. Vincent [Lesser Antilles].)

Habitat.—Mountain forest, rarely in lowland forest.
Distribution.—*Resident* on St. Vincent, in the Lesser Antilles.

Amazona imperialis Richmond. IMPERIAL PARROT.

Psittacus augustus (not Shaw, 1792) Vigors, 1837, Proc. Zool. Soc. London (1836), p. 80. (South America, error = Dominica.)
Amazona imperialis (Ridgway MS) Richmond, 1899, Auk, 16, p. 186 (in text). New name for *Psittacus augustus* Vigors, preoccupied.

Habitat.—Mountain forest at higher elevations.
Distribution.—*Resident* on Dominica, in the Lesser Antilles, where surviving in small numbers.

Order CUCULIFORMES: Cuckoos and Allies

Family CUCULIDAE: Cuckoos, Roadrunners and Anis

Subfamily CUCULINAE: Old World Cuckoos

Genus CUCULUS Linnaeus

Cuculus Linnaeus, 1758, Syst. Nat., ed. 10, 1, p. 110. Type, by tautonymy, *Cuculus canorus* Linnaeus (*Cuculus,* prebinomial specific name, in synonymy).

Cuculus canorus Linnaeus. COMMON CUCKOO. [388.2.]

Cuculus canorus Linnaeus, 1758, Syst. Nat., ed. 10, 1, p. 110. (in Europa = Sweden.)

Habitat.—Open woodland, forest edge and clearings, taiga, open country with scattered trees and, occasionally, treeless regions with bushy growth.

Distribution.—*Breeds* from the British Isles, Scandinavia, northern Russia and northern Siberia south to northern Africa, the Mediterranean region, Asia Minor, the Himalayas, Burma, Southeast Asia and eastern China.

Winters from the Sahara (rarely Sudan), India and Southeast Asia south to South Africa, the East Indies, New Guinea and the Philippines, casually to the eastern Atlantic islands, Ceylon, and the Bonin, Moluccas and Palau islands in the western Pacific.

In migration occurs in the Mediterranean region, Arabia, the Ryukyu Islands and Formosa, ranging casually to the western and central Aleutian (Buldir, Kiska, Amchitka, Adak) and Pribilof (St. Paul) islands.

Casual on the western Alaskan mainland (Tutakoke River mouth), Iceland and the Faroe Islands. Accidental in Massachusetts (Martha's Vineyard) and the Lesser Antilles (Barbados).

Notes.—Known in Old World literature as the CUCKOO. Some authors regard *C. canorus* and the African *C. gularis* Stephens, 1815, as conspecific; they constitute a superspecies.

Cuculus saturatus Blyth. ORIENTAL CUCKOO. [388.1.]

Cuculus saturatus (Hodgson MS) Blyth, 1843, J. Asiat. Soc. Bengal, 12, p. 942. (Nepal.)

Habitat.—Forested regions, primarily coniferous, less frequently deciduous woodland or mixed coniferous-deciduous areas, locally in montane forest.

Distribution.—*Breeds* from central Russia, central Siberia, Anadyrland and Kamchatka south to the Himalayas, northern Burma, southern China, Formosa and Japan.

Winters from the Malay Peninsula and Philippines south through the East Indies and New Guinea to northern and eastern Australia and Lord Howe Island.

In migration occurs on islands of the western Pacific from the Ryukyu and Bonins southward.

Casual in western and southwestern Alaska (Wales, St. Lawrence Island, the Pribilofs, and Rat Island in the Aleutians).

Notes.—Also known as HIMALAYAN CUCKOO.

Subfamily COCCYZINAE: New World Cuckoos

Genus **COCCYZUS** Vieillot

Coccyzus Vieillot, 1816, Analyse, p. 28. Type, by monotypy, "Coucou de la Caroline" Buffon = *Cuculus americanus* Linnaeus.

[Coccyzus pumilus Strickland. DWARF CUCKOO.] See Appendix A.

Coccyzus erythropthalmus (Wilson). BLACK-BILLED CUCKOO. [388.]

Cuculus erythropthalmus Wilson, 1811, Am. Ornithol., 4, p. 16, pl. 28, fig. 2. (No locality given = probably near Philadelphia, Pennsylvania.)

Habitat.—Forest and open woodland, both deciduous and coniferous (breeding); scrub (arid or humid) as well as forest, although most frequently in lowland humid regions (nonbreeding).

Distribution.—*Breeds* from east-central and southeastern Alberta, southern Saskatchewan, southern Manitoba, northern Minnesota, central Ontario, southwestern Quebec, New Brunswick, Prince Edward Island and Nova Scotia south, at least locally, to southeastern Wyoming, eastern Colorado, Nebraska, Kansas, eastern Oklahoma, north-central Texas (once successfully in southern Texas), northern Arkansas, Tennessee, northern Alabama and the Carolinas.

Winters in South America (also Trinidad) from northern Colombia and northern Venezuela south to Ecuador, northern Peru and central Bolivia.

Migrates regularly through the southeastern United States; irregularly through Mexico (recorded from Sinaloa and Tamaulipas southward, mostly in Gulf-Caribbean lowlands, including Cozumel Island) and Middle America (not recorded El Salvador); and casually west to the Pacific region from southern British Columbia south to central California, Arizona and New Mexico, and through the Bahamas (Grand Bahama, New Providence) and the Antilles (recorded Cuba, the Isle of Pines, Jamaica, Puerto Rico and Barbuda).

Casual or accidental in Newfoundland, Paraguay, northern Argentina, Greenland, the British Isles, continental Europe and the Azores.

Coccyzus americanus (Linnaeus). YELLOW-BILLED CUCKOO. [387.]

Cuculus americanus Linnaeus, 1758, Syst. Nat., ed. 10, 1, p. 111. Based on "The Cuckoo of Carolina" Catesby, Nat. Hist. Carolina, 1, p. 9, pl. 9. (in Carolina = South Carolina.)

Habitat.—Open woodland, especially where undergrowth is thick, parks and riparian woodland (breeding); forest, woodland and scrub (nonbreeding).

Distribution.—*Breeds* from interior California (rarely north to western Washington, questionably to southwestern British Columbia), northern Utah, northern Colorado, the Dakotas, southern Manitoba (rarely), Minnesota, southern Ontario, southwestern Quebec and southern New Brunswick south to southern Baja California, southern Arizona, Coahuila, Chihuahua, Nuevo León, Tamaulipas, the Gulf coast and Florida Keys, sporadically farther south in Mexico (recorded Zacatecas and the state of Yucatán) and the Greater Antilles (Cuba, Jamaica, Hispaniola, Gonâve Island, Puerto Rico, and St. Croix in the Virgin Islands), probably also in the Bahamas (Great Inagua) and Lesser Antilles (St. Kitts).

Winters from northern South America (also Tobago and Trinidad) south to eastern Peru, Bolivia and northern Argentina.

Migrates regularly through the southern United States, Middle America and the West Indies.

Casual or accidental north to central Alberta, southern Saskatchewan, Labrador, Newfoundland and Nova Scotia, and in Bermuda, Greenland, the British Isles, continental Europe and the Azores.

Notes.—Some authors suggest that *C. americanus* and the South American *C. euleri* Cabanis, 1873, constitute a superspecies.

Coccyzus minor (Gmelin). MANGROVE CUCKOO. [386.]

Cuculus minor Gmelin, 1788, Syst. Nat., 1 (1), p. 411. Based mainly on "Petit Vieillard" Buffon, Hist. Nat. Ois., 6, p. 401, and the "Mangrove Cuckoo" Latham, Gen. Synop. Birds, 1 (2), p. 537. (in Cayenna = Cayenne.)

Habitat.—Open woodland, lowland forest edge, scrub, deciduous forest and mangroves (Tropical and, rarely, Subtropical zones).

Distribution.—*Breeds* from Sinaloa south on the Pacific slope of Middle America to western Panama (Veraguas); from Tamaulipas south in the Gulf-Caribbean lowlands of Middle America (including Holbox, Mujeres and Cozumel islands off the Yucatan Peninsula, and the Bay Islands off Honduras) to eastern Nicaragua; and from southern Florida (Tampa Bay and Miami areas southward in coastal areas, including the Florida Keys) and the Bahamas south throughout the Antilles (rare in Cuba, except on cays, not recorded Isle of Pines) and islands in the Caribbean Sea (Cayman, Swan, Providencia and San Andrés) to Venezuela (also Netherlands Antilles and Trinidad), the Guianas and northern Brazil.

Winters throughout the breeding range, and occurs, at least casually, elsewhere in peninsular Florida (including the interior) and south to central Panama (Canal Zone and the Pearl Islands).

Accidental in southeastern Texas (Port Bolivar, also sight reports elsewhere).

Notes.—*C. minor* and *C. ferrugineus* are considered to be closely related and conspecific (or members of a superspecies) by some authors, although this is questioned by others. In addition, the suggestion that the South American *C. melacoryphus* Vieillot, 1817, also belongs in this superspecies has been made, but others do not support such a treatment.

Coccyzus ferrugineus Gould. COCOS CUCKOO.

Coccyzus ferrugineus Gould, 1843, Proc. Zool. Soc. London, p. 105. (Cocos Island.)

Habitat.—Forest, open woodland, second growth and, occasionally, scrub.

Distribution.—*Resident* on Cocos Island, off Costa Rica.

Notes.—See comments under *C. minor*.

[Coccyzus lansbergi Bonaparte. GRAY-CAPPED CUCKOO.] See Appendix A.

Genus SAUROTHERA Vieillot

Saurothera Vieillot, 1816, Analyse, p. 28. Type, by monotypy, "Coucou à longbec" Buffon = *Cuculus vetula* Linnaeus.

Saurothera merlini d'Orbigny. GREAT LIZARD-CUCKOO.

Saurothera merlini d'Orbigny, 1839, *in* La Sagra, Hist. Fis. Pol. Nat. Cuba, Ois., p. 152 [p. 115 in Spanish edition], pl. 25. (Cuba.)

Habitat.—Open woodland, especially in thickets or dense undergrowth.

Distribution.—*Resident* in the Bahamas (Andros, New Providence and Eleuthera), and on Cuba (including Cayo Santa María and Cayo Coco) and the Isle of Pines.

Notes.—All species of the genus *Saurothera* appear to constitute a superspecies.

Saurothera vieilloti Bonaparte. PUERTO RICAN LIZARD-CUCKOO.

Saurothera vetula (not Linnaeus, 1758) Vieillot, 1819, Nouv. Dict. Hist. Nat., nouv. éd., 32, p. 348. (Porto Rico = Puerto Rico.)

Saurothera vieilloti Bonaparte, 1850, Consp. Gen. Avium, 1 (1), p. 97. New name for *Saurothera vetula* Vieillot, preoccupied.

Habitat.—Open woodland, primarily with heavy undergrowth, brushy hillsides and coffee plantations.
Distribution.—*Resident* on Puerto Rico and (formerly) Vieques Island, possibly at one time on St. Thomas in the Virgin Islands.
Notes.—See comments under *S. merlini.*

Saurothera longirostris (Hermann). HISPANIOLAN LIZARD-CUCKOO.

Cuculus longirostris Hermann, 1783, Tabula Affinit. Anim., p. 186. (Hispaniola.)

Habitat.—Woodland with dense undergrowth and thickets.
Distribution.—*Resident* on Hispaniola (including Gonâve, Tortue and Saona islands).
Notes.—See comments under *S. merlini.*

Saurothera vetula (Linnaeus). JAMAICAN LIZARD-CUCKOO.

Cuculus Vetula Linnaeus, 1758, Syst. Nat., ed. 10, 1, p. 111. Based mainly on *Cuculus major* Sloane, Voy. Jamaica, 2, p. 312, pl. 258. (in Jamaica.)

Habitat.—Open hilly woodland with dense undergrowth, and arid lowland woodland.
Distribution.—*Resident* on Jamaica.
Notes.—See comments under *S. merlini.*

Genus HYETORNIS Sclater

Ptiloleptis (not *Ptiloleptus* Swainson, 1837, emended to *Ptiloleptis* by G. R. Gray, 1849) Bonaparte, 1854, Ateneo Ital., 2, p. 121. Type, by monotypy, *Cuculus pluvialis* Gmelin.
Hyetornis Sclater, 1862, Cat. Collect. Am. Birds, pp. xiii, 321. New name for *Ptiloleptis* Bonaparte, preoccupied.

Hyetornis pluvialis (Gmelin). CHESTNUT-BELLIED CUCKOO.

Cuculus pluvialis Gmelin, 1788, Syst. Nat., 1 (1), p. 411. Based in part on the "Old man or rainbird" Sloane, Voy. Jamaica, 2, p. 321, pl. 258, fig. 1. (in Jamaica.)

Habitat.—Thickets in open woodland or scrub in hills or mountains.
Distribution.—*Resident* on Jamaica.
Notes.—*H. pluvialis* and *H. rufigularis* appear to constitute a superspecies.

Hyetornis rufigularis (Hartlaub). BAY-BREASTED CUCKOO.

Coccyzus rufigularis "Herz. c. Württemb." Hartlaub, 1852, Naumannia, 2, p. 55. (Mountain forests of Spanish Santo Domingo = Dominican Republic.)

Habitat.—Heavily forested hills and mountains, also arid lowland scrub.

Distribution.—*Resident* on Hispaniola (primarily the Dominican Republic, rare in Haiti) and Gonâve Island.

Notes.—See comments under *H. pluvialis.*

Genus PIAYA Lesson

Piaya Lesson, 1830, Traité Ornithol., livr. 2, p. 139. Type, by original designation, *Cuculus cayanus* Gmelin [=Linnaeus].

Piaya cayana (Linnaeus). SQUIRREL CUCKOO.

Cuculus cayanus Linnaeus, 1766, Syst. Nat., ed. 12, 1, p. 170. Based on "Le Coucou de Cayenne" Brisson, Ornithologie, 4, p. 122, pl. 8, fig. 2. (in Cayana = Cayenne.)

Habitat.—Open woodland, forest edge, second-growth woodland, scrubby areas, thickets, plantations, and open country with scattered trees (Tropical and Subtropical zones).

Distribution.—*Resident* from southern Sonora, southern Chihuahua, Durango, Zacatecas, southern San Luis Potosí and southern Tamaulipas south through Middle America (doubtfully recorded from Holbox and Mujeres islands, but casual on Isla Cancun, off Quintana Roo), and in South America from Colombia, Venezuela (also Trinidad) and the Guianas south, west of the Andes to northwestern Peru and east of the Andes to eastern Peru, Bolivia, northern Argentina and Uruguay.

Piaya minuta (Vieillot). LITTLE CUCKOO.

Coccyzus minutus Vieillot, 1817, Nouv. Dict. Hist. Nat., nouv. éd., 8, p. 275. Based in part on "Le petit Coucou de Cayenne" Brisson, Ornithologie, 4, p. 124, pl. 16, fig. 2. (No locality given = Cayenne.)

Habitat.—Thickets, shrubby areas and dense undergrowth, generally near water (Tropical Zone).

Distribution.—*Resident* from eastern Panama (Canal Zone and eastern Panamá province eastward), Colombia and Venezuela (also Trinidad) south, east of the Andes, to eastern Peru, northern Bolivia and Amazonian Brazil.

Subfamily NEOMORPHINAE: Ground-Cuckoos and Roadrunners

Genus TAPERA Thunberg

Tapera Thunberg, 1819, Göteborgs Kungl. Vetensk. Vitterhets-Samh. Handl., 3, p. 1. Type, by monotypy, *Tapera brasiliensis* Thunberg = *Cuculus naevius* Linnaeus.

Tapera naevia (Linnaeus). STRIPED CUCKOO.

Cuculus nævius Linnaeus, 1766, Syst. Nat., ed. 12, 1, p. 170. Based on "Le Coucou tacheté de Cayenne" Brisson, Ornithologie, 4, p. 127, pl. 9, fig. 1. (in Cayania = Cayenne.)

Habitat.—Dense second-growth areas, thickets, brushy regions, fields and scrub (Tropical and lower Subtropical zones).

Distribution.—*Resident* from southern Mexico (Veracruz, Oaxaca, Tabasco, Chiapas and southern Quintana Roo) south along both slopes of Middle America, and in South America from Colombia, Venezuela (also Margarita Island and Trinidad) and the Guianas south, west of the Andes to southwestern Ecuador and east of the Andes to eastern Peru, Bolivia, northern Argentina and southern Brazil.

Genus DROMOCOCCYX Wied

Dromococcyx Wied, 1832, Beitr. Naturgesch. Bras., 4 (1), p. 351. Type, by monotypy, *Macropus phasianellus* Spix.

Dromococcyx phasianellus (Spix). PHEASANT CUCKOO.

Macropus phasianellus Spix, 1824, Avium Spec. Nov. Bras., 1, p. 53, pl. 42. (forest of Rio Tonantins, Amazon Valley, Brazil.)

Habitat.—Dense undergrowth and thickets of deciduous forest and second-growth woodland, forest edge and scrubby growth (Tropical Zone.)

Distribution.—*Resident* from southern Mexico (Veracruz, Oaxaca, Chiapas and the Yucatan Peninsula) south through Middle America (not recorded Belize), and in South America from Colombia, Venezuela and the Guianas south, east of the Andes, to eastern Colombia, northern Bolivia, Paraguay, northeastern Argentina and southeastern Brazil.

Genus MOROCOCCYX Sclater

Morococcyx Sclater, 1862, Cat. Collect. Am. Birds, p. 322. Type, by monotypy, *Coccyzus erythropyga* Lesson.

Morococcyx erythropygus (Lesson). LESSER GROUND-CUCKOO.

Coccyzus erythropyga Lesson, 1842, Rev. Zool. [Paris], 5, p. 210. (San-Carlos, Centre Amérique = San Carlos, Nicaragua.)

Habitat.—Deciduous woodland undergrowth, thickets, shrubby growth, scrub, and edges of fields and pastures in tangled growth, primarily in arid regions (Tropical Zone).

Distribution.—*Resident* on the Pacific slope of Middle America from southern Sinaloa south to northwestern Costa Rica (Guanacaste), occurring also in the arid interior valleys on the Caribbean slope of Guatemala (Motagua) and Honduras (Quimistán, Sula, Comayagua and Aguán).

Genus GEOCOCCYX Wagler

Geococcyx Wagler, 1831, Isis von Oken, col. 524. Type, by monotypy, *Geococcyx variegata* Wagler = *Saurothera californiana* Lesson.

Geococcyx velox (Wagner). LESSER ROADRUNNER.

Cuculus velox A. Wagner, 1836, Gelehrte Anz., München, 3, col. 96. (Mexico = outskirts of Mexico City.)

Habitat.—Arid semi-open country with tangles, thickets and scrubby undergrowth, including open deciduous forest, pine-oak woodland and savanna (Tropical and Subtropical zones).

Distribution.—*Resident* in western Mexico from extreme southern Sonora south to the Isthmus of Tehuantepec, and in the interior of Middle America from central Mexico (Michoacán, state of México, Morelos, Puebla and west-central Veracruz, with an isolated population in the state of Yucatán) south through Guatemala, El Salvador and Honduras to central Nicaragua.

Geococcyx californianus (Lesson). GREATER ROADRUNNER. [385.]

Saurothera Californiana Lesson, 1829, Compl. Oeuvres Buffon, 6, p. 420. (Californie = San Diego, California.)

Habitat.—Desert scrub, chaparral, edges of cultivated lands, and arid open situations with scattered brush, locally in cedar glades and pine-oak woodland (Tropical and Subtropical zones).

Distribution.—*Resident* from northern California, western and central Nevada, southern Utah, Colorado, southern Kansas, central and eastern Oklahoma, southwestern Missouri, western Arkansas and north-central Louisiana south to southern Baja California, Sinaloa, Durango, Zacatecas, northeastern Jalisco, eastern Michoacán, the state of México, Distrito Federal, Puebla, Veracruz, Tamaulipas and the Gulf coast of Texas.

Notes.—Often called the ROADRUNNER in American literature.

Genus NEOMORPHUS Gloger

Neomorphus Gloger, 1827, *in* Froriep, Notizen, 16, col. 278, note. Type, by original designation, *Coccyzus geoffroyi* Temminck.

Neomorphus geoffroyi (Temminck). RUFOUS-VENTED GROUND-CUCKOO.

Coccyzus geoffroyi Temminck, 1820, Planches Color., livr. 2, pl. 7. (No locality given = Para, Brazil.)

Habitat.—Humid lowland and foothill forest (Tropical and lower Subtropical zones).

Distribution.—*Resident* in Nicaragua (Caribbean slope), Costa Rica (primarily Caribbean slope, on Pacific drainage in Cordillera de Guanacaste) and Panama (both slopes), and in South America from Colombia south, east of the Andes, to eastern Peru, northern Bolivia and Amazonian Brazil.

Subfamily CROTOPHAGINAE: Anis

Genus CROTOPHAGA Linnaeus

Crotophaga Linnaeus, 1758, Syst. Nat., ed. 10, 1, p. 105. Type, by monotypy, *Crotophaga ani* Linnaeus.

Crotophaga major Gmelin. GREATER ANI.

Crotophaga major Gmelin, 1788, Syst. Nat., 1 (1), p. 363. Based in part on "Le grand Bout-de-petun" Brisson, Ornithologie, 4, p. 180, pl. 18, fig. 2, and Daubenton, Planches Enlum., pl. 102, fig. 1. (in Cayenna = Cayenne.)

Habitat.—Thickets and second growth (generally near water), swamps and marshes (Tropical Zone, locally to Temperate Zone).

Distribution.—*Resident* from eastern Panama (on the Caribbean slope from western Colón eastward, on the Pacific from the Canal Zone eastward), Colombia, Venezuela (also Trinidad) and the Guianas south, west of the Andes to western Colombia and east of the Andes virtually throughout to northern Argentina; several specimens taken along the Río Tamesí, southern Tamaulipas, suggest a resident population in northeastern Mexico (Colson, 1978, Auk, 95, pp. 766–767).

Crotophaga ani Linnaeus. SMOOTH-BILLED ANI. [383.]

> *Crotophaga Ani* Linnaeus, 1758, Syst. Nat., ed. 10, 1, p. 105. Based mainly on the "Razor-billed Blackbird" Catesby, Nat. Hist. Carolina, 2, app., p. 3, pl. 3, and Sloane, Voy. Jamaica, 2, p. 298, pl. 256, fig. 1. (in America, Africa = Jamaica.)

Habitat.—Open situations with brush or scrub, fields, plantations, gardens and forest clearings (Tropical and lower Subtropical zones).

Distribution.—*Resident* in central and southern Florida (Tampa Bay and Merritt Island region southward, most abundantly from Lake Okeechobee area to Dade County); from the Bahamas south throughout the Antilles (including the Cayman Islands); on islands off Quintana Roo (Holbox and Cozumel), Honduras (Swan and Bay islands) and Nicaragua (Corn, Providencia and San Andrés); and in southwestern Costa Rica (Pacific slope north to the Gulf of Nicoya region), Panama (both slopes, including Coiba and the Pearl islands), and South America from Colombia, Venezuela (also Margarita Island, Tobago and Trinidad) and the Guianas south, west of the Andes to western Ecuador and east of the Andes virtually throughout to northern Argentina.

Casual north along the Atlantic coast to North Carolina, in southern Louisiana and northern Florida, and to the mainland of Honduras (Trujillo region, where possibly breeding). Accidental in New Jersey (Petty Island in the Delaware River).

Crotophaga sulcirostris Swainson. GROOVE-BILLED ANI. [384.]

> *Crotophaga sulcirostris* Swainson, 1827, Philos. Mag., new ser., 1, p. 440. (Table land. Temiscaltepec = Temascaltepec, state of México.)

Habitat.—Open and partly open country, including scrub, thickets, cultivated lands, savanna and second growth (Tropical and Subtropical zones).

Distribution.—*Resident* in southern Baja California (Cape district, formerly); from southern Sonora, central and southern (casually western and southeastern) Texas and southern Louisiana (rarely, one breeding record, Plaquemines Parish) south along both slopes of Middle America (including Mujeres, Holbox and Cozumel islands off Quintana Roo) and along both coasts of South America to extreme northern Chile and Guyana (also the Netherlands Antilles); and in northwestern Argentina.

Wanders regularly east along the Gulf coast to peninsular Florida, and casually northward to southern California, southern Nevada, central Arizona, central New Mexico, Colorado, South Dakota, Minnesota, Wisconsin, Michigan, southern Ontario, Ohio and Maryland. Reports from Trinidad are erroneous.

Order STRIGIFORMES: Owls

Family TYTONIDAE: Barn-Owls

Genus TYTO Billberg

Tyto Billberg, 1828, Synop. Faunae Scand., ed. 2, 1 (2), tab. A. Type, by monotypy, *Strix flammea* auct. = *Strix alba* Scopoli.

Tyto alba (Scopoli). COMMON BARN-OWL. [365.]

Strix alba Scopoli, 1769, Annus I, Hist.-Nat., p. 21. (Ex Foro Juli = Friuli, northern Italy.)

Habitat.—Open and partly open country in a wide variety of situations, often around human habitation, breeding in buildings, caves, crevices on cliffs, burrows and hollow trees, rarely in trees with dense foliage, such as palms (Tropical to Temperate zones).

Distribution.—*Resident* in the Americas from southwestern British Columbia, western Washington, Oregon, southern Idaho, Montana, North Dakota, southern Minnesota, southern Wisconsin, southern Michigan, southern Ontario, New York, southern Vermont and Massachusetts south through the United States and Middle America (including many islands around Baja California and in the Gulf of California, the Tres Marías Islands, Bay Islands off Honduras, and Pearl Islands off Panama), Bermuda, the Bahamas, Greater Antilles (except Puerto Rico and the Virgin Islands) and Lesser Antilles (Dominica, St. Vincent, Grenada and the Grenadines), and in South America from Colombia, Venezuela (also the Netherlands Antilles, Tobago and Trinidad) south to Tierra del Fuego; and in the Old World from the British Isles, Baltic countries, southern Russia and southern Siberia south throughout most of Eurasia and Africa to southern Africa, Madagascar, the Malay Peninsula, the East Indies (except Sumatra, Borneo and the Philippines) and Australia, and east in the western Pacific to the Society Islands. Northernmost populations in North America are partially migratory, wintering south to southern Mexico and the West Indies.

Wanders casually north to southern Alberta, southern Saskatchewan, southern Manitoba, northern Minnesota, southern Quebec, New Brunswick, Newfoundland and Nova Scotia. Accidental in Alaska (Delta Junction).

Introduced and established in the Hawaiian Islands (in 1958, now on all main islands from Kauai eastward) and on Lord Howe Island.

Notes.—Known in most literature as the BARN OWL. *T. alba* and the closely related *T. glaucops* are regarded as species since sympatry occurs on Hispaniola. Some authors suggest that the populations in the Australian region may constitute a separate species, *T. delicatula* (Gould, 1837), as apparently both North American and Australian forms have become established on Lord Howe Island without evidence of interbreeding.

Tyto glaucops (Kaup). ASHY-FACED BARN-OWL.

Strix glaucops Kaup, 1853, *in* Jardine, Contrib. Ornithol. (1852), p. 118. (Jamaica, error = Hispaniola.)

Habitat.—Open woodland and scrub, breeding in limestone caves and sinkholes, foraging also around old buildings and ruins.
Distribution.—*Resident* on Hispaniola.
Notes.—Also known as HISPANIOLAN BARN-OWL. See comments under *T. alba.*

Family **STRIGIDAE**: Typical Owls

Genus **OTUS** Pennant

Otus Pennant, 1769, Indian Zool., p. 3. Type, by monotypy, *Otus bakkamoena* Pennant.
Gymnasio Bonaparte, 1854, Rev. Mag. Zool., ser. 2, 6, p. 543. Type, by monotypy, *Strix nudipes* Daudin.

Notes.—See comments under *Gymnoglaux.*

Otus sunia (Hodgson). ORIENTAL SCOPS-OWL. [374.1.]

Strix sunia Hodgson, 1836, Asiat. Res., 19, p. 175. (Nepal.)

Habitat & Distribution.—*Breeds* in forest and woodland from Mongolia, Manchuria, Amurland, Sakhalin and Japan south to northern China, Korea, the Ryukyu Islands, and Seven Islands of Izu, and *winters* from southeastern China, the Ryukyus and Japan south to Southeast Asia and the Seven Islands of Izu.

Accidental in Alaska in the Aleutian Islands on Buldir (5 June 1977; Day, *et al.,* 1979, Auk, 96, p. 189) and Amchitka (late June 1979; Roberson, 1980, Rare Birds W. Coast, p. 230).

Notes.—*O. sunia* and other Old World forms are sometimes merged in the Eurasian *O. scops* (Linnaeus, 1758) [COMMON SCOPS-OWL], but studies of vocalizations and behavior indicate their specific status. See also comments under *O. flammeolus.*

Otus flammeolus (Kaup). FLAMMULATED OWL. [374.]

Scops (*Megascops*) *flammeola* "Licht." Kaup, 1853, *in* Jardine, Contrib. Ornithol. (1852), p. 111. (Mexico.)

Habitat.—Montane forest, primarily ponderosa pine association, in migration widely through wooded areas in lowlands and mountains (upper Subtropical and Temperate zones).

Distribution.—*Breeds* locally from southern British Columbia (Kamloops, Penticton), north-central Washington, eastern Oregon, southern Idaho and northern Colorado south to southern California, southern Arizona, southern New Mexico and western Texas (Guadalupe and Chisos mountains); also in southeastern Coahuila (probably), Nuevo León (La Esperanza), the state of México (Chimalpa) and Veracruz (Las Vigas).

Winters from central Mexico (Sinaloa, Jalisco, Michoacán and Distrito Federal) south in the highlands to Guatemala and El Salvador, casually north to southern California.

In migration occurs east to Montana, central Colorado, eastern New Mexico and western Texas.

Casual or accidental in southeastern Texas (Port Aransas), Louisiana (Baton

Rouge), Alabama (Shelby County), Florida (Reddington Beach) and the Gulf of Mexico (ca. 75 miles southeast of Galveston, Texas).

Notes.—Also known as FLAMMULATED SCREECH-OWL. *O. scops* and *O. flammeolus* are closely related and have been considered conspecific by some authors; differences in vocalizations suggest specific treatment, and consideration as a superspecies seems the preferred option (see Marshall, 1978, A. O. U. Ornithol. Monogr., no. 25, p. 8).

Otus asio (Linnaeus). EASTERN SCREECH-OWL. [373.]

Strix Asio Linnaeus, 1758, Syst. Nat., ed. 10, 1, p. 92. Based on "The Little Owl" Catesby, Nat. Hist. Carolina, 1, p. 7, pl. 7. (in America = South Carolina.)

Habitat.—Open woodland, deciduous forest, parklands, residential areas in towns, scrub, and riparian woodland in drier regions.

Distribution.—*Resident* from southern Saskatchewan (probably), southern Manitoba, northern Minnesota, northern Michigan, southern Ontario, southwestern Quebec and Maine south through the eastern United States to eastern San Luis Potosí, southern Texas, the Gulf coast and southern Florida (Florida Keys), and west to eastern Montana, the Dakotas, eastern Colorado, Kansas, western Oklahoma and west-central (casually extreme western) Texas. Recorded in summer (and probably breeding) in central Alberta.

Casual in Nova Scotia (Indian Lake), with sight reports from New Brunswick.

Notes.—Formerly known as the SCREECH OWL. Relationships of North and Middle American *Otus* are discussed in Marshall (1967, W. Found. Vertebr. Zool., Monogr., no. 1, pp. 1–72), in which the four groups of *O. asio* are recognized on the basis of vocalizations and behavior as "incipient species"; these groups are now considered to be allospecies of a superspecies. Long distance dispersal apparently accounts for overlap and mixed pairs in marginally poor habitat along the Arkansas River in Colorado and the Rio Grande in Texas; the overlap does not appear to represent hybridization. If these four species (*O. asio* and the following three species) are treated as a single species, *O. asio,* COMMON SCREECH-OWL is the appropriate English name.

Otus kennicottii (Elliot). WESTERN SCREECH-OWL. [373.2.]

Scops Kennicottii Elliot, 1867, Proc. Acad. Nat. Sci. Philadelphia, 19, p. 99. (Sitka, Alaska.)

Habitat.—Woodland, especially oak and riparian woodland, and scrub (Subtropical and Temperate zones).

Distribution.—*Resident* from south-coastal and southeastern Alaska (west to Cordova), coastal and southern British Columbia, northern Idaho, western Montana, southeastern Colorado and extreme western Oklahoma south to southern Baja California, northern Sinaloa, in the Mexican highlands through Chihuahua and Coahuila as far as the Distrito Federal, and to western Texas (east to Big Bend).

Notes.—Also known as KENNICOTT'S SCREECH-OWL. Populations of this species in southern Sonora, western Chihuahua and Sinaloa have been treated by some authors as a separate species, *O. vinaceus* (Brewster, 1888) [VINACEOUS

SCREECH-OWL], but differences in voice and behavior are lacking and intergradation occurs (see A. H. and L. Miller, 1951, Condor, 53, pp. 172–176). See also comments under *O. asio.*

Otus seductus Moore. BALSAS SCREECH-OWL.

> *Otus vinaceus seductus* Moore, 1941, Proc. Biol. Soc. Wash., 54, p. 156. (5 miles northeast of Apatzingán, Michoacán, altitude 1000 feet.)

Habitat.—Deciduous woodland, mesquite and heavy second growth (Tropical and lower Subtropical zones).
Distribution.—*Resident* in the lowlands of Colima, and in the Río Balsas drainage of Michoacán and western Guerrero.
Notes.—See comments under *O. asio.*

Otus cooperi (Ridgway). PACIFIC SCREECH-OWL.

> *Scops cooperi* Ridgway, 1878, Proc. U.S. Natl. Mus., 1, p. 116. (Santa Ana, Costa Rica.)

Habitat.—Open woodland, swamp forest and mangroves (Tropical and Subtropical zones).
Distribution.—*Resident* along the Pacific coast of Middle America from Oaxaca (Puerto Angel region, Nejapa) south to northwestern Costa Rica (Guanacaste region).
Notes.—Also known as COOPER'S SCREECH-OWL. See comments under *O. asio.*

Otus trichopsis (Wagler). WHISKERED SCREECH-OWL. [373.1.]

> *Scops trichopsis* Wagler, 1832, Isis von Oken, col. 276. (Mexico = mountains of southwestern Puebla.)

Habitat.—Montane pine-oak association (Subtropical and lower Temperate zones).
Distribution.—*Resident* from southeastern Arizona, northeastern Sonora, Chihuahua, Durango, San Luis Potosí and Nuevo León south through the mountains of Mexico (west to Sinaloa, Nayarit, Jalisco, Michoacán and Guerrero, and east to west-central Veracruz), Guatemala, El Salvador and Honduras to northern Nicaragua.
Casual in southwestern New Mexico (Peloncillo Mountains).
Notes.—Also known as WHISKERED OWL or SPOTTED SCREECH-OWL.

Otus guatemalae (Sharpe). VERMICULATED SCREECH-OWL.

> *Scops brasilianus* Subsp. β. *Scops guatemalæ* Sharpe, 1875, Cat. Birds Br. Mus., 2, pp. ix, 112, pl. 9. (Central America, from Veraguas northwards to Mexico = Guatemala.)

Habitat.—Humid lowland and montane forest, pine-oak association, lowland deciduous forest (both humid and arid), open woodland and plantations (Tropical and Subtropical zones).
Distribution.—*Resident* [*guatemalae* group] from southeastern Sonora and Tamaulipas south on both slopes of Mexico to Chiapas and the Yucatan Peninsula

(including Cozumel Island), and thence south, mostly in the highlands, through Guatemala (including Petén) and Honduras to north-central Nicaragua; and [*vermiculatus* group] locally from northeastern Costa Rica and Panama south to northern Venezuela, Colombia, Ecuador and Bolivia.

Notes.—The two groups are sometimes regarded as distinct species, *O. guatemalae* [MIDDLE AMERICAN SCREECH-OWL] and *O. vermiculatus* (Ridgway, 1887) [VERMICULATED SCREECH-OWL].

Otus choliba (Vieillot). TROPICAL SCREECH-OWL.

Strix choliba Vieillot, 1817, Nouv. Dict. Hist. Nat., nouv. éd., 7, p. 39. Based on "Chóliba" Azara, Apunt. Hist. Nat. Páx. Parag., 2, p. 218 (no. 48). (Paraguay.)

Habitat.—Open woodland, second growth, forest border and clearings, open country with scattered trees, parklands and residential areas (Tropical and Subtropical zones).

Distribution.—*Resident* from central Costa Rica (San José region) south through Panama (including the Pearl Islands), and in South America from Colombia and Venezuela (also Margarita Island and Trinidad) south, east of the Andes, to eastern Peru, Bolivia, northern Argentina and Paraguay; erroneously recorded from Honduras.

Otus barbarus (Sclater and Salvin). BEARDED SCREECH-OWL.

Scops barbarus Sclater and Salvin, 1868, Proc. Zool. Soc. London, p. 56. (Santa Barbara, Vera Paz, Guatemala.)

Habitat.—Open woodland in humid montane and pine forest (Subtropical and Temperate zones).

Distribution.—*Resident* in the mountains of Chiapas and northern Guatemala.

Notes.—Also known as BRIDLED SCREECH-OWL.

Otus clarkii Kelso and Kelso. BARE-SHANKED SCREECH-OWL.

Otus clarkii L. and E. H. Kelso, 1935, Biol. Leaflet, no. 5, [not paged]. (Calobre, Panama.)

Habitat.—Humid montane forest, forest edge and hedgerows (Subtropical and lower Temperate zones).

Distribution.—*Resident* in the mountains of Costa Rica (Cordillera Central eastward), Panama (recorded from western Chiriquí, Veraguas and eastern Darién) and extreme northwestern Colombia.

Notes.—Also known as BARE-LEGGED SCREECH-OWL. Once called *Otus nudipes* in the literature, based on *Bubo nudipes* Vieillot, 1807, now regarded as a *nomen dubium*.

Otus nudipes (Daudin). PUERTO RICAN SCREECH-OWL.

Strix nudipes Daudin, 1800, Traité Ornithol., 2, p. 199. (Porto Rico and Cayenne = Puerto Rico.)

Habitat.—Dense woodland, thickets and caves.

Distribution.—*Resident* on Puerto Rico (including Vieques and Culebra islands) and in the Virgin Islands (St. Thomas, St. John, Tortola, Virgin Gorda and St. Croix).
Notes.—Also known as PUERTO RICAN BARE-LEGGED OWL.

Genus GYMNOGLAUX Cabanis

Gymnoglaux Cabanis, 1855, J. Ornithol., 3, p. 466. Type, by monotypy, *Noctua nudipes* Lembeye (not *Strix nudipes* Daudin) = *Gymnoglaux lawrencii* Sclater and Salvin.

Notes.—Some authors merge this genus in *Otus.*

Gymnoglaux lawrencii Sclater and Salvin. BARE-LEGGED OWL.

Gymnoglaux lawrencii Sclater and Salvin, 1868, Proc. Zool. Soc. London, p. 327, pl. 29. (Cuba = Remedios, Cuba.)

Habitat.—Densely foliaged trees, thickets and caves.
Distribution.—*Resident* on Cuba and the Isle of Pines.

Genus LOPHOSTRIX Lesson

Lophostrix Lesson, 1836, Compl. Ouevres Buffon, 7, p. 261. Type, by monotypy, *Strix griseata* Latham = *Strix cristata* Daudin.

Lophostrix cristata (Daudin). CRESTED OWL.

Strix cristata Daudin, 1800, Traité Ornithol., 2, p. 307. Based on "La Chouette à aigrette blanche" Levaillant, Ois. Afr., 1, p. 43. (Guiana.)

Habitat.—Humid lowland and foothill forest, and second-growth woodland (Tropical and lower Subtropical zones).
Distribution.—*Resident* from southern Mexico (Veracruz, Oaxaca and Chiapas) south through Middle America (not recorded Belize), and in South America from Colombia, western Venezuela and the Guianas south, east of the Andes, to eastern Peru, central Bolivia and Amazonian Brazil.

Genus PULSATRIX Kaup

Pulsatrix Kaup, 1848, Isis von Oken, col. 771. Type, by monotypy, *Strix torquata* Daudin = *Strix perspicillata* Latham.

Pulsatrix perspicillata (Latham). SPECTACLED OWL.

Strix perspicillata Latham, 1790, Index Ornithol., 1, p. 58. Based on the "Spectacle Owl" Latham, Gen. Synop. Birds, suppl., 1, p. 50, pl. 107. (in Cayana = Cayenne.)

Habitat.—Humid lowland and foothill forest, second-growth woodland and plantations (Tropical and lower Subtropical zones).
Distribution.—*Resident* from southern Mexico (Veracruz, Oaxaca and Chiapas) south through Middle America, and in South America from Colombia, Venezuela (also Trinidad) and the Guianas south, west of the Andes to western Ecuador and

east of the Andes to eastern Peru, Bolivia, northwestern Argentina, Paraguay and southeastern Brazil.

Genus **BUBO** Duméril

Bubo Duméril, 1806, Zool. Anal., p. 34. Type, by tautonymy, *Strix bubo* Linnaeus.

Bubo virginianus (Gmelin). GREAT HORNED OWL. [375.]

Strix virginiana Gmelin, 1788, Syst. Nat., 1 (1), p. 287. Based mainly on the "Virginia Eared Owl" Latham, Gen. Synop. Birds, 1 (1), p. 119. (in omni America, etc. = Virginia.)

Habitat.—A wide variety of forested habitats, moist or arid, deciduous or evergreen lowland forest to open temperate woodland, including second-growth forest, swamps, orchards, parklands, riverine forest, brushy hillsides and semidesert, nesting primarily in large nests of other species, sometimes on cliffs, in barns or on artificial platforms (Tropical to Paramo zones, most commonly Subtropical and Temperate zones).

Distribution.—*Breeds* from western and central Alaska, central Yukon, northwestern and southern Mackenzie, southern Keewatin, northern Manitoba, northern Ontario, northern Quebec, Labrador and Newfoundland south throughout the Americas (except the West Indies and most other islands) to Tierra del Fuego.

Winters generally throughout the breeding range, with the northernmost populations being partially migratory, wintering south to southern Canada and the northern United States.

Genus **NYCTEA** Stephens

Nyctea Stephens, 1826, *in* Shaw, Gen. Zool., 13 (2), p. 62. Type, by tautonymy, *Strix erminea* Shaw = *Strix nyctea* Linnaeus = *Strix scandiaca* Linnaeus.

Nyctea scandiaca (Linnaeus). SNOWY OWL. [376.]

Strix scandiaca Linnaeus, 1758, Syst. Nat., ed. 10, 1, p. 92. (in Alpibus Lapponiæ = Lapland.)

Habitat.—Tundra, primarily where mounds, hillocks or rocks are present, nesting on the ground, in winter and migration occurring also in open country such as prairie, marshes, fields, pastures and sandy beaches.

Distribution.—*Breeds* in North America in the western Aleutians (Attu, Buldir), on Hall Island (in the Bering Sea), and from northern Alaska, northern Yukon (Herschel Island), and Prince Patrick and northern Ellesmere islands south to coastal western Alaska (to Hooper Bay), northern Mackenzie, southern Keewatin, northeastern Manitoba (Churchill), Southampton and Belcher islands, northern Quebec and northern Labrador; and in the Palearctic in northern Greenland, and from northern Scandinavia, northern Russia, southern Novaya Zemlya and northern Siberia south to the British Isles (rarely), southern Scandinavia, the limits of tundra in Eurasia, and the Commander Islands.

Winters irregularly from the breeding range in North America south to southern Canada, Minnesota and New York, casually or sporadically to central California (Santa Cruz County), southern Nevada, Utah, Colorado, Oklahoma, central and southeastern Texas, the Gulf states and Georgia (sight reports from central Florida); and in Eurasia south to Iceland, the British Isles, northern continental Europe, central Russia, northern China and Sakhalin.

Casual or accidental in Bermuda, the Azores, Mediterranean region, Iran, northwestern India and Japan.

Genus SURNIA Duméril

Surnia Duméril, 1806, Zool. Anal., p. 34. Type, by subsequent designation (G. R. Gray, 1840), *Strix funerea* Gmelin = *Strix ulula* Linnaeus.

Surnia ulula (Linnaeus). NORTHERN HAWK-OWL. [377.]

Strix Ulula Linnaeus, 1758, Syst. Nat., ed. 10, 1, p. 93. (in Europa = Sweden.)

Habitat.—Open coniferous or mixed coniferous-deciduous forest, forest edge and clearings, old deciduous forest burns, dense brushy areas (especially tamarack), swamps, scrubby second-growth woodland and muskeg, nesting in hollow trees and, occasionally, in old crow nests.

Distribution.—*Breeds* in North America from the limit of trees in western and central Alaska, central Yukon, northwestern and central Mackenzie, southern Keewatin, northern Manitoba, northern Ontario, northern Quebec, central Labrador and Newfoundland south to south-coastal Alaska (Kodiak Island), southern British Columbia, south-central Alberta, central Saskatchewan, southern Manitoba, northern Minnesota, south-central Ontario, northern Michigan (Isle Royale), southern Quebec and New Brunswick; and in Eurasia from northern Scandinavia, northern Russia and northern Siberia south to central Russia, northern Mongolia, northern Manchuria and Sakhalin.

Winters from the breeding range southward, in North America irregularly to southern Canada and northern Minnesota, casually to western Oregon, Idaho, Montana, North Dakota, Iowa, Wisconsin, southern Michigan, northern Ohio, Pennsylvania and New Jersey; and in Eurasia to the British Isles, continental Europe and southern Russia.

Accidental in Nebraska (Raymond).

Notes.—Known widely as the HAWK OWL.

Genus GLAUCIDIUM Boie

Glaucidium Boie, 1826, Isis von Oken, col. 970. Type, by subsequent designation (G. R. Gray, 1840), *Strix passerina* Linnaeus.

Glaucidium gnoma Wagler. NORTHERN PYGMY-OWL. [379.]

Glaucidium Gnoma Wagler, 1832, Isis von Oken, col. 275. (Mexico.)

Habitat.—Forested regions, both dense and open situations, in coniferous, hardwood, mixed and pine-oak associations, primarily in humid habitats, less frequently in arid ones, and foraging in open situations such as meadows adjacent to forest (Subtropical and Temperate zones).

Distribution.—*Resident* from central (and probably northern) British Columbia (absent from Queen Charlotte Islands), southwestern Alberta and western Montana south, mostly in mountainous regions, to southern California, the interior of Mexico, Guatemala and central Honduras, extending east as far as central Colorado, central New Mexico and extreme western Texas; also in the Cape district of southern Baja California. Recorded rarely but regularly (and possibly breeding) in southeastern Alaska (west to Yakutat).

Notes.—Relationships between the various New World species of *Glaucidium* are presently not well understood. A superspecific relationship between *G. gnoma* and *G. jardinii* has been proposed. Within *G. gnoma,* particularly in Arizona, populations in close proximity display differences in ecology (a northern form in coniferous forest, a southern one in pine-oak) and vocalizations, suggesting that two sibling species, *G. gnoma* and *G. pinicola* Nelson, 1910, are involved; further study is required to determine relationships.

Glaucidium jardinii (Bonaparte). ANDEAN PYGMY-OWL.

Palœnopsis jardinii Bonaparte, 1855, C. R. Acad. Sci. Paris, 41, p. 654. (Andes of Quito, Ecuador.)

Habitat.—Dense montane moist forest, forest edge and tangled undergrowth (Subtropical and Temperate zones).

Distribution.—*Resident* in the mountains of central Costa Rica and Panama (recorded Chiriquí and Veraguas); and in the Andes of South America from Colombia and western Venezuela south to Peru and central Bolivia.

Notes.—Also known as MOUNTAIN PYGMY-OWL. See comments under *G. gnoma.*

Glaucidium minutissimum (Wied). LEAST PYGMY-OWL.

Strix minutissima Wied, 1830, Beitr. Naturgesch. Bras., 3 (1), p. 242. (Interior of the Province of Bahia, Brazil.)

Habitat.—Humid lowland and foothill forest and forest edge, in western Mexico in lowland deciduous and gallery forest, locally in eastern Mexico to humid montane forest (Tropical to lower Subtropical zones, locally to upper Subtropical Zone).

Distribution.—*Resident* in the Pacific lowlands of Mexico from southern Sinaloa to south-central Oaxaca (Puerto Escondido area); on the Gulf-Caribbean slope of Middle America (not recorded Yucatan Peninsula or Nicaragua) to Costa Rica, Panama (also Pacific slope in eastern Panamá province, Canal Zone and Darién) and northwestern Colombia; and locally in eastern South America in Guyana, southeastern Peru, Paraguay, and central and northeastern Brazil.

Notes.—The populations on the Pacific slope of Mexico may constitute a distinct species, *G. palmarum* Nelson, 1901; in addition, the affinities of two races, *G. m. sanchezi* Lowery and Newman, 1949, and *G. m. occultum* Moore, 1947, are uncertain. Further study of this complex is required to determine relationships. See also comments under *G. gnoma.*

Glaucidium brasilianum (Gmelin). FERRUGINOUS PYGMY-OWL. [380.]

Strix brasiliana Gmelin, 1788, Syst. Nat., 1 (1), p. 289. Based on "Le Hibou de Brésil" Brisson, Ornithologie, 1, p. 499. (in Brasilia = Ceara, Brazil.)

Habitat.—Open woodland, second growth, coffee plantations, scrubby pastures, thorn scrub, partially cleared lands, and open situations with scattered trees and bushes, primarily in arid habitats (Tropical and lower Subtropical zones).

Distribution.—*Resident* from south-central Arizona (north to Phoenix area), Sonora, Chihuahua, Coahuila, Nuevo León and southern Texas (north to Starr and Kenedy counties) south through Mexico (including Isla Cancun off Quintana Roo), Belize, Guatemala (Pacific slope and arid interior valleys), El Salvador, Honduras, Nicaragua, Costa Rica (Pacific slope, very rare on Caribbean drainage) and Panama (Pacific slope east to western Panamá province), and in South America from the coastal lowlands of Colombia, Venezuela (also Margarita Island and Trinidad) and the Guianas south, east of the Andes to eastern Peru, Bolivia, central Argentina and Uruguay (also on Pacific coast of Peru and northern Chile).

Notes.—Also known as FERRUGINOUS OWL. Patagonian *G. nanum* (King, 1827) variously has been treated as conspecific or as forming a superspecies with *G. brasilianum*. See also comments under *G. gnoma*.

Glaucidium siju (d'Orbigny). CUBAN PYGMY-OWL.

Noctua siju d'Orbigny, 1839, *in* La Sagra, Hist. Fis. Pol. Nat. Cuba, Ois., p. 41, pl. 3. (Cuba.)

Habitat.—Open woodland and forest edge.
Distribution.—*Resident* on Cuba and the Isle of Pines.
Notes.—See comments under *G. gnoma*.

Genus MICRATHENE Coues

Micrathene Coues, 1866, Proc. Acad. Nat. Sci. Philadelphia, 18, p. 51. Type, by original designation, *Athene whitneyi* Cooper.
Micropallas Coues, 1889, Auk, 6, p. 71. Type, by original designation, *Athene whitneyi* Cooper.

Micrathene whitneyi (Cooper). ELF OWL. [381.]

Athene whitneyi Cooper, 1861, Proc. Calif. Acad. Sci., ser. 1, 2, p. 118. (Fort Mojave, latitude 35° [N.], Colorado Valley [Arizona].)

Habitat.—Desert with giant cacti, oak woodland and riparian woodland, especially with sycamores (Tropical and lower Subtropical zones).

Distribution.—*Breeds* from extreme southern Nevada (Colorado River, opposite Fort Mohave, Arizona), southeastern California (formerly west to central Riverside County), central Arizona, southwestern New Mexico, western Texas (Big Bend), Coahuila, Nuevo León and southern Texas (lower Rio Grande Valley) south to Sonora, Guanajuato and Puebla, probably elsewhere in central Mexico; also in southern Baja California (Cape district) and the Revillagigedo Islands (Socorro).

Winters from southern Sinaloa, Michoacán and Morelos south to Guerrero and northern Oaxaca, certainly also elsewhere in central Mexico; resident on Socorro Island and in Baja California, where recorded north to lat. 28°10′N., possibly only as a vagrant.

In migration occurs casually in east-central New Mexico.

Genus ATHENE Boie

Athene Boie, 1822, Isis von Oken, col. 549. Type, by subsequent designation (G. R. Gray, 1841), *A. noctua* (Retz.) Boie, Pl. enl. 439. *Str. passerina* Auct. = *Strix noctua* Scopoli.

Speotyto Gloger, 1842, Gemein. Hanb. Hilfsb. Naturgesch. (1841), p. 226. Type, by monotypy, *Strix cunicularia* Molina.

Athene cunicularia (Molina). BURROWING OWL. [378.]

Strix Cunicularia Molina, 1782, Saggio Stor. Nat. Chili, p. 263. (Chili = Chile.)

Habitat.—Open grasslands, especially prairie, plains and savanna, sometimes in open areas such as vacant lots near human habitation or airports, nesting in mammal burrows in the ground (Tropical to Paramo zones).

Distribution.—*Breeds* from southern interior British Columbia, southern Alberta, southern Saskatchewan and southern Manitoba south through eastern Washington, central Oregon and California (including the Farallon and Channel islands) to Baja California (including many coastal islands, and on Guadalupe Island), east to western Minnesota, northwestern Iowa, western Missouri, Oklahoma, eastern Texas and Louisiana (Baton Rouge), and south to central Mexico (including Isla Clarión in the Revillagigedo group, but southern limits of the breeding range in the interior in Mexico not known); in Florida (north to Suwannee and Duval counties), the Bahamas, western Cuba (western Pinar del Rio), eastern Cuba (near Guantánamo), Hispaniola (including Gonâve and Beata islands) and, at least formerly, the northern Lesser Antilles (St. Kitts, Nevis, Antigua, Redonda and Marie Galante); and locally in South America from Colombia and Venezuela (including Margarita Island) south to northern Tierra del Fuego.

Winters in North America and Middle America in general through the breeding range, except for the northern portions in the Great Basin and Great Plains regions, and regularly south to southern Mexico, Guatemala and El Salvador, casually to Honduras (Monte Redondo), Costa Rica (Los Cuadros on Volcán Irazú) and Panama (Divalá in Chiriquí); and through the breeding range in the West Indies and South America, casually to Cuba.

Casual north and east in eastern North America to Wisconsin, Michigan, southern Ontario, southern Quebec, Maine, New Brunswick (sight record), Massachusetts and North Carolina, and in the Gulf states to Alabama and northwestern Florida.

Notes.—Often placed in the monotypic genus *Speotyto*.

Genus CICCABA Wagler

Ciccaba Wagler, 1832, Isis von Oken, col. 1222. Type, by monotypy, *Ciccaba huhula* = *Strix huhula* Daudin.

Ciccaba virgata (Cassin). MOTTLED OWL.

Syrnium virgatum Cassin, 1849, Proc. Acad. Nat. Sci. Philadelphia, 4 (1848), p. 124. (South America = Bogotá, Colombia.)

Habitat.—Dense forest, open woodland and second growth, both in arid and humid regions (Tropical and Subtropical zones).

Distribution.—*Resident* from southern Sonora, Sinaloa, Nayarit, Jalisco, Guanajuato, San Luis Potosí, southern Nuevo León and Tamaulipas south through Middle America (including the Yucatan Peninsula), and in South America from Colombia, Venezuela (also Trinidad) and the Guianas south, west of the Andes to western Ecuador and east of the Andes to Bolivia, Paraguay and northeastern Argentina.

Notes.—Also known as MOTTLED WOOD-OWL.

Ciccaba nigrolineata Sclater. BLACK-AND-WHITE OWL.

Ciccaba nigrolineata Sclater, 1859, Proc. Zool. Soc. London, p. 131. (In Mexico Meridionali = Oaxaca.)

Habitat.—Humid lowland and foothill forest and forest edge, less frequently in deciduous woodland and mangrove swamps (Tropical and lower Subtropical zones).

Distribution.—*Resident* from eastern and southern Mexico (southeastern San Luis Potosí, Veracruz, Oaxaca, Chiapas and southern Quintana Roo) south locally through Middle America, and in South America from Colombia east to northwestern Venezuela and south, west of the Andes, to western Ecuador and northwestern Peru.

Notes.—*C. nigrolineata* and the South American *C. huhula* (Daudin, 1800) are regarded as conspecific by some authors; they constitute at least a superspecies.

Genus **STRIX** Linnaeus

Strix Linnaeus, 1758, Syst. Nat., ed. 10, 1, p. 92. Type, by tautonymy, *Strix stridula* Linnaeus (*Strix,* prebinomial specific name, in synonymy) = *Strix aluco* Linnaeus.

Strix occidentalis (Xántus de Vesey). SPOTTED OWL. [369.]

Syrnium occidentale Xántus de Vesey, 1860, Proc. Acad. Nat. Sci. Philadelphia, 11 (1859), p. 193. (Fort Tejon, California.)

Habitat.—Dense forest, both coniferous (primarily fir) and hardwood, the latter especially in shaded, steep-walled canyons (Temperate Zone).

Distribution.—*Resident* in the mountains and in humid coastal forest from southwestern British Columbia (north to Atka Lake, east to Manning Provincial Park) south through western Washington and western Oregon to southern California (San Diego County) and, probably, northern Baja California (Sierra San Pedro Mártir); and in the Rocky Mountain region from southern Utah (Zion Canyon and Navajo Mountain) and central Colorado south through the mountains of Arizona, New Mexico, extreme western Texas (Guadalupe Mountains), northern Sonora, Chihuahua and Nuevo León to Jalisco, Michoacán and Guanajuato.

Notes.—Some authors consider *S. occidentalis* and *S. varia* (along with *S. fulvescens*) as constituting a superspecies.

Strix varia Barton. BARRED OWL. [368.]

Strix varius Barton, 1799, Fragm. Nat. Hist. Pa., p. 11. (Philadelphia, Pennsylvania.)

Habitat.—Dense woodland and forest (coniferous or hardwood), swamps, wooded river valleys, and cabbage palm-live oak hammocks, especially where bordering streams, marshes and meadows (Subtropical and Temperate zones).

Distribution.—*Resident* from northern Washington, southern and eastern British Columbia, and extreme northwestern Montana (Lincoln County) east across central Alberta and central Saskatchewan, and from southern Manitoba, central Ontario, southern Quebec (including Anticosti Island), New Brunswick, Prince Edward Island and Nova Scotia south to central and southern Texas, the Gulf coast and southern Florida, and west to southeastern South Dakota (formerly), eastern Nebraska, central Kansas and central Oklahoma; and in the Central Plateau of Mexico from Durango south to Guerrero (Mount Teotepec) and Oaxaca (La Parada and Cerro San Felipe), and east to San Luis Potosí, Puebla and Veracruz. Recorded in summer (and probably breeding) in southeastern Alaska, southwestern British Columbia and northeastern Oregon.

Northernmost populations are partially migratory, individuals occasionally ranging to the Gulf coast.

Notes.—*S. varia* and *S. fulvescens* are closely related and constitute a superspecies; they are considered conspecific by some authors. See also comments under *S. occidentalis*.

Strix fulvescens (Sclater and Salvin). FULVOUS OWL.

Syrnium fulvescens Sclater and Salvin, 1868, Proc. Zool. Soc. London, p. 58. (Guatemala.)

Habitat.—Humid montane forest and pine-oak association (Subtropical and lower Temperate zones).

Distribution.—*Resident* in the mountains of Oaxaca (Totontepec), Chiapas, Guatemala, El Salvador and Honduras.

Notes.—See comments under *S. varia*.

Strix nebulosa Forster. GREAT GRAY OWL. [370.]

Strix nebulosa J. R. Forster, 1772, Philos. Trans. R. Soc. London, 62, p. 424. (Severn River [northwestern Ontario].)

Habitat.—Dense coniferous and hardwood forest, especially pine, spruce, paper birch and poplar, nesting primarily in old hawk nests, in migration and winter also in second growth, especially near water, foraging in wet meadows.

Distribution.—*Breeds* in North America from central Alaska, northern Yukon, northwestern and central Mackenzie, northern Manitoba and northern Ontario south locally in the interior to the mountains of southwestern Oregon, California (central Sierra Nevada), northern Idaho, western Montana, northwestern Wyoming, central Alberta, central Saskatchewan, southern Manitoba, northern Minnesota, northern Wisconsin and south-central Ontario; and in Eurasia from northern Scandinavia, northern Russia and northern Siberia south to central Russia, northern Mongolia, northern Manchuria, Amurland and Sakhalin. Recorded in summer (and possibly breeding) in southern Quebec.

Winters generally through the breeding range, in central and eastern North America wandering south irregularly to southern Montana, North Dakota, southern Minnesota, southern Wisconsin, northern Michigan, southern Ontario and central New York, casually as far as southern Idaho, Nebraska, Iowa, Indiana, Ohio, and from southern and eastern Quebec, New Brunswick and Nova Scotia south to Pennsylvania and New Jersey.

Genus ASIO Brisson

Asio Brisson, 1760, Ornithologie, 1, pp. 28, 477. Type, by tautonymy, *Asio* Brisson = *Strix otus* Linnaeus.
Rhinoptynx Kaup, 1851, Arch. Naturgesch., 17, p. 107. Type, by subsequent

designation (Sharpe, 1875), *Otus mexicanus* Cuv. = *Bubo clamator* Vieillot.

Asio otus (Linnaeus). LONG-EARED OWL. [366.]

Strix Otus Linnaeus, 1758, Syst. Nat., ed. 10, 1, p. 92. (in Europa = Sweden.)

Habitat.—Coniferous or mixed coniferous-deciduous forest, especially near water, less frequently in hardwoods or second growth, roosting in very dense, thick cover, less commonly in caves or cracks in canyon walls.

Distribution.—*Breeds* in North America from southern and eastern British Columbia, northern Yukon, southwestern Mackenzie, northern Saskatchewan, central Manitoba, central Ontario, southern Quebec, New Brunswick, Prince Edward Island and Nova Scotia south to northwestern Baja California (lat. 30°N.), southern Arizona, southern New Mexico, northern Nuevo León, western and central Texas, central Oklahoma, Arkansas, Missouri, central Illinois, western and northern Indiana, northern Ohio, Pennsylvania (also in the mountains to western Virginia), New York and New England; and in Eurasia from the British Isles, Scandinavia, northern Russia and northern Siberia south to the Azores, Canary Islands, northwestern Africa, southern Europe, Asia Minor, Iran, the Himalayas, Manchuria, Formosa and Korea.

Winters in North America from southern Canada south to northern Baja California (casually to Los Coronados, Cedros and Tiburón islands), Jalisco, the state of México, Distrito Federal, Puebla, San Luis Potosí, southern Texas, the Gulf coast and Georgia, casually to Florida, Bermuda and Cuba; and in the Old World from the breeding range south to northern Africa, Iraq, India and southern China.

Casual or accidental in southeastern Alaska (Taku River), Labrador (Red Bay) and western Cuba.

Asio stygius (Wagler). STYGIAN OWL.

Nyctalops stygius Wagler, 1832, Isis von Oken, col. 1222. (Brazil or South Africa = Minas Gerais, Brazil.)

Habitat.—Humid or semi-arid forest (Tropical to Temperate zones).

Distribution.—*Resident* locally in Middle America in northeastern Sinaloa, northwestern Durango, Guerrero (Omilteme), Veracruz (Mirador), Chiapas (Volcán Tacaná), Guatemala (Cobán), Belize and north-central Nicaragua; in the Greater Antilles (Cuba, the Isle of Pines, Hispaniola and Gonâve Island); and locally in South America in Colombia, western Venezuela, Ecuador, Brazil, Paraguay and northern Argentina. Recorded also (and possibly resident) on Cozumel Island, Quintana Roo.

Asio clamator (Vieillot). STRIPED OWL.

Bubo Clamator Vieillot, 1808, Hist. Nat. Ois. Am. Sept., 1 (1807), pl. 20. (depuis Caienne jusq'à la Baie d'Hudson = Cayenne.)

Habitat.—Open grassy and shrubby areas, savanna, forest edge and lowland moist forest, generally in open woodland situations (Tropical Zone).

Distribution.—*Resident* locally on the Gulf-Caribbean slope in northern Oaxaca, Veracruz, Guatemala, Honduras and Nicaragua, on the Pacific slope in El Salvador, on both slopes of Costa Rica and Panama, and in South America from eastern Colombia, Venezuela (also Tobago) and the Guianas south, east of the Andes, to eastern Peru, Bolivia, northern Argentina and Uruguay.

Notes.—Frequently placed in the monotypic genus *Rhinoptynx.*

Asio flammeus (Pontoppidan). SHORT-EARED OWL. [367.]

Strix flammea Pontoppidan, 1763, Dan. Atlas, 1, p. 617, pl. 25. (Sweden.)

Habitat.—Open country, including prairie, meadows, tundra, moorlands, marshes, savanna and open woodland, in the Hawaiian Islands also around towns, nesting on the ground.

Distribution.—*Breeds* in the Hawaiian Islands (main islands from Kauai eastward), and on Ponape in the Caroline Islands; in North America from northern Alaska, northern Yukon, northern Mackenzie, central Keewatin, southern Baffin Island (probably), northern Quebec, northern Labrador and Newfoundland south to the eastern Aleutian Islands (west to Unalaska), southern Alaska, central (and formerly southern) California, northern Nevada, Utah, northeastern Colorado, Kansas, Missouri, southern Illinois, northern Indiana, northern Ohio, Pennsylvania, New Jersey and northern (formerly coastal) Virginia; in the Greater Antilles (Cuba, Hispaniola and Puerto Rico); and in Eurasia from Iceland, the British Isles, Scandinavia, northern Russia and northern Siberia south to southern Europe, Afghanistan, Transbaicalia, northern Mongolia, northern Manchuria, Anadyrland, Sakhalin, the northern Kurile Islands and Kamchatka.

Winters generally in the breeding range, in the Hawaiian Islands ranging casually to the western islands (Kure, Midway, and casually east to French Frigate Shoals); in North America and Middle America mostly from southern Canada south to southern Baja California (casually to Los Coronados Islands and Isla Tiburón), Oaxaca, Puebla, Veracruz, the Gulf coast and southern Florida; and in the Old World south to northwestern Africa, the Mediterranean region, northeastern Africa, Asia Minor, Ceylon, the Malay Peninsula, southern China and Japan, casually to the Azores, eastern Atlantic islands, Borneo, the Philippines and Ryukyu Islands.

Casual or accidental in the Revillagigedo Islands (Clarión), Guatemala (Volcán de Agua), the Bahamas (Grand Turk), Lesser Antilles (St. Barthélemy), Bermuda and Greenland.

Genus **PSEUDOSCOPS** Kaup

Pseudoscops Kaup, 1848, Isis von Oken, col. 769. Type, by monotypy, *Ephialtes grammicus* Gosse.

Pseudoscops grammicus (Gosse). JAMAICAN OWL.

Ephialtes grammicus Gosse, 1847, Birds Jamaica, p. 19 (footnote). (Bluefields Mountains and Tait-Shafton, Jamaica = Tait-Shafton.)

Habitat.—Open woodland and open country with scattered trees.
Distribution.—*Resident* on Jamaica.

Genus **AEGOLIUS** Kaup

Aegolius Kaup, 1829, Skizz. Entw.-Ges. Eur. Thierw., p. 34. Type, by monotypy, *Strix tengmalmi* Gmelin = *Strix funereus* Linnaeus.

Aegolius funereus (Linnaeus). BOREAL OWL. [371.]

> *Strix funereus* Linnaeus, 1758, Syst. Nat., ed. 10, 1, p. 93. (in Europa = Sweden.)

Habitat.—Dense coniferous forest, mixed coniferous-hardwood forest, and thickets of alder, aspen or stunted spruce, most commonly in proximity to open grassy situations, nesting mostly in old woodpecker holes in paper birch and poplar.

Distribution.—*Breeds* in North America to tree line from central Alaska, central Yukon, southern Mackenzie, northern Saskatchewan, northern Manitoba, northern Ontario, central (and probably northern) Quebec, Labrador and Newfoundland (probably) south to southern Alaska (Kodiak Island), northern British Columbia, central Alberta, central Saskatchewan, southern Manitoba, northeastern Minnesota (near Grand Marais), western and central Ontario, southern Quebec (Magdalen Islands) and New Brunswick (Grand Manan), also in northwestern Wyoming (Yellowstone and Grand Teton) and Colorado (Rocky Mountain National Park); and in Eurasia from northern Scandinavia, northern Russia and northern Siberia south to the mountains of southern Europe, the western Himalayas, western China, Sakhalin and Kamchatka.

Winters generally in the breeding range, in North America south irregularly to southern British Columbia, central Montana, North Dakota, southern Minnesota, central Wisconsin, southern Michigan, southern Ontario, New York and New England, casually to southern Oregon, Idaho, Colorado, Nebraska, Illinois, Pennsylvania and New Jersey; and in Eurasia to southern Europe, Ussuriland, the Kurile Islands and Japan.

Accidental in the Pribilofs (St. Paul).

Notes.—Known in Old World literature as TENGMALM'S OWL.

Aegolius acadicus (Gmelin). NORTHERN SAW-WHET OWL. [372.]

> *Strix acadica* Gmelin, 1788, Syst. Nat., 1 (1), p. 296. Based on the "Acadian Owl" Latham, Gen. Synop. Birds, 1 (1), p. 149, pl. 5, fig. 2. (in America septentrionali = Nova Scotia.)

Habitat.—Dense coniferous or mixed coniferous-hardwood forest, cedar groves, alder thickets and tamarack bogs, occurring in migration and winter also in dense second growth, brushy areas, arid scrub and open buildings.

Distribution.—*Breeds* from southern Alaska (west to the base of the Alaska Peninsula), central British Columbia (including the Queen Charlotte Islands), central Alberta, central Saskatchewan, central Manitoba, central Ontario, southern Quebec (possibly also Anticosti Island), northern New Brunswick, Prince Edward Island and Nova Scotia south to the mountains of southern California (also on Santa Cruz and Santa Catalina islands), locally in the highlands of Mexico to Oaxaca (Cerro San Felipe), and to extreme western Texas, central Oklahoma, central Missouri, southern Wisconsin, southern Michigan, central Ohio, West Virginia, western Maryland and New York (Long Island); also in the mountains of eastern Tennessee and western North Carolina.

Winters generally throughout the breeding range, south irregularly or casually to desert regions of southern California and southern Arizona, to the Gulf coast (eastern Texas eastward), and through the Atlantic states to central Florida.

Casual or accidental on islands in the Bering Sea (St. Lawrence Island, and St. Paul in the Pribilofs), Newfoundland and Bermuda.

Notes.—*A. acadicus* and *A. ridgwayi* are closely related and have been considered conspecific [SAW-WHET OWL] by a few authors; they constitute a superspecies.

Aegolius ridgwayi (Alfaro). UNSPOTTED SAW-WHET OWL.

Cryptoglaux ridgwayi Alfaro, 1905, Proc. Biol. Soc. Wash., 18, p. 217. (Cerro de la Candelaria, near Escasú, Costa Rica.)

Habitat.—Open pine-oak woodland and moist montane forest edge, also recorded from farm buildings (Subtropical and lower Temperate zones).

Distribution.—*Resident* locally in Chiapas (Volcán Tacaná), Guatemala (Sacapulas, Quetzaltenango and Soloma), El Salvador (Los Esesmiles) and Costa Rica (Volcán Irazú, and Candelaria and Dota mountains). The accuracy of locality of a specimen reportedly taken in Oaxaca (Amatepec) has recently been questioned; occurrence of this species west of the Isthmus of Tehuantepec requires confirmation.

Notes.—See comments under *A. acadicus.*

Order **CAPRIMULGIFORMES**: Goatsuckers, Oilbirds and Allies

Family **CAPRIMULGIDAE**: Goatsuckers

Subfamily CHORDEILINAE: Nighthawks

Genus **LUROCALIS** Cassin

Lucrocalis Cassin, 1851, Proc. Acad. Nat. Sci. Philadelphia, 5, p. 189. Type, by subsequent designation (G. R. Gray, 1855), *Caprimulgus nattereri* Temminck = *Caprimulgus semitorquatus* Gmelin.

Lurocalis semitorquatus (Gmelin). SHORT-TAILED NIGHTHAWK.

Caprimulgus semitorquatus Gmelin, 1789, Syst. Nat., 1 (2), p. 1031. Based on the "White-collared Goatsucker" Latham, Gen. Synop. Birds, 2 (2), p. 599. (in Cayenna = Cayenne.)

Habitat.—Humid lowland and foothill forest (up to montane forest in South America), foraging in partly open situations adjacent to forest (Tropical and lower Subtropical zones, in South America to Temperate Zone).

Distribution.—*Resident* from northeastern Nicaragua (Río Banbana) south through Costa Rica (entire Caribbean slope, and Pacific southwest) and Panama (both slopes, including Isla Cébaco), and in South America from Colombia, Venezuela (also Trinidad) and the Guianas south to central and eastern Peru, central Bolivia, northern Argentina and central Brazil.

Notes.—Also known as SEMICOLLARED NIGHTHAWK. The Amazonian and Andean forms in South America are often treated as separate species, *L. rufiventris* Taczanowski, 1884, and *L. nattereri* (Temminck, 1822), respectively.

Genus **CHORDEILES** Swainson

Chordeiles [subgenus] Swainson, 1832, *in* Swainson and Richardson, Fauna Bor.-Am., 2 (1831), pp. 337, 496. Type, by original designation, *Caprimulgus virginianus* Gmelin = *Caprimulgus minor* Forster.

Chordeiles acutipennis (Hermann). LESSER NIGHTHAWK. [421.]

Caprimulgus acutipennis Hermann, 1783, Tabula Affinit. Anim., p. 230. Based mainly on "Crapaud-volant ou Tette-chevre de la Guiane" Daubenton, Planches Enlum., pl. 732. (Cayenne.)

Habitat.—Open country, desert regions, scrub, savanna and cultivated areas, primarily in arid habitats (Tropical and Subtropical zones).

Distribution.—*Breeds* from central interior California, southern Nevada, extreme southwestern Utah, central Arizona, central New Mexico, and central and southeastern Texas south to southern Baja California, and through the lowlands of both slopes of Mexico (including the Yucatan Peninsula and Cozumel Island) to Belize and Guatemala, also locally in Honduras (arid interior valleys on Caribbean drainage), Nicaragua (Tipitapa), Costa Rica (Pacific slope of Guanacaste, and Puerto Cortés area) and Panama (Coclé and western Panamá province); and in South America from Colombia, Venezuela (also Margarita Island, Tobago and Trinidad) and the Guianas south, generally throughout, to Peru, central Bolivia, Paraguay and southern Brazil.

Winters from southern Baja California, central Sinaloa, Durango and Veracruz (casually from southern California and southwestern Arizona) south through Middle America and South America to the limits of the breeding range, casually to Chile.

Migrates regularly through Middle America (including the Bay Islands off Honduras), most commonly on the Pacific slope, ranging casually east to southern Louisiana.

Casual or accidental in Colorado (Trinidad), north-central New Mexico, Oklahoma (Boise City), Ontario (Point Pelee), Alabama (Dauphin Island), Florida (St. George Island and Dry Tortugas) and Bermuda.

Notes.—Also known as TRILLING NIGHTHAWK.

Chordeiles minor (Forster). COMMON NIGHTHAWK. [420.]

Caprimulgus minor J. R. Forster, 1771, Cat. Anim. N. Am., p. 13. Based on "The Whip-poor Will" Catesby, Nat. Hist. Carolina, 2, app., p. 16. (No locality given = South Carolina.)

Habitat.—A wide variety of open and semi-open situations, especially in savanna, grasslands, fields, and around human habitation, including cities and towns, frequently breeding on flat gravel roofs of buildings (Tropical to Temperate zones).

Distribution.—*Breeds* from southern Yukon, southern Mackenzie, northern Saskatchewan, northern Manitoba, northern Ontario, central Quebec, southern Labrador and Nova Scotia south to southern British Columbia (including Vancouver Island), southern California (San Bernardino Mountains), southern Nevada, southern Arizona, northeastern Sonora, Chihuahua, Texas, Tamaulipas, the Gulf coast and southern Florida, and south locally in Middle America through Mexico (recorded Durango, and in eastern Mexico south to Chiapas and the Yucatan Peninsula), the pine savanna of Belize and the Mosquitia of eastern Honduras and Nicaragua, and Costa Rica and Panama (east to eastern Panamá province).

Winters throughout South America south to northern Argentina.

In migration occurs throughout Middle America and the West Indies, including most islands in the Caribbean Sea and those off Venezuela, and (in fall) in southeastern Alaska.

Casual north to south-coastal, central and northern Alaska, northern Yukon, Melville Island, coastal Labrador, Newfoundland and Greenland; in Bermuda and Europe; and at sea near the Azores.

Notes.—Also known as BOOMING NIGHTHAWK. *C. minor* and *C. gundlachii* are often treated as conspecific, despite differences in vocalizations (but see Eisenmann, 1962, Am. Mus. Novit., no. 2094, pp. 9–10); they constitute a superspecies.

Chordeiles gundlachii Lawrence. ANTILLEAN NIGHTHAWK. [420.1.]

> *Chordeiles gundlachii* Lawrence, 1857, Ann. Lyc. Nat. Hist. N.Y., 6, p. 165. (Cuba.)

Habitat.—Open and semi-open situations.

Distribution.—*Breeds* in the Florida Keys (Stock Island, near Key West), the Bahamas, Greater Antilles (east to the Virgin Islands, including small cays off Cuba, Gonâve and Tortue) and Cayman Islands. Occurs in summer also on the southern Florida mainland.

Winters presumably in South America.

In migration recorded in the Swan Islands, in the western Caribbean Sea.

Casual in summer in Louisiana (New Orleans).

Notes.—See comments under *C. minor*.

Subfamily CAPRIMULGINAE: Nightjars

Genus **NYCTIDROMUS** Gould

> *Nyctidromus* Gould, 1838, Icones Avium, pt. 2, pl. [12] and text. Type, by monotypy, *Nyctidromus derbyanus* Gould = *Caprimulgus albicollis* Gmelin.

Nyctidromus albicollis (Gmelin). COMMON PAURAQUE. [419.]

> *Caprimulgus albicollis* Gmelin, 1789, Syst. Nat., 1 (2), p. 1030. Based on the "White-throated Goatsucker" Latham, Gen. Synop. Birds, 2 (2), p. 596. (in Cayenna = Cayenne.)

Habitat.—Open woodland, forest edge and clearings, shrubby areas, second growth, arid scrub, roadsides and plantations, less commonly in denser forest (Tropical and Subtropical zones).

Distribution.—*Resident* from Sinaloa, southern Texas (McMullen and Refugio counties, probably north to Zavala, Frio and De Witt counties), Nuevo León and Tamaulipas south along both slopes of Middle America (including the Tres Marias, Mujeres and Cozumel islands off Mexico, and the Pearl Islands off Panama), and in South America from Colombia, Venezuela (also Trinidad) and the Guianas south, west of the Andes to northwestern Peru and east of the Andes to eastern Peru, Bolivia, northern Argentina and southern Brazil.

Notes.—Formerly known as the PAURAQUE.

Genus **PHALAENOPTILUS** Ridgway.

> *Phalænoptilus* Ridgway, 1880, Proc. U.S. Natl. Mus., 3, p. 5. Type, by original designation, *Caprimulgus nuttallii* Audubon.

Phalaenoptilus nuttallii (Audubon). COMMON POORWILL. [418.]

> *Caprimulgus Nuttallii* Audubon, 1844, Birds Am. (octavo ed.), 7, p. 350, pl. 495. (upper Missouri = between Fort Pierre and mouth of the Cheyenne River, South Dakota.)

Habitat.—Scrubby and bushy areas, prairie, desert, rocky canyons, open woodland and broken forest, primarily in arid or semi-arid habitats.

Distribution.—*Breeds* from southern interior British Columbia, Montana, southeastern Alberta, southwestern Saskatchewan (probably), southwestern (and formerly also southeastern) South Dakota and Nebraska south through eastern Washington, central and eastern Oregon and California to southern Baja California, Jalisco, Durango, San Luis Potosí and Coahuila, and east to eastern Kansas, northwestern Oklahoma and central Texas.

Winters in southern parts of the breeding range in California and Arizona (probably also farther east), sometimes in a torpid condition, and south to the · limits of the breeding range in Mexico.

Accidental in southern Manitoba (Treesbank), Minnesota (Swift County) and eastern Oklahoma (Oklahoma City).

Notes.—Formerly known as the POORWILL.

Genus SIPHONORHIS Sclater

> *Siphonorhis* Sclater, 1861, Proc. Zool. Soc. London, p. 77. Type, by original designation, *Caprimulgus americanus* Linnaeus.

†**Siphonorhis americanus** (Linnaeus). JAMAICAN PAURAQUE.

> *Caprimulgus americanus* Linnaeus, 1758, Syst. Nat., ed. 10, 1, p. 193. Based on the "Small wood owl" Sloane, Voy. Jamaica, 2, p. 296, pl. 255, fig. 1. (in America calidiore = Jamaica.)

Habitat.—Scrubby woods and partly open situations in arid or semi-arid regions.

Distribution.—EXTINCT. Formerly *resident* on Jamaica; last collected in Trelawny in September 1859.

Notes.—*S. americanus* and *S. brewsteri* are closely related and constitute a superspecies.

Siphonorhis brewsteri (Chapman). LEAST PAURAQUE.

> *Microsiphonorhis brewsteri* Chapman, 1917, Bull. Am. Mus. Nat. Hist., 37, p. 329. (Túbano, Province of Azua, Dominican Republic.)

Habitat.—Semi-arid situations in the lowlands, especially in scrubby woodland.

Distribution.—*Resident* locally on Hispaniola (including Gonâve Island).

Notes.—See comments under *S. americanus.*

Genus NYCTIPHRYNUS Bonaparte

> *Nyctiphrynus* Bonaparte, 1857, Riv. Contemp., 9, p. 215. Type, by subsequent designation (Oberholser, 1914), *Caprimulgus ocellatus* Tschudi.

Otophanes Brewster, 1888, Auk, 5, p. 88. Type, by original designation, *Otophanes mcleodii* Brewster.
Nyctagreus Nelson, 1901, Proc. Biol. Soc. Wash., 14, p. 171. Type, by original designation, *Caprimulgus yucatanicus* Hartert.

Nyctiphrynus mcleodii (Brewster). EARED POORWILL.

Otophanes mcleodii Brewster, 1888, Auk, 5, p. 89. (Sierra Madre of Chihuahua, Mexico.)

Habitat.—Open oak woodland and pine-oak association in semi-arid situations (upper Tropical and lower Subtropical zones).
Distribution.—*Resident* locally in Chihuahua (including near the Sonora-Chihuahua border), Jalisco, Colima and Guerrero.
Casual (possibly resident) in Oaxaca (San Gabriel Mixtepec).
Notes.—Often placed in the genus *Otophanes.*

Nyctiphrynus yucatanicus (Hartert). YUCATAN POORWILL.

Caprimulgus yucatanicus Hartert, 1892, Cat. Birds Br. Mus., 16, pp. xv, 525, 575. (Tizimin, Yucatan.)

Habitat.—Open woodland and partly open situations in arid and semi-arid lowlands, foraging at night in open areas (Tropical Zone).
Distribution.—*Resident* in the Yucatan Peninsula, northern Guatemala (Petén) and Belize.
Notes.—Often placed in the genus *Otophanes.*

Nyctiphrynus ocellatus (Tschudi). OCELLATED POORWILL.

Caprimulgus ocellatus Tschudi, 1844, Arch. Naturgesch., 10, p. 268. (Republica Peruana = Peru.)

Habitat.—Humid lowland forest (Tropical Zone).
Distribution.—*Resident* (presumably) in northern Nicaragua (where known from a single specimen taken at Peña Blanca, Depto. de Jinotega); and in South America west of the Andes from western Colombia to western Ecuador, and east of the Andes from eastern Peru, northern Bolivia and Amazonian Brazil south to Paraguay and northeastern Argentina; a sight report for Panama (Canal Zone) requires confirmation.

Genus **CAPRIMULGUS** Linnaeus

Caprimulgus Linnaeus, 1758, Syst. Nat., ed. 10, 1, p. 193. Type, by tautonymy, *Caprimulgus europaeus* Linnaeus (*Caprimulgus,* prebinomial specific name, in synonymy).
Antrostomus Bonaparte, 1838, Geogr. Comp. List, p. 8. Type, by subsequent designation (G. R. Gray, 1840), *Caprimulgus carolinensis* Gmelin.
Antiurus Ridgway, 1912, Proc. Biol. Soc. Wash., 25, p. 98. Type, by original designation, *Stenopsis maculicaudus* Lawrence.
Setochalcis Oberholser, 1914, Bull. U.S. Natl. Mus., no. 86, p. 11. Type, by original designation, *Caprimulgus vociferus* Wilson.

Caprimulgus carolinensis Gmelin. CHUCK-WILL'S-WIDOW. [416.]

Caprimulgus carolinensis Gmelin, 1789, Syst. Nat., 1 (2), p. 1028. Based mainly on "The Goat Sucker of Carolina" Catesby, Nat. Hist. Carolina, 1, p. 8, pl. 8. (in Virginia et Carolina = South Carolina.)

Habitat.—Deciduous forest, pine-oak association and live-oak groves, in migration and winter also in open woodland, scrub and palmetto thickets.

Distribution.—*Breeds* from eastern Kansas, southern Iowa, central Illinois, central Indiana, extreme southern Ontario, central and eastern Ohio, central West Virginia (probably), Maryland, New Jersey and southern New York (Long Island) and (probably) Massachusetts (Martha's Vineyard) south to south-central and southeastern Texas, the Gulf coast, southern Florida and the northern Bahamas (Andros, one record). Recorded sporadically in summer north to southern Wisconsin, southern Michigan and Pennsylvania.

Winters from southeastern Texas and Louisiana south through Middle America (reported on the Gulf-Caribbean slope of eastern Mexico and the Pacific slope of Oaxaca, on both slopes south of Mexico, but not recorded Belize) to Colombia, and from northern Florida and the Bahamas south through the Greater Antilles (east to the Virgin Islands).

Casual in Maine, New Brunswick, Nova Scotia and Venezuela.

Notes.—Some authors suggest that *C. carolinensis* and *C. rufus* (plus *C. otiosus*) constitute a superspecies.

Caprimulgus rufus Boddaert. RUFOUS NIGHTJAR.

Caprimulgus rufus Boddaert, 1783, Table Planches Enlum., p. 46. Based on "Crapaud-Volant ou Tette-Chèvre de Cayenne" Daubenton, Planches Enlum., pl. 735. (Cayenne.)

Habitat.—Open woodland, second growth and forest edge in lowlands and foothills (Tropical and lower Subtropical zones).

Distribution.—*Resident* from southeastern Costa Rica south through Panama (primarily the Pacific slope, including Isla Coiba), and in South America from Colombia, Venezuela (also Trinidad) and the Guianas south, east of the Andes to Bolivia, northern Argentina, Paraguay and southern Brazil.

Notes.—Smaller forms of this species occurring from Costa Rica to Venezuela may represent a distinct species, *C. minimus* Griscom and Greenway, 1937 [RUDDY NIGHTJAR], with the large *C. rufus* ranging from the Guianas southward. See also comments under *C. carolinensis* and *C. otiosus.*

Caprimulgus otiosus (Bangs). ST. LUCIA NIGHTJAR.

Antrostomus rufus otiosus Bangs, 1911, Proc. Biol. Soc. Wash., 24, p. 188. (St. Lucia, West Indies.)

Habitat.—Open woodland in lowlands (Tropical Zone).

Distribution.—*Resident* in the Lesser Antilles (St. Lucia) and (presumably) northern Venezuela (recorded Zulia, Aragua and Miranga).

Notes.—The distributional status of this species in Venezuela is uncertain, and thus its taxonomic status is unresolved. Specimens from Venezuela, all taken between August and May, possibly represent transients from St. Lucia but generally average smaller in size; more probably they constitute a resident population.

Various authors have considered *C. otiosus* to be a subspecies of *C. rufus*; however, it seems best to retain *C. otiosus* as specifically distinct until its status is determined. See also comments under *C. carolinensis* and *C. rufus*.

Caprimulgus cubanensis (Lawrence). GREATER ANTILLEAN NIGHTJAR.

Antrostomus Cubanensis Lawrence, 1860, Ann. Lyc. Nat. Hist. N.Y., 7, p. 260. (Cienaga de Zapata, and on the coast of Manzanillo, Cuba.)

Habitat.—Open woodland, especially along borders of swamps.

Distribution.—*Resident* on Cuba, the Isle of Pines and Hispaniola.

Notes.—Differences in vocalizations suggest that the population on Hispaniola may represent a species, *C. ekmani* (Lönnberg, 1929) [HISPANIOLAN NIGHTJAR], distinct from the form on Cuba and the Isle of Pines, *C. cubanensis* [CUBAN NIGHTJAR].

Caprimulgus salvini Hartert. TAWNY-COLLARED NIGHTJAR.

Antrostomus macromystax (not *Caprimulgus macromystax* Wagler, 1831) Baird, Brewer and Ridgway, 1874, Hist. N. Am. Birds, 2, p. 409. (Mirador, Vera Cruz.)

Caprimulgus salvini Hartert, 1892, Ibis, p. 287. New name for *Antrostomus macromystax* Baird, Brewer and Ridgway, preoccupied.

Habitat.—Open woodland in lowlands (Tropical Zone).

Distribution.—*Resident* [*salvini* group] from Nuevo León and southern Tamaulipas south through eastern San Luis Potosí and Veracruz to northern Oaxaca and Chiapas; and [*badius* group] in the Yucatan Peninsula (including Cozumel Island), Belize (including Half Moon Cay, possibly as a vagrant) and Guatemala (presumably the Caribbean lowlands).

One record [*salvini* group] from Nicaragua (Matagalpa), probably representing a vagrant.

Notes.—Distinct vocalizations attributed to the *badius* group suggest that the groups may represent separate species, *C. salvini* and *C. badius* (Bangs and Peck, 1908) [YUCATAN NIGHTJAR]. *C. salvini* is considered by some authors as conspecific with the South American *C. sericocaudatus* (Cassin, 1849) [SILKY-TAILED NIGHTJAR], with which it forms a superspecies.

Caprimulgus ridgwayi (Nelson). BUFF-COLLARED NIGHTJAR. [416.1.]

Antrostomus ridgwayi Nelson, 1897, Auk, 14, p. 50. (Tlalkisala, Guerrero, Mexico.)

Habitat.—Open woodland, including scrub, second-growth woodland, deciduous forest, and hillsides with scattered trees, more frequently in arid situations (Tropical and Subtropical zones).

Distribution.—*Resident* from southern Sonora, Sinaloa and Durango south through western Mexico and the southern portions of the Central Plateau to Morelos, Oaxaca and Chiapas; and in the Motagua Valley of Guatemala, the interior of Honduras, and central Nicaragua. Recorded in summer (and probably breeding) in southeastern Arizona and extreme southwestern New Mexico (Guadalupe Canyon).

Notes.—Also known as RIDGWAY'S WHIP-POOR-WILL.

Caprimulgus vociferus Wilson. WHIP-POOR-WILL. [417.]

Caprimulgus vociferus Wilson, 1812, Am. Ornithol., 5, p. 71, pl. 41, figs. 1–3. (Pennsylvania = Philadelphia.)

Habitat.—Forest and open woodland, both arid and humid, from lowland moist and deciduous forest to montane forest and pine-oak association, breeding in the tropics primarily in the mountain habitats (Tropical to Temperate zones).

Distribution.—*Breeds* from southern California (north to Los Angeles and San Bernardino counties, rare and local), southern Nevada, central Arizona, central Mexico and extreme western Texas south through the highlands of Mexico, Guatemala and El Salvador to Honduras; and from north-central Saskatchewan, southern Manitoba, southern Ontario, southern Quebec, New Brunswick and Nova Scotia south, east of the Great Plains (west to southeastern South Dakota, eastern Nebraska, eastern Kansas and northeastern Oklahoma) to extreme northeastern Texas, northern Louisiana, northern Mississippi, north-central Alabama, central Georgia, northwestern South Carolina, east-central North Carolina and eastern Virginia.

Winters from northern Mexico (Sonora eastward), southern Texas, the Gulf coast and east-central South Carolina (casually farther north, on the Atlantic coast to New Jersey) south through Middle America to western Panama (western Chiriquí), casually to southern California and Cuba.

Casual in southern Baja California, southern Alberta, southwestern Saskatchewan, Utah (possibly breeds), Colorado and northern Quebec. Accidental in southeastern Alaska (Kupreanof Island).

Notes.—*C. vociferus* and *C. noctitherus,* considered conspecific by some authors, may constitute at least a superspecies.

Caprimulgus noctitherus (Wetmore). PUERTO RICAN NIGHTJAR.

Setochalcis noctitherus Wetmore, 1919, Proc. Biol. Soc. Wash., 32, p. 235. (Bayamón, Puerto Rico.)

Habitat.—Heavily wooded areas in dry lowland forest.

Distribution.—*Resident* on Puerto Rico, where now restricted to the southwestern portion of the island.

Notes.—Also known as PUERTO RICAN WHIP-POOR-WILL. See comments under *C. vociferus.*

Caprimulgus saturatus (Salvin). DUSKY NIGHTJAR.

Antrostomus saturatus Salvin, 1870, Proc. Zool. Soc. London, p. 203. (Volcán de Chiriquí, Panama.)

Habitat.—Open montane forest and woodland, forest clearings and edge, and second growth, foraging in more open situations adjacent to forest (Subtropical and Temperate zones).

Distribution.—*Resident* in the central highlands of Costa Rica, and in western Panama (vicinity of Volcán Barú, western Chiriquí).

Caprimulgus cayennensis Gmelin. WHITE-TAILED NIGHTJAR.

Caprimulgus cayennensis Gmelin, 1789, Syst. Nat., 1 (2), p. 1031. Based mainly on "Engoulevent de Cayenne" Buffon, Hist. Nat. Ois., 6, p. 545, and the "White-necked Goatsucker" Latham, Gen. Synop. Birds, 2 (2), p. 599. (in Cayennae cultis = Cayenne.)

Habitat.—Open situations, especially grassy hillsides with scattered bushes, and savanna (Tropical and Subtropical zones).

Distribution.—*Resident* in the Lesser Antilles (Martinique); and in Costa Rica and Panama, and in South America from northern Colombia, Venezuela (also islands from the Netherlands Antilles to Tobago and Trinidad) and the Guianas south, east of the Andes, to northern Brazil.

Accidental in Puerto Rico (sight report).

Caprimulgus maculicaudus (Lawrence). SPOT-TAILED NIGHTJAR.

Stenopsis maculicaudus Lawrence, 1862, Ann. Lyc. Nat. Hist. N.Y., 7, p. 459. (Para [Brazil].)

Habitat.—Grasslands and savanna (Tropical Zone).

Distribution.—*Breeds* locally in the Gulf-Caribbean lowlands of southern Mexico (southern Veracruz, northeastern Oaxaca and northern Chiapas), and in the Mosquitia of northeastern Nicaragua (probably also eastern Honduras); and in South America from eastern Colombia, Venezuela and the Guianas south, east of the Andes, to southeastern Peru, east-central Bolivia and southeastern Brazil.

Apparently at least partly migratory from the Middle American breeding grounds, as there are few records during the nonbreeding season; recorded also from central Honduras (Lake Yojoa), probably as a transient. Presumably resident in the South American portion of the breeding range.

Caprimulgus indicus Latham. JUNGLE NIGHTJAR. [416.2.]

Caprimulgus indicus Latham, 1790, Index Ornithol., 2, p. 588. Based on the "Indian Goatsucker" Latham, Gen. Synop. Birds, suppl., 1, p. 196. (in India.)

Habitat & Distribution.—*Breeds* in open woodland and forest from Manchuria and Japan south to India, Ceylon and eastern China, and *winters* in a variety of woodland and partly open habitats from the Himalayas, eastern China and Japan south to the East Indies and New Guinea.

Casual in the Kurile Islands and Sakhalin. Accidental in Alaska (Buldir Island in the Aleutians, 31 May 1977; Day, *et al.*, 1979, Auk, 96, p. 189).

Notes.—Also known as GRAY NIGHTJAR.

Family NYCTIBIIDAE: Potoos

Genus NYCTIBIUS Vieillot

Nyctibius Vieillot, 1816, Analyse, p. 38. Type, by monotypy, "Grand Engoulevent de Cayenne" Buffon = *Caprimulgus grandis* Gmelin.

Nyctibius grandis (Gmelin). GREAT POTOO.

Caprimulgus grandis Gmelin, 1789, Syst. Nat., 1 (2), p. 1029. Based mainly on "Le grand Tette-chévre tacheté du Brésil" Brisson, Ornithologie, 2, p. 485, and the "Grand Goatsucker" Latham, Gen. Synop. Birds, 2 (2), p. 590. (in Cayenna = Cayenne.)

Habitat.—Dense lowland forest, forest edge and clearings, less commonly in open meadows (Tropical Zone).

Distribution.—*Resident* locally in Guatemala (Polochic and Salinas rivers), eastern Honduras (Olancho), Nicaragua (San Emilio), Costa Rica and Panama (Caribbean lowlands throughout, and Pacific lowlands in eastern Panamá province and Darién), and in South America from Colombia, Venezuela and the Guianas south, east of the Andes, to eastern Peru, east-central Bolivia and southeastern Brazil.

Nyctibius griseus (Gmelin). COMMON POTOO.

> *Caprimulgus griseus* Gmelin, 1789, Syst. Nat., 1 (2), p. 1029. Based on "Engoulevent gris" Buffon, Hist. Nat. Ois., 6, p. 548, and the "Grey Goatsucker" Latham, Gen. Synop. Birds, 2 (2), p. 592. (in Cayenna = Cayenne.)

Habitat.—Open woodland, forest edge, clearings, and areas with scattered trees, also sometimes around human settlements (Tropical and lower Subtropical zones).

Distribution.—*Resident* from southern Sinaloa, southern San Luis Potosí and southern Tamaulipas south along both slopes of Middle America (including Isla Roatán in the Bay Islands, Honduras), and in South America from Colombia, Venezuela (also Trinidad) and the Guianas south, west of the Andes to western Ecuador and east of the Andes to eastern Peru, Bolivia, northern Argentina and Uruguay; and in the Greater Antilles (Jamaica, Hispaniola and Gonâve Island, also a sight report from Mona Island off Puerto Rico).

Notes.—Also known as LESSER POTOO. Two groups within the species may be defined on the basis of differences in vocalizations and are regarded as separate species by some authors, *N. jamaicensis* (Gmelin, 1789) [JAMAICAN POTOO], occurring in the West Indies and from Mexico south on the Gulf-Caribbean slope to Honduras and on the Pacific slope to central Costa Rica, and *N. griseus* [GRAY POTOO], ranging from eastern Nicaragua southward. Further studies are needed to determine the status of these two groups.

Family STEATORNITHIDAE: Oilbirds

Genus STEATORNIS Humboldt

> *Steatornis* Humboldt, 1814, *in* Humboldt and Bonpland, Voy. Inter. Am., 1, p. 416. Type, by monotypy, "Guacharo" = *Steatornis caripensis* Humboldt.

Steatornis caripensis Humboldt. OILBIRD.

> *Steatornis caripensis* Humboldt, 1817, Bull. Sci. Soc. Philom. Paris, p. 52. (caverns of Caripe, Cumaná, Venezuela.)

Habitat & Distribution.—*Resident* from Colombia, Venezuela (also Trinidad) and the Guianas south to Peru and northwestern Bolivia, nesting and roosting in caves, and foraging at night for oil palm fruits (its exclusive food) in open woodland where palms occur.

Casual (although probably resident) in Panama (Río Tacarcuna, eastern Darién, 19 March 1954, and Canal Zone, 11 May 1974).

Order **APODIFORMES**: Swifts and Hummingbirds

Notes.—The degree of relationship between the swifts and hummingbirds has yet to be established (see Sibley and Ahlquist, 1962, Peabody Mus. Nat. Hist. Bull., 39, pp. 198–206).

Family **APODIDAE**: Swifts

Subfamily CYPSELOIDINAE: Cypseloidine Swifts

Genus **CYPSELOIDES** Streubel

Cypseloides Streubel, 1848, Isis von Oken, col. 366. Type, by subsequent designation (Sclater, 1865), *Hemiprocne fumigata* Streubel.

Cypseloides niger (Gmelin). BLACK SWIFT. [422.]

Hirundo nigra Gmelin, 1789, Syst. Nat., 1 (2), p. 1025. Based on "Le Martinet de S. Domingue" Brisson, Ornithologie, 2, p. 514, pl. 46, fig. 3. (in insulae S. Dominici et Cayennae = Hispaniola.)

Habitat.—Primarily montane areas (except in the most northern part of the range), nesting in crevices or shallow caves in steep rock faces and canyons, usually near or behind waterfalls (occasionally in seacaves), foraging over both forest and open areas in montane habitats (Subtropical and Temperate zones).

Distribution.—*Breeds* locally from southeastern Alaska (north to the Stikine River), northwestern and central British Columbia, and southwestern Alberta south through the Pacific states to southern California; in northwestern Montana, Colorado, central Utah (Provo Canyon) and north-central New Mexico (probably); locally from Nayarit, Puebla and Veracruz south through southern Mexico, Guatemala and Honduras to Costa Rica; and in the Antilles (Cuba, Jamaica, Hispaniola, Puerto Rico, Montserrat, Guadeloupe, Dominica, Martinique, St. Lucia and St. Vincent).

Winters in Mexico (presumably), through the breeding range from Chiapas to Costa Rica, and in the Greater Antilles (except Puerto Rico); sight reports from northern South America (Trinidad and Guyana) may pertain to other species.

In migration occurs from California, Arizona (casually) and New Mexico south through Mexico (including Baja California, with records at sea in the Pacific off Chiapas and Guatemala), and through the Virgin Islands and Lesser Antilles.

Casual in south-coastal Alaska (Wooded Islands), also sight reports from Texas and the Florida Keys (Dry Tortugas).

Cypseloides cryptus Zimmer. WHITE-CHINNED SWIFT.

Cypseloides cryptus Zimmer, 1945, Auk, 62, p. 588. (Inca Mine, Río Tavara, Perú.)

Habitat.—Forested regions, both lowlands and highlands, ranging also over more open habitats (Tropical and Subtropical zones).

Distribution.—*Breeds* presumably in South America (recorded Colombia, Venezuela, Guyana, Ecuador and eastern Peru), possibly in Middle America; recorded locally from the Caribbean slope in Belize, Honduras (San Esteban), Nicaragua (El Recreo), Costa Rica (San José, and the Térraba region) and Panama (San Blas and Isla Coiba).

Cypseloides cherriei Ridgway. SPOT-FRONTED SWIFT.

Cypseloides cherriei Ridgway, 1893, Proc. U.S. Natl. Mus., 16, p. 44. (Volcán de Irazú, Costa Rica.)

Habitat.—Montane areas, nesting on rock ledges near waterfalls (Subtropical Zone).

Distribution.—Known only from Costa Rica (Volcán de Irazú, and Puntarenas province), Colombia (Santander) and Venezuela (Aragua, where nesting has been verified).

Cypseloides rutilus (Vieillot). CHESTNUT-COLLARED SWIFT.

Hirundo rutila Vieillot, 1817, Nouv. Dict. Hist. Nat., nouv. éd., 14, p. 528. (No locality given = Trinidad.)

Habitat.— Lowland and montane forest, nesting on rock faces near or behind waterfalls (occasionally in seacaves), foraging also over open country (Tropical and Subtropical zones).

Distribution.—*Resident* from eastern Sinaloa, Durango, Zacatecas, Puebla and Veracruz south through Middle America (not reported Nicaragua), and in South America from Colombia, Venezuela (also Trinidad), Guyana and French Guiana (probably) south, on the eastern slope of the Andes, to eastern Peru and western Bolivia. Possibly migratory in part, especially the northern Middle American populations.

Notes.—Sometimes placed in the genus *Chaetura.*

Genus STREPTOPROCNE Oberholser

Streptoprocne Oberholser, 1906, Proc. Biol. Soc. Wash., 19, p. 69. Type, by original designation, *Hirundo zonaris* Shaw.
Semicollum [subgenus] Brooke, 1970, Durban Mus. Novit., 9, p. 16. Type, by original designation, *Acanthylis semicollaris* de Saussure.

Streptoprocne zonaris (Shaw). WHITE-COLLARED SWIFT. [422.1.]

Hirundo zonaris Shaw, 1796, *in* J. F. Miller, Cimelia Phys., p. 100, pl. 44. (No locality given = Chapada, Mato Grosso, Brazil.)

Habitat.—Forest and open country, lowlands and highlands, nesting on cliffs near or behind waterfalls (Tropical to Temperate zones).

Distribution.—*Resident* from Guerrero, San Luis Potosí and Tamaulipas south through Middle America (including Isla Coiba off Panama), and in South America from Colombia, Venezuela and the Guianas south to Peru, Bolivia, northwestern Argentina, and central and southeastern Brazil; and in the Greater Antilles (Cuba, Jamaica, Hispaniola, Tortue Island, and possibly also the Isle of Pines).

Wanders irregularly north in the Lesser Antilles to Grenada and the Grenadines. Accidental in western Florida (western Escambia County) and the northern Lesser

Antilles (Saba), also sight reports from southern Texas (Rockport) and Vieques Island (off Puerto Rico).

Notes.—In the West Indies known as Antillean Cloud Swift.

Streptoprocne semicollaris (de Saussure). White-naped Swift.

Acanthylis semicollaris de Saussure, 1859, Rev. Mag. Zool., ser. 2, 11, p. 118. (les grandes forêts, du Mexique = San Joaquin, near City of Mexico.)

Habitat.—Forest and partly open country, lowlands and highlands, nesting on ledges in caves (Tropical to lower Temperate zones).

Distribution.—*Resident* in northern and central Mexico (recorded Sinaloa, Chihuahua, Nayarit, Hidalgo, Morelos and the state of México).

Notes.—Relationships of this species are uncertain; it is sometimes placed in the genus *Aerornis* W. Bertoni, 1901.

Subfamily CHAETURINAE: Chaeturine Swifts

Genus **CHAETURA** Stephens

Chætura Stephens, 1826, *in* Shaw, Gen. Zool. 13 (2), p. 76. Type, by subsequent designation (Swainson, 1829), *Chaetura pelasgia* [sic] = *Hirundo pelagica* Linnaeus.

Chaetura pelagica (Linnaeus). Chimney Swift. [423.]

Hirundo pelagica Linnaeus, 1758, Syst. Nat., ed. 10, 11, p. 192. Based on "The American Swallow" Catesby, Nat. Hist. Carolina, 2, app., p. 8, pl. 8. (in America = South Carolina.)

Habitat.—Open situations and woodland, especially around human habitation, now nesting and roosting primarily in chimneys, originally on cliffs or in hollow trees.

Distribution.—*Breeds* in eastern North America east of the Rocky Mountains from east-central Saskatchewan, southern Manitoba, central Ontario, southern Quebec, New Brunswick, Prince Edward Island, Nova Scotia and Newfoundland (probably) south to eastern New Mexico, south-central and southern Texas, the Gulf coast and south-central Florida, with one confirmed breeding record for southern California (Ventura, 1977); recently recorded in summer (and probably breeding) elsewhere in southern California and Arizona.

Winters in western Peru, and in the upper Amazon basin of eastern Peru, northern Chile and northwestern Brazil.

Migrates regularly through the lowlands of eastern Mexico, the Caribbean slope of Middle America (including Cozumel Island, the Bay Islands off Honduras, and Taboga Island off Panama, casually on the Pacific slope of eastern Panama), Colombia and western Venezuela, casually west to Montana, Utah, California (primarily southern portion), Arizona and New Mexico, and through the Bahamas, Greater Antilles (recorded Cuba, Jamaica, Hispaniola and Tortue Island), and the Cayman Islands.

Casual or accidental in Alaska (St. George Island in the Pribilofs), Bermuda and Greenland; sight reports from Alberta are questionable.

Notes.—*C. pelagica, C. vauxi* and *C. chapmani* may constitute a superspecies.

Chaetura vauxi (Townsend). VAUX'S SWIFT. [424.]

Cypcelus [sic] *Vauxi* J. K. Townsend, 1839, Narr. Journey Rocky Mount., etc., p. 348. (Columbia River = Fort Vancouver, Washington.)

Habitat.—Forested regions, foraging and migrating also over open country (Tropical to Temperate zones).

Distribution.—*Breeds* in western North America from southeastern Alaska, northwestern and southern British Columbia, northern Idaho and western Montana south, chiefly from the Cascades and Sierra Nevada westward, to central California (Santa Cruz County); in southwestern Tamaulipas and southeastern San Luis Potosí; on the Yucatan Peninsula (including Cozumel Island); from Oaxaca, Veracruz and Chiapas south to Panama (including Coiba and the Pearl islands); and in northern Venezuela (Lara to Monagas). Recorded in summer (and probably breeding) in western Mexico from Sinaloa and Nayarit to Jalisco.

Winters from central Mexico (casually from central California) south throughout the breeding range in Middle America, and in Venezuela; casual in winter in southern Louisiana and western Florida (Tallahassee).

In migration occurs east of the breeding range from Idaho, Nevada and Utah south through the southwestern United States, Baja California and western Mexico.

Notes.—Populations from southern Mexico southward have often been treated as a separate species, *C. richmondi* Ridgway, 1910 [DUSKY-BACKED SWIFT]; further, the form in the Yucatan Peninsula and on Cozumel Island was formerly considered by some authors to be a distinct species, *C. gaumeri* Lawrence, 1882 [YUCATAN SWIFT], but intergradation between *gaumeri* and *richmondi* is now known to occur. See also comments under *C. pelagica*.

Chaetura chapmani Hellmayr. CHAPMAN'S SWIFT.

Chœtura chapmani Hellmayr, 1907, Bull. Br. Ornithol. Club, 19, p. 62. (Caparo, Trinidad.)

Habitat & Distribution.—*Resident* in forested and partly open regions (Tropical to lower Temperate zones) from eastern Colombia, Venezuela (also Trinidad) and the Guianas south locally to southwestern and northeastern Brazil, the southernmost population migratory northward.

Ranges casually to (and possibly resident in) central Panama (Gatun, Canal Zone, 11 July 1911, and Mandinga, San Blas, 30 January 1957).

Notes.—Also known as DARK-BREASTED SWIFT. See comments under *C. pelagica*.

Chaetura brachyura (Jardine). SHORT-TAILED SWIFT.

Acanthylis brachyura Jardine, 1846, Ann. Mag. Nat. Hist., ser. 1, 18, p. 120. (Tobago.)

Habitat.—Lowland forest, savanna and mangroves, foraging also over open country and human settlements (Tropical Zone).

Distribution.—*Resident* in the Lesser Antilles (St. Vincent, the population apparently partly migratory), and from Panama (Canal Zone and Darién), Colombia, Venezuela (also Tobago and Trinidad) and the Guianas south, east of the Andes to eastern Peru and central Brazil; also west of the Andes in southwestern Ecuador and northwestern Peru.

Accidental in the Virgin Islands (St. Croix). Reports from Grenada are regarded as doubtful.

Chaetura andrei Berlepsch and Hartert. ASHY-TAILED SWIFT.

Chaetura andrei Berlepsch and Hartert, 1902, Novit. Zool., 9, p. 91. (Caicara, Orinoco River, Venezuela.)

Habitat & Distribution.—*Breeds* in lowland forest in central Venezuela and Surinam, and from eastern Brazil south to Paraguay, northern Argentina and southern Brazil, ranging in winter from the breeding range north, at least casually, to Venezuela and Colombia.

Accidental in Panama (Juan Díaz, western Panamá province, 4 August 1923; Rogers, 1939, Auk, 56, p. 82), also an additional sight report from western Panama (Herrera).

Notes.—Also known as ANDRE'S SWIFT.

Chaetura spinicauda (Temminck). BAND-RUMPED SWIFT.

Cypselus spinicaudus Temminck, 1839, Planches Color., livr. 102, Tabl. Méth., p. 57. Based on "Hirondelle à queue pointue de Cayenne" Daubenton, Planches Enlum., pl. 726, fig. 1. (Cayenne.)

Habitat.—Lowland and foothill forest, foraging also over open country (Tropical and lower Subtropical zones).

Distribution.—*Resident* in southwestern Costa Rica (El General, Térraba and Golfo Dulce Regions) and Panama, and in South America from Colombia, Venezuela (also Trinidad) and the Guianas south, west of the Andes to western Colombia and east of the Andes to the Guianas and Amazonian Brazil.

Chaetura cinereiventris Sclater. GRAY-RUMPED SWIFT.

Chætura cinereiventris Sclater, 1862, Cat. Collect. Am. Birds, p. 283. (Bahia, Brazil.)

Habitat.—Primarily in montane forest and open woodland, foraging also over open situations in lowlands and foothills (Tropical and Subtropical zones).

Distribution.—*Resident* in the Lesser Antilles (Grenada); from the Caribbean slope of Nicaragua and Costa Rica south to western Panama (western Bocas del Toro); and in South America from Colombia, Venezuela (also Trinidad) and the Guianas south, at least locally, west of the Andes to western Ecuador and east of the Andes to eastern Peru, Paraguay, northeastern Argentina and southeastern Brazil.

Notes.—*C. cinereiventris* and *C. martinica* constitute a superspecies; they are considered conspecific by some authors.

Chaetura martinica (Hermann). LESSER ANTILLEAN SWIFT.

Hirundo martinica Hermann, 1783, Tabula Affinit. Anim., p. 229. (Martinique, West Indies.)

Habitat.—Mountain forest, ranging to sea level over woodland or open country.
Distribution.—*Resident* in the Lesser Antilles (Guadeloupe, Dominica, Martinique, St. Lucia and St. Vincent); doubtfully recorded from Nevis (sight record). Reports from Trinidad are erroneous, being based on specimens actually taken on Dominica.
Notes.—See comments under *C. cinereiventris.*

Genus HIRUNDAPUS Hodgson

Hirund-apus Hodgson, 1837, J. Asiat. Soc. Bengal, 5 (1836), p. 780. Type, by original designation, *Cypselus* (*Chaetura*) *nudipes* Hodgson.

Hirundapus caudacutus (Latham). WHITE-THROATED NEEDLETAIL. [422.2.]

Hirundo caudacuta Latham, 1801?, Index Ornithol., suppl., p. 57. (Nova Hollandia = New South Wales, Australia.)

Habitat & Distribution.—*Breeds* in the bottoms of hollow trees in montane forested regions in the Himalayas, and from Siberia south to Mongolia, Manchuria, Korea and Japan, and *winters* over forested regions and open country from India and Formosa south to Australia and Tasmania.
Accidental in the Aleutians on Shemya (21 May 1974; White and Baird, 1977, Auk, 94, p. 389) and Attu (24 May 1978; Roberson, 1980, Rare Birds W. Coast, p. 236), and in Europe and New Zealand.
Notes.—Also known as WHITE-THROATED NEEDLE-TAILED SWIFT.

[Genus AERODRAMUS Oberholser]

Aerodramus Oberholser, 1906, Proc. Acad. Nat. Sci. Philadelphia, 58, pp. 179, 182. Type, by original designation, *Collocalia innominata* Hume = *Hirundo fuciphaga* Thunberg.

Notes.—This genus is often merged in *Collocalia* G. R. Gray, 1840.

[Aerodramus vanikorensis (Quoy and Gaimard). GRAY SWIFTLET.] See Appendix B.

Subfamily APODINAE: Apodine Swifts

Genus APUS Scopoli

Apus Scopoli, 1777, Introd. Hist. Nat., p. 483. Type, by tautonymy, *Hirundo apus* Linnaeus.

Apus apus (Linnaeus). COMMON SWIFT. [424.2.]

Hirundo Apus Linnaeus, 1758, Syst. Nat., ed. 10, 1, p. 192. (in Europæ altis = Sweden.)

Habitat & Distribution.—*Breeds* in tree cavities and in cliffs and buildings from northern Eurasia south to northern Africa, Arabia, Iraq, the Himalayas and northeastern China, and *winters* in the southern half of Africa.

Accidental in Alaska (St. Paul Island, in the Pribilofs, 28 June 1950; Kenyon and Phillips, 1965, Auk, 82, p. 633); a sight report from Barbados is questionable.

Notes.—Known in Old World literature as the SWIFT. A resident African form, *A. barbatus* (Sclater, 1865), is sometimes considered conspecific with *A. apus*; they constitute a superspecies.

Apus pacificus (Latham). FORK-TAILED SWIFT. [424.1.]

> *Hirundo pacifica* Latham, 1801?, Index Ornithol., suppl., p. lviii. (Nova Hollandia = New South Wales, Australia.)

Habitat.—A wide variety of habitats from seacoasts to mountains, generally breeding in colonies on cliffs, and in caves, buildings or tree cavities, migrating and wintering in both forested and open habitats.

Distribution.—*Breeds* from eastern Siberia, Kamchatka and the Commander Islands south to northern India, the Malay Peninsula and southern China.

Winters from the Himalayas and Malay Peninsula south to New Guinea, Australia and New Zealand.

In migration ranges casually (primarily in summer and fall) to the Pribilof (St. George, St. Paul) and western Aleutian (Agattu, Shemya) islands.

Accidental in the Seychelles.

Notes.—Also known as WHITE-RUMPED SWIFT, a name now generally restricted to the African species *A. caffer* (Lichtenstein, 1823).

Apus melba (Linnaeus). ALPINE SWIFT.

> *Hirundo Melba* Linnaeus, 1758, Syst. Nat., ed. 10, 1, p. 192. (ad fretum Herculeam = Gibraltar.)

Habitat & Distribution.—*Breeds* in cliffs and buildings from southern Europe and India south to southern Africa, Madagascar and Ceylon, and *winters* generally throughout the breeding range, the northernmost populations being partly migratory.

Accidental in the Lesser Antilles (Barbados, September 1955, after a hurricane; Bond, 1959, Birds W. Indies, 4th Suppl., p. 11).

Genus AERONAUTES Hartert

> *Aëronautes* Hartert, 1892, Cat. Birds Br. Mus., 16, pp. xiii, 436, 459. Type, by monotypy, *Cypselus melanoleucus* Baird = *Acanthylis saxatalis* Woodhouse.

Aeronautes saxatalis (Woodhouse). WHITE-THROATED SWIFT. [425.]

> *Acanthylis saxatalis* Woodhouse, 1853, *in* Sitgreaves, Rep. Exped. Zuni Colo. Rivers, p. 64. (Inscription Rock, New Mexico.)

Habitat.—Primarily mountainous country, especially near cliffs and canyons where breeding occurs, occasionally nesting in buildings and on seacliffs, foraging over forest and open situations in a variety of habitats (Subtropical and Temperate zones).

Distribution.—*Breeds* from southern British Columbia, Idaho, Montana and southwestern South Dakota south through the Pacific and southwestern states (including the Channel Islands off California) to southern Baja California (a questionable sight record of nesting on Guadalupe Island in 1892, unreported there since 1922), east to western Nebraska, northeastern and central New Mexico, and western Texas (to Val Verde County), and south through the interior of Mexico to Guatemala, El Salvador and Honduras.

Winters from central California, central Arizona and, rarely, southern New Mexico (casually farther north) south to the limits of the breeding range in Middle America.

Casual in eastern and southern Texas. Accidental in Kansas (Manhattan), Michigan (Hillsdale) and Arkansas (Hot Springs).

Genus **PANYPTILA** Cabanis

Panyptila Cabanis, 1847, Arch. Naturgesch., 13, p. 345. Type, by original designation, *Hirundo cayennensis* Gmelin.

Panyptila cayennensis (Gmelin). LESSER SWALLOW-TAILED SWIFT.

Hirundo cayennensis Gmelin, 1789, Syst. Nat., 1 (2), p. 1024. Based on "Le Martinet à collier blanc" Buffon, Hist. Nat. Ois., 6, p. 671, and "Martinet à collier de Cayenne" Daubenton, Planches Enlum., pl. 725, fig. 2. (in Cayenna = Cayenne.)

Habitat.—Humid lowland forest, foraging high over open and forested situations and towns, and occasionally nesting on buildings as well as on cliffs and trees (Tropical Zone).

Distribution.—*Resident* from Veracruz (Presidio), Oaxaca and Chiapas (Palenque) south locally on the Caribbean slope of Belize, Honduras and Nicaragua, in Costa Rica (Caribbean slope, and Golfo Dulce region on the Pacific) and Panama (both slopes), and in South America from Colombia, Venezuela (also Tobago and Trinidad) and the Guianas south, east of the Andes, to eastern Peru and east-central Brazil.

Panyptila sanctihieronymi Salvin. GREAT SWALLOW-TAILED SWIFT.

Panyptila sancti-hieronymi Salvin, 1863, Proc. Zool. Soc. London, p. 190, pl. 23. (San Geronimo, Vera Paz, Guatemala.)

Habitat.—Montane forest, breeding in humid areas, foraging also over open situations at moderate elevations, including over towns (Subtropical and Temperate zones).

Distribution.—*Resident* in the highlands of southern Mexico (Michoacán, Guerrero, Oaxaca and Chiapas), Guatemala and Honduras.

Casual in north-central Nicaragua (El Corozo, Depto. de Nueva Segovia), also sight reports for Costa Rica.

Genus **TACHORNIS** Gosse

Tachornis Gosse, 1847, Birds Jamaica, p. 58 (footnote). Type, by monotypy, *Tachornis phoenicobia* Gosse.

Tachornis phoenicobia Gosse. ANTILLEAN PALM SWIFT. [425.1.]

Tachornis phoenicobia Gosse, 1847, Birds Jamaica, p. 58 (footnote). (Jamaica.)

Habitat.—Lowlands, most commonly around human settlements, nesting in colonies in palm trees.

Distribution.—*Resident* on Cuba, the Isle of Pines, Hispaniola (including Saona and Beata islands, and Île-à-Vache) and Jamaica.

Casual in the Florida Keys (Key West), also a sight report for Puerto Rico.

Family TROCHILIDAE: Hummingbirds

Notes.—Generic limits and relationships within this family are subjects of much controversy and are currently under study.

Genus GLAUCIS Boie

Glaucis Boie, 1831, Isis von Oken, col. 545. Type, by subsequent designation (G. R. Gray, 1840), *G. braziliensis* (Lath.) = *Trochilus hirsutus* Gmelin.

Notes.—See comments under *Threnetes.*

Glaucis aenea Lawrence. BRONZY HERMIT.

Glaucis æneus Lawrence, 1868, Proc. Acad. Nat. Sci. Philadelphia, 19 (1867), p. 232. (Costa Rica.)

Habitat.—Undergrowth and thickets bordering humid lowland forest, forest clearings, dense second growth and banana plantations, occasionally mangroves (Tropical Zone).

Distribution.—*Resident* from the Caribbean slope of Nicaragua south through Costa Rica (both slopes) to western Panama (Bocas del Toro, Chiriquí and western Veraguas); and the Pacific coast of Colombia and northwestern Ecuador.

Notes.—*G. aenea* and *G. hirsuta* are closely related and constitute a superspecies; they are regarded as conspecific by some authors.

Glaucis hirsuta (Gmelin). RUFOUS-BREASTED HERMIT.

Trochilus hirsutus Gmelin, 1788, Syst. Nat., 1 (1), p. 490. Based in part on "Le Colibry du Brésil" Brisson, Ornithologie, 3, p. 670. (in Brasilia = northeastern Brazil.)

Habitat.—Dense undergrowth and thickets of humid forest edge, forest clearings, second growth and banana plantations (Tropical Zone).

Distribution.—*Resident* from central Panama (Coclé and western Panamá province eastward), Colombia, Venezuela (also Tobago and Trinidad) and the Guianas south, east of the Andes, to eastern Peru, northern Bolivia and central Brazil; and in the Lesser Antilles (Grenada).

Notes.—Also known as HAIRY HERMIT. See comments under *G. aenea.*

Genus **THRENETES** Gould

Threnetes Gould, 1852, Monogr. Trochil., pt. 4, pl. [14 and 15]. Type, by subsequent designation (G. R. Gray, 1855), *Trochilus leucurus* Linnaeus.

Notes.—Sometimes merged in the genus *Glaucis.*

Threnetes ruckeri (Bourcier). BAND-TAILED BARBTHROAT.

> *Trochilus Ruckeri* Bourcier, 1847, Proc. Zool. Soc. London, p. 46. (No locality given = Esmeraldas, Ecuador.)

Habitat.—Undergrowth of humid lowland forest and dense woodland, forest edge and thickets (Tropical Zone).

Distribution.—*Resident* on the Caribbean slope of Belize, eastern Guatemala, Honduras and Nicaragua, and from Costa Rica (both slopes, except dry northwest) and Panama south through Colombia to western Venezuela and northwestern Ecuador.

Genus **PHAETHORNIS** Swainson

Phæthornis Swainson, 1827, Philos. Mag., new ser., 1, p. 441. Type, by original designation, *"Troch. superciliosus* of Authors" = *Trochilus superciliosus* Linnaeus.

Phaethornis guy (Lesson). GREEN HERMIT.

> *Trochilus Guy* Lesson, 1833, Les Trochil., p. 119, Index, p. xiv. (Brazil, error = Venezuela.)

Habitat.—Humid foothill and montane forest, forest edge and second-growth woodland, primarily in undergrowth or understory (upper Tropical and Subtropical zones).

Distribution.—*Resident* in Costa Rica and Panama, and in South America from Colombia and northern Venezuela (also Trinidad) south, west of the Andes to western Colombia and east of the Andes to southeastern Peru.

Phaethornis superciliosus (Linnaeus). LONG-TAILED HERMIT.

> *Trochilus superciliosus* Linnaeus, 1766, Syst. Nat., ed. 12, 1, p. 189. Based on "Le Colibry a longue queue de Cayenne" Brisson, Ornithologie, 3, p. 686, pl. 35, fig. 5. (in Cayania = Cayenne.)

Habitat.—Undergrowth of humid lowland and deciduous (occasionally montane) forest, forest edge and second-growth woodland (Tropical and lower Subtropical zones).

Distribution.—*Resident* on the Pacific slope from Nayarit south to western Oaxaca; and on the Caribbean slope from Veracruz, Oaxaca and Chiapas south through Central America to Nicaragua, on both slopes of Costa Rica and Panama, and in South America from northern Colombia and southern Venezuela south, east of the Andes, to eastern Peru, Bolivia and Amazonian Brazil.

Notes.—The relationships between *P. superciliosus* and *P. malaris* (Nordmann, 1835), which are sympatric in Cayenne, are uncertain; some authors have treated them as conspecific, or Middle American populations have been assigned to one or the other form.

Phaethornis anthophilus (Bourcier). PALE-BELLIED HERMIT.

Trochilus anthophilus Bourcier, 1843, Rev. Zool. [Paris], 6, p. 71. (la vallée supérieure de la Madeleine, région tempérée, la Colombie = upper Magdalena Valley, Colombia.)

Habitat.—Undergrowth of lowland and foothill forest, forest edge, clearings, thickets and plantations, less frequently in forest than congeners (Tropical and lower Subtropical zones).

Distribution.—*Resident* from eastern Panama (eastern San Blas, eastern Panamá province, and the Pearl Islands) east through northern Colombia to northern Venezuela.

Phaethornis longuemareus (Lesson). LITTLE HERMIT.

Trochilus Longuemareus Lesson, 1832, Les Trochil., p. 15; 1833, p. 160, pl. 2, 62. (Cayenne.)

Habitat.—Undergrowth of humid lowland and foothill forest, forest edge and dense second growth, also in similar situations in deciduous forest in more arid regions, and in plantations (Tropical and lower Subtropical zones).

Distribution.—*Resident* on the Gulf-Caribbean slope of Middle America from Veracruz, Campeche and Quintana Roo south through northern Oaxaca, Tabasco, Chiapas, Belize and eastern Guatemala to Honduras, on both slopes of Nicaragua (rare on Pacific slope), Costa Rica (rare in dry northwest) and Panama, and in South America from Colombia and Venezuela (also Trinidad) south, west of the Andes to western Ecuador and east of the Andes to eastern Peru and northern Amazonian Brazil.

Genus **EUTOXERES** Reichenbach

Eutoxeres Reichenbach, 1849, Avium Syst. Nat., pl. XL [generic description only]; species added, Gould, 1851, Monogr. Trochil., pt. 2, pl. [5 and 6]. Type, by subsequent designation (G. R. Gray, 1855), *Trochilus aquila* "Lodd." = Bourcier.

Eutoxeres aquila (Bourcier). WHITE-TIPPED SICKLEBILL.

Trochilus Aquila (Loddiges MS) Bourcier, 1847, Proc. Zool. Soc. London, p. 42. (Nouvelle Grenade, les environs de Bogota = vicinity of Bogotá, Colombia.)

Habitat.—Undergrowth of humid forest, forest edge and thickets (upper Tropical and lower Subtropical zones).

Distribution.—*Resident* from central Costa Rica south locally through Panama, and in South America west of the Andes from western Colombia south to western Ecuador and east of the Andes from southeastern Colombia south to northeastern Peru.

Genus **ANDRODON** Gould

Androdon Gould, 1863, Ann. Mag. Nat. Hist., ser. 3, 12, p. 247. Type, by monotypy, *Androdon aequatorialis* Gould.

Androdon aequatorialis Gould. TOOTH-BILLED HUMMINGBIRD.

Androdon æquatorialis Gould, 1863, Ann. Mag. Nat. Hist., ser. 3, 12, p. 247. (Ecuador.)

Habitat.—Humid forest, forest edge, clearings and open woodland (Tropical and Subtropical zones).

Distribution.—*Resident* from eastern Panama (eastern Darién) and Colombia (east to Magdalena Valley) south along the Pacific coast to western Ecuador.

Genus DORYFERA Gould

Doryfera Gould, 1847, Proc. Zool. Soc. London, p. 95. Type, by subsequent designation (G. R. Gray, 1855), *Trochilus ludoviciae* Bourcier and Mulsant.

Doryfera ludoviciae (Bourcier and Mulsant). GREEN-FRONTED LANCE-BILL.

Trochilus ludoviciæ Bourcier and Mulsant, 1847, Ann. Sci. Phys. Nat. Agric. Inc. Soc. R., etc., Lyon, 10, p. 136. (Colombia = Buena Vista, 4500 feet, Eastern Andes above Villavicencio, Colombia.)

Habitat.—Humid montane forest and forest edge (Subtropical Zone).

Distribution.—*Resident* in the highlands of central Costa Rica (primarily the Caribbean slope of the Cordillera Central) and Panama (Chiriquí, Veraguas and eastern Darién); and in the Andes of South America from Colombia and western Venezuela south to Peru and western Bolivia.

Genus PHAEOCHROA Gould

Phæochroa Gould, 1861, Introd. Trochil., p. 54. Type, by subsequent designation (Elliot, 1879), *Trochilus cuvierii* De Lattre and Bourcier.

Notes.—Some authors merge *Phaeochroa* in *Campylopterus.*

Phaeochroa cuvierii (De Lattre and Bourcier). SCALY-BREASTED HUMMINGBIRD.

Trochilus Cuvierii De Lattre and Bourcier, 1846, Rev. Zool. [Paris], 9, p. 310. (isthme de Panama et Teleman, Amérique centrale.)

Habitat.—Undergrowth of open woodland, forest edge, clearings, scrub, thickets and gardens (Tropical Zone).

Distribution.—*Resident* on the Caribbean slope from Belize to northeastern Costa Rica (Puerto Viejo de Sarapiquí), and from central Costa Rica (primarily on the Pacific slope) south through Panama (both slopes, and on Isla Coiba) to northern Colombia.

Notes.—The northern Middle American populations south to northeastern Costa Rica are sometimes recognized as a distinct species, *P. roberti* (Salvin, 1861) [ROBERT'S HUMMINGBIRD].

Genus CAMPYLOPTERUS Swainson

Campylopterus Swainson, 1827, Zool. J., 3, p. 358. Type, by subsequent designation (G. R. Gray, 1840), *C. latipennis* (Lath.) = *Trochilus largipennis* Boddaert.

Notes.—See comments under *Phaeochroa.*

Campylopterus curvipennis (Lichtenstein). WEDGE-TAILED SABREWING.

Trochilus curvipennis Lichtenstein, 1830, Preis.-Verz. Säugeth. Vögel, etc., Mex., p. 1, no. 32. (Mexico.)

Habitat.—Humid lowland and foothill forest, forest edge and open woodland (Tropical and lower Subtropical zones).

Distribution.—*Resident* on the Gulf-Caribbean slope from southern San Luis Potosí and southwestern Tamaulipas south through Veracruz, northeastern Puebla, northern Oaxaca, Tabasco, northeastern Chiapas and the Yucatan Peninsula to central Guatemala (Petén and Alta Verapaz) and Belize; also in eastern Honduras (Olancho).

Notes.—Also known as CURVE-WINGED SABREWING. The morphologically distinct form from the Yucatan Peninsula and northern Central America has been treated as a separate species, *C. pampa* (Lesson, 1832) [WEDGE-TAILED SABREWING], although intergradation with *C. curvipennis* [CURVE-WINGED SABREWING] in Campeche has been reported. *C. curvipennis* and *C. excellens* are treated as conspecific by many authors; they constitute a superspecies. Further study of this complex is needed.

Campylopterus excellens (Wetmore). LONG-TAILED SABREWING.

Pampa pampa excellens Wetmore, 1941, Proc. Biol. Soc. Wash., 54, p. 207. (Volcán San Martín, 3300 feet, Tuxtla Mountains, Vera Cruz, México.)

Habitat.—Humid lowland and foothill forest and open woodland (Tropical and lower Subtropical zones).

Distribution.—*Resident* in southern Veracruz (Sierra de Tuxtla and Jesús Carranza).

Notes.—For recognition of *C. excellens* as a distinct species, see Lowery and Dalquest, 1951, Univ. Kans. Publ., Mus. Nat. Hist., 3, pp. 583–586. See also comments under *C. curvipennis*.

Campylopterus rufus Lesson. RUFOUS SABREWING.

Campylopterus rufus Lesson, 1840, Rev. Zool. [Paris], 3, p. 73. (No locality given = Guatemala.)

Habitat.—Humid montane forest, forest edge, scrub, fields and coffee plantations, in nonbreeding season also to forest at lower elevations (upper Tropical and Subtropical zones).

Distribution.—*Resident* in eastern Oaxaca (Sierra Madre de Chiapas), Chiapas, central Guatemala and El Salvador.

Campylopterus hemileucurus (Lichtenstein). VIOLET SABREWING.

Trochilus hemileucurus Lichtenstein, 1830, Preis.-Verz. Säugeth. Vögel, etc., Mex., p. 1, no. 33. (Mexico.)

Habitat.—Humid forest, forest edge, clearings and fields (upper Tropical and Subtropical, occasionally lower Tropical zones).

Distribution.—*Resident* in the highlands of Middle America from southern Mexico (Guerrero, Veracruz, Oaxaca, Tabasco and Chiapas) and Belize south to western Panama (Chiriquí and Veraguas), ranging in nonbreeding season to lower elevations, occasionally to sea level.

Genus **FLORISUGA** Bonaparte

Florisuga Bonaparte, March 1850, Consp. Gen. Avium, 1 (1), p. 73. Type, by subsequent designation (Bonaparte, April 1850), *Trochilus mellivorus* Linnaeus.

Florisuga mellivora (Linnaeus). WHITE-NECKED JACOBIN.

Trochilus mellivorus Linnaeus, 1758, Syst. Nat., ed. 10, 1, p. 121. Based on "The White-belly'd Humming Bird" Edwards, Nat. Hist. Birds, 1, p. 35, pl. 35, upper fig. (in India, error = Surinam.)

Habitat.—Humid lowland forest, forest edge, clearings, second-growth woodland and plantations (Tropical and, locally, lower Subtropical zones).

Distribution.—*Resident* on the Gulf-Caribbean slope of Middle America from Veracruz and northern Oaxaca south through Chiapas, northern Guatemala and Belize to Honduras, on both slopes of Nicaragua, Costa Rica (rare in dry northwest) and Panama, and in South America from Colombia, Venezuela (also Tobago and Trinidad) and the Guianas south, west of the Andes to western Ecuador and east of the Andes to eastern Peru, Bolivia and Amazonian Brazil.

Accidental in the southern Lesser Antilles (Carriacou) and Netherlands Antilles.

Genus **COLIBRI** Spix

Colibri Spix, 1824, Avium Spec. Nov. Bras., 1, p. 80. Type, by subsequent designation (G. R. Gray, 1855), *Trochilus serrirostris* Vieillot.

Notes.—See comments under *Lampornis.*

Colibri delphinae (Lesson). BROWN VIOLET-EAR.

Ornismya Delphinæ Lesson, 1839, Rev. Zool. [Paris], 2, p. 44. (No locality given = Santa Fé de Bogotá, Colombia.)

Habitat.—Humid forest, forest edge, clearings, second growth and plantations, more frequently in partly open situations than in dense forest (Tropical and Subtropical zones).

Distribution.—*Resident* locally on the Caribbean slope of Middle America from Belize and eastern Guatemala south to Costa Rica and Panama (locally in highlands on both slopes), and in South America from Colombia, Venezuela (also Trinidad) and the Guianas south, west of the Andes to western Ecuador and east of the Andes to eastern Peru and Bolivia, also in northern and eastern Brazil.

Colibri thalassinus (Swainson). GREEN VIOLET-EAR. [427.1.]

Trochilus thalassinus Swainson, 1827, Philos. Mag., new ser., 1, p. 441. (Temiscaltipec, Mexico = Temascaltepec, state of México.)

Habitat.—Forest edge, brushy hillsides and pine-oak woodland, rarely in humid forest (upper Tropical and Subtropical zones, in South America also Temperate Zone).

Distribution.—*Resident* from Jalisco, Guanajuato, San Luis Potosí and Veracruz south through the highlands of Middle America (not recorded Nicaragua) to western Panama (Chiriquí and Veraguas); and in South America from Colombia and northern Venezuela south, west of the Andes to western Ecuador and east of the Andes to eastern Peru and northern Bolivia.

Casual in south-central and southern Texas (Hays County, the Austin area, Padre Island, and the lower Rio Grande Valley). Accidental in California (Mt. Pinos, Kern County).

Notes.—The populations from Costa Rica southward have sometimes been separated as a distinct species, *C. cyanotus* (Bourcier, 1843) [MOUNTAIN VIO-LET-EAR].

Genus **ANTHRACOTHORAX** Boie

Anthracothorax Boie, 1831, Isis von Oken, col. 545. Type, by subsequent designation (Elliot, 1879), *Trochilus violicauda* Boddaert = *Trochilus viridigula* Boddaert.

[**Anthracothorax viridigula** (Boddaert). GREEN-THROATED MANGO.] See Appendix A.

Anthracothorax prevostii (Lesson). GREEN-BREASTED MANGO.

Trochilus prevostii Lesson, 1832, Hist. Nat. Colibris, livr. 13, p. 87, pl. 24. (South America.)

Habitat.—Open situations with scattered trees, edge of scrubby woodland, agricultural lands and mangroves, especially common in coastal areas (Tropical Zone).

Distribution.—Resident [*prevostii* group] from Oaxaca, San Luis Potosí and southern Tamaulipas south along both coasts of Middle America (including the Yucatan Peninsula and larger islands offshore, Hunting Cay off Belize, the Bay Islands off Honduras, and Providencia and San Andrés islands in the Caribbean Sea off Nicaragua) to Costa Rica, and in northern Venezuela; [*veraguensis* group] in the Pacific lowlands of western Panama from Chiriquí east to southern Coclé, also recorded on on the Caribbean slope of the Canal Zone; and [*iridescens* group] the arid Pacific lowlands from western Colombia south to northwestern Peru.

Notes.—Also known as PREVOST'S MANGO. The populations in Panama are often regarded as a distinct species, *A. veraguensis* Reichenbach, 1855 [VERAGUAS MANGO]; the *iridescens* group is regarded as a subspecies, *A. p. iridescens* (Gould, 1861), or by some authors as a subspecies of *A. nigricollis*. The latter species and *A. prevostii* are closely related and are regarded as conspecific by some; they constitute a superspecies.

Anthracothorax nigricollis (Vieillot). BLACK-THROATED MANGO.

Trochilus nigricollis Vieillot, 1817, Nouv. Dict. Hist. Nat., nouv. éd., 7, p. 349. (Brazil.)

Habitat.—Forest edge, second growth, open woodland, clearings, plantations and gardens (Tropical and lower Subtropical zones).

Distribution.—Resident in Panama (from southern Veraguas on the Pacific slope, and the Canal Zone on the Caribbean eastward), and in South America from Colombia, Venezuela (also Tobago and Trinidad) and the Guianas south, east of the Andes, to eastern Peru, Bolivia, Paraguay and northeastern Argentina.

Notes.—See comments under *A. prevostii*.

Anthracothorax mango (Linnaeus). JAMAICAN MANGO.

Trochilus Mango Linnaeus, 1758, Syst. Nat., ed. 10, 1, p. 121. Based on *Mellivora mango* Albin, Nat. Hist. Birds, 2, p. 45, pl. 49, fig. 1. (in Jamaica.)

Habitat.—Open woodland and partly open situations, especially in more arid habitats.

Distribution.—*Resident* on Jamaica.

Anthracothorax dominicus (Linnaeus). ANTILLEAN MANGO.

Trochilus dominicus Linnaeus, 1766, Syst. Nat., ed. 12, 1, p. 191. Based on "Le Colibry de S. Domingue" Brisson, Ornithologie, 3, p. 672, pl. 35, fig. 4. (in Dominica = Hispaniola.)

Habitat.—Woodland and open situations in lowlands, in both arid and humid habitats, and in plantations and gardens.

Distribution.—*Resident* on Hispaniola (including Gonâve, Tortue and Beata islands, and Île-à-Vache), in central and western Puerto Rico (including Vieques, Culebra and Culebrita islands), and in the Virgin Islands (St. Thomas, formerly on St. John and Anegada).

Anthracothorax viridis (Audebert and Vieillot). GREEN MANGO.

Trochilus viridis Audebert and Vieillot, 1801, Ois. Dorés, 1, p. 34, pl. 15. (Îles de l'Amérique Septentrionale = Puerto Rico.)

Habitat.—Open woodland, partly open situations and plantations in uplands.

Distribution.—*Resident* on Puerto Rico.

Genus EULAMPIS Boie

Eulampis Boie, 1831, Isis von Oken, col. 547. Type, by subsequent designation (G. R. Gray, 1840), *E. aurata* (Audebert) *i.e.* Gmelin = *Trochilus jugularis* Linnaeus.

Anthracothorax γ *Sericotes* Reichenbach, 1854, J. Ornithol., 1, Beil. zu Extrah., p. 11. Type, by subsequent designation (G. R. Gray, 1855), *Trochilus holo-*
sericeus Linnaeus.

Eulampis jugularis (Linnaeus). PURPLE-THROATED CARIB.

Trochilus jugularis Linnaeus, 1766, Syst. Nat., ed. 12, 1, p. 190. Based on the "Red-breasted Humming-bird" Edwards, Glean. Nat. Hist., 2, p. 118, pl. 266, fig. 1. (in Cayenna, Surinamo, error = Lesser Antilles.)

Habitat.—Montane forest, forest edge, clearings and banana plantations.

Distribution.—*Resident* in the Lesser Antilles (Saba, St. Estatius, St. Kitts, Nevis, Montserrat, Antigua, Guadeloupe, Dominica, Martinique, St. Lucia and St. Vincent).

Casual in Barbuda, Désirade, Îles des Saintes and Bequia, also sight records for Barbados and Grenada.

Notes.—Also known as GARNET-THROATED HUMMINGBIRD, a name now restricted to *Lamprolaima rhami.*

Eulampis holosericeus (Linnaeus). GREEN-THROATED CARIB.

Trochilus holosericeus Linnaeus, 1758, Syst. Nat., ed. 10, 1, p. 120. Based on "The Black-belly'd Green Humming Bird" Edwards, Nat. Hist. Birds, 1, p. 36, pl. 36. (in America = Lesser Antilles.)

Habitat.—Open woodland, second growth and partly open situations, mostly in lowlands, less frequently in montane forest clearings.

Distribution.—*Resident* in Puerto Rico (primarily eastern), the Virgin Islands, and Lesser Antilles (virtually throughout south to Grenada); reports from Tobago are apparently without basis.

Notes.—Also known as EMERALD-THROATED HUMMINGBIRD. Often placed in the monotypic genus *Sericotes*.

[Genus **CHRYSOLAMPIS** Boie]

Chrysolampis Boie, 1831, Isis von Oken, col. 546. Type, by subsequent designation (G. R. Gray, 1840), *Trochilus* "*moschita*" [=*mosquitus*] Linnaeus.

Notes.—Some authors suggest that *Chrysolampis* be merged in *Orthorhynchus*.

[**Chrysolampis mosquitus** (Linnaeus). RUBY-TOPAZ HUMMINGBIRD.] See Appendix A.

Genus **ORTHORHYNCHUS** Lacépède

Orthorhynchus Lacépède, 1799, Tabl. Mamm. Ois., p. 9. Type, by subsequent designation (G. R. Gray, 1840), *Trochilus cristatus* Linnaeus.

Notes.—See comments under *Chrysolampis*.

Orthorhynchus cristatus (Linnaeus). ANTILLEAN CRESTED HUMMINGBIRD.

Trochilus cristatus Linnaeus, 1758, Syst. Nat., ed. 10, 1, p. 121. Based on "The Crested Humming Bird" Edwards, Nat. Hist. Birds, 1, p. 37, pl. 37. (in America = Barbados, Lesser Antilles.)

Habitat.—Open situations, woodland, forest edge, clearings and around human habitation, more frequently in lowlands, less commonly in montane habitats.

Distribution.—*Resident* in Puerto Rico (including on Vieques and Culebra islands), the Virgin Islands and Lesser Antilles (virtually throughout south to Grenada).

A specimen obtained in Texas (Galveston Island, February 1967) is questionably a natural vagrant.

Genus **KLAIS** Reichenbach

Basilinna β Klais Reichenbach, 1854, J. Ornithol., 1, Beil. zu Extrah., p. 13. Type, by monotypy, *Trochilus guimeti* Bourcier.

Klais guimeti (Bourcier). VIOLET-HEADED HUMMINGBIRD.

Trochilus Guimeti Bourcier, 1843, Rev. Zool. [Paris], 6, p. 72. (à Caracas, capitale de Vénezuéla, la Colombie = Caracas, Venezuela.)

Habitat.—Humid forest edge, open woodland, clearings and second growth (upper Tropical and Subtropical zones, rarely lower Tropical Zone).

Distribution.—*Resident* on the Caribbean slope of eastern Honduras (west to the Sula Valley) and Nicaragua, in Costa Rica (Caribbean slope and, in the southwestern region, the Pacific lowlands) and Panama (both slopes), and in South America from northern Colombia and western Venezuela south, east of the Andes, to eastern Peru, northwestern Bolivia and extreme western Brazil.

Genus **ABEILLIA** Bonaparte

Abeillia Bonaparte, 1850, Consp. Gen. Avium, 1 (1), p. 79. Type, by original designation, *Abeillia typica* Bonaparte = *Ornismya abeillei* Lesson and De Lattre.

Abeillia abeillei (Lesson and De Lattre). EMERALD-CHINNED HUMMING-BIRD.

Ornismya Abeillei Lesson and De Lattre, 1839, Rev. Zool. [Paris], 2, p. 16. (Jalapa [Veracruz].)

Habitat.—Humid forest, forest edge and clearings, most frequently in montane situations, less commonly (primarily in nonbreeding season) in lowland forest (Tropical and Subtropical zones).

Distribution.—*Resident* from Veracruz, Oaxaca and Chiapas south through the highlands of Guatemala, El Salvador and Honduras to north-central Nicaragua.

Notes.—Also known as ABEILLE'S HUMMINGBIRD.

Genus **LOPHORNIS** Lesson

Lophornis Lesson, 1829, Hist. Nat. Ois.-Mouches, p. xxxvii. Type, by subsequent designation (G. R. Gray, 1840), *L. ornata* (L.) Less. Ois. M., pl. 41 = *Trochilus ornatus* Boddaert.

Paphosia Mulsant and J. and E. Verreaux, 1866, Mém. Soc. Imp. Sci. Nat. Cherbourg, 12, p. 219. Type, by monotypy, *Ornismya helenae* De Lattre.

Lophornis delattrei (Lesson). RUFOUS-CRESTED COQUETTE.

Ornismya (Lophorinus) De Lattrei Lesson, 1839, Rev. Zool. [Paris], 2, p. 19. (No locality given = Peru.)

Habitat.—Humid forest edge, clearings and open woodland (Tropical and Subtropical zones).

Distribution.—*Resident* locally in central Costa Rica (San José region, possibly only a vagrant from the south) and Panama (throughout, but most frequent in central Panama); in northern Colombia (Magdalena Valley); and in eastern Peru and east-central Bolivia.

Lophornis helenae (De Lattre). BLACK-CRESTED COQUETTE.

Ornismya Helenæ De Lattre, 1843, Rev. Zool. [Paris], 6, p. 133. (Vera-Pax, propte, Petinck in republica Guatimala = Vera Paz, Guatemala.)

Habitat.—Humid forest edge, clearings, second growth, open woodland, scrub and plantations (Tropical and lower Subtropical zones).

Distribution.—*Resident* on the Caribbean slope of Middle America from Veracruz, northern Oaxaca and Chiapas south to central Costa Rica (on Caribbean slope, also a vagrant to the vicinity of San José and the Pacific slope). Reports from southern Texas are erroneous.

Notes.—This species and the following are often placed in the genus *Paphosia*.

Lophornis adorabilis Salvin. WHITE-CRESTED COQUETTE.

Lophornis adorabilis Salvin, 1870, Proc. Zool. Soc. London, p. 207. (Bugaba, Chiriquí, Panama.)

Habitat.—Forest edge, open woodland, second growth and scrub (upper Tropical and Subtropical zones).

Distribution.—*Resident* in central and southwestern Costa Rica (north to the Cordillera Central) and extreme western Panama (western Chiriquí); a report from Isla Cébaco, Panama, is considered doubtful.

Notes.—Also known as ADORABLE COQUETTE. See comments under *L. helenae.*

Genus DISCOSURA Bonaparte

Discosura Bonaparte, 1850, Consp. Gen. Avium, 1 (1), p. 84. Type, by subsequent designation (G. R. Gray, 1855), *Trochilus longicaudus* Gmelin.
Popelairia Reichenbach, 1854, J. Ornithol., 1, Beil. zu Extrah., p. 12. Type, by monotypy, *Popelairia tricholopha* Reichenbach = *Trochilus popelairii* Du Bus de Gisignies.

Discosura conversii (Bourcier and Mulsant). GREEN THORNTAIL.

Trochilus Conversii Bourcier and Mulsant, 1846, Ann. Sci. Phys. Nat. Agric. Ind. Soc. R., etc., Lyon, 9, p. 313, pl. [9]. (Bogotá, Colombia.)

Habitat.—Humid forest edge, clearings, open woodland and scrub (upper Tropical and Subtropical zones).

Distribution.—*Resident* in Costa Rica (Caribbean slope north to the Cordillera Central), locally in Panama (recorded eastern Chiriquí, Veraguas, Coclé, the Canal Zone, eastern Panamá province and eastern Darién), and on the Pacific slope of western Colombia and western Ecuador.

Notes.—Often placed in the genus *Popelairia.*

Genus CHLOROSTILBON Gould

Chlorostilbon Gould, 1853, Monogr. Trochil., pt. 5, pl. [14] and text. Type, by monotypy, *Chlorostilbon prasinus* Gould (not other authors) = *Trochilus pucherani* Bourcier = *Ornismya aureo-ventris* d'Orbigny and Lafresnaye.
Chlorestes δ Riccordia Reichenbach, 1854, J. Ornithol., 1, Beil. zu Extrah., p. 8. Type, by subsequent designation (G. R. Gray, 1855), *Riccordia ramondii* Reichenbach = *Ornismya ricordii* Gervais.

Chlorostilbon canivetii (Lesson). FORK-TAILED EMERALD.

Ornismya canivetii Lesson, 1832, Hist. Nat. Colibris, livr. 13, pp. 174, 177, pl. 37, 38. (Brazil, error = Jalapa, Veracruz.)

Habitat.—Open situations, scrub, plantations and gardens, most frequently in lowland habitats (Tropical and Subtropical zones).

Distribution.—*Resident* from Sinaloa, Durango, Nayarit, Jalisco, Michoacán, the state of México, San Luis Potosí and southern Tamaulipas south along both slopes of Middle America (including islands off Quintana Roo, and the Bay and Hog islands off Honduras) to Nicaragua and northwestern Costa Rica (Guanacaste and the central plateau region).

Notes.—Some authors consider *C. canivetii* and *C. assimilis* to be conspecific with the South American *C. mellisugus* (Linnaeus, 1758) [BLUE-TAILED EMERALD]; in view of the uncertainty of specific limits throughout this genus, it seems best to regard these three forms as allospecies of a superspecies.

Chlorostilbon assimilis Lawrence. GARDEN EMERALD.

> *Chlorostilbon assimilis* Lawrence, 1861, Ann. Lyc. Nat. Hist. N.Y., 7, p. 292. (Atlantic side of the Isthmus of Panama, along the line of the Panama Railroad.)

Habitat.—Open and partly open country in lowlands and foothills, including forest clearings, plantations and gardens (Tropical and lower Subtropical zones).

Distribution.—*Resident* in southwestern Costa Rica (north to the Térraba region) and Panama (Pacific slope east to the Canal Zone and western Panamá province, including Coiba, Pearl and many smaller islands).

Notes.—Also known as ALLIED EMERALD. See comments under *C. canivetii.*

Chlorostilbon ricordii (Gervais). CUBAN EMERALD.

> *Ornismya Ricordii* Gervais, 1835, Mag. Zool. [Paris], 5, cl. 2, pl. 41, 42. (Santiago de Cuba = Santiago, Cuba.)

Habitat.—Open woodland, open situations with scattered trees, and gardens.

Distribution.—*Resident* in the Bahamas (Abaco, including offshore cays, Grand Bahama, Andros and Green Cay), and on Cuba (including offshore cays) and the Isle of Pines.

Casual elsewhere in the Bahamas (New Providence), also sight reports for southern and east-central Florida.

Notes.—*C. ricordii, C. swainsonii* and *C. maugaeus* constitute a superspecies; in addition, some authors who treat this group as conspecific, and the *C. mellisugus* complex as forming but a single additional species, would hold that these enlarged two species constitute a single superspecies.

Chlorostilbon swainsonii (Lesson). HISPANIOLAN EMERALD.

> *Ornismya Swainsonii* Lesson, 1829, Hist. Nat., Ois.-Mouches, p. "xvij" [=xvii]; 1830, p. 197, pl. 70. (le Brésil, error = Hispaniola.)

Habitat.—Open forest, forest edge and scrub, primarily in mountains, less commonly in lowlands and open situations.

Distribution.—*Resident* on Hispaniola; reports from Gonâve Island are unsubstantiated.

Notes.—See comments under *C. ricordii.*

Chlorostilbon maugaeus (Audebert and Vieillot). PUERTO RICAN EMERALD.

Trochilus Maugæus Audebert and Vieillot, 1801, Ois. Dorés, 1, pp. 77, 79, pl. 37, 38. (Puerto Rico.)

Habitat.—Open forest, plantations, partly open situations and mangroves.
Distribution.—*Resident* on Puerto Rico.
Notes.—See comments under *C. ricordii.*

Genus CYNANTHUS Swainson

Cynanthus Swainson, 1827, Philos. Mag., new ser., 1, p. 441. Type, by subsequent designation (Stone, 1907), *Cynanthus latirostris* Swainson.

Cynanthus sordidus (Gould). DUSKY HUMMINGBIRD.

Cyanomyia (?) *sordida* Gould, 1859, Ann. Mag. Nat. Hist., ser. 3, 4, p. 97. (Oaxaca, Mexico.)

Habitat.—Arid scrub, second growth, plantations and gardens (Subtropical and lower Temperate zones).
Distribution.—*Resident* from Jalisco, Michoacán, the state of México and Hidalgo south to Oaxaca and Puebla.

Cynanthus latirostris Swainson. BROAD-BILLED HUMMINGBIRD. [441.]

Cynanthus latirostris Swainson, 1827, Philos. Mag., new ser., 1, p. 441. (Tableland of Mexico = valley of México, near Mexico City.)

Habitat.—Arid scrub, open deciduous forest, semi-desert and other open situations in arid habitats (Tropical and lower Subtropical zones).
Distribution.—*Breeds* from western Sonora, southeastern Arizona, southwestern New Mexico (Guadalupe Canyon), northern Chihuahua, western Texas (Brewster County) and Tamaulipas south through Mexico (including the Tres Marias Islands) to Oaxaca and Chiapas, and east to northern Veracruz, Hidalgo and Puebla.

Winters from central Sonora, Chihuahua, Coahuila and Tamaulipas south through the breeding range, casually north to southern Arizona.

Casual north to central and southern California (to Alameda County), central Arizona, central New Mexico (sight records) and southern Texas. Accidental in Utah (Springdale) and western Florida (near Pensacola).

Notes.—Some authors have suggested that the southern form from Guerrero, Oaxaca and Chiapas represents a distinct species, *C. doubledayi* (Bourcier, 1847) [DOUBLEDAY'S HUMMINGBIRD].

Genus CYANOPHAIA Reichenbach

Cyanophaia Reichenbach, 1854, J. Ornithol., 1, Beil. zu Extrah., p. 10. Type, by subsequent designation (G. R. Gray, 1855), *Trochilus bicolor* "Linn." [=Gmelin].

Cyanophaia bicolor (Gmelin). BLUE-HEADED HUMMINGBIRD.

Trochilus bicolor Gmelin, 1788, Syst. Nat., 1 (1), p. 496. Based in part on "Saphir-émeraude" Buffon, Hist. Nat. Ois., 6, p. 26, and the "Sapphire and Emerald Humming-bird" Latham, Gen. Synop. Birds, 1 (2), p. 775. (in Guadeloupe, error = Dominica.)

Habitat.—Forest and partly open country in mountains.

Distribution.—*Resident* on Dominica and Martinique, in the Lesser Antilles.

Genus THALURANIA Gould

Thalurania Gould, 1848, Proc. Zool. Soc. London, p. 13. Type, by subsequent designation (G. R. Gray, 1855), *Trochilus furcatus* Gmelin.

Notes.—See comments under *Damophila.*

Thalurania colombica (Bourcier). CROWNED WOODNYMPH.

Ornismya Colombica Bourcier, 1843, Rev. Zool. [Paris], 6, p. 2. (la Colombie = San Agustín, Magdalena Valley, Colombia.)

Habitat.—Humid lowland forest, forest edge, clearings, second-growth woodland, partly open situations and plantations (Tropical, rarely lower subtropical zones).

Distribution.—*Resident* in western Mexico (Nayarit, western Jalisco and Colima); and from Guatemala and Belize south along the Caribbean slope of northern Middle America to Nicaragua, on both slopes of Costa Rica and Panama, and in northern Colombia and western Venezuela.

Notes.—Various distinct populations have been recognized by authors as separate species: *T. ridgwayi* Nelson, 1900 [MEXICAN WOODNYMPH], of western Mexico; *T. townsendi* Ridgway, 1888 [BLUE-CROWNED WOODNYMPH], of Middle America south to western Panama; and *T. fannyi* (De Lattre and Bourcier, 1846) [GREEN-CROWNED WOODNYMPH], of eastern Panama and northwestern Colombia. Other authors regard *T. colombica* and the South American *T. furcata* (Gmelin, 1789) [COMMON WOODNYMPH] as conspecific; they constitute a superspecies.

Genus PANTERPE Cabanis and Heine

Panterpe Cabanis and Heine, 1860, Mus. Heineanum, 3, p. 43 (footnote). Type, by original designation, *Panterpe insignis* Cabanis and Heine.

Panterpe insignis Cabanis and Heine. FIERY-THROATED HUMMINGBIRD.

Panterpe insignis Cabanis and Heine, 1860, Mus. Heineanum, 3, p. 43 (footnote). (Costa Rica.)

Habitat.—Forest edge, open scrub, meadows, clearings and second-growth woodland (Subtropical and Temperate zones).

Distribution.—*Resident* in Costa Rica (cordilleras de Talamanca and Central) and western Panama (western Chiriquí and western Bocas del Toro).

Genus **DAMOPHILA** Reichenbach

Damophila Reichenbach, 1854, J. Ornithol., 1, Beil. zu Extrah., p. 7. Type, by subsequent designation (Elliot, 1879), *T. julie* Bourcier = *Ornismyia julie* Bourcier.

Notes.—Some authors merge this genus in *Thalurania.*

Damophila julie (Bourcier). VIOLET-BELLIED HUMMINGBIRD.

Ornismyia Julie Bourcier, 1842, Rev. Zool. [Paris], 5, p. 373. (Tunja en Colombie = Tunja, Colombia.)

Habitat.—Humid lowland forest edge, clearings and second-growth woodland (Tropical Zone).

Distribution.—*Resident* in central and eastern Panama (from northern Coclé and the Canal Zone eastward), western Colombia and western Ecuador; specimens reported from "Costa Rica" are regarded as probably mislabeled.

Genus **LEPIDOPYGA** Reichenbach

Agyrtria γ *Lepidopyga* Reichenbach, 1855, Trochil. Enum., p. 7. Type, by subsequent designation (Ridgway, 1911), *Trochilus goudoti* Bourcier.

Lepidopyga coeruleogularis (Gould). SAPPHIRE-THROATED HUMMINGBIRD.

Trochilus (————?) *cœruleogularis* Gould, 1851, Proc. Zool. Soc. London (1850), p. 163. (Near David, on the north side of the Cordillera, Veragua [Chiriquí, Panama].)

Habitat.—Clearings, partly open situations, brushy areas, gardens and mangroves (Tropical Zone).

Distribution.—*Resident* in Panama (the Pacific lowlands from Chiriquí eastward, including Isla Coiba, and the Caribbean lowlands in the Canal Zone and San Blas) and northern Colombia; an old specimen from "Costa Rica" is regarded as probably mislabeled.

Genus **HYLOCHARIS** Boie

Hylocharis Boie, 1831, Isis von Oken, col. 546. Type, by subsequent designation (G. R. Gray, 1840), *H. sapphirina* (Gm.) Boie = *Trochilus sapphirinus* Gmelin.

Basilinna Boie, 1831, Isis von Oken, col. 546. Type, by subsequent designation (G. R. Gray, 1855), *Trochilus leucotis* Vieillot.

Hylocharis grayi (De Lattre and Bourcier). BLUE-HEADED SAPPHIRE.

Trochilus Grayi De Lattre and Bourcier, 1846, Rev. Zool. [Paris], 9, p. 307. (Popayán, Nouvelle-Grenade [=Colombia].)

Habitat.—Open woodland, forest edge, scrub and mangroves, in both humid and semi-arid situations (Tropical and lower Subtropical zones).

Distribution.—*Resident* from extreme eastern Panama (near Jaque in southern Darién) south through western and central Colombia to northwestern Ecuador.

Hylocharis eliciae (Bourcier and Mulsant). BLUE-THROATED GOLDENTAIL.

Trochilus Eliciæ Bourcier and Mulsant, 1846, Ann. Sci. Phys. Nat. Agric. Ind. Soc. R., etc., Lyon, 9, p. 314. (No locality given.)

Habitat.—Open woodland, forest edge and clearings, and open situations with scattered trees, both in humid and semi-arid habitats (Tropical and lower Subtropical zones).

Distribution.—*Resident* from southern Mexico (recorded Veracruz and Chiapas) south along both slopes of Central America (not recorded Belize) to western Panama (east to Canal Zone and western Panamá province, also Isla Coiba).

Hylocharis leucotis (Vieillot). WHITE-EARED HUMMINGBIRD. [440.1.]

Trochilus leucotis Vieillot, 1818, Nouv. Dict. Hist. Nat., nouv. éd., 23, p. 428. (au Brésil, error = Orizaba, Veracruz.)

Distribution.—*Resident* from Sonora, Chihuahua, Coahuila, Nuevo León and Tamaulipas south through the highlands of Mexico, Guatemala, El Salvador and Honduras to north-central Nicaragua. Recorded irregularly in summer (and probably breeding) in the mountains of southern Arizona, southwestern New Mexico (Animas Mountains) and western Texas (Big Bend); northernmost populations are partially migratory.

Notes.—*H. leucotis* and *H. xantusii* may constitute a superspecies.

Hylocharis xantusii (Lawrence). XANTUS' HUMMINGBIRD. [440.]

Amazilia Xantusii Lawrence, 1860, Ann. Lyc. Nat. Hist. N.Y., 7, p. 109. (Cape St. Lucas, South California = San Nicolás, 10 miles northeast of Cape San Lucas, Baja California).

Habitat.—Open montane forest (especially oak), clearings, brushy hillsides and canyons, second growth, and arid lowland scrub (Tropical to Temperate zones).

Distribution.—*Resident* in southern Baja California, casually north to lat. 29°N., including islands in the Gulf of California north to Isla San José.

Notes.—Also known as BLACK-FRONTED HUMMINGBIRD. See comments under *H. leucotis.*

Genus GOLDMANIA Nelson

Goldmania Nelson, 1911, Smithson. Misc. Collect., 56, no. 21, p. 1. Type, by original designation, *Goldmania violiceps* Nelson.

Goldmania violiceps Nelson. VIOLET-CAPPED HUMMINGBIRD.

Goldmania violiceps Nelson, 1911, Smithson. Misc. Collect., 56, no. 21, p. 1. (Cerro Azul, 3000 feet, northwest of Chepo, Panamá.)

Habitat.—Humid montane forest and forest edge, primarily in low undergrowth (Subtropical Zone).

Distribution.—*Resident* in eastern Panama (eastern Colón, eastern Panamá province and eastern Darién) and extreme northwestern Colombia.

Genus GOETHALSIA Nelson

Goethalsia Nelson, 1912, Smithson. Misc. Collect., 60, no. 3, p. 6. Type, by original designation, *Goethalsia bella* Nelson.

Goethalsia bella Nelson. RUFOUS-CHEEKED HUMMINGBIRD.

Goethalsia bella Nelson, 1912, Smithson. Misc. Collect., 60, no. 3, p. 7. (Cana, at 2000 feet altitude, eastern Panama.)

Habitat.—Foothills and highlands, nothing further known concerning habitat (upper Tropical and Subtropical zones).
Distribution.—*Resident* in extreme eastern Panama (cerros Pirre and Sapo in eastern Darién) and adjacent northwestern Colombia (Alturas del Nique in Chocó).
Notes.—Also known as PIRRE HUMMINGBIRD.

Genus TROCHILUS Linnaeus

Trochilus Linnaeus, 1758, Syst. Nat., ed. 10, 1, p. 119. Type, by subsequent designation (G. R. Gray, 1840), *Trochilus polytmus* Linnaeus.

Trochilus polytmus Linnaeus. STREAMERTAIL.

Trochilus Polytmus Linnaeus, 1758, Syst. Nat., ed. 10, 1, p. 120. Based mainly on *Polytmus viridans aureo varie splendens,* etc. Brown, Jamaica, p. 145, and the "Long-tailed Black-cap Humming Bird" Edwards, Nat. Hist. Birds, 1, p. 34, pl. 34. (in America = Jamaica.)

Habitat.—Open woodland and partly open situations from lowlands to mountains, more frequently in humid habitats, less commonly in semi-arid regions.
Distribution.—*Resident* on Jamaica.
Notes.—Populations in extreme eastern Jamaica (John Crow Mountains, and east of the Morant River) differ from those elsewhere in bill color, display and vocalizations, with an apparent narrow hybrid zone between them; some authors suggest that these be recognized as distinct species, *T. polytmus* [WESTERN STREAMERTAIL] and *T. scitulus* (Brewster and Bangs, 1901) [EASTERN STREAMERTAIL]. For recent discussions, see Schuchmann (1978, Ardea, 66, pp. 156–172) and Gill and F. J. and C. Stokes (1973, Condor, 75, pp. 170–176).

Genus AMAZILIA Lesson

Amazilia Lesson, 1843, Echo Monde Savant, sér. 2, 7, col. 757. Type, by subsequent designation (Stone, 1918), *Ornismia cinnamomea* Less[on] (=*O. rutila* De Lattre) = *Ornismya rutila* De Lattre.
Saucerottia Bonaparte, 1850, Consp. Gen. Avium, 1 (1), p. 77. Type, by original designation, *Saucerottia typica* Bonaparte = *Trochilus saucerrottei* De Lattre and Bourcier.
Polyerata Heine, 1863, J. Ornithol., 11, p. 194. Type, by monotypy, *Trochilus amabilis* Gould.

Amazilia candida (Bourcier and Mulsant). WHITE-BELLIED EMERALD.

Trochilus candidus Bourcier and Mulsant, 1846, Ann. Sci. Phys. Nat. Agric. Ind. Soc. R., etc., Lyon, 9, p. 326. (Cobán, Guatemala.)

Habitat.—Humid forest edge, clearings, open woodland, brushy areas and plantations (Tropical and lower Subtropical zones).

Distribution.—*Resident* from San Luis Potosí and northern Veracruz south along the Gulf-Caribbean slope of Middle America (including the Yucatan Peninsula, also Pacific lowlands of Guatemala) to Honduras, and on both slopes of Nicaragua and, probably only as a vagrant, Costa Rica (south to Osa Peninsula).

[Amazilia chionopectus (Gould). WHITE-CHESTED EMERALD.] See Appendix B.

Amazilia luciae (Lawrence). HONDURAN EMERALD.

Thaumatias Luciæ Lawrence, 1867, Proc. Acad. Nat. Sci. Philadelphia, 19, p. 233. (Honduras.)

Habitat.—Unknown, localities generally in the humid lowlands (Tropical Zone).
Distribution.—*Resident* in Honduras (Caribbean lowlands from Cofradía east to Catacamas).

Amazilia amabilis (Gould). BLUE-CHESTED HUMMINGBIRD.

Trochilus (——?) *amabilis* Gould, 1853, Proc. Zool. Soc. London (1851), p. 115. (New Grenada = Colombia.)

Habitat.—Humid forest edge, second-growth woodland and clearings (Tropical and lower Subtropical zones).

Distribution.—*Resident* on the Caribbean slope of Nicaragua and Costa Rica, and in Panama (Caribbean slope throughout, and Pacific slope from eastern Panamá province eastward), Colombia (east to the Magdalena Valley, and south along the Pacific coast) and western Ecuador.

Notes.—*A. amabilis* and *A. decora* constitute a superspecies; they are considered conspecific by some authors.

Amazilia decora (Salvin). CHARMING HUMMINGBIRD.

Polyerata decora Salvin, 1891, Ann. Mag. Nat. Hist., ser. 6, 7, p. 377. (western slopes of the Volcano of Chiriqui [Panama].)

Habitat.—Humid forest, forest edge, clearings and open woodland (Tropical and lower Subtropical zones).

Distribution.—*Resident* on the Pacific slope of southwestern Costa Rica (El General-Térraba-Golfo Dulce region) and extreme western Panama (western Chiriquí).

Notes.—See comments under *A. amabilis.*

Amazilia boucardi (Mulsant). MANGROVE HUMMINGBIRD.

Arena Boucardi Mulsant, 1877, Descr. Esp. Nouv. Trochil., p. 6. (Punta Arenas, Costa Rica.)

Habitat.—Mangroves and adjacent partly open situations (Tropical Zone).
Distribution.—*Resident* on the Pacific coast of Costa Rica (Gulf of Nicoya to Golfo Dulce region).
Notes.—Also known as BOUCARD'S HUMMINGBIRD.

Amazilia cyanocephala (Lesson). AZURE-CROWNED HUMMINGBIRD.

Ornismya cyanocephalus Lesson, 1829, Hist. Nat. Ois.-Mouches, p. xlv. (Le Brésil, error = Veracruz, Veracruz.)

Habitat.—Open woodland and forest edge, primarily pine and pine-oak association, locally in lowland pine savanna (Tropical and Subtropical zones).
Distribution.—*Breeds* from southern Tamaulipas south, primarily in the highlands, through Veracruz, Oaxaca, Chiapas, southern Quintana Roo, central and eastern Guatemala, Belize, El Salvador and Honduras to north-central Nicaragua; and in the lowland pine savanna of eastern Honduras and northeastern Nicaragua.

Winters generally in the breeding range, occurring also in lowland habitats (recorded San Luis Potosí and northern Quintana Roo).

Notes.—Also known as RED-BILLED AZURECROWN. *A. microrhyncha* (Elliot, 1876) [SMALL-BILLED AZURECROWN], is now regarded as being based on an aberrant or possibly juvenile specimen of *A. cyanocephala.*

Amazilia cyanifrons (Bourcier). INDIGO-CAPPED HUMMINGBIRD.

Trochilus cyanifrons Bourcier, 1843, Rev. Zool. [Paris], 6, p. 100. (Ybagué, Nouvelle-Grenade = Ibague, Colombia.)

Habitat.—Forest, forest edge and open woodland (Tropical and Subtropical zones).
Distribution.—*Resident* in northeastern Colombia (Atlántico and the Magdalena Valley to Notre de Santander); one specimen known from northwestern Costa Rica (Volcán Miravalles).
Notes.—Also known as BLUE-FRONTED HUMMINGBIRD. This form is known from Middle America only from the single specimen taken in Costa Rica and described as a new species, *A. alfaroana* Underwood, 1896, Ibis, p. 441. The type closely resembles *A. cyanifrons* and does not appear to be be a hybrid between any Middle American species of *Amazilia.* The unique specimen of *alfaroana* is tentatively considered to represent a subspecies of *A. cyanifrons*; its status can be clarified only by additional data.

Amazilia beryllina (Lichtenstein). BERYLLINE HUMMINGBIRD. [438.1.]

Trochilus beryllinus Lichtenstein, 1830, Preis.-Verz. Säugeth. Vögel, etc., Mex., p. 1. (México = Temascaltepec, state of México.)

Habitat.—Open woodland, primarily pine and pine-oak association, ranging in nonbreeding season into arid scrub, deciduous forest and humid montane forest (Tropical and Subtropical zones).
Distribution.—*Resident* from Sonora and southern Chihuahua south through western Mexico (east to Durango, Guanajuato, Tlaxcala, Puebla and west-central Veracruz), Guatemala and El Salvador to central Honduras.

Casual in southeastern Arizona (Huachuca, where breeding once, and Chiricahua mountains).

Notes.—Hybridization between *A. beryllina* and *A. cyanura* has been reported from south-central Guatemala (Patulul) and El Salvador. *A. sumichrasti* Salvin, 1891, is based on an aberrant individual of *A. beryllina* taken at Santa Efigenia, Oaxaca.

Amazilia cyanura Gould. BLUE-TAILED HUMMINGBIRD.

Amazilia cyanura Gould, 1859, Monogr. Trochil., pt. 18, pl. [12] and text. (Realejo, Nicaragua.)

Habitat.—Open woodland, forest edge, clearings and scrub, primarily in arid habitats but also locally in humid situations (Tropical and lower Subtropical zones).

Distribution.—*Resident* on the Pacific slope from Chiapas to western Nicaragua (also locally on the Caribbean slope of Honduras).

Casual in Costa Rica (near San José and Finca La Selva), possibly a rare and local resident.

Notes.—*A. cyanura* and *A. saucerrottei* appear to constitute a superspecies. See also comments under *A. beryllina*.

Amazilia saucerrottei (De Lattre and Bourcier). STEELY-VENTED HUM-MINGBIRD.

Trochilus Saucerrottei De Lattre and Bourcier, 1846, Rev. Zool. [Paris], 9, p. 311. (Caly, Nouvelle-Grenade = Cali, Colombia.)

Habitat.—Open woodland, forest edge, clearings, second growth and plantations (Tropical to Temperate zones).

Distribution.—*Resident* in Middle America from western and southern Nicaragua south to southern Costa Rica (primarily on the Pacific slope and in the central plateau, south to the Dota region); and in South America in Colombia and northwestern Venezuela.

Casual in Caribbean Costa Rica (Carrillo).

Notes.—Also known as BLUE-VENTED HUMMINGBIRD. See comments under *A. cyanura*.

[Amazilia tobaci (Gmelin). COPPER-RUMPED HUMMINGBIRD.] See Appendix B.

Amazilia edward (De Lattre and Bourcier). SNOWY-BELLIED HUMMING-BIRD.

Trochilus Edward De Lattre and Bourcier, 1846, Rev. Zool. [Paris], 9, p. 308. (isthme de Panama.)

Habitat.—Open woodland, clearings and gardens (Tropical and Subtropical zones).

Distribution.—*Resident* in southwestern Costa Rica (El General-Térraba-Golfo Dulce region) and Panama (east to Darién, primarily on the Pacific slope, and including the Pearl, Coiba, Taboga, Taboguilla and Uravá islands).

Notes.—Also known as SNOWY-BREASTED HUMMINGBIRD. The form from Costa Rica and western Panama is sometimes regarded as a distinct species, *A. niveo-*

venter (Gould, 1851), but intergradation with *A. edward* occurs in central Panama; with *niveoventer* treated as a species, *A. edward* has been called WHITE-BELLIED HUMMINGBIRD.

Amazilia tzacatl (De la Llave). RUFOUS-TAILED HUMMINGBIRD. [438.]

> *Trochilus Tzacatl* De la Llave, 1833, Registro Trimestre, 2, no. 5, p. 48. (México.)

Habitat.—Humid forest edge, open woodland, clearings, second growth, plantations and gardens (Tropical and lower Subtropical zones).

Distribution.—*Resident* from southern Tamaulipas south in the Gulf-Caribbean lowlands of eastern Mexico (west to northern Oaxaca and Chiapas, and including the Yucatan Peninsula), Guatemala (locally also on Pacific slope), Belize, Honduras and Nicaragua, and on both slopes of Costa Rica (rare in the arid northwest) and Panama (including many islands off Pacific coast, and Isla Escudo de Veraguas off the Caribbean coast), and in South America from Colombia (including Gorgona Island) to east to northwestern Venezuela and south to western Ecuador.

Accidental in southern Texas (Brownsville).

Notes.—Also known as RIEFFER'S HUMMINGBIRD. The population on Isla Escudo de Veraguas, Panama, has sometimes been regarded as a distinct species, *A. handleyi* Wetmore, 1963 [ESCUDO HUMMINGBIRD].

Amazilia yucatanensis (Cabot). BUFF-BELLIED HUMMINGBIRD. [439.]

> *Trochilus yucatanensis* Cabot, 1845, Proc. Boston Soc. Nat. Hist., 2, p. 74. (Yucatán.)

Habitat.—Open woodland, second growth, clearings, scrub, plantations and gardens (Tropical Zone).

Distribution.—*Resident* from Coahuila, Nuevo León and southern Texas (lower Rio Grande Valley) south in the Gulf-Caribbean lowlands (including the Yucatan Peninsula) to northern Guatemala (Petén), Belize and, at least casually, northern Honduras (Cofradía).

Casual north to central and eastern Texas, and southern Louisiana (New Orleans area, Sabine).

Notes.—Also known as FAWN-BREASTED or YUCATAN HUMMINGBIRD.

Amazilia rutila (De Lattre). CINNAMON HUMMINGBIRD.

> *Ornismya cinnamomea* (not *Ornismya cinnamomeus* Gervais, 1835) Lesson, 1842, Rev. Zool. [Paris], 5, p. 175. (Acapulco [Guerrero].)
> *Ornismya rutila* De Lattre, 1843, Echo Monde Savant, ser. 2, 7, col. 1069. New name for *Ornismya cinnamomea* Lesson, preoccupied.

Habitat.—Open deciduous forest, forest edge, clearings, second growth, arid scrub, plantations and gardens, in arid or semi-arid situations (Tropical and lower Subtropical zones).

Distribution.—*Resident* on the Pacific slope of Middle America (including the Tres Marias Islands) from central Sinaloa south to central Costa Rica; and on the Caribbean slope on the Yucatan Peninsula (including Holbox, Contoy, Mujeres and Cancun islands, and Cayo Culebra), in Belize (including offshore cays), in the arid interior valleys of Guatemala and Honduras, and in the Mosquitia of eastern Honduras and northeastern Nicaragua.

Amazilia violiceps (Gould). VIOLET-CROWNED HUMMINGBIRD. [439.1.]

Cyanomyia violiceps Gould, 1859, Ann. Mag. Nat. Hist., ser. 3, 4, p. 97. (Atlixco, Puebla, México.)

Habitat.—Scrub, open woodland, forest edge, riparian groves and plantations, generally in arid or semi-arid situations (Subtropical and lower Temperate zones).

Distribution.—*Resident* from northern Sonora, southern Arizona (Huachuca and Chiricahua mountains), southwestern New Mexico (Guadalupe Canyon) and western Chihuahua south to Oaxaca, Puebla and Hidalgo.

Casual or accidental in southern California (Santa Paula, Ventura County), central Arizona (Tucson) and Veracruz.

Notes.—The name *A. verticalis* (W. Deppe, 1830), often used for this species, has been relegated to the synonymy of *A. cyanocephala* (see Phillips, 1965, Rev. Soc. Mex. Hist. Nat., 25 (1964), pp. 217–223). *A. violiceps* and *A. viridifrons* are sometimes considered conspecific, but sympatry in Guerrero and Oaxaca without intergradation seems to support their status as full species.

Amazilia viridifrons (Elliot). GREEN-FRONTED HUMMINGBIRD.

Cyanomyia viridifrons Elliot, 1871, Ann. Mag. Nat. Hist., ser. 4, 8, p. 267. (Putla, [Oaxaca,] Mexico.)

Habitat.—Open woodland, forest edge and scrub, in arid situations (Tropical and lower Temperate zones).

Distribution.—*Resident* on the Pacific slope of southern Mexico from central Guerrero south through Oaxaca to Chiapas (east to Tonalá and Ocozocoautla).

Notes.—See comments under *A. violiceps.*

Genus **EUPHERUSA** Gould

Eupherusa Gould, 1857, Monogr. Trochil., pt. 14, pl. [12] and text. Type, by monotypy, *Ornismya eximia* De Lattre.

Eupherusa eximia (De Lattre). STRIPE-TAILED HUMMINGBIRD.

Ornismya eximia De Lattre, 1843, Echo Monde Savant, sér. 2, 7, col. 1069. (Guatemala = Cobán.)

Habitat.—Humid forest, open woodland, forest edge and clearings (Tropical and Subtropical zones).

Distribution.—*Resident* on the Gulf-Caribbean slope from eastern Mexico (Puebla, Veracruz, northern Oaxaca and Chiapas) south through eastern Guatemala, Belize and Honduras to north-central Nicaragua, and in the interior highlands of Costa Rica and western Panama (east to Veraguas).

Notes.—Relationships between *E. eximia, E. cyanophrys* and *E. poliocerca* are uncertain; present data indicate they are probably allospecies of a superspecies.

Eupherusa cyanophrys Rowley and Orr. BLUE-CAPPED HUMMINGBIRD.

Eupherusa cyanophrys Rowley and Orr, 1964, Condor, 66, p. 82. (11 miles south of Juchatengo, 4700 feet, Oaxaca, México.)

Habitat.—Open woodland, humid montane forest and forest edge (Subtropical Zone).

Distribution.—*Resident* in central Oaxaca (Sierra de Miahuatlán).

Notes.—Also known as OAXACA HUMMINGBIRD. See comments under *E. eximia.*

Eupherusa poliocerca Elliot. WHITE-TAILED HUMMINGBIRD.

Eupherusa poliocerca Elliot, 1871, Ann. Mag. Nat. Hist., ser. 4, 8, p. 266. (Putla, [Oaxaca,] Mexico.)

Habitat.—Open woodland, forest edge and clearings, in semi-arid situations (Subtropical Zone).

Distribution.—*Resident* in Guerrero and western Oaxaca (Putla de Guerrero and Río Jalatengo). Reports of this species from Chinantla, Puebla, probably pertain to *E. eximia.*

Notes.—See comments under *E. eximia.*

Eupherusa nigriventris Lawrence. BLACK-BELLIED HUMMINGBIRD.

Eupherusa nigriventris Lawrence, 1868, Proc. Acad. Nat. Sci. Philadelphia, 19 (1867), p. 232. (Costa Rica.)

Habitat.—Humid montane forest, generally in understory within forest, less frequently in forest edge and clearings (Subtropical Zone).

Distribution.—*Resident* in Costa Rica (primarily central highlands) and western Panama (east to Veraguas, mostly on the Caribbean slope).

Genus ELVIRA Mulsant, Verreaux and Verreaux

Elvira Mulsant, and J. and E. Verreaux, 1866, Mém. Soc. Imp. Sci. Nat. Cherbourg, 12, p. 176. Type, by monotypy, *Trochilus* (*Thaumatias*) *chionura* Gould.

Elvira chionura (Gould). WHITE-TAILED EMERALD.

Trochilus (*Thaumatias?*) *chionura* Gould, 1851, Proc. Zool. Soc. London (1850), p. 162. (Chiriqui near David, province of Veragua, at an altitude of from 2000 to 3000 feet [Chiriquí, Panamá].)

Habitat.—Humid forest, forest edge and clearings (Subtropical Zone).

Distribution.—*Resident* in the highlands of southwestern Costa Rica (north to the Dota Mountains) and western Panama (Chiriquí, Veraguas and eastern Coclé).

Elvira cupreiceps (Lawrence). COPPERY-HEADED EMERALD.

Eupherusa cupreiceps Lawrence, 1867, Ann. Lyc. Nat. Hist. N.Y., 8, p. 348. (Barranca, Costa Rica.)

Habitat.—Humid montane forest, forest edge and, rarely, partly open situations (Subtropical Zone).

Distribution.—*Resident* in the highlands of Costa Rica (primarily on the Caribbean slope of the Cordillera Central, and in the cordilleras de Tilarán and Guanacaste).

Genus **MICROCHERA** Gould

Microchera Gould, 1858, Monogr. Trochil., pt. 16, pl. [12] and text. Type, by original designation, *Mellisuga albo-coronata* Lawrence.

Microchera albocoronata (Lawrence). SNOWCAP.

Mellisuga albo-coronata Lawrence, 1855, Ann. Lyc. Nat. Hist. N.Y., 6, p. 137, pl. 4. (Belen, Veraguas, New Grenada [=Panama].)

Habitat.—Forest edge, undergrowth, clearings, open woodland, thickets and plantations (Tropical and lower Subtropical zones).

Distribution.—*Resident* on the Caribbean slope of eastern Honduras (Olancho, sight records), Nicaragua, Costa Rica and western Panama (Veraguas, western Colón and western Panamá province).

Genus **CHALYBURA** Reichenbach

Agyrtria δ *Chalybura* Reichenbach, 1854, J. Ornithol., 1, Beil. zu Extrah., p. 10. Type, by subsequent designation (Elliot, 1879), *Trochilus buffonii* Lesson.

Chalybura buffonii (Lesson). WHITE-VENTED PLUMELETEER.

Trochilus Buffonii Lesson, 1832, Les Trochil., p. 31, pl. 5. (Brazil, error = Bogotá region, Colombia.)

Habitat.—Open woodland, second growth, forest edge, clearings, plantations and swampy areas (Tropical Zone).

Distribution.—*Resident* in Panama (from western Panamá province on the Pacific slope to and the Canal Zone in the Caribbean lowlands eastward), and in South America from Colombia east to central Venezuela (to Miranda and Guárico) and south to southwestern Ecuador.

Notes.—The populations in southwestern Ecuador and in eastern Colombia are often recognized as distinct species, *C. intermedia* E. and C. Hartert, 1894, and *C. caeruleogaster* (Gould), 1847, respectively.

Chalybura urochrysia (Gould). BRONZE-TAILED PLUMELETEER.

Hypuroptila urochrysia Gould, 1861, Monogr. Trochil., pt. 22, pl. [7] and text. (neighborhood of Panamá, error = western Colombia.)

Habitat.—Humid lowland forest, primarily in undergrowth, also in forest edge, clearings and, less frequently, open woodland and second growth (Tropical Zone).

Distribution.—*Resident* on the Caribbean slope of extreme eastern Honduras (Gracias a Dios), Nicaragua and Costa Rica, and from Panama (locally on both slopes) and western Colombia south to northwestern Ecuador.

Notes.—The form from Nicaragua and Costa Rica has often been recognized as a full species. *C. melanorrhoa* Salvin, 1865 [BLACK-VENTED PLUMELETEER], but free interbreeding with *C. urochrysia* occurs in northwestern Panama (see Eisenmann and Howell, 1962, Condor, 64, pp. 300–310).

Genus **LAMPORNIS** Swainson

Lampornis Swainson, 1827, Philos. Mag., new ser., 1, p. 442. Type, by monotypy, *Lampornis amethystinus* Swainson.

Notes.—It has been suggested that this genus is closely related to (or congeneric with) *Colibri,* but most authors disagree.

Lampornis viridipallens (Bourcier and Mulsant). GREEN-THROATED MOUNTAIN-GEM.

Trochilus Viridi-pallens Bourcier and Mulsant, 1846, Ann. Sci. Phys. Nat. Agric. Ind. Soc. R., etc., Lyon, 9, p. 321. (Cobán, Vera Paz, Guatemala.)

Habitat.—Humid montane forest, pine-oak association, scrub and brushy areas (Subtropical and lower Temperate zones).

Distribution.—*Resident* in the highlands of extreme eastern Oaxaca (Sierra Madre de Chiapas), Chiapas, Guatemala, El Salvador and western Honduras (west of the Comayagua-Ulúa river valley).

Notes.—*L. viridipallens* and *L. sybillae* are considered conspecific by some authors; they are best regarded as allospecies of a superspecies.

Lampornis sybillae (Salvin and Godman). GREEN-BREASTED MOUNTAIN-GEM.

Delattria sybillæ Salvin and Godman, 1892, Ibis, p. 327. (Matagalpa, Nicaragua.)

Habitat.—Humid montane forest, forest edge and clearings, less frequently oak woodland and brushy areas (Subtropical and lower Temperate zones).

Distribution.—*Resident* in the highlands of eastern Honduras (east of the Comayagua-Ulúa river valley) and north-central Nicaragua.

Notes.—See comments under *L. viridipallens.*

Lampornis amethystinus Swainson. AMETHYST-THROATED HUMMINGBIRD.

Lampornis amethystinus Swainson, 1827, Philos. Mag., new ser., 1, p. 442. (Temiscaltipec [=Temascaltepec] and Real del Monte, [state of México,] Mexico.)

Habitat.—Humid montane forest, forest edge, oak woodland and brushy areas (Subtropical and lower Temperate zones).

Distribution.—*Resident* from Nayarit, Jalisco, San Luis Potosí and southern Tamaulipas south through the highlands of southern Mexico, Guatemala and El Salvador to central Honduras.

Notes.—Irregularly distributed populations from Michoacán to Oaxaca consisting of bluish-throated rather than pink-throated males may represent a species, *L. margaritae* (Salvin and Godman, 1889) [MARGARET'S HUMMINGBIRD], distinct from *L. amethystinus.*

Lampornis clemenciae (Lesson). BLUE-THROATED HUMMINGBIRD. [427.]

Ornismya Clemenciae Lesson, 1829, Hist. Nat. Ois.-Mouches, p. xlv; 1830, p. 216, pl. 80. (le Mexique = Mexico.)

Habitat.—Open woodland, second growth and shrubby areas, primarily in pine-oak and deciduous woodland, sometimes nesting under bridges, in caves or on buildings, in migration also visiting flowers in open situations and gardens (Subtropical and lower Temperate zones).

Distribution.—*Breeds* from northern Sonora, southeastern Arizona (Huachuca and Chiricahua mountains), Chihuahua and western Texas south through Coahuila, Durango and western Mexico to Oaxaca (east to the Isthmus of Tehuantepec). Recorded in summer (sight reports) in Utah, Colorado and northern New Mexico.

Winters from southern Sonora (casually southern Arizona) and Chihuahua south through the breeding range in Mexico.

In migration occurs casually east to southwestern New Mexico and southern Texas (Rockport and Corpus Christi area southward).

Casual in south-central California (a female mated to either *Calypte anna* or *Archilochus alexandri* raised young in 1977 and 1978 at Three Rivers, Tulare County).

Lampornis hemileucus (Salvin). WHITE-BELLIED MOUNTAIN-GEM.

Oreopyra hemileuca Salvin, 1865, Proc. Zool. Soc. London (1864), p. 584. (Turrialba and Tucurruquí, Costa Rica.)

Habitat.—Humid montane forest, forest edge and clearings (Subtropical Zone).

Distribution.—*Resident* in Costa Rica (in the Tilarán, Central and Talamanca cordilleras) and western Panama (recorded Chiriquí and Veraguas).

Lampornis calolaema (Salvin). PURPLE-THROATED MOUNTAIN-GEM.

Oreopyra calolæma Salvin, 1865, Proc. Zool. Soc. London (1864), p. 584. (Volcán de Cartago = Volcán de Irazú, Costa Rica).

Habitat.—Humid forest edge and clearings, open woodland and second growth (Subtropical and lower Temperate zones).

Distribution.—*Resident* in the highlands of western Nicaragua (Volcán Mombacho), Costa Rica (from the Cordillera de Guanacaste south to the Dota region and the northern tip of the Cordillera de Talamanca) and western Panama (Volcán de Chiriquí region of western Chiriquí).

Notes.—Relationships within the *L. calolaema-castaneoventris* complex are not well understood. It has been suggested by some authors that the purple-throated males (*calolaema*) and white-throated males (*castaneoventris*) are morphs of the same species; some introgression occurs in areas where both types are found, although they tend to maintain their distinctness. Until the matter is resolved, it seems best to treat the forms as separate species with limited hybridization in the areas of sympatry. If the entire complex is regarded as a single species, the name VARIABLE MOUNTAIN-GEM may be used.

Lampornis castaneoventris (Gould). WHITE-THROATED MOUNTAIN-GEM.

Trochilus (——?) *castaneoventris* Gould, 1851, Proc. Zool. Soc. London (1850), p. 163. (Cordillera of Chiriqui, at an altitude of 6000 feet [Panama].)

Habitat.—Humid forest, much less frequently recorded in forest edge, clearings or open woodland (Subtropical and lower Temperate zones).

Distribution.—*Resident* in the highlands of southern Costa Rica (north to the

Dota region and Cordillera de Talamanca) and western Panama (east to Veraguas and western Coclé).

Notes.—The Costa Rican populations are sometimes regarded as a distinct species, *L. cinereicauda* (Lawrence, 1867) [GRAY-TAILED MOUNTAIN-GEM]. See also comments under *L. calolaema.*

Genus LAMPROLAIMA Reichenbach

Heliodoxa δ *Lamprolaima* Reichenbach, 1854, J. Ornithol., 1, Beil. zu Extrah., p. 9. Type, by subsequent designation (G. R. Gray, 1855), *Ornismya rhami* Lesson.

Lamprolaima rhami (Lesson). GARNET-THROATED HUMMINGBIRD.

Ornismya Rhami Lesson, 1838, Rev. Zool. [Paris], 1, p. 315. (Mexico.)

Habitat.—Humid montane forest, forest edge, clearings, pine-oak woodland and brushy areas (Subtropical and lower Temperate zones).

Distribution.—*Resident* from Guerrero, the state of México, and western Veracruz south through Oaxaca, Chiapas, Guatemala and El Salvador to Honduras.

Genus HELIODOXA Gould

Heliodoxa Gould, 1850, Proc. Zool. Soc. London (1849), p. 95. Type, by subsequent designation (Bonaparte, 1850), *Trochilus leadbeateri* Bourcier.

Notes.—See comments under *Eugenes.*

Heliodoxa jacula Gould. GREEN-CROWNED BRILLIANT.

Heliodoxa jacula Gould, 1850, Proc. Zool. Soc. London (1849), p. 96. (Santa Fé de Bogota [Colombia].)

Habitat.—Humid montane forest, forest edge and clearings (Subtropical Zone).

Distribution.—*Resident* from Costa Rica (north to the Cordillera Central, primarily on Caribbean slope) south locally through Panama (recorded east to Veraguas, in eastern Panamá province, and in eastern Darién) and northern Colombia to western Ecuador.

Genus EUGENES Gould

Eugenes Gould, 1856, Monogr. Trochil., pt. 12, pl. [7] and text. Type, by monotypy, *Trochilus fulgens* Swainson.

Notes.—By some authors merged in *Heliodoxa.*

Eugenes fulgens (Swainson). MAGNIFICENT HUMMINGBIRD. [426.]

Trochilus fulgens Swainson, 1827, Philos. Mag., new ser., 1, p. 441. (Temiscaltipec, Mexico = Temascaltepec, state of México.)

Habitat.—Humid montane forest (primarily in edge and clearings), pastures, open woodland, pine-oak association and scrubby areas (Subtropical and Temperate zones).

Distribution.—*Breeds* [*fulgens* group] in western Colorado, and from southeastern Arizona (north to Graham and Santa Catalina mountains), southwestern (and proabably also north-central) New Mexico, and western Texas (Culberson, Jeff Davis and Brewster counties) south through the highlands of Mexico, Guatemala, western El Salvador and Honduras to north-central Nicaragua.

Winters [*fulgens* group] from Sonora and Chihuahua south through the breeding range in Middle America.

Resident [*spectabilis* group] in the mountains from central Costa Rica to western Panama (western Chiriquí).

Casual [*fulgens* group] north to Utah (Springdale), northern New Mexico (Cedar Crest), northeastern Kansas (Linn County) and south-central Texas (San Antonio).

Notes.—Also known as RIVOLI'S HUMMINGBIRD. The two groups are sometimes regarded as separate species, *E. fulgens* [MAGNIFICENT or RIVOLI'S HUMMINGBIRD] and *E. spectabilis* (Lawrence, 1867) [ADMIRABLE HUMMINGBIRD].

Genus HAPLOPHAEDIA Simon

Haplophædia Simon, 1918, Not. Travaux Sci., p. 39. Type, by monotypy, *Trochilus aureliae* Bourcier and Mulsant.

Haplophaedia aureliae (Bourcier and Mulsant). GREENISH PUFFLEG.

Trochilus Aureliæ Bourcier and Mulsant, 1846, Ann. Sci. Phys. Nat. Agric. Ind. Soc. R., etc., Lyon, 9, p. 315, pl. 10. (Bogotá, Colombia.)

Habitat.—Undergrowth of humid montane forest (upper Tropical and Subtropical zones).

Distribution.—*Resident* in eastern Panama (in eastern Darién on cerros Pirre, Malí and Tacarcuna); and in the Andes of South America from Colombia south to Peru and northern Bolivia.

Genus HELIOTHRYX Boie

Heliothryx Boie, 1831, Isis von Oken, col. 547. Type, by subsequent designation (G. R. Gray, 1840), *H. aurita* (L.) = *Trochilus auritus* Gmelin.

Heliothryx barroti (Bourcier). PURPLE-CROWNED FAIRY.

Trochilus Barroti Bourcier, 1843, Rev. Zool. [Paris], 6, p. 72. (Carthagène = Cartagena, Colombia.)

Habitat.—Humid lowland and foothill forest, forest edge, clearings, open woodland, shrubby areas and plantations (Tropical and lower Subtropical zones).

Distribution.—*Resident* on the Gulf-Caribbean slope from Tabasco (Tenosique) south through eastern Guatemala, Belize and Honduras to Nicaragua, on both slopes of Costa Rica (except the arid northwest) and Panama, and from northern Colombia south, west of the Andes, to southwestern Ecuador.

Notes.—*H. barroti* and *H. aurita* (Gmelin, 1788), of South America, are sometimes regarded as conspecific; they constitute a superspecies.

Genus HELIOMASTER Bonaparte

Heliomaster Bonaparte, March 1850, Consp. Gen. Avium, 1 (1), p. 70. Type, by subsequent designation (Bonaparte, April 1850), *Orn. angel.* = *Ornismya angelae* Lesson = *Trochilus furcifer* Shaw.

Heliomaster longirostris (Audebert and Vieillot). LONG-BILLED STAR-THROAT.

Trochilus longirostris Audebert and Vieillot, 1801, Ois. Dorés, 1, p. 107, pl. 59. (West Indies = Trinidad.)

Habitat.—Open woodland, second growth, forest edge, clearings, shrubby areas and plantations, more frequently in humid situations (Tropical and Subtropical zones).

Distribution.—*Resident* on both slopes of Middle America from eastern Oaxaca (locally in the Sierra Madre de Chiapas) and Veracruz south (exclusive of the Yucatan Peninsula) through Middle America (rare on Pacific slope from Honduras to northwestern Costa Rica), and in South America from Colombia, Venezuela (also Trinidad) and the Guianas south, west of the Andes to northwestern Peru and east of the Andes to Bolivia and central Brazil. A report from Guerrero is considered doubtful.

Heliomaster constantii (De Lattre). PLAIN-CAPPED STARTHROAT. [426.1.]

Ornismya Constantii De Lattre, 1843, Echo Monde Savant, sér. 2, 7, col. 1069, in text. (Guatemala, error = Bolson, Costa Rica.)

Habitat.—Open woodland, deciduous forest, arid scrub and plantations (Tropical Zone).

Distribution.—*Resident* from southern Sonora south on the Pacific slope of Middle America to Costa Rica (primarily the Guanacaste region in the northwest, rarely in the El General-Térraba region in the southwest).

Casual in southeastern Arizona (north to Phoenix).

Notes.—Also known as CONSTANT'S STARTHROAT.

Genus CALLIPHLOX Boie

Calliphlox Boie, 1831, Isis von Oken, col. 544. Type, by subsequent designation (G. R. Gray, 1855), *Trochilus amethystinus* Gm. = Boddaert.
Philodice Mulsant, and J. and E. Verreaux, 1866, Mém. Soc. Imp. Sci. Nat. Cherbourg, 12, p. 230.

Calliphlox evelynae (Bourcier). BAHAMA WOODSTAR. [437.1.]

Trochilus Evelynæ Bourcier, 1847, Proc. Zool. Soc. London, p. 44. (Nassau, New Providence [Bahamas].)

Habitat.—Scrubby woodland, open situations with scattered trees, and gardens.
Distribution.—*Resident* throughout the Bahama Islands.

Casual in southern Florida (Lantana, Homestead, Miami area).

Notes.—Often treated in the genus *Philodice.*

Calliphlox bryantae (Lawrence). MAGENTA-THROATED WOODSTAR.

Doricha bryantæ Lawrence, 1867, Ann. Lyc. Nat. Hist. N.Y., 8, p. 483. (Costa Rica).

Habitat.—Forest edge, clearings, shrubby areas, pastures and partly cleared lands (Subtropical and lower Temperate zones).

Distribution.—*Resident* in the highlands of Costa Rica (from the Cordillera de

Guanacaste to the central plateau near San José and the Dota Mountains) and western Panama (Chiriquí and Veraguas).

Notes.—Also known as COSTA RICAN WOODSTAR. Frequently placed in the genus *Philodice.*

Genus DORICHA Reichenbach

Calliphlox β *Doricha* Reichenbach, 1854, J. Ornithol., 1, Beil. zu Extrah., p. 12. Type, by monotypy, *Trochilus enicurus* Vieillot.

Doricha enicura (Vieillot). SLENDER SHEARTAIL.

Trochilus enicurus Vieillot, 1818, Nouv. Dict. Hist. Nat., nouv. éd., 23, p. 429. (Brazil, error = Guatemala.)

Habitat.—Brushy areas, second growth, open woodland and forest edge (Subtropical Zone).

Distribution.—*Resident* in the highlands of Chiapas, Guatemala, El Salvador and western Honduras (east to La Paz).

Doricha eliza (Lesson and De Lattre). MEXICAN SHEARTAIL.

Trochilus Eliza Lesson and De Lattre, 1839, Rev. Zool. [Paris], 2, p. 20. (Pas du Taureau, entra la Vera Cruz et Jalapa = Paso del Toro, Veracruz.)

Habitat.—Open woodland, clearings and scrubby areas, generally in arid and semi-arid situations (Tropical Zone).

Distribution.—*Resident* in two disjunct areas of southeastern Mexico (in central Veracruz, where rare, and the coastal scrub of the Yucatan Peninsula, including Holbox Island, also a sight record for Isla Cancun).

Genus TILMATURA Reichenbach

Tilmatura Reichenbach, 1855, Trochil. Enum., p. 5. Type, by monotypy, *Trochilus lepidus* Reichenbach = *Ornismya dupontii* Lesson.

Tilmatura dupontii (Lesson). SPARKLING-TAILED HUMMINGBIRD.

Ornismya dupontii Lesson, 1832, Hist. Nat. Colibris, livr. 13, p. 100, pl. 1. (México.)

Habitat.—Open woodlands, pine-oak association, clearings and shrubby areas (Subtropical and lower Temperate zones).

Distribution.—*Resident* in the highlands from Sinaloa, Jalisco, Colima, Michoacán, the state of México, Distrito Federal, Morelos and western Veracruz south through Guerrero, Oaxaca, Chiapas, Guatemala, El Salvador and Honduras to north-central Nicaragua.

Genus CALOTHORAX Gray

Calothorax G. R. Gray, 1840, List Genera Birds, p. 13. Type, by original designation, *C. cyanopogon* (Lesson) = *Cynanthus lucifer* Swainson.

Calothorax lucifer (Swainson). LUCIFER HUMMINGBIRD. [437.]

Cynanthus Lucifer Swainson, 1827, Philos. Mag., new ser., 1, p. 442. (Temiscaltipec, Mexico = Temascaltepec, state of México.)

Habitat.—Scrub, semi-desert, brushy hillsides, and cleared lands with scattered bushes, primarily in arid habitats (upper Tropical and Subtropical zones).

Distribution.—*Breeds* from southern Arizona (Cochise County), western Texas (Brewster County) and Nuevo León south in the highlands of Mexico to Guanajuato, possibly in Morelos and Puebla.

Winters from northern Mexico south to the limits of the breeding range, casually to western Veracruz, Oaxaca and Chiapas.

Casual elsewhere in southern Arizona, also sight reports from southern New Mexico and southern Texas (east to Hays, Bee and Aransas counties).

Notes.—*C. lucifer* and *C. pulcher* appear to constitute a superspecies.

Calothorax pulcher Gould. BEAUTIFUL HUMMINGBIRD.

Calothorax pulcher Gould, 1859, Ann. Mag. Nat. Hist., ser. 3, 4, p. 97. (Oaxaca.)

Habitat.—Arid scrub, brushy areas and partly open situations (Subtropical and lower Temperate zones).

Distribution.—*Resident* from Guerrero, the Distrito Federal, Morelos and Puebla south through Oaxaca to Chiapas (east to Comitán).

Notes.—See comments under *C. lucifer*.

Genus ARCHILOCHUS Reichenbach

Selasphorus β Archilochus Reichenbach, 1854, J. Ornithol., 1, Beil. zu Extrah., p. 13. Type, by monotypy, *Trochilus alexandri* Bourcier [=Bourcier and Mulsant].

Notes.—See comments under *Calypte*.

Archilochus colubris (Linnaeus). RUBY-THROATED HUMMINGBIRD. [428.].

Trochilus Colubris Linnaeus, 1758, Syst. Nat., ed. 10, 1, p. 120. Based mainly on "The Hummingbird" Catesby, Nat. Hist. Carolina, 1, p. 65, pl. 65. (in America, imprimis septentrionali = South Carolina.)

Habitat.—Deciduous or mixed woodland, second growth, parks, and open situations with scattered trees, foraging in meadows and gardens, in migration and winter in a wide variety of woodland and open habitats.

Distribution.—*Breeds* from central Alberta, central Saskatchewan, southern Manitoba, southern Ontario, southern Quebec, New Brunswick, Prince Edward Island and Nova Scotia south, east of the Rocky Mountains, to southern Texas, the Gulf coast and southern Florida, and west to the eastern Dakotas, central Nebraska, central Kansas, central Oklahoma and central Texas.

Winters from southern Sinaloa, Guanajuato, San Luis Potosí, Nuevo León and southern Texas south through Middle America (including Cozumel and Holbox islands) to central Costa Rica (south of Nicaragua most commonly on the Pacific slope), casually to western Panama (Chiriquí and western Panamá province); also in southern Florida, casually to southern Alabama, northern Florida and western Cuba.

Casual north to southwestern British Columbia, northern Manitoba, northern Ontario, Labrador and Newfoundland, and in the Bahamas (New Providence) and Bermuda; reports from Jamaica, Hispaniola and Puerto Rico are questionable. Accidental in Alaska (St. Michael).

Notes.—Although the breeding ranges of *A. colubris* and *A. alexandri* overlap slightly in central Texas, it seems best to regard these species as constituting a superspecies.

Archilochus alexandri (Bourcier and Mulsant). BLACK-CHINNED HUMMINGBIRD. [429.]

> *Trochilus Alexandri* Bourcier and Mulsant, 1846, Ann. Sci. Phys. Nat. Agric. Ind. Soc. R., etc., Lyon, 9, p. 330. (Sierra Madre [Occidental], Mexico.)

Habitat.—Open woodland, scrub, desert washes, riparian woodland, chaparral, parks and gardens, most frequently in arid regions.

Distribution.—*Breeds* from southwestern British Colombia (probably), Washington, central Idaho and northwestern Montana south to northern Baja California, northern Sonora, northwestern Chihuahua, northern Coahuila (probably) and southern Texas, and east to western Wyoming, eastern Colorado, eastern New Mexico and central Texas (to Dallas, Navarro and Hidalgo counties).

Winters from northern Mexico and southern Texas (casually) south to southern Baja California, Guerrero, Morelos and Veracruz, casually east to southern Louisiana and northwestern Florida.

Casual in southern Alberta, southern Saskatchewan (sight records), Wyoming, western Oklahoma, and elsewhere in Florida (south to Florida Keys). Accidental in Massachusetts (Cohasset).

Notes.—See comments under *A. colubris.*

Genus MELLISUGA Brisson

> *Mellisuga* Brisson, 1760, Ornithologie, 1, p. 40; 3, p. 694. Type, by tautonymy, *Mellisuga* Brisson = *Trochilus minimus* Linnaeus.

Mellisuga minima (Linnaeus). VERVAIN HUMMINGBIRD.

> *Trochilus minimus* Linnaeus, 1758, Syst. Nat., ed. 10, 1, p. 121. Based on "The Least Humming-bird" Edwards, Nat. Hist. Birds, 2, p. 105, pl. 105. (in America = Jamaica.)

Habitat.—A wide variety of open and partly open sitautions, absent from forest.

Distribution.—*Resident* on Jamaica and Hispaniola (including Gonâve, Tortue, Saona and Catalina islands, and Île-à-Vache).

Accidental in Puerto Rico (sight report).

Mellisuga helenae (Lembeye). BEE HUMMINGBIRD.

> *Orthorhynchus helenæ* (Gundlach MS) Lembeye, 1850, Aves Isla Cuba, p. 70, pl. 10, fig. 2. (Cárdenas, Cuba.)

Habitat.—Open woodland, shrubby areas and gardens, occasionally open country.

Distribution.—*Resident* on Cuba and the Isle of Pines.

Notes.—Sometimes placed in the genus *Calypte.*

Genus **CALYPTE** Gould

Calypte Gould, 1856, Monogr. Trochil., pt. 11, pl. [5–7] and text. Type, by subsequent designation (Baird, Brewer and Ridgway, 1875), *Ornismya costae* Bourcier.

Notes.—Some authors merge *Calypte* in *Archilochus.*

Calypte anna (Lesson). ANNA'S HUMMINGBIRD. [431.]

Ornismya Anna Lesson, 1829, Hist. Nat. Ois.-Mouches, p. "xxxj" [=xxxi]; 1830, p. 205, pl. 74. (La Californie = San Francisco, California.)

Habitat.—Open woodland, chaparral, scrubby areas, and partly open situations, foraging also in gardens and meadows, ascending to montane regions in summer postbreeding season.

Distribution.—*Breeds* in western Washington (Seattle, Tacoma), western Oregon, California (west of the Sierra Nevada from Humboldt, Shasta and Tehama counties southward), northwestern Baja California (Sierra San Pedro Mártir and San Quintín) and southern Arizona (north to Phoenix and Superior). Recorded in summer (and probably breeding) in southwestern British Columbia (Vancouver Island) and western Texas (Davis Mountains).

Winters from southwestern Oregon south to central Baja California, and east to southern Arizona, northern Sonora and northern Chihuahua, casually north to south-coastal Alaska, central British Columbia and western Montana, and east to central New Mexico, northern Coahuila, and east-central and southeastern Texas.

Casual or accidental in southern Alberta (Calgary), Oklahoma (Tulsa) and southwestern Louisiana (Cameron Parish).

Calypte costae (Bourcier). COSTA'S HUMMINGBIRD. [430.]

Ornismya Costae Bourcier, 1839, Rev. Zool. [Paris], 2, p. 294. (la Californie = Magdalena Bay, Baja California.)

Habitat.—Desert and semi-desert, arid brushy foothills and chaparral, in migration and winter also in adjacent mountains and in open meadows and gardens.

Distribution.—*Breeds* from central California (north to Monterey, Merced and Inyo counties), southern Nevada and southwestern Utah (Beaverdam Mountains) south to southern Baja California (including the Channel Islands off California, and islands off both coasts of Baja California), Sonora (including Tiburón and San Esteban islands), southern Arizona and southwestern New Mexico.

Winters from southern California and southern Arizona south to Sinaloa, casually north to southwestern British Columbia (Vancouver Island, sight record), western Washington, Oregon, central Nevada (Toiyabe Mountains) and northern Utah, and east to central Texas (Hays County, also sight records east to Aransas County).

Genus STELLULA Gould

Stellula Gould, 1861, Introd. Trochil., p. 90. Type, by monotypy, *Trochilus calliope* Gould.

Stellula calliope (Gould). CALLIOPE HUMMINGBIRD. [436.]

Trochilus (Calothorax) Calliope Gould, 1847, Proc. Zool. Soc. London, p. 11. (Mexico = Real del Monte, Hidalgo.)

Habitat.—Open montane forest, mountain meadows, and willow and alder thickets, in migration and winter also in chaparral, lowland brushy areas, deserts and semi-desert regions.

Distribution.—*Breeds* in the mountains from central interior British Columbia and southwestern Alberta south through Washington, Oregon, Nevada and California to northern Baja California (Sierra San Pedro Mártir), and east to northern Wyoming, western Colorado and Utah.

Winters from Baja California, Sonora and Sinaloa south to Michoacán, Guerrero and Distrito Federal, and east to Aguascalientes and Guanajuato.

Migrates regularly through the southwestern United States, and casually east to southwestern Saskatchewan, Nebraska, Kansas, and western and central Texas. Accidental in Oaxaca (Río Molino).

Genus ATTHIS Reichenbach

Trochilus δ Atthis Reichenbach, 1854, J. Ornithol., 1, Beil. zu Extrah., p. 12. Type, by subsequent designation (G. R. Gray, 1855), *Ornismya heloisa* Lesson and De Lattre.

Atthis heloisa (Lesson and De Lattre). BUMBLEBEE HUMMINGBIRD. [435.]

Ornysmya Heloisa Lesson and De Lattre, 1839, Rev. Zool. [Paris], 2, p. 15. (Jalapa et Quatepu = Coátepec, Veracruz.)

Habitat.—Pine-oak assocation and humid montane forest, forest edge, clearings and brushy areas in montane situations (Subtropical and lower Temperate zones).

Distribution.—*Resident* in the highlands from southwestern Chihuahua, southeastern Sinaloa, Nayarit, Jalisco, Guanajuato, San Luis Potosí, Nuevo León and southern Tamaulipas south to Oaxaca (east to the Isthmus of Tehuantepec) and western Veracruz.

Accidental in Arizona (Huachuca Mountains).

Notes.—Also known as HELOISE'S HUMMINGBIRD. *A. heloisa* and *A. ellioti* are considered conspecific by some authors; they constitute at least a superspecies.

Atthis ellioti Ridgway. WINE-THROATED HUMMINGBIRD.

Atthis ellioti Ridgway, 1878, Proc. U.S. Natl. Mus., 1, pp. 8, 9, and fig. (Volcán de Fuego, Guatemala.)

Habitat.—Humid montane forest, forest edge, clearings, pine-oak woodland and scrubby areas near forest (Subtropical and Temperate zones).

Distribution.—*Resident* in the highlands of Chiapas, Guatemala, El Salvador (Volcán de Santa Ana) and Honduras.

Notes.—See comments under *A. heloisa.*

Genus ACESTRURA Gould

Acestrura Gould, 1861, Introd. Trochil., p. 91. Type, by subsequent designation (Elliot, 1879), *Ornismya mulsanti* Bourcier.

Acestrura heliodor (Bourcier). GORGETED WOODSTAR.

Ornismya heliodor Bourcier, 1840, Rev. Zool. [Paris], 3, p. 275. (Santa-Fé de Bogota [Colombia].)

Habitat & Distribution.—*Resident* in humid montane forest, forest edge and scrub in the mountains of Colombia (Santa Marta Mountains, and Eastern and Central Andes), northwestern Venezuela and northwestern Ecuador.

Possibly resident in eastern Panama, where known from a single specimen (Cana, Cerro Pirre, eastern Darién, 13 April 1938; Wetmore, 1968, Smithson. Misc. Collect., 150 (2), p. 373).

Genus SELASPHORUS Swainson

Selasphorus Swainson, 1832, *in* Swainson and Richardson, Fauna Bor.-Am., 2 (1831), pp. 324, 496. Type, by subsequent designation (G. R. Gray, 1840), *Trochilus rufus* Gmelin.
Platurornis Oberholser, 1974, Bird Life Texas, 2, p. 986. Type, by original designation, *Selasphorus platycercus* = *Trochilus platycercus* Swainson.

Selasphorus platycercus (Swainson). BROAD-TAILED HUMMINGBIRD. [432.]

Trochilus platycercus Swainson, 1827, Philos. Mag., new ser., 1, p. 441. (No locality given = Mexico.)

Habitat.—Open woodland, especially pinyon-juniper and pine-oak association, brushy hillsides, montane scrub and thickets, in migration and winter also open situations in lowlands where flowering shrubs are present (Subtropical and Temperate zones).

Distribution.—*Breeds* in the mountains from north-central Idaho (Latah County), northern Utah and northern Wyoming south to southeastern California, northeastern Sonora, Guanajuato, the state of México, Distrito Federal, Hidalgo, Nuevo León and western Texas (east to Bandera County); and in eastern Chiapas (Teopisca) and Guatemala (rare in eastern mountains).

Winters from the highlands of northern Mexico south to western Veracruz and Oaxaca (east to the Isthmus of Tehuantepec); and in the breeding range in Chiapas and Guatemala.

In migration occurs casually east to Nebraska, central Kansas, and eastern and southeastern Texas, and west to southwestern California.

Casual, primarily in summer, north to Oregon and Montana, and in fall and winter east to Louisiana (Baton Rouge, New Orleans).

Selasphorus rufus (Gmelin). RUFOUS HUMMINGBIRD. [433.]

Trochilus rufus Gmelin, 1788, Syst. Nat., 1 (1), p. 497. Based mainly on the "Ruffed Honeysucker" Pennant, Arct. Zool., 2, p. 290. (in sinu Americae Natka = Nootka Sound, Vancouver Island, British Columbia.)

Habitat.—Coniferous forest, second growth, thickets and brushy hillsides, foraging in adjacent scrubby areas and meadows, in migration and winter in open situations where flowers are present.

Distribution.—*Breeds* from southern Alaska (west to Prince William Sound, probably to Cook Inlet), southern Yukon, western and southern British Columbia (including the Queen Charlotte Islands), southwestern Alberta and western Montana south, primarily in the mountains, to northwestern California (probably), eastern Oregon and central Idaho.

Winters in coastal southern California (rarely), and from Sinaloa, Chihuahua, southern Texas and the Gulf coast (in small numbers regularly from southeastern Texas east to western Florida) south to Oaxaca, the state of México, Distrito Federal and western Veracruz.

Migrates regularly through the southwestern United States, Baja California and northern Mexico, casually east to eastern Alberta, southern Saskatchewan, southern Manitoba, South Dakota, Nebraska, Kansas, Missouri, Oklahoma and Texas.

Casual east across the Great Lakes region (recorded Minnesota, Wisconsin, Michigan, southern Ontario and northern New York), and along the Atlantic coast (from Nova Scotia south to central Georgia and southern Florida). Accidental on Big Diomede Island.

Notes.—*S. rufus* and *S. sasin* constitute a superspecies.

Selasphorus sasin (Lesson). ALLEN'S HUMMINGBIRD. [434.]

Ornismya Sasin Lesson, 1829, Hist. Nat. Ois.-Mouches, p. xxx; 1830, p. 190, pl. 66, 67. (La Californie, la côte N.-O. d'Amérique = San Francisco, California.)

Habitat.—Chaparral, thickets, brushy hillsides and open coniferous woodland, in migration and winter also in open situations with flowering shrubs.

Distribution.—*Breeds* from southwestern Oregon south through coastal California to Santa Barbara County.

Winters from Baja California and Sinaloa south to Aguascalientes, Guanajuato and Distrito Federal.

Migrates through southern California and northern Baja California (including Los Coronados and Cedros islands), and east, at least casually, to southern Arizona, southeastern Texas (numerous sight records, specimen from Houston, and bird in hand examined at Corpus Christi) and southern Louisiana (east to Reserve).

Resident in southern California in the Channel Islands and on the Palos Verdes Peninsula (in Los Angeles County).

Accidental in Washington (Seattle); a report from British Columbia (Victoria) is based on photographs that do not eliminate *S. rufus*.

Notes.—See comments under *S. rufus*.

Selasphorus flammula Salvin. VOLCANO HUMMINGBIRD.

Selasphorus flammula Salvin, 1865, Proc. Zool. Soc. London (1864), p. 586. (Volcán de Cartago [=Irazú], Costa Rica.)

Habitat.—Forest edge, clearings, brushy areas and highland pastures (upper Subtropical and Temperate zones).

Distribution.—*Resident* in the highlands of Costa Rica (Cordillera Central south along the Cordillera de Talamanca) and western Panama (Volcán Barú in western Chiriquí).

Notes.—There has been much confusion regarding the status and distribution of the forms of this species. As presently understood, the mauve-gorgeted race *flammula* breeds on the Irazú-Turrialba massifs in central Costa Rica; *S. torridus* Salvin, 1870 [HELIOTROPE-THROATED HUMMINGBIRD], based on dull-gorgeted males, breeds the length of the Cordillera de Talamanca and is now considered a subspecies of *flammula* (formerly it was considered but a color morph). The red-gorgeted form *S. simoni* Carriker, 1910 [CERISE-THROATED HUMMINGBIRD], breeds on Volcán Poás and Volcán Barba of the northern Cordillera Central and (formerly?) the Cerros de Escazú south of San José; *simoni* is divergent in morphology (but not in displays) and was previously considered a distinct species related to *S. ardens*, but it appears to be just a distinct subspecies of *flammula*. If any of the preceding are regarded as specifically distinct, ROSE-THROATED HUMMINGBIRD would be the appropriate English name for *S. flammula*. See also comments under *S. ardens*.

Selasphorus ardens Salvin. GLOW-THROATED HUMMINGBIRD.

> *Selasphorus ardens* Salvin, 1870, Proc. Zool. Soc. London, p. 209. (Calovévora and Castilla, Panama.)

Habitat.—Forest edge, clearings and brushy areas (Subtropical Zone).
Distribution.—*Resident* in the mountains of western Panama in eastern Chiriquí (Cerro Flores) and Veraguas (Santa Fé, Castillo and Calovévora).
Notes.—This species has been considered closely related to *S. flammula* on the basis of gorget color and measurements, but in wing and tail morphology (and presumably displays) is in reality much more similar to *S. scintilla*, with which it may constitute a superspecies. See also comments under *S. flammula*.

Selasphorus scintilla (Gould). SCINTILLANT HUMMINGBIRD.

> *Trochilus* (*Selosphorus*) *scintilla* Gould, 1851, Proc. Zool. Soc. London (1850), p. 162. (Volcano of Chiriqui, at an altitude of 9000 feet [Panama].)

Habitat.—Humid montane forest, forest edge, clearings, shrubby areas, highland meadows and gardens (Subtropical and lower Temperate zones).
Distribution.—*Resident* in the mountains of central Costa Rica (Cordillera Central south along the Pacific slope of the Cordillera de Talamanca, and north, at least casually, to the Cordillera de Tilarán) and western Panama (western Chiriquí).
Notes.—See also comments under *S. ardens*.

Order TROGONIFORMES: Trogons

Notes.—Sometimes merged in the Coraciiformes.

Family TROGONIDAE: Trogons

Genus PRIOTELUS Gray

Temnurus (not Lesson, 1831) Swainson, 1837, Class. Birds, 2, p. 337. Type, by monotypy, *T. albicollis* Pl. col. 326 = *Trogon temnurus* Temminck.
Priotelus G. R. Gray, 1840, List Genera Birds, p. 10. New name for *Temnurus* Swainson, preoccupied.
Temnotrogon Bonaparte, 1854, Ateneo Ital., 2, p. 129. Type, by monotypy, *Trogon roseigaster* Vieillot.

Priotelus temnurus (Temminck). CUBAN TROGON.

Trogon temnurus Temminck, 1825, Planches Color., livr. 55, pl. 326. (Havana, Cuba.)

Habitat.—Forested regions, most frequently in mountains.
Distribution.—*Resident* on Cuba and the Isle of Pines.

Priotelus roseigaster (Vieillot). HISPANIOLAN TROGON.

Trogon roseigaster Vieillot, 1817, Nouv. Dict. Hist. Nat., nouv. éd., 8, p. 314. (Santo Domingo and México = Hispaniola.)

Habitat.—Primarily in mountain forest, locally in coastal mangroves.
Distribution.—*Resident* on Hispaniola.
Notes.—Often placed in the monotypic genus *Temnotrogon.*

Genus **TROGON** Brisson

Trogon Brisson, 1760, Ornithologie, 1, p. 42; 4, p. 164. Type, by subsequent designation (Stone, 1907), *Trogon viridis* Linnaeus.

Trogon melanocephalus Gould. BLACK-HEADED TROGON.

Trogon melanocephala Gould, 1835, Monogr. Trogonidae, ed. 1, pt. 2, pl. [6] and text. (State of Tamaulipas, Mexico.)

Habitat.—Open woodland, scrub, bushy and thicketed areas, partially cleared lands with scattered trees, and plantations, in both humid and semi-arid regions, the latter mostly on the Pacific slope of Middle America (Tropical and lower Subtropical zones).
Distribution.—*Resident* on the Gulf-Caribbean slope from Tamaulipas and the Pacific slope from El Salvador south in Middle America (including the Yucatan Peninsula and islands off Quintana Roo), to Costa Rica (mostly in the northeastern and northwestern portions).
Notes.—See comments under *T. citreolus.*

Trogon citreolus Gould. CITREOLINE TROGON.

Trogon citreolus Gould, 1835, Proc. Zool. Soc. London, p. 30. (No locality given = Mexico.)

Habitat.—Open woodland, deciduous forest, scrub and plantations, primarily in arid or semi-arid regions (Tropical and lower Subtropical zones).
Distribution.—*Resident* on the Pacific slope from Sinaloa to Oaxaca and central Chiapas.
Notes.—Although *T. citreolus* and *T. melanocephalus* are considered conspecific by some authors, the nature of the distinct differences between the two forms in pattern of tail and color of iris and orbital skin suggest probable isolating mechanisms; they are best regarded as constituting a superspecies.

Trogon viridis Linnaeus. WHITE-TAILED TROGON.

Trogon viridis Linnaeus, 1766, Syst. Nat., ed. 12, 1, p. 167. Based on "Le Couroucou verd de Cayenne" Brisson, Ornithologie, 4, p. 168, pl. 17, fig. 1. (in Cayania = Cayenne.)

Habitat.—Humid lowland and foothill forest, forest edge, clearings, second-growth woodland and plantations (Tropical and lower Subtropical zones).

Distribution.—*Resident* in Panama (west on the Caribbean slope nearly to the Costa Rican border, and on the Pacific to eastern Panamá province), and in South America from Colombia, Venezuela (also Trinidad) and the Guianas south, west of the Andes to western Ecuador and east of the Andes to eastern Peru, northern Bolivia and south-central Brazil.

Notes.—Some authors consider *T. viridis* and *T. bairdii* to be conspecific; they constitute a superspecies. For use of the name *T. viridis* instead of *T. strigilatus* Linnaeus, 1766, see Zimmer, 1948, Am. Mus. Novit., no. 1380, p. 26.

Trogon bairdii Lawrence. BAIRD'S TROGON.

Trogon bairdii Lawrence, 1868, Ann. Lyc. Nat. Hist. N.Y., 9, p. 119. (San Mateo, Costa Rica.)

Habitat.—Humid lowland and foothill forest, forest edge and adjacent open woodland, but more common in forest proper (Tropical and lower Subtropical zones).

Distribution.—*Resident* on the Pacific slope of southwestern Costa Rica (north to the region around Río Grande de Tárcoles) and western Panama (western Chiriquí).

Notes.—See comments under *T. viridis.*

Trogon violaceus Gmelin. VIOLACEOUS TROGON.

Trogon violaceus Gmelin, 1788, Syst. Nat., 1 (1), p. 404. Based mainly on "Couroucou à chaperon violet" Buffon, Hist. Nat. Ois., 6, p. 294, and the "Violet-headed Curucui" Latham, Gen. Synop. Birds, 1 (2), p. 491. (No locality given = Surinam.)

Habitat.—Forest edge, clearings, open woodland and second growth, especially near streams, more commonly in humid lowlands, less frequently in semi-arid deciduous woodland and scrub (Tropical and lower Subtropical zones).

Distribution.—*Resident* from San Luis Potosí, Puebla, Veracruz and Oaxaca south along both slopes of Middle America (including the Yucatan Peninsula), and in South America from Colombia, Venezuela (also Trinidad) and the Guianas south, west of the Andes to western Ecuador and east of the Andes to eastern Peru, northern Bolivia and Amazonian Brazil. A report from "near City of Mexico" is regarded as erroneous.

Notes.—The Middle American and northwestern South American populations are sometimes regarded as a separate species, *T. caligatus* Gould, 1838 [GARTERED TROGON].

Trogon mexicanus Swainson. MOUNTAIN TROGON.

Trogon Mexicanus Swainson, 1827, Philos. Mag., new ser., 1, p. 440. (Temiscaltipec, Mexico = Temascaltepec, state of México.)

Habitat.—Open pine woodland, pine-oak association and humid montane forest (Subtropical and Temperate zones).

Distribution.—*Resident* from eastern Sinaloa, southern Chihuahua, Durango, Zacatecas, San Luis Potosí and southern Tamaulipas south through the mountains of Mexico and Guatemala to central Honduras.

Notes.—Also known as MEXICAN TROGON.

Trogon elegans Gould. ELEGANT TROGON. [389.]

Trogon elegans Gould, 1834, Proc. Zool. Soc. London, p. 26. (apud Guatimala, in Mexico = Guatemala.)

Habitat.—Open woodland, pine-oak association, scrubby woodland and second growth, primarily in arid or semi-arid situations, less frequently in humid woodland (Tropical to lower Temperate zones).

Distribution.—*Resident* from southern Arizona (Chiricahua, Huachuca and Atascosa mountains, formerly Santa Catalina Mountains), Sonora, northwestern Chihuahua, Durango, Zacatecas, Nuevo León and Tamaulipas south through Mexico (including María Madre and María Magdalena in the Tres Marias Islands) to Guerrero, Veracruz and Oaxaca (west of the Isthmus of Tehuantepec); and in southern and eastern Guatemala (Motagua Valley and Pacific lowlands), El Salvador, Honduras (interior valleys and Pacific lowlands), Nicaragua (Pacific slope) and northwestern Costa Rica (Guanacaste). Northernmost populations are partially migratory, the species being casual in Arizona in winter.

Casual in southwestern New Mexico and southern Texas (Big Bend and lower Rio Grande Valley).

Notes.—The populations of the southwestern United States and Mexico have sometimes been regarded as a separate species, *T. ambiguus* Gould, 1835 [COPPERY-TAILED TROGON].

Trogon collaris Vieillot. COLLARED TROGON.

Trogon collaris Vieillot, 1817, Nouv. Dict. Hist. Nat., nouv. éd., 8, p. 320. (Cayenne.)

Habitat.—Humid forest, forest edge and open woodland, in Middle America more frequent in foothills and mountains (Tropical and Subtropical zones).

Distribution.—*Resident* from San Luis Potosí, Puebla, Veracruz and Oaxaca south along both slopes of Middle America (including the Yucatan Peninsula, but on the Pacific slope of Central America from Guatemala to northwestern Costa Rica confined entirely to highland regions), and in South America from Colombia, Venezuela (also Tobago and Trinidad) and the Guianas south, west of the Andes to northwestern Ecuador and east of the Andes to eastern Peru, northern Bolivia and east-central Brazil.

Notes.—The Middle American form is sometimes regarded as a distinct species, *T. puella* Gould, 1845 [BAR-TAILED TROGON].

Trogon aurantiiventris Gould. ORANGE-BELLIED TROGON.

Trogon aurantiiventris Gould, 1856, Proc. Zool. Soc. London, p. 107. (near David, Veragua [=Chiriquí, Panama].)

Habitat.—Humid montane forest and forest edge, rarely in clearings or open woodland (Subtropical and lower Temperate zones).

Distribution.—*Resident* in the mountains of Costa Rica and western Panama (east to Veraguas).

Trogon rufus Gmelin. BLACK-THROATED TROGON.

Trogon rufus Gmelin, 1788, Syst. Nat. 1 (1), p. 404. Based mainly on "Couroucou à queue rousse de Cayenne" Buffon, Hist. Nat. Ois., 6, p. 293, and Daubenton, Planches Enlum., pl. 736. (in Cayenna = Cayenne.)

Habitat.—Humid lowland forest, forest edge, clearings, open woodland and second growth (Tropical Zone).

Distribution.—*Resident* on the Caribbean slope of Honduras (east of the Sula Valley) and Nicaragua, on both slopes of Costa Rica (except the dry northwest) and Panama, and in South America from Colombia, Venezuela and the Guianas south, west of the Andes to western Ecuador and east of the Andes to eastern Peru, central and southern Brazil, extreme northeastern Argentina and eastern Paraguay.

Notes.—Also known as GRACEFUL TROGON.

Trogon melanurus Swainson. BLACK-TAILED TROGON.

Trogon melanurus Swainson, 1838, Anim. Menag. (1837), p. 329. (Demerara [Guyana].)

Habitat.—Humid lowland forest and forest edge (Tropical Zone).

Distribution.—*Resident* from central Panama (the Canal Zone eastward), Colombia, Venezuela and the Guianas south, west of the Andes to northwestern Peru and east of the Andes to eastern Peru, northern Bolivia and Amazonian Brazil.

Notes.—Some authors suggest that the form in Panama and northern Colombia represents a distinct species, *T. macroura* Gould, 1838 [LARGE-TAILED TROGON].

Trogon massena Gould. SLATY-TAILED TROGON.

Trogon massena Gould, 1838, Monogr. Trogonidae, ed. 1, pt. 3, pl. [4] and text. (México.)

Habitat.—Humid lowland and foothill forest, forest edge, second-growth woodland and mangroves (Tropical and lower Subtropical zones).

Distribution.—*Resident* on the Gulf-Caribbean slope of southeastern Mexico (Veracruz, northern Oaxaca, Tabasco, Chiapas, Campeche and Quintana Roo), Belize, Guatemala and Honduras, on both slopes of Nicaragua, Costa Rica (absent from the dry northwest) and Panama, and on the Pacific slope of Colombia and northwestern Ecuador.

Notes.—Also known as MASSENA TROGON.

Trogon clathratus Salvin. LATTICE-TAILED TROGON.

Trogon clathratus Salvin, 1866, Proc. Zool. Soc. London, p. 75. (Santa Fé de Veragua, Panamá = Calovévora, Veraguas, Panama.)

Habitat.—Humid lowland and foothill forest, rarely in forest edge (Tropical and lower Subtropical zones).

Distribution.—*Resident* on the Caribbean slope of Costa Rica and Panama

(Bocas del Toro, Veraguas and Coclé, locally also on the Pacific slope in Chiriquí and Veraguas).

Genus EUPTILOTIS Gould

Euptilotis (not *Euptilotus* Reichenbach, 1850) Gould, 1858, Monogr. Trogon-idae, ed. 2, pt. 1, pl. 4 and text. Type, by original designation, *Trogon neoxenus* Gould.

Euptilotis neoxenus (Gould). EARED TROGON. [389.1.]

Trogon neoxenus Gould, 1838, Monogr. Trogonidae, ed. 1, pt. 3, pl. [10] and text. (Mexico.)

Habitat.—Montane pine forest (Temperate Zone).

Distribution.—*Resident* in the mountains of northwestern Chihuahua, Sinaloa, Durango, Zacatecas, Nayarit and Michoacán.

Recorded since 1977 (in fall and winter, and probably resident) in southern Arizona (Huachuca and Chiricahua mountains), also a sight report for south-western New Mexico (Animas Mountains).

Genus PHAROMACHRUS de la Llave

Pharomachrus de la Llave, 1832, Registro Trimestre, 1, p. 48. Type, by monotypy, *Pharomachrus mocinno* de la Llave.

Pharomachrus auriceps (Gould). GOLDEN-HEADED QUETZAL.

Trogon (*Calurus*) *auriceps* Gould, 1842, Ann. Mag., Nat. Hist., ser. 1, 9, p. 238. (the Cordillerian Andes.)

Habitat.—Humid montane and foothill forest, less frequently forest edge and clearings (upper Tropical and Subtropical zones).

Distribution.—*Resident* in eastern Panama (Cerro Pirre in eastern Darién); and in South America in the Andes from Colombia and northwestern Venezuela south to eastern Peru and northern Bolivia.

Notes.—By some considered to be conspecific with *P. pavoninus* (Spix, 1824) [PAVONINE QUETZAL], which has a complementary range chiefly east of that of *P. auriceps* in South America; they constitute a superspecies.

Pharomachrus mocinno de la Llave. RESPLENDENT QUETZAL.

Pharomachrus Mocinno de la Llave, 1832, Registro Trimestre, 1, p. 48. (Gua-temala and Chiapas.)

Habitat.—Humid montane forest, forest edge, clearings, and open situations with scattered trees adjacent to forest (Subtropical and lower Temperate zones).

Distribution.—*Resident* in the mountains of eastern Oaxaca (Sierra Madre de Chiapas), Chiapas, Guatemala, El Salvador, Honduras, north-central Nicaragua, Costa Rica (except the Cordillera de Guanacaste) and western Panama (east to Veraguas, at least formerly).

Notes.—Some authors have considered the Andean form, *P. antisianus* (d'Or-bigny, 1837) [CRESTED QUETZAL], as conspecific with *P. mocinno*; they constitute a superspecies. For use of *"mocinno"* instead of the emended *"mocino"*, see Eisenmann, 1959, Auk, 76, p. 108.

Order **CORACIIFORMES**: Kingfishers, Rollers, Hornbills and Allies

Notes.—This order may be polyphyletic. The arrangement used here is subject to modification.

Suborder UPUPAE: Hoopoes and Allies

Family **UPUPIDAE**: Hoopoes

Genus **UPUPA** Linnaeus

Upupa Linnaeus, 1758, Syst. Nat., ed. 10, 1, p. 117. Type, by tautonymy, *Upupa epops* Linnaeus (*Upupa,* prebinomial specific name, in synonymy).

Upupa epops Linnaeus. HOOPOE. [391.1.]

Upupa epops Linnaeus, 1758, Syst. Nat., ed. 10, 1, p. 117. (in Europæ sylvis = Sweden.)

Habitat & Distribution.—*Breeds* in open and partly open situations from northern Eurasia south to southern Africa, Madagascar, India and Southeast Asia, and *winters* from southern Europe, India and southern China south through the remainder of the breeding range.

Accidental in western Alaska (Old Chevak, Yukon-Kuskokwim Delta, 2–3 September 1975; Dau and Paniyak, 1977, Auk, 94, p. 601).

Notes.—Includes the African race regarded by some authors as a species, *U. africana* Bechstein, 1811 [AFRICAN HOOPOE], distinct from *U. epops* [COMMON HOOPOE].

Suborder ALCEDINES: Todies, Motmots and Kingfishers

Superfamily TODOIDEA: Todies and Motmots

Family **TODIDAE**: Todies

Genus **TODUS** Brisson

Todus Brisson, 1760, Ornithologie, 1, p. 44; 4, p. 528. Type, by tautonymy, *Alcedo todus* Linnaeus.

Todus multicolor Gould. CUBAN TODY.

Todus multicolor Gould, 1837, Icones Avium, pt. 1, pl. [12] and text. (No locality given = western Cuba.)

Habitat.—Forest and open woodland, especially along streams.
Distribution.—*Resident* on Cuba and the Isle of Pines.

Todus subulatus Gray. BROAD-BILLED TODY.

> *Todus subulatus* "Gould" G. R. Gray, 1847, Genera Birds, 1, pl. 22. (No locality given.)

Habitat.—Lowland open woodland, second growth and scrub, primarily in semi-arid situations.
Distribution.—*Resident* on Hispaniola (including Gonâve Island).
Notes.—Also known as HISPANIOLAN TODY.

Todus angustirostris Lafresnaye. NARROW-BILLED TODY.

> *Todus angustirostris* Lafresnaye, 1851, Rev. Mag. Zool., ser, 2, 3, p. 478. (in Sancti-Dominicensis insulâ = Hispaniola.)

Habitat.—Dense mountain undergrowth, forest edge and shrubbery.
Distribution.—*Resident* in the mountains of Hispaniola (locally also at low elevations in the Dominican Republic).

Todus todus (Linnaeus). JAMAICAN TODY.

> *Alcedo Todus* Linnaeus, 1758, Syst. Nat., ed. 10, 1, p. 116. Based mainly on "The Green Sparrow, or Green Humming Bird" Edwards, Nat. Hist. Birds, 3, p. 121, pl. 121, upper fig.. (in America = Jamaica.)

Habitat.—Open woodland, second growth and scrubby undergrowth, mostly in wooded hills and mountains.
Distribution.—*Resident* on Jamaica.

Todus mexicanus Lesson. PUERTO RICAN TODY.

> *Todus mexicanus* Lesson, 1838, Ann. Sci. Nat. (Zool.), sér. 2, 9, p. 167, note 1. (Mexico, particularly Tampico, error = Puerto Rico.)

Habitat.—Forest undergrowth, open woodland and scrub, from semi-arid lowlands to humid mountain slopes.
Distribution.—*Resident* on Puerto Rico.

Family MOMOTIDAE: Motmots

Genus HYLOMANES Lichtenstein

> *Hylomanes* Lichtenstein, 1839, Abh. Phys. Kl. Akad. Wiss. Berlin (1838), p. 449, pl. 4. Type, by monotypy, *Hylomanes momotula* Lichtenstein.

Hylomanes momotula Lichtenstein. TODY MOTMOT.

> *Hylomanes momotula* Lichtenstein, 1839, Abh. Phys. Kl. Akad. Wiss. Berlin (1838), p. 449, pl. 4. (Valle Real, México.)

Habitat.—Humid lowland and foothill forest (Tropical and lower Subtropical zones).
Distribution.—*Resident* from Veracruz and northern Oaxaca south on the Gulf-Caribbean slope (except the Yucatan Peninsula) to Nicaragua (recorded only at

Peña Blanca, Depto. de Jinotega), locally on the Pacific slope of Guatemala, and in Costa Rica (most frequently on the Pacific slope of Cordillera de Guanacaste), Panama (local, recorded Veraguas, Colón, eastern Panamá province and Darién) and western Colombia.

Genus ASPATHA Sharpe

Aspatha Sharpe, 1892, Cat. Birds Br. Mus., 17, pp. x, 313, 331. Type, by monotypy, *Prionites gularis* Lafresnaye.

Aspatha gularis (Lafresnaye). BLUE-THROATED MOTMOT.

Prionites gularis Lafresnaye, 1840, Rev. Zool. [Paris], 3, p. 130. (Guatimala = Guatemala.)

Habitat.—Humid montane forest, less frequently in pine-oak association and brush (Subtropical and lower Temperate zones).

Distribution.—*Resident* in the mountains of eastern Oaxaca (Sierra Madre de Chiapas), Chiapas, Guatemala, El Salvador and Honduras.

Genus MOMOTUS Brisson

Momotus Brisson, 1760, Ornithologie, 1, p. 44; 4, p. 465. Type, by tautonymy, *Momotus* Brisson = *Ramphastos momota* Linnaeus.

Momotus momota (Linnaeus). BLUE-CROWNED MOTMOT.

Ramphastos Momota Linnaeus, 1766, Syst. Nat., ed. 12, 1, p. 152. (in America meridionali = Cayenne.)

Habitat.—Open woodland, forest edge, clearings, second growth, scrub and plantations, generally in humid habitats (Tropical and Subtropical zones).

Distribution.—*Resident* from Nuevo León and Tamaulipas on the Gulf-Caribbean and Chiapas (locally) on the Pacific south along both slopes of Middle America (including the Yucatan Peninsula), and in South America from Colombia, Venezuela (also Tobago and Trinidad) and the Guianas south, west of the Andes to northwestern Peru and east of the Andes to eastern Peru, Bolivia, northern Argentina, Paraguay and south-central Brazil.

Notes.—Throughout the extensive range of this species, various morphologically distinct groups exist, which are sometimes recognized as separate species; in Middle America, two groups are involved, *M. lessonii* Lesson, 1842 [LESSON'S MOTMOT], occurring south to western Panama, and *M. subrufescens* Sclater, 1853 [TAWNY-BELLIED MOTMOT], found from eastern Panama to northern Venezuela.

Momotus mexicanus Swainson. RUSSET-CROWNED MOTMOT.

Momotus Mexicanus Swainson, 1827, Philos. Mag., new ser., 1, p. 442. (Temiscaltipec, Mexico = Temascaltepec, state of México.)

Habitat.—Open woodland, second growth, scrub and plantations, primarily in semi-arid situations (Tropical and lower Subtropical zones).

Distribution.—*Resident* in western and interior Mexico from southern Sonora, southwestern Chihuahua, Durango and Zacatecas south to Morelos, western Puebla, Oaxaca and Chiapas; and in the interior of Guatemala (upper Motagua Valley).

Genus BARYPHTHENGUS Cabanis and Heine

Baryphthengus Cabanis and Heine, 1859, Mus. Heineanum, 2, p. 114. Type, by subsequent designation (Sharpe, 1892), *Baryphonus ruficapillus* Vieillot.

Baryphthengus ruficapillus (Vieillot). RUFOUS MOTMOT.

Baryphonus ruficapillus Vieillot, 1818, Nouv. Dict. Hist. Nat., nouv. éd., 21, p. 315. (No locality given = southeastern Mexico.)

Habitat.—Humid forest, forest edge, clearings, second growth and plantations, especially near streams (Tropical and lower Subtropical zones).

Distribution.—*Resident* [*martii* group] on the Caribbean slope of northeastern Honduras (Gracias a Dios), Nicaragua and Costa Rica, on both slopes of Panama, and in South America from Colombia south, west of the Andes to western Ecuador and east of the Andes through eastern Ecuador to eastern Peru, Bolivia and Amazonian Brazil; and [*ruficapillus* group] in southern and eastern Brazil, northeastern Argentina and eastern Paraguay.

Notes.—The two groups are sometimes considered separate species, *B. martii* (Spix, 1824) [RUFOUS MOTMOT] and *B. ruficapillus* [RUFOUS-CAPPED MOTMOT].

Genus ELECTRON Gistel

Crypticus (not Latreille, 1817) Swainson, 1837, Class. Birds, 2, p. 338. Type, by monotypy, *C. platyrhynchus* Ill. of Orn. iii. pl. 106 = *Momotus platyrhynchus* Leadbeater.
Electron Gistel, 1848, Naturgesch. Thierr. Höhere Schulen, p. viii. New name for *Crypticus* Swainson, preoccupied.

Electron carinatum (Du Bus). KEEL-BILLED MOTMOT.

Prionites carinatus Du Bus, 1847, Bull. Acad. R. Sci. Lett. Beaux-Arts Belg., 14, p. 108. (Guatemala.)

Habitat.—Humid lowland and montane forest (Tropical and Subtropical zones).

Distribution.—*Resident* locally on the Caribbean slope from southeastern Mexico (recorded Veracruz and Tabasco, possibly also Oaxaca) south through Central America to northeastern Costa Rica.

Electron platyrhynchum (Leadbeater). BROAD-BILLED MOTMOT.

Momotus platyrhynchus Leadbeater, 1829, Trans. Linn. Soc. London, 16, p. 92. (Brazil, error = western Ecuador.)

Habitat.—Humid forest, forest edge, clearings, open woodland and second growth (Tropical and Subtropical zones).

Distribution.—*Resident* in eastern Honduras (Lancetilla, Olancho), Nicaragua (Caribbean slope), Costa Rica (mostly Caribbean slope, locally on Pacific drainage), Panama (both slopes), and in South America from Colombia south, west of the Andes to western Ecuador and east of the Andes to eastern Peru, east-central Bolivia and central Brazil.

Genus **EUMOMOTA** Sclater

Eumomota Sclater, 1858, Proc. Zool. Soc. London (1857), p. 257. Type, by monotypy, *Prionites superciliaris* Jardine and Selby = *Pyronites superciliosus* Sandbach.

Eumomota superciliosa (Sandbach). TURQUOISE-BROWNED MOTMOT.

Pyronites superciliosus Sandbach, 1837, Athenaeum, no. 517, p. 698. (México = Campeche.)

Habitat.—Open woodland, scrubby areas, plantations, open situations with scattered trees, and fencerows in cultivated areas, generally in arid or semi-arid situations (Tropical Zone).

Distribution.—*Resident* in the Gulf-Caribbean lowlands of southeastern Mexico (from southern Veracruz and Tabasco through the Yucatan Peninsula); in the Pacific lowlands of Middle America from Oaxaca south to central Costa Rica (south to Quepos); and in the interior valleys of Guatemala (Motagua and Río Negro drainages) and Honduras (locally spreading to Caribbean lowlands).

Superfamily **ALCEDINOIDEA**: Kingfishers

Family **ALCEDINIDAE**: Kingfishers

Subfamily **CERYLINAE**: Typical Kingfishers

Genus **CERYLE** Boie

Ceryle Boie, 1828, Isis von Oken, col. 316. Type, by subsequent designation (G. R. Gray, 1840), *C. rudis* (Gm.) = *Alcedo rudis* Linnaeus.

Subgenus **MEGACERYLE** Kaup

Megaceryle Kaup, 1848, Verh. Naturhist. Ver. Grossherz. Hessen, 2, p. 68. Type, by subsequent designation (Sharpe, 1871), *Alcedo guttata* Vigors = *Ceryle guttulata* Stejneger.
Streptoceryle Bonaparte, 1854, Ateneo Ital., 2, p. 320. Type, by subsequent designation (G. R. Gray, 1855), *Alcedo torquata* Linnaeus.

Ceryle torquata (Linnaeus). RINGED KINGFISHER. [390.1.]

Alcedo torquata Linnaeus, 1766, Syst. Nat., ed. 12, 1, p. 180. Based mainly on "Le Martin-pescheur hupé du Mexique" Brisson, Ornithologie, 4, p. 518, pl. 41, fig. 1. (in Martinica, Mexico = Mexico.)

Habitat.—Lakes, rivers, streams, lagoons and coastal regions (Tropical to lower Temperates zones).

Distribution.—*Resident* from southern Sinaloa, Nuevo León, southern Texas (lower Rio Grande Valley west to Webb County) and Tamaulipas south along both slopes of Middle America (including islands off the Pacific coast from the Tres Marias south to the Pearl islands), and throughout most of South America from Colombia, Venezuela (also Margarita Island and Trinidad) and the Guianas south to Tierra del Fuego; also in the Lesser Antilles (Guadeloupe, Dominica and Martinique, doubtfully recorded from Grenada and St. Kitts).

Casual in western Texas (Big Bend), and north to central and southeastern Texas (Travis and Nueces counties), also a sight report from Puerto Rico.

Ceryle alcyon (Linnaeus). BELTED KINGFISHER. [390.]

> *Alcedo alcyon* Linnaeus, 1758, Syst. Nat., ed. 10, 1, p. 115. Based mainly on the "Kingfisher" Catesby, Nat. Hist. Carolina, 1, p. 69, pl. 69. (in America = South Carolina.)

Habitat.—Primarily along watercourses, both fresh-water and marine, including lakes, streams, wooded creeks and rivers, seacoasts, bays, estuaries and mangroves.

Distribution.—*Breeds* from western and central Alaska, central Yukon, British Columbia (including the Queen Charlotte and Vancouver islands), western and south-central Mackenzie, northern Saskatchewan, central (and probably northern) Manitoba, northern Ontario, central Quebec, east-central Labrador and Newfoundland south to southern California, southern Arizona, southern New Mexico, southern Texas, the Gulf coast and central Florida.

Winters from south-coastal and southeastern Alaska, central and southern British Columbia, western Montana, Wyoming, Colorado, Nebraska, southern Minnesota, the southern Great Lakes region, New York and New England south throughout the continental United States, Middle America (including offshore islands from western Mexico to Cocos and the Pearl islands), the West Indies and Bermuda to northern South America (recorded Colombia, Venezuela, Guyana and most islands off Venezuela) and the Galapagos Islands.

Casual in the Hawaiian Islands, the eastern Aleutians, northern Alaska (Point Barrow), Greenland, Iceland, the British Isles, continental Europe and the Azores.

Genus **CHLOROCERYLE** Kaup

> *Chloroceryle* [subgenus] Kaup, 1848, Verh. Naturhist. Ver. Grossherz. Hessen, 2, p. 68. Type, by subsequent designation (Sharpe, 1871), *Alcedo superciliosa* Linnaeus = *Alcedo aenea* Pallas.

Chloroceryle amazona (Latham). AMAZON KINGFISHER.

> *Alcedo amazona* Latham, 1790, Index Ornithol., 1, p. 257. Based on the "Amazonian Kingfisher" Latham, Gen. Synop. Birds, suppl., 1, p. 116. (in Cayana = Cayenne.)

Habitat.—Rivers, lakes, forest streams and ponds in forest and savanna (Tropical and lower Subtropical zones).

Distribution.—*Resident* from Nayarit, southeastern San Luis Potosí and southern Tamaulipas south along both slopes of Middle America (except Campeche, doubtfully recorded in the state of Yucatán), and in South America from Colombia, Venezuela (also Tobago and Trinidad), and the Guianas south, mostly east of the Andes, to eastern Peru, Bolivia, northern Argentina and Uruguay.

Chloroceryle americana (Gmelin). GREEN KINGFISHER. [391.]

> *Alcedo americana* Gmelin, 1788, Syst. Nat., 1 (1), p. 451. Based on "Martin-pescheur du Brésil" Brisson, Ornithologie, 4, p. 510, and "Martin-pecheur

vert et blanc de Cayenne" Daubenton, Planches Enlum., pl. 591. (in Cayenna = Cayenne.)

Habitat.—Streams, rivers, lakes, marshes, swamps, mangroves and rarely rocky
seacoasts (Tropical and Subtropical zones).

Distribution.—*Resident* from Sonora, Chihuahua, northern Coahuila and central Texas south, primarily in the lowlands, along both slopes of Middle America
(including Isla Coiba off Panama), and in South America from Colombia, Venezuela (also Tobago and Trinidad) and the Guianas south, west of the Andes to
northern Chile and east of the Andes to central Argentina.

Casual north to southern Arizona, and north-central and eastern Texas.

Chloroceryle inda (Linnaeus). Green-and-rufous Kingfisher.

Alcedo inda Linnaeus, 1766, Syst. Nat., ed. 12, 1, p. 179. Based on the
"Spotted King's-fisher" Edwards, Glean. Nat. Hist., 3, p. 262, pl. 335. (in
India occidentali, error = Guyana.)

Habitat.—Forest streams, swamps and mangroves (Tropical Zone).

Distribution.—*Resident* locally on the Caribbean slope of southeastern Nicaragua and Costa Rica, on both slopes of Panama (including the Pearl Islands),
and in South America from Colombia, Venezuela and the Guianas south, west
of the Andes to western Ecuador and east of the Andes to eastern Peru, east-
central Bolivia and central Brazil.

Chloroceryle aenea (Pallas). American Pygmy Kingfisher.

Alcedo (*aenea*) Pallas, 1764, *in* Vroeg, Cat. Raissoné Ois., Adumbr., p. 1, no.
54. (Surinam.)

Habitat.—Forest streams, swamps and mangroves.

Distribution.—*Resident* from Oaxaca, southeastern San Luis Potosí and Veracruz south in the lowlands of both slopes of Middle America (including Cozumel
Island off Quintana Roo, the Bay Islands off Honduras, and Isla Coiba off Panama),
and in South America from Colombia, Venezuela (also Trinidad) and the Guianas
south, west of the Andes to western Ecuador and east of the Andes to eastern
Peru, east-central Bolivia and central Brazil.

Notes.—Known in most literature as Pygmy Kingfisher.

Order PICIFORMES: Puffbirds, Toucans, Woodpeckers and Allies

Notes.—This order may be polyphyletic.

Suborder GALBULAE: Puffbirds and Jacamars

Notes.—This suborder may belong in the Coraciiformes.

Family BUCCONIDAE: Puffbirds

Genus BUCCO Brisson

Bucco Brisson, 1760, Ornithologie, 1, p. 42; 4, pp. 91, 92. Type, by tautonymy,
Bucco Brisson = *Bucco capensis* Linnaeus.

Nystalus Cabanis and Heine, 1863, Mus. Heineanum, 1, p. 139. Type, by subsequent designation (Sclater, 1882), *Alcedo maculata* Gmelin.

Notharchus Cabanis and Heine, 1863, Mus. Heineanum, 1, pp. 146, 149. Type, by subsequent designation (Sclater, 1882), *Bucco hyperrhynchus* Sclater = *Bucco macrorhynchos* Gmelin.

Bucco radiatus Sclater. BARRED PUFFBIRD.

Bucco radiatus Sclater, 1854, Proc. Zool. Soc. London (1853), p. 122, pl. 50–51. (in Nova Grenada = Magdalena Valley, Colombia.)

Habitat.—Humid lowland and foothill forest and forest edge (Tropical and lower Subtropical zones).

Distribution.—*Resident* from western Panama (west to Coclé and western Panamá province, possibly to Veraguas) and northern Colombia south through western Colombia to western Ecuador.

Notes.—This species is frequently placed in the genus *Nystalus*. *B. radiatus* and the Amazonian *B. chacuru* (Vieillot, 1816) may constitute a superspecies.

Bucco macrorhynchos Gmelin. WHITE-NECKED PUFFBIRD.

Bucco macrorhynchos Gmelin, 1788, Syst. Nat., 1 (1), p. 406. Based in part on "Le plus grande Barbu à gros bec de Cayenne" Daubenton, Planches Enlum., pl. 689. (in Cayenna = Cayenne.)

Habitat.—Open woodland, second growth, forest edge, plantations and savanna, more frequently in humid situations, less commonly in semi-arid habitats (Tropical and lower Subtropical zones).

Distribution.—*Resident* from southern Mexico (west-central Veracruz, Oaxaca, Chiapas, southern Campeche and southern Quintana Roo) south along both slopes of Middle America, and in South America from Colombia, Venezuela and the Guianas south, west of the Andes to western Ecuador and east of the Andes to eastern Peru, Bolivia, Paraguay, northeastern Argentina and southern Brazil.

Notes.—This and the following two species are often placed in the genus *Notharchus*. Some authors consider the form in the southern portion of the South American range to represent a separate species, *B. swainsoni* G. R. Gray, 1846 [BUFF-BELLIED PUFFBIRD].

Bucco pectoralis Gray. BLACK-BREASTED PUFFBIRD.

Bucco pectoralis G. R. Gray, 1846. Genera Birds, 1, pl. 26. (No locality given.)

Habitat.—Humid lowland forest and forest edge (Tropical Zone).

Distribution.—*Resident* in eastern Panama (west to the Canal Zone, mostly on the Pacific drainage), and in South America from northern Colombia south, west of the Andes, to western Ecuador.

Notes.—See comments under *N. macrorhynchos*.

Bucco tectus Boddaert. PIED PUFFBIRD.

Bucco tectus Boddaert, 1783, Table Planches Enlum., p. 43. Based on "Barbu à plastron noir" Daubenton, Planches Enlum., pl. 688, fig. 2. (Cayenne.)

Habitat.—Humid lowland forest edge, clearings, plantations and open situations with scattered trees, usually near water (Tropical Zone).

Distribution.—*Resident* on the Caribbean slope of Costa Rica (from Río Sarapiquí drainage southward), in Panama (throughout the Caribbean slope, on the Pacific known from eastern Panamá province and Darién), and in South America from Colombia, southern Venezuela and the Guianas south, east of the Andes, to eastern Peru and Amazonian Brazil.

Notes.—See comments under *N. macrorhynchos.*

Genus MALACOPTILA Gray

Malacoptila G. R. Gray, 1841, List Genera Birds, ed. 2, p. 13. Type, by subsequent designation (G. R. Gray, 1846), *Bucco fuscus* Gmelin.

Malacoptila panamensis Lafresnaye. WHITE-WHISKERED PUFFBIRD.

Malacoptila panamensis Lafresnaye, 1847, Rev. Zool. [Paris], 10, p. 79. (Panamá.)

Habitat.—Humid lowland and foothill forest, forest edge (especially overgrown borders) and dense second growth (Tropical and lower Subtropical zones).

Distribution.—*Resident* on the Gulf-Caribbean slope from southeastern Mexico (recorded Tabasco and Chiapas) south to Nicaragua, on both slopes of Costa Rica (absent from the drier portions of Guanacaste in the northwest) and Panama, and in South America from northern Colombia south, west of the Andes, to western Ecuador.

Notes.—*M. panamensis* and the South American *M. mystacalis* (Lafresnaye, 1850) appear to constitute a superspecies.

Genus MICROMONACHA Sclater

Micromonacha Sclater, 1881, Monogr. Jacamars Puff-birds, pt. 5, p. 131, pl. 44. Type, by monotypy, *Bucco lanceolata* Deville.

Micromonacha lanceolata (Deville). LANCEOLATED MONKLET.

Bucco lanceolata Deville, 1849, Rev. Mag. Zool., ser. 2, 1, p. 56. (Pampa del Sacramento, mission de Sarayacu [upper Amazon].)

Habitat.—Humid lowland forest (Tropical Zone).

Distribution.—*Resident* locally in Costa Rica (northern slope of Cordillera Central), Panama (one record from Caribbean slope of western Veraguas) and western Colombia (Nariño); also in South America east of the Andes in eastern Colombia, eastern Ecuador, eastern Peru and western Amazonian Brazil.

Genus NONNULA Sclater

Nonnula Sclater, 1854, Proc. Zool. Soc. London (1853), p. 124. Type, by original designation, *Bucco rubecula* Spix.

Nonnula ruficapilla (Tschudi). GRAY-CHEEKED NUNLET.

Lypornix ruficapilla Tschudi, 1844, Arch. Naturgesch., 10, p. 300. (Republica Peruana = Vitoc Valley, Peru.)

Habitat.—Humid lowland forest, forest edge, clearings and second-growth woodland (Tropical Zone).

Distribution.—*Resident* [*frontalis* group] in central and eastern Panama (west to northern Coclé and the Canal Zone) and northern Colombia; and [*ruficapilla* group] in eastern Peru and western Brazil.

Notes.—The two groups are often regarded as distinct species, *N. frontalis* (Sclater, 1854) [GRAY-CHEEKED NUNLET] and *N. ruficapilla* [RUFOUS-CAPPED NUNLET].

Genus MONASA Vieillot

Monasa Vieillot, 1816, Analyse, p. 27. Type, by monotypy, "Coucou noir de Cayenne" Buffon = *Cuculus ater* Boddaert.

Monasa morphoeus (Hahn and Küster). WHITE-FRONTED NUNBIRD.

Bucco Morphœus "Wagler" Hahn and Küster, 1823, Vögel Asien, Afr., etc., lief. 14, pl. 2 and text. (Brazil.)

Habitat.—Humid lowland forest, forest edge, clearings, second-growth woodland, and plantations (Tropical Zone).

Distribution.—*Resident* in the Caribbean lowlands of eastern Honduras (Olancho), Nicaragua, Costa Rica and western Panama (western Bocas del Toro); and from eastern Panama (both slopes, west to the Canal Zone), northern and western Colombia, and southwestern Venezuela south, east of the Andes, to eastern Peru, northern Bolivia, and central and southeastern Brazil.

Family GALBULIDAE: Jacamars

Genus BRACHYGALBA Bonaparte

Brachygalba Bonaparte, 1854, Ateneo Ital., 2, p. 129. Type, by subsequent designation (G. R. Gray, 1855), *Galbula albogularis* Spix.

Brachygalba salmoni Sclater and Salvin. DUSKY-BACKED JACAMAR.

Brachygalba salmoni Sclater and Salvin, 1879, Proc. Zool. Soc. London, p. 535. (Rio Neche [=Nechí], Antioquia, Colombia.)

Habitat.—Humid lowland forest and forest edge, especially near streams (Tropical Zone).

Distribution.—*Resident* in extreme eastern Panama (eastern Darién) and northwestern Colombia.

Notes.—*B. salmoni* and three South American species, *B. albogularis* (Spix, 1824), *B. goeringi* Sclater and Salvin, 1869, and *B. lugubris* (Swainson, 1838), appear to constitute a superspecies.

Genus GALBULA Brisson

Galbula Brisson, 1760, Ornithologie, 1, p. 42; 4, p. 86. Type, by tautonymy, *Galbula* Brisson = *Alcedo galbula* Linnaeus.

Galbula ruficauda Cuvier. RUFOUS-TAILED JACAMAR.

Galbula ruficauda Cuvier, 1817, Règne Anim., 1 (1816), p. 420. Based on Levaillant, Hist. Nat. Ois. Paradis Rolliers, 2, pl. 50, (Guiana.)

Habitat.—Humid forest, forest edge, clearings, dense second growth, plantations and thick scrub, especially near streams (Tropical and lower Subtropical zones).

Distribution.—*Resident* [*melanogenia* group] from Veracruz and northern Oaxaca south on the Gulf-Caribbean slope of Middle America (except the Yucatan Peninsula) to Nicaragua, on both slopes of Costa Rica (except the dry northwest) and western Panama (western Chiriquí and western Bocas del Toro), and in eastern Panama (Darién), western Colombia and western Ecuador; and [*ruficauda* group] from eastern Panama (eastern Panamá province and eastern Darién), northern Colombia, Venezuela (also Tobago and Trinidad) and the Guianas south to eastern Colombia, and from Amazonian Brazil south to northern Bolivia, northeastern Argentina, Paraguay and southeastern Brazil.

Notes.—The form *melanogenia* is regarded by some authors as a species, *G. melanogenia* Sclater, 1853 [BLACK-CHINNED JACAMAR], distinct from *G. ruficauda*; intergradation between the two occurs in eastern Panama and northwestern Colombia. *G. ruficauda* appears to be part of a large superspecies including the following South American allospecies: *G. galbula* (Linnaeus, 1766); *G. tombacea* Spix, 1824; *G. cyanescens* Deville, 1849; and *G. pastazae* Taczanowski and Berlepsch, 1885.

Genus JACAMEROPS Lesson

Jacamerops Lesson, 1830, Traité Ornithol., livr. 3, p. 234. Type, by monotypy, *Alcedo grandis* Gmelin = *Alcedo aurea* Müller.

Jacamerops aurea (Müller). GREAT JACAMAR.

Alcedo aurea P. L. S. Müller, 1776, Natursyst., Suppl., p. 94. Based on the "Long-tailed Kingfisher" Vosmaer, Beschr. Missch. Am. Langst. Ys-Vogel. (Berbice, British Guiana.)

Habitat.—Humid lowland forest, shaded forest edge, and (rarely) dense second growth, often near streams (Tropical Zone).

Distribution.—*Resident* in Costa Rica (Caribbean slope west to the Sarapiquí region) and Panama (both slopes), and in South America from Colombia, Venezuela and the Guianas south, west of the Andes to western Ecuador and east of the Andes to eastern Peru, northern Bolivia and Amazonian Brazil.

Suborder PICI: Barbets, Woodpeckers and Allies

Family CAPITONIDAE: Barbets

Genus CAPITO Vieillot

Capito Vieillot, 1816, Analyse, p. 27. Type, by monotypy, "Tamatia à tête et gorge rouges" Buffon = *Bucco niger* P. L. S. Müller.

Capito maculicoronatus Lawrence. SPOT-CROWNED BARBET.

Capito maculicoronatus Lawrence, 1861, Ann. Lyc. Nat. Hist. N.Y., 7, p. 300. (Atlantic side of the Isthmus of Panama, along the line of the Panama Railroad = Canal Zone.)

Habitat.—Humid lowland forest and forest edge (Tropical Zone).

Distribution.—*Resident* in Panama (west to Veraguas on the Caribbean slope and to eastern Panamá province on the Pacific) and western Colombia.

Notes.—*C. maculicoronatus* and *C. squamatus* Salvin, 1876, appear to constitute a superspecies.

Genus EUBUCCO Bonaparte

Eubucco Bonaparte, 1850, Consp. Gen. Avium, 1 (1), p. 142. Type, by subsequent designation (G. R. Gray, 1855), *Capito richardsoni* G. R. Gray.

Eubucco bourcierii (Lafresnaye). RED-HEADED BARBET.

Micropogon Bourcierii Lafresnaye, 1845, Rev. Zool. [Paris], 8, p. 179. (Bogotá, Colombia.)

Habitat.—Humid forest, forest edge, second growth and clearings (upper Tropical and Subtropical zones).

Distribution.—*Resident* in the highlands of Costa Rica (north to the Cordillera Central) and Panama (recorded east to Veraguas, in San Blas, and in eastern Darién); and in South America in the Andes from Colombia and western Venezuela south to northeastern Peru.

Notes.—*E. bourcierii* and the closely related *E. tucinkae* (Seilern, 1913) of southeastern Peru constitute a superspecies.

Genus SEMNORNIS Richmond

Tetragonops Anonymous [=Jardine] (not Gerstäcker, Feb./Mch. 1855, Coleoptera) Oct. 1855, Edinburgh New Philos. J., new ser., 2, p. 404. Type, by monotypy, *Tetragonops ramphastinus* Jardine.

Pan (not Oken, 1816, Mammalia) Richmond, 1899, Auk, 16, p. 77. New name for *Tetragonops* Jardine, preoccupied.

Semnornis Richmond, 1900, Auk, 17, p. 179. New name for *Pan* Richmond, preoccupied.

Semnornis frantzii (Sclater). PRONG-BILLED BARBET.

Tetragonops frantzii Sclater, 1864, Ibis, p. 371, pl. 10. (in int. reipubl. Costa Rica = near San José, Costa Rica.)

Habitat.—Humid montane forest, forest edge, open woodland and pastures with scattered trees (Subtropical and lower Temperate zones).

Distribution.—*Resident* in the mountains of Costa Rica (north to the Cordillera de Tilarán, and primarily on the Caribbean slope) and western Panama (east to Veraguas).

Family RAMPHASTIDAE: Toucans

Genus AULACORHYNCHUS Gould

Aulacorhynchus Gould, 1835, Proc. Zool. Soc. London (1834), p. 147. Type, by subsequent designation (G. R. Gray, 1840), *A. sulcatus* (Swains.) = *Pteroglossus sulcatus* Swainson.

Aulacorhynchus prasinus (Gould). EMERALD TOUCANET.

Pteroglossus prasinus "Licht." Gould, 1834, Proc. Zool. Soc. London, p. 78. (México = Valle Real.)

Habitat.—Humid forest, forest edge, clearings and open woodland (upper Tropical to lower Temperate zones).

Distribution.—*Resident* [*prasinus* group] in the highlands of Middle America from San Luis Potosí, Hidalgo, Puebla, Veracruz, Oaxaca, Chiapas and Quintana Roo south through Central America to north-central Nicaragua, and in the Andes of South America from Colombia and western Venezuela south to eastern Peru; and [*caeruleogularis* group] in Costa Rica and Panama (east to Coclé and western Panamá province, and in eastern Darién).

Notes.—The two groups are sometimes recognized as separate species, *A. prasinus* and *A. caeruleogularis* (Gould, 1854) [BLUE-THROATED TOUCANET].

Genus **PTEROGLOSSUS** Illiger

Pteroglossus Illiger, 1811, Prodromus, p. 202. Type, by subsequent designation (G. R. Gray, 1840), *Ramphastos aracari* Linnaeus.

Pteroglossus torquatus (Gmelin). COLLARED ARACARI.

Ramphastos torquatus Gmelin, 1788, Syst. Nat., 1 (1), p. 354. Based in part on "Le Toucan a collier du Mexique" Brisson, Ornithologie, 4, p. 421, and the "Collared Toucan" Latham, Gen. Synop. Birds, 1 (1), p. 330. (in novae Hispaniae maritimis = Veracruz.)

Habitat.—Lowland and foothill forest, forest edge, clearings, open woodland, second growth and plantations (Tropical and lower Subtropical zones).

Distribution.—*Resident* from Veracruz, Oaxaca, Chiapas and the Yucatan Peninsula south along both slopes of Middle America (except the Pacific slope in Costa Rica and Panama from the Gulf of Nicoya east to western Panamá province), and in northern South America from Colombia east to northern Venezuela and south to western Ecuador.

Notes.—*P. torquatus* and *P. frantzii* are closely related and considered conspecific by some authors (for contrary opinion, see Slud, 1964, Bull. Am. Mus. Nat. Hist., 128, pp. 184–185). South American populations of *P. torquatus* are treated by some authors as distinct species, *P. sanguineus* Gould, 1854 [STRIPE-BILLED ARACARI], a form that ranges into extreme eastern Panama (eastern Darién), and *P. erythropygius* Gould, 1843 [PALE-BILLED ARACARI], although *torquatus* and *sanguineus* freely interbreed in a narrow zone in northwestern Colombia. This entire group, along with the South American *P. castanotis* Gould, 1834, *P. aracari* (Linnaeus, 1758) and *P. pleuricinctus* Gould, 1836, appears to constitute a superspecies.

Pteroglossus frantzii Cabanis. FIERY-BILLED ARACARI.

Pteroglossus Frantzii Cabanis, 1861, Sitzungsber. Ges. Naturforsch. Freunde Berlin, 13 November. (Costa Rica = Aguacate, Costa Rica.)

Habitat.—Forest and open woodland, forest edge, clearings, plantations and second-growth woodland (Tropical and lower Subtropical zones).

Distribution.—*Resident* on the Pacific slope of Costa Rica (west to the Gulf of Nicoya) and western Panama (east to Veraguas).

Notes.—See comments under *P. torquatus.*

Genus SELENIDERA Gould

Selenidera Gould, 1837, Icones Avium, pt. 1, pl. [7] and text. Type, by subsequent designation (G. R. Gray, 1840), *S. gouldii* (Natt.) = *Pteroglossus gouldii* Natterer.

Selenidera spectabilis Cassin. YELLOW-EARED TOUCANET.

Selenidera spectabilis Cassin, 1857, Proc. Acad. Nat. Sci. Philadelphia, 9, p. 214. (Cucuyos de Veragua, Panamá.)

Habitat.—Humid forest, forest edge, clearings and, less frequently, second growth and open woodland (Tropical and lower Subtropical zones).

Distribution.—*Resident* on the Caribbean slope of Honduras (west to the Sula Valley), Nicaragua, Costa Rica (locally on Pacific drainage), Panama (also in Pacific lowlands but less widely distributed there than on Caribbean slope) and northwestern Colombia.

Notes.—All six recognized species of the genus, which includes the South American forms *S. maculirostris* (Lichtenstein, 1823), *S. gouldii* (Natterer, 1837), *S. reinwardtii* (Wagler, 1827), *S. nattereri* (Gould, 1835) and *S. culik* (Wagler, 1827), appear to constitute a superspecies.

Genus RAMPHASTOS Linnaeus

Ramphastos Linnaeus, 1758, Syst. Nat., ed. 10, 1, p. 103. Type, by subsequent designation (Vigors, 1826), *Ramphastos erythrorhynchus* Gmelin = *Ramphastos tucanus* Linnaeus.

Ramphastos sulfuratus Lesson. KEEL-BILLED TOUCAN.

Ramphastos sulfuratus Lesson, 1830, Traité Ornithol., livr. 3, p. 173. (le Mexique = Mexico.)

Habitat.—Humid lowland and foothill forest, forest edge, clearings, second-growth woodland and plantations (Tropical and lower Subtropical zones).

Distribution.—*Resident* on the Gulf-Caribbean slope from southeastern San Luis Potosí, Puebla, Veracruz, northern Oaxaca, Tabasco, Chiapas and the Yucatan Peninsula south to Honduras, on both slopes (although locally distributed on the Pacific) of Nicaragua, Costa Rica and Panama, and in northern Colombia and northwestern Venezuela.

Notes.—*R. sulfuratus* and the South American species *R. dicolorus* Linnaeus, 1776, *R. vitellinus* Lichtenstein, 1823, and *R. brevis* appear to constitute a superspecies.

[Ramphastos brevis Meyer de Schauensee. CHOCO TOUCAN.] See Appendix B.

Ramphastos swainsonii Gould. CHESTNUT-MANDIBLED TOUCAN.

Ramphastos Swainsonii Gould, 1833, Proc. Zool. Soc. London, p. 69. (in montosis Columbiæ = mountains of Colombia.)

Habitat.—Humid forest, forest edge and clearings (Tropical and lower Subtropical zones).

Distribution.—*Resident* in eastern Honduras (Olancho, Mosquitia), Nicaragua (Caribbean slope), Costa Rica (absent from dry northwest and most of central plateau), Panama (absent from Pacific slope from eastern Chiriquí east to western Panamá province) and northern Colombia.

Notes.—*R. swainsonii* and the South American *R. ambiguus* Swainson, 1823, are sometimes considered conspecific; with a single species concept, YELLOW-BREASTED TOUCAN is the appropriate English name. These two allospecies plus the South American *R. tucanus* Linnaeus, 1758, appear to constitute a superspecies.

Family PICIDAE: Woodpeckers and Allies

Subfamily JYNGINAE: Wrynecks

Genus JYNX Linnaeus

Jynx Linnaeus, 1758, Syst. Nat., ed. 10, 1, p. 112. Type, by monotypy, *Jynx torquilla* Linnaeus.

Jynx torquilla Linnaeus. EURASIAN WRYNECK. [415.1.]

Jynx Torquilla Linnaeus, 1758, Syst. Nat., ed. 10, 1, p. 112. (in Europa = Sweden.)

Habitat & Distribution.—*Breeds* in open woodland and second growth from northern Eurasia south to northwestern Africa, the Mediterranean region and central Asia, and *winters* from central Eurasia south to northern tropical Africa, India, Southeast Asia, southern China and southern Japan.

Accidental in Alaska (Wales, 8 September 1945; Bailey, 1947, Auk, 64, p. 456) and Formosa.

Notes.—Known in Old World literature as the WRYNECK.

Subfamily PICUMNINAE: Piculets

Tribe PICUMNINI: Typical Piculets

Genus PICUMNUS Temminck

Picumnus Temminck, 1825, Planches Color., livr. 62, text to pl. 371. Type, by subsequent designation (G. R. Gray, 1840), *Picus minutissimus* (Gm.) = *Picumnus buffoni* Lafresnaye = *Picus exilis* Lichtenstein.

Picumnus olivaceus Lafresnaye. OLIVACEOUS PICULET.

Picumnus olivaceus Lafresnaye, 1845, Rev. Zool. [Paris], 8, p. 7. (Bogotá, Colombia.)

Habitat.—Open woodland with dense undergrowth, forest edge, brushy clearings, dense second growth, and plantations (Tropical and Subtropical zones).

Distribution.—*Resident* locally on the Caribbean slope of eastern Guatemala, Honduras and Nicaragua, in southwestern Costa Rica (Golfo Dulce region) and

Panama (Pacific slope from Chiriquí to Los Santos, and both slopes from Canal Zone eastward), and in northern South America from Colombia east to northwestern Venezuela and south to western Ecuador.

Tribe NESOCTITINI: Antillean Piculets

Genus NESOCTITES Hargitt

Nesoctites Hargitt, 1890, Cat. Birds Br. Mus., 18, pp. xv, 8, 552. Type, by original designation, *Picumnus micromegas* Sundevall.

Nesoctites micromegas (Sundevall). ANTILLEAN PICULET.

Picumnus micromegas Sundevall, 1866, Consp. Avium Picinarum, p. 95. (Brazil, error = Hispaniola.)

Habitat.—Forest and open woodland, from lowland to montane situations, most commonly in semi-arid habitats, less frequently in humid ones.
Distribution.—*Resident* on Hispaniola (including Gonâve Island).

Subfamily PICINAE: Woodpeckers

Genus MELANERPES Swainson

Melanerpes Swainson, 1832, *in* Swainson and Richardson, Fauna Bor.-Am., 2 (1831), pp. 300, 303, 310, 316. Type, by monotypy, *Picus erythrocephalus* Linnaeus.
Centurus Swainson, 1837, Class. Birds, 2, p. 310. Type, by subsequent designation (G. R. Gray, 1840), *C. carolinus* (L.) = *Picus carolinus* Linnaeus.
Tripsurus Swainson, 1837, Class. Birds, 2, p. 311. Type, by monotypy, *T. flavifrons* Spix, pl. 52 = *Picus flavifrons* Vieillot.
Asyndesmus Coues, 1866, Proc. Acad. Nat. Sci. Philadelphia, 17, p. 55. Type, by original designation, *Picus torquatus* Wilson = *Picus lewis* Gray.
Balanosphyra Ridgway, 1911, Proc. Biol. Soc. Wash., 24, p. 34. Type, by original designation, *Picus formicivorus* Swainson.
Chryserpes W. Miller, 1915, Bull. Am. Mus. Nat. Hist., 34, p. 517. Type, by original designation, *Picus striatus* Müller.

Melanerpes lewis (Gray). LEWIS' WOODPECKER. [408.]

Picus torquatus (not Boddaert, 1783) Wilson, 1811, Am. Ornithol., 3, p. 31, pl. 20, fig. 3. (No locality given = Montana, about lat. 46°N.)
Picus Lewis "Drap[iez]." G. R. Gray, 1849, Genera Birds, 3, app., p. 22. New name for *Picus torquatus* Wilson, preoccupied.

Habitat.—Open forest and woodland, often logged or burned, including oak, coniferous forest (primarily ponderosa pine), riparian woodland and orchards, less commonly in pinyon-juniper.
Distribution.—*Breeds* from southern British Columbia (including Vancouver Island), southwestern Alberta, Montana, southwestern South Dakota and northwestern Nebraska south to south-central California (San Luis Obispo and Kern counties), central Arizona, southern New Mexico and eastern Colorado.
Winters from northern Oregon (rarely southern British Columbia), southern

Idaho, central Colorado and south-central Nebraska south irregularly to northern Baja California, Sonora (including Isla Tiburón), northern Chihuahua, southern New Mexico and western Texas.

Casual east to central and southern Saskatchewan, southern Manitoba, Minnesota, Wisconsin, southern Ontario, Illinois, Missouri, Arkansas and central Texas. Accidental in Rhode Island and Massachusetts.

Notes.—Often placed in the monotypic genus *Asyndesmus*.

Melanerpes herminieri (Lesson). GUADELOUPE WOODPECKER.

Picus Herminieri Lesson, 1830, Traité Ornithol., livr. 3, p. 228. (l'Amérique du nord, error = Guadeloupe, Lesser Antilles.)

Habitat.—Woodland and edge, most commonly in hilly regions.

Distribution.—*Resident* on Guadeloupe, in the Lesser Antilles.

Melanerpes portoricensis (Daudin). PUERTO RICAN WOODPECKER.

Picus portoricensis Daudin, 1803, Ann. Mus. Hist. Nat. [Paris], 2, p. 286, pl. 51. (Puerto Rico.)

Habitat.—Woodland, and coffee and coconut plantations.

Distribution.—*Resident* on Puerto Rico (including Vieques Island), formerly also in the Virgin Islands on St. Thomas.

Melanerpes erythrocephalus (Linnaeus). RED-HEADED WOODPECKER. [406.]

Picus erythrocephalus Linnaeus, 1758, Syst. Nat., ed. 10, 1, p. 113. Based on "The Red-headed Wood-pecker" Catesby, Nat. Hist. Carolina, 1, p. 20, pl. 20. (in America = South Carolina.)

Habitat.—Open woodland (especially with beech or oak), open situations with scattered trees, parks, cultivated areas and gardens.

Distribution.—*Breeds* from southern Saskatchewan, southern Manitoba, western and southern Ontario, southwestern Quebec (rarely), southern New Hampshire and southern New Brunswick (at least formerly) south to central Texas, the Gulf coast and Florida (except the southernmost portion), extending west to central Montana, eastern Wyoming, eastern Colorado and central New Mexico, rarely to northeastern Utah. Occurs in summer (and probably breeds) in southeastern Alberta.

Winters regularly through the southern two-thirds of the breeding range, rarely or casually north to the limits of the breeding range.

Casual or accidental in southern British Columbia, southern Alberta, central Saskatchewan, Idaho, southeastern California (Imperial County; a deteriorated specimen found in Los Angeles County was likely transported by car), Arizona and the Florida Keys (Dry Tortugas).

Melanerpes formicivorus (Swainson). ACORN WOODPECKER. [407.]

Picus formicivorus Swainson, 1827, Philos. Mag., new ser., 1, p. 439. (Temiscaltipec, Mexico = Temascaltepec, state of México.)

Habitat.—Oaks, either in unmixed open woodland or mixed with conifers (Subtropical to Temperate, locally also in Tropical zones).

Distribution.—*Resident* west of the Cascades and Sierra Nevada from northwestern Oregon south through California (including Santa Catalina and Santa Cruz islands, and locally east of the Sierras in Lassen County) to southern Baja California; from northern Arizona, northern New Mexico, western Texas, Nuevo León and southwestern Tamaulipas south through the highlands of Middle America (including also the Mosquitia of eastern Honduras and northeastern Nicaragua) to extreme western Panama (western Chiriquí); and in South America in the northern Andes of Colombia.

Casual north to south-central Washington and southern Utah, and east to central Texas.

Melanerpes chrysauchen Salvin. GOLDEN-NAPED WOODPECKER.

Melanerpes chrysauchen Salvin, 1870, Proc. Zool. Soc. London, p. 213. (Bogaba, [Chiriquí,] Panama.)

Habitat.—Humid lowland and foothill forest, forest edge and shaded second growth (Tropical and lower Subtropical zones).

Distribution.—*Resident* in southwestern Costa Rica (west to the Gulf of Nicoya) and western Panama (Pacific slope of Chiriquí and Veraguas); also in northern Colombia (Magdalena Valley).

Notes.—The isolated Colombian form is sometimes regarded as a distinct species, *M. pulcher* Sclater, 1870. *M. chrysauchen, M., pucherani,* and the South American *M. flavifrons* (Vieillot, 1818) and *M. cruentatus* (Boddaert, 1783) appear to constitute a superspecies; this complex is sometimes placed in the genus *Tripsurus*.

Melanerpes pucherani (Malherbe). BLACK-CHEEKED WOODPECKER.

Zebrapicus Pucherani Malherbe, 1849, Rev. Mag. Zool., ser. 2, 1, p. 542. (Tobago, error = Colombia.)

Habitat.—Humid lowland and foothill forest, forest edge, clearings, partially cleared lands, and plantations (Tropical and lower Subtropical zones).

Distribution.—*Resident* from southeastern Mexico (Puebla, Veracruz, Tabasco, Oaxaca and Chiapas) south along the Caribbean slope of Central America to Costa Rica (where also rare and local on the Pacific drainage in the northwest), and in Panama (Caribbean slope throughout and on the Pacific from Veraguas eastward), Colombia (the Pacific slope and lower Cauca Valley) and western Ecuador (Pacific lowlands).

Notes.—Also known as PUCHERAN'S WOODPECKER. See comments under *M. chrysauchen.*

Melanerpes striatus (Müller). HISPANIOLAN WOODPECKER.

Picas [sic] *striatus* P. L. S. Müller, 1776, Natursyst., Suppl., p. 91. (Santo Domingo.)

Habitat.—Forest, woodland, mangroves, orchards and desert scrub.

Distribution.—*Resident* on Hispaniola.

Notes.—Sometimes placed in the monotypic genus *Chryserpes*; other authors would treat this and all following species of *Melanerpes* in the genus *Centurus*.

Melanerpes radiolatus (Wagler). JAMAICAN WOODPECKER.

Picus radiolatus Wagler, 1827, Syst. Avium., 1, Genus *Picus*, sp. 39. (Jamaica.)

Habitat.—Forest and open woodland, from lowlands to mountains, and from plantations to humid forest.
Distribution.—*Resident* on Jamaica.
Notes.—See comments under *M. striatus.*

Melanerpes chrysogenys (Vigors). GOLDEN-CHEEKED WOODPECKER.

Picus chrysogenys Vigors, 1839, *in* Beechey, Zool. Voy. "Blossom," p. 24. (No locality given = either Mazatlán, Sinaloa, or San Blas or Tepic, Nayarit.)

Habitat.—Forest, open woodland and plantations, in humid or semi-arid situations (Tropical and lower Subtropical zones).
Distribution.—*Resident* from Sinaloa south in the Pacific lowlands to Oaxaca (east to Bahía Santa Cruz), and in the interior of western Mexico to eastern Michoacán, northern Guerrero, Morelos and extreme southwestern Puebla.
Notes.—See comments under *M. striatus.*

Melanerpes hypopolius (Wagler). GRAY-BREASTED WOODPECKER.

Picus hypopolius Wagler, 1829, Isis von Oken, col. 514. (México = Tehuacán and Tecuapán, Puebla.)

Habitat.—Scrub and open woodland, generally in arid and semi-arid situations (Tropical and Subtropical zones).
Distribution.—*Resident* from northwestern Guerrero, the state of México, Tlaxcala and Puebla south on the Pacific slope to central Oaxaca (east to vicinity of San Pedro Totolapan).
Notes.—Although considered conspecific with *M. uropygialis* by a few authors, *M. hypopolius* rather appears to be more closely related to *M. chrysogenys.* See also comments under *M. striatus.*

Melanerpes pygmaeus (Ridgway). RED-VENTED WOODPECKER.

Centurus rubriventris pygmæus Ridgway, 1885, Proc. U.S. Natl. Mus., 8, p. 576. (Cozumel Island.)

Habitat.—Coastal scrub, deciduous forest and second growth (Tropical Zone).
Distribution.—*Resident* on the Yucatan Peninsula (including Cozumel Island), in Belize (vicinity of Belize City), and on Guanaja Island (in the Bay Islands, off Honduras).
Notes.—Also known as YUCATAN WOODPECKER. *M. pygmaeus* and *M. rubricapillus* are closely related and considered conspecific by some authors; they constitute a superspecies. See also comments under *M. striatus.*

Melanerpes rubricapillus (Cabanis). RED-CROWNED WOODPECKER.

Centurus rubricapillus Cabanis, 1862, J. Ornithol., 10, p. 328. (Barranquilla, Colombia.)

Habitat.—Open woodland, scrub, second growth, partially cleared lands, plantations, parks, gardens and mangroves (Tropical and lower Subtropical zones).

Distribution.—*Resident* from southwestern Costa Rica (Cordillera de Talamanca southward) south and east through Panama (both slopes, including Isla Coiba, the Pearl Islands, and other small islets off the Pacific coast), northern Colombia and northern Venezuela (also islands of Margarita, Patos and Tobago) to Guyana and Surinam.

Notes.—See comments under *M. pygmaeus* and *M. striatus.*

Melanerpes hoffmannii (Cabanis). HOFFMANN'S WOODPECKER.

Centurus Hoffmannii Cabanis, 1862, J. Ornithol., 10, p. 322. (Costa Rica.)

Habitat.—Open woodland, scrub, savanna, agricultural lands and parks, most frequently in arid and semi-arid situations (Tropical and lower Subtropical zones).

Distribution.—*Resident* in the Pacific lowlands of southern Honduras (Río Pespire southeastward) and Nicaragua, and in Costa Rica in the arid northwest (Guanacaste) and central plateau (Cordillera Central area, locally on the Caribbean drainage).

Notes.—Hybridizes locally with *M. aurifrons* along the Río Pespire in southern Honduras, and considered conspecific with the latter by some authors. See also comments under *M. striatus* and *M. aurifrons.*

Melanerpes uropygialis (Baird). GILA WOODPECKER. [411.]

Centurus uropygialis Baird, 1854, Proc. Acad. Nat. Sci. Philadelphia, 7, p. 120. (Bill Williams Fork of Colorado River, New Mexico [=Arizona].)

Habitat.—Desert (especially saguaro and other large cacti), semi-desert, riparian woodland and towns, in arid regions (Tropical and lower Subtropical zones).

Distribution.—*Resident* from southeastern California (Imperial and lower Colorado River valleys), extreme southern Nevada (opposite Fort Mohave, Arizona), central Arizona and southwestern New Mexico south through Baja California, Sonora (including Isla Tiburón), southwestern Chihuahua, Sinaloa, Durango, Nayarit and Zacatecas to Jalisco and Aguascalientes.

Notes.—See comments under *M. striatus, M. hypopolius* and *M. aurifrons.*

Melanerpes aurifrons (Wagler). GOLDEN-FRONTED WOODPECKER. [410.]

Picus aurifrons "Lichtenst." Wagler, 1829, Isis von Oken, col. 512. (México = Ismiquilpam, Hidalgo.)

Habitat.—Open woodland (including pine), scrub, semi-desert, second growth, towns and parks, in both arid and humid habitats but generally avoiding very humid regions (Tropical and Subtropical zones).

Distribution.—*Resident* from southwestern Oklahoma and north-central Texas south through central Texas (west to the Big Bend region), Mexico (west to central Chihuahua, eastern Durango, Zacatecas, central Jalisco and Michoacán, and including Cozumel Island), Guatemala, Belize (including Turneffe Islands), El Salvador and Honduras (including Utila, Roatán and Barbareta islands in the Bay Islands, but absent from northeastern Honduras and from the Pacific lowlands east of the Río Pespire) to north-central Nicaragua.

Casual in southeastern New Mexico (sight reports). Accidental in Michigan (Cheboygan) and Florida (Pensacola).

Notes.—Hybridizes locally with *M. uropygialis* in western Mexico. *M. aurifrons, M. carolinus, M. hoffmannii, M. uropygialis* and *M. superciliaris* appear to constitute a superspecies. See also comments under *M. striatus* and *M. hoffmannii.*

Melanerpes carolinus (Linnaeus). RED-BELLIED WOODPECKER. [409.]

Picus carolinus Linnaeus, 1758, Syst. Nat., ed. 10, 1, p. 113. Based on the "Red-bellied Wood-pecker" Catesby, Nat. Hist. Carolina, 1, p. 19, pl. 19. (in America septentrionali = South Carolina.)

Habitat.—Open woodland (primarily deciduous, less commonly coniferous), second growth, riverine forest, swamps, parks and towns.

Distribution.—*Resident* from southeastern Minnesota, south-central Wisconsin, southern Michigan, southern Ontario, central New York and Massachusetts south to central Texas, the Gulf coast and southern Florida (including the Florida Keys), and west to Iowa, eastern Nebraska, western Kansas, central Oklahoma and north-central Texas.

Casual north to southern Alberta, southern Saskatchewan, northeastern Montana, southern Manitoba, southern Quebec, New Hampshire and Nova Scotia, and west to eastern New Mexico.

Notes.—See comments under *M. striatus* and *M. aurifrons.*

Melanerpes superciliaris (Temminck). WEST INDIAN WOODPECKER.

Picus superciliaris Temminck, 1827, Planches Color., livr. 73, pl 433. (Cuba.)

Habitat.—Woodland and palm groves.

Distribution.—*Resident* in the Bahamas (Grand Bahama, Abaco and San Salvador), and on Cuba (including cayos de San Felipe, Largo and Cantiles), the Isle of Pines and Grand Cayman.

Notes.—Also known as GREAT or WEST INDIAN RED-BELLIED WOODPECKER. See comments under *M. striatus* and *M. aurifrons.*

Genus SPHYRAPICUS Baird

Sphyrapicus Baird, 1858, *in* Baird, Cassin and Lawrence, Rep. Explor. Surv. R. R. Pac., 9, pp. xviii, xxviii, 80, 101. Type, by original designation, *Picus varius* Linnaeus.

Sphyrapicus varius (Linnaeus). YELLOW-BELLIED SAPSUCKER. [402.]

Picus varius Linnaeus, 1766, Syst. Nat., ed. 12, 1, p. 176. Based mainly on "The yellow belly'd Wood-pecker" Catesby, Nat. Hist. Carolina, 1, p. 21, pl. 21. (in America septentrionali = South Carolina.)

Habitat.—Deciduous or mixed deciduous-coniferous forest (*varius* group), or primarily coniferous forest including aspen (*nuchalis* group), in migration and winter also in a variety of forest and open woodland habitats, parks, orchards and gardens.

Distribution.—*Breeds* [*varius* group] from extreme eastern Alaska, southwestern Yukon, southwestern Mackenzie, northwestern and central Saskatchewan, central Manitoba, north-central Ontario, southern Quebec (including Anticosti Island), southern Labrador and central Newfoundland south to northeastern British Columbia, central Alberta, central and southeastern Saskatchewan, eastern North Dakota, eastern South Dakota, Iowa, northeastern Missouri, central Illinois, northwestern Indiana, northern Ohio, western Pennsylvania, northwestern Connecticut, western Massachusetts and New Hampshire, and locally in the Appalachians south to eastern Tennessee and western North Carolina; and [*nuchalis* group] in the Rocky Mountain region from south-central British Columbia, southwestern Alberta and western Montana south, east of the Cascades, to east-central California, southern Nevada, central Arizona, southern New Mexico and extreme western Texas (Davis and Guadalupe mountains).

Winters [*varius* group] from Missouri, Illinois, Indiana, the Ohio Valley and New Jersey (rarely farther north) south through Texas, the southeastern United States, Middle America (except northwestern Mexico north of Sinaloa and west of Coahuila), the Bahamas and the Antilles (south to Dominica, but rare east of Hispaniola and in the Lesser Antilles) to central Panama (east to the Canal Zone) and the Netherlands Antilles; and [*nuchalis* group] from southern California (casually from Oregon), southern Nevada, central Arizona and central New Mexico south to southern Baja California, Jalisco, Durango, Coahuila and Nuevo León.

Casual or accidental [*varius* group] in south-coastal Alaska, California, Arizona, New Mexico, Colorado, Wyoming, Bermuda and Greenland; and [*nuchalis* group] in Saskatchewan, Kansas, Nebraska, Oklahoma, southwestern Louisiana, Guatemala and Honduras.

Notes.—Some authors consider *S. nuchalis* Baird, 1858 [RED-NAPED SAPSUCK-ER, 402.1], as a species distinct from *S. varius*; others consider *S. ruber* to be conspecific with *S. varius*. Limited and localized hybridization occurs among the three groups. The entire complex constitutes a superspecies. See also comments under *S. thyroideus*.

Sphyrapicus ruber (Gmelin). RED-BREASTED SAPSUCKER. [403.]

Picus ruber Gmelin, 1788, Syst. Nat., 1 (1), p. 429. Based on the "Red-breasted Woodpecker" Latham, Gen. Synop. Birds, 1 (2), p. 562. (in Cayenna, error = Nootka Sound, Vancouver Island.)

Habitat.—Aspen-pine association and coniferous forest, including humid coastal lowlands, in migration and winter also in open woodland and parks.

Distribution.—*Breeds* from southeastern Alaska, and coastal and central interior British Columbia (including the Queen Charlotte and Vancouver islands), south, west of the Cascades, to northwestern California (Mendocino County), and in the Sierra Nevada to east-central California (Kern County) and extreme western Nevada (Lake Tahoe region); and locally in the mountains of southern California (from Mount Pinos to the San Jacinto Mountains) and southern Nevada. Recorded in summer (and possibly breeding) in western Arizona (Mohave County).

Winters throughout the breeding range (except for interior British Columbia) and south through most of California (west of the deserts) to northern Baja California.

Casual in south-coastal Alaska (west to Kodiak Island) and southern Arizona.

Notes.—See comments under *S. varius.*

Sphyrapicus thyroideus (Cassin). WILLIAMSON'S SAPSUCKER. [404.]

Picus thyroideus Cassin, 1852, Proc. Acad. Nat. Sci. Philadelphia, 5 (1851), p. 349. (California = Georgetown, about twelve miles from Sutter's Mill, Eldorado County, California.)

Habitat.—Montane coniferous forest, especially fir and lodgepole pine, in migration and winter also in lowland forest.

Distribution.—*Breeds* from extreme southern interior British Columbia, Idaho, western Montana and Wyoming south in the mountains to northern and east-central California (also locally in southern California from Ventura to San Diego counties), central Arizona and southern New Mexico, probably also in northern Baja California (Sierra San Pedro Mártir).

Winters generally from the breeding range (extending to lower elevations) south to northern Baja California, Jalisco and Michoacán, and east to western Texas, Chihuahua, Durango and Zacatecas.

Casual or accidental east to southern Alberta, southern Saskatchewan, Oklahoma (Cimarron County) and west-central Texas, also sight reports from Minnesota, South Dakota, Kansas and east-central Texas.

Notes.—*S. thyroideus* occasionally hybridizes with *S. varius* (*nuchalis*).

Genus XIPHIDIOPICUS Bonaparte

Xiphidiopicus Bonaparte, 1854, Ateneo Ital., 2, p. 126. Type, by monotypy, *Picus percussus* Temminck.

Xiphidiopicus percussus (Temminck). CUBAN GREEN WOODPECKER.

Picus percussus Temminck, 1826, Planches Color., livr. 66, pl. 390, 424. (Cuba.)

Habitat.—Woodland, forest edge and gardens, in both humid and arid areas.

Distribution.—*Resident* on Cuba (including Cayo Cantiles and Jardines de la Reina) and the Isle of Pines.

Genus PICOIDES Lacépède

Picoïdes Lacépède, 1799, Tabl. Mamm. Ois., p. 7. Type, by subsequent designation (G. R. Gray, 1840), *Picus tridactylus* Linnaeus.

Dendrocopos C. L. Koch, 1816, Syst. Baier. Zool., 1, pp. xxvii, 72, pl. 1A, fig. a. Type, by subsequent designation (Hargitt, 1890), *D. major* = *Picus major* Linnaeus.

Dryobates Boie, 1826, Isis von Oken, p. 977. Type, by monotypy, *Picus pubescens* Linnaeus.

Phrenopicus Bonaparte, 1854, Ateneo Ital., 2, p. 123. Type, by subsequent designation (G. R. Gray, 1855), *Picus querulus* Wilson = *Picus borealis* Vieillot.

Xenopicus Baird, 1858, *in* Baird, Cassin and Lawrence, Rep. Explor. Surv. R. R. Pac., 9, pp. xviii, xxviii, 83, 96. Type, by monotypy, *Leuconerpes albolarvatus* Cassin.

Picoides scalaris (Wagler). LADDER-BACKED WOODPECKER. [396.]

> *Picus scalaris* Wagler, 1829, Isis von Oken, col. 511. (Mexico = central Veracruz.)

Habitat.—Deserts, arid scrub, riparian woodland, pinyon-juniper woodland, pine-oak association and pine savanna (Tropical to Temperate zones).

Distribution.—*Resident* from southern interior California (north to Los Angeles and Kern counties), southern Nevada, southwestern Utah, northwestern and central Arizona, central and northeastern New Mexico, southeastern Colorado, southwestern Kansas and western Oklahoma south through Texas (except the eastern portion) and most of Mexico (including Baja California, islands in the Gulf of California, the Tres Marias Islands, and Holbox and Cancun islands off Quintana Roo) to Chiapas, the Yucatan Peninsula and Belize; and locally in Honduras (the interior, Pacific lowlands, and presumably the Mosquitia in the northeast) and northeastern Nicaragua (Mosquitia).

Casual in south-central California and eastern Texas, and on Cozumel Island (off Quintana Roo).

Notes.—*P. scalaris* and *P. nuttallii* hybridize sporadically and constitute a superspecies.

Picoides nuttallii (Gambel). NUTTALL'S WOODPECKER. [397.]

> *Picus Nuttalii* [sic] Gambel, 1843, Proc. Acad. Nat. Sci. Philadelphia, 1, p. 259. (near the Pueblo de los Angelos [sic], Upper California = Los Angeles, California.)

Habitat.—Oak woodland, chaparral and riparian (especially willow-cottonwood) woodland.

Distribution.—*Resident* from northern California (Humboldt County) south, west of the deserts and the Sierra divide, to northwestern Baja California.

Casual or accidental in southern Oregon (possibly breeds), southeastern California (Salton Sea) and Arizona (Phoenix).

Notes.—See comments under *P. scalaris*.

Picoides pubescens (Linnaeus). DOWNY WOODPECKER. [394.]

> *Picus pubescens* Linnaeus, 1766, Syst. Nat., ed. 12, 1, p. 175. Based on "The smaller Spotted Woodpecker" Catesby, Nat. Hist. Carolina, 1, p. 21, pl. 21. (in America septentrionali = South Carolina.)

Habitat.—Deciduous and mixed deciduous-coniferous woodland, second growth, parks, orchards and riparian woodland.

Distribution.—*Breeds* from western and central Alaska, southern Yukon, southwestern Mackenzie, northern Alberta, northern Saskatchewan, central Manitoba, northern Ontario, southern Quebec (including Anticosti Island) and Newfoundland south to southern California (except the southeastern deserts), central Arizona, south-central New Mexico, central Texas, the Gulf coast and southern Florida (except the Florida Keys).

Winters throughout the breeding range, but more northern populations are mostly migratory, occurring irregularly southward.

Casual on the Queen Charlotte Islands (British Columbia). Accidental in the British Isles.

Picoides villosus (Linnaeus). HAIRY WOODPECKER. [393.]

Picus villosus Linnaeus, 1766, Syst. Nat., ed. 12, 1, p. 175. Based on "The Hairy Wood-pecker" Catesby, Nat. Hist. Carolina, 1, p. 19, pl. 19. (in America septentrionali = New Jersey.)

Habitat.—Deciduous or coniferous forest, open woodland, well-wooded towns and parks, and open situations with scattered trees (Subtropical and Temperate zones).

Distribution.—*Breeds* from western and central Alaska, central Yukon, southwestern and south-central Mackenzie, northern Saskatchewan, northern Manitoba, northern Ontario, southern Quebec (including Anticosti Island) and Newfoundland south throughout most of North America (including the Queen Charlotte and Vancouver islands) to northern Baja California, through the highlands of Middle America (except Belize) to western Panama (Chiriquí and Bocas del Toro), and to the Gulf coast, southern Florida (except the Florida Keys) and the Bahamas (Grand Bahama, Mores Island, Abaco, New Providence and Andros).

Winters generally throughout the breeding range, with the more northern populations partially migratory southward.

Accidental on Mona Island, off Puerto Rico (sight report).

Picoides stricklandi (Malherbe). STRICKLAND'S WOODPECKER. [398.]

Picus (Leuconotopicus) Stricklandi Malherbe, 1845, Rev. Zool. [Paris], 8, p. 373. (du Mexique = Mt. Orizaba massif, Veracruz.)

Habitat.—Open woodland, primarily in oak [*arizonae* group] or pine [*stricklandi* group], in mountains and canyons (upper Subtropical and Temperate zones).

Distribution.—*Resident* [*arizonae* group] from southeastern Arizona (Boboquivari, Santa Catalina and Pinaleño mountains) and extreme southwestern New Mexico (Peloncillo and Animas mountains) south in the Sierra Madre Occidental to Jalisco and Michoacán; and [*stricklandi* group] in the high mountains of the state of México, Distrito Federal, Morelos, Puebla and west-central Veracruz.

Notes.—Also known as BROWN-BACKED WOODPECKER, but this name is properly restricted to the African *P. obsoletus* (Wagler, 1829). The two groups have sometimes been regarded as distinct species, *P. arizonae* (Hargitt, 1886) [ARIZONA WOODPECKER] and *P. stricklandi* [BROWN-BARRED WOODPECKER].

Picoides borealis (Vieillot). RED-COCKADED WOODPECKER. [395.]

Picus borealis Vieillot, 1808, Hist. Nat. Ois. Am. Sept., 2 (1807), p. 66, pl. 122. (dans le nord des États-Unis, error = southern United States.)

Habitat.—Open mature pine woodland, rarely in deciduous woodland near pine or in mixed woodland.

Distribution.—*Resident* locally from eastern Oklahoma, southern Missouri (formerly), northern Arkansas, northern Mississippi, northern Alabama, northern Georgia, southeastern Virginia and southern Maryland (Dorchester County) south to eastern Texas, the Gulf coast and southern Florida, and north in the Cumberland Plateau through eastern Tennessee to eastern Kentucky (Daniel Boone National Forest). Recorded in summer (and possibly breeding) in central Maryland (Anne Arundel County).

Accidental in Pennsylvania and New Jersey.

Picoides albolarvatus (Cassin). WHITE-HEADED WOODPECKER. [399.]

Leuconerpes albolarvatus Cassin, 1850, Proc. Acad. Nat. Sci. Philadelphia, 5, p. 106. (near Sutter's Mill, California = Oregon Canyon, near George-town, 12 miles from Sutter's Mill.)

Habitat.—Montane coniferous forest, primarily pine and fir.

Distribution.—*Resident* from southern interior British Columbia (Anarchist Mountains), north-central Washington and northern Idaho south through Oregon (east of the Cascades) to southern California (absent from the humid coastal coniferous forest) and west-central Nevada.

Casual in coastal and desert areas of southern California.

Picoides tridactylus (Linnaeus). THREE-TOED WOODPECKER. [401.]

Picus tridactylus Linnaeus, 1758, Syst. Nat., ed. 10, 1, p. 114. (in Svecia ad Alpes Lapponicas, Dalekarlicas . . . = mountains of Sweden.)

Habitat.—Coniferous forest (primarily spruce), less frequently mixed conifer-ous-deciduous forest, occasionally in willow thickets along streams.

Distribution.—*Resident,* often locally, in North America from northwestern and central Alaska, central Yukon, northwestern and central Mackenzie, northern Saskatchewan, northern Manitoba, northern Ontario, northern Quebec, northern Labrador and Newfoundland south to western and southern Alaska, southern British Columbia (including Vancouver Island), central Washington and southern Oregon, in the Rocky Mountains to eastern Nevada, central Arizona and south-central New Mexico, and to southwestern and central Alberta, central Saskatch-ewan, southern Manitoba, northeastern Minnesota, central Ontario, northern New York, northern Vermont, northern New Hampshire, northern Maine, northern New Brunswick and southern Quebec (Anticosti Island); and in Eurasia from northern Scandinavia, northern Russia and northern Siberia south to northern Mongolia, Manchuria, Ussuriland, northern Korea, Sakhalin and Japan, also lo-cally in the mountains of southern Europe and western China.

Wanders casually or irregularly north to southwestern Keewatin, and south to Nebraska, southern Minnesota, southern Wisconsin, Michigan, southern Ontario, Pennsylvania, Delaware, Massachusetts and Nova Scotia.

Notes.—Also known as NORTHERN THREE-TOED WOODPECKER.

Picoides arcticus (Swainson). BLACK-BACKED WOODPECKER. [400.]

Picus (Apternus) arcticus Swainson, 1832, *in* Swainson and Richardson, Fauna Bor.-Am., 2 (1831), p. 313. (near the sources of the Athabasca River, lat. 57° [N.], on the eastern declivity of the Rocky Mountains.)

Habitat.—Coniferous forest (primarily spruce and fir), especially windfalls and burned areas with standing dead trees, less frequently in mixed coniferous-decid-uous forest, in winter rarely in deciduous woodland.

Distribution.—*Resident,* often locally, from western and central Alaska, south-ern Yukon, west-central and southern Mackenzie, northern Saskatchewan, north-ern Manitoba, northern Ontario, central Quebec, central Labrador and Newfound-land south to southeastern British Columbia, through the Cascade, Siskiyou and Warner mountains and Sierra Nevada of Washington and Oregon to central Cal-ifornia (about lat. 37°30′ N.) and west-central Nevada, through Montana to northwestern Wyoming and southwestern South Dakota, and to southwestern and central Alberta, central Saskatchewan, central and southeastern Manitoba, northern Minnesota, northeastern Wisconsin, north-central Michigan, southeastern Ontario, northern New York, northern Vermont, northern New Hampshire and northern Maine.

Wanders irregularly south in winter to Nebraska, Illinois, Indiana, Ohio, Pennsylvania, West Virginia, New Jersey and Delaware. An old record from Florida is highly questionable.

Notes.—Also known as ARCTIC or BLACK-BACKED THREE-TOED WOODPECKER.

Genus VENILIORNIS Bonaparte

Veniliornis Bonaparte, 1854, Ateneo Ital., 2, p. 125. Type, by subsequent designation (G. R. Gray, 1855), *Picus sanguineus* Lichtenstein.

Veniliornis fumigatus (d'Orbigny). SMOKY-BROWN WOODPECKER.

Picus fumigatus d'Orbigny, 1840, Voy. Am. Mérid., 4, Ois., livr. 61, pl. 65, fig. 1; 1847, livr. 89, p. 380. (Province of Corrientes, Argentina in lat. 28°S., and Santa Cruz de la Sierra and Province of Chiquitos in Bolivia = Yungas, Bolivia.)

Habitat.—Second-growth woodland, humid forest edge, clearings, tall thickets, and coffee plantations (Tropical and Subtropical zones).

Distribution.—*Resident* from Nayarit, Jalisco, the state of México, San Luis Potosí and Tamaulipas south along both slopes of Middle America to western Panama (east to Veraguas); and from extreme eastern Panama (eastern Darién) east through Colombia to northern Venezuela, and south along the western slope of the Andes to western Peru and the eastern slope to eastern Peru, Bolivia and northwestern Argentina.

Veniliornis kirkii (Malherbe). RED-RUMPED WOODPECKER.

Picus (*Chloropicus*) *Kirkii* Malherbe, 1845, Rev. Zool. [Paris], 8, p. 400. (Tobago.)

Habitat.—Forest edge, clearings, open woodland, second growth, less frequently savanna and plantations, rarely in forest interior (Tropical and Subtropical zones).

Distribution.—*Resident* locally in southwestern Costa Rica (lower Térraba valley) and Panama (recorded western Chiriquí, Veraguas, eastern Panamá province, Isla Coiba, eastern San Blas and eastern Darién), and in South America from northern Colombia east to northern Venezuela (also Tobago and Trinidad), and south, west of the Andes, to western Ecuador.

Notes.—*V. kirkii* and the South American *V. affinis* (Swainson, 1821), *V. maculifrons* (Spix, 1824) and *V. cassinii* (Malherbe, 1861) appear to constitute a superspecies.

Genus PICULUS Spix

Piculus Spix, 1824, Avium Spec. Nov. Bras., 1, p. [3] of index. Type, by subsequent designation (Oberholser, 1923), *Piculus macrocephalus* Spix = *Picus chrysochloros* Vieillot.

Piculus leucolaemus (Natterer and Malherbe). RUFOUS-WINGED WOOD-
PECKER.

Picus leucolæmus Natterer and Malherbe, 1845, Mém. Soc. R. Sci. Liége, 2,
p. 68. (Brazil.)

Habitat.—Humid lowland and foothill forest, forest edge, clearings, open woodland, second growth and plantations (Tropical and lower Subtropical zones).

Distribution.—Resident [*simplex* group] on the Caribbean slope of Honduras
(east of the Sula Valley) and Nicaragua, in Costa Rica (Caribbean slope and Pacific
southwest) and, at least formerly, in western Panama (east to Veraguas); [*callopterus* group] on both slopes of Panama (on the Caribbean from Veraguas eastward,
the Pacific from eastern Panamá province eastward); and [*leucolaemus* group] in
South America west of the Andes from western Colombia south to northwestern
Ecuador, and east of the Andes from eastern Colombia south to eastern Peru,
northern Bolivia and western Amazonian Brazil.

Notes.—The three groups are often recognized as distinct species, *P. simplex*
(Salvin, 1870) [RUFOUS-WINGED WOODPECKER], *P. callopterus* (Lawrence, 1862)
[STRIPE-CHEEKED WOODPECKER] and *P. leucolaemus* [WHITE-THROATED WOOD-
PECKER], or as two species, *P. simplex* as one, with *callopterus* regarded as a
subspecies of *P. leucolaemus.*

Piculus chrysochloros (Vieillot). GOLDEN-GREEN WOODPECKER.

Picus chrysochloros Vieillot, 1818, Nouv. Dict. Hist. Nat., nouv. éd., 26, p.
98. Based on "Carpintero Verde dorado" Azara, Apunt. Hist. Nat. Páx,
Parag., 2, p. 318 (no. 256). (Paraguay and Brazil.)

Habitat.—Humid forest, forest edge, open woodland, swampy forest, and open
situations with scattered trees (Tropical Zone).

Distribution.—Resident from eastern Panama (eastern Panamá province and
eastern Darién) east across northern Colombia and northwestern and southern
Venezuela to the Guianas, and south, east of the Andes, to northeastern Peru,
thence east across Brazil (generally south of the Río Negro and the Amazon) and
south to southeastern Bolivia, north-central Argentina, Paraguay and southeastern
Brazil.

Notes.—*P. chrysochloros* and the South American *P. aurulentus* (Temminck,
1823) appear to constitute a superspecies.

Piculus rubiginosus (Swainson). GOLDEN-OLIVE WOODPECKER.

Picus rubiginosus Swainson, 1820, Zool. Illus., ser. 1, 1 (3), pl. 14 and text.
("Spanish Main" = Caracas, Venezuela.)

Habitat.—Open woodland, forest edge, second growth, pine-oak association,
scrub and pine savanna, primarily in humid situations, less frequently in arid
habitats (Tropical and Subtropical zones).

Distribution.—Resident [*aeruginosus* group] from southern Nuevo Léon and
Tamaulipas south through eastern San Luis Potosí to northeastern Puebla and
northern Veracruz (reports from Guerrero and Oaxaca are erroneous); and [*rubiginosus* group] from eastern Oaxaca, eastern Veracruz, Tabasco, Chiapas and
the Yucatan Peninsula south along both slopes of Middle America, and in South

America from Colombia east through Venezuela (also Tobago and Trinidad) to the Guianas and south, west of the Andes to northwestern Peru and east of the Andes to eastern Peru, Bolivia and northwestern Argentina.

Notes.—The two groups are often regarded as distinct species, *P. aeruginosus* (Malherbe, 1862) [BRONZE-WINGED WOODPECKER] and *P. rubiginosus*. *P. rubiginosus* and *P. auricularis* constitute a superspecies; some authors consider them conspecific.

Piculus auricularis (Salvin and Godman). GRAY-CROWNED WOODPECKER.

Chloronerpes auricularis Salvin and Godman, 1889, Ibis, p. 381. (Xautipa, Sierra Madre del Sur in the State of Guerrero.)

Habitat.—Open lowland and foothill forest, humid montane forest and pine-oak association (upper Tropical and Subtropical zones).
Distribution.—*Resident* on the Pacific slope from southeastern Sonora south to Oaxaca (west of the Isthmus of Tehuantepec).
Notes.—See comments under *P. rubiginosus.*

Genus **COLAPTES** Vigors

Colaptes Vigors, 1826, Trans. Linn. Soc. London, 14, p. 457 (note). Type, by original designation, *Cuculus auratus* Linnaeus.
Chrysoptilus Swainson, 1832, *in* Swainson and Richardson, Fauna Bor.-Am., 2 (1831), p. 300. Type, by subsequent designation (G. R. Gray, 1840), *C. cayanensis* (Gm.) Swainson, pl. enl. 613 = *Picus punctigula* Boddaert.
Nesoceleus Sclater and Salvin, 1873, Nomencl. Avium Neotrop., pp. 101, 155. Type, by original designation, *Colaptes fernandinae* Vigors.

Colaptes punctigula (Boddaert). SPOT-BREASTED WOODPECKER.

Picus punctigula Boddaert, 1783, Table Planches Enlum., p. 37. Based on Daubenton, Planches Enlum., pl. 613. (Cayenne.)

Habitat.—Open woodland, second growth, mangroves, palm savanna, humid forest edge, and open situations with scattered trees (Tropical Zone).
Distribution.—*Resident* in Panama (on the Pacific slope from eastern Panamá province east to Darién), and in South America from northern Colombia, Venezuela and the Guianas south, east of the Andes, to eastern Peru, northern Bolivia, and western and central Amazonian Brazil.
Notes.—*C. punctigula* and the South American *C. melanochloros* (Gmelin, 1788) appear to constitute a superspecies. This species is often placed in the genus *Chrysoptilus.*

Colaptes auratus (Linnaeus). NORTHERN FLICKER. [412.]

Cuculus auratus Linnaeus, 1758, Syst. Nat., ed. 10, 1, p. 112. Based on "The Golden-winged Wood-pecker" Catesby, Nat. Hist. Carolina, 1, p. 18, pl. 18. (in Carolina = South Carolina.)

Habitat.—Forest, both deciduous and coniferous, open woodland, open situations with scattered trees and snags, riparian woodland, pine-oak association, parks and (*chrysoides* group) desert, primarily with saguaro or other large cacti present (Subtropical and Temperate zones).

Distribution.—*Breeds* [*auratus* group] from central Alaska, central Yukon, northwestern and southern Mackenzie, northern Manitoba, northern Ontario, north-central Quebec, south-central Labrador and Newfoundland south through central and eastern British Columbia, west-central and southwestern Alberta, eastern Montana and eastern North America (east of the Rocky Mountains) to central and eastern Texas, the Gulf coast and southern Florida (including the upper Florida Keys); and [*cafer* group] from southeastern Alaska, coastal and southern British Columbia (including the Queen Charlotte and Vancouver islands), west-central and southern Alberta, and southwestern Saskatchewan south (from the western edge of the Great Plains westward) to northern Baja California (formerly also on Guadalupe Island), the Mexican border and western Texas, and in the interior highlands of Mexico to Oaxaca and west-central Veracruz (west of the Isthmus of Tehuantepec).

Winters [*auratus* group] from southern Canada (rarely to the northern limits of the breeding range) south through the remainder of the breeding range to southern Texas, the Gulf coast and southern Florida (including the Florida Keys), rarely to the Pacific states from Washington south to California and Arizona; and [*cafer* group] generally throughout the breeding range and east to eastern Kansas, eastern Oklahoma, and eastern and southern Texas, the northern populations being largely migratory.

Resident [*chrysocaulosus* group] in Cuba and on Grand Cayman; [*chrysoides* group] from southeastern California, northeastern Baja California and central Arizona south to southern Baja California and through Sonora (including Isla Tiburón) to northern Sinaloa; and [*mexicanoides* group] in the highlands of Middle America from Chiapas south through Guatemala, El Salvador and Honduras to north-central Nicaragua.

Casual [*auratus* group] north to the Arctic and Bering coasts of Alaska, islands in the Bering Sea, northern Quebec and Newfoundland; and [*cafer* group] east to northern Alberta, southern Keewatin, Manitoba, Minnesota, Iowa, western Missouri and Arkansas. Accidental [*auratus* group] in England; and [*cafer* group] in Pennsylvania, New Jersey and Florida.

Notes.—Also known as COMMON FLICKER. The three northern groups have often been treated as separate species, *C. auratus* [YELLOW-SHAFTED FLICKER, 412], *C. cafer* (Gmelin, 1788) [RED-SHAFTED FLICKER, 413] and *C. chrysoides* (Malherbe, 1852) [GILDED FLICKER, 414], although intergradation between them occurs; the other two groups, which are disjunct, have been treated as races of the preceding, *mexicanoides* in *C. cafer* and *chrysocaulosus* in *C. auratus*.

Colaptes fernandinae Vigors. FERNANDINA'S WOODPECKER.

Colaptes Fernandinæ Vigors, 1827, Zool. J., 3, p. 445. (near Habana, Cuba.)

Habitat.—Primarily palm groves in open, low country.
Distribution.—*Resident* on Cuba.
Notes.—Often placed in the monotypic genus *Nesoceleus*.

Genus CELEUS Boie

Celeus Boie, 1831, Isis von Oken, col. 542. Type, by subsequent designation (G. R. Gray, 1840), *C. flavescens* (Gm.) = *Picus flavescens* Gmelin.

Celeus loricatus (Reichenbach). CINNAMON WOODPECKER.

Meiglyptes loricatus Reichenbach, 1854, Handb. Spec. Ornithol., cont. xii, Scansoriae C. Picinae, p. 405, pl. DCLXXXI, fig. 4495, 4496. (Peru.)

Habitat.—Humid lowland forest and forest edge (Tropical Zone).

Distribution.—*Resident* on the Caribbean slope of Nicaragua (one record, Eden) and Costa Rica, and from Panama (Caribbean slope throughout, and Pacific slope from the Canal Zone eastward) east through northern Colombia to the Magdalena Valley, and south along the Pacific coast to northwestern Ecuador.

[Celeus immaculatus Berlepsch. IMMACULATE WOODPECKER.] See Appendix B.

Celeus castaneus (Wagler). CHESTNUT-COLORED WOODPECKER.

Picus castaneus Wagler, 1829. Isis von Oken, col. 515. (No locality given = Veracruz.)

Habitat.—Humid lowland and foothill forest, forest edge, clearings, second-growth woodland, and open situations with scattered trees (Tropical and lower Subtropical zones).

Distribution.—*Resident* on the Gulf-Caribbean slope from southern Mexico (Veracruz, northern Oaxaca, Tabasco, Chiapas and the Yucatan Peninsula) south to extreme western Panama (western Bocas del Toro).

Notes.—*C. castaneus* and the South American *C. elegans* (P. L. S. Müller, 1776), *C. lugubris* (Malherbe, 1851) and *C. flavescens* (Gmelin, 1788) appear to constitute a superspecies.

Genus **DRYOCOPUS** Boie

Dryocopus Boie, 1826, Isis von Oken, col. 977. Type, by monotypy, *Picus martius* Linnaeus.

Hylatomus Baird, 1858, *in* Baird, Cassin and Lawrence, Rep. Explor. Surv. R. R. Pac., 9, pp. xxviii, 107. Type, by monotypy, *Picus pileatus* Linnaeus.

Dryocopus lineatus (Linnaeus). LINEATED WOODPECKER.

Picus lineatus Linnaeus, 1766, Syst. Nat., ed. 12, 1, p. 174. Based on "Le Pic noir hupé de Cayenne" Brisson, Ornithologie, 4, p. 31, pl. 1, fig. 2. (in Cayana = Cayenne.)

Habitat.—Open woodland, forest edge, second growth, partially cleared lands and plantations, rarely in dense forest, in both humid and semi-arid habitats (Tropical and lower Subtropical zones).

Distribution.—*Resident* from extreme southeastern Sonora, southeastern Nuevo León and central Tamaulipas south along both slopes of Middle America (including the Yucatan Peninsula and Isla Cancun), and in South America from Colombia, Venezuela (also Trinidad) and the Guianas south, west of the Andes to northwestern Peru and east of the Andes to eastern Peru, Bolivia, northwestern and northeastern Argentina, Paraguay and southern Brazil.

Notes.—*D. lineatus, D. pileatus* and the South American *D. schulzi* (Cabanis, 1883) appear to constitute a superspecies; hybrids between *D. lineatus* and *D. schulzi* are known.

Dryocopus pileatus (Linnaeus). PILEATED WOODPECKER. [405.]

Picus pileatus Linnaeus, 1758, Syst. Nat., ed. 10, 1, p. 113. Based mainly on "The larger red-crested Wood-pecker" Catesby, Nat. Hist. Carolina, 1, p. 17, pl. 17. (in America = South Carolina.)

Habitat.—Deciduous and coniferous forest, open woodland, second growth, and (locally) parks and wooded residential areas of towns.

Distribution.—*Resident* from southern and eastern British Columbia (including Vancouver Island), southwestern Mackenzie, northern Alberta, northwestern and central Saskatchewan, central Manitoba, central Ontario, southern Quebec (including Anticosti Island), New Brunswick, Prince Edward Island (formerly) and Nova Scotia south through Alberta (except southeastern), Washington, south-central Idaho, western Montana and Oregon to northern California (the coast range to Santa Cruz County, and the Sierra Nevada to Kern County), and south (west to the eastern Dakotas, Iowa, Missouri, eastern Kansas and Oklahoma) to east-central Texas, the Gulf coast and southern Florida (Key Largo).

Casual in southeastern Alberta, southeastern Utah and eastern Nebraska (sight reports from southwestern New Mexico).

Notes.—See comments under *D. lineatus.*

Genus CAMPEPHILUS Gray

Campephilus G. R. Gray, 1840, List Genera Birds, p. 54. Type, by original designation, *Picus principalis* Linnaeus.

Phlœoceastes Cabanis, 1862, J. Ornithol., 10, pp. 175, 176. Type, by original designation, *Ph. robustus* (Ill. Licht.) = *Picus robustus* Lichtenstein.

Campephilus haematogaster (Tschudi). CRIMSON-BELLIED WOODPECKER.

Picus hœmatogaster Tschudi, 1844, Arch. Naturgesch., 10, p. 302. (Republica Peruana = Peru.)

Habitat.—Humid forest, forest edge and clearings (Tropical and lower Subtropical zones, in South America also to upper Subtropical Zone).

Distribution.—*Resident* in Panama (from Bocas del Toro on the Caribbean and eastern Panamá province on the Pacific eastward), and in South America from Colombia south, west of the Andes to western Ecuador and east of the Andes to eastern Peru.

Notes.—The form in Panama and South America west of the Andes has sometimes been treated as a species, *C. splendens* Hargitt, 1889 [SPLENDID WOOD-PECKER], distinct from *C. haematogaster.*

Campephilus melanoleucos (Gmelin). CRIMSON-CRESTED WOODPECKER.

Picus melanoleucos Gmelin, 1788, Syst. Nat., 1 (1), p. 426. Based on the "Buff-crested Woodpecker" Latham, Gen. Synop. Birds, 1 (2), p. 558, pl. 25. (in Surinamo = Surinam.)

Habitat.—Humid forest, forest edge, clearings, second growth, open woodland, plantations and swamps (Tropical and Subtropical, occasionally lower Temperate zones).

Distribution.—*Resident* in Panama (from central Bocas del Toro and eastern

Chiriquí eastward), and in South America from Colombia, Venezuela (also Trinidad) and the Guianas south, east of the Andes, to eastern Peru, Bolivia, extreme northern Argentina, Paraguay and central Brazil.

Notes.—*C. melanoleucos, C. guatemalensis* and the South American *C. gayaquilensis* (Lesson, 1845) constitute a superspecies; they have been considered conspecific by some authors.

Campephilus guatemalensis (Hartlaub). PALE-BILLED WOODPECKER.

Picus guatemalensis Hartlaub, 1844, Rev. Zool. [Paris], 7, p. 214. (Guatemala.)

Habitat.—Forest, forest edge, clearings, open woodland, second growth and plantations, more commonly in humid habitats but occurring also in semi-arid regions (Tropical and lower Subtropical zones, locally or occasionally to upper Subtropical Zone).

Distribution.—*Resident* from extreme southeastern Sonora, San Luis Potosí and southern Tamaulipas south along both slopes of Middle America to extreme western Panama (western Bocas del Toro and western Chiriquí).

Notes.—Also known as FLINT-BILLED or GUATEMALAN IVORY-BILLED WOODPECKER. See comments under *C. melanoleucos.*

Campephilus principalis (Linnaeus). IVORY-BILLED WOODPECKER. [392.]

Picus principalis Linnaeus, 1758, Syst. Nat., ed. 10, 1, p. 113. Based on "The Largest White-bill Woodpecker" Catesby, Nat. Hist. Carolina, 1, p. 16, pl. 16. (in America septentrionali = South Carolina.)

Habitat.—Formerly occurred in the United States largely in mature lowland deciduous forest, especially swamps, and less frequently in pines, in Cuba in both montane and lower forest (pine and deciduous); in recent years reported from secondary deciduous woodland and partially cleared pinelands.

Distribution.—*Resident* formerly from eastern Texas, southeastern Oklahoma, northeastern Arkansas, southeastern Missouri, southern Illinois, southern Indiana, Kentucky and southeastern North Carolina south to the Gulf coast and southern Florida; and throughout Cuba.

Nearing extinction, with unverified reports in recent years from eastern Texas (Big Thicket region), Louisiana (Atchafalaya basin), South Carolina, southern Georgia, northern Florida and eastern Cuba (Sierra de Moa).

Notes.—The Cuban form has been considered by some authors to be a distinct species, *C. bairdii* Cassin, 1863. *C. principalis* and *C. imperialis* appear to constitute a superspecies.

Campephilus imperialis (Gould). IMPERIAL WOODPECKER.

Picus imperialis Gould, 1832, Proc. Zool. Soc. London, Comm. Sci. Corresp., pt. 2, p. 140. (California, error = Jalisco.)

Habitat.—Montane pine forest and pine-oak association (upper Subtropical and Temperate zones).

Distribution.—*Resident* formerly from northeastern Sonora and western Chihuahua south through the Sierra Madre Occidental to western Durango, west-central Zacatecas, northeastern Nayarit, central Jalisco and northern Michoacán.

Unreported since 1956–1957 (sight records) and possibly extinct, but some may survive in remote areas of Chihuahua and western Durango.
Notes.—See comments under *C. principalis.*

Order **PASSERIFORMES**: Passerine Birds

Suborder TYRANNI: Suboscines

Superfamily FURNARIOIDEA: Ovenbirds, Woodcreepers, Antbirds and Allies

Family **FURNARIIDAE**: Ovenbirds

Notes.—See comments under Dendrocolaptidae.

Genus **SYNALLAXIS** Vieillot

Synallaxis Vieillot, 1818, Nouv. Dict. Hist. Nat., nouv. éd., 24 (1817), p. 117 (generic characters only); 1819, 32, p. 310 (species added). Type, by subsequent designation (G. R. Gray, 1840), *Synallaxis ruficapilla* Vieillot.

Synallaxis albescens Temminck. PALE-BREASTED SPINETAIL.

Synallaxis albescens Temminck, 1823, Planches Color., livr. 38, pl. 227, fig. 2. (Brazil = Cimeterio do Lambari, near Sorocaba, São Paulo.)

Habitat.—Grasslands with scattered bushes, savanna, wet meadows and semi-arid scrub, in South America also forest edge, coffee plantations, mangroves and reed beds (Tropical and lower Subtropical zones).
Distribution.—*Resident* locally in southwestern Costa Rica (Térraba region and Osa Peninsula) and on the Pacific slope of Panama (Chiriquí east to eastern Panamá province), and in South America from northern Colombia east through Venezuela (also Margarita Island and Trinidad) to the Guianas and south, east of the Andes, to eastern Peru, Bolivia, northern Argentina, and central and south-eastern Brazil.

Synallaxis brachyura Lafresnaye. SLATY SPINETAIL.

Synnallaxis [sic] *brachyurus* Lafresnaye, 1843, Rev. Zool. [Paris], 6, p. 290. (de Colombie = Bogotá, Colombia.)

Habitat.—Thickets and dense undergrowth at woodland edge, ditches and stream borders, and shrubby growth around clearings, primarily in humid habitats (Tropical Zone).
Distribution.—*Resident* on the Caribbean slope of Honduras (east of the Sula Valley) and Nicaragua, locally on both slopes of Costa Rica (absent from dry northwest) and Panama, and in western Colombia and western Ecuador; also in east-central Brazil (southern Goiás).
Notes.—The isolated population in eastern Brazil may constitute a distinct species, *S. jaraguana* Pinto, 1936. *S. brachyura* and the South American *S. albigularis* Sclater, 1859, appear to constitute a superspecies.

Synallaxis erythrothorax Sclater. RUFOUS-BREASTED SPINETAIL.

Synallaxis erythrothorax Sclater, 1855, Proc. Zool. Soc. London, p. 75, pl. 86. (in America Centrali: Coban et Honduras = Honduras.)

Habitat.—Brushy areas, shrubby growth, thickets and fencerows, in humid habitats (Tropical Zone).

Distribution.—*Resident* in the Gulf-Caribbean lowlands from Veracruz, northern Oaxaca, Tabasco, Chiapas and the Yucatan Peninsula south to northern Honduras (east to Tela and south to Lake Yojoa); and in the Pacific lowlands from southwestern Chiapas south to El Salvador.

Genus **CRANIOLEUCA** Reichenbach

Cranioleuca Reichenbach, 1853, Handb. Spec. Ornithol., cont. x, Scansoriae A. Sittinae, p. 167. Type, by monotypy, *Synallaxis albiceps* d'Orbigny and Lafresnaye.

Notes.—Merged by some authors in *Certhiaxis* Lesson, 1844.

Cranioleuca erythrops (Sclater). RED-FACED SPINETAIL.

Synallaxis erythrops Sclater, 1860, Proc. Zool. Soc. London, p. 66. (In rep. Equatoriana = Pallatanga, Ecuador.)

Habitat.—Humid montane forest (mostly edge and clearings) and bordering thickets (Subtropical and lower Temperate zones).

Distribution.—*Resident* in Costa Rica (from the central highlands southward), Panama (recorded Chiriquí, Veraguas and eastern Darién), and the Western and Central Andes of Colombia and western Ecuador.

Cranioleuca vulpina (Pelzeln). RUSTY-BACKED SPINETAIL.

Synallaxis vulpina "Natterer" Pelzeln, 1856, Sitzungsb. K. Akad. Wiss. Wien, Math.-Naturwiss. Kl., 20, p. 162. (Brazil = Engeho do Gama, Rio Guaporé, Mato Grosso.)

Habitat.—Open woodland (on Isla Coiba), in South America in reedbeds, tangled undergrowth, brushy areas and savanna, often near watercourses (Tropical Zone).

Distribution.—*Resident* [*dissita* group] on Isla Coiba, Panama; and [*vulpina* group] in South America from eastern Colombia and Venezuela south, east of the Andes, to eastern Peru, northern Bolivia, and central and southeastern Brazil.

Notes.—The two widely disjunct groups may represent distinct species, *C. vulpina* and *C. dissita* Wetmore, 1957 [COIBA SPINETAIL].

Genus **XENERPESTES** Berlepsch

Xenerpestes Berlepsch, 1886, Ibis, pp. 53, 54. Type, by monotypy, *Xenerpestes minlosi* Berlepsch.

Notes.—The relationships of this peculiar genus are uncertain; the suggestion has been made that it might be a formicariid related to *Terenura* or *Herpsilochmus*.

Xenerpestes minlosi Berlepsch. DOUBLE-BANDED GRAYTAIL.

Xenerpestes minlosi Berlepsch, 1886, Ibis, pp. 53, 54, pl. 4. (near Bucaramanga, Colombia.)

Habitat.—Humid lowland forest and forest edge (Tropical Zone).
Distribution.—*Resident* in eastern Panama (eastern Panamá province and Darién), and western and northern Colombia.
Notes.—Also known as DOUBLE-BANDED SOFTTAIL.

Genus **PREMNOPLEX** Cherrie

Premnoplex Cherrie, 1891, Proc. U.S. Natl. Mus., 14, p. 339. Type, by original designation, *Margarornis brunnescens* "Lawr." = Sclater.

Notes.—Merged by some authors in *Margarornis*.

Premnoplex brunnescens (Sclater). SPOTTED BARBTAIL.

Margarornis brunnescens Sclater, 1856, Proc. Zool. Soc. London, p. 27, pl. 116. (Bogota [Colombia].)

Habitat.—Humid montane forest and forest edge (Subtropical and lower Temperate zones).
Distribution.—*Resident* in Costa Rica (north to the Cordillera de Tilarán) and Panama (recorded Chiriquí, Bocas del Toro, Veraguas, western Panamá province and Darién), and in South America in the mountains of northern Venezuela (east to Miranda) and the Andes from Colombia south to central Peru.
Notes.—*P. tatei* (Chapman, 1925), of northeastern Venezuela (west to Anzoátegui), is regarded by some authors as conspecific with *P. brunnescens*; these two species constitute a superspecies.

Genus **MARGARORNIS** Reichenbach

Margarornis Reichenbach, 1853, Handb. Spec. Ornithol., cont. x, Scansoriae A. Sittinae, pp. 146, 179. Type, by subsequent designation (G. R. Gray, 1855), *Sittasomus perlatus* Lesson.

Notes.—See comments under *Premnoplex*.

Margarornis bellulus Nelson. BEAUTIFUL TREERUNNER.

Margarornis bellulus Nelson, 1912, Smithson. Misc. Collect., 60, no. 3, p. 12. (Mount Pirri, at 4500 feet altitude, near head of Rio Limon, eastern Panama.)

Habitat.—Humid montane forest (Subtropical Zone).
Distribution.—*Resident* in eastern Panama (Cerro Pirre and Cerro Mali, eastern Darién).
Notes.—*M. bellulus* and the South American *M. squamiger* (d'Orbigny and Lafresnaye, 1838) appear to constitute a superspecies.

Margarornis rubiginosus Lawrence. RUDDY TREERUNNER.

Margarornis rubiginosa Lawrence, 1865, Ann. Lyc. Nat. Hist. N.Y., 8, p. 128. (San Jose, Costa Rica.)

Habitat.—Humid montane forest edge, clearings, open woodland and, less frequently, in forest interior (Subtropical and Temperate zones).

Distribution.—*Resident* in Costa Rica (north to Cordillera de Guanacaste) and western Panama (Chiriquí and Veraguas).

Notes.—*M. rubiginosus* and the South American *M. stellatus* Sclater and Salvin, 1873, appear to constitute a superspecies.

Genus PSEUDOCOLAPTES Reichenbach

Pseudocolaptes Reichenbach, 1853, Handb. Spec. Ornithol., cont. x, Scansoriae A. Sittinae, pp. 148, 209. Type, by subsequent designation (G. R. Gray, 1855), *Anabates auritus* "Lichtenstein" [=Tschudi] = *Anabates boissonneautii* Lafresnaye.

Pseudocolaptes lawrencii Ridgway. BUFFY TUFTEDCHEEK.

Pseudocolaptes lawrencii Ridgway, 1878, Proc. U.S. Natl. Mus., 1, pp. 253, 254. (La Palma and Navarro, 3500–5000 feet, Costa Rica.)

Habitat.—Humid forest edge, clearings and open woodland (Subtropical and Temperate zones).

Distribution.—*Resident* in Costa Rica (from the central highlands southward) and western Panama (Chiriquí, western Bocas del Toro and Veraguas); and in the Western Andes of Colombia and Ecuador.

Notes.—Some authors consider *P. lawrencii* and the South American *P. boissonneautii* (Lafresnaye, 1840) as conspecific; they constitute a superspecies.

Genus HYLOCTISTES Ridgway

Hyloctistes Ridgway, 1909, Proc. Biol. Soc. Wash., 22, p. 72. Type, by original designation, *Philydor virgatus* Lawrence.

Notes.—See comments under *Philydor.*

Hyloctistes subulatus (Spix). STRIPED WOODHAUNTER.

Sphenura subulata Spix, 1824, Avium Spec. Nov. Bras., 1, p. 26, pl. 36, fig. 1. (No locality given = Rio Solimões, Brazil.)

Habitat.—Humid lowland forest (Tropical Zone).

Distribution.—*Resident* in eastern Nicaragua (Caribbean lowlands), Costa Rica (absent from dry northwest), Panama (locally throughout), and in South America from Colombia and southern Venezuela south, west of the Andes to western Ecuador and east of the Andes to southeastern Peru and Amazonian Brazil.

Genus SYNDACTYLA Reichenbach

Syndactyla Reichenbach, 1853, Handb. Spec. Ornithol., cont. x, Scansoriae A. Sittinae, p. 171. Type, by monotypy, *Xenops rufosuperciliatus* Lafresnaye.

Notes.—See comments under *Philydor.*

Syndactyla subalaris (Sclater). LINEATED FOLIAGE-GLEANER.

Anabates subalaris Sclater, 1859, Proc. Zool. Soc. London, p. 141. (Pallatanga, Ecuador.)

Habitat.—Humid foothill and montane forest and forest edge (upper Tropical and Subtropical zones).

Distribution.—*Resident* in Costa Rica (central highlands southward) and Panama (locally, recorded Chiriquí, Veraguas and Darién), and in South America from Colombia and northwestern Venezuela south in the Andes to western Ecuador and eastern Peru.

Notes.—*S. subalaris* and *S. guttulata* (Sclater, 1858), of northern Venezuela, appear to constitute a superspecies.

Genus ANABACERTHIA Lafresnaye

Anabacerthia Lafresnaye, 1842, Dict. Univ. Hist. Nat., 1 (1840), p. 412. Type, by monotypy, *Anabacerthia striaticollis* Lafresnaye.

Notes.—See comments under *Philydor.*

Anabacerthia variegaticeps (Sclater). SPECTACLED FOLIAGE-GLEANER.

Anabazenops variegaticeps Sclater, 1857, Proc. Zool. Soc. London (1856), p. 289. (Cordova [=Córdoba] in the State of Vera Cruz, Southern Mexico.)

Habitat.—Humid foothill and montane forest (upper Tropical and Subtropical zones).

Distribution.—*Resident* locally in the highlands of Guerrero, western Veracruz, Oaxaca, Chiapas, Guatemala, Honduras, Costa Rica and western Panama (western Chiriquí); and on the west slope of the Western Andes in Colombia and Ecuador.

Notes.—Also known as SCALY-THROATED FOLIAGE-GLEANER. The South American populations have sometimes been regarded as a distinct species, *A. temporalis* (Sclater, 1859). *A. variegaticeps* and the South American *A. striaticollis* Lafresnaye, 1842, have been regarded as conspecific by some authors; they constitute a superspecies.

Genus PHILYDOR Spix

Philydor Spix, 1824, Avium Spec. Nov. Bras., 1, p. 73. Type, by subsequent designation (G. R. Gray, 1855), *Anabates atricapillus* Wied.

Notes.—Some authors merge *Hyloctistes, Syndactyla* and *Anabacerthia* in *Philydor.*

Philydor erythrocercus (Pelzeln). RUFOUS-RUMPED FOLIAGE-GLEANER.

Anabates erythrocercus Pelzeln, 1859, Sitzungsb. K. Akad. Wiss. Wien, Math.-Naturwiss. Kl., 34, pp. 105, 128. (Barra do Rio Negro = Manaus, Brazil.)

Habitat.—Humid lowland forest (Tropical Zone).

Distribution.—*Resident* [*fuscipennis* group] in Panama (locally on both slopes west to Veraguas), western Colombia and western Ecuador; and [*erythrocercus* group] in South America from southeastern Colombia south, east of the Andes, to southeastern Peru and northern Bolivia, and eastward over Amazonian and central Brazil to eastern Brazil, also in the Guianas.

Notes.—Some authors regard the two groups as separate species, *P. fuscipennis* Salvin, 1866 [SLATY-WINGED FOLIAGE-GLEANER] and *P. erythrocercus,* suggesting that the former may be more closely related to the South American *P. pyrrhodes* (Cabanis, 1848) [CINNAMON-RUMPED FOLIAGE-GLEANER] than to *erythrocercus*.

Philydor rufus (Vieillot). BUFF-FRONTED FOLIAGE-GLEANER.

> *Dendrocopus rufus* Vieillot, 1818, Nouv. Dict. Hist. Nat., nouv. éd., 26, p. 119. (Brazil = Rio de Janeiro.)

Habitat.—Humid foothill and montane forest and forest edge (upper Tropical and Subtropical zones).

Distribution.—*Resident* in the highlands of Costa Rica (primarily in the central highlands and Dota Mountains) and western Panama (western Chiriquí and Bocas del Toro); and disjunctly in South America in the northern Andes (the Eastern and Western Andes of Colombia, south on the west slope of the latter to northwestern Ecuador), in northern and south-central Venezuela, and from eastern Peru east through northern Bolivia and central Brazil to eastern Brazil, and south to eastern Paraguay, northeastern Argentina and southern Brazil.

Genus **AUTOMOLUS** Reichenbach

> *Automolus* Reichenbach, 1853, Handb. Spec. Ornithol., cont. x, Scansoriae A. Sittinae, pp. 146, 173. Type, by monotypy, *Sphenura sulphurascens* Lichtenstein.

Automolus ochrolaemus (Tschudi). BUFF-THROATED FOLIAGE-GLEANER.

> *Anabates ochrolæmus* Tschudi, 1844, Arch Naturgesch., 10, p. 295. (Republica Peruana = Peru.)

Habitat.—Humid lowland and foothill forest, and dense second-growth woodland (Tropical and lower Subtropical zones).

Distribution.—*Resident* on the Gulf-Caribbean slope of southern Mexico (recorded Oaxaca, Veracruz, Tabasco and Chiapas), Guatemala (one record also from interior highlands), Belize, Honduras and Nicaragua, on both slopes of Costa Rica (absent from dry northwest) and Panama, and in South America from northern Colombia east across southern Venezuela to the Guianas, and south, west of the Andes to northwestern Ecuador and east of the Andes to eastern Peru, northern Bolivia and Amazonian Brazil.

Notes.—Populations from Middle America south to western Ecuador are sometimes regarded as a distinct species, *A. pallidigularis* Lawrence, 1862 [PALE-THROATED FOLIAGE-GLEANER].

Automolus rubiginosus (Sclater). RUDDY FOLIAGE-GLEANER.

> *Anabates rubiginosus* Sclater, 1857, Proc. Zool. Soc. London (1856), p. 288. (Cordova [=Córdoba] in the State of Vera Cruz, Southern Mexico.)

Habitat.—Humid montane forest, in South America also humid lowland forest (upper Tropical and Subtropical zones, in South America in Tropical Zone).

Distribution.—*Resident* locally in the highlands of Mexico (recorded southern San Luis Potosí, Veracruz, Guerrero, Oaxaca and Chiapas), Guatemala, El Salvador, Honduras, north-central Nicaragua, southwestern Costa Rica, and Panama (recorded Chiriquí and eastern Darién); and in South America from northern Colombia east through southern Venezuela and extreme northern Brazil to French Guiana, and in the Andes south on the western slope to western Ecuador and on the eastern slope to eastern Peru and northwestern Bolivia.

Notes.—Populations from eastern Panama, western Colombia and western Ecuador are sometimes considered a distinct species, *A. nigricauda* Hartert, 1898 [BLACK-TAILED FOLIAGE-GLEANER].

Genus THRIPADECTES Sclater

Thripadectes Sclater, 1862, Cat. Collect. Am. Birds, p. 157. Type, by monotypy, *Anabates flammulatus* Eyton.

Thripadectes rufobrunneus (Lawrence). STREAK-BREASTED TREEHUNTER.

Philydor rufobrunneus Lawrence, 1865, Ann. Lyc. Nat. Hist. N.Y., 8, p. 127. (San Jose, Costa Rica.)

Habitat.—Humid foothill and montane forest, mostly in dense undergrowth and thickets (upper Tropical and Subtropical zones).

Distribution.—*Resident* in the highlands of Costa Rica (primarily on the Caribbean slope of the central highlands, also recorded in the Dota Mountains and Cordillera de Talamanca) and western Panama (Chiriquí, Bocas del Toro and Veraguas).

Genus XENOPS Illiger

Xenops Illiger, 1811, Prodromus, p. 213. Type, by monotypy, *Xenops genibarbis* Illiger.

Xenops minutus (Sparrman). PLAIN XENOPS.

Turdus minutus Sparrman, 1788, Mus. Carlson., fasc. 3, pl. 68. (No locality given = Rio de Janeiro, Brazil.)

Habitat.—Humid forest, forest edge, clearings, second-growth woodland and plantations (Tropical and lower Subtropical zones).

Distribution.—*Resident* on the Gulf-Caribbean slope of Middle America from southern Mexico (Veracruz, northern Oaxaca, Tabasco, Chiapas, Campeche and Quintana Roo) south to Nicaragua, on both slopes of Costa Rica (rare in dry northwest) and Panama, and in South America from Colombia, Venezuela and the Guianas south, west of the Andes to western Ecuador and east of the Andes to eastern Peru, central Bolivia, eastern Paraguay, northeastern Argentina (Misiones) and central Brazil.

Xenops rutilans Temminck. STREAKED XENOPS.

Xenops rutilans Temminck, 1821, Planches Color., livr. 12, pl. 72, fig. 2. (Brazil.)

Habitat.—Humid forest and forest edge (Subtropical Zone, in South America also Tropical Zone).

Distribution.—*Resident* locally in the highlands of Costa Rica (central highlands southward) and Panama (western Chiriquí and eastern Darién), and in South America from Colombia, Venezuela (also Trinidad) and the Guianas south, west of the Andes to northwestern Peru and east of the Andes to eastern Peru, Bolivia, northwestern and extreme northeastern Argentina, eastern Paraguay and southern Brazil.

Genus SCLERURUS Swainson

Sclerurus Swainson, 1827, Zool. J., 3, p. 356. Type, by subsequent designation (Cabanis, 1847), *Thamnophilus caudacutus* Vieillot.

Notes.—Members of this genus have often been known by the group name LEAFSCRAPER.

Sclerurus mexicanus Sclater. TAWNY-THROATED LEAFTOSSER.

Sclerurus mexicanus Sclater, 1857, Proc. Zool. Soc. London (1856), p. 290. (Cordova [=Córdoba] in the State of Vera Cruz, Southern Mexico.)

Habitat.—Understory of humid forest, in Middle America primarily in montane forest (Tropical and Subtropical zones).
Distribution.—*Resident* locally in southeastern Mexico (recorded Veracruz, eastern Puebla, northern Oaxaca and Chiapas), Guatemala, Honduras, Costa Rica and Panama, and in South America from northern and eastern Colombia east across southern Venezuela to the Guianas, and south, west of the Andes to northwestern Peru and east of the Andes to eastern Peru and northern Bolivia, thence eastward through central Brazil (south of the Amazon) to eastern Brazil.

Sclerurus albigularis Sclater and Salvin. GRAY-THROATED LEAFTOSSER.

Sclerurus albigularis Sclater and Salvin, 1869, Proc. Zool. Soc. London (1868), pp. 627, 630. (Venezuela = Cumbre de Valencia.)

Habitat.—Humid foothill and montane forest (upper Tropical and Subtropical zones).
Distribution.—*Resident* locally in the highlands of Costa Rica (recorded from cordilleras de Guanacaste and Central) and western Panama (western Chiriquí); and in South America in northern and eastern Colombia and northern Venezuela (also Tobago and Trinidad), and east of the Andes south to northern Peru and northern Bolivia.

Sclerurus guatemalensis (Hartlaub). SCALY-THROATED LEAFTOSSER.

Tinactor guatemalensis Hartlaub, 1844, Rev. Zool. [Paris], 7, p. 370. (No locality given = Guatemala.)

Habitat.—Understory of humid lowland forest (Tropical, rarely lower Subtropical zones).
Distribution.—*Resident* on the Gulf-Caribbean slope from southern Mexico (Veracruz, Tabasco, northern Oaxaca, Chiapas and Quintana Roo) south to Nicaragua, and on both slopes from Costa Rica (absent from dry northwest) and Panama south to Colombia (east to the Magdalena Valley and south to the Baudó mountains).

Genus LOCHMIAS Swainson

Lochmias Swainson, 1827, Zool. J., 3, p. 355. Type, by subsequent designation (Swainson, 1836), *Lochmias squamulata* Swainson = *Myiothera nematura* Lichtenstein.

Lochmias nematura (Lichtenstein). STREAMSIDE LOCHMIAS.

Myiothera nematura Lichtenstein, 1823, Verz. Doubl. Zool. Mus. Berlin, p. 43. (São Paulo, Brazil.)

Habitat.—Humid forest, generally in dense undergrowth along mountain streams (upper Tropical and Subtropical zones).

Distribution.—*Resident* locally in eastern Panama (eastern Darién), in the mountains of northern and extreme southern Venezuela, and from eastern Colombia south (primarily on the east slope of the Eastern Andes) to eastern Peru and Bolivia, thence eastward over central Brazil (Mato Grosso to Goiás and Minas Gerais) and south to Paraguay, northeastern Argentina, Uruguay and southern Brazil.

Notes.—Also known as SHARP-TAILED STREAMCREEPER.

Family DENDROCOLAPTIDAE: Woodcreepers

Notes.—Sometimes treated as the subfamily Dendrocolaptinae of the Furnariidae. The group name WOODHEWER is occasionally used for members of this family.

Genus DENDROCINCLA Gray

Dendrocincla G. R. Gray, 1840, List Genera Birds, p. 18. Type, by original designation, *D. turdinus* (Licht.) = *Dendrocopus fuliginosus* Vieillot.

Dendrocincla fuliginosa (Vieillot). PLAIN-BROWN WOODCREEPER.

Dendrocopus fuliginosus Vieillot, 1818, Nouv. Dict. Hist. Nat., nouv. éd., 26, p. 117. Based on Levaillant, Hist. Nat. Promerops, pl. 28. (Cayenne.)

Habitat.—Humid lowland and foothill forest, second-growth woodland and mangroves (Tropical and lower Subtropical zones).

Distribution.—*Resident* on the Caribbean slope of southeastern Honduras (Río Segovia [=Coco]), Nicaragua and Costa Rica (locally also on Pacific drainage in northwest), on both slopes of Panama, and in South America from Colombia, Venezuela (also Tobago and Trinidad) and the Guianas south, west of the Andes to western Ecuador and east of the Andes through eastern Ecuador and most of Brazil to east-central Peru, Bolivia, Paraguay, extreme northeastern Argentina and southern Brazil.

Notes.—The northern populations, including those in Middle America, have sometimes been considered as a species, *D. meruloides* (Lafresnaye, 1851) [PLAIN-BROWN WOODCREEPER], distinct from *D. fuliginosa* [LINE-THROATED WOODCREEPER].

Dendrocincla anabatina Sclater. TAWNY-WINGED WOODCREEPER.

Dendrocincla anabatina Sclater, 1859, Proc. Zool. Soc. London, p. 54, pl. 150. (Omoa, Honduras.)

Habitat.—Humid lowland and foothill forest and mangroves (Tropical and lower Subtropical zones).

Distribution.—*Resident* on the Gulf-Caribbean slope from southeastern Mexico (Veracruz, northern Oaxaca, Tabasco, Chiapas and the Yucatan Peninsula) south to Nicaragua; and on the Pacific slope of southwestern Costa Rica (north to the Gulf of Nicoya) and extreme western Panama (western Chiriquí).

Dendrocincla homochroa (Sclater). RUDDY WOODCREEPER.

Dendromanes homochrous Sclater, 1859, Proc. Zool. Soc. London, p. 382. (Teotalcingo, Oaxaca.)

Habitat.—Forest, forest edge, clearings, second-growth woodland and dense scrub, in both humid and semi-arid situations (Tropical and Subtropical zones).

Distribution.—*Resident* locally on both slopes from Oaxaca, Chiapas and the Yucatan Peninsula (including Cozumel and Mujeres islands) south through Middle America (not recorded El Salvador) to eastern Panama and northwestern Colombia (Chocó); and in extreme northeastern Colombia and northern Venezuela.

Genus SITTASOMUS Swainson

Sittasomus Swainson, 1827, Zool. J., 3, p. 355. Type, by original designation, *Dendrocolaptes sylviellus* Temminck = *Dendrocopus griseicapillus* Vieillot.

Sittasomus griseicapillus (Vieillot). OLIVACEOUS WOODCREEPER.

Dendrocopus griseicapillus Vieillot, 1818, Nouv. Dict. Hist. Nat., nouv. éd., 26, p. 119. Based on "trepadore palido y roxo" Azara, Apunt. Hist. Nat. Pax. Parag. (Paraguay = Concepción del Paraguay.)

Habitat.—Humid lowland and foothill forest, forest edge open woodland, second growth and coffee plantations (Tropical and Subtropical zones).

Distribution.—*Resident* from Jalisco, San Luis Potosí and southwestern Tamaulipas south along both slopes of Middle America to Panama (where local, primarily on the Pacific drainage), and in South America virtually throughout from Colombia, Venezuela (also Tobago) and the Guianas south, west of the Andes to northwestern Peru and east of the Andes to eastern Peru, Bolivia, northern Argentina and southern Brazil (not recorded Uruguay).

Genus DECONYCHURA Cherrie

Deconychura Cherrie, 1891, Proc. U.S. Natl. Mus., 14, p. 338. Type, by original designation, *Deconychura typica* Cherrie = *Dendrocincla longicauda* Pelzeln.

Deconychura longicauda (Pelzeln). LONG-TAILED WOODCREEPER.

Dendrocincla longicauda "Natterer" Pelzeln, 1868, Ornithol. Bras., 1, pp. 42, 60. (Borba, Marabitanas, Barre do Rio Negro = Manaus, Brazil.)

Habitat.—Humid lowland and foothill forest (Tropical and lower Subtropical zones).

Distribution.—*Resident* locally in southeastern Honduras (Olancho), Costa Rica (Caribbean slope of Cordillera Central, and southwestern region from the Gulf of Nicoya southward) and Panama (western Chiriquí, and from eastern Panamá province and the Canal Zone eastward), and widely in South America from northern Colombia, southern Venezuela and the Guianas south, east of the Andes, to eastern Peru and central Brazil.

Notes.—The Middle American forms have sometimes been regarded as a distinct species, *D. typica* Cherrie, 1891 [CHERRIE'S WOODCREEPER].

Genus GLYPHORHYNCHUS Wied

Glyphorhynchus Wied, 1831, Beitr. Naturgesch. Bras., 3 (2), p. 1149. Type, by monotypy, *Glyphorhynchus ruficaudus* Wied = *Dendrocolaptes cuneatus* Lichtenstein = *Neops spirurus* Vieillot.

Glyphorhynchus spirurus (Vieillot). WEDGE-BILLED WOODCREEPER.

Neops spirurus Vieillot, 1819, Nouv. Dict. Hist. Nat., nouv. éd., 31, p. 338. Based on Levaillant, Hist. Nat. Promerops, pl. 31, fig. 1. (South America = Cayenne.)

Habitat.—Humid lowland and foothill forest, forest edge, second growth woodland, brushy scrub and plantations (Tropical and lower Subtropical zones).

Distribution.—*Resident* on the Gulf-Caribbean slope of Middle America from southern Mexico (Veracruz, northern Oaxaca and Chiapas) south to Nicaragua, in Costa Rica (primarily Caribbean slope, less commonly in the Pacific southwest) and Panama (mostly Caribbean slope, locally on Pacific), and in South America from Colombia, Venezuela and the Guianas south, east of the Andes, to eastern Peru, northern Bolivia and central Brazil.

Genus XIPHOCOLAPTES Lesson

Xiphocolaptes Lesson, 1840, Rev. Zool. [Paris], 3, p. 269. Type, by subsequent designation (G. R. Gray, 1855), *Dendrocopus albicollis* Vieillot.

Xiphocolaptes promeropirhynchus (Lesson). STRONG-BILLED WOOD-CREEPER.

Dendrocolaptes promeropirhynchus Lesson, 1840, Rev. Zool. [Paris], 3, p. 270. (No locality given = Bogotá, Colombia.)

Habitat.—Humid foothill and montane forest, pine-oak association and coffee plantation, rarely in humid lowland forest (Subtropical and lower Temperate zones, occasionally to Tropical Zone).

Distribution.—*Resident* in the highlands from Guerrero, San Luis Potosí and Veracruz south through Oaxaca, Chiapas and northern Central America to north-central Nicaragua; locally in Costa Rica (Caribbean slope of Cordillera Central) and western Panama (western Chiriquí and Veraguas); and in South America from northern Colombia east across northern Venezuela to Guyana, and south in the Andes to Peru and Bolivia.

Notes.—Some authors consider the Amazonian form, *X. orenocensis* Berlepsch and Hartert, 1902, to be conspecific with *X. promeropirhynchus*; they constitute a superspecies.

Genus DENDROCOLAPTES Hermann

Dendrocolaptes Hermann, 1804, Observ. Zool., p. 135. Type, by subsequent designation (G. R. Gray, 1840), "*D. cayanensis* (Gm.), Pl. enl. 621" = *Picus certhia* Boddaert.

Dendrocolaptes certhia (Boddaert). BARRED WOODCREEPER.

Picus certhia Boddaert, 1783, Table Planches Enlum., p. 38. Based on Daubenton, Planches Enlum., pl. 621. (Cayenne.)

Habitat.—Humid lowland and foothill forest, forest edge, clearings, second growth woodland and plantations (Tropical and lower Subtropical zones).

Distribution.—*Resident* from southern Mexico (primarily the Gulf-Caribbean slope from Veracruz and northern Oaxaca south through Tabasco, Chiapas, southern Campeche and Quintana Roo, locally on the Pacific slope of Oaxaca) south through Middle America (primarily Caribbean slope, rare and local on Pacific slope) to Costa Rica (Caribbean slope and Pacific southwest, rare in dry northwest) and Panama (absent from dry Pacific region), and in South America from Colombia, southern Venezuela and the Guianas south, west of the Andes to northwestern Ecuador and east of the Andes to eastern Peru, northern Bolivia, and Amazonian and eastern Brazil.

Dendrocolaptes picumnus Lichtenstein. BLACK-BANDED WOODCREEPER.

Dendrocolaptes Picumnus Lichtenstein, 1820, Abh. Phys. Kl. Akad. Wiss. Berlin (1818–19), p. 202. Based on Levaillant, Hist. Nat. Promerops, pl. 26. (Cayenne.)

Habitat.—Humid foothill and montane forest, forest edge, pine-oak association and plantations, in South America also in humid lowland forest (Subtropical and lower Temperate zones, in South America to Tropical Zone).

Distribution.—*Resident* in the highlands of Middle America from Chiapas south through Guatemala to Honduras, and locally in Costa Rica (primarily Cordillera Central and the Dota Mountains) and western Panama (western Chiriquí and Veraguas); and in South America from northern Colombia, Venezuela and the Guianas south, primarily east of the Andes, to eastern Peru, Bolivia, northwestern Argentina, Paraguay, and central and eastern Brazil.

Notes.—Includes two South American forms regarded by some authors as separate species, *D. pallescens* Pelzeln, 1868, and *D. transfasciatus* Todd, 1925. *D. picumnus* and the South American *D. platyrostris* Spix, 1824, may constitute a superspecies.

Genus **XIPHORHYNCHUS** Swainson

Xiphorhynchus Swainson, June 1827, Philos. Mag., new ser., 1, p. 440. Type, by subsequent designation (Oberholser, 1905), *Xiphorhynchus flavigaster* Swainson.

Dendroplex Swainson, Dec. 1827, Zool. J., 3, p. 354. Type, by subsequent designation (Swainson, 1837), "*D. guttatus* Spix, 1, 91, f. 1" = *Dendrocolaptes ocellatus* Spix.

Xiphorhynchus picus (Gmelin). STRAIGHT-BILLED WOODCREEPER.

Oriolus Picus Gmelin, 1788, Syst. Nat., 1 (1), p. 384. Based on "Talapiot" Daubenton, Planches Enlum., pl. 605, and the "Climbing Oriole" Latham, Gen. Synop. Birds, 1 (2), p. 453. (in Gujanae = Cayenne.)

Habitat.—Humid forest edge, open woodland, mangroves, swamps, scrub, plantations and parks (Tropical Zone).

Distribution.—*Resident* in Panama (on the Pacific slope from the Azuero Peninsula eastward, locally on the Caribbean slope in the Canal Zone), and in South America from northern Colombia east to Venezuela (also Margarita Island and Trinidad) and the Guianas, and south, east of the Andes, to eastern Peru, northern Bolivia and Amazonian Brazil.

Notes.—The northern populations from Panama east to northern Venezuela are recognized by some authors as a species, *X. picirostris* (Lafresnaye, 1847) [PLAIN-THROATED WOODCREEPER], distinct from *X. picus*. This complex is sometimes placed in the genus *Dendroplex.*

Xiphorhynchus guttatus (Lichtenstein). BUFF-THROATED WOODCREEPER.

Dendrocolaptes guttatus Lichtenstein, 1820, Abh. Phys. Kl. Akad. Wiss. Berlin (1818–19), p. 201. (No locality given = Bahia, Brazil.)

Habitat.—Humid lowland and foothill forest edge, second-growth woodland, mangroves, semi-arid scrub and plantations (Tropical and lower Subtropical zones).

Distribution.—*Resident* on the Caribbean slope of eastern Guatemala (lower Río Motagua valley), Honduras and Nicaragua, on both slopes of Costa Rica and Panama, and in South America from northern Colombia east to Venezuela (also Tobago and Trinidad) and the Guianas, and south, east of the Andes, to eastern Peru, northern Bolivia and Brazil (north of the Amazon eastward to Pará, and south along the coast to Rio de Janeiro, and south of the Amazon east to the Rio Madeira).

Notes.—Includes *X. susurrans* (Jardine, 1847), and *X. polystictus* (Salvin and Godman, 1883), recognized by some authors as distinct species.

Xiphorhynchus flavigaster Swainson. IVORY-BILLED WOODCREEPER.

Xiphorhynchus flavigaster Swainson, 1827, Philos. Mag., new ser., 1, p. 440. (Temiscaltipec, Mexico = Temascaltepec, state of México.)

Habitat.—Humid lowland and foothill forest edge, clearings, open woodland, pine-oak association, plantations and semi-arid scrub, less frequently in humid montane forest (Tropical and Subtropical zones).

Distribution.—*Resident* on both slopes of Middle America from southern Sonora, Sinaloa, western Durango, eastern San Luis Potosí and southern Tamaulipas south to Honduras, then largely confined to the Pacific slope in Nicaragua and Costa Rica (south to Nicoya Peninsula).

Notes.—*X. striatigularis* (Richmond, 1900), based on the unique type from Tamaulipas, is here regarded as an aberrant individual of *X. flavigaster.*

Xiphorhynchus lachrymosus (Lawrence). BLACK-STRIPED WOODCREEPER.

Dendrornis lachrymosus Lawrence, 1862, Ann. Lyc. Nat. Hist. N.Y., 7, p. 467. (Atlantic side of the Isthmus of Panama, along the line of the Panama Railroad = Lion Hill, Canal Zone.)

Habitat.—Humid lowland and foothill forest, forest edge and mangroves (Tropical and lower Subtropical zones).

Distribution.—*Resident* from eastern Nicaragua south through Costa Rica (absent from dry northwest) and Panama (more widespread on Carribbean slope) to western Colombia and northwestern Ecuador.

Xiphorhynchus erythropygius (Sclater). SPOTTED WOODCREEPER.

Dendrornis erythropygia Sclater, 1859, Proc. Zool. Soc. London, p. 366. (In Stat. Verae Crucis et Oaxaca reipubl. Mexicanae = Jalapa, Veracruz.)

Habitat.—Humid montane forest, forest edge and second-growth woodland, in southern parts of range also in lowland forest (Subtropical and lower Temperate zones, from Nicaragua southward also in Tropical Zone).

Distribution.—*Resident* in the highlands from Guerrero, Oaxaca, southeastern San Luis Potosí, Veracruz and Chiapas south through northern Central America to north-central Nicaragua, and in lowlands as well as highlands from eastern Nicaragua south through Costa Rica, Panama and western Colombia to western Ecuador.

Notes.—Populations from eastern Nicaragua southward, occurring commonly in lowland habitats, are sometimes recognized as a species, *X. aequatorialis* (Berlepsch and Taczanowski, 1884) [SPOT-THROATED WOODCREEPER], distinct from *X. erythropygius*. The widespread South American species, *X. triangularis* (Lafresnaye, 1842), and *X. erythropygius* are regarded as conspecific by some authors; they constitute a superspecies.

Genus LEPIDOCOLAPTES Reichenbach

Lepidocolaptes Reichenbach, 1853, Handb. Spec. Ornithol., cont. x, Scansoriae A. Sittinae, p. 183. Type, by subsequent designation (G. R. Gray, 1855), *Dendrocolaptes squamatus* Lichtenstein.

Lepidocolaptes leucogaster (Swainson). WHITE-STRIPED WOODCREEPER.

Xiphorhynchus leucogaster Swainson, 1827, Philos. Mag., new ser., 1, p. 440. (Temiscaltipec, Mexico = Temascaltepec, state of México.)

Habitat.—Open forest, second-growth woodland, pine-oak association and scrub (Tropical to Temperate zones).

Distribution.—*Resident* from extreme southeastern Sonora, southern Chihuahua, Durango, Zacatecas and western San Luis Potosí south to Oaxaca, Puebla and western Veracruz.

Lepidocolaptes souleyetii (Des Murs). STREAK-HEADED WOODCREEPER.

Dendrocolaptes Souleyetii (Lafresnaye MS) Des Murs, 1849, Iconogr. Ornithol., livr. 12, pl. 70 and text. (Perú = Payta, Peru.)

Habitat.—Forest edge, open woodland, plantations, parks, and locally savanna (Tropical and lower Subtropical zones).

Distribution.—*Resident* from southern Mexico (Guerrero, Oaxaca, Veracruz, Tabasco, Chiapas, southern Campeche and southern portions of the state of Yucatán) south through Middle America, and in South America from northern and eastern Colombia, northern Venezuela and Guyana south, west of the Andes to northwestern Peru and east of the Andes to northern Brazil.

Lepidocolaptes affinis (Lafresnaye). SPOT-CROWNED WOODCREEPER.

Dendrocolaptes affinis Lafresnaye, 1839, Rev. Zool. [Paris], 2, p. 100. (Mexico.)

Habitat.—Humid montane forest, forest edge, open woodland, second growth and coffee plantations (Subtropical and Temperate zones).

Distribution.—*Resident* from Guerrero, the state of México, Hidalgo, southeastern San Luis Potosí and southwestern Tamaulipas south through western Veracruz, Puebla, Chiapas and Central America (except Belize) to western Panama (Chiriquí); and in South America from the mountains of Colombia and northern Venezuela south in the Andes to eastern Peru and northern Bolivia.

Notes.—The South American populations are sometimes recognized as a distinct species, *L. lacrymiger* (Des Murs, 1849).

Genus CAMPYLORHAMPHUS Bertoni

Campylorhamphus Bertoni, 1901, An. Cien. Parag., ser. 1, no. 1, p. 70. Type, by monotypy, *Campylorhamphus longirostris* Bertoni = *Dendrocopus falcularius* Vieillot.

Campylorhamphus trochilirostris (Lichtenstein). RED-BILLED SCYTHEBILL.

Dendrocolaptes trochilirostris Lichtenstein, 1820, Abh. Phys. Kl. Akad. Wiss. Berlin (1818–19), p. 207, pl. 3. (Brazil = Bahia, Brazil.)

Habitat.—Humid forest edge, clearings, open woodland and second growth (Tropical and Subtropical zones).

Distribution.—*Resident* in Panama (from northern Coclé and eastern Panamá province eastward), and in South America from Colombia, Venezuela and the Guianas south, west of the Andes to northwestern Peru and east of the Andes to eastern Peru, Bolivia, northern Argentina, Paraguay, and central and eastern Brazil.

Notes.—*C. trochilirostris* and the southeastern South American *C. falcularius* (Vieillot, 1823) have sometimes been considered as conspecific.

Campylorhamphus pusillus (Sclater). BROWN-BILLED SCYTHEBILL.

Xiphorhynchus pusillus Sclater, 1860, Proc. Zool. Soc. London, p. 278, footnote. (In Nov. Granada int. = Bogotá, Colombia.)

Habitat.—Humid forest and forest edge (upper Tropical to Temperate zones).

Distribution.—*Resident* locally in Costa Rica (Caribbean slope of highlands from Cordillera de Tilarán southward, and in Pacific southwest) and Panama, and in South America from northern Colombia east to western Venezuela and south, west of the Andes, to western Ecuador; also in Guyana.

Family FORMICARIIDAE: Antbirds

Subfamily THAMNOPHILINAE: Typical Antbirds

Genus CYMBILAIMUS Gray

Cymbilaimus G. R. Gray, 1840, List Genera Birds, p. 36. Type, by original designation, *C. lineatus* (Leach) = *Lanius lineatus* Leach.

Cymbilaimus lineatus (Leach). FASCIATED ANTSHRIKE.

Lanius lineatus Leach, 1814, Zool. Misc., 1, p. 20, pl. 6. (Berbice, British Guiana.)

Habitat.—Undergrowth of humid lowland and foothill forest, forest edge, shrubby second growth, and thickets (Tropical and lower Subtropical zones).

Distribution.—*Resident* on the Caribbean slope of extreme southeastern Honduras (Olancho), Nicaragua and Costa Rica, throughout Panama (except the Azuero Peninsula), and in South America from Colombia, Venezuela and the Guianas south, east of the Andes, to eastern Peru, northern Bolivia and Amazonian Brazil.

Genus TARABA Lesson

Taraba Lesson, 1831, Traité Ornithol., livr. 5 (1830), p. 375. Type, by subsequent designation (Sherborn, 1931), *Tamnophilus* [sic] *magnus* Wied = *Thamnophilus major* Vieillot.

Taraba major (Vieillot). GREAT ANTSHRIKE.

Thamnophilus major Vieillot, 1816, Nouv. Dict. Hist. Nat., nouv. éd., 3, p. 313. Based on "Batara major" Azara, Apunt. Hist. Nat. Pax. Parag., 2, p. 195 (no. 211). (Paraguay.)

Habitat.—Undergrowth of humid lowland forest, forest edge, clearings, shrubby second growth, thickets, brushy fields, dense grassy areas, and occasionally semiarid habitats (Tropical, rarely Subtropical zones).

Distribution.—*Resident* on the Gulf-Caribbean slope from southeastern Mexico (Veracruz, northern Oaxaca, Tabasco and Chiapas) south through northern Central America to Nicaragua, on both slopes of Costa Rica (rare in dry northwest) and Panama, and in South America from Colombia, Venezuela (also Trinidad) and the Guianas south, west of the Andes to northwestern Peru and east of the Andes to eastern Peru, Bolivia, northern Argentina, Uruguay and southeastern Brazil.

Genus THAMNOPHILUS Vieillot

Thamnophilus Vieillot, 1816, Analyse, p. 40. Type, by subsequent designation (Swainson, 1824), *Lanius doliatus* Linnaeus.

Thamnophilus doliatus (Linnaeus). BARRED ANTSHRIKE.

Lanius doliatus Linnaeus, 1764, Mus. Adolphi Friderici, 2, Prodr., p. 12. (No locality given = Surinam.)

Habitat.—Shrubby undergrowth, thickets, second-growth woodland, forest understory, savanna, gardens and mangroves (Tropical Zone).

Distribution.—*Resident* from eastern San Luis Potosí, southern Tamaulipas, Veracruz, eastern Puebla and Oaxaca south along both slopes of Central America (including the Yucatan Peninsula and Cozumel Island) through Panama (including Coiba and the Pearl islands, but rare on the Caribbean slope), and in South America from Colombia, Venezuela (also Margarita Island, Tobago and Trinidad) and the Guianas south, west of the Andes to northwestern Peru and east of the Andes to eastern Peru, Bolivia, Paraguay, northeastern Argentina (Formosa), and central and eastern Brazil.

Notes.—*T. doliatus, T. multistriatus,* and possibly also the South American *T. palliatus* (Lichtenstein, 1823), constitute a superspecies.

[**Thamnophilus multistriatus** Lafresnaye. BAR-CRESTED ANTSHRIKE.] See Appendix B.

Thamnophilus nigriceps Sclater. BLACK ANTSHRIKE.

Thamnophilus nigriceps Sclater, 1869, Proc. Zool. Soc. London (1868), p. 571. (Bogotá, Colombia, error = probably Barranquilla.)

Habitat.—Shrubby undergrowth of humid forest edge and clearings, and heavy second growth (Tropical Zone).

Distribution.—*Resident* in eastern Panama (eastern Panamá province and Darién) and northern Colombia.

Thamnophilus bridgesi Sclater. BLACK-HOODED ANTSHRIKE.

Thamnophilus bridgesi Sclater, 1856, Proc. Zool. Soc. London, p. 141. (river David, in the vicinity of the Town of David in the Province of Chiriqui in the State of Panama.)

Habitat.—Scrubby undergrowth of humid lowland and foothill forest, forest edge and clearings, thickets, and second-growth woodland (Tropical and lower Subtropical zones).

Distribution.—*Resident* on the Pacific slope of southwestern Costa Rica (rarely north to southern Guanacaste) and western Panama (east to the Azuero Peninsula).

Thamnophilus punctatus (Shaw). SLATY ANTSHRIKE.

Lanius punctatus Shaw, 1809, Gen. Zool., 7 (2), p. 327. Based on "Le Tachet" Levaillant, Hist. Nat. Ois. Afr., 2, p. 113, pl. 77, fig. 1. (Cayenne.)

Habitat.—Humid lowland and foothill forest, primarily in undergrowth, and second-growth woodland (Tropical and lower Subtropical zones).

Distribution.—*Resident* on the Caribbean slope from Belize and Guatemala south to Costa Rica, in Panama (entire Caribbean slope and Pacific slope from Coclé eastward), and in South America from Colombia (also Gorgona Island), Venezuela and the Guianas south, west of the Andes to western Ecuador and east of the Andes to northeastern Peru, northern Bolivia, and central and southeastern Brazil.

Genus XENORNIS Chapman

Xenornis Chapman, 1924, Am. Mus. Novit., no. 123, p. 1. Type, by original designation, *Xenornis setifrons* Chapman.

Xenornis setifrons Chapman. SPINY-FACED ANTSHRIKE.

Xenornis setifrons Chapman, 1924, Am. Mus. Novit., no. 123, p. 1. (Tacarcuna, 2050 feet, eastern Panama.)

Habitat.—Dense undergrowth in humid lowland and foothill forest (Tropical and lower Subtropical zones).

Distribution.—*Resident* in eastern Panama in eastern San Blas (Armila) and eastern Darién (Cerro Tacarcuna foothills), and in northwestern Colombia in Chocó (Río Baudó).

Notes.—Also known as SPECKLED or SPECKLE-BREASTED ANTSHRIKE, and GRAY-FACED ANTBIRD.

Genus **THAMNISTES** Sclater and Salvin

Thamnistes Sclater and Salvin, 1860, Proc. Zool. Soc. London, p. 299. Type, by original designation, *Thamnistes anabatinus* Sclater and Salvin.

Thamnistes anabatinus Sclater and Salvin. RUSSET ANTSHRIKE.

Thamnistes anabatinus Sclater and Salvin, 1860, Proc. Zool. Soc. London, p. 299. (In prov. Veræ Pacis regionale calida = Vera Paz, Guatemala.)

Habitat.—Humid lowland and foothill forest, primarily in undergrowth, less commonly in dense second-growth woodland (upper Tropical and Subtropical zones).

Distribution.—*Resident* on the Gulf-Caribbean slope from Tabasco south through northern Central America to Nicaragua, on both slopes of Costa Rica (absent from dry northwest) and Panama, and in South America on the Pacific slope of Colombia and locally from western Venezuela and eastern Colombia south, east of the Andes, to southeastern Peru and northern Bolivia.

Notes.—Also known as TAWNY ANTSHRIKE.

Genus **DYSITHAMNUS** Cabanis

Dysithamnus Cabanis, 1847, Arch. Naturgesch., 13, p. 223. Type, by subsequent designation (G. R. Gray, 1855), *Myothera strictothorax* [sic] Temminck.

Dysithamnus mentalis (Temminck). PLAIN ANTVIREO.

Myothera mentalis Temminck, 1823, Planches Color., livr. 30, pl. 179, fig. 3. (Brazil = Curytiba, Paraná, Brazil.)

Habitat.—Humid foothill and montane forest, primarily in undergrowth, less commonly in dense second-growth woodland (upper Tropical and Subtropical zones).

Distribution.—*Resident* in Middle America locally from Campeche, northern Guatemala and Belize south, mostly on the Caribbean slope, through Honduras and Costa Rica (not recorded Nicaragua) to Panama (throughout on both slopes), and in South America from Colombia and Venezuela (also Tobago and Trinidad) south, west of the Andes to northwestern Peru and east of the Andes to eastern Peru, northern Bolivia, eastern Paraguay and northeastern Argentina, and eastward across central Brazil to eastern and southeastern Brazil.

Dysithamnus striaticeps Lawrence. STREAK-CROWNED ANTVIREO.

Dysithamnus striaticeps Lawrence, 1865, Ann. Lyc. Nat. Hist. N.Y., 8, p. 130. (Angostura, Costa Rica.)

Habitat.—Humid lowland and foothill forest and heavy second growth (Tropical and lower Subtropical zones).

Distribution.—*Resident* on the Caribbean slope of extreme southeastern Honduras (Arenal), Nicaragua and Costa Rica, occurring locally also on the Pacific slope along the Cordillera de Guanacaste in northwestern Costa Rica.

A report from western Panama (Río Sixaola) is erroneous, being based on a specimen of *D. puncticeps.*

Notes.—*D. striaticeps* and *D. puncticeps* are closely related and appear to constitute a superspecies.

Dysithamnus puncticeps Salvin. SPOT-CROWNED ANTVIREO.

Dysithamnus puncticeps Salvin, 1866, Proc. Zool. Soc. London, p. 72. (Veragua, Caribbean lowlands of Panamá.)

Habitat.—Humid lowland forest, primarily in undergrowth (Tropical Zone).

Distribution.—*Resident* in extreme southeastern Costa Rica (Caribbean lowlands), Panama (entire Caribbean lowlands, and the Pacific lowlands in Darién), northern and western Colombia, and western Ecuador.

Notes.—See comments under *D. striaticeps.*

Genus **MYRMOTHERULA** Sclater

Myrmotherula Sclater, 1858, Proc. Zool. Soc. London, p. 234. Type, by subsequent designation (Sclater, 1890), *M[uscicapa]. pygmaea* Gmelin = *Muscicapa brachyura* Hermann.

Myrmotherula brachyura (Hermann). PYGMY ANTWREN.

Muscic[apae] brachyurae [nom. pl.] Hermann, 1783, Tabula Affinit. Anim., p. 229. Based on "Le petit Gobe-mouche tacheté, de Cayenne" Buffon, Hist. Nat. Ois., 4, p. 554, and Daubenton, Planches Enlum., pl. 831, fig. 2. (Cayenne.)

Habitat.—Humid forest edge, clearings and thick brush, often near streams (Tropical Zone).

Distribution.—*Resident* in central and eastern Panama (Canal Zone eastward on both slopes), and in South America from Colombia, southern Venezuela and the Guianas south, east of the Andes, to eastern Peru, northern Bolivia and Amazonian Brazil.

Notes.—The populations in Panama and western Colombia may prove to be a species, *M. ignota* Griscom, 1929 [GRISCOM'S ANTWREN], distinct from *M. brachyura.* Some authors suggest that *ignota* is more closely related to and perhaps conspecific with an Amazonian form, *M. obscura* Zimmer, 1932, in which case the combined species would be known by the name *M. ignota* [SHORT-BILLED ANTWREN]. If more than one species is recognized in this complex, all would be considered allospecies of a superspecies.

Myrmotherula surinamensis (Gmelin). STREAKED ANTWREN.

Sitta surinamensis Gmelin, 1788, Syst. Nat., 1 (1), p. 442. Based on the "Surinam Nuthatch" Latham, Gen. Synop. Birds, 1 (2), p. 654, pl. 28. (in Surinamo = Surinam.)

Habitat.—Humid lowland forest edge, clearings and second-growth woodland, primarily in undergrowth and often near water (Tropical Zone).

Distribution.—*Resident* from Panama (entire Caribbean slope, and Pacific drainage west to western Panamá province) east across Colombia and southern

Venezuela to the Guianas, and south, west of the Andes to western Ecuador and east of the Andes to eastern Peru, thence eastward over Amazonian and central Brazil to eastern Brazil.

Myrmotherula fulviventris Lawrence. CHECKER-THROATED ANTWREN.

Myrmetherula [sic] *fulviventris* Lawrence, 1862, Ann. Lyc. Nat. Hist. N.Y., 7, p. 468. (on the Atlantic side of the Isthmus of Panama, along the line of the Panama Railroad = Lion Hill, Canal Zone.)

Habitat.—Humid lowland and foothill forest and dense second-growth woodland, primarily in undergrowth (Tropical and lower Subtropical zones).

Distribution.—*Resident* on the Caribbean slope of eastern Honduras (Olancho, Gracias a Dios), Nicaragua and Costa Rica, in Panama (both slopes, the Pacific from Veraguas eastward), and in South America in central and western Colombia, and western Ecuador.

Myrmotherula axillaris (Vieillot). WHITE-FLANKED ANTWREN.

Myrmothera axillaris Vieillot, 1817, Nouv. Dict. Hist. Nat., nouv. éd., 12, p. 113. ("La Guyane" = Cayenne.)

Habitat.—Humid lowland forest, forest edge, clearings and second-growth woodland, occasionally in dense undergrowth (Tropical Zone).

Distribution.—*Resident* on the Caribbean slope of northeastern Honduras (Gracias a Dios), Nicaragua and Costa Rica, in Panama (both slopes, the Pacific from western Panamá province eastward), and in South America from Colombia, Venezuela (also Trinidad) and the Guianas south, west of the Andes to western Ecuador and east of the Andes in to eastern Peru, northern Bolivia, and Amazonian and southeastern Brazil.

Myrmotherula schisticolor (Lawrence). SLATY ANTWREN.

Formicivora schisticolor Lawrence, 1865, Ann. Lyc. Nat. Hist. N.Y., 8, p. 172. (Turrialba, Costa Rica.)

Habitat.—Humid foothill and montane forest, forest edge and second-growth woodland, primarily in undergrowth (Tropical and Subtropical zones).

Distribution.—*Resident* in the highlands from Chiapas south through Guatemala and Honduras to north-central Nicaragua; in lowlands and foothills of eastern Nicaragua, Costa Rica and western Panama (east to western Panamá province); and in South America in the mountains from northern Venezuela and Colombia south to western Ecuador and eastern Peru.

Genus HERPSILOCHMUS Cabanis

Herpsilochmus Cabanis, 1847, Arch. Naturgesch, 12, p. 224. Type, by subsequent designation (G. R. Gray, 1855), *Myiothera pileata* Lichtenstein.

Herpsilochmus rufimarginatus (Temminck). RUFOUS-WINGED ANTWREN.

Myiothera rufimarginata Temminck, 1822, Planches Color., livr. 22, pl. 132, figs. 1–2. (Brazil = Rio de Janeiro.)

Habitat.—Humid lowland and foothill forest, forest edge and second-growth woodland (Tropical and lower Subtropical zones).

Distribution.—*Resident* locally in eastern Panama (recorded in eastern Panamá province and Darién), and in South America from Colombia and Venezuela south, east of the Andes, to eastern Peru, northern Bolivia, eastern Paraguay, northeastern Argentina, and eastern and southern Brazil.

Genus **MICRORHOPIAS** Sclater

Microrhopias Sclater, 1862, Cat. Collect. Am. Birds, p. 182. Type, by subsequent designation (Sclater, 1890), *F. quixensis* = *Thamnophilus quixensis* Cornalia.

Microrhopias quixensis (Cornalia). DOT-WINGED ANTWREN.

Thamnophilus quixensis Cornalia, 1849, Vertebr. Synop. Mus. Mediolanense Osculati, pp. 6, 12. (eastern Ecuador.)

Habitat.—Humid lowland forest edge, clearings and second-growth woodland, generally in heavy undergrowth, less frequently in humid forest interior (Tropical Zone).

Distribution.—*Resident* on the Gulf-Caribbean slope from southeastern Mexico (southern Veracruz, northern Oaxaca, Tabasco, Chiapas and southern Quintana Roo) south through northern Central America to Nicaragua, on both slopes of Costa Rica (absent from the dry northwest) and Panama, and in South America west of the Andes in western Colombia and western Ecuador, and east of the Andes from southeastern Colombia south to eastern Peru and northern Bolivia, thence eastward over Amazonian and central Brazil, also in French Guiana.

Notes.—It is not certain that all forms of *Microrhopias* are conspecific with *quixensis*; if not, the Middle America races would be assigned to the species *M. boucardi* (Sclater, 1858) [BOUCARD'S ANTWREN].

Genus **FORMICIVORA** Swainson

Formicivora Swainson, 1824, Zool. J., 1, p. 301, in text. Type, by subsequent designation (G. R. Gray, 1840), *Formicivora nigricollis* Swainson = *Turdus griseus* Boddaert.

Formicivora grisea (Boddaert). WHITE-FRINGED ANTWREN.

Turdus grieseus [sic] Boddaert, 1783, Table Planches Enlum., p. 39. Based on "Le Grisin, de Cayenne" Daubenton, Planches Enlum., pl. 643, fig. 1. (Cayenne.)

Habitat.—Arid scrub, cactus and thornbush, less frequently in thickets and dense undergrowth in forested regions, second-growth situations and mangroves (Tropical Zone).

Distribution.—*Resident* in the Pearl Islands, Panama; and in South America from northern Colombia, Venezuela (also Margarita and Chacachacare islands, and Tobago) and the Guianas south, east of the Andes, to eastern Colombia, and Amazonian, central and southeastern Brazil.

Notes.—Also known as BLACK-BREASTED ANTWREN.

Genus **TERENURA** Cabanis and Heine

Terenura Cabanis and Heine, 1859, Mus. Heineanum, 2, p. 11. Type, by monotypy, *Myiothera maculata* Wied.

Terenura callinota (Sclater). RUFOUS-RUMPED ANTWREN.

Formicivora callinota Sclater, 1855, Proc. Zool. Soc. London, p. 89, pl. 96. (Santa Fé di Bogota [Colombia].)

Habitat.—Humid montane forest (Subtropical Zone).

Distribution.—*Resident* locally in the highlands of Costa Rica (Caribbean slope of Cordillera Central) and Panama (recorded Chiriquí, Veraguas and eastern Darién); and in South America in Surinam, Guyana (Acary Mountains), western Venezuela (Sierra de Perijá), and on the slopes of the Andes from Colombia south to western Ecuador and eastern Peru.

Genus **CERCOMACRA** Sclater

Cercomacra Sclater, 1858, Proc. Zool. Soc. London, p. 244. Type, by subsequent designation (Sclater, 1890), *Cercomacra caerulescens* Sclater = *Cercomacra brasiliana* Hellmayr.

Cercomacra tyrannina (Sclater). DUSKY ANTBIRD.

Pyriglena tyrannina Sclater, 1855, Proc. Zool. Soc. London, p. 90, pl. 98. (Santa Fé di Bogota [Colombia].)

Habitat.—Humid lowland and foothill forest edge, clearings and second-growth woodland, mostly in dense undergrowth and shrubby thickets (Tropical and lower Subtropical zones).

Distribution.—*Resident* on the Gulf-Caribbean slope from southeastern Mexico (Veracruz, northern Oaxaca, Tabasco, Chiapas, Campeche and southern Quintana Roo) south to Honduras, on both slopes of Nicaragua (absent from Pacific northwest), Costa Rica (rare in dry northwest) and Panama, and in South America from Colombia, Venezuela and the Guianas south, west of the Andes to western Ecuador and east of the Andes to eastern Ecuador, and Amazonian and eastern Brazil.

Notes.—Also known as TYRANNINE ANTBIRD.

Cercomacra nigricans Sclater. JET ANTBIRD.

Cercomacra nigricans Sclater, 1858, Proc. Zool. Soc. London, p. 245. (New Grenada, S. Martha; Bogota = Santa Marta, Colombia.)

Habitat.—Humid lowland forest edge and dense second-growth woodland, primarily in thickets and tangled undergrowth (Tropical Zone).

Distribution.—*Resident* in Panama (on the Caribbean slope from western Colón east to western San Blas, on the Pacific from Veraguas east to Darién, and in the Pearl Islands), and in South America from northern Colombia and northern Venezuela south, west of the Andes to western Ecuador and east of the Andes to eastern Colombia and northern Brazil (Rio Branco).

Genus GYMNOCICHLA Sclater

Gymnocichla Sclater, 1858, Proc. Zool. Soc. London, p. 274. Type, by monotypy, *Myiothera nudiceps* Cassin.

Gymnocichla nudiceps (Cassin). BARE-CROWNED ANTBIRD.

Myiothera nudiceps Cassin, 1850, Proc. Acad. Nat. Sci. Philadelphia, 5, p. 106, pl. 6. (Panama.)

Habitat.—Humid lowland and foothill forest edge, clearings and second-growth woodland, primarily in dense undergrowth and thickets (Tropical and lower Subtropical zones).

Distribution.—*Resident* on the Caribbean slope of eastern Guatemala (including Petén), Belize, Honduras and Nicaragua, on both slopes of Costa Rica (absent from dry northwest) and Panama (Caribbean slope throughout, local on Pacific), and in northern Colombia.

Genus MYRMECIZA Gray

Myrmeciza G. R. Gray, 1841, List Genera Birds, ed. 2, p. 34. Type, by original designation, *Drymophila longipes* Swainson.

Myrmeciza longipes (Swainson). WHITE-BELLIED ANTBIRD.

Drymophila longipes Swainson, 1825, Zool. J., 2, p. 152. ("some part of Brazil", error = Trinidad.)

Habitat.—Primarily in dense undergrowth of humid lowland forest, forest edge, clearings, second-growth woodland and, less frequently, drier woodland (Tropical Zone).

Distribution.—*Resident* from central Panama (west to southern Coclé in the Pacific lowlands, locally on the Caribbean slope in the Canal Zone) east across northern Colombia to Venezuela (also Trinidad) and Guyana, and south to eastern Colombia and northern Brazil (north of the Amazon).

Myrmeciza exsul Sclater. CHESTNUT-BACKED ANTBIRD.

Myrmeciza exsul Sclater, 1858, Proc. Zool. Soc. London, p. 540. (Panamá and Nicaragua.)

Habitat.—Humid lowland and foothill forest, forest edge and dense second-growth woodland, generally in undergrowth (Tropical and lower Subtropical zones).

Distribution.—*Resident* in Nicaragua (Caribbean slope), Costa Rica (absent from dry northwest), Panama (both slopes), northern and western Colombia (possibly also eastern Colombia), and western Ecuador.

Notes.—Populations from eastern Panama (eastern Darién) south to western Colombia have sometimes been regarded as a distinct species, *M. maculifer* (Hellmayr, 1906) [WING-SPOTTED ANTBIRD], but intergradation occurs in western Darién.

Myrmeciza laemosticta Salvin. DULL-MANTLED ANTBIRD.

Myrmeciza læmosticta Salvin, 1865, Proc. Zool. Soc. London (1864), p. 582. (Tucurriquí, Costa Rica.)

Habitat.—Humid lowland and foothill forest and dense second growth, primarily in undergrowth (Tropical and lower Subtropical zones).

Distribution.—*Resident* in Costa Rica (Caribbean slope, from the Cordillera de Guanacaste southward), Panama (locally on both slopes), and in South America from northern Colombia east to western Venezuela and south, west of the Andes, to northwestern Ecuador.

Myrmeciza immaculata (Lafresnaye). IMMACULATE ANTBIRD.

Thamnophilus immaculatus Lafresnaye, 1845, Rev. Zool. [Paris], 8, p. 340. (Bogotá, Colombia.)

Habitat.—Humid forest and forest edge, mostly in heavy undergrowth (upper Tropical and Subtropical zones).

Distribution.—*Resident* in Costa Rica (Cordillera de Talamanca, Cordillera Central, and Dota Mountains), Panama (recorded Bocas del Toro, Chiriquí, Veraguas and Darién), and in South America from northern Colombia and northwestern Venezuela south, west of the Andes to western Ecuador and east of the Andes to eastern Colombia.

Genus HYLOPHYLAX Ridgway

Hylophylax Ridgway, 1909, Proc. Biol. Soc. Wash., 22, p. 70. Type, by original designation, *Conopophaga naevioides* Lafresnaye.

Hylophylax naevioides (Lafresnaye). SPOTTED ANTBIRD.

Conopophaga nævioides Lafresnaye, 1847, Rev. Zool. [Paris], 10, p. 69. (No locality given = Panama.)

Habitat.—Humid lowland and foothill forest and dense second-growth woodland, primarily in undergrowth (Tropical and lower Subtropical zones).

Distribution.—*Resident* in eastern Honduras (west to La Ceiba), eastern Nicaragua, Costa Rica (absent from dry northwest), Panama (both slopes), northern and western Colombia, and western Ecuador.

Notes.—*H. naevioides* and the South American *H. naevia* (Gmelin, 1789), found east of the Andes, appear to constitute a superspecies.

Genus MYRMORNIS Hermann

Myrmornis Hermann, 1783, Tabula Affinit. Anim., pp. 180, 210, 235. Type, by subsequent designation (Hellmayr, 1924), "Fourmilier proprement dit" Buffon = *Formicarius torquatus* Boddaert.

Myrmornis torquata (Boddaert). WING-BANDED ANTBIRD.

Formicarius torquatus Boddaert, 1783, Table Planches Enlum., p. 43. Based on Daubenton, Planches Enlum., pl. 700, fig. 1. (Cayenne.)

Habitat.—Undergrowth of humid lowland forest (Tropical Zone).

Distribution.—*Resident* [*stictoptera* group] locally in eastern Nicaragua (Caribbean lowlands), central and eastern Panama (west in the Caribbean lowlands to the Canal Zone, in the Pacific to eastern Panamá province), and northern and western Colombia; and [*torquata* group] in South America east of the Andes from eastern Colombia, southern Venezuela and the Guianas south to eastern Ecuador and Amazonian and central Brazil.

Notes.—Also known as WING-BANDED ANTPITTA and WING-BANDED ANT-THRUSH. Some authors regard the two groups as separate species, *M. stictoptera* (Salvin, 1893) [BUFF-BANDED ANTBIRD] and *M. torquata*.

Genus GYMNOPITHYS Bonaparte

Gymnopithys Bonaparte, 1857, Bull. Soc. Linn. Normandie, 2, p. 35. Type, by monotypy, *Gymnopithys pectoralis* "Schiff, *ex* Lath." = *Turdus pectoralis* Latham = *Turdus rufigula* Boddaert.

Gymnopithys leucaspis (Sclater). BICOLORED ANTBIRD.

Myrmeciza leucaspis Sclater, 1855, Proc. Zool. Soc. London (1854), p. 253, pl. 70. (In Peruvia Chamicurros; in Nova Grenada; at Rio Negro, Cobati = Villavicencio, Colombia.)

Habitat.—Undergrowth of humid lowland forest and heavy second growth (Tropical Zone).

Distribution.—*Resident* [*bicolor* group] in northern and eastern Honduras (west to the Sula Valley), Nicaragua (Caribbean lowlands), Costa Rica (absent from dry northwest), Panama (both slopes), north-central and western Colombia, and western Ecuador; and [*leucaspis* group] in South America east of the Andes in eastern Colombia, eastern Ecuador, northeastern Peru and northwestern Brazil (east to Rio Negro).

Notes.—Some authors recognize the two groups as distinct species, *G. bicolor* (Lawrence, 1863) [BICOLORED ANTBIRD] and *G. leucaspis* [WHITE-CHEEKED ANTBIRD].

Genus PHAENOSTICTUS Ridgway

Phænostictus Ridgway, 1909, Proc. Biol. Soc. Wash., 22, p. 70. Type, by original designation, *Phlegopsis macleannani* [sic] Lawrence.

Phaenostictus mcleannani (Lawrence). OCELLATED ANTBIRD.

Phlogopsis MeLeannani [sic] Lawrence, 1860, Ann. Lyc. Nat. Hist. N.Y., 7, p. 285. (Isthmus of Panama, Lion Hill, Canal Zone.)

Habitat.—Undergrowth of humid lowland and foothill forest (Tropical and lower Subtropical zones).

Distribution.—*Resident* in eastern Honduras (Olancho, Gracias a Dios), eastern Nicaragua (Caribbean slope), Costa Rica (primarily Caribbean slope), Panama (both slopes), north-central and western Colombia, and northwestern Ecuador.

Notes.—Also known as OCELLATED ANTTHRUSH.

Subfamily FORMICARIINAE: Antthrushes and Antpittas

Genus FORMICARIUS Boddaert

Formicarius Boddaert, 1783, Table Planches Enlum., pp. 43, 44, 50. Type, by subsequent designation (G. R. Gray, 1840), *Formicarius cayanensis* Boddaert = *Formicarius colma* Boddaert.

Formicarius analis (d'Orbigny and Lafresnaye). BLACK-FACED ANT-THRUSH.

Myothera analis d'Orbigny and Lafresnaye, 1837, Mag. Zool. [Paris], 7, cl. 2, pl. 77–79, p. 14. (Yuracares et Chiquitos, Bolivia.)

Habitat.—Humid forest and second-growth woodland, generally on the ground (Tropical and Subtropical zones).

Distribution.—*Resident* on the Gulf-Caribbean slope from southeastern Mexico (southern Veracruz, northern Oaxaca, Tabasco, Chiapas and the Yucatan Peninsula) south to Nicaragua, on both slopes of Costa Rica (absent from dry northwest) and Panama, and in South America from northern Colombia, Venezuela (also Trinidad) and the Guianas south, east of the Andes, to eastern Peru, northern Bolivia, and central and eastern Brazil.

Formicarius nigricapillus Ridgway. BLACK-HEADED ANTTHRUSH.

Formicarius nigricapillus Ridgway, 1893, Proc. U.S. Natl. Mus., 16, pp. 670, 675. (Buena Vista, Costa Rica.)

Habitat.—Humid forest, usually on the ground (upper Tropical and lower Subtropical zones).

Distribution.—*Resident* locally in Costa Rica (primarily on the Caribbean slope of the Guanacaste, Central and Talamanca cordilleras) and western Panama (east to Veraguas and western Panamá province); also along the Pacific slope of western Colombia and western Ecuador.

Formicarius rufipectus Salvin. RUFOUS-BREASTED ANTTHRUSH.

Formicarius rufipectus Salvin, 1866, Proc. Zool. Soc. London, p. 73, pl. 8 (Santiago de Veraguas, Panamá.)

Habitat.—Humid forest and heavy second growth in hilly regions, primarily on the ground (upper Tropical to lower Temperate zones).

Distribution.—*Resident* locally in the highlands of Costa Rica (Caribbean slope of Cordillera Central, and Cordillera de Talamanca) and Panama (Chiriquí, Veraguas and eastern Darién), and in South America on the west slope of the Andes from Colombia to western Ecuador and the east slope from northwestern Venezuela to eastern Peru.

Genus **PITTASOMA** Cassin

Pittasoma Cassin, 1860, Proc. Acad. Nat. Sci. Philadelphia, 12, p. 189. Type, by monotypy, *Pittasoma michleri* Cassin.

Pittasoma michleri Cassin. BLACK-CROWNED ANTPITTA.

Pittasoma Michleri Cassin, 1860, Proc. Acad. Nat. Sci. Philadelphia, 12, p. 189. (River Truando, New Grenada [=Colombia].)

Habitat.—Humid lowland and foothill forest, in understory and on the ground (Tropical and lower Subtropical zones).

Distribution.—*Resident* locally in Costa Rica (Caribbean slope from the Cordillera Central southeastward), Panama (both slopes, more common in eastern Panama) and extreme northwestern Colombia (Chocó).

Genus **GRALLARIA** Vieillot

Grallaria Vieillot, 1816, Analyse, p. 43. Type, by monotypy, "Roi des Four-milliers" Buffon = *Formicarius varius* Boddaert.

Notes.—See comments under *Hylopezus.*

Grallaria guatimalensis Prévost and Des Murs. SCALED ANTPITTA.

Grallaria guatimalensis Prévost and Des Murs, 1846, Voy. Venus, Atlas, Zool., Ois. (1842), pl. 4. (Guatemala.)

Habitat.—Humid forest and heavy second growth woodland, generally in dense understory or on the ground (upper Tropical to lower Temperate zones).

Distribution.—*Resident* in the highlands and on the Gulf-Caribbean slope from Jalisco, Michoacán, the state of México, Morelos, Veracruz and Tabasco south through Guerrero, Oaxaca, Chiapas, Guatemala, El Salvador and Honduras to north-central Nicaragua; in the highlands of Costa Rica (primarily on Caribbean drainage) and Panama (recorded Bocas del Toro, Chiriquí, Veraguas and eastern Darién); and in South America in southern Venezuela (also Trinidad) and adjacent northern Brazil, and from northern Colombia south, on the west slope of the Andes to western Ecuador and on the east slope to eastern Peru and northern Bolivia.

Genus **HYLOPEZUS** Ridgway

Hylopezus Ridgway, 1909, Proc. Biol. Soc. Wash., 22, p. 71. Type, by original designation, *Grallaria perspicillata* Lawrence.

Notes.—For recognition of this genus as distinct from *Grallaria,* see Lowery and O'Neill, 1969, Auk, 86, pp. 1–12.

Hylopezus perspicillatus (Lawrence). SPECTACLED ANTPITTA.

Grallaria perspicillata Lawrence, 1861, Ann. Lyc. Nat. Hist. N.Y., 7, p. 303. (New Grenada, Isthmus of Panama.)

Habitat.—Humid lowland and foothill forest, generally on the ground (Tropical and lower Subtropical zones).

Distribution.—*Resident* in northeastern Honduras (Gracias a Dios), Nicaragua (Caribbean slope), Costa Rica (absent from dry northwest), Panama (more common on Caribbean slope), north-central and western Colombia, and western Ecuador.

Notes.—Also known as STREAK-CHESTED ANTPITTA. Often placed in the genus *Grallaria.*

Hylopezus fulviventris (Sclater). FULVOUS-BELLIED ANTPITTA.

Grallaria fulviventris Sclater, 1858, Proc. Zool. Soc. London, p. 68. (Rio Napo in the Republic of Ecuador.)

Habitat.—Humid lowland and foothill forest edge and second-growth woodland, generally in dense undergrowth or thickets (Tropical and lower Subtropical zones).

Distribution.—*Resident* on the Caribbean slope of northeastern Honduras (Olancho), Nicaragua and Costa Rica, in Panama (locally in western Bocas del Toro and eastern Darién), and in Colombia and Ecuador both east and west of the Andes.

Notes.—Often placed in the genus *Grallaria*.

Genus GRALLARICULA Sclater

Grallaricula Sclater, 1858, Proc. Zool. Soc. London, p. 283. Type, by subsequent designation (Sclater, 1890), *Grallaria flavirostris* Sclater.

Grallaricula flavirostris (Sclater). OCHRE-BREASTED ANTPITTA.

Grallaria flavirostris Sclater, 1858, Proc. Zool. Soc. London, p. 68. (Rio Napo in the Republic of Ecuador.)

Habitat.—Humid foothill and montane forest, in dense understory (upper Tropical and Subtropical zones).

Distribution.—*Resident* locally in the highlands of Costa Rica (in the Dota Mountains and Cordillera de Talamanca, and on the Caribbean slope of the Cordillera Central) and Panama (recorded Chiriquí, Bocas del Toro, Veraguas and eastern Darién), and in South America from Colombia south,west of the Andes to western Ecuador and east of the Andes to northeastern Peru and northern Bolivia.

Family RHINOCRYPTIDAE: Tapaculos

Genus SCYTALOPUS Gould

Scytalopus Gould, 1837, Proc. Zool. Soc. London (1836), p. 89. Type, by subsequent designation (G. R. Gray, 1840), *Sylvia magellanicus* (Lath.) = *Motacilla magellanica* Gmelin.

Scytalopus panamensis Chapman. PALE-THROATED TAPACULO.

Scytalopus panamensis Chapman, 1915, Auk, 32, p. 420. (Tacarcuna, 3600 ft., eastern Panama.)

Habitat.—Humid montane forest, in understory or on the ground (Subtropical Zone).

Distribution.—*Resident* in extreme eastern Panama (cerros Tacarcuna and Malí, eastern Darién).

Notes.—*S. panamensis* and *S. vicinior* are sometimes regarded as conspecific; they constitute a superspecies.

Scytalopus vicinior Zimmer. NARINO TAPACULO.

Scytalopus panamensis vicinior Zimmer, 1939, Am. Mus. Novit., no. 1044, p. 11. (Ricaurte, altitude 5000–6000 feet, Narino, western Colombia.)

Habitat.—*Resident* in extreme eastern Panama (Cerro Pirre, eastern Darién), and in the Western and Central Andes from western Colombia south to northwestern Ecuador.

Notes.—See comments under *S. panamensis*.

Scytalopus argentifrons Ridgway. SILVERY-FRONTED TAPACULO.

Scytalopus argentifrons Ridgway, 1891, Proc. U.S. Natl. Mus., 14, p. 475. (Volcan de Irazú, Costa Rica.)

Habitat. — Undergrowth and dense brushy edges of humid montane forest (Subtropical and lower Temperate zones).

Distribution. — *Resident* in the highlands of Costa Rica (northwest to Cordillera de Tilarán) and western Panama (Chiriquí and Veraguas).

Notes. — The populations in Panama have sometimes been treated as a distinct species, *S. chiriquensis* Griscom, 1924, but see Wetmore, 1972, Smithson. Misc. Collect., 150 (3), p. 259.

Superfamily TYRANNOIDEA: Tyrant Flycatchers and Allies

Notes. — The limits of the families in this superfamily are difficult to define. The sequence and placement of genera used here are essentially those of Traylor (1979, *in* Peters, Birds World, vol. 8).

Family TYRANNIDAE: Tyrant Flycatchers

Subfamily ELAENIINAE: Tyrannulets, Elaenias and Allies

Genus PHYLLOMYIAS Cabanis and Heine

Phyllomyias Cabanis and Heine, 1859, Mus. Heineanum, 2, p. 57. Type, by subsequent designation (Sclater, 1888), "*P. brevirostris*" = *Platyrhynchus brevirostris* Spix = *Pipra fasciata* Thunberg.
Tyranniscus Cabanis and Heine, 1859, Mus. Heineanum, 2, p. 57. Type, by monotypy, *Tyrannulus nigricapillus* [sic] Lafresnaye.
Acrochordopus Berlepsch and Hellmayr, 1905, J. Ornithol., 53, p. 26. Type, by monotypy, *Phyllomyias subviridis* Pelzeln = *Phyllomyias burmeisteri* Cabanis and Heine.

Phyllomyias burmeisteri Cabanis and Heine. ROUGH-LEGGED TYRANNULET.

Phyllomyias Burmeisteri Cabanis and Heine, 1859, Mus. Heineanum, 2, p. 57. (Brasilien = Rio de Janeiro, Brazil.)

Habitat. — Humid foothill and montane forest edge, clearings and open woodland (upper Tropical and Subtropical zones).

Distribution. — *Resident* [*zeledoni* group] in the highlands of central Costa Rica (Cordillera Central and Dota Mountains) and western Panama (Chiriquí); [*leucogonys* group] in the mountains from eastern Colombia and Venezuela south along the eastern slope of the Andes to southeastern Peru; and [*burmeisteri* group] in eastern Bolivia and northwestern Argentina, and from eastern Paraguay across extreme northeastern Argentina to southeastern Brazil.

Notes. — Some authors consider the three groups as separate species, *P. zeledoni* (Lawrence, 1869) [ZELEDON'S TYRANNULET], *P. leucogonys* (Sclater and Salvin, 1871) [WHITE-FRONTED TYRANNULET], and *P. burmeisteri*; others merge *leucogonys* in *P. zeledoni* [WHITE-FRONTED TYRANNULET], recognizing two species. This species is often treated in the genus *Acrochordopus*.

Phyllomyias griseiceps (Sclater and Salvin). Sooty-headed Tyrannulet.

Tyranniscus griseiceps Sclater and Salvin, 1871, Proc. Zool. Soc. London (1870), pp. 841, 843. (Babahoyo and Pallatanga, Ecuador, and Lake of Valencia, Venezuela = Babahoyo, Ecuador.)

Habitat.—Humid lowland forest edge, clearings, open woodland, thickets and plantations (Tropical Zone).

Distribution.—*Resident* locally in extreme eastern Panama (eastern Darién, also a single report from eastern Panamá province), and in South America from Colombia and Venezuela south, west of the Andes to western Ecuador and east of the Andes to central Peru and Amazonian Brazil.

Notes.—Also known as Sooty-crested or Crested Tyrannulet.

Genus ZIMMERIUS Traylor

Zimmerius Traylor, 1977, Bull. Mus. Comp. Zool. Harv., 148, p. 147. Type, by original designation, *Tyrannulus chrysops* Sclater = *Elaenia viridiflavus* Tschudi.

Zimmerius vilissimus (Sclater and Salvin). Paltry Tyrannulet.

Elainia vilissima Sclater and Salvin, 1859, Ibis, p. 122, pl. 4, fig. 1. (Central America = Cobán, Vera Paz, Guatemala.)

Habitat.—Open second-growth woodland, humid forest edge, clearings and plantations (Tropical to lower Temperate zones).

Distribution.—*Resident* in eastern Chiapas (highlands), Guatemala (primarily highlands, rare in Petén), El Salvador (Balsam Range), Honduras (humid Caribbean lowlands), Nicaragua, Costa Rica (throughout, except dry northwest), Panama, northern Colombia and northern Venezuela (mountains).

Notes.—Formerly placed in the genus *Tyranniscus* Cabanis and Heine, 1859.

Genus ORNITHION Harlaub

Ornithion Hartlaub, 1853, J. Ornithol., 1, p. 35. Type, by monotypy, *Ornithion inerme* Hartlaub.
Microtriccus Ridgway, 1905, Proc. Biol. Soc. Wash., 18, p. 210. Type, by original designation, *Tyrannulus semiflavus* Sclater and Salvin.

Ornithion semiflavum (Sclater and Salvin). Yellow-bellied Tyrannulet.

Tyrannulus semiflavus Sclater and Salvin, 1860, Proc. Zool. Soc. London, p. 300. (In prov. Veræ Pacis regione calida = Choctum, Vera Paz, Guatemala.)

Habitat.—Humid lowland forest, forest edge and shaded second-growth woodland (Tropical Zone).

Distribution.—*Resident* in the Gulf-Caribbean lowlands from southern Mexico (northern Oaxaca, southern Veracruz, Tabasco and northern Chiapas) south to Nicaragua, and in Costa Rica (primarily Pacific slope southward, locally on Caribbean slope in Alajuela province).

Notes.—*O. semiflavum* and *O. brunneicapillum* are closely related and considered conspecific by some authors, but probable sympatry has recently been reported from northern Costa Rica; they constitute a superspecies. These two species are treated by some authors in the genus *Microtriccus*.

Ornithion brunneicapillum (Lawrence). BROWN-CAPPED TYRANNULET.

Tyrannulus brunneicapillus Lawrence, 1862, Ibis, p. 12. (Isthmus of Panama = Lion Hill, Canal Zone.)

Habitat.—Humid lowland and foothill forest, forest edge, clearings, second-growth woodland and, occasionally, open situations with scattered trees (Tropical and lower Subtropical zones).

Distribution.—*Resident* in Costa Rica (Caribbean slope north to Alajuela province) and Panama (Caribbean slope throughout, Pacific from Canal Zone eastward), and in South America from northern Colombia south to western Ecuador and east to northern Venezuela.

Notes.—See comments under *O. semiflavum.*

Genus CAMPTOSTOMA Sclater

Camptostoma Sclater, 1857, Proc. Zool. Soc. London, p. 203. Type, by monotypy, *Camptostoma imberbe* Sclater.

Camptostoma imberbe Sclater. NORTHERN BEARDLESS-TYRANNULET. [472.]

Camptostoma imberbe Sclater, 1857, Proc. Zool. Soc. London, p. 203. (in vicinitate urbis S[an]. Andres Tuxtla, [Veracruz,] in rep. Mexicana.)

Habitat.—Arid scrub, thickets, mesquite, forest edge, and open riparian woodland (Tropical and Subtropical zones).

Distribution.—*Breeds* from Sonora, southeastern Arizona, southwestern New Mexico (Guadalupe Canyon), Zacatecas, Nuevo León and southern Texas (north to Kenedy County) south along both slopes of Middle America to Nicaragua (Pacific slope only) and northern Costa Rica (primarily Guanacaste, locally on the Caribbean slope in the Río Frío region).

Winters from northern Mexico (casually southern Arizona) south throughout the remainder of the breeding range.

In migration recorded from the Tres Marias Islands, off Nayarit, where possibly also breeding.

Notes.—Also known as BEARDLESS FLYCATCHER. *C. imberbe* and the closely related *C. obsoletum* are considered conspecific by some authors, but both breed in the Tempisque region of Costa Rica; they constitute a superspecies.

Camptostoma obsoletum (Temminck). SOUTHERN BEARDLESS-TYRANNULET.

Muscicapa obsoleta (Natterer MS) Temminck, 1824, Planches Color., livr. 46, pl. 275, fig. 1. (Brazil = Curitiba, Paraná, Brazil.)

Habitat.—Scrub, shrubby areas, second-growth woodland and humid forest edge (Tropical and lower Subtropical zones).

Distribution.—*Resident* in southwestern Costa Rica (Pacific slope north to the Tempisque Valley) and Panama (Pacific slope throughout, including Coiba, Cébaco and the Pearl islands, locally on the Caribbean slope in Colón, Canal Zone and San Blas), and in South America from Colombia, Venezuela (also Trinidad) and the Guianas south, west of the Andes to central Peru and east of the Andes to eastern Peru, northern and eastern Bolivia, northern Argentina and southern Brazil.

Notes.—See comments under *C. imberbe.*

Genus PHAEOMYIAS Berlepsch

Phaeomyias Berlepsch, 1902, Novit. Zool., 9, p. 41. Type, by subsequent designation (Chubb, 1921), "*P. imcompta*" = *Elainea incomta* Cabanis and Heine = *Platyrhynchus murinus* Spix.

Phaeomyias murina (Spix). MOUSE-COLORED TYRANNULET.

Platyrhynchus murinus Spix, 1825, Avium Spec. Nov. Bras., 2, p. 14, pl. 16, fig. 2. (Brazil = Rio São Francisco, northern Bahia.)

Habitat.—Arid scrub, thorn bush, second growth, savanna, mangroves, thickets and, less frequently, humid forest edge (Tropical and lower Subtropical zones).

Distribution.—*Resident* in western and central Panama (Pacific slope from Chiriquí east to eastern Panamá province), and in South America from Colombia, Venezuela (also Trinidad and Monos Island) and the Guianas south, west of the Andes to western Peru and east of the Andes to eastern Peru, northern and eastern Bolivia, northwestern Argentina, Paraguay, and central and eastern Brazil.

Genus SUBLEGATUS Sclater and Salvin

Sublegatus Sclater and Salvin, 1869, Proc. Zool. Soc. London (1868), p. 923. Type, by monotypy, *Sublegatus glaber* Sclater and Salvin = *Muscipeta modesta* Wied.

Sublegatus modestus (Wied). SCRUB FLYCATCHER.

Muscipeta modesta Wied, 1831, Beitr. Naturgesch. Bras., 3 (2), p. 923. (Camamú and Bahia, Brazil.)

Habitat.—Arid scrub, open woodland, thorn scrub, mangroves, swamps, savanna and forest edge (Tropical Zone).

Distribution.—*Resident* [*arenarum* group] in the Pacific lowlands of south-central Costa Rica (around Gulf of Nicoya) and Panama (including Coiba, Cébaco, Taboga and the Pearl islands), and in South America from northern Colombia, Venezuela (also islands from Netherlands Antilles east to Trinidad) and the Guianas south, east of the Andes, to eastern Peru and Amazonian Brazil; and [*modestus* group] in southern South America from southeastern Peru, eastern Paraguay, and southern and eastern Brazil south through Uruguay to northern Argentina, with the southernmost populations partially migratory north to eastern Peru and Amazonian Brazil.

Notes.—The two groups are sometimes regarded as separate species, *S. arenarum* (Salvin, 1863) [SCRUB FLYCATCHER] and *S. modestus* [SHORT-BILLED FLYCATCHER].

Genus TYRANNULUS Vieillot

Tyrannulus Vieillot, 1816, Analyse, p. 31. Type, by monotypy, "Roitelet-Mésange" Buffon = *Sylvia elata* Latham.

Tyrannulus elatus (Latham). YELLOW-CROWNED TYRANNULET.

Sylvia elata Latham, 1790, Index Ornithol., 2, p. 549. Based on "Le Roitelet Mesange" Buffon, Hist. Nat. Ois., 5, p. 375, and "Mesange huppée de Cayenne" Daubenton, Planches Enlum., pl. 708, fig. 2. (in Cayanæ uliginosis = Cayenne.)

Habitat.—Humid forest edge, open woodland, clearings, second growth and gardens (Tropical Zone).

Distribution.—*Resident* in southwestern Costa Rica (Golfo Dulce region) and Panama (Pacific slope throughout, Caribbean slope from Coclé eastward), and in South America from Colombia, Venezuela and the Guianas south, west of the Andes to western Ecuador and east of the Andes to eastern Peru, northern Bolivia and Amazonian Brazil.

Genus MYIOPAGIS Salvin and Godman

Myiopagis Salvin and Godman, 1888, Biol. Cent.-Am., Aves, 2, p. 26. Type, by original designation, *Elainea placens* Sclater = *Sylvia viridicata* Vieillot.

Myiopagis gaimardii (d'Orbigny). FOREST ELAENIA.

Muscicapara Gaimardii d'Orbigny, 1840, Voy. Am. Mérid., 4, Ois., livr. 3, p. 326. (Yuracares, Bolivia.)

Habitat.—Humid lowland forest, forest edge, second-growth woodland, thorny scrub and marshes (Tropical Zone).

Distribution.—*Resident* from central Panama (west on the Caribbean slope to Coclé, on Pacific slope to the Canal Zone) east across northern Colombia and Venezuela (also Trinidad and Chacachacare Island) to the Guianas, and south, east of the Andes, to eastern Peru, nothern Bolivia, and Amazonian and central Brazil.

Myiopagis caniceps (Swainson). GRAY ELAENIA.

Tyrannula caniceps Swainson, 1836?, Ornithol. Drawings, pt. 4, pl. 49. (Brazil = Santo Amaro, Reconcavo de Baía, Brazil.)

Habitat.—Humid lowland and foothill forest (Tropical and lower Subtropical zones).

Distribution.—*Resident* locally in eastern Panama (eastern Darién, also sight reports from the Canal Zone), western Colombia and western Ecuador; also in northwestern Venezuela, and from southeastern Colombia and southern Venezuela south, east of the Andes, to eastern Peru, Paraguay, extreme northeastern Argentina, and central and eastern Brazil.

Myiopagis cotta (Gosse). JAMAICAN ELAENIA.

Elania [sic] *cotta* Gosse, 1849, Ann. Mag. Nat. Hist., ser. 2, 3, p. 257. (Jamaica.)

Habitat.—Forest, open woodland and shrubby areas, both in mountains and lowlands, more commonly in the former.

Distribution.—*Resident* on Jamaica.

Notes.—Also known as JAMAICAN YELLOW-CROWNED ELAENIA.

Myiopagis viridicata (Vieillot). GREENISH ELAENIA.

Sylvia viridicata Vieillot, 1817, Nouv. Dict. Hist. Nat., nouv. éd., 11, p. 171. Based on "Contramaestre Pardo verdoso corona amarilla" Azara, Apunt. Hist. Nat. Páx. Parag., 2, p. 57 (no. 156). (Paraguay.)

Habitat.—Humid lowland forest edge, open woodland, clearings, and open situations with scattered trees (Tropical and lower Subtropical zones).

Distribution.—*Resident* from Nayarit, Durango, San Luis Potosí and southern Tamaulipas south along both slopes of Mexico (including the Tres Marias Islands and Yucatan Peninsula, but a record from Isla Mujeres is unverified) and Central America (throughout, but in Costa Rica confined primarily to the Pacific slope) to Panama (Pacific slope throughout, including Coiba and the Pearl islands, locally on the Caribbean slope in Colón and the Canal Zone), and in South America from western Colombia south, west of the Andes, to western Ecuador (including Puna Island), and locally from Venezuela and southeastern Colombia south, east of the Andes, to southeastern Peru, central Bolivia, northern Argentina, and south-central and eastern Brazil.

Genus **ELAENIA** Sundevall

Elænia Sundevall, 1836, Vetensk.-Akad. Handl. (1835), p. 89. Type, by subsequent designation (G. R. Gray, 1855), *Muscicapa pagana* Lichtenstein = *Pipra flavogaster* Thunberg.

Elaenia martinica (Linnaeus). CARIBBEAN ELAENIA.

Muscicapa martinica Linnaeus, 1766, Syst. Nat., ed. 12, 1, p. 325. Based on "Le Gobe-mouche hupé de la Martinique" Brisson, Ornithologie, 2, p. 362, pl. 36, fig. 2. (in Martinica = Martinique.)

Habitat.—On islands, where found in forest, woodland and scrub, most commonly in open or semi-open habitats.

Distribution.—*Resident* in the Cayman, Providencia and San Andrés islands in the Caribbean Sea, on islands off the Yucatan Peninsula and Belize (Cozumel, Mujeres and Cayo Culebra, probably also Holbox, formerly Banco Chinchorro, Half Moon Cay and Glover's Reef), and from Puerto Rico (including Vieques, Culebra and Culebrita islands) and the Virgin Islands south through the Lesser Antilles to Grenada (apparently absent from the Grenadines), Trinidad and the Netherlands Antilles.

Casual on the mainland of Belize (Belize City).

Elaenia flavogaster (Thunberg). YELLOW-BELLIED ELAENIA.

Pipra flavogaster Thunberg, 1822, Mém. Acad. Imp. Sci. St. Pétersbourg, 8, pp. 283, 286. (Brazil = probably Rio de Janeiro.)

Habitat.—Open woodland, second growth, savanna, shrubby areas and gardens, in both humid and arid habitats (Tropical and Subtropical zones).

Distribution.—*Resident* from central Veracruz, northern Oaxaca and Chiapas south along both slopes of Middle America (including the Yucatan Peninsula, Isla Mujeres off Quintana Roo, and the Pearl, Taboga, Coiba and smaller islands off Panama), and in South America from Colombia, Venezuela (also Margarita and Patos islands) and the Guianas south, west of the Andes to northwestern Peru and east of the Andes (absent from eastern Colombia, eastern Ecuador and most of eastern Peru) to southeastern Peru, northern and eastern Bolivia, northwestern and northeastern Argentina, Paraguay and southern Brazil; also the southern Lesser Antilles (Grenada, the Grenadines and St. Vincent), Tobago and Trinidad.

Notes.—Some authors consider *E. flavogaster* and the South American *E. spectabilis* Pelzeln, 1868, as conspecific despite apparent overlap in Brazil; they appear to constitute a superspecies.

Elaenia chiriquensis Lawrence. LESSER ELAENIA.

Elainea Chiriquensis Lawrence, 1867, Ann. Lyc. Nat. Hist. N.Y., 8, p. 176. (near David, Chiriqui, New Granada [=Panama].)

Habitat.—Scrub, open woodland, second growth, shrubby areas and savanna (Tropical and Subtropical zones).

Distribution.—*Resident* in central (vicinity of Cartago) and southwestern Costa Rica (El General-Térraba regions), in Panama (Caribbean slope in Colón and the Canal Zone, Pacific slope east to eastern Panamá province, and Coiba, Cébaco and the Pearl islands), and in South America from Colombia, Venezuela and the Guianas south, west of the Andes to northwestern Ecuador and east of the Andes to eastern Peru, central Bolivia, Paraguay, and central and southeastern Brazil.

Accidental on Bonaire, in the Netherlands Antilles; a record from Miravalles, in northwestern Costa Rica, probably represents a vagrant.

Elaenia frantzii Lawrence. MOUNTAIN ELAENIA.

Elainea frantzii Lawrence, 1867, Ann. Lyc. Nat. Hist. N.Y., 8, p. 172. (San Jose, Costa Rica.)

Habitat.—Humid montane forest edge, clearings, scrubby areas, farmland and, less frequently, more open portions of humid montane forest (Subtropical and Temperate zones).

Distribution.—*Resident* in the mountains of central Guatemala, Honduras, north-central and southwestern Nicaragua, Costa Rica, western Panama (Chiriquí, Veraguas and western Herrera), Colombia and western Venezuela.

Notes.—Some authors consider *E. frantzii* and the South American *E. obscura* (Lafresnaye and d'Orbigny, 1837) to be conspecific; they constitute a superspecies.

Elaenia fallax Sclater. GREATER ANTILLEAN ELAENIA.

Elainea fallax Sclater, 1861, Proc. Zool. Soc. London, p. 76 (footnote). (Jamaica.)

Habitat.—Humid forest edge, open pine woodland, and thickets in partly open situations, primarily in mountains.

Distribution.—*Resident* on Jamaica (primarily in Blue Mountains, less frequently in hills of St. Ann and Trelawny) and Hispaniola (high elevations).

Genus **SERPOPHAGA** Gould

Serpophaga Gould, 1839, *in* Darwin, Zool. Voy. Beagle, 3 (9), p. 49. Type, by subsequent designation (G. R. Gray, 1855), *Serpophaga albocoronatus* [sic] Gould = *Sylvia subcristata* Vieillot.

Serpophaga cinerea (Tschudi). TORRENT TYRANNULET.

Leptopogon cinereus Tschudi, 1844, Arch. Naturgesch., 10, p. 276. (Republica Peruana = vicinity of Tarma, Depto. Junín, Peru.)

Habitat.—Along rocky torrents in humid montane regions (Subtropical Zone).
Distribution.—*Resident* in the highlands of Costa Rica (central highlands southward) and western Panama (east to Veraguas); and in South America in the Andes from Colombia and northwestern Venezuela south to Peru (also along the central coast) and northern Bolivia.

Genus MIONECTES Cabanis

Mionectes Cabanis, 1844, Arch. Naturgesch., 10, p. 275. Type, by original designation, *M. poliocephalus* Tsch[udi]. = *Muscicapa striaticollis* d'Orbigny and Lafresnaye.
Pipromorpha G. R. Gray, 1855, Cat. Genera Subgenera Birds, p. 146. Type, by monotypy, *Muscicapa oleagina* [sic] Lichtenstein.

Mionectes olivaceus Lawrence. OLIVE-STRIPED FLYCATCHER.

Mionectes olivaceus Lawrence, 1868, Ann. Lyc. Nat. Hist. N.Y., 9, p. 111. (Barranca and Dota, Costa Rica = Barranca, Costa Rica.)

Habitat.—Understory of humid forest, forest edge, clearings, second-growth woodland, shrubby growth and plantations (Tropical and Subtropical zones).
Distribution.—*Resident* in Costa Rica (on both slopes of highlands, most commonly on Caribbean, to lowlands mainly in the nonbreeding season) and Panama (Caribbean slope throughout, Pacific slope west to the Canal Zone), and in South America from Colombia and northern Venezuela (also Trinidad) south, west of the Andes to northwestern Ecuador and east of the Andes to central Peru.

Mionectes oleagineus (Lichtenstein). OCHRE-BELLIED FLYCATCHER.

Muscicapa oleaginea Lichtenstein, 1823, Verz. Doubl. Zool. Mus. Berlin, p. 55. (Bahia, Brazil.)

Habitat.—Humid lowland and foothill forest, forest edge, second growth, open woodland, shrubby growth and plantations (Tropical and lower Subtropical zones).
Distribution.—*Resident* from eastern Puebla, central Veracruz, northern and eastern Oaxaca, Tabasco, Chiapas and the Yucatan Peninsula (including Isla Mujeres) south along both slopes of Central America to Panama (including Coiba, Cébaco and the Pearl islands), and in South America from Colombia, Venezuela (also Tobago and Trinidad) and the Guianas south, west of the Andes to western Ecuador and east of the Andes to eastern Peru, Bolivia, and Amazonian and eastern Brazil.
Notes.—Formerly placed in the genus *Pipromorpha*.

Genus LEPTOPOGON Cabanis

Leptopogon Cabanis, 1844, Arch. Naturgesch, 10, p. 275. Type, by subsequent designation (G. R. Gray, 1855), *Leptopogon superciliaris* Tsch[udi].

Leptopogon amaurocephalus Tschudi. SEPIA-CAPPED FLYCATCHER.

Leptopogon amaurocephalus (Cabanis MS) Tschudi, 1846, Unters. Fauna Peru, lief. 6, Ornithol., p. 162 (footnote). (São Paulo, Brazil.)

Habitat.—Humid lowland and foothill forest, forest edge, open woodland and plantations (Tropical and lower Subtropical zones).

Distribution.—*Resident* on the Gulf-Caribbean slope from southern Mexico (northern Oaxaca, southern Veracruz, Tabasco and Chiapas) south to Nicaragua, on both slopes of Costa Rica (rare, occurring primarily in foothills), and in western and central Panama (Pacific slope east to eastern Panamá province, including Isla Coiba, locally also on the Caribbean slope in the Canal Zone); from northern and eastern Colombia east across Venezuela to Surinam; and from eastern Peru and Brazil (south of the Amazon) south to central Bolivia, northern Argentina and Paraguay.

Leptopogon superciliaris Tschudi. SLATY-CAPPED FLYCATCHER.

Leptopogon superciliaris Tschudi, 1844, Arch. Naturgesch., 10, p. 275. (Republica Peruana = Montaña de Vitoc, Peru.)

Habitat.—Humid foothill and montane forest, forest edge, dense second-growth woodland, and shaded plantations (upper Tropical and Subtropical zones).

Distribution.—*Resident* in the highlands of Costa Rica and Panama (recorded western Chiriquí, Veraguas and eastern Darién), and in South America from the Andes of Colombia east across northern Venezuela (also Trinidad) and south, west of the Andes to western Ecuador and east of the Andes to eastern Peru and northern Bolivia; also locally in extreme southern Venezuela (Amazonas).

Genus CAPSIEMPIS Cabanis and Heine

Capsiempis Cabanis and Heine, 1859, Mus. Heineanum, 2, p. 56. Type, by original designation, *Muscicapa flaveola* Lichtenstein.

Notes.—This genus is sometimes merged in *Phylloscartes.*

Capsiempis flaveola (Lichtenstein). YELLOW TYRANNULET.

Muscicapa flaveola Lichtenstein, 1823, Verz. Doubl. Zool. Mus. Berlin, p. 56. (Bahia, Brazil.)

Habitat.—Thickets, brushy areas, overgrown pastures, and borders of forest and open woodland, locally also in thorn scrub and mangroves (Tropical Zone).

Distribution.—*Resident* in Nicaragua (Caribbean slope), Costa Rica (Caribbean slope and Pacific southwest) and Panama (locally east to eastern Colón and eastern Panamá province, also Isla Coiba), and in South America from Colombia, Venezuela and the Guianas south, east of the Andes, to northeastern Ecuador, thence east across Brazil and southward to eastern Bolivia, Paraguay, extreme northeastern Argentina and southeastern Brazil.

Genus PHYLLOSCARTES Cabanis and Heine

Phylloscartes Cabanis and Heine, 1859, Mus. Heineanum, 2, p. 52. Type, by monotypy, *Muscicapa ventralis* Temminck.

Notes.—See comments under *Capsiempis.*

Phylloscartes flavovirens (Lawrence). YELLOW-GREEN TYRANNULET.

Leptopogon flavovirens Lawrence, 1862, Ann. Lyc. Nat. Hist. N.Y., 7, p. 472. (Atlantic side of the Isthmus of Panama, along the line of the Panama Railroad = Atlantic slope, Canal Zone.)

Habitat.—Humid second-growth woodland in lowlands (Tropical Zone).

Distribution.—*Resident* locally in Panama (Pacific lowlands from the Canal Zone east to eastern Darién, Caribbean slope in the Canal Zone).

Notes.—*P. flavovirens* and the South American *P. ventralis* (Temminck, 1824) [MOTTLE-CHEEKED TYRANNULET] constitute a superspecies; they are considered conspecific by some authors.

Phylloscartes superciliaris (Sclater and Salvin). RUFOUS-BROWED TY-RANNULET.

Leptotriccus superciliaris Sclater and Salvin, 1869, Proc. Zool. Soc. London (1868), p. 389. (Chitrá, Veragua, Panama.)

Habitat.—Humid montane forest, forest edge and, less frequently, dense vegetation in partly open situations (Subtropical Zone).

Distribution.—*Resident* locally in Costa Rica (Caribbean slope of Cordillera de Tilarán southward), Panama (recorded Chiriquí, Veraguas and eastern Darién), Colombia ("Bogotá" only) and northwestern Venezuela (Zulia).

Notes.—Sometimes placed in the South American genus *Mecocerculus* Sclater, 1862.

Genus PSEUDOTRICCUS Taczanowski and Berlepsch

Pseudotriccus Taczanowski and Berlepsch, 1885, Proc. Zool. Soc. London, p. 88. Type, by monotypy, *Pseudotriccus pelzelni* Taczanowski and Berlepsch.

Pseudotriccus pelzelni Taczanowski and Berlepsch. BRONZE-OLIVE PYGMY-TYRANT.

Pseudotriccus pelzelni Taczanowski and Berlepsch, 1885, Proc. Zool. Soc. London, p. 88. (Machay and [Hacienda] Mapoto, Tungurahua, Ecuador.)

Habitat.—Undergrowth of humid montane forest (Subtropical, less frequently, upper Tropical zones).

Distribution.—*Resident* in the highlands of extreme eastern Panama (cerros Pirre and Tacarcuna, eastern Darién), and in South America from Colombia south, west of the Andes to northwestern Ecuador and east of the Andes to eastern Peru.

Notes.—Also known as STREAK-CROWNED PYGMY-TYRANT.

Genus MYIORNIS Bertoni

Myiornis Bertoni, 1901, Aves Nuev. Parag., p. 129. Type, by monotypy, *Euscarthmus minutus* Bertoni = *Platyrhynchos auricularis* Vieillot.
Perissotriccus Oberholser, 1902, Proc. U.S. Natl. Mus., 25, p. 64. Type, by original designation, *Todirostrum ecaudatum* Lafresnaye and d'Orbigny.

Myiornis atricapillus (Lawrence). BLACK-CAPPED PYGMY-TYRANT.

Orchilus atricapillus Lawrence, 1875, Ibis, p. 385. (Angostura and Volcan de Irazu, Costa Rica = Talamanca, Costa Rica.)

Habitat.—Humid lowland forest, forest edge and second-growth woodland (Tropical Zone).

Distribution.—*Resident* in Costa Rica (Caribbean lowlands), Panama (Caribbean slope, locally also on Pacific slope in eastern Panamá province and eastern Darién), western Colombia and western Ecuador.

Notes.—*M. atricapillus* and the South American *M. ecaudatus* (Lafresnaye and d'Orbigny, 1837) [SHORT-TAILED PYGMY-TYRANT] are closely related and considered conspecific by some authors; they constitute at least a superspecies. These two species are sometimes placed in the genus *Perissotriccus*.

Genus LOPHOTRICCUS Berlepsch

Lophotriccus Berlepsch, 1884, Proc. Zool. Soc. London (1883), p. 533. Type, by subsequent designation (Sharpe, 1884), *Lophotriccus squamicristatus* (Lafr.) = *Todirostrum squamaecrista* Lafresnaye.

Lophotriccus pileatus (Tschudi). SCALE-CRESTED PYGMY-TYRANT.

Euscarthmus pileatus Tschudi, 1844, Arch. Naturgesch., 10, p. 273. (Republica Peruana = valley of Vitoc, Depto. Junín, Peru.)

Habitat.—Understory of humid forest edge and second-growth woodland, forest clearings, brushy undergrowth, and open situations with scattered small trees (upper Tropical and Subtropical zones, in South America also lower Tropical Zone).

Distribution.—*Resident* in the foothills and highlands of Costa Rica (both slopes) and Panama, and in South America from Colombia and northern Venezuela south, west of the Andes to western Ecuador and east of the Andes to eastern Peru; also in southwestern Brazil.

Genus ATALOTRICCUS Ridgway

Atalotriccus Ridgway, 1905, Proc. Biol. Soc. Wash., 18, p. 208. Type, by original designation, *Colopterus pilaris* Cabanis.

Atalotriccus pilaris (Cabanis). PALE-EYED PYGMY-TYRANT.

Colopterus pilaris Cabanis, 1847, Arch. Naturgesch., 13, p. 253, pl. 5, fig. 4. (environs of Cartagena, Bolívar, Colombia.)

Habitat.—Arid scrub, thorn bush, thickets, and small trees and bushes near water (Tropical, occasionally lower Subtropical zones).

Distribution.—*Resident* on the Pacific slope of western and central Panama (western Chiriquí east to eastern Panamá province); and in South America in northern Colombia, Venezuela and Guyana.

Notes.—Also known as WHITE-EYED PYGMY-TYRANT.

Genus ONCOSTOMA Sclater

Oncostoma Sclater, 1862, Cat. Collect. Am. Birds, p. 208. Type, by monotypy, *Todirostrum cinereigulare* Sclater.

Oncostoma cinereigulare (Sclater). NORTHERN BENTBILL.

Todirostrum cinereigulare Sclater, 1857, Proc. Zool. Soc. London (1856), p. 295. (Cordova [=Córdoba] in the State of Vera Cruz, Southern Mexico.)

Habitat.—Humid lowland forest edge, thickets, undergrowth of second-growth woodland, and brushy areas near forest (Tropical Zone).

Distribution.—*Resident* from central Veracruz and northern and eastern Oaxaca south along both slopes of Middle America (including the Yucatan Peninsula) to western Panama (western Bocas del Toro and western Chiriquí; an old specimen from "Canal Zone" is probably mislabeled); and in extreme northwestern Colombia (Antioquia).

Notes.—*O. cinereigulare* and *O. olivaceum* constitute a superspecies; they are regarded as conspecific by some authors. With treatment as a single species, the English name would be BENTBILL.

Oncostoma olivaceum (Lawrence). SOUTHERN BENTBILL.

Todirostrum olivaceum Lawrence, 1862, Ibis, p. 12. (Isthmus of Panama = Lion Hill, Canal Zone.)

Habitat.—Thickets and undergrowth of humid forest edge and second-growth woodland (Tropical Zone).

Distribution.—*Resident* in eastern Panama (west on the Caribbean slope to Coclé and the Pacific slope to the Canal Zone) and northern Colombia.

Notes.—See comments under *O. cinereigulare.*

Genus **TODIROSTRUM** Lesson

Todirostrum Lesson, 1831, Traité Ornithol., livr. 5 (1830), p. 384. Type, by subsequent designation (G. R. Gray, 1840), *T. cinereum* = *Todus cinereus* Linnaeus.

Todirostrum sylvia (Desmarest). SLATE-HEADED TODY-FLYCATCHER.

Todus sylvia Desmarest, 1806, Hist. Nat. Tangaras, Manakins, Todiers, livr. 10, pl. 71. (No locality given = probably Cayenne.)

Habitat.—Dense thickets, brushy growth and low second growth, mostly in humid lowlands and foothills, locally in drier habitats (Tropical and lower Subtropical zones).

Distribution.—*Resident* on the Gulf-Caribbean slope from northern Mexico (southern Veracruz, northern Oaxaca, Tabasco, northern Chiapas and Quintana Roo) south through northern Central America to Honduras, on both slopes of Nicaragua, Costa Rica (most commonly on Pacific slope from Gulf of Nicoya southward, less commonly on Caribbean slope) and Panama (Pacific slope east to eastern Panamá province, on Caribbean slope east to the Canal Zone), and in South America from Colombia across northwestern and southern Venezuela to the Guianas, and south to northern Amazonian Brazil.

Todirostrum cinereum (Linnaeus). COMMON TODY-FLYCATCHER.

Todus cinereus Linnaeus, 1766, Syst. Nat., ed. 12, 1, p. 178. Based on "The Grey and Yellow Flycatcher" Edwards, Glean. Nat. Hist., 2, p. 110, pl. 262, fig. 1. (in Surinamo = Surinam.)

Habitat.—Open woodland, thickets, brushy areas, scrub, gardens and forest border, primarily in humid lowlands and foothills (Tropical and lower Subtropical zones).

Distribution.—*Resident* from southeastern Mexico (central Veracruz, northern Oaxaca, Tabasco, Chiapas, Campeche and Quintana Roo, including Isla Mujeres) south on both slopes of Middle America (including Isla Coiba off Panama), and in South America from Colombia, Venezuela and the Guianas south, west of the Andes to northwestern Peru and east of the Andes to eastern Peru, northern and eastern Bolivia, and southern Brazil.

Notes.—The distinct form from northwestern Venezuela, *T. viridanum* Hellmayr, 1927, is sometimes regarded as conspecific with *T. cinereum*; they constitute a superspecies.

Todirostrum nigriceps Sclater. BLACK-HEADED TODY-FLYCATCHER.

Todirostrum nigriceps Sclater, 1855, Proc. Zool. Soc. London, p. 66, pl. 84, fig. 1. (Santa Martha in Nov. Grenada = Sierra Nevada de Santa Marta, Colombia.)

Habitat.—Humid lowland forest edge, clearings, open woodland, second growth, plantations and scrub (Tropical Zone).

Distribution.—*Resident* in Costa Rica (primarily Caribbean lowlands, locally on Pacific drainage of Cordillera de Guanacaste) and Panama (Caribbean slope generally throughout, Pacific slope from the Canal Zone eastward), and in South America in Colombia, northwestern Venezuela and western Ecuador.

Notes.—*T. nigriceps* is considered by some authors to be conspecific with the South American *T. chrysocrotaphum* Strickland, 1850 [PAINTED TODY-FLYCATCHER]; they constitute a superspecies.

Genus CNIPODECTES Sclater and Salvin

Cnipodectes Sclater and Salvin, 1873, Proc. Zool. Soc. London, p. 281. Type, by monotypy, *Cyclorhynchus subbrunneus* Sclater.

Cnipodectes subbrunneus (Sclater). BROWNISH FLYCATCHER.

Cyclorhynchus subbrunneus Sclater, 1860, Proc. Zool. Soc. London, p. 282. (In rep. Equator = Babahoyo, Los Ríos, Ecuador.)

Habitat.—Undergrowth of humid lowland forest and second-growth woodland (Tropical Zone).

Distribution.—*Resident* in Panama (from Coclé on the Caribbean slope and the Canal Zone on the Pacific slope eastward), and in South America from Colombia south, west of the Andes to western Ecuador and east of the Andes to northeastern Peru and western Brazil.

Genus RHYNCHOCYCLUS Cabanis and Heine

Cyclorhynchus (not *Cyclorrhynchus* Kaup, 1829) Sundevall, 1836. Vetensk.-Akad. Handl. (1835), p. 83. Type, by monotypy, *Platyrhynchus olivaceus* Temminck. *Nomen oblitum.*
Rhynchocyclus Cabanis and Heine, 1859, Mus. Heineanum, 2, p. 56. New name for *Cyclorhynchus* Sundevall.

Rhynchocyclus brevirostris (Cabanis). EYE-RINGED FLATBILL.

Cyclorhynchus brevirostris Cabanis, 1847, Arch. Naturgesch., 13, p. 249. (Xalapa, Mexico = Jalapa, Veracruz.)

Habitat.—Humid forest, forest edge and shaded second-growth woodland (Tropical and Subtropical zones).

Distribution.—*Resident* from southern Mexico (eastern Oaxaca, Puebla and central Veracruz southward, including the Yucatan Peninsula, primarily in lowlands) south on both slopes of Middle America (not recorded Pacific slope of Guatemala) to Nicaragua, in Costa Rica (Caribbean slope and Pacific southwest) and Panama (locally on both slopes, not recorded between western Panamá province and eastern Darién), and in western Colombia and northwestern Ecuador.

Rhynchocyclus olivaceus (Temminck). OLIVACEOUS FLATBILL.

Platyrhynchos olivaceus Temminck, 1820, Planches Color., livr. 2, pl. 12, fig. 1. (Brésil = Rio de Janeiro, Brazil.)

Habitat.—Humid lowland forest, forest edge, second-growth woodland, swamps and plantations (Tropical Zone).

Distribution.—*Resident* in Panama (on Caribbean slope west to western Colón, on Pacific slope west to the Canal Zone, one old record from "Veragua" in western Panama), and in South America from northern Colombia, Venezuela and the Guianas south, east of the Andes, to eastern Peru, northern Bolivia, and central and southeastern Brazil.

Genus TOLMOMYIAS Hellmayr

Tolmomyias Hellmayr, 1927, Field Mus. Nat. Hist. Publ., Zool. Ser., 13 (5), p. 273. Type, by original designation, *Platyrhynchus sulphurescens* Spix.

Tolmomyias sulphurescens (Spix). YELLOW-OLIVE FLYCATCHER.

Platyrhynchus sulphurescens Spix, 1825, Avium Spec. Nov. Bras., 2, p. 10, pl. 12, fig. 1. (Rio de Janeiro and Piauí, Brazil = Rio de Janeiro.)

Habitat.—Open woodland, second growth, humid forest edge and plantations (Tropical and Subtropical zones).

Distribution.—*Resident* from northern and eastern Oaxaca and central Veracruz south through Middle America (both slopes, including the Yucatan Peninsula), and in South America from Colombia, Venezuela (also Trinidad) and the Guianas south, west of the Andes to northwestern Peru and east of the Andes to northern Argentina and southern Brazil (not recorded Uruguay).

Tolmomyias assimilis (Pelzeln). YELLOW-MARGINED FLYCATCHER.

Rhynchocyclus assimilis Pelzeln, 1868, Ornithol. Bras., 2, pp. 110, 181. (Engenho do Gama, S. Vicente, Borba, Rio Negro, and Barra do Rio Negro, n. Brazil = Borba, Rio Madeira.)

Habitat.—Humid forest, forest edge, clearings, and open situations with scattered trees adjacent to forest (Tropical and Subtropical zones).

Distribution.—*Resident* in Costa Rica (Caribbean slope throughout) and Panama (both slopes, but rare and local on the Pacific slope west of the Canal Zone), and in South America from Colombia, southern Venezuela and the Guianas south, west of the Andes to northwestern Ecuador and east of the Andes to eastern Peru, northern Bolivia, and central and eastern Brazil.

Notes.—Also known as YELLOW-MARGINED FLATBILL.

Genus **PLATYRINCHUS** Desmarest

Platyrinchus Desmarest, 1805, Hist. Nat. Tangaras, Manakins, Todiers, livr. 4, p. [2] of text to pl. [72]. Type, by tautonymy, *Platyrinchus fuscus* Desmarest = *Todus platyrhynchos* Gmelin.

Platyrinchus cancrominus Sclater and Salvin. STUB-TAILED SPADEBILL.

Platyrhynchus cancrominus Sclater and Salvin, 1860, Proc. Zool. Soc. London, p. 299. (In prov. Veræ Pacis regione calida, et in Mexico Merid. statu Veræ Crucis = Choctum, Vera Paz, Guatemala.)

Habitat.—Undergrowth of humid lowland and foothill forest, forest edge, heavy second growth and deciduous woodland (Tropical and lower Subtropical zones).

Distribution.—*Resident* from southern Mexico (central Veracruz, northern and eastern Oaxaca, Tabasco, Chiapas, southern Campeche and southern Quintana Roo) south along both slopes of Central America to Nicaragua and northwestern and central Costa Rica (Pacific slope south to the Río Pirrís area).

Notes.—Some authors consider *P. cancrominus* conspecific with *P. mystaceus,* but see Slud (1964, Bull. Am. Mus. Nat. Hist., 128, pp. 260–261); they constitute a superspecies.

Platyrinchus mystaceus Vieillot. WHITE-THROATED SPADEBILL.

Platyrhynchus mystaceus Vieillot, 1818, Nouv. Dict. Hist. Nat., nouv. éd., 27, p. 14. Based on "Tachuri Bigotillos" Azara, Apunt. Hist. Nat. Páx. Parag., 2, p. 93 (no. 173). (Paraguay = San Ignacio Guazú, southern Paraguay.)

Habitat.—Understory in humid forest, forest edge, heavy second growth and, less frequently, open brush (Tropical and Subtropical zones).

Distribution.—*Resident* in Costa Rica (Caribbean slope throughout, and Pacific slope of central highlands from the Dota Mountains eastward) and western and extreme eastern Panama (unrecorded between Cerro Campana and eastern Darién), and in South America from Colombia, Venezuela (also Tobago and Trinidad) and the Guianas south, west of the Andes to western Ecuador and east of the Andes to eastern Peru, northern Bolivia, eastern Paraguay, extreme northeastern Argentina and southern Brazil.

Notes.—See comments under *P. cancrominus.*

Platyrinchus coronatus Sclater. GOLDEN-CROWNED SPADEBILL.

Platyrhynchus coronatus (Verreaux MS) Sclater, 1858, Proc. Zool. Soc. London, p. 71. (Rio Napo in the Republic of Ecuador.)

Habitat.—Understory in humid lowland and foothill forest and heavy second growth (Tropical and lower Subtropical zones).

Distribution.—*Resident* on the Caribbean slope of Honduras (west to the Sula Valley) and Nicaragua, in Costa Rica (Caribbean slope and Pacific southwest) and Panama (both slopes, more widespread on the Caribbean), and in South America west of the Andes in western Colombia and western Ecuador, and east of the Andes from southeastern Colombia, southern Venezuela and the Guianas south to eastern Peru and Amazonian Brazil.

Subfamily FLUVICOLINAE: Fluvicoline Flycatchers

Genus ONYCHORHYNCHUS Fischer von Waldheim

Onychorhynchus Fischer von Waldheim, 1810, Descr. Obj. Rares Mus. Hist. Nat. Univ. Imp. Moscou, 1, p. 1, pl. 1. Type, by monotypy, *Todus regius* "Linn. Gmel." = *Muscicapa coronata* Müller.

Onychorhynchus coronatus (Müller). ROYAL FLYCATCHER.

Muscicapa coronata P. L. S. Müller, 1776, Natursyst., Suppl., p. 168. Based on Daubenton, Planches Enlum., pl. 289. (Cayenne.)

Habitat.—Understory of tall, humid (less frequently subhumid) forest edge, clearings, second-growth woodland and plantations, especially along forest streams (Tropical and lower Subtropical zones).

Distribution.—*Resident* [*mexicanus* group] from central Veracruz and central Oaxaca south along both slopes of Middle America (including the Yucatan Peninsula, most commonly on the Gulf-Caribbean slope south through Nicaragua, and on the Pacific drainage in Costa Rica) to northern Colombia and northwestern Venezuela; and [*coronatus* group] in South America from eastern Colombia and southern Venezuela south, east of the Andes, to northern Peru, northern Bolivia, and Amazonian and southeastern Brazil, also west of the Andes in western Ecuador and extreme northwestern Peru.

Notes.—The two groups are sometimes regarded as separate species, *O. mexicanus* (Sclater, 1857) [NORTHERN ROYAL-FLYCATCHER] and *O. coronatus* [AMAZONIAN ROYAL-FLYCATCHER].

Genus TERENOTRICCUS Ridgway

Terenotriccus Ridgway, 1905, Proc. Biol. Soc. Wash., 18, p. 207. Type, by original designation, *Myiobius fulvigularis* Salvin and Godman = *Myiobius erythrurus* Cabanis.

Terenotriccus erythrurus (Cabanis). RUDDY-TAILED FLYCATCHER.

Myiobius erythrurus Cabanis, 1847, Arch. Naturgesch., 13, p. 249, pl. 5, fig. 1. (Guiana, Cayenne = Cayenne.)

Habitat.—Humid lowland forest, forest edge, clearings, second-growth woodland and, less frequently, in open situations with scattered trees (Tropical and lower Subtropical zones).

Distribution.—*Resident* on the Gulf-Caribbean slope of Tabasco (near Tenosique), Guatemala, Belize, Honduras and Nicaragua, on both slopes of Costa Rica (absent from the dry northwest) and Panama, and in South America from northern Colombia, Venezuela and the Guianas south, east of the Andes, to eastern Peru, northern Bolivia, and Amazonian and central Brazil.

Genus MYIOBIUS Darwin

Tyrannula (not Vieillot, 1816) Swainson, 1827, Zool. J., 3. p. 358. Type, by monotypy, *Muscicapa barbata* Swainson [= Gmelin].
Myiobius (Gray MS) Darwin, 1839, Zool. Voy. Beagle, 3 (9), p. 46. New name for *Tyrannula* Swainson, preoccupied.

Myiobius villosus Sclater. TAWNY-BREASTED FLYCATCHER.

Myiobius villosus Sclater, 1860, Proc. Zool. Soc. London, p. 93. (in rep. Ecuat., part. = Nanegal, Pichincha, Ecuador.)

Habitat.—Humid foothill and montane forest, clearings, forest edge and second-growth woodland (upper Tropical and Subtropical zones).

Distribution.—*Resident* from extreme eastern Panama (Cerro Tacarcuna in eastern Darién), Colombia and northwestern Venezuela south, west of the Andes to northwestern Ecuador and east of the Andes to eastern Peru and northwestern Bolivia.

Myiobius sulphureipygius (Sclater). SULPHUR-RUMPED FLYCATCHER.

Tyrannula sulphureipygia Sclater, 1857, Proc. Zool. Soc. London (1856), p. 296. (Cordova [=Córdoba] in the State of Vera Cruz, Southern Mexico.)

Habitat.—Understory of humid lowland and foothill forest and shaded second growth (Tropical and lower Subtropical zones).

Distribution.—*Resident* from southern Mexico (central Veracruz, northern Oaxaca, Tabasco, Chiapas, southern Campeche and southern Quintana Roo, with one old record from Cozumel Island) south on the Gulf-Caribbean slope of northern Central America to Nicaragua, on both slopes of Costa Rica (absent from the dry northwest) and Panama, and in South America in the Pacific lowlands of western Colombia and western Ecuador.

Notes.—Closely related to and sometimes considered conspecific with the South American *M. barbatus* (Gmelin, 1789); they constitute at least a superspecies.

Myiobius atricaudus Lawrence. BLACK-TAILED FLYCATCHER.

Myiobius atricaudus Lawrence, 1863, Ibis, p. 183. (Isthmus of Panama = Lion Hill, Canal Zone.)

Habitat.—Humid lowland forest edge, and undergrowth of heavy second-growth woodland and clearings (Tropical Zone).

Distribution.—*Resident* in Costa Rica (Pacific southwest, locally in the Tempisque basin in the Pacific northwest), Panama (both slopes), northern and western Colombia, western Ecuador and extreme northwestern Peru; also in South America east of the Andes from southeastern Ecuador, extreme southern Venezuela and Amazonian Brazil south to eastern Peru, and central and southern Brazil.

Genus **MYIOPHOBUS** Reichenbach

Myiophobus Reichenbach, 1850, Avium Syst. Nat., pl. 67. Type, by subsequent designation (G. R. Gray, 1855), *Muscicapa ferruginea* Swainson = *Muscicapa fasciata* Müller.

Myiophobus fasciatus (Müller). BRAN-COLORED FLYCATCHER.

Muscicapa fasciata P. L. S. Müller, 1776, Natursyst., Suppl., p. 172. Based on Daubenton, Planches Enlum., pl. 574, fig. 3. (Cayenne.)

Habitat.—Brushy areas, overgrown fields and pastures, open shrubby areas, and open woodland (Tropical and lower Subtropical zones).

Distribution.—*Resident* in southwestern Costa Rica (El General-Térraba region), western and central Panama (Pacific slope east to eastern Panamá province, Caribbean slope in the Canal Zone and adjacent Colón, and in the Pearl Islands), and in South America from northern Colombia south, west of the Andes to northern Chile, and east of the Andes in northern Venezuela (also Trinidad and Chacachacare Island) and the Guianas, and from central and eastern Peru east across central and eastern Brazil, thence southward through Paraguay and Uruguay to central Argentina.

Genus APHANOTRICCUS Ridgway

Aphanotriccus Ridgway, 1905, Proc. Biol. Soc. Wash., 18, p. 207. Type, by original designation, *Myiobius capitalis* Salvin.
Prædo Nelson, 1912, Smithson. Misc. Collect., 60, no. 3, p. 14. Type, by original designation, *Praedo audax* Nelson.

Aphanotriccus capitalis (Salvin). TAWNY-CHESTED FLYCATCHER.

Myiobius capitalis Salvin, 1865, Proc. Zool. Soc. London (1864), p. 583. (Tucurrique, Costa Rica.)

Habitat.—Overgrown humid forest edge, dense second growth and bamboo thickets, especially along streams, rarely inside forest (upper Tropical and Subtropical zones).
Distribution.—*Resident* on the Caribbean slope of eastern Nicaragua and northeastern and east-central Costa Rica.

Aphanotriccus audax (Nelson). BLACK-BILLED FLYCATCHER.

Prædo audax Nelson, 1912, Smithson. Misc. Collect., 60, no. 3, p. 15. (Cana, at 2,000 feet altitude, eastern Panamá.)

Habitat.—Undergrowth of humid lowland forest (Tropical Zone).
Distribution.—*Resident* locally in eastern Panama (near Puerto San Antonio and Majé in eastern Panamá province, and near Cana and on Cerro Pirre in eastern Darién), and in northwestern Colombia (in Córdoba).
Notes.—Often placed in the monotypic genus *Praedo*.

Genus XENOTRICCUS Dwight and Griscom

Xenotriccus Dwight and Griscom, 1927, Am. Mus. Novit., no. 254, p. 1. Type, by original designation, *Xenotriccus callizonus* Dwight and Griscom.
Aechmolophus Zimmer, 1938, Auk, 55, p. 663. Type, by original designation, *Aechmolophus mexicanus* Zimmer.

Xenotriccus callizonus Dwight and Griscom. BELTED FLYCATCHER.

Xenotriccus callizonus Dwight and Griscom, 1927, Am. Mus. Novit., no. 254, p. 2. (Panajachel, 5,500 ft., Lake Atitlán, Guatemala.)

Habitat.—Brushy hillsides, generally near water (Subtropical Zone.)
Distribution.—*Resident* locally in Chiapas (Ocozocuautla, Chichimá), Guatemala (Lake Atitlán, Baja Verapaz) and El Salvador (Depto. de Santa Ana).

Xenotriccus mexicanus (Zimmer). PILEATED FLYCATCHER.

Aechmolophus mexicanus Zimmer, 1938, Auk, 55, p. 664. (Cuernavaca, altitude 5000 feet, [Guerrero,] Mexico.)

Habitat.—Arid scrub, especially mesquite or oak-thorn (Subtropical and lower Temperate zones).

Distribution.—*Resident* from eastern Michoacán south through the highlands of Guerrero, Morelos and southwestern Puebla to central Oaxaca.

Notes.—Formerly placed in the monotypic genus *Aechmolophus.*

Genus **MITREPHANES** Coues

Mitrephorus (not Schönherr, 1837) Sclater, 1859, Proc. Zool. Soc. London, p. 44. Type, by subsequent designation (Sclater, 1888), *Mitrephorus phaeocercus* Sclater.
Mitrephanes Coues, 1882, Bull. Nuttall Ornithol. Club, 7, p. 55. New name for *Mitrephorus* Sclater, preoccupied.

Mitrephanes phaeocercus (Sclater). TUFTED FLYCATCHER.

Mitrephorus phæocercus Sclater, 1859, Proc. Zool. Soc. London, p. 44. (In Mexico merid. et in Guatemala = Córdoba, Veracruz.)

Habitat.—Humid forest edge, clearings, pine-oak association and brushy hillsides (upper Tropical to lower Temperate zones).

Distribution.—*Resident* in the highlands from northeastern Sonora, western Chihuahua, Sinaloa, Durango, western Zacatecas, southern San Luis Potosi and southern Tamaulipas south through the interior of Mexico (also to coastal areas in Jalisco), Guatemala, El Salvador and Honduras to north-central Nicaragua; from central Costa Rica south locally through Panama (Chiriquí, Veraguas, Coclé and eastern Darién) and western Colombia to northwestern Ecuador; and in the Andes from northern Peru south to eastern Bolivia.

Notes.—The Andean form in Peru and Bolivia is sometimes regarded as a separate species, *M. olivaceus* Berlepsch and Stolzmann, 1894.

Genus **CONTOPUS** Cabanis

Syrichta (not *Syrichtus* Boisduval, 1833) Bonaparte, 1854, Ann. Sci. Nat. (Zool.), sér. 4, 1, p. 133. Type, by monotypy, *Tyrannula ardosiaca* Lafresnaye = *Tyrannus fumigatus* d'Orbigny and Lafresnaye. *Nomen nudum.*
Contopus Cabanis, 1855, J. Ornithol., 3, p. 479. Type, by original designation, *Muscicapa virens* Linnaeus.
Blacicus Cabanis, 1855, J. Ornithol., 3, p. 480. Type, by original designation, *Muscipeta caribaea* d'Orbigny.
Syrichtha Bonaparte, 1857, Bull. Soc. Linn. Normandie, 2, p. 36. Type, by monotypy, *Syrichta curtipes* Bonaparte ex Swainson = *Platyrhynchus cinereus* Spix.
Myiochanes Cabanis and Heine, 1859, Mus. Heineanum, 2, p. 71. New name for *Syrichta* Bonaparte.
Syrichta G. R. Gray, 1869, Handl. Genera Spec. Birds, 1, p. 362. Type, by original designation, *Tyrannula ardosiaca* Lafresnaye = *Tyrannus fumigatus* d'Orbigny and Lafresnaye.

Nuttallornis Ridgway, 1887, Man. N. Am. Birds, p. 337. Type, by monotypy, *C. borealis* (Swainson) = *Tyrannus borealis* Swainson.

Contopus borealis (Swainson). OLIVE-SIDED FLYCATCHER. [459.]

Tyrannus borealis Swainson, 1832, *in* Swainson and Richardson, Fauna Bor.-Am., 2 (1831), p. 141, pl. 35. (Cumberland House [=Carlton House], lat. 54°, banks of the Saskatchewan [Canada].)

Habitat.—Forest and woodland, especially in burned-over areas with standing dead trees, breeding in taiga, subalpine coniferous forest and mixed coniferous-deciduous forest, in migration and winter in a variety of forest, woodland and open situations with scattered trees, especially where tall dead snags are present.

Distribution.—*Breeds* from western and central Alaska, central Yukon, west-central and southern Mackenzie, northern Saskatchewan, north-central Manitoba, northern Ontario, south-central Quebec, southern Labrador and central Newfoundland south to northern Baja California, southern California, southern Nevada, central Arizona, southern New Mexico and western Texas, and, east of the Rocky Mountains, to central Saskatchewan, southern Manitoba, northeastern North Dakota, central Minnesota, northern Wisconsin, northern Michigan, southern Ontario, northeastern Ohio and Massachusetts, also locally in the Appalachians south through New York, Pennsylvania, eastern West Virginia and southwestern Virginia to eastern Tennessee and western North Carolina.

Winters in the mountains of South America from Colombia and Venezuela (also Trinidad) south through Ecuador to southeastern Peru, irregularly in Middle America as far north as Oaxaca and Belize, and casually in southern California.

Migrates regularly through most of the western United States and Middle America, less commonly in the eastern United States, casually along the southern Atlantic coast and in peninsular Florida.

Casual or accidental in northern Alaska (Point Barrow), Bermuda, the Netherlands Antilles, Surinam, Amazonian Brazil and Greenland.

Notes.—Formerly placed in the monotypic genus *Nuttallornis.*

Contopus pertinax Cabanis and Heine. GREATER PEWEE. [460.]

Contopus pertinax (Lichtenstein MS) Cabanis and Heine, 1859, Mus. Heineanum, 2, p. 72. (Xalapa = Jalapa, Veracruz.)

Habitat.—Highland pine, pine-oak association, riparian woodland and humid montane forest edge (Subtropical and Temperate zones).

Distribution.—*Breeds* from central Arizona, southwestern New Mexico, central Chihuahua, southern Coahuila, central Nuevo León and southern Tamaulipas south in the highlands of Mexico and northern Central America (including Belize) to north-central Nicaragua.

Winters from northern Mexico (casually southern Arizona) south through the breeding range in Middle America.

In migration occurs casually in western Texas.

Casual in southern California (north to the Monterey area) and Colorado (Port Lyon).

Notes.—Also known as COUES' FLYCATCHER. *C. pertinax, C. lugubris* and the South American *C. fumigatus* (Lafresnaye and d'Orbigny, 1837), and especially the latter two, are closely related and considered conspecific by some authors; the three species constitute a superspecies. Some authors treat *C. pertinax* as *C. musicus* (Swainson), based on *Tyrannula musica* Swainson, 1827, a name generally regarded as unidentifiable.

Contopus lugubris Lawrence. DARK PEWEE.

Contopus lugubris Lawrence, 1865, Ann. Lyc. Nat. Hist. N.Y., 8, p. 134. (Barranca, Costa Rica.)

Habitat.—Humid montane forest edge, open woodland and clearings (Subtropical and Temperate zones).

Distribution.—*Resident* in the mountains of Costa Rica (from the Cordillera de Tilarán southward) and extreme western Panama (western Chiriquí).

Notes.—See comments under *C. pertinax.*

Contopus ochraceus Sclater and Salvin. OCHRACEOUS PEWEE.

Contopus ochraceus Sclater and Salvin, 1869, Proc. Zool. Soc. London, p. 419. (Costa Rica.)

Habitat.—Humid montane forest (Temperate Zone).

Distribution.—*Resident* locally at high elevations in Costa Rica (Irazú and Turrialba volcanoes, and near Empalme in the Cordillera de Talamanca) and, probably, extreme western Panama (one specimen known from "Chiriquí", regarded as questionable for locality, and sight records from Cerro Punta, Chiriquí).

Contopus sordidulus Sclater. WESTERN WOOD-PEWEE. [462.]

Contopus sordidulus Sclater, 1859, Proc. Zool. Soc. London, p. 43. (In Mexico meridionali et Guatemala = Orizaba, Veracruz.)

Habitat.—Forest, forest edge and woodland, especially coniferous or mixed coniferous-deciduous forest, and poplar or riparian woodland (Subtropical and Temperate zones, in nonbreeding season also Tropical Zone).

Distribution.—*Breeds* from east-central Alaska, southern Yukon, southern Mackenzie, northern Alberta, northwestern and east-central Saskatchewan, south-central Manitoba and northwestern Minnesota (Roseau County) south to southern Baja California and in the interior highlands of Mexico and Guatemala to Honduras and (possibly) north-central Nicaragua, and east to central North Dakota, western South Dakota, western Kansas, western Texas and southern Tamaulipas. Breeding reports from Costa Rica and Panama are unverified; one from Colombia is erroneous (pertaining to *C. cinereus*).

Winters from Colombia and Venezuela south to Peru and Bolivia, casually north to Costa Rica.

Migrates regularly east to western Kansas, and south through Middle America, occurring in lowlands on both slopes as well as in highlands.

Casual or accidental in northern Alaska (Point Barrow, Umiat), Maryland, Massachusetts, southwestern Louisiana, Mississippi, Jamaica and Belize, with reports (based on identification by call) from Iowa, Wisconsin and southern Ontario.

Notes.—This species was formerly known as *C. richardsonii,* based on *Tyrannula Richardsonii* Swainson, 1832, now regarded as a synonym of *Sayornis phoebe* (see Phillips and Parkes, 1955, Condor, 57, p. 244). See also comments under *C. virens.*

Contopus virens (Linnaeus). EASTERN WOOD-PEWEE. [461.]

Muscicapa virens Linnaeus, 1766, Syst. Nat., ed. 12, 1, p. 327. Based on "Le Gobe-mouche condré de la Caroline" Brisson, Ornithologie, 2, p. 368. (in Carolina ad ripas = South Carolina.)

Habitat.—Forest, woodland, scrub, parks, and open situations with scattered trees, breeding in deciduous or mixed deciduous-coniferous forest and forest edge, and in open woodland.

Distribution.—*Breeds* from southeastern Saskatchewan, southern Manitoba, western and southern Ontario, southern Quebec, northern Maine, New Brunswick, Prince Edward Island and Nova Scotia (including Cape Breton Island) south to Texas, the Gulf coast and central Florida, and west to the eastern Dakotas, eastern Nebraska, eastern Kansas, central Oklahoma and south-central Texas.

Winters from Colombia and Venezuela south to Peru and western Brazil, casually north to Costa Rica.

Migrates through the eastern United States, Gulf-Caribbean lowlands of Mexico, and along both slopes from Chiapas, Guatemala and Belize south through Middle America (more abundantly on the Caribbean slope, including most offshore islands), casually through the western Bahamas (New Providence, Grand Bahama, Eleuthera, Mayaguana), western Cuba, the Isle of Pines, Jamaica, Grand Cayman, and islands of the western Caribbean (Swan, Providencia and San Andrés islands, and Albuquerque Cay).

Casual or accidental off Labrador (200 miles at sea), and in eastern Colorado, Arizona, Bermuda and Barbados; a photographic record for California (Farallon Islands) is questionable.

Notes.—*C. virens* and *C. sordidulus* are considered conspecific by some authors; they constitute a superspecies; with conspecific treatment, WOOD PEWEE would be the appropriate English name.

Contopus cinereus (Spix). TROPICAL PEWEE.

Platyrhynchus cinereus Spix, 1825, Avium Spec. Nov. Bras., 2, p. 11, pl. 13, fig. 2. ("in sylvis flum. Amazonum," error = Rio de Janeiro, Brazil.)

Habitat.—Scrubby areas, second-growth woodland, open situations with scattered trees, forest edge, plantations and mangroves (Tropical and lower Subtropical zones, locally in South America to lower Temperate Zone).

Distribution.—*Resident* from eastern Oaxaca and southern Veracruz south along both slopes of Middle America (including Cozumel and Cancun islands off Quintana Roo, and Isla Coiba off Panama) to northern Colombia, northern Venezuela (also Trinidad) and the Guianas, and south in the Andes to Peru; also locally in arid southwestern Ecuador, in extreme southern Venezuela and adjacent northern Brazil, and from central and eastern Brazil south to eastern Bolivia, northern Argentina, Paraguay and southern Brazil.

Contopus caribaeus (d'Orbigny). GREATER ANTILLEAN PEWEE.

Muscipeta caribaea d'Orbigny, 1839, *in* La Sagra, Hist. Fis. Pol. Nat. Cuba, Ois., p. 92. (Cuba = Holguín, Oriente Prov., Cuba.)

Habitat.—Forest, forest edge, open woodland, scrub, brushy areas and mangroves, from mountains to arid lowlands.

Distribution.—*Resident* in the northern Bahama Islands (Grand Bahama, Abaco, New Providence, Eleuthera and Cat islands), and on Cuba (including cays off the coast of both Cuba and the Isle of Pines), Jamaica and Hispaniola (including Gonâve Island).

Accidental on Mona Island (off Puerto Rico).

Notes.—*C. caribaeus* and *C. latirostris* appear to constitute a superspecies.

Contopus latirostris (Verreaux). LESSER ANTILLEAN PEWEE.

Myiobius latirostris Verreaux, 1866, Bull. Nouv. Arch. Mus. Hist. Nat. [Paris], 2, p. 22, pl. 3, fig. 2. (Sainte Lucie, dans la Nouvelle Grenade = St. Lucia, in the Lesser Antilles.)

Habitat.—Mountain forest, wooded hills and coffee plantations, locally on Puerto Rico also in semi-arid, coastal scrub.

Distribution.—*Resident* on Puerto Rico (primarily western and central portions) and in the northern Lesser Antilles (St. Lucia, Martinique, Dominica and Guadeloupe).

Notes.—See comments under *C. caribaeus.*

Genus **EMPIDONAX** Cabanis

Empidonax Cabanis, 1855, J. Ornithol., 3, p. 480. Type, by monotypy, *Empidonax pusillus* Cabanis = *Platyrhynchos virescens* Vieillot.

Empidonax flaviventris (Baird and Baird). YELLOW-BELLIED FLYCATCHER. [463.]

Tyrannula flaviventris W. M. and S. F. Baird, 1843, Proc. Acad. Nat. Sci. Philadelphia, 1, p. 283. ([near Carlisle,] Cumberland Co., Pa.)

Habitat.—Forest, forest edge, clearings, second-growth woodland and swamps, breeding in boreal coniferous forest (primarily spruce, fir, jack pine and tamarack), in winter commonly in humid lowland forest and open woodland.

Distribution.—*Breeds* from northern British Columbia, west-central and southern Mackenzie, northern Saskatchewan, northern Manitoba, northern Ontario, central Quebec, southern Labrador and Newfoundland south to central Alberta, central Saskatchewan, northern North Dakota, northern Minnesota, northern Wisconsin, northern Michigan, southern Ontario, northeastern Pennsylvania, central New York, New Brunswick, Prince Edward Island and Nova Scotia, with isolated breeding in western Virginia (Mt. Rogers, since 1977).

Winters in Middle America from southern Tamaulipas, southeastern San Luis Potosí and Puebla on the Gulf-Caribbean slope and eastern Oaxaca on the Pacific slope south to western Panama (casually east to the Canal Zone and Darién).

Migrates regularly through the eastern United States west to the central Great Plains and central Texas, uncommonly through the Gulf and South Atlantic states from South Carolina to eastern Louisiana, and casually through eastern New Mexico, western Texas and peninsular Florida.

Casual in east-central Alaska. Accidental in California (Farallon Islands), Arizona (Tucson), Cuba and Greenland.

Empidonax virescens (Vieillot). ACADIAN FLYCATCHER. [465.]

Muscicapa querula (not Vieillot, 1807) Wilson, 1810, Am. Ornithol., 2, p. 77, pl. 13, fig. 3. (No locality given = near Philadelphia, Pennsylvania.)

Platyrhynchos virescens Vieillot, 1818, Nouv. Dict. Hist. Nat., nouv. éd., 27, p. 22. New name for *Muscicapa querula* Wilson, preoccupied.

Habitat.—Humid deciduous forest (primarily mature), woodland, thickets, second growth and plantations.

Distribution.—*Breeds* from southeastern South Dakota, northern Iowa, extreme southeastern Minnesota, southern Wisconsin, southern Michigan, extreme southern Ontario, northeastern Pennsylvania, southern New York, Massachusetts, Vermont and (probably) southern New Hampshire south to central and southern Texas (west to Tom Greene County), the Gulf coast and central Florida, and west to eastern Nebraska, central Kansas and central Oklahoma.

Winters on the Caribbean slope of Nicaragua, on both slopes (more commonly on the Caribbean) of Costa Rica and Panama (including Taboguilla and the Pearl islands), and in northern and western Colombia, northern Venezuela and western Ecuador.

In migration occurs regularly (but uncommonly recorded) on the Gulf-Caribbean slope of Middle America from northeastern Mexico south to Costa Rica, and casually west to western South Dakota (at least formerly) and western Nebraska, and through the Bahamas (recorded from Grand Bahama, New Providence and Cay Lobos) and western Cuba.

Accidental in southeastern British Columbia (Barriere area) and Arizona (Tucson).

Empidonax alnorum Brewster. ALDER FLYCATCHER. [466.1.]

Empidonax traillii alnorum Brewster, 1895, Auk, 12, p. 161. (Upton, Maine.)

Habitat.—Brushy and scrubby growth, thickets, deciduous forest edge, open second growth, and swamps, breeding in damp thickets of alder and various shrubs, in bogs, along marshy borders of lakes, and in brush along stream banks, in winter also in open woodland.

Distribution.—*Breeds* from central Alaska, central Yukon, northwestern and southern Mackenzie, northern Alberta, northern Saskatchewan, northern Manitoba, northern Ontario, central and eastern Quebec, southern Labrador and southern Newfoundland south to southern Alaska, south-central British Columbia, southern Alberta, southern Saskatchewan, northern North Dakota, south-central Minnesota, central Michigan, southern Ontario, south-central Ohio, western Maryland, eastern Pennsylvania, southern New York and Connecticut; and in the Appalachians south to eastern Tennessee, western Virginia and western North Carolina. Recorded in summer (and possibly breeding) in southeastern Iowa, northeastern Missouri and northern Indiana.

Winters presumably in South America (definitely recorded only in Peru, on the basis of call); individuals of the "*traillii* complex" have been reported in South America from Colombia and northwestern Venezuela south, east of the Andes, to eastern Peru, Bolivia and northern Argentina.

In migration reported irregularly in the eastern United States, casually west to Colorado; presumably migrates through Middle America (mostly Caribbean slope, reported from Costa Rica), as few records of the complex exist for the West Indies.

Casual in northern Alaska, Cuba, the Isles of Pines (possibly referable to *E. traillii*) and Bermuda.

Notes.—*E. alnorum* and *E. traillii* are closely related, virtually indistinguishable morphologically, differing primarily in vocalizations and ecology; formerly recognized as a single species, *E. traillii* [TRAILL'S FLYCATCHER, 466], the two are now considered as constituting a superspecies [="*traillii* complex"].

Empidonax traillii (Audubon). WILLOW FLYCATCHER. [466.]

> *Muscicapa Traillii* Audubon, 1828, Birds Am. (folio), 1, pl. 45 (1831, Ornithol. Biogr., 1, p. 236). (woods along the prairie lands of the Arkansas River = Fort of Arkansas [Arkansas Post], Arkansas.)

Habitat.—Thickets, scrubby and brushy areas, open second growth, swamps and open woodland, breeding primarily in swampy thickets, especially of willow and buttonbush.

Distribution.—*Breeds* from central British Columbia, southern Alberta, southern Saskatchewan, southwestern Manitoba, northern North Dakota, western and southern Minnesota, southern Wisconsin, central Michigan, southern Ontario, southern Quebec, central Maine and Nova Scotia south to southern California (local, formerly widespread), northern Baja California (at least formerly), southern Arizona, southern New Mexico, western and central Texas, northeastern Oklahoma, Arkansas, central Tennessee, northern Georgia, western North Carolina, and central and eastern Virginia.

Winters in Middle America from Veracruz and Oaxaca (at least casually) south to Panama (where recorded by vocalizations as well as by specimens).

In migration recorded widely in the southern United States, presumably occurring as a regular migrant through Middle America south to the limits of the wintering range.

Casual north to New Brunswick.

Notes.—Sometimes treated as *E. brewsteri* Oberholser, 1918, but *traillii* clearly pertains to this species and has priority. See also comments under *E. alnorum*.

Empidonax albigularis Sclater and Salvin. WHITE-THROATED FLYCATCHER.

> *Empidonax albigularis* Sclater and Salvin, 1859, Ibis, p. 122. (Dueñas [Guatemala].)

Habitat.—Brushy fields, grassy areas, scrub and second growth (Subtropical and lower Temperate zones, in winter also to Tropical Zone).

Distribution.—*Breeds* in the highlands from southwestern Chihuahua, Durango, Zacatecas, San Luis Potosí and southern Tamaulipas south through interior Mexico, Guatemala and Honduras to north-central Nicaragua; and in central Costa Rica (vicinity of Cartago) and western Panama (Chiriquí).

Winters from Jalisco, Guanajuato and Hidalgo south through the breeding range, descending into lowlands (recorded near sea level in Veracruz, Oaxaca, Belize, Guatemala and Honduras), casually to Costa Rica and central Panama (recorded Bocas del Toro and the Canal Zone).

Empidonax euleri (Cabanis). EULER'S FLYCATCHER.

> *Empidochanes Euleri* Cabanis, 1868, J. Ornithol., 16, p. 195. (Cantagallo, Rio de Janeiro, Brazil.)

Habitat.—Humid forest, open woodland and plantations (Tropical and lower Subtropical zones).

Distribution.—*Resident* in the southern Lesser Antilles (on Grenada, where possibly extirpated); and in South America from eastern Colombia across northern Venezuela (also Trinidad) to Surinam (one record), and south, east of the Andes, to eastern Peru, thence eastward over Amazonian Brazil to eastern Brazil and south to eastern Bolivia, Paraguay, northern Argentina and Uruguay. Southern breeding populations migrate northward to Colombia and Venezuela.

Notes.—Relationships within this species are not well understood. The northern forms, including that on Grenada, are sometimes recognized as a distinct species, *E. lawrencei* Allen, 1889 [LAWRENCE'S FLYCATCHER].

Empidonax minimus (Baird and Baird). LEAST FLYCATCHER. [467.]

Tyrannula minima W. M. and S. F. Baird, 1843, Proc. Acad. Nat. Sci. Philadelphia, 1, p. 284. ([near Carlisle,] Cumberland Co., Pa.)

Habitat.—Open woodland and brushy areas, breeding in poplar woodland, deciduous scrub, forest edge, parks and gardens.

Distribution.—*Breeds* from southern Yukon, west-central and southern Mackenzie, northern Alberta, northern Saskatchewan, north-central Manitoba, northern Ontario, southern Quebec, New Brunswick, Prince Edward Island and Nova Scotia south to southern British Columbia, central Montana, northeastern Wyoming, central and southeastern South Dakota, eastern Nebraska, southwestern Missouri, central Illinois, south-central Indiana, northern Ohio, Pennsylvania, central New Jersey and, in the Appalachians, through West Virginia, western Maryland, western Virginia, eastern Tennessee and western North Carolina to northwestern Georgia. Recorded in summer (and possibly breeding) in northeastern Washington and eastern Kentucky.

Winters from southern Sonora and southern Tamaulipas south along both slopes of Middle America to Honduras and northern Nicaragua, casually to Costa Rica and central Panama (east to the Canal Zone); also casually in southern California, southern Texas and Florida.

Migrates commonly through the south-central United States from the Mississippi Valley and northern Gulf states west to the Rockies and through most of Mexico (except the northwestern portion), casually (or regularly in small numbers), primarily in the fall, from southwestern British Columbia south through California (including the Farallon Islands), southern Nevada, western Arizona and Sonora, and in the southeastern United States through the South Atlantic and southern Gulf states.

Accidental in the Cayman Islands (Grand Cayman).

Empidonax hammondii (Xántus de Vesey). HAMMOND'S FLYCATCHER. [468.]

Tyrannula hammondii Xántus de Vesey, 1858, Proc. Acad. Nat. Sci. Philadelphia, 10, p. 117. (Fort Tejon, California.)

Habitat.—Cool forest and woodland, breeding primarily in dense fir, in migration and winter through deserts and in scrub, pine and pine-oak association.

Distribution.—*Breeds* from east-central Alaska, southern Yukon, northern British Columbia, southwestern Alberta, western and south-central Montana, and northwestern Wyoming south to southeastern Alaska, and through British Columbia and the Pacific states to east-central California (south to Tulare County), east-central Nevada, central Utah, northeastern Arizona, western Colorado and north-central New Mexico.

Winters from southeastern Arizona (casually southern California), western Chihuahua, southern Coahuila, central Nuevo León and central Tamaulipas south through the highlands of Mexico, Guatemala and El Salvador to Honduras and (probably) north-central Nicaragua; reports from Peru are unfounded.

Migrates regularly through the southwestern United States (east to western Texas) and northern Mexico, casually east to western Nebraska, west-central Kansas, western Oklahoma and central Texas.

Accidental in northern Alaska (Sadlerochit River), Pennsylvania (Schnecksville) and Louisiana (Woodworth).

Empidonax oberholseri Phillips. DUSKY FLYCATCHER. [469.]

Empidonax oberholseri Phillips, 1939, Auk, 56, p. 311. (Hart Prairie, San Francisco Mountain, Arizona.)

Habitat.—Scrub, brushy areas, thickets and open areas with scattered trees, breeding in aspen groves, willow thickets, open coniferous forest and mountain chaparral, especially in areas near water, in migration and winter also through open woodland and deserts.

Distribution.—*Breeds* from southwestern Yukon south through northwestern and central British Columbia to north-central Washington, thence eastward through southern Alberta to southwestern Saskatchewan, and south (except in coastal areas of Washington and Oregon) to southern California, southern Nevada, southwestern Utah, central Arizona, and central and northeastern New Mexico, and east to southeastern Montana, western South Dakota (Black Hills) and central Colorado.

Winters from southern California (casually), southern Arizona, Sonora, northwestern Durango, southern Coahuila, central Nuevo León and central Tamaulipas south, mostly in the highlands, to Guerrero and Oaxaca, casually south to northwestern Guatemala (Huehuetenango).

Migrates regularly through the southwestern United States (east to southwestern Kansas and western Texas), casually through the coastal areas of Washington and Oregon, to Baja California, and east to central and southern Texas.

Accidental in northern Alaska (Icy Cape) and Pennsylvania (Kutztown).

Notes.—Formerly known as *E. wrightii* [WRIGHT'S FLYCATCHER]; all records of *E. wrightii* prior to 1939 and most prior to 1957 pertain to *E. oberholseri.*

Empidonax wrightii Baird. GRAY FLYCATCHER. [469.1.]

Empidonax wrightii Baird, 1858, *in* Baird, Cassin and Lawrence, Rep. Explor. Surv. R. R. Pac., 9, p. 200 (in text). (El Paso, Texas.)

Habitat.—Arid woodland and brushy areas, breeding in sagebrush, pinyon-juniper woodland and, less frequently, open pine-oak association, in migration and winter also in arid scrub, riparian woodland and mesquite.

Distribution.—*Breeds* from south-central Washington, central and eastern Oregon, south-central Idaho, southern Wyoming, northeastern Utah and central Colorado south to south-central California (San Bernardino County), southern Nevada, central Arizona and south-central New Mexico.

Winters from southern California (rarely), central Arizona, southern Coahuila and central Tamaulipas south to southern Baja California, Jalisco, northern Michoacán, the state of Mexico and Puebla, casually to central Oaxaca.

Migrates regularly through the southwestern United States east to eastern New Mexico and western Texas, casually to southwestern Kansas, and through northern Mexico.

Casual in northern Wyoming. Accidental in Ontario (Toronto) and Massachusetts (Littleton).

Notes.—Formerly known as *E. griseus* Brewster, 1889. See also comments under *E. oberholseri*.

Empidonax affinis (Swainson). PINE FLYCATCHER.

Empidonax affinis Swainson, 1827, Philos. Mag., new ser., 1, p. 367. (Maritime parts of Mexico = Temascaltepec, state of México.)

Habitat.—Pine and pine-oak woodland, less frequently humid montane forest (Subtropical and Temperate zones).

Distribution.—*Breeds* from northern Sinaloa, central Chihuahua, southern Coahuila, Zacatecas and San Luis Potosí south in the Mexican highlands to central Oaxaca, Puebla and west-central Veracruz.

Winters generally throughout the breeding range and south in the highlands to central Guatemala.

Empidonax difficilis Baird. WESTERN FLYCATCHER. [464.]

Empidonax difficilis Baird, 1858, *in* Baird, Cassin and Lawrence, Rep. Explor. Surv. R. R. Pac., 9, pp. xxx, 198 (in text). (west coast of United States, Fort Steilacoom, Shoalwater Bay, Washington, Fort Tejon, California = Fort Steilacoom, Washington.)

Habitat.—Humid coniferous and montane forest, dense second-growth woodland, and pine-oak association, breeding along streams with nest placed in cliffs, rock walls, earth banks or buildings, wintering also to humid lowland forest (Subtropical and Temperate zones).

Distribution.—*Breeds* from southeastern Alaska, northwestern and central British Columbia (including the Queen Charlotte and Vancouver islands), southwestern Alberta, northern Idaho, western Montana, Wyoming and western South Dakota south to southwestern California (generally west of the Sierra Nevada), central Nevada, and central and southeastern Arizona, in the mountains of northern and southern Baja California, and in the Mexican highlands to Oaxaca (west of the Isthmus of Tehuantepec), Puebla and west-central Veracruz, and east to western Nebraska (rarely), central Colorado, central New Mexico and western Texas.

Winters from southern Baja California and northern Mexico (casually to southern California and southern Arizona) south through the breeding range, occurring also in lowlands areas south to the Isthmus of Tehuantepec; reports from Chiapas, Guatemala and Honduras are based on *E. flavescens*.

In migration recorded casually in the Tres Marias Islands (off Nayarit), eastern New Mexico and southwestern Kansas.

Notes.—*E. difficilis* and *E. flavescens* are closely related and considered conspecific by some authors; they constitute a superspecies.

Empidonax flavescens Lawrence. YELLOWISH FLYCATCHER.

Empidonax flavescens Lawrence, 1865, Ann. Lyc. Nat. Hist. N.Y., 8, p. 133. (Barranca, Costa Rica.)

Habitat.—Humid montane forest and forest edge, occasionally in moist canyons in pine-oak association (Subtropical and lower Temperate zones).

Distribution.—*Resident* in the highlands of southeastern Veracruz (Sierra de Tuxtla), eastern Oaxaca (Sierra Madre de Chiapas), Guatemala, El Salvador, Honduras, north-central Nicaragua, Costa Rica and western Panama (Chiriquí and Veraguas).

Notes.—See comments under *E. difficilis*.

Empidonax fulvifrons (Giraud). BUFF-BREASTED FLYCATCHER. [470.]

Muscicapa fulvifrons Giraud, 1841, Descr. Sixteen New Spec. N. Am. Birds, pl. 4, fig. 2. (Texas, error = Miquiahuana, Tamaulipas.)

Habitat.—Pine, pine-oak association and riparian woodland, in winter occasionally in open deciduous woodland (Subtropical and lower Temperate zones, in winter casually to Tropical Zone).

Distribution.—*Breeds* from east-central and southeastern Arizona (formerly to Prescott in central Arizona), west-central New Mexico (at least formerly), northeastern Sonora, Chihuahua, Durango, Zacatecas, San Luis Potosí, Guanajuato and Hidalgo south through the highlands of Mexico, Guatemala and El Salvador to central Honduras.

Winters from Sonora and Chihuahua south through the breeding range, occurring also in adjacent lowlands.

Empidonax atriceps Salvin. BLACK-CAPPED FLYCATCHER.

Empidonax atriceps Salvin, 1870, Proc. Zool. Soc. London, p. 198. (Volcán de Chiriquí, Panama.)

Habitat.—Brushy clearing and forest edge in humid highlands (upper Subtropical and Temperate zones).

Distribution.—*Resident* in the mountains of Costa Rica (Cordillera Central, Dota Mountains and Cordillera de Talamanca) and western Panama (Chiriquí and Bocas del Toro).

Genus **NESOTRICCUS** Townsend

Nesotriccus C. H. Townsend, 1895, Bull. Mus. Comp. Zool. Harv., 27, p. 124. Type, by original designation, *Nesotriccus ridgwayi* Townsend.

Notes.—Skull characters suggest placement of this genus in the Elaeniinae, probably near *Phaeomyias* (*fide* Lanyon).

Nesotriccus ridgwayi Townsend. COCOS FLYCATCHER.

Nesotriccus Ridgwayi C. H. Townsend, 1895, Bull. Mus. Comp. Zool. Harv., 27, p. 124. (Cocos Island.)

Habitat.—Forest, scrub, woodland and tangled undergrowth.
Distribution.—*Resident* on Cocos Island, off Costa Rica.

Genus **SAYORNIS** Bonaparte

Sayornis Bonaparte, 1854, C. R. Acad. Sci. Paris, 38, p. 657. Type, by monotypy, *Sayornis nigricans* Bonaparte = *Tyrannula nigricans* Swainson.

Sayornis nigricans (Swainson). BLACK PHOEBE. [458.]

Tyrannula nigricans Swainson, 1827, Philos. Mag., new ser., 1, p. 367. (Table land of Mexico = Valley of Mexico.)

Habitat.—Usually near water, especially along streams in a variety of situations from open to wooded, nesting in rocky canyon walls, in coastal cliffs, and under bridges or on other man-made structures (Tropical to Temperate zones).

Distribution.—*Breeds* from northwestern California, southern Nevada, southwestern Utah, central Arizona, south-central Colorado (Pueblo, 1972–1974), central New Mexico, and western and west-central Texas (east to Crockett and Val Verde counties) south to southern Baja California and, mostly in the highlands, through Middle America (except the Yucatan Peninsula) and South America east to northern Venezuela and south through Colombia, Ecuador, Peru and Bolivia to northwestern Argentina.

Partially migratory, northern populations wandering after the breeding season and tropical ones descending to lower elevations.

Casual north to southern British Columbia (Vancouver), western Washington and Oregon, and east to southeastern Texas and Florida, also a sight report for Minnesota.

Notes.—Birds from central Panama south through South America have sometimes been regarded as a distinct species, *S. latirostris* (Cabanis and Heine, 1859) [WHITE-WINGED PHOEBE].

Sayornis phoebe (Latham). EASTERN PHOEBE. [456.]

Muscicapa Phœbe Latham, 1790, Index Ornithol., 2, p. 489. Based on the "Dusky Fly-catcher" Pennant, Arct. Zool., 2, p. 389, and the "Phoebe Flycatcher" Latham, Gen. Synop. Birds, suppl., 1, p. 173. (in America septentrionali, Noveboraco = New York).

Habitat.—Open woodland, situations with scattered trees, and farmlands, usually near water, nesting on cliffs, under bridges and eaves, and sometimes inside buildings.

Distribution.—*Breeds* from northeastern British Columbia, west-central and southern Mackenzie, northern Saskatchewan, northern Manitoba, western and central Ontario, southwestern Quebec, central New Brunswick and southern Nova Scotia south to southern Alberta, southwestern South Dakota, southeastern Colorado, central New Mexico, central and northeastern Texas, northwestern Louisiana, Arkansas, southwestern Tennessee, northeastern Mississippi, central Alabama, northern Georgia, western South Carolina and North Carolina.

Winters from Chihuahua, central Texas, the Gulf states and Virginia (casually from Oklahoma, southern Missouri, the Ohio Valley, southern Ontario and New England) south to Oaxaca, Veracruz and southern Florida.

Casual west to the Pacific coast from southwestern Yukon and southern British Columbia to Baja California and Arizona, on St. Pierre (off Newfoundland), and to Quintana Roo, Cuba, the Bahamas (Grand Bahama, Bimini) and Bermuda, also sight repots for Sonora and Sinaloa.

Sayornis saya (Bonaparte). SAY'S PHOEBE. [457.]

Muscicapa saya Bonaparte, 1825, Am. Ornithol., 1, p. 20, pl. 11, fig. 3. (Arkansaw River, about twenty miles from the Rocky Mountains = near Pueblo, Colorado.)

Habitat.—Arid scrub, desert and partly open situations in arid habitats, nesting frequently on cliffs and in abandoned mine and ranch buildings, ranging into more humid open country in nonbreeding season.

Distribution.—*Breeds* from western and northern Alaska, northern Yukon, northwestern and central Mackenzie, central Alberta, central Saskatchewan and southwestern Manitoba south to southern California (absent or very rare west of the coastal ranges from southern Alaska to central California), northern Baja California, Michoacán, Guanajuato and Hidalgo, and east to the central Dakotas, northwestern Iowa, east-central Nebraska, central Kansas, western Oklahoma, western and northern Texas, Nuevo León and San Luis Potosí.

Winters from northern California, northern Arizona, central (rarely northern) New Mexico and central Texas south (including islands off southern California) to southern Baja California, Oaxaca and Veracruz.

In migration occurs rarely in the coastal areas of southeastern Alaska, British Columbia, Washington and Oregon, and casually east to western Iowa, western Missouri, Arkansas and eastern Texas.

Casual or accidental in south-coastal Alaska; east across the northern United States (south to Iowa, Illinois and the Ohio Valley), southern Ontario and southern Quebec to Nova Scotia, New England, Pennsylvania and New Jersey; and east along the Gulf coast to east-central Florida.

Genus **PYROCEPHALUS** Gould

Pyrocephalus Gould, 1839, *in* Darwin, Zool. Voy. Beagle, 3 (9), p. 44. Type, by subsequent designation (G. R. Gray, 1840), "*P. coronatus* (L) Gould" = *Pyrocephalus major* Pelzeln = *Muscicapa rubinus* Boddaert.

Pyrocephalus rubinus (Boddaert). VERMILION FLYCATCHER. [471.]

Muscicapa rubinus Boddaert, 1783, Table Planches Enlum., p. 42. Based on Daubenton, Planches Enlum., pl. 675, fig. 2. (riviere des Amazones = Teffé, Brazil.)

Habitat.—Arid scrub, desert, savanna, cultivated lands, and riparian woodland edge (Tropical to Temperate zones).

Distribution.—*Breeds* from southern California (north to San Bernardino County), southern Nevada, central Arizona, central (rarely northern) New Mexico, western Oklahoma, and western and central Texas south through Mexico (including Baja California and the Yucatan Peninsula) to northern Guatemala (Petén) and Belize; in the lowland pine savanna of the Mosquitia of eastern Honduras and northeastern Nicaragua; in the Galapagos Islands; from northern Colombia east across northern Venezuela to Guyana and south, west of the Andes, to extreme northern Chile; in north-central Brazil; and from northern Argentina and Paraguay south to central Argentina and Uruguay.

Winters from southern California, southern Nevada, northern Arizona, central New Mexico, central Texas and the Gulf coast (east to south-central Florida) south through the breeding range in Middle America, casually to central Guatemala, northern Honduras and southern Florida; and in South America where the more northern populations (including that of the Galapagos Islands) are essentially resident while the southern ones from Peru and Paraguay southward migrate northward, east of the Andes, to eastern Colombia and Amazonian Brazil.

In North America casual north and east to central California, Colorado, South Dakota, central Minnesota, northern Illinois, southern Ontario, Ohio, West Virginia, Kentucky, Tennessee and Georgia; also in Panama (western Panamá province and the Canal Zone), presumably individuals of South American origin.

Genus FLUVICOLA Swainson

Fluvicola Swainson, 1827, Zool. J., 3, p. 172. Type, by subsequent designation (Swainson, 1831), *Fluvicola cursoria* Swainson = *Lanius nengeta* Linnaeus.

Fluvicola pica (Boddaert). PIED WATER-TYRANT.

Muscicapa Pica Boddaert, 1783, Table Planches Enlum., p. 42. Based on Daubenton, Planches Enlum., pl. 675, fig. 1. (Cayenne.)

Habitat.—Fresh-water marshes, ponds, swamps, stream banks, reedbeds and adjacent brushy areas (Tropical Zone).

Distribution.—*Resident* locally in Panama (eastern Panamá province, Canal Zone and Darién), and in South America from northern Colombia east across northern and central Venezuela (also Trinidad) to the Guianas, and south, east of the Andes, to eastern Peru and northern Bolivia, thence eastward across Amazonian Brazil (mostly south of the Amazon) to eastern Brazil and south to northern Argentina and Uruguay.

Notes.—The southern form from eastern Peru eastward and southward may represent a distinct species, *F. albiventer* (Spix, 1825).

Genus COLONIA Gray

Colonia J. E. Gray, 1827, *in* Cuvier and Griffith, Anim. Kingdom, 6, p. 336. Type, by monotypy, *Muscicapa colonus* Vieillot.

Colonia colonus (Vieillot). LONG-TAILED TYRANT.

Muscicapa colonus Vieillot, 1818, Nouv. Dict. Hist. Nat., nouv. éd., 21, p. 448. Based on "Suiriri El Colón" Azara, Apunt. Hist. Nat. Páx. Parag., 2, p. 114 (no. 180). (Paraguay.)

Habitat.—Humid lowland and foothill forest, forest edge, and areas of scattered trees near water (Tropical and lower Subtropical zones).

Distribution.—*Resident* on the Caribbean slope of northeastern Honduras (Olancho, Gracias a Dios), Nicaragua and Costa Rica, on both slopes of Panama, and in South America from Colombia, southern Venezuela and the Guianas south, west of the Andes to western Ecuador and east of the Andes to eastern Peru, central Bolivia, Paraguay, extreme northeastern Argentina and southern Brazil.

[Genus MACHETORNIS Gray]

Chrysolophus (not Gray, 1834) Swainson, 1837, Class. Birds, 2, p. 225. Type, by monotypy, *C. ambulans.* Spix, II, pl. 23 = *Tyrannus rixosus* Vieillot.

Machetornis G. R. Gray, 1841, List. Gen. Birds, ed. 2, p. 41. New name for *Chrysolophus,* Vieillot, preoccupied.

[**Machetornis rixosus** (Vieillot). CATTLE TYRANT.] See Appendix A.

Subfamily TYRANNINAE: Tyrannine Flycatchers

Genus ATTILA Lesson

Attila Lesson, 1831, Traité Ornithol., livr. 5 (1830), p. 360. Type, by monotypy, *Attila brasiliensis* Lesson = *Muscicapa spadicea* Gmelin.

Notes.—The genera *Attila, Rhytipterna* and *Laniocera* have often been placed in the Cotingidae, but recent studies by various workers indicate a relationship with the Tyrannidae (but see also comments under *Laniocera*).

Attila spadiceus (Gmelin). BRIGHT-RUMPED ATTILA.

Muscicapa spadicea Gmelin, 1789, Syst. Nat., 1 (2), p. 937. Based on the "Yellow-rumped Flycatcher" Latham, Gen. Synop. Birds, 2 (1), p. 354 (in Cayenna = Cayenne.)

Habitat.—Humid forest, forest edge, clearings and second-growth woodland (Tropical and Subtropical zones).

Distribution.—*Resident* from extreme southern Sonora, Sinaloa, western Durango, Nayarit, Jalisco, Colima, Michoacán, the state of México, San Luis Potosí and Veracruz south along both slopes of Middle America (including the Yucatan Peninsula, Cozumel and other islands off Quintana Roo, and Coiba and Parida islands off Panama), and in South America from Colombia, Venezuela (also Trinidad) and the Guianas south, west of the Andes to western Ecuador and east of the Andes to eastern Peru, northern and eastern Bolivia, and Amazonian and coastal southeastern Brazil.

Genus LANIOCERA Lesson

Laniocera Lesson, 1840, Rev. Zool. [Paris], 3, p. 353. Type, by monotypy, *Laniocera sanguinaria* Lesson = *Ampelis hypopyrra* Vieillot.

Notes.—Recent examination of characters of the skull and syrinx suggest that this genus is not properly placed in the Tyranninae (*fide* Lanyon); its relationships remain uncertain. See also comments under *Attila.*

Laniocera rufescens (Sclater). SPECKLED MOURNER.

Lipaugus rufescens Sclater, 1858, Proc. Zool. Soc. London (1857), p. 276. (In rep. Guatimalensi prope urbem Coban = Cobán, Vera Paz, Guatemala.)

Habitat.—Humid lowland forest and dense, second-growth woodland (Tropical Zone).

Distribution.—*Resident* locally on the Gulf-Caribbean slope from southern Mexico (Chiapas) south through Central America to Costa Rica (also one record from central Pacific lowlands) and Panama (Caribbean slope throughout, and Pacific slope from the Canal Zone eastward), and in northern and western Colombia and northwestern Ecuador.

Notes.—*L. rufescens* and the South American *L. hypopyrra* (Vieillot, 1817) may constitute a superspecies.

Genus **RHYTIPTERNA** Reichenbach

Rhytipterna Reichenbach, 1850, Avium Syst. Nat., pl. 65. Type, by subsequent designation (G. R. Gray, 1855), *Tyrannus calcaratus* Swainson = *Muscicapa simplex* Lichtenstein.

Notes.—See comments under *Attila.*

Rhytipterna holerythra (Sclater and Salvin). RUFOUS MOURNER.

Lipaugus holerythra Sclater and Salvin, 1861, Proc. Zool. Soc. London (1860), p. 300. (Choctum, Vera Paz, Guatemala.)

Habitat.—Humid lowland and foothill forest and forest edge, second growth, partly cleared woodland, and plantations (Tropical and lower Subtropical zones).

Distribution.—*Resident* from southeastern Mexico (Veracruz, northern Oaxaca and Chiapas) south on the Gulf-Caribbean slope of northern Central America to Nicaragua, on both slopes of Costa Rica (absent from dry northwest) and Panama (more widespread on Caribbean slope), and in northern and western Colombia and northwestern Ecuador.

Notes.—*R. holerythra* and the South American *R. simplex* (Lichtenstein, 1823) appear to constitute a superspecies.

Genus **SIRYSTES** Cabanis and Heine

Sirystes Cabanis and Heine, 1859, Mus. Heineanum, 2, p. 75. Type, by monotypy, *Muscicapa sibilator* Vieillot.

Sirystes sibilator (Vieillot). SIRYSTES.

Muscicapa sibilator Vieillot, 1818, Nouv. Dict. Hist. Nat., nouv. éd., 21, p. 457. Based on "Suiriri Pitador" Azara, Apunt. Hist. Nat. Páx. Parag., 2, p. 135 (no. 191). (Paraguay.)

Habitat.—Humid lowland and foothill forest (Tropical and lower Subtropical zones).

Distribution.—*Resident* in Panama (Veraguas, and from the Canal Zone eastward), and in South America from northern Colombia and southwestern Venezuela south, east of the Andes, to eastern Peru and northern Bolivia, thence eastward across Amazonian Brazil and southern Surinam to eastern Brazil, and south to southern Paraguay, extreme northeastern Argentina and southern Brazil.

Genus **MYIARCHUS** Cabanis

Myiarchus Cabanis, 1844, Arch. Naturgesch., 10, p. 272. Type, by subsequent designation (G. R. Gray, 1855), *Muscicapa ferox* Gmelin.

Hylonax Ridgway, 1905, Proc. Biol. Soc. Wash., 18, p. 210. Type, by original designation, *Myiarchus validus* Cabanis.

Myiarchus yucatanensis Lawrence. YUCATAN FLYCATCHER.

Myiarchus yucatanensis Lawrence, 1871, Proc. Acad. Nat. Sci. Philadelphia, 22, p. 235. (Yucatan = Merida, state of Yucatán.)

Habitat.—Open deciduous forest, forest edge, second-growth woodland and partly cleared lands (Tropical Zone).

Distribution.—*Resident* on the Yucatan Peninsula (Campeche, the state of Yucatán, and Quintana Roo) and Cozumel Island, with reports (based on vocalizations) from Belize (Gallon Jug).

Myiarchus barbirostris (Swainson). SAD FLYCATCHER.

> *Tyrannula barbirostris* Swainson, 1827, Philos. Mag., new ser., 1, p. 367. (Mexico, error = Jamaica.)

Habitat.—Open woodland and mountain forest.

Distribution.—*Resident* on Jamaica.

Notes.—See comments under *M. tuberculifer.*

Myiarchus tuberculifer (d'Orbigny and Lafresnaye). DUSKY-CAPPED FLYCATCHER. [455.]

> *Tyrannus tuberculifer* d'Orbigny and Lafresnaye, 1837, Mag. Zool. [Paris], 7, cl. 2, pl. 77–79, p. 43. (Guarayos, [Santa Cruz], Bolivia.)

Habitat.—Open forest, forest edge, second-growth woodland, parks and plantations, primarily in humid regions, less frequently in arid situations (Tropical and Subtropical zones).

Distribution.—*Breeds* from northern Sonora, southeastern Arizona, southwestern New Mexico, Chihuahua, Coahuila, central Nuevo León and central Tamaulipas south along both slopes of Middle America (including the Tres Marias Islands off Nayarit, the Yucatan Peninsula and Cozumel Island off Quintana Roo, and most islands off the Pacific coast of Panama), and in South America from Colombia, Venezuela (also Trinidad) and the Guianas south, west of the Andes to northwestern Peru and east of the Andes to eastern Peru, eastern Bolivia, northwestern Argentina, Paraguay and southeastern Brazil.

Winters from southern Sonora, Durango, southern Nuevo León and southern Tamaulipas south through the breeding range, the populations in the southwestern United States, extreme northern Mexico, and the Yucatan Peninsula being migratory, the remaining mostly sedentary; also the southernmost populations in South America are migratory, ranging northward in winter.

In migration occurs casually in western Texas.

Casual in California (north to Santa Cruz County and Death Valley regions), Colorado, Baja California (Sierra Laguna), and on Isla Isabela (off Nayarit).

Notes.—Also known as OLIVACEOUS FLYCATCHER. *M. tuberculifer* and *M. barbirostris* are closely related and have been considered as conspecific by some authors, but see Lanyon (1967, Bull. Am. Mus. Nat. Hist., 136, pp. 342–346); they constitute a superspecies.

Myiarchus panamensis Lawrence. PANAMA FLYCATCHER.

> *Myiarchus panamensis* Lawrence, 1860, Ann. Lyc. Nat. Hist. N.Y., 7, p. 284. (Isthmus of Panama.)

Habitat.—Open woodland, forest edge, partly cleared lands, scrubby areas and mangroves (Tropical and lower Subtropical zones).

Distribution.—*Resident* in Costa Rica (Pacific coast from the Gulf of Nicoya southward, primarily in mangroves), Panama (both slopes, including Coiba, Taboga and the Pearl islands), northern Colombia and northwestern Venezuela.

Notes.—Closely related to the widespread South American *M. ferox* (Gmelin, 1789) [SHORT-CRESTED FLYCATCHER], from which it differs primarily in vocalizations. *M. panamensis* and *M. ferox* constitute a superspecies.

Myiarchus cinerascens (Lawrence). ASH-THROATED FLYCATCHER. [454.]

> *Tyrannula cinerascens* Lawrence, 1851, Ann. Lyc. Nat. Hist. N.Y., 5, p. 121. (Western Texas.)

Habitat.—Desert scrub, pinyon-juniper and oak woodland, chaparral, thorn scrub and riparian woodland, in winter also in open deciduous woodland.

Distribution.—*Breeds* from northwestern Oregon, eastern Washington, southern Idaho, northern Utah, southern Wyoming, Colorado, western Kansas, New Mexico, and northern and central Texas south to southern Baja California, southern Sonora, and in the Mexican highlands to northern Jalisco, northern Michoacán (at least formerly), northern Guanajuato, southern San Luis Potosí and southern Tamaulipas.

Winters from southern California, central Arizona, Chihuahua, Nuevo León and southern Tamaulipas (casually farther north in the breeding range) south throughout most of western and interior Mexico and interior Guatemala, and on the Pacific slope to Honduras, casually to Nicaragua and northern Costa Rica (San Carlos).

Casual north to southern British Columbia and Montana; east to Illinois and the northeastern Atlantic region (recorded New York and Massachusetts south to Maryland, also sight records to Quebec, Maine, Virginia and North Carolina); and southeast along the Gulf coast to southern Alabama and western Florida.

Notes.—*M. cinerascens* and *M. nuttingi* constitute a superspecies. See also comments under *M. crinitus.*

Myiarchus nuttingi Ridgway. NUTTING'S FLYCATCHER. [453.1.]

> *Myiarchus nuttingi* Ridgway, 1883, *in* Nutting, Proc. U.S. Natl. Mus., 5 (1882), p. 394. (Hacienda La Palma, Golfo de Nicoya, western Costa Rica.)

Habitat.—Arid scrub, open thorn and deciduous woodland, and areas with scattered trees (Tropical and Subtropical zones).

Distribution.—*Resident* from central Sonora and southwestern Chihuahua south along the Pacific slope of Mexico (also through the interior in the state of México, Morelos and Puebla, and to the Gulf drainage in southern San Luis Potosí and Hidalgo), and in the Pacific lowlands and interior valleys of Guatemala, El Salvador, Honduras, Nicaragua and northwestern Costa Rica.

Accidental in Arizona (Roosevelt); a report from Baja California pertains to *M. cinerascens.*

Notes.—Also known as PALE-THROATED FLYCATCHER. See comments under *M. cinerascens* and *M. crinitus.*

Myiarchus crinitus (Linnaeus). GREAT CRESTED FLYCATCHER. [452.]

> *Turdus crinitus* Linnaeus, 1758, Syst. Nat., ed. 10, 1, p. 170. Based on "The Crested Fly-catcher" Catesby, Nat. Hist. Carolina 1, p. 52, pl. 52. (in America = South Carolina.)

Habitat.—Deciduous forest, open woodland, parks and orchards, in winter mostly in lowland forest and woodland.

Distribution.—*Breeds* from east-central Alberta, central and southeastern Saskatchewan, southern Manitoba, western and southern Ontario, southwestern Quebec, northern Maine, central New Brunswick and southern Nova Scotia south to central and southeastern Texas, the Gulf coast and southern Florida, and west to the eastern Dakotas, eastern Nebraska, western Kansas and west-central Oklahoma.

Winters in central and southern Florida and Cuba, and from southern Veracruz, Oaxaca and the Yucatan Peninsula south along both slopes of Middle America (more commonly on the Gulf-Caribbean) to western and northern Colombia and northern Venezuela.

In migration occurs regularly through eastern New Mexico and eastern Mexico (west at least to Nuevo León and Guanajuato), casually west to Montana, Wyoming and Colorado.

Casual or accidental in northern Mackenzie (Coppermine), California (primarily the Farallon Islands and coastal areas) and southern Arizona (Huachuca Mountains), also sight reports from the Bahamas (New Providence, Eleuthera) and Puerto Rico.

Notes.—*M. crinitus, M. cinerascens, M. nuttingi, M. tyrannulus* and *M. nugator* are closely related; some authors would consider *M. crinitus* and *M. tyrannulus* as constituting a superspecies, others would align *crinitus* with the *cinerascens-nuttingi* complex. It seems best for the present not to consider superspecies within this group, except for *cinerascens-nuttingi* and *tyrannulus-nugator* groups.

Myiarchus tyrannulus (Müller). BROWN-CRESTED FLYCATCHER. [453.]

Muscicapa tyrannulus P. L. S. Müller, 1776, Natursyst., Suppl., p. 169. Based on Daubenton, Planches Enlum., pl. 571, fig. 1. (Cayenne.)

Habitat.—Open woodland, situations with scattered trees, plantations, riparian woodland, second growth, scrub and mangroves, primarily in arid or semi-arid habitats (Tropical and lower Subtropical zones).

Distribution.—*Breeds* [*magister* group] from southeastern California (north to San Bernardino County), extreme southern Nevada, southwestern Utah, Arizona and southwestern New Mexico south along the Pacific slope of Mexico (including the Tres Marias Islands) to central Chiapas (and east to western Durango, Zacatecas, Morelos and southwestern Puebla), and from eastern Coahuila and southern Texas (north to Bexar County) south on the Gulf-Caribbean slope (including the Yucatan Peninsula, and Cozumel and Cancun islands) to northern Honduras (also the Bay Islands), thence across the Sula Valley of Honduras to the Pacific lowlands of Central America (from El Salvador to northwestern Costa Rica).

Winters [*magister* group] from northern Mexico south through the breeding range (wandering outside this range in Mexico and Guatemala), and rarely in southern Florida.

Resident [*tyrannulus* group] in South America from northern Colombia, Venezuela (also from Aruba east to Tobago and Trinidad) and the Guianas southeast to the lower Amazon basin and eastern Brazil, thence south and west across central and southeastern Brazil to southeastern Peru, Bolivia and northern Argentina; also in northwestern Peru.

Casual [*magister* group] in southern Louisiana. Accidental [*magister* group] in British Columbia (Vancouver).

Notes.—Also known as WIED'S CRESTED FLYCATCHER. Some authors consider the Middle American group to represent a species, *M. magister* Ridgway, 1884, distinct from the South American *M. tyrannulus*; populations from the Pacific slope of northern Central America have sometimes been regarded as a species, *M. brachyurus* Ridgway, 1887 [OMETEPE FLYCATCHER], but intergradation with *tyrannulus* occurs in Honduras. The Lesser Antillean *M. nugator* has only recently been recognized as a distinct species (Lanyon, 1967, Bull. Am. Must. Nat. Hist., 136, pp. 359–362); this species and *M. tyrannulus* constitute a superspecies. See also comments under *M. crinitus*.

Myiarchus nugator Riley. GRENADA FLYCATCHER.

> *Myiarchus oberi nugator* Riley, 1905, Smithson. Misc. Collect., 47, p. 275. (Grenada, West Indies.)

Habitat.—Open woodland, second growth, and situations with scattered trees.
Distribution.—*Resident* in the southern Lesser Antilles (Grenada, the Grenadines and St. Vincent).
Notes.—See comments under *M. tyrannulus.*

Myiarchus validus Cabanis. RUFOUS-TAILED FLYCATCHER.

> *Myiarchus validus* Cabanis, 1847, Arch. Naturgesch., 13, p. 351. ("one of the West Indian islands" = Jamaica.)

Habitat.—Wooded hills and mountains.
Distribution.—*Resident* on Jamaica.
Notes.—Sometimes placed in the monotypic genus *Hylonax.*

Myiarchus sagrae (Gundlach). LA SAGRA'S FLYCATCHER. [455.1.]

> *Muscicapa sagræ* Gundlach, 1852, J. Boston Soc. Nat. Hist., 6, p. 313. (Cuba.)

Habitat.—Open woodland, second growth and mangroves.
Distribution.—*Resident* in the Bahama Islands (common throughout the northern islands, irregularly in the southern ones, absent from Turks and Caicos), and on Cuba, the Isle of Pines and Grand Cayman.
Accidental in Alabama (Oroville, Dallas County).
Notes.—Formerly regarded as a race of *M. stolidus,* but see Lanyon (1967, Bull. Am. Mus. Nat. Hist., 136, pp. 335–339); *M. stolidus, M. sagrae, M. antillarum* and *M. oberi* are considered to constitute a superspecies.

Myiarchus stolidus (Gosse). STOLID FLYCATCHER.

> *Myiobius stolidus* Gosse, 1847, Birds Jamaica, p. 168 (footnote). (Jamaica.)

Habitat.—Open woodland, second growth and mangroves, primarily at low elevations.
Distribution.—*Resident* on Jamaica and Hispaniola (including Gonâve, Tortue, Grande Cayemite and Beata islands).
Notes.—See comments under *M. sagrae.*

Myiarchus antillarum (Bryant). PUERTO RICAN FLYCATCHER.

Tyrannus antillarum Bryant, 1866, Proc. Boston Soc. Nat. Hist., 10, p. 249. (Porto Rico.)

Habitat.—Open woodland and mangroves.
Distribution.—*Resident* on Puerto Rico (including Vieques and Culebra islands), and in the Virgin Islands (St. Thomas, St. John, Tortola and Virgin Gorda).
Notes.—Usually considered a subspecies of *M. stolidus,* but see Lanyon (1967, Bull. Am. Mus. Nat. Hist., 136, pp. 352–354). See also comments under *M. sagrae.*

Myiarchus oberi Lawrence. LESSER ANTILLEAN FLYCATCHER.

Myiarchus oberi Lawrence, 1878, Ann. N.Y. Acad. Sci., 1 (1877), p. 48. (Dominica.)

Habitat.—Open woodland and partly cleared lands.
Distribution.—*Resident* in the Lesser Antilles (St. Kitts, Nevis, Barbuda, Guadeloupe, Dominica, Martinique and St. Lucia).
Notes.—Sometimes considered allied to or a subspecies of *M. tyrannulus,* but relationships appear to be with *M. stolidus* (Lanyon, 1967, Bull. Am. Mus. Nat. Hist., 136, pp. 354–359). See also comments under *M. sagrae.*

Genus **DELTARHYNCHUS** Ridgway

Deltarhynchus Ridgway, 1893, Proc. U.S. Natl. Mus., 16, p. 606. Type, by original designation, *Myiarchus flammulatus* Lawrence.

Deltarhynchus flammulatus (Lawrence). FLAMMULATED FLYCATCHER.

Myiarchus flammulatus Lawrence, 1875, Ann. Lyc. Nat. Hist. N.Y., 11, p. 71. (Cacoprieto, Tehuantepec [=Oaxaca], Mexico.)

Habitat.—Deciduous forest, open woodland and scrub, primarily in semi-arid situations (Tropical Zone).
Distribution.—*Resident* in the Pacific lowlands from Sinaloa south to western Chiapas.

Genus **PITANGUS** Swainson

Pitangus Swainson, 1827, Zool. J., 3, p. 165. Type, by original designation, *Tyrannus sulphuratus* Vieillot = *Lanius sulphuratus* Linnaeus.

Pitangus lictor (Lichtenstein). LESSER KISKADEE.

Lanius Lictor Lichtenstein, 1823, Verz. Doubl. Zool. Mus. Berlin, p. 49. (Pará, Brazil.)

Habitat.—Shrubby growth, gallery forest, marshes, mangroves and low trees, invariably near water (Tropical Zone).
Distribution.—*Resident* in eastern Panama (west to the Canal Zone), and in South America from Colombia and Venezuela south, east of the Andes, to eastern Peru, northern Bolivia and southern Brazil.
Casual in western Panama (western Bocas del Toro).

Pitangus sulphuratus (Linnaeus). GREAT KISKADEE. [449.]

Lanius sulphuratus Linnaeus, 1766, Syst. Nat., ed. 12, 1, p. 137. Based on "La Pie-griesche jaune de Cayenne" Brisson, Ornithologie, 2, p. 176, pl. 16, fig. 4. (in Cayania = Cayenne.)

Habitat.—Partly open country with scattered trees, second-growth woodland, shrubby areas and savanna, especially near water, also around human habitation (Tropical and lower Subtropical zones).

Distribution.—*Resident* from southern Sonora, Sinaloa, Durango, Zacatecas, Nuevo León and southern Texas (north to Webb County and the Corpus Christi area) south along both slopes of Middle America (including the Yucatan Peninsula and Isla Cancun, off Quintana Roo), and in South America from Colombia, Venezuela (also Trinidad) and the Guianas south, east of the Andes, to central Argentina.

Introduced and established (from Trinidad stock) on Bermuda.

Casual north to southern Arizona (near Tucson), central and southeastern Texas, and southern Louisiana, also sight reports for New Jersey and Florida (possibly based on escaped individuals); a bird remaining from 1957 to 1959 in southern California almost certainly was an escape.

Notes.—Also known as KISKADEE FLYCATCHER.

Genus MEGARYNCHUS Thunberg

Megarynchus Thunberg, 1824, Dissert. Megaryncho Schaerstrom, p. 2. Type, by subsequent designation (Heine, 1859), *Lanius pitangua* Linnaeus.

Megarynchus pitangua (Linnaeus). BOAT-BILLED FLYCATCHER.

Lanius Pitangva [sic] Linnaeus, 1766, Syst. Nat., ed. 12, 1, p. 136. Based in part on "La Tyran du Brésil" Brisson, Ornithologie, 2, p. 401, pl. 36, fig. 5. (in Brasilia = Rio de Janeiro, Brazil.)

Habitat.—Open woodland, forest edge, clearings, second growth and plantations, especially in the vicinity of water (Tropical and Subtropical zones).

Distribution.—*Resident* from southern Sinaloa, southern San Luis Potosí and southern Tamaulipas south along both slopes of Middle America (including Isla Cébaco, off Panama), and in South America from Colombia, Venezuela (also Trinidad) and the Guianas south, west of the Andes to northwestern Peru and east of the Andes to northern Argentina and southern Brazil.

Casual on Isla Cancun, off Quintana Roo.

Genus MYIOZETETES Sclater

Myiozetetes Sclater, 1859, Proc. Zool. Soc. London, p. 46. Type, by original designation, *Elainia cayennensis,* Auct. = *Musciapa cayanensis* Linnaeus.

Myiozetetes cayanensis (Linnaeus). RUSTY-MARGINED FLYCATCHER.

Muscicapa cayanensis Linnaeus, 1766, Syst. Nat., ed. 12, 1, p. 327. Based on "Le Gobe-mouche de Cayenne" Brisson, Ornithologie, 2, p. 404, pl. 38, fig. 4. (in Cayana = Cayenne.)

Habitat.—Open country with scattered trees, second growth, scrub, forest edge and clearings, and along watercourses (Tropical and lower Subtropical zones).

Distribution.—*Resident* in Panama (west on the Caribbean slope to the Canal Zone, and on the Pacific to eastern Chiriquí), and in South America from Colombia, Venezuela and the Guianas south, west of the Andes to southwestern Ecuador and east of the Andes across Amazonian Brazil to eastern Bolivia and central and southeastern Brazil.

Myiozetetes similis (Spix). SOCIAL FLYCATCHER.

Muscicapa similis Spix, 1825, Avium Spec. Nov. Bras., 2, p. 18. (Amazon Valley = mouth of the Rio Madeira, Brazil.)

Habitat.—Open country with scattered trees, scrubby growth, forest edge, plantations, around human habitation, and along watercourses (Tropical and lower Subtropical zones).

Distribution.—*Resident* [*texensis* group] from southern Sonora, Sinaloa, western Durango, Zacatecas, southeastern San Luis Potosí and southern Tamaulipas south along both slopes of Middle America (including Isla Cancun, off Quintana Roo) to Costa Rica (except southwestern portion); and [*similis* group] from southwestern Costa Rica (Golfo Dulce region southward) to central Panama (east to eastern Colón and eastern Panamá province), and in South America from Colombia and Venezuela south, west of the Andes to northwestern Peru and east of the Andes to eastern Peru, Bolivia, Paraguay, extreme northeastern Argentina and southern Brazil, with the southernmost breeding populations in South America migratory northward in nonbreeding season.

Notes.—Because of differences in vocalizations, the two groups are sometimes regarded as distinct species, *M. texensis* (Giraud, 1841) [VERMILION-CROWNED FLYCATCHER] and *M. similis* [SOCIAL FLYCATCHER.].

Myiozetetes granadensis Lawrence. GRAY-CAPPED FLYCATCHER.

Myiozetetes granadensis Lawrence, 1862, Ibis, p. 11. (Isthmus of Panama = Lion Hill, Canal Zone.)

Habitat.—Open country with scattered trees, shrubby areas, plantations and clearings, most frequently near water, occasionally in mangroves (Tropical and lower Subtropical zones).

Distribution.—*Resident* on the Caribbean slope of eastern Honduras (Olancho, Gracias a Dios) and Nicaragua, on both slopes of Costa Rica and Panama (more commonly on the Caribbean), and in South America from Colombia and southern Venezuela south, west of the Andes to northwestern Peru and east of the Andes to eastern Peru, northern Bolivia and western Brazil.

Genus CORYPHOTRICCUS Ridgway

Coryphotriccus Ridgway, 1906, Proc. Biol. Soc. Wash., 19, p. 115. Type, by original designation, *Pitangus albovittatus* Lawrence.

Coryphotriccus albovittatus (Lawrence). WHITE-RINGED FLYCATCHER.

Pitangus albovittatus Lawrence, 1862, Ibis, p. 11. (Isthmus of Panama = Canal Zone.)

Habitat.—Humid lowland and foothill forest, forest edge, clearings, and second-growth woodland and plantations (Tropical and lower Subtropical zones).

Distribution.—*Resident* [*albovittatus* group] in eastern Honduras (Olancho, Gracias a Dios), Costa Rica (Caribbean slope), central and eastern Panama (west to the Canal Zone and eastern Panamá province), western Colombia and northwestern Ecuador; and [*parvus* group] in South America east of the Andes in southern Venezuela, the Guianas, southeastern Colombia and northern Brazil.

Notes.—Often placed in the genus *Conopias* Cabanis and Heine, 1859. The two groups are often regarded as distinct species, *C. albovittatus* and *C. parvus* (Pelzeln, 1868).

Genus **MYIODYNASTES** Bonaparte

Myiodynastes Bonaparte, 1857, Bull. Soc. Linn. Normandie, 2, p. 35. Type, by monotypy, *Myiodynastes audax* Bp. ex. Gm. = *Muscicapa audax* Gmelin = *Muscicapa maculata* Müller.

Myiodynastes hemichrysus (Cabanis). GOLDEN-BELLIED FLYCATCHER.

Hypermitres hemichrysus Cabanis, 1861, J. Ornithol., 9, p. 247. (Los Frailes, Costa Rica.)

Habitat.—Humid montane forest edge and clearings, especially near water, rarely in heavy forest (upper Tropical and Subtropical zones).

Distribution.—*Resident* in the highlands of Costa Rica (Tilarán, Central and Talamanca cordilleras) and western Panama (east to Veraguas).

Notes.—*M. hemichrysus* and *M. chrysocephalus* constitute a superspecies; they are considered conspecific by some authors.

Myiodynastes chrysocephalus (Tschudi). GOLDEN-CROWNED FLYCATCHER.

Scaphorhynchus chrysocephalus Tschudi, 1844, Arch. Naturgesch., 10, p. 272. (Republica Peruana = Chanchamayo, Depto. de Junín, Peru.)

Habitat.—Humid montane forest edge and clearings, often near water (upper Tropical and Subtropical zones).

Distribution.—*Resident* in extreme eastern Panama (cerros Pirre and Malí, eastern Darién), and in the mountains of South America from Colombia and northern Venezuela south, west of the Andes to western Ecuador and east of the Andes to eastern Peru.

Notes.—See comments under *M. hemichrysus*.

Myiodynastes maculatus (Müller). STREAKED FLYCATCHER.

Muscicapa maculata P. L. S. Müller, 1776, Natursyst., Suppl., p. 169. Based on "Gobe-mouche tachetée de Cayenne" Daubenton, Planches Enlum., p. 453, fig. 2. (Cayenne.)

Habitat.—Humid forest edge, clearings, second-growth woodland, plantations and mangroves (Tropical and lower Subtropical zones).

Distribution.—*Breeds* on the Gulf-Caribbean slope from southern San Luis Potosí and southern Tamaulipas south through southeastern Mexico (including Puebla, northern Oaxaca and the Yucatan Peninsula), northern Guatemala and

Belize to Honduras; and in Costa Rica (Pacific slope from Gulf of Nicoya southward) and Panama (both slopes, and Coiba, Cébaco and the Pearl islands), and in South America from Colombia, Venezuela (also Margarita Island, Tobago and Trinidad) and the Guianas south, west of the Andes to central Peru and east of the Andes to northern Argentina and southern Brazil.

Winters from Costa Rica and Panama south through the breeding range in South America to Peru, Bolivia and southern Brazil, while the southernmost breeding populations migrate north to northern South America.

Accidental in Chile.

Notes.—The southern South American breeding populations from southern Peru, Bolivia and southern Brazil southward, which migrate northward in the winter, are sometimes regarded as a distinct species, *M. solitarius* (Vieillot, 1819).

Myiodynastes luteiventris Sclater. SULPHUR-BELLIED FLYCATCHER. [451.]

Myiodynastes luteiventris Sclater, 1859, Proc. Zool. Soc. London, p. 42. (In Mexico merid., Guatemala, et America centrali = Orizaba, Veracruz.)

Habitat.—Open woodland, forest edge, clearings, plantations and scrub, in extreme northern part of range breeding primarily in sycamore-walnut canyons (Tropical and Subtropical zones).

Distribution.—*Breeds* from southeastern Arizona, eastern Sonora, western Chihuahua, Nuevo León and Tamaulipas south along both slopes of Middle America (including the Yucatan Peninsula) to central Costa Rica.

Winters in South America east of the Andes in Peru and Bolivia.

Migrates regularly through all of Middle America, northern and eastern Colombia, and eastern Ecuador.

Casual in southern California (north to Santa Barbara County), southwestern New Mexico, and western and southern Texas, also sight reports for southwestern Louisiana, southern Mississippi and southern Florida (although some of these could possibly refer to *M. maculatus*).

Genus LEGATUS Sclater

Legatus Sclater, 1859, Proc. Zool. Soc. London, p. 46. Type, by original designation, *Legatus albicollis* (Vieillot) = *Tyrannus albicollis* Vieillot = *Platyrhynchos leucophaius* Vieillot.

Legatus leucophaius (Vieillot). PIRATIC FLYCATCHER.

Platyrhynchos leucophaius Vieillot, 1818, Nouv. Dict. Hist. Nat., nouv. éd., 27, p. 11. (l'Amérique méridionale = Cayenne.)

Habitat.—Humid forest edge, open woodland, clearings and plantations (Tropical and lower Subtropical zones).

Distribution.—*Breeds* from southeastern Mexico (southern San Luis Potosí, Veracruz, Puebla, Oaxaca, Tabasco, Chiapas and southern Quintana Roo) south on the Gulf-Caribbean coast of northern Central America to Nicaragua, on both slopes of Costa Rica and Panama, and in South America from Colombia, Venezuela (also Trinidad) and the Guianas south, west of the Andes to northwestern Ecuador and east of the Andes to northern Argentina, Uruguay and southern Brazil.

Winters generally throughout the breeding range in South America, recorded only casually anywhere in Middle America between October and March.

Genus EMPIDONOMUS Cabanis and Heine

Empidonomus Cabanis and Heine, 1859, Mus. Heineanum, 2, p. 76. Type, by monotypy, *Muscicapa varia* Vieillot.

Empidonomus varius (Vieillot). VARIEGATED FLYCATCHER. [451.1.]

Muscicapa varia Vieillot, 1818, Nouv. Dict. Hist. Nat., nouv. éd., 21, p. 458. Based on "Suiriri Chorreado debaxo" Azara, Apunt. Hist. Nat. Páx. Parag., 2, p. 125 (no. 187). (Paraguay.)

Habitat & Distribution.—*Resident* in open woodland and second growth throughout most of South America east of the Andes, the southernmost populations migrating northward in winter as far as the northern South American coast and Trinidad.

Accidental in Maine (Biddeford Pool, 5–11 November 1977, photograph; Abbott and Finch, 1978, Am. Birds, 32, pp. 161–163).

Genus TYRANNUS Lacépède

Tyrannus Lacépède, 1799, Tabl. Mamm. Ois., p. 5. Type, by tautonymy, *Lanius tyrannus* Linnaeus.

Muscivora Lacépède, 1799, Tabl. Mamm. Ois., p. 5. Type, by subsequent designation (Fischer, 1831), *Muscicapa forficata* Gmelin.

Tolmarchus Ridgway, 1905, Proc. Biol. Soc. Wash., 18, p. 209. Type, by original designation, *Pitangus taylori* Sclater = *Tyrannus caudifasciatus* d'Orbigny.

Tyrannus melancholicus Vieillot. TROPICAL KINGBIRD. [446.]

Tyrannus melancholicus Vieillot, 1819, Nouv. Dict. Hist. Nat., nouv. éd., 35, p. 84. Based on "Suiriri-guazú" Azara, Apunt. Hist. Nat. Páx. Parag., 2, p. 152 (no. 198). (Paraguay.)

Habitat.—Situations with scattered trees, savanna, open woodland, forest edge, plantations, residential areas and agricultural lands (Tropical to Temperate zones).

Distribution.—*Breeds* from southeastern (rarely central) Arizona, Sonora, eastern San Luis Potosí and southern Tamaulipas south on both slopes of Middle America (including the Tres Marias Islands, Yucatan Peninsula, and most islands off the Middle American coast), and in South America from Colombia, Venezuela (also Netherlands Antilles east to Tobago, Trinidad and probably Grenada) and the Guianas south, west of the Andes to central Peru and east of the Andes to central Argentina.

Winters from Sonora and northeastern Mexico south through the Middle America and South American breeding range; the southernmost populations in South America are partly migratory northward.

Casual (mostly in fall and winter) along the Pacific coast from southern British Columbia (including Vancouver Island) south to southern California, and in southern Texas (Brownsville) and Cuba; accidental in Maine (Scarborough). Sight (or photographic) records for southeastern Louisiana, the Gulf coast (east to southern

Florida and the Florida Keys), Nova Scotia and Massachusetts may pertain to either this species or *T. couchii.*

Notes.—Populations in Arizona and western Mexico (south to Guerrero) are sometimes regarded as a separate species, *T. occidentalis* Hartert and Goodson, 1917 [WEST MEXICAN KINGBIRD, 446.2], but recent studies do not confirm such a status. *T. melancholicus* and *T. couchii* have been considered conspecific but these forms are widely sympatric (with limited hybridization) in eastern and southern Mexico (Traylor, 1979, Auk, 96, pp. 221–233).

Tyrannus couchii Baird. COUCH'S KINGBIRD. [446.1.]

> *Tyrannus couchii* Baird, 1858, *in* Baird, Cassin and Lawrence, Rep. Explor. Surv. R. R. Pac., 9, pp. xxx, 170, 175. (New Leon and San Diego, [Nuevo León,] Mexico.)

Habitat.—Situations with scattered trees, open woodland, and areas around human habitation (Tropical and lower Subtropical zones).

Distribution.—*Resident* from southern Texas (north to Webb and Kenedy counties), Nuevo León and Tamaulipas south on the Gulf-Caribbean slope of eastern Mexico (including the Yucatan Peninsula and most islands off the coast) to northern Guatemala (Petén) and Belize.

Casual in southeastern Texas and Louisiana; sight reports along the Gulf coast east to Florida likely pertain to this species but possibly represent *T. melancholicus.*

Notes.—Also known as THORNSCRUB KINGBIRD. See comments under *T. melancholicus.*

Tyrannus vociferans Swainson. CASSIN'S KINGBIRD. [448.]

> *Tyrannus vociferans* Swainson, 1826, Q. J. Sci. Lit. Arts R. Inst., 20, p. 273. (Temascáltepec, [state of] México.)

Habitat.—Dry savanna, open scrub, and pinyon-juniper-oak woodland, in winter also in highland pine-oak association and dry scrub.

Distribution.—*Breeds* from central California, southern Nevada, northern Arizona, southern Utah, Colorado, eastern Wyoming, southeastern Montana, Colorado, western Oklahoma and western Texas south to northwestern Baja California, and through the Mexican highlands to Michoacán, Oaxaca, Puebla and central Tamaulipas.

Winters from central California (irregularly), southern Baja California and northern Mexico south to central Guatemala, casually to Honduras (Comayagüela).

In migration occurs casually east to western South Dakota, northwestern Nebraska, southwestern Kansas, Arkansas and southwestern Louisiana.

Casual or accidental in Oregon, Ontario and Massachusetts (also sight report for Virginia).

Tyrannus crassirostris Swainson. THICK-BILLED KINGBIRD. [455.1.]

> *Tyrannus crassirostris* Swainson, 1826, Q. J. Sci. Lit. Arts R. Inst., 20, p. 273. (Mexico = Acapulco, Guerrero.)

Habitat.—Arid scrub, savanna, riparian woodland, clearings in deciduous forest, and open situations with scattered trees (Tropical and lower Subtropical zones).

Distribution.—*Breeds* from southeastern Arizona (Patagonia, Guadalupe Mountains), extreme southwestern New Mexico (Guadalupe Canyon), Sonora, southwestern Chihuahua, Sinaloa and western Durango south to Guerrero, the state of México, Morelos, southern Puebla and western Oaxaca.

Winters from Sonora south through the breeding range to Chiapas, casually to western Guatemala (Escuintla).

Casual in California (north to San Francisco). Accidental in southwestern British Columbia (Vancouver Island) and western Texas (Big Bend).

Tyrannus verticalis Say. WESTERN KINGBIRD. [447.]

> *Tyrannus verticalis* Say, 1823, *in* Long, Exped. Rocky Mount., 2, p. 60. (Ash River, near Rocky Mts. = near La Junta, Colorado.)

Habitat.—Open and partly open country, especially savanna, agricultural lands, and areas with scattered trees.

Distribution.—*Breeds* from southern interior British Columbia, southern Alberta, southern Saskatchewan, southern Manitoba and western Minnesota south to northern Baja California, Sonora, northwestern Chihuahua, southern New Mexico, and southern and south-central Texas, rarely or sporadically eastward to southern Wisconsin, northern Illinois, southern Michigan, southern Ontario, western Missouri, central Arkansas and southwestern Louisiana.

Winters from southern Mexico (casually north to northern Mexico and southern Texas) south through Middle America (except the Yucatan Peninsula and Belize) to central and southwestern Costa Rica, and in small numbers along the Atlantic and Gulf coasts from South Carolina to southern Florida and west to southern Louisiana.

In migration occurs regularly in small numbers (chiefly in fall) to northeastern North America from southern Quebec, New Brunswick and Nova Scotia south to North Carolina, casually in the Bahamas (New Providence, also sight reports from Grand Bahama, Bimini and Eleuthera) and Swan Islands (western Caribbean Sea).

Casual, primarily in summer, north to central Alaska and the northern portions of the Canadian provinces (east to Ontario and Newfoundland). Accidental on Bathurst Island.

Tyrannus tyrannus (Linnaeus). EASTERN KINGBIRD. [444.]

> *Lanius Tyrannus* Linnaeus, 1758, Syst. Nat., ed. 10, 1, p. 94. Based mainly on "The Tyrant" Catesby, Nat. Hist. Carolina, 1, p. 55, pl. 55. (in America septentrionali = South Carolina.)

Habitat.—Forest edge, open situations with scattered trees and shrubs, cultivated lands with bushes and fencerows, and parks, in winter more closely associated with forest clearings and borders.

Distribution.—*Breeds* from southwestern and north-central British Columbia (including Vancouver Island), southern Mackenzie, northern Saskatchewan, central Manitoba, central Ontario, southern Quebec, New Brunswick, Prince Edward Island and Nova Scotia south to western Washington, Oregon (east of the coast ranges), northeastern California (locally), northern Nevada (at least formerly), northern Utah, Colorado, northwestern and central New Mexico, central and eastern Texas, the Gulf coast and southern Florida. Occurs rarely but regularly in summer (and probably breeding) in southeastern Alaska.

Winters from Colombia (casually from Honduras) south to northern Chile and northern Argentina.

In migration occurs in eastern Mexico, and from Oaxaca (Isthmus of Tehuantepec) and the Yucatan Peninsula south on both slopes of Middle America (including most islands) to northwestern South America, casually through California, Arizona, Bermuda, the Bahamas, Cuba, the Isle of Pines, Puerto Rico, and the Swan, Providencia and San Andrés islands in the Caribbean Sea.

Casual north to northern and western Alaska (including Nunivak and the Pribilof islands), southern Yukon, the northern Hudson Bay region, central Quebec, Labrador, Newfoundland and southern Greenland, and east in South America to eastern Venezuela, Guyana, Surinam and central Brazil.

Tyrannus dominicensis (Gmelin). GRAY KINGBIRD. [445.]

Lanius Tyrannus β dominicensis Gmelin, 1788, Syst. Nat., 1 (1), p. 302. Based largely on "Le Tyran de S. Domingue" Brisson, Ornithologie, 2, p. 394, pl. 38, fig. 2. (in insula S. Dominici et Jamaica = Hispaniola.)

Habitat.—Open situations with scattered trees, most frequently in insular or coastal areas, including in mangroves and along beaches (Tropical and, less frequently, Subtropical zones).

Distribution.—*Breeds* along the Atlantic and Gulf coasts from South Carolina (at least formerly) south to the Florida Keys, and west to southern Alabama and islands off the coast of Mississippi; throughout the West Indies, and on islands off South America from the Netherlands Antilles east to Tobago and Trinidad; and sporadically in northern Colombia and northern Venezuela.

Winters from Hispaniola and Puerto Rico (casually from southern Florida) south through the Lesser Antilles and on islands off northern Venezuela, and from central Panama east across Colombia and Venezuela to the Guianas.

Casual along the Atlantic coast north to Massachusetts (sight records to New Brunswick and Nova Scotia), west along the Gulf coast to southeastern Texas, on islands off the Yucatan Peninsula, in the Swan Islands (Caribbean Sea), and in Nicaragua (also sight reports from Caribbean Costa Rica). Accidental in British Columbia (Vancouver Island) and Bermuda.

Tyrannus caudifasciatus d'Orbigny. LOGGERHEAD KINGBIRD. [445.2.]

Tyrannus caudifasciatus d'Orbigny, 1839, *in* La Sagra, Hist. Fis. Pol. Nat. Cuba, Ois., p. 70 [p. 82 in French ed.], pl. 12. (Cuba.)

Habitat.—Open woodland, less frequently in open situations with scattered trees.

Distribution.—*Resident* in the northern Bahama Islands (Grand Bahama, Abaco, Andros and New Providence) and Greater Antilles (east to Puerto Rico, including Vieques and the Cayman islands).

Casual in southern Florida (Monroe and Dade counties, also a sight report for Merritt Island).

Notes.—This species is often placed in the monotypic genus *Tolmarchus*.

Tyrannus cubensis Richmond. GIANT KINGBIRD.

> *Tyrannus magnirostris* (not Swainson, 1831) d'Orbigny, 1839, *in* La Sagra, Hist. Fis. Pol. Nat. Cuba, Ois., p. 69 [p. 80 in French ed.], pl. 13. (Cuba.)
> *Tyrannus cubensis* Richmond, 1898, Auk, 15, p. 330. New name for *Tyrannus magnirostris* d'Orbigny, preoccupied.

Habitat.—Woodland, especially pine, and borders of swamps.

Distribution.—*Resident* on Cuba and the Isle of Pines, formerly in the southern Bahamas (Great Inagua and Caicos islands).

Accidental on Isla Mujeres (off Quintana Roo).

Tyrannus forficatus (Gmelin). SCISSOR-TAILED FLYCATCHER. [443.]

> *Muscicapa forficata* Gmelin, 1789, Syst. Nat., 1 (2), p. 931. Based mainly on the "Swallow-tailed Flycatcher" Latham, Gen. Synop. Birds, 2(1), p. 356. (in nova Hispania = Mexico.)

Habitat.—Generally open country, most commonly dry grasslands, cultivated lands, scrub and savanna, occurring in migration in both wet and dry situations but more frequently in the latter.

Distribution.—*Breeds* from eastern New Mexico, southeastern Colorado, southern Nebraska, north-central Missouri, central Arkansas and western Louisiana south to northern Nuevo León and southern Texas; also isolated breeding reports from northeastern Mississippi (Tupelo, 1975), central Tennessee (Murfreesboro, 1978) and central Iowa (Ames, 1979).

Winters in southern Louisiana (casually) and southern Florida, and in Middle America from Veracruz and Oaxaca south, primarily on the Pacific slope, to central Costa Rica, rarely to western Panama (east to the Canal Zone).

In migration occurs throughout most of Mexico (except the northwestern portion and Baja California) and sparingly (but regularly) along the Gulf coast from Louisiana to southern Florida.

Casual throughout most of North America north and west of the breeding range from southern British Columbia, Alberta, Saskatchewan, Manitoba, Minnesota, Wisconsin, Michigan, southern Ontario, southern Quebec, New Brunswick and Nova Scotia south to southern California, Arizona, the Gulf states, Bahamas (Grand Bahama, San Salvador), western Cuba and Puerto Rico.

Notes.—This and the following species were formerly placed in the genus *Muscivora*.

Tyrannus savana Vieillot. FORK-TAILED FLYCATCHER. [442.]

> *Muscicapa Tyrannus* (not *Lanius tyrannus* Linnaeus, 1758) Linnaeus, 1766, Syst. Nat., ed. 12, 1, p. 325. Based on "Le Tyran a queue fourchue" Brisson, Ornithologie, 2, p. 395, pl. 39, fig. 3. (in Canada, Surinamo = Surinam.)
> *Tyrannus savana* Vieillot, 1808, Hist. Nat. Ois. Am. Sept., 1 (1807), p. 72, pl. 43. New name for *Muscicapa tyrannus* Linnaeus, preoccupied.

Habitat.—Open situations, primarily savanna, less frequently scrub, cultivated areas and sparsely wooded regions (Tropical and Subtropical zones).

Distribution.—*Breeds* locally (mostly on the Gulf-Caribbean slope) from southeastern Mexico (Veracruz and Tabasco, possibly also northern Oaxaca, northern Chiapas, Campeche and Quintana Roo) south to central Panama (eastern Panamá province and the Canal Zone); and in South America in northern and central Colombia and northern Venezuela, also locally from central Brazil south to central Argentina and Uruguay.

Winters irregularly through Middle America from the breeding range in southeastern Mexico south to central Panama; widely in South America from Colombia, Venezuela (also Curaçao, Tobago, Trinidad) and the Guianas south, east of the Andes, to Peru, Bolivia, northern Argentina and southern Brazil; and casually in the southern Lesser Antilles (Barbados, Grenada and the Grenadines).

Casual north in eastern North America to southern Canada, primarily along the Atlantic coast (recorded Wisconsin, Michigan, southern Ontario, New Brunswick, Nova Scotia, New England, New York, Pennsylvania, New Jersey, Maryland, South Carolina, Florida and Mississippi); also in southern Texas, Bermuda, Cuba, St. Martin (in the Lesser Antilles), and elsewhere in Panama (Taboga and Coiba islands, and San Blas). Accidental in the Falkland Islands; a record from California (old specimen) is probably erroneous.

Notes.—Formerly known as *Muscivora tyrannus* (Linnaeus, 1766). One New Jersey specimen (possibly mislabeled) has been referred to the race breeding in Venezuela and Colombia, *T. s. sanctaemartae* (Zimmer, 1937); all other specimens taken north of Mexico, as well as those in the southern Lesser Antilles, have been identified as pertaining to *T. s. savana,* the subspecies breeding in southern South America.

Subfamily TITYRINAE: Tityras and Becards

Notes.—Formerly included in the Cotingidae.

Genus **PACHYRAMPHUS** Gray

Pachyramphus G. R. Gray, 1840, List Genera Birds, p. 31. Type, by original designation, *Psaris cuvierii* Swainson = *Tityra viridis* Vieillot.
Platypsaris [subgenus] Sclater, 1857, Proc. Zool. Soc. London, p. 72. Type, by subsequent designation (Sclater, 1888), *Pachyrhynchus aglaiae* Lafresnaye.

Pachyramphus versicolor (Hartlaub). BARRED BECARD.

Vireo versicolor Hartlaub, 1843, Rev. Zool. [Paris], 6, p. 289. (du la Nouvelle-Grenade = Bogotá, Colombia.)

Habitat.—Humid montane forest, forest edge, clearings, open woodland and, less frequently, bushes in open situations (Subtropical and lower Subtropical zones).

Distribution.—*Resident* in the mountains of Costa Rica (mostly in the Cordillera Central and Dota Mountains) and western Panama (western Chiriquí); in northwestern Venezuela; from Colombia south, west of the Andes, to northwestern Ecuador; and, east of the Andes, in eastern Peru and northern Bolivia.

Pachyramphus rufus (Boddaert). CINEREOUS BECARD.

Muscicapa rufa Boddaert, 1783, Table Planches Enlum., p. 27. Based on "Le Gobemouche roux, de Cayenne" Daubenton, Planches Enlum., pl. 453, fig. 1. (Cayenne.)

Habitat.—Forest, open woodland, mangroves, brushy areas, and sometimes open fields (Tropical and lower Subtropical zones).

Distribution.—*Resident* locally in central Panama (recorded certainly from the Canal Zone and eastern Panamá province, a doubtful record from "Veragua"), and in South America from central and northern Colombia east across northern Venezuela to the Guianas, and south, east of the Andes, to northeastern Peru, thence eastward across Amazonian Brazil to Pará (including Marajó and Mexiana islands).

Notes.—*P. rufus* and *P. spodiurus* Sclater, 1860, of western Ecuador and northwestern Peru, appear to constitute a superspecies.

Pachyramphus cinnamomeus Lawrence. CINNAMON BECARD.

Pachyramphus cinnamomeus Lawrence, 1861, Ann. Lyc. Nat. Hist. N.Y., 7, p. 295. (on the Atlantic side of the Isthmus of Panama, along the line of Panama Railroad = Lion Hill, Canal Zone.)

Habitat.—Humid forest edge, second-growth woodland, clearings, plantations and mangroves, less frequently in forest interior (Tropical and lower Subtropical zones).

Distribution.—*Resident* from southeastern Mexico (northern Oaxaca, Tabasco and Chiapas) south on the Gulf-Caribbean slope of northern Central America to Nicaragua, on both slopes of Costa Rica (absent from the dry northwest) and Panama (more commonly on the Caribbean slope), and in South America in northern and western Colombia, northwestern Venezuela and northwestern Ecuador.

Notes.—*P. cinnamomeus* and the South American *P. castaneus* (Jardine and Selby, 1827) appear to constitute a superspecies.

Pachyramphus polychopterus (Vieillot). WHITE-WINGED BECARD.

Platyrhynchus polychopterus Vieillot, 1818, Nouv. Dict. Hist. Nat., nouv. éd., 27, p. 10. (Nouvelle-Hollande, error = Bahia, Brazil.)

Habitat.—Forest edge, clearings, second-growth and open woodland, mangroves and plantations, mostly in humid habitats (Tropical and lower Subtropical zones).

Distribution.—*Resident* on the Caribbean slope of eastern Guatemala and Honduras, on both slopes of Nicaragua, Costa Rica (less commonly in the dry northwest) and Panama, and in South America from Colombia, Venezuela (also Tobago and Trinidad) and the Guianas south, mostly east of the Andes, to eastern Peru, northern and eastern Bolivia, northern Argentina, Uruguay and southern Brazil. Southernmost populations in South America are partially migratory northward in nonbreeding season.

Pachyramphus albogriseus Sclater. BLACK-AND-WHITE BECARD.

Pachyrhamphus albo-griseus Sclater, 1857, Proc. Zool. Soc. London, p. 78. (New Grenada, Bogota = Bogotá, Colombia.)

Habitat.—Open forest, forest edge, second-growth woodland and clearings, primarily in semi-arid situations (Tropical and Subtropical zones).

Distribution.—*Resident* in Costa Rica and western Panama (Chiriquí and Veraguas, records elsewhere are unverified); and in South America from northern Colombia east to northern Venezuela and south, west of the Andes, to northwestern Peru. The old record of this species from Nicaragua pertains to *P. polychopterus*.

Notes.—*P. albogriseus* and the South American *P. marginatus* (Lichtenstein, 1823) appear to constitute a superspecies.

Pachyramphus major (Cabanis). GRAY-COLLARED BECARD.

Bathmidurus major Cabanis, 1847, Arch. Naturgesch., 13, p. 246. (Xalapa [=Jalapa], Vera Cruz, Mexico.)

Habitat.—Humid montane forest, forest edge, pine-oak woodland, second growth, and lowland deciduous forest (Subtropical Zone, in Tropical Zone in drier habitats).

Distribution.—*Resident* from Sinaloa, western Durango, San Luis Potosí, Nuevo León and Tamaulipas south on both slopes of Middle America (including the Yucatan Peninsula), and from Chiapas in the interior highlands, to El Salvador, Honduras and north-central Nicaragua.

Pachyramphus aglaiae (Lafresnaye). ROSE-THROATED BECARD. [441.1.]

Platyrhynchus Aglaiæ Lafresnaye, 1839, Rev. Zool. [Paris], 2, p. 98. (Mexico = Jalapa, Veracruz.)

Habitat.—Open forest, woodland, scrubby areas, open areas with scattered trees, plantations and mangroves, mostly in semi-arid regions but also less commonly in humid areas (Tropical and Subtropical zones).

Distribution.—*Breeds* from southeastern Arizona, northeastern Sonora, western Chihuahua, northeastern Coahuila, Nuevo León and southern Texas (Cameron and Hidalgo counties) south along both slopes of Middle America (including the Tres Marias Islands, Yucatan Peninsula and Cozumel Island) to Costa Rica (primarily in the dry northwest south to the Gulf of Nicoya, casually in the northeast), also sight reports for southwestern New Mexico and western Panama (Chiriquí), which probably represent vagrant individuals.

Winters from northern Mexico south throughout the remainder of the breeding range.

Notes.—*P. aglaiae, P. homochrous, P. niger* and two South American species, *P. validus* (Lichtenstein, 1823) [=*P. rufus* (Vieillot, 1816)] and *P. minor* (Lesson, 1830), appear to constitute a superspecies; these species also have been placed in the past in the genus *Platypsaris*.

Pachyramphus homochrous Sclater. ONE-COLORED BECARD.

Pachyramphus homochrous Sclater, 1859, Proc. Zool. Soc. London, p. 142. (Pallatanga, Ecuador.)

Habitat.—Lowland forest, forest edge and open woodland (Tropical Zone).

Distribution.—*Resident* locally from central Panama (the Caribbean slope in the Canal Zone, both slopes of eastern Panamá province, and in the Pacific lowlands of Darién) east across northern Colombia to northwestern Venezuela and south, west of the Andes, to northwestern Peru.

Notes.—See comments under *P. aglaiae.*

Pachyramphus niger (Gmelin). JAMAICAN BECARD.

Lanius niger Gmelin, 1788, Syst. Nat., 1 (1), p. 301. Based on the "Black Shrike" Latham, Gen. Synop. Birds, 1 (2), p. 187. (in Jamaica.)

Habitat.—Forest and open woodland, primarily in mountainous regions.
Distribution.—*Resident* on Jamaica.
Notes.—See comments under *P. aglaiae*.

Genus TITYRA Vieillot

Tityra Vieillot, 1816, Analyse, p. 39. Type, by monotypy, "Bécarde" Buffon = *Lanius cayanus* Linnaeus.
Erator [subgenus] Kaup, 1852, Proc. Zool. Soc. London (1851), p. 47. Type, by subsequent designation (G. R. Gray, 1855), *Lanius inquisitor* Lichtenstein.

Tityra semifasciata (Spix). MASKED TITYRA.

Pachyrhynchus semifasciatus Spix, 1825, Avium Spec. Nov. Bras., 2, p. 32, pl. 44, figs. 2 (Pará, Brazil.)

Habitat.—Open forest, forest edge, tall secondary forest, open woodland and plantations (Tropical and lower Subtropical zones).
Distribution.—*Resident* from southern Sonora, Sinaloa, Guanajuato, San Luis Potosí and Tamaulipas south along both slopes of Middle America (including the Yucatan Peninsula) to Panama (including Cébaco and Coiba islands), and in South America from Colombia, northern Venezuela (also Trinidad) and the Guianas south, west of the Andes to western Ecuador and east of the Andes to eastern Peru, thence eastward over Amazonian Brazil to Para and northern Maranhão.

Tityra inquisitor (Lichtenstein). BLACK-CROWNED TITYRA.

Lanius inquisitor (Olfers MS) Lichtenstein, 1823, Verz. Doubl. Zool. Mus. Berlin, p. 50. (São Paulo, Brazil.)

Habitat.—Forest, second-growth woodland and plantations, most frequently in humid situations (Tropical and lower Subtropical zones).
Distribution.—*Resident* from eastern Mexico (San Luis Potosí, Veracruz, eastern Puebla, northern Oaxaca, Tabasco, Chiapas and the Yucatan Peninsula) south on the Caribbean slope of northern Central America to Nicaragua, on both slopes of Costa Rica and Panama, and in South America from Colombia, Venezuela and the Guianas south, west of the Andes to western Ecuador and east of the Andes to eastern Peru, northern and eastern Bolivia, Paraguay, northeastern Argentina and southern Brazil.
Notes.—Often placed in the genus *Erator*.

Family COTINGIDAE: Cotingas

Genus LIPAUGUS Boie

Lipangus [typo. error = *Lipaugus*] Boie, 1828, Isis von Oken, col. 318. Type, by subsequent designation (G. R. Gray, 1840), *Muscicapa plumbea* Licht. = *Muscicapa vociferans* Wied.

Lipaugus unirufus Sclater. RUFOUS PIHA.

Lipaugus unirufus Sclater, 1859, Proc. Zool. Soc. London, p. 385. (Playa Vicente, Oaxaca, Mexico, and Coban, Vera Paz, Guatemala = Playa Vicente, Oaxaca.)

Habitat.—Humid lowland and foothill forest, forest edge and second-growth woodland (Tropical and lower Subtropical zones).

Distribution.—*Resident* from southeastern Mexico (southern Veracruz, northern Oaxaca, Tabasco and Chiapas) south on the Caribbean slope of northern Central America to Nicaragua, on both slopes of Costa Rica (absent from the dry northwest) and Panama (more commonly on the Caribbean slope), and in western Colombia and western Ecuador.

Notes.—*L. unirufus* and the South American *L. vociferans* (Wied, 1820) may constitute a superspecies.

Genus **COTINGA** Brisson

Cotinga Brisson, 1760, Ornithologie, 2, p. 339. Type, by tautonymy, *Cotinga* Brisson = *Ampelis cotinga* Linnaeus.

Cotinga amabilis Gould. LOVELY COTINGA.

Cotinga amabilis Gould, 1857, Proc. Zool. Soc. London, p. 64, pl. 123. (Guatemala = Verapaz, Guatemala.)

Habitat.—Humid lowland and foothill forest, forest edge and second-growth woodland (Tropical and lower Subtropical zones).

Distribution.—*Resident* from southern Mexico (southern Veracruz, northern Oaxaca and northern Chiapas) south on the Caribbean slope of Central America to southeastern Costa Rica.

Notes.—*C. amabilis, C. ridgwayi* and *C. nattererii* are closely related and constitute a superspecies; some authors would consider them conspecific [BLUE COTINGA]. These three species are also related to the South American *C. cotinga* (Linnaeus, 1766), *C. maculata* (P. L. S. Müller, 1776) and *C. maynana* (Linnaeus, 1766); all six may constitute a superspecies.

Cotinga ridgwayi Ridgway. TURQUOISE COTINGA.

Cotinga ridgwayi (Zeledón MS) Ridgway, 1887, Proc. U.S. Natl. Mus., 10, p. 1, pl. 6, fig. 3. (Pozo Azul, Costa Rica.)

Habitat.—Humid lowland and foothill forest, forest edge, second growth, and open woodland (Tropical and lower Subtropical zones).

Distribution.—*Resident* on the Pacific slope of southwestern Costa Rica (northwest to the Gulf of Nicoya) and extreme southwestern Panama (western Chiriquí).

Notes.—See comments under *C. amabilis.*

Cotinga nattererii (Boissonneau). BLUE COTINGA.

Ampelis Nattererii Boissonneau, 1840, Rev. Zool. [Paris], 3, p. 2. (Santa-Fé de Bogota [Colombia].)

Habitat.—Humid lowland forest, forest edge and second-growth woodland (Tropical Zone).

Distribution.—*Resident* from central Panama (west to the Canal Zone) east across Colombia to northwestern Venezuela, and south, west of the Andes, to northwestern Ecuador.

Notes.—Also known as NATTERER'S COTINGA. See comments under *C. amabilis.*

Genus CARPODECTES Salvin

Carpodectes Salvin, 1865, Proc. Zool. Soc. London (1864), p. 583. Type, by original designation, *Carpodectes nitidus* Salvin.

Carpodectes hopkei Berlepsch. BLACK-TIPPED COTINGA.

Carpodectes hopkei Berlepsch, 1897, Ornithol. Monatsber., 5, p. 174. (San José, Río Dagua, Colombia.)

Habitat.—Humid lowland and foothill forest and forest edge (Tropical and lower Subtropical zones).

Distribution.—*Resident* in extreme eastern Panama (eastern Darién), western Colombia and northwestern Ecuador.

Notes.—Considered by some to be part of the superspecies formed by *C. antoniae* and *C. nitidus.*

Carpodectes antoniae Ridgway. YELLOW-BILLED COTINGA.

Carpodectes antoniæ (Zeledón MS) Ridgway. 1884, Ibis, p. 27, pl. 2. (Pirris, South-western Costa Rica.)

Habitat.—Coastal mangroves and adjacent tall forest (Tropical Zone).

Distribution.—*Resident* in the Pacific lowlands of southwestern Costa Rica (northwest to the Gulf of Nicoya) and extreme western Panama (western Chiriquí).

Notes.—Also known as ANTONIA'S COTINGA. *C. antoniae* and *C. nitidus* constitute a superspecies; they are considered conspecific by some authors. With a single species treatment, WHITE COTINGA would be the appropriate English name.

Carpodectes nitidus Salvin. SNOWY COTINGA.

Carpodectes nitidus Salvin, 1865, Proc. Zool. Soc. London (1864), p. 583, pl. "36" [=35]. (Tucurique [=Tucurriquí], Costa Rica.)

Habitat.—Humid lowland and foothill forest, forest edge, second growth and plantations (Tropical and lower Subtropical zones).

Distribution.—*Resident* on the Caribbean slope from northern Honduras (east of the Sula Valley) south to extreme western Panama (western Bocas del Toro).

Notes.—See comments under *C. antoniae.*

Genus QUERULA Vieillot

Querula Vieillot, 1816, Analyse, p. 37. Type, by monotypy, "Piauhau" Buffon = *Muscicapa purpurata* Müller.

Querula purpurata (Müller). PURPLE-THROATED FRUITCROW.

Muscicapa purpurata P. L. S. Müller, 1776, Natursyst., Suppl., p. 169, Based on "Gobe-Mouche noir à gorge pourpre de Cayenne" Daubenton, Planches Enlum., pl. 381. (Cayenne.)

Habitat.—Humid lowland forest, forest edge, second-growth woodland, clearings and plantations (Tropical Zone).

Distribution.—*Resident* in Costa Rica (entire Caribbean lowlands), Panama (Caribbean slope throughout, and Pacific slope from the Canal Zone eastward), and South America from Colombia, southern Venezuela and the Guianas south, west of the Andes to western Ecuador and east of the Andes to eastern Peru, northern Bolivia and Amazonian Brazil.

Genus CEPHALOPTERUS Geoffroy Saint-Hilaire

Cephalopterus Geoffroy Saint-Hilaire, 1809, Ann. Mus. Hist. Nat. [Paris], 13, pp. 235, 238. Type, by original designation, *Cephalopterus ornatus* Geoffroy Saint-Hilaire.

Cephalopterus glabricollis Gould. BARE-NECKED UMBRELLABIRD.

Cephalopterus glabricollis Gould, 1851, Proc. Zool. Soc. London (1850), p. 92, pl. 20. (Cordillera de Chiriqué in Veragua, at an elevation of 8000 feet [Panama].)

Habitat.—Humid forest and forest edge, less frequently in clearings or partly cleared lands (Subtropical Zone, to Tropical Zone in nonbreeding season).

Distribution.—*Resident* in Costa Rica (Tilarán, Central and possibly Guanacaste cordilleras, and the Dota Mountains, descending to the Caribbean lowlands in nonbreeding season) and western Panama (highlands of Bocas del Toro, Chiriquí and Veraguas, to lower elevations in nonbreeding season).

Notes.—*C. glabricollis* and *C. penduliger* Sclater, 1859, of western Colombia and western Ecuador, are sometimes regarded as conspecific with the South American *C. ornatus* Geoffroy Saint-Hilaire, 1809; the three constitute a superspecies.

Genus PROCNIAS Illiger

Procnias Illiger, 1811, Prodromus, p. 228. Type, by subsequent designation (G. R. Gray, 1840), *P. variegatus* (L.) Ill. = *Ampelis variegata* Gmelin = *Ampelis averano* Hermann.

Procnias tricarunculata (Verreaux and Verreaux). THREE-WATTLED BELL-BIRD.

Casmarhynchus tricarunculatus J. and E. Verreaux, 1853, Rev. Mag. Zool., ser. 2, 5, p. 193. (Bocos del toro (Nouvelle-Grenade) = Bocas del Toro, western Panama.)

Habitat.—Humid forest, breeding in montane forest, in nonbreeding season to lowland forest (Subtropical and lower Temperate zones, in nonbreeding season to Tropical Zone).

Distribution.—*Breeds,* and largely *resident,* in the highlands of eastern Honduras (Olancho), Nicaragua, Costa Rica and western Panama (Bocas del Toro, Chiriquí and Veraguas, possibly also to the Azuero Peninsula), in nonbreeding season descending to the adjacent Caribbean lowlands (also Pacific lowlands in Panama, and ranging east to the Canal Zone).

Notes.—*P. tricarunculata* and three South American species, *P. alba* (Hermann, 1783), *P. nudicollis* (Vieillot, 1817) and *P. averano* (Hermann, 1783), may constitute a superspecies.

Family **PIPRIDAE**: Manakins

Genus **SCHIFFORNIS** Bonaparte

Schiffornis Bonaparte, 1854, Ateneo Ital., 2, p. 314. Type, by monotypy, *Muscicapa turdina* Wied.

Notes.—Relationships of this genus are uncertain; it may be a cotingid.

Schiffornis turdinus (Wied). THRUSHLIKE MANAKIN.

Muscicapa turdina Wied, 1831, Beitr. Naturgesch. Bras., 3(2), p. 817. (eastern Brazil = Bahia.)

Habitat.—Humid forest, forest edge and dense second-growth woodland, generally in understory (Tropical and Subtropical zones).
Distribution.—*Resident* [*veraepacis* group] from southeastern Mexico (southern Veracruz, northern Oaxaca, Tabasco, Chiapas, Campeche and Quintana Roo), south on the Caribbean slope of northern Central America to Nicaragua, on both slopes of Costa Rica (absent from the dry northwest) and western Panama (west of the Canal Zone); and [*turdinus* group] in central and eastern Panama (Canal Zone eastward), and in South America from Colombia, southern Venezuela and the Guianas south, west of the Andes to western Ecuador and east of the Andes to eastern Peru, northern Bolivia, and central and southeastern Brazil.
Notes.—Because of the apparent overlap of races in eastern Panama and northeastern Colombia, some authors suggest that the two groups are distinct species, *S. veraepacis* (Sclater and Salvin, 1860) [BROWN MANAKIN] and *S. turdinus* [THRUSHLIKE MANAKIN]. *S. turdinus* and the southeastern South American *S. virescens* (Lafresnaye, 1824) may represent a superspecies despite marginal overlap.

Genus **SAPAYOA** Hartert

Sapayoa Hartert, 1903, Novit. Zool., 10, p. 117. Type, by original designation, *Sapayoa aenigma* Hartert.

Notes.—The systematic position of this genus is uncertain; relationships with the Tyrannidae, Cotingidae or even the Eurylaimidae have been suggested.

Sapayoa aenigma Hartert. BROAD-BILLED MANAKIN.

Sapayoa aenigma Hartert, 1903, Novit. Zool., 10, p. 117. (Río Sapayo [=Sapallo Grande], prov. Esmeraldas, Ecuador.)

Habitat.—Humid lowland forest, usually near water (Tropical Zone).
Distribution.—*Resident* in eastern Panama (west to the Canal Zone), western Colombia and northwestern Ecuador.

Genus **PIPRITES** Cabanis

Piprites Cabanis, 1847, Arch. Naturgesch., 13, p. 234. Type, by monotypy, *Pipra pileata* Temminck.

Piprites griseiceps Salvin. GRAY-HEADED MANAKIN.

Piprites griseiceps Salvin, 1865, Proc. Zool. Soc. London (1864), p. 583. (Tucurruque [=Tucurriquí], Costa Rica.)

Habitat.—Understory in humid lowland forest and dense second-growth woodland (Tropical Zone).

Distribution.—*Resident* on the Caribbean slope of eastern Guatemala (near Izabal), eastern Honduras (Olancho), Nicaragua and Costa Rica (south to Suretka).

Notes.—*P. griseiceps* and the South American *P. chloris* (Temminck, 1822) appear to constitute a superspecies.

Genus CHLOROPIPO Cabanis and Heine

Chloropipo Cabanis and Heine, 1859, Mus. Heineanum, 2, p. 90 (note 2). Type, by original designation, *Chloropipo flavicollis* Cabanis and Heine = *Pipra flavicapilla* Sclater.

Chloropipo holochlora Sclater. GREEN MANAKIN.

Chloropipo holochlora Sclater, 1888, Cat. Birds Br. Mus., 14, pp. xvi, 281, 287. (Colombia and Amazonia = Bogotá, Colombia.)

Habitat.—Undergrowth of humid lowland and foothill forest (Tropical and lower Subtropical zones).

Distribution.—*Resident* in eastern Panama (eastern San Blas and eastern Darién), and in South America from northern Colombia south, west of the Andes to western Ecuador and east of the Andes to eastern Peru.

Notes.—*C. holochlora* and the South American *C. uniformis* Salvin and Godman, 1884, appear to constitute a superspecies.

Genus MANACUS Brisson

Manacus Brisson, 1760, Ornithologie, 4, p. 442. Type, by tautonymy, *Manacus* Brisson = *Pipra manacus* Linnaeus.

Manacus candei (Parzudaki). WHITE-COLLARED MANAKIN.

Pipra Candei Parzudaki, 1841, Rev. Zool. [Paris], 4, p. 306. (à Truxillo, dans la baie de Honduras = Trujillo, Honduras.)

Habitat.—*Resident* from southeastern Mexico (southern Veracruz, northern Oaxaca, Tabasco, Chiapas, southern Campeche and southern Quintana Roo) south on the Caribbean slope of Central America to extreme western Panama (western Bocas del Toro).

Notes.—Some authors consider *M. candei* conspecific with *M. vitellinus,* with which it constitutes a superspecies, but the two appear to be sympatric in western Panama; with the broader treatment of *M. vitellinus,* COLLARED MANAKIN may be used for the species. See also comments under *M. vitellinus.*

Manacus vitellinus (Gould). GOLDEN-COLLARED MANAKIN.

Pipra vitellina Gould, 1843, Proc. Zool. Soc. London, p. 103. (Panamá = Panama City, Panama.)

Habitat.—Undergrowth of humid forest, forest edge and dense second-growth woodland (Tropical and lower Subtropical zones).

Distribution.—*Resident* [*aurantiacus* group] on the Pacific slope of southwestern

Costa Rica (west to the Gulf of Nicoya) and western Panama (east to the Azuero Peninsula); and [*vitellinus* group] in Panama (the entire Caribbean coast, including Bastimentos and Escudo de Veraguas islands, and the Pacific coast from eastern Veraguas eastward), and in northwestern and north-central Colombia.

Notes.—A highly variable population in extreme western Bocas del Toro, western Panama, has sometimes been regarded as a distinct species. *M. cerritus* Peters, 1927 [ALMIRANTE MANAKIN], but this form intergrades with *M. vitellinus* in western Panama. The distinct Pacific slope form in Costa Rica and western Panama is often regarded as a separate species, *M. aurantiacus* (Salvin, 1870) [ORANGE-COLLARED MANAKIN.]. Limited hybridization between *M. vitellinus* and the South American *M. manacus* (Linnaeus, 1766) [WHITE-BEARDED MANAKIN] is known from western Colombia; some authors regard these two and the Middle American *M. candei* as one species [BEARDED MANAKIN], but they are treated here as allospecies of a superspecies complex. See also comments under *M. candei.*

Genus CORAPIPO Bonaparte

Corapipo Bonaparte, 1854, Ateneo Ital., 2, p. 316. Type, by monotypy, *Pipra gutturalis* Linnaeus.

Corapipo leucorrhoa (Sclater). WHITE-RUFFED MANAKIN.

Pipra leucorrhoa Sclater, 1863, Proc. Zool. Soc. London, p. 63. (New Granada = Bucaramanga, Santander, Colombia.)

Habitat.—Humid forest, forest edge and second-growth woodland, primarily in undergrowth (upper Tropical and Subtropical zones, in South America to lower Tropical Zone).

Distribution.—*Resident* [*altera* group] in foothills and highlands from eastern Honduras (Olancho) south through eastern Nicaragua, Costa Rica and Panama to northwestern Colombia; and [*leucorrhoa* group] in South America in eastern Colombia (west to the Cauca Valley) and northwestern Venezuela.

Notes.—The two groups are often recognized as distinct species, *C. altera* Hellmayr, 1906 [WHITE-RUFFED MANAKIN], and *C. leucorrhoa* [WHITE-BIBBED MANAKIN].

Genus CHIROXIPHIA Cabanis

Chiroxiphia Cabanis, 1847, Arch. Naturgesch., 13, p. 235. Type, by subsequent designation (G. R. Gray, 1855), *Pipra caudata* Shaw and Nodder.

Chiroxiphia lanceolata (Wagler). LANCE-TAILED MANAKIN.

Pipra lanceolata Wagler, 1830, Isis von Oken, col. 931. (Guiane sive Cajenna, error = Cerro Turumiquire, Sucre, Venezuela.)

Habitat.—Thick scrub, open woodland, second growth and plantations, usually in relatively dry regions (Tropical and lower Subtropical zones).

Distribution.—*Resident* in extreme southwestern Costa Rica (Golfo Dulce region), on the Pacific slope of Panama (locally also on the Caribbean slope in the Canal Zone, and on Cébaco and Coiba islands), and in northern Venezuela (including Margarita Island).

Notes.—*C. lanceolata* and *C. linearis* are considered by some authors to be conspecific with the South American *C. pareola* (Linnaeus, 1766) [BLUE-BACKED MANAKIN]; the three constitute a superspecies.

Chiroxiphia linearis (Bonaparte). LONG-TAILED MANAKIN.

Pipra linearis Bonaparte, 1838, Proc. Zool. Soc. London (1837), p. 113. (Mexico = Santa Efigenia, Oaxaca.)

Habitat.—Undergrowth of forest edge and clearings, second-growth woodland, thickets and scrubby areas, mostly in dry forest, less frequently in humid areas (Tropical and Subtropical zones).

Distribution.—*Resident* on the Pacific slope from Oaxaca (west to Chivela) south to Costa Rica (east to the Dota Mountains, possibly also the Térraba region).

Notes.—See comments under *C. lanceolata.*

Genus PIPRA Linneaus

Pipra Linnaeus, 1764, Mus. Adolphi Friderici, 2, Prodr., p. 32. Type, by subsequent designation (G. R. Gray, 1840), *Pipra aureola* Linnaeus.

Pipra pipra (Linnaeus). WHITE-CROWNED MANAKIN.

Parus Pipra Linnaeus, 1758, Syst. Nat., ed. 10, 1, p. 190. Based mainly on the "Cacotototl" Seba, Thes., 2, p. 102, pl. 96, fig. 5. (in Indiis, error = Surinam.)

Habitat.—Understory of humid forest and dense second-growth woodland (Subtropical Zone, in South America also Tropical Zone).

Distribution.—*Resident* locally in Costa Rica (primarily on Caribbean slope of Talamanca and Central cordilleras) and Panama (eastern Chiriquí, both slopes of Veraguas, and the Caribbean slope of Coclé), and in South America from northern and central Colombia, southern Venezuela and the Guianas south, east of the Andes, to northeastern Peru and Amazonian and coastal southeastern Brazil.

Pipra coronata Spix. BLUE-CROWNED MANAKIN.

Pipra coronata Spix, 1825, Avium Spec. Nov. Bras., 2, p. 5, pl. 7, fig. 1. (ad pagum St. Pauli in sylviis fl. Solimoëns = São Paulo de Olivença, Rio Solimões, Brazil.)

Habitat.—Understory of humid forest and dense second-growth woodland (Tropical and Subtropical zones).

Distribution.—*Resident* locally in Costa Rica (west to the Gulf of Nicoya on the Pacific slope, and in the Sixaola region in the southeast) and Panama (western portion east to Veraguas, and on both slopes from the Canal Zone eastward), and in South America from Colombia and southern Venezuela south, west of the Andes to northwestern Ecuador and east of the Andes to eastern Peru, northern Bolivia, and the western and central portions of Amazonian Brazil.

Notes.—*P. coronata* and the South American *P. isidorei* Sclater, 1852, *P. coeruleocapilla* Tschudi, 1844, *P. nattereri* Sclater, 1865, *P. vilasboasi* Sick, 1959, *P. iris* Schinz, 1851, and *P. serena* Linnaeus, 1766, appear to constitute a superspecies.

Pipra erythrocephala (Linnaeus). GOLDEN-HEADED MANAKIN.

Parus erythrocephalus Linnaeus, 1758, Syst. Nat., ed. 10, 1, p. 191. Based on *Parus auricapillus* Klein, Hist. Avium, p. 86, and "The Golden-headed Black Titmouse" Edwards, Nat. Hist. Birds, 1, p. 21, pl. 21, lower fig. (in America australi = Surinam.)

Habitat.—Humid forest, forest edge and second-growth woodland (Tropical and Subtropical zones).

Distribution.—*Resident* in eastern Panama (from eastern San Blas and eastern Panamá province eastward), and in South America from Colombia, Venezuela (also Trinidad) and the Guianas south, mostly east of the Andes, to eastern Peru and Amazonian Brazil (north of the Amazon).

Notes.—*P. erythrocephala, P. mentalis* and three South American species, *P. rubrocapilla* Temminck, 1821, *P. chloromeros* Tschudi, 1844, and *P. cornuta* Spix, 1825, appear to constitute a superspecies.

Pipra mentalis Sclater. RED-CAPPED MANAKIN.

Pipra mentalis Sclater, 1857, Proc. Zool. Soc. London (1856), p. 299, pl. 121. (Cordova [=Córdoba] in the State of Vera Cruz, Southern Mexico.)

Habitat.—Humid lowland and foothill forest, forest edge and second-growth woodland (Tropical and lower Subtropical zones).

Distribution.—*Resident* from southeastern Mexico (southern Veracruz, northern Oaxaca, Tabasco, Chiapas and the Yucatan Peninsula) south on the Caribbean slope of northern Central America to Nicaragua, on both slopes of Costa Rica (absent from the dry northwest) and Panama (east on the Caribbean slope to western San Blas, and on the Pacific to eastern Panamá province), and in western Colombia and northwestern Ecuador.

Notes.—Also known as YELLOW-THIGHED MANAKIN. See comments under *P. erythrocephala.*

Family OXYRUNCIDAE: Sharpbills

Genus OXYRUNCUS Temminck

Oxyruncus Temminck, 1820, Man. Ornithol., ed. 2, 1, p. lxxx [generic character only, no type-species indicated]. Type, by monotypy, *Oxyrhynchus flammiceps* Temminck = *Oxyrhynchus cristatus* Swainson.

Oxyruncus cristatus Swainson. SHARPBILL.

Oxyrhynchus [sic] *cristatus* Swainson, 1821, Zool. Illus., ser. 1, 1 (9), pl. 49. (Brazil.)

Habitat.—Humid forest, forest edge and dense second-growth woodland (Subtropical Zone, in South America also Tropical Zone).

Distribution.—*Resident* (with disjunct distribution) in Costa Rica (Caribbean slope of northwestern and central highlands, and Dota Mountains), Panama (recorded western Chiriquí, Veraguas and eastern Darién), southern Venezuela, Guyana, Surinam, eastern Peru, eastern and southeastern Brazil, and Paraguay.

Suborder PASSERES: Oscines

Family ALAUDIDAE: Larks

Genus ALAUDA Linnaeus

Alauda Linnaeus, 1758, Syst. Nat., ed. 10, 1, p. 165. Type, by subsequent designation (Selby, 1825), *Alauda arvensis* Linnaeus.

Alauda arvensis Linnaeus. EURASIAN SKYLARK. [473.]

Alauda arvensis Linnaeus, 1758, Syst. Nat., ed. 10, 1, p. 165. (in Europæ apricis = Uppsala, Sweden.)

Habitat.—Open country, grasslands, tundra, marshy and sandy areas, and wide forest clearings.

Distribution.—*Breeds* from the British Isles, Scandinavia, northern Russia and northern Siberia south to northwestern Africa, the northern Mediterranean region, Asia Minor, northern China, Korea and Japan.

Winters from the breeding range (except the northern portions) south to northern Africa, the Persian Gulf and eastern China.

In migration ranges regularly to the western Aleutian Islands (Attu, Agattu, Shemya), and casually to St. Lawrence Island and the Pribilofs (St. George, where possibly has bred).

Introduced and established in the Hawaiian Islands (main islands from Niihau eastward), British Columbia (Vancouver Island, with recent spread to the adjacent mainland and to San Juan Island, Washington), New York (Brooklyn in 1887, where extirpated by1913), Australia and New Zealand. Birds introduced elsewhere in North America did not become established.

Accidental in the western Hawaiian Islands (Kure), Bermuda, Madeira and the Canary Islands. An individual, which was photographed and extensively studied, wintered for three successive years (1978–1980) at Point Reyes, California; European experts have identified this bird as *A. arvensis,* probably one of the Asiatic races.

Notes.—Also known as EUROPEAN or COMMON SKYLARK, and, in Old World literature, as the SKY LARK. North American introductions, the many in the Hawaiian Islands (with one exception), and the vagrant individual reported from Bermuda pertain to the European race, *A. a. arvensis*; transients through Alaska, the report from Kure, and probably the California individual, are referable to the Siberian *A. a. pekinensis* Swinhoe, 1863. One Hawaiian introduction (in 1934) was of the Japanese form, the relationships of which are uncertain; it may be a full species, *A. japonica* Temminck and Schlegel, 1848 [JAPANESE SKYLARK], a subspecies of the Asiatic species *A. gulgula* Franklin, 1831, or, as here regarded, a race of *A. arvensis.*

Genus EREMOPHILA Boie

Eremophila Boie, 1828, Isis von Oken, col. 322. Type, by subsequent designation (Sharpe, 1874), *O. alpestris* = *Alauda alpestris* Linnaeus.

Otocoris Bonaparte, 1838, Nuovi Ann. Sci. Nat. Bologna, 2, p. 407. Type, by monotypy, *Phileremos cornutus* Bonaparte = *Alauda cornuta* Wilson = *Alauda alpestris* Linnaeus.

Eremophila alpestris (Linnaeus). HORNED LARK. [474.]

Alauda alpestris Linnaeus, 1758, Syst. Nat., ed. 10, 1, p. 166. Based mainly on "The Lark" Catesby, Nat. Hist. Carolina, 1, p. 32, pl. 32. (in America septentrionali = coast of South Carolina.)

Habitat.—Grassland, tundra, sandy regions, desert playas, grazed pastures, stubble fields, open cultivated areas and, rarely, open areas in forest (Subtropical to Temperate, locally Tropical zones).

Distribution.—*Breeds* in North America from western and northern Alaska, the Arctic coast of northern Canada, Prince Patrick, Devon and northern Baffin islands, northern Quebec, northern Labrador and Newfoundland south to southern Baja California (including many islands), central Sonora, in the Central Plateau region to western Veracruz and Oaxaca (also to sea level in the Isthmus of Tehuantepec), the Gulf coast (from northwestern Tamaulipas to southwestern Louisiana), northwestern Louisiana, central Missouri, southern Tennessee, extreme northern Alabama and North Carolina; in South America in the Eastern Andes of Colombia (near Bogotá); and in Eurasia from the Arctic coast south to extreme northern Africa, Asia Minor, the Himalayas and Japan.

Winters in North America from southern Canada (British Columbia east to Newfoundland) south throughout the breeding range, and, locally or irregularly, to the Gulf coast and southern Florida; in Colombia; and in Eurasia in the breeding range except for the more northern portions.

Accidental in Greenland, the western Aleutians (Shemya) and Bermuda.

Notes.—Known in the Old World as SHORE LARK. *E. alpestris* and the North African *E. bilopha* (Temminck, 1823) are closely related; they constitute a superspecies. At least one Eurasian race, *E. a. flava* (Gmelin, 1789), occurs casually as a migrant in western Alaska (St. Lawrence Island).

Family **HIRUNDINIDAE**: Swallows

Subfamily HIRUNDININAE: Typical Swallows

Genus **PROGNE** Boie

Progne Boie, 1826, Isis von Oken, col. 971. Type, by monotypy, *Hirundo purpurea* "Gm. Wils. pl. 39, fig. 2" = *Hirundo subis* Linnaeus.

Notes.—See comments under *Phaeoprogne*.

Progne subis (Linnaeus). PURPLE MARTIN. [611.]

Hirundo subis Linnaeus, 1758, Syst. Nat., ed. 10, 1, p. 192. Based on "The Great American Martin" Edwards, Nat. Hist. Birds, 3, p. 120, pl. 120. (ad sinum Hudsonis = Hudson Bay.)

Habitat.—A wide variety of open and partly open situations, frequently near water or around towns, nesting in tree holes and bird houses (Subtropical and Temperate zones, in winter also Tropical Zone).

Distribution.—*Breeds* from southwestern British Columbia, western Washington, western Oregon, northern California, northern Arizona, central Utah, eastern Idaho, northeastern and east-central British Columbia, central Alberta, central

Saskatchewan, southern Manitoba, western and southern Ontario, southern Quebec, New Brunswick, Prince Edward Island (possibly) and central Nova Scotia south (except in desert regions) to southern Baja California and Isla Tiburón (off Sonora), in the Mexican highlands to Michoacán, Guanajuato and San Luis Potosí, and to southern Texas, the Gulf coast and southern Florida (except the Florida Keys).

Winters in South America from Colombia, Venezuela and the Guianas south, east of the Andes, to northern Bolivia and southeastern Brazil, casually in Florida.

In migration occurs regularly in Middle America (both slopes, rarely on the Pacific slope south of Nicaragua) and the Florida Keys, and casually through the Bahamas and Greater Antilles (recorded Cuba, Grand Cayman and Hispaniola, also a sight report for Puerto Rico).

Casual north to the Pribilof Islands (St. Paul), western and northern Alaska, central Yukon, northwestern Ontario and northern Nova Scotia. Accidental in Bermuda and the British Isles.

Notes.—Species limits in this complex are uncertain. Some authors treat *P. subis, P. cryptoleuca, P. dominicensis, P. sinaloae* and *P. chalybea* as conspecific; these five, along with the South American *P. modesta* complex (including *P. elegans*), constitute a superspecies. See also comments under these other species.

Progne cryptoleuca Baird. CUBAN MARTIN. [611.1.]

Progne cryptoleuca Baird, 1865, Rev. Am. Birds, 1, p. 277. (Cuba and Florida Keys? = Remedios, Cuba.)

Habitat.—Open and partly open situations, frequently near water or around towns.

Distribution.—*Breeds* on Cuba and the Isle of Pines.

Winter range unknown. Three specimens taken at Quiriguá and one from Gualán, in the Caribbean lowlands of Guatemala, and reported as *P. cryptoleuca* are referable to *P. chalybea*; another individual from Belize is referable to *P. subis*.

Casual in southern Florida (Cape Florida, Key West, Clearwater).

Notes.—Variously treated as a full species, a race of *P. dominicensis,* or a race of *P. subis*; see further comments under these species.

Progne dominicensis (Gmelin). CARIBBEAN MARTIN. [611.3.]

Hirundo dominicensis Gmelin, 1789, Syst. Nat., 1 (2), p. 1025. Based on "L'Hirondelle de S. Domingue" Brisson, Ornithologie, 2, p. 493, and "Hirondelle d'Amerique" Daubenton, Planches Enlum., pl. 545, fig. 1. (in insula S. Dominici = Hispaniola.)

Habitat.—Open and partly open situations, frequently along seacoasts, near fresh-water habitats, or around towns.

Distribution.—*Breeds* in the Greater Antilles (from Jamaica and Hispaniola eastward, absent from Cuba and the Isle of Pines), Lesser Antilles and Tobago.

Winters presumably in South America (no West Indian records in November or December).

Casual or accidental on Bermuda and in the Bahamas (Mayaguana, Great Inagua and Grand Turk).

Notes.—*P. dominicensis* and *P. sinaloae* are often considered conspecific

[SNOWY-BELLIED MARTIN], but the morphological similarity in these widely disjunct populations may be convergence. See also comments under *P. subis.*

Progne sinaloae Nelson. SINALOA MARTIN.

Progne sinaloæ Nelson, 1898, Proc. Biol. Soc. Wash., 12, p. 59. (Plomosas, Sinaloa.)

Habitat.—Pine-oak association and partly open situations in montane habitats (Subtropical and lower Temperate zones).

Distribution.—*Breeds* in the Sierra Madre Occidental of western Mexico from southeastern Sonora and southwestern Chihuahua south through Sinaloa, northern Nayarit and northwestern Jalisco to northern Michoacán.

Winter range unknown.

In migration recorded in northern Guatemala (Petén).

Notes.—This species has been treated as a race of *P. subis,* but the latter and *P. sinaloae* breed sympatrically in western Mexico without extensive hybridization (one possibly hybrid specimen reported). See also comments under *P. subis* and *P. dominicensis.*

Progne chalybea (Gmelin). GRAY-BREASTED MARTIN. [611.2.]

Hirundo chalybea Gmelin, 1789, Syst. Nat., 1 (2), p. 1026. Based mostly on "L'Hirondelle de Cayenne" Brisson, Ornithologie, 2, p. 495, pl. 46, fig. 1. (in Cayenna = Cayenne.)

Habitat.—Open and partly open situations, commonly near water or around human habitation (Tropical and Subtropical zones).

Distribution.—*Breeds* from Nayarit, Coahuila, Nuevo León and Tamaulipas south along both slopes of Middle America (including Isla Coiba off Panama), and in South America from Colombia, Venezuela (also Trinidad) and the Guianas south, west of the Andes to northwestern Peru and east of the Andes to eastern Peru, eastern Bolivia, northern Argentina and southern Brazil.

Winters sparingly in the northern parts of the breeding range, becoming more abundant and regular from Costa Rica and Panama south through South America to northern Bolivia and central Brazil (southernmost breeding populations also migratory, ranging north as far as Venezuela and Amazonian Brazil).

Casual in southern Texas (Rio Grande City, Hidalgo) and Tobago.

Notes.—See comments under *P. subis.*

Progne elegans Baird. SOUTHERN MARTIN. [611.4.]

Progne elegans Baird, 1865, Rev. Am. Birds, 1, p. 275, note. (Rio Bermejo, Argentina.)

Habitat & Distribution.—*Breeds* in open or partly open country from Bolivia, Paraguay and Uruguay south to central Argentina, and *winters* north to eastern Peru, Colombia and Amazonian Brazil, casually to eastern Panama (Puerto Olbadía, San Blas, also summer sight records of dark martins in eastern Panamá province and the Canal Zone probably pertaining to this species).

Accidental in southern Florida (Key West, 14 August 1890; Eisenmann and Haverschmidt, 1970, Condor, 72, pp. 368–369) and the Falkland Islands.

Notes.—Resident South American species *P. modesta* Gould, 1838 [GALAPAGOS

MARTIN], from the Galapagos Islands, and *P. murphyi* Chapman, 1925 [PERUVIAN MARTIN], from the coast of Peru and Chile, are regarded by some authors as conspecific with *P. elegans*. See also comments under *P. subis*.

Genus PHAEOPROGNE Baird

Phæoprogne Baird, 1865, Rev. Am. Birds, 1, pp. 272, 283. Type, by subsequent designation (Sharpe, 1885), *Hirundo tapera* Linnaeus.

Notes.—By some authors merged in *Progne*.

Phaeoprogne tapera (Linnaeus). BROWN-CHESTED MARTIN.

Hirundo Tapera Linnaeus, 1766, Syst. Nat., ed. 12, 1, p. 345. Based on "L'Hirondelle d'Amérique" Brisson, Ornithologie, 2, p. 502, pl. 45, fig. 3. (in America = Pernambuco, eastern Brazil.)

Habitat.—Forested regions, open situations and cultivated lands, especially near water, nesting in holes in the ground, in migration and winter in a wide variety of open and partly open situations in lowland areas (Tropical Zone).

Distribution.—*Breeds* from northern and eastern Colombia, Venezuela and the Guianas south, east of the Andes, to eastern Peru, Bolivia, northern Argentina, Uruguay and southern Brazil; also west of the Andes in southwestern Ecuador and northwestern Peru.

Winters from southern Bolivia and southern Brazil northward to northern South America and Panama (both slopes, irregularly westward to western Bocas del Toro and western Chiriquí), also a sight report from central Costa Rica.

Genus TACHYCINETA Cabanis

Tachycineta Cabanis, 1850, Mus. Heineanum, 1 (1851), p. 48. Type, by original designation, *Hirundo thalassina* Swainson.

Callichelidon (Bryant MS) Baird, 1865, Rev. Am. Birds, 1, pp. 271 [in key, as "*Callochelidon*"], 303. Type, by original designation, *Hirundo cyaneoviridis* Bryant.

Kalochelidon [subgenus] H. Bryant, 1867, Proc. Boston Soc. Nat. Hist., 11 (1866), p. 95. Type, by monotypy, *Hirundo euchrysea* var. *dominicensis* Bryant = *Hirundo sclateri* Cory = *Hirundo euchrysea* Gosse.

Iridoprocne [subgenus] Coues, 1878, Birds Colo. Valley, p. 412. Type, by original designation, *Hirundo bicolor* Vieillot.

Lamprochelidon Ridgway, 1903, Proc. Biol. Soc. Wash., 16, p. 106. Type, by original designation, *Hirundo euchrysea* Gosse.

Leucochelidon [subgenus] Brooke, 1974, Durban Mus. Novit., 10, p. 135. Type, by original designation, *Petrochelidon meyeni* Cabanis = *Hirundo leucopyga* Meyen.

Tachycineta bicolor (Vieillot). TREE SWALLOW. [614.]

Hirundo bicolor Vieillot, 1808, Hist. Nat. Ois. Am. Sept., 1 (1807), p. 61, pl. 31. (Centre des États-Unis = New York.)

Habitat.—Open situations near water, including streams, lakes, ponds, marshes and coastal regions, breeding in tree cavities or nest boxes near water, less frequently in open woodland away from water.

Distribution.—*Breeds* from western and central Alaska, central Yukon, northwestern and southern Mackenzie, northern Saskatchewan, northern Manitoba, northern Ontario, northern Quebec, central Labrador and Newfoundland south to southwestern Alaska (Cold Bay), along the Pacific coast to southern California, central Nevada, central Arizona, south-central New Mexico, south-central Texas (formerly), northeastern Louisiana, west-central Mississippi, Tennessee and North Carolina, generally sporadic or irregular as a breeder east of the Rocky Mountain states and south of the upper Mississippi and Ohio valleys, or along the Atlantic coast south of Massachusetts. Nonbreeding individuals occur in summer in northern Alaska.

Winters from southern California, southwestern Arizona, northern Mexico, Texas, the Gulf coast, and the Atlantic coast from New York (casually farther north) south along the Pacific coast of Mexico at least to southern Baja California and Colima, in the interior and along the Gulf-Caribbean coast of Middle America to Honduras (also the Swan Islands), Nicaragua and central Costa Rica (casually to western Panama and the Canal Zone), and to southern Florida, the Bahamas (New Providence) and Greater Antilles (including the Cayman Islands).

Casual or accidental on Wrangel Island, in the Pribilof and Aleutian islands, along the Arctic coast (from northern Yukon and Banks Islands east to Keewatin), and in Bermuda, Greenland, the British Isles, Colombia, Guyana, and off Trinidad.

Notes.—*T. bicolor* and *T. albilinea* are sometimes placed in the genus *Iridoprocne*.

Tachycineta albilinea (Lawrence). MANGROVE SWALLOW.

Petrochelidon albilinea Lawrence, 1863, Ann. Lyc. Nat. Hist. N.Y., 8, p. 2. (on the Atlantic side of the Isthmus of Panama, along the line of Panama Railroad = Canal Zone.)

Habitat.—Open areas near water, primarily around rivers, lakes, ponds, marshes and mangroves, less frequently over nearby meadows and fields, rarely along ocean beaches (Tropical Zone).

Distribution.—*Resident* [*albilinea* group] from southern Sonora, southeastern San Luis Potosí and southern Tamaulipas south along both slopes of Middle America (including the Yucatan Peninsula and most islands nearby) to eastern Panama (east on the Caribbean coast to eastern Colón, and on the Pacific to eastern Darién, including Isla Coiba); and [*stolzmanni* group] along the coast of northern Peru.

Notes.—Some authors regard the two groups as distinct species, *T. albilinea* and *T. stolzmanni* (Philippi, 1902). See also comments under *T. bicolor*.

Tachycineta euchrysea (Gosse). GOLDEN SWALLOW.

Hirundo euchrysea Gosse, 1847, Birds Jamaica, p. 68 (footnote). (higher mountains in the very centre of Jamaica, as in Manchester, and St. Ann's.)

Habitat.—Mountains, primarily in open areas, less frequently over forested regions.

Distribution.—*Resident* locally on Jamaica (where very rare) and Hispaniola.
Notes.—Often placed in the monotypic genus *Kalochelidon.*

Tachycineta thalassina (Swainson). VIOLET-GREEN SWALLOW. [615.]

Hirundo thalassinus Swainson, 1827, Philos. Mag., new ser., 1, p. 366. (Real del Monte, [Hidalgo,] Mexico.)

Habitat.—Open coniferous, deciduous or mixed forest and woodland, primarily in highlands, nesting in holes in cliff crevices, tree cavities or nest boxes, in migration and winter also meadows, fields and watercourses, more commonly in highland regions.

Distribution.—*Breeds* from central Alaska, central Yukon, extreme southwestern Mackenzie, northern British Columbia, southwestern Alberta, southwestern Saskatchewan, central Montana, western South Dakota and western Nebraska south to southern Alaska (west to the Alaska Peninsula), southern Baja California, coastal Sonora, in the Mexican highlands to Oaxaca and Veracruz, and to western Texas.

Winters from central coastal and southern California, Sonora, Chihuahua and Coahuila south in the interior of Middle America to Honduras, casually or irregularly to Costa Rica and western Panama (Chiriquí and western Panamá province).

Casual or accidental in the Aleutian Islands (Shemya, Unalaska), and east to southern Manitoba, North Dakota, Missouri and central Texas, also sight reports from Minnesota, Nova Scotia, New Hampshire, Oklahoma and Florida; an old record from Yucatán is questionable.

Tachycineta cyaneoviridis (Bryant). BAHAMA SWALLOW. [615.1.]

Hirundo cyaneoviridis H. Bryant, 1859, Proc. Boston Soc. Nat. Hist., 7, p. 111. (Nassau [New Providence, Bahamas].)

Habitat.—Open and partly open situations, nesting in pine woodland, locally on buildings in towns.

Distribution.—*Breeds* on the northern Bahama Islands (Grand Bahama, Great Abaco, Andros and New Providence). Summered once in the lower Florida Keys (Sugarloaf Key, 1974).

Winters, at least sparingly, throughout the Bahama Islands and in eastern Cuba.

In migration occurs irregularly in the lower Florida Keys and on Dry Tortugas, casually to southern Florida (recorded north to Tarpon Springs).

Notes.—Frequently placed in the monotypic genus *Callichelidon.*

Genus PYGOCHELIDON Baird

Pygochelidon Baird, 1865, Rev. Am. Birds, 1, pp. 270, 306. Type, by original designation, *Hirundo cyanoleuca* Vieillot.

Pygochelidon cyanoleuca (Vieillot). BLUE-AND-WHITE SWALLOW.

Hirundo cyanoleuca Vieillot, 1817, Nouv. Dict. Hist. Nat., nouv. éd., 14, p. 509. Based on "Golondrina Timoneles negros" Azara, Apunt. Hist. Nat. Páx. Parag., 2, p. 508 (no. 303). (Paraguay.)

Habitat.—Open and partly open situations, often around towns, in Middle

America primarily in highlands (Tropical to Temperate zones, mostly Subtropical Zone in Middle America).

Distribution.—*Breeds* [*patagonica* group] from central Chile and central (possibly north-central) Argentina south to Tierra del Fuego.

Winters [*patagonica* group] from northern Chile and northern Argentina north regularly to northern South America and central Panama (west to the Canal Zone), casually to Nicaragua and Chiapas (a report from Honduras is erroneous).

Resident [*cyanoleuca* group] in the foothills and highlands of Costa Rica (northwest to the Cordillera de Guanacaste) and western Panama (Chiriquí, Veraguas and western Panamá province); and in South America from Colombia, Venezuela (also Trinidad) and the Guianas south to Peru, Bolivia, northwestern Argentina, Paraguay, Uruguay and southern Brazil.

Notes.—Some authors regard the two groups as distinct species, *P. cyanoleuca* and *P. patagonica* (d'Orbigny and Lafresnaye, 1837) [PATAGONIAN SWALLOW]. This species is sometimes treated in the genus *Notiochelidon,* or occasionally placed in the South American genus *Atticora* Boie, 1844.

Genus **NOTICHELIDON** Baird

Notiochelidon Baird, 1865, Rev. Am. Birds, 1, pp. 270, 306. Type, by original designation, *Atticora pileata* Gould.

Notiochelidon pileata (Gould). BLACK-CAPPED SWALLOW.

Atticora pileata Gould, 1858, Proc. Zool. Soc. London, p. 355. (Guatemala.)

Habitat.—Open woodland, forest edge, partly open situations, and cultivated regions, primarily in interior highlands (Subtropical and Temperate zones).

Distribution.—*Resident* in the mountains of Chiapas, Guatemala and El Salvador.

Casual in nonbreeding season in western Honduras (La Esperanza).

Notes.—Also known as COBAN SWALLOW.

Genus **NEOCHELIDON** Sclater

Microchelidon (not Reichenbach, 1853) Sclater, 1862, Cat. Collect. Am. Birds, p. 39. Type, by monotypy, *Petrochelidon tibialis* Cassin.
Neochelidon Sclater, 1862, Cat. Collect. Am. Birds, p. [xvi]. New name for *Microchelidon* Sclater, preoccupied.

Neochelidon tibialis (Cassin). WHITE-THIGHED SWALLOW.

Petrochelidon ? *tibialis* Cassin, 1853, Proc. Acad. Nat. Sci. Philadelphia, 6, p. 370. (probably Brazil = Rio de Janeiro, Brazil.)

Habitat.—Humid lowland forest clearings, forest edge, scrub, partly open situations, along streams, and around villages (Tropical Zone).

Distribution.—*Resident* in Panama (west to Coclé, the Canal Zone and western Panamá province), and in South America locally from Colombia east through southern Venezuela to Surinam, and south, east of the Andes, to eastern Ecuador, southeastern Peru, and Amazonian and southeastern Brazil.

Genus **STELGIDOPTERYX** Baird

Stelgidopteryx [subgenus] Baird, 1858, *in* Baird, Cassin and Lawrence, Rep. Explor. Surv. R. R. Pac., 9, pp. xxxiv, 312. Type, by monotypy, *Hirundo serripennis* Audubon.

Stelgidopteryx serripennis (Audubon). NORTHERN ROUGH-WINGED SWALLOW. [617.]

> *Hirundo serripennis* Audubon, 1838, Ornithol Biogr., 4, p. 593. (Charleston, South Carolina.)

Habitat.—Open and partly open situations, especially along watercourses with steep banks, and roadside cuts, where nesting in burrows, also locally [*ridgwayi* group] in caves and old buildings.

Distribution.—*Breeds* [*serripennis* group] from southeastern Alaska (rarely), central British Columbia, southern Alberta, southern Saskatchewan, southern Manitoba, western and southern Ontario, southwestern Quebec, central Maine and southwestern New Brunswick south to southern Baja California, Oaxaca, Veracruz, in the Middle American highlands through Chiapas, Guatemala, western Belize, El Salvador, Honduras and Nicaragua to Costa Rica, and to southern Texas, the Gulf coast, and south-central and southwestern Florida.

Winters [*serripennis* group] from northern Mexico, southern Texas, southern Louisiana and southern Florida (casually South Carolina) south through the breeding range in Mexico and Central America, and lowlands to Panama; breeding populations from the lowlands and central interior of Mexico southward are generally sedentary.

In migration [*serripennis* group] occurs in the northwestern Bahama Islands, Cuba, Jamaica, and the Cayman and Swan islands, casually to southwestern and south-coastal Alaska.

Resident [*ridgwayi* group] on the Yucatan Peninsula.

Casual or accidental [*serripennis* group] in northern Alaska (Barrow) and southern Yukon, also sight reports from the Revillagigedos (Socorro Island) and Virgin Islands (St. John).

Notes.—Some authors treat the two groups as distinct species, *S. serripennis* [NORTHERN ROUGH-WINGED SWALLOW] and *S. ridgwayi* Nelson, 1901 [YUCATAN ROUGH-WINGED SWALLOW]. *S. serripennis* and *S. ruficollis* were formerly considered conspecific [ROUGH-WINGED SWALLOW], but sympatric breeding has recently been reported in Costa Rica (see Stiles, 1981, Auk, 98, pp. 282–293).

Stelgidopteryx ruficollis (Vieillot). SOUTHERN ROUGH-WINGED SWALLOW.

> *Hirundo ruficollis* Vieillot, 1817, Nouv. Dict. Hist. Nat., nouv. éd., 14, p. 523. (Brazil.)

Habitat.—Open and partly open situations, especially along watercourses with steep banks, and roadside cuts, where nesting in burrows (Tropical to Temperate zones).

Distribution.—*Resident* in the lowlands from eastern Honduras (Olancho) south through Nicaragua (Caribbean slope), Costa Rica (both slopes, on the Pacific northwest to the Gulf of Nicoya) and Panama, and in South America from Colombia, Venezuela (also Trinidad) and the Guianas south, west of the Andes to northwestern Peru and east of the Andes to central Argentina.

Notes.—See comments under *S. serripennis*.

Genus **RIPARIA** Forster

Riparia T. Forster, 1817, Synop. Cat. Br. Birds, p. 17. Type, by monotypy, *Riparia europaea* Forster = *Hirundo riparia* Linnaeus.

Riparia riparia (Linnaeus). BANK SWALLOW. [616.]

Hirundo riparia Linnaeus, 1758, Syst. Nat., ed. 10, 1, p. 192. (in Europæ collibus arenosis abruptis = Sweden.)

Habitat.—Open and partly open situations, frequently near flowing water, nesting in burrows in sand, dirt or gravel banks and cuts.

Distribution.—*Breeds* in North America from western and central Alaska, central Yukon, northwestern and south-central Mackenzie, northern Saskatchewan, northern Manitoba, northern Ontario, central Quebec, southern Labrador and southwestern Newfoundland south to southern Alaska (west to the eastern Aleutians), southern California (but rare west of the coast ranges from British Columbia to Oregon), western Nevada, northern Utah, Colorado, southern New Mexico, southern Texas, Arkansas, Tennessee, northern Alabama, central West Virginia, eastern Virginia, and (casually) northwestern North Carolina and south-central South Carolina; and in Eurasia from the Hebrides, Orkneys, northern Scandinavia, northern Russia and Siberia south to the Mediterranean region, Palestine, Iran, Afghanistan, northern India, southeastern China and Japan.

Winters in central and eastern Panama (at least rarely), and in South America from Colombia, Venezuela and the Guianas south, primarily east of the Andes, to Peru, northern Argentina and Paraguay, casually to northern Chile; and in the Old World from the Mediterranean region, Near East, northern India and eastern China south to tropical and eastern Africa, Madagascar, Arabia, southern India, Southeast Asia, Borneo and the Philippines.

Migrates in the Americas widely through the southern United States, Middle America, the West Indies (rare in the Lesser Antilles), and northern South America (including the Netherlands Antilles east to Tobago and Trinidad); and in the Old World through the eastern Atlantic islands in addition to the region between breeding and wintering ranges.

Casual or accidental in the Pribilof, western Aleutian and Commander islands, on Victoria and Melville islands, and on Bermuda.

Notes.—Known in Old World literature as SAND MARTIN.

Genus **HIRUNDO** Linnaeus

Hirundo Linnaeus, 1758, Syst. Nat., ed. 10, 1, p. 191. Type, by subsequent designation (G. R. Gray, 1840), *Hirundo rustica* Linnaeus.

Petrochelidon Cabanis, 1850, Mus. Heineanum, 1 (1851), p. 47. Type, by subsequent designation (G. R. Gray, 1855), *Hirundo melanogaster* Swainson = *Hirundo pyrrhonota* Vieillot.

Hirundo pyrrhonota Vieillot. CLIFF SWALLOW. [612.]

Hirundo pyrrhonota Vieillot, 1817, Nouv. Dict. Hist. Nat., nouv. éd., 14, p. 519. (Paraguay.)

Habitat.—Open country, less frequently partly open situations, most frequently in the vicinity of water, nesting on cliffs, bridges, dams, buildings and, occasionally, in caves.

Distribution.—*Breeds* from western and central Alaska, central Yukon, northern Mackenzie, central Keewatin, northern Manitoba, northern Ontario, southern Quebec (including Anticosti Island), New Brunswick, Prince Edward Island and Nova Scotia south to south-coastal and southern Alaska, northern Baja California, Oaxaca, Veracruz, the Gulf coast (east to southwestern Louisiana), northern portion of the Gulf states (east to Georgia), and to western South Carolina and southern North Carolina, also in the Lake Okeechobee region of southern Florida; now scarce and local in the eastern portion of the breeding range.

Winters in South America from Paraguay, and central and southeastern Brazil south to central Argentina.

Migrates regularly through the southeastern United States, Middle America and northern South America (recorded Colombia, Venezuela and the Netherlands Antilles), rarely through the northwestern Bahama Islands, Cuba and the Virgin Islands.

Casual or accidental on Wrangel Island, and in northern Alaska, the Aleutians, Barbados, Chile, Tierra del Fuego and southern Greenland.

Notes.—This and the following species are often placed in the genus *Petrochelidon.*

Hirundo fulva Vieillot. CAVE SWALLOW. [612.1.]

Hirundo fulva Vieillot, 1808, Hist. Nat. Ois. Am. Sept., 1 (1807), p. 62, pl. 32. (Saint-Domingue = Hispaniola.)

Habitat.—Open country, less commonly partly open situations, frequently near water, nesting in caves, sinkholes and culverts.

Distribution.—*Breeds* from southeastern New Mexico (Carlsbad Caverns), and western and south-central Texas (east to Kerr County) south to southern Chihuahua, Coahuila and San Luis Potosí; in southern Mexico (central Chiapas, the state of Yucatán, and Quintana Roo); in the Greater Antilles east to Puerto Rico (including Gonâve, Tortue and Vieques islands, and Île-à-Vache); and in South America in southwestern Ecuador and northwestern Peru.

Winter range of northern populations unknown; breeding populations in southern Mexico, the Greater Antilles and South America are essentially resident, although the Cuban populations decrease in winter, and vagrants are recorded regularly in southern (casually northern) Florida and casually north to Nova Scotia (Seal Island, Sable Island).

In migration recorded in Tamaulipas and Chiapas (an old specimen record from Costa Rica has been questioned), also sight reports from Panama (eastern Panamá province).

Casual or accidental in Arizona (Tucson) and the Virgin Islands.

Notes.—The isolated South American form has sometimes been regarded as a distinct species, *H. rufocollaris* Peale, 1848. See also comments under *H. pyrrhonota.*

Hirundo rustica Linnaeus. BARN SWALLOW. [613.]

Hirundo rustica Linnaeus, 1758, Syst. Nat., ed. 10, 1, p. 191. (in Europæ domibus intra tectum = Sweden.)

Habitat.—Open situations, less frequently in partly open habitats, frequently near water, nesting in sheltered areas in buildings, under bridges, or in caves.

Distribution.—*Breeds* in North America from south-coastal and southeastern (formerly north-central) Alaska, southern Yukon, western Mackenzie, northwestern and east-central Saskatchewan, central Manitoba, northern Ontario, southern Quebec and southern Newfoundland south to Baja California, Jalisco, Michoacán, the state of México, Distrito Federal, central Puebla, northern Veracruz, the Gulf coast, north-central Florida and southern North Carolina (casually southeastern Georgia); and in Eurasia from Iceland, the British Isles, Faroe Islands, Scandinavia, northern Russia and northern Siberia south to the Mediterranean region, northern Africa, the Near East, Arabia, Iran, the Himalayas, China, Formosa and Japan.

Winters in the Americas from Panama (casually north to the southwestern United States, northern Mexico and southern Florida), Puerto Rico and the Lesser Antilles south throughout South America to Tierra del Fuego; and in the Old World south to tropical Africa, the East Indies, northern Australia and Micronesia.

Migrates through Middle America, the West Indies, and islands off the eastern Atlantic and western Pacific oceans and along continental coasts, as well as throughout continental areas between the breeding and wintering ranges, casually also through the Aleutians.

Casual or accidental in the western Hawaiian Islands; north to northern Alaska, to St. Lawrence, Pribilof, Aleutian, Victoria, Cornwallis and Mansel islands, and to northern Mackenzie, southern Keewatin and southern Labrador; and in Bermuda, southern Greenland, Tristan da Cunha and the Falkland Islands.

Notes.—*H. rustica* and the African *H. lucida* Hartlaub, 1858, are closely related and considered conspecific by some authors; they constitute a superspecies.

Genus DELICHON Horsfield and Moore

Delichon "Hodgs." Horsfield and Moore, 1854, Cat. Birds Mus. Hon. E. India Co., 1 (1856), p. 384. Type, by monotypy, *Delichon nipalensis* Horsfield and Moore.

Delichon urbica (Linnaeus). COMMON HOUSE-MARTIN. [615.2.]

Hirundo urbica Linnaeus, 1758, Syst. Nat., ed. 10, 1, p. 192. (in Europa = Sweden.)

Habitat & Distribution.—*Breeds* widely through most of Eurasia south to northern Africa, the Himalayas and China, commonly nesting on houses, and *winters* south to southern Africa, India and Southeast Asia, casually to Greenland, Iceland and the eastern Atlantic islands.

Accidental in Alaska (Nome, and St. Paul in the Pribilofs, 6–7 and 12 June 1974; Hall and Cardiff, 1978, Auk, 95, p. 429), and in Bermuda (Devonshire Parish, 9 August 1957; Wingate, 1958, Auk, 75, pp. 359–360).

Notes.—Known in Old World literature as the HOUSE MARTIN.

Family CORVIDAE: Jays, Magpies and Crows

Notes.—Recent studies have indicated that the division of this family into subfamilies is not warranted.

Genus PERISOREUS Bonaparte

Perisoreus Bonaparte, 1831, G. Arcad. Sci. Lett. Arti [Rome], 49, p. 42. Type, by subsequent designation (G. R. Gray, 1840), *Corvus canadensis* Linnaeus.

Perisoreus canadensis (Linnaeus). GRAY JAY. [484.]

Corvus canadensis Linnaeus, 1766, Syst. Nat., ed. 12, 1, p. 158. Based on "Le Geay brun de Canada" Brisson, Ornithologie, 2, p. 54, pl. 4, fig. 2. (in Canada = Quebec.)

Habitat.—Coniferous and mixed coniferous-deciduous forest (primarily spruce), including open and partly open woodland and around bogs.

Distribution.—*Breeds* from western and central Alaska, central Yukon, northern Mackenzie, southwestern Keewatin, northern Manitoba, northern Ontario, northern Quebec, northern Labrador and Newfoundland south to southern Alaska (west to the Alaska Peninsula, but absent from humid coastal forests of south-coastal and southeastern Alaska), British Columbia (including Vancouver Island, but absent from the Queen Charlotte Islands), northern California, eastern Oregon, central Idaho, central Utah, east-central Arizona (White Mountains), north-central New Mexico, east-central Colorado and southwestern South Dakota (Black Hills), and (east of the Rocky Mountains) to central Saskatchewan, southern Manitoba, northern Minnesota, northern Wisconsin, northern Michigan, southern Ontario, northern New York, northern New England, New Brunswick and Nova Scotia.

Winters generally throughout the breeding range, casually or irregularly south to northwestern Nebraska, central Minnesota, southeastern Wisconsin, central Michigan, southern Pennsylvania, central New York, Connecticut and Massachusetts.

Notes.—*P. canadensis* and the Old World *P. infaustus* (Linnaeus, 1758) appear to constitute a superspecies.

Genus CYANOCITTA Strickland

Cyanocitta Strickland, 1845, Ann. Mag. Nat. Hist., ser. 1, 15, pp. 260, 261. Type, by original designation, *Corvus cristatus* Linnaeus.

Cyanocitta stelleri (Gmelin). STELLER'S JAY. [478.]

Corvus Stelleri Gmelin, 1788, Syst. Nat., 1 (1), p. 370. Based on "Steller's Crow" Latham, Gen. Synop. Birds, 1 (1), p. 387. (in sinu Natka Americae borealis = Nootka Sound, Vancouver Island, British Columbia.)

Habitat.—Primarily coniferous and mixed coniferous-deciduous forest, including humid coniferous forest in northwestern North America, and arid pine-oak association in the Middle American highlands, occurring less frequently in open woodland, orchards and gardens (upper Subtropical and Temperate zones).

Distribution.—*Resident* from south-coastal and southeastern Alaska (west to the Kenai Peninsula), western and southeastern British Columbia, southwestern Alberta, western Montana, Wyoming, northern Colorado and western Nebraska south to southern California, Arizona, through the highlands of Middle America (except Belize) to north-central Nicaragua, and east to east-central Colorado, central New Mexico and western Texas (Davis and Guadalupe mountains).

Casual east to southern Saskatchewan, southwestern South Dakota, southwestern Kansas and central Texas, and south to extreme northwestern Baja California. Accidental in southeastern Quebec (Cap Rouge).

Notes.—*C. stelleri* and *C. cristata* hybridize infrequently in eastern Colorado; they may constitute a superspecies, although authors disagree on the level of relationship.

Cyanocitta cristata (Linnaeus). BLUE JAY. [477.]

Corvus cristatus Linnaeus, 1758, Syst. Nat., ed. 10, 1, p. 106. Based on "The Blew Jay" Catesby, Nat. Hist. Carolina, 1, p. 15, pl. 15. (in America septentrionali = South Carolina.)

Habitat.—Primarily forest (deciduous, mixed deciduous-coniferous or fir), open woodland, parks and residential areas, less frequently in open situations with scattered trees.

Distribution.—*Resident* from extreme east-central British Columbia, central and southeastern Alberta, central Saskatchewan, central Manitoba, southern Ontario, southern Quebec, New Brunswick, Prince Edward Island, Nova Scotia and Newfoundland south to central and southeastern Texas, the Gulf coast and southern Florida (except the Florida Keys), and west to eastern Montana, eastern Wyoming, eastern Colorado and east-central New Mexico.

Northern populations are partly migratory to the southern parts of the breeding range (casually to the Florida Keys), and irregular or casual west to southwestern British Columbia, western Washington, central Oregon, California (mostly northern), west-central Nevada, Idaho, Utah, Montana, northeastern Arizona and western New Mexico.

Accidental on Bermuda.

Notes.—See comments under *C. stelleri*.

Genus CALOCITTA Gray

Calocitta G. R. Gray, 1841, List Genera Birds, ed. 2, p. 50. Type, by original designation, *Pica bullockii* Wagler = *Pica formosa* Swainson.

Calocitta colliei (Vigors). BLACK-THROATED MAGPIE-JAY.

Pica colliei Vigors, 1829, Zool. J., 4 (1828), p. 353, pl. 12. (San Blas, Nayarit, Mexico.)

Habitat.—Arid scrub, deciduous forest, and riparian or open woodland (Tropical and lower Subtropical zones).

Distribution.—*Resident* on the Pacific slope from southern Sonora and western Chihuahua south to Nayarit, Jalisco and (possibly) Guanajuato.

A report from southeastern Arizona (Douglas) is almost certainly based on an escaped individual.

Notes.—*C. colliei* and *C. formosa* constitute a superspecies; they are considered conspecific by some authors. If treated as a single species, MAGPIE JAY is the appropriate English name.

Calocitta formosa (Swainson). WHITE-THROATED MAGPIE-JAY.

Pica formosa Swainson, 1827, Philos. Mag., new ser., 1, p. 437. (Temiscaltipec, Mexico = Temascaltepec, state of México.)

Habitat.—Arid deciduous forest, scrub and riparian woodland (Tropical and lower Subtropical zones).

Distribution.—*Resident* on the Pacific slope from Colima, Michoacán and western Puebla south to northwestern Costa Rica (Gulf of Nicoya region), also in arid interior valleys on the Gulf-Caribbean drainage in eastern Oaxaca, Chiapas, Guatemala (Motagua Valley) and Honduras.

Notes.—See comments under *C. colliei*.

Genus CYANOCORAX Boie

Cyanocorax Boie, 1826, Isis von Oken, col. 975. Type, by monotypy, *Corvus pileatus* Temminck = *Pica chrysops* Vieillot.

Psilorhinus Rüppell, 1837, Mus. Senckenb., 2 (2), p. 188. Type, by monotypy, *Psilorhinus mexicanus* Rüppell = *Pica morio* Wagler.

Cissilopha Bonaparte, 1850, Consp. Gen. Avium, 1 (2), p. 380. Type, by monotypy, *Garrulus sanblasianus* Lafresnaye = *Pica san-blasiana* Lafresnaye.

Xanthoura Bonaparte, 1850, Consp. Gen. Avium, 1 (2), p. 380. Type, by subsequent designation (G. R. Gray, 1855), *Corvus peruvianus* Gmelin = *Corvus yncas* Bonaparte.

Cyanocorax dickeyi Moore. TUFTED JAY.

Cyanocorax dickeyi Moore, 1935, Auk, 52, p. 275, pl. 13. (Rancho Batel, 5 miles N.E. of Santa Lucia, altitude 5200 ft., Sinaloa, Mexico.)

Habitat.—Humid montane forest, foraging also in riparian woodland and pine-oak association (Subtropical and Temperate zones).

Distribution.—*Resident* in the mountains of southeastern Sinaloa, northeastern Nayarit and southwestern Durango.

Cyanocorax affinis Pelzeln. BLACK-CHESTED JAY.

Cyanocorax affinis Pelzeln, 1856, Sitzungsber. K. Akad. Wiss. Wien, Math.-Naturwiss. Kl., 20, p. 164. (Bogotá, Colombia.)

Habitat.—Humid lowland and foothill forest, forest edge, second-growth woodland, riparian forest and, less frequently, dry deciduous woodland (Tropical and lower Subtropical zones).

Distribution.—*Resident* in southeastern Costa Rica (Sixaola region), Panama (both slopes), northern and eastern Colombia, and northwestern Venezuela.

Cyanocorax yncas (Boddaert). GREEN JAY. [483.]

Corvus yncas Boddaert, 1783, Table Planches Enlum., p. 38. Based on Daubenton, Planches Enlum., pl. 625. (Peru = Chilpes, Depto. de Junín.)

Habitat.—Humid forest, forest edge, dense second growth, clearings, plantations, pine-oak association and, less commonly, open situations with scattered trees (Tropical and Subtropical zones).

Distribution.—*Resident* from Nayarit, Nuevo León and southern Texas south in Middle America on the Pacific slope to western Guatemala, and on the Gulf-Caribbean slope to Belize, eastern Guatemala and north-central Honduras (to the Tela region and Valle del Aguán); and in South America from northern Colombia and northern Venezuela south, east of the Andes, to eastern Peru and northern Bolivia.

Notes.—The distinctive Middle American group has sometimes been treated as a species, *C. luxuosus* (Lesson, 1839) [GREEN JAY], separate from the South American *C. yncas* [INCA JAY]. Sometimes treated in the genus *Xanthoura*.

Cyanocorax morio (Wagler). BROWN JAY. [483.2.]

Pica morio Wagler, 1829, Isis von Oken, col. 751. (Mexico = Alvarado, Veracruz.)

Habitat.—Open woodland, forest edge, second-growth woodland, clearings and plantations, primarily in humid habitats (Tropical to lower Temperate zones).

Distribution.—*Resident* from extreme southern Texas (Starr County), Nuevo León and Tamaulipas south on the Gulf-Caribbean slope of Middle America to western Panama (recorded Bocas del Toro and western Colón), locally also on the Pacific drainage in central Costa Rica.

Casual on Isla Cancun, off Quintana Roo.

Notes.—Two distinct color morphs are regarded as separate species by some authors, *C. morio* [PLAIN-TIPPED BROWN-JAY] and *C. mexicanus* (Rüppell, 1837) [WHITE-TIPPED BROWN-JAY], the former occurring south to Tabasco, the latter north to central Veracruz; evidence strongly supports the treatment of the two forms as morphs of a single species. Frequently treated in the genus *Psilorhinus*.

Cyanocorax melanocyaneus (Hartlaub). BUSHY-CRESTED JAY.

Garrulus (Cyanocorax) melanocyaneus Hartlaub, 1844, Rev. Zool. [Paris], 7, p. 215. (Guatemala.)

Habitat.—Humid forest, forest edge, pine-oak association, open woodland and scrub, primarily in montane situations, less frequently in humid lowland or arid habitats (Subtropical and lower Temperate zones, occasionally Tropical Zone).

Distribution.—*Resident* in the highlands (rarely lowlands) of Guatemala, El Salvador, Honduras and north-central Nicaragua.

Notes.—*C. melanocyaneus* is closely allied to the *C. sanblasianus-yucatanicus* superspecies; a reasonable treatment might be to consider these three species and *C. beecheii* as constituting a superspecies. This complex is often placed in the genus *Cissilopha*.

Cyanocorax sanblasianus (Lafresnaye). SAN BLAS JAY. [483.1.]

Pica San-Blasiana Lafresnaye, 1842, Mag. Zool. [Paris], ser. 2, 4, Ois., pl. 28, p. 1 and plate. (à Acapulco et à San Blas sur la côte ouest du Mexique = Acapulco, Guerrero.)

Habitat.—Open woodland, coastal scrub and mangroves (Tropical and lower Subtropical zones).

Distribution.—*Resident* on the Pacific slope from Nayarit south to central coastal Guerrero.

Accidental in Arizona (Tucson), flock of eight individuals, possibly the result of an escaped group.

Notes.—Also known as BLACK-AND-BLUE JAY. *C. sanblasianus* and *C. yucatanicus* constitute a superspecies; they are considered conspecific by some authors. See also comments under *C. melanocyaneus*.

Cyanocorax yucatanicus (Dubois). YUCATAN JAY.

Cyanocitta yucatanica Dubois, 1875, Bull. Acad. R. Sci. Lett. Beaux-Arts Belg., ser. 2, 40, p. 797. (Yucatan.)

Habitat.—Deciduous forest and coastal scrub (Tropical Zone).
Distribution.—*Resident* in Tabasco, the Yucatan Peninsula, northern Guatemala (Petén) and Belize.
Notes.—See comments under *C. melanocyaneus* and *C. sanblasianus.*

Cyanocorax beecheii (Vigors). PURPLISH-BACKED JAY.

Pica Beecheii Vigors, 1829, Zool. J., 4 (1828), p. 353. (Montereale = Mazatlán, Sinaloa, or San Blas, Nayarit.)

Habitat.—Arid scrub and thorn forest (Tropical and lower Subtropical zones).
Distribution.—*Resident* on the Pacific slope in Sonora, Sinaloa and Nayarit.
Notes.—See comments under *C. melanocyaneus.*

Genus CYANOLYCA Cabanis

Cyanolyca Cabanis, 1851, Mus. Heineanum, 1, p. 233. Type, by subsequent designation (G. R. Gray, 1855), *Cyanocorax armillatus* G. R. Gray = *Garrulus viridi-cyanus* Lafresnaye and d'Orbigny.

Cyanolyca cucullata (Ridgway). AZURE-HOODED JAY.

Cyanocorax cucullatus Ridgway, 1885, Proc. U.S. Natl. Mus., 8, p. 23. (Navarro, Costa Rica.)

Habitat.—Humid montane forest, forest edge, clearings, plantations and, locally, oak woodland (Subtropical and lower Temperate zones).
Distribution.—*Resident* locally in the mountains, primarily on the Gulf-Caribbean slope, in eastern Mexico (southeastern San Luis Potosí, Veracruz, eastern Oaxaca and interior Chiapas), Guatemala, western Honduras (east to the Sula Valley), Costa Rica and western Panama (east to Veraguas).
Notes.—*C. cucullata* and the South American *C. pulchra* (Lawrence, 1876) appear to constitute a superspecies.

Cyanolyca pumilo (Strickland). BLACK-THROATED JAY.

Cyanocorax pumilo Strickland, 1849, *in* Jardine, Contrib. Ornithol., p. 122 (in text). (Guatemala = probably Antigua, Depto. Sacatepéquez.)

Habitat.—Humid montane forest and pine-oak association (Subtropical and lower Temperate zones).
Distribution.—*Resident* in the mountains of Chiapas, Guatemala, El Salvador and Honduras; an old report from Belize is unsatisfactory.

Cyanolyca nana (Du Bus de Gisignies). DWARF JAY.

Cyanocorax nanus Du Bus de Gisignies, 1847, Bull. Acad. R. Sci. Lett. Beaux-Arts Belg., 14, p. 103. (Le Mexique = Mexico.)

Habitat.—Humid montane pine-oak and fir forest (upper Subtropical and Temperate zones).

Distribution.—*Resident,* at least formerly, in the mountains of Veracruz, Puebla and Oaxaca, now possibly restricted to the latter state; reports from the state of México are open to question.

Cyanolyca argentigula (Lawrence). SILVERY-THROATED JAY.

Cyanocitta argentigula Lawrence, 1875, Ann. Lyc. Nat. Hist. N.Y., 11, p. 88. (Talamanca, Costa Rica = near Pico Blanco, above Sipurio, Costa Rica.)

Habitat.—Humid montane forest and forest edge (Subtropical and lower Temperate zones).

Distribution.—*Resident* in the mountains of Costa Rica (Cordillera Central on slopes of Irazú and Turrialba volcanoes, and the Cordillera de Talamanca) and western Panama (western Chiriquí).

Notes.—*C. argentigula* and *C. mirabilis* have been considered by some authors as constituting a superspecies.

Cyanolyca mirabilis Nelson. WHITE-THROATED JAY.

Cyanolyca mirabilis Nelson, 1903, Proc. Biol. Soc. Wash., 16, p. 154. (Omilteme, Guerrero.)

Habitat.—Humid pine-oak association and (probably) montane forest (upper Subtropical and Temperate zones).

Distribution.—*Resident* in the mountains of Guerrero (Sierra Madre del Sur) and Oaxaca (Sierra de Miahuatlán and Sierra de Yucuyacua).

Notes.—Also known as OMILTEME JAY. See comments under *C. argentigula.*

Genus APHELOCOMA Cabanis

Aphelocoma Cabanis, 1851, Mus. Heineanum, 1, p. 221. Type, by subsequent designation (Baird, 1858), *Garrulus californicus* Vigors = *Corvus coerulescens* Bosc.
Sieberocitta [subgenus] Coues, 1903, Key N. Am. Birds, ed. 5, 1, p. 497. Type, by original designation, *Cyanocitta ultramarina arizonae* Ridgway = *Corvus ultramarinus* Bonaparte.

Aphelocoma coerulescens (Bosc). SCRUB JAY. [481.]

Corvus coerulescens Bosc, 1795, Bull. Sci. Soc. Philom. Paris, 1 (1791–1799), p. 87. (in Amer[ica]. Septentrional[e]. = Florida.)

Habitat.—Scrub (especially oak, pinyon and juniper), brush, chaparral and pine-oak association, in nonbreeding season also in riparian woodland, gardens, orchards and lowland brushy areas (Subtropical and Temperate zones).

Distribution.—*Resident* [*californica* group] from southwestern Washington south through western and central Oregon, California, and northwestern and west-central Nevada to southern Baja California; [*insularis* group] on Santa Cruz in the Channel Islands, California; [*woodhouseii* group] from southeastern Oregon, southern Idaho, southern Wyoming, western and southern Colorado, and western Oklahoma south to southern Arizona, in the Mexican highlands to Oaxaca (west of the Isthmus of Tehuantepec), Puebla and west-central Veracruz, and to western and west-central Texas (east to the Edwards Plateau); and [*coerulescens* group] in peninsular Florida, formerly from Dixie, Gilchrist, Alachua and Duval counties south to Collier and Dade counties (absent in the east-central interior from Osceola County southward), the range now much reduced, especially in the southern portion.

Casual [group uncertain] in southwestern British Columbia (Langley); [*woodhouseii* group] in eastern Washington, southwestern Nebraska, central Kansas and the Texas Panhandle; and [*coerulescens* group] in southeastern Georgia (Jekyll Island), with a report from Key West regarded as erroneous.

Notes.—The four groups are considered by a few authors as distinct species, *A. californica* (Vigors, 1839) [CALIFORNIA JAY, 481], *A. insularis* Henshaw, 1886 [SANTA CRUZ JAY, 481.1], *A. woodhouseii* (Baird, 1858) [WOODHOUSE'S JAY, 480] and *A. coerulescens* [FLORIDA JAY, 479].

Aphelocoma ultramarina (Bonaparte). GRAY-BREASTED JAY. [482.]

Corvus ultramarinus Bonaparte, 1825, J. Acad. Nat. Sci. Philadelphia, 4, p. 387. (No locality given = Temascaltepec, state of México.)

Habitat.—Oak woodland, pine-oak association, juniper, scrub and, rarely, lowland riparian woodland (Subtropical and Temperate zones).

Distribution.—*Resident* from central Arizona, southwestern New Mexico, northern Chihuahua, western Texas (Brewster County), northern Coahuila, central Nuevo León and west-central Tamaulipas south in the Mexican highlands to Colima, northern Michoacán, the state of México, northern Morelos, Puebla and west-central Veracruz.

Accidental in southern Kansas (Clark County).

Notes.—Also known as ULTRAMARINE or MEXICAN JAY.

Aphelocoma unicolor (Du Bus de Gisignies). UNICOLORED JAY.

Cyanocorax unicolor Du Bus de Gisignies, 1847, Bull. Acad. R. Sci. Lett. Beaux-Arts Belg., 14, p. 103. (le Mexique = San Cristóbal [=Ciudad de Las Cacas], Chiapas.)

Habitat.—Humid montane forest and pine-oak association, less frequently in dense second growth (Subtropical and lower Temperate zones).

Distribution.—*Resident* in the mountains of south-central Guerrero (Mount Teotepec), the state of México (formerly), western Puebla (Pinal, at least formerly), Oaxaca (Sierra de Juárez and Sierra de Zempoaltepec), Chiapas, Guatemala, El Salvador (Los Esesmiles) and Honduras.

Genus **GYMNORHINUS** Wied

Gymnorhinus Wied, 1841, Reise N.-Am., 2, p. 21. Type, by monotypy, *Gymnorhinus cyanocephalus* Wied.

Gymnorhinus cyanocephalus Wied. PINYON JAY. [492.]

Gymnorhinus cyanocephalus Wied, 1841, Reise N.-Am., 2, p. 22. (am Maria-River = between the Marias and Yellowstone rivers, Montana.)

Habitat.—Pinyon-juniper woodland, less frequently pine, in nonbreeding season also scrub oak and sagebrush.

Distribution.—*Breeds* from central Oregon, southern Idaho, east-central Montana and western South Dakota south through California (primarily the eastern and southern mountains) to northern Baja California (Sierra Juárez and Sierra San Pedro Mártir), southern Nevada, northwestern and east-central Arizona, central (probably also southern) New Mexico and western Oklahoma.

Winters throughout the breeding range and irregularly from northwestern Oregon, southern Washington, northern Idaho and northwestern Montana south to southeastern Arizona, northern Chihuahua and central Texas, and east to western Nebraska and western Kansas, casually to North Dakota and to the Channel Islands (off California).

Casual to southwestern Saskatchewan.

Genus NUCIFRAGA Brisson

Nucifraga Brisson, 1760, Ornithologie, 1, p. 30; 2, p. 58. Type, by tautonymy, *Nucifraga* Brisson = *Corvus caryocatactes* Linnaeus.

Nucifraga columbiana (Wilson). CLARK'S NUTCRACKER. [491.]

Corvus columbianus Wilson, 1811, Am. Ornithol., 3, pp. xv, 29, pl. 20, fig. 2. (shores of the Columbia = Clearwater River, about two miles north of Kamiah, Idaho.)

Habitat.—Open coniferous forest, forest edge and clearings, primarily in mountains, in winter also in lowlands.

Distribution.—*Resident* from central British Columbia, southwestern Alberta, western and central Montana, and western and southeastern Wyoming south through the mountains of central Washington, eastern Oregon, central and eastern California, and Nevada to northern Baja California (Sierra San Pedro Mártir), and in the Rockies to east-central Arizona and southern New Mexico.

Wanders irregularly north to central and southern Alaska, southern Yukon, central Alberta, southern Saskatchewan and southern Manitoba, and south to coastal Oregon, southwestern California, southern Arizona, northern Sonora (Sierra de la Madera), western Texas and northern Nuevo León (Cerro Potosí), and east to southwestern South Dakota, Nebraska and Kansas.

Casual or accidental east to Minnesota, Iowa, Wisconsin, Michigan, southern Ontario, Pennsylvania, Illinois, Missouri, Arkansas and southeastern Texas, and south to southwestern Durango (Sierra Madre Occidental).

Genus PICA Brisson

Pica Brisson, 1760, Ornithologie, 1, p. 20; 2, p. 35. Type, by tautonymy, *Pica* Brisson = *Corvus pica* Linnaeus.

Pica pica (Linnaeus). BLACK-BILLED MAGPIE. [475.]

Corvus Pica Linnaeus, 1758, Syst. Nat., ed. 10, 1, p. 106. (in Europa = Uppsala, Sweden.)

Habitat.—Open country (including grasslands), open situations with scattered trees, shrubby areas, riparian and open woodland, forest edge and farmlands, in either arid or humid habitats.

Distribution.—*Resident* in North America from south-coastal and southern Alaska (west to the Alaska Peninsula), southern Yukon, northern Alberta, central Saskatchewan, central Manitoba and western Ontario south (absent from coastal areas and regions west of the Cascade and Sierra Nevada ranges from southeastern

Alaska southward) to northeastern and east-central California (to Inyo County), south-central Nevada, south-central Utah, extreme northeastern Arizona (Apache County, formerly more widespread), northern New Mexico, western and northeastern Oklahoma and western Kansas; and in the Old World from the British Isles, Scandinavia, northern Russia and central Siberia south to the Mediterranean region, northwestern Africa, the Near East, Iran, the Himalayas, Southeast Asia, eastern China, Formosa and Japan.

Wanders casually or irregularly from northern (Umiat) and west-central Alaska, central Yukon, central Mackenzie, northern Saskatchewan, northern Manitoba, central Ontario and southern Quebec, and south to western Washington, east-central California (southern California reports probably pertain to escaped individuals), southern Nevada, northern Arizona, southern New Mexico, western Texas, northern Missouri, Iowa and Minnesota; accidental on Banks Islands. Also occurs casually or accidentally farther east, but many records pertain to escaped individuals; recorded from Wisconsin, Michigan, southern Ontario, New York and New Brunswick south to Illinois, Ohio, West Virginia (breeding reported in the Canaan Valley) and Pennsylvania (breeding reported in Pittsburgh area), also in South Carolina and Florida.

Notes.—Known in Old World literature as the MAGPIE. *P. pica* and *P. nuttalli* are closely related and considered conspecific by some authors; they constitute a superspecies.

Pica nuttalli (Audubon). YELLOW-BILLED MAGPIE. [476.]

Corvus Nutalli [sic] Audubon, 1837, Birds Am. (folio), 4, pl. 362, fig. 1. (Upper California, around the village of Sta. Barbara.)

Habitat.—Broken oak woodland interspersed with grasslands or cultivated lands, open riparian woodland, and savanna.

Distribution.—*Resident* in California in the Sacramento and San Joaquin valleys (from Shasta County south to Kern County), and in valleys of the coast ranges from San Francisco Bay south to Santa Barbara County (formerly to Ventura County).

Casual north to near the Oregon border in northern California (Siskiyou County).

Notes.—See comments under *P. pica.*

[Genus UROCISSA Cabanis]

Urocissa Cabanis, 1850, Mus. Heineanum, 1 (1851), p. 87. Type, by subsequent designation (G. R. Gray, 1855), *Cuculus sinensis* Linnaeus = *Corvus erythrorhynchus* Boddaert.

[Urocissa erythrorhyncha (Boddaert). RED-BILLED BLUE-MAGPIE.] See Appendix B.

Genus CORVUS Linnaeus

Corvus Linnaeus, 1758, Syst. Nat., ed. 10, 1, p. 105. Type, by tautonymy, *Corvus corax* Linnaeus (*Corvus,* prebinomial specific name, in synonymy).

[Corvus frugilegus Linnaeus. EURASIAN ROOK.] See Appendix B.

[**Corvus corone** Linnaeus. CARRION CROW.] See Appendix B.

Corvus brachyrhynchos Brehm. AMERICAN CROW. [488.]

Corvus brachyrhynchos C. L. Brehm, 1822, Beitr. Vögelkd., 2, p. 56. (Nordlichen Amerika = Boston, Massachusetts.)

Habitat.—Open forest and woodland for nesting and roosting, open and partly open country for foraging, including agricultural lands, urban areas, orchards and tidal flats, primarily in humid situations, restricted mostly to riparian forest and adjacent areas in arid regions.

Distribution.—*Breeds* from north-central British Columbia, southwestern Mackenzie, northern Saskatchewan, northern Manitoba, northern Ontario, central Quebec and southern Newfoundland south (except in Pacific coastal areas south to northwestern Washington) to northern Baja California (to lat. 32°S.), central Arizona, southern New Mexico, central and southeastern Texas, the Gulf coast and southern Florida (except the Florida Keys).

Winters from southern Canada (British Columbia east to Nova Scotia) south throughout the breeding range, and to the Florida Keys.

Introduced and established on Bermuda.

Casual in eastern Keewatin and northwestern Sonora.

Notes.—Also known as COMMON CROW. *C. brachyrhynchos* and *C. caurinus* are closely related and considered conspecific by some authors; they constitute a superspecies. Although a few authors consider *C. brachyrhynchos* and the Old World *C. corone* to be closely related (or even conspecific), the relationships of the latter appear to be with other Old World species.

Corvus caurinus Baird. NORTHWESTERN CROW. [489.]

Corvus caurinus Baird, 1858, *in* Baird, Cassin and Lawrence, Rep. Explor. Surv. R. R. Pac., 9, pp. xliii, 559, 569. (Washington Territory and northwestern coast = Fort Steilacoom, Washington.)

Habitat.—Coastal tidelands near coniferous woodland or forest edge, foraging also in adjacent croplands and around human habitation.

Distribution.—*Resident* along the Pacific coast from south-coastal and southeastern Alaska (west to Kodiak Island) south through British Columbia (including the Queen Charlotte and Vancouver islands) to northwestern Washington (Puget Sound area).

Wanders, at least casually, south to northwestern Oregon (Portland area).

Notes.—This species is apparently not closely related to the ecologically similar *C. ossifragus*. See also comments under *C. brachyrhynchos*.

Corvus palmarum Württemberg. PALM CROW.

Corvus palmarum Württemberg, 1835, Erste Reise N. Am., p. 68. (vicinity of Cibao Mountains, Dominican Republic.)

Habitat.—Woodland, in both lowlands and mountains, most commonly in highland pine forest.

Distribution.—*Resident* on Cuba (locally in Pinar del Río and Camagüey provinces, formerly more widespread) and Hispaniola (mostly in the mountains).

Corvus nasicus Temminck. CUBAN CROW.

Corvus nasicus Temminck, 1826, Planches Color., livr. 70, p. 413. (Cuba.)

Habitat.—Forest and woodland, also around towns and villages.

Distribution.—*Resident* on Cuba and the Isle of Pines, and in the southern Bahama Islands (Providenciales, North Caicos and Grand Caicos).

Notes.—*C. nasicus* and *C. leucognaphalus* are closely related and considered conspecific by some authors; they constitute a superspecies.

Corvus leucognaphalus Daudin. WHITE-NECKED CROW.

Corvus leucognaphalus Daudin, 1800, Traité Ornithol., 2, p. 231. (Puerto Rico.)

Habitat.—Wooded regions in lowlands and mountains, especially in pine forest.

Distribution.—*Resident* on Hispaniola and, at least formerly, Puerto Rico (where probably extinct, not recorded since 1963).

Casual on Gonâve and Saona islands.

Notes.—See comments under *C. nasicus.*

Corvus jamaicensis Gmelin. JAMAICAN CROW.

Corvus jamaicensis Gmelin, 1788, Syst. Nat., 1 (1), p. 367. Based largely on the "Chattering Crow" Latham, Gen. Synop. Birds, 1 (1), p. 377. (in Jamaicae montanis = Jamaica.)

Habitat.—Woodland, forest and parks, generally in partly open situations.

Distribution.—*Resident* on Jamaica.

Corvus imparatus Peters. MEXICAN CROW. [489.1.]

Corvus imparatus Peters, 1929, Proc. Biol. Soc. Wash., 42, p. 123. New name for *Corvus mexicanus* Auct. (not Gmelin) [= *Quiscalus mexicanus*]. (Rio La Cruz, Tamaulipas, Mexico.)

Habitat.—Arid scrub, riparian woodland, cultivated lands, and around human habitation, especially garbage dumps (Tropical Zone).

Distribution.—*Resident* on the Pacific coast from Sonora south to Colima; and on the Gulf coast from Nuevo León and Tamaulipas south to San Luis Potosí and northern Veracruz.

Regular postbreeding vagrant to southern Texas (north to Starr and Kenedy counties).

Casual in the Tres Marias Islands (María Madre Island).

Notes.—The Pacific coast populations, differing only in voice, have been regarded by some authors as a full species. *C. sinaloae* Davis, 1958 [SINALOA CROW]. Although *C. imparatus* and *C. ossifragus* are thought to be closely related or even conspecific by some authors, they apparently do not warrant treatment as a superspecies.

Corvus ossifragus Wilson. FISH CROW. [490.]

Corvus ossifragus Wilson, 1812, Am. Ornithol., 5, p. 27, pl. 37, fig. 2. (Great Egg-Harbor = Beasley's Point, New Jersey.)

Habitat.—Beaches, bays, inlets, lagoons, swamps and, less frequently, deciduous or coniferous woodland, in inland situations occurring primarily in bald-cypress swamps and along major watercourses.

Distribution.—*Resident* from New York (northwest to Ithaca) and Massachusetts south along the Atlantic-Gulf coast to southern Florida, and west to southern Texas; inland along major river systems to northwestern Louisiana, east-central Oklahoma, southeastern Missouri, southern Illinois, southwestern Kentucky, western Tennessee, central Georgia, western South Carolina, northwestern North Carolina, central Virginia, central Maryland, extreme eastern West Virginia and central Pennsylvania.

Casual in southern Maine (Portland).

Notes.—See comments under *C. caurinus* and *C. imparatus.*

Corvus hawaiiensis Peale. HAWAIIAN CROW. [489.2.]

Corvus tropicus (not Gmelin, 1788) Kerr, 1792, Anim. Kingdom, 1 (2), p. 640. (Hawaii.)

Corvus hawaiiensis Peale, 1848, U.S. Explor. Exped., 8, p. 106. (a few miles inland from the village of Kaawaloa, Hawaii.)

Habitat.—Upland forest and forest edge, and grazed lands.

Distribution.—*Resident* in the Hawaiian Islands on Hawaii, where now very much reduced in numbers and restricted to the Hualalai, and western and southern slopes of Mauna Loa.

Notes.—Also known as the ALALA.

Corvus cryptoleucus Couch. CHIHUAHUAN RAVEN. [487.]

Corvus cryptoleucus Couch, 1854, Proc. Acad. Nat. Sci. Philadelphia, 7, p. 66. (State of Tamaulipas, Mexico = Charco Escondido, Tamaulipas.)

Habitat.—Arid and semi-arid grassland, scrub and desert, especially in yucca-mesquite association (Tropical and Subtropical zones).

Distribution.—*Resident* from northern Sonora, south-central and southeastern Arizona, central and northeastern New Mexico, northeastern Colorado and south-central Nebraska south to Michoacán, Guanajuato, San Luis Potosí and Tamaulipas, and east to western Kansas, western Oklahoma, and central and southern Texas. Northeastern populations, especially those in Nebraska and Kansas, are migratory southward in winter.

Notes.—Formerly known as WHITE-NECKED RAVEN, a name now restricted to the African *C. albicollis* Latham, 1790.

Corvus corax Linnaeus. COMMON RAVEN. [486.]

Corvus Corax Linnaeus, 1758, Syst. Nat., ed. 10, 1, p. 105. (in Europa = Sweden.)

Habitat.—A wide variety of situations from lowlands to mountains, open country to forested regions, and humid regions to desert, but most frequently in mountainous or hilly areas, especially in vicinity of cliffs, a preferred nesting site (Tropical to Temperate zones).

Distribution.—*Resident* in North America from western and northern Alaska (including islands in the Bering Sea, but absent from the Arctic coast) and northern

Canada (throughout, including Arctic islands north to Prince Patrick and southern Ellesmere) south to the Aleutians (west to Attu), southern Baja California (including the Revillagigedo Islands, and islands in the Gulf of California), through Mexico and the highlands of Guatemala, El Salvador and Honduras to north-central Nicaragua, east to the eastern edge of the Rockies, western Oklahoma and central Texas, and, east of the Rockies, south to central Saskatchewan, southern Manitoba, northeastern Minnesota, northern Wisconsin, northern Michigan, southern Ontario, northern New York, Vermont, New Hampshire, southeastern Maine, New Brunswick, Nova Scotia and Newfoundland, also locally in the Appalachians of western Pennsylvania, West Virginia, western Maryland, eastern Kentucky, western Virginia, eastern Tennessee, western North Carolina and north-western Georgia; and in the Palearctic from Greenland, Iceland and Scandinavia east across the Arctic coasts to northern Siberia, and south to the Canary Islands, northwestern Africa, the Mediterranean region, Near East, Iran, and Himalayas, Manchuria and Japan. Formerly also bred locally south to northern Arkansas and northeastern Alabama.

Wanders sporadically or casually south throughout the Great Plains and to the southern shores of the Great Lakes, southern New York, New Jersey and southern New England, also to lower elevations in the Appalachians in central (formerly coastal) Virginia and western South Carolina.

Notes.—Also known as NORTHERN or HOLARCTIC RAVEN, and, in Old World literature, as the RAVEN. *C. corax* and the Old World *C. ruficollis* Lesson, 1830, appear to constitute a superspecies.

Family **PARIDAE**: Titmice

Notes.—The families Remizidae and Aegithalidae were formerly included in the Paridae; their true relationships are uncertain, so they are placed after the Paridae pending new evidence.

Genus **PARUS** Linnaeus

Parus Linnaeus, 1758, Syst. Nat., ed. 10, 1, p. 189. Type, by subsequent designation (G. R. Gray, 1840), *Parus major* Linnaeus.
Baeolophus Cabanis, 1850, Mus. Heineanum, 1 (1851), p. 91. Type, by monotypy, *Parus bicolor* Linnaeus.

Parus atricapillus Linnaeus. BLACK-CAPPED CHICKADEE. [735.]

Parus atricapillus Linnaeus, 1766, Syst. Nat., ed. 12, 1, p. 341. Based on "Le Mésange a teste [=tête] noire de Canada" Brisson, Ornithologie, 3, p. 553, pl. 29, fig. 1. (in Canada = Quebec City, Quebec.)

Habitat.—Deciduous or mixed deciduous-coniferous woodland, tall thickets, open woodland and parks.
Distribution.—*Resident* from western and central Alaska, southern Yukon, southwestern Mackenzie, northern Saskatchewan, north-central Manitoba, north-central Ontario, southern Quebec (including Anticosti Island) and Newfoundland south to southern Alaska (west to the Alaska Peninsula, and the Shumagin and Kodiak islands), northwestern California, southern Oregon, northeastern Nevada, southern Utah, central New Mexico, Kansas, northeastern Oklahoma, central Missouri, south-central Illinois, central Indiana, central Ohio, southern Pennsylvania and northern New Jersey, and in the Appalachians at higher elevations

through West Virginia, western Maryland and western Virginia to eastern Tennessee and western North Carolina.

Wanders irregularly south in winter to northern Arizona, central New Mexico, central Texas (questionably), Oklahoma, southeastern Missouri, central Kentucky, eastern Virginia and southeastern New Jersey.

Casual in Alaska on Nunivak Island, and at Wales and Point Barrow.

Notes.—*P. atricapillus* and *P. carolinensis* hybridize on a limited basis in the zone of contact in the midwestern states (Kansas east to Illinois) and in the southern Appalachians. *P. atricapillus* and *P. carolinensis* appear to constitute a superspecies; the Old World *P. montanus* Conrad von Baldenstein, 1827, may also belong in this superspecies. See also comments under *P. sclateri.*

Parus carolinensis Audubon. CAROLINA CHICKADEE. [736.]

> *Parus carolinensis* Audubon, 1834, Ornithol. Biogr., 2, p. 341. (Charleston in South Carolina [and] not far from New Orleans = Charleston, South Carolina.)

Habitat.—Deciduous woodland, forest clearings and edge, swamps, thickets, second-growth woodland, parks and brushy areas.

Distribution.—*Resident* from southern Kansas, central Missouri, central Illinois, central Indiana, central Ohio, southern Pennsylvania and central New Jersey south to central and southeastern Texas, the Gulf coast and northern peninsular Florida.

Wanders casually northward to southern Iowa, northern Illinois and southeastern Michigan, and south to central Florida.

Notes.—See comments under *P. atricapillus* and *P. sclateri.*

Parus sclateri Kleinschmidt. MEXICAN CHICKADEE. [737.]

> *Parus meridionalis* (not Lilljeborg, 1852) Sclater, 1857, Proc. Zool. Soc. London (1856), p. 293. (El Jacale in the State of Vera Cruz [or Puebla], Southern Mexico.)
>
> *Parus sclateri* Kleinschmidt, 1897, J. Ornithol., 45, p. 133. New name for *Parus meridionalis* Sclater, preoccupied.

Habitat.—Montane pine, spruce-fir and pine-oak forest, primarily in mesic habitats, in nonbreeding season also in more arid pine-oak association (Subtropical and Temperate zones).

Distribution.—*Resident* from northeastern Sonora, extreme southeastern Arizona (Chiricahua Mountains), southwestern New Mexico (Animas Mountains, casually Peloncillo Mountains), central Chihuahua, southern Coahuila and southern Nuevo León south in the Mexican highlands to central Oaxaca (west to the Isthmus of Tehuantepec) and western Veracruz.

Notes.—*P. sclateri* and *P. gambeli* may constitute a superspecies, which appears to have affinities with the *P. atricapillus-carolinensis-montanus* superspecies.

Parus gambeli Ridgway. MOUNTAIN CHICKADEE. [738.]

> *Parus montanus* (not Conrad von Baldenstein, 1827) Gambel, 1843, Proc. Acad. Nat. Sci. Philadelphia, 1, p. 259. (about a-day's journey [west] from Santa Fe, in New Mexico.)
>
> *Parus gambeli* Ridgway, 1886, A. O. U. Check-list N. Am. Birds, ed. 1, p. 335. New names for *Parus montanus* Gambel, preoccupied.

Habitat.—Montane coniferous forest, primarily pine, spruce-fir and locally pinyon-juniper, in nonbreeding season also in pine-oak association and riparian woodland.

Distribution.—*Resident* from northwestern and central British Columbia, southwestern Alberta, western and south-central Montana, and Colorado south (except for most of the coast ranges) to northern Baja California (Sierra Juárez and Sierra San Pedro Mártir), southern California, southern Nevada, central and southeastern Arizona (except mountains along the Mexican border), southern New Mexico and extreme western Texas (Davis and Guadalupe mountains). Recorded in summer (and possibly breeding) in southeastern Alaska (Warm Pass Valley) and southern Yukon.

Casual (mostly in winter) elsewhere in extreme southeastern Alaska, to the coastal ranges of Washington, Oregon and California, and east to southwestern Saskatchewan, southwestern South Dakota, western Nebraska, southwestern Kansas, and the Panhandle of western Texas.

Notes.—See comments under *P. sclateri.*

Parus cinctus Boddaert. SIBERIAN TIT. [739.]

Parus cinctus Boddaert, 1783, Table Planches Enlum., p. 44. Based on "Mésange de Sibérie" Daubenton, Planches Enlum., pl. 708, fig. 3. (Sibérie = Siberia.)

Habitat.—Boreal coniferous forest, primarily spruce, most commonly in stream basins, also locally in willow and aspen thickets.

Distribution.—*Resident* from northern Alaska east across northern Yukon (Old Crow) to northwestern Mackenzie (Aklavik, Fort Anderson), and south locally to western and central Alaska (Nulato, central Alaska Range); and in Eurasia from Scandinavia, northern Russia and northern Siberia south to northern Mongolia, Transbaicalia, northern Amurland, Kamchatka and Anadyrland.

Notes.—Also known as GRAY-HEADED or SIBERIAN CHICKADEE. *P. cinctus, P. hudsonicus* and *P. rufescens* may constitute a superspecies.

Parus hudsonicus Forster. BOREAL CHICKADEE. [740.]

Parus Hudsonicus J. R. Forster, 1772, Philos. Trans. R. Soc. London, 62, pp. 408, 430. (Severn River [west coast of Hudson Bay, Canada].)

Habitat.—Boreal coniferous (primarily spruce) and mixed coniferous-deciduous woodland, rarely in deciduous thickets and woodland.

Distribution.—*Resident* from western and central Alaska, central Yukon, northwestern and south-central Mackenzie, northern Saskatchewan, northern Manitoba, northern Ontario, northern Quebec, Labrador and Newfoundland south to southern Alaska (west to the Alaska Peninsula), British Columbia (east of the coast ranges), extreme north-central Washington, northwestern Montana, southwestern and central Alberta, central Saskatchewan, southern Manitoba, northern Minnesota, northern Michigan, Ontario (except extreme southern part), northern New York, northern Vermont, northern New Hampshire, New Brunswick, Maine and Nova Scotia.

Wanders irregularly after the breeding season north to southwestern Keewatin, and south to South Dakota, Iowa, Illinois, Indiana, Ohio, West Virginia, northern Virginia, Maryland and New Jersey.

Notes.—Also known as BROWN-CAPPED CHICKADEE. See comments under *P. cinctus*.

Parus rufescens Townsend. CHESTNUT-BACKED CHICKADEE. [741.]

Parus rufescens J. K. Townsend, 1837, J. Acad. Nat. Sci. Philadelphia, 7, p. 190. (forests of the Columbia River = Fort Vancouver, Washington.)

Habitat.—Coniferous and mixed coniferous-deciduous forest, primarily in humid regions, less frequently in pine forest, oak woodland, pine-oak association, and thickets.

Distribution.—*Resident* from south-central and southeastern Alaska (west to the Prince William Sound region), western British Columbia (including the Queen Charlotte and Vancouver islands), northern Idaho, western Alberta (locally) and northwestern Montana south through the coast ranges to southern California (San Luis Obispo and Santa Barbara counties), and through the Cascades and Sierra Nevada to central California (Mariposa County).

Wanders irregularly after the breeding season inland to southeastern British Columbia.

Notes.—See comments under *P. cinctus*.

Parus wollweberi (Bonaparte). BRIDLED TITMOUSE. [734.]

Lophophanes wollweberi Bonaparte, 1850, C. R. Acad. Sci. Paris, 31, p. 478. (en Mexico Zacatecas = Zacatecas, Zacatecas.)

Habitat.—Oak woodland and pine-oak association, occasionally also in cottonwood-willow-mesquite habitat, in winter also in riparian woodland (Subtropical and lower Temperate zones).

Distribution.—*Resident* from north-central Sonora, central and southeastern Arizona (north to the Mogollon Plateau), southwestern New Mexico, northwestern and central Chihuahua, northern Durango, Zacatecas, central Nuevo León and western Tamaulipas south in the Mexican highlands to central Oaxaca (west of the Isthmus of Tehuantepec) and western Veracruz.

Accidental in southwestern Arizona (Bill Williams Delta).

Parus varius Temminck and Schlegel. VARIED TIT. [734.1.]

Parus varius Temminck and Schlegel, 1848, *in* Siebold, Fauna Jpn., Aves, p. 71, pl. 35. (Japon = Honshu, Japan.)

Habitat.—Deciduous forest, mixed coniferous-deciduous forest, and open woodland.

Distribution.—*Resident* from southeastern Manchuria, Korea, Japan and the southern Kurile Islands south to Formosa, the Ryukyu Islands, Seven Islands of Izu, and other small islands south of Japan.

Introduced in the Hawaiian Islands about 1890 (on Kauai, Oahu, Maui and Hawaii) and established (at least formerly) on Kauai and Oahu; numbers diminished during the 1940's, and it is probably extirpated (last reported in the 1960's), although small numbers may persist in the Kokee area of Kauai and the Koolau Mountains of Oahu.

Parus inornatus Gambel. PLAIN TITMOUSE. [733.]

> *Parus inornatus* Gambel, 1845, Proc. Acad. Nat. Sci. Philadelphia, 2, p. 265. (Upper California = near Monterey, California.)

Habitat—Pinyon-juniper and oak woodland.

Distribution.—*Resident* from southern Oregon, northeastern Nevada, southeastern Idaho, southern Wyoming, central Colorado and western Oklahoma south to southern Baja California (absent from most of central Baja California), southeastern California, central and southeastern Arizona, extreme northeastern Sonora, southern New Mexico and extreme western Texas (El Paso to Guadalupe Mountains).

Notes.—*P. inornatus* and *P. bicolor* appear to constitute a superspecies.

Parus bicolor Linnaeus. TUFTED TITMOUSE. [731.]

> *Parus bicolor* Linnaeus, 1766, Syst. Nat., ed. 12, 1, p. 340. Based on "The Crested Titmouse" Catesby, Nat. Hist. Carolina, 1, p. 57, pl. 57. (in America septentrionali = South Carolina.)

Habitat.—Forest, woodland, scrub and partly open situations with scattered trees, from deciduous and mixed deciduous-coniferous woodland in the northeast to oak-juniper scrub, mesquite and riparian woodland in the southwest, also in parks and around human habitation where trees are present.

Distribution.—*Resident* [*bicolor* group] from northeastern Nebraska, central and eastern Iowa, southeastern Minnesota, southern Wisconsin, southern Michigan, extreme southern Ontario, northern Ohio, northwestern Pennsylvania, central New York, southern Vermont, western Massachusetts and southwestern Connecticut south to eastern Texas (formerly to San Angelo, San Antonio and Corpus Christi areas), the Gulf coast and southern Florida, and west to central Kansas and eastern Oklahoma; and [*atricristatus* group] from western and northern Texas (north to Randall and Armstrong counties, and east to Grimes, Lavaca and Calhoun counties) south through Coahuila, Nuevo León, Tamaulipas and eastern San Luis Potosí to Hidalgo and northern Veracruz.

Wanders [*bicolor* group] irregularly northward to South Dakota, northern Minnesota, southwestern Quebec, Rhode Island and Maine.

Accidental [*atricristatus* group] in Massachusetts (Weymouth).

Notes.—The two groups have been regarded as distinct species, *P. bicolor* [TUFTED TITMOUSE, 731] and *P. atricristatus* Cassin, 1850 [BLACK-CRESTED TITMOUSE, 732], but they interbreed freely in a narrow zone through east-central Texas. See also comments under *P. inornatus.*

Family **REMIZIDAE**: Penduline Tits and Verdins

Notes.—See comments under Paridae.

Genus **AURIPARUS** Baird

> *Auriparus* Baird, 1864, Rev. Am. Birds, 1, p. 85. Type, by original designation, *Aegithalus flaviceps* Sundevall.

Auriparus flaviceps (Sundevall). VERDIN. [746.]

Aegithalus flaviceps Sundevall, 1850, Kongl. Svensk. Vet.-Akad. Forh., 7, p. 129 (note). (e Sitka in America bor. occid., vel e California = probably near Loreto, lat. 26°N., Baja California.)

Habitat.—Desert and arid brush, primarily in mesquite and creosote-bush.

Distribution.—*Resident* from northeastern Baja California, southern California (north to Kern and Inyo counties), southern Nevada, northern Arizona, southwestern Utah, central New Mexico and central Texas (east to Callahan, Williamson and Calhoun counties) south to southern Baja California (including many Pacific and Gulf coastal islands), Jalisco, Guanajuato, Querétaro, Hidalgo and Tamaulipas.

Casual in southwestern California (northern San Diego County) and southwestern Oklahoma (Jackson County).

Family AEGITHALIDAE: Long-tailed Tits and Bushtits

Notes.—See comments under Paridae.

Genus PSALTRIPARUS Bonaparte

Psaltriparus Bonaparte, 1850, C. R. Acad. Sci. Paris, 31, p. 478. Type, by monotypy, *Psaltriparus personatus* Bonaparte = *Parus melanotis* Hartlaub = *Parus minimus* Townsend.

Psaltriparus minimus (Townsend). BUSHTIT. [743.]

Parus minimus J. K. Townsend, 1837, J. Acad. Nat. Sci. Philadelphia, 7, p. 190. (forests of Columbia River = probably near Fort Vancouver, Washington.)

Habitat.—Woodland and scrub (especially oak), pinyon-juniper, chaparral and pine-oak association (Subtropical and Temperate zones).

Distribution.—*Resident* from extreme southwestern British Columbia (Vancouver region), western Washington, western and southern Oregon, southwestern Idaho, northern Nevada, north-central Utah, southwestern Wyoming, north-central Colorado, western Oklahoma (Kenton) and central Texas (east to Bosque and Travis counties) south to southern Baja California (absent from most of central Baja California), southern California (absent from or casual in the southeastern portion north to the Salton Sea area), central and southeastern Arizona, and the highlands of Mexico to central Guatemala.

Casual in central Kansas (Hays).

Notes.—Populations from northeastern Sonora, southwestern New Mexico and western Texas southward, in which adult males are black-eared, have sometimes been regarded as a species, *P. melanotis* (Hartlaub, 1844) [BLACK-EARED BUSHTIT, 745], distinct from the northern *P. minimus* [COMMON BUSHTIT, 743], which ranges south to central Sonora, southern Arizona, southern New Mexico, and western and central Texas; that the difference in the two groups is a case of polymorphism is now well established. A few authors also consider the gray-headed forms of interior western North America to be a species, *P. plumbeus* (Baird, 1854) [LEAD-COLORED BUSHTIT, 744], distinct from the brown-headed form, *P. minimus,* occurring west of the Cascades and Sierra Nevada.

Family **SITTIDAE**: Nuthatches

Subfamily SITTINAE: Typical Nuthatches

Genus **SITTA** Linnaeus

Sitta Linnaeus, 1758, Syst. Nat., ed. 10, 1, p. 115. Type, by monotypy, *Sitta europaea* Linnaeus.

Sitta canadensis Linnaeus. RED-BREASTED NUTHATCH. [728.]

Sitta canadensis Linnaeus, 1766, Syst. Nat., ed. 12, 1, p. 177. Based on "Le Torchepot de Canada" Brisson, Ornithologie, 3, p. 592, pl. 29, fig. 4. (in Canada.)

Habitat.—Coniferous (mostly spruce and fir), mixed coniferous-deciduous forest, and aspen woodland, in migration and winter also in deciduous forest, open woodland, parks, scrub and riparian woodland.

Distribution.—*Breeds* from south-coastal and southeastern Alaska (west to the Kenai Peninsula and Kodiak Island), southern Yukon, southwestern Mackenzie, northwestern Saskatchewan, central Manitoba, western and north-central Ontario, south-central Quebec, Labrador and Newfoundland south to southern California (including casually on Santa Cruz Island), central and southeastern Arizona, southern New Mexico, central Colorado, Wyoming, western South Dakota, southwestern North Dakota, southern Saskatchewan, southern Manitoba, north-central and eastern Minnesota, southern Wisconsin, southern Michigan, southern Ontario, north-central Ohio, in the Appalachians to eastern Tennessee and western North Carolina, and to southeastern Pennsylvania (probably), southern New Jersey and southern New York (including Long Island); also on Guadalupe Island, off Baja California. Isolated cases of breeding have been reported from Kansas (Riley County), Iowa (Des Moines), Missouri (Kansas City) and Indiana (Terre Haute).

Winters throughout most of the breeding range except at the higher latitudes and elevations, irregularly south to northern Baja California, southern Arizona, southern New Mexico, southern Texas, the Gulf coast and central Florida.

Casual north to western and central Alaska and northern Manitoba, and to Bermuda.

Notes.—*S. canadensis* and the Asiatic *S. villosa* Verreaux, 1865, appear to constitute a superspecies; possibly they are conspecific. The treatment by a few authors of *S. canadensis* and the Old World *S. whiteheadi* Sharpe, 1884, and *S. yunnanensis* Ogilvie-Grant, 1900, as closely related has been questioned.

Sitta carolinensis Latham. WHITE-BREASTED NUTHATCH. [727.]

Sitta carolinensis Latham, 1790, Index Ornithol., 1, p. 262. Based mainly on "Le Torchepot de la Caroline" Brisson, Ornithologie, 3, p. 596. (in America, Jamaica; Europæa minor = South Carolina.)

Habitat.—Forest, primarily deciduous and mixed deciduous-coniferous, locally in coniferous, more frequently in open woodland, pinyon-juniper, clearings, forest edge, parks, and partly open situations with scattered trees (upper Subtropical and Temperate zones).

Distribution. — *Resident* from northwestern Washington, southern interior British Columbia, central Alberta, central Montana, southeastern Saskatchewan, southern Manitoba, southwestern Ontario, northern Minnesota, northern Wisconsin, northern Michigan, southern Ontario, southwestern Quebec, New Brunswick, Prince Edward Island and Nova Scotia south to southern Baja California (absent from most of central Baja California), southern California, southern Nevada, central and southeastern Arizona, in the highlands of Mexico to central Oaxaca, Puebla and western Veracruz, and to western and east-central Texas, the Gulf coast and northern (formerly central) Florida; absent from most of the Great Plains from southern Alberta and southwestern Saskatchewan south through the western portions of the plains states to northern and west-central Texas.

Casual in southwestern British Columbia, the Great Plains region, and southern Texas.

Notes. — A few authors regard *S. carolinensis* and the Old World *S. leucopsis* Gould, 1850, to be closely related.

Sitta pygmaea Vigors. PYGMY NUTHATCH. [730.]

Sitta pygmaea Vigors, 1839, *in* Beechey, Zool. Voy. "Blossom," p. 25, pl. 4. (Monterey, [California.])

Habitat. — Pine forest and woodland, especially ponderosa pine, less frequently pinyon-juniper.

Distribution. — *Resident* from southern interior British Columbia, northern Idaho, western Montana, central Wyoming and southwestern South Dakota south (west to the Cascades) to northern Baja California (including the coast ranges from west-central California southward, and coastal forests from Mendocino to San Luis Obispo counties), southern Nevada, central and southeastern Arizona, in the mountains of Mexico to Michoacán, the state of México, Morelos, Puebla and west-central Veracruz, and to central New Mexico, extreme western Texas (Davis and Guadalupe mountains) and extreme western Oklahoma (Panhandle).

Casual to southwestern British Columbia (Vancouver Island), central Montana, western South Dakota, southeastern Nebraska, central Iowa, eastern Kansas, and northern and northeastern Texas.

Notes. — *S. pygmaea* and *S. pusilla* are closely related and considered conspecific by some authors; they constitute a superspecies.

Sitta pusilla Latham. BROWN-HEADED NUTHATCH. [729.]

Sitta pusilla Latham, 1790, Index Ornithol., 1, p. 263. Based largely on "Le petit Torchepot de la Caroline" Brisson, Ornithologie, 3, p. 598. (in Carolina, Jamaica = South Carolina.)

Habitat. — Pine forest and pine-oak woodland, foraging less frequently in deciduous scrub, along fence rows, and in open situations with scattered trees.

Distribution. — *Resident* from southeastern Oklahoma, central Arkansas, the northern portions of the Gulf states, northern Georgia, extreme eastern Tennessee, western North Carolina, south-central and eastern Virginia, southern Maryland and southern Delaware south to eastern Texas (west to the Houston area), the Gulf coast and southern Florida; also in the northern Bahama Islands (Grand Bahama).

Casual or accidental north to Iowa (Lee County), Missouri (Ink), Wisconsin (Milwaukee), New York (Elmira) and New Jersey (Haddonfield).

Notes.—See comments under *S. pygmaea.*

Family CERTHIIDAE: Creepers

Subfamily CERTHIINAE: Typical Creepers

Genus CERTHIA Linnaeus

Certhia Linnaeus, 1758, Syst. Nat., ed. 10, 1, p. 118. Type, by tautonymy, *Certhia familiaris* Linnaeus (*Certhia,* prebinomial specific name, in synonymy).

Certhia americana Bonaparte. BROWN CREEPER. [726.]

Certhia familiaris (not Linnaeus, 1758) Audubon, 1838, Birds Am. (folio), 4, p. 419. (North America.)

Certhia Americana Bonaparte, 1838, Geogr. Comp. List, p. 11. New name for *Certhia familiaris* Audubon, preoccupied.

Habitat.—Coniferous and deciduous forest, more frequently in northern or montane habitats, locally in lowland situations, and in Middle America primarily in montane pine or pine-oak association; in migration and winter also in open woodland, scrub and parks (Subtropical and Temperate zones).

Distribution.—*Breeds* from southwestern, central and southeastern Alaska, central British Columbia (including the Queen Charlotte and Vancouver islands), central Alberta, central Saskatchewan, central Manitoba, central Ontario, southern Quebec (including Anticosti Island) and Newfoundland south to southern California, southern Nevada, central and southeastern Arizona, in the mountains of Middle America through Mexico, Guatemala and Honduras to north-central Nicaragua, to extreme western Texas (Guadalupe Mountains), southeastern Nebraska, southern Iowa, southeastern Missouri, southern Illinois, central Michigan, southern Ontario, eastern Ohio, West Virginia, in the Appalachians to eastern Tennessee and western North Carolina, and to the lowlands of Virginia, Maryland and Delaware. Recorded in summer (and possibly breeding) north to southern Yukon and northern Manitoba, and south to northern Arkansas, western Kentucky and central Indiana.

Winters generally throughout the breeding range, withdrawing from the higher latitude and altitudes, and south throughout the eastern United States to southern Texas, the Gulf coast and central Florida.

Notes.—*C. americana* has usually been regarded as conspecific with the Eurasian *C. familiaris* Linnaeus, 1758 [EUROPEAN TREE-CREEPER or, in Old World literature, the TREE CREEPER]; however, recent studies of vocalizations suggest a relationship, at least of the western North American populations, to another Old World species, *C. brachydactyla* C. L. Brehm, 1820 [SHORT-TOED TREE-CREEPER]. Until relationships in the entire complex are studied, it seems best to retain all three forms as species.

Family PYCNONOTIDAE: Bulbuls

Genus PYCNONOTUS Boie

Brachypus (not Meyer, 1814) Swainson, 1824, Zool. J., 1, p. 305. Type, by subsequent designation (Rand and Deignan, 1960), "Le Curouge" Levaillant = *Turdus cafer* Linnaeus.

Pycnonotus "Kuhl" Boie, 1826, Isis von Oken, col. 973. Type, by monotypy, *Turdus capensis* Linnaeus.

Pycnonotus cafer (Linnaeus). RED-VENTED BULBUL. [726.2.]

Turdus cafer Linnaeus, 1766, Syst. Nat., ed. 12, 1, p. 295. Based on "Le Merle dupé du Cap de Bonne Espérance" Brisson, Ornithologie, 2, p. 257, pl. 20, fig. 2. (ad Cap. b. spei, error = Ceylon.)

Habitat.—Scrub, brushy areas, second growth, gardens, urban residential areas, and now in the Hawaiian Islands penetrating into native forest.

Distribution.—*Resident* from Pakistan and the Himalayas south through India to Ceylon, central Burma and western Yunnan.

Introduced and established in the Hawaiian Islands (in 1966, on Oahu), and in the Fiji, Samoa, Tahiti and other Pacific islands.

Notes.—Two other Eurasian species, *P. leucogenys* (J. E. Gray, 1835) and *P. aurigaster* (Vieillot, 1818), are closely allied with *P. cafer,* forming zones of hybridization in areas of sympatry.

Pycnonotus jocosus (Linnaeus). RED-WHISKERED BULBUL. [726.1.]

Lanius jocosus Linnaeus, 1758, Syst. Nat., ed. 10, 1, p. 95. (in China = Canton, Kwangtung, China.)

Habitat.—Forest edge and clearings, second-growth woodland, brushy areas, cultivated lands, villages, and suburban residential areas.

Distribution.—*Resident* from India and southern China south to southern Laos and Cambodia; also in the Andaman Islands.

Introduced and established in the Hawaiian Islands (in 1967, on Oahu), southern Florida (Dade County), Australia (New South Wales) and the Nicobar Islands.

Family TROGLODYTIDAE: Wrens

Genus DONACOBIUS Swainson

Donacobius Swainson, 1832, Zool. Illus., ser. 2, 2, text to pl. 72. Type, by monotypy, *Donacobius vociferans* Swainson = *Turdus atricapilla* Linnaeus.

Notes.—Formerly placed in the Mimidae, but recent studies indicate that this genus is properly placed in the Troglodytidae, probably closest to *Campylorhynchus.*

Donacobius atricapillus (Linnaeus). BLACK-CAPPED DONACOBIUS.

Turdus atricapilla Linnaeus, 1766, Syst. Nat., ed. 12, 1, p. 295. Based on "Le Merle á teste [=tête] noire du Cap de Bonne Espérance" Brisson, Ornithologie, 6, suppl., p. 47, pl. 3, fig. 2. (ad Cap. b. spei, error = eastern Brazil.)

Habitat.—Marshes, swamps, flooded forest, stream borders and open country with low vegetation (Tropical and lower Subtropical zones).

Distribution.—*Resident* in eastern Panama (lower Río Tiura and around El Real, in eastern Darién) and northern Colombia (south to the Río Atrato and east to the Santa Marta lowlands), and in South America east of the Andes from southeastern Colombia, Venezuela and the Guianas south to eastern Peru, Bolivia, Paraguay, northeastern Argentina and south-central Brazil.

Notes.—Also known as BLACK-CAPPED MOCKINGTHRUSH.

Genus CAMPYLORHYNCHUS Spix

Campylorhynchus Spix, 1824, Avium Spec. Nov. Bras., 1, p. 77. Type, by subsequent designation (G. R. Gray, 1840), *C. variegatus* (Gm.) = *Opetiorhynchus turdinus* Wied.

Campylorhynchus albobrunneus (Lawrence). WHITE-HEADED WREN.

Heleodytes albo-brunneus Lawrence, 1862, Ibis, p. 10. (line of the Panama Railroad, near the summit of the Atlantic slope, Isthmus of Panama = Canal Zone.)

Habitat.—Humid lowland forest edge, dense second growth, and clearings (Tropical Zone).

Distribution.—*Resident* locally in Panama (west to western Colón in the Caribbean lowlands, and to the Canal Zone on the Pacific slope; one old record from "Veraguas") and western Colombia (west of the Andes).

Notes.—*C. albobrunneus* is sometimes considered conspecific with the South American *C. turdinus* (Wied, 1821) [THRUSHLIKE WREN], a species widely distributed east of the Andes; the basis for this treatment is a highly variable, apparently intermediate population of *C. albobrunneus* in southwestern Colombia, which may represent hybridization with *C. turdinus* but possibly is a result of hybridization with *C. zonatus* instead. At present, it seems best to treat *C. albobrunneus* and *C. turdinus* as allospecies of a superspecies.

Campylorhynchus zonatus (Lesson). BAND-BACKED WREN.

Picolaptes zonatus Lesson, 1832, Cent. Zool., p. 210, pl. 70. (la Californie, error = Orizaba, Veracruz.)

Habitat.—Highly variable in different regions, from lowlands to mountains, in forest edge, second growth, clearings, pine-oak association, plantations and scrub, in both humid and arid habitats (Tropical to Subtropical zones).

Distribution.—*Resident* from eastern and southern Mexico (eastern San Luis Potosí, Veracruz, northern Puebla, Oaxaca, Tabasco, Chiapas and southern Campeche) south along both slopes of Middle America to north-central Nicaragua, and in Costa Rica and western Panama (east to central Bocas del Toro and the Pacific slope of Veraguas); in northern Colombia; and in northwestern Ecuador.

Notes.—*C. zonatus, C. megalopterus* and two South American species, *C. nuchalis* Cabanis, 1847, and *C. fasciatus* (Swainson, 1837), appear to constitute a superspecies. See also comments under *C. albobrunneus*.

Campylorhynchus megalopterus Lafresnaye. GRAY-BARRED WREN.

Campylorhynchus megalopterus Lafresnaye, 1845, Rev. Zool [Paris], 8, p. 339. (Mexique = Mexico.)

Habitat.—Montane coniferous forest (primarily pine) and humid montane pine-oak association (Temperate Zone).

Distribution.—*Resident* in the mountains of Mexico from southern Jalisco east through Michoacán, the state of México, Morelos and western Puebla to southwestern Veracruz and Oaxaca (east to Mount Zempoaltepec).

Notes.—See comments under *C. zonatus*.

Campylorhynchus chiapensis Salvin and Godman. GIANT WREN.

Campylorhynchus chiapensis Salvin and Godman, 1891, Ibis, p. 609. (Tonala, State of Chiapas, Mexico.)

Habitat.—Humid lowland forest, forest edge, scrub, clearings, and hedgerows adjacent to forest (Tropical Zone).

Distribution.—*Resident* in the Pacific lowlands of Chiapas (Tonalá to Escuintla).

Notes.—Some authors consider *C. chiapensis* to be conspecific with the South American *C. griseus* (Swainson, 1837); they constitute at least a superspecies.

Campylorhynchus rufinucha (Lesson). RUFOUS-NAPED WREN.

Picolaptes rufinucha Lesson, 1838, Ann. Sci. Nat. (Zool.), sér. 2, 9, p. 168. (Vera-Cruz, Mexico.)

Habitat.—Scrub, thickets, forest edge, open second-growth woodland, brushy areas and cultivated lands, primarily in arid or semi-arid habitats (Tropical Zone).

Distribution.—*Resident* in the Pacific lowlands of Middle America from Colima to northwestern Costa Rica (Guanacaste), and locally in interior valleys on the Gulf-Caribbean drainage in central Veracruz, northeastern Oaxaca, Guatemala (Motagua Valley) and Honduras (Sula Valley).

Campylorhynchus gularis Sclater. SPOTTED WREN.

Campylorhynchus gularis Sclater, 1861, Proc. Zool. Soc. London (1860), p. 462. (in Mexico = Bolaños, Jalisco.)

Habitat.—Pine-oak woodland, forest edge, and open situations with scattered trees, primarily in semi-arid habitats (upper Tropical and Subtropical zones).

Distribution.—*Resident* on the Pacific slope from north-central Sonora and southwestern Chihuahua, and on the Gulf slope from southwestern Tamaulipas, south to Michoacán, the state of México, Querétaro and northern Hidalgo.

Campylorhynchus jocosus Sclater. BOUCARD'S WREN.

Campylorhynchus jocosus Sclater, 1859, Proc. Zool. Soc. London, p. 371. (State of Oaxaca, South-western Mexico.)

Habitat.—Pine-oak association and oak scrub, primarily in arid country (upper Tropical to Subtropical zones).

Distribution.—*Resident* in the highlands from Guerrero, Morelos, Distrito Federal and southern Puebla south to central Oaxaca (Sierra de Miahuatlán and Sierra de Yucuyacua).

Notes.—*C. jocosus*, *C. yucatanicus* and *C. brunneicapillus* appear to constitute a superspecies.

Campylorhynchus yucatanicus (Hellmayr). YUCATAN WREN.

Heleodytes brunneicapillus yucatanicus Hellmayr, 1934, Field Mus. Nat. Hist. Publ., Zool. Ser., 13 (7), p. 150. (Río Lagartos, Yucatán, Mexico.)

Habitat.—Desert scrub and brushy thickets, primarily with *Opuntia,* in coastal lowlands (Tropical Zone).

Distribution.—*Resident* along the coast of the Yucatan Peninsula (state of Yucatán).

Notes.—Some authors consider *C. yucatanicus* and *C. brunneicapillus* to be conspecific. See also comments under *C. jocosus*.

Campylorhynchus brunneicapillus (Lafresnaye). CACTUS WREN. [713.]

Picolaptes brunneicapillus Lafresnaye, 1835, Mag. Zool. [Paris], 5, cl. 2, pl. 47. (Californie, error = coast region of southern Sonora.)

Habitat.—Desert (especially with cholla cactus or yucca), mesquite, arid scrub, and in trees in towns in arid regions (Tropical to Subtropical zones).

Distribution.—*Resident* from southern California (north to Ventura and Inyo counties), southern Nevada, southwestern Utah, central Arizona, central New Mexico, and central and southern Texas south to southern Baja California, the Pacific lowlands to northwestern Sinaloa (including Isla Tiburón, off Sonora), and in the Mexican highlands to Michoacán, the state of México and Hidalgo.

Casual north to east-central California (Mono County).

Notes.—See comments under *C. jocosus* and *C. yucatanicus.*

Genus SALPINCTES Cabanis

Salpinctes Cabanis, 1847, Arch. Naturgesch., 13, p. 323. Type, by subsequent designation (G. R. Gray, 1855), *Troglodytes obsoleta* Say.

Notes.—See comments under *Catherpes.*

Salpinctes obsoletus (Say). ROCK WREN. [715.]

Troglodytes obsoleta Say, 1823, *in* Long, Exped. Rocky Mount., 2, p. 4 (note). (Northern part of Douglas Co., Colorado, near junction of Plum Creek with South Platte River.)

Habitat.—Primarily in arid or semi-arid areas with exposed rocks, canyons and cliffs, usually with some brushy vegetation, also around man-made concrete or stone structures (Subtropical and Temperate zones).

Distribution.—*Breeds* from south-central British Columbia, southern Alberta, southern Saskatchewan, western North Dakota and western South Dakota south (east of the coast ranges in Washington, Oregon and northern California) to the Cape region of southern Baja California (including most coastal islands, Guadalupe Island, and, formerly, San Benedicto in the Revillagigedo Islands), in the highlands of Middle America to northwestern Costa Rica (restricted to Pacific slope volcanic peaks in El Salvador, Nicaragua and northwestern Costa Rica), and east to western Nebraska, western Kansas, western Oklahoma, central and southern Texas, and southwestern Tamaulipas.

Winters from northern California, southern Nevada, southern Utah, northern New Mexico and north-central Texas south through the southern portions of the breeding range, wandering to lower elevations, casually wintering north to Oregon, Montana and Wyoming.

Casual in summer north to northwestern Mackenzie, northern Alberta and northern Manitoba, and in migration and winter west of the coast ranges (from southern British Columbia to northern California), and east to Minnesota, Iowa, eastern Nebraska, eastern Kansas, central Oklahoma and eastern Texas. Casual or accidental east to Michigan, southern Ontario, Indiana, central Kentucky, western Tennessee and Arkansas, and in Nova Scotia (Seal Island), Massachusetts (Rockport) and Alabama (Dauphin Island); many (or possibly most) of these eastern records pertain to individuals transported accidentally in railroad boxcars.

Genus CATHERPES Baird

Catherpes Baird, 1858, *in* Baird, Cassin and Lawrence, Rep. Explor. Surv. R. R. Pac., 9, pp. xix, xxxvi, 354, 356. Type, by original designation, *Thryothorus mexicanus* Swainson.

Notes.—Some authors merge this genus with *Salpinctes.*

Catherpes mexicanus (Swainson). CANYON WREN. [717.]

Thryothorus Mexicanus Swainson, 1829, Zool. Illus., ser. 2, 1, no. 3, pl. 11 and text. (Real del Monte [Hidalgo], Mexico.)

Habitat.—Cliffs, steep-sided canyons, rocky outcrops and boulder piles, usually in arid regions (Tropical and Subtropical zones).

Distribution.—*Resident* from eastern Washington, southern interior British Columbia, west-central Idaho, Wyoming, southeastern Montana and southwestern South Dakota south (east of the Cascades and coast ranges in Oregon and California, but including coastal areas south of Santa Cruz County) to southern Baja California (including Ildefonso and Espíritu Santo islands, and Isla Tiburón off Sonora), southern Arizona, in the Mexican highlands to Oaxaca, central Chiapas and western Veracruz, and east to western Oklahoma and east-central Texas (McLennan County).

Casual on Santa Cruz Island (off southern California) and Los Coronados Islands (off northern Baja California).

Genus HYLORCHILUS Nelson

Hylorchilus Nelson, 1897, Auk, 14, p. 71. Type, by original designation, *Catherpes sumichrasti* Lawrence.

Hylorchilus sumichrasti (Lawrence). SLENDER-BILLED WREN.

Catherpes sumichrasti Lawrence, 1871, Proc. Acad. Nat. Sci. Philadelphia, 22, p. 233. (Mato Bejuco, Vera Cruz.)

Habitat.—Dense humid lowland forest, generally in areas with rocky outcrops (Tropical Zone).

Distribution.—*Resident* locally in the lowlands of west-central Veracruz (Motzorongo, Presidio), extreme northwestern Oaxaca (San Miguel Soyaltepec, Temascal) and western Chiapas (Ocozocoautla).

Genus THRYOTHORUS Vieillot

Thriothorus [sic] Vieillot, 1816, Analyse, pp. 45, 70 (corrected to *Thryothorus*). Type, by monotypy, "Troglodyte des roseaux" Vieillot, Ois. Amér. Sept. = *Troglodytes arundinaceus* Vieillot = *Sylvia ludoviciana* Latham.

Thryothorus spadix (Bangs). SOOTY-HEADED WREN.

Pheugopedius spadix Bangs, 1910, Proc. Biol. Soc. Wash., 23, p. 74. (Naranjito, Río Dagua, Valle, Colombia.)

Habitat.—Humid foothill forest (upper Tropical and lower Subtropical zones).
Distribution.—*Resident* in extreme eastern Panama (eastern Darién) and western Colombia.
Notes.—*T. spadix* and *T. atrogularis* are closely related and considered conspecific by some authors; they constitute a superspecies.

Thryothorus atrogularis Salvin. BLACK-THROATED WREN.

Thryothorus atrogularis Salvin, 1865, Proc. Zool. Soc. London (1864), p. 580. (Tucurrique, Costa Rica.)

Habitat.—Dense second-growth woodland, dense undergrowth in humid forest edge or clearings, overgrown tangles, and swampy woodland (Tropical and lower Subtropical zones).
Distribution.—*Resident* on the Caribbean slope from Nicaragua south through Costa Rica to extreme western Panama (western Bocas del Toro).
Notes.—See comments under *T. spadix*.

Thryothorus fasciatoventris Lafresnaye. BLACK-BELLIED WREN.

Thriothorus [sic] *fasciato-ventris* Lafresnaye, 1845, Rev. Zool. [Paris], 8, p. 337. ("Bogotá," Colombia.)

Habitat.—Thickets and dense undergrowth of open woodland or forest edge, usually in the vicinity of streams (Tropical Zone).
Distribution.—*Resident* on the Pacific slope from Costa Rica (northwest to the Gulf of Nicoya) to western Panama (Chiriquí, one old record from "Veragua"), and on both slopes from central Panama (Canal Zone) east to northern Colombia.

Thryothorus nigricapillus Sclater. BAY WREN.

Thryothorus nigricapillus Sclater, 1861, Proc. Zool. Soc. London (1860), p. 84. (Nanegal [alt. *ca.* 4,000 ft.], Pichincha, Ecuador.)

Habitat.—Rank undergrowth along streams and roadsides through humid lowland and foothill forest, and in overgrown clearings (Tropical and lower Subtropical zones).
Distribution.—*Resident* [*castaneus* group] on the Caribbean slope of eastern Nicaragua, Costa Rica and Panama (including Isla Escudo de Veraguas, off Bocas del Toro), and on the Pacific slope of Panama from Veraguas east to central Darién; and [*nigricapillus* group] in extreme eastern Panama (eastern Darién), western Colombia and western Ecuador.
Notes.—The two groups are sometimes recognized as distinct species, *T. castaneus* Lawrence, 1861 [BAY WREN], and *T. nigricapillus* [BLACK-CAPPED WREN]. *T. nigricapillus* and *T. semibadius* constitute a superspecies; they are considered conspecific by some authors.

Thryothorus semibadius Salvin. RIVERSIDE WREN.

Thryothorus semibadius Salvin, 1870, Proc. Zool. Soc. London, p. 181. (Bugaba, Chiriquí, Panama.)

Habitat.—Undergrowth of humid lowland forest edge and clearings, dense shrubbery and thickets, usually along streams, occasionally in brushy thickets away from water, and in mangroves (Tropical Zone).

Distribution.—*Resident* in the Pacific lowlands of southwestern Costa Rica (El General-Térraba region) and extreme western Panama (western Chiriquí).

Notes.—See comments under *T. nigricapillus.*

Thryothorus leucopogon (Salvadori and Festa). STRIPE-THROATED WREN.

Thryophilus leucopogon Salvadori and Festa, 1899, Bull. Mus. Zool. Anat. Comp. Torino, 14, no. 357, p. 6. (Río Peripa, Pichincha, Ecuador.)

Habitat.—Undergrowth of humid lowland forest (Tropical Zone).

Distribution.—*Resident* in extreme eastern Panama (eastern San Blas and eastern Darién), western Colombia and northwestern Ecuador.

Notes.—Some authors regard *T. leucopogon* and *T. thoracicus* conspecific; they constitute a superspecies.

Thryothorus thoracicus Salvin. STRIPE-BREASTED WREN.

Thryothorus thoracicus Salvin, 1865, Proc. Zool. Soc. London (1864), p. 580. (Tucurrique, Costa Rica.)

Habitat.—Undergrowth of humid lowland and foothill forest, forest edge, dense second growth, and thickets (Tropical and lower Subtropical zones).

Distribution.—*Resident* on the Caribbean slope of Nicaragua, Costa Rica (locally also on the Pacific slope of the Cordillera de Guanacaste) and western Panama (east to Coclé, rarely to the Canal Zone, also locally in the Pacific foothills of Veraguas).

Notes.—See comments under *T. leucopogon.*

Thryothorus rutilus Vieillot. RUFOUS-BREASTED WREN.

Thryothorus rutilus Vieillot, 1819, Nouv. Dict. Hist. Nat., nouv. éd., 34, p. 55. (l'Amérique septentrionale = Trinidad.)

Habitat.—Thickets, undergrowth and overgrown borders of forest, clearings and second-growth woodland, usually in humid or semi-humid habitats (Tropical and lower Subtropical zones).

Distribution.—*Resident* on the Pacific slope of Costa Rica (west to the Gulf of Nicoya) and western Panama (east to eastern Panamá province, also on the Caribbean slope of the Canal Zone); and in South America east of the Andes in Colombia and northern Venezuela (also Tobago and Trinidad).

Notes.—*T. rutilus* and *T. maculipectus* are regarded by a few authors as conspecific [SPECKLED WREN]; they constitute a superspecies.

Thryothorus maculipectus Lafresnaye. SPOT-BREASTED WREN.

> *Thriothorus* [sic] *maculipectus* Lafresnaye, 1845, Rev. Zool. [Paris], 8, p. 338. (Mexique = Veracruz.)

Habitat.—Thickets and undergrowth of forest, forest edge, clearings and second-growth woodland, in areas of either evergreen or deciduous forest (Tropical Zone).

Distribution.—*Resident* from eastern Nuevo León, eastern San Luis Potosí and central Tamaulipas south in the Gulf-Caribbean lowlands of Middle America (including the Yucatan Peninsula and Isla Cancun) to northeastern Costa Rica, and on the Pacific slope in Chiapas, Guatemala and El Salvador.

Notes.—See comments under *T. rutilus.*

Thryothorus rufalbus Lafresnaye. RUFOUS-AND-WHITE WREN.

> *Thryothorus rufalbus* Lafresnaye, 1845, Rev. Zool. [Paris], 8, p. 337. (Mexique, error = Guatemala.)

Habitat.—Thickets and undergrowth of forest, forest edge, clearings and second-growth woodland, in regions of either humid or seasonally dry forest (Tropical and lower Subtropical zones).

Distribution.—*Resident* on the Pacific slope of Middle America from extreme southwestern Chiapas south to western Panama (east to eastern Panamá province), locally also on the Caribbean slope in Guatemala, Honduras, Costa Rica and central Panama (Canal Zone).

Notes.—Some authors consider the Colombian *T. nicefori* Meyer de Schauensee, 1946, to be conspecific with *T. rufalbus*; they constitute a superspecies.

Thryothorus sinaloa (Baird). SINALOA WREN.

> *Thryophilus sinaloa* Baird, 1864, Rev. Am. Birds, 1, pp. 122, 130. (Mazatlán, Sinaloa, Mexico.)

Habitat.—Scrub, thickets, brushy areas, open deciduous woodland and mangroves (Tropical and Subtropical zones).

Distribution.—*Resident* on the Pacific slope from southeastern Sonora and southwestern Chihuahua south through western Durango and coastal states to extreme western Oaxaca (Putla de Guerrero region).

Notes.—Also known as BAR-VENTED WREN.

Thryothorus pleurostictus Sclater. BANDED WREN.

> *Thryothorus pleurostictus* Sclater, 1860, Ibis, p. 30. (Vera Paz, Guatemala = Gualán, Zacapa, Guatemala.)

Habitat.—Arid scrub, thickets, scrubby woodland and brushy ravines (Tropical and Subtropical zones).

Distribution.—*Resident* on the Pacific slope of Middle America from Michoacán, the southwestern portion of the state of México, Morelos and western Puebla south to northwestern Costa Rica (Guanacaste region, locally also on the Pacific slope of the central plateau).

Thryothorus ludovicianus (Latham). CAROLINA WREN. [718.]

> *Sylvia ludoviciana* Latham, 1790, Index Ornithol., 2, p. 548. Based on "Roitelet de la Louisiane" Daubenton, Planches Enlum., pl. 730, fig. 1. (in Louisiana = along the Mississippi River at New Orleans.)

Habitat.—Open deciduous woodland, mostly in undergrowth and thickets, and in parks and residential areas, locally in humid forest edge and clearings (Tropical and Subtropical zones, and, north of Mexico, Temperate Zone).

Distribution.—*Resident* [*ludovicianus* group] from eastern Nebraska, northern Iowa, southeastern Minnesota, southern Wisconsin, southern Michigan, southern Ontario, extreme southwestern Quebec, central New York, southern Vermont and Massachusetts south to eastern Mexico (eastern Coahuila, Nuevo León, eastern San Luis Potosí and Tamaulipas), the Gulf coast (including islands off the coast of Mississippi and northwestern Florida) and southern Florida (to Key Largo), and west to central Kansas, central Oklahoma and central Texas; and [*albinucha* group] in southeastern Mexico (Tabasco and the Yucatan Peninsula), northern Guatemala (Petén) and Belize, and locally in the interior of Guatemala (Sacapulas) and Nicaragua (Metapa [= Darío]).

Wanders casually [*ludovicianus* group] west and north to central New Mexico, eastern Colorado, eastern Wyoming, South Dakota, southern Manitoba, northern Michigan, New Brunswick, southeastern Quebec (Magdalen Islands) and Nova Scotia (sight reports), and south to Key West, Florida.

Notes.—The two groups have sometimes been regarded as distinct species, *T. ludovicianus* and *T. albinucha* (Cabot, 1847) [WHITE-BROWED WREN].

Thryothorus felix Sclater. HAPPY WREN.

> *Thryothorus felix* Sclater, 1859, Proc. Zool. Soc. London, p. 371. ([Santa Catarina] Juquila, Oaxaca, South-western Mexico.)

Habitat.—Scrub, thickets, brushy roadsides, and undergrowth of open deciduous forest, usually in arid or semi-arid regions (Tropical and lower Subtropical zones).

Distribution.—*Resident* on the Pacific slope from southern Sonora, Sinaloa and western Durango south to the state of México, Morelos, western Puebla and central Oaxaca (east to the Puerto Angel region); also in the Tres Marias Islands (María Madre and María Magdalena).

Thryothorus leucotis Lafresnaye. BUFF-BREASTED WREN.

> *Thryothorus leucotis* Lafresnaye, 1845, Rev. Zool. [Paris], 8, p. 338. (in Colombia aut Mexico = Honda, Río Magdalena, Tolima, Colombia.)

Habitat.—Undergrowth of humid and deciduous forest edge, clearings, secondgrowth woodland and mangroves, especially near streams (Tropical Zone).

Distribution.—*Resident* from in eastern Panama (west to the Canal Zone, and including the Pearl Islands), and in South America from northern Colombia, Venezuela and the Guianas south, east of the Andes, to central Peru and Amazonian and central Brazil.

Notes.—*T. leucotis* and the South American *T. superciliaris* (Lawrence, 1869) are closely related and constitute a superspecies; *T. modestus* appears to be part of this species group and is regarded by some authors as a member of the *T. leucotis* superspecies containing all three species.

Thryothorus modestus Cabanis. PLAIN WREN.

> *Thryothorus modestus* Cabanis, 1860, J. Ornithol., 8, p. 409. (San Jose, Costa Rica.)

Habitat.—Undergrowth in open woodland, thickets and brushy areas in primarily arid regions, and in gardens and plantations, also ranging into humid forest undergrowth, mangroves, and canebrakes along rivers (Tropical and Subtropical zones).

Distribution.—*Resident* [*modestus* group] on the Pacific slope of Middle America from extreme eastern Oaxaca (Sierra Madre de Chiapas) south to Costa Rica (locally also on the Caribbean slope in interior valleys of Chiapas, Guatemala and Honduras, and in the Mosquitia of northeastern Honduras) and Panama, where occurring on both slopes (except the extreme northwestern portion) east to eastern Colón and eastern Panamá province; and [*zeledoni* group] on the Caribbean slope from southeastern Nicaragua south to extreme northwestern Panama (western Bocas del Toro).

Notes.—Some authors regard the two groups as distinct species, *T. modestus* and *T. zeledoni* (Ridgway, 1878) [CANEBRAKE WREN]. See also comments under *T. leucotis*.

Genus THRYOMANES Sclater

> *Thryomanes* Sclater, 1862, Cat. Collect. Am. Birds, p. 22. Type, by monotypy, *Troglodytes bewickii* Audubon.

Thryomanes bewickii (Audubon). BEWICK'S WREN. [719.]

> *Troglodytes Bewickii* Audubon, 1827, Birds Am. (folio), 1, pl. 18 (1831, Ornithol. Biogr., 1, p. 96). (Five miles from St. Francisville, Louisiana.)

Habitat.—Brushy areas, thickets and scrub in open country, open and riparian woodland, and chaparral, more commonly in arid regions but locally also in humid areas (Subtropical and Temperate zones).

Distribution.—*Breeds* from southwestern British Columbia, western and central Washington, western and southern Oregon, northern California, west-central and southern Nevada, southern Utah, southern Wyoming, central Colorado, Kansas, eastern Nebraska, southern Iowa, southeastern Minnesota, southern Wisconsin, southern Michigan, southern Ontario, northern Ohio, central Pennsylvania and southeastern New York south to southern Baja California (including some islands off the coast of southern California south, formerly, to Guadalupe Island, where extirpated between 1892 and 1906), northern Sonora, in the Mexican highlands to central Oaxaca, western Puebla and west-central Veracruz, and to southern Tamaulipas, central Texas, northern Arkansas, the northern portions of the Gulf states, central Georgia and central South Carolina; in recent years scarce and local throughout the eastern portion of the breeding range.

Winters from the northern limits of the breeding range (west of the Rockies), southern Kansas, southern Missouri, the lower Ohio Valley, Tennessee and North

Carolina south to the limits of the breeding range in Mexico, the Gulf coast and central Florida.

Casual north to South Dakota, northern New York and northern New England.

Thryomanes sissonii (Grayson). SOCORRO WREN.

Thryothorus sissonii Grayson, 1868, Calif. Farmer J. Useful Sci., 29, p. 7. (Isla Socorro, Islas de Revillagigedo, Colima, Mexico.)

Habitat.—Arid scrub.

Distribution.—*Resident* on Socorro Island, in the Revillagigedo Islands, off western Mexico.

Genus **FERMINIA** Barbour

Ferminia Barbour, 1926, Proc. N. Engl. Zool. Club, 9, p. 74. Type, by original designation, *Ferminia cerverai* Barbour.

Ferminia cerverai Barbour. ZAPATA WREN.

Ferminia cerverai Barbour, 1926, Proc. N. Engl. Zool. Club, 9, p. 74. (Santo Tomás, Ciénaga de Zapata, Las Villas, Cuba.)

Habitat.—Dense shrubbery in swampy areas.

Distribution.—*Resident* in the Ciénaga de Zapata in the vicinity of Santo Tomás, western Cuba; rare and possibly extinct, unreported during a search in 1980.

Genus **TROGLODYTES** Vieillot

Troglodytes Vieillot, 1808, Hist. Nat. Ois. Am. Sept., 2 (1807), p. 52. Type, by subsequent designation (Baird, 1858), *Troglodytes aedon* Vieillot.
Nannus Billberg, 1828, Synop. Faunae Scand., ed. 2, 1 (2), p. 57, tab. A. Type, by monotypy, *Motacilla troglodytes* Linnaeus.

Troglodytes aedon Vieillot. HOUSE WREN. [721.]

Troglodytes aëdon Vieillot, 1808, Hist. Nat. Ois. Am. Sept., 2 (1807), p. 52, pl. 107. (No locality given = New York City.)

Habitat.—Thickets, shrubbery and brushy areas in partly open situations, open woodland, farmlands, chaparral, and around human habitations, also [*brunneicollis* group] in humid montane forest, forest edge, clearings and pine-oak association, and [*musculus* group] from arid to humid forest, woodland and scrub habitats, including mangroves (Tropical to Temperate zones).

Distribution.—*Breeds* [*aedon* group] from southern and east-central British Columbia, northern Alberta, central Saskatchewan, southern Manitoba, central Ontario, southwestern Quebec, Maine and New Brunswick south to northern Baja California, southern California, southern Nevada, central and southeastern Arizona, southern New Mexico, western and northern Texas, central Arkansas, southern Tennessee, northeastern Georgia, western South Carolina and eastern North Carolina; and [*brunneicollis* group] from northern Sonora, southeastern Arizona (Huachuca and Santa Rita mountains), central Chihuahua, northern Coahuila, central Nuevo León and southwestern Tamaulipas south in the mountains of Mexico to Oaxaca (west to the Isthmus of Tehuantepec) and west-central Veracruz.

Winters [*aedon* group] from southern California, southern Nevada, northern Arizona, southern New Mexico, northern Texas, southern Arkansas, the northern portions of the Gulf states, and coastal Maryland (casually farther north) south to southern Baja California, throughout Mexico to Oaxaca and Veracruz, and to the Gulf coast and southern Florida; and [*brunneicollis* group] from northern Mexico south throughout the remainder of the breeding range.

Resident [*musculus* group] from eastern Oaxaca (probably also southern Veracruz), Tabasco, Chiapas and the Yucatan Peninsula (including Isla Cancun) south through Middle America (scarce or absent from arid Pacific lowlands, but present on Coiba and the Pearl islands off Panama), and in virtually all of South America from Colombia, Venezuela (also Tobago and Trinidad) and the Guianas south to central Chile and central Argentina (also the Falkland Islands); [*martinicensis* group] in the Lesser Antilles on Guadeloupe, Dominica, St. Lucia (surviving in small numbers in the northeastern coastal lowlands), St. Vincent and Grenada (vocalizations suggest Grenada birds may be part of *musculus* group), formerly also on Martinique; and [*beani* group] on Cozumel Island, off Quintana Roo.

Casual or accidental [*aedon* group] north to northern Manitoba, Prince Edward Island and Nova Scotia, and to western Cuba (near Havana) and the Bahama Islands (South Bimini, New Providence, Exuma).

Notes.—In view of the uncertainty of publication dates during the year 1808, replacement of the well established name *T. aedon* with *T. domesticus,* based on *Sylvia domestica* Wilson, 1808, seems unwarranted. Species limits within this complex are not well understood. The five groups listed have been recognized by at least some authors as full species, *T. aedon* [NORTHERN HOUSE-WREN, 721], *T. brunneicollis* Sclater, 1858 [BROWN-THROATED WREN, 721.1], *T. musculus* Naumann, 1823 [SOUTHERN HOUSE-WREN], *T. martinicensis* (Sclater, 1866) [ANTILLEAN HOUSE-WREN] and *T. beani* Ridgway, 1885 [COZUMEL WREN]. *T. aedon* and *T. brunneicollis* intergrade through intermediate breeding populations in southern Arizona, but intergradation between *brunneicollis* and *musculus* in an area of close approach in eastern Oaxaca has not been definitely established; *T. beani* appears to be part of the Antillean *T. martinicensis* complex, generally associated with *T. musculus* forms occupying Tobago and Trinidad. See also comments under *T. ochraceus.*

Troglodytes tanneri Townsend. CLARION WREN.

Troglodytes tanneri C. H. Townsend, 1890, Proc. U.S. Natl. Mus., 13, p. 133. (Isla Clarión, Islas de Revillagigedo, Colima, Mexico.)

Habitat.—Brush, scrub and open woodland.
Distribution.—*Resident* on Isla Clarión, in the Revillagigedo Islands, off western Mexico.

Troglodytes rufociliatus Sharpe. RUFOUS-BROWED WREN.

Troglodytes brunneicollis Subsp. α. *Troglodytes rufociliatus* Sharpe, 1881, Cat. Birds Br. Mus., 6, pp. xii, 262. (Upper Chirostemon Forest, alt. 10,000 ft., Volcan de Fuego, [Sacatepéquez], Guatemala.)

Habitat.—Humid montane forest, forest edge, clearings and brushy areas in pine-oak woodland (Subtropical and Temperate zones).

Distribution.—*Resident* in the mountains of Chiapas, Guatemala, El Salvador and Honduras.

Notes.—See comments under *T. ochraceus.*

Troglodytes ochraceus Ridgway. OCHRACEOUS WREN.

Troglodytes (?) *ochraceus* Ridgway, 1882, Proc. U.S. Natl. Mus., 4 (1881), p.. 334. (Volcán Irazú, Cartago, Costa Rica.)

Habitat.—Humid montane forest, forest edge, open woodland and undergrowth in clearings (Subtropical to Temperate zones).

Distribution.—*Resident* in the mountains of Costa Rica (north to Cordillera de Tilarán) and Panama (Chiriquí, Veraguas, and cerros Pirre and Campana in eastern Darién).

Notes.—*T. ochraceus, T. rufociliatus,* the Colombian *T. monticola* Bangs, 1899, and the South American *T. solstitialis* Sclater, 1859, are closely related and considered conspecific by some authors [MOUNTAIN WREN]; they constitute a superspecies. The matter of relationship is further complicated since some authors consider *T. rufociliatus* to be closely related to and possibly conspecific with the *brunneicollis* group of *T. aedon.*

Troglodytes troglodytes (Linnaeus). WINTER WREN. [722.]

Motacilla Troglodytes Linnaeus, 1758, Syst. Nat., ed. 10, 1, p. 188. (in Europa = Sweden.)

Habitat.—Coniferous forest (especially spruce and fir), primarily with dense understory and near water, and in open areas with low cover along rocky coasts, cliffs, islands or high mountain regions, including moors and steppes; in migration and winter also in deciduous forest and woodland with understory, thickets, hedgerows, gardens and brushy fields.

Distribution.—*Resident* in North America from coastal southern and southeastern Alaska (including the Pribilof Islands, and throughout most of the Aleutians), northern British Columbia, northern Alberta, central Saskatchewan, central Manitoba, central Ontario, central Quebec, southern Labrador and Newfoundland south to central California (San Luis Obispo County, and the western slope of the central Sierra Nevada), northeastern Oregon, central Idaho, western Montana, southwestern Alberta, southeastern Manitoba, east-central Minnesota, southern Wisconsin, central Michigan, southern Ontario, north-central Ohio (probably), in the Appalachians through eastern West Virginia, western Virginia, eastern Tennessee and western North Carolina to northeastern Georgia, and to northern Pennsylvania, northern New Jersey and southeastern New York; and in the Palearctic from Iceland, the Faroe Islands, Shetlands, British Isles, northern Scandinavia, northern Russia and central Siberia south to northwestern Africa, the Mediterranean region, Near East, Iran, northern India, central China and Japan. Recorded in summer (and probably breeding) in southern Yukon, south-central Mackenzie and northern Indiana.

Winters in North America from southern Alaska (including the Pribilof and Aleutian islands), British Columbia, southwestern Alberta, western Montana, northeast Colorado, southern Nebraska, central Iowa, central Illinois, southern Michigan, southern Ontario, central New York and Massachusetts (casually farther north) south to southern California, central and southeastern Arizona, southern New Mexico, southern Texas, the Gulf coast and central (formerly southern) Florida; and in the Old World generally throughout the breeding range, although the extreme northern populations usually migrate southward.

Accidental in northern Alaska (Point Barrow).

Notes.—Known in Old World literature as the WREN; HOLARCTIC and NORTHERN WREN have also been used for this species.

Genus CISTOTHORUS Cabanis

Cistothorus Cabanis, 1850, Mus. Heineanum, 1 (1851), p. 77. Type, by subsequent designation (G. R. Gray, 1855), *Troglodytes stellaris* Naumann = *Sylvia platensis* Latham.

Telmatodytes Cabanis, 1850, Mus. Heineanum, 1 (1851), p. 78. Type, by subsequent designation (Baird, 1858), *Certhia palustris* Wilson.

Cistothorus platensis (Latham). SEDGE WREN. [724.]

Sylvia platensis Latham, 1790, Index Ornithol., 2, p. 548. Based on "Le Roitelet de Buenos-Ayres" Daubenton, Planches Enlum., pl. 730, fig. 2. (in Bonaria = Buenos Aires, Argentina.)

Habitat.—Grasslands and savanna, especially where wet or boggy, and sedge marshes, in South America in dry grasslands, and locally in North America in dry, cultivated grain fields; in migration and winter also in brushy grasslands (Tropical to Paramo zones).

Distribution.—*Breeds* [*stellaris* group] in North America from extreme east-central Alberta, central Saskatchewan, southern Manitoba, western and southern Ontario, northern Michigan, extreme southwestern Quebec, central Maine and southern New Brunswick south to east-central Arkansas, southern Illinois, central Kentucky, west-central West Virginia and southeastern Virginia, and west to central North Dakota, eastern South Dakota, eastern Nebraska, northeastern Colorado (possibly) and eastern Kansas.

Winters [*stellaris* group] in North America from western Tennessee and Maryland (casually farther north) south to southeastern New Mexico, western and southern Texas, San Luis Potosí, Tamaulipas, the Gulf coast and southern Florida.

Resident [*stellaris* group] locally in Middle America in Michoacán (Lake Pátzcuaro region), Veracruz, Chiapas, Guatemala (central highlands), Honduras (Siguatepeque, and the Mosquitia pine savanna), north-central and northeastern Nicaragua, Costa Rica (vicinity of Cartago) and western Panama (western Chiriquí); and [*platensis* group] in South America locally in the Andes from Colombia south to Argentina and Chile, and in the eastern lowlands from eastern Brazil and Paraguay south to Tierra del Fuego (including the Falkland Islands), with the southernmost breeding populations in Chile and Argentina being migratory northward in winter.

Casual [*stellaris* group] in California and Wyoming, also sight reports from Arizona.

Notes.—Also known as SHORT-BILLED MARSH-WREN. The two groups are sometimes regarded as distinct species, *C. stellaris* (J. F. Naumann, 1823) [SEDGE WREN] and *C. platensis* [GRASS WREN]. *C. platensis* and two species with restricted ranges in the high Andes of Venezuela and Colombia, *C. meridae* Hellmayr, 1907, and *C. apolinari* Chapman, 1914, respectively, constitute a superspecies.

Cistothorus palustris (Wilson). MARSH WREN. [725.]

Certhia palustris Wilson, 1810, Am. Ornithol., 2, p. 58, pl. 12, fig. 4. (Borders of the Schuylkill or Delaware [rivers, Philadelphia, Pennsylvania].)

Habitat.—Fresh-water and brackish marshes in cattails, tule, bulrush and reeds.

Distribution.—*Breeds* from southwestern and east-central British Columbia, northern Alberta, central Saskatchewan, southern Manitoba, western and southern Ontario, northern Michigan, southwestern Quebec, southern Maine and eastern New Brunswick south to southern California, northeastern Baja California, northwestern Sonora, southwestern Arizona, southern Nevada, south-central Utah, extreme northwestern New Mexico, extreme western and southern Texas, the Gulf coast (east to the Tampa Bay region, formerly farther south along the Gulf coast of peninsular Florida), and east-central Florida (St. John's River, formerly to New Smyrna Beach), generally very local in distribution in the interior of North America; also locally in the state of México.

Winters in coastal areas throughout the breeding range, and in the interior from the southern United States (casually north to South Dakota, southern Illinois and the Great Lakes region) south to southern Baja California, Michoacán, the state of México and Veracruz.

Accidental in Nova Scotia and Greenland.

Notes.—Also known as LONG-BILLED MARSH-WREN. Placed by many authors in the monotypic genus *Telmatodytes*.

Genus UROPSILA Sclater and Salvin

Uropsila Sclater and Salvin, 1873, Nomencl. Avium Neotrop., pp. 7, 155. Type, by original designation, *Troglodytes leucogastra* Gould.

Uropsila leucogastra (Gould). WHITE-BELLIED WREN.

Troglodytes leucogastra Gould, 1837, Proc. Zool. Soc. London (1836), p. 89. (Taumalipas, in Mexico = Tamaulipas, Mexico.)

Habitat.—Thickets and dense undergrowth in humid lowland forest, dense second growth and, locally, arid coastal scrub (Tropical Zone).

Distribution.—*Resident* in the Pacific lowlands from Colima to central Guerrero (Acapulco); on the Gulf-Caribbean slope from eastern San Luis Potosí and southern Tamaulipas south through Veracruz, northeastern Puebla, northern Oaxaca, Tabasco, northern Chiapas, and the Yucatan Peninsula to northern Guatemala (Petén) and Belize; and locally in north-central Honduras (Coyoles).

Genus THRYORCHILUS Oberholser

Thryorchilus Oberholser, 1904, Proc. U.S. Natl. Mus., 27, p. 198. Type, by original designation, *Troglodytes browni* Bangs.

Thryorchilus browni (Bangs). TIMBERLINE WREN.

Troglodytes browni Bangs, 1902, Proc. N. Engl. Zool. Club, 3, p. 53. (Volcán de Chiriquí, alt. 10,000 ft., Chiriquí, Panama.)

Habitat.—Dense brushy scrub and bamboo thickets bordering montane forest or above timberline (Temperate Zone).

Distribution.—*Resident* in the high mountains of Costa Rica (Cordillera de Talamanca, and on the Irazú-Turrialba massif in the Cordillera Central) and western Panama (Volcán Barú in western Chiriquí).

Notes.—Although some authors place this species in the genus *Troglodytes,* others suggest affinities with *Henicorhina;* the relationships of this wren remain uncertain.

Genus **HENICORHINA** Sclater and Salvin

Heterorhina (not Westwood, 1845) Baird, 1864, Rev. Am. Birds, 1, p. 115. Type, by original designation, *Scytalopus prostheleucus* Sclater = *Cyphorhinus leucosticta* Cabanis.
Henicorhina Sclater and Salvin, 1868, Proc. Zool. Soc. London, p. 170. New name for *Heterorhina* Baird, preoccupied.

Henicorhina leucosticta (Cabanis). WHITE-BREASTED WOOD-WREN.

Cyphorhinus leucosticta Cabanis, 1847, Arch. Naturgesch., 13, p. 206. (Guiana and Mexico = Guiana.)

Habitat.—Understory of humid lowland and foothill forest (Tropical and lower Subtropical zones).

Distribution.—*Resident* from eastern San Luis Potosí, Hidalgo and northern Veracruz south on the Gulf-Caribbean slope of Middle America (including the Yucatan Peninsula, and locally also on the Pacific slope in extreme southern Chiapas and Guatemala) to Nicaragua, on both slopes of Costa Rica (absent from the dry northwest) and Panama, and in South America from northern Colombia, southern Venezuela, Guyana and Surinam south, east of the Andes, to eastern Eccdor and northeastern Peru.

Notes.—*H. leucosticta* and *H. leucophrys* are obvious altitudinal representatives of one another and are viewed by some authors as constituting a superspecies despite local sympatry.

Henicorhina leucophrys (Tschudi). GRAY-BREASTED WOOD-WREN.

Troglodytes leucophrys Tschudi, 1844, Arch. Naturgesch., 10, p. 282. (Republica Peruana = Peru.)

Habitat.—Undergrowth and thickets of humid montane forest edge, overgrown clearings, and dense second growth (Subtropical and Temperate zones).

Distribution.—*Resident* in the highlands from southwestern Jalisco, western Michoacán, Guerrero, eastern San Luis Potosí, Puebla and central Veracruz south through Oaxaca, Chiapas and Guatemala to El Salvador and Honduras; in Costa Rica and Panama (recorded Chiriquí, Veraguas, western Panamá province and eastern Darién); and in South America from Colombia and northern Venezuela south, west of the Andes to western Ecuador and east of the Andes to eastern Peru and northern Bolivia.

Notes.—See comments under *H. leucosticta.*

Genus **MICROCERCULUS** Sclater

Microcerculus Sclater, 1862, Cat. Collect. Am. Birds, p. 19. Type, by subsequent designation (Baird, 1864), *Turdus bambla* Boddaert = *Formicarius bambla* Boddaert.

Microcerculus marginatus (Sclater). NIGHTINGALE WREN.

Heterocnemis marginatus Sclater, 1855, Proc. Zool. Soc. London, p. 37, pl. 6. (Santa Fé di Bogota [Colombia].)

Habitat.—Understory of humid forest, especially on steep, forested hillsides, in ravines, and in dense undergrowth along streams (Tropical and Subtropical zones).

Distribution.—Resident [*philomela* group] from northern Chiapas south through the Gulf-Caribbean lowlands of Guatemala and Honduras to Nicaragua, and from Costa Rica (highlands, and lowlands of Caribbean slope and Pacific southwest) and Panama (foothills and Caribbean slope throughout, in Pacific lowlands west to eastern Panamá province) to northern and western Colombia, northwestern Venezuela and western Ecuador; and [*marginatus* group] in South America east of the Andes from northern Venezuela and eastern Colombia south to eastern Peru, northern Bolivia and Amazonian Brazil.

Notes.—Some authors regard the two groups as distinct species, *M. philomela* (Salvin, 1861) [NIGHTINGALE WREN] and *M. marginatus* [SCALY-BREASTED WREN]. To further complicate matters, the song type changes abruptly in central Costa Rica, one type occurring north of Volcán de Turrialba, the other to the south, suggesting that two species may be involved within the *philomela* group, the northern *M. philomela* [NIGHTINGALE WREN] and the southern *M. luscinia* Salvin, 1866 [WHISTLING WREN].

Genus **CYPHORHINUS** Cabanis

Cyphorhinus Cabanis, 1844, Arch. Naturgesch., 10, p. 282. Type, by monotypy, *Cyphorhinus thoracicus* Tschudi.

Cyphorhinus phaeocephalus Sclater. SONG WREN.

Cyphorhinus phæocephalus Sclater, 1860, Proc. Zool. Soc. London, p. 291. (In rep. Equator. Occ. = Esmeraldas, Esmeraldas, Ecuador.)

Habitat.—Undergrowth of humid lowland and foothill forest, less frequently in tall, shaded second growth and thickets adjacent to forest (Tropical and lower Subtropical zones).

Distribution.—Resident on the Caribbean slope of northeastern Honduras (Gracias a Dios) and Nicaragua, on both slopes of Costa Rica (Caribbean slope throughout, and on the Pacific slope of Cordillera de Guanacaste and in the Pacific southwest) and Panama (Caribbean slope throughout, Pacific slope west to western Panamá province), and in western Colombia and western Ecuador.

Notes.—*C. phaeocephalus* and the South American *C. aradus* (Hermann, 1783) constitute a superspecies; they are considered conspecific by some authors.

Family **CINCLIDAE**: Dippers

Notes.—The relationships of this family are uncertain.

Genus **CINCLUS** Borkhausen

Cinclus Borkhausen, 1797, Dtsch. Fauna, 1, p. 300. Type, by monotypy, *Cinclus hydrophilus* Borkhausen = *Sturnus cinclus* Linnaeus.

Cinclus mexicanus Swainson. AMERICAN DIPPER. [701.]

Cinclus Mexicanus Swainson, 1827, Philos. Mag., new ser., 1, p. 368. (Mexico = Temascaltepec, state of México.)

Habitat.—Montane streams, primarily swift-flowing, less frequently along mountain ponds and lakes, in winter occasionally to rocky seacoasts (Subtropical and Temperate zones).

Distribution.—*Resident* from western and northeastern Alaska (Sadlerochit Springs), north-central Yukon, northern British Columbia, southwestern Alberta, north-central Montana and southwestern South Dakota south to the Aleutian Islands (Unalaska, Unimak), southern California, southern Nevada, north-central and southeastern Arizona, southern New Mexico, and in the mountains of northern Middle America through Mexico, Guatemala and Honduras to north-central Nicaragua; also in the mountains of Costa Rica and western Panama (Chiriquí and Veraguas).

Casual in southern Mackenzie, southwestern Saskatchewan, the Channel Islands (off southern California), and western and central Texas. Accidental in northeastern Minnesota (Cook County).

Notes.—Also known as NORTH AMERICAN DIPPER.

Family MUSCICAPIDAE: Muscicapids

Notes.—See Introduction (p. xviii) for a summary of the treatment of this family.

Subfamily SYLVIINAE: Old World Warblers, Kinglets and Gnatcatchers

Tribe SYLVIINI: Old World Warblers and Kinglets

Notes.—Includes *Regulus,* considered in the subfamily Regulinae in the 5th edition.

Genus CETTIA Bonaparte

Cettia Bonaparte, 1834, Iconogr. Fauna Ital., 1, text to pl. 29. Type, by original designation, *Sylvia cetti* Marmora [=Temminck].

Cettia diphone (Kittlitz). JAPANESE BUSH-WARBLER. [746.1.]

Sylvia diphone Kittlitz, 1831, Mém. Acad. Imp. Sci. St.-Pétersbourg, 1, p. 27, pl. 14. (Bonin Islands.)

Habitat.—Dense brush and undergrowth, tall grass, and bamboo scrub, in the Hawaiian Islands also in upper native forest, particularly on steep slopes.

Distribution.—*Resident* in Sakhalin, the Kurile Islands, Japan, and the Ryukyu, Bonin and Volcano islands. Northernmost populations are migratory south to the Japanese islands.

Introduced and established in the Hawaiian Islands (in 1929, now widespread on Oahu, recently recorded on Molokai, Lanai and Maui).

Notes.—Some authors consider *C. canturians* (Swinhoe, 1860) [MANCHURIAN or CHINESE BUSH-WARBLER] as conspecific with *C. diphone*; they constitute a superspecies. *C. diphone* has often been treated in the Hawaiian literature as *Horeites cantans* (Temminck and Schlegel, 1847).

Genus LOCUSTELLA Kaup

Locustella Kaup, 1829, Skizz. Entw.-Ges. Eur. Thierw., p. 115. Type, by monotypy, *Sylvia locustella* Latham = *Motacilla naevia* Boddaert.

Locustella ochotensis (Middendorff). MIDDENDORFF'S GRASSHOPPER-WARBLER. [747.1.]

Sylvia (*Locustella*) *Ochotensis* Middendorff, 1853, Reise Sib., 2 (2), p. 185, pl. 16, fig. 7. (Uds' Kój Ostrog = Idskoe, Khabarovsk, Sea of Okhotsk.)

Habitat & Distribution.—*Breeds* in dense grassy and bushy areas from Kamchatka and Sakhalin south to Japan and Korea, and *winters* in the Philippines and Greater Sunda Islands.

Casual in Alaska (Nunivak, St. Lawrence and Near islands, and Attu in the Aleutians) and the Commander Islands.

Notes.—Also known as MIDDENDORFF'S WARBLER. By some authors considered conspecific with eastern Eurasian *L. certhiola* (Pallas, 1811) [PALLAS' GRASSHOPPER-WARBLER]; the two species, along with *L. pleskei* Taczanowski, 1889, of Korea and islands south of Japan, constitute a superspecies.

Genus ACROCEPHALUS Naumann and Naumann

Acrocephalus J. A. and J. F. Naumann, 1811, Naturgesch. Land-Wasser-Vögel Dtsch., suppl., pt. 4, p. 199. Type, by subsequent designation (G. R. Gray, 1840), *Turdus arundinaceus* Linnaeus.

Acrocephalus familiaris (Rothschild). MILLERBIRD. [746.2.]

Tatare familiaris Rothschild, 1892, Ann. Mag. Nat. Hist., ser. 6, 10, p. 109. (Laysan Island, Sandwich Group.)

Habitat.—Dense low vegetation and grass.

Distribution.—*Resident* in the western Hawaiian Islands (on Nihoa, formerly also Laysan, where extirpated between 1913 and 1923).

Notes.—Some authors suggest that the form on Nihoa represents a species, *A. kingi* Wetmore, 1924 [NIHOA MILLERBIRD, 746.3], distinct from that formerly on Laysan [LAYSAN MILLERBIRD, 746.2]. The relationships of the species remain in doubt; it does not seem to be close to other members of the genus *Acrocephalus*.

Genus PHYLLOSCOPUS Boie

Phylloscopus Boie, 1826, Isis von Oken, col. 972. Type, by monotypy, *Sylvia trochilus* Latham = *Motacilla trochilus* Linnaeus.

[Phylloscopus trochilus (Linnaeus). WILLOW WARBLER.] See Appendix B.

Phylloscopus sibilatrix (Bechstein). WOOD WARBLER. [747.3.]

Motacilla Sibilatrix Bechstein, 1793, Der Naturforscher, Halle, 27, p. 47. (mountains of Thuringia.)

Habitat & Distribution.—*Breeds* in forest and woodland throughout much of Europe and Russia, and *winters* in tropical Africa and Asia Minor, casually to the Canary Islands and Madeira.

Accidental in Alaska (Shemya Island, in the Aleutians, 9 October 1978; Gibson, 1981, Condor, 83, p. 72).

Phylloscopus fuscatus (Blyth). DUSKY WARBLER. [747.4.]

Phillopneuste fuscata Blyth, 1842, J. Asiat. Soc. Bengal, 11, p. 113. (Calcutta, India.)

Habitat & Distribution.—*Breeds* in bushes and scrub in hilly or mountainous areas from Anadyrland and the Sea of Okhotsk south to Mongolia and the eastern Himalayas, and *winters* from India east to Southeast Asia and southern China.

Accidental in Alaska (Shemya Island, in the Aleutians, 18-23 September 1978; Gibson, 1981, Condor, 83, p. 72) and California (Farallon Islands, 27 September 1980; Am. Birds, 35: 223, 1981), also an additional sight report from Gambell, St. Lawrence Island, Alaska (King *et al.,* 1978, Am. Birds, 32, pp. 158–159).

Phylloscopus borealis (Blasius). ARCTIC WARBLER. [747.]

Phyllopneuste borealis Blasius, 1858, Naumannia, 8, p. 313. (ochotzkischen Meere = Sea of Okhotsk.)

Habitat.—Open coniferous or mixed coniferous-deciduous forest, and in medium to tall shrublands.

Distribution.—*Breeds* in western Alaska from the Noatak River and western and central Brooks Range south to southwestern Alaska, the base of the Alaska Peninsula, the Alaska Range, and Susitna River highlands; and in Eurasia from Finland, northern Russia and northern Siberia south to central Russia, Mongolia, Amurland, Ussuriland, Japan and Kamchatka. Recorded in summer north to Barrow, and on St. Lawrence and St. Matthew islands.

Winters from Southeast Asia and southeastern China south to the East Indies, Philippines and Moluccas.

In migration occurs in eastern Asia and the Commander Islands, casually in the Aleutians.

Notes.—Also known as ARCTIC WILLOW-WARBLER. Specimens representing Asiatic breeding populations have been taken in migration in the Aleutians (Attu, Shemya and Amchitka).

Genus REGULUS Cuvier

Regulus Cuvier, 1800, Leçons Anat. Comp., 1, table ii. Type, by monotypy, "Roitelets" = *Motacilla regulus* Linnaeus.
Orchilus Morris, 1837, *in* Wood, Naturalist, 2, p. 124. Type, by subsequent designation (Oberholser, 1974), *Orchilus cristatus* Wood = *Motacilla regulus* Linnaeus.

Subgenus REGULUS Cuvier

Regulus satrapa Lichtenstein. GOLDEN-CROWNED KINGLET. [748.]

Regulus satrapa Lichtenstein, 1823, Verz. Doubl. Zool. Mus. Berlin, p. 35. (Am. sept. = North America.)

Habitat.—Coniferous forest and woodland (especially spruce), in migration and winter also deciduous woodland, scrub and brush.

Distribution.—*Breeds* from southern Alaska (west to the base of the Alaska Peninsula), southern Yukon, northern Alberta, northern Saskatchewan, northern Manitoba, central Ontario, southern Quebec (including Anticosti Island), Prince Edward Island, Nova Scotia and Newfoundland south in the coastal and interior mountains to southern and eastern California (to the San Bernardino and San Jacinto mountains), extreme western and northeastern Nevada (absent from central region), southern Utah, central and southeastern Arizona, south-central New Mexico, in the highlands through Mexico to western Guatemala, and east of the Rockies to central Saskatchewan (probably), southern Manitoba, northern and east-central Minnesota, north-central Michigan, southern Ontario, New York, in the mountains to eastern Tennessee and western North Carolina, and to southeastern Pennsylvania, northern New Jersey, central Massachusetts and southern Maine.

Winters from south-coastal Alaska (Kodiak Island) and southern Canada (British Columbia, southern Saskatchewan, southern Manitoba, southern Ontario, New Brunswick and Newfoundland) south to northern Baja California, through the breeding range to Guatemala (rarely to lowland regions in Mexico), and to northern Tamaulipas, the Gulf coast and central Florida.

Accidental in Bermuda.

Subgenus CORTHYLIO Cabanis

Corthylio Cabanis, 1853, J. Ornithol., 1, p. 83. Type, by subsequent designation (Baird, Brewer and Ridgway, 1874), *Motacilla calendula* Linnaeus.

Regulus calendula (Linnaeus). RUBY-CROWNED KINGLET. [749.]

Motacilla Calendula Linnaeus, 1766, Syst. Nat., ed. 12, 1, p. 337. Based on "The Ruby-crowned Wren" Edwards, Glean. Nat. Hist., 1, p. 95, pl. 254, fig. 2. (in Pensylvania = Philadelphia.)

Habitat.—Coniferous forest, mixed coniferous-deciduous woodland, and muskeg, in migration and winter also deciduous forest, open woodland, brush and scrub.

Distribution.—*Breeds* from northwestern and north-central Alaska, central Yukon, northwestern and southern Mackenzie, northern Saskatchewan, northern Manitoba, northern Ontario, northern Quebec, Labrador and Newfoundland south to southern Alaska (west to the base of the Alaska Peninsula), in the mountains to southern California (San Bernardino, San Jacinto and White mountains), central and southern Arizona, south-central New Mexico and east-central Colorado, and east of the Rockies to central Alberta, central Saskatchewan, southern Manitoba, northeastern (casually central) Minnesota, north-central Wisconsin, northern Michigan, southern Ontario, northern New York, southern Quebec, northern Maine and Nova Scotia; also resident on Guadalupe Island, off Baja California.

Winters from southern British Columbia, Idaho, northern Arizona, northern New Mexico, Nebraska, Iowa, Illinois, southern Ontario and New Jersey (rarely along the northern edge, casually recorded farther north in winter) south to southern Baja California, throughout most of Mexico to western Guatemala, and to

southern Texas, the Gulf coast and southern Florida (including the Florida Keys), casually to western Cuba and the northwestern Bahama Islands.
Accidental in Greenland; also a sight report from Jamaica.

Tribe RAMPHOCAENINI: Gnatwrens

Genus MICROBATES Sclater and Salvin

Microbates Sclater and Salvin, 1873, Nomencl. Avium Neotrop., pp. 72, 155. Type, by original designation, *Microbates torquatus* Sclater and Salvin = *Rhamphocaenus collaris* Pelzeln.

Notes.—Some authors merge this genus in *Ramphocaenus.*

Microbates cinereiventris (Sclater). TAWNY-FACED GNATWREN.

Ramphocænus cinereiventris Sclater, 1855, Proc. Zool. Soc. London, p. 76, pl. 87. (in rep. Novæ Grenadæ, Pasto = Buenaventura, Colombia.)

Habitat.—Humid lowland forest, primarily in undergrowth and dense borders, shaded second growth, and thick bushy growth (Tropical and lower Subtropical zones).
Distribution.—*Resident* on the Caribbean slope of southeastern Nicaragua and Costa Rica, on both slopes of Panama (more widespread on the Caribbean), and in South America from Colombia south, west of the Andes to western Ecuador and east of the Andes to southeastern Peru.
Notes.—Also known as HALF-COLLARED GNATWREN.

Genus RAMPHOCAENUS Vieillot

Ramphocænus Vieillot, 1819, Nouv. Dict. Hist. Nat., nouv. éd., 29, p. 5. Type, by monotypy, *Ramphocaenus melanurus* Vieillot.

Ramphocaenus melanurus Vieillot. LONG-BILLED GNATWREN.

Ramphocænus melanurus Vieillot, 1819, Nouv. Dict. Hist. Nat., nouv. éd., 29, p. 6. (Brésil = Rio de Janeiro, Brazil.)

Habitat.—Humid forest undergrowth, clearings, forest edge, second growth, scrubby woodland and tangled brush (Tropical and lower Subtropical zones).
Distribution.—*Resident* from central Oaxaca and southern Veracruz south along both slopes of Middle America (including the Yucatan Peninsula), and in South America from Colombia, Venezuela and the Guianas south, east of the Andes, to northeastern Peru and central and southeastern Brazil.
Notes.—The Middle American populations south to Colombia are sometimes regarded as a species, *R. rufiventris* (Bonaparte, 1838) [LONG-BILLED GNATWREN], distinct from the South American *R. melanurus* [STRAIGHT-BILLED GNATWREN].

Tribe POLIOPTILINI: Gnatcatchers

Notes.—Formerly considered a subfamily, the Polioptilinae, of the Sylviidae.

Genus POLIOPTILA Sclater

Polioptila Sclater, 1855, Proc. Zool. Soc. London, p. 11. Type, by subsequent designation (Baird, 1864), *Motacilla caerulea* Linnaeus.

Polioptila caerulea (Linnaeus). BLUE-GRAY GNATCATCHER. [751.]

Motacilla cærulea Linnaeus, 1766, Syst. Nat., ed. 12, 1, p. 337. Based on the "Little Blue-grey Flycatcher" Edwards, Glean. Nat. Hist., 2, p. 194, pl. 302. (in Pensylvania = Philadelphia.)

Habitat.—Deciduous forest, open woodland, second growth, scrub, brushy areas and chaparral (Tropical to lower Temperate zones).

Distribution.—*Breeds* from southern Oregon (casually), northern California, southern Idaho (casually), western and central Nevada, central Utah, Colorado, Nebraska, southeastern South Dakota (possibly), western Iowa, southeastern Minnesota, southern Wisconsin, southern Michigan, extreme southern Ontario, southwestern Quebec, central New York, central Vermont, southern New Hampshire and southern Maine south to southern Baja California, throughout most of Mexico (including the Yucatan Peninsula and Cozumel Island) to southern Chiapas and (probably) western Guatemala, and to southeastern Texas, the Gulf coast, southern Florida and the Bahama Islands (south to Grand Turk).

Winters from southern California, southern Nevada, western and central Arizona, southern New Mexico (rarely), central Texas, the southern portions of the Gulf states, and on the Atlantic coast from Virginia (casually farther north) south throughout Mexico to Guatemala and Honduras (including the Bay Islands), and to the western Greater Antilles (Cuba, the Isle of Pines and Cayman Islands) and the Bahamas.

Casual north to southwestern British Columbia, southern Alberta, North Dakota, New Brunswick and Nova Scotia.

Polioptila lembeyei (Gundlach). CUBAN GNATCATCHER.

Culicivora lembeyei Gundlach, 1858, Ann. Lyc. Nat. Hist. N.Y., 6, p. 273. (Eastern part of Cuba.)

Habitat.—Semi-arid scrub near coastal areas.

Distribution.—*Resident* in Cuba (central and eastern Camagüey and Las Villas provinces east to the Guantánamo region, also on Cayo Coco and probably Cayo Romano, off Camagüey).

Polioptila melanura Lawrence. BLACK-TAILED GNATCATCHER. [752.]

Polioptila melanura Lawrence, 1857, Ann. Lyc. Nat. Hist. N.Y., 6, p. 168. (Texas, California = Rio Grande Valley, Texas.)

Habitat.—Desert brush and scrub, especially in mesquite and creosote-bush, also [*californica* group] in coastal sagebrush and thorn forest (Tropical and Subtropical zones).

Distribution.—*Resident* [*californica* group] from southwestern California (north to Los Angeles County, formerly to Ventura County) and northwestern Baja California south locally to southern Baja California (including Santa Margarita and Espíritu Santo islands); and [*melanura* group] from northeastern (and possibly east-central) Baja California, southeastern California (north to southern Inyo County), southern Nevada, western and central Arizona, southern (rarely central) New Mexico, and western and southern Texas (Rio Grande Valley) south to southern Sonora (including Isla Tiburón), southern Durango, Jalisco, Guanajuato, San Luis Potosí and Tamaulipas.

Notes.—Differences in morphology and vocalizations suggest that the two groups may be distinct species, *P. californica* Brewster, 1881 [BLACK-TAILED GNATCATCH-ER, 753], and *P. melanura* [PLUMBEOUS GNATCATCHER, 752].

Polioptila nigriceps Baird. BLACK-CAPPED GNATCATCHER. [753.1.]

> *Polioptila nigriceps* Baird, 1864, Rev. Am. Birds, 1, p. 69. (Mazatlán, Sinaloa, Mexico.)

Habitat.—Riparian woodland and associated brushy areas, especially mesquite (Tropical and lower Subtropical zones).

Distribution.—*Resident* from extreme southern Arizona (Nogales area, Santa Rita Mountains), southern Sonora and southwestern Chihuahua south through Sinaloa, western Durango, Nayarit and Jalisco to Colima.

Notes.—Although considered conspecific with *P. albiloris* by some authors, *P. nigriceps* differs in plumage sequence as well as morphology, and shows no approach to *albiloris* in the region of geographic proximity in western Mexico.

Polioptila albiloris Sclater and Salvin. WHITE-LORED GNATCATCHER.

> *Polioptila albiloris* Sclater and Salvin, 1860, Proc. Zool. Soc. London, p. 298. (In rep. Guatimalensi in valle fl. Motagua = Motagua Valley, Zacapa, Guatemala.)

Habitat.—Deciduous woodland, arid scrub, brush and, less commonly, riparian woodland, primarily in arid or semi-arid regions (Tropical and Subtropical zones).

Distribution.—*Resident* in the Pacific lowlands and arid interior valleys from Michoacán, Guerrero, Oaxaca, western Puebla and Chiapas south through Central America to northwestern Costa Rica (south to the Gulf of Nicoya region); also on the Yucatan Peninsula in the state of Yucatán (doubtfully recorded also from Cozumel Island).

Notes.—Although closely related to *P. plumbea*, *P. albiloris* differs in appearance, voice and habitat, and occurs sympatrically with *plumbea* at several locations. See also comments under *P. nigriceps*.

Polioptila plumbea (Gmelin). TROPICAL GNATCATCHER.

> *Todus plumbeus* Gmelin, 1788, Syst. Nat., 1 (1), p. 444. Based on the "Plumbeous Tody" Latham, Gen. Synop. Birds, 1 (2), p. 661. (in Surinamo = Surinam.)

Habitat.—Humid forest edge, clearings, open woodland, second growth, scrub and savanna (Tropical and lower Subtropical zones).

Distribution.—*Resident* on the Gulf-Caribbean slope of Campeche, Quintana Roo, Guatemala, Belize, Honduras and Nicaragua, on both slopes of Costa Rica (uncommon in the dry northwest) and Panama (including Isla Coiba, also sight records from the Pearl Islands), and in South America from Colombia, Venezuela (also Margarita Island) and the Guianas south, west of the Andes to western Peru and east of the Andes to central Peru and Amazonian and eastern Brazil.

Notes.—The Peruvian form found at higher elevations is sometimes regarded as a distinct species, *P. maior* Hellmayr, 1900. The relationship of *P. plumbea* to the southwestern South American *P. lactea* Sharpe, 1885, is uncertain; a few authors have suggested conspecificity. See also comments under *P. albiloris*.

Polioptila schistaceigula Hartert. SLATE-THROATED GNATCATCHER.

Polioptila schistaceigula Hartert, 1898, Bull. Br. Ornithol. Club, 7, p. 30. (Cachabi [=Cachaví], 500 ft., [Esmeraldas,] North Ecuador.)

Habitat.—Humid lowland forest, forest edge and second growth (Tropical Zone).

Distribution.—*Resident* from eastern Panama (recorded in eastern Panamá province above Madden Lake, and in eastern Darién on Cerro Quía) south through northern and western Colombia (also in Cundimarca east of the Andes) to northwestern Ecuador.

Notes.—The relationship of *P. schistaceigula* with the northeastern South American *P. guianensis* Todd, 1920, is uncertain; conspecificity has been suggested by a few authors.

Subfamily MUSCICAPINAE: Old World Flycatchers and Allies

Genus **FICEDULA** Brisson

Ficedula Brisson, 1760, Ornithologie, 3, p. 369. Type, by tautonymy, *Ficedula* Brisson = *Ficedula hypoleuca* Pallas.

Notes.—Some authors merge this genus in *Muscicapa.*

Ficedula parva (Bechstein). RED-BREASTED FLYCATCHER. [771.]

Muscicapa parva Bechstein, 1794, *in* Latham, Allg. Uebers. Vögel, 2 (1), p. 356, fig. on title page vol. 3. (Thüringerwald.)

Habitat & Distribution.—*Breeds* in undergrowth of mixed deciduous-coniferous woodland from central Europe, Russia and Siberia south to northern Iran, the northern Himalayas, northern Mongolia, Anadyrland and Kamchatka, and *winters* in India and Ceylon, migrating through western Asia and China.

Accidental in Alaska in the Aleutians (Shemya) and on St. Lawrence Island (Gambell), 1 June and 5 June 1977, respectively (Gibson and Hall, 1978, Auk, 95, p. 429).

Notes.—Also known as RED-THROATED FLYCATCHER. Includes the Himalayan form, sometimes regarded as a distinct species, *F. subrubra* (Hartert and Steinbacher, 1934).

Genus **MUSCICAPA** Brisson

Muscicapa Brisson, 1760, Ornithologie, 1, p. 32. Type, by tautonymy, *Muscicapa* Brisson = *Motacilla striata* Pallas.

Notes.—See comments under *Ficedula.*

Muscicapa sibirica Gmelin. SIBERIAN FLYCATCHER. [772.]

Muscicapa sibirica Gmelin, 1789, Syst. Nat., 1 (2), p. 936. Based on the "Dun Fly-catcher" Pennant, Arct. Zool., 2, p. 390, and Latham, Gen. Synop. Birds, 2 (1), p. 351. (Circa lacum Baical, et in orientali Sibiria ad Camtschatcam usque = near Lake Baikal.)

Habitat & Distribution.—*Breeds* in open forest of mountains and taiga from central Siberia south to the Himalayas, northern China, Japan, Kamchatka and the Kurile Islands, and *winters* south to northern India, Southeast Asia and southern China.

Accidental in Alaska (Shemya Island, in the Aleutians, 13 September 1977; Gibson, 1981, Condor, 83, p. 73) and Bermuda (Sandy's Parish, 29 September 1980, D. B. Wingate, specimen in A. M. N. H.).

Notes.—Also known as SOOTY FLYCATCHER, a name now generally restricted to the African *Artomyias fuliginosa* (J. & E. Verreaux, 1855).

Muscicapa griseisticta (Swinhoe). GRAY-SPOTTED FLYCATCHER. [773.]

> *Hemichelidon griseisticta* Swinhoe, 1861, Ibis, p. 330. (Amoy and Takoo, eastern China.)

Habitat.—Open forest of the taiga (breeding); wooded areas and scrub (nonbreeding).

Distribution.—*Breeds* from eastern Siberia and Kamchatka south to eastern Manchuria, Ussuriland, Sakhalin and the Kurile Islands.

Winters from eastern China, Formosa and the Philippines south to Celebes, New Guinea, and islands of this general region.

Migrates through northern China, Japan and the Ryukyu Islands, ranging casually to the Commander Islands and (in spring) the western Aleutians (Attu, Shemya, Buldir and Amchitka).

Subfamily MONARCHINAE: Monarch Flycatchers

Notes.—The birds of this subfamily may not belong in the muscicapid assemblage.

Genus CHASIEMPIS Cabanis

Chasiempis Cabanis, 1847, Arch. Naturgesch., 13, p. 207. Type, by monotypy, *Muscicapa sandvichensis* Latham = *Muscicapa sandwichensis* Gmelin.

Chasiempis sandwichensis (Gmelin). ELEPAIO. [770.]

> *Muscicapa sandwichensis* Gmelin, 1789, Syst. Nat., 1 (2), p. 945. Based on the "Sandwich Fly-catcher" Latham, Gen. Synop. Birds, 2 (1), p. 344. (in insulis Sandwich = Hawaii.)

Habitat.—Forested areas, especially in regions of high rainfall.
Distribution.—*Resident* in the Hawaiian Islands (Kauai, Oahu and Hawaii).

Subfamily TURDINAE: Solitaires, Thrushes and Allies

Notes.—Sometimes considered a family, the Turdidae.

Genus LUSCINIA Forster

Luscinia T. Forster, 1817, Synop. Cat. Br. Birds, p. 14. Type, by monotypy, *Sylvia luscinia* Forster = *Luscinia megarhynchos* Brehm.

Notes.—*Luscinia* is sometimes merged with the Old World genus *Erithacus* Cuvier, 1800.

Luscinia calliope (Pallas). SIBERIAN RUBYTHROAT. [764.1.]

Motacilla Calliope Pallas, 1776, Reise Versch. Prov. Russ. Reichs, 3, p. 697. (a Jenisea usque ad Lenam = between the Yenisei and Lena rivers.)

Habitat.—Open shrubby areas in mixed or coniferous forest near streams.

Distribution.—*Breeds* from Siberia (the Urals east to Anadyrland and Kamchatka) south to Mongolia, Transbaicalia, Amurland, Sakhalin, Japan and the Kurile Islands.

Winters from India, Southeast Asia and southern China south to Malaya, the Philippines and Formosa.

In migration through eastern China, Korea, Japan, the Ryukyu Islands, and rarely (but regularly) through the western Aleutians (Near Islands, casually east to Amchitka) and Commander Islands, casually to the Pribilofs (St. Paul) and St. Lawrence Island.

Casual west to western Europe.

Luscinia svecica (Linnaeus). BLUETHROAT. [764.]

Motacilla svecica Linnaeus, 1758, Syst. Nat., ed. 10, 1, p. 187. (in Europæ alpinis = Sweden and Lappland.)

Habitat.—Bushes, undergrowth and scrub in Arctic tundra, swamps, dense or open forest, and open country.

Distribution.—*Breeds* from northern Scandinavia, northern Russia, northern Siberia, and northern and western Alaska (from the central Brooks Range west and south to the Seward Peninsula) south to western and central Europe, Iran, Turkestan, the northern Himalayas and Manchuria.

Winters in northern Africa (from Morocco east to northeastern Africa), the Near East, India and Southeast Asia.

In migration through western Alaska (St. Lawrence Island, and casually on the mainland south to St. Michael), the British Isles, western and southern Europe, and southwestern and eastern Asia.

Accidental in Yukon (Babbage River).

Genus **COPSYCHUS** Wagler

Copsychus Wagler, 1827, Syst. Avium, 1, note to genus *Gracula,* p. 306. Type, by subsequent designation (G. R. Gray, 1840), *Gracula saularis* Linnaeus.

[Copsychus saularis (Linnaeus). MAGPIE ROBIN.] See Appendix B.

Copsychus malabaricus (Scopoli). WHITE-RUMPED SHAMA. [769.]

Muscicapa (*malabarica*) Scopoli, 1786, Del. Flor. Faun. Insubr., fasc. 2, p. 96. (Mahé, Malabar.)

Habitat.—Thickets and dense undergrowth in forest and second growth, less commonly in overgrown gardens.

Distribution.—*Resident* from India, Southeast Asia and southwestern China south to Ceylon, the Andaman and Greater Sunda islands, and Hainan.

Introduced and established in the Hawaiian Islands (in 1931, now on Kauai and Oahu).

Notes.—Also known as SHAMA THRUSH.

Genus OENANTHE Vieillot

Oenanthe Vieillot, 1816, Analyse, p. 43. Type, by monotypy, "Motteux" Buffon = *Turdus leucurus* Gmelin.

Oenanthe oenanthe (Linnaeus). NORTHERN WHEATEAR. [765.]

Motacilla Oenanthe Linnaeus, 1758, Syst. Nat., ed. 10, 1, p. 186. (in Europæ apricis lapidosis = Sweden.)

Habitat.—Open country, stony or barren localities with or without bushes, tundra, steppe and desert, in migration and winter also in meadows and cultivated fields.

Distribution.—*Breeds* in North America from northern Alaska, northern Yukon and northwestern Mackenzie south to western and south-coastal Alaska (to the Kenai Peninsula) and southern Yukon, and from central Ellesmere Island south to the Boothia Peninsula (possibly), southeastern Keewatin, White Island, eastern and southern Baffin Island, northern Quebec and Labrador; and in the Palearctic from Greenland, Jan Mayen, Iceland, Spitsbergen, the British Isles, northern Scandinavia, northern Russia (including Novaya Zemlya) and northern Siberia south to northern Africa, Asia Minor, the northwestern Himalayas, Turkestan, Mongolia and Manchuria.

Winters from northern Africa, Arabia, India, Mongolia and northern China south to southern Africa (at least casually), and rarely to eastern China and the Philippines.

In migration occurs regularly in western Alaska and on islands in the Bering Sea, casually in the Aleutians, Pribilofs and southeastern Alaska (Juneau).

Casual or accidental along the Pacific coast in British Columbia (Victoria), Oregon (Malheur) and northern California (Farallon Islands and Humboldt County); in northeastern North America from southern Ontario, New York, southern Quebec, New Brunswick, Nova Scotia and Newfoundland south through New England to New Jersey, Pennsylvania and Virginia; and in Colorado (Boulder), Louisiana (New Orleans), Florida (south to Collier County), Bermuda, Cuba (Santiago de Cuba), Barbados and the Netherlands Antilles, also sight reports for northeastern Manitoba, Michigan and Puerto Rico.

Notes.—Known in Old World literature as the WHEATEAR.

[Genus SAXICOLA Bechstein]

Saxicola Bechstein, 1803, Ornithol. Taschenb. Dtsch., 1 (1802), p. 216. Type, by subsequent designation (Swainson, 1827), *Motacilla rubicola* Linnaeus = *Motacilla torquata* Linnaeus.

[Saxicola rubetra (Linnaeus). EUROPEAN WHINCHAT.] See Appendix B.

[Saxicola torquata (Linnaeus). STONECHAT.] See Appendix B.

Genus SIALIA Swainson

Sialia Swainson, 1827, Philos. Mag., new ser., 1, p. 369. Type, by monotypy, *Sialia azurea* Swainson = *Motacilla sialis* Linnaeus.

Sialia sialis (Linnaeus). EASTERN BLUEBIRD. [766.]

Motacilla Sialis Linnaeus, 1758, Syst. Nat., ed. 10, 1, p. 187. Based mainly on "The Blew Bird" Catesby, Nat. Hist. Carolina, 1, p. 47, pl. 47. (in Bermudis & America calidiore = South Carolina.)

Habitat.—Forest edge, open woodland, and partly open situations with scattered trees, from coniferous or deciduous forest to riparian woodland but most frequently in pine-oak association, in the tropics also in pine woodland or pine savanna (Tropical to Temperate zones).

Distribution.—*Breeds* from southern Saskatchewan, southern (casually northwestern) Manitoba, central Ontario, southern Quebec, New Brunswick and southwestern Nova Scotia south, west to the Dakotas, central Nebraska, western Kansas, central Oklahoma, Texas (except for High Plains and Trans-Pecos) and southeastern New Mexico (casually to the eastern foothills of the Rockies in eastern Montana, eastern Wyoming and eastern Colorado), through the highlands of Mexico, Guatemala, El Salvador and Honduras to north-central Nicaragua (also in the lowland pine savanna of northeastern Honduras and northern Nicaragua), and to southern Tamaulipas, southern Texas, the Gulf coast and southern Florida; also in southeastern Arizona (Nogales and Patagonia east to Huachuca and Chiricahua mountains), and in Bermuda.

Winters from the middle portions of the eastern United States (casually north to the northern states, southern Ontario, southern Quebec and New England) south throughout the breeding range, casually to the lowlands of eastern Mexico (Veracruz) and to western Cuba; most of the populations from the Gulf states southward are sedentary.

In migration occurs irregularly west to the foothills of the Rockies from Montana south to central New Mexico.

Casual north to southern Alberta, north-central and southern Quebec (including Anticosti Island), and Prince Edward Island.

Sialia mexicana Swainson. WESTERN BLUEBIRD. [767.]

Sialia Mexicana Swainson, 1832, *in* Swainson and Richardson, Fauna Bor.-Am., 2 (1831), p. 202. (table land of Mexico.)

Habitat.—Open coniferous, deciduous and mixed forest, partly open situations with scattered trees, savanna, and riparian woodland (Subtropical and Temperate zones).

Distribution.—*Resident* from southern British Columbia, western and south-central Montana, and north-central Colorado south through the mountains to northern Baja California (Sierra Juárez and Sierra San Pedro Mártir), western and southern Nevada, southern Utah, western and southeastern Arizona, and northeastern Sonora, in the highlands of Mexico to Michoacán, the state of México, Morelos, Puebla and west-central Veracruz, and east to southwestern Tamaulipas, Nuevo León, western (Trans-Pecos) Texas and central New Mexico.

Wanders in winter to lowland areas throughout the breeding range, and to islands off California (Santa Catalina and San Clemente, at least casually) and Baja California (Todos Santos), rarely north to southern British Columbia, south to southeastern California, and east to central Texas.

Casual in Oklahoma (Kenton), also sight records from Kansas.

Sialia currucoides (Bechstein). MOUNTAIN BLUEBIRD. [768.]

Motacilla s. *Sylvia Currucoides* (Borkhausen MS) Bechstein, 1798, *in* Latham, Allg. Uebers. Vögel, 3 (2), p. 546, pl. 121. (Virginien = western America.)

Habitat.—Open coniferous forest, subalpine meadows, and pinyon-juniper woodland, in migration and winter also in grasslands, plains, open brushy areas and agricultural lands.

Distribution.—*Breeds* from east-central Alaska (Fairbanks, Eagle, Chisana), southern Yukon, north-central Alberta, central Saskatchewan and western Manitoba south in the mountains (eastern slopes of coast ranges, and in the Sierra Nevada and Rocky Mountains) to southern California (to San Bernardino Mountains), central and southeastern Nevada, northern and east-central Arizona, and southern New Mexico, and east to northeastern North Dakota, western South Dakota, western Nebraska and central Oklahoma (Cleveland County). Recorded in summer (and possibly breeding) in southern Mackenzie.

Winters from southern British Columbia and western Montana south to northern Baja California (including islands off California and Baja California south to Guadalupe Island), Sinaloa, Michoacán, Guanajuato, Nuevo León and southern Texas, and east, at least casually, to eastern Kansas, western Oklahoma and central Texas.

Casual in western and northern Alaska (Nunivak Island and Point Barrow) and northern Manitoba (Churchill); east across Minnesota, Iowa, Wisconsin, Missouri and southern Ontario to New York (east to Long Island) and Pennsylvania; and in the Gulf region through eastern Texas to eastern Louisiana (Baton Rouge region) and Mississippi (Grenada Dam).

Genus **MYADESTES** Swainson

Myadestes Swainson, 1838, Naturalists' Libr., Ornithol., 10 (Flycatchers), p. 132. Type, by monotypy, *Myidestes* [sic] *genibarbis* Swainson.

Notes.—See comments under *Phaeornis.*

Myadestes townsendi (Audubon). TOWNSEND'S SOLITAIRE. [754.]

Ptilogony's [sic] *Townsendi* Audubon, 1838, Birds Am. (folio), 4, pl. 419, fig. 2 (1839, Ornithol. Biogr., 5, p. 206). (Columbia River = Astoria, Oregon.)

Habitat.—Montane and subalpine coniferous forest, rocky cliffs, and adjacent brushy areas and thickets (breeding); open woodland, pinyon-juniper association, chaparral, desert and riparian woodland (nonbreeding).

Distribution.—*Breeds* from east-central, south-coastal and southeastern Alaska, southern Yukon, and west-central and southwestern Mackenzie south in the mountains to southern California (to Santa Rosa and San Bernardino mountains), northern and east-central Arizona, and central New Mexico, in the mountains of Mexico to Durango, Jalisco and Zacatecas, and east to southwestern Alberta, southwestern Saskatchewan, western and southern Montana, northeastern Wyoming, southwestern South Dakota and northwestern Nebraska.

Winters from southern British Columbia (casually north to Alaska), southern Alberta, Montana and South Dakota south to northern Baja California, Sonora, and southern limits of the breeding range in Mexico, and east to western Missouri, western Oklahoma and central Texas.

Casual on Guadalupe Island (off Baja California), and east across Minnesota,

Iowa, Wisconsin, northern Illinois, southern Michigan, southern Ontario, northern Ohio, southern Quebec, New York and New Brunswick to Nova Scotia, New Hampshire and Rhode Island.

Myadestes obscurus Lafresnaye. BROWN-BACKED SOLITAIRE.

Myadestes obscurus Lafresnaye, 1839, Rev. Zool. [Paris], 2, p. 98. (Mexico = probably Veracruz.)

Habitat.—Humid montane forest and pine-oak association, less frequently semi-arid oak woodland (Subtropical Zone).

Distribution.—*Resident* from southeastern Sonora, southern Chihuahua, Sinaloa, Durango, Nayarit (including the Tres Marias Islands), Jalisco, Guanajuato, San Luis Potosí, central Nuevo León and southern Tamaulipas south through the mountains of Mexico, Guatemala and El Salvador to central Honduras (east to the Comayagua Valley).

Myadestes elisabeth (Lembeye). CUBAN SOLITAIRE.

Muscicapa elisabeth Lembeye, 1850, Aves Isla Cuba, p. 39, pl. 5, fig. 3. (Cuba.)

Habitat.—Forested hills and mountains (Cuba) and dense lowland woodland (Isle of Pines).

Distribution.—*Resident* in the mountains of western Cuba (Pinar del Río province) and eastern Cuba (Oriente province), and on the Isle of Pines (vicinity of Ciénaga de Lanier).

Myadestes genibarbis Swainson. RUFOUS-THROATED SOLITAIRE.

Myidestes [sic] *genibarbis* Swainson, 1838, *in* Jardine, Naturalists' Libr., Ornithol., 10 (Flycatchers), p. 134, pl. 13. (Africa or India, error = Martinique.)

Habitat.—Primarily mountain forest, less frequently humid lowland forest.

Distribution.—*Resident* on Jamaica and Hispaniola, and in the Lesser Antilles (Dominica, Martinique, St. Lucia and St. Vincent).

Myadestes melanops Salvin. BLACK-FACED SOLITAIRE.

Myiadestes melanops Salvin, 1865, Proc. Zool. Soc. London (1864), p. 580, pl. 36. (Tucurrique, Costa Rica.)

Habitat.—Humid foothill and montane forest (upper Tropical and Subtropical zones).

Distribution.—*Resident* in the mountains of Costa Rica (more commonly on the Caribbean slope) and western Panama (east on both slopes to Veraguas).

Notes.—*M. melanops* and *M. coloratus* are considered by some authors to be conspecific with the Andean *M. ralloides* (d'Orbigny, 1840) [ANDEAN SOLITAIRE]; the three species constitute a superspecies.

Myadestes coloratus Nelson. VARIED SOLITAIRE.

Myadestes coloratus Nelson, 1912, Smithson. Misc. Collect., 60, no. 3, p. 23. (Mount Pirri, at 5000 feet altitude, near head of Rio Limon, eastern Panama.)

Habitat.—Humid foothill and montane forest and forest edge (upper Tropical and Subtropical zones).
Distribution.—*Resident* in extreme eastern Panama (cerros Tacarcuna, Pirre and Quía, in eastern Darién) and extreme northwestern Colombia.
Notes.—See comments under *M. melanops.*

Myadestes unicolor Sclater. SLATE-COLORED SOLITAIRE.

Myiadestes unicolor Sclater, 1857, Proc. Zool. Soc. London (1856), p. 299. (Cordova [=Córdoba] in the State of Vera Cruz, Southern Mexico.)

Habitat.—Humid foothill and montane forest and dense pine-oak woodland, in winter also to humid lowland forest (upper Tropical and Subtropical zones, reaching lower Tropical Zone in winter).
Distribution.—*Resident* (some postbreeding downslope movement) in the mountains from Hidalgo, Puebla, Oaxaca and eastern Veracruz south through Chiapas, Guatemala, northern El Salvador (Los Esesmiles) and Honduras to north-central Nicaragua.

Genus PHAEORNIS Sclater

Phaeornis Sclater, 1859, Ibis, p. 327. Type, by monotypy, *Taenioptera obscura* = *Muscicapa obscura* Gmelin.

Notes.—By some authors merged in *Myadestes.*

Phaeornis obscurus (Gmelin). HAWAIIAN THRUSH. [754.1.]

Muscicapa obscura Gmelin, 1789, Syst. Nat., 1 (2), p. 945. Based on the "Dusky Fly-catcher" Latham, Gen. Synop. Birds, 2 (1), p. 344. (in insulis Sandwich = Hawaii.)

Habitat.—Forest, preferably dense, native forest, more common at higher elevations where also found in subalpine or alpine scrub.
Distribution.—*Resident* in the Hawaiian Islands on Kauai (rare), Molokai (rare) and Hawaii (common), formerly also on Lanai and Oahu.
Notes.—Also improperly known as OMAO, a name that should pertain only to the race on Hawaii.

Phaeornis palmeri Rothschild. SMALL KAUAI THRUSH. [754.2.]

Phaeornis palmeri Rothschild, 1893, Avifauna Laysan, p. 67. (Halemanu, Kauai.)

Habitat.—Ohia forest.
Distribution.—*Resident* in the Hawaiian Islands on Kauai, where surviving in small numbers in the Alakai Swamp region.
Notes.—Also known as PUAIOHI.

Genus CATHARUS Bonaparte

Catharus Bonaparte, 1850, Consp. Gen. Avium, 1 (2), p. 278. Type, by monotypy, *Turdus immaculatus* Bonaparte = *Turdus aurantiirostris* Hartlaub.

Notes.—See comments under *Hylocichla.*

Catharus gracilirostris Salvin. BLACK-BILLED NIGHTINGALE-THRUSH.

Catharus gracilirostris Salvin, 1865, Proc. Zool. Soc. London (1864), p. 580. (Volcán de Cartago, Costa Rica.)

Habitat.—Humid montane forest, forest edge, cleared pastureland, and scrub (upper Subtropical and Temperate zones).

Distribution.—*Resident* in the mountains of Costa Rica (Cordillera Central and Cordillera de Talamanca) and extreme western Panama (western Chiriquí).

Catharus aurantiirostris (Hartlaub). ORANGE-BILLED NIGHTINGALE-THRUSH.

Turdus aurantiirostris Hartlaub, 1850, Rev. Zool. [Paris], ser. 2, 1, p. 158. (Venezuela = Caracas.)

Habitat.—Humid forest edge, dense second growth, thickets, brushy areas, plantations and gardens (upper Tropical and Subtropical zones).

Distribution.—*Resident* from Sinaloa, southwestern Chihuahua, Durango, Nayarit, Jalisco, Guanajuato, southeastern San Luis Potosí and southwestern Tamaulipas south through Middle America (except the Yucatan Peninsula and Belize) to western Panama (Chiriquí and Veraguas), and in South America locally in western and northern Colombia, and northern Venezuela (also Trinidad).

Notes.—The morphologically distinct populations in southwestern Costa Rica, western Panama and western Colombia have sometimes been regarded as a distinct species, *C. griseiceps* Salvin, 1866 [GRAY-HEADED NIGHTINGALE-THRUSH].

Catharus fuscater (Lafresnaye). SLATY-BACKED NIGHTINGALE-THRUSH.

Myioturdus fuscater Lafresnaye, 1845, Rev. Zool. [Paris], 8, p. 341. (Bogotá, Colombia.)

Habitat.—Humid montane forest undergrowth (Subtropical Zone).

Distribution.—*Resident* in the mountains of Costa Rica (primarily on the Caribbean slope) and Panama (recorded Chiriquí, Veraguas, eastern Panamá province and eastern Darién), and in the mountains of South America from northern Colombia and northwestern Venezuela south through the Andes to eastern Peru and west-central Bolivia.

Catharus occidentalis Sclater. RUSSET NIGHTINGALE-THRUSH.

Catharus occidentalis Sclater, 1859, Proc. Zool. Soc. London, p. 323. (Western Mexico, Oaxaca, Totontepec = Totontepec, Oaxaca.)

Habitat.—Humid montane forest and pine-oak association, primarily in undergrowth and dense borders (Subtropical and lower Temperate zones).

Distribution.—*Resident* [*olivascens* group] in the Sierra Madre Occidental of western Chihuahua, eastern Sinaloa and northwestern Durango; and [*occidentalis* group] in the mountains from southern Durango, Nayarit, Michoacán, Guanajuato, eastern Coahuila, southern Nuevo León, southwestern Tamaulipas and eastern San Luis Potosí south to west-central Veracruz and central Oaxaca (east to Mount Zempoaltepec and the Río Molino areas).

Notes.—The two groups are sometimes regarded as distinct species, *C. olivascens* Nelson, 1899 [OLIVE NIGHTINGALE-THRUSH], and *C. occidentalis*. See also comments under *C. frantzii*.

Catharus frantzii Cabanis. RUDDY-CAPPED NIGHTINGALE-THRUSH.

Catharus Frantzii Cabanis, 1861, J. Ornithol., 8 (1860), p. 323. (Volcán de Irazú, Costa Rica.)

Habitat.—Humid montane forest and pine-oak association, primarily in dense edge and undergrowth (Subtropical and lower Temperate zones).

Distribution.—*Resident* in the mountains from western Jalisco, Michoacán, southeastern San Luis Potosí and Hidalgo south through Middle America (except the Yucatan Peninsula and Belize) to western Panama (western Chiriquí).

Notes.—Formerly regarded as a race of *C. occidentalis,* but the two species are quite distinct and widely sympatric in central Mexico.

Catharus mexicanus (Bonaparte). BLACK-HEADED NIGHTINGALE-THRUSH.

Malacocychla mexicana Bonaparte, 1856, C. R. Acad. Sci. Paris, 43, p. 998. (Jalapa, Veracruz, Mexico.)

Habitat.—Humid foothill and montane forest, undergrowth of forest edge, shaded second growth, and woodland patches, locally also in humid lowland forest (Tropical and Subtropical zones).

Distribution.—*Resident* in eastern and southern Mexico (recorded Tamaulipas, Hidalgo, Veracruz, the state of México, Puebla, northern Oaxaca and Chiapas), eastern Guatemala, Honduras, Nicaragua (north-central highlands, and locally in Caribbean lowlands), Costa Rica and western Panama (east to Veraguas).

Catharus dryas (Gould). SPOTTED NIGHTINGALE-THRUSH.

Malacocichla dryas Gould, 1855, Proc. Zool. Soc. London (1854), p. 285, pl. 75. (Guatemala.)

Habitat.—Humid montane forest, primarily in undergrowth, thickets and dense forest edge (upper Tropical and Subtropical zones).

Distribution.—*Resident* in the mountains of eastern Oaxaca (Sierra Madre de Chiapas), Chiapas, Guatemala and Honduras (east to the Tegucigalpa region); and in South America on the west slope of the Andes from western Ecuador to central Peru, and from northeastern Colombia and northwestern Venezuela south on the east slope of the Andes to eastern Peru, Bolivia and northern Argentina (Jujuy).

Catharus fuscescens (Stephens). VEERY. [756.]

Turdus Fuscescens Stephens, 1817, *in* Shaw, Gen. Zool., 10 (1), p. 182. (Pensylvania.)

Habitat.—Poplar, aspen or other swampy forest, especially in more open areas with shrubby understory, also in second growth, willow or alder shrubbery near water, in migration and winter also in lowland forest, woodland and scrub.

Distribution.—*Breeds* from south-central and southeastern British Columbia, central Alberta, central Saskatchewan, southern Manitoba, southern Ontario, southern Quebec (including Magdalen and possibly also Anticosti islands), New Brunswick, central Nova Scotia and southwestern Newfoundland south to central Oregon, northeastern Nevada, southern Idaho, southeastern Wyoming, south-central Colorado, northeastern South Dakota, Iowa, northern Illinois, north-central Indiana and northern Ohio, in the mountains through West Virginia, western and central Maryland, eastern Kentucky, western and central Virginia, eastern Tennessee and western North Carolina to northwestern Georgia, and in the Atlantic region to eastern Pennsylvania, central New Jersey and the District of Columbia; also in east-central Arizona (Springerville area).

Winters in South America from northern Colombia east across Venezuela (also Trinidad) to Guyana, and south to Amazonian and central Brazil.

Migrates primarily through the southeastern United States west to the Rocky Mountains, eastern New Mexico, and central and southern Texas, and through eastern Mexico (recorded Veracruz, the state of Yucatán, Cayos Arcas off Campeche, and Cozumel Island off Quintana Roo), northern Guatemala (Tikal), northern Honduras (Bay Islands), Costa Rica (Caribbean lowlands and San José), Panama (rare but regular in fall in Caribbean lowlands in the west, casually on Pacific slope), islands of the western Caribbean Sea (Providencia, San Andrés), Cuba, Jamaica and the Bahamas.

Casual or accidental in California, central Bolivia, the British Isles, Sweden and continental Europe, also sight reports for the Virgin Islands (St. John).

Notes.—*C. fuscescens* and the following three species were formerly included in the genus *Hylocichla*.

Catharus minimus (Lafresnaye). GRAY-CHEEKED THRUSH. [757.]

Turdus minimus Lafresnaye, 1848, Rev. Zool. [Paris], 11, p. 5. (ad Bogotam, in Nova-Granada = Bogotá, Colombia.)

Habitat.—Coniferous forest (primarily spruce) and tall shrubby areas in taiga, in migration and winter also in deciduous forest, open woodland, second growth and scrub.

Distribution.—*Breeds* from northeastern Siberia (Chukotski Peninsula and Anadyrland), northern Alaska, northern Yukon, northern Mackenzie, southern Keewatin, northern Quebec, Labrador and Newfoundland south to southern Alaska (west to the Alaska Peninsula and Kodiak Island, possibly also on St. Lawrence Island in the Bering Sea), northwestern British Columbia, southern Mackenzie, northern Alberta (probably), northeastern Saskatchewan, northern Manitoba, extreme northwestern Ontario, central and southeastern Quebec (including Magdalen Islands), eastern New York (Catskill and Adirondack mountains), Massachusetts (Mount Greylock), central Vermont, northern New Hampshire, central Maine, New Brunswick and northern Nova Scotia (Seal and Mud islands).

Winters in South America from Colombia, Venezuela (also Trinidad) and Guyana south to northern Peru and northwestern Brazil, casually in Hispaniola and north in Middle America (mostly on the Caribbean slope) to Costa Rica.

Migrates primarily through eastern North America west to the Great Plains and eastern Texas (casually to Montana, Wyoming, Colorado and New Mexico), the Bahamas and Greater Antilles, less frequently through the Swan Islands and southern Central America (Costa Rica and Panama, most commonly in fall), and rarely through southeastern Mexico (recorded Tabasco, Chiapas, Campeche, and Cozumel Island off Quintana Roo), Guatemala (Petén), Belize (including Half Moon Cay) and northern Honduras (including the Bay Islands).

Casual or accidental in California (primarily in the Farallon Islands), Arizona

(Chiricahua Mountains), northeastern Keewatin, Martinique, Greenland, the British Isles and continental Europe, also a sight report for the Aleutian Islands (Shemya).

Notes.—See comments under *C. fuscescens.*

Catharus ustulatus (Nuttall). SWAINSON'S THRUSH. [758.]

> *Turdus ustulatus* Nuttall, 1840, Man. Ornithol. U.S. Can., ed. 2, 1, pp. vi, 400, 830. (forests of the Oregon = Fort Vancouver, Washington.)

Habitat.—Dense tall shrubbery, coniferous woodland (especially spruce), aspen-poplar forest, second growth, and willow or alder thickets, in migration and winter also deciduous forest, open woodland, humid lowland forest, scrub and brushy areas.

Distribution.—*Breeds* from western and central Alaska, central Yukon, western and southern Mackenzie, northern Saskatchewan, north-central Manitoba, northern Ontario, central Quebec, southern Labrador and Newfoundland south to southern Alaska (west to the Alaska Peninsula), southern and east-central California, central Nevada, central Utah, north-central New Mexico, extreme northern Nebraska, eastern Wyoming, eastern Montana, southwestern and central Saskatchewan, southern Manitoba, northern Minnesota, northern Wisconsin, northern Michigan, southern Ontario, southern Quebec, southern New York, northern Pennsylvania, southern Vermont, central New Hampshire and southern Maine; also in eastern West Virginia, western Virginia (Mount Rogers), and (formerly) western Maryland.

Winters from Nayarit and southern Tamaulipas (casually from southern Texas and the Gulf coast) south through Middle America and South America east to Guyana and western Brazil, and south to Peru, Bolivia, northwestern Argentina and Paraguay.

Migrates through southern Canada, the United States (rare in southwestern portion) and Middle America (rare in Baja California and northwestern Mexico), less frequently through the Bahamas (Grand Bahama, New Providence), western Cuba, the Isle of Pines, Hispaniola, Jamaica, the Swan Islands, and Isla Providencia (in the western Caribbean Sea).

Casual or accidental on Meighen Island (Franklin District), and in Bermuda, the British Isles, continental Europe and the Ukraine.

Notes.—Also known as OLIVE-BACKED or RUSSET-BACKED THRUSH. See comments under *C. fuscescens.*

Catharus guttatus (Pallas). HERMIT THRUSH. [759.]

> *Muscicapa guttata* Pallas, 1811, Zoogr. Rosso-Asiat., 1, p. 465. (in insulis Americae vicinis praesertim Kadiak = Kodiak Island, Alaska.)

Habitat.—Open humid coniferous and mixed coniferous-deciduous forest and forest edge, and dry sandy and sparse jack-pine, less frequently in deciduous forest and thickets, in migration and winter also chaparral, riparian woodland, arid pine-oak association, and desert scrub.

Distribution.—*Breeds* from western and central Alaska, southern Yukon, southern Mackenzie, northern Saskatchewan, northern Manitoba, northern Ontario, central Quebec, southern Labrador and Newfoundland south to southern Alaska (west to the Alaska Peninsula, and Shumagin and Kodiak islands), in the mountains to southern California (to San Bernardino Mountains), southern Nevada, central and southeastern Arizona, southern New Mexico and extreme western Texas, and east of the Rockies to central Alberta, central Saskatchewan, southern Manitoba, north-central and northeastern Minnesota, central Wisconsin, north-central Michigan, southern Ontario, northeastern Ohio, central Pennsylvania, eastern West Virginia, western Virginia (Mount Rogers), western Maryland, southern New Jersey and southern New York (including Long Island); also isolated breeding in the Black Hills of southwestern South Dakota.

Winters from southern British Columbia, the northern United States, southern Ontario and New England (casually or irregularly in the northern portions of the breeding range) south to southern Baja California (including islands), through Mexico (mostly in the interior, not recorded Yucatan Peninsula) to Guatemala and El Salvador, and to southern Texas, the Gulf coast, southern Florida and the northern Bahamas (south to New Providence and Cat islands).

Casual or accidental on Southampton Island (The Post) and Bermuda, and in the British Isles.

Notes.—See comments under *C. fuscescens.*

Genus HYLOCICHLA Baird

Hylocichla Baird, 1864, Rev. Am. Birds, 1, p. 12. Type, by original designation, *Turdus mustelinus* Gmelin.

Notes.—Some authors merge *Hylocichla* with *Catharus,* but relationships of the former may be with *Turdus.*

Hylocichla mustelina (Gmelin). WOOD THRUSH. [755.]

Turdus mustelinus Gmelin, 1789, Syst. Nat., 1 (2), p. 817. Based on the "Tawny Thrush" Latham, Gen. Synop. Birds, 2 (1), p. 29. (in Noveboraco = New York.)

Habitat.—Deciduous forest and woodland, primarily more mature forest, in migration and winter also forest and woodland of various types from humid lowland to arid or humid montane forest, also scrub and thickets, more frequently in lowland situations.

Distribution.—*Breeds* from southeastern North Dakota, central Minnesota, central Wisconsin, northern Michigan, southern Ontario, southwestern Quebec, northern Vermont, central New Hampshire, southwestern Maine, New Brunswick and Nova Scotia south to east-central Texas, the Gulf coast and northern Florida (Panhandle east to Jacksonville area), and west to eastern South Dakota, central Nebraska, central Kansas and eastern Oklahoma; casual breeding to southern Manitoba, southwestern North Dakota and central South Dakota.

Winters from southern (rarely eastern) Texas south through eastern Mexico (including the Yucatan Peninsula and islands) and Middle America (primarily Caribbean slope, but recorded in El Salvador and rarely on the Pacific slope from Oaxaca southward) to Panama (most common in Bocas del Toro and Chiriquí) and northwestern Colombia (Chocó).

In migration occurs casually in Cuba and the Bahama Islands (New Providence, Grand Bahama, Cay Lobos).

Casual in western North America from Oregon, Utah, Montana, Saskatchewan and Manitoba south to California, Arizona and New Mexico. Accidental in Bermuda, Puerto Rico, Curaçao and Guyana.

Genus **TURDUS** Linnaeus

Turdus Linnaeus, 1758, Syst. Nat., ed. 10, 1, p. 168. Type, by subsequent designation (G. R. Gray, 1840), *Turdus viscivorus* Linnaeus.

Mimocichla [subgenus] Sclater, 1859, Proc. Zool. Soc. London, p. 336. Type, by subsequent designation (Baird, 1864), *Turdus rubripes* Temminck = *Turdus plumbeus* Linnaeus.

Notes.—See comments under *Hylocichla*.

Turdus merula Linnaeus. EURASIAN BLACKBIRD. [761.1.]

Turdus Merula Linnaeus, 1758, Syst. Nat., ed. 10, 1, p. 170. (in Europæ sylvis = Sweden.)

Habitat & Distribution.—*Resident* (or partly migratory) in woodland, forest, scrub and gardens virtually throughout Eurasia south to northwestern Africa, the Mediterranean region, Asia Minor, India, Southeast Asia and China.

Accidental in Quebec (Outremont, island of Montreal, 23 November 1970; McNeil and Cyr, 1971, Auk, 88, pp. 919-920); a specimen collected at Oakland, California, in 1891 is regarded as an escape.

Introduced and established in Australia and New Zealand, and on associated islands.

Notes.—Also known as EUROPEAN BLACKBIRD and, in Old World literature, the BLACKBIRD.

Turdus obscurus Gmelin. EYE-BROWED THRUSH. [761.3.]

Turdus obscurus Gmelin, 1789, Syst. Nat., 1 (2), p. 816. Based on the "Dark Thrush" Latham, Gen. Synop. Birds, 2 (1), p. 31. (in Sibiriae silvis, ultra lacum Baical = Lake Baikal.)

Habitat.—Dense coniferous and mixed coniferous-deciduous woodland, usually near water, in migration and winter also deciduous woodland and scrub.

Distribution.—*Breeds* from northern Siberia and Kamchatka south to northern Mongolia, Sakhalin, the Kurile Islands and Japan (Honshu).

Winters from India, Southeast Asia, southeastern China and Formosa south to the Andaman Islands, Java, Borneo, the Philippines and Palau Islands.

Migrates through Mongolia, Manchuria, eastern China, Korea, Japan and the Ryukyu Islands, ranging rarely but regularly (mostly in spring) to the western Aleutians (Near Islands, casually east to Amchitka), and casually to the Pribilofs and Alaska mainland (Wales, Barrow).

Casual in western Europe.

Turdus naumanni Temminck. DUSKY THRUSH. [761.4.]

Turdus naumanni Temminck, 1820, Man. Ornithol., ed. 2, 1, p. 170. (en Silésie et en Autriche . . . en Hongrie, etc., error = Siberia.)

Habitat.—Open coniferous forest, forest edge and deciduous scrub, in migration and winter also woodland and brushy areas.

Distribution.—*Breeds* [*eunomus* group] from northern Siberia east to Kamchatka; and [*naumanni* group] from southern Siberia east to Lake Baikal, northern Manchuria, Amurland and the Sea of Okhotsk.

Winters [*eunomus* group] from Japan and the Ryukyu Islands south to southern China and Formosa, rarely west to Southeast Asia and India; and [*naumanni* group] from southern Manchuria, northern China and Korea south to eastern China, rarely to Formosa and the Ryukyu Islands.

In migration [*eunomus* group] ranges casually (in spring) to Alaska (St. Lawrence Island, Barrow, and Attu and Shemya in the western Aleutians), and to the British Isles, western Europe and the Commander Islands.

Notes.—The two groups are sometimes regarded as distinct species, *T. eunomus* Temminck, 1831 [Dusky Thrush], and *T. naumanni* [Naumann's Thrush].

Turdus pilaris Linnaeus. Fieldfare. [761.2.]

Turdus pilaris Linnaeus, 1758, Syst. Nat., ed. 10, 1, p. 168. (in Europa = Sweden.)

Habitat.—Coniferous and mixed coniferous-deciduous woodland, and birch, alder or willow thickets, in migration and winter also open country in meadows, tundra and marshes, as well as in gardens, parks and cultivated lands.

Distribution.—*Breeds* from southern Greenland, Scandinavia, northern Russia and northern Siberia south to central Europe, central Russia, southern Siberia and Lake Baikal, occasionally in the Faroe Islands.

Winters from Iceland, the Faroe Islands, British Isles, southern Scandinavia and central Europe south to the Mediterranean region, Asia Minor, Iran, Turkestan and northwestern India, casually to the eastern Atlantic islands and northern Africa.

Casual or accidental in Alaska (Point Barrow), Keewatin (Foxe Basin), Franklin District (Jens Munk Island), Ontario (Point Pelee), Quebec (Rigaud) and Connecticut (Stamford), also sight reports for Ontario, Newfoundland, Nova Scotia, New York and Delaware.

Turdus iliacus Linnaeus. Redwing. [760.]

Turdus iliacus Linnaeus, 1766, Syst. Nat., ed. 12, 1, p. 292. (in Europa = Sweden.)

Habitat & Distribution.—*Breeds* in forest and woodland from Iceland across northern Eurasia to central Siberia, and *winters* south to the British Isles, continental Europe and the Mediterranean region, in migration casually to Greenland.

Accidental in Newfoundland (St. Anthony, 25 June–11 July 1980, photograph; Montevecchi, Mactavish and Kirkham, 1981, Am. Birds, 35, p. 147); an additional sight report from Jamaica Bay, Long Island, New York (1959) may be based on an escape from captivity.

Notes.—*T. iliacus* is sometimes known as *T. musicus* Linnaeus, 1758, but the latter name has been suppressed by the International Commission on Zoological Nomenclature.

Turdus nigrescens Cabanis. Sooty Robin.

Turdus nigrescens Cabanis, 1860, J. Ornithol., 8, p. 324. (Volcán de Irazú, Costa Rica.)

Habitat.—Parklike pastures, scrub and forest clearings in mountains (Subtropical and Temperate zones).

Distribution.—*Resident* in the mountains of Costa Rica (cordilleras de Tilarán, Central and de Talamanca) and extreme western Panama (western Chiriquí).

Notes.—This and most following species of the genus *Turdus* (through *T. assimilis*) known as ROBIN are called THRUSH by some authors.

Turdus infuscatus (Lafresnaye). BLACK ROBIN.

Merula infuscata Lafresnaye, 1844, Rev. Zool. [Paris], 7, p. 41. (du Mexique = Mexico.)

Habitat.—Humid montane forest, pine-oak association and oak woodland (Subtropical and Temperate zones).

Distribution.—*Resident* in the mountains from Guerrero, the state of México, eastern San Luis Potosí and southwestern Tamaulipas south through Veracruz, Oaxaca, Chiapas, Guatemala and El Salvador to central Honduras.

Notes.—Treated by a few authors as conspecific with the South American *T. serranus* Tschudi, 1844 [GLOSSY-BLACK THRUSH]. See also comments under *T. nigrescens.*

Turdus plebejus Cabanis. MOUNTAIN ROBIN.

Turdus plebejus Cabanis, 1861, J. Ornithol., 8 (1860), p. 323. (Costa Rica.)

Habitat.—Humid montane forest edge, clearings, open woodland and parklike pastures (Subtropical and lower Temperate zones).

Distribution.—*Resident* in the mountains from eastern Chiapas (Mount Ovando, Volcán Tacaná) south through Guatemala, El Salvador, Honduras, north-central Nicaragua and Costa Rica to western Panama (Chiriquí and Bocas del Toro).

Notes.—A few authors consider this species as conspecific with the South American *T. ignobilis* Sclater, 1857 [BLACK-BILLED ROBIN]. See also comments under *T. nigrescens.*

Turdus fumigatus Lichtenstein. COCOA THRUSH.

Turdus fumigatus Lichtenstein, 1823, Verz. Doubl. Zool. Mus. Berlin, p. 38. (Brazil = Rio Espirito Santo.)

Habitat.—Montane forest and plantations, in South America also in second growth, open woodland and lowland forest (Tropical and lower Subtropical zones).

Distribution.—*Resident* in the Lesser Antilles (St. Vincent and Grenada), and in South America from eastern Colombia, Venezuela (also Trinidad) and the Guianas south to eastern Bolivia and central and eastern Brazil.

Notes.—Considered by some authors to be conspecific with *T. obsoletus,* but the two are sympatric at a number of Amazonian localities; the two groups appear to constitute a superspecies. A few authors also suggest that the Lesser Antillean populations may represent a species, *T. personus* (Barbour, 1911), distinct from *T. fumigatus.*

Turdus obsoletus Lawrence. PALE-VENTED THRUSH.

Turdus obsoletus Lawrence, 1862, Ann. Lyc. Nat. Hist. N.Y., 7, p. 470. (Atlantic side of the Isthmus of Panama, along the line of the Panama Railroad = Canal Zone.)

Habitat.—Humid lowland and foothill forest, forest edge, clearings, second growth, open woodland and plantations (Tropical and lower Subtropical zones).

Distribution.—*Resident* [*obsoletus* group] from central Costa Rica (Caribbean slope of Cordillera Central and Cordillera de Talamanca) south through Panama (locally in foothills east to the Canal Zone, and in eastern Darién) and western Colombia to western Ecuador; and [*hauxwelli* group] in South America from central and eastern Colombia, and southern Venezuela south, east of the Andes, to eastern Peru, northern Bolivia and upper Amazonian Brazil.

Notes.—Some authors regard the two groups as species, *T. obsoletus* and *T. hauxwelli* Lawrence, 1869 [HAUXWELL'S THRUSH], but populations on the eastern slope of the Western Andes in Colombia appear to be intermediate. See also comments under *T. fumigatus.*

Turdus grayi Bonaparte. CLAY-COLORED ROBIN. [762.1.]

Turdus Grayi Bonaparte, 1838, Proc. Zool. Soc. London (1837), p. 118. (Guatamala = Alta Vera Paz, Guatemala.)

Habitat.—Open woodland, clearings, second growth, scrub, plantations and gardens (Tropical and lower Subtropical zones).

Distribution.—*Resident* from Guerrero, the state of México, Hidalgo, eastern San Luis Potosí, central Nuevo León and southern Tamaulipas south along both slopes of Middle America to northern Colombia.

Casual in southern Texas (lower Rio Grande Valley), also one record for eastern Texas (Walker County).

Notes.—Also known as GRAY'S THRUSH. *T. grayi* and *T. nudigenis* are considered by a few authors to be conspecific; they appear to constitute a superspecies. See also comments under *T. nigrescens.*

Turdus nudigenis Lafresnaye. BARE-EYED THRUSH.

Turdus nudigenis Lafresnaye, 1848, Rev. Zool. [Paris], 11, p. 4. (Caracas [Venezuela].)

Habitat.—Open forest and woodland, second growth, plantations and gardens (Tropical and lower Subtropical zones).

Distribution.—*Resident* in the Lesser Antilles (Martinique, St. Lucia, St. Vincent, the Grenadines and Grenada), and in South America from eastern Colombia, Venezuela (also Tobago, Trinidad, and Margarita and Patos islands) and the Guianas south, east of the Andes, to northern Brazil.

An attempted introduction on Barbados was unsuccessful.

Notes.—See comments under *T. grayi.*

Turdus jamaicensis Gmelin. WHITE-EYED THRUSH.

Turdus jamaicensis Gmelin, 1789, Syst. Nat., 1 (2), p. 809. Based on the "Jamaica Thrush" Latham, Gen. Synop. Birds, 2 (1), p. 20. (in Jamaica.)

Habitat.—Mountain forest and wooded hills, rarely in lowland woodland.

Distribution.—*Resident* on Jamaica.

Turdus assimilis Cabanis. WHITE-THROATED ROBIN.

Turdus assimilis Cabanis, 1850, Mus. Heineanum, 1 (1851), p. 4. (Xalapa = Jalapa, Veracruz.)

Habitat.—Humid forest, forest edge and dense second growth, rarely in open woodland (Tropical and Subtropical zones).

Distribution.—*Resident* from southeastern Sonora, southwestern Chihuahua, Sinaloa, western Durango, Nayarit, Jalisco, Michoacán, the state of México, Hidalgo, eastern San Luis Potosí and southern Tamaulipas south along both slopes of Middle America (including Isla Coiba off Panama, but absent from the Yucatan Peninsula) and western Colombia to western Ecuador.

Notes.—*T. assimilis* and the South American *T. albicollis* Vieillot, 1818 [WHITE-NECKED ROBIN], are considered conspecific by many authors; they constitute a superspecies. The populations of *T. assimilis* from eastern Panama (eastern Darién) south to Ecuador are sometimes considered a distinct species, *T. daguae* Berlepsch, 1897 [DAGUA ROBIN]. See also comments under *T. nigrescens*.

Turdus rufopalliatus Lafresnaye. RUFOUS-BACKED ROBIN. [762.2.]

> *Turdus rufo-palliatus* Lafresnaye, 1840, Rev. Zool. [Paris], 3, p. 259. (al Monterey en Californie, error = Acapulco, Guerrero.)

Habitat.—Deciduous forest, arid scrub and riparian woodland, in nonbreeding season also open woodland, brush and lowland forest (Tropical and Subtropical zones).

Distribution.—*Resident* [*rufopalliatus* group] from southern Sonora south through Sinaloa, western Durango, Nayarit, Jalisco, Colima, Michoacán, the state of México, Distrito Federal, Morelos and Guerrero to western Puebla and Oaxaca (west to the Isthmus of Tehuantepec); and [*graysoni* group] in the Tres Marias Islands and, probably, coastal Nayarit (San Blas region).

Casual [*rufopalliatus* group] north to southern California (Death Valley, Imperial Valley), southern Arizona (north to Phoenix area) and western Texas (Langtry, Big Bend, several sight reports also from Santa Ana).

Notes.—Recent evidence (Phillips, 1981, Wilson Bull., 93, pp. 301–309) suggests that the two groups represent distinct species, *T. rufopalliatus* [RUFOUS-BACKED ROBIN] and *T. graysoni* (Ridgway, 1882) [GRAYSON'S ROBIN], with the latter resident (rather than a casual vagrant) in coastal Nayarit and thus sympatric with the former.

Turdus rufitorques Hartlaub. RUFOUS-COLLARED ROBIN.

> *Turdus (Merula) rufitorques* Hartlaub, 1844, Rev. Zool. [Paris], 7, p. 214. (Guatemala.)

Habitat.—Humid montane forest, forest edge, pine-oak association and highland brushy areas (Subtropical and lower Temperate zones).

Distribution.—*Resident* in the mountains of Chiapas, Guatemala, El Salvador and western Honduras (Güise).

Notes.—*T. rufitorques* and *T. migratorius* appear to constitute a superspecies.

Turdus migratorius Linnaeus. AMERICAN ROBIN. [761.]

> *Turdus migratorius* Linnaeus, 1766, Syst. Nat., ed. 12, 1, p. 292. Based mainly on "The Fieldfare of Carolina" Catesby, Nat. Hist. Carolina, 1, p. 29, pl. 29. (in America septentrionali = South Carolina.)

Habitat.—Forest (coniferous and deciduous, lowland and montane), woodland, scrub, parks, thickets, gardens, cultivated lands and savanna (Subtropical and Temperate zones).

Distribution.—*Breeds* [*migratorius* group] from western and northern Alaska, northern Yukon, northern Mackenzie, southern Keewatin, northern Manitoba, northern Ontario, northern Quebec, Labrador and Newfoundland south to southern Alaska (west to the Alaska Peninsula and Kodiak Island), southern California (except interior and southeastern desert regions), southern Nevada, central and southeastern Arizona, northern Sonora, in the mountains of Mexico to Oaxaca (west of the Isthmus of Tehuantepec), and to southeastern Texas, the Gulf coast and central Florida.

Winters [*migratorius* group] from southern Alaska (casually), southwestern British Columbia, the northern United States (at least irregularly in the northernmost states) and Newfoundland south to southern Baja California (casually to Guadalupe Island), throughout Mexico (rarely to the Yucatan Peninsula and Isla Holbox) to Guatemala, and to southern Texas, the Gulf coast, southern Florida, Bermuda and (at least irregularly) western Cuba, casually to the northern Bahama Islands (south to San Salvador).

Resident [*confinis* group] in the mountains of southern Baja California (Cape San Lucas district).

Casual or accidental [*migratorius* group] in the Pribilofs (St. Paul), Aleutians (Amchitka), Greenland, the British Isles and continental Europe, also sight reports from Jamaica, Mona Island and Puerto Rico.

Notes.—Formerly known in American literature as the ROBIN. The two groups are sometimes considered as separate species, *T. migratorius* and *T. confinis* Baird, 1864 [SAN LUCAS ROBIN]. See also comments under *T. rufitorques.*

Turdus swalesi (Wetmore). LA SELLE THRUSH.

Haplocichla swalesi Wetmore, 1927, Proc. Biol. Soc. Wash., 40, p. 55. (Massif de la Selle, 6,000 ft., Haiti.)

Habitat.—Dense mountain shrubbery, moist forest and pine woodland.

Distribution.—*Resident* in the mountains of Hispaniola (Morne La Selle east to Sierra de Baoruco).

Turdus aurantius Gmelin. WHITE-CHINNED THRUSH.

Turdus aurantius Gmelin, 1789, Syst. Nat., 1 (2), p. 832. Based largely on "Le Merle de la Jamaique" Brisson, Ornithologie, 2, p. 277. (in Jamaicae montibus silvosis = Jamaica.)

Habitat.—Woodland and gardens, primarily in hilly or mountainous areas.
Distribution.—*Resident* on Jamaica.

†Turdus ravidus (Cory). GRAND CAYMAN THRUSH.

Mimocichla ravida Cory, 1886, Auk, 3, p. 499. (Island of Grand Cayman, West Indies.)

Distribution.—EXTINCT. Formerly *resident* on Grand Cayman, in the Cayman

Islands. Last recorded in 1938 on the eastern part of the island; several recent thorough searches have had negative results.

Notes.— *T. ravidus* and *T. plumbeus* are sometimes placed in the genus *Mimocichla*; the two species appear to constitute a superspecies.

Turdus plumbeus Linnaeus. RED-LEGGED THRUSH.

Turdus plumbeus Linnaeus, 1758, Syst. Nat., ed. 10, 1, p. 169. Based on "The Red-leg'd Thrush" Catesby, Nat. Hist. Carolina, 1, p. 30, pl. 30. (in America = Andros and Eleuthera islands, Bahamas.)

Habitat.— Forest, open woodland, plantations and gardens.

Distribution.— *Resident* in the northern Bahama Islands (south to Andros, Exuma Cays and Cat Island, also a sight report from Great Inagua), Cuba (and nearby cays), the Isle of Pines, Cayman Islands (Cayman Brac, with reports from Grand Cayman based on an escaped individual), Hispaniola (including Gonâve, Tortue and Saona islands), Puerto Rico, Dominica (in the Lesser Antilles), and (formerly) the Swan Islands (in the western Caribbean Sea).

Notes.— A few authors have considered the populations from Hispaniola eastward to Puerto Rico and Dominica to represent a species, *T. ardosiaceus* Vieillot, 1823 [EASTERN RED-LEGGED THRUSH], distinct from *T. plumbeus* [WESTERN RED-LEGGED THRUSH]. See also comments under *T. ravidus*.

Genus CICHLHERMINIA Bonaparte

Cichlherminia Bonaparte, 1854, C. R. Acad. Sci. Paris, 38, p. 2. Type, by subsequent designation (G. R. Gray, 1855), *Turdus lherminieri* Lafresnaye.

Cichlherminia lherminieri (Lafresnaye). FOREST THRUSH.

Turdus L'Herminieri Lafresnaye, 1844, Rev. Zool. [Paris], 7, p. 167. (Guadeloupe.)

Habitat.— Forest and undergrowth of forest edge.

Distribution.— *Resident* in the Lesser Antilles (Montserrat, Guadeloupe, Dominica and St. Lucia).

Genus IXOREUS Bonaparte

Ixoreus Bonaparte, 1854, C. R. Acad. Sci. Paris, 38, p. 3 (note). Type, by original designation, *Turdus naevius* Gmelin.
Hesperocichla Baird, 1864, Rev. Am. Birds, 1, p. 12. Type, by monotypy, *Turdus naevius* Gmelin.

Notes.— This genus and *Ridgwayia* are sometimes merged in the Old World genus *Zoothera* Vigors, 1832.

Ixoreus naevius (Gmelin). VARIED THRUSH. [763.]

Turdus naevius Gmelin, 1789, Syst. Nat., 1 (2), p. 817. Based on the "Spotted Thrush" Latham, Gen. Synop. Birds, 2 (1), p. 27. (in sinu Americae Natca = Nootka Sound, Vancouver Island, British Columbia.)

Habitat.—Humid coastal and interior montane coniferous forest, deciduous forest with dense understory, and tall shrubs (especially alder), in migration and winter also open woodland and chaparral.

Distribution.—*Breeds* from western and northern Alaska, northern Yukon, and northwestern and western Mackenzie south through central and southern Alaska (west to the base of the Alaska Peninsula and Kodiak Island), British Columbia (including the Queen Charlotte and Vancouver islands), southwestern Alberta, northwestern Montana, northern Idaho, Washington and Oregon (except southeastern portion) to extreme northwestern California (Del Norte and Humboldt counties).

Winters from southern Alaska (coastally west to Kodiak Island), southern British Columbia and northern Idaho south through Washington, Oregon and California to northern Baja California.

Casual widely in central and northeastern North America from southern Alberta, southern Saskatchewan, North Dakota, Minnesota, Wisconsin, Michigan, southern Ontario, southwestern Quebec, New Brunswick, Maine and Nova Scotia south to southern Arizona, central and southeastern New Mexico, central and eastern Texas, Oklahoma, Kansas, Nebraska, Iowa, Illinois, Indiana, Ohio, Pennsylvania, and in Atlantic coastal states from Maryland south to southern Florida; also on Guadalupe Island, off southern Baja California.

Genus **RIDGWAYIA** Stejneger

Ridgwayia Stejneger, 1883, Proc. U.S. Natl. Mus., 5 (1882), p. 460. Type, by original designation, *Turdus pinicola* Sclater.

Notes.—See comments under *Ixoreus.*

Ridgwayia pinicola (Sclater). Aztec Thrush. [763.1.]

Turdus pinicola Sclater, 1859, Proc. Zool. Soc. London, p. 334. (Pine-forests of the tableland above Jalapa, [Veracruz,] Southern Mexico.)

Habitat.—Humid montane forest and pine-oak woodland (Subtropical and Temperate zones).

Distribution.—*Resident* in the mountains from southern Chihuahua and west-central Coahuila south through Sinaloa, Durango, Nayarit, Jalisco, Michoacán, Guerrero, the Distrito Federal, Hidalgo and Puebla to west-central Veracruz and central Oaxaca (west to the Isthmus of Tehuantepec).

Casual in southern Arizona (Huachuca and Santa Rita mountains), western Texas (Chisos Mountains) and eastern San Luis Potosí (near El Naranjo), also a sight report for southeastern Texas (Port Aransas).

Subfamily TIMALIINAE: Babblers

Notes.—Sometimes considered a family, the Timaliidae.

Genus **GARRULAX** Lesson

Garrulax Lesson, 1831, Traité Ornithol., livr. 8, p. 647. Type, by subsequent designation (Ripley, 1961), *Garrulax rufifrons* Lesson.

Garrulax pectoralis (Gould). GREATER NECKLACED LAUGHING-THRUSH. [742.3.]

Ianthocincla pectoralis Gould, 1836, Proc. Zool. Soc. London (1835), p. 186. (in Nepaliâ = Nepal.)

Habitat.—Forest undergrowth, dense second growth and brush.

Distribution.—*Resident* from the Himalayan region of southwestern China and Nepal southeast to northern Burma, northern Thailand, northern Laos and southeastern China (including Hainan).

Introduced and established in the Hawaiian Islands (since 1967, on Kauai).

Notes.—Also known as BLACK-GORGETED LAUGHING-THRUSH.

[Garrulax caerulatus (Hodgson). GRAY-SIDED LAUGHING-THRUSH.] See Appendix B.

Garrulax canorus (Linnaeus). MELODIOUS LAUGHING-THRUSH. [742.2.]

Turdus Canorus Linnaeus, 1758, Syst. Nat., ed. 10, 1, p. 169. Based on "The Brown Indian Thrush" Edwards, Nat. Hist. Birds, 4, p. 184, pl. 184, and Albin, Nat. Hist. Birds, 3, p. 18, pl. 19. (in Benghala, China = Amoy, Fukien, China.)

Habitat.—Forest undergrowth, brush, thickets and scrub.

Distribution.—*Resident* from central to southeastern China (including Formosa and Hainan).

Introduced and established in the Hawaiian Islands (in 1900), where common on Kauai, and uncommon or local on Oahu, Maui and Hawaii.

Notes.—Also known as HWA-MEI, CHINESE THRUSH or SPECTACLED LAUGHING-THRUSH.

Genus **LEIOTHRIX** Swainson

Leiothrix Swainson, 1832, *in* Swainson and Richardson, Fauna Bor.-Am., 2 (1831), pp. 233, 490. Type, by original designation, *Parus furcatus* Temm[inck]. Pl. Col. = *Sylvia lutea* Scopoli.

Leiothrix lutea (Scopoli). RED-BILLED LEIOTHRIX. [742.1.]

Sylvia (*lutea*) Scopoli, 1786, Del. Flor. Faun. Insubr., fasc. 2, p. 96. (China = mountains of Anhwei, China.)

Habitat.—Undergrowth, brushy areas and dense second growth, in forested regions.

Distribution.—*Resident* in the Himalayas from Nepal and northern India east to northern Burma and central China.

Introduced and established in the Hawaiian Islands (in 1918, now common on Molokai, Maui and Hawaii, formerly common but now rare on Kauai and Oahu).

Notes.—Also known as PEKIN NIGHTINGALE, PEKIN ROBIN or JAPANESE HILL-ROBIN.

Genus **CHAMAEA** Gambel

Chamæa Gambel, 1847, Proc. Acad. Nat. Sci. Philadelphia, 3, p. 154. Type, by original designation, *Parus fasciatus* Gambel.

Notes.—This genus was formerly placed in the monotypic family Chamaeidae.

Chamaea fasciata (Gambel). WRENTIT. [742.]

Parus fasciatus Gambel, 1845, Proc. Acad. Nat. Sci. Philadelphia, 2, p. 265. (California = Monterey.)

Habitat.—Chaparral and brushy areas, primarily in lowlands.
Distribution.—*Resident* in coastal areas from northwestern Oregon south to northwestern Baja California (south to lat. 30°N.), and in interior areas of northern and central California.

Family **MIMIDAE**: Mockingbirds, Thrashers and Allies

Notes.—See comments under the genus *Donacobius.*

Genus **DUMETELLA** S.D.W.

Dumetella S.D.W., 1837, Analyst, 5, p. 206. Type, by monotypy, *Turdus felivox* Vieillot = *Muscicapa carolinensis* Linnaeus.
Lucar Coues, 1875, Proc. Acad. Nat. Sci. Philadelphia, 27, p. 349. Type, by monotypy, *Muscicapa carolinensis* Linnaeus.

Notes.—See comments under *Melanoptila.*

Dumetella carolinensis (Linnaeus). GRAY CATBIRD. [704.]

Muscicapa carolinensis Linnaeus, 1766, Syst. Nat., ed. 12, 1, p. 328. Based mainly on "The Cat-Bird" Catesby, Nat. Hist. Carolina, 1, p. 66, pl. 66. (in Carolina = Virginia.)

Habitat.—Thickets, dense brushy and shrubby areas, undergrowth of forest edge, hedgerows and gardens.
Distribution.—*Breeds* from southern British Columbia (except Vancouver Island), central Alberta, central Saskatchewan, southern Manitoba, southern Ontario, southwestern Quebec, New Brunswick, Prince Edward Island and Nova Scotia south to central New Mexico, north-central and eastern Texas, the central portions of the Gulf states, and northern Florida (Tallahassee, Jacksonville), and west to northern and south-central Washington, south-central and eastern Oregon, north-central Utah, and central and northeastern Arizona; also in Bermuda.
Winters from north-central and eastern Texas, southeastern Arkansas, the central portions of the Gulf states, central Georgia, and in the Atlantic coastal lowlands from Long Island (casually north to South Dakota, the northern United States from Minnesota eastward, and southern Ontario) south along the Gulf-Caribbean slope of Middle America (casually recorded from the interior of Guatemala, Honduras and Costa Rica) to central Panama (east to the Canal Zone), and in Bermuda, the Greater Antilles (Cuba, the Isle of Pines and Cayman Islands, rarely Jamaica,

Hispaniola and Tortue Island) and islands in the western Caribbean Sea (San Andrés and Providencia).

Casual in western Oregon, California, Nevada, the Lesser Antilles (Anguilla) and northern Colombia, also sight reports from Newfoundland. Accidental in James Bay (North Twin Island) and Germany.

Notes.—Also known as COMMON or NORTHERN CATBIRD.

Genus MELANOPTILA Sclater

Melanoptila Sclater, 1858, Proc. Zool. Soc. London (1857), p. 275. Type, by monotypy, *Melanoptila glabrirostris* Sclater.

Notes.—This genus is sometimes merged in *Dumetella.*

Melanoptila glabrirostris Sclater. BLACK CATBIRD.

Melanoptila glabrirostris Sclater, 1858, Proc. Zool. Soc. London (1857), p. 275. (In rep. Honduras, prope urbem Omoa = Omoa, Honduras.)

Habitat.—Thickets, dense brush, undergrowth in open deciduous forest and, rarely, humid forest edge (Tropical Zone).

Distribution.—*Resident* in the Yucatan Peninsula (including Cozumel, Holbox and Mujeres islands, and Cayo Culebra), northern Guatemala (Petén), Belize and extreme northern Honduras (Omoa).

Genus MIMUS Boie

Mimus Boie, 1826, Isis von Oken, col. 972. Type, by monotypy, *Turdus polyglottos* Linnaeus.

Mimus polyglottos (Linnaeus). NORTHERN MOCKINGBIRD. [703.]

Turdus polyglottos Linnaeus, 1758, Syst. Nat., ed. 10, 1, p. 169. Based mainly on "The Mock-Bird" Catesby, Nat. Hist. Carolina, 1, p. 27, pl. 27. (in Virginia.)

Habitat.—A variety of open and partly open situations from areas of scattered brush or trees to forest edge and semi-desert (absent from forest interior), especially in scrub, thickets, gardens, towns, and around cultivated areas (Tropical to Temperate zones).

Distribution.—*Resident* regularly from northern California, eastern Oregon, northwestern Nevada, northern Utah, southeastern Wyoming, southwestern South Dakota, eastern Nebraska, southern Iowa, central Illinois, central Indiana, northern Ohio, southern Pennsylvania, southern New York and southern New England, sporadically or locally north to southern Alberta, southern Saskatchewan, southern Manitoba, central and northeastern Minnesota, southern Wisconsin, southern Michigan, southern Ontario, southwestern Quebec, Nova Scotia and Newfoundland, south to southern Baja California (including many offshore islands), through Mexico (including the Tres Marias Islands, and on Socorro Island in the Revillagigedos) to Oaxaca and Veracruz, and to southeastern Texas, the Gulf coast, southern Florida (including the Florida Keys), the Bahama Islands and Greater Antilles (east to Anegada in the Virgin Islands, and recently on Little Cayman in the Cayman Islands).

Northern populations are partially migratory.

Introduced and established in the Hawaiian Islands (main islands from Kauai eastward, wandering casually west to French Frigate Shoals), and in Bermuda; an introduced population in Barbados, in the Lesser Antilles, has become extirpated.

Casual north to British Columbia, southwestern Keewatin, northern Ontario and Prince Edward Island.

Notes.—*M. polyglottos* and *M. gilvus* are closely related and hybridize, at least occasionally, in Oaxaca and Veracruz; constituting a superspecies, they are considered conspecific by some authors.

Mimus gilvus (Vieillot). TROPICAL MOCKINGBIRD.

Turdus gilvus Vieillot, 1808, Hist. Nat. Ois. Am. Sept., 2 (1807), p. 15, pl. 68 bis. (la Guiane et les contrées les plus chaudes de l'Amérique septentrionale = French Guiana.)

Habitat.—Partly open situations, especially arid and thorn scrub, and around parks and towns, absent from forest (Tropical and Subtropical zones).

Distribution.—*Resident* in southern Mexico (Gulf-Caribbean slope from eastern Oaxaca and southern Veracruz south through Tabasco to eastern Chiapas and the Yucatan Peninsula, including Mujeres, Holbox and Cozumel islands), Guatemala (Petén, the arid interior valleys, and locally on the northwestern Pacific slope), Belize and Honduras (primarily the arid interior valleys, and locally on the northwestern Pacific slope), Belize and Honduras (primarily the arid interior and Pacific lowlands); on Isla San Andrés in the western Caribbean Sea; in the southern Lesser Antilles (from Guadeloupe, Désirade and Antigua southward); and in South America from northern Colombia, Venezuela (also islands from the Netherlands Antilles east to Tobago and Trinidad) and the Guianas south to northern Amazonian Brazil and along the coast to southeastern Brazil.

Introduced and established in central Panama (Canal Zone and adjacent regions of Colón and Panamá provinces); introductions on Barbados and Nevis, in the Lesser Antilles, have been extirpated.

Notes.—The form on Isla San Andrés is sometimes treated as a distinct species, *M. magnirostris* Cory, 1887 [ST. ANDREW MOCKINGBIRD]. See also comments under *M. polyglottos.*

Mimus gundlachii Cabanis. BAHAMA MOCKINGBIRD. [703.1.]

Mimus Gundlachii Cabanis, 1855, J. Ornithol., 3, p. 470. (Cuba.)

Habitat.—Arid and semi-arid scrub, and around villages and towns.

Distribution.—*Resident* in the Bahama Islands, on cays off the northern coast of Cuba, and in the arid coast of southern Jamaica.

Casual in the Florida Keys (Dry Tortugas, also sight reports for Key West and Elliott Key).

Genus **OREOSCOPTES** Baird

Oreoscoptes Baird, 1858, *in* Baird, Cassin and Lawrence, Rep. Explor. Surv. R. R. Pac., 9, pp. xix, xxxv, 346. Type, by monotypy, *Orpheus montanus* Townsend.

Oreoscoptes montanus (Townsend). SAGE THRASHER. [702.]

Orpheus montanus C. K. Townsend, 1837, J. Acad. Nat. Sci. Philadelphia, 7, p. 192. (Plains of the Rocky Mountains = Sandy Creek, lat 42°N., long. 109°30′W., Wyoming.)

Habitat.—Sagebrush plains, in migration and winter also arid scrub, brush and thickets, primarily in arid or semi-arid situations, rarely around towns.

Distribution.—*Breeds* from extreme southern British Columbia, central Idaho, south-central Montana (with an isolated colony in southwestern Saskatchewan), northern and southeastern Wyoming, and Colorado south through eastern Washington, eastern Oregon, east-central California (Inyo County, formerly to Ventura and San Bernardino counties), southern Nevada, southern Utah, northeastern Arizona, west-central and northern New Mexico, northern Texas (possibly), western Oklahoma and (casually) southwestern Kansas.

Winters from central California (rarely), southern Nevada, northern Arizona, central (rarely western) New Mexico and central Texas south to southern Baja California, northern Sonora, Chihuahua, Durango, Guanajuato, northern Nuevo León, northern Tamaulipas and southern Texas.

In migration occurs casually west to western Washington and western Oregon, north to Alberta and northern Montana, and east to the Dakotas, western Nebraska, western Kansas, and along the Gulf coast from eastern Texas to northwestern Florida (recorded east to Gilchrist County).

Casual east across the Great Lakes region (Wisconsin, northern Illinois, southern Ontario) to the Atlantic coastal region (recorded from Massachusetts south to North Carolina), and on Guadalupe Island (off southern Baja California).

Genus **MIMODES** Ridgway

Mimodes Ridgway, 1883, Proc. U.S. Natl. Mus., 5 (1882), p. 45. Type, by monotypy, *Harporhynchus graysoni* Lawrence.

Mimodes graysoni (Lawrence). SOCORRO MOCKINGBIRD.

Harporhynchus graysoni (Baird MS) Lawrence, 1871, Ann. Lyc. Nat. Hist. N.Y., 10, p. 1. (Socorro Island, Mexico.)

Habitat.—Arid scrub.
Distribution.—*Resident* on Socorro Island, in the Revillagigedo Islands, off western Mexico.
Notes.—Formerly known as SOCORRO THRASHER.

Genus **TOXOSTOMA** Wagler

Toxostoma Wagler, 1831, Isis von Oken, col. 528. Type, by monotypy, *Toxostoma vetula* Wagler = *Orpheus curvirostre* Swainson.

Toxostoma rufum (Linnaeus). BROWN THRASHER. [705.]

Turdus rufus Linnaeus, 1758, Syst. Nat., ed. 10, 1, p. 169. Based on the "Fox-coloured Thrush" Catesby, Nat. Hist. Carolina, 1, p. 28, pl. 28. (in America septentrionali & meridionali = South Carolina.)

Habitat.—Thickets and bushy areas in deciduous forest clearings and forest edge, shrubby areas and gardens, in migration and winter also scrub.

Distribution.—*Breeds* from southeastern Alberta, central Saskatchewan, southern Manitoba, southern Ontario, southwestern Quebec, Vermont, New Hampshire, southwestern Maine and New Brunswick south to east-central Texas (south to Nueces County), the Gulf coast and southern Florida (to the upper Keys), and west to western Montana, eastern Wyoming, eastern Colorado, northeastern New Mexico and western Kansas.

Winters from eastern New Mexico, northern Texas, eastern Oklahoma, Arkansas, western Tennessee, central Kentucky, North Carolina and southern Maryland (casually north to southern Ontario, and the northern United States from Minnesota eastward) south to southeastern Texas, the Gulf coast and southern Florida.

Casual from southwestern British Columbia, Washington, Idaho and Utah south to southern California, southern Arizona, northern Sonora, western New Mexico and western Texas, and to Nova Scotia, the Bahama Islands (Grand Bahama, Harbour Island) and western Cuba. Accidental in Alaska (Point Barrow), southern Hudson Bay, Newfoundland, Bermuda and Germany.

Notes.—*T. rufum, T. longirostre* and *T. guttatum* are considered conspecific by some authors; they constitute a superspecies.

Toxostoma longirostre (Lafresnaye). LONG-BILLED THRASHER. [706.]

Orpheus longirostris Lafresnaye, 1838, Rev. Zool. [Paris], 1, p. 55. (du Mexique et de la Californie = Mexico.)

Habitat.—Thickets and brushy areas, especially in bottomland willow, scrub and mesquite (Subtropical Zone).

Distribution.—*Resident* from eastern Coahuila, northern Nuevo León and southern Texas (north to the San Antonio area) south to eastern San Luis Potosí, northern Querétaro, northeastern Hidalgo, northeastern Puebla and central Veracruz (south to Córdoba).

Notes.—See comments under *T. rufum.*

Toxostoma guttatum (Ridgway). COZUMEL THRASHER.

Harporhynchus guttatus Ridgway, 1885, Proc. Biol. Soc. Wash., 3, p. 21. (Cozumel Island, Yucatan.)

Habitat.—Thick undergrowth bordering fields (Tropical Zone).

Distribution.—*Resident* on Cozumel Island, off Quintana Roo.

Notes.—See comments under *T. rufum.*

Toxostoma cinereum (Xántus de Vesey). GRAY THRASHER.

Harporhynchus cinereus Xántus de Vesey, 1860, Proc. Acad. Nat. Sci. Philadelphia, 11 (1859), p. 298. (Cape St. Lucas, Lower California.)

Habitat.—Desert scrub (Tropical Zone).

Distribution.—*Resident* in Baja California from lat. 31°7′N. (on the Pacific coast) and Animas Bay (on the east coast) south to Cape San Lucas.

Notes.—*T. cinereum* and *T. bendirei* appear to constitute a superspecies.

Toxostoma bendirei (Coues). BENDIRE'S THRASHER. [708.]

Harporhynchus Bendirei Coues, 1873, Am. Nat., 7, p. 330 (footnote). (Tucson, Ariz[ona].)

Habitat.—Desert, especially areas of tall vegetation, cholla cactus, creosote bush and yucca, and in juniper woodland.

Distribution.—*Breeds* from southeastern California (north to the Mojave Desert in eastern San Bernardino and north-central Riverside counties), southern Nevada, southern Utah, and western and central New Mexico (east to Sandoval and Socorro counties) south to southern Sonora; also one breeding record for southeastern Colorado (Otero County).

Winters from southern Arizona and extreme southwestern New Mexico south through Sonora to southern Sinaloa.

Casual north to central California (Sacramento County and the Farallon Islands) and north-central Utah.

Notes.—See comments under *T. cinereum.*

Toxostoma ocellatum (Sclater). OCELLATED THRASHER.

Harporhynchus ocellatus Sclater, 1862, Proc. Zool. Soc. London, p. 18, pl. iii. (Oaxaca.)

Habitat.—Oak scrub, bushy areas in arid pine-oak association and adjacent humid pine-oak forest, and in arid scrub adjoining oak woodland (Subtropical and Temperate zones).

Distribution.—*Resident* in the interior of central Mexico from Guanajuato and Hidalgo south through the state of México, Puebla and west-central Veracruz to central Oaxaca.

Notes.—*T. ocellatum* and *T. curvirostre* appear to constitute a superspecies.

Toxostoma curvirostre (Swainson). CURVE-BILLED THRASHER. [707.]

Orpheus curvirostris Swainson, 1827, Philos. Mag., new ser., 1, p. 369. (Table land, Mexico).

Habitat.—Thorn brush and scrub, semi-desert (especially where mesquite or cholla cactus is present), shrubby areas, open brushy woodland, and around towns (upper Tropical and Subtropical zones).

Distribution.—*Resident* from central and southeastern Arizona, central and northeastern New Mexico, southeastern Colorado, extreme western Oklahoma, extreme southwestern Kansas, and western and central Texas (east to Travis and Refugio counties) south to Nayarit (including San Esteban and Tiburón islands off Sonora), through the Mexican Plateau to central Oaxaca and Veracruz, and to central Tamaulipas.

Wanders casually to southeastern California, South Dakota, Nebraska, Kansas, Iowa, western Oklahoma, eastern Texas and southern Louisiana; also southern Wisconsin (Buffalo County, three consecutive winters). Accidental in western Florida (Santa Rosa County, male in breeding condition probably mated to a *T. rufum*).

Notes.—See comments under *T. ocellatum.*

Toxostoma redivivum (Gambel). CALIFORNIA THRASHER. [710.]

Harpes rediviva Gambel, 1845, Proc. Acad. Nat. Sci. Philadelphia, 2, p. 264. (near Monterey, in Upper California.)

Habitat.—Lowland and coastal chaparral, and riparian woodland thickets.

Distribution.—*Resident* in California north to Humboldt and Shasta counties (west of the Cascades-Sierra Nevada and the deserts), and in northwestern Baja California (south to lat. 30°N.).

Casual in southwestern Oregon (Medford).

Notes.—*T. redivivum* and *T. dorsale* appear to constitute a superspecies.

Toxostoma dorsale Henry. CRISSAL THRASHER. [712.]

Toxostoma dorsalis Henry, 1858, Proc. Acad. Nat. Sci. Philadelphia, 10, p. 117. (Fort Thorn [Doña Ana County, New Mexico].)

Habitat.—Desert scrub, mesquite, tall riparian brush and, locally, chaparral.

Distribution.—*Resident* from southeastern California (north to Inyo County), southern Nevada, southwestern Utah, northwestern and central Arizona, central New Mexico and western Texas south to northeastern Baja California, central Sonora and central Chihuahua, and locally south in the Mexican Plateau to central Mexico (recorded Coahuila, Zacatecas, San Luis Potosí and Hidalgo).

Notes.—While it is clear from evidence external to the original description (see Hubbard, 1976, Nemouria, no. 20, pp. 1–7) that the name intended to be given in Henry's paper was *T. crissalis* and not *dorsalis,* the present International Code of Zoological Nomenclature, Article 32 (a) (ii), restricts usage to the latter; a ruling by the Commission on a petition to supplant *T. dorsale* with *T. crissale* is pending. See also comments under *T. redivivum.*

Toxostoma lecontei Lawrence. LE CONTE'S THRASHER. [711.]

Toxostoma Le Contei Lawrence, 1851, Ann. Lyc. Nat. Hist. N.Y., 5, p. 121. (California near the junction of the Gila and Colorado Rivers = Fort Yuma, California.)

Habitat.—Desert scrub, particularly creosote bush associations.

Distribution.—*Resident* in southern California (the Carrizo Plain of eastern San Luis Obispo County, and the San Joaquin Valley desert in Kern County, formerly north to Fresno County); and from eastern California (east of the Sierra Nevada north to southern Mono and Inyo counties), southern Nevada, southwestern Utah, and western and south-central Arizona south to northeastern Baja California and northwestern Sonora; and in west-central Baja California (Pacific coast from lat. 29°N. south to lat. 26°N.).

Genus RAMPHOCINCLUS Lafresnaye

Ramphocinclus Lafresnaye, 1843, Rev. Zool. [Paris], 6, p. 66. Type, by original designation, *Turdus brachyurus* Vieillot.

Ramphocinclus brachyurus (Vieillot). WHITE-BREASTED THRASHER.

Turdus brachyurus Vieillot, 1818, Nouv. Dict. Hist. Nat., nouv. éd., 20, p. 255. (Martinique.)

Habitat.—Semi-arid woodland.
Distribution.—*Resident* on Martinique and St. Lucia, in the Lesser Antilles.
Notes.—This species appears not to be closely related to *Cinclocerthia ruficauda*, although the two have been considered congeneric by some authors.

Genus **MELANOTIS** Bonaparte

Melanotis Bonaparte, 1850, Consp. Gen. Avium, 1 (2), p. 276. Type, by monotypy, *Turdus melanotis* Temminck = *Orpheus caerulescens* Swainson.

Melanotis caerulescens (Swainson). BLUE MOCKINGBIRD.

Orpheus cærulescens Swainson, 1827, Philos. Mag., new ser., 1, p. 369. (Table land, Mexico.)

Habitat.—Scrub, pine-oak association and montane forest, in both arid and humid regions, wandering to humid lowland forest in the nonbreeding season (upper Tropical to lower Temperate zones).
Distribution.—*Resident* from southern Sonora, southwestern Chihuahua, western Durango, Sinaloa, Nayarit (including the Tres Marias Islands), Jalisco, Guanajuato, eastern San Luis Potosí and southern Tamaulipas south to eastern Oaxaca and central Veracruz.
Casual in western Chiapas (Ocozocoautla).
Notes.—*M. caerulescens* and *M. hypoleucus* constitute a superspecies.

Melanotis hypoleucus Hartlaub. BLUE-AND-WHITE MOCKINGBIRD.

Melanotis hypoleucus Hartlaub, 1852, Rev. Mag. Zool., ser. 2, 4, p. 460. (Guatemala.)

Habitat.—Brush, dense undergrowth and second-growth woodland, mostly in humid montane regions (Subtropical and lower Temperate zones).
Distribution.—*Resident* in the mountains of Chiapas, Guatemala, El Salvador and western Honduras (east to the Tegucigalpa region).
Notes.—See comments under *M. caerulescens*.

Genus **MARGAROPS** Sclater

Cichalopia (not Bonaparte, 1854) Bonaparte, 1857, Rev. Mag. Zool., ser. 2, 9, p. 205. Type, by original designation, *Turdus densirostris* Vieillot = *Turdus fuscatus* Vieillot.
Margarops Sclater, 1859, Proc. Zool. Soc. London, p. 335. New name for *Cichalopia* Bonaparte, 1857, preoccupied.
Allenia Cory, 1891, Auk, 8, p. 42. Type, by original designation, *Turdus montanus* Lafresnaye = *Muscicapa fusca* Müller.

Margarops fuscus (Müller). SCALY-BREASTED THRASHER.

Muscicapa fusca P. L. S. Müller, 1776, Natursyst., Suppl., p. 170. (Martinique.)

Habitat.—Forest, woodland, and around settlements.

Distribution.—*Resident* in the Lesser Antilles (Saba, St. Eustatius and Barbuda south to Grenada and Barbados, possibly extirpated on Barbuda and Grenada). Casual in the Grenadines.

Notes.—Often treated in the monotypic genus *Allenia.*

Margarops fuscatus (Vieillot). PEARLY-EYED THRASHER.

Turdus fuscatus Vieillot, 1808, Hist. Nat. Ois. Am. Sept., 2 (1807), p. 1, pl. 57 bis. (les grande îles Antilles et particulièrement à Porto-Ricco et à Saint-Domingue = Puerto Rico.)

Habitat.—Forest and scrubby woodland, both montane and lowland.

Distribution.—*Resident* in the southern Bahama Islands (north to Eleuthera), Hispaniola (questionably on the mainland, but found on Beata Island), Puerto Rico (including Mona, Desecheo, Vieques, Culebra and Culebrita islands), the Virgin Islands and Lesser Antilles (south to St. Lucia); and on islands north of Venezuela from Bonaire east to Los Hermanos.

Accidental (possibly formerly resident) on Barbados.

Genus CINCLOCERTHIA Gray

Stenorhynchus (not Lamarck, 1819) Gould, 1836, Proc. Zool. Soc. London (1835), p. 186. Type, by monotypy, *Stenorhynchus ruficauda* Gould.
Cinclocerthia G. R. Gray, 1840, List Genera Birds, p. 17. New name for *Stenorhynchus* Gould, preoccupied.

Cinclocerthia ruficauda (Gould). TREMBLER.

Stenorhynchus ruficauda Gould, 1836, Proc. Zool. Soc. London (1835), p. 186. (No locality given = Dominica.)

Habitat.—Primarily humid forest, less frequently second growth and open woodland.

Distribution.—*Resident* in the Lesser Antilles (Saba, St. Eustatius, St. Kitts, Nevis, Montserrat, Guadeloupe, Dominica, Martinique, St. Lucia and St. Vincent).

Accidental on St. Thomas, in the Virgin Islands (sight report).

Notes.—See comments under *Ramphocinclus brachyurus.*

Family PRUNELLIDAE: Accentors

Genus PRUNELLA Vieillot

Prunella Vieillot, 1816, Analyse, p. 43. Type, by monotypy, "Fauvette de haie" Buffon = *Motacilla modularis* Linnaeus.

Prunella montanella (Pallas). SIBERIAN ACCENTOR. [749.1.]

Motacilla montanella Pallas, 1776, Reise Versch. Prov. Russ. Reichs, 3, p. 695. (in Dauuriam = Dauria.)

Habitat & Distribution.—*Breeds* in forest and shrubby areas in the mountains of Siberia, and *winters* from southern Manchuria and Japan south to central China, *in migration* occurring through Mongolia.

Casual in fall in Alaska (Nunivak Island, 3 October 1927; St. Lawrence Island, 13 October 1936; Point Barrow, fall 1951; and Shemya in the Aleutians, 17 and 24 September 1978).

Notes.—Also known as MOUNTAIN ACCENTOR.

Family **MOTACILLIDAE**: Wagtails and Pipits

Genus **MOTACILLA** Linnaeus

Motacilla Linnaeus, 1758, Syst. Nat., ed. 10, 1, p. 184. Type, by tautonymy, *Motacilla alba* Linnaeus (*Motacilla,* prebinomial specific name, listed in synonymy).

Motacilla flava Linnaeus. YELLOW WAGTAIL. [696.]

Motacilla flava Linnaeus, 1758, Syst. Nat., ed. 10, 1, p. 185. (in Europa = Sweden.)

Habitat.—Wet meadows, shrubby tundra, moorlands and seacoasts, in winter also in open grasslands and cultivated fields.

Distribution.—*Breeds* in North America in northern and western Alaska (south to St. Lawrence and Nunivak islands, and on the mainland to the Nushagak River), northern Yukon and northwestern Mackenzie; and in the Palearctic from the British Isles, southern Scandinavia, northern Russia and northern Siberia south to northwestern Africa, the Mediterranean region, Asia Minor, Iran, Turkestan, northern Mongolia, central Manchuria, Kamchatka, and the Kurile and Commander islands.

Winters in the Old World from northern Africa, India, Southeast Asia, eastern China and the Philippines south to southern Africa, the East Indies and (rarely) northern Australia.

Migrates regularly through coastal western Alaska and the western Aleutians, and in the Old World throughout Europe, the Mediterranean region and Asia (except unsuitable regions in central Asia and the Himalayas), including Japan and Korea.

Casual in the eastern Aleutians, central and south-coastal Alaska, Iceland, the Faroe Islands, northern Scandinavia, the eastern Atlantic islands and New Guinea, also sight reports for central coastal California.

Notes.—Variation in this species is complex, and relationships between morphologically distinguishable groups are uncertain; should groups be recognized as species, North American populations and records would pertain to the eastern Eurasian *M. tschutschensis* Gmelin, 1789.

Motacilla cinerea Tunstall. GRAY WAGTAIL [696.1.]

Motacilla Cinerea Tunstall, 1771, Ornithol. Br., p. 2. Based on the "Gray Water Wagtail" Pennant, Br. Zool., and "La Bergeronette jaune" Brisson, Ornithologie, 3, p. 471, pl. 23, fig. 3. (No locality given = Wycliffe, Yorkshire, England.)

Habitat.—Along watercourses, most frequently swift flowing streams in mountainous country, less frequently along seashores or sluggish streams, in open country such as pastures and meadows, and around human habitation.

Distribution.—*Breeds* from the British Isles, southern Scandinavia, central Russia and central Siberia south to the eastern Atlantic islands, northwestern Africa, the Mediterranean region, Asia Minor, Iran, the Himalayas, northern Mongolia, Manchuria, northern Korea and Japan.

Winters from northern Africa, Arabia, Iraq, southern Iran, Afghanistan, India, Southeast Asia, southern China and Formosa south to central Africa, Ceylon, the Malay Peninsula, East Indies and western New Guinea.

In migration ranges casually (primarily in spring) to the Pribilofs (St. Paul), St. Lawrence Island, the Aleutians (Attu, Agattu, Shemya, Buldir and Amchitka) and Commander Islands, also a sight report for northwestern Mackenzie.

Motacilla alba Linnaeus. WHITE WAGTAIL. [694.]

Motacilla alba Linnaeus, 1758, Syst. Nat., ed. 10, 1, p. 185. (in Europa = Sweden.)

Habitat.—Open country from tundra and desert edge to margins of watercourses, also in towns, villages and, in the Old World, cultivated areas.

Distribution.—*Breeds* in North America in western Alaska from Cape Lisburne south to St. Lawrence Island and Norton Sound, probably farther south; and in the Old World from Greenland, Iceland and northern Eurasia south to southern Africa, Arabia, Asia Minor, Iran, the Himalayas, Southeast Asia, eastern China, southern Ussuriland and northern Kamchatka.

Winters from the southern parts of the breeding range in Eurasia south to southern Africa, the coasts of the Indian Ocean, East Indies and Philippines.

In migration occurs in the eastern Atlantic islands, and on islands from Japan south to the Philippines.

Casual or accidental in the Pribilofs, central Alaska (Fairbanks) and Baja California (La Paz); an old report from northern Quebec is questionable. See further comments under *M. lugens.*

Notes.—Known in the Old World as PIED WAGTAIL. The resident African forms are sometimes regarded as a separate species, *M. aguimp* Dumont, 1821. *M. alba* and *M. lugens* are sympatric with limited hybridization in Kamchatka and southern Ussuriland (Kistchinski and Lobkov, 1979, Moskov. Obs. I Spyt. Prirody, Otd. Biol., Biull., nov. ser., 5, pp. 11–23); they formerly were considered conspecific. *M. alba, M. lugens* and the Japanese *M. grandis* Sharpe, 1885, appear to constitute a superspecies.

Motacilla lugens Gloger. BLACK-BACKED WAGTAIL. [695.1.]

Motacilla lugens Gloger, 1829, Isis von Oken, col. 771. (Kamchatka.)

Habitat.—Primarily near seacoasts, also in forest edge, second-growth woodland, and around towns and human habitation.

Distribution.—*Breeds* from southern Ussuriland, Sakhalin, Kamchatka and (possibly) the Commander Islands south to the Kurile Islands and northern Japan.

Winters from eastern China, Korea and Japan south to southeastern China, Formosa, the Seven Islands of Izu and Bonin Islands.

In migration occurs in Manchuria, northeastern China, and (mostly in spring) the western Aleutian Islands (Near Islands, casually east to Amchitka and Adak).

Casual or accidental on St. Lawrence Island, and in southeastern Alaska (Glacier Bay), Oregon (Eugene) and California (Tiburon, Watsonville); additional sight reports or photographs of individuals in the Aleutians, southeastern Alaska, southwestern British Columbia, western Washington, and elsewhere in Oregon and California are indeterminate as to species (see Morlan, 1981, Cont. Birdlife, 2, pp. 37–50).

Notes.—See comments under *M. alba.*

Genus ANTHUS Bechstein

Anthus Bechstein, 1805, Gemein. Naturgesch. Dtsch., ed. 2, 2, p. 302. Type, by subsequent designation (Sharpe, 1885), *Alauda trivialis* Linnaeus.

Anthus trivialis (Linnaeus). BROWN TREE-PIPIT. [698.2.]

Alauda trivialis Linnaeus, 1758, Syst. Nat., ed. 10, 1, p. 166. (in Svecia = Sweden.)

Habitat & Distribution.—*Breeds* in open and partly open situations with scattered trees and bushes through most of Eurasia, and *winters* south to tropical Africa and India.

Accidental in Alaska (Cape Prince of Wales, 23 June 1972, Kessel; Roberson, 1980, Rare Birds W. Coast, p. 334).

Notes.—Known in Old World literature as the TREE PIPIT.

Anthus hodgsoni Richmond. OLIVE TREE-PIPIT. [698.3.]

Anthus maculatus (not Vieillot, 1818) "Hodgson" Jerdon, 1864, Birds India, "3" [=2 (2)], p. 873. (India = Bengal.)

Anthus hodgsoni Richmond, 1907, *in* Blackwelder, Publ. Carnegie Inst., no. 54, 1 (2), p. 493. New name for *Anthus maculatus* Jerdon, preoccupied.

Habitat.—Taiga, pine forest and montane forest, including clearings and adjacent meadows.

Distribution.—*Breeds* from northeastern Russia and central Siberia south to the Himalayas, western China, Mongolia, Japan and the Kurile Islands.

Winters from India, Southeast Asia, eastern China, Korea and Japan south to southeastern China, the Philippines, Formosa and the Ryukyu Islands.

In migration ranges casually to the western Aleutians (Attu, Shemya and Buldir) and St. Lawrence Island.

Accidental in Nevada (Reno).

Notes.—Also known as OLIVE-BACKED PIPIT, or INDIAN, ORIENTAL or CHINESE TREE-PIPIT.

Anthus gustavi Swinhoe. PECHORA PIPIT. [698.1.]

Anthus gustavi Swinhoe, 1863, Proc. Zool. Soc. London, p. 90. (Amoy, [China].)

Habitat.—Woody and shrubby tundra, swampy scrub and wet meadows, in migration and winter also in open country and cultivated lands.

Distribution.—*Breeds* from northeastern Siberia (east to the Bering Strait) south to southern Ussuriland and the Commander Islands.

Winters from eastern China, Korea and the Ryukyu Islands south to the East Indies and Moluccas.

In migration ranges casually to the Pribilofs (St. Paul), St. Lawrence Island and the western Aleutians (Attu).
Casual in the Shetlands and Turkestan.

[Anthus pratensis (Linnaeus). MEADOW PIPIT.] See Appendix B.

Anthus cervinus (Pallas). RED-THROATED PIPIT. [699.]

> *Motacilla cervina* Pallas, 1811, Zoogr. Rosso-Asiat., 1, p. 511. (Siberia near the Kolyma, and Kamchatka = Kolyma.)

Habitat.—Rocky areas with mat tundra in coastal mountains, and, in the Old World, wet grassy areas in tundra, in migration and winter in open grasslands and cultivated areas, most frequently near water.

Distribution.—*Breeds* in North America in western Alaska on St. Lawrence Island and on the mainland from Cape Lisburne south to Wales, probably also on Little Diomede and Sledge islands; and in Eurasia from northern Scandinavia east across northern Russia and northern Siberia to the Chukotski Peninsula, possibly also Kamchatka and the Kurile Islands.

Winters in the Old World from northern Africa east across Asia Minor, Iran and India to southeastern China, and south to central Africa (regularly?), Southeast Asia, the East Indies and Philippines.

Migrates through the western Aleutian islands (east to Shemya and Buldir), central and southern California (primarily in fall along coasts and in the Channel Islands), and in the Old World through central Eurasia from Italy east to Sakhalin, Korea, the Ryukyu Islands and Formosa, rarely through the Faroe Islands and British Isles.

Casual or accidental in the Hawaiian Islands (Kure), Pribilofs (St. Paul), Gulf of Alaska (Middleton Island), Washington (American Camp) and southern Baja California (San José del Cabo).

Anthus spinoletta (Linnaeus). WATER PIPIT. [697.]

> *Alauda Spinoletta* Linnaeus, 1758, Syst. Nat., ed. 10, 1, p. 166. (in Italia = Italy.)

Habitat.—Tundra, rocky Arctic slopes, alpine meadows and, in the Old World, rocky seacoasts and islands (breeding); seacoasts, beaches, mudflats, wet meadows, sandy areas and cultivated fields (nonbreeding).

Distribution.—*Breeds* in North America throughout Alaska (including the eastern Aleutian Islands), from northern Yukon south through British Columbia, southwestern Alberta, Washington and western Montana, locally on mountain tops from Oregon, Utah and Colorado south to California (the Sierra Nevada, and on Mt. San Gorgonio), northern Arizona (San Francisco and White mountains) and central New Mexico, and from the Canadian Arctic islands (northern Banks east to northern Baffin islands) south to south-central and southeastern Mackenzie, southern Keewatin, northern Manitoba, northern Ontario, southern Labrador, Newfoundland and, locally, southeastern Quebec (Gaspe Peninsula) and northern Maine (Mt. Katahdin); and in the Palearctic locally along rocky seacoasts from Greenland, the Faroe Islands, British Isles, Scandinavia and northern Siberia south to southern Europe, Asia Minor, Iran, Turkestan, northern Mongolia, Sakhalin, Kamchatka and the Kurile Islands.

Winters in North America from the southern United States (in coastal areas north to southern British Columbia and New York, casually in the interior and northeast as far as southern Canada, and in Alaska in the Aleutians and on Kodiak Island) south to Guatemala, El Salvador, southern Mexico (including the Yucatan Peninsula), the Gulf coast and southern Florida; and in Eurasia from the Faroe Islands, British Isles and southern Scandinavia south to the Mediterranean region, northwestern Africa and Arabia, and east across Asia Minor, Iran and India to eastern China and Southeast Asia.

Migrates regularly throughout North America and Eurasia between the breeding and wintering ranges, including Japan and the Ryukyu Islands.

Casual or accidental in the Hawaiian Islands (Kure), Bermuda, the Bahama Islands (south to San Salvador), Jamaica, and islands in the Caribbean Sea (Swan, Providencia and San Andrés).

Notes.—The distinct group of subspecies breeding around northern European seacoasts is known in Old World literature as ROCK PIPIT.

Anthus spragueii (Audubon). SPRAGUE'S PIPIT. [700.]

Alauda Spragueii Audubon, 1844, Birds Am. (octavo ed.), 7, p. 334, pl. 486. (Near Ft. Union [western North Dakota].)

Habitat.—Prairies and short-grass plains, in migration and winter also in pastures and weedy fields.

Distribution.—*Breeds* from north-central Alberta, central Saskatchewan, and west-central and southern Manitoba south to Montana, western South Dakota, North Dakota and northwestern Minnesota.

Winters from south-central and southeastern Arizona, southern New Mexico, central and eastern Texas, Arkansas, northwestern Mississippi and southern Louisiana south through Mexico (except the northwestern portion) to Michoacán, Puebla and Veracruz.

Migrates primarily through the eastern Great Plains, casually west (primarily in fall) to southwestern Alberta, California and northwestern Mexico.

Casual in Michigan, southern Ontario, Ohio, and the Gulf and southern Atlantic states (Mississippi east and north to South Carolina), also sight reports from Illinois, Maine, Virginia, North Carolina and (questionably) the Bahama Islands.

Notes.—Although a close relationship between *A. spragueii* and the South American *A. furcatus* Lafresnaye and d'Orbigny, 1837, has been suggested, the affinities of *A. spragueii* remain uncertain.

Anthus lutescens Pucheran. YELLOWISH PIPIT.

Anthus lutescens Pucheran, 1855, Arch. Mus. Nat. Hist. Paris, 7, p. 343. (Brésil = vicinity of Rio de Janeiro.)

Habitat.—Short-grass savanna and fields, damp pastures, and open situations near water (Tropical Zone).

Distribution.—*Resident* on the Pacific slope of Panama (western Chiriquí east to the Canal Zone and eastern Panamá province); and in South America west of the Andes in coastal Peru and northern Chile, and locally east of the Andes from eastern Colombia, Venezuela and the Guianas south to central Argentina, Uruguay and southeastern Brazil.

Notes.—*A. chii* Vieillot, 1818, is sometimes used for this species, but this name is now regarded as unidentifiable.

Family **BOMBYCILLIDAE**: Waxwings

Notes.—Some authors include the Ptilogonatidae and Dulidae in the Bombycillidae.

Genus **BOMBYCILLA** Vieillot

Bombycilla Vieillot, 1808, Hist. Nat. Ois. Am. Sept., 1 (1807), p. 88. Type, by monotypy, *Bombycilla cedrorum* Vieillot.

Bombycilla garrulus (Linnaeus). BOHEMIAN WAXWING. [618.]

Lanius Garrulus Linnaeus, 1758, Syst. Nat., ed. 10, 1, p. 95. (in Europa & America boreali = Sweden.)

Habitat.—Open coniferous or deciduous forest, muskeg and, less frequently, mixed coniferous-deciduous woodland, in migration and winter also open woodland and parks.

Distribution.—*Breeds* in North America from western and northern Alaska, central Yukon, northwestern and southern Mackenzie, northern Saskatchewan and northern Manitoba south to southwestern and south-coastal Alaska (west to the base of the Alaska Peninsula), and through interior British Columbia and northern and southwestern Alberta to central Washington, northern Idaho and northwestern Montana; and in Eurasia from northern Scandinavia east across northern Russia to northern Siberia.

Winters in North America from central, south-coastal and southeastern Alaska, northern British Columbia, southwestern Mackenzie, central Alberta, central Saskatchewan, southern Manitoba, southern Ontario, southwestern Quebec, Prince Edward Island (probably), New Brunswick, Nova Scotia and Newfoundland south irregularly or sporadically to southern California, southern Arizona, southern New Mexico, northern Texas, northwestern Arkansas, southern Illinois, central Indiana, central Ohio, West Virginia, Pennsylvania and New Jersey, also sight reports south to southern Texas and Virginia; and in Eurasia from the breeding range south to the British Isles, central and southeastern Europe, Asia Minor, Iran, Turkestan, Mongolia, Manchuria, Ussuriland, Korea, Japan and the Kurile Islands.

Casual in the Pribilofs (St. Paul), Aleutians (Amchitka), Greenland, Iceland, the Faroe Islands, Mediterranean region and islands off Japan (south to the Volcano Islands).

Notes.—Also known as GREATER WAXWING and, in Old World literature, as the WAXWING.

Bombycilla cedrorum Vieillot. CEDAR WAXWING. [619.]

Bombycilla cedrorum Vieillot, 1808, Hist. Nat. Ois. Am. Sept., 1 (1807), p. 88, pl. 57. (Amérique depuis le Canada jusqu'au Mexique = eastern North America.)

Habitat.—A wide variety of open woodland types, either deciduous or coniferous, forest edge, second growth, parks, orchards and gardens, in migration and winter occurring wherever there are trees.

Distribution.—*Breeds* from southeastern Alaska, north-central British Columbia, northern Alberta, northern Saskatchewan, northern Manitoba, northern Ontario, central Quebec, New Brunswick, Prince Edward Island, Nova Scotia and Newfoundland south to northern California (Del Norte and Humboldt counties, one breeding record in southern California in Orange County), northern Utah (rarely), Colorado, western Oklahoma, Kansas, central Missouri, southern Illinois, central Kentucky, eastern Tennessee, northern Alabama, northern Georgia and northwestern South Carolina. Recorded in summer (and breeding suggested) in north-central New Mexico and south-central Texas (San Antonio).

Winters from southern British Columbia, central Alberta, central Saskatchewan, southern Manitoba, southern Ontario, New York, New England, New Brunswick and Nova Scotia south through the continental United States (casual in the northwestern states) and Middle America to central Panama (the Canal Zone and Pearl Islands), irregularly to the Bahama Islands and Greater Antilles (including the Cayman Islands).

Casual in the Lesser Antilles (Guadeloupe and Dominica), northern Colombia and northern Venezuela.

Family **PTILOGONATIDAE**: Silky-flycatchers

Notes.—See comments under Bombycillidae.

Genus **PHAINOPTILA** Salvin

Phainoptila Salvin, 1877, Proc. Zool. Soc. London, p. 367. Type, by original designation, *Phainoptila melanoxantha* Salvin.

Phainoptila melanoxantha Salvin. BLACK-AND-YELLOW SILKY-FLY-CATCHER.

Phainoptila melanoxantha Salvin, 1877, Proc. Zool. Soc. London, p. 367. (Costa Rica = San Francisco, Costa Rica.)

Habitat.—Humid montane forest and forest edge (Subtropical and Temperate zones).

Distribution.—*Resident* in the mountains of Costa Rica (Cordillera de Guanacaste to Cordillera de Talamanca) and western Panama (east to Veraguas).

Genus **PTILOGONYS** Swainson

Ptilogonys Swainson, 1824, Cat. Exhib. Mod. Mex., app., p. 4. Type, by monotypy, *Ptilogonys cinereus* Swainson.

Ptilogonys cinereus Swainson. GRAY SILKY-FLYCATCHER.

Ptilogonys cinereus Swainson, 1824, Cat. Exhib. Mod. Mex., app., p. 4. (Mexico = Temascaltepec, state of México.)

Habitat.—Open pine-oak association, juniper scrub and, rarely, arid scrub (Subtropical and Temperate zones).

Distribution.—*Resident* in the highlands from Sinaloa, southern Chihuahua, western Durango, Zacatecas, central Nuevo León and southwestern Tamaulipas south to central Guatemala.

Notes.—Also known as MEXICAN PTILOGONYS.

Ptilogonys caudatus Cabanis. LONG-TAILED SILKY-FLYCATCHER.

Ptilogonys caudatus Cabanis, 1861, J. Ornithol., 8 (1860), p. 402. (Irazú, Costa Rica.)

Habitat.—Open and cut-over woodland, pastures with scattered trees, and humid forest edge (Subtropical and Temperate zones).

Distribution.—*Resident* in the mountains of Costa Rica (north to the Cordillera Central) and western Panama (western Chiriquí).

Genus PHAINOPEPLA Baird

Phainopepla Baird, 1858, *in* Baird, Cassin and Lawrence, Rep. Explor. Surv. R. R. Pac., 9, pp. xix, xxxiv, 923. Type, by original designation, *Ptilogonys nitens* Swainson.

Phainopepla nitens (Swainson). PHAINOPEPLA. [620.]

Ptilogonys nitens Swainson, 1837, Anim. Menag. (1838), p. 285. (Mexico.)

Habitat.—Desert scrub, mesquite, juniper and oak woodland, tall brush, riparian woodland and orchards (Tropical to Temperate zones).

Distribution.—*Breeds* from central California (north irregularly to the San Francisco region and upper Sacramento Valley), southern Nevada, southern Utah, southern New Mexico and western Texas south to southern Baja California, Sonora, western Durango, Coahuila, Nuevo León and San Luis Potosí, possibly farther south on the Mexican Plateau.

Winters from southern (casually central and southwestern) California, southern Nevada, central Arizona, southern New Mexico, and western and southern Texas south to extreme northwestern Oaxaca, Puebla and west-central Veracruz.

Casual or accidental in southern Oregon, north-central Colorado, southern Ontario (Wallacetown, London) and Rhode Island (Block Island), also sight reports for Massachusetts.

Family DULIDAE: Palmchats

Notes.—See comments under Bombycillidae.

Genus DULUS Vieillot

Dulus Vieillot, 1816, Analyse, p. 42. Type, by monotypy, "Tanagra esclave" Buffon = *Tanagra dominica* Linnaeus.

Dulus dominicus (Linnaeus). PALMCHAT.

Tanagra dominica Linnaeus, 1766, Syst. Nat., ed. 12, 1, p. 316. Based on "Le Tangara de S. Domingue" Brisson, Ornithologie, 3, p. 37, pl. 2, fig. 4. (in Dominica = Santo Domingo, Hispaniola.)

Habitat.—Partly open situations with scattered trees, rarely in open woodland, nesting primarily in royal palm.
Distribution.—*Resident* on Hispaniola (including Gonâve Island).

Family **LANIIDAE**: Shrikes

Subfamily LANIINAE: Typical Shrikes

Genus **LANIUS** Linnaeus

Lanius Linnaeus, 1758, Syst. Nat., ed. 10, 1, p. 93. Type, by subsequent designation (Swainson, 1824), *Lanius excubitor* Linnaeus.

Lanius cristatus Linnaeus. BROWN SHRIKE. [622.1.]

> *Lanius cristatus* Linnaeus, 1758, Syst. Nat., ed. 10, 1, p. 93. (in Benghala = Bengal.)

Habitat & Distribution.—*Breeds* in deciduous and coniferous woodland from northern Siberia south to Mongolia, Manchuria and Japan, and *winters* from India east to eastern China, and south to Southeast Asia and the East Indies.

Accidental in Alaska (Shemya Island in the Aleutians, 10 October 1978; Gibson, 1981, Condor, 83, p. 73), also a sight report for St. Lawrence Island (Gambell, 4–6 June 1977; King *et al.,* 1978, Am. Birds, 32, p. 158).

Notes.—Also known as RED-TAILED SHRIKE. The Shemya specimen has been referred to *L. c. lucionensis* Linnaeus, 1766, a race breeding from Korea southward and separated from Alaska by several other subspecies. Some authors consider *L. cristatus* and the Old World *L. collurio* Linnaeus, 1758 [RED-BACKED SHRIKE] to be conspecific; they constitute a superspecies.

Lanius excubitor Linnaeus. NORTHERN SHRIKE. [621.]

> *Lanius Excubitor* Linnaeus, 1758, Syst. Nat., ed. 10, 1, p. 94. (in Europa = Sweden.)

Habitat.—Open deciduous or coniferous woodland, taiga, thickets, bogs, scrub and, locally, semi-desert, in migration and winter also in open situations with scattered trees, savanna and cultivated lands.

Distribution.—*Breeds* in North America from western and northern Alaska, northern Yukon, northwestern and southern Mackenzie, and southwestern Keewatin south to southern Alaska (west to the Alaska Peninsula), northern British Columbia, northern Alberta and northern Manitoba, and from northern Quebec south to central Quebec and southern Labrador; and in the Old World from northern Scandinavia, northern Russia and northern Siberia south to the Canary Islands, northern Africa (just south of the Sahara), Arabia, Iran, India, northern Mongolia, Amurland, Kamchatka and the Kurile Islands.

Winters in North America from central Alaska and the southern portions of the breeding range in Canada south to central California, central Nevada, Utah, central New Mexico, southern Kansas, central Missouri, northern Illinois, northern Indiana, central Ohio, Pennsylvania and New Jersey, casually to the Aleutians, southern California, southern Arizona, southern New Mexico, northern and north-central Texas, central Oklahoma, Arkansas, central Kentucky, North Carolina and

Bermuda; and in Eurasia throughout the breeding range, the northern populations being partly migratory.

Notes.—Also known as GREAT GRAY SHRIKE. Conspecificity between *L. excubitor* and *L. ludovicianus* has been suggested by a few authors; these two, along with the Asiatic *L. sphenocercus* Cabanis, 1873, constitute a superspecies.

Lanius ludovicianus Linnaeus. LOGGERHEAD SHRIKE. [622.]

> *Lanius ludovicianus* Linnaeus, 1766, Syst. Nat., ed. 12, 1, p. 134. Based on "La Pie-grieche de la Louisiane" Brisson, Ornithologie, 2, p. 162, pl. 15, fig. 2. (in Ludovicia = Louisiana.)

Habitat.—Open country with scattered trees and shrubs, savanna, desert scrub and, occasionally, open woodland, often found on poles, wires or fenceposts (Tropical to Temperate zones).

Distribution.—*Breeds* from California (except the northwestern portion, but including the Channel Islands), eastern Oregon, eastern Washington, central Alberta, central Saskatchewan, southern Manitoba, southern Ontario, southwestern Quebec, central New York and Pennsylvania (formerly from central Maine, southwestern New Brunswick and Nova Scotia) south to southern Baja California (including Cedros Island), throughout Mexico to Oaxaca and Veracruz, and to the Gulf coast and southern Florida; in recent years scarce and local in the northeastern portion of the breeding range.

Winters from central Washington, eastern Oregon, California, southern Nevada, northern Arizona, northern New Mexico and, east of the Rockies, the southern half of the breeding range (casually north to the Canadian border) south to the southern limits of the breeding range.

Casual from southern British Columbia south, west of the Cascades, to northwestern California.

Notes.—See comments under *L. excubitor.*

Family STURNIDAE: Starlings and Allies

Subfamily STURNINAE: Starlings

Genus STURNUS Linnaeus

> *Sturnus* Linnaeus, 1758, Syst. Nat., ed. 10, 1, p. 167. Type, by tautonymy, *Sturnus vulgaris* Linnaeus (*Sturnus,* prebinomial specific name, in synonymy).

Sturnus vulgaris Linnaeus. EUROPEAN STARLING. [493.]

> *Sturnus vulgaris* Linnaeus, 1758, Syst. Nat., ed. 10, 1, p. 167. (in Europa, Africa = Sweden.)

Habitat.—A variety of situations from open to wooded, generally avoiding only heavily forested areas, and in cultivated regions and urban areas.

Distribution.—*Breeds* from Iceland, the Faroe and Shetland islands, northern Scandinavia, northern Russia and central Siberia south to the Azores, southern Europe, Asia Minor, Iran, the Himalayas, northern Mongolia and Lake Baikal.

Winters from the breeding range south to northern Africa, India and northeastern China.

Casual in Labrador (about 1878) and Greenland.

Introduced in the United States (New York City, 1890); now *breeds* from east-central and southeastern Alaska, southern Yukon, northern British Columbia, southern Mackenzie, central Saskatchewan, northern Manitoba, northern Ontario, northern Quebec, southern Labrador and Newfoundland south to northern Baja California, southern Arizona, southern New Mexico, southern Texas, the Gulf coast and southern Florida (to Key West), and *winters* throughout the breeding range and south to Guanajuato, Veracruz, the Bahama Islands (south to Grand Turk) and eastern Cuba. Also introduced and established on Jamaica and Puerto Rico, and in South Africa, Australia, New Zealand and Polynesia. Reported casually in the Hawaiian Islands (Oahu, possibly also Hawaii), on Bermuda, and in the summer north to western and northern Alaska, northern Mackenzie and Southampton Island; an individual recorded in Panama (Canal Zone) was questionably a natural vagrant.

Notes.—Formerly known as the STARLING; also known as COMMON STARLING. *S. vulgaris* and *S. unicolor* Temminck, 1820, of the Mediterranean region, are closely related and considered conspecific by some authors; they constitute a superspecies.

Genus **ACRIDOTHERES** Vieillot

Acridotheres Vieillot, 1816, Analyse, p. 42. Type, by subsequent designation (G. R. Gray, 1840), *Paradisaea tristis* Linnaeus.

Acridotheres tristis (Linnaeus). COMMON MYNA. [493.2.]

Paradisœa tristis Linnaeus, 1766, Syst. Nat., ed. 12, 1, p. 167. Based on "Le Merle des Philippines" Brisson, Ornithologie, 2, p. 278, pl. 26, fig. 1. (in Philippinis, error = Pondichéry.)

Habitat.—Open country and plains, primarily in the vicinity of human habitation.

Distribution.—*Resident* from eastern Iran, Turkestan and the Himalayas south to India, Ceylon, Southeast Asia and the Andaman Islands.

Introduced and established in the Hawaiian Islands (in 1865, now abundant on all main islands from Kauai eastward, and recently on Midway), South Africa, Malaya, Australia, New Zealand, and on many islands in the South Atlantic, Indian and Pacific oceans.

Notes.—Also known as INDIAN or HOUSE MYNA.

[**Acridotheres javanicus** Cabanis. WHITE-VENTED MYNA.] See Appendix B.

Acridotheres cristatellus (Linnaeus). CRESTED MYNA. [493.1.]

Gracula cristatella Linnaeus, 1758, Syst. Nat., ed. 10, 1, p. 109. Based on "The Chinese Starling or Blackbird" Edwards, Nat. Hist. Birds, 1, p. 19, pl. 19. (in China.)

Habitat.—Open country, cultivated lands, and around human habitation.
Distribution.—*Resident* in central and southern China, Hainan, Formosa and northern Indochina.

Introduced and established in southwestern British Columbia (Vancouver region), Japan and the Philippines (Luzon). Recorded casually in western Washington and northwestern Oregon (Portland), possibly based on local escapes.

Notes.—*A. cristatellus* and the central Asiatic *A. grandis* Moore, 1858, appear to constitute a superspecies.

Genus **GRACULA** Linnaeus

Gracula Linnaeus, 1758, Syst. Nat., ed. 10, 1, p. 108. Type, by subsequent designation (G. R. Gray, 1840), *Gracula religiosa* Linnaeus.

Gracula religiosa Linnaeus. HILL MYNA.

Gracula religiosa Linnaeus, 1758, Syst. Nat., ed. 10, 1, p. 108. (in Asia = Java.)

Habitat.—Forest, second growth and scrub.

Distribution.—*Resident* from India, Southeast Asia, extreme southern China and Hainan south to the Andaman and Nicobar islands, and the East Indies (east to Palawan and Alor).

Introduced and established in Puerto Rico (casual vagrant to Mona and Vieques islands), and in the Indian Ocean on Christmas Island; escapes in the Hawaiian Islands (Oahu, 1960, 1961) and southern Florida (Palm Beach and Dade counties) have persisted for years without definite evidence of establishment.

Notes.—Also known as TALKING or INDIAN HILL MYNA and, in Old World literature, as the GRACKLE.

Family **MELIPHAGIDAE**: Honeyeaters

Genus **MOHO** Lesson

Moho Lesson, 1831, Traité Ornithol., livr. 5 (1830), p. 302. Type, by monotypy, *Merops fasciculatus* Latham = *Gracula nobilis* Merrem.

Moho braccatus Cassin. KAUAI OO. [622.1.]

Mohoa [sic] *braccata* Cassin, 1855, Proc. Acad. Nat. Sci. Philadelphia, 7, p. 440. (Sandwich Islands = Kauai, Hawaiian Islands.)

Habitat.—Thick, undisturbed native forest.

Distribution.—*Resident* on Kauai, in the Hawaiian Islands (surviving in small numbers in the Alakai Swamp region).

†Moho apicalis Gould. OAHU OO. [622.2.]

Moho apicalis Gould, 1860, Proc. Zool. Soc. London, p. 381. (Owhyhee = Oahu, Hawaiian Islands.)

Habitat.—Presumably forest.

Distribution.—EXTINCT. Formerly *resident* on Oahu, in the Hawaiian Islands (disappeared in a short period after 1837).

Notes.—*M. apicalis*, *M. bishopi* and *M. nobilis* may constitute a superspecies.

Moho bishopi (Rothschild). BISHOP'S OO. [622.3.]

Acrulocercus bishopi Rothschild, 1893, Bull. Br. Ornithol. Club, 1, p. 41. (Island of Molokai.)

Habitat.—Forest, primarily ohia.

Distribution.—Formerly *resident* on Molokai, in the Hawaiian Islands (last reported in 1904); possibly persisting in small numbers on Maui, with sightings up to 1901, local reports in the 1970's, and a brief but rather convincing sighting on Haleakala on 10 May 1981 (Stephen Sabo).

Notes.—Also known as MOLOKAI OO. See comments under *M. apicalis.*

†Moho nobilis (Merrem). HAWAII OO. [622.4.]

Gracula nobilis Merrem, 1786, Avium Rar. Icones Descr., 1, fasc. 1, p. 7, pl. 2. (Insulæ Sanduicenses = island of Hawaii.)

Habitat.—Heavy forest.

Distribution.—EXTINCT. Formerly *resident* on Hawaii, in the Hawaiian Islands (last definite record in 1898).

Notes.—See comments under *M. apicalis.*

Genus CHAETOPTILA Sclater

Chætoptila Sclater, 1871, Ibis, p. 358. Type, by original designation, *Entomyza angustipluma* Cassin [=Peale].

†Chaetoptila angustipluma (Peale). KIOEA. [622.5.]

Entomiza? angustipluma Peale, 1848, U.S. Explor. Exped., 8, p. 147. (Hawaii.)

Habitat.—Forest.

Distribution.—EXTINCT. Formerly *resident* on Hawaii, in the Hawaiian Islands (last reported in 1859).

Family ZOSTEROPIDAE: White-eyes

Genus ZOSTEROPS Vigors and Horsfield

Zosterops Vigors and Horsfield, 1826, Trans. Linn. Soc. London, 15, p. 234. Type, by subsequent designation (Lesson, 1828), *Motacilla maderaspatana* Linnaeus.

Zosterops japonicus Temminck and Schlegel. JAPANESE WHITE-EYE. [622.6.]

Zosterops japonicus Temminck and Schlegel, 1847, *in* Siebold, Fauna Jpn., Aves, p. 57, pl. 22. (Japon = Decima, Nagasaki, Japan.)

Habitat.—Forest, second growth and scrub, from sea level to the upper limit of forest, also cultivated lands and gardens.

Distribution.—*Resident* from eastern China, Formosa and Japan south to northern Indochina, southern China, Hainan and, through the Ryukyu and Volcano islands, to the northern Philippines.

Introduced and established in the Hawaiian Islands (in 1929, now widespread and common on the main islands from Kauai eastward) and Bonin Islands.

Notes.—Also known as CHINESE WHITE-EYE. *Z. japonicus* is sometimes regarded as conspecific with *Z. palpebrosus* (Temminck, 1824), of India and Southeast Asia, but the two species overlap in southern China. A pair of some race of the, *Z. palpebrosus* complex escaped from the San Diego Zoo in the early 1970's, and a small but apparently increasing population is now present in the San Diego area, although attempts are being made to control its establishment and spread.

Family **VIREONIDAE**: Vireos

Subfamily VIREONINAE: Typical Vireos

Genus **VIREO** Vieillot

Vireo Vieillot, 1808, Hist. Nat. Ois. Am. Sept., 1 (1807), p. 83. Type, by subsequent designation (Gadow, 1883), *Vireo musicus* Vieillot = *Muscicapa noveboracensis* Gmelin = *Tanagra grisea* Boddaert.

Subgenus VIREO Vieillot

Neochloe Sclater, 1858, Proc. Zool. Soc. London (1857), p. 213. Type, by monotypy, *Neochloe brevipennis* Sclater.

Vireo brevipennis (Sclater). SLATY VIREO.

Neochloe brevipennis Sclater, 1858, Proc. Zool. Soc. London (1857), p. 213. (Orizaba, [Veracruz,] Southern Mexico.)

Habitat.—Pine-oak association and oak scrub (Subtropical and lower Temperate zones).
Distribution.—*Resident* in the highlands of Jalisco, Guerrero, Morelos, Oaxaca and Veracruz.
Notes.—Sometimes placed in the monotypic genus *Neochloe.*

Vireo griseus (Boddaert). WHITE-EYED VIREO. [631.]

Tanagra grisea Boddaert, 1783, Table Planches Enlum., p. 45. Based on "Tanagra olive, de la Louisiane" Daubenton, Planches Enlum., pl. 714, fig. 1. (Louisiana = New Orleans.)

Habitat.—Thickets, undergrowth, scrub and brushy woodland (Tropical to lower Temperate zones).
Distribution.—*Breeds* [*griseus* group] from central Iowa, southern Wisconsin, southern Michigan, southern Ontario (rarely), southern New York and southern Massachusetts south to eastern San Luis Potosí, northern Hidalgo, extreme northern Veracruz, Tamaulipas, southern Texas, the Gulf coast, southern Florida (including the Florida Keys) and Bermuda, and west to eastern Nebraska, eastern Kansas, central Oklahoma, central Texas and Coahuila; and [*perquisitor* group] in northeastern Puebla and north-central Veracruz.
Winters [*griseus* group] from southern Texas, the Gulf coast, South Carolina, the Bahama Islands (east to San Salvador) and Bermuda south along the Gulf-

Caribbean slope of Mexico (including the Yucatan Peninsula, also on the Pacific slope in Oaxaca), Belize, Guatemala, Honduras and (rarely) northern Nicaragua, on Cuba and the Isle of Pines, and in the Cayman (Grand Cayman) and Swan islands; and [*perquisitor* group] presumably in the breeding range.

Casual [*griseus* group] north to southern Manitoba, southern Minnesota, southern Quebec, Maine and Nova Scotia, west to California, Utah, Arizona (Tucson area), Colorado, southern New Mexico, Chihuahua and North Dakota, and south to Costa Rica (Punta Cahuita), Panama (Almirante), Puerto Rico (including Mona Island) and the Virgin Islands (St. John).

Notes.—The two groups are often recognized as distinct species, *V. griseus* and *V. perquisitor* Nelson, 1900 [VERACRUZ VIREO]. Species and superspecies boundaries in the "white-eyed vireo" complex (all species from *V. griseus* through *V. nanus*) are poorly understood, and their accurate definition awaits further research.

Vireo crassirostris (Bryant). THICK-BILLED VIREO.

> *Lanivireo crassirostris* Bryant, 1859, Proc. Boston Soc. Nat. Hist., 7, p. 112. (New Providence, Bahama Islands.)

Habitat.—Scrub, shrubbery and undergrowth.

Distribution.—*Resident* in the Bahamas (virtually throughout, even on small islands) and Cayman Islands (Grand Cayman and Cayman Brac, recently extirpated on Little Cayman), on Tortue Island (off Hispaniola), and on Providencia and Santa Catalina islands (in the western Caribbean Sea).

Casual in southern Florida (sight records for Hypoluxo Island, Lantana, Dry Tortugas and Flamingo).

Notes.—See comments under *V. griseus.*

Vireo pallens Salvin. MANGROVE VIREO.

> *Vireo pallens* Salvin, 1863, Proc. Zool. Soc. London, p. 188. (Realejo, Nicaragua and Punta Arenas, Costa Rica = Punta Arenas, Costa Rica.)

Habitat.—Mangroves and swampy thickets near mangroves, locally in Caribbean lowlands in swamps away from coastal regions (Tropical Zone).

Distribution.—*Resident* along the Pacific coast from southwestern Sonora south to Nayarit, and from Guatemala south to Costa Rica (to the Gulf of Nicoya); and on the Gulf-Caribbean coast from the Yucatan Peninsula (including Holbox and Mujeres islands) and eastern Guatemala (Petén) south through Belize (including Soldier Cay) and Honduras (including the Bay Islands) to Nicaragua.

Notes.—Considered by a few authors to be conspecific with *V. griseus.* See also comments under *V. griseus.*

Vireo bairdi Ridgway. COZUMEL VIREO.

> *Vireo bairdi* Ridgway, 1885, Proc. Biol. Soc. Wash., 3, p. 22. (Cozumel Island, Yucatan.)

Habitat.—Heavy underbrush of deciduous forest (Tropical Zone).
Distribution.—*Resident* on Cozumel Island, off Quintana Roo.
Notes.—See comments under *V. griseus.*

Vireo caribaeus Bond and Meyer de Schauensee. St. Andrew Vireo.

> *Vireo caribaeus* Bond and Meyer de Schauensee, 1942, Not. Nat., Acad. Nat. Sci. Philadelphia, no. 96, p. 1. (St. Andrew's [=San Andrés] Island, Colombia.)

Habitat.—Shrubbery and mangroves.
Distribution.—*Resident* on Isla San Andrés, in the western Caribbean Sea.
Notes.—Sometimes regarded as a race of *V. pallens* or *V. modestus.* See also comments under *V. griseus.*

Vireo modestus Sclater. Jamaican Vireo.

> *Vireo modestus* Sclater, 1860, Proc. Zool. Soc. London, p. 462. (In ins. Jamaica.)

Habitat.—Low trees and shrubbery, in both semi-arid and humid regions in both lowlands and mountains.
Distribution.—*Resident* on Jamaica.
Notes.—Also known as Jamaican White-eyed Vireo. See comments under *V. griseus* and *V. caribaeus.*

Vireo gundlachii Lembeye. Cuban Vireo.

> *Vireo gundlachii* Lembeye, 1850, Aves Isla Cuba, p. 29, pl. 5, fig. 1. (Cuba = Cienfuegos, Cuba.)

Habitat.—Undergrowth in woodland and second growth, in both semi-arid and humid regions.
Distribution.—*Resident* on Cuba (including many cays) and the Isle of Pines.
Notes.—See comments under *V. griseus.*

Vireo latimeri Baird. Puerto Rican Vireo.

> *Vireo latimeri* Baird, 1866, Rev. Am. Birds, 1, p. 364. (north side of Puerto Rico.)

Habitat.—Undergrowth on limestone hills, coastal shrubbery and coffee plantations.
Distribution.—*Resident* on Puerto Rico (except the eastern portion).
Notes.—See comments under *V. griseus.*

Vireo nanus (Lawrence). Flat-billed Vireo.

> *Empidonax nanus* Lawrence, 1875, Ibis, p. 386. (St. Domingo = Dominican Republic.)

Habitat.—Primarily semi-arid lowland scrub, less commonly in more humid hilly country.
Distribution.—*Resident* on Hispaniola (including Gonâve Island).
Notes.—See comments under *V. griseus.*

Vireo bellii Audubon. BELL'S VIREO. [633.]

Vireo bellii Audubon, 1844, Birds Am. (octavo ed.), 7, p. 333, pl. 485. (short distance below Black Snake Hills = near St. Joseph, Missouri.)

Habitat.—Dense brush, mesquite, streamside thickets, and scrub oak, in arid regions but often near water, in migration and winter also in other types of open woodland and open brush (Tropical and Subtropical zones).

Distribution.—*Breeds* from coastal southern and interior California (north to Santa Barbara and Inyo counties, now scarce and local, formerly also in the interior to Tehama County), southern Nevada, southwestern Utah, northwestern and east-central Arizona, southern New Mexico, eastern Colorado, central Nebraska, eastern South Dakota, south-central North Dakota, southeastern Minnesota, southern Wisconsin, northeastern Illinois and northwestern Indiana south to northern Baja California, southern Sonora, southern Durango, Zacatecas, southern Nuevo León, southern Tamaulipas, southern and eastern Texas, northwestern Louisiana, Arkansas, southwestern Tennessee, southwestern Kentucky, southern Indiana and western Ohio.

Winters from southern Baja California, southern Sonora and Veracruz (casually north to extreme southern California, southern Arizona, southern Texas, Louisiana and southern Florida) south along both slopes of Middle America to Honduras, casually to north-central Nicaragua.

In migration occurs regularly in northern Mexico, casually (mostly in fall) along the Gulf coast east to western Florida.

Casual north to central coastal California, Wyoming, southern Michigan and southern Ontario, and east to New York (Long Island) and New Jersey.

Vireo atricapillus Woodhouse. BLACK-CAPPED VIREO. [630.]

Vireo atricapilla Woodhouse, 1852, Proc. Acad. Nat. Sci. Philadelphia, 6, p. 60. (Rio San Pedro, 208 miles from San Antonio, on road to El Paso del Norte, Texas = Devils River, near Sonora, Sutton County, Texas.)

Habitat.—Dense low thickets and oak scrub, mostly on rocky hillsides, in winter also semi-arid tropical scrub.

Distribution.—*Breeds* from south-central Kansas (Comanche County, formerly) south through central Oklahoma and central Texas (east to Dallas, Waco, Austin and San Antonio areas, and west to Abilene, San Angelo and Big Bend) to central Coahuila (Sierra del Carmen).

Winters from southern Sonora, Sinaloa and Durango south to Guerrero and Oaxaca.

Migrates through central Mexico (east to the state of México and Tamaulipas), casually through western and southern Texas.

Casual north to eastern Nebraska and northeastern Kansas, also a sight report for southeastern Louisiana.

Vireo nelsoni Bond. DWARF VIREO.

Vireo nanus (not *Empidonax nanus* Lawrence) Nelson, 1898, Proc. Biol. Soc. Wash., 12, p. 59. (Querendaro, Michoacan, Mexico.)
Vireo nelsoni Bond, 1936, Auk, 53, p. 458. New name for *Vireo nanus* Nelson, preoccupied.

Habitat.—Arid scrub, in migration to scrubby areas at higher elevations (Subtropical Zone, to lower Temperate Zone in winter).

Distribution.—*Breeds* in the highlands from Jalisco, Guanajuato and Querétaro south through Michoacán and the state of México to Oaxaca.

Winters presumably mostly in the breeding range (ascending in migration to higher elevations), ranging north at least to Sinaloa.

Subgenus LANIVIREO Baird

Lanivireo Baird, 1858, *in* Baird, Cassin and Lawrence, Rep. Explor. Surv. R. R. Pac., 9, pp. xix, "xxxxv" [=xxxv], 329. Type, by original designation, *Vireo flavifrons* Vieillot.

Solivireo Oberholser, 1974, Bird Life Tex., 2, p. 997. Type, by original designation, *Muscicapa solitaria* Wilson.

Vireo vicinior Coues. GRAY VIREO. [634.]

Vireo vicinior Coues, 1866, Proc. Acad. Nat. Sci. Philadelphia, 18, p. 75. (Fort Whipple, Arizona.)

Habitat.—Thorn scrub, oak-juniper woodland, pinyon-juniper, dry chaparral, mesquite and riparian willows, in migration and winter also desert and arid scrub.

Distribution.—*Breeds* locally from southern California (north to San Bernardino County), southern Nevada, southern Utah, and northwestern and central New Mexico south to northwestern Baja California, central and southeastern Arizona, southern New Mexico, western Texas (Panhandle, and east to Irion County) and northwestern Coahuila (Sierra del Carmen); also in western Oklahoma (Kenton).

Winters in southern Baja California, southern Arizona (rarely), Sonora (including Tiburón and San Esteban islands) and western Texas (Big Bend region).

In migration occurs in Baja California and Durango.

Casual north to central Utah. Accidental in Wisconsin (Sheboygan County).

Vireo osburni (Sclater). BLUE MOUNTAIN VIREO.

Laletes osburni Sclater, 1861, Proc. Zool. Soc. London, p. 72, pl. 14, fig. 2. (Freeman's Hall, Trelawny Parish, Jamaica.)

Habitat.—Low growth in montane forest, upland woodland and coffee plantations.

Distribution.—*Resident* in the hills and mountains of Jamaica (most commonly in the Blue Mountains).

Vireo solitarius (Wilson). SOLITARY VIREO. [629.]

Muscicapa solitaria Wilson, 1810, Am. Ornithol., 2, p. 143, pl. 17, fig. 6. (Bartram's woods, near Philadelphia [Pennsylvania].)

Habitat.—Mixed coniferous-deciduous woodland, humid montane forest, pine-oak association, oak forest and pinyon-juniper, in migration and winter also in a variety of forest, woodland, scrub and thicket habitats (Subtropical and Temperate zones).

Distribution.—*Breeds* from southern and northeastern British Columbia, southwestern Mackenzie, northern Alberta, northern Saskatchewan, central Manitoba, central Ontario, southern Quebec, New Brunswick, Prince Edward Island, Nova Scotia and southwestern Newfoundland south to southern California (also in the Sierra San Pedro Mártir and the Cape district of Baja California), southern Nevada, central and southeastern Arizona, through the highlands of Mexico and northern Central America (including Belize) to central Honduras, through the Rockies to southern New Mexico and western Texas, east of the Rockies to central Alberta, central Saskatchewan, north-central North Dakota, north-central and northeastern Minnesota, southern Wisconsin, northern Illinois, south-central Indiana, south-central Ohio, eastern Pennsylvania, northern New Jersey and Massachusetts, and in the Appalachian and Piedmont region to eastern Tennessee, northeastern Alabama, central Georgia, northwestern South Carolina, central North Carolina, central Virginia and western Maryland.

Winters from southern California, northern Mexico, central Texas, the northern portions of the Gulf states, and North Carolina (casually farther north) south through Middle America (mostly in the breeding range, where breeding populations are largely resident) to Costa Rica (also sight reports for western Chiriquí, Panama), and to the Gulf coast, southern Florida, Cuba and the Isle of Pines.

In migration occurs casually through the northern Bahama Islands (Eleuthera, New Providence), also a sight report for Jamaica.

Notes.—Recent studies suggest that more than one species may be presently included under *V. solitarius*; delineation of species limits will have to await publication of pertinent data.

Vireo flavifrons Vieillot. YELLOW-THROATED VIREO. [628.]

> *Vireo flavifrons* Vieillot, 1808, Hist. Nat. Ois. Am. Sept., 1 (1807), p. 85, pl. 54. (États Unis = eastern United States.)

Habitat.—Primarily open deciduous forest and woodland, riparian woodland and, less frequently, mixed deciduous-coniferous forest, in migration and winter also a wide variety of forest, woodland, second-growth and mangrove habitats.

Distribution.—*Breeds* from southern Manitoba, Minnesota (except northeastern), central Wisconsin, central Michigan, southern Ontario, southwestern Quebec, northern New Hampshire and southwestern Maine south to eastern Texas, the Gulf coast and central Florida, and west to the eastern Dakotas, eastern Nebraska, eastern Kansas, eastern Oklahoma and west-central Texas.

Winters from eastern Oaxaca, southern Veracruz and southern Florida (casually from southern Texas and northern Florida) south through Middle America (including the Yucatan Peninsula and Cozumel Island), Cuba, the Isle of Pines and Bahama Islands to Colombia and northern Venezuela, casually in the Virgin Islands (St. Thomas, St. John).

Migrates regularly through eastern North America east of the Rockies and eastern Mexico, casually through western North America from central California, Nevada, Utah, Colorado and western Texas southward.

Casual north to central Saskatchewan, western Ontario and Nova Scotia. Accidental in Bermuda, the Lesser Antilles (St. Vincent, Barbados), Tobago, and Chacachacare Island (off Trinidad).

Vireo carmioli Baird. YELLOW-WINGED VIREO.

> *Vireo carmioli* Baird, 1866, Rev. Am. Birds, 1, p. 356. (Dota [=Santa María de Dota], San José, Costa Rica).

Habitat.—Montane forest edge, open woodland, and partly open situations with scattered trees (upper Subtropical and Temperate zones).

Distribution.—*Resident* in the mountains of Costa Rica (Cordillera Central, Dota Mountains, and Cordillera de Talamanca) and western Panama (western Chiriquí).

Notes.—Also known as CARMIOL'S VIREO.

Vireo huttoni Cassin. HUTTON'S VIREO. [632.]

Vireo Huttoni Cassin, 1851, Proc. Acad. Nat. Sci. Philadelphia, 5, p. 150, pl. 10, fig. 1. (Monterey and Georgetown, California = Monterey, California.)

Habitat.—Pine-oak association, oak woodland and riparian woodland, primarily in low trees and scrub (Subtropical and Temperate zones).

Distribution.—*Resident* from southwestern British Columbia (including Vancouver Island) south through western Washington, western Oregon and California (west of the Sierra Nevada divide) to northwestern Baja California; in the Cape district of southern Baja California; and from central Arizona, southwestern New Mexico and extreme western Texas (Chisos Mountains) south through the highlands of Mexico to western Guatemala.

Casual to the desert region of southeastern California and southwestern Arizona.

Subgenus VIREOSYLVA Bonaparte

Vireosylva Bonaparte, 1838, Geogr. Comp. List, p. 26. Type, by subsequent designation (G. R. Gray, 1841), *Muscicapa olivacea* Linnaeus.

Melodivireo Oberholser, 1974, Bird Life Tex., 2, p. 998. Type, by original designation, *Muscicapa gilva* Vieillot.

Vireo hypochryseus Sclater. GOLDEN VIREO.

Vireo hypochryseus Sclater, 1863, Proc. Zool. Soc. London (1862), p. 369, pl. 46. (Mexico.)

Habitat.—Deciduous forest, brushy slopes, arid scrub and riparian woodland (Tropical Zone).

Distribution.—*Resident* in the Pacific lowlands from southern Sonora south to Oaxaca (west of the Isthmus of Tehuantepec); also in the Tres Marias Islands, off Nayarit.

Vireo gilvus (Vieillot). WARBLING VIREO. [627.]

Muscicapa gilva Vieillot, 1808, Hist. Nat. Ois. Am. Sept., 1 (1807), p. 65, pl. 34. (État de New-Yorck = New York.)

Habitat.—Open deciduous and mixed deciduous-coniferous woodland, riparian forest and thickets, pine-oak association, orchards, and parks, in migration and winter in a wide variety of forest, woodland and scrub habitats (Subtropical and Temperate zones).

Distribution.—*Breeds* from southeastern Alaska, northern British Columbia, west-central and southwestern Mackenzie, northern Alberta, central Saskatchewan, southern Manitoba, western Ontario, northern Minnesota, northern Michigan, southern Ontario, extreme southwestern Quebec, Maine and New Brunswick south to southern California (also in the Victoria Mountains of southern Baja

California), southern Nevada, central and southeastern Arizona, in the highlands of Mexico (Sierra Madre Occidental) to the state of México, Morelos and central Oaxaca, to southern New Mexico and western Texas, and, east of the Rockies, to southeastern Texas (casually), southern Louisiana, central Mississippi, northern Alabama, southeastern Tennessee, western North Carolina and Virginia.

Winters from southern Sonora and Veracruz (casually from southern California and southern Arizona) south through Mexico and Guatemala to El Salvador, rarely to the Pacific slopes of Honduras and Nicaragua, also a sight report for northeastern Costa Rica.

Migrates regularly through the south-central United States and eastern Mexico, rarely through the southeastern states east to southern Florida.

Casual in south-coastal Alaska (Anchorage, Middleton Island), Nova Scotia (Seal Island) and Newfoundland (Great Codroy).

Notes.—Relationships between *V. gilvus* and *V. leucophrys* remain uncertain; considered conspecific by some authors, they constitute at least a superspecies.

Vireo leucophrys (Lafresnaye). BROWN-CAPPED VIREO.

Hylophilus leucophrys Lafresnaye, 1844, Rev. Zool. [Paris], 7, p. 81. (Colombie = Colombia.)

Habitat.—Humid montane forest edge, clearings, second growth, thickets and pine-oak association (Subtropical and Temperate zones).

Distribution.—*Resident* in the highlands from eastern San Luis Potosí and southern Tamaulipas south through Hidalgo, Puebla, Veracruz, eastern Oaxaca, Chiapas and Guatemala to Honduras; in the mountains of Costa Rica and western Panama (east to Veraguas); and from eastern Panama (Darién), Colombia and northern Venezuela south in the mountains through Ecuador and Peru to northwestern Bolivia.

Notes.—See comments under *V. gilvus.*

Vireo philadelphicus (Cassin). PHILADELPHIA VIREO. [626.]

Vireosylva philadelphica Cassin, 1851, Proc. Acad. Nat. Sci. Philadelphia, 5, p. 153, pl. 10, fig. 2. (Bingham's woods, near Philadelphia, Pennsylvania.)

Habitat.—Open deciduous or mixed deciduous-coniferous woodland, forest edge, second growth, parks, and alder and willow thickets, especially near streams, in migration and winter in a wide variety of open woodland and partly open situations with scattered trees.

Distribution.—*Breeds* from east-central British Columbia, northern Alberta, northwestern Saskatchewan, central Manitoba, central Ontario, central Quebec, New Brunswick and southwestern Newfoundland (not known to breed in Nova Scotia) south to south-central Alberta, central Saskatchewan, southern Manitoba, north-central North Dakota, northeastern Minnesota, southern Ontario, southern Quebec, northern New Hampshire, northern Vermont and central Maine. Reported in summer (and possibly breeding) in northern Michigan.

Winters from Guatemala and the Yucatan Peninsula (at least casually, and rarely farther north in Mexico) south to central Panama (Canal Zone), rarely to northern Colombia.

Migrates primarily east of the Rockies and west of the Appalachians, rarely along the Pacific coast from southwestern British Columbia southward (occurs regularly in small numbers in California in the fall and casually in spring in eastern and south-central regions of the state), and rarely through the southeastern United States south to the Gulf coasts and southern Florida.

Casual in Nova Scotia, the northern Rockies (Montana, Colorado), the south-western United States (southern Arizona, southern New Mexico and western Texas), the Bahama Islands (Eleuthera, New Providence), Cuba and Jamaica.

Vireo olivaceus (Linnaeus). RED-EYED VIREO. [624.]

> *Muscicapa olivacea* Linnaeus, 1766, Syst. Nat., ed. 12, 1, p. 327. Based mainly on "The Red Ey'd Flycatcher" Catesby, Nat. Hist. Carolina, 1, p. 54, pl. 54. (in America septentrionali = South Carolina.)

Habitat.—Open deciduous (less frequently coniferous) forest, second-growth woodland, scrub, thickets, gardens and mangroves, in migration and winter in a variety of open forest, woodland, scrub and brush habitats (Tropical and Subtropical zones [*flavoviridis* group], to Temperate Zone in North America).

Distribution.—*Breeds* [*olivaceus* group] from southeastern Alaska (probably), southwestern and northeastern British Columbia, west-central and southwestern Mackenzie, northern Alberta, northwestern and central Saskatchewan, north-central Manitoba, central Ontario, south-central Quebec (including Anticosti and Magdalen islands), New Brunswick, Prince Edward Island, Nova Scotia and southern Newfoundland south to northern Oregon, northern Idaho, southwestern and central Montana, Wyoming, eastern Colorado, western Oklahoma, south-central and eastern Texas, the Gulf coast and southern Florida; [*flavoviridis* group] from central Sonora, central Nuevo León and southern Texas (lower Rio Grande Valley) south along both slopes of Middle America (including the Tres Marias Islands, off Nayarit) to Costa Rica and Panama (Pacific slope east to the Canal Zone, including Coiba and the Pearl islands); and [*chivi* group] in South America from Colombia, Venezuela (also Margarita Island, Tobago and Trinidad) and the Guianas south, west of the Andes to western Ecuador and east of the Andes to eastern Peru, Bolivia and central Argentina, also on Fernando de Noronha (off Brazil).

Winters [*olivaceus* group] in South America east of the Andes in the Amazon basin of eastern Colombia, southern Venezuela, eastern Ecuador, eastern Peru and western Brazil; [*flavoviridis* group] in South America in southeastern Peru and central Bolivia, probably elsewhere in the Amazon basin; and [*chivi* group] in the northern part of the breeding range south to the Amazon basin.

Migrates [*olivaceus* group] through eastern North America (east of the Rockies), the Gulf-Caribbean slope of Mexico, Bahama Islands, Cuba, the Isle of Pines, Jamaica, along both slopes of Middle America (from Chiapas southward) and northern South America, regularly through California (more commonly in fall), casually elsewhere in western North America south of the breeding range; and [*flavoviridis* group] through Middle America and Colombia.

Casual or accidental [*olivaceus* group] in south-coastal Alaska (Anchorage, Middleton Island), Bermuda, Chile, Greenland and the British Isles; and [*flavoviridis* group] in central coastal and southern California (also the Farallon Islands), southern Arizona (sight records), Quebec (Godbout), Florida (Pensacola), the Lesser Antilles (St. Lucia, Barbados) and Venezuela.

Notes.—Specific limits in this complex are uncertain; the three groups are often recognized as distinct species, *V. olivaceus* [RED-EYED VIREO, 624], *V. flavoviridis*

(Cassin, 1851) [YELLOW-GREEN VIREO, 625] and *V. chivi* (Vieillot, 1817) [CHIVI VIREO], with the resident population on Fernando de Noronha being recognized by a few authors as a species, *V. gracilirostris* Sharpe, 1890, distinct from *V. chivi. V. olivaceus, V. altiloquus* and *V. magister* are also closely related and may constitute a superspecies.

Vireo altiloquus (Vieillot). BLACK-WHISKERED VIREO. [623.]

> *Muscicapa altiloqua* Vieillot, 1808, Hist. Nat. Ois. Am. Sept., 1 (1807), p. 67, pl. 38. (Jamaica, Saine-Domingue, etc. = St. Thomas, Virgin Islands.)

Habitat.—Mangroves, open woodland, mango and avocado groves, and residential areas, in migration and winter also lowland forest, woodland, scrub, and partly open situations with scattered trees.

Distribution.—*Breeds* in central and southern Florida (Cedar Keys and New Smyrna Beach southward), the Bahama Islands, through the Antilles (including Little Cayman and Cayman Brac in the Cayman Islands), islands of the western Caribbean Sea (Providencia, Santa Catalina and San Andrés), and islands off the north coast of Venezuela (Netherlands Antilles east to Margarita Island).

Winters in South America from eastern Colombia, Venezuela and the Guianas south, east of the Andes, to northeastern Peru and Amazonian Brazil, rarely on Hispaniola, Puerto Rico, and in the northern Lesser Antilles, casually on the Caribbean slope of Panama.

In migration recorded along the Gulf coast from western Florida to southern Louisiana (where summer reports suggest possible breeding), and on Trinidad.

Casual in Texas (Galveston), Belize (Half Moon Cay), Costa Rica (Punta Cahuita) and Tobago; an old record from Honduras is without basis.

Notes.—See comments under *V. olivaceus.*

Vireo magister (Lawrence). YUCATAN VIREO.

> *Vireosylvia* [sic] *magister* (Baird MS) Lawrence, 1871, Ann. Lyc. Nat. Hist. N.Y., 10, p. 20. (Belize, Br. Honduras.)

Habitat.—Mangroves, low deciduous forest, coastal scrub and gardens (Tropical Zone).

Distribution.—*Resident* in the Cayman Islands (Grand Cayman), on the Yucatan Peninsula (including Mujeres, Holbox and Cozumel islands) south to Belize (including small cays offshore), and on the Bay and Hog islands off the Caribbean coast of Honduras.

Notes.—See comments under *V. olivaceus.*

Genus HYLOPHILUS Temminck

> *Hylophilus* Temminck, 1822, Planches Color, livr. 29, pl. 173. Type, by subsequent designation (G. R. Gray, 1840), *Hylophilus poicilotis* Temminck.

Hylophilus flavipes Lafresnaye. SCRUB GREENLET.

> *Hylophilus flavipes* Lafresnaye, 1845, Rev. Zool. [Paris], 8, p. 342. ("Bogotá," Colombia.)

Habitat.—Arid scrub, thickets, mangroves, second growth and deciduous woodland (Tropical Zone).

Distribution.—*Resident* on the Pacific slope of Panama (also Isla Coiba, and the Caribbean slope in the Canal Zone), and in South America from northern and eastern Colombia east through Venezuela (also Margarita Island and Tobago).

Notes.—The populations in Panama are sometimes regarded as a distinct species, *H. viridiflavus* Lawrence, 1862 [YELLOW-GREEN GREENLET]. *H. flavipes* and *H. olivaceus* Tschudi, 1844, of eastern Ecuador and Peru, are sometimes considered conspecific; they constitute a superspecies.

Hylophilus ochraceiceps Sclater. TAWNY-CROWNED GREENLET.

Hylophilus ochraceiceps Sclater, 1859, Proc. Zool. Soc. London, p. 375. (Playa Vicente, Oaxaca.)

Habitat.—Humid lowland and foothill forest, forest edge and second-growth woodland (Tropical and lower Subtropical zones).

Distribution.—*Resident* from northeastern Oaxaca and southern Veracruz south on the Gulf-Caribbean slope (except the Yucatan Peninsula) to Nicaragua, on both slopes of Costa Rica (absent from the dry northwest) and Panama, and in South America from Colombia, Venezuela and the Guianas south, west of the Andes to western Ecuador and east of the Andes to eastern Peru, central Bolivia, and Amazonian and central Brazil.

Hylophilus aurantiifrons Lawrence. GOLDEN-FRONTED GREENLET.

Hylophilus aurantiifrons Lawrence, 1862, Ann. Lyc. Nat. Hist. N.Y., 7, p. 324. (Atlantic slope, along the line of the Panama Railroad = Canal Zone.)

Habitat.—Humid forest edge, clearings, second growth, deciduous woodland, scrub and mangroves (Tropical Zone).

Distribution.—*Resident* from eastern Panama (west to western Panamá province on the Pacific slope, and in the Canal Zone on the Caribbean slope) east across northern Colombia to northern Venezuela (also Trinidad).

Hylophilus decurtatus (Bonaparte). LESSER GREENLET.

Sylvicola decurtata Bonaparte, 1838, Proc. Zool. Soc. London (1837), p. 118. (Guatamala = Guatemala.)

Habitat.—Lowland forest, forest edge, clearings, open woodland and plantations (Tropical Zone).

Distribution.—*Resident* [*decurtatus* group] from eastern San Luis Potosí, Veracruz, northeastern Puebla, northern Oaxaca and Chiapas south along both slopes of Middle America (except the state of Yucatán) to central Panama (east to the Canal Zone); and [*minor* group] from eastern Panama (west to the Canal Zone) south through northern and western Colombia to western Ecuador.

Notes.—Although the two groups are often recognized as separate species, *H. decuratatus* [GRAY-HEADED GREENLET] and *H. minor* Berlepsch and Taczanowski, 1884 [LESSER GREENLET], they intergrade through eastern Panamá province and the Canal Zone.

Subfamily VIREOLANIINAE: Shrike-Vireos

Notes.—Considered a family, the Vireolaniidae, by some authors.

Genus VIREOLANIUS Bonaparte

Vireolanius (Du Bus de Gisignies MS) Bonaparte, 1850, Consp. Gen. Avium, 1 (2), p. 330. Type, by monotypy, *Vireolanius melitophrys* Bonaparte. *Smaragdolanius* Griscom, 1930, Am. Mus. Novit., no. 438, p. 3. Type, by original designation, *Vireolanius pulchellus* Sclater and Salvin.

Vireolanius melitophrys Bonaparte. CHESTNUT-SIDED SHRIKE-VIREO.

Vireolanius melitophrys (Du Bus de Gisignies MS) Bonaparte, 1850, Consp. Gen. Avium, 1 (2), p. 330. (Mexico = Jico, near Jalapa, Veracruz.)

Habitat.—Oak forest, open woodland and second growth (Subtropical and lower Temperate zones).

Distribution.—*Resident* in the highlands from Jalisco, San Luis Potosí and Veracruz south to western Guatemala.

Vireolanius pulchellus Sclater and Salvin. GREEN SHRIKE-VIREO.

Vireolanius pulchellus Sclater and Salvin, 1859, Ibis, p. 12. (Guatemala.)

Habitat.—Humid lowland and foothill forest, forest edge and second-growth woodland (Tropical and lower Subtropical zones).

Distribution.—*Resident* from Veracruz, northern Oaxaca and Chiapas south on the Gulf-Caribbean slope of Central America to Nicaragua, and on both slopes of Costa Rica (except the dry northwest) and Panama (east to the Canal Zone and eastern Panamá province).

Notes.—Some authors regard *V. pulchellus* and *V. eximius* to be conspecific; they constitute a superspecies. These two species are frequently placed in the genus *Smaragdolanius*.

Vireolanius eximius Baird. YELLOW-BROWED SHRIKE-VIREO.

Vireolanius eximius Baird, 1866, Rev. Am. Birds, 1, p. 398. ("Bogotá," Colombia.)

Habitat.—Humid lowland and foothill forest (Tropical and lower Subtropical zones).

Distribution.—*Resident* in extreme eastern Panama (Cana, eastern Darién), northern Colombia and western Venezuela.

Notes.—See comments under *V. pulchellus*.

Subfamily CYCLARHINAE: Peppershrikes

Notes.—Considered a family, the Cyclarhidae, by some authors.

Genus CYCLARHIS Swainson

Cyclarhis Swainson, 1824, Zool. J., 1, p. 294. Type, by monotypy, *Tanagra gujanensis* Gmelin.

Cyclarhis gujanensis (Gmelin). RUFOUS-BROWED PEPPERSHRIKE.

Tanagra gujanensis Gmelin, 1789, Syst. Nat., 1 (2), p. 893. Based on "Verderoux" Buffon, Hist. Nat. Ois, 5, p. 27. (in Gujanae silvis ingentibus = French Guiana.)

Habitat.—Humid forest edge and clearings, second growth, deciduous woodland, scrub and plantations (Tropical and Subtropical zones).

Distribution.—*Resident* from San Luis Potosí, southern Tamaulipas, Veracruz, Hidalgo, Puebla, northern Oaxaca and Chiapas south on both slopes of Middle America (including the Yucatan Peninsula, and Cancun and Cozumel islands) to Panama (including Isla Coiba), and in South America from northern and eastern Colombia, Venezuela (also Trinidad) and the Guianas south, east of the Andes, to eastern Peru, Bolivia, central Argentina and southern Brazil.

Notes.—The populations from southeastern Brazil and northeastern Argentina are sometimes recognized as a distinct species, *C. ochrocephala* Tschudi, 1845.

Family **EMBERIZIDAE**: Emberizids

Notes.—See Preface (p. xviii) for a summary of the treatment of this family.

Subfamily PARULINAE: Wood-Warblers

Genus **VERMIVORA** Swainson

Vermivora Swainson, 1827, Philos. Mag., new ser., 1, p. 434. Type, by monotypy, *Sylvia solitaria* Wilson = *Certhia pinus* Linnaeus.
Helminthophaga (not Bechstein, 1803) Cabanis, 1850, Mus. Heineanum, 1 (1851), p. 20. Type, by original designation, *Motacilla chrysoptera* Linnaeus.
Helminthophila Ridgway, 1882, Bull. Nuttall Ornithol. Club, 7, p. 53. New name for *Helminthophaga* Cabanis, preoccupied.

Notes.—The genera *Vermivora, Parula* and *Dendroica* are closely related and weakly differentiated; some authors merge all in *Vermivora*. See also comments under *Helmitheros vermivorus*.

Vermivora bachmanii (Audubon). BACHMAN'S WARBLER. [640.]

Sylvia Bachmanii Audubon, 1833, Birds Am. (folio), 2, pl. 185 (1834, Ornithol. Biogr., 2, p. 483). (a few miles from Charleston [=Edisto River], in South Carolina.)

Habitat.—Moist deciduous woodland and swamp, in migration and winter also open woodland, pine and scrub.

Distribution.—Possibly extinct. *Bred* formerly in northeastern Arkansas, southeastern Missouri, south-central Kentucky, central Alabama and southeastern South Carolina. Recorded in summer (and possibly breeding) from northeastern Oklahoma, western Arkansas, south-central Missouri, northern Kentucky and Virginia south to Louisiana, Mississippi and southern Alabama.

Wintered on Cuba and the Isle of Pines.

In migration recorded from the Gulf coast (west to Louisiana), Florida Keys and Bahama Islands (Cay Sal).

Although a few are still reported on the basis of song or sightings, the last confirmed report was in 1962.

Vermivora pinus (Linnaeus). BLUE-WINGED WARBLER. [641.]

> *Certhia Pinus* Linnaeus, 1766, Syst. Nat., ed. 12, 1, p. 187. Based largely on "The Pine-Creeper" Edwards, Glean. Nat. Hist., 2, p. 140, pl. 277. (in America septentrionali = Philadelphia, Pennsylvania.)

Habitat.—Brushy hillsides, second growth, partly open situations with saplings, and bogs, in migration and winter in a variety of brushy areas, scrub and open woodland.

Distribution.—*Breeds* from eastern Nebraska, central Iowa, southeastern Minnesota, southern Wisconsin, southern Michigan, northern Ohio, extreme southern Ontario, central New York, southern Vermont, Massachusetts and southern Maine south to northwestern Arkansas, east-central Missouri, central Tennessee, northern Alabama, northern Georgia, western South Carolina, western North Carolina, northern Virginia, central Maryland and Delaware.

Winters from Oaxaca, Puebla and Veracruz south through Middle America (both slopes, including the Yucatan Peninsula, but less commonly on the Pacific drainage) to central Panama (east to the Canal Zone and eastern Panamá province).

Migrates commonly through the eastern United States (west to the eastern Great Plains and eastern and southern Texas, but rare in the extreme southeast) and eastern Mexico (Gulf slope), rarely through Cuba, Jamaica, Hispaniola and the Bahama Islands.

Casual north to southern Saskatchewan, South Dakota, southwestern Quebec, Maine and Nova Scotia, west to California, southern Arizona, New Mexico and western Texas and south to northern Colombia, also a sight report in the Virgin Islands (St. John).

Notes.—Hybridizes regularly and extensively with *V. chrysoptera* in a dynamic situation, producing variable hybrids that have resulted in the naming of two extreme types, *V. "leucobronchialis"* and *V. "lawrencii"* (see Appendix C). There generally has resulted a replacement of *V. chrysoptera* by *V. pinus,* the extent of interbreeding diminishing with this shift, but the situation is complex and locally variable.

Vermivora chrysoptera (Linnaeus). GOLDEN-WINGED WARBLER. [642.]

> *Motacilla chrysoptera* Linnaeus, 1766, Syst. Nat., ed. 12, 1, p. 333. Based on "The Golden-winged Fly-catcher" Edwards, Glean. Nat. Hist., 2, p. 189, pl. 299. (in Pensylvania = near Philadelphia, Pennsylvania.)

Habitat.—Open deciduous woodland, second growth, brushy pastures, and bogs, in migration and winter in a variety of open woodland, pine-oak association and scrub.

Distribution.—*Breeds* from northeastern North Dakota, southern Manitoba, central Minnesota, northern Wisconsin, northern Michigan, southern Ontario, extreme southwestern Quebec, northern New York, southern Vermont and eastern Massachusetts south to southeastern Iowa, northern Illinois, northern Indiana, southern Ohio, eastern Kentucky, eastern Tennessee, northern Georgia, northwestern South Carolina, western Virginia, north-central Maryland, southeastern Pennsylvania and southern Connecticut; breeding range in the northeast and Appalachians decreasing in recent years. Recorded in summer (and possibly breeding) north to Maine.

Winters from the Yucatan Peninsula and Guatemala south through Middle America (mostly on the Caribbean drainage north of Panama) to northern and eastern Colombia and northern Venezuela, and rarely in the Greater Antilles (east to Puerto Rico).

Migrates through eastern North America east of the Rockies (rare along the Great Plains and in the extreme southeast) south to south-central Texas and the Gulf coast, recorded rarely in eastern Mexico (Gulf-Caribbean slope), Cuba and the northwestern Bahama Islands.

Casual in southern Saskatchewan, California, Arizona, Colorado, New Mexico, western Texas, New Brunswick and Nova Scotia.

Notes.—See comments under *V. pinus.*

Vermivora peregrina (Wilson). TENNESSEE WARBLER. [647.]

Sylvia peregrina Wilson, 1811, Am. Ornithol., 3, p. 83, pl. 25, fig. 2. (banks of the Cumberland River in Tennessee.)

Habitat.—Coniferous and deciduous woodland, alder and willow thickets, and open deciduous second growth, in migration and winter in a variety of forest, woodland, scrub and thicket habitats.

Distribution.—*Breeds* from southeastern Alaska, southern Yukon, northwestern and southern Mackenzie, northern Saskatchewan, northern Manitoba, northern Ontario, north-central Quebec, southern Labrador and western Newfoundland south to south-central British Columbia, southwestern and south-central Alberta, northwestern Montana, south-central Saskatchewan, southern Manitoba, northern Minnesota, northern Wisconsin, northern Michigan, south-central Ontario, northeastern New York, southern Vermont, central New Hampshire, southern Maine and Nova Scotia.

Winters From Oaxaca and Veracruz (casually farther north) south through Middle America (including islands off the Caribbean coast) to Colombia, northern Venezuela and Ecuador (sight record).

Migrates regularly through eastern North America east of the Rockies, eastern Mexico, the Bahama Islands, Greater Antilles (east to Hispaniola), and islands in the western Caribbean Sea (Providencia, San Andrés), also rarely but regularly through California (more commonly in fall).

Casual elsewhere in western North America from southwestern British Columbia and Colorado south to northern Baja California, northern Sonora, southeastern Arizona, southern New Mexico and western Texas, also in central Alaska and the British Isles. Accidental on Clipperton Island, and in the Revillagigedo Islands (Socorro, sight report), Bermuda and Greenland.

Vermivora celata (Say). ORANGE-CROWNED WARBLER. [646.]

Sylvia celatus Say, 1823, *in* Long, Exped. Rocky Mount., 1, p. 169 (note). (Engineer Cantonment near Council Bluff = Omaha, Nebraska.)

Habitat.—Deciduous and mixed deciduous-coniferous woodland, shrublands, chaparral, and riparian thickets and woodland, in migration and winter in a variety of brushy and shrubby areas, woodland and forest edge.

Distribution.—*Breeds* from western and central Alaska, central Yukon, northwestern and southern Mackenzie, northern Alberta, northern Saskatchewan, northern Manitoba, northern Ontario, central Quebec and southern Labrador south to southern Alaska (west to the Alaska Peninsula and Kodiak Island), southwestern and central California (including the Channel Islands), islands off northwestern Baja California (Los Coronados and Todos Santos), south-central Nevada, central Utah, southeastern Arizona, southern New Mexico and extreme western Texas (Guadalupe Mountains), and, east of the Rockies, to southern Saskatchewan, southern Manitoba, northeastern North Dakota (probably), central Ontario and south-central Quebec.

Winters from coastal and southern California, central Arizona, southern New Mexico (rarely), Texas, the southern portions of the Gulf states, and South Carolina (casually north to the northern United States) south to southern Baja California, Guatemala, Belize, the Yucatan Peninsula and southern Florida.

Migrates regularly through the United States west of the Appalachians, rarely through the eastern states.

Casual north to northern Alaska and northern Mackenzie, in the Maritime Provinces, and in the northern Bahama Islands. Accidental in Costa Rica (Limón) and Greenland.

Vermivora ruficapilla (Wilson). NASHVILLE WARBLER. [645.]

Sylvia ruficapilla Wilson, 1811, Am. Ornithol., 3, p. 120, pl. 27, fig. 3. (near Nashville, Tennessee.)

Habitat.—Open deciduous or coniferous woodland, second growth, and forest-bordered bogs, in migration and winter in a variety of woodland, scrub and thicket habitats.

Distribution.—*Breeds* from southern interior British Columbia, southern Alberta (rarely) and northwestern Montana south through Washington (except western portion), Oregon and central Idaho to northwestern and south-central California, and extreme west-central Nevada; and from central Saskatchewan, central Manitoba, central Ontario, southern Quebec (including Anticosti and Magdalen islands), New Brunswick, Prince Edward Island and Nova Scotia south to southern Manitoba, northern and east-central Minnesota, southern Wisconsin, northeastern Illinois, southern Michigan, northeastern Ohio, northeastern West Virginia, western Maryland, southeastern Pennsylvania, northern New Jersey, southeastern New York, southern Connecticut and Rhode Island. Recorded in summer (and probably breeding) in southwestern Newfoundland.

Winters from southern Sonora, Durango, Nuevo León and southern Texas south through Mexico (but doubtfully recorded Yucatan Peninsula) to Guatemala, Belize, El Salvador and central Honduras; also rarely in southern (casually northern) California, southern Florida, the Bahama Islands, Cuba and Jamaica.

Migrates regularly through California, Arizona, New Mexico, and the central United States from the Plains states east to the Appalachians, rarely through Baja California, the Rockies, and the southeastern United States.

Accidental in Bermuda and Greenland, also sight reports from southern Alaska (Middleton Island) and Panama (Chiriquí).

Notes.—*V. ruficapilla, V. virginiae* and *V. crissalis* are closely related and constitute a superspecies; some authors merge them under *V. ruficapilla* [GRAY-HEADED WARBLER].

Vermivora virginiae (Baird). VIRGINIA'S WARBLER. [644.]

Helminthophaga virginiae Baird, 1860, *in* Baird, Cassin and Lawrence, Birds N. Am., p. xi, Atlas, pl. 79, fig. 1. (Cantonment [=Fort] Burgwyn, N.M.)

Habitat.—Arid montane woodland, oak thickets, pinyon-juniper, coniferous scrub, and chaparral, in migration and winter also in open woodland, second growth, thickets and arid scrub.

Distribution.—*Breeds* from east-central California (Mono and Inyo counties), central Nevada, southeastern Idaho, southern Wyoming and north-central Colorado south to south-central California (San Bernardino County), southern Nevada, central and southeastern Arizona, southern New Mexico and extreme western Texas (Guadalupe Mountains).

Winters from Jalisco and Guanajuato south to Morelos and Oaxaca.

In migration occurs from southern California, Arizona, New Mexico, and western and northern Texas south through northern Mexico (except Baja California), casually in southern coastal California and east to western Kansas, western Oklahoma and southeastern Texas.

Casual or accidental in Oregon (Eugene, Hart Mountain), coastal northern California, Ontario (Point Pelee) and New Jersey (Island Beach), also a sight report for Illinois.

Notes.—See comments under *V. ruficapilla.*

Vermivora crissalis (Salvin and Godman). COLIMA WARBLER. [647.1.]

Helminthophila crissalis Salvin and Godman, 1889, Ibis, p. 380. (Sierra Nevada de Colima, Mexico.)

Habitat.—Thickets and scrubby woodland, primarily oak, maple, cypress and juniper scrub in hilly areas, in migration and winter in open woodland, thickets and scrub.

Distribution.—*Breeds* in extreme western Texas (Chisos Mountains), southern Coahuila (Diamante Pass, Sierra Guadalupe), western Nuevo León (Cerro Potosí) and southwestern Tamaulipas (Miquihuana).

Winters from southern Sinaloa south through Jalisco, Colima and Michoacán to Guerrero.

Casual in southern Texas (Santa Ana, sight report).

Notes.—See comments under *V. ruficapilla.*

Vermivora luciae (Cooper). LUCY'S WARBLER. [643.]

Helminthophaga luciæ J. G. Cooper, 1861, Proc. Calif. Acad. Sci., ser. 1, 2, p. 120. (Fort Mojave, near lat. 35° in the Colorado Valley [Arizona].)

Habitat.—Mesquite, scrub and riparian woodland in desert regions, in migration and winter also in arid brush and thickets.

Distribution.—*Breeds* from southeastern California (north to Inyo County), southern Nevada, Utah and (at least formerly) southwestern Colorado south to northeastern Baja California, southern Arizona and northern Sonora, and east across southern New Mexico to extreme western Texas (Hudspeth and Presidio counties).

Winters in western Mexico from Jalisco south to Guerrero.

In migration occurs in northwestern Mexico, rarely in southern California (casually north to Point Reyes and the Farallon Islands). Accidental in southern Louisiana (Buras) and Massachusetts (Ipswich).

Genus PARULA Bonaparte

Parula Bonaparte, 1838, Geogr. Comp. List, p. 20. Type, by monotypy, *Sylvia americana* Latham = *Parus americanus* Linnaeus.
Oreothlypis Ridgway, 1884, Auk, 1, p. 169. Type, by original designation, *Compsothlypis gutturalis* Cabanis.

Notes.—See comments under *Vermivora*.

Parula americana (Linnaeus). NORTHERN PARULA. [648.]

Parus americanus Linnaeus, 1758, Syst. Nat., ed. 10, 1, p. 190. Based on "The Finch-Creeper" Catesby, Nat. Hist. Carolina, 1, p. 64, pl. 64. (in America septentrionali = South Carolina.)

Habitat.—Open deciduous or coniferous forest, woodland and swamp, in migration and winter also humid lowland forest, second growth, scrub and brushy areas.

Distribution.—*Breeds* from southeastern Manitoba, central Ontario, southern Quebec, New Brunswick, Prince Edward Island and Nova Scotia south to south-central and southern Texas (San Antonio area and Hidalgo County), the Gulf coast and southern Florida (to Collier County), and west to the eastern edge of the Plains states; and rarely in New Mexico (near Bernalillo, 1977) and California (Point Lobos in 1952, Point Reyes in 1977).

Winters from southern Tamaulipas (sparingly), Veracruz and Oaxaca (casually from southern California, southern Arizona and northern Sonora) south through Mexico (primarily on the Gulf-Caribbean drainage and offshore islands) to Guatemala and Belize, rarely to Nicaragua and Costa Rica, also sight reports from the Caribbean coast of Panama; and from central Florida and the Bahama Islands south throughout the West Indies to Tobago, casually to Curaçao and Isla Los Roques, off Venezuela.

Migrates primarily through eastern North America and northeastern Mexico, rarely but regularly to California, casually elsewhere in western North America (from Washington, Alberta, Saskatchewan, Montana and Wyoming southward).

Casual or accidental in Bermuda, Greenland, Iceland and the British Isles.

Notes.—*P. americana* and *P. pitiayumi* are regarded as conspecific by some authors [PARULA WARBLER]; they constitute a superspecies.

Parula pitiayumi (Vieillot). TROPICAL PARULA. [649.]

Sylvia pitiayumi Vieillot, 1817, Nouv. Dict. Hist. Nat., nouv. éd., 11, p. 276. Based on "Pico de Punzon del celeste pecho de oro" Azara, Apunt. Hist. Nat. Páx. Parag., 1, p. 421 (no. 109). (Paraguay.)

Habitat.—Humid forest, forest edge, second growth, deciduous woodland and, less frequently, scrub (Tropical and Subtropical zones).

Distribution.—*Resident* from southern Sonora, southwestern Chihuahua, Sinaloa, western Durango, Nayarit (including the Tres Marias and Isabela islands), Jalisco, San Luis Potosí, Nuevo León and southern Texas (lower Rio Grande

Valley) south locally through Middle America to Panama (including Isla Coiba), and in South America from Colombia, Venezuela (also Margarita Island, Tobago and Trinidad) and the Guianas south, west of the Andes to northwestern Peru and east of the Andes to eastern Peru, Bolivia, northern Argentina and Brazil; also on Socorro Island, in the Revillagigedo group, off western Mexico.

Casual in southern Baja California.

Notes.—Also known as OLIVE-BACKED WARBLER. The resident population on Socorro Island has sometimes been treated as a distinct species, *P. graysoni* (Ridgway, 1887) [SOCORRO WARBLER]. See also comments under *P. americana*.

Parula superciliosa (Hartlaub). CRESCENT-CHESTED WARBLER.

Conirostrum superciliosum Hartlaub, 1844, Rev. Zool. [Paris], 7, p. 215. (Guatemala.)

Habitat.—Humid montane forest, pine-oak association and deciduous woodland (Subtropical and lower Temperate zones).

Distribution.—*Resident* in the highlands from southern Chihuahua, eastern Sinaloa, western Durango, Nayarit, Jalisco, San Luis Potosí, central Nuevo León and western Tamaulipas south through Mexico, Guatemala, El Salvador and Honduras to north-central Nicaragua.

Notes.—Also known as HARTLAUB'S or SPOT-BREASTED WARBLER. Often treated in the genus *Vermivora*.

Parula gutturalis (Cabanis). FLAME-THROATED WARBLER.

Compsothlypis gutturalis Cabanis, 1860, J. Ornithol., 8, p. 329. (Irazú, Costa Rica.)

Habitat.—Humid montane forest edge, clearings, open woodland and scrub (Subtropical and lower Temperate zones).

Distribution.—*Resident* in the highlands of Costa Rica (Cordillera Central, Dota Mountains and Cordillera de Talamanca) and western Panama (Chiriquí).

Notes.—Often placed in the genus *Vermivora,* occasionally in the monotypic genus *Oreothlypis.*

Genus **DENDROICA** Gray

Dendroica G. R. Gray, 1842, List Genera Birds, app., p. 8. Type, by original designation, *Motacilla coronata* Linnaeus.

Notes.—See comments under *Vermivora* and *Catharopeza.*

Dendroica petechia (Linnaeus). YELLOW WARBLER. [652.]

Motacilla petechia Linnaeus, 1766, Syst. Nat., ed. 12, 1, p. 334. Based on "The Yellow Red-pole" Edwards, Glean. Nat. Hist., 1, p. 99, pl. 256, fig. 2. (in America septentrionali = Barbados.)

Habitat.—[*aestiva* group] Open scrub, second-growth woodland, thickets, farmlands and gardens, especially near water, in migration and winter also open woodland, plantations, brushy areas and forest edge (Tropical to Temperate zones); and [*petechia* and *erithachorides* groups] mangroves, scrub and thickets (Tropical Zone).

Distribution.— *Breeds* [*aestiva* group] from northwestern and north-central Alaska, northern Yukon, northwestern and central Mackenzie, northern Saskatchewan, northern Manitoba, northern Ontario, central Quebec, southern Labrador and Newfoundland south to southern Alaska (west to the Alaska Peninsula and Unimak Island), northern Baja California, through Mexico to northern Guerrero, Puebla and southeastern San Luis Potosí, and to central and northeastern Texas, central Oklahoma, northern Arkansas, northern Mississippi, central Alabama, central Georgia and central South Carolina.

Winters [*aestiva* group] from southern California, southwestern Arizona, northern Mexico, southern Florida and the Bahama Islands south through Middle America, the West Indies and South America (mostly east of the Andes) to Peru, Bolivia and Amazonian Brazil (including most insular areas within this range).

Resident [*petechia* group] from southern Florida (Florida Bay area and the Florida Keys) and the Bahama Islands south throughout the West Indies (south to St. Lucia and Barbados, and including the Cayman, Providencia and San Andrés islands) to the northern coast of Venezuela (west to Falcón) and islands offshore (also Tobago and Trinidad), and on Cozumel Island (off Quintana Roo); and [*erithachorides* group] from southern Baja California (north to lat. 27°N.), Sonora and southern Tamaulipas south along both coasts of Middle America (including the Bay Islands off Honduras, and Cocos Island off Costa Rica) to eastern Panama (on the Pacific coast east only to western Darién, but including Escudo, Coiba and the Pearl islands), along the west coast of South America from northwestern Colombia south to central Peru (also the Galapagos Islands), and east along the northern coast of Colombia to northwestern Venezuela (east to Paraguana Peninsula).

Casual or accidental [*aestiva* group] in northern Alaska, islands in the Bering Sea (Nunivak and the Pribilofs), Baffin Island and the British Isles; and [*erithachorides* group] in the Revillagigedo Islands (Socorro, sight report) and southeastern Texas (Rockport).

Notes.— The three groups are sometimes recognized as distinct species, *D. aestiva* (Gmelin, 1789) [YELLOW WARBLER, 652], *D. petechia* [GOLDEN WARBLER, 652.1] and *D. erithachorides* Baird, 1858 [MANGROVE WARBLER, 653].

Dendroica pensylvanica (Linnaeus). CHESTNUT-SIDED WARBLER. [659.]

Motacilla pensylvanica Linnaeus, 1766, Syst. Nat., ed. 12, 1, p. 333. Based on "The Red-throated Fly-catcher" Edwards, Glean. Nat. Hist., 2, p. 193, pl. 301. (in Pensylvania= Philadelphia.)

Habitat.— Open deciduous woodland, forest edge, second growth and brushy areas, in migration and winter also in a variety of forest, woodland, scrub and thicket habitats.

Distribution.— *Breeds* from east-central Alberta, central Saskatchewan, central Manitoba, central Ontario, southern Quebec, New Brunswick, Prince Edward Island and Nova Scotia south to eastern Colorado, north-central North Dakota, eastern Nebraska, Iowa, Missouri (formerly), northern Illinois, northern Indiana and central Ohio, in the Appalachians south through West Virginia, eastern Kentucky, western Virginia, eastern Tennessee and western North Carolina to north-central Georgia and northwestern South Carolina, and to central Maryland, southeastern Pennsylvania, central New Jersey, southern New York, Massachusetts and Maine.

Winters from Oaxaca, Chiapas and Guatemala (casually farther north) south through Middle America (primarily on the Caribbean slope north of Costa Rica) to eastern Panama, casually to northern Colombia, Venezuela and Trinidad.

Migrates primarily through the eastern United States (east of the Rockies), Bahama Islands, Greater Antilles (Cuba and Jamaica, sight reports also from Hispaniola, Puerto Rico and the Virgin Islands) and eastern Mexico (also recorded once from Nayarit, otherwise not recorded Pacific slope north of Oaxaca), rarely through western North America from southern British Columbia, Idaho and Montana south to southern California, southern Arizona and New Mexico.

Casual or accidental in Bermuda, Barbados and Greenland, with a sight report from southern Alaska (Middleton Island).

Dendroica magnolia (Wilson). MAGNOLIA WARBLER. [657.]

Sylvia magnolia Wilson, 1811, Am. Ornithol., 3, p. 63, pl. 23, fig. 2. (the Little Miami, near its junction with the Ohio . . . [and] not far from fort Adams on the Mississippi = Fort Adams, Mississippi.)

Habitat.—Open coniferous (mostly spruce and fir) or mixed coniferous-deciduous woodland, forest edge and second growth, in migration and winter also in a variety of open forest, woodland, scrub and thicket habitats.

Distribution.—*Breeds* from northeastern British Columbia, west-central and southern Mackenzie, northwestern Saskatchewan, north-central Manitoba, central Ontario, south-central and eastern Quebec (including Anticosti and Magdalen islands) and southern Newfoundland south to south-central British Columbia, south-central Alberta, central Saskatchewan, southern Manitoba, northeastern Minnesota, central Wisconsin, central Michigan, southern Ontario, north-central and northeastern Ohio, southeastern West Virginia, western Virginia, western Maryland, northeastern Pennsylvania, northwestern New Jersey and Connecticut.

Winters from Oaxaca, Puebla, San Luis Potosí, central Veracruz, the Greater Antilles and Bahama Islands (casually north to southern California, southwestern Arizona, northern Sonora, southern Texas, the Gulf coast and Virginia) south through Middle America to central Panama (east to Canal Zone and eastern Panamá province), and east in the West Indies (at least rarely) to the Virgin Islands.

Migrates primarily through eastern North America east of the Rockies, rarely (but apparently regularly) to California, and casually elsewhere in western North America (recorded in the Pacific states from southeastern Alaska to Oregon, and in Montana, Colorado, New Mexico, southern Arizona and Nevada).

Casual or accidental in western and northern Alaska, Barbados, northwestern Colombia and Greenland.

Notes.—*Dendroica lutea,* based on *Muscicapa lutea* Linnaeus, 1776, has been officially suppressed (Int. Comm. Zool. Nomencl., 1956, Opin. Decl. Rend., 13, pp. 205–232).

Dendroica tigrina (Gmelin). CAPE MAY WARBLER. [650.]

Motacilla tigrina Gmelin, 1789, Syst. Nat., 1 (2), p. 985. Based on "Le Figuier brun de Canada" Brisson, Ornithologie, 3, p. 515, pl. 27, fig. 4. (in Canada.)

Habitat.—Open boreal coniferous forest, forest edge and open woodland, in migration and winter also in a variety of forest, woodland, scrub and thicket habitats.

Distribution.—*Breeds* from northeastern British Columbia, southwestern and south-central Mackenzie, northern Alberta, northern Saskatchewan, central Manitoba, central Ontario, southern Quebec, New Brunswick, Prince Edward Island and Nova Scotia south to central Alberta, central Saskatchewan, southeastern Manitoba, northwestern North Dakota, northeastern Minnesota, northern Wisconsin, northern Michigan (probably), southern Ontario, northeastern New York, east-central Vermont, northern New Hampshire and east-central Maine. Recorded in summer (and possibly breeding) in southern Michigan and on Anticosti Island (Quebec).

Winters in central and southern Florida, the West Indies (primarily the Bahamas and Greater Antilles, less commonly in the Lesser Antilles), casually to Middle America (recorded Yucatan Peninsula, Belize, the Bay Islands off Honduras, Nicaragua, Costa Rica and Panama); recorded casually in winter also in southern California, southern Arizona, and the central and eastern United States.

Migrates primarily through the midwestern, eastern and southeastern states, rarely (occurring mostly in spring) south of Arkansas and Tennessee and west of Alabama, also rarely to California.

Casual north to northern Alaska, elsewhere in western North America south to southern Nevada, southern Arizona, New Mexico, Chihuahua and Texas, and to Isla Providencia (in the western Caribbean Sea), Tobago, and islands off Venezuela (Los Roques, La Orchila), also a sight report for Great Britain.

Dendroica caerulescens (Gmelin). BLACK-THROATED BLUE WARBLER. [654.]

Motacilla caerulescens Gmelin, 1789, Syst. Nat., 1 (2), p. 960. Based on "La Fauvette bleuâtre de St. Domingue" Buffon, Hist. Nat. Ois., 5, p. 164. (in insula S. Dominici = Hispaniola.)

Habitat.—Understory of deciduous or mixed deciduous-coniferous woodland, second growth and partially cleared forest, in migration and winter also in other forest types, open woodland and scrub.

Distribution.—*Breeds* from western and central Ontario, southern Quebec, New Brunswick, Prince Edward Island and Nova Scotia south to northeastern Minnesota, northern Wisconsin, central Michigan, southern Ontario, north-central and northeastern Ohio, in the Appalachians through West Virginia, western Maryland, eastern Kentucky, western Virginia, eastern Tennessee and western North Carolina to northeastern Georgia and northwestern South Carolina, and to northeastern Pennsylvania, northern New Jersey, southern New York and southern New England. Recorded in summer (and possibly breeding) in southern Manitoba, and on Anticosti and Magdalen islands.

Winters from southern Florida and the Bahama Islands south through the Greater Antilles (east to St. Croix in the Virgin Islands, and including the Cayman Islands), casually in southern California, on Cozumel Island (off Quintana Roo), and in the Swan Islands, Guatemala (Caribbean lowlands), Belize, Costa Rica, Colombia and Venezuela, also sight reports from Costa Rica.

Migrates through eastern North America east of the Rockies (west to eastern Texas), rarely to California, and casually elsewhere in western North America (recorded from Oregon, Alberta, Saskatchewan and Wyoming south to southern Baja California, southern Arizona, southern New Mexico and southern Texas).

Casual in the Lesser Antilles (Guadeloupe, Dominica).

Dendroica coronata (Linnaeus). YELLOW-RUMPED WARBLER. [655.]

Motacilla coronata Linnaeus, 1766, Syst. Nat., ed. 12, 1, p. 333. Based on "The Golden-crowned Fly-catcher" Edwards, Glean. Nat. Hist., 2, p. 187, pl. 298. (in Pensylvania = Philadelphia.)

Habitat.—Coniferous and deciduous forest, and open woodland, in migration and winter also open forest, woodland, second growth, scrub, thickets, parks and gardens.

Distribution.—*Breeds* [*coronata* group] from western and central Alaska, central Yukon, northwestern and central Mackenzie, southwestern Keewatin (probably), northern Manitoba, northern Ontario, northern Quebec, north-central Labrador and Newfoundland south to southern Alaska, northern British Columbia, central and southwestern Alberta, central and southeastern Saskatchewan, southwestern North Dakota (probably), northern Minnesota, northern Wisconsin, central Michigan, southern Ontario, in the Appalachians to eastern West Virginia and northwestern Virginia, and to eastern Pennsylvania, extreme northeastern Maryland and Massachusetts; and [*auduboni* group] from central British Columbia, southern Alberta, southwestern Saskatchewan, central and southeastern Montana, and western South Dakota south to northern Baja California, southern California, southern Arizona, western Chihuahua, southern New Mexico and extreme western Texas (Guadalupe Mountains), also in the mountains of western Durango, eastern Chiapas (Volcán Tacaná) and western Guatemala, and one reported breeding from northwestern Nebraska. Recorded in summer (and possibly breeding) [*coronata* group] in southeastern West Virginia and [*auduboni* group] in southeastern Alaska.

Winters [*coronata* group] from southwestern British Columbia, the Pacific states, southern Arizona, Colorado, and from Kansas east across the central United States and southern Ontario to New England (casually farther north) south through the southern United States, Middle America and the West Indies to eastern Panama (including the Pearl Islands, as well as islands off Middle America in the western Caribbean Sea) and Barbados; and [*auduboni* group] from southwestern British Columbia, southeastern Washington, Idaho, Colorado, and central and southeastern Texas south (more commonly in the highlands) to southern Baja California and the Revillagigedo Islands (Socorro), and through Mexico to Guatemala and western Honduras.

Migrates [*coronata* group] primarily through North America east of the Rockies and in the Pacific northwest, less commonly elsewhere in western North America; and [*auduboni* group] through western North America east to the western Plains states (casually to Minnesota, Missouri, Arkansas and eastern Texas).

Casual or accidental [*coronata* group] north to King William and Southampton islands, and in Tobago, Colombia, Venezuela, Greenland, the British Isles and Siberia (Chukotski Peninsula); and [*auduboni* group] on Attu in the Aleutian Islands, and in northeastern North America from southern Ontario, southern Quebec and Massachusetts south to Pennsylvania, New Jersey and North Carolina (sight records to Florida). Reports [*auduboni* group] from Costa Rica are regarded as erroneous, although a sight report for western Panama (Chiriquí) is well documented.

Notes.—The two groups have often been regarded as distinct species, *D. coronata* [MYRTLE WARBLER, 655] and *D. auduboni* (J. K. Townsend, 1837) [AUDUBON'S WARBLER, 656]; intergradation occurs from southeastern Alaska southeast across central British Columbia to southern Alberta.

Dendroica nigrescens (Townsend). BLACK-THROATED GRAY WARBLER. [665.]

> *Sylvia nigrescens* J. K. Townsend, 1837, J. Acad. Nat. Sci. Philadelphia, 7, p. 191. (No locality given = near Fort William, Portland, Oregon.)

Habitat.—Open coniferous or mixed coniferous-deciduous woodland with brushy undergrowth, pinyon-juniper, pike-oak association, and oak scrub, in migration and winter also in a variety of forest, woodland, scrub and thicket habitats.

Distribution.—*Breeds* from southwestern British Columbia, western Washington, central Oregon, southwestern Idaho, northern Utah, southern Wyoming, and northwestern and central Colorado south, primarily in mountains, to northern Baja California, southern California, central and southeastern Arizona, northeastern Sonora, southern New Mexico and (probably) extreme western Texas (Guadalupe Mountains).

Winters from coastal southern (casually northern) California, southern Arizona and (rarely) southern Texas south to Oaxaca and Veracruz.

In migration occurs regularly east to western Kansas.

Casual north to Alberta and Saskatchewan, across the northeastern region from Minnesota, Wisconsin, Michigan, southern Ontario, New York, Massachusetts and Nova Scotia south to Ohio, Pennsylvania, New Jersey and Virginia, and through the Gulf states from eastern Texas east to southeastern Georgia and southern Florida, also sight reports from other midwestern and eastern states, and from Guatemala (Dueñas).

Dendroica townsendi (Townsend). TOWNSEND'S WARBLER. [668.]

> *Sylvia Townsendi* (Nuttall MS) J. K. Townsend, 1837, J. Acad. Nat. Sci. Philadelphia, 7, p. 191. (forests of the Columbia River = Fort Vancouver, Washington.)

Habitat.—Tall coniferous and mixed coniferous-deciduous forest, in migration and winter also humid forest, pine-oak association, open woodland, second growth and scrub, primarily in montane situations.

Distribution.—*Breeds* from east-central Alaska, southern Yukon, northern British Columbia, southwestern Alberta and southwestern Saskatchewan south to south-coastal and southeastern Alaska, northwestern Washington, and inland to central and southeastern Washington, central and northeastern Oregon, northern Idaho, northwestern and south-central Montana, and northwestern Wyoming.

Winters in central and (rarely) southern California, and from northern Mexico (Sonora east to Nuevo León) south through the highlands of Mexico and Central America (except Belize) to Costa Rica.

Migrates primarily through the western United States east to the Rockies and western Texas, rarely through the Mexican lowlands.

Casual or accidental in the western Aleutians (Shemya), northern Alaska (Point Barrow), the Revillagigedo Islands (Socorro), Great Plains region (central Alberta and Minnesota south to Nebraska, Kansas and Illinois), the northeastern region (from New York, New Hampshire and Nova Scotia south to Pennsylvania, New Jersey and Massachusetts, also sight reports from southern Ontario and North Carolina), the Gulf states from eastern Texas east to Mississippi (sight reports from Florida), and western Panama (Chiriquí).

Notes.—*D. townsendi, D. occidentalis, D. virens* and *D. chrysoparia* appear to constitute a superspecies.

Dendroica occidentalis (Townsend). HERMIT WARBLER. [669.]

Sylvia occidentalis J. K. Townsend, 1837, J. Acad. Nat. Sci. Philadelphia, 7, p. 190. (forests of the Columbia River = Fort Vancouver, Washington.)

Habitat.—Coniferous forest, in migration in a variety of forest, woodland and scrub habitats, in winter primarily in montane forest and pine-oak association.

Distribution.—*Breeds* from southwestern Washington south through the coast ranges and Sierra Nevada to southern California (to Santa Cruz, Los Angeles and San Bernardino counties) and west-central Nevada.

Winters locally in coastal California (Point Reyes southward), and from Sinaloa and Durango south through the highlands of Mexico and Central America (except Belize) to north-central Nicaragua.

Migrates through the southwestern states (California and southern Arizona east to southern New Mexico and, rarely, western Texas), Baja California and most of Mexico (except the Yucatan Peninsula).

Casual along the Gulf coast from southeastern Texas to southwestern Louisiana. Accidental in Kansas (Finney County), Minnesota (Cambridge), Missouri (Maryville) and Nova Scotia, also sight reports for Colorado, Massachusetts, Connecticut, Costa Rica and western Panama (Chiriquí).

Notes.—See comments under *D. townsendi*.

Dendroica virens (Gmelin). BLACK-THROATED GREEN WARBLER. [667.]

Motacilla virens Gmelin, 1789, Syst. Nat., 1 (2), p. 985. Based on "The Black-throated Green Fly-catcher" Edwards, Glean. Nat. Hist., 2, p. 190, pl. 300. (in Pensilvania = Philadelphia.)

Habitat.—Open coniferous (primarily balsam fir) or mixed deciduous-coniferous woodland, forest edge and second growth, in migration and winter in a variety of open forest (lowland or highland), woodland, second growth, scrub and thickets, but in Middle America in winter confined mostly to montane regions.

Distribution.—*Breeds* from east-central British Columbia (probably), northern Alberta, north-central Saskatchewan, central Manitoba, central Ontario, southern Quebec, southern Labrador and Newfoundland south to central Alberta, central Saskatchewan, southern Manitoba, northern and east-central Minnesota, central Wisconsin, southern Michigan, south-central and eastern Ohio, eastern Kentucky, eastern Tennessee, central Alabama, northern Georgia, western South Carolina, western North Carolina, western Virginia, western Maryland, eastern Pennsylvania, central New Jersey and southern New York; also in the coastal plains from southeastern Virginia to eastern South Carolina.

Winters from Nuevo León, southern and southeastern Texas, southern Florida and the Bahama Islands south through eastern and southern Mexico (west to San Luis Potosí, Hidalgo, Morelos, Puebla and Oaxaca), Central America, Cuba, the Isle of Pines and Jamaica (casually east to the Virgin Islands) to central Panama (east to the Canal Zone and eastern Panamá province).

Migrates primarily through North America east of the Rockies and through Middle America (including both lowlands from Oaxaca southward), rarely to

California, Arizona and New Mexico, casually elsewhere in western North America north to Washington, southern Alberta and southern Saskatchewan.

Casual or accidental in southeastern Alaska (Chichagof Island), the Revillagigedo Islands (Socorro), Bermuda, the Lesser Antilles (Barbuda, Guadeloupe, Dominica, Barbados), Colombia, Venezuela, Greenland and Europe.

Notes.—See comments under *D. townsendi.*

Dendroica chrysoparia Sclater and Salvin. GOLDEN-CHEEKED WARBLER. [666.]

Dendrœca chrysoparia Sclater and Salvin, 1860, Proc. Zool. Soc. London, p. 298. (In reip. Guatemalensis provincia Veræ Pacis, inter montes = Vera Paz, Guatemala.)

Habitat.—Oak-cedar association, in migration in a variety of open woodland, scrub and thicket habitats, in winter known only from montane pine-oak association.

Distribution.—*Breeds* in central Texas from Dallas County south to the Edwards Plateau region (south to Medina and Bexar counties, and west to Real and Kerr counties).

Winters in the highlands of Guatemala, Honduras and north-central Nicaragua.

In migration rarely recorded in Mexico (reported Coahuila, Nuevo León, Tamaulipas and Chiapas; a record from Puebla is questionable, one from Sinaloa is erroneous).

Accidental in California (Farallon Islands) and Florida (Pinellas County), also a sight report from eastern Texas.

Notes.—See comments under *D. townsendi.*

Dendroica fusca (Müller). BLACKBURNIAN WARBLER. [662.]

Motacilla fusca P. L. S. Müller, 1776, Natursyst., Suppl., p. 175. (Guyana = French Guiana.)

Habitat.—Coniferous (primarily balsam fir) and mixed coniferous-deciduous forest, open woodland and second growth, in migration and winter in a variety of forest, woodland, scrub and thicket habitats.

Distribution.—*Breeds* from central Alberta (probably), central Saskatchewan, central Manitoba, central Ontario, southern Quebec, New Brunswick, Prince Edward Island and Nova Scotia south to southern Manitoba, central Minnesota, central Wisconsin, central Michigan, southern Ontario, northeastern Ohio, Pennsylvania, in the Appalachians through West Virginia, western Maryland, eastern Kentucky, western Virginia, eastern Tennessee and western North Carolina to north-central Georgia and northwestern South Carolina, and to southeastern New York and Massachusetts. Recorded in summer (and possibly breeding) in north-central Colorado, northern Ontario and central Quebec.

Winters from Costa Rica, Panama, Colombia and northern Venezuela south through Ecuador to central Peru and Bolivia.

Migrates regularly through the eastern United States (west to the Plains states and eastern Texas), Bahama Islands, Greater Antilles (except Jamaica, but including the Cayman Islands), eastern Mexico, both slopes of Middle America from Oaxaca and Veracruz southward (more frequently on the Caribbean slope), islands in the western Caribbean Sea (Swan, Providencia and San Andrés), and the Netherlands Antilles, also rarely to California (primarily in coastal areas).

Casual in east-central British Columbia, Washington, Montana, Colorado, Arizona, New Mexico, Bermuda, the Lesser Antilles (Barbados, Grenada) and Tobago.

Dendroica dominica (Linnaeus). YELLOW-THROATED WARBLER. [663.]

> *Motacilla dominica* Linnaeus, 1766, Syst. Nat., ed. 12, 1, p. 334. Based mainly on "Le Figuier cendré de S. Domingue" Brisson, Ornithologie, 3, p. 520, pl. 27, fig. 3. (in Jamaica, Dominica = Hispaniola.)

Habitat.—Pine forest, sycamore-baldcypress swamp and riparian woodland, in migration and winter in a variety of woodland, scrub, brush and thicket situations but most frequently in pine woodland if such habitat is available.

Distribution.—*Breeds* from central Oklahoma, southeastern Kansas, central Missouri, extreme southeastern Iowa, central Illinois, central Indiana, central Ohio, central Pennsylvania and central New Jersey south to south-central and eastern Texas (west to San Antonio region), the Gulf coast, central Florida and the northern Bahama Islands (Grand Bahama, Abaco); formerly bred north to northern Missouri, northern Illinois, southern Michigan and northern Ohio.

Winters from southeastern Texas, the Gulf coast and South Carolina (casually farther north) south through Middle America (primarily the Gulf-Caribbean slope and, in northern Central America, in the interior highlands), the Greater Antilles (east to the Virgin Islands) and Bahama Islands to Costa Rica (casually to Panama).

In migration occurs rarely west to Colorado and New Mexico, casually to southern Arizona and California.

Casual or accidental north to Montana, Minnesota, Wisconsin, southern Ontario, southern Quebec, New York, New Brunswick, Nova Scotia and Newfoundland, and to the Lesser Antilles (Montserrat, Guadeloupe), also sight reports for Saskatchewan, Nevada and Colombia.

Notes.—*D. dominica, D. graciae* and *D. adelaidae* constitute a superspecies; *D. pityophila* also appears to be most closely related to *D. graciae* and to belong to this group, but it is sympatric with *D. dominica* in the Bahamas.

Dendroica graciae Baird. GRACE'S WARBLER. [664.]

> *Dendroica graciæ* (Coues MS) Baird, 1865, Rev. Am. Birds, 1, p. 210. (Fort Whipple, near Prescott, Arizona.)

Habitat.—Pine forest, pine-oak association and pine savanna (Tropical to Temperate zones).

Distribution.—*Breeds* from southern Nevada, southern Utah, southwestern Colorado, northern New Mexico and western Texas (Guadalupe and Davis mountains) south through the mountains of western Mexico (east to western Chihuahua, Durango and western Zacatecas), Guatemala, El Salvador and Honduras to north-central Nicaragua; also in the lowland pine savanna of Belize, eastern Honduras and northeastern Nicaragua.

Winters from Sonora and Chihuahua south through the breeding range (occurring east at least to Morelos), being generally resident from central Mexico southward.

Casual in southern California (Santa Barbara County in winter, Clark Mountain and the San Bernardino Mountains in summer).

Notes.—See comments under *D. dominica.*

Dendroica adelaidae Baird. ADELAIDE'S WARBLER.

Dendroica adelaidæ Baird, 1865, Rev. Am. Birds, 1, p. 212. (Puerto Rico.)

Habitat.—Lowland thickets, on St. Lucia also in montane forest.

Distribution.—*Resident* on Puerto Rico (including Vieques Island), and in the Lesser Antilles on Barbuda and St. Lucia.

Notes.—See comments under *D. dominica.*

Dendroica pityophila (Gundlach). OLIVE-CAPPED WARBLER.

Sylvicola pityophila Gundlach, 1858, Ann. Lyc. Nat. Hist. N.Y., 6, p. 160. (Cuba.)

Habitat.—Pine barrens.

Distribution.—*Resident* in the northern Bahama Islands (Grand Bahama and Abaco) and Cuba (Pinar del Río and Oreinte provinces).

Dendroica pinus (Wilson). PINE WARBLER. [671.]

Sylvia pinus Wilson, 1811, Am. Ornithol., 3, p. 25, pl. 19, fig. 4. (Southern States = Georgia.)

Habitat.—Pine forest and pine woodland, in migration and winter also uncommonly in deciduous forest, woodland, scrub and thickets.

Distribution.—*Breeds* from southern Manitoba, western Ontario, northeastern Minnesota, northern Wisconsin, northern Michigan, east-central Ontario, southwestern Quebec and central Maine south to eastern Texas (west to Bastrop and Matagorda counties), the Gulf coast, southern Florida (to Everglades National Park) and the northern Bahama Islands (Grand Bahama, Abaco, Andros and New Providence), and west to southwestern Wisconsin, northeastern Illinois, Missouri and southeastern Oklahoma; also on Hispaniola.

Winters in the southeastern United States (casually north to the southern Great Lakes region, New York and New England) south to southern Texas, extreme northern Tamaulipas (Matamoras), the Gulf coast, southern Florida, and through the breeding range in the Bahamas and on Hispaniola.

Casual north to New Brunswick, Prince Edward Island and Nova Scotia, west to southeastern Alberta, southern Saskatchewan, Montana, Wyoming, Colorado, western Kansas and central Texas, and to California (primarily coastal region), the Florida Keys, Cay Sal (in the southern Bahamas) and Bermuda. Accidental in Greenland, also sight reports from New Mexico and Costa Rica.

Dendroica kirtlandii (Baird). KIRTLAND'S WARBLER. [670.]

Sylvicola kirtlandii Baird, 1852, Ann. Lyc. Nat. Hist. N.Y., 5, p. 217, pl. 6. (near Cleveland, Ohio.)

Habitat.—Scrubby jack-pine, in winter in low scrub, thickets, and (rarely) deciduous woodland.

Distribution.—*Breeds* in central Michigan from Otsego, extreme southwestern

Presque Isle and Alpena counties south to Kalkaska, northwestern Clare, Roscommon, Ogemaw and Iosco counties. Recorded in summer (and possibly breeding) in west-central Wisconsin (Jackson County) and southern Ontario (Petawawa).
Winters throughout the Bahamas.

In migration recorded from Illinois (Chicago), western Ohio (Cincinnati, Tiffin and Magee Marsh), western Pennsylvania (Westmoreland County) and southwestern Quebec (Kazabazua), also sight records from Minnesota, Kentucky, West Virginia, Alabama, Georgia, Florida and Veracruz; recorded (prior to 1901) from northern Michigan, Missouri, Virginia and southern Florida.

Dendroica discolor (Vieillot). PRAIRIE WARBLER. [673.]

Sylvia discolor Vieillot, 1808, Hist. Nat. Ois. Am. Sept., 2 (1807), p. 37, pl. 98. (États-Unis et les grandes Îles Antilles = New York.)

Habitat.—Brushy second growth, dry scrub, low pine-juniper and mangroves, in migration and winter also in a variety of woodland, second growth, brush and thicket situations.

Distribution.—*Breeds* from eastern Nebraska, eastern Kansas, central Missouri, northern Illinois, central Wisconsin, northern Michigan, southern Ontario, southern Pennsylvania, southeastern New York, Massachusetts and southern New Hampshire south to eastern Oklahoma, extreme eastern Texas, the Gulf coast (except southern Mississippi, southwestern Alabama) and southern Florida (except northwestern region north and west of Cedar Keys and Gainesville).

Winters from central Florida (casually from southern Texas, the Gulf coast and Virginia) and the Bahama Islands south throughout the West Indies to islands off the coast of northern Middle America (off Quintana Roo, Belize and Honduras), also a sight report from the pine savanna of Caribbean Nicaragua.

In migration occurs casually west to the Plains states and central Texas, and in California (primarily coastal areas).

Casual or accidental north to southern Quebec and New Brunswick, and to Colorado, Oaxaca (Pacific slope), El Salvador and Bermuda, also sight reports for southern Arizona, New Mexico, South Dakota, Nova Scotia, Guatemala (off the Pacific coast), Costa Rica, Panama and Trinidad.

Notes.—*D. discolor* and *D. vitellina* are closely related and considered conspecific by some authors; they constitute a superspecies.

Dendroica vitellina Cory. VITELLINE WARBLER.

Dendroica vitellina Cory, 1886, Auk, 3, p. 497. (Island of Grand Cayman, West Indies.)

Habitat.—Scrubby thickets.

Distribution.—*Resident* in the Cayman (including Grand Cayman, Little Cayman and Cayman Brac) and Swan (especially Little Swan) islands, in the Caribbean Sea.

Notes.—See comments under *D. discolor.*

Dendroica palmarum (Gmelin). PALM WARBLER. [672.]

Motacilla palmarum Gmelin, 1789, Syst. Nat., 1 (2), p. 951. Based on the "Bimbelé ou fausse Linotte" Buffon, Hist. Nat. Ois., 5, p. 330. (in insula S. Dominici = Hispaniola.)

Habitat.—Bogs, open boreal coniferous forest, and partly open situations with scattered trees and heavy undergrowth, usually near water, in migration and winter in a variety of woodland, second growth and thicket habitats, on the ground in savanna and open fields, and in mangroves.

Distribution.—*Breeds* from west-central and southern Mackenzie, northern Alberta, northern Saskatchewan, northern Manitoba, northern Ontario, south-central Quebec, southern Labrador and Newfoundland south to northeastern British Columbia, central Alberta, central Saskatchewan, southern Manitoba, northeastern Minnesota, northern Wisconsin, central Michigan, southern Ontario, southern Quebec, New Brunswick, Maine and Nova Scotia.

Winters from north-central Texas, the Gulf coast and South Carolina (casually north to Missouri, the Ohio Valley and New England) south to southern Texas, southern Florida, the Bahama Islands, Greater Antilles (east to the Virgin Islands), islands in the western Caribbean Sea, and the Yucatan Peninsula (including islands offshore and off Belize); also, apparently regularly, in coastal California, the Pacific lowlands of Oaxaca, and the lowland pine savanna of eastern Honduras and northeastern Nicaragua.

Migrates primarily through the central United States (from the Plains states eastward to the Atlantic seaboard, but uncommon in New England), regularly through coastal California, and casually elsewhere in western North America (from British Columbia, Montana and Wyoming south to northern Baja California, southern Arizona and New Mexico).

Casual in Panama (Canal Zone and eastern Panamá province), Bermuda and the Netherlands Antilles, also sight reports for Alaska and Costa Rica.

Dendroica castanea (Wilson). BAY-BREASTED WARBLER. [660.]

Sylvia castanea Wilson, 1810, Am. Ornithol., 2, p. 97, pl. 14, fig. 4. (Pennsylvania.)

Habitat.—Boreal coniferous forest (especially balsam fir), occasionally adjoining second growth or deciduous scrub, in migration and winter in a variety of forest, woodland, scrub and thicket habitats.

Distribution.—*Breeds* from southwestern Mackenzie, northern Alberta, north-central Saskatchewan, central Manitoba, central Ontario, central Quebec, New Brunswick, Prince Edward Island, Nova Scotia and Newfoundland (probably) south to northeastern British Columbia, central Alberta, south-central Saskatchewan, southern Manitoba, northeastern Minnesota, northern Wisconsin, northern Michigan (probably), southern Ontario, southern Quebec, northeastern New York, central Vermont, New Hampshire and southern Maine.

Winters from Panama (Caribbean slope throughout, Pacific slope from eastern Veraguas eastward) east through Colombia to northwestern Venezuela (also to Curaçao, Tortuga Island and Trinidad), recorded casually north to the southern United States.

Migrates primarily through the eastern United States (west to the eastern Plains states, and eastern and southern Texas, but rare in peninsular Florida), Cuba, Jamaica, islands in the western Caribbean Sea (Providencia, San Andrés), and Middle America (from the Yucatan Peninsula south to Panama), rarely (mostly along the coast) in western North America from Oregon and Idaho south to southern California, southern Arizona and New Mexico.

Casual on Clipperton and the Revillagigedo islands, in eastern Mexico (recorded

Tamaulipas and Tabasco), on Bermuda, and in the eastern Greater Antilles (recorded Hispaniola, Mona Island, Puerto Rico, and St. Croix in the Virgin Islands), Lesser Antilles (St. Vincent, Barbados) and Greenland, also sight reports for central Alaska and Ecuador.

Dendroica striata (Forster). BLACKPOLL WARBLER. [661.]

Muscicapa striata J. R. Forster, 1772, Philos. Trans. R. Soc. London, 62, pp. 406, 428. (Severn River = Fort Severn, west coast of Hudson Bay.)

Habitat.—Boreal coniferous forest (primarily spruce) and woodland, mixed coniferous-deciduous second growth, tall shrubs, and alder thickets, in migration and winter in a variety of forest, woodland, scrub and brushy habitats.

Distribution.—*Breeds* from western and north-central Alaska, central Yukon, northern Mackenzie, southern Keewatin, northern Manitoba, northern Ontario, northern Quebec, northern Labrador and Newfoundland south to southern Alaska (west to the Alaska Peninsula), south-central British Columbia, southwestern and central Alberta, north-central Saskatchewan, central Manitoba, north-central Ontario, southern Quebec, eastern New York, northwestern Massachusetts, central New Hampshire, east-central Maine and Nova Scotia.

Winters from Colombia, Venezuela and the Guianas south, mostly east of the Andes, to eastern Peru, northern Argentina and southern Brazil.

Migrates primarily in spring through the West Indies, Bahama Islands and eastern North America (west to central and southern Texas, and the eastern Plains states); and in fall mostly across northeastern North America to New England and the Maritime Provinces, thence at sea over Bermuda and the Lesser Antilles (north, at least irregularly, to Puerto Rico and the Virgin Islands) to northern South America (including islands north of Venezuela), also regularly in California.

Casual elsewhere in western North America from southwestern British Columbia, Utah and New Mexico south to northern Baja California, southern Arizona and Chihuahua, and in Costa Rica. Accidental on Cornwallis Island, and in Oaxaca (Tehuantepec City), Panama (Bocas del Toro), Chile, the Galapagos Islands, Greenland and the British Isles.

Notes.—*Dendroica breviunguis,* based on *Alauda* (*Anthus*) *breviunguis* Spix, 1824, sometimes used for this species, is not valid since *Muscicapa striata* Forster is unaffected by *Motacilla striata* Pallas, 1764, the latter species now currently placed in the Old World genus *Muscicapa.*

Dendroica cerulea (Wilson). CERULEAN WARBLER. [658.]

Sylvia cerulea Wilson, 1810, Am. Ornithol., 2, p. 141, pl. 17, fig. 5. (Pennsylvania = Philadelphia.)

Habitat.—Mature deciduous forest, in migration and winter in a variety of forest, woodland, second growth and scrub habitats.

Distribution.—*Breeds* from southeastern Nebraska, northern Iowa, central and southeastern Minnesota, southern Wisconsin, southern Michigan, southern Ontario, southwestern Quebec, western and southeastern New York, northwestern Vermont and central Connecticut south to eastern Oklahoma, north-central Texas (to Dallas area), southern Arkansas, southeastern Louisiana (probably), central Mississippi, central Alabama and central Georgia, and east to northern New Jersey, northern Delaware, eastern Maryland, central Virginia and central North Carolina.

Winters from Colombia and Venezuela south, mostly east of the Andes, to eastern Peru and northern Bolivia.

Migrates through the southeastern United States (west to central and southern Texas, rare in Florida), Cuba, the Isle of Pines, Jamaica and, uncommonly, along the Caribbean slope and offshore islands from the Yucatan Peninsula south to Panama (also the Pearl Islands, off Pacific Panama, but not recorded Nicaragua), casually through the Bahama Islands (recorded Cay Lobos, New Providence).

Casual north to southwestern Manitoba, North Dakota, northern Minnesota, New Hampshire and Maine, in western North America to California, northern Baja California, southern Nevada, Colorado and New Mexico, and in Veracruz.

Dendroica plumbea Lawrence. PLUMBEOUS WARBLER.

> *Dendrœca plumbea* Lawrence, 1878, Ann. N.Y. Acad. Sci., 1 (1877), p. 47. (Dominica.)

Habitat.—Forest and lowland arid scrub.
Distribution.—*Resident* in the Lesser Antilles (Dominica, Marie Galante, Guadeloupe and Terre-de-Haut, possibly only a casual vagrant to the latter).
Notes.—*D. plumbea, D. pharetra* and *D. angelae* appear to constitute a super-species.

Dendroica pharetra (Gosse). ARROW-HEADED WARBLER.

> *Sylvicola pharetra* Gosse, 1847, Birds Jamaica, p. 163. (Bognie woods, on the top of Bluefields Peak, Jamaica.)

Habitat.—Montane forest and humid ravines, mostly in forest undergrowth.
Distribution.—*Resident* on Jamaica.
Notes.—See comments under *D. plumbea.*

Dendroica angelae Kepler and Parkes. ELFIN WOODS WARBLER.

> *Dendroica angelae* Kepler and Parkes, 1972, Auk, 89, p. 3. (ridge between the Río Sabana and Río Espíritu Santo valleys, approximately 2.5 km west of Highway 191 on the El Toro trail, Sierra de Luquillo, Puerto Rico [elevation 780 m].)

Habitat.—Humid montane elfin woodland and dense forest at lower elevations.
Distribution.—*Resident* on Puerto Rico (Sierra de Luquillo, Maricao).
Notes.—See comments under *D. plumbea.*

Genus CATHAROPEZA Sclater

> *Catharopeza* Sclater, 1880, Ibis, pp. 40, 73, 74. Type, by original designation, *Leucopeza bishopi* Lawrence.

Notes.—By some authors merged in *Dendroica.*

Catharopeza bishopi (Lawrence). WHISTLING WARBLER.

> *Leucopeza bishopi* Lawrence, 1878, Ann. N.Y. Acad. Sci., 1 (1877), p. 151. (St. Vincent.)

Habitat.—Montane forest, primarily in undergrowth.
Distribution.—*Resident* on St. Vincent, in the Lesser Antilles.

Genus MNIOTILTA Vieillot

Mniotilta Vieillot, 1816, Analyse, p. 45. Type, by monotypy, "Figuier varié" Buffon = *Motacilla varia* Linnaeus.

Mniotilta varia (Linnaeus). BLACK-AND-WHITE WARBLER. [636.]

Motacilla varia Linnaeus, 1766, Syst. Nat., ed. 12, 1, p. 333. Based on the "Small Black and White Creeper" Sloane, Voy. Jamaica, 2, p. 309, pl. 265, fig. 1, and "Le Figuier varié de S. Domingue" Brisson, Ornithologie, 3, p. 529, pl. 27, fig. 5. (in Jamaica, Dominica = Hispaniola.)

Habitat.—Deciduous and mixed deciduous-coniferous forest and woodland, in migration and winter in a variety of forest, woodland, second growth and scrub situations.

Distribution.—*Breeds* from west-central and southwestern Mackenzie, northern Alberta, central Saskatchewan, central Manitoba, north-central Ontario, southern Quebec and Newfoundland south (at least locally) to northeastern British Columbia, central Alberta, southern Saskatchewan, eastern Montana, southwestern South Dakota, central Nebraska, central Kansas, south-central and eastern Texas, northern and southeastern Louisiana, central Mississippi, central Alabama, central Georgia, central South Carolina and southeastern North Carolina. Recorded in summer in California and southern Arizona.

Winters from southern and coastal northern California (rarely), southern Arizona (rarely), Coahuila, Nuevo León, southern Texas, northwestern and north-central Florida and the Bahama Islands (casually farther north) south through Middle America and the West Indies (less commonly in the Lesser Antilles) to Colombia, Venezuela (also the Netherlands Antilles and Trinidad) and eastern Ecuador.

Migrates most commonly east of the Rockies, regularly (but rarely) through Bermuda and in western North America from southwestern British Columbia, Idaho, and Montana southward.

Casual or accidental in northern Alaska (Colville River delta) and the British Isles.

Genus SETOPHAGA Swainson

Setophaga Swainson, 1827, Philos. Mag., new ser., 1, p. 368. Type, by subsequent designation (Swainson, 1827), *Motacilla ruticilla* Linnaeus.

Setophaga ruticilla (Linnaeus). AMERICAN REDSTART. [687.]

Motacilla Ruticilla Linnaeus, 1758, Syst. Nat., ed. 10, 1, p. 186. Based mostly on "The Red-start" Catesby, Nat. Hist. Carolina, 1, p. 67, pl. 67, and "The Small American Redstart" Edwards, Nat. Hist. Birds, 1, p. 80, pl. 80. (in America = Virginia.)

Habitat.—Open deciduous and mixed deciduous-coniferous woodland, second growth and tall shrubbery, in migration and winter in a variety of forest, woodland, scrub and thicket habitats.

Distribution.—*Breeds* from southeastern Alaska, southern Yukon, west-central and southern Mackenzie, north-central Saskatchewan, north-central Manitoba, northern Ontario, central Quebec, southern Labrador and Newfoundland south, at least locally (or formerly), to south-central British Columbia, central Washington, eastern Oregon, northwestern California (Humboldt County), Idaho, northern Utah, east-central Arizona, New Mexico (probably), eastern Oklahoma, eastern Texas, northern and southeastern Louisiana, central Mississippi, southern Alabama, northwestern Florida, southern Georgia, central South Carolina, central North Carolina and southern Virginia; absent as a breeding bird through most of the Great Plains regions.

Winters from southern Baja California, Sinaloa, Veracruz, central Florida and the Bahama Islands (rarely from southern California, southern Texas and the Gulf coast, casually farther north) south through Middle America and the West Indies, and in South America from Colombia, Venezuela (also islands from the Netherlands Antilles east to Tobago and Trinidad) and the Guianas south, west of the Andes to northwestern Ecuador and east of the Andes to eastern Ecuador and northwestern Brazil.

Migrates through North America (more commonly in the eastern portion) between the breeding and wintering ranges.

Casual north to northern and south-coastal Alaska, northern Mackenzie, Banks Island and northern Quebec, in the Revillagigedo Islands (San Benedicto, sight report), on Bermuda, at sea near the Azores, and in the British Isles.

Genus **PROTONOTARIA** Baird

Protonotaria Baird, 1858, *in* Baird, Cassin and Lawrence, Rep. Explor. Surv. R. R. Pac., 9, pp. xix, xxxi, 235, 239. Type, by monotypy, *Motacilla protonotarius* Gmelin = *Motacilla citrea* Boddaert.

Protonotaria citrea (Boddaert). PROTHONOTARY WARBLER. [637.]

Motacilla citrea Boddaert, 1783, Table Planches Enlum., p. 44. Based on "Figuier à ventre et tête jaunes de la Louisiane" Daubenton, Planches Enlum., pl. 704, fig. 2. (Louisiana.)

Habitat.—Swamps and wet lowland forest, in migration and winter also dry woodland, scrub, thickets and mangroves.

Distribution.—*Breeds* from east-central and southeastern Minnesota, south-central Wisconsin, southern Michigan, southern Ontario, central New York and northern New Jersey south to south-central and eastern Texas (west to Medina County), the Gulf coast and central (possibly also southern) Florida, and west to eastern Oklahoma, eastern Kansas and central Oklahoma.

Winters from the Yucatan Peninsula south on the Caribbean slope of Middle America (including nearby islands) to Nicaragua, on both slopes of Costa Rica and Panama, and in South America from Colombia east to northern Venezuela (also islands from the Netherlands Antilles east to Tobago and Trinidad), rarely in the Virgin Islands, and casually east to Surinam and north in the Antilles.

Migrates through the southeastern United States (west to central and southern Texas), the West Indies, and islands in the western Caribbean Sea, casually on Bermuda.

Casual north to southern Quebec, Maine and Nova Scotia, in western North America from southern Washington, Oregon, Nevada and Colorado south to southern California, southern Arizona and southern New Mexico, and in Jalisco and Hispaniola, also a sight report for southern Saskatchewan.

Genus HELMITHEROS Rafinesque

Helmitheros Rafinesque, 1819, J. Phys. Chim. Hist. Nat., 88, p. 418. Type, by original designation, *Helmitheros migratorius* Rafinesque = *Motacilla vermivora* Gmelin.

Notes.—See comments under *Limnothlypis.*

Helmitheros vermivorus (Gmelin). WORM-EATING WARBLER. [639.]

Motacilla vermivora Gmelin, 1789, Syst. Nat., 1 (2), p. 951. Based mainly on "The Worm-eater" Edwards, Glean. Nat. Hist., 2, p. 200, pl. 305. (in Pensilvania = Philadelphia.)

Habitat.—Undergrowth of deciduous forest, and damp, bushy ravines, in migration and winter also in a variety of forest, woodland, scrub and thicket situations.

Distribution.—*Breeds* from northeastern Kansas, southeastern Nebraska, northern Missouri, southeastern Iowa (rarely), central (rarely northern) Illinois, central Indiana, southern and east-central Ohio, central Pennsylvania, central and southeastern New York, western Massachusetts and southern Connecticut south to southeastern Oklahoma, northeastern Texas, south-central Louisiana, central and northwestern Arkansas, western Tennessee, south-central Alabama, extreme northwestern Florida, northern Georgia, northwestern South Carolina and northeastern North Carolina. Recorded in summer (and possibly breeding) north to Wisconsin, southern Michigan, southern Ontario, southern Quebec and Maine.

Winters from Veracruz, Chiapas and the Yucatan Peninsula south through Middle America (primarily on the Caribbean slope north of central Costa Rica) to central Panama (east to the Canal Zone and eastern Panamá province), and in the Bahama Islands and Greater Antilles (east to the Virgin Islands).

Migrates through the southeastern United States (west to central and southern Texas), eastern Mexico (mostly Gulf slope), islands in the western Caribbean Sea (Swan, Providencia), and casually in California and Nevada.

Casual in southern Saskatchewan, North Dakota, eastern South Dakota, Minnesota and Bermuda.

Notes.—*Vermivora americ* Linnaeus, 1776 (both genus and species), has been officially suppressed (Int. Comm. Zool. Nomencl., 1956, Opin. Decl. Rend., 13, pp. 205–232).

Genus LIMNOTHLYPIS Stone

Limnothlypis Stone, 1914, Science, new ser., 40, p. 26. Type, by original designation, *Sylvia swainsonii* Audubon.

Notes.—Some authors merge this genus in *Helmitheros.*

Limnothlypis swainsonii (Audubon). SWAINSON'S WARBLER. [638.]

Sylvia Swainsonii Audubon, 1834, Birds Am. (folio), 2, pl. 198 (1834, Ornithol. Biogr., 2, p. 563). (Edisto River, near Charleston in South Carolina.)

Habitat.—Undergrowth of moist lowland forest and woodland, canebrakes and swamps, in migration and winter also in lowland scrub, thickets and mangroves.

Distribution.—*Breeds* locally from northeastern Oklahoma, southern Missouri, southern Illionis, southwestern Indiana, southwestern and eastern Kentucky, southern Ohio, western West Virginia, western and southern Virginia, and southern Delaware south to east-central Texas (west to Brazos County, possibly to Bastrop County), the Gulf coast (from southeastern Louisiana eastward) and northern Florida.

Winters in the northern Bahama Islands (Grand Bahama, New Providence, Cay Lobos), Cuba, the Cayman Islands, Jamaica, the Yucatan Peninsula and Belize.

Migrates through the southeastern United States (west to southern Texas), eastern Mexico (recorded Tamaulipas and Veracruz), and the Swan Islands.

Casual north to eastern Colorado, southern Nebraska, eastern Kansas, northern Illinois, eastern Ohio, Pennsylvania and southern New York (including Long Island), also sight reports for Puerto Rico. Accidental in east-central Arizona (Eagar) and Nova Scotia (Seal Island).

Genus **SEIURUS** Swainson

Seiurus Swainson, 1827, Philos. Mag., new ser., 1, p. 369. Type, by subsequent designation (Swainson, 1827), *Motacilla aurocapilla* Linnaeus.

Seiurus aurocapillus (Linnaeus). OVENBIRD. [674.]

Motacilla aurocapilla Linnaeus, 1766, Syst. Nat., ed. 12, 1, p. 334. Based on "The Golden-crowned Thrush" Edwards, Glean. Nat. Hist., 5, p. 91, pl. 252. (in Pensylvania, error = at sea, apparently off Haiti.)

Habitat.—Deciduous forest, rarely humid deciduous-coniferous woodland, in migration and winter in a variety of forest, woodland, second growth and scrubby habitats.

Distribution.—*Breeds* from northeastern British Columbia, southern Mackenzie, northern Alberta, central Saskatchewan, central (probably also northern) Manitoba, central Ontario, central Quebec (including Anticosti and Magdalen islands) and Newfoundland south to southern Alberta, southwestern Saskatchewan, southern Montana, central and southeastern Colorado, Nebraska, eastern Kansas, southeastern Oklahoma, northern Arkansas, southwestern Tennessee, northern Alabama, northern Georgia, western South Carolina, and central and northeastern North Carolina.

Winters from Sinaloa, southern Texas, the Gulf coast and South Carolina (casually north to southern California, the Great Lakes region and New England) south through Middle America (both slopes, more commonly on the Gulf-Caribbean) and the West Indies to Panama (casual east of the Canal Zone and eastern Panamá province) and northern Venezuela (also the Netherlands Antilles, Tobago and Trinidad), casually in Colombia.

Migrates primarily through eastern North America from the Rockies eastward, rarely to California, casual elsewhere in western North America from southwestern British Columbia, Washington, Idaho and Montana south to Baja California, northwestern Mexico and western Texas.

Casual or accidental in Alaska (Prudhoe Bay), on Guadalupe Island (off Baja California), and in Bermuda, Greenland and the British Isles.

Seiurus noveboracensis (Gmelin). NORTHERN WATERTHRUSH. [675.]

Motacilla noveboracensis Gmelin, 1789, Syst. Nat., 1 (2), p. 958. Based on "The New York Warbler" Latham, Gen. Synop. Birds, 2 (2), p. 436. (in Louisiana, et Noveboraci sepibus = New York.)

Habitat.—Thickets near water, swamps and bogs, in migration and winter in forest, woodland, scrub, brushy areas and mangroves, generally near water.

Distribution.—*Breeds* from western and north-central Alaska, central Yukon, northwestern and southern Mackenzie, northern Saskatchewan, northern Manitoba, northern Ontario, northern Quebec, central Labrador and Newfoundland south to southern Alaska (west to the base of the Alaska Peninsula), central British Columbia, northwestern Washington, northern Idaho, western Montana, southwestern and central Alberta, southeastern Saskatchewan, southern Manitoba, northern North Dakota, northeastern Minnesota, northern Wisconsin, central Michigan, southern Ontario, northeastern Ohio, southeastern West Virginia, Pennsylvania, New York and Massachusetts; one breeding record from north-central North Carolina (Caswell County). Recorded in summer (and probably breeding) in eastern Oregon, Colorado and northern Nebraska.

Winters from southern California (rarely), southern Baja California, Sinaloa, San Luis Potosí, Tamaulipas, southern Florida, the Bahama Islands and Bermuda (casually north to British Columbia, the Gulf coast and Virginia) south through Middle America and the West Indies, and in northern South America from Colombia, Venezuela (also all islands from Netherlands Antilles east to Tobago and Trinidad) and the Guianas south, west of the Andes to northwestern Ecuador and east of the Andes to eastern Ecuador and northeastern Peru.

Migrates regularly through North America between the breeding and wintering ranges.

Casual in northern Alaska, Banks Island, Greenland, the British Isles, continental Europe and Siberia (Chukotski Peninsula).

Seiurus motacilla (Vieillot). LOUISIANA WATERTHRUSH. [676.]

Turdus motacilla Vieillot, 1808, Hist. Nat. Ois. Am. Sept., 2 (1807), p. 9, pl. 65. (Kentucky.)

Habitat.—Humid forest, woodland and ravines along streams, and in swamps, in migration and winter also in riparian woodland, scrub and thickets, generally in the vicinity of water.

Distribution.—*Breeds* from eastern Nebraska, north-central Iowa, east-central and southeastern Minnesota, central Wisconsin, southern Michigan, southern Ontario, central New York, central Vermont, central New Hampshire and southern Maine south to eastern Kansas, eastern Oklahoma, eastern Texas, central Louisiana, southern Mississippi, southern Alabama, northern Florida (Gainesville area), central and southwestern Georgia, central South Carolina, and central and northeastern North Carolina.

Winters from Sonora, Nuevo León, Tamaulipas, southern Florida, the Bahama Islands and Bermuda (casually north to southeastern Arizona and Maryland) south through Middle America (both slopes, although more commonly on the Gulf-Caribbean) and the West Indies (south to St. Vincent in the Lesser Antilles) to eastern Panama, northeastern Colombia and northern Venezuela (also Trinidad).

Migrates primarily through the southeastern United States (west to central and southern Texas) and northern Mexico.

Casual north to southern Quebec, Maine and Nova Scotia, and in California, Baja California, Colorado and New Mexico, also a sight (and song) report for North Dakota.

Genus **OPORORNIS** Baird

Oporornis Baird, 1858, *in* Baird, Cassin and Lawrence, Rep. Explor. Surv. R. R. Pac., 9, pp. xix, xxxii, 240, 246. Type, by original designation, *Sylvia agilis* Wilson.

Notes.—Some authors merge this genus in *Geothlypis.*

Oporornis formosus (Wilson). KENTUCKY WARBLER. [677.]

Sylvia formosa Wilson, 1811, Am. Ornithol., 3, p. 85, pl. 25, fig. 3. (Kentucky.)

Habitat.—Humid deciduous forest, dense second growth and swamps, in migration and winter also in open forest, woodland, scrub and thickets.

Distribution.—*Breeds* from southeastern Nebraska, central Iowa, southwestern Wisconsin, northeastern Illinois, central Indiana, north-central Ohio, southern Pennsylvania, northern New Jersey, southeastern New York and southwestern Connecticut south to south-central and eastern Texas (west to Kerrville), the Gulf coast (east to northwestern Florida), central Georgia and South Carolina, and west to eastern Kansas and central Oklahoma.

Winters from Nayarit (rarely), Oaxaca, Veracruz and the Yucatan Peninsula south through Middle America (primarily the Caribbean slope, rare and local on the Pacific slope north of central Costa Rica) to northern Colombia and northern Venezuela, casually in Puerto Rico and the Virgin Islands.

Migrates primarily through the southeastern United States (west to eastern New Mexico and western Texas), northeastern Mexico, the Greater Antilles (east to the Virgin Islands) and Bahama Islands.

Casual north to northern Iowa, Minnesota, central Wisconsin, northern Michigan, southern Ontario, central New York, northern New England and Nova Scotia, in western North America from California (especially the Farallon Islands) east through southern Arizona and northern Sonora to southern New Mexico, and in the Lesser Antilles (Guadeloupe), also sight reports for Saskatchewan, North Dakota, Nevada and southern Quebec.

Oporornis agilis (Wilson). CONNECTICUT WARBLER. [678.]

Sylvia agilis Wilson, 1812, Am. Ornithol., 5, p. 64, pl. 39, fig. 4. (Connecticut.)

Habitat.—Spruce and tamarack bogs, less frequently open poplar woodland, in migration and winter in a variety of forest, woodland, scrub and thicket habitats.

Distribution.—*Breeds* from east-central British Columbia east across central Alberta, central Saskatchewan, central Manitoba and north-central Ontario to west-central Quebec, and south to southern Manitoba, northern Minnesota, northern Wisconsin, central Michigan and south-central Ontario.

Winters from northeastern Colombia south to Amazonian and central Brazil.

Migrates through the Atlantic states (primarily in fall, rarely north to southern New England and Nova Scotia), the east-central United States west of the Appalachians and east of the Plains states (mostly in spring, casually west to eastern Texas), and in both seasons through the southeastern states, Bahama Islands, Netherlands Antilles and Venezuela.

Casual in California, southern Arizona, Kansas, Montana, western Panama (Bocas del Toro), the Greater Antilles (Hispaniola, and Mona Island off Puerto Rico), and the Lesser Antilles (St. Martin), also sight reports for islands off Belize and Caribbean Honduras.

Oporornis philadelphia (Wilson). MOURNING WARBLER. [679.]

Sylvia Philadelphia Wilson, 1810, Am. Ornithol., 2, p. 101, pl. 14, fig. 6. (within a few miles of Philadelphia, Pennsylvania.)

Habitat.—Shrubbery and bushes of open deciduous woodland and second growth, and margins of bogs and marshes, in migration and winter in thickets, weedy areas, scrub and woodland undergrowth, primarily in humid regions.

Distribution.—*Breeds* from northeastern and central Alberta, central Saskatchewan, central Manitoba, central Ontario, south-central and southeastern Quebec, and Newfoundland south to southern Manitoba, northeastern North Dakota, central Minnesota, central Wisconsin, northeastern Illinois (at least formerly), southern Michigan and northern Ohio, in the higher Appalachians to eastern West Virginia and northwestern Virginia, and to northeastern Pennsylvania, southeastern New York and central Massachusetts.

Winters from southern Nicaragua south through Costa Rica and Panama to Colombia (except southwestern portion), eastern Ecuador and southern Venezuela.

Migrates primarily through the Mississippi and Ohio valleys (west to the Plains states and central Texas, casually to Colorado, eastern New Mexico and western Texas), rarely the southeastern states (casually in Florida), and regularly through eastern Mexico (recorded also Pacific slope of Oaxaca) and northern Middle America (more frequently in highlands, rarely in Caribbean lowlands in spring).

Casual or accidental in California, southeastern Arizona, Hispaniola, Puerto Rico, Curaçao and Greenland, also sight reports from the Bahama Islands (New Providence) and Vieques Island (off Puerto Rico).

Notes.—*O. philadelphia* and *O. tolmiei* are closely related, apparently hybridizing in central Alberta; they constitute a superspecies and are considered conspecific by some authors.

Oporornis tolmiei (Townsend). MACGILLIVRAY'S WARBLER. [680.]

Sylvia Tolmiei J. K. Townsend, 1839, Narr. Journey Rocky Mount., etc., p. 343. (the Columbia = Fort Vancouver, Washington.)

Habitat.—Coniferous forest undergrowth and edge, brushy hillsides, riparian thickets, and chaparral, in migration and winter in a variety of open woodland undergrowth, scrubby areas and thickets.

Distribution.—*Breeds* from southeastern Alaska, southwestern Yukon, northern British Columbia, southern Alberta, northwestern Saskatchewan, eastern Montana and southwestern South Dakota south, primarily in the mountains, to southern California, central Arizona and southern New Mexico; also reported breeding on Cerro Potosí, Nuevo León.

Winters from southern Baja California, southern Sonora, Chihuahua, Coahuila and Nuevo León (casually farther north) south, mostly in the highlands, through

Middle America (except Belize) to western Panama (Chiriquí, casually east to the Canal Zone).

Migrates primarily through western North America from the Rockies and central Texas westward, casually east to Minnesota, central South Dakota, eastern Kansas, eastern Texas and Louisiana.

Casual or accidental in northern and south-coastal Alaska, southern Ontario and Massachusetts.

Notes.—See comments under *O. philadelphia.*

Genus **GEOTHLYPIS** Cabanis

Trichas (not Gloger, March 1827) Swainson, June 1827, Philos. Mag., new ser., 1, p. 433. Type, by monotypy, *Trichas personatus* Swainson = *Turdus trichas* Linnaeus.

Geothlypis Cabanis, 1847, Arch. Naturgesch., 13, pp. 316, 349. New name for *Trichas* Swainson, preoccupied.

Chamæthlypis Ridgway, 1887, Man. N. Am. Birds, p. 225. Type, by original designation, *Geothlypis poliocephala* Baird.

Notes.—See comments under *Oporornis.*

Geothlypis trichas (Linnaeus). COMMON YELLOWTHROAT. [681.]

Turdus Trichas Linnaeus, 1766, Syst. Nat., ed. 12, 1, p. 293. Based on "The Maryland Yellow-Throat" Edwards, Glean. Nat. Hist., 1, p. 56, pl. 257, fig. 2. (in America septentrionali = Maryland.)

Habitat.—Marshes (especially cattail), thickets near water, bogs, brushy pastures, old fields and, locally, undergrowth of humid forest, in migration and winter also in brushy and shrubby areas in both moist and arid regions (Tropical to Temperate zones).

Distribution.—*Breeds* from southeastern Alaska (west and north to Glacier Bay), southern Yukon, northern British Columbia, northern Alberta, central Saskatchewan, north-central Manitoba, central Ontario, central Quebec and Newfoundland south to northern Baja California, in Mexico to Oaxaca and Veracruz (west of the Isthmus of Tehuantepec), and to southern Texas, the Gulf coast and southern Florida.

Winters from northern California, southern Arizona, southern New Mexico (rarely), southern Texas, the Gulf states and South Carolina (casually farther north) south through Middle America, the Greater Antilles (east to the Virgin Islands) and Bahama Islands to central Panama (east to the Canal Zone and eastern Panamá province, casually to Darién), and casually to northern Colombia and the Lesser Antilles (Dominica); questionably reported from northern Venezuela and Tobago.

In migration recorded also on islands in the western Caribbean Sea, and on Bermuda.

Casual in central and south-coastal Alaska. Accidental in Greenland.

Notes.—Breeding populations around Lake Chapala, Jalisco, are sometimes treated as a separate species, *G. chapalensis* Nelson, 1903 [CHAPALA YELLOWTHROAT.]. *G. rostrata* is apparently closely related to *G. trichas* and considered conspecific with it by some authors; a few authors would also merge *G. flavovelata* and *G. beldingi* in *G. trichas.* Species limits within the genus are generally poorly understood and require further study. The four species in this complex constitute a superspecies.

Geothlypis beldingi Ridgway. BELDING'S YELLOWTHROAT.

Geothlypis beldingi Ridgway, 1883, Proc. U.S. Natl. Mus., 5 (1882), p. 344. (San José del Cabo, Baja California.)

Habitat.—Marshes.
Distribution.—*Resident* in southern Baja California (north to lat 28°N.).
Notes.—See comments under *G. trichas.*

Geothlypis flavovelata Ridgway. ALTAMIRA YELLOWTHROAT.

Geothlypis flavovelata Ridgway, 1896, Proc. U.S. Natl. Mus., 18 (1895), p. 119. (Alta Mira, near Tampico, Tamaulipas, Mexico.)

Habitat.—Marshes.
Distribution.—*Resident* in southern Tamaulipas, extreme eastern San Luis Potosí and northern Veracruz.
Notes.—Also known as YELLOW-CROWNED YELLOWTHROAT. See comments under *G. trichas.*

Geothlypis rostrata Bryant. BAHAMA YELLOWTHROAT.

Geothlypis rostratus Bryant, 1867, Proc. Boston Soc. Nat. Hist., 11 (1866), p. 67. (Nassau, New Providence, Bahamas.)

Habitat.—Brush, scrub and thickets.
Distribution.—*Resident* in the northern Bahama Islands (Grand Bahama, Little Abaco and Great Abaco south to Cat and Long islands, and Little Inagua), with a report (bird briefly examined in the hand before escaping) from southern Florida (Loxahatchee).
Notes.—See comments under *G. trichas.*

Geothlypis semiflava Sclater. OLIVE-CROWNED YELLOWTHROAT.

Geothlypis semiflava Sclater, 1860, Proc. Zool. Soc. London, p. 273. (In rep. Equator = Babahoyo, Ecuador.)

Habitat.—Tall grass, bamboo thickets and low bushes, primarily near water (Tropical and lower Subtropical zones).
Distribution.—*Resident* in Middle America from northeastern Honduras (Río Segovia [=Coco]) south in the Caribbean lowlands of Nicaragua and Costa Rica (locally also on the Pacific slope in the Arenal region) to western Panama (Bocas del Toro); and in South America in western Colombia and western Ecuador.

Geothlypis speciosa Sclater. BLACK-POLLED YELLOWTHROAT.

Geothlypis speciosa Sclater, 1859, Proc. Zool. Soc. London (1858), p. 447. (In Mexico = headwaters of the Río Lerma, state of México.)

Habitat.—Highland marshes and wetlands (Subtropical and Temperate zones).
Distribution.—*Resident* in the highlands of eastern Michoacán (Lago Patzcuaro, Lago Cuitzeo), southern Guanajuato (Lago Yuriria, Presa Solis), the state of México (upper Río Lerma, Lago Zumpango) and Distrito Federal (Lago Texcoco).

Geothlypis nelsoni Richmond. HOODED YELLOWTHROAT.

> *Geothlypis cucullata* Salvin and Godman, 1889, Ibis, p. 237. (Cofre de Perote, Jalapa, [Veracruz,] Mexico.) Not *Sylvia cucullata* Latham, 1790 = *Geothlypis aequinoctialis* (Gmelin).
> *Geothlypis nelsoni* Richmond, 1900, Auk, 17, p. 179. New name for *G. cucullata* Salvin and Godman, preoccupied.

Habitat.—Undergrowth of pine-oak association, and wet, brushy areas (Subtropical and Temperate zones).
Distribution.—*Resident* from southeastern Coahuila and central Nuevo León south through eastern San Luis Potosí, Hidalgo, Puebla, central Veracruz and Distrito Federal to western and central Oaxaca.

Geothlypis aequinoctialis (Gmelin). MASKED YELLOWTHROAT.

> *Motacilla aequinoctialis* Gmelin, 1789, Syst. Nat., 1 (2), p. 972. Based on "Figuier olive de Cayenne" Daubenton, Planches Enlum., pl. 685, fig. 1. (in Cayenna = Cayenne.)

Habitat.—Damp meadows, low marshy growth, savanna and dense underbrush, usually near water (Tropical Zone, in Panama known only from upper Tropical Zone).
Distribution.—*Resident* [*chiriquensis* group] in southwestern Costa Rica (Cañas Gordas district) and western Panama (Volcán de Chiriquí, in western Chiriquí); [*auricularis* group] on the Pacific slope from western Ecuador to central Peru; and [*aequinoctialis* group] from eastern Colombia, Venezuela (also Trinidad) and the Guianas south, east of the Andes, to eastern Peru, Bolivia, northern Argentina and Uruguay.
Notes.—The three groups are sometimes recognized as distinct species, *G. chiriquensis* Salvin, 1872 [CHIRIQUI YELLOWTHROAT], *G. auricularis* Salvin, 1884 [BLACK-LORED YELLOWTHROAT] and *G: aequinoctialis* [MASKED YELLOWTHROAT].

Geothlypis poliocephala Baird. GRAY-CROWNED YELLOWTHROAT. [682.1.]

> *Geothlypis poliocephala* Baird, 1865, Rev. Am. Birds., 1, p. 225. (Mazatlán, Sinaloa.)

Habitat.—Grassy areas, dense undergrowth in partly open situations, brushy fields, weedy areas, shrubby clearings and hedgerows (Tropical and Subtropical zones).
Distribution.—*Resident* from northern Sinaloa, Tamaulipas and (formerly) southern Texas (lower Rio Grande Valley) south along both slopes of Middle America to western Panama (western Chiriquí).
Notes.—Also known as GROUND CHAT. Placed by some authors in the monotypic genus *Chamaethlypis*.

Genus **MICROLIGEA** Cory

Ligea (not Illiger, 1801 [Crustacea], nor Drybowski, 1876 [Mollusca]) Cory, 1884, Auk, 1, p. 1. Type, by original designation, *Ligea palustris* Cory.

Ligia (not Weber, 1795 [Crustacea], Fabricius, 1798 [Crustacea], nor Dupre, 1829 [Lepidoptera]) Cory, 1884, Birds Haiti San Domingo, p. 34. Emendation of *Ligea,* Cory, preoccupied.

Microligea Cory, 1884, Auk, 1, p. 290. New name for *Ligea* Cory and *Ligia* Cory, preoccupied.

Notes.—See comments under *Xenoligea.*

Microligea palustris (Cory). Green-tailed Ground Warbler.

Ligea palustris Cory, 1884, Auk, 1, p. 1, pl. 1. (Santo Domingo = Río Villa, Dominican Republic.)

Habitat.—Dense thickets, more commonly in humid montane regions, less frequently in semi-arid lowlands.

Distribution.—*Resident* on Hispaniola (in Haiti confined to high elevations in Massif de la Selle, more widespread in the Dominican Republic), including Beata Island.

Notes.—Also known as Gray-breasted Ground Warbler.

Genus **TERETISTRIS** Cabanis

Teretistris Cabanis, 1855, J. Ornithol., 3, pp. 475, 476. Type, by original designation, *Anabates fernandinae* Lembeye.

Teretistris fernandinae (Lembeye). Yellow-headed Warbler.

Anabates fernandinæ Lembeye, 1850, Aves Isla Cuba, p. 66, pl. 5, fig. 2. (Cuba = western Cuba.)

Habitat.—Forest undergrowth and scrubby thickets.

Distribution.—*Resident* in western Cuba (east to southwestern Las Villas and western Matanzas provinces) and the Isle of Pines.

Teretistris fornsi Gundlach. Oriente Warbler.

Teretistris fornsi Gundlach, 1858, Ann. Lyc. Nat. Hist. N.Y., 6, p. 274. (eastern part of Cuba.)

Habitat.—Undergrowth and brushy areas from semi-arid coastal districts to humid mountains.

Distribution.—*Resident* in eastern Cuba (ranging west along the north coast to eastern Matanzas province).

Genus **LEUCOPEZA** Sclater

Leucopeza Sclater, 1876, Proc. Zool. Soc. London, p. 14. Type, by monotypy, *Leucopeza semperi* Sclater.

Leucopeza semperi Sclater. SEMPER'S WARBLER.

Leucopeza semperi Sclater, 1876, Proc. Zool. Soc. London, p. 14, pl. 2. (St. Lucia.).

Habitat.—Undergrowth of mountain forest.
Distribution.—*Resident* in the highlands of St. Lucia (in the Lesser Antilles), where now very rare and local.

Genus WILSONIA Bonaparte

Wilsonia Bonaparte, 1838, Geogr. Comp. List, p. 23. Type, by subsequent designation (Ridgway, 1881), *Motacilla mitrata* Gmelin=*Muscicapa citrina* Boddaert.

Wilsonia citrina (Boddaert). HOODED WARBLER. [684.]

Muscicapa Citrina Boddaert, 1783, Table Planches Enlum., p. 41. Based on "Gobe-mouche de la Louisiane" Daubenton, Planches Enlum., pl. 666, fig. 2. (Louisiana.)

Habitat.—Understory of mature deciduous forest, especially along streams and ravine edges, and thickets in riverine forest, in migration and winter in a variety of woodland undergrowth, scrubby areas and thickets.

Distribution.—*Breeds* from extreme southeastern Nebraska (rarely), central and northeastern Iowa (rarely), central (rarely northern) Illinois, southern Michigan, southern Ontario, northwestern Pennsylvania, central and southeastern New York, southern Connecticut and Rhode Island south to eastern Texas (south to Matagorda County), the Gulf coast and northern peninsular Florida, and west to eastern Kansas (casually) and eastern Oklahoma.

Winters from Nayarit (rarely), Oaxaca and southern Tamaulipas (casually farther north) south along both slopes of Middle America (rare on Pacific slope south of Honduras) to Panama (east to the Canal Zone, including Isla Coiba).

Migrates regularly through the eastern Plains states (west to eastern New Mexico and western Texas), southeastern states, the Antilles (east to the Virgin Islands, and casually to Saba and Martinique), Bahama Islands, Bermuda, and islands in the western Caribbean Sea, rarely to California.

Casual elsewhere in western North America from Washington, Oregon, Nevada, Colorado, eastern Wyoming and North Dakota south to southern Arizona (summer records, possibly breeding) and southern New Mexico; north to southern Minnesota, Wisconsin, southern Quebec, New Brunswick and Nova Scotia; and in Trinidad; also a sight report for the British Isles.

Wilsonia pusilla (Wilson). WILSON'S WARBLER. [685.]

Muscicapa pusilla Wilson, 1811, Am. Ornithol., 3, p. 103, pl. 26, fig. 4. (southern States, . . . lower parts . . . of New Jersey and Delaware = southern New Jersey.)

Habitat.—Shrubby and brushy areas (especially near water), bogs, and thickets in riparian woodland, in boreal and montane regions (breeding); a variety of open woodland, thickets, brushy and scrubby areas and forest undergrowth, in both lowland and highland habitats (nonbreeding).

Distribution.—*Breeds* from western and northern Alaska, northern Yukon, northwestern and east-central Mackenzie, northwestern Saskatchewan, northern Manitoba, northern Ontario, northern Quebec, central Labrador and Newfoundland south to southern Alaska (west to the Alaska Peninsula and Unimak Island), through British Columbia and the mountains of the western states to southern California, west-central and northeastern Nevada, south-central Utah, southwestern Colorado and north-central New Mexico, and to southwestern and east-central Alberta, central Saskatchewan, southern Manitoba, northern Minnesota (possibly), south-central Ontario, southern Quebec, extreme northeastern New York, northern Vermont, central Maine and central Nova Scotia.

Winters from coastal California (rarely), southern Baja California, southern Sonora, southern Texas, southern Louisiana (rarely) and Florida (casually farther north) south through Middle America (except the Yucatan Peninsula) to western Panama (Chiriquí), rarely to central Panama.

Migrates regularly through North America west of the Appalachians, less commonly through the Atlantic and southeastern states, rarely through the Bahama Islands (Grand Bahama, New Providence) and the Greater Antilles (Cuba, Jamaica and Puerto Rico).

Accidental in northern Baffin Island.

Notes.—Also known as PILEOLATED or BLACK-CAPPED WARBLER.

Wilsonia canadensis (Linnaeus). CANADA WARBLER. [686.]

> *Muscicapa canadensis* Linnaeus, 1766, Syst. Nat., ed. 12, 1, p. 327. Based on "Le Gobe-mouche cendré de Canada" Brisson, Ornithologie, 2, p. 406, pl. 39, fig. 4. (in Canada.)

Habitat.—Woodland undergrowth (especially aspen-poplar), bogs, and tall shrubbery along streams, in migration and winter in a variety of forest, woodland, scrub and thickets habitats, mostly in humid regions.

Distribution.—*Breeds* from northern and central Alberta, central Saskatchewan, central Manitoba, north-central Ontario, southern Quebec (including Anticosti Island), New Brunswick, Prince Edward Island and Nova Scotia south to southern Manitoba, northern Minnesota, southern Wisconsin, northern Illinois, central Michigan and central Ohio, through the Appalachians to eastern Kentucky, eastern Tennessee, northwestern Goergia, western North Carolina, western Virginia, western Maryland and east-central Pennsylvania, and to northern New Jersey, southeastern New York and southern New England.

Winters in South America (casually in Middle America north to Oaxaca, Belize and Honduras) from northern Colombia and Venezuela south, mostly east of the Andes, to eastern Peru and northern Brazil.

Migrates mostly through North America east of the Rockies (rare in the southeastern states), Middle America (rare on Pacific slope of Mexico north of Oaxaca) and, rarely, to California (mostly in fall in coastal regions).

Casual elsewhere in western North America in Nevada, Arizona and New Mexico, and in the Bahama Islands (Grand Bahama, New Providence, Exuma) and Greater Antilles (Cuba, Jamaica, Puerto Rico and the Virgin Islands). Accidental in Alaska (Barrow), the Lesser Antilles (Guadeloupe) and Greenland.

Genus **CARDELLINA** Bonaparte

Cardellina (Du Bus de Gisignies MS) Bonaparte, 1850, Consp. Gen. Avium, 1 (2), p. 312. Type, by subsequent designation (Baird, 1865), *Cardellina amicta* Du Bus de Gisignies = *Muscicapa rubrifrons* Giraud.

Cardellina rubrifrons (Giraud). RED-FACED WARBLER. [690.]

Muscicapa rubrifrons Giraud, 1841, Descr. Sixteen New Spec. N. Am. Birds., pl. [7], fig. 1 and text. (Texas, error = Mexico.)

Habitat.—Montane fir, pine and pine-oak woodland, in migration and winter in humid montane forest, pine-oak association and riparian woodland, rarely in open woodland in lowland habitats (Subtropical and lower Temperate zones).

Distribution.—*Breeds* from central Arizona and southwestern New Mexico south through Sonora, western Chihuahua and Sinaloa to western Durango.

Winters from Sinaloa and Durango south through the highlands of Mexico (ranging east to west-central Veracruz) and Guatemala to El Salvador and western Honduras.

Casual in southern California (possibly breeds) and central New Mexico, also sight reports for southern Nevada and western Texas.

Genus **ERGATICUS** Baird

Ergaticus Baird, 1865, Rev. Am. Birds., 1, pp. 237, 264. Type, by original designation, *Setophaga rubra* Swainson.

Ergaticus ruber (Swainson). RED WARBLER.

Setophaga rubra Swainson, 1827, Philos. Mag., new ser., 1, p. 368. (woods of Valladolid, Mexico = Morelia, Michoacán.)

Habitat.—Pine forest and pine-oak association (upper Subtropical and Temperate zones, to lower Subtropical Zone in winter).

Distribution.—*Resident* in the mountains of southwestern Chihuahua, eastern Sinaloa and western Durango, and from Jalisco, Michoacán and Guerrero east to Hidalgo, eastern Puebla, central Veracruz and central Oaxaca, ranging in winter to lower elevations.

Notes.—*E. ruber* and *E. versicolor* are regarded as conspecific by some authors; they constitute a superspecies.

Ergaticus versicolor (Salvin). PINK-HEADED WARBLER.

Cardellina versicolor Salvin, 1863, Proc. Zool. Soc. London, p. 188, pl. 24, fig. 1. (Volcán de Fuego, Totonicapam and Chilasco, Guatemala = Chilasco, Guatemala.)

Habitat.—Humid montane forest, pine-oak woodland and adjacent second growth (Subtropical and Temperate zones).

Distribution.—*Resident* in the mountains of central and eastern Chiapas, and western Guatemala (east to the Sierra de las Minas).

Notes.—See comments under *E. ruber*.

Genus **MYIOBORUS** Baird

Erythrosoma [subgenus] Swainson, 1832, *in* Swainson and Richardson, Fauna Bor.-Am., 2 (1831), p. 201. Type, by subsequent designation (Richmond, 1917), *Setophaga picta* Swainson. *Nomen oblitum.*
Myioborus Baird, 1865, Rev. Am. Birds., 1, pp. 237, 257. Type, by original designation, *Setophaga verticalis* Lafresnaye and d'Orbigny = *Setophaga miniata* Swainson.

Myioborus pictus (Swainson). PAINTED REDSTART. [688.]

Setophaga picta Swainson, 1829, Zool. Illus., ser. 2, 1, pl. 3 and text. (Real del Monte, Hidalgo, Mexico.)

Habitat.—Oak and pine forest, pinyon-juniper woodland, and pine-oak association, in migration and winter rarely in deciduous woodland and lowland forest (upper Tropical to lower Temperate zones).

Distribution.—*Breeds* from northwestern and central Arizona, southwestern New Mexico, western Texas (Chisos Mountains) and central Nuevo León south through the mountains of Middle America to north-central Nicaragua; summers casually in southern California (attempted breeding in Laguna Mountains in 1974, recorded also in San Bernardino Mountains and Clark Mountain).

Winters from eastern Sonora, central Chihuahua, central Nuevo León and central Tamaulipas south through the remainder of the breeding range.

Casual in California (north to Tulare County), southern Utah, and northern and eastern New Mexico. Accidental in Ohio (Middleburg Heights), southern Ontario (Pickering Township), New York (Dansville), Massachusetts (Marblehead Neck) and Louisiana (New Orleans), also sight reports for British Columbia (Vancouver), Colorado (Lyons), Wisconsin (Madison), and central and southeastern Texas.

Notes.—Formerly placed in the genus *Setophaga*.

Myioborus miniatus (Swainson). SLATE-THROATED REDSTART. [689.]

Setophaga miniata Swainson, 1827, Philos. Mag., new ser., 1, p. 368. (woods of Valladolid, Mexico = Morelia, Michoacán.)

Habitat.—Humid montane forest, forest edge, open woodland, second growth and pine-oak association (upper Tropical and Subtropical zones).

Distribution.—*Resident* from southern Sonora, southern Chihuahua, Durango, Zacatecas and San Luis Potosí south through the mountains of Mexico, Guatemala and El Salvador to Honduras; in Costa Rica and western Panama (Chiriquí and Veraguas, reported also from eastern Panamá province); and from eastern Panama (Darién) east across Colombia and Venezuela to Guyana and extreme northwestern Brazil, and south in the Andes to Peru and northern Bolivia.

Accidental in southeastern New Mexico (Lea County) and southern Arizona (Miller Canyon, sight record also from Cave Creek Canyon).

Myioborus torquatus (Baird). COLLARED REDSTART.

Setophaga torquata Baird, 1865, Rev. Am. Birds., 1, p. 261. (San José, Costa Rica.)

Habitat.—Humid montane forest edge, clearings, second-growth woodland, shrubby areas, and thickets near forest (upper Subtropical and Temperate zones).

Distribution.—*Resident* in the mountains of Costa Rica (northwest to the Cordillera de Tilarán) and western Panama (Chiriquí and adjacent Bocas del Toro).

Genus EUTHLYPIS Cabanis

Euthlypis Cabanis, 1850, Mus. Heineanum, 1 (1851), p. 18. Type, by original designation, *Euthlypis lachrymosa* Cabanis = *Basileuterus lachrymosa* Bonaparte.

Euthlypis lachrymosa (Bonaparte). FAN-TAILED WARBLER. [688.1.]

Basileuterus lachrymosa (Lichtenstein MS) Bonaparte, 1850, Consp. Gen. Avium, 1 (2), p. 314. (Mexico = Laguna Huetulacán, Veracruz.)

Habitat.—Tropical deciduous forest, riparian woodland, humid lowland and montane forest, second growth and scrub (Tropical and Subtropical zones).

Distribution.—*Resident* from southern Sonora, eastern San Luis Potosí and southern Tamaulipas south on the Gulf slope of Mexico to Veracruz and northern Oaxaca, and on the Pacific slope of Mexico, Guatemala, El Salvador and Honduras (locally also in interior valleys) to central Nicaragua.

Accidental in northern Baja California (Santo Domingo) and southern Arizona (Guadalupe Mountains).

Genus BASILEUTERUS Cabanis

Basileuterus Cabanis, 1849, *in* Schomburgk, Reisen Brit.-Guiana, 3 (1848), p. 666. Type, by monotypy, *Basileuterus vermivorus* Cabanis = *Setophaga auricapilla* Swainson = *Sylvia culicivora* Deppe.

Notes.—See comments under *Phaeothlypis*.

Basileuterus culicivorus (Deppe). GOLDEN-CROWNED WARBLER. [692.]

Sylvia culicivora W. Deppe, 1830, Preis. Verz. Säugeth. Vögel, etc., Mex., p. 2. (Mexico = Jalapa, Veracruz.)

Habitat.—Humid forest, forest edge, clearings, deciduous woodland, second growth and coffee plantations (Tropical and Subtropical zones).

Distribution.—*Resident* [*culicivorus* group] in Nayarit and Jalisco, and from Nuevo León and Tamaulipas south on the Gulf-Caribbean slope of San Luis Potosí, Veracruz, Hidalgo, Puebla, Veracruz, Tabasco, southern Campeche and southern Quintana Roo, and on both slopes from Oaxaca south through Chiapas and Central America to western Panama (Chiriquí, Veraguas and Herrera); [*cabanisi* group] in the Santa Marta Mountains and Andes of Colombia and northern Venezuela; and [*auricapillus* group] from the eastern slope of the Eastern Andes in Colombia east across southern Venezuela to Trinidad and the Guianas, and south through Brazil, eastern Bolivia, Paraguay and Uruguay to northern Argentina.

Casual [*culicivorus* group] in southern Texas (Brownsville, also a sight report from Starr County).

Notes.—The three groups are sometimes considered separate species, *B. culicivorus* [STRIPE-CROWNED WARBLER], *B. cabanisi* Berlepsch, 1879 [CABANIS' WARBLER], and *B. auricapillus* (Swainson, 1838) [GOLDEN-CROWNED WARBLER].

Basileuterus rufifrons (Swainson). RUFOUS-CAPPED WARBLER. [692.1.]

Setophaga rufifrons Swainson, 1837, Anim. Menag. (1838), p. 294. (Mexico = Real del Arriba, state of México.)

Habitat.—Forest edge, clearings, open woodland, second growth, scrub, plantations and brushy areas (Tropical and Subtropical zones).

Distribution.—*Resident* [*rufifrons* group] from northern Sonora, western Chihuahua, Sinaloa, western Durango, Nayarit, Jalisco, Guanajuato, San Luis Potosí, central Nuevo León and western Tamaulipas south through Mexico (except the Yucatan Peninsula) to Belize and northern and central Guatemala; and [*delattrii* group] from western Guatemala, El Salvador and Honduras south through Nicaragua, Costa Rica, Panama (including Isla Coiba) and northern Colombia to northwestern Venezuela.

Casual [*rufifrons* group] in southern Arizona (Cave Creek Canyon, with attempted nesting in 1977), and western and southern Texas (Brewster, Webb and Kendall counties, also a sight report from Starr County).

Notes.—The two groups are often considered as separate species, *B. rufifrons* [RUFOUS-CAPPED WARBLER] and *B. delattrii* Bonaparte, 1854 [CHESTNUT-CAPPED WARBLER], but intergradation occurs in Guatemala, El Salvador and Honduras.

Basileuterus belli (Giraud). GOLDEN-BROWED WARBLER.

Muscicapa belli Giraud, 1841, Descr. Sixteen New Spec. N. Am. Birds, pl. [4], fig. 2 and text. (Texas, error = Mount Orizaba, Veracruz.)

Habitat.—Humid montane forest, and dense or brushy pine-oak association (Subtropical and Temperate zones).

Distribution.—*Resident* from southeastern Sinaloa, western Durango, Nayarit, Jalisco, Michoacán, the state of México, Hidalgo, eastern San Luis Potosí and southwestern Tamaulipas south through the mountains of southern Mexico, Guatemala and El Salvador to central Honduras.

Notes.—Also known as BELL'S WARBLER.

Basileuterus melanogenys Baird. BLACK-CHEEKED WARBLER.

Basileuterus melanogenys Baird, 1865, Rev. Am. Birds, 1, p. 248. ("San José ?," Costa Rica.)

Habitat.—Humid montane forest undergrowth, forest edge, open woodland and scrub (Subtropical and Temperate zones).

Distribution.—*Resident* in the mountains of Costa Rica (Cordillera Central southward) and western Panama (Chiriquí and Veraguas).

Notes.—*B. melanogenys* and *B. ignotus* constitute a superspecies; they are considered conspecific by some authors.

Basileuterus ignotus Nelson. PIRRE WARBLER.

Basileuterus melanogenys ignotus Nelson, 1912, Smithson. Misc. Collect., 60, no. 3, p. 21. (Mount Pirri, at 5200 feet altitude, near head of Rio Limon, [Darién,] eastern Panama.)

Habitat.—Humid montane forest undergrowth and edge (Subtropical and lower Temperate zones).

Distribution.—*Resident* in the mountains of eastern Panama (Cerro Pirre and Cerro Tacarcuna, eastern Darién).

Notes.—See comments under *B. melanogenys.*

Basileuterus tristriatus (Tschudi). THREE-STRIPED WARBLER.

Myiodioctes tristriatus Tschudi, 1844, Arch. Naturgesch., 10, p. 283. (Republica Peruana = San Pedro plantation, near Lurín, error [=valley of Vitoc, Depto. de Junín].)

Habitat.—Humid forest undergrowth, edge, second growth, scrub, thickets and plantations (upper Tropical and Subtropical zones).

Distribution.—*Resident* in the mountains of Costa Rica (north to Cordillera de Tilarán) and western Panama (east to Veraguas); and from eastern Panama (eastern Panamá province and Darién), Colombia and northern Venezuela south, primarily east of the Andes, through eastern Ecuador to eastern Peru and northern Bolivia.

Genus PHAEOTHLYPIS Todd

Phaeothlypis Todd, 1929, Proc. U.S. Natl. Mus., 74, art. 7, p. 8. Type, by original designation, *Muscicapa fulvicauda* Spix.

Notes.—Merged by some authors in *Basileuterus.*

Phaeothlypis fulvicauda (Spix). BUFF-RUMPED WARBLER.

Muscicapa fulvicauda Spix, 1825, Avium Spec. Nov. Bras., 2, p. 20, pl. 28, fig. 2. (No locality given = São Paulo de Olivença, Rio Solimões, Brazil.)

Habitat.—Along streams and rivers, usually rocky and rapid-flowing, in humid lowland forest and second-growth woodland, and in mangroves (Tropical Zone).

Distribution.—*Resident* on the Caribbean slope of Honduras (west to the Sula Valley) and Nicaragua, on both slopes of Costa Rica (except the dry northwest) and Panama, and in South America from Colombia south, west of the Andes to northwestern Peru and east of the Andes to eastern Ecuador, eastern Peru and extreme western Amazonian Brazil.

Notes.—*P. fulvicauda* and *P. rivularis* (Wied, 1821) [RIVER WARBLER], of eastern South America, are considered conspecific by some authors; they constitute a superspecies.

Genus ZELEDONIA Ridgway

Zeledonia Ridgway, 1889, Proc. U.S. Natl. Mus., 11 (1888), p. 537. Type, by monotypy, *Zeledonia coronata* Ridgway.

Notes.—Formerly considered related to the muscicapid assemblage (with turdine affinities) and placed in the monotypic family Zeledoniidae, but now regarded as a paruline (see Sibley, 1968, Postilla, no. 125, pp. 1–12, and Hunt, 1971, Auk, 88, pp. 1–20).

Zeledonia coronata Ridgway. WRENTHRUSH.

Zeledonia coronata Ridgway, 1889, Proc. U.S. Natl. Mus., 11 (1888), p. 538. (Laguna del Volcán de Poás, Costa Rica.)

Habitat.—Dense thickets and brushy areas, especially ravines, in humid mountainous country (Subtropical and Temperate zones).

Distribution.—*Resident* in the highlands of Costa Rica (north to Cordillera de Tilarán) and western Panama (western Chiriquí and Veraguas).

Genus **ICTERIA** Vieillot

Icteria Vieillot, 1808, Hist. Nat. Ois. Am. Sept., 1 (1807), pp. iv, 85. Type, by monotypy, *Icteria dumicola* Vieillot = *Turdus virens* Linnaeus.

Notes.—Allocation of the genus is in doubt; it may not be paruline.

Icteria virens (Linnaeus). YELLOW-BREASTED CHAT. [683.]

Turdus virens Linnaeus, 1758, Syst. Nat., ed. 10, 1, p. 171. Based on "The yellow brested Chat" Catesby, Nat. Hist. Carolina, 1, p. 50, pl. 50. (in America = South Carolina, 200 or 300 miles from the sea.)

Habitat.—Second growth, thickets, brushy areas, scrub, woodland undergrowth and fencerows (Tropical to Temperate zones).

Distribution.—*Breeds* from southern British Columbia, southern Alberta, southern Saskatchewan, North Dakota, southern Minnesota, southern Wisconsin, southern Michigan, southern Ontario, central New York, southern Vermont and southern New Hampshire south to south-central Baja California, Jalisco, the state of México, southern Tamaulipas, the Gulf coast and north-central Florida.

Winters from southern Baja California, southern Sinaloa, southern Texas and southern Florida (casually from California, the Great Lakes region, New York and New England) south through Middle America to western Panama (western Bocas del Toro, also a sight report from Cerro Campana).

In migration occurs casually in the northern Bahama Islands (Grand Bahama, Abaco, Bimini, Andros) and Cuba.

Casual north to southern Manitoba, northern Michigan, southern Quebec, New Brunswick, Nova Scotia and Newfoundland.

Genus **GRANATELLUS** Bonaparte

Granatellus (Du Bus de Gisignies MS) Bonaparte, 1850, Consp. Gen. Avium, 1 (2), p. 312. Type, by monotypy, *Granatellus venustus* Bonaparte.

Notes.—Systematic position uncertain; it may not be paruline.

Granatellus venustus Bonaparte. RED-BREASTED CHAT.

Granatellus venustus (Du Bus de Gisignies MS) Bonaparte, 1850, Consp. Gen. Avium, 1 (2), p. 312. (Mexico = Comitán, Chiapas.)

Habitat.—Deciduous forest, second growth, arid scrub and brush (Tropical and lower Subtropical zones).

Distribution.—*Resident* in the Pacific lowlands of Mexico from northern Sinaloa south to Chiapas (also Isla María Madre, in the Tres Marias Islands). Wanders in winter into foothills to western Durango.

Notes.—The form from the Tres Marias Islands is sometimes regarded as a distinct species, *G. francescae* Baird, 1865 [TRES MARIAS CHAT]. *G. venustus, G. sallaei* and the South American *G. pelzelni* Sclater, 1865, appear to constitute a superspecies.

Granatellus sallaei (Bonaparte). GRAY-THROATED CHAT.

Setophaga sallæi (Bonaparte and Sclater MS) Bonaparte, 1856, C. R. Acad. Sci. Paris, 42, p. 957. (southern Mexico = Córdoba, Veracruz.)

Habitat.—Deciduous forest, second growth and brushy areas (Tropical Zone).
Distribution.—*Resident* from southern Veracruz and the Yucatan Peninsula south in the Gulf-Caribbean lowlands of Tabasco, northern Oaxaca and northern Chiapas to northern Guatemala and Belize.
Notes.—See comments under *G. venustus.*

Genus **XENOLIGEA** Bond

Xenoligea [subgenus] Bond, 1967, Birds W. Indies, 12th Suppl., p. 20. Type, by original designation, *Microligea montana* Chapman.

Notes.—By some authors merged with *Microligea,* but the species *montana* appears to have thraupine affinities while *Microligea palustris* seems to be paruline, possibly close to the genus *Dendroica.*

Xenoligea montana (Chapman). WHITE-WINGED WARBLER.

Microligea montana Chapman, 1917, Bull. Am. Mus. Nat. Hist., 37, p. 330. (Mt. Tina, Azua, Santo Domingo.)

Habitat.—Montain forest undergrowth and adjacent thickets.
Distribution.—*Resident* in the higher mountains of Hispaniola.
Notes.—Also known as WHITE-WINGED GROUND WARBLER.

Genus **PEUCEDRAMUS** Henshaw

Peucedramus Henshaw, 1875, Ann. Rep. Geogr. Explor. West 100th Merid., p. 201. Type, by original designation, *Sylvia olivacea* Giraud = *Sylvia taeniata* Du Bus de Gisignies.

Notes.—Systematic position uncertain; this genus may prove to be sylviine (Muscicapidae) rather than paruline.

Peucedramus taeniatus (Du Bus de Gisignies). OLIVE WARBLER. [651.]

Sylvia tæniata Du Bus de Gisignies, 1847, Bull. Acad. R. Sci. Lett. Beaux-Arts Belg., 14, p. 104. (Mexico = San Cristóbal, Chiapas.)

Distribution.—*Breeds* from central and southeastern Arizona, southwestern New Mexico, northern Chihuahua, northern Coahuila, southern Nuevo León and western Tamaulipas south through the highlands of Mexico, Guatemala, El Salvador and Honduras to north-central Nicaragua.
Winters primarily through the breeding range, although most individuals migrate southward from the breeding range in Arizona and New Mexico; recorded in winter also in Nayarit.
Casual in western Texas (sight reports for El Paso and Big Bend).

Subfamily COEREBINAE: Bananaquits

Genus **COEREBA** Vieillot

Cœreba Vieillot, 1808, Hist. Nat. Ois. Am. Sept., 2 (1807), p. 70. Type, by monotypy, *Certhia flaveola* Linnaeus.

Notes.—Formerly considered, along with several genera now treated as thraupine or emberizine, in a distinct family, the Coerebidae; presently considered a distinct monotypic subfamily close to the Parulinae.

Coereba flaveola (Linnaeus). BANANAQUIT. [635.]

Certhia flaveola Linnaeus, 1758, Syst. Nat., ed. 10, 1, p. 119. Based mainly on "Luscinia s. Philomela e fusco & luteo varia" Sloane, Voy. Jamaica, 2, p. 307, pl. 259, fig. 3, and "The Black and Yellow Creeper" Edwards, Nat. Hist. Birds, 3, p. 122, pl. 122, upper fig. (in America = Jamaica.)

Habitat.—A wide variety of habitats from arid thorn scrub to humid montane forest, mangroves and gardens, generally wherever flowering trees or shrubs are found (Tropical to lower Temperate zones).

Distribution.—*Resident* throughout the West Indies (including many small cays throughout, and islands in the western Caribbean Sea, but absent from Cuba and the Swan Islands); and from central Veracruz, Oaxaca and Chiapas (also the islands of Holbox, Cancun, Cozumel and Cayo Culebra, but absent from the Yucatan Peninsula) south through the Gulf-Caribbean lowlands of northern Central America to Nicaragua, on both slopes of Costa Rica (except the dry northwest) and Panama (including Coiba and the Pearl islands), and in South America from Colombia (including Isla Gorgona), Venezuela (also the Netherlands Antilles east to Tobago and Trinidad) and the Guinas south, west of the Andes to northwestern Peru and east of the Andes to eastern Peru, Bolivia, Paraguay, extreme northeastern Argentina and southern Brazil.

Casual in southern Florida (north to Brevard County, most frequently recorded in Palm Beach and Broward counties, including at least two reports of attempted but unsuccessful breeding) and off Cuba (Cayo Tío Pepe, Gibara).

Notes.—The breeding population in the Bahama Islands, from which the Florida and Cuba vagrants originated, has sometimes been recognized as a separate species, *C. bahamensis* (Reichenbach, 1853) [BAHAMA BANANAQUIT or HONEYCREEPER].

Subfamily THRAUPINAE: Tanagers

Tribe THRAUPINI: Typical Tanagers

Genus **CONIROSTRUM** Lafresnaye and d'Orbigny

Conirostrum Lafresnaye and d'Orbigny, 1838, Mag. Zool. [Paris], 8, cl. 2, pl. 77–79, p. 25. Type, by monotypy, *Conirostrum cinereum* Lafresnaye and d'Orbigny.

Notes.—Affinities uncertain, possibly emberizine if not thraupine.

Conirostrum leucogenys (Lafresnaye). WHITE-EARED CONEBILL.

Dacnis Leucogenys Lafresnaye, 1852, Rev. Mag. Zool., ser. 2, 4, p. 470. (Colombiâ = Bogotá.)

Habitat.—Humid lowland forest edge, clearings, second-growth woodland, and fields in partly open situations with scattered trees (Tropical Zone).

Distribution.—*Resident* from eastern Panama (eastern Panamá province in the Bayano River valley, and Darién) east across northern Colombia to northern Venezuela.

Genus TANGARA Brisson

Tangara Brisson, 1760, Ornithologie, 3, p. 3. Type, by tautonymy, *Tangara* Brisson = *Aglaia paradisea* Swainson = *Aglaia chilensis* Vigors.

Tangara inornata (Gould). PLAIN-COLORED TANAGER.

Calliste inornata Gould, 1855, Proc. Zool. Soc. London, p. 158. (Santa Fé di Bogota [Colombia].)

Habitat.—Humid lowland forest edge, clearings, second-growth woodland, and partly open situations with scattered trees (Tropical Zone).

Distribution.—*Resident* in Costa Rica (Caribbean slope only, north to Sarapiquí region), Panama (entire Caribbean slope, and Pacific slope from western Panamá province eastward) and northern Colombia.

Tangara cabanisi (Sclater). AZURE-RUMPED TANAGER.

Calliste s. Callispiza Sclateri (not *Calliste sclateri* Lafresnaye, 1854) Cabanis, 1866, J. Ornithol., 14, p. 163. (Costa Cuca, western Guatemala.)
Calliste cabanisi Sclater, 1868, Ibis, p. 71, pl. 3. New name for *Calliste sclateri* Cabanis, preoccupied.

Habitat.—Humid montane forest edge (Subtropical Zone).

Distribution.—*Resident* in the highlands of Chiapas (Mount Ovando and Cacahuatlán) and western Guatemala (Costa Cuca region).

Notes.—Also known as CABANIS' TANAGER.

Tangara palmeri (Hellmayr). GRAY-AND-GOLD TANAGER.

Calospiza palmeri Hellmayr, 1909, Rev. Fr. Ornithol., 1, p. 49. (Sipi, Rio Sipi, Choco, Colombia.)

Habitat.—Humid lowland and foothill forest and forest edge (Tropical and lower Subtropical zones).

Distribution.—*Resident* in eastern Panama (cerros Sapo, Quía and Tacarcuna, in eastern Darién), western Colombia and northwestern Ecuador.

Tangara florida (Sclater and Salvin). EMERALD TANAGER.

Calliste florida Sclater and Salvin, 1869, Proc. Zool. Soc. London, p. 416, pl. 28. (Costa Rica.)

Habitat.—Humid foothill forest edge, adjacent second-growth woodland and mature scrub (upper Tropical and lower Subtropical zones).

Distribution.—*Resident* in the highlands of Costa Rica (primarily in the Cordillera Central), Panama (entire Caribbean slope, and Pacific slope from eastern Panamá province eastward) and western Colombia, also a sight report for western Ecuador.

Tangara icterocephala (Bonaparte). SILVER-THROATED TANAGER.

Calliste icterocephala Bonaparte, 1851, C. R. Acad. Sci. Paris, 32, p. 76. (Ecuador = valley of Punta Playa, south of Quito.)

Habitat.—Humid foothill and montane forest and forest edge (upper Tropical and Subtropical zones).

Distribution.—*Resident* in the highlands of Costa Rica (north to Cordillera de Guanacaste, more frequently found on Caribbean slope), Panama (both slopes), western Colombia and western Ecuador.

Tangara guttata (Cabanis). SPECKLED TANAGER.

Callispiza guttata Cabanis, 1850, Mus. Heineanum, 1 (1851), p. 26, (Roraima, Guiana = Cerro Roraima, Bolívar, Venezuela.)

Habitat.—Humid foothill and montane forest edge, second-growth woodland, clearings and plantations (upper Tropical and Subtropical zones).

Distribution.—*Resident* in Costa Rica (from the Cordillera Central southward), Panama (entire Caribbean slope, and Pacific slope in Chiriquí and from eastern Panamá province eastward), and South America from northern Colombia and Venezuela (also Trinidad) south, east of the Andes, to southeastern Colombia and extreme northern Brazil.

Notes.—Although sometimes called *T. chrysophrys* (Sclater, 1851), the name *T. guttata* clearly has priority (see Storer, 1970, *in* Peters, Birds World, 13, p. 370, footnote). See also comments under *Chlorothraupis olivacea.*

Tangara gyrola (Linnaeus). BAY-HEADED TANAGER.

Fringilla Gyrola Linnaeus, 1758, Syst. Nat., ed. 10, 1, p. 181. Based on "The Red-headed Green-Finch" Edwards, Nat. Hist. Birds, 1, p. 23, pl. 23. (in America = Surinam.)

Habitat.—Humid forest, forest edge, second-growth woodland and plantations (Tropical and Subtropical zones).

Distribution.—*Resident* in Costa Rica (north to the Cordillera Central), Panama (both slopes), and in South America from Colombia, Venezuela (also Trinidad) and the Guianas south, west of the Andes to western Ecuador and east of the Andes to eastern Peru, northern Bolivia, and Amazonian and eastern Brazil.

Notes.—Some authors suggest that distinct morphological differences indicate that three species might be recognized in this complex: *T. gyrola*, in the Guianas and southeastern Venezuela; *T. viridissima* (Lafresnaye, 1847), in northeastern Colombia, northern Venezuela and Trinidad; and *T. gyroloides* (Lafresnaye, 1847) [=*T. albertinae* (Pelzeln, 1877)], in the remainder of the range, including the Middle American populations [BAY-AND-BLUE TANAGER].

Tangara lavinia (Cassin). RUFOUS-WINGED TANAGER.

Calliste Lavinia Cassin, 1858, Proc. Acad. Nat. Sci. Philadelphia, 10, p. 178. (Isthmus of Darien, New Grenada [=Panama].)

Habitat.—Humid lowland and foothill forest, forest edge and second-growth woodland (Tropical and lower Subtropical zones).

Distribution.—*Resident* from eastern Guatemala (Santo Tomás) south on the Caribbean slope of Central America to Costa Rica, on both slopes of Panama (entire Caribbean slope, and Pacific slope in eastern Panamá province and Darién), and in western Colombia (including Gorgona Island) and western Ecuador.

Tangara cucullata (Swainson). LESSER ANTILLEAN TANAGER.

Aglaia Cucullata Swainson, 1834, Ornithol. Drawings, pt. 1, pl. 7. (No locality given = Grenada, Lesser Antilles.)

Habitat.—Forest, forest edge and second growth.

Distribution.—*Resident* on St. Vincent and Grenada, in the Lesser Antilles.

Notes.—Also known as HOODED TANAGER, a name now generally applied to the South American *Nemosia pileata* (Boddaert, 1783). Some authors consider *T. cucullata* and the South American *T. cayana* (Linnaeus, 1766) [RUFOUS-CROWNED TANAGER] to be conspecific; they constitute a superspecies.

Tangara larvata (Du Bus de Gisignies). GOLDEN-MASKED TANAGER.

Calliste larvata Du Bus de Gisignies, 1846, Esquisses Ornithol., livr. 2, pl. 9. (Tabasco, Mexico.)

Habitat.—Humid lowland and foothill forest edge, second-growth woodland and plantations (Tropical and lower Subtropical zones).

Distribution.—*Resident* from northern Oaxaca, Tabasco and Chiapas south on the Gulf-Caribbean slope of Central America to Nicaragua, on both slopes of Costa Rica (absent from the dry northwest) and Panama (entire Caribbean slope, and Pacific slope in Chiriquí and from eastern Panamá province eastward), and in western Colombia and western Ecuador.

Notes.—Also known as GOLDEN-HOODED TANAGER. Some authors consider *T. larvata* and the South American *T. nigrocincta* (Bonaparte, 1838) [BLACK-BANDED TANAGER] to be conspecific; these two, plus the South American *T. cyanicollis* (d'Orbigny and Lafresnaye, 1837), constitute a superspecies. With *T. larvata* merged in *T. nigrocincta,* MASKED TANAGER is the appropriate English name.

Tangara dowii (Salvin). SPANGLE-CHEEKED TANAGER.

Calliste dowii Salvin, 1863, Proc. Zool. Soc. London, p. 168. (San José [=Rancho Redondo de San José], Costa Rica.)

Habitat.—Humid montane forest, forest edge, and adjacent open woodland (Subtropical and lower Temperate zones).

Distribution.—*Resident* in the mountains of Costa Rica (north to the Cordillera de Tilarán) and western Panama (east to Veraguas).

Notes.—Some authors regard *T. dowii* and *T. fucosa* as conspecific; they constitute a superspecies. With a single species concept, SPANGLE-CHEEKED TANAGER is the appropriate English name.

Tangara fucosa Nelson. GREEN-NAPED TANAGER.

Tangara fucosus Nelson, 1912, Smithson. Misc. Collect., 60, no. 3, p. 17. (Mount Pirri, at 5,000 feet altitude, near head of Rio Limon, eastern Panama.)

Habitat.—Humid montane forest and forest edge (Subtropical Zone).
Distribution.—*Resident* in extreme eastern Panama (on Cerro Malí and Cerro Pirre, in eastern Darién).
Notes.—See comments under *T. dowii.*

Genus **DACNIS** Cuvier

Dacnis Cuvier, 1817, Règne Anim., 1 (1816), p. 395. Type, by monotypy, *Motacilla cayana* Linnaeus.

Notes.—The genera *Dacnis, Chlorophanes* and *Cyanerpes,* formerly placed in the family Coerebidae, are now considered to be thraupines related to the genus *Tangara.*

Dacnis venusta Lawrence. SCARLET-THIGHED DACNIS.

Dacnis venusta Lawrence, 1862, Ann. Lyc. Nat. Hist. N.Y., 7, p. 464. (Atlantic side of the Isthmus of Panama, along the line of the Panama Railroad = Canal Zone.)

Habitat.—Humid forest edge and adjacent open woodland (Tropical and Subtropical zones).
Distribution.—*Resident* on both slopes of Costa Rica (north to the Cordillera de Guanacaste) and Panama, and in western Colombia and northwestern Ecuador; presence in the lower Tropical Zone in Costa Rica and Panama appears to be primarily in the nonbreeding season.

Dacnis cayana (Linnaeus). BLUE DACNIS.

Motacilla cayana Linnaeus, 1766, Syst. Nat., ed. 12, 1, p. 336. Based in part on "Le Pipit bleu de Cayenne" Brisson, Ornithologie, 3, p. 534, pl. 28, fig. 1. (in Cayana = Cayenne.)

Habitat.—Humid open woodland, second growth, forest edge, clearings, parks, plantations and scrubby areas (Tropical Zone).
Distribution.—*Resident* on the Caribbean slope of northeastern Honduras (Olancho, Gracias a Dios), Nicaragua, on both slopes of Costa Rica (except the dry northwest) and Panama, and in South America from Colombia, Venezuela (also Trinidad) and the Guianas south, west of the Andes to western Ecuador and east of the Andes to eastern Peru, northern and eastern Bolivia, Paraguay, northeastern Argentina and southern Brazil.

Dacnis viguieri Salvin and Godman. VIRIDIAN DACNIS.

Dacnis viguieri (Oustalet MS) Salvin and Godman, 1883, Biol. Cent.-Am. Aves, p. 246, pl. 15A, fig. 3. (Isthmus of Panama, on the shores of the Gulf of Darien.)

Habitat.—Humid lowland forest and forest edge (Tropical Zone).

Distribution.—*Resident* in extreme eastern Panama (Jaqué, in southeastern Darién) and northwestern Colombia (northern Chocó and Córdoba).

Genus CHLOROPHANES Reichenbach

Chlorophanes Reichenbach, 1853, Hand. Spec. Ornithol., cont. xi, Scansoriae B. Tenuirostres, p. 233. Type, by monotypy, *Coereba atricapilla* Vieillot = *Motacilla spiza* Linnaeus.

Notes.—See comments under *Dacnis.*

Chlorophanes spiza (Linnaeus). GREEN HONEYCREEPER.

Motacilla Spiza Linnaeus, 1758, Syst. Nat., ed. 10, 1, p. 188. Based on "The Green Black-cap Fly-catcher" Edwards, Nat. Hist. Birds, 1, p. 25, pl. 25, upper fig. (in Surinami = Surinam.)

Habitat.—Humid lowland and foothill forest edge, clearings, second-growth woodland, plantations and savanna (Tropical and lower Subtropical zones).

Distribution.—*Resident* from northeastern Oaxaca (Montebello), Chiapas and southern Campeche (Pacaytún) south on the Gulf-Caribbean slope of Central America to Nicaragua, on both slopes of Costa Rica (except the dry northwest) and Panama, and in South America from Colombia, Venezuela (also Trinidad) and the Guianas south, west of the Andes to northwestern Peru and east of the Andes to eastern Peru, central Bolivia, and central and southeastern Brazil.

Genus CYANERPES Oberholser

Cyanerpes Oberholser, 1899, Auk, 16, p. 32. Type, by original designation, *Certhia cyanea* Linnaeus.

Notes.—See comments under *Dacnis.*

Cyanerpes lucidus (Sclater and Salvin). SHINING HONEYCREEPER.

Cœreba lucida Sclater and Salvin, 1859, Ibis, p. 14. (Guatemala.)

Habitat.—Humid lowland and foothill forest, forest edge, and adjacent second-growth woodland (Tropical and lower Subtropical zones).

Distribution.—*Resident* locally on the Caribbean slope of Chiapas (Tumbalá, Santa Rosa), Guatemala (Verapaz), Belize, Honduras (Omoa, La Ceiba) and Nicaragua, on both slopes of Costa Rica (except the dry northwest) and Panama, and in extreme northwestern Colombia (Chocó).

Notes.—Sometimes regarded as conspecific with *C. caeruleus,* but sympatry is reported from northwestern Colombia; *C. lucidus* and *C. caeruleus* constitute a superspecies. If but a single species is recognized, the English name YELLOW-LEGGED HONEYCREEPER is appropriate.

Cyanerpes caeruleus (Linnaeus). PURPLE HONEYCREEPER.

Certhia cærulea Linnaeus, 1758, Syst. Nat., ed. 10, 1, p. 118. Based on "The Blue Creeper" Edwards, Nat. Hist. Birds, 1, p. 21, pl. 21, upper fig. (Surinami = Surinam.)

Habitat.—Humid lowland and foothill forest, second-growth woodland, clearings, plantations, parks and swamps (Tropical and lower Subtropical zones).

Distribution.—*Resident* in extreme eastern Panama (Jaqué and Cerro Quía, in eastern Darién), and in South America from Colombia, Venezuela (also Trinidad) and the Guianas south, west of the Andes to western Ecuador and east of the Andes to eastern Peru, northern Bolivia, and Amazonian and eastern Brazil.

Notes.—See comments under *C. lucidus.*

Cyanerpes cyaneus (Linnaeus). RED-LEGGED HONEYCREEPER.

Certhia cyanea Linnaeus, 1766, Syst. Nat., ed. 12, 1, p. 188. Based in part on "The Black and Blue Creeper" Edwards, Glean. Nat. Hist., 2, p. 114, pl. 264, upper fig. (in Brasilia, Cayania = Surinam.)

Habitat.—Humid forest edge and clearings, open woodland, second growth, plantations, parks and shrubby areas (Tropical and Subtropical zones).

Distribution.—*Resident* from eastern San Luis Potosí, Veracruz, Puebla and Oaxaca south along both slopes of Middle America (including the Yucatan Peninsula, and Coiba and the Pearl islands off Panama), and in South America from Colombia, Venezuela (also Margarita Island and Trinidad) and the Guianas south, west of the Andes to western Ecuador and east of the Andes to eastern Peru, northern Bolivia, and central and eastern Brazil; also on Cuba (possibly introduced), where formerly widespread but now confined to Oriente province).

Records from Jamaica and Bonaire (in the Netherlands Antilles) are probably based on escaped cage birds.

Genus CHLOROPHONIA Bonaparte

Chlorophonia Bonaparte, 1851, Rev. Mag. Zool., ser. 2, 3, p. 137. Type, by subsequent designation (G. R. Gray, 1855), *Tanagra viridis* Vieillot = *Pipra cyanea* Vieillot.

Chlorophonia occipitalis (Du Bus de Gisignies). BLUE-CROWNED CHLORO-PHONIA.

Euphonia occipitalis Du Bus de Gisignies, 1847, Esquisses Ornithol., livr. 3, pl. 14. (Le Mexique = Mexico.)

Habitat.—Humid montane forest, adjacent heavy second growth, and plantations, descending in nonbreeding season to humid lowland forest (Subtropical Zone, to Tropical Zone in nonbreeding season).

Distribution.—*Resident* from central Veracruz and Oaxaca south through Chiapas, Guatemala, El Salvador and Honduras to north-central Nicaragua.

Notes.—*C. occipitalis* and *C. callophrys* constitute a superspecies; they are considered conspecific by some authors. With a single species concept, BLUE-CROWNED CHLOROPHONIA would be the proper English name.

Chlorophonia callophrys (Cabanis). GOLDEN-BROWED CHLOROPHONIA.

Triglyphidia callophrys Cabanis, 1860, J. Ornithol., 8, p. 331. (Costa Rica.)

Habitat.—Humid montane forest edge and partly cleared lands (upper Tropical and Subtropical zones).

Distribution.—*Resident* in the highlands of Costa Rica (north to the Cordillera de Guanacaste) and western Panama (Chiriquí and Veraguas), descending to lower elevations in nonbreeding season.

Notes.—See comments under *C. occipitalis.*

Genus EUPHONIA Desmarest

Euphonia Desmarest, 1806, Hist. Nat. Tangaras, Manakins, Todiers, livr. 10, table [pl. 27]. Type, by monotypy, *Euphonia olivacea* Desmarest = *Euphonia minuta* Cabanis.

Pyrrhuphonia Bonaparte, 1850, C. R. Acad. Sci. Paris, 31, p. 423. Type, by subsequent designation (G. R. Gray, 1855), *Fringilla jamaica* Linnaeus.

Notes.—The generic name *Tanagra* Linnaeus, 1764, has been suppressed for the purposes of the Law of Priority (but not the Law of Homonymy) by the International Commission on Zoological Nomenclature (1968, Bull. Zool. Nomencl., 25, p. 74).

Euphonia jamaica (Linnaeus). JAMAICAN EUPHONIA.

Fringilla jamaica Linnaeus, 1766, Syst. Nat., ed. 12, 1, p. 323. Based mainly on *Passer Coeruleofuscus* Sloane, Voy. Jamaica, 2, p. 311, pl. 257, fig. 3. (in Jamaica.)

Habitat.—Partly open country with scattered trees, open woodland, forest edge and shrubbery.

Distribution.—*Resident* on Jamaica.

Notes.—Often placed in the monotypic genus *Pyrrhuphonia.*

Euphonia affinis (Lesson). SCRUB EUPHONIA.

Tanagra (Euphonia) affinis Lesson, 1842, Rev. Zool. [Paris], 5, p. 175. (Realejo [Nicaragua].)

Habitat.—Open woodland, forest edge, clearings, second growth, partly open situations with scattered trees, and cultivated lands (Tropical Zone).

Distribution.—*Resident* [*godmani* group] in the Pacific lowlands from southeastern Sonora south to central Guerrero; and [*affinis* group] from eastern San Luis Potosí, southern Tamaulipas, Veracruz, Puebla and Oaxaca south along both slopes of Middle America (including the Yucatan Peninsula and Cozumel Island) to Honduras, and in the Pacific lowlands through western Nicaragua to northwestern Costa Rica (Guanacaste).

Notes.—Also known as LESSON'S or BLACK-THROATED EUPHONIA. Some authors suggest that the two groups represent distinct species, *E. godmani* Brewster, 1889 [PALE-VENTED EUPHONIA], and *E. affinis* [SCRUB EUPHONIA].

Euphonia luteicapilla (Cabanis). YELLOW-CROWNED EUPHONIA.

Phonasca luteicapilla Cabanis, 1860, J. Ornithol., 8, p. 332. (Costa Rica.)

Habitat.—Scrub, savanna, shrubby areas, partly open situations with scattered trees, and, occasionally, open woodland and forest edge (Tropical and lower Subtropical zones).

Distribution.—*Resident* in eastern Nicaragua, Costa Rica (both slopes, except the dry northwest) and Panama (east to the Canal Zone and western Darién).

Euphonia laniirostris d'Orbigny and Lafresnaye. THICK-BILLED EUPHONIA.

Euphonia laniirostris d'Orbigny and Lafresnaye, 1837, Mag. Zool. [Paris], 7, cl. 2, pl. 77–79, p. 30. (Yuracares, Bolivia.)

Habitat.—Humid forest edge, clearings, second-growth woodland, gardens, plantations and savanna (Tropical and Subtropical zones).

Distribution.—*Resident* in Costa Rica (primarily the humid southwest), Panama (both slopes), and South America from Colombia and northern Venezuela south, west of the Andes to western Peru and east of the Andes to eastern Peru and northern Bolivia, thence east across Amazonian and central Brazil to eastern Brazil.

Euphonia hirundinacea Bonaparte. YELLOW-THROATED EUPHONIA.

> *Euphonia hirundinacea* Bonaparte, 1838, Proc. Zool. Soc. London (1837), p. 117. (Guatamala = Guatemala.)

Habitat.—Open woodland, forest edge, clearings, partly open situations with scattered trees, second-growth woodland, and plantations (Tropical and lower Subtropical zones).

Distribution.—*Resident* from eastern San Luis Potosí, southern Tamaulipas, Veracruz, Puebla and Oaxaca south along both slopes of Middle America (including the Yucatan Peninsula) to Costa Rica (most commonly in the dry northwest) and extreme western Panama (western Chiriquí).

Notes.—Also known as BONAPARTE'S EUPHONIA. With the use of *Euphonia* instead of the suppressed *Tanagra*, *E. hirundinacea* Bonaparte is no longer preoccupied by *Tanagra hirundinacea* Lesson, 1831; thus the frequently used *T. lauta* Bangs and Penard, 1919, becomes a synonym of *E. hirundinacea*.

Euphonia musica (Gmelin). ANTILLEAN EUPHONIA.

> *Pipra musica* Gmelin, 1789, Syst. Nat., 1 (2), p. 1004. Based on "L'Organiste" Daubenton, Planches Enlum., pl. 809, fig. 1. (in insula S. Dominici = Hispaniola.)

Habitat.—Woodland and forest edge, more commonly in mountainous regions.

Distribution.—*Resident* on Hispaniola (including Gonâve Island) and Puerto Rico, and in the Lesser Antilles (Barbuda, Antigua, Montserrat, Guadeloupe, Dominica, Martinique, St. Lucia, St. Vincent and Grenada).

Casual elsewhere in the Lesser Antilles (Saba, St. Barthélemy, Terre-de-haut, Bequia).

Notes.—*E. musica*, *E. elegantissima* and the South American *E. aureata* (Vieillot, 1822) are considered conspecific by some authors; they constitute a superspecies. With a single species concept, BLUE-HOODED EUPHONIA would be the appropriate English name.

Euphonia elegantissima (Bonaparte). BLUE-HOODED EUPHONIA.

> *Pipra elegantissima* Bonaparte, 1838, Proc. Zool. Soc. London (1837), p. 112. (Mexico.)

Habitat.—Humid foothill and montane forest edge, clearings, pine-oak association, oak scrub and plantations (upper Tropical and Subtropical zones).

Distribution.—*Resident* from southeastern Sonora, southwestern Chihuahua, Sinaloa, western Durango, Nayarit, Jalisco, Guanajuato, San Luis Potosí, central Nuevo León and southern Tamaulipas south through the highlands of Middle America to western Panama (Chiriquí and Veraguas).

Notes.—See comments under *E. musica*.

Euphonia fulvicrissa Sclater. FULVOUS-VENTED EUPHONIA.

Euphonia fulvicrissa Sclater, 1857, Proc. Zool. Soc. London (1856), p. 276. ("S[anta]. Martha in New Grenada" = locality uncertain.)

Habitat.—Humid lowland forest edge and clearings, and shrubby areas (Tropical Zone).

Distribution.—*Resident* from central Panama (west to western Panamá province, formerly to Chiriquí) south through central and western Colombia (west of the Eastern Andes) to northwestern Ecuador.

Euphonia imitans (Hellmayr). SPOT-CROWNED EUPHONIA.

Tanagra imitans Hellmayr, 1936, Field Mus. Nat. Hist. Publ., Zool. Ser., 13 (9), p. 63. (El Pózo, Río Térraba, Costa Rica.)

Habitat.—Humid lowland and foothill forest edge, and second-growth woodland (Tropical and lower Subtropical zones).

Distribution.—*Resident* in southwestern Costa Rica (Pacific slope west to the Gulf of Nicoya) and extreme western Panama (western Chiriquí).

Accidental in central Costa Rica (San José, possibly an escaped cage bird; a record from Miravalles is erroneous).

Notes.—Also known as TAWNY-BELLIED EUPHONIA.

Euphonia gouldi Sclater. OLIVE-BACKED EUPHONIA.

Euphonia Gouldi Sclater, 1857, Proc. Zool. Soc. London, p. 66, pl. 24. (In Guatimala et Mexico Meridionali = Guatemala.)

Habitat.—Humid lowland forest, forest edge, second-growth woodland and plantations (Tropical Zone).

Distribution.—*Resident* from central Veracruz, northern Oaxaca, Tabasco, Chiapas and southern Quintana Roo south in the Gulf-Caribbean lowlands of Central America to Costa Rica (also known from the Pacific slope of the Cordillera de Guanacaste) and western Panama (Bocas del Toro and western Veraguas).

Notes.—Also known as GOULD'S EUPHONIA.

[**Euphonia mesochrysa** Salvadori. BRONZE-GREEN EUPHONIA.] See Appendix B.

Euphonia minuta Cabanis. WHITE-VENTED EUPHONIA.

Euphonia minuta Cabanis, 1849, *in* Schomburgk, Reisen Br.-Guiana, 3 (1848), p. 671. (British Guiana.)

Habitat.—Humid lowland and foothill forest, forest edge, second-growth woodland and scrub (Tropical and lower Subtropical zones).

Distribution.—*Resident* locally on the Gulf-Caribbean slope of Chiapas (Palenque), Guatemala (Cobán), Belize and Nicaragua, and widely on both slopes of Costa Rica (except the dry northwest) and Panama (more widespread on the Caribbean slope), and in South America from Colombia, Venezuela and the Guianas south, west of the Andes to western Ecuador and east of the Andes to eastern Peru and northern Bolivia, thence east across Amazonian Brazil to eastern Brazil.

Notes.—The name *E. olivacea* Desmarest, 1806, has been suppressed for the purposes of the Law of Priority (but not the Law of Homonymy) by the International Commission of Zoological Nomenclature (1968, Bull. Zool. Nomencl., 25, p. 74).

Euphonia anneae Cassin. TAWNY-CAPPED EUPHONIA.

Euphonia Anneæ Cassin, 1865, Proc. Acad. Nat. Sci. Philadelphia. 17, p. 172. (Santa Rosa, Costa Rica.)

Habitat.—Humid forest edge and second-growth woodland (upper Tropical and Subtropical zones).

Distribution.—*Resident* in Costa Rica (Caribbean slope, north to the Cordillera de Guanacaste), Panama (locally on both slopes) and extreme northwestern Colombia (Gulf of Urabá region).

Euphonia xanthogaster (Sundevall). ORANGE-BELLIED EUPHONIA.

Euphone xanthogaster Sundevall, 1834, Vetensk.-Akad. Handl. (1833), p. 310, pl. 10, fig. 1. (Brazil = Rio de Janeiro.)

Habitat.—Humid forest, forest edge and second-growth woodland (Tropical and Subtropical zones).

Distribution.—*Resident* from eastern Panama (eastern Darién), Colombia, Venezuela and Guyana south, west of the Andes to western Ecuador and east of the Andes to eastern Peru and northern Bolivia, thence east across Amazonian and central Brazil to eastern and southeastern Brazil.

Genus THRAUPIS Boie

Thraupis Boie, 1826, Isis von Oken, col. 974. Type, by virtual monotypy, *Tanagra archiepiscopus* Desmarest = *Tanagra ornata* Sparrman.

Thraupis episcopus (Linnaeus). BLUE-GRAY TANAGER.

Tanagra Episcopus Linnaeus, 1766, Syst. Nat., ed. 12, 1, p. 316. Based on "L'Evesque" Brisson, Ornithologie, 3, p. 40, pl. 1, fig. 2. (in Brasilia, error = probably Cayenne.)

Habitat.—Open woodland, forest edge, clearings, plantations, second growth, parks and gardens (Tropical and Subtropical zones).

Distribution.—*Resident* from Guanajuato, San Luis Potosí, Veracruz, Puebla, Oaxaca, Tabasco, Chiapas, southern Campeche and southern Quintana Roo south along both slopes of Central America to Panama (including Coiba, Escudo de Veraguas, and the Pearl Islands), and in South America from Colombia, Venezuela (also Tobago and Trinidad) and the Guianas south, west of the Andes to northwestern Peru and east of the Andes to eastern Peru, northwestern Bolivia and Amazonian Brazil.

Introduced about 1960 in southern Florida (southern Broward and Dade counties) but has apparently disappeared in recent years.

Notes.—Formerly called *T. virens* (Linnaeus, 1766); *T. episcopus* has been ruled to have priority by the International Commission on Zoological Nomenclature (1968, Bull. Zool. Nomencl., 25, p. 74).

Thraupis abbas (Deppe). YELLOW-WINGED TANAGER.

Tanagra Abbas (Lichtenstein MS) W. Deppe, 1830, Preis.-Verz. Säugeth. Vögel, etc., Mex., p. 2. (Jalapa, Veracruz.)

Habitat.—Forest edge and clearings, open woodland, mature scrub and parks (Tropical and Subtropical zones).

Distribution.—*Resident* from eastern San Luis Potosí, Veracruz, the state of México, Puebla and Oaxaca south along both slopes of Middle America (including the Yucatan Peninsula) to Honduras and eastern Nicaragua (Zelaya).

Notes.—Also known as ABBOT'S TANAGER.

Thraupis palmarum (Wied). PALM TANAGER.

Tanagra palmarum Wied, 1821, Reise Bras., 2, p. 76. (Canavieras, Bahia, Brazil.)

Habitat.—Open woodland, forest edge, clearings, parks, plantations, and partly open situations with scattered trees (Tropical and occasionally lower Subtropical zones).

Distribution.—*Resident* in southeastern Honduras (Olancho) and eastern Nicaragua, on both slopes of Costa Rica (rare in the dry northwest) and Panama (except for dry Pacific slope from Veraguas to western Panamá province), and in South America from Colombia, Venezuela (also Margarita and Patos islands, and Trinidad) and the Guianas south, west of the Andes to western Ecuador and east of the Andes to eastern Peru, northern Bolivia, Paraguay and southern Brazil.

Genus SPINDALIS Jardine and Selby

Spindalis Jardine and Selby, 1837, Illus. Ornithol., new ser., pt. 2, pl. 9. Type, by monotypy, *Spindalis bilineatus* Jardine and Selby = *Tanagra nigricephala* Jameson = *Fringilla zena* Linnaeus.

Spindalis zena (Linnaeus). STRIPE-HEADED TANAGER. [610.1.]

Fringilla Zena Linnaeus, 1758, Syst. Nat., ed. 10, 1, p. 181. Based on "The Bahama Finch" Catesby, Nat. Hist. Carolina, 1, p. 42, pl. 42. (Bahama Islands = New Providence.)

Habitat.—Second growth, open woodland, scrub and shrubby areas, especially in hilly country.

Distribution.—*Resident* throughout the Bahama Islands, in the Greater Antilles (east to Puerto Rico, including the Isle of Pines, Grand Cayman, and Gonâve Island off Hispaniola), and on Cozumel Island (off Quintana Roo).

Ranges irregularly to southern Florida (north to the Palm Beach area).

Notes.—Because of distinct morphological differences in females, some authors have suggested that three species should be recognized, *S. dominicensis* (Bryant, 1866) from Hispaniola, Gonâve Island and Puerto Rico, *S. nigricephala* (Jameson, 1835) from Jamaica, and *S. zena* in the remainder of the range (including the Florida vagrants).

Genus **BUTHRAUPIS** Cabanis

Buthraupis Cabanis, 1850, Mus. Heineanum, 1 (1851), p. 29. Type, by subsequent designation (G. R. Gray, 1855), *Tanagra montana* Lafresnaye = *Aglaia montana* d'Orbigny and Lafresnaye.
Bangsia Penard, 1919, Auk, 36, p. 539. Type, by original designation, *Buthraupis arcaei caeruleigularis* Cherrie [=Ridgway] = *Buthraupis arcaei* Sclater and Salvin.

Buthraupis arcaei Sclater and Salvin. BLUE-AND-GOLD TANAGER.

Buthraupis arcæi Sclater and Salvin, 1869, Proc. Zool. Soc. London, p. 439, pl. 31. (Cordillera del Chucú, Veraguas, Panama.)

Habitat.—Humid lowland and foothill forest and forest edge (Tropical and lower Subtropical zones).
Distribution.—*Resident* in Costa Rica (the Caribbean slope north to the Cordillera de Tilarán) and western Panama (in Chiriquí, on both slopes in Veraguas, and in the Cerro Jefe area of eastern Panamá province).
Notes.—Often placed in the genus *Bangsia*.

Genus **CHLOROTHRAUPIS** Salvin and Godman

Chlorothraupis (Ridgway MS) Salvin and Godman, 1883, Biol. Cent.-Am., Aves, 1, p. 297. Type, by subsequent designation (Ridgway, 1884), *Phoenicothraupis carmioli* Lawrence.

Chlorothraupis carmioli (Lawrence). OLIVE TANAGER.

Phænicothraupis carmioli Lawrence, 1868, Ann. Lyc. Nat. Hist. N.Y., 9, p. 100. (Angostura, Costa Rica.)

Habitat.—Humid lowland and foothill forest undergrowth and edge (Tropical and lower Subtropical zones).
Distribution.—*Resident* in eastern Nicaragua (Caribbean slope), Costa Rica (Caribbean slope, locally on Pacific slope in low passes) and Panama (entire Caribbean slope, and Pacific slope from eastern Panamá province to Darién, generally north and east of the valleys of Río Chepo and Río Chucunaque); and in South America from southeastern Colombia south, east of the Andes, to eastern Peru and northwestern Bolivia.
Notes.—Also known as CARMIOL'S TANAGER. *C. carmioli* and *C. olivacea* are considered conspecific by some authors; they constitute at least a superspecies.

Chlorothraupis olivacea (Cassin). LEMON-BROWED TANAGER.

Orthogonys olivaceus Cassin, 1860, Proc. Acad. Nat. Sci. Philadelphia, 12, p. 140. (Cordilleras Mountains, on the River Truando, New Granada = Río Truandó, northwestern Colombia.)

Habitat.—Undergrowth of humid lowland forest and forest edge (Tropical Zone).
Distribution.—*Resident* in extreme eastern Panama (eastern Darién, generally south and west of the valleys of Río Chepo and Río Chucunaque), western Colombia and northwestern Ecuador.

Notes.—Formerly known as YELLOW-BROWED TANAGER, a name confusingly applied also to *Tangara guttata*. See also comments under *C. carmioli.*

Genus EUCOMETIS Sclater

Comarophagus (not Boie, 1826) Bonaparte, 1851, C. R. Acad. Sci. Paris, 32, p. 81. Type, by subsequent designation (G. R. Gray, 1855), *Tanagra penicillata* Spix.
Eucometis Sclater, 1856, Proc. Zool. Soc. London, p. 117. New name for *Comarophagus* Bonaparte, preoccupied.

Eucometis penicillata (Spix). GRAY-HEADED TANAGER.

Tanagra penicillata Spix, 1825, Avium Spec. Nov. Bras., 2, p. 36, pl. 49, fig. 1. (No locality given = Fonte Bôa, Rio Solimões, Brazil.)

Habitat.—Humid lowland and foothill forest undergrowth, forest edge, dense second-growth woodland, and heavy scrub (Tropical and lower Subtropical zones).
Distribution.—*Resident* from Veracruz, northern Oaxaca and the Yucatan Peninsula) south along the Gulf-Caribbean slope to Honduras, on both slopes of Nicaragua (rare on Pacific slope), Costa Rica (primarily Pacific slope, locally on Caribbean drainage) and Panama (Pacific slope throughout, on Caribbean slope from the Canal Zone eastward), and in South America from northern Colombia, Venezuela and the Guianas south, east of the Andes, to eastern Peru, northern Bolivia, northern Paraguay, and central and eastern Brazil.

Genus LANIO Vieillot

Lanio Vieillot, 1816, Analyse, p. 40. Type, by original designation, "Tangara mordoré" Buffon = *Tangara fulva* Boddaert.

Lanio aurantius Lafresnaye. BLACK-THROATED SHRIKE-TANAGER.

Lanio Aurantius Lafresnaye, 1846, Rev. Zool. [Paris], 9, p. 204. (in Colombiâ, error = Guatemala.)

Habitat.—Humid lowland forest (Tropical Zone).
Distribution.—*Resident* from central Veracruz and northern Oaxaca south on the Gulf-Caribbean slope of Tabasco, Chiapas, southern Campeche, southern Quintana Roo, Guatemala and Belize to northern Honduras (east to the La Ceiba region).
Notes.—Some authors consider *L. aurantius* and *L. leucothorax* to be conspecific; they constitute a superspecies. With the single species treatment, GREAT SHRIKE-TANAGER would be the appropriate English name.

Lanio leucothorax Salvin. WHITE-THROATED SHRIKE-TANAGER.

Lanio leucothorax Salvin, 1865, Proc. Zool. Soc. London (1864), p. 581. (Tucurriqui, Costa Rica.)

Habitat.—Humid lowland and foothill forest (Tropical and lower Subtropical zones).

Distribution.—*Resident* from eastern Honduras (Olancho) south through Nicaragua (Caribbean slope) and Costa Rica (both slopes, absent from the dry northwest) to western Panama (western Bocas del Toro, Chiriquí and Veraguas).

Notes.—See comments under *L. aurantius.*

Genus HETEROSPINGUS Ridgway

Heterospingus Ridgway, 1898, Auk, 15, p. 225. Type, by original designation, *Tachyphonus rubrifrons* Lawrence.

Heterospingus rubrifrons (Lawrence). SULPHUR-RUMPED TANAGER.

Tachyphonus rubrifrons Lawrence, 1865, Proc. Acad. Nat. Sci. Philadelphia, 17, p. 106. (Line of the Pan[ama]. R[ail]. Road, near Lion Hill Station = Lion Hill, Canal Zone.)

Habitat.—Humid lowland forest and forest edge (Tropical Zone).

Distribution.—*Resident* in eastern Costa Rica (Caribbean lowlands west to the Río Reventazón) and Panama (entire Caribbean slope, and Pacific lowlands in eastern Panamá province and Darién).

Notes.—Some authors consider *H. rubrifrons* and *H. xanthopygius* to be conspecific; they constitute a superspecies.

Heterospingus xanthopygius (Sclater). SCARLET-BROWED TANAGER.

Tachyphonus xanthopygius Sclater, 1855, Proc. Zool. Soc. London (1854), p. 158, pl. 69. (in Nov. Grenada = Bogotá, Colombia.)

Habitat.—Humid lowland forest and forest edge (Tropical Zone).

Distribution.—*Resident* in eastern Panama (El Real, Jaqué, Pucro and Cana, in eastern Darién), western Colombia and western Ecuador.

Notes.—See comments under *H. rubrifrons.*

Genus TACHYPHONUS Vieillot

Tachyphonus Vieillot, 1816, Analyse, p. 33. Type, by monotypy, "Tangara noir" Buffon = *Tangara rufa* Boddaert.

Tachyphonus luctuosus d'Orbigny and Lafresnaye. WHITE-SHOULDERED TANAGER.

Tachyphonus luctuosus d'Orbigny and Lafresnaye, 1837, Mag. Zool. [Paris], 7, cl. 2, pl. 77–79, p. 29. (Guarayos [Bolivia].)

Habitat.—Humid forest clearings, forest edge, second growth, open woodland and scrub (Tropical and Subtropical zones).

Distribution.—*Resident* from eastern Honduras (Caribbean slope west to La Ceiba region) south through Nicaragua (Caribbean slope) and Costa Rica (both slopes, absent from the dry northwest) to Panama (Caribbean slope in western Bocas del Toro and from Coclé eastward, and Pacific slope in western Chiriquí and from the Canal Zone eastward), and in South America from Colombia, Venezuela (also Trinidad) and the Guianas south, west of the Andes to western Ecuador and east of the Andes to eastern Peru, northern Bolivia, and central and eastern Brazil.

Tachyphonus delatrii Lafresnaye. TAWNY-CRESTED TANAGER.

> *Tachyphonus Delatrii* Lafresnaye, 1847, Rev. Zool. [Paris], 10, p. 72. (St-Bonaventure = Buenaventura, Colombia.)

Habitat.—Humid lowland and foothill forest, forest edge and second-growth woodland (Tropical and lower Subtropical zones).

Distribution.—*Resident* from eastern Honduras (sight report), eastern Nicaragua (Caribbean slope) south through Costa Rica (primarily Caribbean slope), Panama (entire Caribbean slope, and Pacific slope in Veraguas and Darién) and western Colombia (including Gorgona Island) to western Ecuador.

Tachyphonus rufus (Boddaert). WHITE-LINED TANAGER.

> *Tangara rufa* Boddaert, 1783, Table Planches Enlum., p. 44. Based on "Le Tangaroux de Cayenne" Daubenton, Planches Enlum., pl. 711. (Cayenne.)

Habitat.—Humid lowland and foothill forest edge, clearings, second growth, open woodland and scrub (Tropical and lower Subtropical zones).

Distribution.—*Resident* in Costa Rica (primarily Caribbean lowlands) and Panama (entire Caribbean slope, on Pacific slope from western Panamá province eastward), and in South America from Colombia, Venezuela (also Margarita Island, Tobago and Trinidad) and the Guianas south, west of the Andes to northwestern Ecuador and east of the Andes to eastern Peru, northern Bolivia, Paraguay, northeastern Argentina and southeastern Brazil.

Genus HABIA Blyth

> *Habia* Blyth, 1840, *in* Cuvier, Anim. Kingdom, p. 184. Type, by subsequent designation (Oberholser, 1922), *Tanagra flammiceps* Temminck = *Saltator rubicus* Vieillot.

Habia rubica (Vieillot). RED-CROWNED ANT-TANAGER.

> *Staltator* [sic] *rubicus* Vieillot, 1817, Nouv. Dict. Hist. Nat., nouv. éd., 14, p. 107. Based on "Habia Roxiza" Azara, Apunt. Hist. Nat. Páx. Parag., 1, p. 351 (no. 85). (Paraguay.)

Habitat.—Humid lowland forest undergrowth and edge, second-growth woodland, scrub, thickets and swampy woodland (Tropical Zone).

Distribution.—*Resident* from Nayarit and southern Tamaulipas south along both slopes of Middle America (including the Yucatan Peninsula) to Nicaragua, in Costa Rica (Pacific lowlands) and Panama (primarily Pacific lowlands, locally on Caribbean slope), and in South America from eastern Colombia (locally also in western Colombia) and northern Venezuela (also Trinidad) south, east of the Andes, to eastern Peru and northern Bolivia, thence east across Amazonian Brazil to Paraguay, extreme northeastern Argentina, and southeastern Brazil.

Habia fuscicauda (Cabanis). RED-THROATED ANT-TANAGER.

> *Phoenicothraupis fuscicauda* Cabanis, 1861, J. Ornithol., 9, p. 86. (Costa Rica.)

Habitat.—Humid lowland and foothill forest edge, clearings, undergrowth in second-growth woodland, plantations and mangroves (Tropical and lower Subtropical zones).

Distribution.—*Resident* from Oaxaca, Puebla, Veracruz, eastern San Luis Potosí and southern Tamaulipas south along both slopes of Middle America (including the Yucatan Peninsula, and Meco and Mujeres islands) to Honduras, and in Nicaragua (Caribbean slope only), Costa Rica (mostly Caribbean slope, absent from Pacific coast south of Río Pirris), Panama (throughout, but rare on Pacific slope in western Panama) and northern Colombia.

Notes.—Also known as DUSKY-TAILED ANT-TANAGER. Some authors consider *H. fuscicauda* to be conspecific with the South American *H. gutturalis* (Sclater, 1854) [SOOTY ANT-TANAGER]; they consistute at least a superspecies. In the combined situation, RED-THROATED ANT-TANAGER is the most appropriate English name.

Habia atrimaxillaris (Dwight and Griscom). BLACK-CHEEKED ANT-TANAGER.

Phœnicothraupis atrimaxillaris Dwight and Griscom, 1924, Am. Mus. Novit., no. 142, p. 4. (Puerto Jimenez, Golfo Dulce, Prov. de Puntarenas, Costa Rica.)

Habitat.—Humid lowland forest undergrowth and shaded second growth (Tropical Zone).

Distribution.—*Resident* in the Pacific lowlands of southwestern Costa Rica (Golfo Dulce region).

Genus **PIRANGA** Vieillot

Piranga Vieillot, 1808, Hist. Nat. Ois. Am. Sept., 1 (1807), p. iv. Type, by monotypy, *Muscicapa rubra* Linnaeus = *Fringilla rubra* Linnaeus.
Spermagra Swainson, 1827, Philos. Mag., new ser., 1, p. 437. Type, by monotypy, *Spermagra erythrocephala* Swainson.

Piranga roseogularis Cabot. ROSE-THROATED TANAGER.

Pyranga roseo-gularis Cabot, 1846, Boston J. Nat. Hist., 5, p. 416. (road from Chemax to Yalahao, Yucatan = Yalahua, Quintana Roo.)

Habitat.—Edge and clearings of humid lowland and deciduous forest (Tropical Zone).

Distribution.—*Resident* in southeastern Mexico (throughout the Yucatan Peninsula, including Cozumel Island) and northern Guatemala (Petén), also a sight report for Belize (Gallon Jug).

Piranga flava (Vieillot). HEPATIC TANAGER. [609.]

Saltator Flavus Vieillot, 1822, *in* Bonnaterre and Vieillot, Tabl. Encycl. Méth., Ornithol., 2, livr. 91, p. 791. Based on "Habia Amarilla" Azara, Apunt. Hist. Nat. Páx. Parag., 1, p. 358 (no. 87). (Paraguay.)

Habitat.—Open coniferous forest (especially pine and pinyon-juniper), montane pine-oak association, riparian woodland, lowland pine savanna and, from Costa Rica southward, also open humid forest, scrub and orchards in both lowlands and highland regions, the migratory northern populations ranging in nonbreeding season to lowland woodland and forest (Tropical to Temperate zones).

Distribution.—*Breeds* [*hepatica* group] from southern California (San Bernardino and Kingston mountains, and Clark Mountain, probably also the New York Mountains), northwestern and central Arizona, western Colorado (probably), northern New Mexico, western Texas, Nuevo León and Tamaulipas south through the highlands of Middle America to northern Nicaragua, and in the lowland pine savanna to northeastern Nicaragua.

Winters [*hepatica* group] from northern Mexico (casually from southern California and southern Arizona) south through the breeding range, occurring also in lowland areas in northern Mexico.

Resident [*lutea* group] from central Costa Rica (Cordillera Central southward), Panama (both slopes), Colombia, Venezuela (also Trinidad), western Guyana and Surinam south, west of the Andes to western Ecuador and east of the Andes to eastern Peru, northwestern Bolivia, and extreme northern Brazil (Sierra Imerí); and [*flava* group] from the Guianas south, east of the Andes, through most of the Brazil, southern Bolivia and Paraguay to northern Argentina and Uruguay.

Casual [*hepatica* group] elsewhere in central and southern California (north to Solano and Inyo counties, and in the Farallon Islands), north to southern Nevada (probably breeds) and southern Wyoming, and east to southeastern Texas. Accidental in Illinois (Beverly).

Notes.—The three groups are sometimes regarded as distinct species, *P. hepatica* Swainson, 1827 [HEPATIC TANAGER], *P. lutea* (Lesson, 1834) [TOOTH-BILLED TANAGER], and *P. flava* [RED TANAGER.].

Piranga rubra (Linnaeus). SUMMER TANAGER. [610.]

> *Fringilla rubra* Linnaeus, 1758, Syst. Nat., ed. 10, 1, p. 181. Based on "The Summer Red-Bird" Catesby, Nat. Hist. Carolina, 1, p. 56, pl. 56. (in America = South Carolina.)

Habitat.—Deciduous forest, open woodland, pine-oak association, riparian woodland and parks, in migration and winter in a wide variety of forest, woodland and scrub habitats.

Distribution.—*Breeds* from southeastern California (west to San Bernardino County, and north to southern Inyo County), southern Nevada, southwestern Utah, central Arizona, central New Mexico, central and northeastern Texas, central Oklahoma, eastern Kansas, southeastern Nebraska, central Iowa (formerly), central (formerly northern) Illinois, southern Wisconsin (formerly), central Indiana, central Ohio, southwestern Pennsylvania, West Virginia, Virginia, eastern Maryland, southern Delaware and southern New Jersey south to northeastern Baja California, southeastern Sonora, northern Durango, southeastern Coahuila, central Nuevo León, southern Texas, the Gulf coast and southern Florida.

Winters from southern Baja California, southern Sinaloa and Veracruz south through Middle America and South America (also Trinidad) west of the Andes to western Ecuador and east of the Andes to eastern Peru, northern Bolivia and Amazonian Brazil, rarely north to coastal (casually northern) California and southern Arizona, casually in the Bahama Islands and Cuba.

In migration occurs regularly through northern Mexico, the Bahama Islands, Cuba, Jamaica, the Cayman Islands, and islands in the western Caribbean Sea (Swan, Providencia and San Andrés).

Casual or accidental north to southern Oregon, Montana, southern Saskatchewan, central Manitoba, Minnesota, Wisconsin, Michigan, southern Ontario, New Brunswick and Nova Scotia, and to Clipperton Island, Bermuda, the Lesser Antilles (Mustique in the Grenadines, and Barbados), Galapagos Islands, Curaçao and the British Isles.

Piranga olivacea (Gmelin). SCARLET TANAGER. [608.]

> *Tanagra olivacea* Gmelin, 1789, Syst. Nat., 1 (2), p. 889. Based primarily on the "Olive Tanager" Latham, Gen. Synop. Birds, 2 (1), p. 218. (in Cayenna et Noveboraco = New York.)

Habitat.—Deciduous forest and mature deciduous woodland, less frequently in mixed deciduous-coniferous forest, in migration and winter in a variety of forest, woodland, scrub and partly open habitats.

Distribution.—*Breeds* from eastern North Dakota, southeastern Manitoba, western Ontario, northeastern Minnesota, northern Michigan, southern Ontario, southwestern Quebec, New Brunswick and central Maine south to central Nebraska, western Kansas, north-central and southeastern Oklahoma, central Arkansas, west-central Tennessee, northern Alabama, northern Georgia, northwestern South Carolina, western North Carolina, central Virginia and Maryland.

Winters from Panama (rarely, in the lowlands) and Colombia south, east of the Andes, through eastern Ecuador and Peru to northwestern Bolivia.

Migrates primarily through the eastern United States (west to eastern New Mexico and central Texas), Middle America (primarily the Gulf-Caribbean slope north of Costa Rica, in Mexico recorded only from Veracruz, Jalisco and the Yucatan Peninsula) and the West Indies, casually west to the eastern slopes of the Rockies, in California and Bermuda, and to the Netherlands Antilles and Isla Los Roques (off Venezuela).

Casual elsewhere in western North America from southern British Columbia, southern Alberta and southern Saskatchewan (possibly breeding) south to Arizona and Colorado, and in northeastern North America north to Prince Edward Island, Nova Scotia and Newfoundland. Accidental in Alaska (Point Barrow) and the British Isles.

Piranga ludoviciana (Wilson). WESTERN TANAGER. [607.]

> *Tanagra ludoviciana* Wilson, 1811, Am. Ornithol., 3, p. 27, pl. 20, fig. 1. (prairies of the Missouri, between the Osage and Mandan nations = about two miles north of Kamiah, Idaho County, Idaho.)

Habitat.—Open coniferous and mixed coniferous-deciduous woodland, primarily in mountains, in migration and winter in a variety of forest, woodland, scrub and partly open habitats, in Middle America mostly in highland pine, pine-oak association, and humid forest edge and clearings.

Distribution.—*Breeds* from southeastern Alaska, northern British Columbia, southern Mackenzie, northern Alberta and central Saskatchewan south to northern Baja California, southern Nevada, southwestern Utah, central and southeastern Arizona, southern New Mexico and western Texas, and east to eastern Montana, western South Dakota, northwestern Nebraska, central Colorado and central New Mexico; one isolated breeding record from southern Wisconsin (Jefferson County, 1877) is questionable.

Winters from southern Baja California, Jalisco and southern Tamaulipas (rarely north to southern Oregon, coastal California, southern Arizona and southern Texas) south through Middle America (mostly highlands, not recorded Belize, doubtfully recorded Yucatan Peninsula) to Costa Rica, casually along the Gulf coast from southeastern Texas east to southern Florida, and to western Panama (western Chiriquí).

In migration occurs regularly east to western Nebraska, western Kansas, western Oklahoma and central Texas.

Casual north to central Alaska and southern Yukon, and across northeastern North America from Minnesota east through Wisconsin, Michigan, southern Ontario and southern Quebec to Maine and Nova Scotia, and south to New York, Pennsylvania, Maryland, Virginia and North Carolina, also sight reports elsewhere in eastern North America. Accidental in northern Alaska (Point Barrow), the Bahama Islands (New Providence) and Cuba (Cárdenas).

Piranga bidentata Swainson. FLAME-COLORED TANAGER.

Pyranga bidentata Swainson, 1827, Philos. Mag., new ser., 1, p. 438. (Temsicaltipec, Mexico = Temascaltepec, state of México.)

Habitat.—Humid montane forest, forest edge and, less frequently dense pine-oak association (Subtropical and Temperate zones).

Distribution.—*Resident* from southern Sonora, southern Chihuahua, central Nuevo León and southern Tamaulipas south through the mountains of Mexico (also the Tres Marias Islands, off Nayarit), Guatemala, El Salvador and Honduras to north-central Nicaragua; and in the mountains of Costa Rica (primarily the Cordillera Central) and western Panama (western Chiriquí).

Notes.—Also known as STREAK-BACKED TANAGER.

Piranga leucoptera Trudeau. WHITE-WINGED TANAGER.

Pyranga leucoptera Trudeau, 1839, J. Acad. Nat. Sci. Philadelphia, 8, p. 160. (Mexico.)

Habitat.—Humid forest, forest edge, clearings, mature second-growth woodland, scrub and plantations (upper Tropical and Subtropical zones).

Distribution.—*Resident* from San Luis Potosí and southern Tamaulipas south (west to Hidalgo, the state of México and Oaxaca) through Middle America (mostly in the highlands, not recorded Yucatan Peninsula) to western Panama (Chiriquí and Veraguas); and in South America from Colombia and Venezuela south, west of the Andes to western Ecuador and east of the Andes to eastern Peru, northwestern Bolivia and extreme northwestern Brazil.

Piranga erythrocephala (Swainson). RED-HEADED TANAGER.

Spermagra erythrocephala Swainson, 1827, Philos. Mag., new ser., 1, p. 437. (Temiscaltipec, Mexico = Temascaltepec, state of México.)

Habitat.—Humid montane forest and pine-oak association, in nonbreeding season also to deciduous forest (Subtropical and lower Temperate zones).

Distribution.—*Resident* from southeastern Sonora and Chihuahua south through Sinaloa, Durango, Nayarit, Jalisco, Guanajuato, Michoacán, the state of México, Morelos and Guerrero to Oaxaca (east to the Isthmus of Tehuantepec).

[Piranga rubriceps Gray. RED-HOODED TANAGER.] See Appendix B.

Genus **RAMPHOCELUS** Desmarest

Ramphocelus Desmarest, 1805, Hist. Nat. Tangaras, Manakins, Todiers, livr. 1, pl. 28 (and text), p. [1]. Type, by subsequent designation (G. R. Gray, 1855), *Tanagra brasilia* [sic] Linnaeus.
Phlogothraupis Sclater and Salvin, 1873, Nomencl. Avium Neotrop., pp. 21, 155. Type, by original designation, *Tanagra (Tachyphonus) sanguinolentus* Lesson.

Ramphocelus sanguinolentus (Lesson). CRIMSON-COLLARED TANAGER.

Tanagra (Tachyphonus) sanguinolentus Lesson, 1831, Cent. Zool., p. 107, pl. 39. (Mexico.)

Habitat.—Humid lowland and foothill forest edge, clearings, shrubby second growth, and thickets (Tropical and lower Subtropical zones).
Distribution.—*Resident* from Veracruz, Tabasco, northern Oaxaca, Chiapas and southern Quintana Roo south on the Gulf-Caribbean slope of Central America to western Panama (Bocas del Toro, Veraguas and western Panamá province, locally also on Pacific slope in Veraguas).
Notes.—Often placed in the monotypic genus *Phlogothraupis.*

Ramphocelus dimidiatus Lafresnaye. CRIMSON-BACKED TANAGER.

Ramphocelus dimidiatus Lafresnaye, 1837, Mag. Zool. [Paris], 7, cl. 2, pl. 81, p. 2. (du sud du Mexique et de Carthagène, Nouvelle-Grenade = Cartagena, Colombia.)

Habitat.—Scrub, shrubby areas, gardens, and humid lowland and foothill forest edge and clearings (Tropical and lower Subtropical zones).
Distribution.—*Resident* in Panama (both slopes west to Chiriquí and Veraguas, including Coiba and the Pearl islands), northern and western Colombia, and western Venezuela.
Notes.—*R. dimidiatus* and the South American *R. melanogaster* (Swainson, 1838), *R. carbo* (Pallas, 1764) and *R. bresilius* (Linnaeus, 1766) appear to constitute a superspecies.

Ramphocelus passerinii Bonaparte. SCARLET-RUMPED TANAGER.

Ramphocelus Passerinii Bonaparte, 1831, Antologia [Florence], 44 (130), p. 164. (in Insula Cuba, error = Guatemala.)

Habitat.—Thickets, gardens, shrubby areas, second growth, and humid forest edge (Tropical and lower Subtropical zones).
Distribution.—*Resident* from Veracruz, Tabasco and Chiapas south on the Gulf-Caribbean slope of Central America to Nicaragua, and on both slopes of Costa

Rica (except the dry northwest) and western Panama (Bocas del Toro and Chiriquí).

Notes.—*R. passerinii* and *R. flammigerus* appear to constitute a superspecies.

Ramphocelus flammigerus (Jardine and Selby). FLAME-RUMPED TANAGER.

Ramphopis flammigerus Jardine and Selby, 1833, Illus. Ornithol., 3, pl. 131. (Columbia River, error = Antioquia, Colombia.)

Habitat.—Shrubby areas, gardens, thickets and humid forest edge, especially near water (Tropical Zone).

Distribution.—*Resident* [*icteronotus* group] in Panama (west to Bocas del Toro and Veraguas, more commonly on the Caribbean slope), western Colombia and western Ecuador; and [*flammigerus* group] in western Colombia (east of the preceding, from the middle Cauca Valley south to Nariño).

Notes.—The two morphologically distinct groups are sometimes regarded as separate species, *R. icteronotus* Bonaparte, 1838 [YELLOW-RUMPED TANAGER], and *R. flammigerus* [FLAME-RUMPED TANAGER], but they intergrade in the Río San Juan region of western Colombia. See also comments under *R. passerinii*.

Genus PHAENICOPHILUS Strickland

Phœnicophilus Strickland, 1851, *in* Jardine, Contrib. Ornithol., 1, p. 104. Type, by original designation, *Phaenicophilus palmarum* (Linn.) = *Turdus palmarum* Linnaeus.

Phaenicophilus palmarum (Linnaeus). BLACK-CROWNED PALM-TANAGER.

Turdus palmarum Linnaeus, 1766, Syst. Nat., ed. 12, 1, p. 295. Based in part on "Le Palmiste a teste [=tête] noire" Brisson, Ornithologie, 2, p. 303, pl. 29, fig. 2. (in Cayennæ Palmis, error = Santo Domingo, Hispaniola.)

Habitat.—Woodland and thickets, in both semi-arid and humid regions, primarily in lowlands.

Distribution.—*Resident* on Hispaniola (except the southern peninsula of Haiti west of the Trouin Valley) and adjacent Saona Island.

Phaenicophilus poliocephalus (Bonaparte). GRAY-CROWNED PALM-TANAGER.

Dulus poliocephalus Bonaparte, 1851, Rev. Mag. Zool., ser. 2, 3, p. 178. (Hispaniola = Haiti.)

Habitat.—Woodland and thickets, mostly in lowland regions.

Distribution.—*Resident* in southwestern Hispaniola (Massif de la Hotte area, in southwestern Haiti) and on adjacent islands (Gonâve, Île-à-Vache and Grand Cayemite).

Genus CALYPTOPHILUS Cory

Calyptophilus Cory, 1884, Auk, 1, p. 3. Type, by monotypy, *Phenoicophilus frugivorus* Cory.

Notes.—Now thought to be more closely related to *Rhodinocichla* than to *Phaenicophilus*.

Calyptophilus frugivorus (Cory). CHAT TANAGER.

Phœnicophilus frugivorus Cory, 1883, Q. J. Boston Zool. Soc., 2, p. 45. (Santo Domingo = Almercen [=Villa Rivas], Dominican Republic.)

Habitat.—Dense mountain thickets, locally also in semi-arid lowland scrub.

Distribution.—*Resident* on Hispaniola [*tertius* group] in southern Haiti (massifs de la Hotte and la Selle); and [*frugivorus* group] in western Dominican Republic (east to Semaná province), and on Gonâve Island.

Notes.—The two groups are considered by some authors to be separate species, *C. tertius* Wetmore, 1929 [WESTERN CHAT-TANAGER], and *C. frugivorus* [EASTERN CHAT-TANAGER.].

Genus **RHODINOCICHLA** Hartlaub

Rhodinocichla Hartlaub, 1853, J. Ornithol., 1, p. 33. Type, by original designation, *Furnarius roseus* Lesson.

Notes.—Systematic position uncertain; may be related to the "paruline" genus *Granatellus.*

Rhodinocichla rosea (Lesson). ROSY THRUSH-TANAGER.

Furnarius roseus Lesson, 1832, Illus. Zool., livr. 2, pl. 5. (du Brésil et du district peu connu de San-Jose, error = Caracas, Venezuela.)

Habitat.—Thickets, dense undergrowth in second-growth woodland, brushy areas and scrub (Tropical and lower Subtropical zones).

Distribution.—*Resident* in the Pacific lowlands of Mexico from Sinaloa to western Michoacán (Coahuayana); on the Pacific slope of southern Middle America from southwestern Costa Rica east to central Panama (to eastern Panamá province, also on the Caribbean slope in Colón and the Canal Zone); and in South America in northern and central Colombia, and northern Venezuela.

Notes.—Also known as ROSE-BREASTED THRUSH-TANAGER.

Genus **MITROSPINGUS** Ridgway

Mitrospingus Ridgway, 1898, Auk, 15, p. 225. Type, by original designation, *Tachyphonus cassini* [sic] Lawrence.

Mitrospingus cassinii (Lawrence). DUSKY-FACED TANAGER.

Tachyphonus Cassinii Lawrence, 1861, Ann. Lyc. Nat. Hist. N.Y., 7, p. 297. (on the Atlantic side of the Isthmus of Panama, along the line of the Panama Railroad = Canal Zone.)

Habitat.—Humid lowland and foothill forest edge, undergrowth of second-growth woodland, thickets adjacent to forest, and plantations (Tropical and lower Subtropical zones).

Distribution.—*Resident* from Costa Rica (Caribbean lowlands) south through Panama (entire Caribbean slope, also in Pacific lowlands in Veraguas, eastern Panamá province and Darién) and the Pacific lowlands of Colombia to northwestern Ecuador.

Genus **CHLOROSPINGUS** Cabanis

Chlorospingus Cabanis, 1851, Mus. Heineanum, 1, p. 139. Type, by virtual monotypy, *Chlorospingus leucophrys* Cabanis = *Arremon ophthalmicus* Du Bus de Gisignies.

Chlorospingus ophthalmicus (Du Bus de Gisignies). COMMON BUSH-TANAGER.

Arremon ophthalmicus Du Bus de Gisignies, 1847, Bull. Acad. R. Sci. Lett. Beaux-Arts Belg., 14, p. 106. (Mexico = Jalapa, Veracruz.)

Habitat.—Humid montane forest, forest edge, clearings, second-growth woodland, shrubby areas and thickets, in nonbreeding season also to lowland forest (upper Tropical and Subtropical zones, in nonbreeding season to lower Tropical Zone, in South America also to lower Temperate Zone).

Distribution.—*Resident* [*ophthalmicus* group] in the highlands from Guerrero, Puebla, Hidalgo, eastern San Luis Potosí and northern Veracruz south through Middle America to western Panama (western Chiriquí and Bocas del Toro), and in South America from the mountains of Colombia and northern Venezuela south through the Andes of Ecuador and Peru to Bolivia and northwestern Argentina; and [*punctulatus* group] in the highlands of western Panama (Veraguas and Coclé).

Notes.—Also known as BROWN-HEADED BUSH-TANAGER. Species limits within the genus are poorly understood. The two groups have sometimes been regarded as separate species, *C. ophthalmicus* [COMMON BUSH-TANAGER] and *C. punctulatus* Sclater and Salvin, 1869 [DOTTED BUSH-TANAGER]; *C. inornatus* is regarded by some authors as a race of *C. ophthalmicus,* while *C. tacarcunae* is considered a race of *C. ophthalmicus* or a race of *C. flavigularis.* Two South American forms, *C. flavopectus* (Lafresnaye, 1840) and *C. cinereocephalus* Taczanowski, 1874, included herein in *C. ophthalmicus,* are sometimes regarded as full species or, in the case of *cinereocephalus,* as a race of the South American *C. semifuscus* Sclater and Salvin, 1873.

Chlorospingus tacarcunae Griscom. TACARCUNA BUSH-TANAGER.

Chlorospingus tacarcunae Griscom, 1924, Am. Mus. Novit., no. 141, p. 11. (Mt. Tacarcuna, east slope, alt. 4600 ft., eastern Panama.)

Habitat.—Humid montane forest, forest edge and brushy second growth (upper Tropical and lower Subtropical zones).

Distribution.—*Resident* in eastern Panama in eastern Panamá province (Cerro Jefe) and eastern Darién (Cerro Tacarcuna).

Notes.—See comments under *C. ophthalmicus.*

Chlorospingus inornatus (Nelson). PIRRE BUSH-TANAGER.

Hylospingus inornatus Nelson, 1912, Smithson. Misc. Collect., 60, no. 3, p. 18. (Mount Pirri, at 5200 feet altitude, eastern Panama.)

Habitat.—Humid montane forest, forest edge and second-growth woodland (upper Tropical and Subtropical zones).

Distribution.—*Resident* in eastern Panama in eastern Darién (Cerro Pirre, Cerro Sapo, and Cana).
Notes.—See comments under *C. ophthalmicus.*

Chlorospingus pileatus Salvin. Sooty-capped Bush-Tanager.

Chlorospingus pileatus Salvin, 1865, Proc. Zool. Soc. London (1864), p. 581. (Volcan de Cartago [=Irazú], Costa Rica.)

Habitat.—Humid montane forest, forest edge, clearings, scrubby second growth, and brushy areas (Subtropical and lower Temperate zones).
Distribution.—*Resident* in the mountains of Costa Rica (north to the Cordillera de Tilarán) and western Panama (Chiriquí and Veraguas).
Notes.—Includes *C. zeledoni* Ridgway, 1905 [Volcano Bush-Tanager], of the Irazú and Turrialba volcanoes in central Costa Rica, now shown to be a color morph of *C. pileatus* (see Johnson and Brush, 1972, Syst. Zool., 21, pp. 245–262).

Chlorospingus flavigularis (Sclater). Yellow-throated Bush-Tanager.

Pipilopsis flavigularis Sclater, 1852, Rev. Mag. Zool., ser. 2, 4, p. 8. (Nouvelle-Grenade = Bogotá, Colombia.)

Habitat.—Humid forest, forest edge and clearings (Tropical and lower Subtropical zones).
Distribution.—*Resident* in western Panama (Bocas del Toro and Veraguas); and in South America from Colombia south, west of the Andes to western Ecuador and east of the Andes to eastern Peru and northwestern Bolivia.
Notes.—Differences in eye color and behavior suggest that the Panama form may represent a species, *C. hypophaeus* Sclater and Salvin, 1868 [Dark-breasted Bush-Tanager], different from the South American *C. flavigularis.* See also comments under *C. ophthalmicus.*

Chlorospingus canigularis (Lafresnaye). Ashy-throated Bush-Tanager.

Tachyphonus canigularis Lafresnaye, 1848, Rev. Zool. [Paris], 11, p. 11. (ad Bogotam, in Colombia = Bogotá, Colombia.)

Habitat.—Humid montane forest, forest edge and clearings (Subtropical Zone).
Distribution.—*Resident* in the mountains of central Costa Rica (primarily Caribbean slope from Río Reventazón to the Cordillera Central) and extreme western Panama (western Bocas del Toro); and in South America from Colombia and northwestern Venezuela south to northwestern Peru and eastern Ecuador.

Genus NESOSPINGUS Sclater

Nesospingus Sclater, 1885, Ibis, p. 273. Type, by monotypy, *Chlorospingus speculiferus* Lawrence.

Nesospingus speculiferus (Lawrence). Puerto Rican Tanager.

Chlorospingus? speculiferus Lawrence, 1875, Ibis, p. 383, pl. 9, fig. 1. (Porto Rico.)

Habitat.—Highland forest and second-growth woodland.
Distribution.—*Resident* in the highlands of Puerto Rico.

Genus HEMITHRAUPIS Cabanis

Hemithraupis Cabanis, 1850, Mus. Heineanum, 1 (1851), p. 21. Type, by original designation, *Hylophilus ruficeps* Wied = *Nemosia ruficapilla* Vieillot.

Hemithraupis flavicollis (Vieillot). YELLOW-BACKED TANAGER.

Nemosia flavicollis Vieillot, 1818, Nouv. Dict. Hist. Nat., nouv. éd., 22, p. 491. (l'Amérique méridionale = Cayenne.)

Habitat.—Humid lowland forest, forest edge and scrub (Tropical and lower Subtropical zones).
Distribution.—*Resident* from extreme eastern Panama (Río Tuira and Cana, in eastern Darién), northern Colombia, southern Venezuela and the Guianas south, east of the Andes, to eastern Peru, northern Bolivia, and Amazonian and southeastern Brazil.

Genus CHRYSOTHLYPIS Berlepsch

Chrysothlypis Berlepsch, 1912, Verh. V Int. Ornithol. Kongr., Berlin (1911), p. 1080. Type, by original designation, *Tachyphonus chrysomelas* Sclater and Salvin.

Chrysothlypis chrysomelas (Sclater and Salvin). BLACK-AND-YELLOW TANAGER.

Tachyphonus chrysomelas Sclater and Salvin, 1869, Proc. Zool. Soc. London, p. 440, pl. 32. (Cordillera del Chucú, Veraguas, Panama.)

Habitat.—Humid foothill forest, forest edge, and adjacent open woodland (upper Tropical and lower Subtropical zones).
Distribution.—*Resident* in Costa Rica (primarily Caribbean slope north to Arenal) and Panama (east to western Panamá province, and in Darién).

Tribe TERSINI: Swallow-Tanagers

Genus TERSINA Vieillot

Tersina Vieillot, 1819, Nouv. Dict. Hist. Nat., nouv. éd., 33, p. 401. Type, by monotypy, *Tersina caerulea* Vieillot = *Hirundo viridis* Illiger.

Notes.—This genus was formerly placed in the monotypic family Tersinidae.

Tersina viridis (Illiger). SWALLOW-TANAGER.

Hirundo viridis Illiger, 1811, Prodromus, p. 229. Based on "L'Hirondelle verte" Temminck, Cat. Syst. Cab. Ornithol., Quadr., p. 245. (Sandwich Islands, error = eastern Brazil.)

Habitat.—Open woodland, second growth, clearings, parks and suburban areas, nesting in holes in earth banks (Tropical and Subtropical zones).

Distribution.—*Resident* in eastern Panama (eastern Panamá province and eastern Darién), and in South America from Colombia, Venezuela and the Guianas south, west of the Andes to western Ecuador and east of the Andes to eastern Peru, northern and eastern Bolivia, Paraguay, northeastern Argentina and southern Brazil. Southernmost populations apparently are migratory, at least in part.

Subfamily CARDINALINAE: Cardinals, Grosbeaks and Allies

Genus **SALTATOR** Vieillot

Saltator Vieillot, 1816, Analyse, p. 32. Type, by monotypy, "Grand Tanagra" Buffon = *Tanagra maxima* Müller.

Saltator albicollis Vieillot. STREAKED SALTATOR.

Saltator albicollis Vieillot, 1817, Nouv. Dict. Hist. Nat., nouv. éd., 14, p. 107. (Cayenne, error = Martinique.)

Habitat.—Open woodland, shrubby areas, scrub, deciduous woodland, thickets and cultivated areas (Tropical and lower Subtropical zones).

Distribution.—*Resident* [*albicollis* group] in the Lesser Antilles (Guadeloupe, Dominica, Martinique and St. Lucia); and [*striatipectus* group] on the Pacific slope of southwestern Costa Rica (El General region) and Panama (including Coiba, Coibita, Taboga and the Pearl islands, and on the Caribbean slope in the Canal Zone), and in South America from northern Colombia and northern Venezuela (also Patos, Monos, Chacachacare islands, and Trinidad) south, west of the Andes, to western Ecuador and western Peru.

Accidental [*albicollis* group] on Nevis, in the Lesser Antilles.

Notes.—Some authors regard the two groups as distinct species, *S. albicollis* [LESSER ANTILLEAN SALTATOR] and *S. striatipectus* Lafresnaye, 1847 [STREAKED SALTATOR].

Saltator coerulescens Vieillot. GRAYISH SALTATOR.

Saltator cœrulescens Vieillot, 1817, Nouv. Dict. Hist. Nat., nouv. éd., 14, p. 105. Based on "Habia Ceja blanca" Azara, Apunt. Hist. Nat. Páx. Parag., 1, p. 344 (no. 81). (Paraguay.)

Habitat.—Open woodland, scrub, second growth, thickets and plantations (Tropical and lower Subtropical zones).

Distribution.—*Resident* [*grandis* group] from Sinaloa, western Durango, eastern San Luis Potosí and southern Tamaulipas south along both slopes of Middle America (including the Yucatan Peninsula, but unrecorded Pacific slope of Nicaragua) to central Costa Rica; and [*coerulescens* group] from northern and eastern Colombia, Venezuela (also Monos and Chacachacare islands, and Trinidad) and the Guianas south, east of the Andes, to eastern Peru, eastern Bolivia, northern Argentina, Uruguay, and central and eastern Brazil.

Notes.—Some authors regard the two groups as distinct species, *S. grandis* (W.

Deppe, 1830) [MIDDLE AMERICAN SALTATOR] and *S. coerulescens* [GRAYISH SALTATOR].

Saltator maximus (Müller). BUFF-THROATED SALTATOR.

Tanagra maxima P. L. S. Müller, 1776, Natursyst., Suppl., p. 159. Based on "Tanagra, des grands bois de Cayenne" Daubenton, Planches Enlum., pl. 205. (Cayenne.)

Habitat.—Humid forest edge, second growth, open woodland, clearings, scrub, swamps and plantations (Tropical and Subtropical zones).

Distribution.—*Resident* from central Veracruz, northern Oaxaca, Tabasco, Chiapas, southern Campeche and southern Quintana Roo south on the Gulf-Caribbean slope of Central America to Nicaragua, on both slopes of Costa Rica (except the dry northwest) and Panama, and in South America from Colombia, Venezuela and the Guianas south, west of the Andes to western Ecuador and east of the Andes to eastern Peru, northern Bolivia, Paraguay, and central and southeastern Brazil.

Saltator atriceps (Lesson). BLACK-HEADED SALTATOR.

Tanagra (Saltator) atriceps Lesson, 1832, Cent. Zool., p. 208, pl. 69. (Mexico = Veracruz.)

Habitat.—Humid lowland and foothill forest edge, second growth, clearings, scrub, thickets and plantations (Tropical and lower Subtropical zones).

Distribution.—*Resident* in central Guerrero (Chilpancingo); and from eastern San Luis Potosí, southern Tamaulipas, Veracruz, eastern Puebla, northern and eastern Oaxaca, Chiapas and the Yucatan Peninsula south along both slopes of Central America to Honduras, and in Nicaragua (Pacific slope only), Costa Rica (primarily Caribbean slope) and Panama (both slopes, east to Darién).

Genus PITYLUS Cuvier

Pitylus Cuvier, 1829, Règne Anim., nouv. éd., 1, p. 413. Type, by subsequent designation (G. R. Gray, 1840), *Loxia grossa* Linnaeus.

Pitylus grossus (Linnaeus). SLATE-COLORED GROSBEAK.

Loxia grossa Linnaeus, 1766, Syst. Nat., ed. 12, 1, p. 307. Based on "Le Gros-bec bleu d'Amérique" Brisson, Ornithologie, 6, suppl., p. 89, pl. 5, fig. 1. (in America = Cayenne.)

Habitat.—Humid lowland and foothill forest, forest, second growth and adjacent scrub (Tropical and lower Subtropical zones).

Distribution.—*Resident* on the Caribbean slope of northeastern Honduras (sight report), Nicaragua and Costa Rica, on both slopes of Panama (more widespread on the Caribbean), and in South America from Colombia, southern Venezuela and the Guianas south, west of the Andes to western Ecuador and east of the Andes to eastern Peru, northwestern Bolivia, and Amazonian and eastern Brazil.

Notes.—Some authors consider *P. grossus* and the South American *P. fuliginosus* (Daudin, 1800) to be conspecific; they constitute a superspecies.

Genus CARYOTHRAUSTES Reichenbach

Caryothraustes Reichenbach, 1850, Avium Syst. Nat., pl. 78. Type, by subsequent designation (Sclater and Salvin, 1869), *"Pitylus"* [=*Coccothraustes*] *viridis* = *Loxia canadensis* Linnaeus.

Notes.—See comments under *Rhodothraupis.*

Caryothraustes poliogaster (Du Bus de Gisignies). BLACK-FACED GROSBEAK.

Pitylus poliogaster Du Bus de Gisignies, 1847, Bull. Acad. R. Sci. Lett. Beaux-Arts Belg., 14, p. 105. (Guatemala.)

Habitat.—Humid lowland and foothill forest, forest edge, and dense second-growth woodland (Tropical and lower Subtropical zones).

Distribution.—*Resident* from southern Veracruz, northern Oaxaca, Tabasco, Chiapas, southern Campeche and southern Quintana Roo south along the Gulf-Caribbean slope of Central America to western Panama (Bocas del Toro, and both slopes of Veraguas, casually or formerly to Coclé, western Panamá province and the Canal Zone).

Notes.—Some authors consider *C. poliogaster* and *C. canadensis* to be conspecific; they constitute a superspecies. With a single species treatment, BLACK-FACED GROSBEAK would be the appropriate English name.

Caryothraustes canadensis (Linnaeus). GREEN GROSBEAK.

Loxia canadensis Linnaeus, 1766, Syst. Nat., ed. 12, 1, p. 304. Based on "Le Gros-bec de Cayenne" Brisson, Ornithologie, 3, p. 229, pl. 11, fig. 3. (in Canada, error = Cayenne.)

Habitat.—Humid lowland and foothill forest, forest edge, second growth, shrubby areas, clearings and suburban regions (Tropical and lower Subtropical zones).

Distribution.—*Resident* in extreme eastern Panama (Cana, in eastern Darién); and in South America from southeastern Colombia, southern Venezuela and the Guianas south through Amazonian and central Brazil to southeastern Brazil.

Notes.—Also known as YELLOW-GREEN GROSBEAK. See comments under *C. poliogaster.*

Genus RHODOTHRAUPIS Ridgway

Rhodothraupis Ridgway, 1898, Auk, 15, p. 226. Type, by original designation, *Fringilla celaeno* Lichtenstein = *Tanagra celaeno* Deppe.

Notes.—Some authors merge this genus in *Caryothraustes.*

Rhodothraupis celaeno (Deppe). CRIMSON-COLLARED GROSBEAK. [594.1.]

Tanagra Celaeno (Lichtenstein MS) W. Deppe, 1830, Preis.-Verz. Säugeth. Vögel, etc., Mex., p. 2. (Mexico = Papantla, Veracruz.)

Habitat.—Brushy woodland, second growth and scrub (Tropical and lower Subtropical zones).

Distribution.—*Resident* from east-central Nuevo León and southern Tamaulipas south through eastern San Luis Potosí and northern Veracruz to northeastern Puebla.

Casual in southern Texas (Hidalgo County).

Genus **CARDINALIS** Bonaparte

Cardinalis Bonaparte, 1838, Proc. Zool. Soc. London (1837), p. 111. Type, by subsequent designation (G. R. Gray, 1840), *Cardinalis virginianus* Bonaparte = *Loxia cardinalis* Linnaeus.

Pyrrhuloxia Bonaparte, 1850, Consp. Gen. Avium, 1 (2), p. 500. Type, by monotypy, *Cardinalis sinuatus* Bonaparte.

Richmondena Mathews and Iredale, 1918, Austral Avian Rec., 3, p. 145. Type, by original designation, *Loxia cardinalis* Linnaeus.

Cardinalis cardinalis (Linnaeus). NORTHERN CARDINAL. [593.]

Loxia cardinalis Linnaeus, 1758, Syst. Nat., ed. 10, 1, p. 172. Based mainly on "The Red-Bird" Catesby, Nat. Hist. Carolina, 1, p. 38, pl. 38. (in America septentrionali = South Carolina.)

Habitat.—Thickets, brushy areas, fields, shrubbery, forest edge, clearings, around human habitation, and, in arid regions, in scrub, riparian thickets, woodland and brush (Tropical to Temperate zones).

Distribution.—*Resident* from cental Baja California, southeastern California, central and southeastern Arizona, southwestern New Mexico, western and northern Texas, western Kansas, central Nebraska, southeastern South Dakota, central Minnesota, northern Wisconsin, southern Ontario, southwestern Quebec, northern New York, Massachusetts and Nova Scotia south to southern Baja California (including Cerralvo, Santa Margarita, Carmen and San José islands), along the Pacific slope of Mexico to Oaxaca (including Tiburón and the Tres Marias islands), in the interior to Guanajuato and Hidalgo, along the Gulf-Caribbean slope to the Yucatan Peninsula (including Cozumel Island), northern Guatemala (Petén) and Belize, and to the Gulf coast and southern Florida (including the Florida Keys); also has bred in southeastern Manitoba (Winnipeg). The range in North America has been gradually expanding northward over the past few decades.

Introduced and established in the Hawaiian Islands (common on all main islands from Kauai eastward), southwestern California (Los Angeles County) and Bermuda.

Casual west and north to central Colorado and southern Saskatchewan.

Notes.—Formerly known as the CARDINAL; also known as COMMON CARDINAL. *C. cardinalis* and the South American *C. phoeniceus* Bonaparte, 1838, constitute a superspecies.

Cardinalis sinuatus Bonaparte. PYRRHULOXIA. [594.]

Cardinalis sinuatus Bonaparte, 1838, Proc. Zool. Soc. London (1837), p. 111. (Western parts of Mexico = Zacatecas.)

Habitat.—Arid brush, thorn scrub, weedy fields and riparian thickets (Tropical and Subtropical zones).

Distribution.—*Resident* from central Baja California (north to lat. 27°N.), Sonora, southern Arizona, southern New Mexico, and western and south-central

Texas south to southern Baja California, northern Nayarit, northeastern Jalisco, northern Michoacán, Querétaro, southern San Luis Potosí and southern Tamaulipas.

Casual north to southern California (Imperial and San Bernardino counties, attempted nesting in latter in 1977), central Arizona, central New Mexico and east-central Texas, also a sight report for Oklahoma (Cimarron County). Reports from Nevada and Puebla are open to question.

Notes.—Frequently placed in the monotypic genus *Pyrrhuloxia*.

Genus **PHEUCTICUS** Reichenbach

Pheucticus Reichenbach, 1850, Avium Syst. Nat., pl. 78. Type, by subsequent designation (G. R. Gray, 1855), *Pitylus aureoventris* d'Orbigny and Lafresnaye.

Hedymeles Cabanis, 1851, Mus. Heineanum, 1, p. 152. Type, by subsequent designation (G. R. Gray, 1855), *Loxia ludoviciana* Linnaeus.

Pheucticus chrysopeplus (Vigors). YELLOW GROSBEAK. [596.1.]

Coccothraustes chrysopeplus Vigors, 1832, Proc. Zool. Soc. London, Comm. Sci. Corresp., pt. 2, p. 4. (Mexico = San Blas, Nayarit.)

Habitat.—Foothill and montane forest edge, second-growth woodland, clearings, scrub and brushy areas (upper Tropical to lower Temperate zones).

Distribution.—*Resident* from southern Sonora, southwestern Chihuahua, Sinaloa and western Durango south in the highlands to Guerrero, Morelos, southwestern Puebla and northwestern Oaxaca; and in southern Chiapas and central Guatemala.

Casual in southern Arizona.

Notes.—Some authors regard *P. chrysopeplus, P. tibialis* and the South American *P. chrysogaster* (Lesson, 1832) as conspecific; they constitute a superspecies. With a single species treatment, YELLOW GROSBEAK is the appropriate English name.

Pheucticus tibialis Lawrence. BLACK-THIGHED GROSBEAK.

Pheucticus tibialis (Baird MS) Lawrence, 1867, Ann. Lyc. Nat. Hist. N.Y., 8, p. 478. ("Eervantes" [=Cervántes], Costa Rica.)

Habitat.—Humid montane forest edge and adjacent woodland (upper Subtropical and Temperate zones).

Distribution.—*Resident* in the mountains of Costa Rica (north to the Cordillera de Tilarán) and western Panama (east to Veraguas).

Notes.—See comments under *P. chrysopeplus.*

Pheucticus ludovicianus (Linnaeus). ROSE-BREASTED GROSBEAK. [595.]

Loxia ludoviciana Linnaeus, 1766, Syst. Nat., ed. 12, 1, p. 306. Based on "Le Gros-bec de la Louisiane" Brisson, Ornithologie, 3, p. 247, pl. 12, fig. 2. (in Ludovicia = Louisiana.)

Habitat.—Deciduous forest (especially poplar and aspen), woodland and second growth, in migration and winter in a variety of forest, woodland and scrub habitats.

Distribution.—*Breeds* from northeastern British Columbia, southwestern and south-central Mackenzie, northern Alberta, central Saskatchewan, southern Manitoba, western and southern Ontario, southwestern Quebec, New Brunswick, Prince Edward Island and Nova Scotia south to central and southeastern Alberta, southern Saskatchewan, north-central North Dakota, eastern South Dakota, eastern Nebraska, central (formerly northwestern) Kansas, central Oklahoma, southern Missouri, southern Illinois, central Indiana, northern Ohio, eastern Kentucky, eastern Tennessee, northern Georgia, western North Carolina, western Virginia, West Virginia and Maryland, casually west to northeastern Wyoming and eastern Colorado.

Winters from Michoacán and San Luis Potosí south through Middle America to northern and eastern Colombia, Venezuela, eastern Ecuador and east-central Peru, rarely in southern Texas, southern Louisiana and western Cuba; recorded occasionally in winter in the breeding range, and in Oregon and California.

Migrates regularly through the southeastern states (west to the Rockies) and northeastern Mexico, irregularly west to California, Utah, Colorado and New Mexico, and through the Bahama Islands, Greater Antilles (east to the Virgin Islands), and islands in the western Caribbean Sea (Swan, Providencia and San Andrés), and casually elsewhere in western North America from southern British Columbia, Idaho and Montana south to Arizona and northwestern Mexico.

Casual or accidental in the Lesser Antilles (Barbuda, Dominica, Barbados), Greenland and the British Isles.

Notes.—*P. ludovicianus* and *P. melanocephalus* hybridize where their ranges overlap in the Great Plains; they constitute a superspecies and are regarded as conspecific by a few authors.

Pheucticus melanocephalus (Swainson). BLACK-HEADED GROSBEAK. [596.]

Guiraca melanocephala Swainson, 1827, Philos. Mag., new ser., 1, p. 438. (Temiscaltipec, Mexico = Temascaltepec, state of México.)

Habitat.—Deciduous forest and woodland, pine-oak association, oak scrub, pinyon-juniper woodland and deciduous thickets (Subtropical and Temperate zones).

Distribution.—*Breeds* from southern British Columbia, southern Alberta, southwestern Saskatchewan, northeastern Montana and northwestern North Dakota south to northern Baja California, southern California, southern Nevada, central and southeastern Arizona and, in the Mexican highlands, to Guerrero and Oaxaca (west of the Isthmus of Tehuantepec), and east to central Nebraska, central Kansas, western Oklahoma, eastern New Mexico and western Texas.

Winters from coastal California (rarely), southern Baja California, northern Mexico, southeastern Texas and (rarely) southern Louisiana south to Oaxaca and Veracruz.

Casual in eastern North America from southern Manitoba, Minnesota, Wisconsin, Michigan, southern Ontario, New York, Maine, New Brunswick and Nova Scotia south to the Gulf coast and Florida (recorded most frequently in New England and along the Atlantic coast south to South Carolina); also a sight report from southern Alaska (Middleton Island), but another for Costa Rica and an old record from the state of Yucatán are highly questionable.

Notes.—See comments under *P. ludovicianus.*

Genus **CYANOCOMPSA** Cabanis

Cyanocompsa Cabanis, 1861, J. Ornithol., 9, p. 4. Type, by original designation, *Fringilla* [*Cyanoloxia*] *parellina* Bonaparte.

Notes.—Some authors merge *Cyanocompsa* and *Guiraca* in *Passerina.*

Cyanocompsa cyanoides (Lafresnaye). BLUE-BLACK GROSBEAK.

Coccoborus cyanoides Lafresnaye, 1847, Rev. Zool. [Paris], 10, p. 74. (Panama.)

Habitat.—Humid lowland and foothill forest undergrowth, forest edge, second growth, open woodland, clearings, plantations and thickets (Tropical and lower Subtropical zones).
Distribution.—*Resident* from southern Veracruz, northern Oaxaca, Tabasco, Chiapas, southern Campeche and southern Quintana Roo south on the Gulf-Caribbean slope of Central America to Nicaragua, on both slopes of Costa Rica (except the dry northwest) and Panama, and in South America from Colombia, Venezuela and the Guianas south, west of the Andes to western Ecuador and east of the Andes to eastern Peru, northern Bolivia and Amazonian Brazil.
A report from Trinidad is regarded as erroneous.

Cyanocompsa parellina (Bonaparte). BLUE BUNTING. [597.1.]

Cyanoloxia parellina (Lichtenstein MS) Bonaparte, 1850, Consp. Gen. Avium, 1(2), p. 502. (Alvarado, Veracruz, Mexico.)

Habitat.—Deciduous forest, forest edge, pine-oak association, clearings, arid scrub, brushy fields and thickets (Tropical and lower Subtropical zones).
Distribution.—*Resident* from central Sinaloa, eastern San Luis Potosí, northern Nuevo León and central Tamaulipas south along both slopes of Mexico (including the Yucatan Peninsula and Isla Mujeres) and Central America to north-central Nicaragua.
Casual or accidental in Texas (Bentsen-Rio Grande State Park area) and southwestern Louisiana (Cameron Parish).

Genus **GUIRACA** Swainson

Guiraca Swainson, 1827, Philos. Mag., new ser., 1, p. 438. Type, by subsequent designation (Swainson, 1827), *Loxia caerulea* "Wilson" [=Linnaeus].

Notes.—See comments under *Cyanocompsa.*

Guiraca caerulea (Linnaeus). BLUE GROSBEAK. [597.]

Loxia cærulea Linnaeus, 1758, Syst. Nat., ed. 10, 1, p. 175. Based on "The blew Gross-bec" Catesby, Nat. Hist. Carolina, 1, p. 39, pl. 39. (in America = South Carolina.)

Habitat.—Partly open situations with scattered trees, riparian woodland, scrub, thickets and cultivated lands, in migration and winter also in second growth, weedy fields and grassy areas (upper Tropical to lower Temperate zones, in non-breeding season also to lower Tropical Zone).

Distribution.—*Breeds* from central interior and southern California (north to Owen's Valley and Mono County), southern Nevada, southern and eastern Utah, southern Colorado, Nebraska (also north through central South Dakota to south-central North Dakota and probably also southwestern Minnesota), Kansas, central Missouri, central Illinois, southern Indiana, southern Ohio, West Virginia, southern Pennsylvania and northern New Jersey south to northern Baja California and southern Arizona, in the highlands and Pacific lowlands of Middle America through Mexico, Guatemala, El Salvador, Honduras and Nicaragua to central Costa Rica, and to southern Tamaulipas, the Gulf coast and central Florida; breeding sporadic and casual in the extreme northeastern parts of the breeding range.

Winters from southern Baja California and northern Mexico (rarely from the Gulf coast and southern Florida, casually elsewhere in the North American breeding range and north to New England) south through Middle America to central Panama (Canal Zone), and (rarely) in Cuba.

Migrates from California and the North American breeding range south over most of Middle America (including the Caribbean lowlands), through the Bahama Islands and Greater Antilles (east to the Virgin Islands), and to the Swan Islands (western Caribbean Sea).

Casual north to Washington, southern Saskatchewan, Minnesota, Wisconsin, southern Michigan, southern Ontario, southern Quebec, New Brunswick and Nova Scotia. Accidental in Ecuador (also sight record from Colombia).

Genus **PASSERINA** Vieillot

Passerina Vieillot, 1816, Analyse, p. 30. Type, by subsequent designation (G. R. Gray, 1840), "Le Ministre" Buffon = *Tanagra cyanea* Linnaeus.

Notes.—See comments under *Cyanocompsa.*

Passerina rositae (Lawrence). ROSE-BELLIED BUNTING.

Cyanospiza rositæ (Sumichrast MS) Lawrence, 1874, Ann. Lyc. Nat. Hist. N.Y., 10, p. 397. (Tehuantepec, Mexico = Cacoprieto, Oaxaca.)

Habitat.—Deciduous forest, riparian woodland and adjacent brush (Tropical Zone).

Distribution.—*Resident* in eastern Oaxaca (Isthmus of Tehuantepec region west to Chivela, Matías Romero and Juchitán) and extreme western Chiapas (La Trinidad).

Notes.—Also known as ROSITA'S BUNTING.

Passerina amoena (Say). LAZULI BUNTING. [599.]

Emberiza amœna Say, 1823, *in* Long, Exped. Rocky Mount., 2, p. 47 (note). (Rocky Mountains, source of the Arkansas = near Canyon City, Colorado.)

Habitat.—Arid brushy areas in canyons, riparian thickets, chaparral and open woodland, in migration and winter also in open grassy and weedy areas.

Distribution.—*Breeds* from southern British Columbia, southern Alberta, southern Saskatchewan, central North Dakota and northeastern South Dakota south to northwestern Baja California, southern California, southern Nevada, central Arizona, central New Mexico and central Texas (Kerr County, with summer records also for Trans-Pecos and the Panhandle), and east to east-central Nebraska, western Kansas and western Oklahoma.

Winters from southern Baja California, southern Arizona and Chihuahua south to Guerrero and central Veracruz.

Migrates regularly through the southwestern United States and northwestern Mexico (including Baja California), rarely west to southwestern British Columbia, north to central Alberta, and east to Minnesota, western Missouri, and eastern and southern Texas.

Casual in eastern North America (recorded Illinois, southern Ontario, Pennsylvania, Maine, Maryland and Florida, also sight reports from Wisconsin, Arkansas and Virginia). Accidental in southern Mackenzie.

Notes.—*P. amoena* and *P. cyanea* hybridize where their ranges overlap in the Great Plains region but are locally sympatric without interbreeding in the Southwest; they constitute a superspecies and are regarded as conspecific by a few authors.

Passerina cyanea (Linnaeus). INDIGO BUNTING. [598.]

Tanagra cyanea Linnaeus, 1766, Syst. Nat., ed. 12, 1, p. 315. Based on "The blew Linnet" Catesby, Nat. Hist. Carolina, 1, p. 45, pl. 45. (in Carolina = South Carolina.)

Habitat.—Deciduous forest edge and clearings, open woodland, second growth, shrubby areas, scrub and cultivated lands, in migration and winter in a variety of open forest, woodland, scrub and open habitats.

Distribution.—*Breeds* from southeastern Saskatchewan, southern Manitoba, northern Minnesota, western and southern Ontario, southwestern Quebec, southern Maine and southern New Brunswick south to southern New Mexico, central and southeastern Texas (south to San Patricio County), the Gulf coast and central Florida, and west to eastern Wyoming, eastern Colorado, western Kansas and central New Mexico; recorded breeding sporadically also in central Colorado, southwestern Utah, central Arizona and southern California.

Winters from Jalisco and San Luis Potosí (rarely from southern Texas, the Gulf coast and Florida, casually in winter elsewhere in the North American breeding range) south through Middle America (including most adjacent islands), the Greater Antilles (east to the Virgin Islands) and Bahama Islands to Panama (rare east of the Canal Zone) and northwestern Colombia.

Migrates through the United States east of the Rockies, Mexico (except the northwestern portion), northern Middle America, the western Greater Antilles and Bahama Islands; uncommonly (but regularly) through California, Baja California, northwestern Mexico, southern Arizona and New Mexico; and casually elsewhere in western North America from southern British Columbia, Idaho, southern Alberta and southern Saskatchewan southward.

Casual north to central Quebec, Nova Scotia, Newfoundland, Iceland and the British Isles (possibly escapes).

Notes.—See comments under *P. amoena*.

Passerina versicolor (Bonaparte). VARIED BUNTING. [600.]

Spiza versicolor Bonaparte, 1838, Proc. Zool. Soc. London (1837), p. 120. (near Temascallepec [=Temascaltepec, state of México].)

Habitat.—Arid thorn brush and thickets, dry washes and arid scrub (Tropical and Subtropical zones).

Distribution.—*Breeds* from southern Baja California (Cape District), northern Sonora, south-central and southeastern Arizona, southern New Mexico (Guadalupe Mountains, Carlsbad Caverns), and western and southern Texas (Culberson and Crockett counties, and the Rio Grande Valley) south through Mexico (except the Yucatan Peninsula) to central Guatemala (Motagua Valley).

Winters from southern Baja California, southern Sonora, southern Chihuahua, central Nuevo León and southern Texas south through the remainder of the breeding range.

Casual north to southern California (to Riverside and Inyo counties), west-central Arizona, west-central New Mexico and south-central Texas.

Passerina leclancherii Lafresnaye. ORANGE-BREASTED BUNTING.

Passerina (Spiza) Leclancherii Lafresnaye, 1840, Rev. Zool. [Paris], 3, p. 260. (Acapulco, [Guerrero,] Mexico.)

Habitat.—Deciduous forest, arid scrub, brush and abandoned fields (Tropical and lower Subtropical zones).

Distribution.—*Resident* on the Pacific slope from Colima, Jalisco and Michoacán south through Guerrero, southern Puebla and Oaxaca to southwestern Chiapas (Arriaga).

An individual netted in southern Texas (Hidalgo County) in 1972 was almost certainly an individual escaped from captivity.

Notes.—Also known as LECLANCHER'S BUNTING.

Passerina ciris (Linnaeus). PAINTED BUNTING. [601.]

Emberiza Ciris Linnaeus, 1758, Syst. Nat., ed. 10, 1, p. 179. Based mainly on "The Painted Finch" Catesby, Nat. Hist. Carolina, 1, p. 44, pl. 44. (in America = South Carolina.)

Habitat.—Partly open situations with scattered brush and trees, riparian thickets and brush, and weedy and shrubby areas, in migration and winter in a variety of open weedy, grassy and scrub habitats, and in open woodland.

Distribution.—*Breeds* from southeastern New Mexico, northern Texas, central Oklahoma, east-central Kansas, southern Missouri and southwestern Tennessee south to southern Chihuahua, northern Coahuila, southern Texas and southern Louisiana, and east along the Gulf coast to southern Alabama (locally to the Apalachicola region of western Florida); and from central South Carolina and southeastern North Carolina south, primarily on barrier islands and the adjacent mainland coast, to central Florida.

Winters from Sinaloa, San Luis Potosí, central Tamaulipas, northern Florida and the northwestern Bahama Islands south through Cuba, Jamaica and Middle America (both slopes) to western Panama (Bocas del Toro and Chiriquí, casually to western Panamá province).

Migrates regularly through the southeastern United States from the breeding range and northern portions of the Gulf states southward, and west (at least formerly) to southeastern Arizona and Sonora, casually to southern California.

Casual north to Oregon, Colorado, Nebraska, Minnesota, Michigan, southern Ontario, New York, New Hampshire, Maine and Nova Scotia; some of these reports are likely based on individuals escaped from captivity. Accidental in Bermuda; a report from the British Isles was almost certainly of an escape.

Genus SPIZA Bonaparte

Spiza Bonaparte, 1824, J. Acad. Nat. Sci. Philadelphia, 4, p. 45. Type, by subsequent designation (Bonaparte, 1827), *Emberiza americana* Gmelin.

Notes.—Affinities of this genus are uncertain; some authors believe it to be an icterine, others an aberrant cardinaline.

Spiza americana (Gmelin). DICKCISSEL. [604.]

Emberiza americana Gmelin, 1789, Syst. Nat., 1 (2), p. 872. Based on the "Black-throated Bunting" Pennant, Arct. Zool., 2, p. 363, pl. 17. (in Noveboraco = New York.)

Habitat.—Grasslands, meadows, savanna, cultivated lands and brushy fields, in migration and winter also in a variety of open country, second growth and scrub.

Distribution.—*Breeds* from eastern Montana, southeastern Saskatchewan, southern Manitoba, northwestern and central Minnesota, northern Wisconsin, central Michigan, southern Ontario, central New York and Massachusetts south to central Colorado, eastern New Mexico (probably), western and southern Texas, southern Louisiana, central Mississippi, central (rarely southern) Alabama, central Georgia and South Carolina, formerly also in the Atlantic lowlands from Massachusetts to North Carolina; breeding sporadic and irregular in eastern portion of range.

Winters from Michoacán south, primarily along the Pacific slope, through Middle America to northern and eastern Colombia, Venezuela (also Trinidad) and the Guianas, locally in small numbers also in coastal lowlands from southern New England south to Florida and west to southern Texas.

Migrates regularly from southern (casually northwestern) California, southern Arizona, New Mexico, the southeastern United States and the Bahama Islands south through Middle America (both slopes), casually through Baja California, Jamaica, Puerto Rico, islands in the western Caribbean Sea (Swan, Providencia, San Andrés and Albuquerque Cay), and the Netherlands Antilles (Aruba).

Casual north to southern British Columbia, southern Alberta, northern Michigan, southern Quebec, southern New Brunswick, Prince Edward Island, Nova Scotia and Newfoundland.

Subfamily EMBERIZINAE: Emberizines

Genus PAROARIA Bonaparte

Paroaria Bonaparte, 1831, G. Arcad. Sci. Lett. Arti [Rome], 52, p. 206. Type, by original designation, *Fringilla cucullata* Vieillot = *Loxia coronata* Miller.

Notes.—Sometimes treated as a cardinaline, but appears to be emberizine, or possibly thraupine of uncertain relationships.

Paroaria coronata (Miller). RED-CRESTED CARDINAL. [592.2.]

> *Loxia coronata* J. F. Miller, 1776, Var. Subj. Nat. Hist., pt. 1, pl. 2. (No locality given = Rio Grande do Sul, Brazil.)

Habitat.—Scrub, brushy areas, parks and residential areas, mostly in humid regions.

Distribution.—*Resident* from eastern Bolivia, Paraguay, Uruguay and extreme southern Brazil south to northern Argentina.

Introduced and established in the Hawaiian Islands in 1928 on Oahu (where now common), presently also on Molokai and, locally, on Kauai, Lanai, Maui and Hawaii.

Notes.—Also known as BRAZILIAN CARDINAL.

Paroaria capitata (d'Orbigny and Lafresnaye). YELLOW-BILLED CARDINAL. [592.3.]

> *Tachyphonus capitatus* d'Orbigny and Lafresnaye, 1837, Mag. Zool. [Paris], 7, cl. 2, pl. 77–79, p. 29. (Corrientes, rep. Argentina.)

Habitat.—Forest and woodland, and adjacent partly open situations with scattered trees, primarily in semi-arid habitats.

Distribution.—*Resident* from southeastern Bolivia, central Brazil (western Mato Grosso) and Paraguay south to northern Argentina.

Introduced and established in the Hawaiian Islands (since 1933, presently in small numbers along the Kona coast of Hawaii).

Genus **LYSURUS** Ridgway

> *Lysurus* Ridgway, 1898, Auk, 15, p. 225. Type, by original designation, *Buarremon crassirostris* Cassin.

Lysurus crassirostris (Cassin). SOOTY-FACED FINCH.

> *Buarremon crassirostris* Cassin, 1865, Proc. Acad. Nat. Sci. Philadelphia, 17, p. 170. (Barranca, Costa Rica.)

Habitat.—Humid montane forest undergrowth, edge, and clearings (Subtropical and lower Temperate zones).

Distribution.—*Resident* in the mountains from central Costa Rica (Aguacate Mountains southward) south through Panama (recorded Chiriquí, Bocas del Toro, Veraguas, Coclé and eastern Darién).

Notes.—*L. crassirostris* and the South American *L. castaneiceps* (Sclater, 1860) [OLIVE FINCH] constitute a superspecies; they are considered conspecific by some authors.

Genus **PSELLIOPHORUS** Ridgway

> *Pselliophorus* Ridgway, 1898, Auk, 15, p. 225. Type, by original designation, *Tachyphonus tibialis* Lawrence.

Notes.—Some authors suggest merger of this genus in *Atlapetes*.

Pselliophorus tibialis (Lawrence). YELLOW-THIGHED FINCH.

Tachyphonus tibialis Lawrence, 1864, Ann. Lyc. Nat. Hist. N.Y., 8, p. 41. (San Jose, Costa Rica.)

Habitat.—Humid montane forest edge and clearings, thickets, brush, and dense second growth (Subtropical and Temperate zones).

Distribution.—*Resident* in the mountains from central Costa Rica (Cordillera Central southward) to extreme western Panama (western Chiriquí).

Notes.—*P. tibialis* and *P. luteoviridis* are closely related and possibly conspecific; they constitute a superspecies.

Pselliophorus luteoviridis Griscom. YELLOW-GREEN FINCH.

Pselliophorus luteoviridis Griscom, 1924, Am. Mus. Novit., no. 141, p. 10. (Cerro Flores, alt. 6000 ft., eastern Chiriqui, Panama.)

Habitat.—Humid montane forest undergrowth, edge and clearings, and adjacent brushy areas (upper Subtropical and Temperate zones).

Distribution.—*Resident* in the mountains of western Panama (eastern Chiriquí and adjacent Veraguas).

Notes.—See comments under *P. tibialis*.

Genus **PEZOPETES** Cabanis

Pezopetes Cabanis, 1860, J. Ornithol., 8, p. 415. Type, by monotypy, *Pezopetes capitalis* Cabanis.

Notes.—Some authors suggest that this genus be merged in *Atlapetes*.

Pezopetes capitalis Cabanis. LARGE-FOOTED FINCH.

Pezopetes capitalis Cabanis, 1860, J. Ornithol., 8, p. 415. (Costa Rica.)

Habitat.—Brushy undergrowth of humid montane forest edge and clearings, thickets, and dense second growth (upper Subtropical and Temperate zones).

Distribution.—*Resident* in the mountains from central Costa Rica (Cordillera Central southward) to extreme western Panama (western Bocas del Toro and western Chiriquí).

Genus **ATLAPETES** Wagler

Atlapetes Wagler, 1831, Isis von Oken, col. 526. Type, by monotypy, *Atlapetes pileatus* Wagler.

Notes.—Members of this genus are sometimes known under the group name ATLAPETES. See also comments under *Pezopetes* and *Pselliophorus*.

Atlapetes albinucha (d'Orbigny and Lafresnaye). WHITE-NAPED BRUSH-FINCH.

Embernagra albinucha d'Orbigny and Lafresnaye, 1838, Rev. Zool. [Paris], 1, p. 165. (Cartagenè, error = Caribbean slope of Mexico.)

Habitat.—Thickets, brush, and undergrowth of humid montane forest (Subtropical and lower Temperate zones).

Distribution.—*Resident* in the highlands on the Gulf slope in Veracruz, Puebla, northern Oaxaca and northern Chiapas, also sight reports from eastern San Luis Potosí. A report from the valley of México is considered doubtful, while those from Colombia are regarded as erroneous.

Notes.—*A. albinucha* and *A. gutturalis* are closely related and sometimes considered conspecific; they constitute a superspecies.

Atlapetes gutturalis (Lafresnaye). YELLOW-THROATED BRUSH-FINCH.

Arremon gutturalis Lafresnaye, 1843, Rev. Zool. [Paris], 6, p. 98. (la Bolivie, error = Colombia.)

Habitat.—Brushy areas, humid montane forest edge, clearings, undergrowth of pine-oak association, dense second growth, and scrub (Subtropical and lower Temperate zones).

Distribution.—*Resident* in the highlands of southern Chiapas, Guatemala, El Salvador, Honduras, north-central Nicaragua, Costa Rica, western Panama (Chiriquí and Veraguas) and Colombia.

Notes.—See comments under *A. albinucha.*

Atlapetes pileatus Wagler. RUFOUS-CAPPED BRUSH-FINCH.

Atlapetes pileatus Wagler, 1831, Isis von Oken, col. 526. (Mexico.)

Habitat.—Undergrowth of humid montane forest and pine-oak association, and adjacent dense brush (Subtropical and Temperate zones).

Distribution.—*Resident* in the Mexican highlands from western Chihuahua, Sinaloa, western Durango, Nayarit, Jalisco, Guanajuato, San Luis Potosí, central Nuevo León and southwestern Tamaulipas south to Oaxaca (west of the Isthmus of Tehuantepec), Puebla and western Veracruz.

Atlapetes brunneinucha (Lafresnaye). CHESTNUT-CAPPED BRUSH-FINCH.

Embernagra brunnei-nucha Lafresnaye, 1839, Rev. Zool. [Paris], 2, p. 97. (Mexico = Jalapa, Veracruz.)

Habitat.—Undergrowth of humid forest, pine-oak association, dense second growth and plantations (upper Tropical to lower Temperate zones).

Distribution.—*Resident* [*apertus* group] in the Sierra de Tuxtla, southern Veracruz; and [*brunneinucha* group] in the highlands from eastern San Luis Potosí and northern Veracruz south through Hidalgo and Puebla to Guerrero, central Oaxaca and central Veracruz, and locally in Chiapas, central Guatemala, northern El Salvador, Honduras, Nicaragua, Costa Rica (Cordillera de Tilarán southward) and Panama (Bocas del Toro, Chiriquí, Veraguas, western Panamá province, and eastern Darién), and in South America from Colombia and northern Venezuela south through Ecuador to southeastern Peru.

Notes.—The two groups are sometimes recognized as distinct species, *A. apertus* Wetmore, 1942 [PLAIN-BREASTED BRUSH-FINCH], and *A. brunneinucha* [CHESTNUT-CAPPED BRUSH-FINCH].

Atlapetes virenticeps (Bonaparte). GREEN-STRIPED BRUSH-FINCH.

Buarremon virenticeps Bonaparte, 1855, C. R. Açad. Sci. Paris, 41, p. 657. (Mexico = Desierto de los Leones, near Ciudad México, Distrito Federal.)

Habitat.—Undergrowth of humid montane forest and pine-oak association (Subtropical and Temperate zones).

Distribution.—*Resident* in the mountains, primarily on the Pacific slope, from southern Sinaloa and western Durango south through Nayarit, Jalisco, Colima and Michoacán to the state of México, Distrito Federal, Morelos and western Puebla.

Notes.—*A. virenticeps, A. atricapillus* and the South American *A. assimilis* (Boissonneau, 1840) [GRAY-STRIPED BRUSH-FINCH] are sometimes considered conspecific with another South American species, *A. torquatus* (Lafresnaye and d'Orbigny, 1837) [STRIPE-HEADED BRUSH-FINCH]; the forms constitute a superspecies. With a single species concept, STRIPED BRUSH-FINCH is the appropriate English name.

Atlapetes atricapillus (Lawrence). BLACK-HEADED BRUSH-FINCH.

Buarremon atricapillus Lawrence, 1874, Ann. Lyc. Nat. Hist. N.Y., 10, p. 396. ("Bogota" = probably northern Colombia.)

Habitat.—Humid foothill and montane forest edge and clearings, dense second growth, and thickets (upper Tropical and Subtropical zones).

Distribution.—*Resident* in the highlands of southwestern Costa Rica (north to the Gulf of Nicoya), Panama (western Chiriquí, eastern Panamá province, and eastern Darién) and northern Colombia.

Notes.—See comments under *A. virenticeps.*

Genus **ARREMON** Vieillot

Arremon Vieillot, 1816, Analyse, p. 32. Type, by monotypy, "L'Oiseau Silencieux" Buffon = *Tanagra taciturna* Hermann.

Notes.—See comments under *Arremonops.*

Arremon aurantiirostris Lafresnaye. ORANGE-BILLED SPARROW.

Arremon aurantiirostris Lafresnaye, 1847, Rev. Zool. [Paris], 10, p. 72. (Panama.)

Habitat.—Undergrowth of humid lowland forest, forest edge, and dense second growth (Tropical Zone).

Distribution.—*Resident* from southern Veracruz, northern Oaxaca, Tabasco and Chiapas south through the Gulf-Caribbean lowlands of Central America to Nicaragua, on both slopes of Costa Rica (except the dry northwest) and Panama, and in northern and western Colombia, and northwestern Ecuador.

Genus **ARREMONOPS** Ridgway

Arremonops Ridgway, 1896, Man. North Am. Birds, ed. 2, pp. 434, 605. Type, by original designation, *Embernagra rufivirgata* Lawrence.

Notes.—Some authors would merge this genus in *Arremon.*

Arremonops rufivirgatus (Lawrence). OLIVE SPARROW. [586.]

Embernagra rufivirgata Lawrence, 1851, Ann. Lyc. Nat. Hist. N.Y., 5, p. 112, pl. 5, fig. 2. (Rio Grande in Texas = Brownsville, Texas.)

Habitat.—Undergrowth of deciduous forest, thickets, thorn scrub, dense second growth, mesquite and riparian brush (Tropical and lower Subtropical zones).

Distribution.—*Resident* [*superciliosus* group] along the Pacific coast from central Sinaloa south to central Oaxaca (west of the Isthmus of Tehuantepec), and in northwestern Costa Rica (Guanacaste); and [*rufivirgatus* group] in the Gulf-Caribbean lowlands from southern Texas (north to Zapata, Bee and Refugio counties), Coahuila and Nuevo León south through eastern Mexico (including the Yucatan Peninsula) to northern Guatemala (Petén) and Belize, and in the Central Valley of Chiapas.

Notes.—Some authors have suggested that the two groups represent distinct species, *A. rufivirgatus* [OLIVE SPARROW] and *A. superciliosus* (Salvin, 1865) [PACIFIC SPARROW]. *A. rufivirgatus* and the South American *A. tocuyensis* Todd, 1912, appear to constitute a superspecies.

Arremonops chloronotus (Salvin). GREEN-BACKED SPARROW.

Embernagra chloronota Salvin, 1861, Proc. Zool. Soc. London, p. 202. (In Prov. Veræ Pacis regione calida = Choctum, Guatemala.)

Habitat.—Undergrowth of open woodland, humid lowland and deciduous forest edge, clearings, second growth, brush and scrub (Tropical Zone).

Distribution.—*Resident* from Tabasco, northern Chiapas and the Yucatan Peninsula (except the northern part of the state of Yucatán) south in the Gulf-Caribbean lowlands through northern Guatemala and Belize to northern Honduras (east to Yoro and Olancho).

Notes.—Although once considered conspecific with *A. conirostris,* differences in morphology, juvenal plumage and vocalizations as well as range overlap in northern Honduras confirm the specific distinctness of *A. chloronotus.*

Arremonops conirostris (Bonaparte). BLACK-STRIPED SPARROW.

Arremon conirostris Bonaparte, 1850, Consp. Gen. Avium, 1 (2), p. 488. (Brasil, error = Colombia.)

Habitat.—Scrub, dense undergrowth, forest edge and clearings, and partly open situations with scattered trees (Tropical and lower Subtropical zones).

Distribution.—*Resident* on the Caribbean slope of Honduras (west to the Sula Valley) and Nicaragua, on both slopes of Costa Rica (rare in the dry northwest) and Panama (including Coiba and the Pearl islands), and in South America from Colombia and Venezuela south, west of the Andes to western Ecuador and east of the Andes to extreme northern Brazil.

Notes.—See comments under *A. chloronotus.*

Genus **MELOZONE** Reichenbach

Melozone Reichenbach, 1850, Avium Syst. Nat., pl. 79. Type, by subsequent designation (Sharpe, 1888), *Pyrgita biarcuata* Prévost and Des Murs.

Melozone kieneri (Bonaparte). RUSTY-CROWNED GROUND-SPARROW.

Pyrgisoma kieneri Bonaparte, 1850, Consp. Gen. Avium, 1 (2), p. 486. (ex Am[erica]. occ[identale]. = San Blas, Nayarit.)

Habitat.—Arid scrub, brush, thickets, and undergrowth of open forest (upper Tropical and Subtropical zones).

Distribution.—*Resident* from southeastern Sonora south through Sinaloa, western Durango, Nayarit, Jalisco, Guanajuato, Colima, Michoacán, the state of México, Morelos and Guerrero, to southwestern Puebla and central Oaxaca.

Notes.—*M. kieneri* and *M. biarcuatum* have been considered conspecific by some authors; they appear to constitute a superspecies.

Melozone biarcuatum (Prévost and Des Murs). PREVOST'S GROUND-SPARROW.

> *Pyrgita biarcuata* Prévost and Des Murs, 1846, Voy. Venus, Atlas, Zool., Ois., pl. 6. (No locality given = Guatemala.)

Habitat.—Brush, scrub, dense undergrowth, meadows and cultivated fields (Subtropical and lower Temperate zones).

Distribution.—*Resident* in the highlands of Chiapas, Guatemala, El Salvador, western Honduras (east to the Sula and Comayagua valleys) and central Costa Rica (Aguacate Mountains east to Turrialba).

Notes.—See comments under *M. kieneri.*

Melozone leucotis Cabanis. WHITE-EARED GROUND-SPARROW.

> *Melozone leucotis* Cabanis, 1860, J. Ornithol., 8, p. 413. (Costa Rica.)

Habitat.—Dense forest understory, forest edge, clearings, scrub and brush (upper Tropical to Temperate zones).

Distribution.—*Resident* in the highlands (primarily on the Pacific slope) of southeastern Chiapas, Guatemala, El Salvador, north-central Nicaragua and central Costa Rica (Cordillera de Tilarán and central highlands).

Genus **PIPILO** Vieillot

> *Pipilo* Vieillot, 1816, Analyse, p. 32. Type, by monotypy, "Pinson aux yeux rouges" Buffon = *Fringilla erythrophthalma* Linnaeus.
>
> *Chlorura* Sclater, 1862, Cat. Collect. Am. Birds, p. 117. Type, by monotypy, *Fringilla chlorura* Audubon.
>
> *Oreospiza* (not Keitel, 1857) Ridgway, 1896, Man. N. Am. Birds, ed. 2, p. 439. Type, by monotypy, *Fringilla chlorura* Audubon.
>
> *Oberholseria* Richmond, 1915, Proc. Biol. Soc. Wash., 28, p. 180. New name for *Oreospiza* Ridgway, preoccupied.

Notes.—The generic name *Hortulanus* Vieillot, 1807, sometimes used for *Pipilo,* is rejected as having no standing.

Pipilo chlorurus (Audubon). GREEN-TAILED TOWHEE. [590.]

> *Fringilla chlorura* Audubon, 1839, Ornithol. Biogr., 5, p. 336. (No locality given = Ross' Creek, ca. 20 miles southwest Blackfoot, Bingham County, Idaho.)

Habitat.—Thickets, chaparral, shrublands and riparian scrub, primarily in mountains in breeding season, to lowland habitats in nonbreeding season.

Distribution.—*Breeds* from southwestern and central Oregon, southeastern Washington, southern Idaho, southwestern Montana, northwestern and southeastern Wyoming, and north-central Colorado south to southern California (primarily interior mountains south to Cuyamaca Mountains), southern Nevada, central Arizona, southern New Mexico and western Texas (Chisos Mountains).

Winters from southern (casually central) California, southern Arizona, southern New Mexico, and western and southern Texas south to southern Baja California, Jalisco, Guanajuato, Querétaro, Morelos, Hidalgo, San Luis Potosí and Tamaulipas.

In migration occurs east to western Kansas, western Oklahoma and west-central Texas.

Casual north to northwestern Washington, southern Saskatchewan and southern Manitoba, and over most of eastern North America from Minnesota, Wisconsin, Michigan, southern Ontario, southwestern Quebec, New Hampshire, Maine and Nova Scotia south to Louisiana, Mississippi, Alabama, Georgia and Cuba.

Notes.—Often treated in the monotypic genus *Chlorura* (or *Oberholseria*).

Pipilo ocai (Lawrence). COLLARED TOWHEE.

Buarremon Ocai Lawrence, 1865, Ann. Lyc. Nat. Hist. N.Y., 8, p. 126. (Jalapa, Mexico = Las Vigas, west of Jalapa, Veracruz.)

Habitat.—Thickets, shrubby slopes, and brushy edges and undergrowth of humid montane forest and pine-oak association (Subtropical and Temperate zones).

Distribution.—*Resident* in the mountains from western Jalisco and extreme northeastern Colima southeast through north-central Michoacán, Guerrero (Sierra Madre del Sur) and eastern Puebla to west-central Veracruz and northern and central Oaxaca.

Notes.—Hybridizes extensively with *P. erythrophthalmus* in western portions of the range but on a limited basis or not at all in the eastern portions.

Pipilo erythrophthalmus (Linnaeus). RUFOUS-SIDED TOWHEE. [587.]

Fringilla erythrophthalma Linnaeus, 1758, Syst. Nat., ed. 10, 1, p. 180. Based on the "Towhee-bird" Catesby, Nat. Hist. Carolina, 1, p. 34, pl. 34. (in America = South Carolina.)

Habitat.—Undergrowth of open woodland, forest edge, second growth, brushy areas, chaparral, and riparian thickets and woodland (Subtropical and Temperate zones).

Distribution.—*Breeds* [*erythrophthalmus* group] from southern Manitoba, northeastern North Dakota, northern Minnesota, northern Wisconsin, northern Michigan, southern Ontario, southwestern Quebec, northern New York, Vermont, central New Hampshire and southwestern Maine south to extreme northeastern Texas (at least formerly), northeastern and south-central Louisiana, the Gulf coast (from Mississippi eastward) and southern Florida, and west to western Iowa, southeastern Nebraska, eastern Kansas and eastern Oklahoma; and [*maculatus* group] from southern British Columbia, southern Alberta and southern Saskatchewan south to southern California (including Santa Cruz, Santa Rosa, Santa Catalina and San Clemente islands), northwestern Baja California (also mountains of southern Baja California and, formerly, Guadalupe Island), southern Nevada, west-central and southern Arizona, and through the Mexican highlands to Chiapas and central Guatemala, and east to the central Dakotas, north-central and western Nebraska, northeastern and central Colorado, eastern New Mexico and extreme western Texas.

Winters [*erythrophthalmus* group] from Nebraska, Iowa, the southern Great Lakes region, southern New York and Massachusetts (rarely farther north) south to southern Texas, the Gulf coast and southern Florida; and [*maculatus* group] from southern British Columbia, Nevada, Utah and Colorado (casually farther north) south to northern Baja California (also in mountains of southern Baja California), northern Sonora, through the Mexican breeding range to central Guatemala, and to south-central Texas.

Resident [*socorroensis* group] on Socorro Island, in the Revillagigedo Islands, off western Mexico.

Casual [*erythrophthalmus* group] north to northern Ontario, southern Quebec, New Brunswick and Nova Scotia, and west to Colorado; and [*maculatus* group] east to Minnesota, Iowa, Illinois and Louisiana, and in Pennsylvania, New York, New Jersey, Alabama and Florida.

Notes.—The two northern groups, although intergrading in riparian habitats in southern Saskatchewan and in the Platte River system in Nebraska, were once regarded as distinct species, *P. erythrophthalmus* [EASTERN TOWHEE, 587] and *P. maculatus* Swainson, 1827 [SPOTTED TOWHEE, 588]; the Socorro Island form, a derivative of the latter group, is occasionally treated as a full species, *P. socorroensis* Grayson, 1867 [SOCORRO TOWHEE]. See also comments under *P. ocai.*

Pipilo fuscus Swainson. BROWN TOWHEE. [591.]

Pipilo fusca Swainson, 1827, Philos. Mag., new ser., 1, p. 434. (Temiscaltepec, Mexico = Temascaltepec, state of México.)

Habitat.—Brushlands, arid scrub, chaparral, mesquite, riparian thickets, and around human habitation (Subtropical and Temperate zones).

Distribution.—*Resident* [*crissalis* group] from southwestern Oregon south through California (from the western slopes of the Sierra Nevada and Argus Range westward, and west of the southeastern desert region) south to southern Baja California; and [*fuscus* group] from western and central Arizona, northern New Mexico, southeastern Colorado, extreme northwestern Oklahoma, and western and central Texas south to northern Sinaloa (including Isla Tiburón, off Sonora), and in the Mexican highlands to Oaxaca (west of the Isthmus of Tehuantepec), west-central Veracruz, Puebla and southwestern Tamaulipas.

Casual [*fuscus* group] in northern Arizona, southwestern Kansas and southern Texas. Accidental [*crissalis* group] on Todos Santos Island, off Baja California.

Notes.—Because of differences in vocalizations and morphology, the two groups are thought by some authors to represent separate species, *P. crissalis* (Vigors, 1839) [CALIFORNIA TOWHEE] and *P. fuscus* [BROWN TOWHEE].

Pipilo aberti Baird. ABERT'S TOWHEE. [592.]

Pipilo aberti Baird, 1852, *in* Baird and Stansbury, Explor. Great Salt Lake Utah, p. 325. ("New Mexico" = Gila Bend, Maricopa County, Arizona.)

Habitat.—Desert scrub, especially near water, and undergrowth of riparian woodland and thickets.

Distribution.—*Resident* from southeastern California (west to Salton Sea), extreme southeastern Nevada, southwestern Utah, central and southeastern Arizona, and southwestern New Mexico south to northeastern Baja California and northwestern Sonora.

A report from extreme western Texas (El Paso) requires verification.

Pipilo albicollis Sclater. WHITE-THROATED TOWHEE.

Pipilo albicollis Sclater, 1858, Proc. Zool. Soc. London, p. 304. (San Miguel de las Peras, Oaxaca, Southern Mexico.)

Habitat.—Arid scrub, and undergrowth of pine-oak association (Subtropical and Temperate zones).

Distribution.—*Resident* in the mountains of eastern Guerrero, southern Puebla and Oaxaca (west of the Isthmus of Tehuantepec).

Notes.—*P. rutilus* W. Deppe, 1830, sometimes used for this species, is now regarded as a synonym of *P. fuscus.*

Genus **VOLATINIA** Reichenbach

Volatinia Reichenbach, 1850, Avium Syst. Nat., pl. 79. Type, by subsequent designation (G. R. Gray, 1855), *Tanagra jacarinia* [sic] Linnaeus.

Volatinia jacarina (Linnaeus). BLUE-BLACK GRASSQUIT.

Tanagra jacarina Linnaeus, 1766, Syst. Nat., ed. 12, 1, p. 314. Based mainly on "Jacarini" Marcgrave, Hist. Nat. Bras., p. 210. (in Brasilia = northeastern Brazil.)

Habitat.—Open situations in grassy or bushy areas, weedy fields, scrub, savanna, second growth and cultivated lands (Tropical, rarely lower Subtropical zones).

Distribution.—*Resident* from southern Sonora, Sinaloa, western Durango, Nayarit, Jalisco, Michoacán, the state of México, Morelos, Puebla, eastern San Luis Potosí and southern Tamaulipas south along both slopes of Middle America (including the Yucatan Peninsula) to Panama (including Coiba and the Pearl islands), and in South America from Colombia, Venezuela (also Margarita Island, Tobago and Trinidad) and the Guianas south, west of the Andes to extreme northern Chile and east of the Andes to eastern Peru, eastern Bolivia, Paraguay and northern Argentina; also on Grenada, in the Lesser Antilles.

Casual on Isla Cancun (off Quintana Roo); an individual captured in Cuba was likely an escaped cage bird.

Genus **SPOROPHILA** Cabanis

Spermophila (not Richardson, 1825) Swainson, 1827, Zool. J., 3, p. 348. Type, by subsequent designation (G. R. Gray, 1840), *Pyrrhula falcirostris* Temminck.

Sporophila Cabanis, 1844, Arch. Naturgesch., 10, p. 291. New name for *Spermophila* Swainson, preoccupied.

Notes.—Some authors would merge *Oryzoborus* in *Sporophila.*

Sporophila schistacea (Lawrence). SLATE-COLORED SEEDEATER.

Spermophila schistacea Lawrence, 1863, Ann. Lyc. Nat. Hist. N.Y., 7, p. 474. (along the line of the Panama Railroad, on the Atlantic side of Isthmus of Panama = Lion Hill, Canal Zone.)

Habitat.—Humid lowland forest edge and clearings, dense second growth, and brushy areas adjacent to forest (Tropical Zone).

Distribution.—*Resident* (presumably) in Oaxaca (known from two specimens from the confluence of the Río Coatzacoalcos and Río Sarabia); and locally in northern Honduras (Lancetilla, Tela), Costa Rica (upper Térraba valley) and Panama (both slopes), and in South America from Colombia, southern Venezuela and the Guianas south, west of the Andes to northwestern Ecuador and east of the Andes to northern and northeastern Brazil, and in northern Bolivia.

Notes.—The Oaxaca specimens, provisionally described as a subspecies of this species, *S.* (? *schistacea*) *subconcolor* Berlioz, 1959, are definitely assigned to *S. schistacea* (Meyer de Schauensee, 1966, Spec. Birds South Am., p. 506).

Sporophila aurita (Bonaparte). VARIABLE SEEDEATER.

Spermophila aurita Bonaparte, 1850, Consp. Gen. Avium, 1 (2), p. 497. (Bras[il]., error = Canal Zone.)

Habitat.—Grassy and shrubby areas of open humid lowland and foothill forest, forest edge, clearings, second growth, scrub and plantations (Tropical and lower Subtropical zones).

Distribution.—*Resident* [*corvina* group] from northern Oaxaca, southern Veracruz and Tabasco south on the Gulf-Caribbean slope of Central America to western Panama (Bocas del Toro); and [*aurita* group] from the Pacific slope of southwestern Costa Rica (north to the Gulf of Nicoya) south through Panama (both slopes, except for Bocas del Toro), western Colombia and western Ecuador to northwestern Peru.

Notes.—Although there are differences in morphology and vocalizations between the two groups, which are sometimes regarded as separate species, *S. aurita* [VARIABLE SEEDEATER] and *S. corvina* (Sclater, 1860) [BLACK SEEDEATER], intergradation occurs in central Panama. Some authors would also merge this complex with the South American *S. americana* (Gmelin, 1789) [WING-BARRED SEEDEATER]; the merged complex would be known as VARIABLE SEEDEATER. Recognition of *S. americana* and *S. aurita* as allospecies of a superspecies complex seems the appropriate treatment.

Sporophila torqueola (Bonaparte). WHITE-COLLARED SEEDEATER. [602.]

Spermophila torqueola Bonaparte, 1850, Consp. Gen. Avium, 1(2), p. 495. (Mexico = Ciudad México.)

Habitat.—Brushy and weedy areas, open situations with scattered scrub or trees, cultivated lands and savanna (Tropical and lower Subtropical zones).

Distribution.—*Resident* [*torqueola* group] on the Pacific slope and in the interior of Mexico from central Sinaloa and western Durango south through Nayarit, Jalisco, Colima, Guanajuato, Michoacán, Guerrero, the state of México, Distrito Federal, Morelos and western Puebla to central Oaxaca (vicinity of Ciudad Oaxaca); and [*morelleti* group] from southern Texas (Rio Grande Valley north to Webb County), Nuevo León and Tamaulipas south on the Gulf-Caribbean slope through eastern San Luis Potosí, Veracruz, northern Oaxaca, Tabasco and the Yucatan Peninsula (including Mujeres, Cozumel and Cancun islands), and on both slopes of Middle America from Chiapas, Guatemala and Belize south to extreme western Panama (Bocas del Toro and Chiriquí).

Notes.—This species is highly variable and relationships between various populations are not well understood. Because of approach of two distinct morphological types in Oaxaca without reported intergradation, some authors suggest that the two groups may represent distinct species, *S. torqueola* [CINNAMON-RUMPED SEEDEATER] and *S. morelleti* (Bonaparte, 1851) [WHITE-COLLARED or MORELLET'S SEEDEATER].

[**Sporophila lineola** (Linnaeus). LINED SEEDEATER.] See Appendix A.

Sporophila nigricollis (Vieillot). YELLOW-BELLIED SEEDEATER.

> *Pyrrhula nigricollis* Vieillot, 1823, *in* Bonnaterre and Vieillot, Tabl. Encycl. Méth., Ornithol., 3, livr. 93, p. 1027. (Brésil = Brazil.)

Habitat.—Open grassy and shrubby areas, savanna, cultivated lands, and forest and woodland edge (Tropical and Subtropical zones).

Distribution.—*Resident* in southwestern Costa Rica (Puntarenas) and Panama (Pacific slope, including Taboga and the Pearl islands, and Caribbean slope in the Canal Zone), and in South America from Colombia, Venezuela (also Chacachacare Island, Tobago and Trinidad), Guyana and Surinam south, east of the Andes, to eastern Peru, northern Bolivia, extreme northeastern Argentina, and central and eastern Brazil; also in the southern Lesser Antilles (Grenada, and Carriacou in the Grenadines).

Accidental in St. Vincent (in the Lesser Antilles).

Sporophila minuta (Linnaeus). RUDDY-BREASTED SEEDEATER.

> *Loxia minuta* Linnaeus, 1758, Syst. Nat., ed. 10, 1, p. 176. (Surinami = Surinam.)

Habitat.—Open grassy and weedy areas, savanna, and forest and woodland edge (Tropical and Subtropical zones).

Distribution.—*Resident* on the Pacific slope from Nayarit south on the Pacific slope of Middle America to Nicaragua; in southwestern Costa Rica (upper Térraba valley) and Panama (Pacific slope throughout, and Caribbean slope in the Canal Zone); and in South America from Colombia, Venezuela (also Tobago and Trinidad) and the Guianas south, west of the Andes to northwestern Ecuador and east of the Andes through Amazonian, central and eastern Brazil to eastern Bolivia, Paraguay, northern Argentina and Uruguay.

Genus **ORYZOBORUS** Cabanis

> *Oryzoborus* Cabanis, 1851, Mus. Heineanum, 1, p. 151. Type, by subsequent designation (G. R. Gray, 1855), *Loxia torrida* "Gmelin" [=Scopoli] = *Loxia angolensis* Linnaeus.

Notes.—See comments under *Sporophila*.

Oryzoborus maximiliani Cabanis. GREAT-BILLED SEED-FINCH.

> *Fringilla crassirostris* (not *Loxia crassirostris* Gmelin, 1789) Wied, 1830, Beitr. Naturgesch. Bras., 3 (1), p. 564. (Rio Espírito Santo, Espírito Santo, and Caravellas, Bahia, Brazil.)

Oryzoborus Maximiliani Cabanis, 1851, Mus. Heineanum, 1, p. 151 (footnote). New name for *Fringilla crassirostris* Wied, preoccupied.

Habitat.—Open grassy or weedy areas (especially near marshes or in damp regions), cultivated lands, and woodland edge (Tropical Zone).

Distribution.—*Resident* [*nuttingi* group] in the Caribbean lowlands of Nicaragua, northern Costa Rica (Laguna de Arenal, near Finca La Selva) and western Panama (Bocas del Toro); [*maximiliani* group] in South America from Colombia, Venezuela (also Trinidad) and the Guianas south, west of the Andes to northwestern Ecuador and east of the Andes across Amazonian and eastern Brazil to central Brazil; and [*atrirostris* group] in eastern Peru and northern Bolivia.

Notes.—Some authors regard the groups as distinct species, *O. nuttingi* Ridgway, 1884 [NICARAGUAN SEED-FINCH], *O. maximiliani* [GREAT-BILLED SEED-FINCH], and *O. atrirostris* Sclater and Salvin, 1878. *O. maximiliani* was formerly considered a race of *O. crassirostris* (Gmelin, 1789) [LARGE-BILLED SEED-FINCH], but the two are widely sympatric in South America east of the Andes and currently regarded as separate species.

Oryzoborus funereus Sclater. THICK-BILLED SEED-FINCH.

Oryzoborus funereus Sclater, 1859, Proc. Zool. Soc. London, p. 378. (Suchapam, Oaxaca.)

Habitat.—Open grassy areas with scattered shrubs or bushes, savanna, and forest edge or clearings (Tropical Zone).

Distribution.—*Resident* from central Veracruz, northern Oaxaca, Tabasco and Chiapas south on the Gulf-Caribbean slope of Central America to Costa Rica (also on Pacific slope in Térraba region), and in Panama (both slopes, including Coiba and the Pearl islands), western Colombia and western Ecuador.

Notes.—*O. funereus* and the South American *O. angolensis* (Linnaeus, 1766) [CHESTNUT-BELLIED SEED-FINCH] are closely related and regarded as conspecific by some authors; they constitute a superspecies. With a single species concept, LESSER SEED-FINCH is the appropriate English name.

Genus AMAUROSPIZA Cabanis

Amaurospiza Cabanis, 1861, J. Ornithol., 9, p. 3. Type, by original designation, *Amaurospiza concolor* Cabanis.
Amaurospizopsis Griscom, 1934, Bull. Mus. Comp. Zool. Harv., 75, p. 412. Type, by original designation, *Amaurospizopsis relictus* Griscom.

Notes.—Systematic position of this genus is uncertain.

Amaurospiza concolor Cabanis. BLUE SEEDEATER.

Amaurospiza concolor Cabanis, 1861, J. Ornithol., 9, p. 3. (Costa Rica = Miravalles, Costa Rica.)

Habitat.—Shrubbery and thickets (especially bamboo) adjacent to humid forest and pine-oak association, and in forest edge and clearings (upper Tropical and Subtropical zones).

Distribution.—*Resident* [*relicta* group] in the mountains of Guerrero, Morelos and Oaxaca (west of the Isthmus of Tehuantepec); and [*concolor* group] locally in Chiapas (Cintalapa, Tuxtla Gutiérrez), El Salvador (Cerro Verde), Honduras (Lago de Yojoa, Arenal), Nicaragua, Costa Rica, Panama (Chiriquí, Veraguas and the Canal Zone), southwestern Colombia and northwestern Ecuador.

Notes.—The two groups are sometimes recognized as distinct species, *A. relicta* (Griscom, 1934) [SLATE-BLUE SEEDEATER] and *A. concolor* [BLUE SEEDEATER].

Genus **MELOPYRRHA** Bonaparte

Melopyrrha Bonaparte, 1853, C. R. Acad. Sci. Paris, 37, p. 924. Type, by subsequent designation (G. R. Gray, 1855), *Loxia nigra* Linnaeus.

Melopyrrha nigra (Linnaeus). CUBAN BULLFINCH.

Loxia nigra Linnaeus, 1758, Syst. Nat., ed. 10, 1, p. 175. Based on "The Little Black Bullfinch" Catesby, Nat. Hist. Carolina, 1, p. 68, pl. 68, and "The Black Bullfinch" Albin, Nat. Hist. Birds, 3, p. 65, pl. 69. (in America australi = Cuba.)

Habitat.—Scrub and woodland.
Distribution.—*Resident* on Cuba (including coastal cays), the Isle of Pines, and Grand Cayman Island.

Genus **TIARIS** Swainson

Tiaris Swainson, 1827, Philos. Mag., new ser., 1, p. 438. Type, by monotypy, *Tiaris pusillus* Swainson = *Emberiza olivacea* Linnaeus.

Tiaris canora (Gmelin). CUBAN GRASSQUIT.

Loxia canora Gmelin, 1789, Syst. Nat., 1 (2), p. 858. Based on the "Brown-cheeked Grosbeak" Latham, Gen. Synop. Birds, 2(1), p. 155. (in nova Hispania, error = Cuba.)

Habitat.—Woodland (including pine) and shrubbery bordering fields.
Distribution.—*Resident* on Cuba and the Isle of Pines (possibly introduced on the latter).
Introduced and established in the Bahama Islands (New Providence).
Several reports from southern Florida are probably based on escaped cage birds; reportedly bred in Dade County in 1960 but no population has become established. An old report from Sombrero Key is based on *T. bicolor*.
Notes.—Also known as MELODIOUS GRASSQUIT.

Tiaris olivacea (Linnaeus). YELLOW-FACED GRASSQUIT. [603.2.]

Emberiza olivacea Linnaeus, 1766, Syst. Nat., ed. 12, 1, p. 309. Based on "Le Bruant de S. Domingue" Brisson, Ornithologie, 3, p. 300, pl. 13, fig. 5. (in Dominica = Hispaniola.)

Habitat.—Open grassy and shrubby areas, fields, second growth, forest and woodland edge and clearings, and around human habitation (Tropical and Subtropical zones).
Distribution.—*Resident* from eastern San Luis Potosí and southern Tamaulipas

south along the Gulf-Caribbean slope of Mexico (including the Yucatan Peninsula, and Cozumel and Holbox islands), Guatemala and Belize, on both slopes of El Salvador and Honduras, in Nicaragua (Caribbean slope only), on both slopes of Costa Rica and Panama (including Isla Coiba), and in western and central Colombia and northwestern Venezuela; also in the Greater Antilles (east to Puerto Rico, and including the Cayman Islands).

Introduced in 1974 and probably established in the Hawaiian Islands (in the highlands of Oahu).

Tiaris bicolor (Linnaeus). BLACK-FACED GRASSQUIT. [603.]

Fringilla bicolor Linnaeus, 1766, Syst. Nat., ed. 12, 1, p. 324. Based on "The Bahama Sparrow" Catesby, Nat. Hist. Carolina, 1, p. 37, pl. 37. (in America = Bahama Islands.)

Habitat.—Open grassy and bushy areas, arid scrub, fields and second growth (Tropical Zone).

Distribution.—*Resident* throughout the West Indies (except Cuba, where confined to cays off Las Villas and Camagüey provinces), on islands in the western Caribbean Sea (Providencia, Santa Catalina and San Andrés), and in northern Colombia and northern Venezuela (including islands from the Netherlands Antilles east to Tobago and Trinidad).

Casual in southern Florida (Palm Beach County south to Sombrero Key), possibly based on escaped individuals.

Genus LOXIPASSER Bryant

Loxipasser Bryant, 1866, Proc. Boston Soc. Nat. Hist., 10, p. 254. Type, by original designation, *Spermophila anoxantha* Gosse.

Loxipasser anoxanthus (Gosse). YELLOW-SHOULDERED GRASSQUIT.

Spermophila anoxantha Gosse, 1847, Birds Jamaica, p. 247 (footnote). (Mount Edgecumbe, Jamaica.)

Habitat.—Shrubbery, forest edge and clearings, more commonly in hills and mountains.

Distribution.—*Resident* on Jamaica.

Notes.—Also known as YELLOW-BACKED FINCH.

Genus LOXIGILLA Lesson

Loxigilla Lesson, 1831, Traité Ornithol., livr. 6, p. 443. Type, by subsequent designation (G. R. Gray, 1855), *Fringilla noctis* Linnaeus.

Loxigilla portoricensis (Daudin). PUERTO RICAN BULLFINCH.

Loxia portoricensis Daudin, 1800, Traité Ornithol., 2, p. 411. (Puerto Rico.)

Habitat.—Woodland (primarily in interior hills, but also in coastal lowlands), arid scrub and mangroves.

Distribution.—*Resident* on Puerto Rico, and formerly also on St. Kitts in the Lesser Antilles (last reported there in 1926).

Loxigilla violacea (Linnaeus). GREATER ANTILLEAN BULLFINCH.

Loxia violacea Linnaeus, 1758, Syst. Nat., ed. 10, 1, p. 176. Based on "The Purple Gross-beak" Catesby, Nat. Hist. Carolina, 1, p. 40, pl. 40. (in America = Bahama Islands.)

Habitat.—Shrubbery, thickets, scrub and dense second growth, on larger islands more commonly in montane forest areas.

Distribution.—*Resident* throughout the Bahama Islands, and in the Greater Antilles on Hispaniola (including Tortue, Gonâve, Saona, Beata and Catalina islands, and Île-à-Vache) and Jamaica; a sight report for southern Florida (Hypoluxo Island) is unverified.

Loxigilla noctis (Linnaeus). LESSER ANTILLEAN BULLFINCH.

Fringilla noctis Linnaeus, 1766, Syst. Nat., ed. 12, 1, p. 320. Based mainly on "Le Pere noir" Brisson, Ornithologie, 3, p. 118, pl. 7, fig. 1. (in Jamaica, Mexico, Martinica = Martinique.)

Habitat.—Shrubbery, forest undergrowth and gardens.

Distribution.—*Resident* in the Virgin Islands (on St. John, since 1971, possibly introduced) and Lesser Antilles (from Anguilla and Saba south to St. Vincent and Barbados, also on Grenada).

Genus EUNEORNIS Fitzinger

Euneornis Fitzinger, 1856, Sitzungsber. K. Akad. Wiss. Wien, Math.-Naturwiss. Kl., 21 (2), p. 316. Type, by original designation, *Motacilla campestris* Linnaeus.

Notes.—Systematic position uncertain; formerly included in the "Coerebidae" or as a thraupine.

Euneornis campestris (Linnaeus). ORANGEQUIT.

Motacilla campestris Linnaeus, 1758, Syst. Nat., ed. 10, 1, p. 184. Based on "The American Hedge-Sparrow" Edwards, Nat. Hist. Birds, 3, p. 122, pl. 122, lower fig. (in Jamaica.)

Habitat.—Open woodland, forest edge and clearings, primarily in the mountains.

Distribution.—*Resident* on Jamaica.

Genus MELANOSPIZA Ridgway

Melanospiza Ridgway, 1897, Proc. U.S. Natl. Mus., 19 (1886), p. 466. Type, by original designation, *Loxigilla richardsoni* Cory.

Melanospiza richardsoni (Cory). ST. LUCIA BLACK FINCH.

Loxigilla richardsoni Cory, 1886, Auk, 3, p. 382. (Mountains of Santa Lucia, West Indies.)

Habitat.—Undergrowth and shrubbery, mostly in mountain clearings, less commonly in arid lowland scrub.

Distribution.—*Resident* on St. Lucia, in the Lesser Antilles.

Genus **PINAROLOXIAS** Sharpe

Pinaroloxias Sharpe, 1885, Cat. Birds Br. Mus., 10, pp. ix, 3, 52. Type, by monotypy, *Cactornis inornata* Gould.

Pinaroloxias inornata (Gould). COCOS FINCH.

Cactornis inornata Gould, 1843, Proc. Zool. Soc. London, p. 104. (Bow Island, Low Archipelago, Polynesia, error = Cocos Island.)

Habitat.—Forest, woodland, open habitats, and around human habitation.
Distribution.—*Resident* on Cocos Island, off Costa Rica.

Genus **HAPLOSPIZA** Cabanis

Haplospiza Cabanis, 1851, Mus. Heineanum, 1, p. 147. Type, by original designation, *Haplospiza unicolor* Cabanis.
Spodiornis Sclater, 1866, Proc. Zool. Soc. London, p. 322. Type, by original designation, *Spodiornis jardinii* Sclater = *Phrygilus rusticus* Tschudi.

Haplospiza rustica (Tschudi). SLATY FINCH.

Phrygilus rusticus (Lichtenstein MS) Tschudi, 1844, Arch. Naturgesch., 10, p. 290. (Republica Peruana = Peru.)

Habitat.—Bushy or shrubby areas in open montane forest, overgrown clearings, and grassy areas adjacent to forest (upper Subtropical and Temperate zones).
Distribution.—*Resident* locally in the highlands of Middle America in Veracruz (Jalapa), Chiapas (Volcán Tacaná), El Salvador, Honduras (El Chorro), Costa Rica (Volcán Irazú, Cartago) and western Panama (western Chiriquí and western Panamá province); and in South America in the mountains from Colombia and Venezuela south to Peru and northwestern Bolivia.
Notes.—Often treated in the monotypic genus *Spodiornis*.

Genus **ACANTHIDOPS** Ridgway

Acanthidops Ridgway, 1882, Proc. U.S. Natl. Mus., 4 (1881), p. 335. Type, by original designation, *Acanthidops bairdii* Ridgway.

Notes.—Closely related to the genus *Haplospiza* and possibly not separable generically from it.

Acanthidops bairdii Ridgway. PEG-BILLED FINCH.

Acanthidops bairdii Ridgway, 1882, Proc. U.S. Natl. Mus., 4 (1881), p. 336. (Volcan de Irazú, Costa Rica.)

Habitat.—Scrubby and bushy growth at high elevations (Temperate Zone).
Distribution.—*Resident* in Costa Rica (the high volcanoes of Poás, Irazú and Turrialba, and in the Dota Mountains).
Casual in western Panama (Cerro Punta, Chiriquí, January–March 1979).

Genus **DIGLOSSA** Wagler

Diglossa Wagler, 1832, Isis von Oken, col. 280. Type, by monotypy, *Diglossa baritula* Wagler.

Notes.—Formerly placed in the family "Coerebidae" or in the Thraupinae.

Diglossa baritula Wagler. CINNAMON-BELLIED FLOWERPIERCER.

Diglossa baritula Wagler, 1832, Isis von Oken, col. 281. (Mexico.)

Habitat.—Humid montane forest, forest edge, clearings, second-growth woodland, pine-oak association, scrub and brushy fields (Subtropical and Temperate zones).

Distribution.—*Resident* in the highlands from Jalisco, Guanajuato, Hidalgo and Veracruz south through southern Mexico, Guatemala and El Salvador to Honduras.

Notes.—Also known as CINNAMON FLOWERPIERCER. Some authors consider *D. baritula* and *D. plumbea* to be conspecific; they constitute a superspecies. With a single species concept, SLATY FLOWERPIERCER is the most appropriate English name.

Diglossa plumbea Cabanis. SLATY FLOWERPIERCER.

Diglossa plumbea Cabanis, 1860, J. Ornithol., 8, p. 411. (Costa Rica.)

Habitat.—Humid montane forest edge and clearings, second growth, scrub and brushy fields (upper Subtropical and Temperate zones).

Distribution.—*Resident* in the mountains of Costa Rica (north to Cordillera de Guanacaste) and western Panama (western Chiriquí and Veraguas).

Notes.—See comments under *D. baritula.*

Genus **SICALIS** Boie

Sicalis Boie, 1828, Isis von Oken, col. 324. Type, by subsequent designation (Cabanis, 1846), *Emberiza brasiliensis* Gmelin = *Fringilla flaveola* Linnaeus.

Sicalis flaveola (Linnaeus). SAFFRON FINCH. [586.1.]

Fringilla flaveola Linnaeus, 1766, Syst. Nat., ed. 12, 1, p. 321. (No locality given = Surinam.)

Habitat.—Open grassland, savanna, open woodland, second growth, and urban and suburban areas (Tropical and lower Subtropical zones).

Distribution.—*Resident* in South America from northern and eastern Colombia, Venezuela and the Guianas south, east of the Andes, through eastern and southern Brazil, eastern Bolivia, Paraguay and Uruguay to central Argentina; and west of the Andes in western Ecuador and northwestern Peru.

Introduced and established in the Hawaiian Islands (since 1966, presently in small numbers on Oahu and Hawaii), central Panama (Canal Zone), Jamaica and Puerto Rico.

Sicalis luteola (Sparrman). GRASSLAND YELLOW-FINCH.

Emberiza luteola Sparrman, 1789, Mus. Carlson., fasc. 4, pl. 93. (No locality given = Surinam.)

Habitat.—Short grasslands and savanna (Tropical, locally to Temperate zones).

Distribution.—*Resident* locally in Middle America in Puebla (Atlixco), Morelos

(Pacific drainage), Veracruz (Orizaba), Chiapas (Palenque), central Guatemala (Dueñas), the Mosquitia of eastern Honduras and northeastern Nicaragua, Costa Rica (Guanacaste) and Panama (Coclé and eastern Panamá province); and in South America from Colombia, western and southern Venezuela (also Trinidad), and the Guianas south, east of and locally in the Andes, to Chile and central Argentina, with the southernmost populations at least partly migratory northward in nonbreeding season.

Introduced and established in the Lesser Antilles on Barbados, from whence it has since spread to the Grenadines (Mustique), St. Vincent, St. Lucia, Martinique, Guadeloupe and Antigua.

Notes.—Also known as YELLOW GRASS-FINCH.

Genus EMBERIZOIDES Temminck

Emberizoïdes Temminck, 1822, Planches Color., livr. 19, text to pl. 114. Type, by subsequent designation (G. R. Gray, 1840), *Emberizoides marginalis* Temminck = *Sylvia herbicola* Vieillot.

Emberizoides herbicola (Vieillot). WEDGE-TAILED GRASS-FINCH.

Sylvia herbicola Vieillot, 1817, Nouv. Dict. Hist. Nat., nouv. éd., 11, p. 192. Based on "Cola aguda encuentro amarillo" Azara, Apunt. Hist. Nat. Páx. Parag., 2, p. 257 (no. 230). (Paraguay.)

Habitat.—Grasslands, savanna, grassy hillsides, and open grassy fields (Tropical and Subtropical zones).

Distribution.—*Resident* locally in southwestern Costa Rica (Térraba region) and western Panama (Chiriquí, Cerro Campana, and the Tocumen-Chepo area in eastern Panamá province); and in South America from Colombia (except the southwestern portion) east across Venezuela and the Guianas, and south through eastern and southern Brazil, eastern Bolivia and Paraguay to northeastern Argentina.

Notes.—Also known as WEDGE-TAILED GROUND-FINCH.

Genus AIMOPHILA Swainson

Aimophila Swainson, 1837, Class. Birds, 2, p. 287. Type, by subsequent designation (G. R. Gray, 1840), *Aimophila rufescens* (Swainson) = *Pipilo rufescens* Swainson.

Notes.—Relationships within this genus are poorly understood, and it is probably polyphyletic as now constituted. See also comments under *Amphispiza*.

Aimophila mystacalis (Hartlaub). BRIDLED SPARROW.

Zonotrichia mystacalis Hartlaub, 1852, Rev. Mag. Zool., ser. 2, 4, p. 3. (Rio Frio entre Puebla et la ville de Mexico = Río Frío, between Puebla and Mexico City.)

Habitat.—Arid scrub, thorn forest and cactus (upper Tropical to lower Temperate zones).

Distribution.—*Resident* in the eastern portion of the state of México, southern Puebla, west-central Veracruz and northern Oaxaca.

Aimophila humeralis (Cabanis). BLACK-CHESTED SPARROW.

Haemophila humeralis (Lichtenstein MS) Cabanis, 1851, Mus. Heineanum, 1, p. 132. (Mexico = Tehotepec, Puebla.)

Habitat.—Arid scrub (Tropical and lower Subtropical zones).

Distribution.—*Resident* from southern Jalisco south through Colima, Michoacán, Guerrero, Morelos and southern Puebla to extreme western Oaxaca (San José Estancia Grande).

Aimophila ruficauda (Bonaparte). STRIPE-HEADED SPARROW.

Chondestes ruficauda Bonaparte, 1853, C. R. Acad. Sci. Paris, 37, p. 918. (Nicaragua.)

Habitat.—Arid scrub, brushy savanna, and thickets bordering fields (Tropical and lower Subtropical zones).

Distribution.—*Resident* along the Pacific slope from southern Durango and Nayarit south through Jalisco, Michoacán, Guerrero, Morelos, southern Puebla, Oaxaca, Chiapas, Guatemala (also in arid interior in Motagua Valley), El Salvador, Honduras and Nicaragua to northwestern Costa Rica (Guanacaste).

Notes.—Also known as RUSSET-TAILED SPARROW.

Aimophila sumichrasti (Lawrence). CINNAMON-TAILED SPARROW.

Hæmophila sumichrasti Lawrence, 1871, Ann. Lyc. Nat. Hist. N.Y., 10, p. 6. (Tuchitan Tehuantepec = Juchitán, Oaxaca.)

Habitat.—Arid scrub (Tropical Zone).

Distribution.—*Resident* on the Pacific slope of Oaxaca (west to Las Tejas) and extreme southwestern Chiapas.

Notes.—Also known as SUMICHRAST'S SPARROW.

Aimophila aestivalis (Lichtenstein). BACHMAN'S SPARROW. [575.]

Fringilla aestivalis Lichtenstein, 1823, Verz. Doubl. Zool. Mus. Berlin, p. 25. (Georgia.)

Habitat.—Open pine woods with scattered bushes or understory, brushy or overgrown hillsides, and overgrown fields with thickets and brambles.

Distribution.—*Breeds* (at least formerly) from south-central Missouri, central and northeastern Illinois, central Indiana, central Ohio, southwestern Pennsylvania and central Maryland south to eastern Oklahoma, eastern Texas, the Gulf coast and south-central Florida; now generally absent (or very local) as a breeding bird in the northeastern portion of the breeding range north of southern Kentucky and North Carolina.

Winters from eastern Texas, the Gulf states and Atlantic coast (from southeastern North Carolina) south through the remainder of the breeding range (casually elsewhere in the northern parts of the breeding range), and to southern Florida.

Casual north to northeastern Kansas, southeastern Michigan, southern Ontario, New York and New Jersey.

Notes.—Also known as PINE-WOODS SPARROW.

Aimophila botterii (Sclater). BOTTERI'S SPARROW. [576.]

Zonotrichia botterii Sclater, 1858, Proc. Zool. Soc. London (1857), p. 214. (vicinity of Orizaba, [Veracruz,] in Southern Mexico.)

Habitat.—Grassland and savanna, especially with scattered bushes or scrub, and coastal prairie (Tropical and Subtropical zones).

Distribution.—*Breeds* from southeastern Arizona, southwestern New Mexico (probably), eastern Sonora, Sinaloa, Durango, Zacatecas, San Luis Potosí, Tamaulipas and extreme southern Texas (lower Rio Grande Valley) south through Mexico to Chiapas and Tabasco, and locally in the state of Yucatán, Guatemala (lowlands of Petén, and central highlands), Belize, eastern Honduras, northwestern and northeastern Nicaragua, and northwestern Costa Rica (base of Cordillera de Guanacaste).

Winters from northern Mexico south throughout the remainder of the breeding range.

Casual in southern Texas just north of the breeding range.

Notes.—Populations in lowland savanna from Tabasco and Petén, Guatemala, south to northeastern Nicaragua, either with or without interior highland populations from Guatemala southward, have sometimes been regarded as a distinct species, *A. petenica* (Salvin, 1863) [PETEN SPARROW]; extensive variability and apparent intergradation in Tabasco and Veracruz suggest strongly that but a single species should be recognized.

Aimophila cassinii (Woodhouse). CASSIN'S SPARROW. [578.]

Zonotrichia Cassinii Woodhouse, 1852, Proc. Acad. Nat. Sci. Philadelphia, 6, p. 60. (near San Antonio, Texas.)

Habitat.—Open grassland and short-grass plains with scattered bushes or shrubs, sagebrush, mesquite or yucca.

Distribution.—*Breeds* from southeastern Arizona, New Mexico (except the northwestern part of state), central and northeastern Colorado, southwestern Nebraska, west-central Kansas and western Oklahoma south to northern Chihuahua, southern Coahuila, northern Tamaulipas, and central and southern Texas. In recent years singing males have appeared sporadically, sometimes in large numbers, from southern California east across southern Arizona, in northwestern New Mexico, and north to central Wyoming and southwestern South Dakota, although breeding has not been confirmed in these regions.

Winters from southeastern Arizona, southern New Mexico (rarely), Sonora Chihuahua, and western and south-central Texas south to southern Sinaloa, Guanajuato, San Luis Potosí and Tamaulipas.

Casual or accidental in California (north to the Farallon Islands), southern Nevada, southern Ontario (Point Pelee), Nova Scotia (Seal Island) and New Jersey (Ocean County).

Aimophila carpalis (Coues). RUFOUS-WINGED SPARROW. [579.]

Peucæa carpalis Coues, 1873, Am. Nat., 7, p. 322 (footnote). (Tucson, Ariz[ona].)

Habitat.—Open flat grassy areas with scattered thorn bush, mixed bunch-grass, mesquite or cholla (Subtropical Zone).

Distribution.—*Resident* from south-central Arizona (north to Tucson area) south through central and southeastern Sonora to central Sinaloa.

Aimophila ruficeps (Cassin). RUFOUS-CROWNED SPARROW. [580.]

Ammodromus ruficeps Cassin, 1852, Proc. Acad. Nat. Sci. Philadelphia, 6, p. 184. (Calaveras River [east of Stockton], California.)

Habitat.—Arid rocky and hilly regions with brush, scattered scrub or stunted trees, and grassy or weedy patches, also in Mexico in arid scrub and pine-oak association (Subtropical and lower Temperate zones).

Distribution.—*Breeds* from central California (north to Sonoma County, and including Santa Cruz, Anacapa and Santa Catalina islands, with an isolated colony in eastern San Bernardino County), southwestern Utah, northwestern and central Arizona, central and northeastern New Mexico, southeastern Colorado, northwestern and central Oklahoma, and north-central Texas south to southern Baja California (including Todos Santos Islands), throughout Mexico to Oaxaca (west of the Isthmus of Tehuantepec), southern Puebla, west-central Veracruz and southern Tamaulipas.

Winters throughout the breeding range except for the northeastern portion, where wintering is usually from northeastern New Mexico, northern Texas and south-central Oklahoma southward.

Casual or accidental in southwestern Kansas (Comanche County), west-central Arkansas (Magazine Mountain) and southeastern Texas.

Aimophila notosticta (Sclater and Salvin). OAXACA SPARROW.

Peucæa notosticta Sclater and Salvin, 1868, Proc. Zool. Soc. London, p. 322. (Mexico = probably Puebla.)

Habitat.—Arid scrub, brushy hillsides and oak scrub (Subtropical Zone).

Distribution.—*Resident* in northwestern and central Oaxaca (south to Ciudad de Oaxaca region) and probably adjacent southwestern Puebla.

Aimophila rufescens (Swainson). RUSTY SPARROW.

Pipilo rufescens Swainson, 1827, Philos. Mag., new ser., 1, p. 434. (Temiscaltipec, Mexico = Temascaltepec, state of México.)

Habitat.—Brushy areas and scrub in both arid and humid pine-oak association and oak woodland, deciduous and humid lowland forest edge, brushy edges of savanna, second-growth woodland, and plantations (Tropical to lower Temperate zones).

Distribution.—*Resident* from north-central and eastern Sonora, western Chihuahua, Sinaloa, northwestern Durango, Nayarit, Jalisco, Guanajuato, eastern San Luis Potosí and southern Tamaulipas south through Mexico (except the Yucatan Peninsula) and Central America to north-central and northeastern Nicaragua and northwestern Costa Rica (base of Cordillera de Guanacaste).

Genus ORITURUS Bonaparte

Oriturus Bonaparte, 1850, Consp. Gen. Avium, 1 (2), p. 469. Type, by subsequent designation (Bonaparte, 1856), *Oriturus mexicanus* Bonaparte = *Aimophila superciliosa* Swainson.

Oriturus superciliosus (Swainson). STRIPED SPARROW.

Aimophila superciliosa Swainson, 1837, Anim. Menag. (1838), p. 314, fig. 63e–g. (Mexico.)

Habitat.—Open grassy and shrubby areas in or near humid montane forest or pine-oak association (upper Subtropical and Temperate zones).

Distribution.—*Resident* from eastern Sonora, Chihuahua, Durango, western Zacatecas, Aguascalientes and San Luis Potosí south to central Oaxaca, Puebla and west-central Veracruz.

Genus **TORREORNIS** Barbour and Peters

Torreornis Barbour and Peters, 1927, Proc. N. Engl. Zool. Club, 9, p. 96. Type, by monotypy, *Torreornis inexpectata* Barbour and Peters.

Torreornis inexpectata Barbour and Peters. ZAPATA SPARROW.

Torreornis inexpectata Barbour and Peters, 1927, Proc. N. Engl. Zool. Club., 9, p. 96. (Santo Tomás, Peninsula de Zapata, Cuba.)

Habitat.—Dense brush and sawgrass in swampy regions, and coastal scrub.

Distribution.—*Resident* locally in southwestern Cuba (Ciénaga de Zapata), southeastern Cuba (near Baitiquiri, Oriente province), and Cayo Coco (off northern Camagüey province).

Genus **SPIZELLA** Bonaparte

Spizella Bonaparte, 1831, G. Arcad. Sci. Lettr. Arti [Rome], 52, p. 205. Type, by original designation, *Fringilla pusilla* Wilson.

Spizella arborea (Wilson). AMERICAN TREE SPARROW. [559.]

Fringilla arborea Wilson, 1810, Am. Ornithol., 2, p. 123, pl. 16, fig. 3. (eastern Pennsylvania.)

Habitat.—Open willow, low shrubbery, scrub conifers, and bogs, in migration and winter also in weedy fields, fencerows, thickets, brushy areas and gardens.

Distribution.—*Breeds* from northern Alaska, northern Yukon, northern Mackenzie, Banks Island (probably), central interior Keewatin, northern Quebec and Labrador south to southern Alaska (Bristol Bay, Alaska Peninsula, and Wrangell Mountains), northwestern British Columbia, southeastern Yukon, west-central and southern Mackenzie, northern Saskatchewan, northern Manitoba, northern Ontario, James Bay and central Quebec.

Winters from south-coastal and southeastern Alaska (rarely), southern Canada (British Columbia east to New Brunswick, Prince Edward Island and Nova Scotia, except southern Manitoba), central Minnesota and northern Michigan (casually farther north) south to eastern Oregon, northern California, central Nevada, northern and east-central Arizona, central and southeastern New Mexico, north-central Texas, Arkansas, Tennessee and North Carolina, casually to coastal and southern California, southern New Mexico, southern Texas, Louisiana, northwestern Mississippi and South Carolina, also a sight report for southwestern Arizona.

In migration occurs regularly throughout central and southern Canada (including Newfoundland), and in central coastal California.

Notes.—Formerly known in American literature as the TREE SPARROW.

Spizella passerina (Bechstein). CHIPPING SPARROW. [560.]

Fringilla passerina (Borkhausen MS) Bechstein, 1798, *in* Latham, Allg. Uebers. Vögel, 3 (2), p. 544, pl. 120, fig. 1. (Canada = City of Quebec, Quebec.)

Habitat.—Open coniferous forest (especially early second growth) and forest edge (especially pine), oak woodland, pine-oak association, thickets and shrubs near woodland, and parks, in migration and winter also in a variety of open woodland, and brushy and shrubby habitats (Tropical to Temperate zones).

Distribution.—*Breeds* from east-central and southeastern Alaska, central Yukon, central Mackenzie, northern Saskatchewan, northern Manitoba, central Ontario, southern Quebec and southwestern Newfoundland south to northern Baja California, southwestern and east-central California, southern Nevada, and central and southeastern Arizona, through the highlands of Mexico and northern Central America to north-central Nicaragua, in the Caribbean lowland pine savanna of Guatemala, Belize, eastern Honduras and northeastern Nicaragua, and to central and eastern Texas, the Gulf coast and northwestern Florida.

Winters from central California, southern Nevada, central Arizona, central New Mexico, northern Texas, Oklahoma, Arkansas, Tennessee, Virginia and Maryland (casually farther north) south throughout Mexico to the Isthmus of Tehuantepec, throughout the breeding range from Oaxaca and Chiapas southward, and to the Gulf coast and southern Florida, casually to the northern Bahama Islands and Cuba.

Casual or accidental in northern Alaska, northern Newfoundland, Costa Rica and Bermuda.

Spizella pallida (Swainson). CLAY-COLORED SPARROW. [561.]

Emberiza pallida Swainson, 1832, *in* Swainson and Richardson, Fauna Bor.-Am., 2 (1831), p. 251. (Carlton-house, Saskatchewan.)

Habitat.—Shrubby areas and thickets, especially near water, tall shrubbery in meadows, bushy openings or burns in open coniferous or deciduous forest, and dry pastures with a few shrubs, in migration and winter also in brushy and weedy fields, fencerows and arid scrub.

Distribution.—*Breeds* from west-central and southern Mackenzie, eastern British Columbia, northwestern and central Saskatchewan, northern Manitoba and central Ontario south to eastern Washington, southern Alberta, central Montana, southeastern Wyoming, eastern Colorado, western Kansas (casually), southern Nebraska, northern Iowa, southern Wisconsin, central and southeastern Michigan, southern Ontario, southwestern Quebec and (sporadically) western New York; recorded in summer (and possibly breeding) in eastern Washington (Spokane Valley), northern Illinois and northern Indiana. Reports of breeding in northern Texas are without foundation.

Winters from southern Baja California, northern Sonora, southern Coahuila, central Nuevo León and central Texas (casually farther north) south through Mexico (mostly in the highlands) to Veracruz, Oaxaca and Chiapas, casually to western Guatemala (Sacapulas).

Migrates regularly west to California (especially southern), southeastern Arizona and New Mexico, and through the Great Plains east to the Mississippi Valley, rarely (most frequently in fall) from New York, Maine and Nova Scotia south through Pennsylvania, West Virginia and the Atlantic states to South Carolina, and casually to the northern Pacific coast (southern British Columbia southward). Casual along the Gulf Coast from Louisiana eastward, in Florida (mostly northwestern portion), and off Quintana Roo (Cozumel Island); reports from the Bahama Islands and Cuba are unverified.

Spizella breweri Cassin. BREWER'S SPARROW. [562.]

> *Spizella Breweri* Cassin, 1856, Proc. Acad. Nat. Sci. Philadelphia, 8, p. 40. (western North America, California, and New Mexico = Black Hills, North Dakota.)

Habitat.—Brushland, especially sagebrush, in migration and winter also in desert scrub and creosote bush.

Distribution.—*Breeds* from southwestern Yukon, northwestern and interior British Columbia, west-central and southern Alberta, southwestern Saskatchewan and southwestern North Dakota south, generally east of the Cascades and the coast ranges, to eastern and southern California (to Mt. Pinos and the San Bernardino Mountains, formerly elsewhere), southern Nevada, central Arizona, northwestern New Mexico, central Colorado, southwestern Kansas, northwestern Nebraska and southwestern South Dakota.

Winters from southern interior (casually central and coastal) California, southern Nevada, western and central Arizona, southern New Mexico, and western and central Texas south to southern Baja California and Sonora (including Isla Tiburón), in the Mexican highlands to Jalisco and Guanajuato, and to southern Texas.

In migration occurs regularly through western Kansas and western Oklahoma, and in coastal California, casually elsewhere in coastal areas from British Columbia southward.

Accidental in Massachusetts (Watertown), also a sight (and sound) report for Minnesota.

Spizella pusilla (Wilson). FIELD SPARROW. [563.]

> *Fringilla pusilla* Wilson, 1810, Am. Ornithol., 2, p. 131, pl. 16, fig. 2. (Pennsylvania = Philadelphia.)

Habitat.—Old fields, brushy hillsides, overgrown pastures, thorn scrub, deciduous forest edge, sparse second growth, and fencerows.

Distribution.—*Breeds* from northwestern and southeastern Montana, northern North Dakota, central Minnesota, north-central Wisconsin, north-central Michigan, southern Ontario, southwestern Quebec, southern Maine and southern New Brunswick south to northeastern Colorado (possibly), western Kansas, western Oklahoma, central and southern Texas (west to Irion County), the Gulf coast (east to northern Florida) and southern Georgia; also in southern Manitoba (Winnipeg).

Winters from Kansas, Missouri, Illinois, southern Michigan, northern Ohio, Pennsylvania and Massachusetts (casually farther north) south to southeastern New Mexico, northern Coahuila, central Nuevo León, northern Tamaulipas, the Gulf coast and southern Florida.

Casual east to southeastern Quebec (including the Magdalen Islands) and Nova

Scotia, and west to Wyoming, California (Farallon Islands), Arizona (Ganado) and central New Mexico.

Notes.—*S. pusilla* and *S. wortheni* are closely related and considered conspecific by some authors; they constitute a superspecies.

Spizella wortheni Ridgway. WORTHEN'S SPARROW. [564.]

> *Spizella wortheni* Ridgway, 1884, Proc. U.S. Natl. Mus., 7, p. 259. (Silver City, New Mexico.)

Habitat.—Arid brush and thorn scrub (upper Tropical and Subtropical zones).

Distribution.—*Breeds* in western Zacatecas and southwestern Tamaulipas, presumably elsewhere in northeastern Mexico.

Recorded also in Coahuila, San Luis Potosí, Puebla and Veracruz, almost certainly a migrant in the latter two states. Accidental in New Mexico (Silver City, 16 June 1884).

Notes.—See comments under *S. pusilla.*

Spizella atrogularis (Cabanis). BLACK-CHINNED SPARROW. [565.]

> *Spinites atrogularis* Cabanis, 1851, Mus. Heineanum, 1, p. 133. (Mexico.)

Habitat.—Chaparral, sagebrush, arid scrub and brushy hillsides (Subtropical and lower Temperate zones).

Distribution.—*Breeds* from central California (north to the San Francisco region and southern Sierra Nevada), southern Nevada, southwestern Utah, central Arizona, central New Mexico, western Texas (Guadalupe and Chisos mountains), central Nuevo León and southwestern Tamaulipas south to northern Baja California, southwestern California and southeastern Arizona, and in the Mexican highlands to Guerrero, Oaxaca (west of the Isthmus of Tehuantepec) and Puebla.

Winters from coastal California (casually), southern Arizona, southern New Mexico, western Texas and Nuevo León south to southern Baja California, and through the remainder of the breeding range in Mexico.

Casual in southwestern Oregon (Medford); sight reports in central and southeastern Texas are questionable.

Genus **POOECETES** Baird

> *Pooecetes* Baird, 1858, *in* Baird, Cassin and Lawrence, Rep. Explor. Surv. R. R. Pac., 9, pp. xx, xxxix [on pp. 439 and 447, as "*Poocœtes*"]. Type, by monotypy, *Fringilla graminea* Gmelin.

Pooecetes gramineus (Gmelin). VESPER SPARROW. [540.]

> *Fringilla graminea* Gmelin, 1789, Syst. Nat., 1 (2), p. 922. Based on the "Grass Finch" Latham, Gen. Synop. Birds, 2 (1), p. 273. (in Noveboraco = New York.)

Habitat.—Plains, prairie, dry shrublands, savanna, weedy pastures, fields, sagebrush, arid scrub and woodland clearings.

Distribution.—*Breeds* from east-central and southern British Columbia, southern Mackenzie, northern Alberta, central Saskatchewan, north-central Manitoba, central and northeastern Ontario, southern Quebec, New Brunswick, Prince Edward Island and Nova Scotia south to western Oregon, eastern and southern California (to Inyo and San Bernardino counties), central Nevada, southwestern Utah, northern and east-central Arizona, central New Mexico, Colorado, Kansas, Missouri, Tennessee and North Carolina, generally local south of northern Illinois, southern Michigan, northern Ohio and (east of the Appalachians) Maryland.

Winters from central California, the southern Great Basin and Rocky Mountain areas, western and central Texas, Arkansas, southern Illinois, Kentucky, West Virginia, southern Pennsylvania and Connecticut (casually farther north) south to southern Baja California, in the Mexican interior to Guerrero, Oaxaca and Veracruz, and to southern Texas, the Gulf coast and central Florida.

Casual in the state of Yucatán, central Guatemala, southern Florida, the Bahama Islands (Grand Bahama) and Bermuda.

Genus **CHONDESTES** Swainson

Chondestes Swainson, 1827, Philos. Mag., new ser., 1, p. 435. Type, by monotypy, *Chondestes strigatus* Swainson = *Fringilla grammaca* Say.

Chondestes grammacus (Say). LARK SPARROW. [552.]

Fringilla grammaca Say, 1823, *in* Long, Exped. Rocky Mount., 1, p. 139. (Prairies on the Missouri between the Kansas and Platte = Bellefontaine, four miles from mouth of Missouri River, Missouri.)

Habitat.—Open situations with scattered bushes and trees, prairie, forest edge, cultivated areas, orchards, fields with bushy borders, and savanna.

Distribution.—*Breeds* from western Oregon, eastern Washington, southern interior British Columbia, southeastern Alberta, southern Saskatchewan, southern Manitoba, northwestern and central Minnesota, north-central Wisconsin, southern Michigan, southern Ontario and central Pennsylvania (formerly) south to southern California (chiefly west of the Sierra Nevada), central Nevada, southern Arizona, northeastern Sonora, southern Chihuahua, Durango, Zacatecas, Nuevo León, northern Tamaulipas, southern and eastern Texas, Louisiana, central Alabama, central North Carolina and western Virginia, with breeding very local and irregular east of the Mississippi Valley.

Winters from central California, southern Arizona, southern New Mexico (rarely), north-central and eastern Texas, the Gulf coast and (casually) the Atlantic coast from New York (and casually farther north in interior North America) south through Mexico to southern Baja California, Chiapas and Veracruz, and (rarely) southern Florida.

Casual in the northeast from southern Quebec, New Brunswick, Nova Scotia and Newfoundland southward, and south to the state of Yucatán, Guatemala, El Salvador, Honduras, Cuba and the northern Bahama Islands (Grand Bahama, Bimini, New Providence).

Genus **AMPHISPIZA** Coues

Amphispiza Coues, 1874, Birds Northwest (Misc. Publ. U.S. Geol. Surv. Terr.), p. 234. Type, by original designation, *Emberiza bilineata* Cassin.

Notes.—Some authors would merge this genus in *Aimophila*.

Amphispiza bilineata (Cassin). BLACK-THROATED SPARROW. [573.]

Emberiza bilineata Cassin, 1850, Proc. Acad. Nat. Sci. Philadelphia, 5, p. 103, pl. 3. (Texas, on the Rio Grande.)

Habitat.—Desert scrub, thorn brush, mesquite and juniper, in migration and winter also occasionally in grassy areas and weedy fields away from desert regions (Tropical and Subtropical zones).

Distribution.—*Breeds* from south-central and southeastern Oregon, southwestern Idaho, southwestern Wyoming, western and southern Colorado, northwestern Oklahoma and north-central Texas south through eastern California (primarily Colorado, Mojave and Great Basin deserts) to southern Baja California (including many islands), northern Jalisco, Guanajuato, Querétaro, Hidalgo, Tamaulipas, and central and southern Texas.

Winters from southern California, southern Nevada, central and southeastern Arizona, southern New Mexico, and central and southern Texas south through the remainder of the breeding range.

Casual in western North America west and north of the breeding range from Washington, southern interior British Columbia and southern Alberta southward. Casual or accidental in eastern North America (recorded from South Dakota, Nebraska and Kansas east through Minnesota, Wisconsin and Illinois to Ohio, along the Atlantic coast in Massachusetts, New Jersey and Virginia, and in the Gulf states in Louisiana and western Florida).

Amphispiza belli (Cassin). SAGE SPARROW. [574.]

Emberiza Belli Cassin, 1850, Proc. Acad. Nat. Sci. Philadelphia, 5, p. 104, pl. 4. (California near Sonoma.)

Habitat.—Sagebrush, salt-bush brushland and chaparral, in migration and winter also in arid plains with sparse bushes, grasslands, and open situations with scattered brush.

Distribution.—*Breeds* from central interior Washington, eastern Oregon, southern Idaho, southwestern Wyoming and northwestern Colorado south to southern California (including San Clemente Island, but absent from the northwestern part of the state), central Baja California, southern Nevada, southwestern Utah, northeastern Arizona and northwestern New Mexico.

Winters from central California, central Nevada, southwestern Utah, northern Arizona and central New Mexico south to central Baja California, northern Sonora, northern Chihuahua and western Texas.

Casual in the Pacific coastal region from southwestern British Columbia southward, and to Montana, eastern Wyoming, eastern Colorado and western Kansas.

Amphispiza quinquestriata (Sclater and Salvin). FIVE-STRIPED SPARROW. [584.2.]

Zonotrichia quinquestriata Sclater and Salvin, 1868, Proc. Zool. Soc. London, p. 323. (Mexico = Bolaños, Jalisco.)

Habitat.—Dense bushy vegetation and grasses on steep hillsides, especially with acacia, mesquite or riparian vegetation (Subtropical Zone).

Distribution.—*Resident* from southeastern Arizona south through eastern Sonora and western Chihuahua to central Sinaloa and western Durango; also in northern Jalisco.

Notes.—This species was formerly placed in the genus *Aimophila*.

Genus CALAMOSPIZA Bonaparte

Calamospiza Bonaparte, 1838, Geogr. Comp. List, p. 30. Type, by monotypy, *Fringilla bicolor* Townsend = *Calamospiza melanocorys* Stejneger.

Calamospiza melanocorys Stejneger. LARK BUNTING. [605.]

Fringilla bicolor (not Linnaeus, 1766) J. K. Townsend, 1837, J. Acad. Nat. Sci. Philadelphia, 7, p. 189. (plains of Platte River = western Nebraska.)
Calamospiza melanocorys Stejneger, 1885, Auk, 2, p. 49. New name for *Fringilla bicolor* Townsend, preoccupied.

Habitat.—Plains, prairies, meadows and sagebrush, in migration and winter also in cultivated lands, brushy areas and desert.

Distribution.—*Breeds* from southern Alberta, southern Saskatchewan, southwestern Manitoba, southeastern North Dakota and southwestern Minnesota south, east of the Rockies, to eastern New Mexico, northern Texas (Panhandle), western Oklahoma, eastern Kansas, and northwestern Missouri; also locally or sporadically in southern California (San Bernardino County), Utah (Murray), southwestern Colorado (Navajo Springs), northwestern New Mexico (Star Lake) and west-central Texas (northern Trans-Pecos and Edwards Plateau).

Winters from southern California, southern Nevada, central Arizona, southern New Mexico and north-central Texas south to southern Baja California, Jalisco, Guanajuato, Hidalgo, Tamaulipas, southern and eastern Texas, and southern Louisiana.

Casual elsewhere in western North America from central British Columbia, central Alberta and Montana southward, and in eastern North America from Wisconsin, southern Ontario, southern Quebec, New Brunswick and Nova Scotia south to the Gulf coast and Florida.

Genus PASSERCULUS Bonaparte

Passerculus Bonaparte, 1838, Geogr. Comp. List, p. 33. Type, by subsequent designation (G. R. Gray, 1840), *Fringilla savanna* Wilson = *Emberiza sandwichensis* Gmelin.

Notes.—Some authors merge *Passerculus* and *Xenospiza* in *Ammodramus*.

Passerculus sandwichensis (Gmelin). SAVANNAH SPARROW. [542.]

Emberiza sandwichensis Gmelin, 1789, Syst. Nat., 1 (2), p. 875. Based on the "Sandwich Bunting" Latham, Gen. Synop. Birds, 2 (1), p. 202. (in Unalaschca et sinu Sandwich = Unalaska, Alaska.)

Habitat.—Open areas, especially grasslands, tundra, meadows, bogs, farmlands, grassy areas with scattered bushes, and marshes, including salt marshes in the *beldingi* and *rostratus* groups (Subtropical and Temperate zones).

Distribution.—*Breeds* [*princeps* group] on Sable Island and the adjacent mainland of Nova Scotia; [*sandwichensis* group] from western and northern Alaska, northern Yukon, northern Mackenzie, northern Keewatin, northern Ontario, islands in James Bay, northern Quebec, northern Labrador and Newfoundland south to southwestern Alaska (including Nunivak Island and the Aleutians west to Amukta), in coastal regions to west-central California (Monterey region), in the interior to central California (locally to San Bernardino County), southern Nevada, southern Utah, east-central Arizona, northern New Mexico, central Colorado, Nebraska, Missouri (at least formerly), Kentucky, eastern Tennessee, western Virginia, western Maryland, southeastern Pennsylvania and northern New Jersey, and locally in the interior highlands of Mexico from Chihuahua and Coahuila south to Guerrero and Puebla, and in southwestern Guatemala; and [*rostratus* group] along the Pacific coast of Baja California from El Rosario south to Magdalena Bay (including the San Benito Islands), and from northeastern Baja California (San Felipe, mouth of the Colorado River) south along the coast of Sonora to northern Sinaloa (lat. 25°N.).

Winters [*princeps* group] along the Atlantic coast from central Nova Scotia south to northeastern Florida; [*sandwichensis* group] from southern British Columbia, southern Nevada, northern Arizona, central New Mexico, Oklahoma, Tennessee, southern Kentucky, and east of the Appalachians, from Massachusetts (casually north to Alaska, the northern United States, southern Ontario and Nova Scotia) south to southern Baja California (including most adjacent islands), throughout most of Mexico (including the Yucatan Peninsula) to Guatemala, Belize and northern Honduras, and to southern Texas, the Gulf coast, southern Florida, the Bahama Islands (south to Rum Cay), Cuba, the Isle of Pines, and Cayman and Swan islands; and [*rostratus* group] in salt marshes from central coastal and southern California (rarely north to the Monterey region and Channel Islands) south to southern Baja California (along both coasts), and the coasts of Sonora and northern Sinaloa.

Resident [*beldingi* group] in salt marshes of coastal southern California (north to Santa Barbara region) and northwestern Baja California (Todos Santos Islands, El Rosario).

Casual or accidental [*sandwichensis* group] in the Pribilofs and western Aleutians (Shemya), north to Seymour, Cornwallis and Southampton islands, in England, and in northeastern Asia (Chukotski Peninsula, Koryak highlands) and Japan, also a sight report for the Hawaiian Islands (Kure).

Notes.—The various groups have been recognized by some authors as separate species, *P. princeps* Maynard, 1872 [IPSWICH SPARROW, 541], *P. sandwichensis* [SAVANNAH SPARROW, 542], *P. beldingi* Ridgway, 1885 [BELDING'S SPARROW, 543], and *P. rostratus* (Cassin, 1852) [LARGE-BILLED SPARROW, 544]; intergradation between the *princeps* and *sandwichensis* groups occurs in Nova Scotia.

Genus **AMMODRAMUS** Swainson

Ammodramus Swainson, 1827, Philos. Mag., new ser., 1, p. 435. Type, by monotypy, *Ammodramus bimaculatus* Swainson = *Fringilla savannarum* Gmelin.

Centronyx Baird, 1858, *in* Baird, Cassin and Lawrence, Rep. Explor. Surv. R. R. Pac., 9, p. 440. Type, by monotypy, *Emberiza bairdii* Audubon.

Ammospiza Oberholser, 1905, Smithson. Misc. Collect., 48, p. 68. Type, by original designation, *Oriolus caudacutus* Gmelin.

Passerherbulus "Maynard" Stone, 1907, Auk, 24, p. 193. Type, by original designation, *Ammodramus lecontei* Audubon = *Emberiza leconteii* Audubon.

Thryospiza Oberholser, 1917, Ohio J. Sci., 17, p. 332. Type, by original designation, *Fringilla maritima* Wilson.
Nemospiza Oberholser, 1917, Ohio J. Sci., 17, p. 335. Type, by original designation, *Emberiza henslowii* Audubon.

Notes.—Generic limits within this group have been treated in a variety of ways in recent years; see comments under each species and also under *Passerculus.*

Ammodramus bairdii (Audubon). BAIRD'S SPARROW. [545.]

Emberiza Bairdii Audubon, 1844, Birds Am. (octavo ed.), 7, p. 359, pl. 500. (Prairie of the upper Missouri = near Old Fort Union, North Dakota.)

Habitat.—Short-grass prairie with scattered low bushes and matted vegetation, in migration and winter also in open grasslands and overgrown fields.
Distribution.—*Breeds* from southeastern Alberta, southern Saskatchewan and southern Manitoba south to central and eastern Montana, southern South Dakota, southeastern North Dakota and west-central Minnesota.

Winters from southeastern Arizona, southern New Mexico (casually) and north-central Texas south to northern Sonora, Durango, Chihuahua, Coahuila and southern Texas.

Migrates regularly through the Plains states from western Kansas east to western Missouri, and south through eastern and southern New Mexico, Texas, and central and western Oklahoma, casually west to western Montana and southern Idaho.

Accidental in California (Farallon Islands and San Diego) and New York (Montauk).

Ammodramus savannarum (Gmelin). GRASSHOPPER SPARROW. [546.]

Fringilla Savannarum Gmelin, 1789, Syst. Nat., 1 (2), p. 921. Based on the "Savanna Finch" Latham, Gen. Synop. Birds, 2 (1), p. 270. (in Jamaicae = Jamaica.)

Habitat.—Prairie, old fields, open grasslands, cultivated fields and savanna (Tropical to Temperate zones).
Distribution.—*Breeds* from eastern Washington, southern interior British Columbia, southern Alberta, southern Saskatchewan, southern Manitoba, northern Minnesota, southern Ontario, southwestern Quebec, northern Vermont, central New Hampshire and southern Maine south to southern California (west of the Sierra Nevada), central Nevada (rare and local), northern Utah, central Colorado, northeastern New Mexico, northern and south-central Texas, Arkansas, northern and east-central Mississippi, central Alabama, central Georgia, central North Carolina and southeastern Virginia; in central peninsular Florida (Kissimmee Prairie region); and in southeastern Arizona and northern Sonora.

Winters from central California (rarely), southern Arizona, southern New Mexico (rarely), Texas, Oklahoma, Arkansas, Tennessee and North Carolina (casually farther north) south through Mexico and northern Central America to north-central Costa Rica.

Resident locally in Middle America in Mexico (the state of México, Veracruz, Oaxaca and Chiapas), Guatemala (Petén and the Caribbean lowlands), Belize, Honduras (interior highlands and eastern pine savanna), northeastern Nicaragua (pine savanna), northwestern Costa Rica, and Panama (Pacific lowlands in western Chiriquí, Coclé and eastern Panamá province); in the Greater Antilles (Jamaica,

Hispaniola and Puerto Rico); and in western Colombia (Cauca Valley), western Ecuador, and the Netherlands Antilles (Curaçao and Bonaire).

Casual west to the Pacific coast from southwestern British Columbia southward, and east to New Brunswick, Prince Edward Island, Nova Scotia and Newfoundland; also in the Swan Islands and northwestern Panama (Bocas del Toro).

Ammodramus henslowii (Audubon). HENSLOW'S SPARROW. [547.]

> *Emberiza Henslowii* Audubon, 1829, Birds Am. (folio), 1, pl. 70 (1831, Ornithol. Biogr., 1, p. 360). (opposite Cincinnati, in state of Kentucky.)

Habitat.—Open fields and meadows with grass interspersed with weeds or shrubby vegetation, especially in damp or low-lying areas, in migration and winter also in grassy areas adjacent to pine woods or second-growth woodland.

Distribution.—*Breeds* from eastern South Dakota, central Minnesota, central Wisconsin, central Michigan, southern Ontario, northern New York, southern Vermont, southern New Hampshire and northeastern Massachusetts south to central Kansas, southwestern and central Missouri, southern Illinois, northern Kentucky, central West Virginia, eastern Virginia and east-central North Carolina; also locally in eastern Texas (Harris County). The breeding range in the northwestern and eastern portions has decreased in recent years.

Winters in coastal states from South Carolina south to southern Florida, and west to eastern and (rarely) southern Texas, casually north to Illinois, Indiana, New England and Nova Scotia.

Notes.—Often treated in the genus *Passerherbulus.*

Ammodramus leconteii (Audubon). LE CONTE'S SPARROW. [548.]

> *Fringilla caudacuta* (not *Oriolus caudacutus* Gmelin) Latham, 1790, Index Ornithol., 1, p. 459. (in Georgiæ americanæ interioribus = interior of Georgia.)
>
> *Emberiza le conteii* Audubon, 1844, Birds Am. (octavo ed.), 7, p. 338, pl. 488. (wet portions of prairies of upper Missouri = Fort Union, North Dakota.)

Habitat.—Moist grass or sedge meadows, damp matted grass and shrubby tangles on edges of marshes and bogs, and areas of moist or dry, tall, rank grass, in migration and winter also in weedy fields, broomsedge and cattails.

Distribution.—*Breeds* from east-central British Columbia, southern Mackenzie, northern Alberta, northern Saskatchewan, central Manitoba, north-central Ontario and west-central Quebec south to southern Alberta, north-central Montana, southern Saskatchewan, northern North Dakota, northwestern and eastern Minnesota, northeastern Wisconsin and northern Michigan, casually south to southeastern South Dakota, northeastern Illinois and southern Ontario.

Winters from west-central Kansas, southern Missouri (rarely), southern Illinois (rarely), western Tennessee, central Alabama, south-central Georgia and South Carolina south to eastern New Mexico (rarely), eastern and southern Texas, the Gulf coast (east to western Florida) and southeastern Georgia.

Migrates regularly through the Great Plains (east to the Mississippi Valley), irregularly through the Ohio Valley, and casually to the east coast from Maine south to southern Florida.

Casual west to Washington, Idaho, Wyoming, Colorado and California, and south to Coahuila (Sabinas).

Notes.—In the past usually treated in the literature as *Passerherbulus caudacutus* (Latham, 1790) or *Ammospiza leconteii.*

Ammodramus caudacutus (Gmelin). SHARP-TAILED SPARROW. [549.]

Oriolus caudacutus Gmelin, 1788, Syst. Nat., 1 (1), p. 394. Based mainly on the "Sharp-tailed Oriole" Latham, Gen. Synop. Birds, 1 (2), p. 448. (in Noveboraco = New York.)

Habitat.—Marshes (both salt and fresh-water) and wet meadows, in migration and winter also in brushy areas and overgrown fields.

Distribution.—*Breeds* from east-central British Columbia, southern Mackenzie, northern Alberta, central Saskatchewan and central Manitoba south to south-central Alberta, southern Saskatchewan, southern Manitoba, western and southeastern North Dakota, southeastern South Dakota and northwestern Minnesota; around James Bay in northern Ontario and northwestern Quebec; and in southeastern Quebec (along the southern shore of St. Lawrence River), and along the Atlantic coast from eastern Quebec (including the Magdalen Islands), Prince Edward Island and Nova Scotia south to North Carolina (Pea Island).

Winters in coastal marshes from New York (casually from Massachusetts) south to southern Florida, along the Gulf coast west to southern Texas, and rarely in coastal California and northwestern Baja California.

Migrates presumably through the interior United States, but recorded only casually from Colorado and the Great Plains east to Michigan, western Pennsylvania and central New York, and virtually unrecorded in the west away from coastal areas.

Notes.—Often treated in the genus *Ammospiza.*

Ammodramus maritimus (Wilson). SEASIDE SPARROW. [550.]

Fringilla maritima Wilson, 1811, Am. Ornithol., 4, p. 68, pl. 34, fig. 2. (sea islands along our Atlantic coast = Great Egg Harbor, New Jersey.)

Habitat.—Salt marshes, especially *Spartina* grass, rushes and tidal reeds, also [*mirabilis* group] marsh prairie (*Muhlenbergia*).

Distribution.—*Breeds* [*maritimus* group] from Massachusetts south along the Atlantic coast to northeastern Florida (south to the St. John's River, formerly to New Smyrna Beach); and along the Gulf coast from western Florida (south to Tampa Bay) west to southeastern Texas (south to Corpus Christi area).

Winters [*maritimus* group] along the Atlantic coast from Massachusetts south through the remainder of the breeding range, casually to southern Florida (Flamingo region); and along the Gulf coast throughout the breeding range and south to the mouth of the Rio Grande.

Resident [*nigrescens* group] formerly along the coast of east-central Florida (eastern Orange and northern Brevard counties), approaching extinction (only a few surviving males in 1981); and [*mirabilis* group] in southern Florida (southwestern Collier, Monroe and southern Dade counties).

Casual [*maritimus* group] north to Maine, southern New Brunswick and Nova Scotia, and inland in North Carolina (Raleigh).

Notes.—The three groups have often been considered as separate species, *A. maritimus* [COMMON SEASIDE-SPARROW, 550], *A. nigrescens* Ridgway, 1873 [DUSKY SEASIDE-SPARROW, 551], and *A. mirabilis* (Howell, 1919) [CAPE SABLE SPARROW or SEASIDE-SPARROW, 551.1]. Often treated in the genus *Ammospiza*.

Genus XENOSPIZA Bangs

Xenospiza Bangs, 1931, Proc. N. Engl. Zool. Club, 12, p. 86. Type, by original designation, *Xenospiza baileyi* Bangs.

Notes.—See comments under *Passerculus*.

Xenospiza baileyi Bangs. SIERRA MADRE SPARROW.

Xenospiza baileyi Bangs, 1931, Proc. N. Engl. Zool. Club, 12, p. 87. (Bolaños, Jalisco, Mexico.)

Habitat.—Bunch grass areas, generally in regions of highland pine (upper Subtropical and Temperate zones).
Distribution.—*Resident* in the highlands of Durango, Jalisco, Morelos and the Distrito Federal.

Genus PASSERELLA Swainson

Passerella Swainson, 1837, Class. Birds, 2, p. 288. Type, by monotypy, *P. iliaca* Wilson, iii. 22. f. 4 = *Fringilla iliaca* Merrem.

Notes.—Some authors merge *Passerella* and *Melospiza* in *Zonotrichia*; a broader generic concept would merge these also in *Junco*.

Passerella iliaca (Merrem). FOX SPARROW. [585.]

Fringilla iliaca Merrem, 1786, Avium Rar. Icones Descr., 2, p. 37, pl. 10. (North America = Quebec.)

Habitat.—Undergrowth of deciduous or coniferous forest, forest edge, woodland thickets, scrub, cut-over lands, chaparral, riparian woodland, streamside shrubbery and montane brushland, in migration and winter also in deciduous forest, open woodland and lowland thickets.
Distribution.—*Breeds* from western and northern Alaska, northern Yukon, northwestern and south-central Mackenzie, southwestern Keewatin, northern Manitoba, northern Ontario, northern Quebec and northern Labrador south to southern Alaska (west to Unalaska in the Aleutians), on the Pacific coast to northwestern Washington, in the western mountains to southern California, central Nevada, central Utah and central Colorado, and, east of the Rockies, to central Alberta, central Saskatchewan, central Manitoba, central Ontario, southern Quebec (including Anticosti and Magdalen islands), northwestern New Brunswick, Nova Scotia and southern Newfoundland.
Winters from southern Alaska (west to Kodiak) and southern British Columbia south through the Pacific states to northern Baja California, and from central Arizona, northern New Mexico, Kansas, southern Iowa, southern Wisconsin, northern Indiana, southern Ontario, southwestern Quebec, New Brunswick, Nova Scotia and southern Newfoundland south to northern Sonora (casually), southern New Mexico, western and southern Texas, the Gulf coast and central Florida.

In migration occurs regularly throughout eastern North America between the breeding and wintering ranges.

Casual or accidental in Bermuda, Greenland, Iceland, the British Isles, continental Europe and Japan.

Genus **MELOSPIZA** Baird

Melospiza Baird, 1858, *in* Baird, Cassin and Lawrence, Rep. Explor. Surv. R. R. Pac., 9, pp. xx, xl, 440, 476. Type, by original designation, *Fringilla melodia* Wilson.

Helospiza Baird, 1858, *in* Baird, Cassin and Lawrence, Rep. Explor. Surv. R. R. Pac., 9, pp. xx, xl, 476. Type, by original designation, *Fringilla palustris* Wilson = *Fringilla georgiana* Latham.

Notes.—See comments under *Passerella.*

Melospiza melodia (Wilson). SONG SPARROW. [581.]

Fringilla melodia Wilson, 1810, Am. Ornithol., 2, p. 125, pl. 16, fig. 4. (Canada to Georgia = Philadelphia, Pennsylvania.)

Habitat.—Brushy, shrubby and deep grassy areas along watercourses and seacoasts, in marshes (cattail, bulrush and salt), and, mostly in northern and eastern portions of the range, in forest, edge, bogs, brushy clearings, thickets, hedgerows, gardens and brushy pastures (upper Subtropical and Temperate zones).

Distribution.—*Breeds* from southern Alaska (including the Aleutian Islands), south-central Yukon, northern British Columbia, south-central Mackenzie, northern Saskatchewan, northern Manitoba, northern Ontario, central Quebec and southwestern Newfoundland south to south-central Baja California and northern Sonora, locally in the Mexican highlands to Michoacán, the state of México, Tlaxcala and Puebla, and to northern New Mexico, northeastern Kansas, north-central Arkansas, southern Tennessee, northeastern Alabama, northern Georgia, and northwestern and coastal South Carolina.

Winters from southern Alaska (resident in the Aleutians), coastal and southern British Columbia, the northern United States, southern Ontario, southwestern Quebec, Prince Edward Island and Nova Scotia south throughout the remainder of the breeding range, and to southern Texas, the Gulf coast and southern Florida.

Casual or accidental in Bermuda, the Bahama Islands (New Providence, Grand Bahama) and British Isles.

Melospiza lincolnii (Audubon). LINCOLN'S SPARROW. [583.]

Fringilla Lincolnii Audubon, 1834, Birds Am. (folio), 2, pl. 193. (Labrador = near mouth of Natashquan River, Quebec.)

Habitat.—Bogs, wet meadows and riparian thickets, mostly in northern and montane areas, in migration and winter also in brushy areas, thickets, hedgerows, understory of open woodland, forest edge, clearings, and scrubby areas.

Distribution.—*Breeds* from western and central Alaska, central Yukon, northwestern and southern Mackenzie, northern Saskatchewan, northern Manitoba, northern Ontario, northern Quebec, central Labrador and Newfoundland south to south-coastal and southeastern Alaska, in the mountains to southern California, extreme west-central Nevada (absent as a breeding bird from most mountains in the Great Basin), east-central Arizona and northern New Mexico, and to south-western and south-central Alberta, central Saskatchewan, southern Manitoba, northeastern Minnesota, northern Wisconsin, central Michigan, southern Ontario, northern New York, northwestern Massachusetts, southern Vermont, northern New Hampshire, central Maine, New Brunswick, Prince Edward Island and Nova Scotia.

Winters from northern California, southern Nevada, Arizona, central New Mexico, Oklahoma, eastern Kansas, central Missouri, southern Kentucky and northern Georgia (casually at Kodiak in southern Alaska, and north to the northern United States) south to southern Baja California, through northern Middle America to El Salvador and Honduras, and to southern Texas, the Gulf coast and central Florida, casually to Costa Rica and Panama (east to the Canal Zone), the Greater Antilles (Cuba and Jamaica, also sight reports from Puerto Rico), southern Florida and the Bahama Islands (south to Little Inagua).

Migrates regularly throughout continental North America between the breeding and wintering ranges.

Accidental in Greenland.

Melospiza georgiana (Latham). SWAMP SPARROW. [584.]

Fringilla georgiana Latham, 1790, Index Ornithol., 1, p. 460. (in Georgiæ americanæ interioribus = interior of Georgia.)

Habitat.—Emergent vegetation around watercourses, marshes, bogs and wet meadows, in migration and winter also in weedy fields, brush, thickets, scrub and forest edge.

Distribution.—*Breeds* from west-central and southern Mackenzie, northern Saskatchewan, northern Manitoba, northern Ontario, central Quebec, southern Labrador and Newfoundland south to northeastern and east-central British Columbia, south-central Alberta, central Saskatchewan, southern Manitoba, the Dakotas, eastern Nebraska, northern Missouri (formerly), northern Illinois, northern Indiana, central Ohio, southeastern West Virginia, Maryland and Delaware.

Winters from eastern Nebraska, Iowa, the Great Lakes region, central New York and Massachusetts (casually farther north) south to western and southern Texas, the Gulf coast and southern Florida, and west across central and southern New Mexico to southeastern Arizona and (rarely) California, irregularly or sporadically to central Mexico (recorded Sonora, Durango, Jalisco, Chihuahua, Coahuila, San Luis Potosí and Tamaulipas).

Casual elsewhere in western North America from southwestern British Columbia and Montana southward, and in Bermuda; a report from the Bahama Islands is questionable. Accidental in Alaska (Anchorage).

Genus **ZONOTRICHIA** Swainson

Zonotrichia [subgenus] Swainson, 1832, *in* Swainson and Richardson, Fauna Bor.-Am., 2 (1831), pp. 254–257, 493. Type, by subsequent designation (Bonaparte, 1832), *Fringilla pensylvanica* Latham = *Fringilla albicollis* Gmelin.

Notes.—See comments under *Passerella.*

Zonotrichia capensis (Müller). RUFOUS-COLLARED SPARROW.

Fringilla capensis P. L. S. Müller, 1776, Natursyst., Suppl., p. 165. Based on "Bruent, du Cap de Bonne-Espérance" Daubenton, Planches Enlum., pl. 386, fig. 2. (Cape of Good Hope, error = Cayenne.)

Habitat.—Partly open situations with scattered bushes, shrubby hillsides, montane thickets, cultivated fields, humid forest edge, open woodland, and around human habitations (Subtropical and Temperate, locally also Tropical zones).

Distribution.—*Resident* in the Greater Antilles in the mountains of Hispaniola; in the highlands of Middle America from Chiapas south through Guatemala and El Salvador to Honduras, and in Costa Rica and western Panama (east to western Panamá province); and in South America at higher elevations from Colombia, Venezuela (also Curaçao and Aruba) and the Guianas south to Peru, and virtually throughout from Bolivia, Paraguay and Brazil south to Tierra del Fuego.

Notes.—Also known as ANDEAN SPARROW.

Zonotrichia albicollis (Gmelin). WHITE-THROATED SPARROW. [558.]

Fringilla albicollis Gmelin, 1789, Syst. Nat., 1 (2), p. 921. Based on the "White-throated Sparrow" Edwards, Glean. Nat. Hist., 2, p. 198, pl. 304. (in Pensilvania = Philadelphia.)

Habitat.—Coniferous and mixed coniferous-deciduous forest, forest edge, clearings, bogs, brush, thickets and open woodland, in migration and winter also in deciduous forest and woodland, scrub, shrubbery and gardens.

Distribution.—*Breeds* from southeastern Yukon, west-central and southern Mackenzie, northern Saskatchewan, northern Manitoba, northern Ontario, north-central Quebec, southern Labrador and Newfoundland south to central interior British Columbia, central Alberta, central and southeastern Saskatchewan, north-central North Dakota, northern and east-central Minnesota, northern Wisconsin, central and southeastern Michigan, northern Ohio, northern West Virginia (irregularly), northern Pennsylvania and northern New Jersey.

Winters from southeastern Iowa, southern Wisconsin, southern Michigan, northern Ohio, Pennsylvania, central New York and Massachusetts (casually north to southern Canada from Manitoba eastward) south to Nuevo León, northern Tamaulipas, southern Texas, the Gulf coast and southern Florida, and west across Texas, New Mexico and southern Arizona to California (virtually statewide) and northern Baja California (casually to Guadalupe Island).

Migrates regularly through North America east of the Rockies, casually through western North America from southern British Columbia and the breeding range southward.

Casual north to northern Alaska, and to the Outer Hebrides, British Isles and continental Europe, also a sight report from Puerto Rico.

Zonotrichia atricapilla (Gmelin). GOLDEN-CROWNED SPARROW. [557.]

Emberiza atricapilla Gmelin, 1789, Syst. Nat., 1 (2), p. 875. Based mainly on the "Black-crowned Bunting" Latham, Gen. Synop. Birds, 2 (1), p. 202, pl. 45. (in Sinu Natka, et insulis Sandwich = Prince William Sound, Alaska.)

Habitat.—Montane thickets and shrubbery, dwarf conifers and brushy canyons, in migration and winter in dense brush, thickets, chaparral and gardens.

Distribution.—*Breeds* from western and north-central Alaska and south-central Yukon south to southern Alaska (west to Unimak in the eastern Aleutian Islands), southern British Columbia, extreme northern Washington (Okanogan County) and southwestern Alberta (Banff).

Winters from southern Alaska (west to Kodiak) and southern British Columbia south, mostly west of the Cascades and Sierra Nevada, to northern Baja California, southern California and southern Arizona, casually east to Utah, Colorado and central New Mexico, and south to southern Baja California (including offshore islands) and northern Sonora.

In migration occurs casually through the Pribilofs and western Aleutians (Attu, Amchitka), and east to southern Alberta, southern Saskatchewan and Idaho.

Casual in northern Alaska and northwestern Mackenzie; in northern North America from Minnesota, Wisconsin, southern Michigan, southern Ontario, New York, Massachusetts and Nova Scotia south to Kansas, Iowa, Illinois, Pennsylvania and New Jersey; along the Gulf coast east to eastern Texas, southern Louisiana and southern Alabama; and in northeastern Siberia. Accidental in Japan, with a sight report for Nayarit.

Zonotrichia leucophrys (Forster). WHITE-CROWNED SPARROW. [554.]

Emberiza leucophrys J. R. Forster, 1772, Philos. Trans. R. Soc. London, 62, p. 340. (Severn River, west shore of Hudson Bay.)

Habitat.—Stunted trees and shrubs, wet meadows with willows, brushy edges of woodland and forest, thickets, chaparral, coastal brushland in the fog belt, gardens and parks, in migration and winter also farmlands and brushy desert areas.

Distribution.—*Breeds* from western and northern Alaska, northern Yukon, northern Mackenzie and central Keewatin south to southern Alaska (west to the Alaska Peninsula), in coastal areas and mountains (somewhat disjunctly in southern portion) to southern California (to Santa Barbara and San Bernardino counties), southern Nevada, northern and east-central Arizona, and northern New Mexico, and from northern Saskatchewan and northern Manitoba east across northern Ontario and northern Quebec to Labrador, northern Newfoundland and south-central Quebec.

Winters from central Alaska (casually), southern British Columbia, Washington, Idaho, Wyoming and the central United States (Kansas east to southern West Virginia, casually farther north) south to southern Baja California, Michoacán, Querétaro, San Luis Potosí, Tamaulipas, southern Texas, the Gulf coast (east to northwestern Florida) and south-central Georgia, less fequently or rarely in eastern coastal areas from Massachusetts south to southern Florida, the Bahama Islands, Cuba and Jamaica, casually to the Yucatan Peninsula.

Migrates regularly through North America between the breeding and wintering ranges and, in the northeast, from southern Ontario eastward (rare in the Maritime Provinces and New England), and south to Pennsylvania, Maryland and Delaware.

Casual or accidental on islands in the Bering Sea (Pribilofs, Nunivak); north to Banks and southern Baffin islands, and to the Melville Peninsula; on Fletcher's Ice Island (in the Arctic Ocean west of northern Ellesmere Island); and in Greenland, the British Isles and Japan. An individual photographed in Panama (Canal Zone) may have been a man-assisted vagrant.

Zonotrichia querula (Nuttall). HARRIS' SPARROW. [553.]

Fringilla querula Nuttall, 1840, Man. Ornithol. U.S. Can., ed. 2, 1, p. 555. (few miles west of Independence, Missouri.)

Habitat.—Woody shrubbery and stunted trees in coniferous forest-tundra ecotone, in migration and winter in thickets, open woodland, forest edge, hedgerows and scrub.

Distribution.—*Breeds* from northwestern and east-central Mackenzie and southern Keewatin south to northeastern Saskatchewan and northern Manitoba.

Winters from southeastern Alaska (Juneau area southward), southern British Columbia, southern Idaho, northern Utah, northern Colorado, northern Nebraska and central Iowa (casually farther north) to southern California (mostly east of the Sierra Nevada), southern Nevada, southern Utah, southern New Mexico, southern Texas, western Louisiana, Arkansas and western Tennessee, also locally in northeastern Saskatchewan (Hasbala and Milton lakes).

In migration occurs regularly through the northern Great Plains region from Alberta, Saskatchewan, Manitoba and Minnesota south to Nebraska and Iowa.

Casual in northern and south-coastal Alaska; elsewhere in western North America from Washington south through coastal areas of California to southern California and east to southern Arizona; and in eastern North America from western and southern Ontario, southern Quebec, Maine and Nova Scotia south to the Gulf coast and central Florida. Accidental on Banks Island.

Genus **JUNCO** Wagler

Junco Wagler, 1831, Isis von Oken, col. 526. Type, by monotypy, *Junco phaeonotus* Wagler.

Notes.—See comments under *Passerella.*

Junco vulcani (Boucard). VOLCANO JUNCO.

Zonotrichia vulcani Boucard, 1878, Proc. Zool. Soc. London, p. 57, pl. 4. (Volcan of Irazu, altitude of 10,000 feet, Costa Rica.)

Habitat.—Thickets, scrubby openings, bushy areas and bare open ground, just below to well above timerline (upper Temperate Zone).

Distribution.—*Resident* on the high mountains of Costa Rica (Irazú and Turrialba volcanoes, and northern portion of Cordillera de Talamanca) and extreme western Panama (Volcán Barú, in western Chiriquí).

Junco hyemalis (Linnaeus). DARK-EYED JUNCO. [567.]

Fringilla hyemalis Linnaeus, 1758, Syst. Nat., ed. 10, 1, p. 183. Based on "The Snow-bird" Catesby, Nat. Hist. Carolina, 1, p. 36, pl. 36. (in America = South Carolina.)

Habitat.—Coniferous and deciduous forest, forest edge, clearings, bogs, open woodland, brushy areas adjacent to forest, and burned-over lands, in migration and winter in a variety of open woodland, brushy and grassy habitats.

Distribution.—*Breeds* [*hyemalis* group] from western and northern Alaska, central Yukon, northwestern and central Mackenzie, southern Keewatin, northern Manitoba, northern Ontario, islands in southern James Bay, northern Quebec,

Labrador and Newfoundland south to southwestern and south-coastal Alaska, southern Yukon, central interior British Columbia, south-central Alberta, south-central Saskatchewan, southern Manitoba, northern and east-central Minnesota, southeastern Wisconsin, central Michigan, southern Ontario and northeastern Ohio, in the Appalachians through eastern Kentucky, western Virginia, eastern Tennessee and western North Carolina to northern Georgia and northwestern South Carolina, and to southeastern New York and southern New England; [*oreganus* group] from south-coastal and southeastern Alaska, coastal and central British Columbia (including the Queen Charlotte Islands), west-central and Southern Alberta, and extreme southwestern Saskatchewan south to central coastal California, and in the mountains to northern Baja California, western Nevada, eastern Oregon, northern Utah, southern Idaho and northwestern Wyoming; [*aikeni* group] from southeastern Montana and western South Dakota south to northeastern Wyoming and northwestern Nebraska; and [*caniceps* group] in the mountains from southern Idaho, northern Utah and southern Wyoming south to eastern California (Clark Mountain and Grapevine Mountains), central Arizona, southern New Mexico and western Texas (Guadalupe Mountains).

Winters [*hyemalis* group] from central (casually) and south-coastal Alaska (west to Kodiak), coastal and southern British Columbia and southern Canada (east to Newfoundland) south to northern Baja California, northern Sonora, central Chihuahua, southern Texas, the Gulf coast and northern (casually southern) Florida; [*oreganus* group] from south-coastal and southeastern Alaska, southern British Columbia and the northwestern United States (east to the Dakotas and Minneosta) south to northern Baja California, northern Sonora, Durango, southern Chihuahua, eastern Texas, Oklahoma and Kansas; [*aikeni* group] from the breeding range south to northern and east-central Arizona (rarely), southern Colorado, northern New Mexico, western Oklahoma and western Kansas; and [*caniceps* group] from Nevada, southern Idaho, southern Wyoming and western Nebraska south to southern California (rarely), northern Sonora, northern Sinaloa, northern Durango, Chihuahua and western Texas.

Resident [*insularis* group] on Guadalupe Island, off Baja California.

Casual or accidental [*hyemalis* group] north to the Arctic coast of Alaska and to islands in the Bering Sea, and to Banks, Southampton and southern Baffin islands, Bermuda, the Bahama Islands (Grand Bahama, New Provindence), Jamaica, the British Isles, continental Europe and eastern Siberia, also sight reports for Puerto Rico and the Virgin Islands (St. Thomas); [*oreganus* group] in the eastern Aleutians (Unalaska), north to Banks Island, and through much of eastern North America from Michigan, southern Ontario, southwestern Quebec, Maine and Nova Scotia south to the Gulf coast (east to southern Louisiana), Tennessee and South Carolina; [*aikeni* group] to southern Idaho, eastern Nebraska, central Oklahoma and northern Texas, and in Michigan (Presque Isle County); and [*caniceps* group] west to the Pacific coast from southern British Columbia south to coastal California, and east to eastern Montana, the Dakotas, Minnesota, Illinois, Arkansas and Louisiana.

Notes.—The various groups of this complex have been treated as species by many authors, *J. hyemalis* [SLATE-COLORED JUNCO, 567], *J. oreganus* (J. K. Townsend, 1837) [OREGON JUNCO, 567.1], *J. aikeni* Ridgway, 1873 [WHITE-WINGED JUNCO, 566], *J. caniceps* (Woodhouse, 1853) [GRAY-HEADED JUNCO, 569], and *J. insularis* Ridgway, 1876 [GUADALUPE JUNCO]. The form *insularis* is an isolated population closest to the *oreganus* group; the remaining groups intergrade in varying degrees. A few authors also treat several distinctive populations within these groups as separate species: *J. mearnsi* Ridgway, 1897 [PINK-SIDED JUNCO, 568], of the *oreganus* group, breeding from southeastern Alberta and southwestern Saskatchewan to eastern Idaho and northwestern Wyoming, and *J. dorsalis* Henry, 1858 [RED-BACKED JUNCO, 569.1], of the *caniceps* group, breeding from northern Arizona and central New Mexico to western Texas.

Junco phaeonotus Wagler. YELLOW-EYED JUNCO. [570.]

Junco phaeonotus Wagler, 1831, Isis von Oken, col. 526. (Mexico.)

Habitat.—Open coniferous forest, pine-oak association and adjacent scrub, brush, pastures and fields (upper Subtropical and Temperate zones).

Distribution.—*Resident* [*phaeonotus* group] from northeastern Sonora, southern Arizona, extreme southwestern New Mexico (Animas, casually Hatchet mountains), Chihuahua, north-central Coahuila, Nuevo León and southwestern Tamaulipas south through the mountains to Oaxaca and western Veracruz (west of the Isthmus of Tehuantepec); [*bairdi* group] in the Cape district of southern Baja California; [*fulvescens* group] in the interior of Chiapas (from vicinity of San Cristóbal south to Teopisca); and [*alticola* group] in the mountains of extreme southeastern Chiapas (Volcán Tacaná area) and western Guatemala.

Notes.—The four groups are sometimes regarded as distinct species, *J. phaeonotus* [MEXICAN JUNCO, 570], *J. bairdi* Ridgway, 1883 [BAIRD'S JUNCO], *J. fulvescens* Nelson, 1897 [CHIAPAS JUNCO], and *J. alticola* Salvin, 1863 [GUATEMALA JUNCO].

Genus CALCARIUS Bechstein

Calcarius Bechstein, 1803, Ornithol. Taschenb. Dtsch., 1 (1802), p. 130. Type, by monotypy, *Fringilla lapponica* Linnaeus.
Rhynchophanes Baird, 1858, *in* Baird, Cassin and Lawrence, Rep. Explor. Surv. R. R. Pac., 9, pp. xx, xxxviii, 432. Type, by monotypy, *Plectrophanes maccownii* [sic] Lawrence.

Notes.—Some authors merge this genus in *Emberiza.*

Calcarius mccownii (Lawrence). McCOWN'S LONGSPUR. [539.]

Plectrophanes McCownii Lawrence, 1851, Ann. Lyc. Nat. Hist. N.Y., 5, p. 122. (high prairies of Western Texas.)

Habitat.—Sparse short-grass plains, plowed and stubble fields, and on bare or nearly bare ground.

Distribution.—*Breeds* from southeastern Alberta, southern Saskatchewan, north-central North Dakota and (formerly) southwestern Minnesota south through Montana to southeastern Wyoming, northeastern Colorado, northwestern Nebraska and central North Dakota.

Winters from southeastern California (rarely), central Arizona, southern (formerly northern) New Mexico, southeastern Colorado (casually), west-central Kansas and central Oklahoma south to northeastern Sonora, Chihuahua, northern Durango, and western and south-central Texas (rare in recent years in eastern portions of range).

In migration occurs rarely in eastern and coastal southern California.

Casual north and west to southern British Columbia, Idaho and Nevada, and east to Illinois, Missouri and eastern Texas. Accidental in Massachusetts (Bridgewater) and Louisiana (New Orleans).

Notes.—Formerly placed in the monotypic genus *Rhynchophanes.*

Calcarius lapponicus (Linnaeus). LAPLAND LONGSPUR. [536.]

> *Fringilla lapponica* Linnaeus, 1758, Syst. Nat., ed. 10, 1, p. 180. (in Lapponia = Lapland.)

Habitat.—Arctic tundra in wet meadows, grassy tussocks and scrub, in migration and winter in weedy and grassy areas, plowed fields and stubble.

Distribution.—*Breeds* in North America from western and northern Alaska, northern Yukon, and Prince Patrick, Melville and northern Ellesmere islands south to islands in the Bering Sea, the Aleutians, south-coastal Alaska (east to the Susitna River highlands and Middleton Island), northern Mackenzie, southern Keewatin, northeastern Manitoba, northern Ontario, northern Quebec and Labrador; and in the Palearctic from Greenland, northern Scandinavia, northern Russia and northern Siberia south to southern Scandinavia, central and eastern Siberia, Kamchatka and the Commander Islands.

Winters in North America from coastal southern Alaska (casually), southern British Columbia, the northern United States, southern Ontario and Nova Scotia south to southeastern California, Utah, Colorado, Oklahoma, Arkansas, Tennessee and Maryland, rarely to coastal California, northern Baja California, southwestern and central Arizona, southern New Mexico, northern and eastern Texas, the Gulf coast and northern Florida; and in the Palearctic from northern Europe and northern Siberia south to central Europe, southern Russia, Mongolia, China, Korea and Japan.

Migrates in North America throughout Alaska and Canada, and in Eurasia throughout the regions between the breeding and wintering ranges, including Iceland.

Accidental in southern Baja California (Isla Cerralvo) and the state of Yucatán (Celestún).

Notes.—In Old World literature known as LAPLAND BUNTING.

Calcarius pictus (Swainson). SMITH'S LONGSPUR. [537.]

> *Emberiza* (*Plectrophanes*) *picta* Swainson, 1832, *in* Swainson and Richardson, Fauna Bor.-Am., 2 (1831), p. 250, pl. 49. (Carlton House, on the banks of the Saskatchewan [River].)

Habitat.—Dry, grassy, and hummocky tundra, in migration and winter in grassy and weedy areas, fields, prairies and airports.

Distribution.—*Breeds* in east-central Alaska (Susitna River highlands, Wrangell Mountains region) and adjacent northwestern British Columbia, and from northern Alaska (Brooks Range) east across northern Yukon and northern and east-central Mackenzie to southern Keewatin, northeastern Manitoba and extreme northern Ontario.

Winters from Kansas and Iowa south to Oklahoma, east-central Texas and northwestern Louisiana.

Migrates primarily through the northern Great Plains (east to Minnesota), casually from central and southern British Columbia east to Montana, and east to Michigan, southern Ontario, Ohio and central Alabama.

Casual or accidental in Arizona, Connecticut, New York, Maryland and South Carolina, also a sight report from North Carolina.

Calcarius ornatus (Townsend). CHESTNUT-COLLARED LONGSPUR. [538.]

Plectrophanes ornata J. K. Townsend, 1837, J. Acad. Nat. Sci. Philadelphia, 7, p. 189. (prairies of Platte River = near forks of Platte River, western Nebraska.)

Habitat.—Short-grass plains and prairies, in migration and winter also in open cultivated fields.

Distribution.—*Breeds* from southern Alberta, southern Saskatchewan and southwestern Manitoba south, east of the Rockies, to northeastern Colorado, western Kansas (formerly), north-central Nebraska and western Minnesota.

Winters from southern California (rarely), northern Arizona, central and northeastern New Mexico, eastern Colorado and central Kansas south to northern Sonora, central Chihuahua, southern Texas and northern Louisiana, casually south to Puebla, Veracruz and the state of México.

In migration occurs regularly west to northern and central California, and Nevada.

Casual elsewhere in western North America from southern and central British Columbia south to southern California and southern Nevada; north to northern Alberta and northern Manitoba; and in eastern North America from Wisconsin, northern Michigan, southern Ontario, New Brunswick, Nova Scotia and Newfoundland south to Missouri, Illinois, southern Ohio, and along the Atlantic coast to Virginia. Accidental in western Florida (Tallahassee).

Genus EMBERIZA Linnaeus

Emberiza Linnaeus, 1758, Syst. Nat., ed. 10, 1, p. 176. Type, by subsequent designation (G. R. Gray, 1840), *Emberiza citrinella* Linnaeus.

Notes.—See comments under *Calcarius.*

Emberiza pusilla Pallas. LITTLE BUNTING. [535.2.]

Emberiza pusilla Pallas, 1776, Reise Versch. Proc. Russ. Reichs, 3, p. 647. (Daurian Range, southern Chita, southeastern Siberia.)

Habitat & Distribution.—*Breeds* in birch and willow scrub in tundra and taiga from northern Finland, northern Russia and northern Siberia south to Lake Baikal, Anadyrland and the Sea of Okhotsk, and *winters* in scrub and cultivated lands in the northern parts of India and Southeast Asia, rarely in the British Isles, continental Europe, North Africa, the Near East and Philippines.

Accidental in Alaska in the Chukchi Sea (280 km northwest of Icy Cape, 6 September 1970; Watson, Angle and Browning, 1974, Auk, 91, p. 417) and in the Aleutian Islands (Shemya, 8 September 1977; Gibson, 1981, Condor, 83, p. 74).

Emberiza rustica Pallas. RUSTIC BUNTING. [535.1.]

Emberiza rustica Pallas, 1776, Reise Versch. Prov. Russ. Reichs, 3, p. 698. (Dauria = Transbaicalia.)

Habitat.—Low bushes and wet grassy areas of taiga, undergrowth of open coniferous-deciduous woodland, and thickets along streams, in migration and winter in scrub, brushy areas, grasslands, open woodland and cultivated lands.

Distribution.—*Breeds* from northern Scandinavia, northern Russia and northern Siberia southeast to southeastern Siberia, northern Sakhalin, the Sea of Okhotsk and Kamchatka.

Winters in eastern China, Japan and, rarely, the Commander Islands.

In migration ranges rarely but regularly to the western Aleutian Islands (Near Islands, casually east to Amchitka), casually to St. Lawrence Island, and rarely to the British Isles and continental Europe, also a questionable sight report from British Columbia (Queen Charlotte Islands).

[Emberiza aureola Pallas. YELLOW-BREASTED BUNTING.] See Appendix B.

Emberiza variabilis Temminck. GRAY BUNTING. [535.3.]

> *Emberiza variabilis* Temminck, 1835, Planches Color., livr. 98, pl. 583, fig. 2. (northern Japan.)

Habitat & Distribution.—*Breeds* in thickets, bamboo, and undergrowth of co-niferous-deciduous woodland in southern Kamchatka, the Kurile Islands, Sakhalin and possibly northern Japan, and *winters* in scrub, thickets and woodland un-dergrowth in Japan and the Ryukyu Islands.

Accidental in Alaska (Shemya, in the Aleutian Islands, 18 May 1977; Gibson and Hall, 1978, Auk, 95, pp. 428–429), also a sight report for Attu.

Emberiza pallasi (Cabanis). PALLAS' REED-BUNTING. [535.4.]

> *Cynchramus Pallasi* Cabanis, 1851, Mus. Heineanum, 1, p. 130 (footnote). Based on *Emberiza schoeniclus* var. β Pallas, Zoogr. Rosso-Asiat., 2, p. 48. (No locality given = near Selenga River, Transbaicalia.)

Habitat & Distribution.—*Breeds* in birch and river thickets in tundra and taiga, and in reed beds, from central and eastern Siberia south to Mongolia and Man-churia, and *winters* from the southern part of the breeding range and Ussuriland south to northern China, Korea and Japan, casually west to the British Isles.

Accidental in northern Alaska (Barrow, 11 June 1968; Pitelka, 1974, Arct. Alp. Res., 6, p. 167) and on St. Lawrence Island (Gambell, 28 May 1973; Johnson, 1976, Syesis, 9, p. 40).

Emberiza schoeniclus (Linnaeus). COMMON REED-BUNTING. [535.5.]

> *Fringilla Schœniclus* Linnaeus, 1758, Syst. Nat., ed. 10, 1, p. 182. (in Europa = Sweden.)

Habitat.—Reed beds, rushes and riparian thickets, in migration and winter also wet meadows, pastures and open country.

Distribution.—*Breeds* from the British Isles, Scandinavia, northern Russia and northern Siberia south to the Mediterranean region, Asia Minor, Iran, Turkestan, southern Siberia, Kamchatka and northern Japan.

Winters from the southern portions of the breeding range south to the Medi-terranean region, Iraq, northwestern India, northeastern China and southern Ja-pan.

In spring migration casually in the western Aleutian Islands (Attu, Shemya, Buldir).

Notes.—Known in Old World literature as the REED BUNTING.

Genus PLECTROPHENAX Stejneger

Plectrophenax Stejneger, 1882, Proc. U.S. Natl. Mus., 5, p. 33. Type, by original designation, *Emberiza nivalis* Linnaeus.

Plectrophenax nivalis (Linnaeus). SNOW BUNTING. [534.]

Emberiza nivalis Linnaeus, 1758, Syst. Nat., ed. 10, 1, p. 176. (in alpibus Lapponiæ, Spitsbergæ ad sinum Hudsonis = Lapland.)

Habitat.—Arctic rocky shores, cliffs, stony escarpments and dry tundra, also nesting in bird houses, empty oil barrels, cabins, and other artificial structures, in migration and winter in grassy or weedy fields, stubble, and along roadsides and shores of lakes and oceans.

Distribution.—*Breeds* in North America from northern Alaska, northern Yukon, northwestern Mackenzie, and Prince Patrick, Ellef Ringnes, Axel Heiberg and northern Ellesmere islands south to southern Alaska (including the Aleutian Islands), extreme northwestern British Columbia, southwestern and central Yukon, east-central Mackenzie, central and southeastern Keewatin, Southampton and Belcher islands, northern Quebec and northern Labrador; and in the Palearctic from Greenland, Spitsbergen, Franz Josef Land, Novaya Zemlya and northern Siberia south to the British Isles, northern Scandinavia, central Siberia, Kamchatka and the Commander Islands.

Winters in North America from west-central and southern Alaska, southern Canada (British Columbia east to southern Labrador and Newfoundland) south to northern (casually southern) California, northern Utah, Colorado, central Kansas, Missouri, northern Kentucky and North Carolina, casually to northeastern New Mexico, Oklahoma, eastern Texas, Arkansas, central Mississippi, Tennessee, Georgia and northeastern Florida; and in the Palearctic from the breeding range south to central continental Europe, the Mediterranean region (casually), Asia Minor (casually), southern Russia, Manchuria, Sakhalin, the Kurile Islands and (casually) Japan.

Casual or accidental in the Hawaiian Islands, northwestern Arizona, the Bahamas (Cat Island), Bermuda, eastern Atlantic islands, and northern Africa.

Notes.—*P. nivalis* and *P. hyperboreus* are closely related and considered conspecific by some authors, with limited hybridization occurring on St. Lawrence Island; they constitute a superspecies.

Plectrophenax hyperboreus Ridgway. MCKAY'S BUNTING. [535.]

Plectrophenax hyperboreus Ridgway, 1884, Proc. U.S. Natl. Mus., 7, p. 68. (St. Michael's, Alaska.)

Habitat.—Open rocky ground, beaches, and shores of tundra pools, in migration and winter in open rocky or sandy areas.

Distribution.—*Breeds* in Alaska on islands in the Bering Sea (Hall and St. Matthew, also rarely on St. Paul in the Pribilofs and on St. Lawrence).

Winters on the coast of western Alaska (Nome to Nushagak, including Nunivak Island), casually to the Aleutians (Adak, Unalaska) and south-coastal Alaska (Kodiak Island, Homer).

Accidental in British Columbia (Vancouver Island), Washington (Ocean Shores) and Oregon (mouth of Columbia River).

Notes.—See comments under *P. nivalis.*

Subfamily ICTERINAE: Icterines

Notes.—Whether the Icterini or Agelaiini is the more derived group is controversial.

Tribe DOLICHONYCHINI: Bobolinks

Genus **DOLICHONYX** Swainson

Dolichonyx Swainson, 1827, Philos. Mag., new ser., 1, p. 435. Type, by monotypy, *Fringilla oryzivora* Linnaeus.

Dolichonyx oryzivorus (Linnaeus). BOBOLINK. [494.]

Fringilla oryzivora Linnaeus, 1758, Syst. Nat., ed. 10, 1, p. 179. Based mainly on "The Rice-Bird" Catesby, Nat. Hist. Carolina, 1, p. 14, pl. 14. (in Cuba, . . . in Carolinam = South Carolina.)

Habitat.—Tall grass areas, flooded meadows, prairie, deep cultivated grains, and alfalfa and clover fields, in migration and winter also in rice fields, marshes and open woody areas.

Distribution.—*Breeds* from southern interior British Columbia, southern Alberta, southern Saskatchewan, southern Manitoba, central Ontario, southern Quebec (including Anticosti Island), New Brunswick, Prince Edward Island and Nova Scotia south to eastern and south-central Washington, eastern Oregon, northeastern Nevada (local), northern Utah, central Colorado, Kansas, northern Missouri, central Illinois, central Ohio, southern Pennsylvania and central New Jersey, and locally to north-central Kentucky, extreme northeastern Tennessee, western North Carolina and western Virginia, also isolated breeding in east-central Arizona; recorded in summer (but without positive evidence of breeding) north to southwestern British Columbia, central Alberta, central Saskatchewan, northern Ontario and eastern Quebec, and south to northeastern California, central Nevada and north-central New Mexico.

Winters in southern South America (mostly east of the Andes) from Peru, eastern Bolivia and central Brazil south to northern Argentina.

Migrates regularly through the southeastern United States (west to the Great Plains and eastern Texas), the West Indies, islands in the Caribbean Sea (Swan, Providencia and San Andrés), the northern coast of South America, Costa Rica (Caribbean lowlands, rarely on Pacific slope), Panama, and northern South America from Colombia, Venezuela (also islands off the northern coast) and the Guianas southward; also rarely through California, southern Nevada, western Arizona and southern New Mexico.

Casual or accidental in Alaska (Point Barrow), Labrador, Newfoundland, the Yucatan Peninsula (state of Yucatán, and Cozumel Island off Quintana Roo), Belize (Northern Two Cays and Half Moon Cay), Honduras (Isla Utila in the Bay Islands), Nicaragua (Río Escondido), Cocos Island (off Costa Rica), Bermuda, the Galapagos Islands, northern Chile, Greenland, the British Isles and Helgoland.

Tribe AGELAIINI: Blackbirds, Meadowlarks, Grackles and Cowbirds

Genus **AGELAIUS** Vieillot

Agelaius Vieillot, 1816, Analyse, p. 33. Type, by original designation, "Troupiale Commandeur" Buffon = *Oriolus phoeniceus* Linnaeus.

Agelaius phoeniceus (Linnaeus). RED-WINGED BLACKBIRD. [498.]

Oriolus phœniceus Linnaeus, 1766, Syst. Nat., ed. 12, 1, p. 161. Based mainly on "The red wing'd Starling" Catesby, Nat. Hist. Carolina, 1, p. 13, pl. 13. (in America septentrionali = Charleston, South Carolina.)

Habitat.—Fresh-water and brackish marshes, bushes and small trees along watercourses, and upland cultivated fields, in migration and winter also in open cultivated lands, plowed fields, pastures and prairie (Tropical to Temperate zones, in Central America restricted to Tropical and lower Subtropical zones).

Distribution.—*Breeds* from east-central, south-coastal and southern Alaska (west to Anchorage and north to Fairbanks), southern Yukon, west-central and southern Mackenzie, northwestern and central Saskatchewan, central Manitoba, central Ontario, southern Quebec (including Anticosti and Magdalen islands), New Brunswick, Prince Edward Island, Nova Scotia and southwestern Newfoundland south to northern Baja California, through Mexico (including the Yucatan Peninsula, and Holbox and Cozumel islands) and along both coasts of Central America to Nicaragua and northern Costa Rica (Guanacaste, Río Frío), and to southern Texas, the Gulf coast and southern Florida; also in the northern Bahama Islands (south to Andros and Eleuthera), western Cuba and the Isle of Pines (Ciénega de Lanier).

Winters from southern British Columbia, Idaho, Colorado, Kansas, Iowa, the southern Great Lakes region, southern Ontario and New England (casually farther north) south throughout the remainder of the breeding range, with the southwestern and most of Middle American populations being sedentary.

Casual north to western and northern Alaska, northern Mackenzie and Victoria Island.

Agelaius tricolor (Audubon). TRICOLORED BLACKBIRD. [500.]

Icterus tricolor Audubon, 1837, Birds Am. (folio), 4, pl. 388, fig. 1 (1839, Ornithol. Biogr., 5, p. 1). (No locality given = Santa Barbara, California.)

Habitat.—Fresh-water marshes of cattails, tule, bulrushes and sedges, in migration and winter also in open cultivated lands and pastures.

Distribution.—*Breeds* from southern Oregon (east of the coast ranges) south through interior California, and along the coast from central California (Sonoma County) south to northwestern Baja California (south to lat. 30°N.).

Winters from northern California (Glenn County southward) south throughout the breeding range and adjacent agricultural areas.

Casual in southeastern California.

Agelaius humeralis (Vigors). TAWNY-SHOULDERED BLACKBIRD. [500.1.]

Leistes humeralis Vigors, 1827, Zool. J., 3, p. 442. (neighborhood of Havana, Cuba.)

Habitat.—Open country, primarily in lowlands, woodland edge, and cultivated lands.

Distribution.—*Resident* in Cuba (including coastal cays) and western Hispaniola (west-central Haiti in vicinity of Port-de-Paix, lower Artibonite River, and St. Marc).

Casual in Florida (Florida Keys, also a sight report from Marathon).

Notes.—*A. humeralis* and *A. xanthomus* appear to constitute a superspecies.

Agelaius xanthomus (Sclater). YELLOW-SHOULDERED BLACKBIRD.

Icterus xanthomus Sclater, 1862, Cat. Collect. Am. Birds., p. 131. (Mexico, error = Puerto Rico.)

Habitat.—Mangroves, trees bordering pastures, plantations, and sea cliffs.
Distribution.—*Resident* on Puerto Rico (presently restricted to the southwestern and northeastern sections, including Mona Island).
Notes.—See comments under *A. humeralis*.

Genus NESOPSAR Sclater

Nesopsar Sclater, 1859, Ibis, p. 457 (footnote). Type, by original designation, *N. nigerrimus* = *Icterus nigerrimus* Osburn.

Nesopsar nigerrimus (Osburn). JAMAICAN BLACKBIRD.

Icterus nigerrimus Osburn, 1859, Zoologist, 17, p. 6662. (lower mountains of Jamaica.)

Habitat.—Humid mountain forest, less frequently in woodland at lower elevations.
Distribution.—*Resident* on Jamaica.

Genus STURNELLA Vieillot

Sturnella Vieillot, 1816, Analyse, p. 34. Type, by monotypy, "Stourne, ou Merle à fer-à-cheval" Buffon = *Alauda magna* Linnaeus.
Leistes Vigors, 1825, Zool. J., 2, p. 191. Type, by original designation, *Oriolus americanus* Gmelin = *Emberiza militaris* Linnaeus.

Sturnella militaris (Linnaeus). RED-BREASTED BLACKBIRD.

Emberiza militaris Linnaeus, 1758, Syst. Nat., ed. 10, 1, p. 178. Based mainly on *Turdus hæmatodos* Linnaeus, Mus. Adolphi Friderici, 1, p. 18. (in America, Asia = Surinam.)

Habitat.—Open country, savanna, partly open situations with scattered trees, cultivated fields, and swamps (Tropical Zone).
Distribution.—*Resident* [*militaris* group] in southwestern Costa Rica (Puntarenas province), Panama (entire Pacific slope, and Caribbean lowlands in Colón and the Canal Zone), and South America from northern Colombia, Venezuela (also Tobago and Trinidad) and the Guianas south, east of the Andes, to northeastern Peru, and Amazonian and central Brazil; and [*superciliaris* group] from southeastern Peru, eastern Bolivia, and southern and eastern Brazil south to northern Argentina.
Notes.—The two groups are sometimes regarded as distinct species, *S. militaris* [RED-BREASTED BLACKBIRD] and *S. superciliaris* (Bonaparte, 1850) [WHITE-BROWED BLACKBIRD]. Often placed in the genus *Leistes*.

Sturnella magna (Linnaeus). EASTERN MEADOWLARK. [501.]

Alauda magna Linnaeus, 1758, Syst. Nat., ed. 10, 1, p. 167. Based on "The Large Lark" Catesby, Nat. Hist. Carolina, 1, p. 33, pl. 33. (in America, Africa = South Carolina.)

Habitat.—Grasslands, savanna, open fields, pastures and cultivated lands (Tropical to Temperate zones).

Distribution.—*Breeds* from northwestern and central Arizona, central New Mexico, northern Texas, northeastern Colorado (probably), central Kansas, central Nebraska, southwestern South Dakota, northern Minnesota, northern Wisconsin, northern Michigan, southern Ontario, southwestern Quebec, Maine, southern New Brunswick and central Nova Scotia south through the southern United States and Middle America (except Baja California) to central Panama (Pacific slope east to eastern Panamá province), and to southern Texas, the Gulf coast, southern Florida, Cuba (including Cayo Coco, off northern Camagüey province) and the Isle of Pines; and in South America from northern and eastern Colombia, Venezuela, Guyana and Surinam south, east of the Andes, to Amazonian Brazil.

Winters from central Arizona, southern New Mexico, northern Texas, Kansas, Nebraska, Iowa, central Wisconsin, central Michigan, southern Ontario, New York, New England and central Nova Scotia (casually farther north) south throughout the remainder of the breeding range, with the West Indian, Middle American and South American populations being essentially sedentary.

Casual north to southern Manitoba, central Ontario, west-central and eastern Quebec, Prince Edward Island and Newfoundland.

Notes.—*S. magna* and *S. neglecta* appear to constitute a superspecies.

Sturnella neglecta Audubon. WESTERN MEADOWLARK. [501.1.]

Sturnella neglecta Audubon, 1844, Birds Am. (octavo ed.), 7, p. 339, pl. 489. (Missouri River above Fort Croghan = Old Fort Union, North Dakota.)

Habitat.—Grasslands, savanna, cultivated fields and pastures (Subtropical and Temperate zones).

Distribution.—*Breeds* from central British Columbia, north-central Alberta, central Saskatchewan, southern Manitoba, western Ontario, northeastern Minnesota, northern Wisconsin, northern Michigan, southern Ontario and northwestern Ohio south to northwestern Baja California, southern California, northwestern Sonora, central and southeastern Arizona, in the Mexican highlands to eastern Jalisco, Guanajuato, San Luis Potosí, southern Nuevo León and western Tamaulipas, and to west-central Texas, northwestern Louisiana, northern Arkansas, southwestern Tennessee, southern Illinois, southern Michigan, central Ohio, western Pennsylvania (possibly) and western New York.

Winters from southern British Columbia, southern Alberta, southern Saskatchewan, southern Manitoba and southern Wisconsin south to southern Baja California, Michoacán, the state of México, Veracruz, southern Texas and the Gulf coast east to northwestern Florida, occurring east regularly to western Kentucky, central Tennessee and Alabama.

Introduced and established in the Hawaiian Islands (on Kauai).

Casual north to southeastern Alaska (one record also from the Brooks Range), southern Mackenzie, northern Alberta, northern Manitoba, northern Ontario and southwestern Quebec, and east to New York and Georgia; singing birds, presumably this species, have been recorded in New England and New Jersey.

Notes.—See comments under *S. magna*.

Genus XANTHOCEPHALUS Bonaparte

Xanthocephalus Bonaparte, 1850, Consp. Gen. Avium, 1 (2), p. 431. Type, by monotypy, *Psarocolius perspicillatus* Wagler = *Icterus xanthocephalus* Bonaparte.

Xanthocephalus xanthocephalus (Bonaparte). YELLOW-HEADED BLACK-BIRD. [497.]

> *Icterus icterocephalus* (not *Oriolus icterocephalus* Linnaeus, 1766 = *Agelaius icterocephalus*) Bonaparte, 1825, Am. Ornithol., 1, p. 27, figs. 1–2. (Pawnee villages on the river Platte = along the Loup River, just west of Fullerton, Nance County, Nebraska.) *Nomen oblitum.*
> *Icterus xanthocephalus* Bonaparte, 1826, J. Acad. Nat. Sci. Philadelphia, 5, p. 223. New name for *Icterus icterocephalus* Bonaparte.

Habitat.—Fresh-water marshes of cattail, tule or bulrushes, in migration and winter also in open cultivated lands, pastures and fields.

Distribution.—*Breeds* from western Oregon, central Washington, central interior British Columbia, northern Alberta, north-central Saskatchewan, central Manitoba, extreme western Ontario, northern Minnesota, northern and east-central Michigan and extreme southern Ontario south to southern California, northeastern Baja California, southwestern and east-central Arizona, central and northeastern New Mexico, northern Texas (Panhandle), northwestern Oklahoma, central Kansas, northwestern Arkansas, southwestern (formerly) and northern Missouri, central Illinois, northwestern Indiana and northwestern Ohio.

Winters from central California, central Arizona, southern New Mexico, and central and southeastern Texas south to southern Baja California, Oaxaca (to Isthmus of Tehuantepec), Puebla and central Veracruz.

Casual north to western and northern Alaska (including in the Arctic Ocean 100 miles west of Point Hope), southern Mackenzie and northern Manitoba, and over eastern North America from southern Quebec and Nova Scotia south to the Gulf coast (eastern Texas eastward) and southern Florida; also recorded Costa Rica (Palo Verde), Panama (eastern Panamá province), Cuba, the northern Bahama Islands (Grand Bahama, San Salvador), Barbados, at sea in the Atlantic Ocean (300 miles northeast of New York City), and in Greenland and Europe.

Genus **DIVES** Deppe

> *Dives* W. Deppe, 1830, Preis.-Verz. Säugeth. Vögel, etc., Mex., p. 1. Type, by tautonymy, *Icterus dives* Deppe.
> *Ptiloxena* Chapman, 1892, Bull. Am. Mus. Nat. Hist., 4, p. 307. Type, by original designation, *Quiscalus atroviolaceus* d'Orbigny.

Dives dives (Deppe). MELODIOUS BLACKBIRD.

> *Icterus dives* W. Deppe, 1830, Preis.-Verz. Säugeth. Vögel, etc., Mex., p. 1. (Mexico.)

Habitat.—Scrub, second growth, woodland edge, and partly open situations with scattered trees, especially near water, and around human habitation (Tropical and lower Subtropical zones).

Distribution.—*Resident* from eastern San Luis Potosí, southern Tamaulipas, Puebla, the state of México and northern Oaxaca south on the Gulf-Caribbean slope of Middle America (including the Yucatan Peninsula) to north-central Nicaragua.

Notes.—Also known as SINGING BLACKBIRD. *D. dives* and the South American *D. warszewiczi* (Cabanis, 1861) and *D. kalinowskii* Berlepsch and Stolzmann, 1892, constitute a superspecies; they are considered conspecific by some authors.

Dives atroviolacea (d'Orbigny). CUBAN BLACKBIRD.

Quiscalus atroviolaceus d'Orbigny, 1839, *in* La Sagra, Hist. Fis. Pol. Nat. Cuba, Ois., p. 121, pl. 19. (Cuba.)

Habitat.—Cultivated areas, woodland edge, and around human habitation.
Distribution.—*Resident* on Cuba; reports from the Isle of Pines are doubtful.
Notes.—Sometimes placed in the monotypic genus *Ptiloxena.*

Genus **EUPHAGUS** Cassin

Euphagus Cassin, 1867, Proc. Acad. Nat. Sci. Philadelphia, 18 (1866), p. 413. Type, by monotypy, *Psarocolius cyanocephalus* Wagler.

Euphagus carolinus (Müller). RUSTY BLACKBIRD. [509.]

Turdus Carolinus P. L. S. Müller, 1776, Natursyst., Suppl., pl. 140. (Carolina.)

Habitat.—Moist woodland (primarily coniferous), bushy bogs and wooded edges of watercourses, in migration and winter also open woodland, scrub, pastures and cultivated lands.
Distribution.—*Breeds* from western and north-central Alaska, northern Yukon, northwestern and central Mackenzie, southern Keewatin, northern Manitoba, northern Ontario, northern Quebec, central Labrador and Newfoundland south to southwestern and south-coastal Alaska, central interior British Columbia, southwestern and south-central Alberta, central Saskatchewan, central Manitoba, south-central Ontario, southern Quebec, northeastern New York, western Massachusetts, central New Hampshire, central Maine and Nova Scotia.

Winters from central (casually) and south-coastal Alaska, southeastern British Columbia, central Alberta, southern Saskatchewan, southern Manitoba, southern Ontario and the northern United States (east of the Rockies) south to central and southeastern Texas, the Gulf coast and northern Florida, and west to Montana, central Colorado and eastern New Mexico, also rarely in coastal California.

In migration occurs regularly through southeastern Alaska, northern British Columbia and eastern California.

Casual elsewhere in western North America from southwestern British Columbia, Idaho and western Montana south to northern Baja California, southern Arizona, southern New Mexico and western Texas, and to islands in the Bering Sea (St. Lawrence, and St. Paul in the Pribilofs) and to southern Florida. Accidental in Siberia and Greenland.

Euphagus cyanocephalus (Wagler). BREWER'S BLACKBIRD. [510.]

Psarocolius cyanocephalus Wagler, 1829, Isis von Oken, col. 758. (Mexico).

Habitat.—Shrubby and bushy areas (especially near water), riparian woodland, aspen parklands, cultivated lands, marshes, and around human habitation, in migration and winter also in pastures and fields.
Distribution.—*Breeds* from southwestern and central interior British Columbia, southwestern Mackenzie, north-central Alberta, central Saskatchewan, southern Manitoba and southern Ontario south to northwestern Baja California, southern California, southern Nevada, central Arizona, southern New Mexico, western and northern Texas, Oklahoma, Colorado, Nebraska, northern Iowa, southern Wis-

consin, northeastern Illinois, northwestern Indiana and southern Michigan. The breeding range has recently expanded along its eastern border.

Winters from southern British Columbia, central Alberta, east-central Montana, the eastern edge of the Rockies, Kansas, Oklahoma, Arkansas, the northern portions of the Gulf states, northern Georgia and western South Carolina (casually farther north) south to southern Baja California, Oaxaca (Isthmus of Tehuantepec), central Veracruz, southern Texas, the Gulf coast and southern Florida.

In migration occurs regularly as far east as the Appalachians from Ohio southward.

Casual north to southern Keewatin and north-central Ontario, and in the northeast from New York, New England and Nova Scotia southward. Accidental in northern Alaska (Barrow) and western Guatemala (Hacienda Chancol).

Genus QUISCALUS Vieillot

Quiscalus Vieillot, 1816, Analyse, p. 36. Type, by subsequent designation (G. R. Gray, 1840), *Gracula quiscala* [sic] Linnaeus.
Cassidix Lesson, 1831, Traité Ornithol., livr. 6, p. 433. Type, by subsequent designation (G. R. Gray, 1840), *Cassidix mexicanus* Lesson = *Corvus mexicanus* Gmelin.
Holoquiscalus Cassin, 1867, Proc. Acad. Nat. Sci. Philadelphia, 18 (1866), p. 404. Type, by subsequent designation (Sclater, 1884), *Quiscalus crassirostris* Swainson.

Quiscalus nicaraguensis Salvin and Godman. NICARAGUAN GRACKLE.

Quiscalus nicaraguensis Salvin and Godman, 1891, Ibis, p. 612. (Momotombo, Lake Managua [Nicaragua].)

Habitat.—Fresh-water marshes, shores of lakes, and adjacent open country and pastures (Tropical Zone).
Distribution.—*Resident* in southwestern Nicaragua (vicinity of Lake Managua and Lake Nicaragua) and northern Costa Rica (Río Frío district).
Notes.—This species is sometimes treated in the genus *Cassidix*.

†Quiscalus palustris (Swainson). SLENDER-BILLED GRACKLE.

Scaphidurus palustris Swainson, 1827, Philos. Mag., new ser., 1, p. 437. (marshes and borders of the lakes round Mexico [City] = marshes at headwater of Río Lerma, state of México.)

Habitat.—Fresh-water marshes and lake margins (lower Temperate Zone).
Distribution.—EXTINCT. Formerly *resident* in marshes in the upper reaches of the Río Lerma, state of México.
Notes.—Although conspecificity with *Q. mexicanus* has been suggested by some authors, the distinctive juvenal plumage indicates continued specific treatment is warranted. This species is often placed in the genus *Cassidix*.

Quiscalus niger (Boddaert). GREATER ANTILLEAN GRACKLE.

Oriolus niger Boddaert, 1783, Table Planches Enlum., p. 31. Based on "Troupiale Noir, de St. Domingue" Daubenton, Planches Enlum., pl. 534. (Santo Domingo = Port au Prince, Haiti.)

Habitat.—Open situations, cultivated lands, pastures, and around human habitation.

Distribution.—*Resident* on Cuba (including nearby cays), the Isle of Pines, Cayman Islands (including Cayman Brac), Jamaica, Hispaniola (including Gonâve, Tortue and Beata islands, and Île-à-Vache) and Puerto Rico (including Vieques Island).

Notes.—*Q. niger* and *Q. lugubris* appear to constitute a superspecies. These two species are often treated in the genus *Holoquiscalus.*

Quiscalus lugubris Swainson. CARIB GRACKLE.

Quiscalus lugubris Swainson, 1837, Anim. Menag. (1838), p. 299, fig. "50c" [=54c]. (Brazil, error = Guyana.)

Habitat.—Open woodland, cultivated lands, pastures, arid scrub, and around human habitation (Tropical Zone).

Distribution.—*Resident* in the Lesser Antilles (Montserrat, Guadeloupe, Marie Galante, Dominica, Martinique, St. Lucia, St. Vincent, Grenada, the Grenadines, and Barbados), Trinidad, northern Venezuela (including islands nearby), the Guianas and extreme northeastern Brazil.

Introduced and established on St. Martin, Barbuda, Antigua, and probably also St. Kitts.

Notes.—Also known as LESSER ANTILLEAN GRACKLE. See comments under *Q. niger.*

Quiscalus mexicanus (Gmelin). GREAT-TAILED GRACKLE. [512.]

Corvus mexicanus Gmelin, 1788, Syst. Nat., 1 (1), p. 375. Based in part on the "Mexican Crow" Latham, Gen. Synop. Birds, 1 (1), p. 396. (in nova Hispania = Veracruz, Veracruz.)

Habitat.—Partly open situations with scattered trees, cultivated lands, pastures, shores of watercourses, swamps, wet thickets, and around human habitation (Tropical and Subtropical zones).

Distribution.—*Resident* from southeastern (locally also central) California, southern Nevada, southern Utah, northern New Mexico, southeastern Colorado, Kansas, southern Nebraska, southwestern Missouri, southwestern Arkansas and southwestern Louisiana south along both slopes of Middle America (including the Yucatan Peninsula, islands and cays off the Yucatan Peninsula and Belize, and the Bay Islands off Honduras) to Costa Rica and Panama (Pacific slope throughout, Caribbean slope in Bocas del Toro, the Canal Zone and San Blas, and widely on islands off the Pacific coast and off San Blas), and along both coasts of South America from Colombia east to northwestern Venezuela and south to Ecuador and northwestern Peru. The breeding range has expanded greatly in the last century, and is apparently continuing to do so.

Casual north to eastern Oregon.

Notes.—Although *Q. mexicanus* and *Q. major* were long considered conspecific, sympatry without interbreeding is known from southwestern Louisiana to southeastern Texas; they should probably be regarded as constituting a superspecies. *Q. mexicanus* and *Q. major* are often placed in the genus *Cassidix.*

Quiscalus major Vieillot. BOAT-TAILED GRACKLE. [513.]

Quiscalus major Vieillot, 1819, Nouv. Dict. Hist. Nat., nouv. éd., 28, p. 487. (Mexico and Louisiana = New Orleans, Orleans Parish, Louisiana.)

Habitat.—Brackish marshes in coastal areas, and adjacent open situations, pastures and cultivated lands.

Distribution.—*Resident* along the Atlantic coast from New York (Long Island) and New Jersey southward, throughout peninsular Florida, and west along the Gulf coast to southeastern Texas (south to Calhoun County).

Casual in Nova Scotia.

Notes.—See comments under *Q. mexicanus.*

Quiscalus quiscula (Linnaeus). COMMON GRACKLE. [511.]

> *Gracula Quiscula* Linnaeus, 1758, Syst. Nat., ed. 10, 1, p. 109. Based mainly on "The Purple Jack-Daw" Catesby, Nat. Hist. Carolina, 1, p. 12, pl. 12. (in America septentrionali = coast of South Carolina.)

Habitat.—Partly open situations with scattered trees, open woodland (coniferous or deciduous), forest edge, and around human habitation, in migration and winter also in open situations, cultivated lands, pastures, fields and marshes.

Distribution.—*Breeds* from northeastern British Columbia, southern Mackenzie, northern Alberta, northwestern and central Saskatchewan, central and northeastern Manitoba, central Ontario, southern Quebec (including Anticosti Island), New Brunswick, Prince Edward Island, Nova Scotia and southwestern Newfoundland south to central and southeastern Texas (south to Corpus Christi region), the Gulf coast and southern Florida (including the Florida Keys), and west to eastern Wyoming, central Colorado, and central and southeastern New Mexico.

Winters from Kansas, Iowa, the southern Great Lakes region, southern Ontario, New England and Nova Scotia (casually farther north) south to southeastern New Mexico, central and southern Texas (rarely also western Texas in the Big Bend region), the Gulf coast and southern Florida.

Casual in western North America from northern and western Alaska south through western British Columbia, Washington, Idaho and Oregon to southern California, and east to Nevada, Utah and western Colorado; reports from northern Tamaulipas are unverified.

Notes.—Although some authors recognize the southeastern *Q. quiscula* [PURPLE GRACKLE, 511] as a species distinct from the more widespread *Q. versicolor* Vieillot, 1819 [BRONZED GRACKLE, 511.1], random and essentially complete interbreeding occurs along a line of junction from Massachusetts to Louisiana.

Genus MOLOTHRUS Swainson

> *Molothrus* Swainson, 1832, *in* Swainson and Richardson, Fauna Bor.-Am., 2 (1831), pp. 275, 277. Type, by original designation, *Fringilla pecoris* Gmelin = *Oriolus ater* Boddaert.
>
> *Tangavius* Lesson, 1839, Rev. Zool. [Paris], 2, p. 41. Type, by monotypy, *Tangavius involucratus* Lesson = *Psarocolius aeneus* Wagler.

Molothrus bonariensis (Gmelin). SHINY COWBIRD.

> *Tanagra bonariensis* Gmelin, 1789, Syst. Nat., 1 (2), p. 898. Based on "Tangavio" Buffon, Hist. Nat. Ois., 4, p. 241, and Daubenton, Planches Enlum., pl. 710. (in Bonaria = Buenos Aires, Argentina.)

Habitat.—Partly open situations with scattered trees, open woodland, cultivated lands, pastures, marshes, and around human habitation (Tropical and Subtropical zones).

Distribution.—*Resident* on Puerto Rico (since 1940's), Vieques Island (where recorded initially about 1860, possibly as an introduction) and Barbados (probably an introduction), since spreading throughout the Antilles west to Hispaniola and south to Grenada; and in eastern Panama (eastern Panamá province, San Blas and Darién), and from Colombia, Venezuela (also Tobago and Trinidad) and the Guianas south over most of South America to central Chile and central Argentina.

Notes.—Also known as GLOSSY COWBIRD.

Molothrus aeneus (Wagler). BRONZED COWBIRD. [496.]

Psarocolius aeneus Wagler, 1829, Isis von Oken, col. 758. (Mexico = Mexico City.)

Habitat.—Partly open situations with scattered trees or scrub, cultivated lands, pastures, and around human habitation (Tropical and Subtropical zones).

Distribution.—*Resident* from extreme southeastern California (lower Colorado River valley), west-central and southern Arizona, southwestern New Mexico, western Chihuahua, and west-central and southern Texas (with an isolated breeding population in the New Orleans area, Louisiana) south through Middle America (including the Yucatan Peninsula, but absent from Baja California) to central Panama (on the Caribbean slope in Bocas del Toro, and east to eastern Panamá province on the Pacific slope). Northern populations are partially migratory, but a few individuals usually winter in the northern portions of the range.

Casual or accidental in southern California (west of the breeding range), central New Mexico, Missouri (Squaw Creek), southern Mississippi, and Florida.

Notes.—Often placed in the genus *Tangavius. M. aeneus* and the South American *M. armenti* Cabanis, 1851, constitute a superspecies; they are considered conspecific by some authors.

Molothrus ater (Boddaert). BROWN-HEADED COWBIRD. [495.]

Oriolus ater Boddaert, 1783, Table Planches Enlum., p. 37. Based on "Troupiale, de la Caroline" Daubenton, Planches Enlum., pl. 606, fig. 1. (Carolina.)

Habitat.—Woodland, forest (primarily deciduous) and forest edge, in migration and winter also in open situations, cultivated lands, fields, pastures and scrub (Tropical to Temperate zones).

Distribution.—*Breeds* from southeastern (and probably south-coastal) Alaska, northern British Columbia, southern Mackenzie, northern Alberta, north-central Saskatchewan, southern Manitoba, central Ontario, southern Quebec, New Brunswick, Prince Edward Island, Nova Scotia and southern Newfoundland south to northern Baja California, Guerrero, Michoacán, Guanajuato, San Luis Potosí, northern Tamaulipas, southern Texas, the Gulf coast and central Florida.

Winters from northern California, central Arizona, southern New Mexico, Kansas, central Missouri, the southern Great Lakes region, southern Ontario, New England, southern New Brunswick and Nova Scotia (casually farther north) south to southern Baja California, Oaxaca (Isthmus of Tehuantepec), central Veracruz, southern Texas, the Gulf coast and southern Florida.

Casual north to western and northern Alaska, northern Manitoba and southern Labrador, and in Bermuda, the Bahama Islands (New Providence, Great Inagua) and Cuba.

Genus **SCAPHIDURA** Swainson

Scaphidura Swainson, 1837, Class. Birds, 2, p. 272. Type, by virtual monotypy, *Scaphidura barita* Swainson = *Oriolus oryzivorus* Gmelin.
Psomocolax Peters, 1929, Proc. Biol. Soc. Wash., 42, p. 123. Type, by original
designation, *Oriolus oryzivorus* Gmelin.

Scaphidura oryzivora (Gmelin). GIANT COWBIRD.

Oriolus oryzivorus Gmelin, 1788, Syst. Nat., 1 (1), p. 386. Based on the "Rice
Oriole" Latham, Gen. Synop. Birds, 1 (2), p. 423. (in Cayenna = Cayenne.)

Habitat.—Partly open situations with scattered trees, cultivated lands, second
growth, open fields and plantations, usually in vicinity of colonies of oropendolas
or caciques (Tropical and lower Subtropical zones).

Distribution.—*Resident* from Veracruz, northern Oaxaca, Tabasco, Chiapas and
southern Quintana Roo south on the Gulf-Caribbean slope of Central America
to Honduras, in Nicaragua (both slopes), Costa Rica (Caribbean slope and central
plateau) and Panama (both slopes, more widespread on Caribbean), and in South
America from Colombia, Venezuela (also Trinidad) and the Guianas south, west
of the Andes to western Ecuador and east of the Andes to eastern Peru, Bolivia,
eastern Paraguay, extreme northeastern Argentina, and central and eastern Brazil.

Notes.—Also known as RICE GRACKLE.

Tribe ICTERINI: Oropendolas, Caciques and American Orioles

Genus **ICTERUS** Brisson

Icterus Brisson, 1760, Ornithologie, 1, p. 30; 2, p. 85. Type, by tautonymy,
Icterus Brisson = *Oriolus icterus* Linnaeus.
Pendulinus Vieillot, 1816, Analyse, p. 33. Type, by subsequent designation
(Sclater, 1883), *Oriolus spurius* Linnaeus.
Bananivorus Bonaparte, 1853, C. R. Acad. Sci. Paris, 37, p. 834. Type, by
original designation, *Oriolus bonana* Linnaeus.
Andriopsar Cassin, 1867, Proc. Acad. Nat. Sci. Philadelphia, 19, p. 49. Type,
by subsequent designation (Sclater, 1883), *Psarocolius gularis* Wagler.

Icterus dominicensis (Linnaeus). BLACK-COWLED ORIOLE.

Oriolus dominicensis Linnaeus, 1766, Syst. Nat., ed. 12, 1, p. 163. Based on
"Le Carouge de S. Domingue" Brisson, Ornithologie, 2, p. 121, pl. 12, fig.
3. (in Dominica = Hispaniola.)

Habitat.—Humid lowland forest edge, open woodland, second growth, plantations, scrub and mangroves (Tropical Zone).

Distribution.—*Resident* [*prosthemelas* group] from southern Veracruz, northern
Oaxaca, Tabasco, Chiapas and the Yucatan Peninsula south through Central
America to extreme western Panama (western Bocas del Toro); and [*dominicensis*
group] in the northern Bahama Islands (Andros, Grand Abaco and Little Abaco),
Cuba, the Isle of Pines, Hispaniola (including Tortue and Gonâve islands, and
Île-à-vache) and Puerto Rico.

An unverified sight report from Nova Scotia is likely based on an escape from captivity.

Notes.—The two groups are sometimes regarded as separate species, *I. prosthemelas* (Strickland, 1850) [BLACK-COWLED ORIOLE] and *I. dominicensis* [GREATER ANTILLEAN ORIOLE]. *I. dominicensis, I. laudabilis, I. oberi, I. bonana* and *I. wagleri* appear to constitute a superspecies.

Icterus laudabilis Sclater. ST. LUCIA ORIOLE.

Icterus laudabilis Sclater, 1871, Proc. Zool. Soc. London, p. 270, pl. 21. (St. Lucia.)

Habitat.—Forest, woodland, and partly open situations with scattered trees, from lowlands to mountains, and in both arid and humid habitats.
Distribution.—*Resident* on St. Lucia, in the Lesser Antilles.
Notes.—See comments under *I. dominicensis.*

Icterus oberi Lawrence. MONTSERRAT ORIOLE.

Icterus oberi Lawrence, 1880, Proc. U.S. Natl. Mus., 3, p. 351. (Montserrat.)

Habitat.—Mountain forest, uncommonly to woodland at lower elevations.
Distribution.—*Resident* on Montserrat, in the Lesser Antilles.
Notes.—See comments under *I. dominicensis.*

Icterus bonana (Linnaeus). MARTINIQUE ORIOLE.

Oriolus Bonana Linnaeus, 1766, Syst. Nat., ed. 12, 1, p. 162. Based primarily on "Le Carouge" Brisson, Ornithologie, 2, p. 115, pl. 12, fig. 2. (in America meridionali = Martinique.)

Habitat.—Forest edge, woodland and plantations.
Distribution.—*Resident* on Martinique, in the Lesser Antilles.
Notes.—See comments under *I. dominicensis.*

Icterus wagleri Sclater. BLACK-VENTED ORIOLE. [504.1.]

Icterus wagleri Sclater, 1857, Proc. Zool. Soc. London, p. 7. (No locality given = Mexico.)

Habitat.—Arid scrub, second growth, woodland edge, and undergrowth of pine-oak association or along ravines (upper Tropical to lower Temperate zones).
Distribution.—*Resident* from southern Sonora, central Chihuahua, Coahuila and Nuevo León south through the highlands of Mexico, Guatemala, El Salvador and Honduras to north-central Nicaragua.
Accidental in Texas (Big Bend, also a sight report for San Ygnacio).
Notes.—Also known as WAGLER'S ORIOLE. See comments under *I. dominicensis.*

Icterus maculialatus Cassin. BAR-WINGED ORIOLE.

Icterus maculialatus Cassin, 1848, Proc. Acad. Nat. Sci. Philadelphia, 3 (1847), p. 332. (near Vera Cruz, Mexico, error = Vera Paz, Guatemala.)

Habitat.—Oak woodland, pine-oak association and second growth (upper Tropical and Subtropical zones).
Distribution.—*Resident* on the Pacific slope from western Chiapas south through Guatemala to El Salvador.

Icterus spurius (Linnaeus). ORCHARD ORIOLE. [506.]

> *Oriolus spurius* Linnaeus, 1766, Syst. Nat., ed. 12, 1, p. 162. Based mainly on "The Bastard Baltimore" Catesby, Nat. Hist. Carolina, 1, p. 48, pl. 48. (in America septentrionali = South Carolina.)

Habitat.—Scrub, second growth, brushy hillsides, partly open situations with scattered trees, open woodland, mesquite and orchards (Subtropical and lower Temperate zones, in winter to Tropical Zone).
Distribution.—*Breeds* [*spurius* group] from southeastern Saskatchewan, southern Manitoba, central Minnesota, central Wisconsin, southern Michigan, southern Ontario, central New York and northern Massachusetts south to eastern Chihuahua, Coahuila, southern Texas, the Gulf coast and central Florida, west to eastern Wyoming, eastern Colorado and southeastern New Mexico, and on the Mexican Plateau from central Durango and Zacatecas to Jalisco, northern Michoacán, the state of México and Hidalgo (probably also in central Sonora); and [*fuertesi* group] in southern Tamaulipas and northern Veracruz.

Winters [*spurius* group] in coastal California (rarely), and from Sinaloa, Guerrero, Puebla and central Veracruz (casually north to the Gulf coast and southern Texas, with occasional reports farther north) south through Middle America (including islands along the coast) to northern Colombia and northwestern Venezuela; and [*fuertesi* group] presumably in central Mexico (recorded Guerrero and Morelos).

In migration [*spurius* group] occurs regularly through Mexico (west to southern Sinaloa), southern Florida (including the Keys) and Cuba, rarely to California, southern Arizona, southern New Mexico, Sonora, the Bahama Islands (Eleuthera), Jamaica and the Swan Islands.

Casual [*spurius* group] west to Washington, Oregon, Wyoming, central Colorado and northern New Mexico, and north to south-central Manitoba, southern Quebec, New Brunswick and Nova Scotia; and [*fuertesi* group] in southern Texas (Brownsville).

Notes.—The two groups are sometimes regarded as distinct species, *I. spurius* [ORCHARD ORIOLE, 506] and *I. fuertesi* Chapman [OCHRE or FUERTES' ORIOLE, 506.1].

Icterus cucullatus Swainson. HOODED ORIOLE. [505.]

> *Icterus cucullatus* Swainson, 1827, Philos. Mag., new ser., 1, p. 436. (Temiscaltipec, Mexico = Temascaltepec, state of México.)

Habitat.—Riparian woodland, palm groves, mesquite, arid scrub, deciduous woodland, and around human habitation (Tropical and Subtropical zones).
Distribution.—*Breeds* from northern coastal and central California, southern Nevada, southwestern Utah, central Arizona, southern New Mexico, and western and southern Texas (one breeding record also from Bell County, in central Texas) south to southern Baja California, and through Mexico to Guerrero, Veracruz,

Tabasco, northern Chiapas and the Yucatan Peninsula (including Mujeres, Holbox, Contoy and Cozumel islands).

Winters from northern Mexico (rarely from southern California, southern Arizona and southern Texas) south through the breeding range in Mexico and to Oaxaca.

Casual north to west-central Oregon and eastern Texas.

Icterus chrysater (Lesson). YELLOW-BACKED ORIOLE.

> *Xanthornus chrysater* Lesson, 1844, Echo Monde Savant, ser. 2, 11, p. 204. (Mexico.)

Habitat.—Forest edge, clearings, scrub, brushy areas, pine-oak association, pine savanna, thorn scrub and plantations (Tropical and Subtropical zones).

Distribution.—*Resident* from Veracruz, northern Chiapas and the Yucatan Peninsula south through the interior of Central America to northern Nicaragua, and, locally, the Gulf-Caribbean lowlands to northeastern Nicaragua; and from Panama (west to Veraguas) east through Colombia to northern Venezuela. Apparently at least partly migratory in El Salvador and probably elsewhere in northern Central America.

Notes.—Includes the lowland form in Panama and Colombia, regarded by some authors as a distinct species, *I. hondae* Chapman, 1914 [HONDA ORIOLE], but the latter intergrades altitudinally with *I. chrysater giraudii* Cassin, 1848.

Icterus auricapillus Cassin. ORANGE-CROWNED ORIOLE.

> *Icterus auricapillus* Cassin, 1848, Proc. Acad. Nat. Sci. Philadelphia, 3 (1847), p. 332. (Mexico and South America = Santa Marta, Colombia.)

Habitat.—Forest and woodland edge, scrub and brush, especially near water, and arid scrub and cultivated areas (Tropical and Subtropical zones).

Distribution.—*Resident* from eastern Panama (eastern Panamá province and Darién) east across northern Colombia to Venezuela.

Icterus mesomelas (Wagler). YELLOW-TAILED ORIOLE.

> *Psarocolius mesomelas* Wagler, 1829, Isis von Oken, col. 755. (Mexico = Chalcaltianges, Veracruz.)

Habitat.—Thickets, brush and scrub, primarily near water, and swamps, less frequently in second growth and forest edge (Tropical Zone).

Distribution.—*Resident* from Veracruz, northern Oaxaca, Tabasco, Chiapas and the Yucatan Peninsula south along the Gulf-Caribbean slope of Middle America to Panama (also on Pacific slope from western Panamá province eastward), and in South America from Colombia and northwestern Venezuela south, west of the Andes, to western Peru.

Icterus icterus (Linnaeus). TROUPIAL.

> *Oriolus Icterus* Linnaeus, 1766, Syst. Nat., ed. 12, 1, p. 161. Based primarily on "Le Troupiale" Brisson, Ornithologie, 2, p. 86, pl. 8, fig. 1. (in America calidiore = Cumaná, Sucre, Venezuela.)

Habitat.—Deciduous woodland, second growth, thorn scrub, thickets and pastures (Tropical Zone).

Distribution.—*Resident* from northern and eastern Colombia, Venezuela (also Aruba, Curaçao and Margarita Island) and southern Guyana south, east of the Andes, to eastern Peru, northeastern Bolivia, Paraguay and southern Brazil.

Introduced and established on Puerto Rico, Mona Island, and St. Thomas (including Water Island) in the Virgin Islands; also reported from Jamaica, St. John, Antigua, Dominica, Grenada and Trinidad, presumably based on escaped cage birds. West Indian introductions were apparently primarily from the Curaçao population.

Notes.—The more southern South American populations are sometimes regarded as species, *I. croconotus* (Wagler, 1829) [ORANGE-BACKED ORIOLE] and *I. jamacaii* (Gmelin, 1788) [CAMPO ORIOLE], distinct from *I. icterus*.

Icterus pustulatus (Wagler). STREAK-BACKED ORIOLE. [505.1.]

> *Psarocolius pustulatus* Wagler, 1829, Isis von Oken, col. 757. (Mexico.)

Habitat.—Deciduous forest edge, open woodland, arid scrub and savanna (Tropical and lower Subtropical zones).

Distribution.—*Resident* [*pustulatus* group] in the Pacific lowlands from Sonora and Chihuahua south to Oaxaca (except southeastern portion); [*graysonii* group] in the Tres Marias Islands, off Nayarit; and [*sclateri* group] on the Pacific slope of southeastern Oaxaca and Chiapas, in the arid interior of Guatemala, and in the Pacific lowlands of El Salvador, Honduras (also arid interior valleys on Caribbean slope), Nicaragua and northwestern Costa Rica (Guanacaste).

Casual in southern California and southern Arizona.

Notes.—The three groups have sometimes been regarded as distinct species, *I. graysonii* Cassin, 1867 [TRES MARIAS ORIOLE], *I. pustulatus* [SCARLET-HEADED ORIOLE, 505.1], and *I. sclateri* Cassin, 1867 [STREAK-BACKED ORIOLE], although the latter two intergrade in the lowlands of southeastern Oaxaca. *I. pustulatus* and *I. nigrogularis* appear to constitute a superspecies.

[Icterus nigrogularis (Hahn). YELLOW ORIOLE.] See Appendix B.

Icterus auratus Bonaparte. ORANGE ORIOLE.

> *Icterus auratus* (Du Bus de Gisignies MS) Bonaparte, 1850, Consp. Gen. Avium, 1 (2), p. 435. (Yucatan.)

Habitat.—Deciduous forest and dense second growth (Tropical Zone).

Distribution.—*Resident* in southeastern Mexico on the Yucatan Peninsula (Campeche, the state of Yucatán, and Quintana Roo).

Icterus leucopteryx (Wagler). JAMAICAN ORIOLE.

> *Oriolus mexicanus* (not Linnaeus, 1766) Leach, 1814, Zool. Misc., 1, p. 8, pl. 2. (St. Andrews, Jamaica.)
> *Psarocolius Leucopteryx* Wagler, 1827, Syst. Avium, sig. 22, genus *Psarocolius,* sp. 16. New name for *Oriolus mexicanus* Leach, preoccupied.

Habitat.—Humid mountain forest, woodland, plantations and gardens.

Distribution.—*Resident* on Jamaica, Grand Cayman (where possibly extinct, not recorded since 1938), and on Isla San Andrés, in the western Caribbean Sea.

Icterus pectoralis (Wagler). SPOT-BREASTED ORIOLE. [503.2.]

> *Psarocolius pectoralis* Wagler, 1829, Isis von Oken, col. 755. (Mexico = Totulapa, Oaxaca.)

Habitat.—Open woodland, deciduous forest, arid scrub and brushy areas (Tropical Zone).

Distribution.—*Resident* in the Pacific lowlands from Colima south to central Costa Rica (vicinity of Puntarenas), and locally in arid interior valleys and on the Caribbean slope of Guatemala and Honduras.

Introduced and established in southeastern Florida (Palm Beach, Broward and Dade counties).

Icterus gularis (Wagler). ALTAMIRA ORIOLE. [503.1.]

> *Psarocolius gularis* Wagler, 1829, Isis von Oken, col. 754. (Mexico = Tehuantepec, Oaxaca.)

Habitat.—Deciduous forest, arid scrub, open woodland, second growth and semi-desert (Tropical and lower Subtropical zones).

Distribution.—*Resident* from extreme southern Texas (lower Rio Grande valley), Nuevo León and eastern San Luis Potosí south in the Gulf-Caribbean slope (including the Yucatan Peninsula) to Belize and (locally) Honduras, and from the state of México and Guerrero south along the Pacific slope to west-central Nicaragua (also locally in arid interior valleys of Guatemala and Honduras).

Notes.—Also known as LICHTENSTEIN'S or BLACK-THROATED ORIOLE.

Icterus graduacauda Lesson. AUDUBON'S ORIOLE. [503.]

> *Icterus graduacauda* Lesson, 1839, Rev. Zool. [Paris], 2, p. 105. (Mexico.)

Habitat.—Scrub, mesquite, riparian thickets, pine-oak association, and humid montane forest edge (upper Tropical and Subtropical zones).

Distribution.—*Resident* from southern Texas (north to Val Verde, Bee and Nueces counties), Nuevo León, Tamaulipas, San Luis Potosí, Nayarit, Jalisco and Guanajuato south through the state of México, Hidalgo, Veracruz, Puebla and Guerrero to Oaxaca (west of the Isthmus of Tehuantepec); old records from Chiapas and Guatemala (Santo Tomás) are questionable.

Notes.—Formerly known as BLACK-HEADED ORIOLE, a name now restricted to an Old World group of species in the genus *Oriolus.*

Icterus galbula (Linnaeus). NORTHERN ORIOLE. [507.]

> *Coracias Galbula* Linnaeus, 1758, Syst. Nat., ed. 10, 1, p. 108. Based on "The Baltimore-Bird" Catesby, Nat. Hist. Carolina, 1, p. 48, pl. 48. (in America = Virginia.)

Habitat.—Open woodland, deciduous forest edge, riparian woodland, partly open situations with scattered trees, orchards, and planted shade trees, in migration and winter also in humid forest edge, second growth and scrub (Subtropical and Temperate zones, in winter to Tropical Zone).

Distribution.—*Breeds* [*galbula* group] from central Alberta, central Saskatchewan, southern Manitoba, western Ontario, northern Michigan, southern Ontario, southwestern Quebec, central Maine, southern New Brunswick and central Nova Scotia south to eastern Texas, central Louisiana, central Mississippi, central Alabama, north-central Georgia, western South Carolina, central North Carolina, central Virginia, Maryland and Delaware, and west to the western edge of the Great Plains (also single breeding records from northeastern Colorado and Key West, Florida); and [*bullockii* group] from southern interior British Columbia, southern Alberta, southwestern Saskatchewan, eastern Montana, southwestern North Dakota and central South Dakota south, east of the coastal areas of Washington and Oregon, to northern Baja California, central Sonora, northern Durango, Coahuila, and central and southern Texas, and east to western Nebraska, western Kansas and western Oklahoma.

Winters [*galbula* group] from Nayarit and Veracruz (casually from coastal California and Sonora) south through Middle America to northern Colombia, northern Venezuela and Trinidad, regularly in small numbers in the Atlantic states north to Virginia, in the Greater Antilles east to the Virgin Islands, and casually elsewhere in eastern North America north to the Great Lakes region, southern Ontario and New England; and [*bullockii* group] regularly in coastal California, and from southern Sinaloa, the state of México and Puebla south to Guatemala (casually to northwestern Costa Rica), in small numbers in the Gulf coast region from eastern and southern Texas east to southern Georgia and Florida, and casually north to central California and southern Arizona.

Migrates [*galbula* group] regularly through the southeastern United States (west to eastern New Mexico and western Texas) and northeastern Mexico, and in coastal California, rarely through the northern Bahama Islands and Yucatan Peninsula, and casually elsewhere in western North America west to Oregon, Arizona and northwestern Mexico; and [*bullockii* group] regularly through western North America (west of the Rockies), including Baja California.

Resident [*abeillei* group] from central Durango, Zacatecas, San Luis Potosí and southern Nuevo León south in the Central Plateau of Mexico to Michoacán, the state of México, Morelos, Puebla and Veracruz (Oaxaca records are open to question).

Casual [*galbula* group] north to northern Manitoba, south-central Ontario, Prince Edward Island, eastern Quebec, Nova Scotia and Newfoundland, and in British Columbia, the Lesser Antilles (Barbados), Greenland and the British Isles; and [*bullockii* group] in southeastern Alaska (Petersburg), and in northeastern North America from Minnesota, southern Ontario, New York, New Brunswick, Maine and Nova Scotia south through New England to New Jersey.

Notes.—The three groups have often been regarded as separate species, *I. galbula* [BALTIMORE ORIOLE, 507], *I. bullockii* (Swainson, 1827) [BULLOCK'S ORIOLE, 508] and *I. abeillei* (Lesson, 1839) [ABEILLE'S or BLACK-BACKED ORIOLE], although the former two intergrade in the southern Great Plains, and the latter two in northern Durango; two species are sometimes recognized, with *galbula* as one species and *abeillei* merged with *bullockii* constituting the other.

Icterus parisorum Bonaparte. SCOTT'S ORIOLE. [504.]

Icterus Parisorum Bonaparte, 1838, Proc. Zool. Soc. London (1837), p. 110. (Mexico.)

Habitat.—Yucca, pinyon-juniper, arid oak scrub and palm oases (upper Tropical to lower Temperate zones).

Distribution.—*Breeds* from southern California (north in the interior to Santa Barbara and Mono counties), southern Nevada, southern Utah, western Colorado, northwestern and central New Mexico, and western Texas (locally east to the Edwards Plateau in Kerr, Kendall and Comal counties) south to southern Baja California, southeastern Sonora, Durango, southeastern Coahuila and, locally, to Michoacán and western Oaxaca.

Winters from southern California (rarely), northern Baja California, southern Sonora, Coahuila and western Nuevo León south to Oaxaca (west of the Isthmus of Tehuantepec), Puebla and Hidalgo.

Casual north to northern California, east-central Utah and central Colorado, southwestern Kansas, and east to Louisiana. Accidental in Washington (Chehalis), Minnesota (Duluth) and southern Ontario (Silver Islet Landing).

Genus AMBLYCERCUS Cabanis

Amblycercus Cabanis, 1851, Mus. Heineanum, 1, p. 186. Type, by monotypy, Amblyramphus prevostii Lesson = Sturnus hoˡᐤsericeus Deppe.

Amblycercus holosericeus (Deppe). YELLOW-BILLED CACIQUE.

Sturnus holosericeus W. Deppe, 1830, Preis.-Verz. Säugeth. Vögel, etc., Mexico, p. 1. (Mexico = Alvarado, Veracruz.)

Habitat.—Undergrowth of humid forest, forest edge, thickets and bamboo (Tropical to Temperate zones).

Distribution.—Resident from San Luis Potosí, Veracruz, Puebla and Oaxaca south along both slopes of Middle America (including the Yucatan Peninsula) to Panama, and in South America from Colombia and northern Venezuela south, west of the Andes to northwestern Peru and east of the Andes to eastern Peru and northern Bolivia.

Notes.—Also known as PREVOST'S CACIQUE. Some authors would place this species in the genus Cacicus.

Genus CACICUS Lacépède

Cacicus Lacépède, 1799, Tabl. Mamm. Ois., p. 6. Type, by subsequent designation (Zimmer, 1930), Oriolus haemorrhous Linnaeus.

Cassiculus Swainson, 1827, Philos. Mag., new ser., 1, p. 436. Type, by original designation, Cassiculus coronatus Swainson = Icterus melanicterus Bonaparte.

Cacicus uropygialis (Lafresnaye). SCARLET-RUMPED CACIQUE.

Cassiculus uropygialis Lafresnaye, 1843, Rev. Zool. [Paris], 6, p. 290. (Colombia = Bogotá.)

Habitat.—Humid lowland and foothill forest, forest edge and second-growth woodland (Tropical and lower Subtropical zones).

Distribution.—Resident [microrhynchus group] on the Caribbean slope of northeastern Honduras (Olancho, Gracias a Dios) and Nicaragua, and on both slopes of Costa Rica (absent from the dry northwest) and Panama (except eastern Darién); [pacificus group] in extreme southeastern Panama (eastern Darién), western Colombia and western Ecuador; and [uropygialis group] in South America from northeastern Colombia and northwestern Venezuela south, east to the Andes, to eastern Ecuador and northeastern Peru.

Notes.—Some authors suggest that the groups represent separate species, *C. microrhynchus* (Sclater and Salvin, 1865) [SMALL-BILLED CACIQUE], *C. pacificus* Chapman, 1915 [PACIFIC CACIQUE], and *C. uropygialis* [CURVE-BILLED CACIQUE].

Cacicus cela (Linnaeus). YELLOW-RUMPED CACIQUE.

Parus Cela Linnaeus, 1758, Syst. Nat., ed. 10, 1, p. 191. Based on *Parus niger, rostro albo* Linnaeus, Mus. Adolphi Friderici, 2, p. . . . (in Indiis, error = Surinam.)

Habitat.—Humid lowland forest, forest edge, clearings, second-growth woodland, plantations, savanna and marshes (Tropical Zone).

Distribution.—*Resident* [*vitellinus* group] in Panama (west on Pacific slope to Veraguas and on Caribbean slope to the Canal Zone) and northern Colombia; and [*cela* group] in western Ecuador and northwestern Peru, and from eastern Colombia, Venezuela (also Trinidad) and the Guianas south, east of the Andes, to eastern Peru, northern Bolivia, and central and eastern Brazil.

Notes.—The two groups are sometimes regarded as distinct species, *C. cela* [YELLOW-RUMPED CACIQUE] and *C. vitellinus* (Lawrence, 1864) [SAFFRON-RUMPED CACIQUE].

Cacicus melanicterus (Bonaparte). YELLOW-WINGED CACIQUE.

Icterus melanicterus Bonaparte, 1825, J. Acad. Nat. Sci. Philadelphia, 4, p. 389. (Mexico = restricted to Temascaltepec, state of México, by van Rossem, 1945, Occas. Pap. Mus. Zool., La. State Univ., no. 21, p. 234, but this locality is certainly erroneous.)

Habitat.—Lowland deciduous forest, open woodland, plantations, and around human habitation (Tropical Zone).

Distribution.—*Resident* in the Pacific lowlands from extreme southern Sonora (at least formerly) south to western Chiapas (Tonalá, Monserrate).

Notes.--Also known as MEXICAN CACIQUE. Often placed in the monotypic genus *Cassiculus*.

Genus PSAROCOLIUS Wagler

Psarocolius Wagler, 1827, Syst. Avium, 1, sig. "22" [=23]. Type, by subsequent designation (G. R. Gray, 1855), *Oriolus cristatus* Gmelin = *Xanthornus decumanus* Pallas.

Subgenus PSAROCOLIUS Wagler

Eucorystes (not Bell, 1862) Sclater, 1883, Ibis, p. 147. Type, by monotypy, *Cassicus* [sic] *wagleri* Gray, 1844.
Zarhynchus Oberholser, 1899, Proc. Acad. Nat. Sci. Philadelphia, 51, p. 215. New name for *Eucorystes* Sclater, preoccupied.

Psarocolius decumanus (Pallas). CRESTED OROPENDOLA.

Xanthornus decumanus Pallas, 1769, Spic. Zool., 1, fasc. 6, p. 1, pl. 1. (America = Surinam.)

Habitat.—Humid lowland and foothill forest, forest edge, and clearings, second-growth woodland, and plantations (Tropical and lower Subtropical zones).

Distribution.—*Resident* in Panama (Pacific slope of western Chiriquí, Veraguas, and from the Canal Zone east to Darién, and on the Caribbean slope recorded only in the Canal Zone), and in South America from northern and eastern Colombia, Venezuela (also Tobago and Trinidad) and the Guianas south, east of the Andes, to eastern Peru, Bolivia, northern Argentina and southern Brazil.

Psarocolius wagleri (Gray). CHESTNUT-HEADED OROPENDOLA.

Cacicus Wagleri G. R. Gray, 1845, Genera Birds, 2, p. 342, pl. 85. (No locality given = "Cobán," Guatemala.)

Habitat.—Humid lowland and foothill forest, forest edge, clearings, second-growth woodland, partly open situations with scattered trees, and plantations (Tropical and lower Subtropical zones).

Distribution.—*Resident* from Veracruz, Tabasco and Chiapas south on the Gulf-Caribbean slope of Central America to Honduras, on both slopes of Nicaragua, Costa Rica (absent from the dry northwest) and Panama, and in western Colombia and northwestern Ecuador.

Notes.—Also known as WAGLER'S OROPENDOLA. Often placed in the monotypic genus *Zarhynchus*.

Subgenus GYMNOSTINOPS Sclater

Gymnostinops Sclater, 1886, Cat. Birds Br. Mus., 11, pp. xvi, 309, 312. Type, by subsequent designation (Ridgway, 1902), *Cacicus montezuma* Lesson.

Psarocolius montezuma (Lesson). MONTEZUMA OROPENDOLA.

Cacicus Montezuma Lesson, 1830, Cent. Zool., livr. 2, p. 33, pl. 7. (Mexico.)

Habitat.—Humid lowland and foothill forest, forest edge, clearings, open woodland, second growth and plantations (Tropical and lower Subtropical zones).

Distribution.—*Resident* from Veracruz, eastern Puebla, northern Oaxaca, Tabasco, Chiapas, Campeche and Quintana Roo south on the Gulf-Caribbean slope of Central America (also on Pacific slope of Nicaragua) to central Panama (east to the Canal Zone).

Notes.—*P. montezuma, P. guatimozinus* and two South American species, *P. cassini* (Richmond, 1898) and *P. bifasciatus* (Spix, 1824), appear to constitute a superspecies.

Psarocolius guatimozinus (Bonaparte). BLACK OROPENDOLA.

Ostinops guatimozinus Bonaparte, 1853, C. R. Acad. Sci. Paris, 37, p. 833. (Guaripata [=Garrapata], middle Rio Magdalena, near Malena, Antioquia, Colombia.)

Habitat.—Humid lowland forest, forest edge, clearings, second-growth woodland, and plantations (Tropical Zone).

Distribution.—*Resident* in eastern Panama (extreme eastern Panamá province and Darién) and northwestern Colombia.

Notes.—See comments under *P. montezuma*.

Family **FRINGILLIDAE**: Fringilline and Cardueline
Finches and Allies

Subfamily FRINGILLINAE: Fringilline Finches

Genus **FRINGILLA** Linnaeus

Fringilla Linnaeus, 1758, Syst. Nat., ed. 10, 1, p. 179. Type, by tautonymy,
Fringilla coelebs Linnaeus (*Fringilla,* prebinomial specific name, in synonymy).

Fringilla coelebs Linnaeus. COMMON CHAFFINCH. [514.3.]

Fringilla cœlebs Linnaeus, 1758, Syst. Nat., ed. 10, 1, p. 179. (in Europa =
Sweden.)

Habitat & Distribution.—*Breeds* in open and partly open country, forest and
woodland throughout Eurasia south to the eastern Atlantic islands, Mediterranean
region, Asia Minor, Iran, southern Russia and western Siberia, with the northernmost populations *wintering* south to northern Africa and southwestern Asia.

Casual or accidental in Maine (Lincoln Center, 3 April 1980), Massachusetts
(Chatham, 1–3 April 1961), Newfoundland (St. John's, 25 February 1967) and
Louisiana (Venice, December 1978). Some of these individuals (particularly the
one in Louisiana) may represent escapes from captivity, but a good case can be
made for natural vagrancy on the part of the northeastern birds (see Am. Birds,
34: 756, 1980).

Notes.—Known in Old World literature as the CHAFFINCH.

Fringilla montifringilla Linnaeus. BRAMBLING. [514.1.]

Fringilla montifringilla Linnaeus, 1758, Syst. Nat., ed. 10, 1, p. 179. (in
Europa = Sweden.)

Habitat.—Mixed deciduous-coniferous forest, forest edge, and birch and willow
scrub, in migration and winter also in woodland and weedy fields.

Distribution.—*Breeds* from northern Scandinavia, northern Russia and northern
Siberia south to southern Scandinavia, central Russia, Transbaicalia, northern
Amurland, Anadyrland, Kamchatka and the Sea of Okhotsk.

Winters from the British Isles and southern portions of the breeding range south
to the Mediterranean region, northern Africa, the Near East, Iran, northwestern
India, Tibet, China, Formosa and Japan, casually to the Faroe Islands, Iceland,
Madeira and the Philippines.

In migration ranges regularly to the western Aleutian Islands (Near Islands,
casually east to Adak), and casually to islands in the Bering Sea (St. Lawrence,
and St. Paul in the Pribilofs), and to western and south-coastal Alaska (Hooper
Bay east to Cordova).

Casual or accidental in northern and southeastern Alaska (Barrow, Juneau),
British Columbia (Graham Island, Vancouver), Oregon (Portland), Nevada (Sut-
cliffe), Montana (Swan Lake), North Dakota (Bismarck), Pennsylvania (Allegheny
County), New York (Kennedy Airport), Massachusetts (Hadley, Richland) and
New Jersey (Stanton, Branchville). Some records, especially those from the north-
eastern states, may be of escaped cage birds.

Subfamily CARDUELINAE: Cardueline Finches

Genus LEUCOSTICTE Swainson

Leucosticte [subgenus] Swainson, 1832, *in* Swainson and Richardson, Fauna Bor.-Am., 2 (1831), p. 265. Type, by monotypy, *Linaria* (*Leucosticte*) *tephrocotis* Swainson = *Passer arctous* Pallas.

Leucosticte arctoa (Pallas). ROSY FINCH. [524.]

Passer arctous Pallas, 1811, Zoogr. Rosso-Asiat., 2, p. 21. (ad Jeniseam [=Yenisei River] et in orientali Sibiria = Russian Altai.)

Habitat.—Barren, rocky or grassy areas and cliffs among glaciers or beyond timberline, in migration and winter also in open situations, fields, cultivated lands, brushy areas, and around human habitation.

Distribution.—*Breeds* [*tephrocotis* group] from western and north-central Alaska (north to the Seward Peninsula and Brooks Range), central Yukon, British Columbia and southwestern Alberta south to southern Alaska (including St. Matthew, Nunivak, and the Pribilof and Aleutian islands), and through the Cascades, Sierra Nevada and Rocky Mountains to northeastern Oregon, east-central California (to Tulare County), central Idaho and northwestern Montana, also in the Commander Islands; [*atrata* group] in the mountains from central Idaho, southwestern and south-central Montana, and northwestern and north-central Wyoming south to southeastern Oregon, northeastern and east-central Nevada (south to the Snake Mountains) and central Utah (to the Tushar and La Sal mountains); [*australis* group] in the mountains from southeastern Wyoming (Medicine Bow Range) south through Colorado to north-central New Mexico (Santa Fe region); and [*arctoa* group] in Asia from the Russia Altai, and southern and eastern Siberia south to Transbaicalia, Lake Baikal, northern Mongolia, the Kurile Islands and Kamchatka.

Winters [*tephrocotis* group] from the Aleutians, southern mainland Alaska (rarely), British Columbia, southern Alberta and southwestern Saskatchewan south to eastern California, central Nevada, central Utah, northern New Mexico and northwestern Nebraska; [*atrata* group] from central Idaho and western and southeastern Wyoming south to eastern California (at least casually), southern Nevada, northern Arizona and northern New Mexico; [*australis* group] generally at lower elevations in the breeding range; and [*arctoa* group] in the breeding range, and south to Manchuria and Japan.

Casual [*tephrocotis* group] east to Manitoba, Minnesota, Wisconsin and Iowa, and south to southern California (Ventura County); and [*atrata* group] in eastern Oregon and eastern Montana. Accidental [*tephrocotis* group] in Ontario (Thunder Bay) and Maine (Gorham); and [*atrata* group] in Ohio (Conneaut).

Notes.—The three American groups are sometimes recognized as distinct species, *L. tephrocotis* (Swainson, 1832) [GRAY-CROWNED ROSY-FINCH, 524], *L. atrata* Ridgway, 1874 [BLACK ROSY-FINCH, 525], and *L. australis* Ridgway, 1874 [BROWN-CAPPED ROSY-FINCH, 526]; intergradation between the *tephrocotis* and *atrata* groups occurs from west-central Idaho to central Montana. Some authors merge the three American groups into a single species, *L. tephrocotis* [AMERICAN ROSY-FINCH], but maintain it as distinct from the Asiatic *L. arctoa* [ASIAN ROSY-FINCH].

Genus PINICOLA Vieillot

Pinicola Vieillot, 1808, Hist. Nat. Ois. Am. Sept., 1 (1807), p. iv, pl. 1, fig. 13. Type, by monotypy, *Pinicola rubra* Vieillot = *Loxia enucleator* Linnaeus.

Pinicola enucleator (Linnaeus). PINE GROSBEAK. [515.]

Loxia Enucleator Linnaeus, 1758, Syst. Nat., ed. 10, 1, p. 171. (in Sveciæ summæ, Canadæ Pinetis = Sweden.)

Habitat.—Open coniferous (less commonly mixed coniferous-deciduous) forest and forest edge, in migration and winter also in deciduous forest, woodland, second growth and shrubbery.

Distribution.—*Breeds* in North America from western and central Alaska, northern Yukon, northwestern and central Mackenzie, northern Manitoba, northern Ontario, northern Quebec, northern Labrador and Newfoundland south to southern Alaska (west to the base of the Alaska Peninsula and Kodiak Island), British Columbia (including the Queen Charlotte and Vancouver islands), central California (southern Sierra Nevada), extreme west-central Nevada, northern and east-central Arizona, northern New Mexico, and, east of the Rockies, to northern Alberta, northern Saskatchewan, central Manitoba, southern Ontario, northern Michigan (probably), southern Quebec, northern New Hampshire, northern Vermont (probably), central Maine and Nova Scotia; and in the Palearctic from northern Scandinavia east across northern Russia to northern Siberia, and south to northern Mongolia, Sakhalin, the Kurile Islands, Kamchatka and Japan.

Winters in North America from western and central Alaska, southern Yukon, southern Mackenzie and southern Canada (east to southern Labrador and Newfoundland) south through the breeding range, casually or sporadically as far as central New Mexico, northern and north-central Texas, northwestern Oklahoma, north-central Arkansas, Missouri, Kentucky, Virginia and the Carolinas; and in the Old World south to northern Europe, the Amur River and Ussuriland, casually to the British Isles and central Europe.

Casual or accidental in the Pribilof, western Aleutian (Attu) and Commander islands, and in Bermuda and Greenland.

Genus CARPODACUS Kaup

Carpodacus Kaup, 1829, Skizz. Entw.-Ges. Eur. Thierw., 1, p. 161. Type, by subsequent designation (G. R. Gray, 1842), *Fringilla rosea* Pallas.

Burrica Ridgway, 1887, Man. N. Am. Birds, p. 390. Type, by original designation, *Fringilla mexicana* Müller.

Notes.—*Erythrina* C. L. Brehm, 1828, is a *nomen nudum.*

Carpodacus erythrinus (Pallas). COMMON ROSEFINCH. [516.1.]

Loxia erythrina Pallas, 1770, Novi Comm. Acad. Sci. Petropol., 14, p. 587, pl. 23, fig. 1. (Volga and Samara Rivers.)

Habitat.—Swampy woods, brushy meadows, thickets, forest edge, clearings, cultivated areas, and around human habitation.

Distribution.—*Breeds* from southern Finland, northern Russia and northern

Siberia south to central Europe, Asia Minor, the Himalayas, Mongolia, northern China, Amurland, the Sea of Okhotsk and Kamchatka.

Winters primarily from India east through Southeast Asia to southern China.

In migration ranges irregularly to the western Aleutians (Attu, Shemya, Buldir), Pribilofs (St. Paul), St. Lawrence Island, the western Alaskan mainland (Yukon-Kuskokwim delta), British Isles, western Europe and Japan.

Notes.—Also known as SCARLET GROSBEAK.

Carpodacus purpureus (Gmelin). PURPLE FINCH. [517.]

Fringilla purpurea Gmelin, 1789, Syst. Nat., 1 (2), p. 923. Based mainly on "The Purple Finch" Catesby, Nat. Hist. Carolina, 1, p. 41, pl. 41. (in Carolina = South Carolina.)

Habitat.—Open coniferous (especially fir and spruce) and mixed coniferous-deciduous forest, forest edge, open woodland and second growth, in migration and winter also in deciduous forest, tall shrubbery, weedy areas, and around human habitation.

Distribution.—*Breeds* from northern and central British Columbia, southern Yukon, southwestern Mackenzie, northern and central Alberta, central Saskatchewan, south-central Manitoba, central Ontario, southern Quebec (including Anticosti Island) and Newfoundland south (west of the Cascades and Sierra Nevada) to northwestern Baja California, and (east of the Great Plains) to central Minnesota, central Wisconsin, central and southeastern Michigan, northern Ohio, West Virginia, central Pennsylvania and southeastern New York.

Winters from southwestern British Columbia south through western Washington, central and western Oregon, and California to northern Baja California, and (rarely) east across central and southern Arizona to southern New Mexico; and from southern Manitoba, southern Ontario, southern Quebec, New Brunswick, Nova Scotia and Newfoundland south to central and southeastern Texas, the Gulf coast, and central (casually southern) Florida.

Casual elsewhere in western North America from eastern Washington, Idaho and Montana south to northern Arizona, New Mexico and extreme western Texas. Accidental north of Labrador (off Resolution Island).

Carpodacus cassinii Baird. CASSIN'S FINCH. [518.]

Carpodacus cassinii Baird, 1854, Proc. Acad. Nat. Sci. Philadelphia, 7, p. 119. (Camp 104, Pueblo Creek, New Mexico = 10 miles east of Gemini Peak, Yavapai County, Arizona.)

Habitat.—Open coniferous forest, in migration and winter also in deciduous woodland, second growth, scrub, brushy areas, and partly open situations with scattered trees.

Distribution.—*Breeds* from southern interior British Columbia, extreme southwestern Alberta, north-central and southeastern Montana, and northern Wyoming south (east of the Cascades and coast ranges) to interior southern California, northern California, southern Nevada, northern Arizona and northern New Mexico.

Winters from southern British Columbia, northwestern Montana and east-central Wyoming south in the interior to northern Baja California, southern Arizona, and in the Mexican highlands to Durango, Zacatecas and Coahuila, casually to coastal and southeastern California, the Tres Marias Islands (off Nayarit), the state of México, and west-central Veracruz.

Casual or irregular east to western Nebraska, western Kansas, western Oklahoma and central Texas.

Notes.—Also known as CASSIN'S PURPLE FINCH.

Carpodacus mexicanus (Müller). HOUSE FINCH. [519.]

Fringilla mexicana P. L. S. Müller, 1776, Natursyst., Suppl., p. 165. (Mexico = valley of México.)

Habitat.—Arid scrub and brush, thornbush, oak-juniper, pine-oak association, chaparral, open woodland, urban areas, cultivated lands and savanna (Subtropical and Temperate zones).

Distribution.—*Breeds* [*mexicanus* group] from southwestern and south-central British Columbia (including Vancouver Island), northern Idaho, western Montana, north-central and southeastern Wyoming, western Nebraska and west-central Kansas south to southern Baja California (including the Channel Islands off California, and most islands off both coasts of Baja California, except Guadalupe and the San Benito islands), central Sonora (including Tiburón and San Pedro Mártir islands), in the Mexican highlands to Oaxaca (west of Isthmus of Tehuantepec) and west-central Veracruz, and to eastern San Luis Potosí, southwestern Tamaulipas, Nuevo León, and western and south-central Texas.

Winters [*mexicanus* group] throughout the breeding range and east to southern Texas.

Resident [*mcgregori* group] formerly on the San Benito Islands, off Baja California, where now extinct (last recorded in 1938), and possibly also on Cedros Island (two records, latest in 1925), where a representative of the *mexicanus* group is now common; and [*amplus* group] on Guadalupe Island, off southern Baja California.

Introduced and established [*mexicanus* group] in the Hawaiian Islands (about 1859, now common on all main islands from Kauai eastward, straggling casually west to Nihoa); and in eastern North America on Long Island, New York (early 1950's), now breeding from Illinois, Indiana, southern Michigan, southern Ontario, southern Quebec, New York, Vermont, Massachusetts, and (probably) Maine and southern New Brunswick south to Missouri, Tennessee, Georgia and South Carolina, and wintering south to Mississippi and Alabama, and north to southern Wisconsin.

Casual [*mexicanus* group] in southern Alberta and North Dakota. Reports from Europe may pertain to escapes from captivity.

Notes.—The three groups are sometimes recognized as distinct species, *C. mexicanus* [COMMON HOUSE-FINCH, 519], *C. mcgregori* Anthony, 1897 [MCGREGOR'S HOUSE-FINCH], and *C. amplus* Ridgway, 1876 [GUADALUPE HOUSE-FINCH].

Genus **LOXIA** Linnaeus

Loxia Linnaeus, 1758, Syst. Nat., ed. 10, 1, p. 171. Type, by tautonymy, *Loxia curvirostra* Linnaeus (*Loxia*, prebinomial specific name, in synonymy).

Loxia curvirostra Linnaeus. RED CROSSBILL. [521.]

Loxia curvirostra Linnaeus, 1758, Syst. Nat., ed. 10, 1, p. 171. (in Europæ = Sweden.)

Habitat.—Coniferous and mixed coniferous-deciduous forest, humid pine-oak association, and lowland pine savanna, in migration and winter also in deciduous forest, woodland, second growth, scrub, weedy fields, shrubbery and gardens (Subtropical and Temperate zones, locally to Tropical Zone in lowland pine savanna).

Distribution.—*Breeds* in North America from south-coastal and southeastern Alaska (west to the base of the Alaska Peninsula and Kodiak Island), southern Yukon, southern Mackenzie, northern Alberta, northwestern and central Saskatchewan, central Manitoba, south-central Ontario, southern Quebec, New Brunswick, Prince Edward Island, Nova Scotia and Newfoundland south to northern Baja California, southern California, southern Nevada, central and southeastern Arizona, in the Middle American highlands through Mexico, Guatemala, El Salvador and Honduras to north-central Nicaragua (also in lowland pine savanna in Belize, eastern Honduras and northeastern Nicaragua), in the Rockies and Plains region east to southeastern Montana, northeastern Wyoming, western South Dakota, northwestern Nebraska, eastern Colorado, northeastern and central New Mexico (probably) and extreme western Texas (Guadalupe Mountains), and to southern Manitoba, central Minnesota, northern Wisconsin, central and southeastern Michigan, southern Ontario, Pennsylvania, West Virginia, western Virginia (also in the Great Smoky Mountains of eastern Tennessee and western North Carolina, possibly northern Georgia), southeastern New York and Massachusetts (with isolated breeding in northeastern Kansas and east-central Mississippi); and in the Old World from the British Isles, northern Scandinavia, northern Russia and northern Siberia south to northwestern Africa, the Mediterranean region, Caucasus, Himalayas, southern China, northern Philippines and Japan.

Winters throughout the breeding range, wandering irregularly and sporadically in the nonbreeding season, occurring in North America south to central Baja California (including Santa Cruz Island off California, and Guadalupe and Cedros islands off Baja California), Sinaloa, southern and eastern Texas, the northern portions of the Gulf states, southern Georgia and central Florida; and in the Old World casually to the Faroe Islands, Iceland, Greenland, Bear Island and Jan Mayen.

Casual in the Pribilof and Aleutian islands, and on St. Lawrence Island and Bermuda.

Notes.—Known in Old World literature as the CROSSBILL.

Loxia leucoptera Gmelin. WHITE-WINGED CROSSBILL. [522.]

Loxia leucoptera Gmelin, 1789, Syst. Nat., 1 (2), p. 844. Based on "The White-winged Crossbill" Latham, Gen. Synop. Birds, 2 (1), p. 108. (in sinu Hudsonis et Noveboraco = Hudson Bay and New York.)

Habitat.—Coniferous forest (especially spruce, fir or larch), mixed coniferous-deciduous woodland, and forest edge, in migration and winter also in deciduous forest and woodland.

Distribution.—*Breeds* in North America from western and central Alaska, northern Yukon, northern and east-central Mackenzie, northern Saskatchewan, central Manitoba, northern Ontario, northern Quebec, north-central Labrador and Newfoundland south to southern Alaska (west to the base of the Alaska Peninsula and Kodiak Island), Washington, northeastern Oregon (with isolated populations breeding irregularly in northern Utah, northwestern Wyoming, and probably north-central New Mexico), western Montana, central and southwestern Alberta, central Saskatchewan, southeastern Manitoba, northern Minnesota, northern Wisconsin, northern Michigan, south-central Ontario, southern Quebec, northeastern New York, northern Vermont, New Hampshire, Maine, New Brunswick and Nova Scotia; in the Greater Antilles in the mountains of Hispaniola (Dominican Republic, and the Massif de La Selle of southeastern Haiti); and in the Palearctic from northern Scandinavia east across northern Russia to northern Siberia, and south to Lake Baikal and Transbaicalia.

Winters in North America throughout the breeding range, wandering irregularly and sporadically south to western Washington, central Oregon, southern Idaho, northern Utah, Colorado, central and northeastern New Mexico, northern Texas (Lubbock), central Oklahoma, Missouri, Kentucky, Virginia and North Carolina; in Hispaniola in the breeding range; and in the Old World irregularly south to central Europe, Sakhalin, Japan, and the Seven Islands of Izu.

Casual in the Bering Sea (Pribilofs, St. Lawrence Island, and at sea), northwestern California, southern Utah, northern Manitoba, southern Baffin Island, Bermuda, Greenland, the Faroe Islands and British Isles, also sight reports for northern Florida and Jamaica.

Genus **CARDUELIS** Brisson

Carduelis Brisson, 1760, Ornithologie, 1, p. 36; 3, p. 53. Type, by tautonymy, *Carduelis* Brisson = *Fringilla carduelis* Linnaeus.

Subgenus ACANTHIS Borkhausen

Acanthis Borkhausen, 1797, Dtsch. Fauna, 1, p. 248. Type, by subsequent designation (Stejneger, 1884), *Fringillaria linaria* Linnaeus = *Fringilla flammea* Linnaeus.

Carduelis flammea (Linnaeus). COMMON REDPOLL. [528.]

Fringilla flammea Linnaeus, 1758, Syst. Nat., ed. 10, 1, p. 182. (in Europa = Norrland, Sweden.)

Habitat.—Forest, scrub and shrubby areas, and open tundra with bushes or dwarf trees, in migration and winter in open woodland, weedy fields, fence rows and cultivated lands.

Distribution.—*Breeds* in North America from western and northern Alaska, northern Yukon, northern Mackenzie, southern Victoria Island, northern Keewatin, northern Quebec, Baffin Island and northern Labrador south to the eastern Aleutians (Unalaska), south-coastal and southeastern Alaska, northwestern British Columbia, central Alberta, northern (casually southern) Saskatchewan, northern Manitoba, northern Ontario, central and southeastern Quebec, and Newfoundland; and in the Palearctic from Greenland, Iceland, northern Scandinavia, northern Russia and northern Siberia south to the British Isles, central Europe (Alps), central Russia, southern Siberia, Amurland, Sakhalin and Kamchatka.

Winters in North America from central Alaska, southern Mackenzie, northern Saskatchewan, northern Manitoba, central Ontario, southern Quebec, central Labrador and Newfoundland south to the northern United States, irregularly or casually to western Oregon, northern California, northern Nevada, northern Utah, central Colorado, Kansas, Missouri, Kentucky and South Carolina (also unverified sight reports for northern Arizona, northern New Mexico and northern Texas); and in the Old World from the southern part of the breeding range south to southern Europe, the northern Mediterranean region, Balkans, Turkestan, Mongolia, eastern China and Japan.

In migration occurs regularly in the Aleutian Islands.

Introduced and established in New Zealand and on Lord Howe Island.

Accidental in Bermuda, also sight reports for the Hawaiian Islands (Kure).

Notes.—Known in Old World literature as the REDPOLL. *C. flammea* and *C. hornemanni* are often placed in the genus *Acanthis*; they appear to constitute a superspecies. See also comments under *C. hornemanni.*

Carduelis hornemanni Holböll. HOARY REDPOLL. [527.]

Carduelis hornemanni Holböll, 1843, *in* Krøyer, Naturhist. Tidskr., 4, p. 398. (Greenland = Ameralikfjord, Greenland.)

Habitat.—Shrubby areas, including sparse low vegetation in open tundra, in migration and winter in open situations, fields and open woodland.

Distribution.—*Breeds* [*exilipes* group] in North America in western and northern Alaska (south to Hooper Bay), northern Yukon, northern and east-central Mackenzie, southern Victoria Island, Keewatin, northeastern Manitoba, Southampton Island and northern Quebec (reported breeding in northern Labrador requires confirmation), and in Eurasia from northern Scandinavia east across northern Russia to northern and eastern Siberia; and [*hornemanni* group] in North America on Ellesmere, Bylot and northern Baffin islands, and in northern Greenland.

Winters [*exilipes* group] in North America in the breeding range (except extreme northern areas) and south, irregularly, to southern Canada (British Columbia eastward), Montana, South Dakota, Minnesota, Wisconsin, northern Illinois, northern Indiana, northern Ohio, New York, Maryland and New England (sight reports from Washington, Nebraska and Virginia need verification), and in the Palearctic irregularly to the British Isles, central Europe, central Asia, Japan, Kamchatka and the Commander Islands; and [*hornemanni* group] in southern Greenland, casually south to northern Manitoba, Keewatin, northern Michigan, southern Ontario, northern Quebec, Labrador and the British Isles.

Notes.—Also known as ARCTIC REDPOLL. The relationships between *C. flammea* and *C. hornemanni* are not totally understood. *C. flammea* and *C. h. exilipes* (Coues, 1862) hybridize extensively in Scandinavia, and recent studies in Alaska suggest that the two forms may be extremes of a single variable species; should this analysis prove to be correct, the morphologically distinct and allopatrically breeding *C. hornemanni* [HORNEMANN'S REDPOLL] may actually represent a species distinct from the *flammea-exilipes* complex. Until the matter is resolved, we are maintaining the present status. See also comments under *C. flammea.*

Subgenus SPINUS Koch

Spinus C. L. Koch, 1816, Syst. Baier. Zool., 1, p. 232. Type, by tautonymy, *Fringilla spinus* Linnaeus.

Loximitris Bryant, 1868, Proc. Boston Soc. Nat. Hist., 11 (1866), p. 93. Type, by monotypy, *Chrysomitris dominicensis* Bryant.

[Carduelis spinus (Linnaeus). EURASIAN SISKIN.] See Appendix B.

Carduelis pinus (Wilson). PINE SISKIN. [533.]

> *Fringilla pinus* Wilson, 1810, Am. Ornithol., 2, p. 133, pl. 17, fig. 1. (Bushhill in the neighborhood of Philadelphia, Pennsylvania.)

Habitat.—Coniferous and mixed coniferous-deciduous forest, woodland, parks and suburban areas, in migration and winter in a variety of woodland and forest habitats, partly open situations with scattered trees, open fields, pastures and savanna (Temperate Zone).

Distribution.—*Breeds* from central and south-coastal Alaska, central Yukon, south-central Mackenzie, northwestern and east-central Saskatchewan, west-central and southern Manitoba, central Ontario, central Quebec, southern Labrador and Newfoundland south to northern Baja California, southern California, southern Nevada, northern and southeastern Arizona, in the western Mexican highlands to Michoacán, the state of México and west-central Veracruz (also in the mountains of interior Chiapas), and, east of the Rockies, to southern New Mexico, western Texas, western Oklahoma, Kansas, Missouri, central Illinois, central Indiana, southern Ontario, northern Ohio, Pennsylvania and southern New Jersey, with nesting irregular and sporadic in southern areas of the range east of the Rockies. Recorded in summer (and probably breeding) in the mountains south to eastern Tennessee and western North Carolina.

Winters throughout the breeding range (rare in more northern portions) and south to northern Baja California, Sonora, Tamaulipas, southern Texas, the Gulf coast and northern Florida (casually to the Florida Keys).

Casual or accidental in the Pribilofs (St. Paul) and eastern Aleutians (Unimak), on St. Lawrence, Bathurst, Cornwallis and Coats islands, and in northern Manitoba, southern Baja California and Bermuda.

Notes.—Often placed in the genus *Spinus* along with all species following through *C. cucullata*. See also comments under *C. atriceps*.

Carduelis atriceps (Salvin). BLACK-CAPPED SISKIN.

> *Chrysomitris atriceps* Salvin, 1863, Proc. Zool. Soc. London, p. 190. (near Quetzaltenango, 8,000 ft., Guatemala.)

Habitat.—Oak and alder growth, adjacent pasture, and pine woodland (Temperate Zone).

Distribution.—*Resident* in the mountains of Chiapas (interior highlands, and Sierra Madre de Chiapas) and Guatemala (Western Highlands).

Notes.—Reportedly hybridizes with *C. pinus* in Chiapas, although the extent and nature of this are not clear. Some authors have considered *C. atriceps* conspecific with *C. pinus*; they are here treated as allospecies of a superspecies. See also comments under *C. pinus*.

Carduelis notata Du Bus de Gisignies. BLACK-HEADED SISKIN.

Carduelis notata Du Bus de Gisignies, 1847, Bull. Acad. R. Sci. Lett. Beaux-Arts Belg., 14, p. 106. (Mexico = Jalapa, Veracruz.)

Habitat.—Pine-oak association, humid montane forest, adjacent weedy areas, pastures, and lowland pine savanna, in winter also in humid lowland forest and adjacent open situations (Tropical to Temperate zones).

Distribution.—*Resident* from southeastern Sonora, western Chihuahua, Sinaloa, Durango, Zacatecas, eastern San Luis Potosí and Veracruz south through the highlands of southern Mexico and northern Central America to north-central Nicaragua (also present in the lowland pine savanna of northeastern Nicaragua and probably also eastern Honduras).

Notes.—See comments under *C. pinus.*

Carduelis xanthogastra (Du Bus de Gisignies). YELLOW-BELLIED SISKIN.

Chrysomitris xanthogastra Du Bus de Gisignies, 1855, Bull. Acad. R. Sci. Lett. Beaux-Arts Belg., 22, p. 152. (Ocaña, Colombia.)

Habitat.—Montane forest edge, clearings, plantations and pastures (upper Tropical and Subtropical zones).

Distribution.—*Resident* in the highlands of Costa Rica (Cordillera Central, Dota Mountains, and Cordillera de Talamanca) and western Panama (western Chiriquí); and in South America from Colombia and northern Venezuela south to southwestern Ecuador, and in central Bolivia.

Notes.—See comments under *C. pinus.*

[Carduelis magellanica (Vieillot). HOODED SISKIN.] See Appendix B.

Carduelis cucullata Swainson. RED SISKIN.

Carduelis cucullata Swainson, 1820, Zool. Illus., ser. 1, 1 (2), pl. 7 and text. ("Spanish Main" = Cumaná, Venezuela.)

Habitat.—Open grassy areas with shrubs and bushes, and scrubby hillsides (upper Tropical Zone.)

Distribution.—*Resident,* at least formerly, in northern Venezuela (also Trinidad, and Monos and Gasparee islands) and northeastern Colombia; recorded in the original range during the last 30 years only in Colombia, perhaps approaching extinction there.

Introduced and established in southeastern Puerto Rico.

Notes.—See comments under *C. pinus.*

Carduelis dominicensis (Bryant). ANTILLEAN SISKIN.

Chrysomitris dominicensis Bryant, 1868, Proc. Boston Soc. Nat. Hist., 11 (1866), p. 93. (Port au Prince, Haiti.)

Habitat.—Mountain pine forest and adjacent scrubby areas, in winter wandering to lowland regions.

Distribution.—*Resident* on Hispaniola (in the Dominican Republic from the province of La Vega westward, and in southeastern Haiti in the Massif de la Selle and probably also Massif de la Hotte).

Notes.—Authors sometimes place this species in *Spinus* or the monotypic genus *Loximitris.*

Subgenus ASTRAGALINUS Cabanis

Astragalinus Cabanis, 1851, Mus. Heineanum, 1, p. 159. Type, by subsequent designation (G. R. Gray, 1855), *Fringilla tristis* Linnaeus.

Carduelis psaltria (Say). LESSER GOLDFINCH. [530.]

> *Fringilla psaltria* Say, 1823, *in* Long, Exped. Rocky Mount., 2, p. 40 (note). (Arkansas River near the mountains = near Colorado Springs, Colorado.)

Habitat.—Partly open situations with scattered trees, woodland edge, second growth, open fields, pastures, and around human habitation (upper Tropical to lower Temperate zones).

Distribution.—*Resident* from southwestern Washington, western Oregon, northern California, northern Utah, northern Colorado, northwestern Oklahoma, and central and southern Texas south to southern Baja California, through Middle America (including the Tres Marias Islands off Nayarit, and Isla Mujeres off Quintana Roo, but in Nicaragua primarily on the Pacific slope), and in South America from Colombia east to Venezuela and south, west of the Andes, to northwestern Peru.

Introduced and established on Cuba (at least formerly).

Casual or accidental in southwestern British Columbia (Huntingdon), eastern Oregon, southern Wyoming, Kansas, Missouri (Kansas City), southwestern Louisiana (Cameron) and Kentucky (Elizabethtown).

Notes.—Also known as DARK-BACKED or ARKANSAS GOLDFINCH. See comments under *C. pinus.*

Carduelis lawrencei Cassin. LAWRENCE'S GOLDFINCH. [531.]

> *Carduelis lawrencei* Cassin, 1852, Proc. Acad. Nat. Sci. Philadelphia, 5 (1850), p. 105. (Sonoma and San Diego, California = Sonoma, California.)

Habitat.—Oak woodland, chaparral, riparian woodland, pinyon-juniper association, and weedy areas in arid regions but usually near water.

Distribution.—*Breeds* from central California south (west of the Sierra Nevada) to southern California, and in northwestern Baja California and western Arizona.

Winters from north-central California, central Arizona, southwestern New Mexico and (at least formerly) extreme western Texas (El Paso area) south to northern Baja California (to lat. 30°S.), northern Sonora and southern Arizona.

Casual in southern Oregon and southern Nevada.

Notes.—See comments under *C. pinus.*

Carduelis tristis (Linnaeus). AMERICAN GOLDFINCH. [529.]

> *Fringilla tristis* Linnaeus, 1758, Syst. Nat., ed. 10, 1, p. 181. Based on "The American Goldfinch" Catesby, Nat. Hist. Carolina, 1, p. 43, pl. 43. (in America septentrionali = South Carolina.)

Habitat.—Weedy fields, cultivated lands, open deciduous and riparian woodland, forest edge, second growth, shrubbery, orchards and farmlands.

Distribution.—*Breeds* from southern British Columbia, north-central Alberta, central Saskatchewan, west-central and southern Manitoba, central Ontario, southern Quebec (including Anticosti Island), New Brunswick, Prince Edward Island, Nova Scotia and southwestern Newfoundland south to southern California (west of the Sierra Nevada and southeastern deserts), northern Baja California, eastern Oregon, central Nevada, southern Colorado, northern New Mexico (probably), central Oklahoma, extreme northeastern Texas, northern Louisiana, northern Mississippi, central Alabama, central Georgia and South Carolina.

Winters from southern British Columbia, the northern United States, southern Manitoba, southern Ontario, New Brunswick and Nova Scotia south to northern Baja California, northern Sonora, southern New Mexico, western and southern Texas, northern Coahuila, Nuevo León, Tamaulipas, Veracruz, the Gulf coast and southern Florida.

Casual north to northern Ontario, northern Quebec and southern Labrador, and in Bermuda, the northern Bahama Islands (Grand Bahama, Abaco, Bimini) and Cuba (Cárdenas).

Notes.—See comments under *C. pinus.*

Subgenus CARDUELIS Brisson

Carduelis carduelis (Linnaeus). EUROPEAN GOLDFINCH. [526.1.]

Fringilla carduelis Linnaeus, 1758, Syst. Nat., ed. 10, 1, p. 180. (in Europæ juniperetis = Sweden.)

Habitat.—Partly open situations with scattered trees, open woodland, weedy areas, pastures, cultivated lands, forest edge, clearings, and around human habitation.

Distribution.—*Resident* from the British Isles, central Scandinavia, central Russia and southern Siberia south to the eastern Atlantic islands, Mediterranean region, northern Africa, the Near East, Himalayas and Mongolia. Northern populations are partially migratory, wintering to the southern parts of the breeding range.

Introduced and established in New York (Long Island, where the population is very low or possibly extirpated), on Bermuda, and in Uruguay and the Australian region; also introduced widely elsewhere in North America (Oregon, Missouri, Ohio, New Jersey, Massachusetts) but not presently established in any of these localities. Occasional reports from North America in these areas and elsewhere (California, Minnesota, Wisconsin, Illinois, and widely in the northeastern United States) probably are based on birds escaped from captivity.

Notes.—Known in Old World literature as the GOLDFINCH.

Carduelis sinica (Linnaeus). ORIENTAL GREENFINCH. [526.2.]

Fringilla sinica Linnaeus, 1766, Syst. Nat., ed. 12, 1, p. 321. Based on "Le Pinçon de la Chine" Brisson, Ornithologie, 3, p. 175, pl. 7, fig. 2. (in China = Macao.)

Habitat.—Open woodland (including pine), and cultivated areas with trees or bushes.

Distribution.—*Breeds* from Amurland, Ussuriland, Sakhalin, the Kurile Islands and Kamchatka south to central and eastern China, Japan, and the Bonin and Volcano islands.

Winters mostly in the southern portions of the breeding range, casually south to Formosa.

In migration ranges casually to the western Aleutian Islands (Attu, Shemya, Buldir).

Notes.—Also known as CHINESE GREENFINCH. This species is often placed in the genus *Chloris,* although it appears to be more closely related to *C. carduelis* than to *C. chloris.*

[Subgenus CHLORIS Cuvier]

Chloris Cuvier, 1800, Leçons Anat. Comp., 1, tab. 2. Type, by tautonymy, *Loxia chloris* Linnaeus.

[**Carduelis chloris** (Linnaeus). EUROPEAN GREENFINCH.] See Appendix B.

Genus SERINUS Koch

Serinus C. L. Koch, 1816, Syst. Baier. Zool., 1, p. 228, pl. 6A, fig. 50. Type, by monotypy, *Serinus hortulanus* Koch = *Fringilla serinus* Linnaeus.

Serinus mozambicus (Müller). YELLOW-FRONTED CANARY. [533.2.]

Fringilla mozambica P. L. S. Müller, 1776, Natursyst., Suppl., p. 163. (Mozambique.)

Habitat.—Open woodland, grasslands, cultivated areas and parks.

Distribution.—*Resident* throughout most of Africa south of the Sahara and east to Ethiopia and Somalia.

Introduced and established in the Hawaiian Islands (since 1964, now in small numbers on Oahu and Hawaii), northeastern Puerto Rico, and the Mascarene Islands (in the Indian Ocean).

Notes.—Also known as GREEN SINGING-FINCH.

Serinus canaria (Linnaeus). COMMON CANARY. [533.1.]

Fringilla Canaria Linnaeus, 1758, Syst. Nat., ed. 10, 1, p. 181. (in Canariis insulis = Canary Islands.)

Habitat.—Open woodland and cultivated districts with trees and shrubs.

Distribution.—*Resident* in the Azores, Madeira and western Canary Islands.

Introduced and established in the Hawaiian Islands (on Midway since at least 1912, presently surviving in small numbers) and on Bermuda. Escaped cage birds occur widely in continental areas of North America and on Puerto Rico but have not established breeding populations.

Notes.—Known in Old World literature as the CANARY.

Genus PYRRHULA Brisson

Pyrrhula Brisson, 1760, Ornithologie, 1, p. 36. Type, by tautonymy, *Pyrrhula* Brisson = *Loxia pyrrhula* Linnaeus.

Pyrrhula pyrrhula (Linnaeus). EURASIAN BULLFINCH. [516.]

Loxia Pyrrhula Linnaeus, 1758, Syst. Nat., ed. 10, 1, p. 171. (in Europæ sylvis = Sweden.)

Habitat.—Coniferous and mixed coniferous-deciduous forest, less commonly open deciduous woodland and parks, in migration and winter also in scrub and partly open situations with scattered trees.

Distribution.—*Breeds* from the British Isles, northern Scandinavia, northern Russia and northern Siberia south to the Azores, southern Europe, the Balkans, northern Iran, northern Mongolia, Ussuriland, Sakhalin, Japan, the Kurile Islands and Kamchatka.

Winters throughout the breeding range and south to Korea, northern China and southern Japan.

In migration ranges casually to Alaska on St. Lawrence and Nunivak islands, in the Aleutians (Attu, Shemya), and to Nulato, Anchorage and Petersburg.

Notes.—Known in Old World literature as the BULLFINCH.

Genus COCCOTHRAUSTES Brisson

Coccothraustes Brisson, 1760, Ornithologie, 1, p. 36, 3, p. 218. Type, by tautonymy, *Coccothraustes* Brisson = *Loxia coccothraustes* Linnaeus.
Hesperiphona Bonaparte, 1850, C. R. Acad. Sci. Paris, 31, p. 424. Type, by original designation, *Fringilla vespertina* Cooper.

Coccothraustes abeillei (Lesson). HOODED GROSBEAK.

Guiraca Abeillei Lesson, 1839, Rev. Zool. [Paris], 2, p. 41. (Mexico.)

Habitat.—Humid montane forest, forest edge, and pine-oak association (Subtropical and Temperate zones).

Distribution.—*Resident* in the mountains of Sinaloa, southern Chihuahua and Durango; in eastern San Luis Potosí and southwestern Tamaulipas; and from Michoacán, the state of México, Morelos, Puebla and west-central Veracruz south through Guerrero, Oaxaca and Chiapas to central Guatemala.

Notes.—Also known as ABEILLE'S GROSBEAK. See comments under *C. vespertinus*.

Coccothraustes vespertinus (Cooper). EVENING GROSBEAK. [514.]

Fringilla vespertina W. Cooper, 1825, Ann. Lyc. Nat. Hist. N.Y., 1, p. 220. (Sault Ste. Marie, near Lake Superior [Michigan].)

Habitat.—Coniferous (primarily spruce and fir) and mixed coniferous-deciduous woodland, second growth, and occasionally parks, in migration and winter in a variety of forest and woodland habitats, and around human habitation (Subtropical and Temperate zones).

Distribution.—*Breeds* from southwestern and north-central British Columbia, northern Alberta, central Saskatchewan, southern Manitoba, central Ontario, southern Quebec (including Anticosti Island), New Brunswick, Prince Edward Island and Nova Scotia south, in the mountains, to central California, west-central and eastern Nevada, central and southeastern Arizona, southern New Mexico, in the Mexican highlands to Michoacán, the state of México, Puebla and west-central

Veracruz, and, east of the Rockies, to north-central and northeastern Minnesota, northern Michigan, southern Ontario, northern New York and Massachusetts.

Winters throughout the breeding range and south, sporadically, to southern California, southern Arizona, Oaxaca (Cerro San Felipe, where possibly resident), western and central Texas, the northern portions of the Gulf states, Georgia and South Carolina, casually to the Gulf coast and central Florida.

Casual in southeastern Alaska, southern Mackenzie and Newfoundland. Accidental in the British Isles (St. Kilda).

Notes.—*C. vespertinus* and *C. abeillei* are often placed in the genus *Hesperiphona.*

Coccothraustes coccothraustes (Linnaeus). HAWFINCH. [514.2.]

> *Loxia Coccothraustes* Linnaeus, 1758, Syst. Nat., ed. 10, 1, p. 171. (in Europa australiori = Italy.)

Habitat.—Mixed deciduous-coniferous or deciduous forest, woodland, parks, bushy areas, scrub and cultivated lands.

Distribution.—*Breeds* from the British Isles, southern Scandinavia, central Russia and central Siberia south to northwestern Africa, the Mediterranean region, Asia Minor, northern Iran, Transbaicalia, Amurland, Manchuria, Ussuriland, Sakhalin and Japan.

Winters throughout the breeding range and south to northern Africa, southern Iran, northwestern India, northern China, and the Ryukyu, Bonin and Volcano islands.

In migration ranges casually (primarily in spring) to St. Lawrence Island, the Aleutians (Attu, Adak) and the Pribilofs (St. Paul).

Subfamily DREPANIDINAE: Hawaiian Honeycreepers

Notes.—In the arrangement of this group, we follow Berger (1981, Hawaiian Birdlife, ed. 2, which was based largely on Pratt, 1979, Univ. Microfilms, CDM-79-21977) uncritically because of the extensive work unpublished and in progress, including studies of fossil material.

Tribe PSITTIROSTRINI: Hawaiian Finches

Genus TELESPYZA Wilson

> *Telespyza* S. B. Wilson, 1890, Ibis, p. 341. Type, by monotypy, *Telespyza cantans* Wilson.

Notes.—Some authors merge the genera from *Telespyza* through *Chloridops* in a single genus *Psittirostra*; others maintain *Psittirostra* as distinct, combining the rest in *Loxioides.*

Telespyza cantans Wilson. LAYSAN FINCH. [774.]

> *Telespyza cantans* S. B. Wilson, 1890, Ibis, p. 341, pl. 9. (Midway Island, North Pacific, error = Laysan Island.)

Habitat.—*Scaevola* thickets, bunch-grass and low bushy areas.

Distribution.—*Resident* on Laysan Island, in the Hawaiian Islands.

Introduced and established on islets in Pearl and Hermes Reef, formerly also on Midway (but since extirpated there).

Notes.—*T. cantans* and *T. ultima* are closely related and constitute a super-species; they are considered conspecific by some authors.

Telespyza ultima Bryan. NIHOA FINCH. [775.]

Telespiza [sic] *ultima* Bryan, 1917, Auk, 34, pp. 70, 71. (Nihoa Island, Hawaiian Group.)

Habitat.—Rock outcroppings and shrub-covered slopes.
Distribution.—*Resident* on Nihoa Island, in the Hawaiian Islands. Introduced but not certainly established on French Frigate Shoals.
Notes.—See comments under *T. cantans.*

Genus PSITTIROSTRA Temminck

Psittirostra Temminck, 1820, Man. Ornithol., ed. 2, 1, p. 70. Type, by monotypy, *Loxia psittacea* Gmelin.

Notes.—See comments under *Telespyza.*

Psittirostra psittacea (Gmelin). OU. [776.]

Loxia psittacea Gmelin, 1789, Syst. Nat., 1 (2), p. 844. Based on the "Parrot-billed Grosbeak" Latham, Gen. Synop. Birds, 2 (1), p. 108, pl. 42. (Sandwich Islands = Hawaii.)

Habitat.—Humid mountain forest, occasionally in drier or lowland forest.
Distribution.—*Resident* in very small numbers in the mountains of Kauai (Alakai Swamp region) and Hawaii (Mauna Loa), formerly also on Oahu (last reported in late 1890's), Molokai (last reported 1907, extirpated before 1948), Lanai (last reported 1923, extirpated by 1932) and Maui (last reported before 1930), in the Hawaiian Islands.

Genus LOXIOIDES Oustalet

Loxioides Oustalet, 1877, Bull. Sci. Soc. Philom. Paris, ser. 7, 1, p. 99. Type, by monotypy, *Psittirostra bailleui* Oustalet.

Notes.—See comments under *Telespyza.*

Loxioides bailleui (Oustalet). PALILA. [777.]

Psittirostra bailleui Oustalet, 1877, Bull. Sci. Soc. Philom. Paris, ser. 7, 1, p. 100. (Hawaii.)

Habitat.—Dry mamane-naio forest at higher elevations.
Distribution.—*Resident* in small numbers in the mountains of Hawaii (slopes of Mauna Kea and, at least formerly, also the western slope of Mauna Loa), in the Hawaiian Islands.

Genus RHODACANTHIS Rothschild

Rhodacanthis Rothschild, 1892, Ann. Mag. Nat. Hist., ser. 6, 10, p. 110. Type, by subsequent designation (Bryan and Greenway, 1944), *Rhodacanthis palmeri* Rothschild.

Notes.—See comments under *Telespyza.*

†Rhodacanthis flaviceps Rothschild. LESSER KOA-FINCH. [778.]

Rhodacanthis flaviceps Rothschild, 1892, Ann. Mag. Nat. Hist., ser. 6, 10, p. 111. (Kona, Hawaii, Sandwich group.)

Habitat.—Humid mountain forest, primarily koa.

Distribution.—EXTINCT. Formerly *resident* at higher elevations in the mountains of the Kona district of Hawaii, in the Hawaiian Islands (last collected in 1891).

Notes.—Also known as YELLOW-HEADED KOA-FINCH.

†Rhodacanthis palmeri Rothschild. GREATER KOA-FINCH. [779.]

Rhodacanthis Palmeri Rothschild, 1892, Ann. Mag. Nat. Hist., ser. 6, 10, p. 111. (Kona, Hawaii, Sandwich Islands.)

Habitat.—Humid mountain forest, primarily koa.

Distribution.—EXTINCT. Formerly *resident* at higher elevations in the mountains of the Kona district of Hawaii, in the Hawaiian Islands (last collected in 1896).

Notes.—Also known as ORANGE KOA-FINCH.

Genus CHLORIDOPS Wilson

Chloridops S. B. Wilson, 1888, Proc. Zool. Soc. London, p. 218. Type, by monotypy, *Chloridops kona* Wilson.

Notes.—See comments under *Telespyza*.

†Chloridops kona Wilson. KONA GROSBEAK. [780.]

Chloridops kona S. B. Wilson, 1888, Proc. Zool. Soc. London, p. 218. (Kona, Hawaii.)

Habitat.—Medium-sized trees (especially naio) on lava flows with little ground cover.

Distribution.—EXTINCT. Formerly *resident* on Hawaii (Kona district), in the Hawaiian Islands.

Notes.—Also known as GROSBEAK FINCH.

Genus PSEUDONESTOR Rothschild

Pseudonestor Rothschild, 1893, Bull. Br. Ornithol. Club, 1, p. 35. Type, by monotypy, *Pseudonestor xanthophrys* Rothschild.

Notes.—Tribal affinities of this genus are uncertain.

Pseudonestor xanthophrys Rothschild. MAUI PARROTBILL. [781.]

Pseudonestor xanthophrys Rothschild, 1893, Bull. Br. Ornithol. Club, 1, p. 36. (Island of Maui, Sandwich Islands.)

Habitat.—Native mountain forest, especially koa.

Distribution.—*Resident* in very small numbers in the mountains of eastern Maui (slopes of Haleakala), in the Hawaiian Islands.

Notes.—Also known as PSEUDONESTOR.

Tribe HEMIGNATHINI: Hawaiian Creepers and Allies

Genus **HEMIGNATHUS** Lichtenstein

Hemignathus Lichtenstein, 1839, Abh. Phys. Kl. Akad. Wiss. Berlin (1838), p. 449. Type, by subsequent designation (G. R. Gray, 1841), *Hemignathus lucidus* Lichtenstein.
Heterorhynchus Lafresnaye, 1839, Mag. Zool. [Paris], 9, pl. 10. Type, by monotypy, *Heterorhynchus olivaceus* Lafresnaye = *Hemignathus lucidus* Lichtenstein.
Viridonia Rothschild, 1892, Ann. Mag. Nat. Hist., ser. 6, 10, p. 112. Type, by monotypy, *Viridonia sagittirostris* Rothschild.

Hemignathus virens (Gmelin). COMMON AMAKIHI. [782.]

> *Certhia virens* Gmelin, 1788, Syst. Nat., 1 (1), p. 479. Based on the "Olive-green Creeper" Latham, Gen. Synop. Birds, 1 (2), p. 740. (in insulis Sandwich = Hawaii.)

Habitat.—Humid ohia forest, drier mamane-naio forest, and subalpine scrub, mostly at higher elevations but seasonally to lowland mixed native-exotic forest.
Distribution.—*Resident* in the Hawaiian Islands [*stejnegeri* group] in the mountains of Kauai; and [*virens* group] in mountain forests on Oahu, Molokai, Lanai (formerly), Maui and Hawaii.
Notes.—Formerly known as the AMAKIHI. Some authors regard the two groups as separate species, *H. virens* and *H. stejnegeri* (S. B. Wilson, 1890) [KAUAI AMAKIHI, 783]. This and the next two species are sometimes placed in the genus *Viridonia*.

Hemignathus parvus (Stejneger). ANIANIAU. [784.]

> *Himatione parva* Stejneger, 1887, Proc. U.S. Natl. Mus., 10, p. 94. (Kauai.)

Habitat.—Humid mountain forest, primarily ohia.
Distribution.—*Resident* in the mountains of Kauai (Kokee, and the Alakai Swamp region), in the Hawaiian Islands.
Notes.—Also known as LESSER AMAKIHI. See comments under *H. virens.*

†**Hemignathus sagittirostris** (Rothschild). GREATER AMAKIHI. [785.]

> *Viridonia sagittirostris* Rothschild, 1892, Ann. Mag. Nat. Hist., ser. 6, 10, p. 112. (Mauna Kea, Hawai[i], Sandwich group.)

Habitat.—Humid mountain forest, especially ohia.
Distribution.—EXTINCT. Formerly *resident* in the mountains of Hawaii (Mauna Kea, and the Wailuku River region), in the Hawaiian Islands.
Notes.—See comments under *H. virens.*

†**Hemignathus obscurus** (Gmelin). HAWAIIAN AKIALOA. [786.]

> *Certhia obscura* Gmelin, 1788, Syst. Nat., 1 (2), p. 470. Based on the "Hook-billed green Creeper" Latham, Gen. Synop. Birds, 1 (2), p. 703, pl. 33, fig. 1. (in insulis Sandwich = Hawaii.)

Habitat.—Humid mountain forests, especially ohia, locally in lowland forest.
Distribution.—EXTINCT. Formerly *resident* in the mountains of Oahu (last

recorded 1837, sight report in 1892), Lanai (last recorded late 1890's) and Hawaii (last recorded in 1890's), in the Hawaiian Islands.

Notes.—*H. obscurus* and *H. procerus* are considered conspecific by some authors [AKIALOA]; they constitute a superspecies.

Hemignathus procerus Cabanis. KAUAI AKIALOA. [787.]

Hemignathus procerus Cabanis, 1889, J. Ornithol., 39, p. 331. (Kauai.)

Habitat.—Humid mountain forest.

Distribution.—*Resident* (at least formerly) in the mountains of Kauai (Alakai Swamp region, now very rare or extinct, last reported in 1967), in the Hawaiian Islands.

Notes.—See comments under *H. obscurus*.

Hemignathus lucidus Lichtenstein. NUKUPUU. [788.]

Hemignathus lucidus Lichtenstein, 1839, Abh. Phys. Kl. Akad. Wiss. Berlin (1838), p. 451, pl. 5. (Oahu.)

Habitat.—Mountain forest, especially ohia and koa.

Distribution.—*Resident* locally in very small numbers on Kauai (Alakai Swamp region) and eastern Maui (slopes of Haleakala), formerly also on Oahu (last recorded in 1860), in the Hawaiian Islands.

Hemignathus munroi Pratt. AKIAPOLAAU. [789.]

Heterorhynchus wilsoni (not *Himatione wilsoni* Rothschild, April 1893) Rothschild, November 1893, Avifauna Laysan, p. 75. (Hawaii.)
Hemignathus munroi Pratt, 1979, Dissert. Abstracts, 40, p. 1581. New name for *Heterorhynchus wilsoni,* preoccupied.

Habitat.—Forest, especially koa or mamane-naio, and adjacent brushy areas, mostly in mountainous regions.

Distribution.—*Resident* in small numbers in widely separated areas on Hawaii (slopes of Mauna Kea and Mauna Loa), in the Hawaiian Islands.

Genus **OREOMYSTIS** Stejneger

Oreomyza (not Pokorny, February 1887, Insecta) Stejneger, April 1887, Proc. U.S. Natl. Mus., 10, p. 99. Type, by original designation, *Oreomyza bairdi* Stejneger.
Oreomystis Stejneger, 1903, Proc. Biol. Soc. Wash., 16, p. 11. New name for *Oreomyza* Stejneger, preoccupied.

Notes.—Some authors merge *Oreomystis* and *Paroreomyza* in *Loxops.*

Oreomystis bairdi (Stejneger). KAUAI CREEPER. [790.]

Oreomyza bairdi Stejneger, 1887, Proc. U.S. Natl. Mus., 10, p. 99. (Kauai.)

Habitat.—Humid mountain forest, especially ohia.

Distribution.—*Resident* in the mountains of Kauai (Kokee, and the Alakai Swamp region), in the Hawaiian Islands.

Notes.—Relationships in the "Hawaiian Creeper" complex (herein split into two genera, *Oreomystis* and *Paroreomyza*) are controversial. Some authors would merge all five species in these two genera into a single one, *Paroreomyza* (or *Loxops*) *maculata(us)* [HAWAIIAN CREEPER]; others would combine *mana* with *bairdi*. At present, it seems best to consider the two species in *Oreomystis* as constituting a superspecies, and of uncertain relationship with the other "creepers."

Oreomystis mana (Wilson). HAWAII CREEPER. [791.]

Himatione mana S. B. Wilson, 1891, Ann. Mag. Nat. Hist., ser. 6, 7, p. 460. (Hawaii.)

Habitat.—Humid forest, especially koa-ohia.

Distribution.—*Resident* on Hawaii (mostly at higher elevations, but in lower forest in the Hilo district), in the Hawaiian Islands.

Notes.—See comments under *O. bairdi.*

Genus **PAROREOMYZA** Perkins

Paroreomyza [subgenus] Perkins, 1901, Ibis, p. 583. Type, by original designation, *Oreomyza* [=*Himatione*] *maculata* Cabanis.

Notes.—See comments under *Oreomystis.*

Paroreomyza montana (Wilson). MAUI CREEPER. [792.]

Himatione montana S. B. Wilson, 1890, Proc. Zool. Soc. London (1889), p. 446. (Lanai.)

Habitat.—Humid mountain forest and adjacent brushy areas.

Distribution.—*Resident* in the mountains of eastern Maui (slope of Haleakala), formerly also on Lanai (last recorded in 1937), in the Hawaiian Islands.

Notes.—Also known as MAUI ALAUWAHIO. See comments under *P. maculata.*

Paroreomyza flammea (Wilson). MOLOKAI CREEPER. [793.]

Loxops flammea S. B. Wilson, 1890, Proc. Zool. Soc. London (1889), p. 445. (Kalae, Molokai.)

Habitat.—Humid mountain forest.

Distribution.—*Resident* (at least formerly) in the mountains of Molokai (now very rare and possibly extinct, last reported in 1962), in the Hawaiian Islands.

Notes.—Also known as KAKAWAHIE. See comments under *P. maculata.*

Paroreomyza maculata (Cabanis). OAHU CREEPER. [794.]

Himatione maculata Cabanis, 1851, Mus. Heineanum, 1, p. 100 (footnote). (Oahu.)

Habitat.—Humid mountain forest.

Distribution.—*Resident* (now very rare and local) in the mountains of Oahu (Waianae and Koolau ranges), in the Hawaiian Islands.

Notes.—Also known as OAHU ALAUWAHIO. *P. maculata, P. flammea* and *P.*

montana are closely related and constitute a superspecies. See also comments under *Oreomystis bairdi.*

Genus **LOXOPS** Cabanis

Loxops Cabanis, 1847, Arch. Naturgesch., 13, p. 330. Type, by original designation, *Fringilla coccinea* Gmelin.

Notes.—See comments under *Oreomystis.*

Loxops coccineus (Gmelin). AKEPA. [795.]

Fringilla coccinea Gmelin, 1789, Syst. Nat., 1 (2), p. 921. Based on the "Scarlet Finch" Latham, Gen. Synop. Birds, 2 (1), p. 270. (in insulis Sandwich = Hawaii.)

Habitat.—Forest (primarily ohia or koa), especially in mountainous regions.
Distribution.—*Resident* in the Hawaiian Islands [*caeruleirostris* group] in the mountains of Kauai (Kokee, and the Alakai Swamp region); and [*coccineus* group] in the mountains of eastern Maui (very rare and local) and Hawaii (uncommon), formerly also on Oahu (not recorded since the early 1900's).
Notes.—The two groups are regarded by some authors as distinct species, *L. caeruleirostris* (S. B. Wilson, 1890) [KAUAI AKEPA, 796] and *L. coccineus* [COMMON AKEPA].

Tribe DREPANIDINI: Mamos, Iiwis and Allies

Genus **CIRIDOPS** Newton

Ciridops Newton, 1892, Nature, 45, p. 469. Type, by monotypy, *Fringilla anna* Dole.

†Ciridops anna (Dole). ULA-AI-HAWANE. [797.]

Fringilla anna Dole, 1878, *in* Thrum, Hawaiian Almanac Annual (1879), p. 49. (Hawaii.)

Habitat.—Mountain forest, especially loulu palm.
Distribution.—EXTINCT. Formerly *resident* in the mountains of Hawaii (Kona and Hilo districts, and Kohala Mountains, last collected in early 1890's), in the Hawaiian Islands.

Genus **VESTIARIA** Jarocki

Vestiaria Jarocki, 1821, Zoologia, 2, p. 75. Type, by monotypy, *Certhia vestiaria* Latham = *Certhia coccinea* Forster.

Notes.—This genus is sometimes merged in *Drepanis.*

Vestiaria coccinea (Forster). IIWI. [798.]

Certhia coccinea J. R. Forster, 1780, Göttinger Mag. Wiss., 1, p. 347. (Hawaiian Islands = probably Kauai.)

Habitat.—Forest, especially ohia, mamane, and where lobelias are present.

Distribution.—*Resident* on Kauai, Oahu (near extirpation), Molokai (very rare), Maui, Lanai (last recorded in 1923) and Hawaii, in the Hawaiian Islands.

Genus DREPANIS Temminck

Drepanis Temminck, 1820, Man. Ornithol., ed. 2, 1, p. 86. Type, by subsequent designation (G. R. Gray, 1840), *Certhia pacifica* Gmelin.

Notes.—See comments under *Vestiaria.*

†Drepanis pacifica (Gmelin). HAWAII MAMO. [799.]

Certhia pacifica Gmelin, 1788, Syst. Nat., 1 (1), p. 470. Based on the "Great Hook-billed Creeper" Latham, Gen. Synop. Birds, 1 (2), p. 703. (in insula amicis maris australis, error = Hawaii.)

Habitat.—Mountain forest, especially ohia.
Distribution.—EXTINCT. Formerly *resident* in the mountains of Hawaii (last recorded in 1898), in the Hawaiian Islands.
Notes.—Frequently known as the MAMO.

†Drepanis funerea Newton. BLACK MAMO. [800.]

Drepanis funerea Newton, 1894, Proc. Zool. Soc. London (1893), p. 690. (Molokai.)

Habitat.—Underbrush of humid mountain forest.
Distribution.—EXTINCT. Formerly *resident* in the mountains of Molokai (last recorded in 1907), in the Hawaiian Islands.
Notes.—Also known as PERKINS' MAMO.

Genus PALMERIA Rothschild

Palmeria Rothschild, 1893, Ibis, p. 113. Type, by monotypy, *Palmeria mirabilis* Rothschild = *Himatione dolei* Wilson.

Palmeria dolei (Wilson). CRESTED HONEYCREEPER. [801.]

Himatione dolei S. B. Wilson, 1891, Proc. Zool. Soc. London, p. 166. (Maui.)

Habitat.—Humid mountain forest, especially ohia.
Distribution.—*Resident* in the mountains of eastern Maui (slopes of Haleakala), formerly also on Molokai (last reported in 1907), in the Hawaiian Islands.
Notes.—Also known as AKOHEKOHE.

Genus HIMATIONE Cabanis

Himatione Cabanis, 1851, Mus. Heineanum, 1, p. 99. Type, by monotypy, *Certhia sanguinea* Gmelin.

Himatione sanguinea (Gmelin). APAPANE. [802.]

Certhia sanguinea Gmelin, 1788, Syst. Nat., 1 (1), p. 479. Based on the "Crimson Creeper" Latham, Gen. Synop. Birds, 1 (2), p. 739. (in insulis Sandwich = Hawaii.)

Habitat.—Native (primarily ohia and ohia-koa) and mixed native-exotic forest at higher (casually lower) elevations, and [*freethii* group] in brushy areas, shrubbery and bunch-grass.

Distribution.—*Resident* [*sanguinea* group] in the mountains in the Hawaiian Islands (all main islands from Kauai eastward); and [*freethii* group] formerly on Laysan Island (extirpated in 1923).

Accidental [*sanguinea* group] on Niihau.

Notes.—Some authors regard the two groups as distinct species, *H. sanguinea* [APAPANE, 802] and *H. freethii* Rothschild, 1892 [LAYSAN HONEYCREEPER, 803].

Genus MELAMPROSOPS Casey and Jacobi

Melamprosops Casey and Jacobi, 1974, Bishop Mus., Occas. Pap., no. 12, p. 217. Type, by original designation, *Melamprosops phaeosoma* Casey and Jacobi.

Notes.—Relationships of this recently discovered genus are uncertain.

Melamprosops phaeosoma Casey and Jacobi. POO-ULI. [804.]

Melamprosops phaeosoma Casey and Jacobi, 1974, Bishop. Mus., Occas. Pap., no. 12, p. 219. (Haleakala Volcano, Maui, Hawaii.)

Habitat.—Humid mountain forest, primarily ohia.

Distribution.—*Resident* in very small numbers in the mountains of Maui (slopes of Haleakala), in the Hawaiian Islands.

Notes.—Known also as BLACK-FACED HONEYCREEPER.

Family PASSERIDAE: Old World Sparrows

Notes.—Sometimes included in the Ploceidae.

Genus PASSER Brisson

Passer Brisson, 1760, Ornithologie, 1, p. 36; 3, p. 71. Type, by subsequent designation (G. R. Gray, 1840), *Passer domesticus* Brisson = *Fringilla domestica* Linnaeus.

Passer domesticus (Linnaeus). HOUSE SPARROW. [688.2.]

Fringilla domestica Linnaeus, 1758, Syst. Nat., ed. 10, 1, p. 183. (in Europa = Sweden.)

Habitat.—Cultivated lands, fields, woodland, forest edge, and around human habitation (Tropical to Temperate zones).

Distribution.—*Resident* from the British Isles, northern Scandinavia, northern Russia and northern Siberia south to northwestern Africa, the Mediterranean region, northeastern Africa, Arabia, India (including Ceylon) and Southeast Asia.

Introduced (initially in 1850 at Brooklyn, New York, with several subsequent introductions elsewhere in the northeast through 1867) and established in North America, presently resident from southern Yukon, central and southeastern British Columbia, southwestern Mackenzie, northwestern and central Saskatchewan, northern Manitoba, northern Ontario, southern Quebec (including Anticosti and Magdalen islands) and Newfoundland south throughout southern Canada, the continental United States, and most of Mexico to Veracruz, Oaxaca and Chiapas, locally in Central America (where range expanding rapidly in recent years) south to Panama (east to eastern Panamá province); also in the Hawaiian Islands (Honolulu in 1871, since spreading throughout all main islands), Bahama Islands (Grand Bahama, New Providence), Cuba (late 1890's), Jamaica (1903–1904), Hispaniola (1978), Puerto Rico (1978), the Virgin Islands (St. Thomas, early 1950's), South America (Ecuador to Chile, and eastern Brazil to Paraguay, Argentina and the Falkland Islands), southern and eastern Africa, islands in the Indian Ocean, Australia and New Zealand.

Passer montanus (Linnaeus). EURASIAN TREE SPARROW. [688.3.]

Fringilla montana Linnaeus, 1758, Syst. Nat., ed. 10, 1, p. 183. (in Europa = Bagnacavallo, Ravenna, Italy.)

Habitat.—Open woodland, fields, cultivated lands, and around human habitation.

Distribution.—*Resident* from the British Isles, northern Scandinavia, northern Russia and northern Siberia south to the Mediterranean region, Iran, Afghanistan, northern India, Southeast Asia, Sumatra, Java, Bali, the Himalayas, Sea of Okhotsk, and on Pacific islands from Sakhalin and the Kuriles south through Japan to Hainan, Formosa, and the Ryukyu Islands.

Introduced and established at St. Louis, Missouri (1870), from whence it has spread into east-central Missouri and western Illinois, with a straggler reported in western Kentucky (Lone Oak); also introduced in Bermuda (no recent records), and established in Borneo, Celebes, the Philippines and Australia.

Notes.—Also known as EUROPEAN TREE SPARROW and, in Old World literature, as the TREE SPARROW.

Family **PLOCEIDAE**: Weavers

Subfamily PLOCEINAE: Typical Weavers

Genus **PLOCEUS** Cuvier

Ploceus Cuvier, 1817, Règne Anim., 1, p. 383. Type, by subsequent designation (G. R. Gray, 1840), *Loxia philippina* Linnaeus.

Ploceus cucullatus (Müller). VILLAGE WEAVER.

Oriolus cucullatus P. L. S. Müller, 1776, Natursyst., Suppl., p. 87. (Senegal.)

Habitat.—Forest, woodland, scrub, brush, vegetation near water, and around human habitation.

Distribution.—*Resident* [*cucullatus* group] in West Africa from Senegal eastward, and across the Congo region to Sudan, Eritrea, Ethiopia, Uganda and western Kenya; [*collaris* group] from Gabon to northern Angola; and [*nigriceps* group] from southern Somalia south through eastern Kenya and Tanzania to southern Africa.

Introduced [*cucullatus* group] and established on Hispaniola (including Saona Island).

Notes.—Also known as BLACK-HEADED WEAVER. The three groups are often regarded as distinct species, *P. cucullatus* [BLACK-HEADED WEAVER], *P. collaris* Vieillot, 1819, and *P. nigriceps* (Layard, 1867).

Genus **EUPLECTES** Swainson

Euplectes Swainson, 1829, Zool. Illus., ser. 2, 1, text to pl. 37. Type, by original designation, "*Loxia*" [=*Emberiza*] *orix* Linnaeus.

Notes.—Members of this genus are sometimes known under the group name BISHOPBIRD.

Euplectes orix (Linnaeus). RED BISHOP.

Emberiza Orix Linnaeus, 1758, Syst. Nat., ed. 10, 1, p. 177. Based on "The Grenadier" Edwards, Nat. Hist. Birds, 4, p. 178, pl. 178. (in Africa interiore = Angola.)

Habitat.—Tall grasslands, cultivated grains and fields.

Distribution.—*Resident* in Africa from Senegal east to Sudan, Ethiopia and Somalia, and south to southern Africa.

Introduced and established on Puerto Rico and Bermuda; introductions in the Hawaiian Islands (Oahu) have not become established.

Notes.—Also known as GRENADIER WEAVER. The northern race occurring from Senegal to the northern Cameroons, and in eastern Zaire, northern Uganda and northwestern Kenya, is sometimes recognized as a full species, *E. franciscanus* (Isert, 1789) [ORANGE BISHOP].

Euplectes afer (Gmelin). YELLOW-CROWNED BISHOP.

Loxia afra Gmelin, 1789, Syst. Nat., 1 (2), p. 857. Based mainly on the "Black-bellied Grosbeak" Latham, Gen. Synop. Birds, 2 (1), p. 155. (in Africa = Senegal.)

Habitat.—Swamps, marshes, and tall grass areas in wet situations, in Puerto Rico also in cultivated lands.

Distribution.—*Resident* in Africa from Senegal east to Sudan, Ethiopia and northern Kenya, and south to southern Africa.

Introduced and established on Puerto Rico; introductions in the Hawaiian Islands (Oahu) have not become established.

Notes.—Also known as GOLDEN or NAPOLEON BISHOP, or NAPOLEON WEAVER.

Family **ESTRILDIDAE**: Estrildid Finches

Subfamily ESTRILDINAE: Estrildine Finches

[Genus **LAGONOSTICTA** Cabanis]

Lagonosticta Cabanis, 1851, Mus. Heineanum, 1, p. 171. Type, by subsequent designation (G. R. Gray, 1855), *Fringilla rubricata* Lichtenstein.

[**Lagonosticta rubricata** (Lichtenstein). AFRICAN FIRE-FINCH.] See Appendix B.

Genus **URAEGINTHUS** Cabanis

Uraeginthus Cabanis, 1851, Mus. Heineanum, 1, p. 171. Type, by subsequent designation (G. R. Gray, 1855), *Fringilla bengalus* Linnaeus.

Uraeginthus bengalus (Linnaeus). RED-CHEEKED CORDONBLEU. [805.]

Fringilla bengalus Linnaeus, 1766, Syst. Nat., ed. 12, 1, p. 323. Based on "Le Bengali" Brisson, Ornithologie, 3, p. 203, pl. 10, fig. 1. (in Bengala, error = Senegal.)

Habitat.—Thornbush, savanna, forest edge, cultivated lands, and around human habitation.

Distribution.—*Resident* in Africa from Senegal east to Sudan, Eritrea and Somalia, and south to Angola, Zambia and Tanzania.

Introduced and established in very small numbers in the Hawaiian Islands (since 1965 on Oahu, where now nearly or actually extirpated, and on Hawaii).

Genus **ESTRILDA** Swainson

Estrilda Swainson, 1827, Zool. J., 3, p. 349. Type, by original designation, *Loxia astrild* Linnaeus.

Notes.—See comments under *Amandava.*

Estrilda caerulescens (Vieillot). LAVENDER WAXBILL. [806.]

Fringilla cærulescens Vieillot, 1817, Nouv. Dict. Hist. Nat., nouv. éd., 12, p. 176. (Zone Torride = Senegal.)

Habitat.—Bush country, scrub, gardens, and around human habitation.

Distribution.—*Resident* in West Africa from Senegal to Nigeria, and inland to western Central African Republic, southwestern Chad and northern Cameroons.

Introduced and established in the Hawaiian Islands (first reported in 1965, now in small numbers on Oahu and Hawaii).

Notes.—Also known as RED-TAILED LAVENDER WAXBILL and LAVENDER FIRE-FINCH.

Estrilda melpoda (Vieillot). ORANGE-CHEEKED WAXBILL. [807.]

Fringilla melpoda Vieillot, 1817, Nouv. Dict. Hist. Nat., nouv. éd., 12, p. 177. (India and west coast of Africa = Senegal.)

Habitat.—Savanna, grasslands, cultivated lands, and around human habitation.

Distribution.—*Resident* in West Africa from Senegal and Gambia east to Chad, and south to Angola and Zambia.

Introduced and established in the Hawaiian Islands (first reported in 1965, now in small numbers on Oahu) and on Puerto Rico.

Estrilda troglodytes (Lichtenstein). BLACK-RUMPED WAXBILL. [808.]

Fringilla Troglodytes Lichtenstein, 1823, Verz. Doubl. Zool. Mus. Berlin, p. 26. (Senegambia.)

Habitat.—Bush country, swampy areas, and brushy habitats.

Distribution.—*Resident* in Africa from Senegal and Gambia east to Sudan, Eritrea and Ethiopia, and south to northeastern Zaire and northwestern Uganda.

Introduced and established in the Hawaiian Islands (first reported in 1965, now in small numbers on Oahu and Hawaii) and on Puerto Rico.

Notes.—Also known as RED-EARED WAXBILL.

Estrilda astrild (Linnaeus). COMMON WAXBILL.

> *Loxia Astrild* Linnaeus, 1758, Syst. Nat., ed. 10, 1, p. 173. Based on "The Wax Bill" Edwards, Nat. Hist. Birds, 4, p. 179, pl. 179, lower fig. (in Canariis, America, Africa = Cape Town, South Africa.)

Habitat.—Open country, grasslands, cultivated lands, open woodland, and around human habitation.

Distribution.—*Resident* throughout Africa south of the Sahara.

Introduced and established in the Hawaiian Islands (Oahu) and Puerto Rico.

Notes.—Also known as the WAXBILL.

Genus AMANDAVA Blyth

> *Amandava* Blyth, 1836, *in* White, Nat. Hist. Selbourne, p. 44, footnote. Type, by monotypy, *Amandava punctata* Blyth = *Fringilla amandava* Linnaeus.

Notes.—Some authors merge this genus in *Estrilda.*

Amandava amandava (Linnaeus). RED AVADAVAT. [809.]

> *Fringilla Amandava* Linnaeus, 1758, Syst. Nat., ed. 10, 1, p. 180. Based on "Amandava" Albin, Nat. Hist. Birds, 3, p. 72, pl. 77. (in india orientali = Calcutta, West Bengal.)

Habitat.—Second growth, grasslands, scrub, reed beds, and cultivated lands.

Distribution.—*Resident* from West Pakistan, India and southern Nepal south through Southeast Asia and Java to the Lesser Sunda Islands (east to Timor).

Introduced and established in the Hawaiian Islands (on Oahu, between 1900 and 1910), and on Puerto Rico, Sumatra and Singapore.

Notes.—Also known as STRAWBERRY FINCH or RED MUNIA.

Genus LONCHURA Sykes

> *Lonchura* Sykes, 1832, Proc. Zool. Soc. London, p. 94. Type, by subsequent designation (G. R. Gray, 1840), *Fringilla nisoria* Temminck = *Loxia punctulata* Linnaeus.
> *Spermestes* Swainson, 1837, Birds W. Afr., 1, p. 201. Type, by monotypy, *Spermestes cucullata* Swainson.
> *Euodice* Reichenbach, 1863, Singvögel, p. 46. Type, by subsequent designation (Sharpe, 1890), *Loxia cantans* Gmelin = *Loxia malabarica* Linnaeus.

Lonchura malabarica (Linnaeus). WARBLING SILVERBILL. [810.]

> *Loxia malabarica* Linnaeus, 1758, Syst. Nat., ed. 10, 1, p. 175. (in Indiis = Malabar.)

Habitat.—Bush country, scrub, brushy areas, and around human habitation.

Distribution.—*Resident* in Africa from Senegal east to Sudan, Ethiopia and Somalia, and south to Kenya and northern Tanzania; in southern Arabia; and from India, Nepal, Sikkim and East Pakistan south to Ceylon.

Introduced and established in the Hawaiian Islands (first reported in 1973 on Hawaii, recently spreading to Maui, Lanai and Molokai), and on Puerto Rico. A pair successfully bred on Merritt Island, Florida, in June 1965 (Am. Birds, 19: 537, 1965, listed as "*Euodice cantans*"), but this species has not become established there.

Notes.—Also known as WHITE-THROATED MUNIA. Often placed in the genus *Euodice.*

Lonchura cucullata (Swainson). BRONZE MANNIKIN.

Spermestes cucullata Swainson, 1837, Birds W. Afr., 1, p. 201. (West Africa = Senegal.)

Habitat.—Open country, bush, cultivated lands, and around human habitation.

Distribution.—*Resident* in Africa from Senegal east to Sudan, Ethiopia and Kenya, and south to Angola, Zambia and Rhodesia (including Zanzibar and other coastal islands in the Gulf of Guinea and along the Indian Ocean).

Introduced and established in Puerto Rico (common in coastal lowlands, but rare in hill country).

Notes.—Also known as BRONZE MUNIA or HOODED WEAVER. Often placed in the genus *Spermestes.*

Lonchura punctulata (Linnaeus). NUTMEG MANNIKIN. [811.]

Loxia punctulata Linnaeus, 1758, Syst. Nat., ed. 10, 1, p. 173. Based on "The Gowry Bird" Edwards, Nat. Hist. Birds, 1, p. 40, pl. 40. (in Asia = Calcutta, India.)

Habitat.—Second growth, scrub, grasslands, cultivated lands, and around human habitation.

Distribution.—*Resident* from India, Nepal, southern China, Hainan and Formosa south to Ceylon, and through Southeast Asia to the East Indies (east to Celebes and Tanimbar) and Philippines.

Introduced and established in the Hawaiian Islands (about 1865, presently widespread on all main islands), in Australia, and on islands in the Indian Ocean. Pairs bred successfully in Fℓ⌐ ⁱ⌐ ⌐t Cocoa Beach in 1964 (Am. Birds, 18: 504–505, 1964) and on Merritt Island in 1965 (Am. Birds, 19: 537, 1965), but no population has become established; also reported (status uncertain) from Hispaniola and Puerto Rico.

Notes.—Also known as SPOTTED MUNIA, SPICE FINCH, RICEBIRD or SCALY-BREASTED MANNIKIN.

Lonchura malacca (Linnaeus). CHESTNUT MANNIKIN. [812.]

Loxia malacca Linnaeus, 1766, Syst. Nat., ed. 12, 1, p. 302. Based mainly on "Le Gros-bec de Java" Brisson, Ornithologie, 3, p. 237, pl. 13, fig. 1. (in China, Java, Malacca, error = Belgaum, India.)

Habitat.—Second growth, scrub, grasslands, cultivated lands, marshes, and around human habitation.

Distribution.—*Resident* from India, Nepal, Southeast Asia, southern China, Hainan and Formosa south to Ceylon, the Greater Sunda Islands and Philippines.

Introduced and established in the Hawaiian Islands (first observed in 1959 on Oahu, presently also occurs on Kauai and possibly Hawaii), on Puerto Rico, and in the Moluccas and Micronesia. A pair bred successfully in 1965 on Merritt Island, Florida (Am. Birds, 19: 537, 1965), but no population became established.

Notes.—Also known as BLACK-HEADED MUNIA or MANNIKIN, CHESTNUT MUNIA or BLACK-HEADED NUN.

Genus **PADDA** Reichenbach

Padda Reichenbach, 1850, Avium Syst. Nat., pl. 76, fig. 4. Type, by monotypy, *Loxia oryzivora* Linnaeus.

Padda oryzivora (Linnaeus). JAVA SPARROW. [813.]

Loxia oryzivora Linnaeus, 1758, Syst. Nat., ed. 10, 1, p. 173. Based in part on "The Cock Padda or Rice-bird" Edwards, Nat. Hist. Birds, 1, p. 41, pl. 41. (in Asia & Æthiopia = Java.)

Habitat.—Scrub, mangroves, cultivated lands, and around human habitation.

Distribution.—*Resident* on Java and Bali, in the East Indies.

Introduced and established in the mid-1960's in the Hawaiian Islands (on Oahu, where locally common; other introductions on Oahu in 1865 did not become established), in southern Florida (Miami region, probably established), on Puerto Rico (San Juan area), and widely elsewhere, especially in Ceylon, Southeast Asia, Celebes, the Lesser Sunda Islands, Philippines and Moluccas.

Notes.—Also known as JAVA FINCH.

Subfamily VIDUINAE: Whydahs

Genus **VIDUA** Cuvier

Vidua Cuvier, 1817, Règne Anim., 1, p. 388. Type, by tautonymy, *Emberiza vidua* Linnaeus = *Fringilla macroura* Pallas.

Vidua macroura (Pallas). PIN-TAILED WHYDAH.

Fringilla macroura Pallas, 1764, *in* Vroeg, Cat. Raissoné Ois., Adumbr., p. 3. (East Indies, error = Angola.)

Habitat.—Arid bush country, grasslands, scrub, cultivated areas, and around human habitation.

Distribution.—*Resident* in Africa from Senegal east to Eritrea, and south to southern Africa, including Zanzibar and other coastal islands.

Introduced and established on Puerto Rico; escapes in the Hawaiian Islands (Oahu) probably bred in the mid-1970's, but the species has not become established.

APPENDIX A

Species recorded in the Check-list area only on the basis of observation and which are accepted by the appropriate regional group are included in Appendix A. For further discussion of sight records, refer to the Preface (pp. xx–xxi).

Diomedea irrorata Salvin. WAVED ALBATROSS.

> *Diomedea irrorata* Salvin, 1883, Proc. Zool. Soc. London, p. 430. (Callao Bay, Peru.)

Habitat & Distribution.—*Breeds* on Hood Island in the Galapagos and on Isla de la Plata off Ecuador, and *ranges* at sea along the coasts of Ecuador and Peru. A specimen was taken just outside the North American area at Octavia Rocks, Colombia, near the Panama-Colombia boundary (8 March 1941, R. C. Murphy).

Sight records.—Panama, west of Piñas Bay, Darién, 26 February 1941, and southwest of the Pearl Islands, 27 September 1964 (Ridgely, 1976, Birds Panama, p. 30).

Notes.—Known also as the GALAPAGOS ALBATROSS.

Macronectes giganteus (Gmelin). ANTARCTIC GIANT-PETREL.

> *Procellaria gigantea* Gmelin, 1789, Syst. Nat., 1 (2), p. 563. Based in part on the "Giant Petrel" Latham, Gen. Synop. Birds, 3 (2), p. 396, pl. 100. (in oceano, potissimum australi, circa Staatenland, Terra del Fuego = Isla los Estados [= Staten Island], off Tierra del Fuego.)

Habitat & Distribution.—*Breeds* in Antarctica and on subantarctic islands, and *ranges* at sea throughout southern oceans. A report from the "coast of Oregon" (immature specimen taken by Townsend) is generally regarded to be in error as to locality (see Stone, 1930, Auk, 47, pp. 414–415, but for conflicting opinion, see also Fisher, 1965, Condor, 67, pp. 355–356).

Sight records.—Hawaiian Islands, Midway, 9 December 1962, dark-phased individual, plus two other probables in December 1959 and December 1961 (Fisher, *loc. cit.*).

Notes.—Also known as GIANT FULMAR or SOUTHERN GIANT-PETREL. The above reports may pertain either to *M. giganteus,* a more southern breeding form, or to the recently recognized *M. halli* Mathews, 1912 [HALL'S or NORTHERN GIANT-PETREL], which breeds on islands in the southern Indian Ocean and off New Zealand. Dark-phased birds in the field and immatures in the hand are not identifiable to species.

Pterodroma rostrata (Peale). TAHITI PETREL.

> *Procellaria rostrata* Peale, 1848, U.S. Explor. Exped., 8, p. 296. (Mountains about 600 feet on Tahiti, Society Islands.)

Habitat & Distribution.—*Breeds* on New Caledonia and in the Society and Marquesas islands, and ranges widely in the South Pacific, occasionally north to Hawaiian waters.

Sight record.—Lat. 19°45′N., long. 153°59′W., ca. 50 miles east of Hawaii, 7 December 1964, W. King. Other sight records in Hawaiian waters were not allocated to species and may have pertained to either *P. rostrata* or *P. alba.*

Pterodroma alba (Gmelin). PHOENIX PETREL.

Procellaria alba Gmelin, 1789, Syst. Nat., 1 (2), p. 565. Based on the "White-breasted Petrel" Latham, Gen. Synop. Birds, 3 (2), p. 400. (in insulis Turturum et nativitatis Christi = Turtle and Christmas islands.)

Habitat & Distribution.—*Breeds* from Christmas Island south to the Tonga and Tuamotu islands, and *ranges* in the tropical Pacific Ocean, occasionally north to Hawaiian waters.

Sight record.—Lat. 17°49′N., long. 153°55′W., ca. 90 miles southeast of Hawaii, 10 November 1964, W. King. See also comments under *P. rostrata.*

Pterodroma solandri (Gould). SOLANDER'S PETREL.

Procellaria Solandri Gould, 1844, Proc. Zool. Soc. London, p. 57. (Australia = Bass Strait.)

Habitat & Distribution.—*Breeds* in the South Pacific from New Zealand waters east to the Tuamotu Islands, and *ranges* south of the Equator in the same general area west to Australia, straggling casually north to the Equator.

Sight record.—Lat. 20°01′N., long. 153°58′W., ca. 50 miles northeast of Hawaii, 7 October 1964, W. King; a report from 60 miles off California (between Cape Mendocino and Point Reyes) apparently pertains to *P. ultima.*

Pterodroma longirostris (Stejneger). STEJNEGER'S PETREL.

Æstrelata longirostris Stejneger, 1893, Proc. U.S. Natl. Mus., 16, p. 618. (Province of Mutzu, Hondo, Japan.)

Habitat & Distribution.—*Breeds* on small islands off New Zealand and on Mas Afuera Island, in the Juan Fernandez group, and *ranges* at sea in the North Pacific to waters off Japan and between the Hawaiian Islands and North America (specimens from lat. 33°6′N., long. 134°W., and lat. 35°40′N., long. 133°10′W., the latter ca. 685 miles west of Piedras Blancas, San Luis Obispo County, California; Moffitt, 1938, Auk, 55, pp. 255–256); however, no specimens have been taken within 200 miles of either the Hawaiian Islands or North American continent.

Sight record.—Davidson Seamount, lat. 35°44′N., long. 122°43′W., ca. 65 miles southwest of Point Sur, Monterey County, California, 17 November 1979, G. McCaskie, J. Dunn and R. Stallcup (Am. Birds, 34:200, 1980).

Notes.—The specimens mentioned above were reported as *P. leucoptera masafuerae* Lönnberg, 1921, presently regarded as a synonym of *P. longirostris*; other reports of *P. leucoptera* in North American waters pertain also to *P. longirostris.*

Oceanites gracilis (Elliot). WHITE-VENTED STORM-PETREL.

Thalassidroma gracilis Elliot, 1859, Ibis, p. 391. (West Coast of America = coast of Chile.)

Habitat & Distribution.—*Breeding* grounds unknown; *ranges* regularly to the Galapagos Islands, and along the Pacific coast of South America from Colombia to Chile.

Sight records.—"Gulf of Panama" and at Humboldt Bay, just south of the Darién border (in Colombia), September 1937, R. Murphy (Wetmore, 1965, Smithson. Misc. Collect., 150 (1), p. 45).

Phalacrocorax bougainvillii (Lesson). GUANAY CORMORANT.

Carbo Bougainvillii Lesson, 1837, *in* Bougainville, J. Navig. Thétis Espérance, 2, p. 331. (Valparaíso, Chile.)

Habitat & Distribution.—*Breeds* on islands off the coast of Peru, central Chile and southern Argentina, and *ranges* north to Colombia and Ecuador.

Sight record.—Panama, off Ensenada de Guayabo Chiquito, southern Darién, 21 May 1941, R. C. Murphy, flock of 100 individuals plus specimens obtained just to the south off Colombia in March and April 1941 (Ridgely, 1976, Birds Panama, p. 39). The reported introduction of this species in 1953 on Isla San Gerónimo, Baja California (see A.O.U., 1957, Check-list N. Am. Birds, ed. 5, p. 34), is erroneous.

Tringa ocrophus Linnaeus. GREEN SANDPIPER.

Tringa Ocrophus Linnaeus, 1758, Syst. Nat., ed. 10, 1, p. 149. (in Europa = Sweden.)

Habitat & Distribution.—*Breeds* in forested regions along brooks and pools in the Palearctic, and *winters* in marshes and flooded areas south to equatorial Africa, southeast Asia and the Philippines.

Sight records.—Alaska, Attu in the western Aleutians, 13 June 1978 and 22 May 1979 (King *et al.,* 1980, Am. Birds, 34, pp. 319–321). Two Canadian records from Hudson Bay (Swainson and Richardson, 1831) and Nova Scotia (Brewer, 1878) are regarded as unsatisfactory (see Godfrey, 1966, Birds Can., p. 146).

Larus cirrocephalus Vieillot. GRAY-HOODED GULL.

Larus cirrocephalus Vieillot, 1818, Nouv. Dict. Hist. Nat., nouv. éd., 21, p. 502. (Brazil = Rio de Janeiro.)

Habitat & Distribution.—*Breeds* on bays, estuaries and lagoons along the Pacific coast of Ecuador and Peru, the Atlantic coast of South America from southern Brazil to central Argentina, and in tropical and southern Africa, and *winters* in coastal areas and on inland lakes near the breeding areas, occasionally north along the coasts of South America and Africa.

Sight record.—Panama, Panama Bay at Panama City, 25 September 1955, M. Moynihan, one adult (Ridgely, 1976, Birds Panama, p. 111).

Larus crassirostris Vieillot. BLACK-TAILED GULL.

Larus crassirostris Vieillot, 1818, Nouv. Dict. Hist. Nat., nouv. éd., 21, p. 508. (Nagasaki, Japan.)

Habitat & Distribution.—*Breeds* on small, rocky, coastal islands from southern Sakhalin, Ussuriland and the Kurile Islands south through Japan to eastern China and Korea, and *winters* along coasts from Japan and Korea south to eastern China, Formosa and the Ryukyu Islands.

Sight record.—Alaska, Attu in the Aleutians, 29 May 1980 (Am. Birds, 34:806–807, 1980). An individual present in San Diego Bay, California, 16–18 November 1954, and collected (Monroe, 1955, Auk, 72, p. 208) is believed to have been a man-assisted vagrant.

Creagrus furcatus (Néboux). SWALLOW-TAILED GULL.

> *Larus furcatus* Néboux, 1846, Voy. Venus, Atlas, Zool., Ois., pl. 10. (rade de Monterey, Haute-Californie, error = Galapagos Islands.)

Habitat & Distribution.—*Resident* in the Galapagos Islands, *ranging* off South America from Colombia to Chile. The type locality of Monterey, California, is regarded as an error.

Sight record.—Panama, northwest of Piñas Bay, Darién, 18 July 1957, one individual (Robins, 1958, Condor, 60, p. 302).

Columba goodsoni Hartert. DUSKY PIGEON.

> *Columba goodsoni* Hartert, 1902, Bull. Br. Ornithol. Club, 12, p. 42. (S[an]. Javier, Pambilar and Carondelet, n.w. Ecuador = Pambilar, Ecuador.)

Habitat & Distribution.—*Resident* in humid lowland forest in western Colombia and western Ecuador.

Sight record.—Panama (upper Tuira valley, Darién, 7 March 1981, two individuals, R. Ridgely, V. Emanuel *et al.*).

Coccyzus pumilus Strickland. DWARF CUCKOO.

> *Coccyzus pumilus* Strickland, 1853, *in* Jardine, Contrib. Ornithol. (1852), p. 28, pl. 82. (Trinidad, error = Venezuela.)

Habitat & Distribution.—*Resident* in open woodland, forest edge and savanna in northern Colombia and northern Venezuela (including Margarita Island).

Sight record.—Panama (Tocumen, eastern Panamá province, 9 January 1979, V. Emanuel, D. Wolf *et al.*; Ridgely, 1981, Birds Panama, rev. ed., p. 366).

Coccyzus lansbergi Bonaparte. GRAY-CAPPED CUCKOO.

> *Coccyzus lansbergi* Bonaparte, 1850, Consp. Gen. Avium, 1 (1), p. 112. (Sta. Fé de Bogotá [Colombia].)

Habitat & Distribution.—*Resident* in open woodland, scrub, and dense brushy undergrowth in northern Colombia and northern Venezuela, migrating, at least in part, south to western Peru. This species was listed from Panama initially by Shelley (1891, Cat. Birds Br. Mus., 19, p. 303), but it seems clear from the comments of Wetmore (1968, Smithson. Misc. Collect., 150 (2), pp. 115–116) that there are no definite records from Panama prior to 1980.

Sight record.—Panama (Tocumen, eastern Panamá province, 10 February 1980, V. Emanuel and M. Braun; Ridgely, 1981, Birds Panama, rev. ed., p. 366).

Anthracothorax viridigula (Boddaert). GREEN-THROATED MANGO.

> *Trochilus viridigula* Boddaert, 1783, Table Planches Enlum., p. 41. Based on Daubenton, Planches Enlum., pl. 671, fig. 1. (Cayenne.)

Habitat & Distribution.—*Resident* in open country, second growth and scrub from eastern Venezuela (also Trinidad) and the Guianas south to northeastern Brazil.

Sight record.—Lesser Antilles, Union Island in the Grenadines, immature individual, A. Clark (Bond, 1956, Birds West Indies, ed. 4, p. 91, footnote).

Chrysolampis mosquitus (Linnaeus). RUBY-TOPAZ HUMMINGBIRD.

Trochilus Mosquitus Linnaeus, 1758, Syst. Nat., ed. 10, 1, p. 120. Based on *Trochilus rectricibus æqualibus ferrugineis* Linnaeus, Mus. Adolphi Friderici, 2, p. . . . (in Indiis, error = Surinam.)

Habitat & Distribution.—*Resident* in open woodland, scrub, second growth and savanna from Colombia, Venezuela (also islands from the Netherlands Antilles east to Tobago and Trinidad) and the Guianas south to central Brazil. An old report from southwestern Costa Rica (San Pedro) is erroneous.

Sight record.—Lesser Antilles, Grenada, 7–8 September 1962 (Groome, 1970, Nat. Hist. Grenada, p. 45).

Machetornis rixosus (Vieillot). CATTLE TYRANT.

Tyrannus rixosus Vieillot, 1819, Nouv. Dict. Hist. Nat., nouv. éd., 35, p. 85. Based on "Suiriri" Azara, Apunt. Hist. Nat. Páx. Parag., 2, p. 148 (no. 197). (Paraguay.)

Habitat & Distribution.—*Resident* in brushy savanna, open fields, scrub and cultivated lands in northern and eastern Colombia and northern Venezuela, and from Bolivia, Paraguay and central Brazil south to northern Argentina and Uruguay, with the southernmost populations migratory northward in winter.

Sight record.—Panama (Cana, Darién, 18 June 1981, P. Scharf and G. Vaucher).

Sporophila lineola (Linnaeus). LINED SEEDEATER.

Loxia Lineola Linnaeus, 1758, Syst. Nat., ed. 10, 1, p. 174. (in Asia, error = Surinam.)

Habitat & Distribution.—*Resident* in open woodland, second growth, savanna and grassy fields in South America from northern and eastern Colombia, Venezuela (also Tobago and Trinidad) and the Guianas south, east of the Andes, to eastern Peru, eastern Bolivia, northern Argentina, Paraguay, and central and southeastern Brazil.

Sight record.—Panama (Yaviza, Darién, 30 April 1979, two pairs, J. Pujals; Ridgely, 1981, Birds Panama, rev. ed., p. 367).

Notes.—The morphologically distinct populations from Tobago and Trinidad are often regarded as a distinct species, *S. bouvronides* (Lesson, 1831) [LESSON'S SEEDEATER], since similar birds appear elsewhere through the range of *S. lineola* (see Schwartz, 1975, Ann. Carnegie Mus., 45, pp. 277–285); should *S. bouvronides* be recognized as a species, it will include the Panama report.

APPENDIX B

Appendix B is the "Hypothetical List" of previous editions (excluding hybrids and forms of doubtful status). Included in this appendix are all species appearing in the fifth edition (or published subsequently) that are not now accepted in the main text for any of the following reasons:

1. The data on which the record is based are either demonstrably erroneous or in all probability erroneous and cannot now be verified, or have been rejected by regional committees evaluating such data.

2. Occurrence in the Check-list area is probably through escape from captivity or through human agency other than intentional introduction, and establishment (according to presently accepted criteria) is not verified although breeding may have been reported.

3. Inclusion in previous editions was based exclusively on records from Greenland, which is outside the area covered by the sixth edition.

Diomedea chrysostoma Forster. GRAY-HEADED ALBATROSS.

> *Diomedea chrysostoma* J. R. Forster, 1785, Mém. Math. Phys. Acad. Sci. Paris, 10, p. 571, pl. 14. (voisinage du cercle polaire antarctique & dans l'Ocean Pacifique = Isla de los Estados, off Tierra del Fuego.)

A southern ocean species, this albatross breeds on islands off Cape Horn, in the South Atlantic, in the southern Indian Ocean and off New Zealand. The records from Oregon (mouth of the Columbia River), California (coast near Golden Gate) and Panama (Bay of Chiriquí) are deemed unsatisfactory (see A.O.U., 1957, Check-list N. Am. Birds, ed. 5, p. 643, and Wetmore, 1965, Smithson. Misc. Collect., 150 (1), pp. 32–33).

Phoebetria palpebrata (Forster). LIGHT-MANTLED ALBATROSS.

> *Diomedea palpebrata* J. R. Forster, 1785, Mém. Math. Phys. Acad. Sci. Paris, 10, p. 571, pl. 15. (depuis le degré quarante-septième de latitude austral jusqu'au soixante-onzième & dix minutes = south of Prince Edward and Marion islands.)

This species, also known as LIGHT-MANTLED SOOTY-ALBATROSS, breeds on subantarctic islands and ranges in southern oceans. A specimen taken by Townsend near the "mouth of the Columbia River, Oregon" is the only report for northern waters; the locality has been regarded as erroneous (A.O.U., 1957, Check-list N. Am. Birds, ed. 5, p. 644).

Procellaria cinerea Gmelin. GRAY PETREL.

> *Procellaria cinerea* Gmelin, 1789, Syst. Nat., 1 (2), p. 563. Based on the "Cinereous Fulmar" Latham, Gen. Synop. Birds, 3 (2), p. 405. (intra circulum Antarcticum = Antarctic seas, lat. 48°S.)

This species, also known as BLACK-TAILED SHEARWATER and frequently placed in the genus *Adamastor,* breeds on islands in the South Pacific, South Atlantic and southern Indian oceans, ranging at sea throughout all southern oceans between lat. 25° and 55°S. A report from California (off Monterey, specimen prior to 1853) is inadequately substantiated.

Fregetta grallaria (Vieillot). WHITE-BELLIED STORM-PETREL.

> *Procellaria grallaria* Vieillot, 1818, Nouv. Dict. Hist. Nat., nouv. éd., 25 (1817), p. 418. (Nouvelle-Hollande = New South Wales, Australia.)

Lawrence (1851, Ann. Lyc. Nat. Hist. N.Y., 5, pp. 117–119) reported the capture of seven individuals in the harbor of St. Marks, Florida; one specimen was preserved and given to the Academy of Natural Sciences at Philadelphia, but its present whereabouts are unknown. The report has been listed under *F. tropica* (Gould, 1844) [BLACK-BELLIED STORM-PETREL] (see A.O.U., 1957, Check-list N. Am. Birds, ed. 5, pp. 25–26) as well as *F. grallaria* (see Palmer, 1962, Handb. N. Am. Birds, 1, pp. 251–254). Since there is confusion as to which of these two southern pelagic species the report pertains, with the one specimen apparently no longer extant, it seems best to consider the record as hypothetical.

Oceanodroma hornbyi (Gray). RINGED STORM-PETREL.

> *Thalassidroma Hornbyi* G. R. Gray, 1854, Proc. Zool. Soc. London (1853), p. 62. (north-west coast of America, error = west coast of South America.)

The type locality originally given for this species, normally found off the Pacific coast of South America from Ecuador to Chile, is deemed in error (see A.O.U., 1957, Check-list N. Am. Birds, ed. 5, p. 644).

Spheniscus mendiculus Sundevall. GALAPAGOS PENGUIN.

> *Spheniscus mendiculus* Sundevall, 1871, Proc. Zool. Soc. London, pp. 126, 129. (Galapagos Islands.)

An immature of this Galapagos endemic was captured alive at Puerto Armuelles, Chiriquí, Panama, in February 1955 (Eisenmann, 1956, Condor, 58, pp. 74–75); since it is unlikely, although not beyond the realm of possibility, that this individual reached Panamanian waters on its own, the occurrence is regarded as a probable result of transport and release by man.

†Phalacrocorax perspicillatus Pallas. PALLAS' CORMORANT.

> *Phalacrocorax perspicillatus* Pallas, 1811, Zoogr. Rosso-Asiat., 2, p. 305. (in Beringii = Bering Island.)

North American records of this species, known only from Bering Island in the Commander Islands and extinct since 1852, are unsatisfactory.

Phalacrocorax gaimardi (Lesson and Garnot). RED-LEGGED CORMORANT.

> *Carbo Gaimardi* Lesson and Garnot, 1828, *in* Duperrey, Voy. Coquille, Zool., Atlas, 1, livr. 7, pl. 48; 1830, livr. 14, p. 601. (Lima, au Pérou = San Lorenzo Island, roadstead of Lima, Peru.)

There is a sight record of this species for Texas (Galveston, 28 December 1946; Oberholser, 1974, Bird Life Texas, 1, p. 94); even if the sighting had been verified through a specimen or photograph, the occurrence of this southern South American species in Texas would have to be the result of an escape from captivity.

Egretta intermedia (Wagler). INTERMEDIATE EGRET.

Ardea intermedia Wagler, 1829, Isis von Oken, col. 659. (Java.)

The specimen of this Old World species, also known as the YELLOW-BILLED or LESSER EGRET, reportedly taken at Vancouver, British Columbia, may actually have been obtained elsewhere, and the species is considered hypothetical for the Americas.

Platalea leucorodia Linnaeus. WHITE SPOONBILL.

Platalea Leucorodia Linnaeus, 1758, Syst. Nat., ed. 10, 1, p. 139. (in Europa = Sweden.)

This widespread Old World species, sometimes called the EUROPEAN SPOONBILL or, in Old World literature, the SPOONBILL, has been included in previous checklists on the basis of several accidental records from Greenland.

Anser anser (Linnaeus). GRAYLAG GOOSE.

Anas Anser Linnaeus, 1758, Syst. Nat., ed. 10, 1, p. 123. Based on "The Laughing-Goose" Edwards, Nat. Hist. Birds, 3, p. 153, pl. 153. (in Europa & America maxime boreali = Sweden.)

An individual of this widespread Eurasian species captured alive on the Housatonic River near Lenox, Massachusetts, 2 December 1932, was considered later to be a domestic bird (Snyder, 1957, Auk, 74, p. 394). More recent sight records, mostly in the eastern United States, are thought also to pertain to escapes from captivity.

Anser indicus Latham. BAR-HEADED GOOSE.

Anser indica Latham, 1790, Index Ornithol., 2, p. 839. (in India; hyeme gregaria; e Thibeto = India in winter, and Tibet.)

Although the wandering of this central Asiatic species to North America is not beyond the realm of possibility, the individual reported from Oregon (Lower Klamath, 18 March 1959, photograph; Scott, 1959, Audubon Field Notes, 13, p. 311) is almost certainly an escape from captivity.

Branta ruficollis (Pallas). RED-BREASTED GOOSE.

Anser ruficollis Pallas, 1769, Spic. Zool., 1, fasc. 6, p. 21, pl. 4. (lower Ob, southern Russia.)

This western Siberian species has been recorded in North America between September and April from California (six reports, 1890's to 1969), Maine (1962) and Texas (1969–1970). It is widely kept by aviculturists, and these records probably pertain to escaped individuals.

Tadorna ferruginea (Pallas). RUDDY SHELDUCK.

Anas ferruginea Pallas, 1764, *in* Vroeg, Cat. Raissoné Ois., Adumbr., p. 5. (No locality given = Tartary.)

This Eurasian species has been recorded casually as a stray in western Greenland. Reports from California, and in eastern North America from Iowa, Ohio, Quebec and Rhode Island south to Kentucky and New Jersey, most likely pertain to escapes from captivity; a record from North Carolina (Waterlily, 1886) is regarded as erroneous.

Tadorna tadorna (Linnaeus). COMMON SHELDUCK.

> *Anas Tadorna* Linnaeus, 1758, Syst. Nat., ed. 10, 1, p. 122. (in Europæ maritimis = Sweden.)

This Eurasian species, known in Old World literature as the SHELDUCK and kept widely in captivity, has been recorded from Massachusetts (Ipswich Bay, 1921) and Delaware (Bombay Hook, 1970–1976), mostly likely escaped individuals; in addition, several other reports of birds definitely known to have escaped have appeared in the literature.

Netta rufina (Pallas). RED-CRESTED POCHARD.

> *Anas rufina* Pallas, 1773, Reise Versch. Prov. Russ. Reichs, 2, p. 713. (in Mari Caspio lacubusque vastissimis deserti Tatarici = Caspian Sea.)

The report of a specimen of this Eurasian species from Long Island Sound (1881) is unsatisfactory; the specimen cannot be located. Sight reports of individuals in eastern North America pertain to individuals escaped from captivity.

Aythya baeri (Radde). BAER'S POCHARD.

> *Anas* (*Fuligula*) *Baeri* Radde, 1863, Reisen Sud. Ost-Sib., 2, p. 376, pl. 15. (in der oberen Salbatsche-Ebene auf dem rechten Amurufer = upper Salbatch Plains, middle Amur River, eastern Siberia.)

This species has been included in the North American avifauna on the basis of two specimens (one still extant) reportedly taken about 1841 by Titian Peale in "Oregon" (= southern British Columbia to Oregon; see Friedmann, 1949, Condor, 51, pp. 43–44). Although the extant specimen is apparently *baeri* (there has been some question as it is not typically plumaged), it is unlikely that this central Asiatic species would wander to the American coast; the possibility of an error in location is substantial. It seems best to consider the species as hypothetical for North America.

Accipiter nisus (Linnaeus). EURASIAN SPARROWHAWK.

> *Falco Nisus* Linnaeus, 1758, Syst. Nat., ed. 10, 1, p. 92. (in Europa = Sweden.)

An immature female of this species, also known as the EUROPEAN or NORTHERN SPARROWHAWK and, in Old World literature, the SPARROW HAWK, was reported from New Jersey (Cape May, 24 October 1978; N. J. Audubon Suppl., 5:11, 1979); the individual photographed is not identifiable as this Old World species, and the record is regarded as hypothetical.

Falco subbuteo Linnaeus. NORTHERN HOBBY.

> *Falco Subbuteo* Linnaeus, 1758, Syst. Nat., ed. 10, 1, p. 89. (in Europa = Sweden.)

A report of an individual of this widespread Eurasian species, known in Old World literature as the HOBBY, from Cordova, Alaska, on 19 September 1977 (Roberson, 1980, Rare Birds W. Coast, p. 481) and deemed "possibly correct" is regarded as unsatisfactory.

Rallus aquaticus Linnaeus. WATER RAIL.

Rallus aquaticus Linnaeus, 1758, Syst. Nat., ed. 10, 1, p. 153. (in Europa = Great Britain.)

This Eurasian species was included in former check-lists on the basis of several stragglers taken in Greenland. There are no known reports from the area treated in the present volume.

Hoploxypterus cayanus (Latham). PIED LAPWING.

Charadrius cayanus Latham, 1790, Index Ornithol., 2, p. 749. Based mainly on "Le Pluvier armé de Cayenne" Buffon, Hist. Nat. Ois., 8, p. 102. (in Cayana = Cayenne.)

The report of this South American species from Honduras, based on a reputed specimen from the "Aloor River" [= Río Ulúa] region (1855–1856), is regarded as unsatisfactory (see Monroe, 1968, A.O.U. Ornithol. Monogr., no. 7, pp. 109–110).

Charadrius veredus Gould. ORIENTAL PLOVER.

Charadrius veredus Gould, 1848, Proc. Zool. Soc. London, p. 38. (Northern Australia.)

This Asiatic species has been reported as a vagrant in Greenland (A.O.U., 1957, Check-list N. Am. Birds, ed. 5, pp. 165–166, footnote, as *C. asiaticus veredus*); there are no North American records.

Haematopus ostralegus Linnaeus. EURASIAN OYSTERCATCHER.

Hæmatopus Ostralegus Linnaeus, 1758, Syst. Nat., ed. 10, 1, p. 152. (in Europæ, Americæ septentrionalis littoribus marinis = Öland Island, Sweden.)

This Old World species, known also as EUROPEAN OYSTERCATCHER and, in Old World literature, as the OYSTERCATCHER, has been included in former check-lists because of records of stragglers in Greenland.

Tringa totanus (Linnaeus). COMMON REDSHANK.

Scolopax Totanus Linnaeus, 1758, Syst. Nat., ed. 10, 1, p. 145. (in Europa = Sweden.)

This species, known in Old World literature as the REDSHANK, breeds in the Palearctic and winters south to southern Africa and the East Indies; it was included in the 5th edition on the basis of a record for Greenland. A sight report from Nova Scotia (Halifax, within a week of 3 January 1960; Audubon Field Notes, 14:82, 1960) is more likely based on *T. erythropus*; another report from Copano Bay, Texas, originally listed as *T. totanus,* definitely pertains to *T. erythropus* (see Oberholser, 1974, Bird Life Texas, 1, pp. 343–344).

Gallinago media (Latham). GREAT SNIPE.

> *Scolopax Media* Latham, 1787, Gen. Synop. Birds, suppl., 1, p. 292. (Lancashire, England.)

This Eurasian species, which winters in Africa, was supposedly photographed in New Jersey (Cape May, 7 September 1963; Audubon Field Notes, 18:21, 1964), but the report has not been verified.

Catharacta chilensis (Bonaparte). CHILEAN SKUA.

> *Stercorarius antarcticus* b. *chilensis* Bonaparte, 1856, Consp. Gen. Avium, 2 (1857), p. 207. (ex Am[erica]. m[eridionale]. = Chile.)

Reports of this South American form in Pacific waters off the coast of North America pertain to *C. maccormicki* (see Devillers, 1977, Auk, 94, pp. 417–429).

Sterna sumatrana Raffles. BLACK-NAPED TERN.

> *Sterna Sumatrana* Raffles, 1822, Trans. Linn. Soc. London, 13 (2), p. 329. (Sumatra.)

This tern ranges throughout much of the Indian Ocean, and in the Pacific from southeastern China and the Ryukyu, Caroline, Gilbert and Phoenix islands south to Australia, New Caledonia and the Loyalty Islands. Old reports from the Hawaiian Islands (Kauai, Hawaii) are erroneous (based on specimens of *S. hirundo*), although pre-recent or subfossil bones have been reported from Hawaii.

Sterna trudeaui Audubon. TRUDEAU'S TERN.

> *Sterna Trudeaui* Audubon, 1838, Birds Am. (folio), 4, pl. 409, fig. 2 (1839, Ornithol. Biogr., 5, p. 125). (Great Egg Harbor, New Jersey.)

This species, known also as SNOWY-CROWNED TERN, breeds in marshes in Chile (province of Cúrico) and Argentina (Santa Fé, Entre Ríos and Buenos Aires provinces) and winters along the coast of Chile and Peru. The type was supposedly taken by Audubon at Great Egg Harbor, New Jersey; the natural occurrence of this species in North America is highly questionable.

Chlidonias hybridus (Pallas). WHISKERED TERN.

> *Sterna hybrida* Pallas, 1811, Zoogr. Rosso-Asiat., 2, p. 338. (circa Jaïcum seu Rhymnum, australem Volgam et ad Sarpae lacus = Southern Volga and Sarpa Lake, southeastern Russia.)

A specimen of this Old World species, known also as MARSH TERN, in the British Museum that is labelled "Barbados" is generally regarded as of doubtful origin (see Hellmayr and Conover, 1948, Field Mus. Nat. Hist. Publ., Zool. Ser., 13 (1), no. 3, p. 292, footnote).

Cepphus carbo Pallas. SPECTACLED GUILLEMOT.

> *Cepphus carbo* Pallas, 1811, Zoogr. Rosso-Asiat., 2, p. 350. (circa insulas Aleuticas, error = Kurile Islands.)

The type locality of this Asiatic species, known also as Sooty Guillemot, is regarded as erroneous; there is no evidence for its occurrence in North American waters.

Nandayus nenday (Vieillot). Black-hooded Parakeet.

> *Psittacus nenday* Vieillot, 1823, in Bonnaterre and Vieillot, Tabl. Encycl. Méth., Ornithol., 3, livr. 93, p. 1400. (Paraguay.)

This southern South American species, known also as Nanday Parakeet or Conure, is widely reported in the United States and Puerto Rico as an escape. There have been several reports of breeding (especially in southern California), and a small population has apparently become established in recent years at Coney Island, Brooklyn, New York.

Forpus xanthopterygius (Spix). Blue-winged Parrotlet.

> *Psittacula xanthopterygius* Spix, 1824, Avium Spec. Nov. Bras., 1, p. 42, pl. 31. (Amazon Basin.)

This South American species has been doubtfully recorded from Panama [as *F. passerinus spengeli* (Hartlaub, 1885)].

Amazona amazonica (Linnaeus). Orange-winged Parrot.

> *Psittacus amazonicus* Linnaeus, 1766, Syst. Nat., ed. 12, 1, p. 147. Based mainly on "Le Perroquet Amazone" Brisson, Ornithologie, 4, p. 256. (in Surinamo = Surinam.)

Small numbers of this recently introduced South American species are now resident and apparently breeding in Puerto Rico (San Juan area); it likely will meet criteria for establishment within the next few years.

Aerodramus vanikorensis (Quoy and Gaimard). Gray Swiftlet.

> *Hirundo vanikorensis* Quoy and Gaimard, 1830, Voy. Astrolabe, Zool., 1, p. 206; Atlas, Ois., pl. 12, fig. 3. (Island and Vanikoro.)

This species, known also (along with related species) as Cave, Uniform or Mossy-nest Swiftlet, ranges from Guam, the Palau Islands and Celebes south to New Guinea, northeastern Australia (Queensland) and the Solomon Islands, and has been introduced in the Hawaiian Islands (on Oahu, from the Guam population in 1962 and 1965), with breeding confirmed in 1978. However, establishment of a stable population is not yet certain, and the identity of the swiftlet now present has not been definitely ascertained. Relationships among species within the genus are uncertain; the Guam (and presumably Hawaiian) form has sometimes been treated as a race of *C. inexpectata* Hume, 1873, a group now generally considered conspecific with *C. fuciphaga* (Thunberg, 1912), which occurs in southeast Asia, the Andaman and Nicobar Islands, Philippines and Greater Sunda Islands.

Amazilia chionopectus (Gould). White-chested Emerald.

> *Thaumatias chionopectus* Gould, 1859, Monogr. Trochil., pt. 18, pl. [8] and text. (Trinidad).

Four specimens of this South American species in the Museum of Comparative Zoology are labeled "Grenada W. I. Peter Gellineau"; since these are of a typical Trinidad "trade skin" make, they are regarded as mislabeled (Ridgway, 1911, Bull. U.S. Natl. Mus., no. 50 (5), p. 431, footnote).

Amazilia tobaci (Gmelin). COPPER-RUMPED HUMMINGBIRD.

> *Trochilus Tobaci* Gmelin, 1788, Syst. Nat., 1 (1), p. 498. Based on the "Tobago Humming-bird" Latham, Gen. Synop. Birds, 1 (2), p. 781. (in insula Tobago.)

This species is known primarily from Tobago, Trinidad and Venezuela. Specimens in the Boucard collection, labeled "Grenada", may have been taken on Tobago (Bond, 1956, Birds W. Indies, ed. 4, p. 91, footnote), and the occurrence of the species in the Lesser Antilles is regarded as doubtful.

Ramphastos brevis Meyer de Schauensee. CHOCO TOUCAN.

> *Ramphastos ambiguus brevis* Meyer de Schauensee, 1945, Proc. Acad. Nat. Sci. Philadelphia, 97, p. 14. (Rio Mechengue (2500 ft.), Cauca, western Colombia.)

This species, distributed along the Pacific lowlands of western Colombia and western Ecuador, was attributed to eastern Panama (as *Ramphastos ambiguus*) by Ridgway (1914, Bull. U.S. Natl. Mus., no. 50 (6), p. 339) on the basis of a specimen in the Museum of Comparative Zoology reported from Loma del León (eastern Darién); Wetmore (1968, Smithson. Misc. Collect., 150 (2), p. 526) and subsequent authors regard the locality as uncertain.

Celeus immaculatus Berlepsch. IMMACULATE WOODPECKER.

> *Celeus immaculatus* Berlepsch, 1880, Ibis, p. 113. (Agua dulce, Panama.)

Both the identity and source of the unique type specimen of *C. immaculatus* have been questioned. The type locality was based on the "make" of the type specimen, a trade skin of uncertain origin. The relationship of *C. immaculatus* appears to be with the South American *C. elegans* or possibly with *C. castaneus*; regardless of the final disposition of this form, the uncertainty of the origin warrants relegation to hypothetical status.

Thamnophilus multistriatus Lafresnaye. BAR-CRESTED ANTSHRIKE.

> *Thamnophilus multistriatus* Lafresnaye, 1844, Rev. Zool. [Paris], 7, p. 82. (Colombie = Bogotá, Colombia.)

This species, known from the northern Andes in extreme western Venezuela and Colombia, was recorded by Sclater (1890, Cat. Birds Br. Mus., 15, p. 211) from Panama; there is apparently no basis for this listing, and the report is regarded as erroneous.

Urocissa erythrorhyncha (Boddaert). RED-BILLED BLUE-MAGPIE.

> *Corvus erythrorynchus* [sic] Boddaert, 1783, Table Planches Enlum., p. 38. Based on the "Geay de la Chine a bec rouge" Daubenton, Planches Enlum., pl. 622. (China = Canton, China.)

This widespread species of southeast Asia became established in the mid-1960's in the Hawaiian Islands (in the Kahaluu Valley on Oahu) through escaped individuals, but apparently has now been extirpated; also introduced in Puerto Rico, but no population has become established.

Corvus frugilegus Linnaeus. EURASIAN ROOK.

Corvus frugilegus Linnaeus, 1758, Syst. Nat., ed. 10, 1, p. 105. (in Europa = Sweden.)

An Old World species, generally called the ROOK, this corvid had been included in earlier check-lists on the basis of a record from southeastern Greenland.

Corvus corone Linnaeus. CARRION CROW.

Corvus Corone Linnaeus, 1758, Syst. Nat., ed. 10, 1, p. 105. (in Europa = England.)

The distinct form of this Eurasian species occurring in Eire, Scotland, and from eastern Europe eastward, formerly treated as a separate species, *C. cornix* Linnaeus, 1758 [HOODED CROW], has been included previously on the basis of a specimen from Greenland.

Phylloscopus trochilus (Linnaeus). WILLOW WARBLER.

Motacilla Trochilus Linnaeus, 1758, Syst. Nat., ed. 10, 1, p. 188. (in Europa = Sweden.)

A specimen, reported as this widespread Eurasian species (which has also straggled to Greenland), was taken at Barrow, Alaska, on 10 June 1952 (Pitelka, 1974, Arct. Alp. Res., 6, pp. 161–184); however, recent examination of the specimen indicates that it is an example of *P. borealis* (see Roberson, 1981, Rare Birds W. Coast, pp. 481–482).

Copsychus saularis (Linnaeus). MAGPIE ROBIN.

Gracula Saularis Linnaeus, 1758, Syst. Nat., ed. 10, 1, p. 109. Based mainly on the "Dialbird" Albin, Nat. Hist. Birds, 3, p. 17, pl. 17–18. (in Asia = Bengal.)

Various introductions of this species in the Hawaiian Islands (Kauai and Oahu) were made between 1922 and 1950, but there is no evidence of establishment; there have been no reliable reports since 1967.

Saxicola rubetra (Linnaeus). EUROPEAN WHINCHAT.

Motacilla Rubetra Linnaeus, 1758, Syst. Nat., ed. 10, 1, p. 186. (in Europa = Sweden.)

A sight report of this European species, known in Old World literature as the WHINCHAT, from Massachusetts (Lincoln, 22 October 1964; Am. Birds, 19:8, 1965) is considered unsatisfactory.

Saxicola torquata (Linnaeus). STONECHAT.

> *Motacilla torquata* Linnaeus, 1766, Syst. Nat., ed. 12, 1, p. 328. (Cape of Good Hope.)

A sight report of this widespread Old World species from Alaska (Gambell, St. Lawrence Island, 6 June 1978; Roberson, 1980, Rare Birds W. Coast, p. 481) is considered unsatisfactory.

Garrulax caerulatus (Hodgson). GRAY-SIDED LAUGHING-THRUSH.

> *Cinclosoma Caerulatus* Hodgson, 1836, Asiat. Res., 19, p. 147. (Nepal.)

Introduced in the Hawaiian Islands (Oahu), this laughing-thrush was frequently recorded during the 1940's and 1950's; a well-substantiated sighting in the same locality in 1978 (Taylor and Collins, 1979, Elepaio, 39, pp. 79–81) suggests that the species is established in small numbers on Oahu, but the specific identification of the recent report has not been verified.

Anthus pratensis (Linnaeus). MEADOW PIPIT.

> *Anthus pratensis* Linnaeus, 1758, Syst. Nat., ed. 10, 1, p. 166. (in Europæ pratis = Sweden.)

This Palearctic species breeds in Greenland and has been included in previous Check-lists on that basis.

Acridotheres javanicus Cabanis. WHITE-VENTED MYNA.

> *Acridotheres javanicus* Cabanis, 1850, Mus. Heineanum, 1 (1851), p. 205. (Java.)

A native of southeast Asia, this species has been introduced in recent years in Puerto Rico (Bayamón area); criteria for establishment will likely be met in the next few years.

Euphonia mesochrysa Salvadori. BRONZE-GREEN EUPHONIA.

> *Euphonia mesochrysa* Salvadori, 1873, Atti R. Accad. Sci. Torino, Cl. Sci. Fis. Math. Nat., 8, p. 193. (No locality given = Bogotá, Colombia.)

The locality "Honduras" on the label of a specimen in the Academy of Natural Sciences at Philadelphia is regarded as erroneous; the species ranges from Colombia to Peru and Bolivia.

Piranga rubriceps Gray. RED-HOODED TANAGER.

> *Pyranga rubriceps* G. R. Gray, 1844, Genera Birds, 2, p. 364, pl. 89, lower fig. (No locality given = Bogotá, Colombia.)

This South American species, also known as GRAY'S TANAGER, is native to western Colombia, Ecuador and northern Peru. A specimen taken about 1871 at Dos Pueblos [= Naples], Santa Barbara County, California, is regarded as a escaped cage bird.

Emberiza aureola Pallas. YELLOW-BREASTED BUNTING.

> *Emberiza Aureola* Pallas, 1773, Reise Versch. Prov. Russ. Reichs, 2, p. 711. (Irtysh River, south-central Siberia.)

A sight report of this Asian species from Alaska (Gambell, St. Lawrence Island, 26–27 June 1978; Roberson, 1980, Rare Birds W. Coast, p. 482) is regarded as unsatisfactory.

Icterus nigrogularis (Hahn). YELLOW ORIOLE.

> *Xanthornus nigrogularis* Hahn, 1819, Vögel Asien, Afr., etc., lief 5, pl. 1. (Jamaica, Mexico, and Cayenne = Brazil.)

There is an old specimen from the "Isthmus of Panama" of this South American species; the locality is regarded as questionable.

Carduelis spinus (Linnaeus). EURASIAN SISKIN.

> *Fringilla Spinus* Linnaeus, 1758, Syst. Nat., ed. 10, 1, p. 181. (in Europæ juniperetis = Sweden.)

Early introductions of this Eurasian species, known in Old World literature as the SISKIN, in Oregon and Ohio were unsuccessful. One individual was seen in Massachusetts (Cambridge, August 1904, W. Brewster; Forbush, 1929, Birds Mass., 3, p. 32) while another was trapped in Maine (Kittery, 24 March 1962; Borror, 1963, Auk, 80, p. 201) and subsequently preserved; these birds are considered to be escapes from captivity. A sight record from Alaska (Attu in the Aleutians, 4 June 1978; Roberson, 1980, Rare Birds W. Coast, p. 482) is considered unsatisfactory.

Carduelis magellanica (Vieillot). HOODED SISKIN.

> *Fringilla magellanica* Vieillot, 1805, Ois. Chant., pl. 30. (southern America and vicinity of Straits of Magellan, error = Buenos Aires, Argentina.)

A specimen of this widespread South American species taken at Henderson, Kentucky, was described and figured by Audubon (1838, Birds Am. (folio), 4, pl. 394, fig. 2; 1839, Ornithol. Biogr., 5, p. 46); it is regarded as an escape from captivity.

Carduelis chloris (Linnaeus). EUROPEAN GREENFINCH.

> *Loxia chloris* Linnaeus, 1758, Syst. Nat., ed. 10, 1, p. 174. (in Europa = Sweden.)

An individual of this European finch, known in Old World literature as the GREENFINCH, was present (and photographed) at St. John, New Brunswick, 31 March–3 April 1977 (Am. Birds, 31:977, 1977); although this sport may represent a natural vagrant, a pattern of such vagrancy in a popular cage-bird species should be demonstrated before the species is removed from hypothetical status.

Lagonosticta rubricata (Lichtenstein). AFRICAN FIRE-FINCH.

Fringilla rubricata Lichtenstein, 1823, Verz. Doubl. Zool. Mus. Berlin, p. 27. (terra Caffrorum = Uitenhage, Cape Province, Africa.)

Successful breeding of escaped pairs of this widespread African species was reported at Pacific Grove, Monterey County, California, in 1965 and 1966 (Am. Birds, 20:90, 598, 1966), but no population became established; it was also introduced in the 1960's in the Hawaiian Islands, where persisting into the mid-1970's, although it has since disappeared.

APPENDIX C

Appendix C contains forms of doubtful status or of hybrid origin that have been given a formal scientific name.

Lophortyx leucoprosopon Reichenow, 1895, Ornithol. Monatsber., 3, p. 11. (Origin unknown).

Known only from a living pair in a private aviary, believed to have been bought from a sailor arriving at Hamburg, Germany, this quail is generally regarded as a hybrid between *Callipepla douglasii* and *C. gambelii.*

Tringa cooperi Baird, 1858, *in* Baird, Cassin and Lawrence, Rep. Explor. Surv. R. R. Pac., 9, p. 716. (Long Island [New York].)

Known from the unique type specimen, taken in May 1833, the COOPER'S SANDPIPER, while certainly a representative of the present genus *Calidris,* remains in undetermined status (Ridgway, 1919, Bull. U.S. Natl. Mus., 50 (8), p. 289).

Larus nelsoni Henshaw, 1884, Auk, 1, p. 250. (St. Michael, Alaska.)

NELSON'S GULL [46] is regarded as a hybrid between *L. hyperboreus* and *L. argentatus* (Dwight, 1925, Bull. Am. Mus. Nat. Hist., 52, p. 249).

Amazilia Ocai Gould, 1859, Ann. Mag. Nat. Hist., ser. 3, 4, p. 96. (Jalapa, Vera Cruz.)

This unique hummingbird is regarded as a hybrid between *Amazilia cyanocephala* and *A. beryllina* (Berlioz, 1932, Ois. Rev. Fr. Ornithol., new ser., 2, p. 531).

Thaumatias lerdi d'Oca, 1875, La Naturaleza, 3, p. 24. (Paso del Mancho, Vera Cruz.)

Of uncertain identity, this form may also represent a hybrid between *Amazilia cyanocephala* and *A. beryllina.*

Saucerottia florenceae van Rossem and Hachisuka, 1938, Trans. San Diego Soc. Nat. Hist., 8, p. 408. (Rancho Santa Barbara, 5000 feet, 20 miles northeast of Guirocoba, Sonora.)

The unique type of FLORENCE'S HUMMINGBIRD is closest to *Amazilia beryllina* and is probably a hybrid between that species and some other unidentified one.

Cyanomyia salvini Brewster, 1893, Auk, 10, p. 214. (Nacosari, Sonora.)

This form, known as SALVIN'S HUMMINGBIRD, is regarded as a hybrid between *Amazilia violiceps* and *Cynanthus latirostris* (Griscom, 1934, Bull. Mus. Comp. Zool. Harv., 75, p. 378).

Amazilis [sic] *bangsi* Ridgway, 1910, Proc. Biol. Soc. Wash., 23, p. 54. (Volcán de Miravalles, Costa Rica.)

This hummingbird is regarded as a hybrid between *Amazilia rutila* and *A. tzacatl* (Bangs, 1930, Bull. Mus. Comp. Zool. Harv., 70, p. 218).

Trochilus violajugulum Jeffries, 1888, Auk, 5, p. 168. (Santa Barbara, California.)

This form is now regarded as a hybrid between *Archilochus alexandri* and *Calypte anna* (Banks and Johnson, 1961, Condor, 63, p. 10).

Phasmornis mystica Oberholser, 1974, Bird Life Texas, 2, p. 485. (Boot Spring, Chisos Mts., Texas.)

Described from the unique type (subsequently lost) as a new species (and genus), the CHISOS HUMMINGBIRD probably represents a hybrid (of unknown parentage) or an aberrant individual of *Archilochus alexandri*.

Selasphorus floresii Gould, 1861, Monogr. Trochil., pt. 23, pl. [10] and text. (Bolaños, Jalisco, México.)

This hummingbird is regarded as a hybrid between *S. sasin* and *Calypte anna.*

Regulus cuvieri Audubon, 1829, Birds Am. (folio), 1, pl. 55 (1831, Ornithol. Biogr., 1, p. 288). (Fatland Ford, about ten miles west of Norristown, Pennsylvania.)

CUVIER'S KINGLET is known only from Audubon's description and plate of a specimen (since lost) taken in June 1812 and of uncertain identity; the drawing may have been based partly on memory and thus be inaccurate.

Vireosylvia propinqua Baird, 1866, Rev. Am. Birds, 1, pp. 345, 348. (Cobán, Vera Paz, Guatemala.)

This form is regarded as a probable hybrid between *Vireo flavifrons* and *V. solitarius.*

Helminthophaga leucobronchialis Brewster, 1874, Am. Sportsman, 5 (3), p. 33. (Newtonville, Massachusetts.)

BREWSTER'S WARBLER is a hybrid form between *Vermivora pinus* and *V. chrysoptera,* displaying the face pattern of *V. pinus*. See also comments under *V. pinus* (page T3).

Helminthophaga Lawrencii Herrick, 1875, Proc. Acad. Nat. Sci. Philadelphia, 26 (1874), p. 220. (bank of the Passaic, near Chatham, New Jersey.)

LAWRENCE'S WARBLER is a hybrid form between *Vermivora pinus* and *V. chrysoptera,* displaying the face pattern of *V. chrysoptera*. See also comments under *V. pinus* (page T3).

Helminthophaga cincinnatiensis Langdon, 1880, J. Cincinnati Soc. Nat. Hist., 3, p. 119. (Madisonville, Hamilton Co., Ohio.)

The CINCINNATI WARBLER is regarded as a hybrid between *Vermivora pinus* and *Oporornis formosus* (Ridgway, 1880, Bull. Nuttall Ornithol. Club, 5, p. 237).

Dendroica potomac Haller, 1940, Cardinal, 5, p. 50. (Berkeley County, twelve miles south of Martinsburg, West Virginia.)

SUTTON'S WARBLER is generally regarded as a hybrid between *D. dominica* and *Parula americana.*

Sylvia carbonata Audubon, 1829, Birds Am. (folio), 1, pl. 60 (1831, Ornithol. Biogr., 1, p. 308). (Near Henderson, Kentucky.)

Audubon's description and plate of two specimens of the CARBONATED WARBLER taken in May 1811 (since lost) are not identifiable with any known species; the plates may have been based partly on memory.

Sylvia montana Wilson, 1812, Am. Ornithol., 5, p. 113, pl. 44, fig. 2. (Near the Blue Mountains, Virginia.)

The BLUE MOUNTAIN WARBLER is known only from the plates of Wilson and Audubon, and is not identifiable as any known species.

Muscicapa minuta (not Gmelin, 1789) Wilson, 1812, Am. Ornithol., 6, p. 62, pl. 50, fig. 5. (New Jersey.)
Sylvania microcephala Ridgway, 1885, Proc. U.S. Natl. Mus., 8, p. 354. New name for *Muscicapa minuta* Wilson, preoccupied.

This odd bird, called the SMALL-HEADED FLYCATCHER, is known only from the works of Wilson and Audubon whose specimens (since lost) came from New Jersey and Kentucky, respectively; it has generally been considered to be a paruline and has never been satisfactorily identified with any known species.

Emberiza townsendi Audubon, 1834, Ornithol. Biogr., 2, p. 183. (near New Garden, Chester County, Pennsylvania.)

TOWNSEND'S BUNTING is known only from the unique type, taken 11 May 1833 by John K. Townsend; it is generally treated in the genus *Spiza,* although its peculiarities cannot be accounted for by hybridism or apparently by individual variation.

Aegiothus (flavirostris var.) *Brewsterii* Ridgway, 1872, Am. Nat., 6, p. 434. (Waltham, Massachusetts.)

BREWSTER'S LINNET is known only from the type, taken 1 November 1870, which possibly is a hybrid between *Carduelis flammeus* and *C. pinus.*

APPENDIX D

Appendix D is a list of deliberately introduced species or escaped captives of which there are records but that are deemed not to have become established nor of sufficient importance to warrant treatment in Appendix B.

Rhynchotus rufescens (Temminck, 1815). RED-WINGED TINAMOU.
Nothoprocta ornata (Taczanowski, 1867). ORNATE TINAMOU.
Nothoprocta perdicaria (Kittlitz, 1830). CHILEAN TINAMOU.
Nothura darwinii Gray, 1867. DARWIN'S NOTHURA.
Nothura maculosa (Temminck, 1815). SPOTTED NOTHURA.
Eudromia elegans Geoffroy Saint-Hilaire, 1832. CRESTED TINAMOU.
Cygnus atratus (Latham, 1790). BLACK SWAN.
Cygnus melanocoryphus (Molina, 1782). BLACK-NECKED SWAN.
Anser cygnoides (Linnaeus, 1758). SWAN GOOSE.
Chenonetta jubata (Latham, 1801). MANED GOOSE.
Tetrao urogallus Linnaeus, 1758. COMMON CAPERCAILLIE.
Lyrurus tetrix (Linnaeus, 1758). EURASIAN BLACK-GROUSE.
Tetrastes bonasia (Linnaeus, 1758). HAZEL GROUSE.
Ammoperdix griseogularis (Brandt, 1843). SEE-SEE PARTRIDGE.
Tetraogallus himalayensis Gray, 1843. HIMALAYAN SNOWCOCK.
Alectoris graeca (Meisner, 1804). ROCK PARTRIDGE.
Alectoris rufa (Linnaeus, 1758). RED-LEGGED PARTRIDGE.
Alectoris barbara (Bonnaterre, 1790). BARBARY PARTRIDGE.
Francolinus pintadeanus (Scopoli, 1786). CHINESE FRANCOLIN.
Francolinus adspersus Waterhouse, 1838. RED-BILLED FRANCOLIN.
Francolinus icterorhynchus Heuglin, 1863. HEUGLIN'S FRANCOLIN.
Francolinus clappertoni Children, 1826. CLAPPERTON'S FRANCOLIN.
Francolinus leucoscepus (Gray, 1867). YELLOW-NECKED SPURFOWL.
Coturnix pectoralis Gould, 1837. STUBBLE QUAIL.
Coturnix chinensis (Linnaeus, 1766). BLUE-BREASTED QUAIL.
Rollulus rouloul (Scopoli, 1786). CRESTED WOOD-PARTRIDGE.
Bambusicola thoracica (Temminck, 1815). CHINESE BAMBOO-PARTRIDGE.
Gallus sonneratii Temminck, 1813. GRAY JUNGLEFOWL.
Lophura nycthemera (Linnaeus, 1758). SILVER PHEASANT.
Syrmaticus reevesii (Gray, 1829). REEVES' PLEASANT.
Syrmaticus soemmerringii (Temminck, 1830). COPPER PHEASANT.
Syrmaticus ellioti (Swinhoe, 1872). ELLIOT'S PHEASANT.
Chrysolophus pictus (Linnaeus, 1758). GOLDEN PHEASANT.
Chrysolophus amherstiae (Leadbeater, 1829). LADY AMHERST PHEASANT.
Turnix varia (Latham, 1801). PAINTED BUTTONQUAIL.
Porphyrio porphyrio (Linnaeus, 1758). PURPLE SWAMPHEN.
Larus novaehollandiae Stephens, 1826. SILVER GULL.
Syrrhaptes paradoxus (Pallas, 1773). PALLAS' SANDGROUSE.
Columba palumbus Linnaeus, 1758. WOOD PIGEON.
Columba corensis Jacquin, 1784. BARE-EYED PIGEON.
Geopelia cuneata (Latham 1801). DIAMOND DOVE.
Geopelia humeralis (Temminck, 1821). BAR-SHOULDERED DOVE.
Chalcophaps indica (Linnaeus, 1758). EMERALD DOVE.
Ocyphaps lophotes (Temminck, 1822). CRESTED PIGEON.
Phaps chalcoptera (Latham, 1790). COMMON BRONZEWING.

Petrophassa plumifera (Gould, 1842). SPINIFEX PIGEON.
Petrophassa smithii (Jardine and Selby, 1830). PARTRIDGE PIGEON.
Gallicolumba luzonica (Scopoli, 1786). BLEEDING-HEART PIGEON.
Leucosarcia melanoleuca (Latham, 1801). WONGA PIGEON.
Caloenas nicobarica (Linnaeus, 1758). NICOBAR PIGEON.
Trichoglossus haematod (Linnaeus, 1771). RAINBOW LORIKEET.
Eolophus roseicapillus (Vieillot, 1817). GALAH.
Cacatua sulphurea (Gmelin, 1788). LESSER SULPHUR-CRESTED COCKATOO.
Cacatua galerita (Latham, 1790). GREATER SULPHUR-CRESTED COCKATOO.
Cacatua moluccensis (Gmelin, 1788). SALMON-CRESTED COCKATOO.
Nymphicus hollandicus (Kerr, 1792). COCKATIEL.
Eclectus roratus (Müller, 1776). ECLECTUS PARROT.
Platycercus adscitus (Latham, 1790). PALE-HEADED ROSELLA.
Agapornis roseicollis (Vieillot, 1818). PEACH-FACED LOVEBIRD.
Agapornis fischeri Reichenow, 1887. FISCHER'S LOVEBIRD.
Agapornis personata Reichenow, 1887. MASKED LOVEBIRD.
Psittacula cyanocephala (Linnaeus, 1766). PLUM-HEADED PARAKEET.
Psittacula roseata Biswas, 1951. BLOSSOM-HEADED PARAKEET.
Psittacus erithacus Linnaeus, 1758. GRAY PARROT.
Pyrrhura melanura (Spix, 1824). MAROON-TAILED PARAKEET.
Pionus maximiliani (Kuhl, 1820). SCALY-HEADED PARROT.
Amazona aestiva (Linnaeus, 1758). TURQUOISE-FRONTED PARROT.
Melanocorypha mongolica (Pallas, 1776). MONGOLIAN LARK.
Lullula arborea (Linnaeus, 1758). WOOD LARK.
Cyanocorax chrysops (Vieillot, 1818). PLUSH-CRESTED JAY.
Grallina cyanoleuca (Latham, 1801). MAGPIE-LARK.
Parus major Linnaeus, 1758. GREAT TIT.
Parus caeruleus Linnaeus, 1758. BLUE TIT.
Sylvia atricapilla (Linnaeus, 1758). BLACKCAP.
Cyanoptila cyanomelana (Temminck, 1829). BLUE-AND-WHITE FLYCATCHER.
Rhipidura leucophrys (Latham, 1790). WILLIE-WAGTAIL.
Erithacus rubecula (Linnaeus, 1758). EUROPEAN ROBIN.
Luscinia akahige (Temminck, 1835). JAPANESE ROBIN.
Luscinia komadori (Temminck, 1835). RYUKYU ROBIN.
Luscinia megarhynchos Brehm, 1831. EUROPEAN NIGHTINGALE.
Turdus philomelos Brehm, 1831. SONG THRUSH.
Garrulax albogularis (Gould, 1836). WHITE-THROATED LAUGHING-THRUSH.
Garrulax leucolophus (Hardwicke, 1815). WHITE-CRESTED LAUGHING-THRUSH.
Garrulax monileger (Hodgson, 1836). LESSER NECKLACED LAUGHING-THRUSH.
Garrulax chinensis (Scopoli, 1786). BLACK-THROATED LAUGHING-THRUSH.
Cinclus cinclus (Linnaeus, 1758). EURASIAN DIPPER.
Prunella modularis (Linnaeus, 1758). DUNNOCK.
Irena puella (Latham, 1790). BLUE-MANTLED FAIRY-BLUEBIRD.
Sturnus nigricollis (Paykull, 1807). BLACK-COLLARED STARLING.
Emberiza citrinella Linnaeus, 1758. YELLOWHAMMER.
Gubernatrix cristata (Vieillot, 1817). YELLOW CARDINAL.
Paroaria dominicana (Linnaeus, 1758). RED-COWLED CARDINAL.
Paroaria gularis (Linnaeus, 1766). RED-CAPPED CARDINAL.
Sturnella loyca (Bonaparte, 1850) [= *Pezites militaris* (Linnaeus, 1771)]. GREATER
  RED-BREASTED MEADOWLARK.

Loxia pytyopsittacus Borkhausen, 1793. PARROT CROSSBILL.
Serinus leucopygius (Sundavell, 1850). WHITE-RUMPED SEEDEATER.
Carduelis cannabina (Linnaeus, 1758). EURASIAN LINNET.
Passer luteus (Lichtenstein, 1823). GOLDEN SPARROW.
Ploceus philippinus (Linnaeus, 1766). BAYA WEAVER.
Emblema guttata (Shaw, 1796). DIAMOND FIRETAIL.
Poephila guttata (Vieillot, 1817). ZEBRA FINCH.
Lagonosticta senegala (Linnaeus, 1766). RED-BILLED FIRE-FINCH.
Uraeginthus angolensis (Linnaeus, 1758). AFRICAN CORDONBLEU.
Uraeginthus cyanocephala (Richmond, 1897). BLUE-CAPPED CORDONBLEU.
Amandava formosa (Latham, 1790). GREEN AVADAVAT.
Amandava subflava (Vieillot, 1819). ZEBRA WAXBILL.
Lonchura nana (Pucheran, 1845). MADAGASCAR MANNIKIN.
Amandina fasciata (Gmelin, 1789). CUT-THROAT FINCH.
Vidua chalybeata (Müller, 1776). VILLAGE INDIGOBIRD.
Vidua paradisaea (Linnaeus, 1758). PARADISE WHYDAH.

A.O.U. NUMBERS

Following the policy of previous check-list editions, we have continued to provide A.O.U. numbers. Originally, the stimulus was to retain stability in the marking of egg sets in collections, but with the increased usage of computers, particularly by federal agencies involved with birds, there is added reason to provide such numbers.

Subsequent to the establishment of the original list in the first edition of the Check-list, radical changes in classification have resulted in the sequence losing much of its taxonomic usefulness; however, groups have tended to remain relatively intact, and it is the intent of the present edition to provide numbers in as taxonomically sound a way as is possible while retaining numbers already established.

Major policy changes in the sixth edition have also caused a change in application of numbers. It is not our intent to provide numbers for Middle American or West Indian birds, and, indeed, such a vast number of new forms would require an essentially new numbering system to accommodate all species. In addition, subspecies are not treated herein and thus will not be considered in the numbering system; in the past, letters were added after the A.O.U. species number (e.g., 581a, 581b, etc.) to indicate subspecies.

A.O.U. numbers are here provided for all species (and groups sometimes considered as species) in the United States and Canada, including the Hawaiian Islands; thus, Greenland, Baja California and Bermuda are removed from the area of consideration. Any number previously assigned by the A.O.U. will remain unchanged (unless two or more numbers now apply to a species, in which case one will be used and the other indicated as an equivalent in the List of A.O.U. Numbers). In the List, any number previously assigned a species not currently recognized as occurring in the United States or Canada will be so indicated. Species currently included in the main body of the Check-list are assigned numbers; species appearing in the Appendices will not be given numbers.

New numbers are added as in the past by providing an additional digit (e.g., 622.1, 622.2, etc.), selecting a number in the appropriate place based on our current classification and availability of a number. Additional three-digit numbers are provided following 768 (the terminal number in the past) to accommodate the muscicapines, monarchines, drepanidines and estrildids, thus bringing the system through number 813. There are ample numbers remaining within the present system to handle future additions, providing the area of coverage is not expanded. Certain federal agencies involved with species from U.S. territories and protectorates (e.g., Guam, Puerto Rico) that are not included in the areas covered by the previous A.O.U. numbering system have provided their own "numbers" for such species. We feel that such piecemeal additions are inconsistent with the geographic coverage of the A.O.U. Check-list and also will cause additional problems within the numbering system. This is especially true of those territories such as Guam that are totally outside the expanded coverage of the sixth edition.

LIST OF A.O.U. NUMBERS

* New AOU number assigned.
# No verified reports for United States/Canada.
× Hybrid or unknown form.
¶ Group or morph sometimes regarded as a species.

1.	Aechmophorus occidentalis	41.	R. brevirostris
*1.1	= 1 [clarkii ¶]	42.	Larus hyperboreus
2.	Podiceps grisegena	42.1	= 42 [L. h. barrovianus]
3.	P. auritus	43.	L. glaucoides
4.	P. nigricollis	*43.1	L. thayeri
5.	Tachybaptus dominicus	44.	L. glaucescens
6.	Podilymbus podiceps	45.	= 43 [L. g. kumlieni]
7.	Gavia immer	×46.	[L. nelsoni—APP. C]
8.	G. adamsii	47.	L. marinus
#9.	= 10 [arctica ¶]	48.	L. schistisagus
10.	G. arctica [pacifica ¶]	49.	L. occidentalis
10.1	= 10 [viridigularis ¶]	*49.1	L. livens
11.	G. stellata	50.	L. fuscus
12.	Fratercula cirrhata	51.	L. argentatus
13.	F. arctica	52.	= 51 [L. a. vegae]
14.	F. corniculata	53.	L. californicus
15.	Cerorhinca monocerata	54.	L. delawarensis
16.	Ptychoramphus aleuticus	#54.1	[L. crassirostris]
17.	Cyclorrhynchus psittacula	*54.2	L. belcheri
18.	Aethia cristatella	55.	L. canus [brachyrhynchus]
19.	A. pygmaea	55.1	L. ridibundus
20.	A. pusilla	#56.	= 55 [L. c. canus]
21.	Synthliboramphus antiquus	*56.1	= 55 [kamtschatschensis ¶]
#22.	[S. wumizusume]	57.	L. heermanni
23.	Brachyramphus marmoratus	58.	L. atricilla
24.	B. brevirostris	59.	L. pipixcan
25.	Synthliboramphus hypoleucus	60.	L. philadelphia
26.	S. craveri	60.1	L. minutus
27.	Cepphus grylle	61.	Rhodostethia rosea
28.	= 27 [C. g. mandtii]	62.	Xema sabini
29.	C. columba	63.	Sterna nilotica
30.	Uria aalge	64.	S. caspia
31.	U. lomvia	65.	S. maxima
32.	Alca torda	66.	S. elegans
33.	Pinguinus impennis	67.	S. sandvicensis
34.	Alle alle	#68.	[S. trudeaui]
35.	Catharcta skua	69.	S. forsteri
#35.1	[C. chilensis]	70.	S. hirundo
*35.2	C. maccormicki	71.	S. paradisaea
36.	Stercorarius pomarinus	72.	S. dougallii
37.	S. parasiticus	73.	S. aleutica
38.	S. longicaudus	74.	S. antillarum
39.	Pagophila eburnea	75.	S. fuscata
40.	Rissa tridactyla	76.	S. anaethetus

*76.1 S. lunata
77.   Chlidonias niger
78.   C. leucopterus
79.   Anous stolidus
*79.1 A. minutus
*79.2 Procelsterna cerulea
*79.3 Gygis alba
80.   Rynchops niger
81.   Diomedea nigripes
*81.1 D. exulans
82.   D. albatrus
82.1 D. immutabilis
#82.2 D. melanophris
82.3 D. cauta
83.   D. chlororhynchos
#84.   [Phoebetria palpebrata]
#85.   [Macronectes giganteus]
86.   Fulmarus glacialis
86.1   = 86 [F. g. rodgersii]
#87.   [F. glacialoides]
88.   Calonectris diomedea
*88.1 C. leucomelas
89.   Puffinus gravis
90.   P. puffinus
91.   P. creatopus
92.   P. lherminieri
92.1 P. assimilis
93.   P. opisthomelas
93.1 P. auricularis [auricularis ¶]
*93.2   = 93.1 [newelli ¶]
94.   = 95.
95.   P. griseus
95.1 P. carneipes
96.   P. tenuirostris
96.1 P. pacificus
96.2 P. bulleri
*96.3 P. nativitatis
#97.   [Procellaria cinerea]
98.   Pterodroma hasitata
#98.1   [P. cahow]
98.2 P. arminjoniana
          [arminjoniana ¶]
98.3 P. cookii
*98.4 P. neglecta
*98.5 P. phaeopygia
*98.6   = 98.2 [heraldica ¶]
*98.7 P. externa
99.   P. inexpectata
*99.1 P. hypoleuca
100.   = 99
*100.1 P. ultima

*100.2 P. nigripennis
101.   Bulweria bulwerii
*101.1 B. fallax
102.   Daption capense
103.   Oceanodroma microsoma
104.   Hydrobates pelagicus
105.   Oceanodroma furcata
105.1   = 106 [O. l. "kaedingi" =
            socorroensis ¶]
105.2   = 106 [socorroensis ¶]
106.   O. leucorhoa [leucorhoa ¶]
#106.1   [O. macrodactyla]
106.2 O. castro
106.3 O. tethys
107.   O. melania
*107.1 O. tristrami
108.   O. homochroa
108.1   = 106 [O. l. willetti]
109.   Oceanites oceanicus
#110.   [Fregetta tropica]
111.   Pelagodroma marina
112.   Phaethon lepturus
113.   P. aethereus
113.1 P. rubricauda
114.   Sula dactylatra
114.1 S. nebouxii
115.   S. leucogaster
115.1   = 115 [S. l. brewsteri]
116.   S. sula
117.   S. bassanus
118.   Anhinga anhinga
119.   Phalacrocorax carbo
120.   P. auritus
121.   P. olivaceus
122.   P. penicillatus
123.   P. pelagicus
124.   P. urile
125.   Pelecanus erythrorhynchos
126.   P. occidentalis
127.   = 126 [P. o. californicus]
128.   Fregata magnificens
*128.1 F. minor
*128.2 F. ariel
129.   Mergus merganser
130.   M. serrator
131.   Lophodytes cucullatus
131.1 Mergellus albellus
132.   Anas platyrhynchos
          [platyrhynchos ¶]
*132.1 A. wyvilliana
*132.2 A. laysanensis

133.　A. rubripes
133.1　= 132 [diazi ¶]
134.　A. fulvigula
*134.1 A. poecilorhyncha
135.　A. strepera
136.　A. penelope
137.　A. americana
137.1 A. falcata
138.　= 139 [crecca ¶]
139.　A. crecca [carolinensis ¶]
139.1 A. formosa
*139.2 A. querquedula
140.　A. discors
141.　A. cyanoptera
#141.1　[Tadorna tadorna]
#141.2　[T. ferruginea]
142.　A. clypeata
143.　A. acuta
143.1 A. bahamensis
144.　Aix sponsa
#145.　[Netta rufina]
146.　Aythya americana
146.1 A. ferina
147.　A. valisineria
148.　A. marila
149.　A. affinis
149.1 A. fuligula
#149.2　[A. baeri]
150.　A. collaris
151.　Bucephala clangula
152.　B. islandica
153.　B. albeola
154.　Clangula hyemalis
155.　Histrionicus histrionicus
156.　Camptorhynchus labradorius
157.　Polysticta stelleri
158.　Somateria fischeri
159.　S. mollissima
160.　= 159 [S. m. dresseri]
161.　= 159 [S. m. v-nigra]
162.　S. spectabilis
163.　Melanitta nigra
#164.　= 165 [fusca ¶]
165.　M. fusca [deglandi ¶]
166.　M. perspicillata
167.　Oxyura jamaicensis
168.　O. dominica
169.　Chen caerulescens
　　　[hyperborea ¶]
169.1　= 169 [caerulescens ¶]
170.　C. rossii

171.　Anser albifrons
171.1 A. fabalis
171.2 A. brachyrhynchus
*171.3 A. erythropus
172.　Branta canadensis
　　　[canadensis ¶]
*172.1　= 172 [leucopareia ¶]
*172.2　= 172 [minima ¶]
*172.3　= 172 [hutchinsii ¶]
173.　B. bernicla [bernicla ¶]
174.　= 173 [nigricans ¶]
175.　B. leucopsis
*175.1 Nesochen sandvicensis
176.　Chen canagica
177.　Dendrocygna autumnalis
178.　D. bicolor
#178.1　[D. viduata]
178.2 Cygnus olor
179.　C. cygnus
180.　C. columbianus
　　　[columbianus ¶]
*180.1　= 180 [bewickii ¶]
181.　C. buccinator
182.　Phoenicopterus ruber
183.　Ajaia ajaja
#183.1　[Platalea leucorodia]
184.　Eudocimus albus
185.　E. ruber
186.　Plegadis falcinellus
187.　P. chihi
188.　Mycteria americana
189.　Jabiru mycteria
190.　Botaurus lentiginosus
191.　Ixobrychus exilis
191.1　= 191 ["neoxenus"]
192.　= 194 [occidentalis ¶]
193.　= 194 [A. h. wardi]
194.　Ardea herodias [herodias ¶]
#195.　[A. cinerea]
196.　Casmerodius albus
196.1 Egretta garzetta
*196.2 E. eulophotes
197.　E. thula
198.　E. rufescens
199.　E. tricolor
200.　E. caerulea
200.1 Bubulcus ibis
201.　Butorides striatus
202.　Nycticorax nycticorax
203.　N. violaceus
204.　Grus americana

205.   = 206 [*G. c. canadensis*]
206.   *G. canadensis* [*tabida*]
*206.1 *G. grus*
207.   *Aramus guarauna*
208.   *Rallus elegans*
209.   = 211 [*R. l. beldingi*]
210.   = 211 [*obsoletus* ¶]
210.1   = 211 [*R. l. levipes*]
211.   *R. longirostris*
        [*longirostris* ¶]
211.1   = 211 [*R. l. scottii*]
#211.2   = 211 [*R. l. caribaeus*]
212.   *R. limicola*
#212.1   [*R. aquaticus*]
*212.2 *Pardirallus maculatus*
#213.   [*Porzana porzana*]
214.   *P. carolina*
*214.1 *P. sandwichensis*
*214.2 *P. palmeri*
215.   *Coturnicops noveboracensis*
216.   *Laterallus jamaicensis*
216.1   = 216 [*L. j. coturniculus*]
217.   *Crex crex*
*217.1 *Neocrex erythrops*
218.   *Porphyrula martinica*
219.   *Gallinula chloropus*
220.   *Fulica atra*
221.   *F. americana*
*221.1 *F. caribaea*
222.   *Phalaropus fulicaria*
223.   *P. lobatus*
224.   *P. tricolor*
225.   *Recurvirostra americana*
226.   *Himantopus mexicanus*
        [*mexicanus* ¶]
*226.1   = 226 [*knudseni* ¶]
227.   *Scolopax rusticola*
228.   *S. minor*
229.   = 230 [*G. g. gallinago*]
*229.1 *Gallinago stenura*
230.   *G. gallinago* [*delicata*]
#230.1   [*G. media*]
230.2 *Lymnocryptes minimus*
231.   *Limnodromus griseus*
232.   *L. scolopaceus*
233.   *Calidris himantopus*
234.   *C. canutus*
234.1 *C. tenuirostris*
235.   *C. maritima*
236.   *C. ptilocnemis* [*couesi*]
237.   = 236 [*ptilocnemis*]

238.   *C. acuminata*
239.   *C. melanotos*
240.   *C. fuscicollis*
241.   *C. bairdii*
*241.1 *C. temminckii*
242.   *C. minutilla*
242.1 *C. subminuta*
242.2 *C. ruficollis*
*242.3 *C. minuta*
243.   *C. alpina*
244.   *C. ferruginea*
245.   *Eurynorhynchus pygmeus*
246.   *Calidris pusilla*
247.   *C. mauri*
248.   *C. alba*
*248.1 *Limicola falcinellus*
249.   *Limosa fedoa*
250.   *L. lapponica*
251.   *L. haemastica*
252.   *L. limosa*
253.   *Tringa nebularia*
#253.1   [*T. totanus*]
*253.2 *T. erythropus*
254.   *T. melanoleuca*
255.   *T. flavipes*
*255.1 *T. stagnatilis*
256.   *T. solitaria*
#257.   [*T. ocrophus*]
257.1 *T. glareola*
258.   *Catoptrophorus semipalmatus*
259.   *Heteroscelus incanus*
259.1 *H. brevipes*
260.   *Philomachus pugnax*
261.   *Bartramia longicauda*
262.   *Tryngites subruficollis*
263.   *Actitis macularia*
*263.1 *A. hypoleucos*
*263.2 *Xenus cinereus*
264.   *Numenius americanus*
264.1 *N. arquata*
265.   *N. phaeopus* [*hudsonicus* ¶]
266.   *N. borealis*
267.   = 265 [*phaeopus* ¶]
268.   *N. tahitiensis*
*268.1 *N. tenuirostris*
*268.2 *N. madagascariensis*
269.   *Vanellus vanellus*
269.1 *Charadrius morinellus*
270.   *Pluvialis squatarola*
271.   *P. apricaria*
272.   *P. dominica* [*dominica* ¶]

*272.1   = 272 [fulva ¶]
273.   Charadrius vociferus
274.   C. semipalmatus
275.   C. hiaticula
276.   C. dubius
277.   C. melodus
278.   C. alexandrinus
279.   C. mongolus
280.   C. wilsonia
281.   C. montanus
282.   Aphriza virgata
283.   Arenaria interpres
284.   A. melanocephala
#285.   [Haematopus ostralegus]
286.   H. palliatus
286.1   = 286 [H. p. frazari]
287.   H. bachmani
288.   Jacana spinosa
288.1 Perdix perdix
288.2 Alectoris chukar
*288.3 Francolinus francolinus
*288.4 F. pondicerianus
*288.5 F. erckelii
*288.6 Coturnix japonica
289.   Colinus virginianus
#290.   = 289 [C. v. cubensis]
291.   = 289 [C. v. ridgwayi]
292.   Oreortyx pictus
293.   Callipepla squamata
294.   C. californica
295.   C. gambelii
296.   Cyrtonyx montezumae
297.   Dendragapus obscurus
        [obscurus ¶]
297.1   = 297 [fuliginosus ¶]
298.   D. canadensis [canadensis ¶]
299.   = 298 [franklinii ¶]
300.   Bonasa umbellus
301.   Lagopus lagopus
302.   L. mutus
302.1   = 302 [L. m. evermanni]
303.   = 302 [L. m. welchi]
304.   L. leucurus
305.   Tympanuchus cupido
306.   = 305 [T. c. cupido]
307.   T. pallidicinctus
308.   T. phasianellus
309.   Centrocercus urophasianus
309.1 Phasianus colchicus
*309.2   = 309.1 [versicolor ¶]
*309.3 Lophura leucomelana

*309.4 Gallus gallus
*309.5 Pavo cristatus
310.   Meleagris gallopavo
311.   Ortalis vetula
*311.1 Pterocles exustus
312.   Columba fasciata
313.   C. flavirostris
313.1 C. livia
314.   C. leucocephala
314.1 C. squamosa
315.   Ectopistes migratorius
315.1 Streptopelia chinensis
315.2 S. risoria
*315.3 Geopelia striata
316.   Zenaida macroura
317.   Z. aurita
318.   Leptotila verreauxi
319.   Zenaida asiatica
320.   Columbina passerina
*320.1 C. talpacoti
321.   C. inca
322.   Geotrygon chrysia
322.1 G. montana
#323.   [Starnoenas cyanocephala]
324.   Gymnogyps californianus
325.   Cathartes aura
326.   Coragyps atratus
#326.1 [Sarcoramphus papa]
327.   Elanoides forficatus
*327.1 Chondrohierax uncinatus
328.   Elanus caeruleus
329.   Ictinia mississippiensis
330.   Rostrhamus sociabilis
331.   Circus cyaneus
332.   Accipiter striatus
333.   A. cooperii
334.   A. gentilis
335.   Parabuteo unicinctus
#336.   [Buteo buteo]
337.   B. jamaicensis
338.   = 337 [harlani ¶]
339.   B. lineatus
340.   B. albonotatus
341.   B. albicaudatus
342.   B. swainsoni
343.   B. platypterus
*343.1 B. magnirostris
344.   B. brachyurus
*344.1 B. solitarius
345.   Buteogallus anthracinus
346.   Buteo nitidus

347. *B. lagopus*
348. *B. regalis*
349. *Aquila chrysaetos*
#350. [*Harpyia harpyja*]
351. *Haliaeetus albicilla*
352. *H. leucocephalus*
352.1 *H. pelagicus*
353. = 354 [*Falco r. candicans*]
354. *F. rusticolus*
355. *F. mexicanus*
356. *F. peregrinus*
357. *F. columbarius*
358. = 357 [*F. c. richardsoni*]
#358.1 = 357 [*F. c. aesalon*]
359. *F. femoralis*
359.1 *F. tinnunculus*
360. *F. sparverius*
#361. =360 [*F. s. cubensis*]
362. *Polyborus plancus* [*cheriway* ¶]
#363. = 362 [*lutosus* ¶]
364. *Pandion haliaetus*
365. *Tyto alba*
366. *Asio otus*
367. *A. flammeus*
368. *Strix varia*
369. *S. occidentalis*
370. *S. nebulosa*
371. *Aegolius funereus*
372. *A. acadicus*
373. *Otus asio* [*asio* ¶]
373.1 *O. trichopsis*
373.2 *O. kennicottii*
374. *O. flammeolus*
*374.1 *O. sunia*
375. *Bubo virginianus*
376. *Nyctea scandiaca*
377. *Surnia ulula*
378. *Athene cunicularia*
379. *Glaucidium gnoma*
379.1 = 379 [*G. g. hoskinsii*]
380. *G. brasilianum*
381. *Micrathene whitneyi*
382. *Conuropsis carolinensis*
382.1 *Rhynchopsitta pachyrhyncha*
*382.2 *Melopsittacus undulatus*
*382.3 *Myiopsitta monachus*
*382.4 *Brotogeris versicolurus*
*382.5 *Amazona viridigenalis*
383. *Crotophaga ani*
384. *C. sulcirostris*
385. *Geococcyx californianus*

386. *Coccyzus minor*
387. *C. americanus*
388. *C. erythropthalmus*
388.1 *Cuculus canorus*
388.2 *C. saturatus*
389. *Trogon elegans*
*389.1 *Euptilotus neoxenus*
390. *Ceryle alcyon*
390.1 *C. torquata*
391. *Chloroceryle americana*
*391.1 *Upupa epops*
392. *Campephilus principalis*
393. *Picoides villosus*
394. *P. pubescens*
395. *P. borealis*
396. *P. scalaris*
397. *P. nuttallii*
398. *P. stricklandi*
399. *P. albolarvatus*
400. *P. arcticus*
401. *P. tridactylus*
402. *Sphyrapicus varius* [*varius* ¶]
*402.1 = 402 [*nuchalis* ¶]
403. *S. ruber*
404. *S. thyroideus*
405. *Dryocopus pileatus*
406. *Melanerpes erythrocephalus*
407. *M. formicivorus*
408. *M. lewis*
409. *M. carolinus*
410. *M. aurifrons*
411. *M. uropygialis*
412. *Colaptes auratus* [*auratus* ¶]
413. = 412 [*cafer* ¶]
414. = 412 [*chrysoides* ¶]
#415. = 412 [*C. a. rufipileus*]
415.1 *Jynx torquilla*
416. *Caprimulgus carolinensis*
*416.1 *C. ridgwayi*
*416.2 *C. indicus*
417. *C. vociferus*
418. *Phalaenoptilus nuttallii*
419. *Nyctidromus albicollis*
420. *Chordeiles minor*
*420.1 *C. gundlachii*
421. *C. acutipennis*
422. *Cypseloides niger*
*422.1 *Streptoprocne zonaris*
*422.2 *Hirundapus caudacutus*
423. *Chaetura pelagica*
424. *C. vauxi*

424.1 *Apus pacificus*
424.2 *A. apus*
425.   *Aeronautes saxatalis*
*425.1 *Tachornis phoenicobia*
426.   *Eugenes fulgens*
*426.1 *Heliomaster constantii*
427.   *Lampornis clemenciae*
*427.1 *Colibri thalassinus*
428.   *Archilochus colubris*
429.   *A. alexandri*
×429.1   [*A. violajugulum*—APP. C]
430.   *Calypte costae*
431.   *C. anna*
×431.1   [*Selasphorus floresii*—
       APP. C]
432.   *S. platycercus*
433.   *S. rufus*
434.   *S. sasin*
435.   *Atthis heloisa*
436.   *Stellula calliope*
437.   *Calothorax lucifer*
*437.1 *Calliphlox evelynae*
438.   *Amazilia tzacatl*
*438.1 *A. beryllina*
439.   *A. yucatanensis*
439.1 *A. violiceps*
#440.   [*Hylocharis xantusii*]
440.1 *H. leucotis*
441.   *Cynanthus latirostris*
441.1 *Pachyramphus aglaiae*
442.   *Tyrannus savana*
443.   *T. forficatus*
444.   *T. tyrannus*
445.   *T. dominicensis*
445.1 *T. crassirostris*
*445.2 *T. caudifasciatus*
446.   *T. melancholicus*
*446.1 *T. couchii*
*446.2   = 446 [*occidentalis* ¶]
447.   *T. verticalis*
448.   *T. vociferans*
449.   *Pitangus sulphuratus*
#450.   [*Myiozetetes similis*]
451.   *Myiodynastes luteiventris*
*451.1 *Empidonomus varius*
452.   *Myiarchus crinitus*
453.   *M. tyrannulus*
453.1 *M. nuttingi*
454.   *M. cinerascens*
455.   *M. tuberculifer*
*455.1 *M. sagrae*

456.   *Sayornis phoebe*
457.   *S. saya*
458.   *S. nigricans*
459.   *Contopus borealis*
460.   *C. pertinax*
461.   *C. virens*
462.   *C. sordidulus*
463.   *Empidonax flaviventris*
464.   *E. difficilis*
#464.1   = 464 [*E. d. cineritius*]
465.   *E. virescens*
466.   *E. traillii*
*466.1 *E. alnorum*
467.   *E. minimus*
468.   *E. hammondii*
469.   *E. oberholseri*
469.1 *E. wrightii*
470.   *E. fulvifrons*
471.   *Pyrocephalus rubinus*
472.   *Camptostoma imberbe*
473.   *Alauda arvensis*
474.   *Eremophila alpestris*
475.   *Pica pica*
476.   *P. nuttalli*
477.   *Cyanocitta cristata*
478.   *C. stelleri*
479.   = 481 [*coerulescens* ¶]
480.   = 481 [*woodhouseii* ¶]
#480.1   = 481 [*A. c. cyanotis*]
480.2   = 481 [*A. c. texana*]
481.   *Aphelocoma coerulescens*
       [*californica* ¶]
481.1   = 481 [*insularis* ¶]
482.   *A. ultramarina*
483.   *Cyanocorax yncas*
#483.1   [*C. sanblasianus*]
*483.2 *C. morio*
484.   *Perisoreus canadensis*
485.   = 484 [*P. c. obscurus*]
486.   *Corvus corax*
487.   *C. cryptoleucus*
488.   *C. brachyrhynchos*
489.   *C. caurinus*
*489.1 *C. imparatus*
*489.2 *C. hawaiiensis*
490.   *C. ossifragus*
#490.1   [*C. frugilegus*]
#490.2   [*C. corone*]
491.   *Nucifraga columbiana*
492.   *Gymnorhinus cyanocephalus*
493.   *Sturnus vulgaris*

493.1 *Acridotheres cristatellus*
*493.2 *A. tristis*
494. *Dolichonyx oryzivorus*
495. *Molothrus ater*
496. *M. aeneus*
497. *Xanthocephalus xanthocepha-lus*
498. *Agelaius phoeniceus*
#499. = [*A. p. gubernator*]
500. *A. tricolor*
500.1 *A. humeralis*
501. *Sturnella magna*
501.1 *S. neglecta*
#502. [*Icterus icterus*]
503. *I. graduacauda*
503.1 *I. gularis*
503.2 *I. pectoralis*
504. *I. parisorum*
*504.1 *I. wagleri*
505. *I. cucullatus*
505.1 *I. pustulatus*
506. *I. spurius* [*spurius* ¶]
*506.1 = 506 [*fuertesi* ¶]
507. *I. galbula* [*galbula* ¶]
508. = 508 [*bullockii* ¶]
509. *Euphagus carolinus*
510. *E. cyanocephalus*
511. *Quiscalus quiscula* [*quiscula* ¶]
511.1 = 511 [*versicolor* ¶]
512. *Q. mexicanus*
513. *Q. major*
514. *Coccothraustes vespertinus*
514.1 *Fringilla montifringilla*
514.2 *Coccothraustes coccothraustes*
*514.3 *Fringilla coelebs*
515. *Pinicola enucleator*
516. *Pyrrhula pyrrhula*
*516.1 *Carpodacus erythrinus*
517. *C. purpureus*
518. *C. cassinii*
519. *C. mexicanus* [*mexicanus* ¶]
#520. = 519 [*amplus* ¶]
#520.1 = 519 [*mcgregori* ¶]
521. *Loxia curvirostra*
522. *L. leucoptera*
523. = 524 [*L. a. griseonucha*]
524. *Leucosticte arctoa* [*tephrocotis* ¶]
525. = 524 [*atrata* ¶]
526. = 524 [*australis* ¶]
526.1 *Carduelis carduelis*

*526.2 *C. sinica*
527. *C. hornemanni*
528. *C. flammea*
529. *C. tristis*
530. *C. psaltria*
531. *C. lawrencei*
#532. [*C. magellanica*]
533. *C. pinus*
*533.1 *Serinus canaria*
*533.2 *S. mozambicus*
534. *Plectrophenax nivalis*
535. *P. hyperboreus*
535.1 *Emberiza rustica*
*535.2 *E. pusilla*
*535.3 *E. variabilis*
*535.4 *E. pallasi*
*535.5 *E. schoeniclus*
536. *Calcarius lapponicus*
537. *C. pictus*
538. *C. ornatus*
539. *C. mccownii*
540. *Pooecetes gramineus*
541. = 542 [*princeps* ¶]
542. *Passerculus sandwichensis* [*sandwichensis* ¶]
543. = 542 [*beldingi* ¶]
544. = 542 [*rostratus* ¶]
#544.1 = 542 [*P. s. sanctorum*]
545. *Ammodramus bairdii*
546. *A. savannarum*
547. *A. henslowii*
548. *A. leconteii*
549. *A. caudacutus*
549.1 = 549 [*A. c. nelsoni*]
550. *A. maritimus* [*maritimus* ¶]
551. = 550 [*nigrescens* ¶]
551.1 = 550 [*mirabilis* ¶]
552. *Chondestes grammacus*
553. *Zonotrichia querula*
554. *Z. leucophrys*
555. = 554 [*Z. l. gambelii*]
556. = 554 [*Z. l. nuttalli*]
557. *Z. atricapilla*
558. *Z. albicollis*
559. *Spizella arborea*
560. *S. passerina*
561. *S. pallida*
562. *S. breweri*
563. *S. pusilla*
564. *S. wortheni*
565. *S. atrogularis*

566.   = 567 [aikeni ¶]
567.   Junco hyemalis [hyemalis ¶]
*567.1   = 567 [oreganus ¶]
568.   = 567 [mearnsi ¶]
568.1   = 567 [J. h. "ridgwayi"]
569.   = 567 [caniceps ¶]
*569.1   = 567 [dorsalis ¶]
570.   J. phaeonotus [phaeonotus ¶]
#571.   = 570 [bairdi ¶]
#571.1   = 567 [J. h. townsendi]
#572.   = 567 [insularis ¶]
573.   Amphispiza bilineata
574.   A. belli
574.1   =574 [A. b. nevadensis]
*574.2 A. quinquestriata
575.   Aimophila aestivalis
576.   A. botterii
#577.   = 576 [A. b. mexicana]
578.   A. cassinii
579.   A. carpalis
580.   A. ruficeps
581.   Melospiza melodia
582.   = 581 [M. m. sanaka]
583.   M. lincolnii
584.   M. georgiana
585.   Passerella iliaca
586.   Arremonops rufivirgatus
*586.1 Sicalis flaveola
587.   Pipilo erythrophthalmus
        [erythrophthalmus ¶]
588.   = 587 [maculatus ¶]
#589.   = 587 [P. e. consobrinus]
590.   P. chlorurus
591.   P. fuscus
591.1   = 591 [P. f. crissalis]
592.   P. aberti
592.1   = 590
*592.2 Paroaria coronata
*592.3 P. capitata
593.   Cardinalis cardinalis
594.   C. sinuatus
*594.1 Rhodothraupis celaeno
595.   Pheucticus ludovicianus
596.   P. melanocephalus
*596.1 P. chrysopeplus
597.   Guiraca caerulea
*597.1 Cyanocompsa parellina
598.   Passerina cyanea
599.   P. amoena
600.   P. versicolor
601.   P. ciris

602.   Sporophila torqueola
603.   Tiaris bicolor
#603.1   [T. canora]
*603.2 T. olivacea
604.   Spiza americana
605.   Calamospiza melanocorys
#606.   [Euphonia elegantissima]
607.   Piranga ludoviciana
608.   P. olivacea
609.   P. flava
610.   P. rubra
*610.1 Spindalis zena
611.   Progne subis
611.1   P. cryptoleuca
611.2   P. chalybea
*611.3 P. elegans
612.   Hirundo pyrrhonota
612.1   H. fulva
613.   H. rustica
613.1   = 613 [H. r. rustica]
614.   Tachycineta bicolor
615.   T. thalassina
615.1   T. cyaneoviridis
615.2   Delichon urbica
616.   Riparia riparia
617.   Stelgidopteryx serripennis
618.   Bombycilla garrulus
619.   B. cedrorum
620.   Phainopepla nitens
621.   Lanius excubitor
*621.1 L. cristatus
622.   L. ludovicianus
*622.1 Moho braccatus
*622.2 M. apicalis
*622.3 M. bishopi
*622.4 M. nobilis
*622.5 Chaetoptila angustipluma
*622.6 Zosterops japonica
623.   Vireo altiloquus
624.   V. olivaceus [olivaceus ¶]
625.   = 624 [flavoviridis ¶]
626.   V. philadelphicus
627.   V. gilvus
628.   V. flavifrons
629.   V. solitarius
630.   V. atricapilla
631.   V. griseus
632.   V. huttoni
633.   V. bellii
634.   V. vicinior
635.   Coereba flaveola

636. *Mniotilta varia*
637. *Protonotaria citrea*
638. *Limnothlypis swainsonii*
639. *Helmitheros vermivorus*
640. *Vermivora bachmanii*
641. *V. pinus*
642. *V. chrysoptera*
643. *V. luciae*
644. *V. virginiae*
645. *V. ruficapilla*
646. *V. celata*
647. *V. peregrina*
647.1 *V. crissalis*
648. *Parula americana*
649. *P. pitiayumi [pitiayumi* ¶]
#649.1   = 649 [*graysoni* ¶]
650. *Dendroica tigrina*
651. *Peucedramus taeniatus*
652. *Dendroica petechia [aestiva* ¶]
*652.1   = 652 [*petechia* ¶]
653.   = 652 [*erithachorides* ¶]
654. *D. caerulescens*
655. *D. coronata [coronata* ¶]
656.   = 655 [*auduboni* ¶]
657. *D. magnolia*
658. *D. cerulea*
659. *D. pensylvanica*
660. *D. castanea*
661. *D. striata*
662. *D. fusca*
663. *D. dominica*
664. *D. graciae*
665. *D. nigrescens*
666. *D. chrysoparia*
667. *D. virens*
668. *D. townsendi*
669. *D. occidentalis*
670. *D. kirtlandii*
671, *D. pinus*
672. *D. palmarum*
673. *D. discolor*
674. *Seiurus aurocapillus*
675. *S. noveboracensis*
676. *S. motacilla*
677. *Oporornis formosus*
678. *O. agilis*
679. *O. philadelphia*
680. *O. tolmiei*
681. *Geothlypis trichas*
#682.   [*G. beldingi*]
682.1 *G. poliocephala*

683. *Icteria virens*
684. *Wilsonia citrina*
685. *W. pusilla*
686. *W. canadensis*
687. *Setophaga ruticilla*
688. *Myioborus pictus*
688.1 *Euthlypis lachrymosa*
688.2 *Passer domesticus*
688.3 *P. montanus*
689. *Myioborus miniatus*
690. *Cardellina rubrifrons*
#691.   [*Ergaticus ruber*]
692. *Basileuterus culicivorus*
*692.1 *B. rufifrons*
#693.   [*B. belli*]
694. *Motacilla alba*
695.   = 694 [*M. a. ocularis*]
695.1 *M. lugens*
696. *M. flava*
*696.1 *M. cinerea*
697. *Anthus spinoletta*
697.1   = 697 [*A. s. japonicus*]
#698. *A. pratensis*
698.1 *A. gustavi*
*698.2 *A. trivialis*
*698.3 *A. hodgsoni*
699. *A. cervinus*
700. *A. spragueii*
701. *Cinclus mexicanus*
702. *Oreoscoptes montanus*
703. *Mimus polyglottos*
*703.1 *M. gundlachii*
704. *Dumetella carolinensis*
705. *Toxostoma rufum*
706. *T. longirostre*
707. *T. curvirostre*
708. *T. bendirei*
#709.   [*T. cinereum*]
710. *T. redivivum*
711. *T. lecontei*
712. *T. dorsale*
713. *Campylorhynchus brunneica-*
       pillus
#714.   = 713 [*C. b. affinis*]
715. *Salpinctes obsoletus*
#716.   = 715 [*S. o. guadeloupensis*]
717. *Catherpes mexicanus*
718. *Thryothorus ludovicianus*
719. *Thryomanes bewickii*
719.1   = 719 [*T. b. leucophrys*]
#720.   = 719 [*T. b. brevicauda*]

721. *Troglodytes aedon* [*aedon* ¶]
721.1 = 721 [*brunneicollis* ¶]
722. *T. troglodytes*
723. = 722 [*T. t. alascensis*]
723.1 = 722 [*T. t. meligerus*]
724. *Cistothorus platensis*
725. *C. palustris*
725.1 = 725 [*C. p. marianae*]
726. *Certhia americana*
*726.1 *Pycnonotus jocosus*
*726.2 *P. cafer*
727. *Sitta carolinensis*
728. *S. canadensis*
729. *S. pusilla*
730. *S. pygmaea*
731. *Parus bicolor* [*bicolor* ¶]
732. = 732 [*atricristatus* ¶]
733. *P. inornatus*
734. *P. wollweberi*
*734.1 *P. varius*
735. *P. atricapillus*
736. *P. carolinensis*
737. *P. sclateri*
738. *P. gambeli*
739. *P. cinctus*
740. *P. hudsonicus*
741. *P. rufescens*
742. *Chamaea fasciata*
*742.1 *Leiothrix lutea*
*742.2 *Garrulax canorus*
*742.3 *G. pectoralis*
743. *Psaltriparus minimus*
744. = 743 [*P. m. plumbeus*]
744.1 = 743 [*P. m. lloydi*]
745. = 743 [*melanotis* ¶]
746. *Auriparus flaviceps*
*746.1 *Cettia diphone*
746.2 *Acrocephalus familiaris*
      [*familiaris* ¶]
*746.3 = 746.2 [*kingi* ¶]
747. *Phylloscopus borealis*
747.1 *Locustella ochotensis*
#747.2 [*Phylloscopus trochilus*]
*747.3 *P. sibilatrix*
*747.4 *P. fuscatus*
748. *Regulus satrapa*
749. *R. calendula*
749.1 *Prunella montanella*
#750. = 749 [*R. c. obscurus*]
751. *Polioptila caerulea*

752. *P. melanura* [*melanura* ¶]
753. = 752 [*californica* ¶]
*753.1 *P. nigriceps*
754. *Myadestes townsendi*
*754.1 *Phaeornis obscurus*
*754.2 *P. palmeri*
755. *Hylocichla mustelina*
756. *Catharus fuscescens*
757. *C. minimus*
758. *C. ustulatus*
759. *C. guttatus*
760. *Turdus iliacus*
761. *T. migratorius* [*migratorius* ¶]
761.1 *T. merula*
761.2 *T. pilaris*
*761.3 *T. obscurus*
*761.4 *T. naumanni*
#762. = 761 [*confinis* ¶]
*762.1 *T. grayi*
*762.2 *T. rufopalliatus*
763. *Ixoreus naevius*
*763.1 *Ridgwayia pinicola*
764. *Luscinia svecica*
764.1 *L. calliope*
765. *Oenanthe oenanthe*
766. *Sialia sialis*
767. *S. mexicana*
768. *S. currucoides*
*769. *Copsychus malabaricus*
*770. *Chasiempis sandwichensis*
*771. *Ficedula parva*
*772. *Muscicapa sibirica*
*773. *M. griseisticta*
*774. *Telespyza cantans*
*775. *T. ultima*
*776. *Psittirostra psittacea*
*777. *Loxioides bailleui*
*778. *Rhodacanthis flaviceps*
*779. *R. palmeri*
*780. *Chloridops kona*
*781. *Pseudonestor xanthophrys*
*782. *Hemignathus virens* [*virens* ¶]
*783. = 782 [*stejnegeri* ¶]
*784. *H. parvus*
*785. *H. sagittirostris*
*786. *H. obscurus*
*787. *H. procerus*
*788. *H. lucidus*
*789. *H. munroi*
*790. *Oreomystis bairdi*

*791.   *O. mana*
*792.   *Paroreomyza montana*
*793.   *P. flammea*
*794.   *P. maculata*
*795.   *Loxops coccineus* [*coccineus* ¶]
*796.   = 795 [*caerulirostris* ¶]
*797.   *Ciridops anna*
*798.   *Vestiaria coccinea*
*799.   *Drepanis pacifica*
*800.   *D. funerea*
*801.   *Palmeria dolei*
*802.   *Himatione sanguinea*
        [*sanguinea* ¶]

*803.   = 802 [*freethii* ¶]
*804.   *Melamprosops phaeosoma*
*805.   *Uraeginthus bengalus*
*806.   *Estrilda caerulescens*
*807.   *E. melpoda*
*808.   *E. troglodytes*
*809.   *Amandava amandava*
*810.   *Lonchura malabarica*
*811.   *L. punctulata*
*812.   *L. malacca*
*813.   *Padda oryzivora*

INDEX